TAX LEGISLATION 2008

Emergency Economic Stabilization Act of 2008

(P.L. 110-343)

As Signed by the President on October 3, 2008

Law, Explanation and Analysis

CCH Editorial Staff Publication

.CCH

a Wolters Kluwer business

ISBN 978-0-8080-1996-1

4025 W. Peterson Ave.
Chicago, IL 60646-6085
1 800 248 3248
www.CCHGroup.com

Printed in the United States of America

Emergency Economic Stabilization Act of 2008
Financial Markets Rescue Plan, AMT Patch, Extenders and More

After a tumultuous week of closed-door meetings, late night press conferences and a strange coexistence of bipartisanship and coalition solidarity, Congress passed and President Bush signed on October 3, 2008, historic financial rescue legislation. The Emergency Economic Stabilization Act of 2008 (P.L. 110-343) provides $700 billion to the Treasury Department for the purchase of certain illiquid assets from troubled institutions. It would be misleading, however, to characterize this legislation as just a banking Act. The Emergency Economic Stabilization Act of 2008 (P.L. 110-343) is also one of the largest tax Acts in recent years. It makes nearly 300 changes to the Internal Revenue Code at a cost of $150 billion. In addition to the major tax provisions that directly address current financial bailout measures, the new law includes a much-anticipated alternative minimum tax (AMT) patch, an extensive package of tax extenders, energy incentives, disaster relief, and more.

Financial Rescue Plan

The centerpiece of the Emergency Economic Stabilization Act of 2008 (P.L. 110-343) is the $700 billion provided to the Treasury Department for the purchase of illiquid assets. The measure gives the Treasury Department $250 billion immediately, and requires the President to certify if an additional $100 billion is necessary. An additional $350 billion may be disbursed subject to Congressional approval. The Treasury Department is required to report on the use of the funds and progress made in addressing the crisis. An oversight board and a special inspector general will also be created to watch over the Treasury Department. The measure also:

1. requires the Treasury Department to modify troubled loans wherever possible to help families keep their homes;

2. directs other federal agencies to modify loans that they own or control;

3. improves the HOPE for Homeowners program by expanding eligibility and increasing the tools available to the Department of Housing and Urban Development to help more families keep their homes; and

4. places certain limits on executive compensation.

The legislation requires companies that sell some of their bad assets to the government to provide warrants so that taxpayers will benefit from any future growth these companies may experience as a result of participation in this program. In addition, the President must submit legislation that would cover any losses to taxpayers resulting from this program by charging a small, broad-based fee to all financial institutions. Finally, the legislation temporarily raises the FDIC insurance cap from $100,000 to $250,000.

Tax Extenders and Energy-Related Incentives

In addition to the provisions related to the controversial rescue plan, the Emergency Economic Stabilization Act of 2008 (P.L. 110-343) contains over 100 tax and accounting provisions that make nearly 300 changes to the Internal Revenue Code. Inserted at the eleventh hour as a "sweetener" designed to entice the House of Representatives into passing the measure, the robust tax package includes:

1. a one-year AMT patch;

2. an extension of a number of individual and business deductions, credits and incentives;

3. disaster relief to those impacted by recent hurricanes and flooding; and

4. a number of energy-related provisions.

The added tax provisions are largely taken from the Renewable Energy and Job Creation Act of 2008 (H.R. 6049), which the Senate passed on September 23, 2008, and are only partially offset. The House of Representatives initially refused to consider the standalone bill because it did not follow House "pay-as-you-go" budget rules. However, with time running out before the elections in November and pressure mounting to address the country's economic crisis, the House of Representatives acquiesced.

About This Work and CCH

Following the passage of the Emergency Economic Stabilization Act of 2008 (P.L. 110-343), CCH is providing practitioners with a single integrated law and explanation of the tax and accounting provisions of:

1. the tax and accounting provisions of the Emergency Economic Stabilization Act of 2008 (P.L. 110-343);

2. the tax provisions of the Federal Aviation Administrative Extension Act of 2008 (P.L. 110-330);

3. the tax provisions of the Fostering Connections to Success and Increasing Adoption Act of 2008 (P.L. 110-351);

4. the tax provisions of the Inmate Tax Fraud Prevention Act of 2008 (H.R. 7082);

5. the tax provisions of the SSI Extension for the Elderly and Disabled Refugees Act of 2008 (P.L. 110-328); and

6. the tax provisions of Michelle's Law (H.R. 2851).

Along with the relevant Internal Revenue Code provisions, as amended by these Acts, and the relevant reports from the Joint Committee on Taxation, the *Emergency Economic Stabilization Act of 2008: Law, Explanation and Analysis* provides a complete practical analysis of the new laws. Other products and tax services relating to the new legislation can be found at CCH's website http://tax.cchgroup.com.

As always, CCH Tax and Accounting remains dedicated to responding to the needs of tax professionals in helping them quickly understand and work with these new laws as they take effect.

Mark A. Luscombe

Principal Analyst

CCH Tax and Accounting

October 2008

Contributors

Stephen J. Bigge, CPA
Virchow, Krause & Co. LLP
Appleton, Wisconsin

Janine H. Bosley, J.D.
Buchanan Ingersoll and Rooney
Washington, D.C.

Kip Dellinger, CPA
Kallman and Co. LLP
Los Angeles, California

Jeffrey D. Eicher, J.D., CPA
Clarion University of Pennsylvania
Clarion, Pennsylvania

Charles R. Goulding, J.D., CPA, MBA
Energy Tax Savers, Inc.
Syosset, New York

Glenn A. Graff, J.D.
Applegate & Thorne-Thomsen, P.C.
Chicago, Illinois

Claudia Hill, EA, MBA
Tax Mam, Inc./TMI Tax Services
Group, Inc.
Cupertino, California

Leo N. Hitt, J.D., LL.M.
Reed Smith LLP
Pittsburgh, Pennsylvania

William C. Hood, J.D., CPA
Central Michigan University
Mount Pleasant, Michigan

Charles C. Hwang, J.D.
Crowell Moring LLP
Washington, D.C.

Robert S. Keebler, CPA, MST
Virchow, Krause & Co. LLP
Appleton, Wisconsin

Arthur H. Kroll, J.D.
KST Consulting Group, Inc.
Hartsdale, New York

Paul C. Lau, CPA, CMA, CFM
Blackman Kallick
Chicago, Illinois

Vincent O'Brien, CPA
Vincent J. O'Brien, CPA, PC
Lynbrook, New York

Pam Perdue, J.D.
Summers, Compton, Wells & Hamburg
St. Louis, Missouri

Jennifer A. Ray, J.D.
Crowell Moring LLP
Washington, D.C.

Donald B. Reynolds, Jr., J.D.
Buchanan Ingersoll and Rooney
Washington, D.C.

Charles P. Rettig, J.D., LL.M.
Hochman, Salkin, Rettig, Toscher & Perez
Beverly Hills, California

Alex Sadler, J.D.
Crowell Moring LLP
Washington, D.C.

Michael Schlesinger, J.D., LL.M.
Schlesinger and Sussman
New York, New York

John A. Sikora, J.D.
Weiss Berzowski Brady LLP
Milwaukee, Wisconsin

Sandy Soltis, CPA, CFP
Blackman Kallick
Chicago, Illinois

Jim Sowell, J.D., LL.M.
KPMG LLP
Washington, D.C.

Robert B. Teuber, J.D.
Weiss Berzowski Brady LLP
Delafield, Wisconsin

Michelle Ward, J.D.
Virchow, Krause & Co. LLP
Appleton, Wisconsin

Robert S. Winters, J.D., MBA
Buchanan Ingersoll & Rooney PC
Washington, D.C.

John Zimmerman, J.D., CPA
Department of Accounting
University of Nevada Las Vegas

CCH Tax and Accounting Publishing
EDITORIAL STAFF

¶1 Features of This Publication

This publication is your complete guide to the tax and accounting-related provisions of the *Emergency Economic Stabilization Act of 2008* (P.L. 110-343), and the tax-related provisions of the *SSI Extension for Elderly and Disabled Refugees Act* (P.L. 110-328), the *Fostering Connections to Success and Increasing Adoptions Act of 2008* (P.L. 110-351), the *Federal Aviation Administration Extension Act of 2008, Part II* (P.L. 110-330), the *Inmate Tax Fraud Prevention Act of 2008* (H.R. 7082), and Michelle's Law (H.R. 2851). The core portion of this publication contains the CCH Explanations of these Acts. The explanations outline all of the law changes and what they mean for you and your clients. The explanations also feature practical guidance, examples, planning opportunities and strategies, as well as pitfalls to be avoided as a result of the law changes.

The law text and Joint Committee on Taxation (JCT) Technical Explanation of H.R. 7060, the *Renewable Energy and Job Creation Act of 2008* (JCX-75-08); the JCT Technical Explanation of Title III (Tax Provisions) of Division A of H.R. 1424, *Emergency Economic Stabilization Act of 2008* (JCX-79-08); the JCT Technical Explanation of H.R. 7006, the *Disaster Tax Relief Act of 2008* (JCX-73-08); the JCT Technical Explanation of H.R. 7005, the *Alternative Minimum Tax Relief Act of 2008* (JCX-71-08); and the House Committee Report accompanying Michelle's Law (H. Rep. No. 110-806) are reproduced following the explanations. Any new or amended Internal Revenue Code sections appear here, with changes highlighted in *italics*. The law text for portions of this Act that did not amend the tax code, appear here. The relevant JCT Technical Explanations that provides the legislative history of each provision follow the law text.

The book also contains numerous other features designed to help you locate and understand the changes made by these Acts. These features include cross references to related materials, detailed effective dates, and numerous finding tables and indexes. A more detailed description of these features appears below.

HIGHLIGHTS

Highlights are quick summaries of the major provisions of the *Emergency Economic Stabilization Act of 2008* (P.L. 110-343), and the tax-related provisions of the *SSI Extension for Elderly and Disabled Refugees Act* (P.L. 110-328), the *Fostering Connections to Success and Increasing Adoptions Act of 2008* (P.L. 110-351), the *Federal Aviation Administration Extension Act of 2008, Part II* (P.L. 110-330), the *Inmate Tax Fraud Prevention Act of 2008* (H.R. 7082), and Michelle's Law (H.R. 2851). The Highlights are arranged by area of interest, such as individual taxpayers, business deductions, tax credits, energy conservation and disaster relief. At the end of each summary is a paragraph reference to the more detailed CCH Explanation on that topic, giving you an easy way to find the portions of the publication that are of most interest to you. *Highlights starts at ¶5.*

TAXPAYERS AFFECTED

The first chapter of the book, *Taxpayers Affected*, contains a detailed look at how the new laws affect specific categories of taxpayers. This chapter provides a quick reference for readers who want to know the immediate impact that the laws will have on their clients. *Taxpayers Affected starts at ¶101.*

CCH EXPLANATIONS

CCH Explanations are designed to give you a complete, accessible understanding of the new law. Explanations are arranged by subject for ease of use. There are two main finding devices you can use to locate explanations on a given topic. These are:

- A detailed table of contents at the beginning of the publication listing all of the CCH Explanations of the new law;
- A table of contents preceding each chapter.

Each CCH Explanation contains special features to aid in your complete understanding of the new law. These include:

- A summary at the beginning of each explanation providing a brief overview of the new law;
- A background or prior law discussion that puts the law changes into perspective;
- Editorial aids, including examples, cautions, planning notes, elections, comments, compliance tips, key rates and figures, and state tax consequences, that highlight the impact of the new laws;
- Charts and examples illustrating the ramifications of specific law changes;
- Captions at the end of each explanation identifying the Code sections added, amended or repealed, as well as the Act sections containing the changes;
- Cross references to the law and JCT Technical Explanation paragraphs related to the explanation;
- A line highlighting the effective date of each law change, marked by an arrow symbol; and
- References at the end of the discussion to related information in the Standard Federal Tax Reporter, Tax Research Consultant and Federal Tax Guide.

The CCH Explanations begin at ¶205.

AMENDED CODE PROVISIONS

Changes to the Internal Revenue Code made by the *Emergency Economic Stabilization Act of 2008* (P.L. 110-343), and the tax-related provisions of the *SSI Extension for Elderly and Disabled Refugees Act* (P.L. 110-328), the *Fostering Connections to Success and Increasing Adoptions Act of 2008* (P.L. 110-351), the *Federal Aviation Administration Extension Act of 2008, Part II* (P.L. 110-330), the *Inmate Tax Fraud Prevention Act of 2008* (H.R. 7082), and Michelle's Law (H.R. 2851), the appear under the heading "Code Sections Added, Amended or Repealed." *Any changed or added law text is set out in italics.* Deleted Code text, or the Code provision prior to amendment, appears in the

Amendment Notes following each reconstructed Code provision. An effective date for each Code change is also provided.

The amendment notes contain cross references to the relevant JCT Technical Explanations and the CCH Explanations that discuss the new law. *The text of the Code begins at ¶5005.*

Sections of these Acts that do not amend the Internal Revenue Code appear in full text following "Code Sections Added, Amended or Repealed." *The text of these provisions appears in Act Section order beginning at ¶7003.*

COMMITTEE REPORTS

The Joint Committee on Taxation (JCT) Technical Explanation of H.R. 7060, the *Renewable Energy and Job Creation Act of 2008* (JCX-75-08); the JCT Technical Explanation of Title III (Tax Provisions) of Division A of H.R. 1424, *Emergency Economic Stabilization Act of 2008* (JCX-79-08); the JCT Technical Explanation of H.R. 7006, the *Disaster Tax Relief Act of 2008* (JCX-73-08); and the JCT Technical Explanation of H.R. 7005, the *Alternative Minimum Tax Relief Act of 2008* (JCX-71-08), explains the intent of Congress regarding the provisions of the *Emergency Economic Stabilization Act of 2008* (P.L. 110-343), and the tax-related provisions of the *SSI Extension for Elderly and Disabled Refugees Act* (P.L. 110-328), the *Fostering Connections to Success and Increasing Adoptions Act of 2008* (P.L. 110-351), the *Federal Aviation Administration Extension Act of 2008, Part II* (P.L. 110-330), and the *Inmate Tax Fraud Prevention Act of 2008* (H.R. 7082). There was no conference report issued for the *Emergency Economic Stabilization Act of 2008.* The relevant portions of the Technical Explanations from the JCT are included in this section to aid the reader's understanding, but may not be cited as the official House, Senate or Conference Committee Report accompanying the *Emergency Economic Stabilization Act of 2008,* the *SSI Extension for Elderly and Disabled Refugees Act,* the *Fostering Connections to Success and Increasing Adoptions Act of 2008,* the *Federal Aviation Administration Extension Act of 2008, Part II* and the *Inmate Tax Fraud Prevention Act of 2008.* At the end of each section, references are provided to the corresponding CCH explanations and the Internal Revenue Code provisions. *The pertinent sections of the Technical Explanation appear in Act Section order beginning at ¶10,010.*

H. Rep. No. 110-806 explains the intent of Congress regarding the tax provisions of Michelle's Law (H.R. 2851). At the end of each section, references are provided to the corresponding CCH explanations and the Internal Revenue Code provisions. *The pertinent sections of H. Rep. No. 110-806 appear in Act Section order beginning at ¶15,010.*

EFFECTIVE DATES

Tables listing the major effective dates provides a reference bridge between Code Sections and Act Sections. The tables also indicate the retroactive or prospective nature of the laws. *The effective dates tables for the Emergency Economic Stabilization Act of 2008 (P.L. 110-343), and the tax-related provisions of the SSI Extension for Elderly and Disabled Refugees Act (P.L. 110-328), the Fostering Connections to Success and Increasing Adoptions Act of 2008 (P.L. 110-351), the Federal Aviation Administration Extension Act of 2008, Part II (P.L. 110-330), the Inmate Tax Fraud Prevention Act of 2008 (H.R. 7082), and Michelle's Law (H.R. 2851) begin at ¶20,001.*

SPECIAL FINDING DEVICES

Other special tables and finding devices in this book include:

- A table cross-referencing Code Sections to the CCH Explanations (*see ¶25,001*);
- A table showing all Code Sections added, amended or repealed (*see ¶25,005*);
- A table showing provisions of other acts that were amended (*see ¶25,010*);
- A table of Act Sections not amending the Internal Revenue Code (*see ¶25,015*); and
- An Act Section amending Code Section table (*see ¶25,020*).

CLIENT LETTERS

Sample client letters allows you to quickly communicate the changes made by the *Emergency Economic Stabilization Act of 2008* to clients and customers (*see ¶27,001*).

¶2 Table of Contents

¶3 Detailed Table of Contents

CHAPTER 4. BUSINESS CREDITS AND OTHER SPECIAL TAXPAYERS

¶3

¶5 Highlights

INDIVIDUAL TAXPAYERS

¶205, ¶210, ¶215   **AMT.** The alternative minimum tax (AMT) exemption amount for individuals is increased for tax years beginning in 2008 while the use of nonrefundable personal tax credits against an individual's regular tax and AMT liability is extended to tax years beginning in 2008. Also, an individual with a long-term unused minimum tax credit for a tax year beginning before January 1, 2013, will have a minimum tax credit allowable for that tax year of not less than the greater of the AMT refundable credit amount (if any) determined in the preceding tax year, or 50 percent of the unused credit.

¶220   **Debt cancellation income exclusion.** The exclusion from gross income for discharges of qualified principal residence indebtedness is extended for three years through calendar year 2012.

¶225   **Charitable distributions from IRAs.** Individuals aged 70 ½ or older can distribute up to $100,000 of their IRA balance to charitable organizations in 2008 and in 2009 without recognizing income and without taking a charitable deduction.

¶230   **Fringe for bike commuters.** Any employee who regularly uses a bicycle to commute to work is entitled to a transportation fringe benefit not to exceed $20 per month.

¶235, ¶240, ¶245, ¶250   **Deductions extended.** Additional standard deduction for real property taxes for nonitemizers may be claimed for any tax year beginning in 2008 or 2009. The election to deduct state and local general sales taxes in lieu of state and local income taxes, the deductions for qualified tuition and related expenses, and for eligible educator expenses have been extended through December 31, 2009.

¶255, ¶260   **Child tax credit.** A taxpayer is eligible for a refundable child credit of 15 percent of his earned income in excess of $8,500, up to the per child credit amount, if the total allowable child tax credit exceeds the total tax liability. The definition of a "qualifying child" is modified with respect to age and joint returns, the tie-breaker rules are clarified, and the child tax credit is tied to the child's dependency exemption.

BUSINESS DEDUCTIONS

¶305, ¶310, ¶315   **15-year MACRS property.** The 15-year modified accelerated cost recovery system (MACRS) recovery period for qualified leasehold improvement property is extended to apply to property placed in service before January 1, 2010. The 15-year recovery period for improvements to a restaurant building is also extended to apply to improvements placed in service in 2008 and 2009. A new category of 15-year MACRS property—"qualified retail improvement property"—is created and thus, has a 15-year recovery period.

¶320   **Farm equipment.** Certain machinery or equipment placed in service in a farming business in 2009, the original use of which begins with the taxpayer in 2009, is treated as five-year MACRS property under the general depreciation system and 10 years under the alternative depreciation system.

¶325   **Motorsports facilities.** The seven-year cost recovery period for motorsports entertainment complexes and related ancillary and support facilities has is extended to property placed in service before January 1, 2010.

¶330   **Cellulosic biofuel.** Taxpayers are allowed to immediately write off 50 percent of the cost of facilities that produce cellulosic biofuel in addition to cellulosic ethanol if such facilities are placed in service after October 3, 2008 and before January 1, 2013.

¶335   **Qualified Indian reservation property.** The MACRS recovery period that apply to qualified Indian reservation property is extended for two years through December 31, 2009.

¶340   **Environmental remediation costs.** The election to deduct environmental remediation costs is extended for two years to cover expenditures paid or incurred before January 1, 2010.

¶345, ¶368   **Film and TV productions.** The election to expense the production costs of a qualifying film and television productions is extended for one year through December 31, 2009. The dollar limitation was modified so that the first $15 million ($20 million for productions in low income communities or distressed area or isolated area of distress) of an otherwise qualified film or television production may be treated as an expense in cases where the aggregate cost of the production exceeds the dollar limitation. Also, the manufacturing deduction rules with respect to film and television production are modified. A qualified film includes any copyrights, trademarks, and other intangibles with respect to the film

¶5

¶350 **Refineries.** The election to expense 50 percent of the cost of eligible qualified refinery property is extended for two more years and the expensing deduction is also available with respect to refineries processing liquid fuel directly from shale or tar sands, for property placed in service after October 3, 2008.

¶355 **Percentage depletion limitation.** The temporary suspension of the taxable income limit on the percentage depletion allowance for oil and gas produced from marginal wells is extended to include tax years beginning after December 31, 2008, and before January 1, 2010.

¶360 **Advanced mine safety equipment.** The election to expense 50 percent of the cost of advanced mine safety equipment is extended for one year, for property placed in service on or before December 31, 2009.

¶365 **Tax incentives for D.C. investments.** The District of Columbia enterprise zone provisions and the D.C. homebuyer credit are extended for two years through December 31, 2009.

¶370, ¶375 **Code Sec. 199 deductions.** The special rule which allows Puerto Rico to be considered part of the United States in determining domestic production gross receipts under Code Sec. 199 is extended for two years. The manufacturing deduction for taxpayers having oil related qualified production activities income for tax years beginning after 2009 must be reduced by three percent of the least of: (1) the taxpayer's oil related qualified production activities income for the tax year; (2) the taxpayer's qualified production activities income for the tax year; or (3) taxable income (determined without regard to the manufacturing deduction).

¶380 **Executive compensation limits.** Certain financial institutions that sell troubled assets to the Treasury Department by means of a public auction are restricted for a period of time from deducting more than $500,000 for executive compensation.

BUSINESS CREDITS AND OTHER SPECIAL TAXPAYERS

¶405 **Research credit.** The credit for increasing research activities termination date is extended for two years through December 31, 2009. However, the orphan drug credit whose credit amount calculation is linked to the research credit, will continue to be effective for periods after December 31, 2009.

¶410 **New markets.** The new markets tax credit is extended through 2009, permitting up to $3.5 billion in qualified equity investments for that calendar year.

¶415   **Railroad track maintenance.** The railroad track maintenance credit is extended to expenditures paid or incurred before 2010. Further, if the credit is determined after 2007, it can be used to offset AMT liability.

¶420   **Mine rescue training team.** The mine rescue training team credit is extended through December 31, 2009.

¶425   **Indian employment.** The Indian employment tax credit is extended for two years through December 31, 2009.

¶430   **American Samoa economic development.** A temporary, four-year credit is provided for qualifying possessions corporations operating in American Samoa.

¶435, ¶440, ¶445, ¶450   **Charitable contributions.** The reduction in shareholder's basis in an S corporation because of the S corporation's charitable contribution shall equal the shareholder's pro rata share of the adjusted basis of the contributed property for contributions made before January 1, 2009. Also the enhanced corporate deduction for charitable contributions of computers, book inventory to public schools or the corporate and noncorporate donations of food inventory is extended for two years through December 31, 2009.

¶455   **Employee compensation.** Compensation from nonqualified deferred compensation plans maintained by foreign corporations will generally become taxable, unless the compensation is deferred 12 months or less after the end of the year that the compensation vests.

¶460   **FUTA.** The temporary FUTA surtax of 0.2 percent of taxable wages is extended through December 31, 2009.

¶465   **Qualifying income.** Certain income related to alternative fuels generated by a publicly traded partnership is treated as qualifying income.

¶470, ¶475   **RIC.** The exemption from the 30-percent tax, collected through withholding, on regulated investment company (RIC) dividends, designated as either an interest-related or short-term capital gain dividends, is extended for two years. Also, the favorable estate tax treatment that excludes a portion of the stock in a RIC owned by a decedent who was a nonresident non-U.S. citizen from the estate is extended for two years through December 31, 2009.

¶480   **Exempt organizations.** The application of special rules that permit the exclusion of certain qualifying payments by a controlled entity to a tax-exempt organization from that tax-exempt organization's unrelated business income is extended until December 31, 2009. Also, the application of the 20-percent valuation misstatement penalty is extended.

¶5

¶485   **Fannie Mae or Freddie Mac preferred stock.** Certain financial institutions will receive ordinary income or loss treatment on the sale or exchange of preferred stock in the Federal National Mortgage Association ("Fannie Mae") or the Federal Home Loan Mortgage Corporation ("Freddie Mac").

ENERGY CONSERVATION

¶505   **Residential energy property credit.** This credit is reinstated for qualified energy property placed in service only in 2009. The credit is expanded to include stoves using renewable plant-derived fuel to heat a taxpayer's residence or the water for the residence (qualified biomass fuel property) and asphalt roofs with cooling granules.

¶510   **Residential alternative energy credit.** This credit is extended for eight years, through 2016. The credit is also expanded to include expenditures for qualified small wind energy property and qualified geothermal heat pump property placed in service in 2008 through 2016.

¶515   **Plug-in electric drive motor vehicle credit.** A new credit against tax applies to new qualified plug-in electric drive motor vehicles placed in service in 2009 through 2014 in the amount of $2,500 plus $417 for each kilowatt hour of traction battery capacity in excess of four kilowatt hours.

¶520   **Alternative fuel vehicle refueling property credit.** This credit is extended through December 31, 2010 and, for purposes of the credit, the definition of a clean-burning fuel is modified to include electricity.

¶525   **Renewable electricity production credit.** This credit is extended through December 31, 2009 for qualified wind and refined coal production facilities, and through December 31, 2010 in the case of other sources. The credit is also modified to include facilities that generate electricity from marine renewables.

¶530   **Energy investment credit.** The 30-percent investment tax credit for solar energy property and qualified fuel cell property and the 10-percent investment tax credit for microturbines are extended through 2016. New 10-percent tax credit for combined heat and power systems and geothermal heat pumps and 30-percent tax credit for small wind energy property are added.

¶535   **Energy efficient homes.** The credit available to contractors for the construction or manufacture of a new energy efficient homes is extended through December 31, 2009.

¶5

¶540   **Energy efficient appliance production credit.** The credit allowed for the manufacture of energy efficient dishwashers, clothes washers, and refrigerators is modified by increasing the credit's standards and amounts, and by extending the credit through 2010.

¶545   **Advanced coal project investment credit.** This credit is increased to 30 percent and the IRS is authorized to allocate an additional $1.25 billion in credits to qualified projects that separate and sequester at least 65 percent of total carbon dioxide emissions.

¶550   **Gasification project credit.** This credit is increased to 30 percent and the IRS is authorized to allocate an additional $250 million in credits to qualified projects that separate and sequester at least 75 percent of total carbon dioxide emissions.

¶555   **Carbon dioxide capture credit.** A new tax credit of $10 per metric ton is added for the capture and transport of carbon dioxide from an industrial source for use in enhanced oil recovery or for permanent storage in a geologic formation.

¶560   **Commercial buildings deduction.** The deduction for costs associated with energy efficient commercial building property is extended for five years and expires with respect to property placed in service after December 31, 2013.

¶565   **Qualified reuse and recycling property.** A 50-percent additional depreciation allowance may be claimed on the adjusted basis of qualified reuse and recycling property acquired and placed in service after August 31, 2008.

¶570   **Smart electric meters.** The new law provides a 10-year recovery period and 150-percent declining balance method for any qualified smart electric meter and any qualified smart electric grid system.

¶575   **Carbon audit.** The Secretary of the Treasury is directed to enter into an agreement with the National Academy of Sciences to undertake a comprehensive review of the Internal Revenue Code to identify tax provisions having the largest effects on carbon and other greenhouse gas emissions, and to estimate and report the magnitude of those effects.

DISASTER RELIEF

¶605   **Casualty losses.** Casualty losses attributable to a federally declared disaster occurring after December 31, 2007, and before January 1, 2010, are deductible without regard to whether the losses exceed 10 percent of a taxpayer's adjusted gross income.

¶610   **NOLs.** A special five-year carryback period for net operating losses (NOLs) is created for qualified disaster losses.

¶615, ¶625   **Election to expense.** A taxpayer can elect to expense qualified disaster expenses after 2007, rather than capitalizing them. Also, the maximum allowable section 179 expense deduction and the investment limitation are both increased for qualified section 179 disaster assistance property placed in service after December 31, 2007, with respect to disasters declared after December 31, 2007

¶620   **Bonus depreciation.** An additional 50-percent depreciation allowance can be claimed for real and personal business property that is purchased to rehabilitate or replace similar property that is destroyed or condemned as a result of a presidentially declared disaster.

¶630   **Charitable contributions.** The annual information reporting requirements for tax exempt entities is expanded to cover information regarding disaster relief and certain charitable contributions.

¶635   **Work opportunity tax credit.** The hiring period for eligibility for the work opportunity tax credit applicable to Hurricane Katrina employees is extended through August 25, 2009.

¶640   **GO Zone rehabilitation credit.** The increased percentages of 13 and 26 percent for claiming the rehabilitation credit on qualified rehabilitated buildings and certified historic structures in the Gulf Opportunity (GO) Zone is extended for one year or until December 31, 2009.

¶645   **Mortgage revenue bond.** At the election of the taxpayer, first-time homebuyer and purchase price limitation requirements for mortgage revenue bonds are waived for a principal residence destroyed in a federally declared disaster area.

¶650   **Hurricane Ike disaster area.** The liberalized tax-exempt bond rules and the increase in the low income housing cap currently available to regions of the Gulf coast struck by hurricanes in 2005 are extended to areas hit by Hurricane Ike in 2008.

¶655   **Midwestern disaster area.** Many of the tax benefits extended to the victims of the Katrina, Wilma and Rita hurricanes are modified and available for victims of the storms that hit the midwestern United States in the summer of 2008.

TAX PRACTICE AND PROCEDURE

¶705   **Tax return preparer penalty.** The definition of "unreasonable position" is revised, and the standards for imposition of the tax return preparer penalty are modified.

¶710   **Refund offsets.** If certain requirements are met, the IRS is required to reduce the amount of any overpayment of federal taxes payable to a taxpayer by the amount of the unemployment compensation debts, and pay the amount by which the overpayment is reduced to the state.

¶715   **Terrorist activities.** The IRS has permanent authority to disclose return information to federal law enforcement or intelligence agencies to apprise the agencies of terrorist activities and when requests for return information by such agencies relate to investigating or analyzing terrorist activities.

¶718   **Prisoner return information.** Effective January 1, 2009, disclosure of return information to the head of the Federal Bureau of Prisons, regarding incarcerated individuals that may have filed, or facilitated the filing, of false returns, may be made to the extent necessary to permit effective tax administration.

¶720   **Undercover operations.** The IRS has permanent authority to use the funds received from an undercover operation to pay for additional expenses of further operations.

¶725, ¶735   **Broker report.** Starting in 2011, brokers required to file information returns on covered securities transactions must report the customer's adjusted basis in the security and whether any gain or loss is long- or short-term. Also, every broker that transfers to a broker a "covered security" in the hands of the transferor broker is required to furnish to the transferee broker a written statement that permits the transferee broker to satisfy the basis and holding-period reporting requirements under new Code Sec. 6045(g).

¶730, ¶740   **Basis of securities.** The determination of the basis of securities is to be done on an account by account basis using existing conventions prescribed by IRS regulations. Also, beginning January 1, 2011, the issuer of a specified security is required to file an information return describing any organizational action which affects the basis of the security and the quantitative effect on the basis of the security resulting from such action.

¶745   **Mark-to-market accounting.** The Securities and Exchange Commission (SEC) is given the authority to suspend the application of Statement of Financial Accounting Standards No. 157, Fair Value Measurements (FAS 157) for any issuer of securities or for any class or category of transaction.

¶750   **Exxon Valdez settlement.** Fishermen and other individuals who receive any settlement or judgment-related income in connection with the civil action for damages from the 1989 Exxon Valdez oil spill may use three-year income averaging for reporting such amounts for federal income tax purposes.

¶5

¶755 **Qualified electric utilities.** Deferral treatment for sales or other dispositions of electric transmission property to independent transmission companies is extended for two years to transactions occurring before January 1, 2010, for sales or dispositions by qualified electric utilities.

BONDS, EXCISE TAXES AND OTHER PROVISIONS

¶805 **Clean renewable energy bonds.** The authorization for non-profit electricity producers to issue clean renewable energy bonds (CREBs) is extended for an additional year, through the end of 2009.

¶810 **Qualified energy conservation bonds.** The issuance of $800 million worth of a new type of tax credit bond called qualified energy conservation bonds was authorized.

¶815 **Qualified zone academy bonds.** The authority of State and local governments to issue qualified zone academy bonds is extended for two additional years, through 2009.

¶820 **Qualified green building.** The authority to issue qualified green building and sustainable design project bonds is extended through September 30, 2012, and the special treatment for current refunding bonds is extended to bonds issued before October 1, 2012.

¶825 **Alternative fuel credits.** The income tax credits, excise tax credits and payment provisions for biodiesel, agri-biodiesel and renewable diesel have been extended through December 31, 2009.

¶830 **Tax on rum.** The $13.25 per proof gallon cover over amount to Puerto Rico and the Virgin Islands for rum brought into the United States is extended for two more years, through December 31, 2009.

¶835 **Aviation excise taxes.** Excise taxes on aviation fuel taxes, airline passenger tickets, and air cargo are extended through March 31, 2009.

¶840 **Wooden arrows.** Shafts used in wooden arrows designed for use by children are now exempt from the Code Sec. 4161(b)(2) excise tax.

¶845 **Heavy truck and trailer tax.** The cost of idling reduction devices such as auxiliary power units, which are designed to eliminate the need for truck engine idling at vehicle rest stops or other temporary parking locations are now exempted from the 12-percent excise tax on heavy trucks and trailers.

¶850   **Excise tax on coal.** The current rates for the excise tax on coal taken from U.S. mines are extended until the earlier of December 31, 2018, or the first December 31 after 2007 of which the Black Lung Disability Trust Fund has repaid, with interest, all amounts borrowed from the General Fund of the Treasury.

¶855   **Oil Spill Fund.** The Oil Spill Liability Trust Fund Tax is extended through December 31, 2017, and increased to 8 cents per barrel for crude oil receive or petroleum products entering the United States through 2016 and 9 cents per barrel for crude oil receive or petroleum products entering the United States in 2017.

¶860, ¶863   **Subpart F exceptions.** The temporary exceptions from subpart F income for certain insurance and insurance investment income and for so-called active financing income are extended through 2009.

¶865   **CFCs.** The look-through rule that applies to dividend, interest, rent and royalty payments received by a controlled foreign corporation from a related corporation is extended for one year.

¶870   **RICs.** The term qualified investment entity will continue to include regulated investment companies (RICs) that are U.S. real property holding companies through December 31, 2009.

¶875   **Foreign tax credit limitations.** The separate foreign tax credit limitations for foreign oil and gas extraction income and foreign oil related income have been eliminated. Both are now combined into one foreign oil basket to which the existing foreign oil and gas extraction income limitation applies.

¶880   **Parity in mental health.** Financial requirements and treatment limitations are added to the existing mental health parity provisions. Also, substance use disorder is added to the coverage of the parity provisions.

¶885   **Health insurance coverage for students.** Group health insurance plans must continue coverage, up to one year, for full-time post secondary students that suffer a serious illness requiring a medical leave that causes them to lose full-time student status.

Taxpayers Affected

1

TAX-EXEMPT ORGANIZATIONS AND GOVERN-MENT ENTITIES

STATE TAX CONSEQUENCES

EMERGENCY ECONOMIC STABILIZATION ACT OF 2008

¶101 Overview

Faced with an almost unprecedented financial crisis, but a controversial rescue plan, Congress decided to add a plethora of tax incentives to promote passage of the Emergency Economic Stabilization Act of 2008 (P.L. 110-343). Spurred by the Senate, the Emergency Economic Act of 2008 includes relief from the alternative minimum tax, tax extenders favored by businesses and individuals, and special provisions for disaster victims.

On the other hand, the legislation includes serious limitations on compensation for executives of financial institutions covered by the government rescue program and on payments from certain offshore deferred compensation plans. Offsets include basis reporting requirements by brokers for publicly traded securities and tighter rules for oil and gas companies paying taxes on overseas income.

INDIVIDUALS

¶103 Overall Effect on Individuals

Many categories of individual taxpayers find themselves the beneficiary or the target of various provisions in the Emergency Economic Stabilization Act of 2008 (P.L. 110-343). From the broadest categories (taxpayers who itemize (¶240) and those who do not (¶235)) to the thinnest of niches (commuters who bike to work (¶230), the estates of nonresident/noncitizens (¶475), and victims of the Exxon Valdez oil spill (¶750)), the Emergency Economic Act of 2008 has a long reach.

Special attention was paid to taxpayers faced with the looming specter of the alternative minimum tax (¶205, ¶210, and ¶215). Disaster victims are another category of taxpayer who receive considerable benefit from the new law (¶605, ¶650, and ¶655). The legislation contains good news for parents entitled to the refundable child tax credit (¶255), IRA owners age 70½ or older wishing to make a charitable contribution (¶225), homeowners who have had their mortgage indebtedness discharged (¶220), and those claiming certain residential energy credits (¶505 and ¶510). Also happy will be those persons paying qualified tuition and related expenses (¶245) and educators who purchase classroom supplies (¶250).

Investors in tax-exempt bonds were not forgotten (¶805, ¶810, ¶815, and ¶820) nor were those who are interested in receiving a tax benefit for the purchase of an alternative fuel vehicle (¶515) or installing an alternative fuel vehicle refueling station (¶520).

Those who may not be so pleased with the Emergency Economic Act of 2008, will be certain executives of entities participating in the government rescue plan for financial institutions (¶380) and those receiving payments from certain offshore deferred compensation plans (¶455). Owners of publicly traded securities may or may not be glad to hear of new basis reporting requirements that will be imposed on their broker dealers (¶725, ¶730, ¶735, and ¶740).

¶105 Effect on Individuals Who Do Not Itemize

Additional standard deduction.—The Emergency Economic Stabilization Act of 2008 (P.L. 110-343) extends a provision allowing an additional standard deduction for real property taxes paid by taxpayers who do not itemize that was enacted earlier this year by the Housing Assistance Tax Act of 2008 (P.L. 110-289) (¶235). The amount of the deduction is the lesser of the amount allowable as a deduction for state and local real property taxes, or $500 ($1,000 for married persons filing a joint return). The provision was set to expire at the end of 2008, but is now extended through 2009. For tax years beginning after December 31, 2007, an additional standard deduction is provided for certain disaster losses (¶605).

¶106 Effect on Individuals Who Itemize

Deduction for state and local sales taxes.—Further extending a provision originally enacted as part of the American Jobs Creation Act of 2004 (P.L. 108-357), and extended through 2007 by the Tax Relief and Health Care Act of 2006 (P.L. 109-432), the Emergency Economic Stabilization Act of 2008 (P.L. 110-343) allows individual taxpayers to elect to take an itemized deduction for state and local general sales taxes instead of the itemized deduction for state and local income taxes (¶240). Extremely popular in states without an income tax, such as Texas and Florida, the new law extends the provision through 2009.

¶107 Effect on Parents and Students

Refundable child credit modified.—The Emergency Economic Stabilization Act of 2008 (P.L. 110-343) lowers the 2008 earned income threshold for purposes of the refundable child tax credit to $8,500 (¶255). Without this amendment, the threshold would have been $12,050. Accordingly, for 2008, if the total amount of a taxpayer's allowable child tax credit exceeds the taxpayer's total tax liability, the taxpayer is eligible for a credit equal to 15 percent of the taxpayer's earned income in excess of $8,500, up to the per child credit amount.

Definition of qualifying child clarified.—The Emergency Economic Act of 2008 adds two new elements to the definition of a qualifying child (¶260). First, the qualifying child must be younger than the taxpayer. Second, with respect to joint returns, a qualifying child cannot file a joint return with a spouse for any tax year beginning during the calendar year in which the taxpayer's tax year begins. However, this second element does not apply if the qualifying child is filing a return solely to obtain a refund. Further clarifications are added to the tiebreaker rules that apply when a single individual is a qualifying child for more than one taxpayer. In addition, for purposes of the child tax credit, a qualifying child must also be the taxpayer's dependent.

Tuition deduction extended.—The above-the-line deduction (Code Sec. 222) for qualified tuition and related expenses is extended through 2009 (¶245). The maximum deduction is $4,000 for taxpayers with an adjusted gross income (AGI) of $65,000 ($130,000 for married persons filing jointly) or below, and $2,000 for taxpayers with an AGI of $80,000 ($160,000 for married persons filing jointly) or less. Taxpayers whose AGI exceeds those amounts are not entitled to a deduction.

Health insurance protection for seriously ill dependent students.—In a separate measure, Michelle's Law (H.R. 2851), Congress added new Code Sec. 9813 to ensure that dependent students who are forced to take a medically necessary leave of absence from their studies do not lose health insurance coverage (¶885). Inspired by the death of a young college student, the new law is intended to apply to all health insurance products whether they were sold to individuals or offered as a work place benefit.

¶108 Effect on Home Buyers and Owners

Special treatment for mortgage discharge.—The Emergency Economic Stabilization Act of 2008 (P.L. 110-343) recognizes the plight of financially strapped homeowners by extending through 2012 a provision allowing that forgiveness of "qualified principal residence indebtedness" will not be included in gross income in a mortgage discharge situation (¶220). The exclusion from gross income will only apply to so much of the amount discharged that exceeds the portion of the debt that is not qualified principal residence indebtedness.

Additonal standard deduction.—The Emergency Economic Act of 2008 also extends through 2009 a provision allowing an additional standard deduction for real property taxes paid by taxpayers who do not itemize (¶235). The amount of the deduction is the lesser of the amount allowable as a deduction for state and local real property taxes, or $500 ($1,000 for married persons filing a joint return).

Energy credits extended.—Homeowners will also be pleased to hear that the credit for residential energy property (Code Sec. 25C) has been reinstated for property placed in service in 2009, however, not for 2008 (¶505). The Code Sec. 25D residential energy efficient property credit for solar electric and solar water heating property is extended through December 31, 2016, and the maximum annual credit limit for qualified solar electric property expenditures has been eliminated after 2008 (¶510). The new law also adds incentives for residential small wind investment and geothermal heat pumps and authorizes taxpayers to use the credit to offset the alternative minimum tax.

First-time home buyers in D.C.—First-time home buyers purchasing in the District of Columbia will benefit from the extension through 2009 of a provision granting them a $5,000 tax credit (¶365).

¶109 Effect on Individuals with Alternative Minimum Taxable Income

AMT relief granted.—In one of the more expensive provisions of the Emergency Economic Stabilization Act of 2008 (P.L. 110-343), the increases in the individual exemption amounts for purposes of alternative minimum tax (AMT) are extended through 2008 (¶205). The exemption amounts are $69,950 for married persons filing a joint return, $46,200 for unmarried individuals, and $34,975 for married persons filing separately.

In addition, nonrefundable personal tax credits are again allowed to the full extent of an individual's regular tax and AMT liability for 2008 (¶210). Also extended and modified to provide quicker relief is a more targeted provision, aimed primarily at taxpayers who exercised incentive stock options at a profit and sold the stock later at a time when the stock price had declined significantly, thus resulting in "phantom" income (¶215).

¶110 Effect on Disaster Victims

Disaster victims generally.—Victims of several recent disasters will receive attention from the new legislation, including victims of federally declared disasters generally. The Emergency Economic Stabilization Act of 2008 (P.L. 110-343) loosens the rules covering casualty losses (¶605) and permits states to issue tax-exempt mortgage revenue bonds to finance low-interest loans to taxpayers for the repair or reconstruction of their homes (¶645).

Midwest storm victims.—Temporary relief is provided for Midwest storm victims, including residents of Arkansas, Illinois, Indiana, Iowa, Kansas, Michigan, Minnesota, Missouri, Nebraska, and Wisconsin (¶655). This temporary relief includes waiver of the 10-percent additional tax on early distributions from a retirement account, liberalized withdrawal and loan rules governing such accounts, as well as suspension of the casualty loss limitations and an additional personal exemption for persons who provide housing for dislocated storm victims.

Additional forms of temporary relief include an employee retention credit, expansion of the Hope Scholarship and Lifetime Learning Credit, and increased flexibility for the Treasury Department to ensure that taxpayers do not lose deductions, tax credits, or filing status as a result of a dislocation caused by these events. Charitable giving incentives, such as the deductibility limits on charitable contributions and the mileage rate for charitable use of a vehicle, are also liberalized. Midwest disaster victims will also be eligible for low-interest loans financed by state-issued tax-exempt mortgage revenue bonds.

Hurricane Ike victims.—The Emergency Economic Act of 2008 also provides tax-exempt bond financing and low-income housing relief for Hurricane Ike victims (¶650).

Exxon Valdez victims.—Victims of the Exxon Valdez oil spill are also the recipients of tax relief in that they will be allowed three years to income average damages recovered as a result of a settlement or judgment from litigation stemming from the incident (¶750). The provision also allows qualifying victims to contribute funds from such recovery to retirement accounts without having the amounts treated as taxable.

¶111 Effect on Executives

Compensation and golden parachutes limited.—CEOs, CFOs, and certain other executives of companies participating in the Troubled Assets Relief Program (TARP) will be impacted by several provisions relating to executive compensation (¶380). For example, in cases where the Treasury has purchased assets directly, the participating entity must comply with rules that limit compensation to such executives and allow a "claw back" provision in order that the entity can recover a bonus or incentive paid to a senior executive officer that was based on statements of earnings, gains, or other criteria that are later proven to be materially inaccurate. So-called golden parachute payments to senior executive officers of these entities will also be prohibited during the period the Treasury holds an equity or debt position in the entity. In cases where the Treasury has purchased assets at auction, a participating entity that has sold more than $300 million in assets is subject to additional limits, including a 20-percent excise tax on golden parachute payments. In addition, the deductibility of compensation to such executives will be limited to $500,000. The TARP authorities period begins October 3, 2008, and extends through 2009.

Other provisions effecting executive compensation include the treatment of certain offshore deferred compensation plans (¶455). This provision taxes individuals on a current basis for deferred compensation received from a "tax indifferent party," such as an offshore corporation that operates in a low or no-tax jurisdiction.

¶112 Effect on Owners of Publicly Traded Securities

Basis reporting requirements.—Although primary responsibility for the reporting of basis on transactions involving publicly traded securities will now fall on the broker dealer community under a new provision added by the Emergency Economic Stabilization Act of 2008 (P.L. 110-343), the result will certainly have an impact on sellers (¶725, ¶730, ¶735, and ¶740). Broker reporting of basis is set to begin in 2011.

¶113 Effect on IRA and Roth IRA Owners

Charitable contributions restored.—The Emergency Economic Stabilization Act of 2008 (P.L. 110-343) restores a popular provision that allows IRA and Roth IRA owners age 70½ and older to make a tax-free charitable contribution of up to $100,000 directly from their IRA (¶225). Qualified charitable distributions are counted toward the IRA owner's required minimum distribution amount, but are not included in the owner's charitable deduction amount for the year because they are not includible in gross income. This provision had expired at the end of 2007, but is now extended through 2009.

¶114 Effect on Primary and Secondary School Educators

Above-the-line deduction extended.—Extended through 2009 is an above-the-line deduction of up to $250 for classroom supplies purchased by teachers, counselors, principals, and classroom aides who work at least 900 hours during the school year (¶250).

¶115 Effect on Tax-Exempt Bond Investors

Investors in tax-exempt bonds will note several changes made by the Emergency Economic Stabilization Act of 2008 (P.L. 110-343). For one, the deadline for issuing clean renewable energy bonds under Code Sec. 54 is extended for one year, to the end of 2009 (¶805). A new category of tax credit bonds, called clean renewable energy bonds, is authorized under new Code Sec. 54C. A national limitation of $800 million on the new bonds will be allocated by the IRS among non-profit electricity generating companies seeking to finance capital investments in clean renewable energy facilities.

A new category of tax credit bonds, qualified energy conservation bonds, is authorized (¶810). A national limitation of $800 million on the new bonds will be allocated by the IRS to the states and large local communities in proportion to their populations. The bond proceeds must be used for qualified conservation purposes.

The qualified zone academy bond program has been extended and modified (¶815). The new law authorizes the issuance of up to $400 million of such bonds through 2009. In addition, the issuance of qualified green building and sustainable design project bonds is extended through September 30, 2012, and the special treatment for current refunding bonds is extended to bonds issued before October 1, 2012 (¶820).

Other changes include waiver of mortgage revenue bond requirements for federally declared disaster areas (¶645) and the allowance of tax-exempt bond financing and low-income housing relief for Hurricane Ike victims (¶650).

¶117 Effect on Estates of Nonresident/Noncitizens

RIC break continued.—Estates of nonresident/noncitizens will benefit from the extension of a provision from the American Jobs Creation Act of 2004 (P.L. 108-357) that treats a portion of stock in a regulated investment company (RIC) as property without the United States and, thus, not includible in the deceased shareholder's gross estate for federal estate tax purposes (¶475). The provision is extended through 2009.

¶118 Effect on Owners of Alternative Powered Vehicles

Credits improved.—With cars such as the Chevy Volt and others coming to market soon, buyers will benefit from a new credit for vehicles using plug-in electric drive motors (¶515). Also, the nonbusiness portion of the new credit will be treated as a personal credit so that the credit may be used to offset the alternative minimum tax.

Extended and modified is a provision that allows a credit for the residential installation of alternative fuel vehicle refueling property (¶520).

¶119 Effect on Bicycle Commuters

Commuters who ride their bicycles to and from work will be entitled to receive a transportation fringe benefit under Code Sec. 132(f) of up to $20 per month (¶230).

¶121 Effect on Individuals Receiving Mental Health Benefits

Effective January 1, 2009, the Emergency Economic Stabilization Act of 2008 (P.L. 110-343) will require that private insurance plans offering mental health benefits as part of the coverage must offer such benefits that are equivalent to other health benefits (¶880).

BUSINESSES

¶131 Effect on Business Generally

The Emergency Economic Stabilization Act of 2008 (P.L. 110-343) is most particularly focused on the financial industry. The many tax provisions inserted into the legislation, particularly the expired tax provisions and the energy provisions, will have a wide ranging impact on many businesses and industry sectors.

The two-year extension of the research credit will be good news to many businesses, but it is not the permanent extension many had hoped for (¶405). The legislation also terminates the alternative incremental credit and modifies the alternative simplified credit. The New Markets Tax Credit is extended (¶410). Also extended and enhanced is the 15-year amortization of leasehold improvements, retail and restaurant property (¶305, ¶310, and ¶315). The expensing of environmental remediation costs is extended for two years (¶340).

In the energy area, the Code Sec. 48 Energy Credit has added combined heat and power system property, increased the credit limit for fuel cell property, removes the prohibition on taking into account public utility property, and allows the credit for AMT purposes (¶530). The legislation provides for a new Code Sec. 48Q Carbon Dioxide Sequestration Credit (¶555). The deduction for energy-efficient commercial buildings is extended through 2013 (¶560). Accelerated depreciation is provided for smart meters and smart grid systems (¶570). Special 50-percent first-year bonus depreciation is provided for reuse and recycling property (¶565). A new credit under Code Sec. 30D is created for qualified plug-in electric drive motor vehicles (¶515).

Important for businesses with health insurance plans is the enactment of a mental health parity requirement (¶880). Transportation fringe benefits are expanded to cover bicycle commuters (¶230). In addition, the imposition of the 0.2 percent temporary Federal Unemployment Tax Act (FUTA) surtax has been extended for one year (¶460).

¶133 Effect on Financial Services Industry

Many of the non-tax provisions of the legislation deal with the government purchase, directly or through auction, of the assets of banks and other financial institutions with mortgage securities and similar assets that have become difficult to value. Non-tax provisions also address the use of mark-to-market accounting. Under the tax provisions, companies participating significantly in the sale of assets to the government will find a new $500,000 limit on the compensation of key executives whose companies sell more than $300 million in assets through government-sponsored auctions (¶380). Companies selling assets directly to the government may also be subject to specially-negotiated limits on executive compensation and claw-backs of remuneration paid based on erroneous financial statements.

Banks and other financial institutions that had invested in Fannie Mae and Freddie Mac in 2008 will be permitted to treat losses on those investments as ordinary losses rather than capital losses (¶485).

¶134 Effect on Securities Brokers

One of the revenue offsets included in the tax portion of the legislation would require broker reporting of basis starting in 2011 (¶725). The new law addresses the determination of basis in securities (¶730), information reporting for transfers of securities (¶735), and returns required for actions affecting basis (¶740).

¶135 Effect on Tax Preparers

Standard lowered.—Effectively providing a "redo" of a provision that has caused controversy in the tax preparer community, the Emergency Economic Stabilization Act of 2008 (P.L. 110-343), modifies the standards for imposition of the tax return preparer penalty for understatement of taxpayer liability (¶705). The new law reduces the preparer standard for undisclosed positions to "substantial authority." The preparer standard for disclosed positions is now "reasonable basis." For listed transactions and reportable transactions with significant avoidance or evasion purposes, a tax return preparer is still required to have a reasonable belief that such a transaction was more likely than not to be sustained on the merits. The provision is effective for returns prepared after May 25, 2007.

¶136 Effect on Commercial Fisherman

Income averaging for oil spill damages.—Commercial fisherman and other victims of the Exxon Valdez oil spill will be allowed three years to income average damages recovered as a result of a settlement or judgment from litigation stemming from the incident (¶750). The provision also allows qualifying victims to contribute funds from such recovery to retirement accounts without having the amounts treated as taxable.

¶137 Effect on Farmers and Ranchers

Five-year property treatment.—Machinery or equipment used in a farming business that is placed in service in 2009 will be treated as five-year property for purposes of claiming Modified Accelerated Cost Recovery System depreciation (¶320).

Food donation limit lifted temporarily.—The 10-percent limitation applicable to qualified donations of food inventory is suspended for contributions by farmers and ranchers on or after October 3, 2008, but before January 1, 2009 (¶445).

¶138 Effect on Regulated Investment Companies

Provisions with respect to interest-related dividends and short-term capital gains dividends of regulated investment companies are extended for two years (¶470). The treatment of stock in a regulated investment company for purposes of determining estates of nonresidents who are not citizens is extended for two years (¶475). The treatment of a regulated investment company investing in real estate as a qualified investment entity with respect to dispositions of investments in U.S. real property is extended for two years (¶870).

¶139 Effect on Insurance Industry

The exempt insurance income provision under the Subpart F exception for active financing income is extended for one year (¶860).

¶141 Effect on Partnerships

The legislation explains the ability of a financial institution that is a partner in a partnership that invested in Fannie Mae or Freddie Mac to treat losses on those investments as an ordinary loss (¶485).

For purposes of determining the current taxation of nonqualified deferred compensation from tax indifferent parties, a partnership is a nonqualified entity unless substantially all of its income is allocated to persons other than foreign persons with respect to whom such income is not subject to a comprehensive foreign income tax, and organizations exempt from U.S. income tax (¶455).

The legislation applies the Code Sec. 48A Qualifying Advanced Coal Project Credit to research partnerships (¶545).

The Code Sec. 199 domestic production activities deduction rules for W-2 wages are modified to provide a special rule for qualified films and to clarify when a partnership or partner will be considered to be directly involved in a film (¶368).

The temporary suspension of charitable contribution limits with respect to Midwest disaster relief is to be made separately by each partner (¶655).

Two provisions address modifications to the definition of qualifying income of publicly-traded partnerships. One includes industrial source carbon dioxide as qualifying income. The other includes certain income and gains with respect to alcohol fuels and mixtures and alternative fuels and mixtures as qualifying income (¶465).

¶142 Effect on C Corporations

The enhanced deduction for contributions of qualified computer equipment by C corporations to educational institutions has been extended for two years (¶440).

¶138

Similarly, the enhanced deduction for contributions of book inventory to schools has been extended (¶450).

¶143 Effect on S Corporations

The new requirements for broker reporting of basis specify that S Corporations are to be treated the same as partnerships (¶725).

The basis adjustment to stock of S Corporations making charitable contributions of property is extended for two years (¶435).

The Code Sec. 199 domestic production activities deduction rules for W-2 wages are modified to provide a special rule for qualified films and to clarify when an S Corporation or S Corporation shareholder will be considered to be directly involved in a film (¶368).

The temporary suspension of charitable contribution limits with respect to Midwest disaster relief is to be made separately by each S Corporation shareholder (¶655).

¶145 Effect on International Business

Nonqualified deferred compensation received from foreign entities and other tax indifferent parties is includible in gross income when there is no substantial risk of forfeiture of the rights to such compensation (¶455). The look-through rule for related controlled foreign corporations is extended for one year (¶865). The treatment of a regulated investment company investing in real estate as a qualified investment entity with respect to dispositions of investments is U. S. real property is extended for two years (¶870). Subpart F exceptions for active financing income involving exempt insurance income and treatment as foreign personal holding company income are extended for one year (¶860). The different treatment of foreign oil and gas extraction income and foreign oil related income under the foreign tax credit is eliminated (¶875).

¶147 Effect on Energy Industry

The extension and expansion of the Code Sec. 45 Credit for Electricity Produced from Renewable Resources will have a wide-ranging impact on the energy industry (¶525). Similarly, the Code Sec. 48 Energy Credit adds combined heat and power system property, small wind turbines, and geothermal heat pumps; increased the credit limit for fuel cell property; removes the prohibition on taking into account public utility property; and allows the credit for AMT purposes (¶530).

The legislation includes an expansion and modification of the Code Sec. 48A Qualifying Advanced Coal Project Credit and the Code Sec. 48B Qualifying Gasification Project Credit (¶545 and ¶550).

The alcohol fuels credit would be limited to U.S. production (¶825).

¶149　Effect on Oil and Gas Producers

The new law limits the Code Sec. 199 deduction for domestic production activities for oil and gas companies to six percent (¶375). It also extends the suspension of the taxable income limit on percentage depletion for oil and natural gas produced from marginal properties through 2008 (¶355). The different treatment of foreign oil and gas extraction income and foreign oil related income under the foreign tax credit is eliminated (¶875). There is also an increase in and extension of the oil spill liability trust fund tax and a change in the termination provision (¶855).

¶151　Effect on Refiners

The election to expense certain refineries is extended for two years and refineries covered are expanded to include those processing fuels from shale and tar sands (¶350). There is also an increase in and extension of the oil spill liability trust fund tax and a change in the termination provision (¶855).

¶153　Effect on Alternative Fuels

The Code Sec. 45 credit for electricity produced from certain alternative resources is modified to address the expansion of biomass facilities (¶525).

The new law includes cellulosic biofuels in place of cellulosic biomass ethanol under the bonus depreciation for biomass ethanol plant property in Code Sec. 168(l) (¶330). The Code Sec. 40A credits for biodiesel and renewable diesel are increased, and agri-biodiesel is defined to include camelina (¶825). The biodiesel fuels and alternative fuels credit are also limited to U.S. production (¶825).

The alternative fuels credit under Code Sec. 6426 is extended and modified to add compressed or liquefied biomass gas (¶825).

¶155　Effect on Mining Industry

The mine rescue team training credit is extended (¶420). The election to expense mine safety equipment is also extended (¶360). An additional authorization is made for a transfer of funds to the Abandoned Mine Reclamation Fund.

¶157　Effect on Coal Industry

The Code Sec. 45 credit for electricity produced from certain renewable resources is extended and the definition of a refined coal facility is modified (¶525). The legislation expands and modifies the Code Sec. 48A Qualifying Advanced Coal Project Credit (¶545). It also expands and modifies the Code Sec. 48B Qualifying Gasification Project Credit (¶550). The legislation provides for a new Code Sec. 45Q Carbon

Dioxide Sequestration Credit (¶555). The increase in the coal excise tax is extended (¶850). A refund of tax is provided to certain producers and exporters of coal (¶850).

¶159 Effect on Electric Utilities

The Code Sec. 45 credit for electricity produced from certain renewable resources is extended to qualified electric utilities (¶525).

¶161 Effect on Renewable Energy Facilities

The Code Sec. 45 credit for electricity produced from certain renewable resources is extended for two years for certain renewable energy facilities (¶525).

¶163 Effect on Wind Energy Industry

The Code Sec. 45 credit for electricity produced from certain renewable resources is extended for one year for wind facilities (¶525). The Code Sec. 48 Energy Credit is expanded to include small wind turbines (¶530). The Code Sec. 25D residential alternative energy credit was also expanded to include small wind turbines (¶510).

¶165 Effect on Trash Industry

The Code Sec. 45 credit for electricity produced from certain renewable resources is clarified with respect to its application to trash facilities (¶525).

¶167 Effect on Hydropower Industry

The Code Sec. 45 credit for electricity produced from certain renewable resources is expanded to apply to marine and hydrokinetic renewables (¶525). The definition of a nonhydroelectric dam is also modified (¶525).

¶169 Effect on Businesses in Disaster Areas

The Work Opportunity Tax Credit for Katrina employees is extended (¶635).

The increased rehabilitation credit for structures in the Gulf Opportunity Zone is extended (¶640).

As was previously done with areas in Kansas damaged by the 2007 tornadoes and storms, Hurricane Katrina-like tax relief has been extended to areas of the Midwest damaged in 2008 by storms, tornadoes and flooding. These relate to tax-exempt bond financing and the low-income housing credit, expensing demolition and clean-up costs, expensing environmental remediation costs, increasing the rehabilitation credit, treatment of net operating losses, housing tax benefits, employee retention credit, credit to holders of tax credit bonds, and special rules for mortgage revenue bonds (¶655).

More limited relief was specifically provided for areas damaged by Hurricane Ike. These include temporary tax-exempt bond financing and low-income housing tax relief (¶650).

In a move to address disaster relief more prospectively, the legislation provides tax relief for disasters, other than the Midwest areas already provided for, from 2008 through 2009 (¶605), to include increased expensing for qualified disaster expenses (¶615), special depreciation for qualified disaster property (¶620), enhanced net operating loss carrybacks (¶610), and waiver of certain mortgage revenue bond requirements (¶645).

¶171 Effect on Automobile Industry

A new credit under Code Sec. 30D is created for qualified plug-in electric drive motor vehicles (¶515).

¶172 Effect on Trucking Industry

An exemption from the heavy truck excise tax is provided for idling reduction units and advanced insulation (¶845).

¶173 Effect on Bicycle Industry

Transportation fringe benefits are expanded to include bicycle commuters (¶230).

¶174 Effect on Railroad Industry

The railroad track maintenance credit is extended for two years and allowed under the alternative minimum tax (¶415).

¶175 Effect on Airline Industry

In separate legislation enacted by Congress, aviation excise taxes were extended (¶835).

¶176   Effect on Real Estate Industry

The energy efficient commercial buildings deduction is extended through 2013 (¶560). Exempt Facility Bonds for qualified green buildings and sustainable design projects are extended to September 30, 2012 (¶820). The treatment of a regulated investment company investing in real estate as a qualified investment entity with respect to dispositions of investments in U. S. real property is extended for two years (¶870). Accelerated depreciation is provided for smart meters and smart grid systems (¶570). Special 50 percent first-year bonus depreciation is provided for reuse and recycling property (¶565).

¶177   Effect on Real Estate Lessees

The 15-year amortization of leasehold improvements has been extended for two years (¶305).

¶178   Effect on Steel Industry

The Code Sec. 45 credit for electricity produced from certain renewable resources is modified to bring within the definition of refined coal certain steel industry fuel (¶525).

¶179   Effect on Appliance Industry

The Code Sec. 45M Energy Efficient Appliance Credit is modified to provide new requirements for dishwashers, clothes washers, and refrigerators (¶540).

¶180   Effect of Motorsport Racing Tracks

The seven-year recovery period for motorsports racing tack facilities is extended for two years (¶325).

¶181   Effect on Restaurant, Food, and Liquor Industries

The 15-year amortization of restaurant improvements has been extended for two years (¶310).

The enhanced deduction for the charitable contribution of food inventory is extended for two years (¶445).

The increase in the limit on cover over of the rum excise tax to Puerto Rico and the Virgin Islands has been extended for two years (¶830).

¶182 Effect on Computer Industry

The enhanced deduction for contributions by C corporations to educational institutions of qualified computer equipment has been extended for two years (¶440).

¶184 Effect on Publishing Industry

The enhanced deduction for the charitable contribution by C corporations to public schools of book inventory is extended for two years (¶450).

¶185 Effect on Retailers

A qualified interior improvement to a building used for retailing and placed in service in 2009 may be depreciated over 15 years (¶315).

¶186 Effect on Film and Television Industry

The legislation provides for an extension and modification of the expensing rules for qualified film and television productions (¶345). The Code Sec. 199 domestic production activities deduction rules for W-2 wages are modified to provide a special rule for qualified films and to clarify when a partnership or S Corporation will be considered to be directly involved in a film (¶368).

¶187 Effect on Arrow Industry

An exemption is provided from the excise tax on arrows for certain toy wooden arrows (¶840).

¶189 Effect on Businesses in the District of Columbia

Tax incentives for investment in the District of Columbia have been extended for two years (¶365).

¶190 Effect on Businesses in Puerto Rico

The Code Sec. 199 domestic production activities deduction with respect to income attributable to domestic production activities in Puerto Rico has been extended for two years (¶370). Also, the increase in the limit on cover over of the rum excise tax to Puerto Rico has been extended for two years (¶830).

¶191 Effect on Businesses in the Virgin Islands

The increase in the limit on cover over of the rum excise tax to the Virgin Islands has been extended for two years (¶830).

¶192 Effect on Businesses in American Samoa

The economic development credit for American Samoa has been extended for two years (¶430).

TAX-EXEMPT ORGANIZATIONS AND GOVERNMENT ENTITIES

¶193 Effect on State and Local Government Entities

New and expanded bond programs.—A new category of tax credit bonds, qualified energy conservation bonds, is authorized (¶810). A national limitation of $800 million on the new bonds will be allocated by the IRS to the states and large local communities in proportion to their populations. The bond proceeds must be used for qualified conservation purposes.

The deadline for issuing clean renewable energy bonds under Code Sec. 54 is extended for one year, to the end of 2009 (¶805). A new category of tax credit bonds, called clean renewable energy bonds, is authorized under new Code Sec. 54C. A national limitation of $800 million on the new bonds will be allocated by the IRS among non-profit electricity generating companies seeking to finance capital investments in clean renewable energy facilities.

The qualified zone academy bond program has been extended and modified (¶815). The new law authorizes the issuance of up to $400 million of such bonds through 2009. In addition, the issuance of qualified green building and sustainable design project bonds is extended through September 30, 2012, and the ability to issue current refunding bonds is extended to October 1, 2012 (¶820).

¶194 Effect on Non-Profit Electricity Generating Companies

A new category of tax credit bonds, called clean renewable energy bonds, is authorized under new Code Sec. 54C. A national limitation of $800 million on the new bonds will be allocated by the IRS among non-profit electricity generating companies seeking to finance capital investments in clean renewable energy facilities (¶805).

¶195 Effect on Controlling Organizations

A favorable provision of the Pension Protection Act of 2006 (P.L. 109-280) dealing with the treatment of payments to controlling organizations is extended through 2009 (¶480). Under that provision, certain qualifying payments by a controlled entity are excluded from the recipient tax-exempt organization's unrelated business taxable income. Also, the 20-percent valuation misstatement penalty is retained.

¶196 Effect on Indian Tribal Governments and Reservations

Modified Accelerated Cost Recovery System (MACRS) recovery periods that apply to qualified Indian reservation property have been extended for two years through December 31, 2009 (¶335).

Special rules govern qualified energy conservation bonds issued by Indian tribal governments (¶810).

The Indian employment tax credit is extended for two years through December 31, 2009 (¶425).

¶197 Effect on the IRS

Terrorist disclosure and undercover provisions permanent.—The authority of the IRS to disclose return information concerning alleged terrorist activities has been made permanent (¶715) as has the IRS's authority to return funds collected through undercover operations in order to offset the costs of such operations (¶720). Returns of prison inmates involved in filing false tax returns may also be disclosed to the head of the Federal Bureau of Prisons, beginning in 2009 (¶718).

Under another provision, the IRS is required to offset overpayments of federal taxes by the amount of unemployment compensation debts resulting from fraud (¶710).

¶198 Effect on the National Academy of Sciences

Carbon audit authorized.—The National Academy of Sciences is directed to undertake a comprehensive review of the Internal Revenue Code with the intent of identifying those provisions that have the greatest impact on carbon and other green house emissions (¶575).

STATE TAX CONSEQUENCES

¶199 Effect on State Tax Law

The provisions included in the Emergency Economic Stabilization Act of 2008 (P.L. 110-343) may have state tax consequences for taxpayers, based on the applicable state law and whether the state law conforms to the Internal Revenue Code (Code), as of a particular date. The state tax consequences of a number of these provisions are summarized, below.

AMT relief

The majority of states do not impose an alternative minimum tax (AMT). Most of the states that impose an AMT based on, or paralleling federal AMT provisions for personal income tax purposes (including California and New York) provide their own exemption amounts. Therefore, the increase in the federal AMT exemption amounts would have no state tax impact (¶205).

Additionally, because the states generally do not adopt federal credits, the increase in the AMT refundable credit amount and the use of nonrefundable personal credits against the AMT would have no impact on state taxation (¶210).

Exclusion of cancellation of debt income for discharged debt on principal residence

The extension through 2012 of the exclusion of cancellation of debt income for discharged debt on a principal residence will impact states that conform to Code Sec. 108, but that have a conformity date that would not cover this extension. States like California, which conforms to the Code, as amended on January 1, 2005, and Kentucky, which conforms to the Code, as amended January 1, 2007, never conformed to the exclusion. Most states conform but have conformity dates that would not incorporate the extension. However, because the exclusion was not due to expire until 2010, most states that update their conformity dates on an annual basis will conform during their next legislative sessions (¶220).

Tax-free distributions from IRAs for charitable purposes

Extending the allowance of tax-free distributions from IRAs for charitable purposes through December 31, 2009, may be problematic in states that do not conform to Code Sec. 170, as currently amended, because the provision expired December 31, 2007. Because most states updated their Code conformity dates to dates after the expiration of the provision, and before this extension, some states may not allow the tax-free distribution for the 2008 tax year. Taxpayers and preparers should check the 2008 personal income tax form instructions for guidance as to whether a state adjustment must be made if a federal tax-free distribution was made in 2008. Most states that update their conformity dates on an annual basis will conform during their next legislative sessions (¶225).

Transportation fringe benefit for bicycle commuters

The inclusion of bicycle commuting reimbursements as an employer-provided transportation fringe benefits will impact states that conform to Code Sec. 132, but that have a conformity date that would not cover this provision. However, because the provision does not take effect until the 2009 tax year, states that conform to the Code annually will most likely conform to the exclusion during their next legislative sessions (¶230).

Additional standard deduction for property taxes for nonitemizers

Because most states, including California, Idaho, Kentucky, and Michigan, have their own standard deduction in lieu of the federal standard deduction (Code Sec. 63(c)), or do not allow a standard deduction (i.e., Connecticut, Illinois, Indiana, Ohio, and Pennsylvania), the additional standard deduction for real property taxes has little if any impact on state taxation, unless the states pass legislation to add a similar state provision for the 2008 and 2009 tax year (¶235).

Election to deduct state and local taxes in lieu of income taxes

The extension of the election to deduct state and local sales taxes in lieu of taking a federal deduction for state and local income taxes as an itemized deduction, may pose a problem in states that do not conform to Code Sec. 164, as currently amended because the provision expired at the end of 2007. The deduction is extended for two years through 2009. Because most states updated their Code conformity dates to dates after the expiration of the provision, and before this extension, some states may not allow the tax-free distribution for the 2008 tax year. Taxpayers and preparers should check the 2008 state personal income tax form instructions for guidance as to whether a state adjustment must be made if the deduction was taken on the federal return in 2008. Special attention should be paid to those states that require an addback of income taxes but do not specifically refer to Code Sec. 164. Those states, if they did not decouple from the sales tax election, may have been forced to allow it and may take advantage of their conformity dates to disallow the deduction in 2008 (¶240).

Tuition and fees and teacher expense deductions

The deduction for tuition and fees and the deduction for teacher expenses expired for tax years after 2007 and most states will not conform to the extensions of these deductions in time for the 2008 tax year. Taxpayers and preparers should check the 2008 personal income tax form instructions for guidance as to whether a state adjustment must be made if the deductions were taken on the federal return in 2008 (¶245, ¶250).

Definition of "qualifying child" for dependency exemption and child tax credit

Most states adopt the federal definition of a "qualifying child" for dependency purposes and in some states, for state child care credits. Because the changes made to the definition under Code Sec. 152 do not take affect until after 2008, states that update their Code conformity dates annually will conform by the time the change takes effect. States like California and Kentucky that do not update their Code conformity dates annually will be out of conformity and legislation or specific guidance may be required to bring these states into conformity with the new definition (¶260).

Enhanced charitable deductions

The extension of the enhanced deductions for contributions of food to charitable organizations, as well as for contributions of books and computer equipment to qualifying schools through 2009, may pose a problem in states that do not conform to Code Sec. 170 as currently amended because the provisions expired at the end of 2007. The deductions are extended through 2009. Because most states updated their

¶199

Code conformity dates to dates after the expiration of the provisions, and before this extension, some states may not allow deductions for the 2008 tax year. Businesses should check the 2008 appropriate state form instructions for guidance as to whether a state adjustment must be made if the deductions were taken on the federal return in 2008 (¶445, ¶450).

Basis adjustment to stock of S corporations making charitable contributions of property

The provision regarding the basis adjustment to an S corporation shareholder's stock if the S corporation makes a charitable contribution of property was extended only for the 2008 tax year. Most states will not conform until after the 2008 tax year. Taxpayers should check the 2008 state S corporation and/or personal income tax form instructions for guidance as to whether a state adjustment must be made for 2008. This may not be an issue unless the shareholder disposes of his or her shares in the S corporation in 2008. For states like California and Kentucky that do not annually update their Code conformity dates, this may result in a difference in basis in future years if the shareholder disposes of his or her interest (¶435).

Tax credits

Generally, states do not incorporate federal credits. Therefore, the business tax credits, the energy conservation credits, and the disaster relief credits will not impact the states. Although a few states (including Arizona, Illinois, Indiana, and New Jersey) have a research credit that is based on Code Sec. 41, the extension and modification of the federal credit should not impact these states (¶405).

Although the states do not incorporate the energy credits, several states have similar independent credits, including Arizona, Colorado, Kansas, Kentucky, Louisiana, Maryland, New York, Oklahoma, Oregon, and Virginia.

Qualifying income of publicly traded partnership

The treatment of certain income related to alternative fuels generated by a publicly traded partnership (PTP), as qualifying income for purposes of determining whether a PTP will be treated as a corporation for federal income tax purposes, will impact states like California, Illinois, New York, and Pennsylvania that follow the federal treatment of PTPs, but with Code conformity dates that do not incorporate this amendment to Code Sec. 7704. States that annually update their Code conformity dates will probably conform during their next legislative sessions. However, because the amendment takes effect on October 3, 2008, for tax years ending after that date, PTPs should check the 2008 state corporate and partnership form instructions for guidance as to whether it will be treated as a PTP or a corporation for state tax purposes (¶465).

Tax treatment of payments to controlling exempt organizations

The two-year extension of the special rules that exclude certain qualifying payments by a controlled entity to a tax-exempt organization from that tax-exempt organization's unrelated business income could impact states that adopt Code Sec. 512, but that have Code conformity dates that would not incorporate the extension. Because the provision originally expired for tax years after 2007, some states will not apply the special rules for the 2008 tax year. Affected taxpayers should check the 2008 appropriate form instructions for guidance as to whether a state adjustment must be made on the 2008 state return (¶480).

Limit on deduction for executive compensation

The limitation on the deduction for executive compensation and golden parachute payments made to executives of financial institutions that sell troubled assets to the Treasury through the Troubled Asset Relief Program will impact states that, because of their Code conformity dates, do not adopt the amendments to Code Secs. 162 or 280G. The deductions would not be limited by those states and thus, amounts not allowed on the federal return could be deducted on the state returns. Because some of the amendments are effective for tax years ending on or after October 3, 2008, adjustments may be required on the 2008 state returns. Affected taxpayers should check the appropriate 2008 state tax return instructions. States that conform to the Code annually will most likely conform to these amendments during their next legislative sessions (¶380).

Treatment of loss from sale of Fannie Mae and Freddie Mac stock

The provision allowing certain financial institutions to take ordinary gains or losses on the sale or exchange of the preferred stock of Fannie Mae or Freddie Mac is problematic because this provision was not codified and the states generally adopt only codified federal law. Therefore, for those financial institutions filing state returns, in the absence of legislation or other guidance, adjustments will probably be required because such gains or losses will be treated as capital gains or losses for state tax purposes. Because the federal treatment applies to tax years after 2007, affected financial institutions should check the appropriate 2008 state tax return instructions (¶485).

Domestic production activities

Many states (including California, Indiana, Massachusetts, and New Jersey) have decoupled from the domestic production activities deduction under Code Sec. 199. States like Virginia that adopt the federal provision, but that have a Code conformity date (e.g., December 31, 2007 in Virginia) would not incorporate the extension of the deduction for income attributable to domestic production activities in Puerto Rico, or the reduction of the deduction for oil and gas taxpayers. However states that conform to the Code annually (including Virginia) will most likely conform to these amendments during their next legislative sessions (¶370, ¶375).

Energy efficient commercial building deduction

The extension of the deduction for energy efficient commercial buildings for five years will impact states that conform to Code Sec. 179D, but that have a conformity date that would not cover this amendment. For example, California conforms to the Code, as amended on January 1, 2005, and Kentucky conforms to the Code, as amended January 1, 2007. States that conform to Code Sec. 179D and that routinely conform to the Code on an annual basis will most likely incorporate the extension in their next legislative sessions. As the provision was not due to expire until 2009, there should be no impact on conforming states for 2008 (¶560).

Depreciation

The special depreciation allowances for qualified refuse and recycling property and for qualified disaster property pose issues, regardless of whether the state has decoupled from bonus depreciation or not. For those states like Delaware, Idaho, and Louisiana that adopt Code Sec. 168, including bonus depreciation, and that conform to the Code as of a specific date, the new provisions will not apply unless or until the

¶199

states update their conformity dates. The majority of states have decoupled from bonus depreciation. However, many states specifically decouple from bonus depreciation allowed under Code Sec. 168(k). As the two new provisions involve new Code Sec. 168(m) and (n), respectively, the prohibition against bonus depreciation would not apply. For those states that decouple from bonus depreciation without specifically mentioning Code Sec. 168(k), the new bonus depreciation provisions would apply if the states' conformity dates allow the adoption of these additional provisions (¶565, ¶620).

Because the depreciation provisions regarding qualified leasehold improvements, restaurant construction and improvements, the seven-year cost recovery period for motor-sports racing facilities, and accelerated depreciation for Indian reservation business property originally expired for tax years after 2007, and the states' Code conformity dates would not adopt the extensions until they update the conformity dates, some states may not allow the deductions for the 2008 tax year. Businesses should check the 2008 appropriate state form instructions for guidance as to whether a state adjustment must be made if the deductions were taken on the federal return in 2008 (¶305, ¶310, ¶325 and ¶335).

The new depreciation provisions for farm business machinery and equipment, retail improvement property, smart electricity meters and grid systems, and facilities that produce cellulosic biofuel will not be adopted in most states that conform to Code Sec. 168 until they update their Code conformity dates to include these provisions (¶315, ¶330 and ¶570).

Expensing elections

The increase in the maximum allowable Code Sec. 179 deduction and the investment limitation, for qualified disaster assistance property for tax years after 2007, will not have an impact in states, including California, Florida, Indiana, New Jersey, and Wisconsin that have decoupled from the federal expensing allowance and limitation, unless they pass legislation to make an exception for disaster property. For states like Connecticut, Illinois, Massachusetts, Michigan, and Pennsylvania that adopt the federal allowance and limitation amounts, whether they adopt this amendment will depend on their Code conformity dates. Those states that update their Code conformity dates annually will most likely conform during their next legislative sessions (¶625).

The new provision under Code Sec. 198A allowing expensing of qualified disaster costs after 2007, will not be adopted by most states until they update their Code conformity dates during their next legislative sessions. Taxpayers should check the 2008 appropriate form instructions for guidance as to whether a state adjustment must be made if the deductions were taken on the federal return in 2008 (¶615).

The extension of the expense election for environmental remediation costs, under Code Sec. 198, may pose a problem in states that do not conform to Code Sec. 198, as currently amended because the provision expired at the end of 2007. The election is extended for two years through 2009. Because most states updated their Code conformity dates to dates after the expiration of the provisions, and before this extension, some states may not allow the expense election for the 2008 tax year. Taxpayers should check the 2008 appropriate state form instructions for guidance as to whether a state adjustment must be made if the election was made on the federal return in 2008 (¶340).

The extensions of the elections to expense film and television production expenses and mine safety equipment expenses take effect after 2008. The extension of the expensing election for certain refinery property applies to property placed in service after October 3, 2008. Therefore, states that update their Code conformity dates annually will be in conformity before the extensions take effect. Those states, like California and Kentucky that do not update their Code conformity dates annually will not conform to the extension of these elections (¶345, ¶350 and ¶360).

Losses attributable to federally declared disasters

Although the majority of states adopt Code Sec. 165, states that do not conform to the Code, as currently amended, will not adopt the special casualty loss rules until they update their conformity dates. For those amendments that are effective after 2007, taxpayers should check the 2008 appropriate state form instructions for guidance as to whether a state adjustment must be made if the disaster loss rules were applied on the federal return in 2008. Most states will conform to the amendments, including the increase in the limitation from $100 to $500, that take affect after 2008 (¶605).

Net operating losses attributable to federally declared disasters

The carryback provision for losses attributable to federally declared disasters will impact states that allow a net operating loss (NOL) carryback. Some states, including Florida, Illinois, Massachusetts, New Jersey, Ohio, and Pennsylvania do not allow NOL carrybacks. Most states, including Delaware, Indiana, Kansas, Louisiana, and Maryland that do allow NOL carrybacks limit the carryback to two or three years. Most of these states have not conformed to prior special carryback periods and in any event, most will be out of conformity until they update their Code conformity dates during their next legislative sessions. Taxpayers should check the 2008 appropriate state form instructions for guidance as to whether a state adjustment must be made if disaster losses were carried back for federal tax purposes in 2008 (¶610).

Temporary tax relief for Midwest storm victims

Most states do not specifically adopt Code Secs. 1400N through 1400T. The temporary extension of the benefits that apply to victims of the recent Midwest storms is uncodified, and in the absence of legislation or other guidance, the states may not adopt the tax relief provisions. Taxpayers should check the 2008 state form instructions for guidance as to whether a state adjustment must be made if disaster relief benefits were claimed for federal tax purposes in 2008 (¶655).

Individual Taxpayers

2

AMT RELIEF

INCOME AND GAINS

DEDUCTIONS

QUALIFYING CHILDREN

AMT RELIEF

¶205 Alternative Minimum Tax Exemption Amount

SUMMARY OF NEW LAW

The alternative minimum tax (AMT) exemption amount for individuals has been increased for tax years beginning in 2008.

BACKGROUND

In addition to all other tax liabilities, an individual is subject to an alternative minimum tax (AMT) to the extent that his or her tentative minimum tax exceeds the amount of regular income tax owed (Code Sec. 55). An individual's tentative minimum tax is generally equal to the sum of: 26 percent of the first $175,000 ($87,500 for a married taxpayer filing a separate return) of the taxpayer's alternative minimum taxable income (AMTI) and 28 percent of the taxpayer's remaining AMTI (Code Sec. 55(b)(1)(A)).

AMTI is the individual's regular taxable income recomputed with certain adjustments and increased by certain tax preferences (Code Sec. 56). However, a specified amount of AMTI is exempt from tax based on the taxpayer's filing status. For example, the exemption amount for tax years prior to 2001 was: (1) $45,000 for married individuals filing a joint return and surviving spouses; (2) $33,750 for unmarried individuals; and (3) $22,500 for married individuals filing separate returns. The exemption amount is phased out by an amount equal to 25 percent of the amount by which the taxpayer's AMTI for the tax year exceeds: (1) $150,000 in the case of married individuals filing a joint return, surviving spouses and corporations; (2) $112,500 in the case of unmarried individuals; and (3) $75,000 in the case of married individuals filing separate returns, or an estate or trust.

Neither the exemption amounts, nor the threshold amounts, are indexed for inflation. Thus, the number of individuals affected by the AMT has increased each tax year. To alleviate this problem, the exemption amounts have been periodically increased by legislation. The latest change increased the exemption amounts for tax years beginning in 2007 to: (1) $66,250 for married individuals filing a joint return and surviving spouses; (2) $44,350 for unmarried individuals; and (3) $33,125 for married individuals filing separate returns (Code Sec. 55(d)(1)). However, for tax years beginning after 2007, the exemption amounts for individuals are scheduled to revert to the amounts that applied prior to 2001.

> **Comment:** The exemption amount for corporations, and estates or trusts, have remained unchanged during this period. The exemption amount is $40,000 for a corporation and $22,500 for an estate or trust.

¶205

NEW LAW EXPLAINED

Extension of AMT exemption amounts.—The alternative minimum tax (AMT) exemption amount for individuals is increased for tax years beginning in 2008, to:

- $69,950 for married individuals filing a joint return and surviving spouses;
- $46,200 for unmarried individuals; and
- $34,975 for married individuals filing separate returns (Code Sec. 55(d)(1)(A) and (B), as amended by the Emergency Economic Stabilization Act of 2008 (P.L. 110-343)).

The $40,000 exemption amount for corporations and the $22,500 exemption amount for estates or trusts remains unchanged for tax years beginning in 2008.

> **Caution:** Absent another legislative extension, for tax years beginning after 2008, the AMT exemption amounts for individuals are scheduled to revert back to the amounts that applied prior to the 2001 tax year. Thus, the exemption amounts would be: (1) $45,000 for married individuals filing a joint return and surviving spouses; (2) $33,750 for unmarried individuals; and (3) $22,500 for married individuals filing separate returns.

Practical Analysis: Vincent O'Brien, President of Vincent J. O'Brien, CPA, PC, Lynbrook, New York, observes that, since many practitioners prepare income tax projections for their clients during the fourth quarter of each year, knowing the higher AMT exemption for 2008 at this time is very useful. (For 2007, the law containing the higher AMT exemption amounts was not enacted until December 26, 2007.)

When preparing such income tax projections, practitioners should review the AMT exemption amount that is used by the planning feature of their tax preparation software. The amount may need to be manually entered unless/until their software packages are updated.

For many middle-class clients, the higher AMT exemption will either reduce or eliminate the AMT to which they would otherwise have been subject, had the AMT exemption levels reverted to $45,000 for a married couple filing a joint return and $33,750 for single or head of household.

It is interesting to note that a big culprit in the expansion of the number of taxpayers subject to the AMT is the fact that the brackets, exemptions and thresholds used to compute the AMT are not automatically indexed for inflation. From 2003 to 2005, the AMT exemption remained unchanged. However, the one-year patch approach to the AMT has resulted in *de facto* inflation indexing of the AMT exemption for 2006 through 2008, since the newly approved exemption amounts for these years have been higher each year.

Nevertheless, the other brackets and thresholds used to compute the AMT have remained unchanged. As a result, the AMT remains a significant planning issue for many practitioners and their clients.

> **Caution:** Although the AMT exemption amounts for individuals are increased for 2008, the threshold levels for the calculation of the phase out remain unchanged. Thus, the exemption amount for tax years beginning in 2008 is still reduced by 25 percent for each $1 of alternative minimum taxable income

¶205

NEW LAW EXPLAINED

(AMTI) in excess of: (1) $150,000 in the case of married individuals filing a joint return, surviving spouses and corporations; (2) $112,500 in the case of unmarried individuals; and (3) $75,000 in the case of married individuals filing separate returns or an estate or a trust.

Practical Analysis: Stephen J. Bigge, CPA, Manager on the Estate Planning Team of Virchow Krause & Co., Appleton, Wisconsin, finds that Division C, Act Sec. 102 of the Emergency Economic Stabilization Act of 2008 (P.L. 110-343) increases the Alternative Minimum Tax ("AMT") exemption from $45,000 for married taxpayers filing jointly ($33,750 for most other taxpayers) to $69,950 ($46,200 for most other taxpayers) in 2008.

Even though the increase in the exemption amount is a welcome relief for taxpayers worried about being subject to AMT in 2008, the Emergency Economic Act of 2008 did nothing to make the AMT exemption increase permanent or address the phase-out of the exemption under Code Sec. 55(d)(3). Accordingly, while the AMT exemption has increased for 2008, most, if not all, married people whose AMT incomes are above $150,000 ($112,500 for single taxpayers) are not going to see much relief from this change.

Practical Analysis: Jeffrey D. Eicher, J.D., CPA, Professor at Clarion University of Pennsylvania, and Leo N. Hitt, J.D., LL.M., Attorney in the Pittsburgh office of Reed Smith, LLP, observe that in Division C, Act Sec. 102 of the Emergency Economic Stabilization Act of 2008 (P.L. 110-343), the exemption amount for noncorporate taxpayers subject to the alternative minimum tax was again increased and extended for an additional year. The exemption amount is increased to $69,950 for joint returns or surviving spouse returns, $46,200 for single returns, and $34,975 for separate returns for married individuals. The exemption amount is scheduled to return to the substantially lower amounts applicable in pre-2001 tax years, beginning in 2009, unless additional legislation in enacted that continues the enhanced exemption.

▶ **Effective date.** The provision applies to tax years beginning after December 31, 2007 (Division C, Act Sec. 102(b) of the Emergency Economic Stabilization Act of 2008 (P.L. 110-343)).

Law source: Law at ¶5170. Committee Reports at ¶10,310.

— Division C, Act Sec. 102(a) of the Emergency Economic Stabilization Act of 2008 (P.L. 110-343), amending Code Sec. 55(d)(1)(A) and (B);

— Division C, Act Sec. 102(b), providing the effective date.

Reporter references: For further information, consult the following CCH reporters.

— Standard Federal Tax Reporter, ¶5101.035 and ¶5101.036

— Tax Research Consultant, FILEIND: 30,400

— Federal Tax Guide, ¶1320 and ¶1430

¶205

¶210 Use of Nonrefundable Personal Credits Against AMT Liability

SUMMARY OF NEW LAW

The use of nonrefundable personal tax credits against an individual's regular tax and alternative minimum tax liability is extended to apply to tax years beginning in 2008.

BACKGROUND

An alternative minimum tax (AMT) is imposed on an individual taxpayer to the extent his or her tentative minimum tax liability exceeds his or her regular income tax liability (Code Sec. 55(a)). An individual's tentative minimum tax liability is the sum of: (1) 26 percent of the first $175,000 ($87,500 for married individuals filing separately) of the taxpayer's alternative minimum taxable income (AMTI) in excess of an exemption amount; and (2) 28 percent of any remaining AMTI in excess of the exemption amount (Code Sec. 55(b)(1)(A)). AMTI is the individual's regular taxable income recomputed with certain adjustments and increased by certain tax preferences (Code Sec. 56).

For tax years beginning before 2008, the amount of nonrefundable personal tax credits available to an individual may be claimed to the extent of the full amount of the taxpayer's combined regular tax and AMT liability. Regular tax liability, however, must first be reduced by the amount of any applicable foreign or U.S. possession tax credit (Code Sec. 26(a)(2)). The nonrefundable personal tax credits include the dependent care credit, the credit for the elderly and disabled, the adoption credit, the child tax credit, the credit for interest on certain home mortgages, the HOPE Scholarship and Lifetime Learning credits, the retirement savings contributions credit, the credit for certain nonbusiness energy property, the credit for residential energy efficient property, and the District of Columbia first-time homebuyer credit.

> **Comment:** An individual is eligible to claim the alternative motor vehicle credit and alternative fuel vehicle refueling property credit for business as well as nonbusiness use. However, the personal use portions of the credits that a taxpayer can claim are limited to the excess of the taxpayer's regular tax liability, reduced by all other nonrefundable credits plus the foreign and possessions tax credit, over his or her tentative minimum tax liability (Code Secs. 30B(g)(2) and 30C(d)(2)). The rule that allows nonrefundable personal credits to be claimed against the sum of the taxpayer's regular and AMT liability for tax years beginning before 2008 does not apply to these credits.

For tax years beginning after 2007, the amount of nonrefundable personal credits that may be claimed by an individual (except for the adoption credit, the child tax credit and the retirement savings contributions credit) is limited to the excess of the taxpayer's regular tax liability over tentative minimum tax liability, determined without regard to the AMT foreign tax credit (Code Sec. 26(a)(1)). Thus, all nonrefundable personal credits (except for the child tax credit, the adoption credit

BACKGROUND

and the retirement savings contributions credit) will only be able to offset regular tax liability and only to the extent it exceeds his or her tentative minimum tax.

> **Comment:** The adoption credit, the child tax credit and the retirement savings contributions credit are allowed to the full extent of the taxpayer's regular tax and AMT liability for any tax years beginning after 2007. Thus, only these three credits may be claimed against both the regular tax and AMT liability for those years.

NEW LAW EXPLAINED

Nonrefundable personal credits allowed against regular tax and AMT liability for tax years beginning in 2008.—For tax years beginning in 2008, the nonrefundable personal tax credits are allowed to the full extent of the taxpayer's regular tax and AMT liability. For this purpose, the regular tax liability is first reduced by the amount of any applicable foreign tax credit (Code Sec. 26(a)(2), as amended by the Emergency Economic Stabilization Act of 2008 (P.L. 110-343)).

> **Practical Analysis:** Claudia A. Hill, EA, M.B.A., Owner and Principal of Tax Mam, Inc., and TMI Tax Services Group, Inc., an association of Enrolled Agents in Cupertino, California, and Editor-in-Chief of the JOURNAL OF TAX PRACTICE & PROCE-DURE, observes that Division C, Act Sec. 101 of the Emergency Economic Stabilization Act of 2008 (P.L. 110-343) was essential to millions of working families who currently benefit from such nonrefundable personal credits as the dependent care credit, credit for the elderly or disabled, education credits and mortgage interest credit. Act Sec. 102 indexed the 2007 exemption amounts for one more year to hold the line for millions of middle-income taxpayers hoping to stay out of AMT. By simply patching the existing AMT exemption amount and re-affirming use of nonrefundable credits, Congress guarantees AMT reform will be on the agenda for 2009.

> **Practical Analysis:** Jeffrey D. Eicher, J.D., CPA, Professor at Clarion University of Pennsylvania, and Leo N. Hitt, J.D., LL.M., Attorney in the Pittsburgh office of Reed Smith, LLP, observe that in Division C, Act Sec. 101 of the Emergency Economic Stabilization Act of 2008 (P.L. 110-343), the temporary provision that permits the offset of nonrefundable personal credits against the sum of an individual's regular income tax and alternative minimum tax is extended for an additional year to years that begin during 2008. This provision was previously extended by Tax Increase Prevention and Reconciliation Act of 2005 (P.L. 109-222) to tax years beginning in 2007.

> **Comment:** This extension does not apply to the personal use portions of the nonrefundable tax credits for alternative motor vehicles and alternative fuel vehicle refueling property. The personal use portion of these credits may only be used against the excess of the taxpayer's regular tax liability, reduced by all

NEW LAW EXPLAINED

other nonrefundable credits plus the foreign or U.S. possession tax credit, over the tentative minimum tax (Code Secs. 30B(g)(2) and 30C(d)(2)).

▶ **Effective date.** The provision applies to tax years beginning after December 31, 2007 (Act Sec. 101(b) of the Emergency Economic Stabilization Act of 2008 (P.L. 110-343)).

Law source: Law at ¶5035. Committee Reports at ¶10,310.

— Division C, Act Sec. 101(a) of the Emergency Economic Stabilization Act of 2008 (P.L. 110-343), amending Code Sec. 26(a)(2);

— Division C, Act Sec. 101(b), providing the effective date.

Reporter references: For further information, consult the following CCH reporters.

— Standard Federal Tax Reporter, ¶3851.021

— Tax Research Consultant, INDIV: 57,200

— Federal Tax Guide, ¶1320 and ¶2050

¶215 AMT Credit Relief for Individuals with Long-Term Unused Credits

SUMMARY OF NEW LAW

If an individual has a long-term unused minimum tax credit for a tax year beginning before January 1, 2013, the minimum tax credit allowable for that tax year will be not less than the greater of (1) the amount (if any) of the AMT refundable credit amount determined for the taxpayer's preceding tax year, or (2) 50 percent of the unused credit.

BACKGROUND

The minimum tax credit for a given tax year is the excess, if any, of the "adjusted net minimum tax" for all prior years over the amount allowed as a minimum tax credit for those years (Code Sec. 53(b)). The minimum tax credit is allowable to the extent the regular tax for the tax year (reduced by certain other nonrefundable credits) exceeds the tentative minimum tax for the year (Code Sec. 53(c)). Unused minimum tax credits are carried forward (but not back) indefinitely as credits against regular tax liability. The minimum tax credit may not be used to offset any future alternative minimum tax (AMT) liability. In calculating the minimum tax credit, an individual's "adjusted net minimum tax" for any given tax year is his or her AMT liability for that year reduced by the amount of AMT that would be attributable to certain AMT adjustments and preference items (Code Sec. 53(d)(1)(B)).

If an individual has a long-term unused minimum tax credit for any tax year beginning before January 1, 2013, the minimum tax credit allowable for that year will not be less than the "AMT refundable credit amount" regardless of the minimum tax

BACKGROUND

credit otherwise allowed to the taxpayer (Code Sec. 53(e)(1)). Also, the additional amount of credit allowed by this provision is refundable (Code Sec. 53(e)(4)).

> **Comment:** This AMT credit relief is intended primarily for individuals who exercised incentive stock options at a profit and sold the stock later when the stock price had significantly declined. Individuals in this situation, would have had to pay an AMT on the profit in the year of the exercise, although they lost a large portion or all of the profit at the time of the stock sale. As a result, such individuals could have ended up with a large amount of minimum tax credit that they may never be able to use even if carried forward.

The AMT refundable credit amount is the greater of: (1) the lesser of $5,000 or the taxpayer's long-term unused minimum tax credit for the tax year; or (2) 20 percent of such credit (Code Sec. 53(e)(2)(A)). The long-term unused minimum tax credit for a tax year is the portion of the minimum tax credit attributable to the adjusted net minimum tax for tax years before the third tax year immediately preceding such tax year. For this purpose, the credits are treated as allowed on a first-in, first-out basis (Code Sec. 53(e)(3)).

The AMT refundable credit amount is phased out at the income levels applicable to the phaseout of the personal exemption deduction. Accordingly, if an individual's adjusted gross income (AGI) for a tax year exceeds certain threshold amounts (based on filing status), the AMT refundable credit amount is reduced by the applicable percentage, which is equal to two percentage points for each $2,500 ($1,250 for married individuals filing separately) by which AGI exceeds the threshold amount (Code Sec. 53(e)(2)(B)(i)).

> **Comment:** The phaseout of the AMT refundable credit begins when AGI exceeds: $239,950 for 2008 for married individuals filing a joint return or a surviving spouse; $159,950 for 2008 for unmarried individuals (not surviving spouse or head of household); $199,950 for 2008 for heads of households; and $119,975 for 2008 for married individuals filing separate returns.

Example 1: In 2010, Bob Williams files a tax return as a head of household. His AGI for the year exceeds the threshold for the phaseout of the personal exemptions, resulting in an applicable percentage of 50 percent. He has a regular tax liability of $45,000 and a tentative AMT liability of $40,000. He is not eligible to claim any credits other than the minimum tax credit. His minimum tax credit for the year is $1.1 million (before application of the limit on the minimum tax credit), of which $1 million is long-term unused minimum tax credit. Generally, the minimum tax credit that Bob could claim would be limited to difference between his regular tax liability for the year over his tentative AMT liability for the year ($5,000).

However, under the refundable credit provision Bob may claim a minimum tax credit of $100,000 in 2010. This is the amount of his AMT refundable credit amount for the tax year (20 percent of his $1 million of long-term unused minimum tax credit reduced by the applicable percentage of 50 percent). The

BACKGROUND

$5,000 credit allowed to Bob without regard to the refundable credit provision is nonrefundable. However, the additional $95,000 of credit allowed under the new rule is treated as a refundable credit. Thus, Bob has an overpayment of $55,000 ($45,000 regular tax, less $5,000 nonrefundable AMT credit, less $95,000 refundable AMT credit). The $55,000 overpayment is allowed as a refund or credit to the taxpayer. The remaining $1 million minimum tax credit is carried forward to future tax years (Joint Committee on Taxation, Technical Explanation of the Tax Relief and Health Care Act of 2006 (P.L. 109-432) (JCX-50-06)).

Example 2: Assume the same facts as in Example 1 above, except that Bob's AGI does not exceed the threshold amount for phaseout of the personal exemption. As a result, his AMT refundable credit amount for 2010 would be $200,000 (20 percent of his $1 million of long-term unused minimum tax credit). His overpayment would be $155,000, and the credit he would carry forward would be $900,000.

NEW LAW EXPLAINED

Increase of AMT refundable credit amount for individuals with long-term unused credits.—The "AMT refundable credit amount" is defined as, with respect to any tax year, the amount (not in excess of the long-term unused minimum tax credit for such tax year) equal to the greater of: (1) 50 percent of the long-term unused minimum tax credit for such tax year, or (2) the amount (if any) of the AMT refundable credit amount determined for the taxpayer's preceding tax year (determined without regard to Code Sec. 53(f)(2)) (Code Sec. 53(e)(2), as amended by the Emergency Economic Stabilization Act of 2008 (P.L. 110-343)).

Practical Analysis: Jeffrey D. Eicher, J.D., CPA, Professor at Clarion University of Pennsylvania, and Leo N. Hitt, J.D., LL.M., Attorney in the Pittsburgh office of Reed Smith, LLP, observe that in Division C, Act Sec. 103(a) of the Emergency Economic Stabilization Act of 2008 (P.L. 110-343), the amount of long-term unused minimum tax credit amount that may be used to offset regular tax and to generate a refund (the "AMT refundable credit amount") is increased from its current threshold of the greatest of (i) 20 percent of the long-term unused minimum tax credit, (ii) the previous year's AMT refundable credit amount before the application of the phaseout for taxpayers with adjusted gross income in excess of certain amounts, or (iii) $5,000. The new limitation is the greater of (a) 50 percent of the long-term unused minimum tax credit or (b) the previous year's AMT refundable credit amount before the application of the phase out for taxpayers with adjusted gross income in excess of certain amounts.

NEW LAW EXPLAINED

In Division C, Act Sec. 103(b) of the Emergency Economic Act of 2008, any underpayment of AMT outstanding on the date of enactment of the Act that is attributable to the exercise of Incentive Stock Options for any tax year ending before January 1, 2008, and any interest or penalty attributable to such an underpayment is abated. Any interest and penalty (but not tax) paid by a taxpayer prior to the enactment of the Emergency Economic Act of 2008 that would have been abated under the preceding sentence will result in an increase in the AMT refundable credit amount and the minimum tax credit for the first two years beginning after December 31, 2007, in the amount of 50 percent of such interest and penalties in each of those years.

For tax years ending before January 1, 2008, any underpayment of outstanding tax which is attributable to the application of Code Sec. 56(b)(3) (and any outstanding interest or penalty associated with such underpayment) is abated. No credit shall be allowed with respect to any abated amount (Code Sec. 53(f)(1), as added by the Emergency Economic Act of 2008).

The alternative minimum tax refundable credit amount, and the minimum tax credit determined under Code Sec. 56(b), for the taxpayer's first two tax years beginning after December 31, 2007, are each increased by 50 percent of the aggregate amount of the interest or penalties paid which would (but for such payment) have been abated (Code Sec. 53(f)(2), as added by the Emergency Economic Act of 2008).

Practical Analysis: Stephen J. Bigge, CPA, Manager on the Estate Planning Team of Virchow Krause & Co., Appleton, Wisconsin, finds that Division C, Act Sec. 103 of the Emergency Economic Stabilization Act of 2008 (P.L. 110-343) expands the "AMT refundable credit amount" from 20 percent of a taxpayer's long-term unused minimum tax credit (*i.e.*, unused AMT credit amount that is more than three tax years old) to 50 percent of a taxpayer's long-term unused minimum tax credit. In addition, Code Sec. 53(f) has been added to provide for the abatement of any outstanding underpayment of tax (including penalties and interest related to the underpayment of tax) associated with the exercise of an Incentive Stock Option ("ISO"). Furthermore, starting in the 2008 tax year and ending in the 2009 tax year, to the extent that a taxpayer has paid underpayment penalties and interest associated with the exercise of an ISO in a prior year, the taxpayer's "AMT refundable credit amount" is increased by the aggregate amount of penalties and interest previously paid.

Practical Analysis: Claudia A. Hill, EA, M.B.A., Owner and Principal of Tax Mam, Inc., and TMI Tax Services Group, Inc., an association of Enrolled Agents in Cupertino, California, and Editor-in-Chief of the JOURNAL OF TAX PRACTICE & PROCEDURE, observes that Division C, Act Sec. 103 of the Emergency Economic Stabilization Act of 2008 (P.L. 110-343) attempts to turn back time to remedy the unintended consequences and injustices experienced by many honest taxpayers who exercised Incentive Stock Options ("ISOs") and recognized phantom income for AMT purposes

¶215

NEW LAW EXPLAINED

during the "dot.com bust" of 2000 and 2001. The phantom income turned into very real income tax liabilities which the individuals either paid or IRS proceeded to attempt to collect through enforcement actions. While Congress had previously made efforts to address this problem when P.L. 109-432 created a refundable amount for long-term unused AMT credit, it fell short. Phase-out limits kept many from receiving any benefit, and it did not address those who had not been able to pay the liability and were still experiencing IRS pressure to do so.

In the National Taxpayer Advocate's June 30, 2008, Report to Congress, Fiscal Year 2009 Objectives, the ISO-AMT problem was included as an Area of Emphasis. In response to a number of influential Senators, on August 26 Commissioner Shulman advised Senator Grassley that IRS had suspended collection of long-term ISO-AMT liabilities pending legislation. For those who had been caught up in this draconian nightmare, this legislation brings much needed relief. For those who personally sacrificed to pay taxes on income they never pocketed and have been waiting ever since to receive the promised credits, the legislation is welcome. It is unfortunate tax equity did not come soon enough to prevent the ISO-AMT financial trauma that caused the loss of homes and marriages, resulting in broken lives and families.

For those who have not been able to pay off their ISO-related AMT liability, including accrued interest and penalties, outstanding amounts are abated at date of enactment. For those who have fully paid and are holding long-term unused AMT credits, the income phase-out limits are eliminated and the period over which they can be refunded is shortened to two years. For taxpayers who were unable to fully and timely pay the original ISO-AMT liability and previously paid penalties and interest, 50 percent of those additions to tax can be added to the AMT credit available for refund for 2008 and 2009. Tax advisors will want to obtain IRS transcripts to confirm such amounts for affected taxpayers as soon as practical. Since recovery of these amounts is addressed as part of the AMT credit carried forward, separate claims will not be needed.

▶ **Effective date.** The provision generally applies to tax years beginning after December 31, 2007 (Division C, Act Sec. 103(c)(1) of the Emergency Economic Stabilization Act of 2008 (P.L. 110-343)). However, the provision relating to abatement of tax, interest and penalties under Code Sec. 53(f)(1) takes effect on October 3, 2008 (Division C, Act Sec. 103(c)(2) of the Emergency Economic Act of 2008).

Law source: Law at ¶5140. Committee Reports at ¶10,320.

— Division C, Act Sec. 103(a) of the Emergency Economic Stabilization Act of 2008 (P.L. 110-343), amending Code Sec. 53(e)(2);

— Division C, Act Sec. 103(b), adding Code Sec. 53(f);

— Division C, Act Sec. 103(c), providing the effective dates.

Reporter references: For further information, consult the following CCH reporters.

— Standard Federal Tax Reporter, ¶4872.01 and ¶37,539.01

— Tax Research Consultant, FILEIND: 30,452

— Federal Tax Guide, ¶2825

¶215

INCOME AND GAINS

¶220 Income Exclusion for Discharges of Acquisition Indebtedness on Principal Residences

SUMMARY OF NEW LAW

The exclusion from gross income for discharges of qualified principal residence indebtedness is extended for three years through calendar year 2012.

BACKGROUND

Taxpayers are generally required to recognize income from the discharge of indebtedness (also referred to as cancellation-of-debt, or "COD" income) (Code Sec. 61(a)(12)). However, there are several exceptions to the general rule of income inclusion: debtors in Title 11 bankruptcy cases, insolvent taxpayers, student-loan debtors, farmers and obligors on certain business real-estate debts may be entitled to forgo the recognition of COD income (Code Sec. 108(a)). Generally, when taxpayers do not recognize COD income, they are required to reduce certain tax attributes, such as net operating loss carryovers or basis in the taxpayer's property (Code Sec. 108(b)). The amount of discharge of indebtedness is generally equal to the difference between the amount of the indebtedness being cancelled and the amount used to satisfy the debt. The COD income rules also apply to the exchange of an old obligation for a new one and a modification of indebtedness that is treated as an exchange of one debt instrument for another.

Congress's response to the early stages of the subprime mortgage crisis, the Mortgage Forgiveness Debt Relief Act of 2007 (P.L. 110-142), created a new exception to the recognition of COD income. The Mortgage Act added new Code Sec. 108(a)(1)(E), which excludes from gross income any income from the discharge (in whole or in part) of "qualified principal residence indebtedness" which occurs in 2007, 2008 or 2009. Qualified principal residence indebtedness is acquisition indebtedness, as defined in the home mortgage interest deduction provisions of Code Sec. 163(h), but with a $2 million dollar limit ($1 million for a married taxpayer filing a separate return) (Code Sec. 108(h)(2)). An individual's acquisition indebtedness is indebtedness with respect to that individual's principal residence if it is incurred in the acquisition, construction, or substantial improvement of such residence and is secured by the residence. Qualified principal residence interest also includes refinancing of such indebtedness to the extent that the amount of the refinancing does not exceed the amount of the refinanced indebtedness.

"Principal residence" has the same meaning for purposes of the exclusion as it does for purposes of Code Sec. 121 (Code Sec. 108(h)(5)). Whether a property qualifies as the taxpayer's principal residence for purposes of Code Sec. 121 depends on all the facts and circumstances of each case. When the taxpayer has more than one property that he or she uses as a residence, the property that the taxpayer uses the majority of the time during the year will be treated as the taxpayer's principal residence for that

¶220

BACKGROUND

year. Other factors taken into account in determining the taxpayer's principal residence include: the taxpayer's place of employment; the principal place where the taxpayer's family lives; the address used by the taxpayer on tax returns, driver's license, automobile registration, and voter registration; the mailing address used by the taxpayer for bills and correspondence; the location of the taxpayer's banks; and the location of religious organizations and recreational clubs with which the taxpayer is affiliated (Reg. § 1.121-1(b)).

Several anti-abuse rules apply to the exclusion of income from the discharge of qualified principal residence indebtedness. For example, the discharge of a loan will not be excluded from gross income if it is as a result of services performed for the lender or other factors unrelated to either the financial condition of the taxpayer or a decline in value of the residence. In addition, if only a portion of discharged indebtedness is qualified principal residence indebtedness, the exclusion applies only to so much of the amount discharged as exceeds the portion of the debt that is not qualified principal residence indebtedness. The basis of the taxpayer's principal residence is reduced (but not below zero) by the amount of qualified principal residence interest that is excluded from income (Code Sec. 108(h)(1)).

The exclusion does not apply to a debtor in a Title 11 bankruptcy case. Rather, the exclusion under Code Sec. 108(a)(1)(A) (exclusion due to bankruptcy) applies. However, the exclusion of debt discharged on a principal residence applies to insolvent taxpayers not involved in Title 11 bankruptcy cases unless the taxpayer elects to have the exclusion of Code Sec. 108(a)(1)(B) (exclusion due to insolvency) apply (Code Sec. 108(a)(2)(C)(2)).

The principal residence indebtedness exclusion added by the Mortgage Act is effective for discharges of indebtedness on principal residences on or after January 1, 2007, and before January 1, 2010.

NEW LAW EXPLAINED

Exclusion for discharge of indebtedness on principal residence extended.—The exclusion from gross income applicable to qualified principal residence indebtedness is extended for three years, and now applies to discharges of indebtedness occurring on or after January 1, 2007, and before January 1, 2013 (Code Sec. 108(a)(1)(E), as amended by Division A, Act Sec. 303(a) of the Emergency Economic Stabilization Act of 2008 (P.L. 110-343)).

> **Practical Analysis:** William C. Hood, J.D., CPA, Professor at Central Michigan University in Mount Pleasant, finds that normally, if a debt is discharged, the debtor must include the amount of the discharge in his or her taxable income. One major exception to this rule relates to debt associated with a taxpayer's principal residence. This exception allows a taxpayer to exclude from taxable income up to $2 million of discharged qualified principal residence indebtedness. The exception was set to expire at the end of 2009. Under Division A, Act Sec. 303 of the Emergency

NEW LAW EXPLAINED

Economic Stabilization Act of 2008 (P.L. 110-343), the qualified principal residence indebtedness exception will continue through 2012.

Practical Analysis: John C. Zimmerman, J.D., CPA, Associate Professor of Accounting at the University of Nevada, Las Vegas, finds that Division A, Act Sec. 303 of the Emergency Economic Stabilization Act of 2008 (P.L. 110-343) now extends the exception of Code Sec. 108(a)(1)(E) to qualified principal residence indebtedness discharged before January 1, 2013. Prior law only allowed the exception if the discharge occurred prior to January 1, 2010.

Code Sec. 108(a)(1)(E) provides an exception to the general rule requiring a taxpayer to recognize income on the discharge of indebtedness if the indebtedness is "qualified principal residence indebtedness." Code Sec. 108(h)(2) allows the taxpayer to exclude from income the discharge of up to $2 million of "qualified principal residence indebtedness." Code Sec. 108(h)(1) provides that the taxpayer must reduce the basis of the residence (but not below zero) by the amount of the discharge.

Qualified principal residence indebtedness is defined in Code Sec. 163(h)(3)(B) as indebtedness that is (1) incurred in acquiring, constructing, or substantially improving any "qualified residence" of the taxpayer, and (2) is secured by the residence. This means the indebtedness is nonrecourse. Code Sec. 108(h)(5) provides that the type of residence to which the discharge applies is a principal residence within the meaning of Code Sec. 121, the place where a taxpayer lives.

Practical Analysis: Michelle Ward, J.D., Senior Consultant on the Estate Planning Team of Virchow Krause & Co., Appleton, Wisconsin, finds that Division A, Act Sec. 303 of the Emergency Economic Stabilization Act of 2008 (P.L. 110-343) extends the exclusion from gross income for the discharge of indebtedness for qualified principal residence indebtedness under Code Sec. 108(a)(1)(E) to January 1, 2013. This is an extension of the previous discharge deadline of January 1, 2010. Such an extension would apply to discharges of indebtedness occurring on or after January 1, 2010. As an example of this exclusion, assume that the taxpayer owns a principal residence subject to a $100,000 mortgage. Assume further that the bank forecloses on the loan and the residence is sold for $90,000, satisfying the mortgage in full. The remaining $10,000 of the mortgage that was discharged will not be subject to income tax under the exception of Code Sec. 108(a)(1)(E).

Practical Analysis: John A. Sikora, J.D., Partner in the Milwaukee and Delafield offices of Weiss Berzowski Brady LLP, notes that Code Sec. 108(a)(1)(E) provides that gross income does not include income from the discharge of a taxpayer's qualified principal residence indebtedness. The provision was added by the Mortgage Forgiveness Debt Relief Act of 2007 (P.L. 110-142) for discharges of indebted-

NEW LAW EXPLAINED

ness on or after January 1, 2007, and before January 1, 2010. The exclusion does not apply to the discharge of a loan if the discharge is on account of services performed for the lender or any other factor not directly related to a decline in the value of the residence or to the financial condition of the taxpayer. The amount excluded from gross income reduces the basis of the principal residence. Qualified principal residence indebtedness is, generally, indebtedness, to the extent not exceeding $2 million ($1 million for a married person filing a separate return), incurred in acquiring, constructing or substantially improving the principal residence of the taxpayer which is secured by the residence. The term also includes debt secured by the principal residence resulting from refinancing such indebtedness to the extent the indebtedness resulting from such refinancing does not exceed the amount of the refinanced indebtedness. Division A, Act Sec. 303 of the Emergency Economic Stabilization Act of 2008 (P.L. 110-343) extends the period for which the provision is effective so that it now applies to discharges of such indebtedness occurring before January 1, 2013.

▶ **Effective date.** The provision applies to discharges of indebtedness occurring on or after January 1, 2010. (Division A, Act Sec. 303(b) of the Emergency Economic Stabilization Act of 2008 (P.L. 110-343)).

Law source: Law at ¶5190. Committee Reports at ¶10,030.

— Division A, Act Sec. 303(a) of the Emergency Economic Stabilization Act of 2008 (P.L. 110-343), amending Code Sec. 108(a)(1)(E);

— Division A, Act Sec. 303(b), providing the effective date.

Reporter references: For further information, consult the following CCH reporters.

— Standard Federal Tax Reporter, ¶7010.048

— Tax Research Consultant, SALES: 12,152.25

— Federal Tax Guide, ¶4235

¶225 Qualified Charitable Distributions from IRAs

SUMMARY OF NEW LAW

Individuals aged 70 1/2 or older can distribute up to $100,000 of their IRA balance to charitable organizations in 2008 and in 2009 without recognizing income and without taking a charitable deduction.

BACKGROUND

In 2006 and 2007, an individual aged 70 1/2 or older can distribute up to $100,000 from his or her IRA to a charitable organization without recognizing income and without having to take a charitable deduction (Code Sec. 408(d)(8)). This rule applies

BACKGROUND

to distributions made after December 31, 2005, through December 31, 2007, directly from traditional IRAs, Roth IRAs or deemed IRAs (not ongoing SEP or SIMPLE IRAs), as well as inherited IRAs if the beneficiary reached the age of 70 1/2 before the distribution (Notice 2007-7, I.R.B. 2007-5, 395). Distributions that are otherwise includible in gross income (Code Sec. 408(d)(8)(B)) and otherwise entirely deductible as charitable contributions (Code Sec. 408(d)(8)(C)) are treated as qualified charitable distributions.

If distributions are made from a traditional IRA that includes both deductible and nondeductible contributions, the distribution is first treated as income, up to the aggregate amount that would otherwise be includible in gross income if all amounts in all of the owner's IRAs were distributed during the same tax year (Code Sec. 408(d)(8)(D)).

Qualified charitable distributions count toward satisfying the IRA owner's minimum distribution requirements. However, such distributions are not taken into account for purposes of determining the IRA owner's charitable deduction.

NEW LAW EXPLAINED

Tax-free treatment of charitable distributions from IRAs extended—The exclusion from gross income provided for qualified charitable distributions of up to $100,000 from traditional, Roth, or deemed IRAs is extended to apply to distributions made in 2008 and 2009 (Code Sec. 408(d)(8)(F) as amended by the Emergency Economic Stabilization Act of 2008 (P.L. 110-343)).

Practical Analysis: Robert S. Keebler, CPA, MST, Partner on the Estate Planning Team of Virchow Krause & Co., Appleton, Wisconsin, finds that Division C, Act Sec. 205 of the Emergency Economic Stabilization Act of 2008 (P.L. 110-343) expands the years that individuals can transfer funds from their individual retirement accounts to charities to include 2008 and 2009. Under Code Sec. 408(d)(8), taxpayers were permitted to make direct IRA distributions to charity without having to include the distribution in gross income. In particular, the tax law permitted up to $100,000 to be contributed each year directly to charity, but individuals were only allowed to do so in 2006 and 2007. The Emergency Economic Act allows for distributions to be made in taxable years beginning after December 31, 2007.

Practical Analysis: Robert B. Teuber, J.D., Attorney in the Milwaukee office of Weiss Berzowski Brady LLP, observes that the Pension Protection Act of 2006 included a provision in Code Sec. 408 that allowed certain IRA distributions to be made to charities without being included in a taxpayer's income. In general, a qualifying IRA distribution (not exceeding $100,000) made directly to certain charities will not be included in a taxpayer's income provided that the owner of the distributing IRA is at least 70 1/2 years old.

¶225

NEW LAW EXPLAINED

The provision was initially effective for the tax years 2006 and 2007. The income exclusion had lapsed by the beginning of 2008, but Division C, Act Sec. 205 of the Emergency Economic Stabilization Act of 2008 (P.L. 110-343) has now reinstituted the income exclusion for the years 2008 and 2009. The extension of this provision will allow for additional tax and estate planning opportunities through 2009.

Planning Note: As a result of the extension, individuals who do not need to take distributions from their IRAs and prefer to avoid tax on the minimum required distributions may again donate up to $100,000 in 2008 and 2009 with no reportable income and no deduction to muddy the waters.

▶ **Effective date.** The provision applies to distributions made in tax years beginning after December 31, 2007 (Division C, Act Sec. 205(b) of the Emergency Economic Stabilization Act of 2008 (P.L. 110-343)).

Law source: Law at ¶5295. Committee Reports at ¶10,370.

— Division C, Act Sec. 205(a) of the Emergency Economic Stabilization Act of 2008 (P.L. 110-343), amending Code Sec. 408(d)(8)(F);

— Division C, Act Sec. 205(b), providing the effective date.

Reporter references: For further information, consult the following CCH reporters.

— Standard Federal Tax Reporter, ¶18,922.0326

— Tax Research Consultant, RETIRE: 66,514

— Federal Tax Guide, ¶11,445 and ¶11,450

¶230 Transportation Fringe Benefit for Bicycle Commuters

SUMMARY OF NEW LAW

Any employee who regularly uses a bicycle to commute to work is entitled to a transportation fringe benefit not to exceed $20 per month.

BACKGROUND

In general, commuting expenses to and from a place of business and home are not deductible. Transportation fringe benefits, though, can turn some commuting expenses into tax-favored benefits. These benefits defray some of an employee's commuting expenses with either pre-tax dollars that reduce otherwise taxable compensation, or with direct, employer-subsidized amounts that are considered tax free.

Qualified transportation fringes include van pooling, transit passes and qualified parking (Code Sec. 132(f)(1)). An employer may provide an employee any one or

BACKGROUND

more of the three benefits (Reg. § 1.132-9(b)). The benefit plan does not have to be in writing (Reg. § 1.132-9(b)). Only individuals who are current employees at the time the employer offers the benefit are eligible recipients of qualified transportation fringe benefits (Reg. § 1.132-9(b)).

The statutory base amounts of $100 for van pooling and transit passes and $175 for qualified parking are adjusted annually for inflation (Code Sec. 132(f)(2)). For 2008, the amount that may be excluded from gross income is $220 per month for qualified parking and $115 per month for van pooling and transit passes (Rev. Proc. 2007-66, I.R.B. 2007-45, 970).

NEW LAW EXPLAINED

Qualified bicycle commuting reimbursement.—The new law adds qualified bike commuting reimbursements to the types of qualified transportation fringe benefits that an employer may provide to an employee who commutes to work using a bike (Code Sec. 132(f)(1)(D), as added by the Emergency Economic Stabilization Act of 2008 (P.L. 110-343)).

The applicable annual limitation in case of any qualified bicycle commuting reimbursement is $20 for every qualified bicycle commuting month for any calendar year (Code Sec. 132(f)(5)(F)(ii), as added by the Emergency Economic Act of 2008). "Qualified bicycle commuting month" refers to any month during which an employee regularly uses a bike for a substantial portion of travel between the employee's residence and place of employment and the employee did not receive any other transportation fringe benefit (Code Sec. 132(f)(5)(F)(iii), as added by the Emergency Economic Act of 2008).

> **Comment:** The applicable annual limitation in case of any qualified bicycle commuting reimbursement is not subject to inflation adjustment. The inflation adjustment applies only to van pooling, transit passes and qualified parking expenses that an employee can exclude from gross income (Code Sec. 132(f)(6)).

A "qualified bicycle commuting reimbursement" refers to any employer reimbursement during the 15-month period starting with the first day of a calendar year to an employee for reasonable expenses incurred by the employee during the calendar year for the purchase of a bike and bike accessories, repair and storage of a bike that is regularly used to ride to and from work (Code Sec. 132(f)(5)(F)(i), as added by Emergency Economic Act of 2008). However, unlike other qualified transportation fringe benefits, the bike commuting fringe may not be provided pursuant to an elective salary reduction agreement (Code Sec. 132(f)(4), as amended by the Emergency Economic Act of 2008). Under such an agreement, no amount is included in an employee's gross income solely because the employee may choose between any qualified transportation fringe benefit and compensation that would otherwise be includable in the gross income of the employee.

Practical Analysis: Michelle Ward, J.D., Senior Consultant on the Estate Planning Team of Virchow Krause & Co., Appleton, Wisconsin, notes that generally, an

¶230

NEW LAW EXPLAINED

amount an employee receives as a fringe benefit must be included in income. An exception exists, however, under Code Sec. 132(f) if the fringe benefit is a "qualified transportation fringe," which includes transit passes and qualified parking. Division B, Act Sec. 211 of the Emergency Economic Stabilization Act of 2008 (P.L. 110-343) would also include "any qualified bicycle commuting reimbursement" in the definition of a qualified transportation fringe. The term "qualified bicycle commuting reimbursement" would mean, with respect to any calendar year, any employer reimbursement during the 15-month period beginning with the first day of such calendar year for reasonable expenses incurred by the employee during such calendar year for the purchase of a bicycle and bicycle improvements, repair and storage, if such bicycle is regularly used for travel between the employee's residence and place of employment. The exclusion limit for an employee for any calendar year would be the product of $20 multiplied by the number of qualified bicycle commuting months during such year. A "qualified bicycle commuting month" means, with respect to any employee, any month during which such employee (1) regularly uses the bicycle for a substantial portion of the travel between the employee's residence and place of employment, and (1) does not receive any benefit described in Code Sec. 132(f)(1)(A),(B), or (C). This additional exception would apply to tax years after December 31, 2008.

Comment: Bike riders have been clamoring for this benefit long before the price of gas soared beyond the $4 a gallon level. Bike riders argued that if the purchasers of hybrid cars get tax savings, then bike riders who do more for the environment should likewise get some tax benefits. Now with gas prices at more than $4 a gallon, even without this fringe benefit, more people have been riding their bikes to work to save on gas. This new fringe benefit, although very minimal, will surely encourage more employees to ride their bikes to work. According to the League of American Bicyclists, more than 500,000 people throughout the United States commute to work by bicycle.

▶ **Effective date.** The provision applies to tax years beginning after December 31, 2008 (Division B, Act Sec. 211(e) of the Emergency Economic Stabilization Act of 2008 (P.L. 110-343)).

Law source: Law at ¶5195. Committee Reports at ¶10,200.

— Division B, Act Sec. 211(a) of the Emergency Economic Stabilization Act of 2008 (P.L. 110-343), adding Code Sec. 132(f)(1)(D);

— Division B, Act Sec. 211(b), adding Code Sec. 132(f)(2)(C);

— Division B, Act Sec. 211(c), adding Code Sec. 132(f)(5)(F);

— Division B, Act Sec. 211(d), amending Code Sec. 132(f)(4);

— Division B, Act Sec. 211(e), providing the effective date.

Reporter references: For further information, consult the following CCH reporters.

— Standard Federal Tax Reporter, ¶7438.054

— Tax Research Consultant, COMPEN: 36,350

— Federal Tax Guide, ¶4672

¶230

DEDUCTIONS

¶235 Additional Standard Deduction for Real Property Taxes for Nonitemizers

SUMMARY OF NEW LAW

Homeowners who claim the basic standard deduction may claim an additional standard deduction for state and local real property taxes, up to $500 ($1,000 for joint returns), for any tax year beginning in 2008 or 2009.

BACKGROUND

The standard deduction is a dollar amount that reduces the amount of taxable income. Taxpayers cannot take the standard deduction if they claim itemized deductions. In some cases, the standard deduction can consist of two parts, the basic standard deduction and an additional standard deduction amount, for age, or blindness, or both. The basic standard deduction and the additional standard deduction amount for age, or blindness, or both are adjusted each year for inflation and varies according to a taxpayer's filing status. Taxpayers who itemize their deductions may deduct state and local taxes paid, including individual income taxes, real property taxes, and personal property taxes. The additional standard deduction for real property taxes was added by the Housing Assistance Tax Act of 2008 (P.L. 110-289) and applies for any tax year beginning in 2008 (Code Sec. 63(c)).

NEW LAW EXPLAINED

Additional standard deduction for real property taxes extended.—Homeowners who claim the basic standard deduction may claim an additional standard deduction for state and local real property taxes for any tax year beginning in 2008 or 2009 (Code Sec. 63(c)(1), as amended by the Emergency Economic Stabilization Act of 2008 (P.L. 110-343)). The real property tax deduction is the lesser of: (1) the amount allowable as a deduction for state and local taxes if the taxpayer claimed itemized deductions, or (2) $500 ($1,000 in the case of joint returns) (Code Sec. 63(c)(7), as amended by the Emergency Economic Act of 2008). Any taxes taken into account when computing adjusted gross income under Code Sec. 62(a) will not be taken into account for purposes of the additional standard deduction for real property taxes.

> **Practical Analysis:** Robert B. Teuber, J.D., Attorney in the Milwaukee office of Weiss Berzowski Brady LLP, observes that the Housing Assistance Tax Act of 2008 increased the standard deduction for nonitemizing taxpayers that pay real property taxes. The increased standard deduction is increased for these taxpayers by the lesser of $500 ($1,000 for joint filers) or the deduction allowed for real property taxes

NEW LAW EXPLAINED

if the taxpayer itemized. Originally, the increase was only allowed for tax years beginning in 2008. Division C, Act Sec. 204 of the Emergency Economic Stabilization Act of 2008 (P.L. 110-343) extends this increased deduction to tax years beginning in 2009.

While the increased deduction is effectively limited to a maximum of $500 ($1,000 for joint filers) and many homeowners may be better suited to itemize their deductions, the extension will provide a small benefit to taxpayers that otherwise have insufficient itemized deductions. Such taxpayers may include those that have paid off (or are close to paying off) their mortgages and have little home mortgage interest expense.

▶ **Effective date.** The provision applies to tax years beginning after December 31, 2008 (Division C, Act Sec. 204 of the Emergency Economic Stabilization Act of 2008 (P.L. 110-343)).

Law source: Law at ¶5185. Committee Reports at ¶10,360.

— Division C, Act Sec. 204(a) of the Emergency Economic Stabilization Act of 2008 (P.L. 110-343), amending Code Sec. 63(c)(1)(C);

— Division C, Act Sec. 204(b), providing the effective date.

Reporter references: For further information, consult the following CCH reporters.

— Standard Federal Tax Reporter, ¶6023.023 and ¶6023.07

— Tax Research Consultant, FILEIND: 12,100

— Federal Tax Guide, ¶6020

¶240 Election to Deduct State and Local General Sales Taxes

SUMMARY OF NEW LAW

The election to deduct state and local general sales taxes in lieu of state and local income taxes is extended through December 31, 2009.

BACKGROUND

Individuals may elect to deduct *either* state and local income taxes or state and local general sales taxes as an itemized deduction on their federal income tax returns (Code Sec. 164(b)(5)). The deduction is *either*:

(1) the total of actual general sales taxes paid as substantiated by accumulated receipts; or

(2) an amount from IRS-generated tables plus, if any, the amount of general sales taxes paid in the purchase of a motor vehicle, boat, or other items as prescribed by the IRS (see IRS Publication 600, State and Local General Sales Taxes).

BACKGROUND

The election to deduct state and local general sales taxes in lieu of state and local income taxes was enacted to apply to tax years beginning in 2004 and 2005 but was extended to apply to 2006 and 2007 calendar tax years (Code Sec. 164(b)(5)(I), as amended by the Tax Relief and Health Care Act of 2006 (P.L. 109-432)).

General sales taxes. For purposes of the deduction, "general sales tax" means a tax imposed at one rate on the retail sales of a broad range of classes of items (Reg. § 1.164-3(f)). Except in the case of a lower rate of tax applicable to food, clothing, medical supplies, and motor vehicles, no deduction is allowed for general sales tax at a rate other than the general rate of tax (Reg. § 1.164-3(g)). If the state sales tax rate for motor vehicles exceeds the general sales tax rate, the excess is disregarded and the general sales tax rate is treated as the rate of tax (Code Sec. 164(b)(5)(F)). Thus, only the amount of tax that is equal to the general sales tax rate is allowed as a deduction.

If the amount of the general sales tax is separately stated, then to the extent it is paid by the consumer to the seller (other than in connection with the consumer's trade or business), the amount is treated as a tax imposed on, and paid by, the consumer (Code Sec. 164(b)(5)(G)). In addition, a *compensating use tax* is treated as a general sales tax provided:

(1) such a tax is complementary to a general sales tax; and

(2) a deduction for sales tax is allowed with respect to similar items sold at retail in the taxing jurisdiction.

The tax must be imposed on the use, storage, or consumption of an item (Reg. § 1.164-3(i)).

NEW LAW EXPLAINED

Election to deduct state and local general sales taxes in lieu of state and local income taxes extended.—The election to deduct state and local general sales taxes in lieu of state and local income taxes is extended to apply to tax years beginning before January 1, 2010 (Code Sec. 164(b)(5)(I), as amended by the Emergency Economic Stabilization Act of 2008 (P.L. 110-343)).

Planning Note: The election to deduct state and local general sales taxes in lieu of state and local income taxes is favorable to taxpayers who live in states that do not impose income taxes or in states in which the sales tax rate exceeds the highest individual income tax rate. For many taxpayers who live in states that impose an income tax, even in those states that impose a higher sales tax, a state and a local general sales tax deduction that is computed using the IRS optional state and certain local sales tax table is usually lower than the state and local income tax deduction. However, if a taxpayer bought big-ticket items such as a motor vehicle, an aircraft or a boat, state and local general sales taxes paid on these will be added to the amount of deduction derived from the optional state and certain local sales tax table.

Compliance Pointer: Taxpayers may elect to deduct sales taxes in lieu of local income taxes on Schedule A of Form 1040. The election may be revoked by filing an amended return for the tax year, if the period of limitation for filing a claim

NEW LAW EXPLAINED

for refund or credit under Code Sec. 6511 has not expired. A taxpayer is permitted to deduct sales taxes in one tax year and local income taxes in another year (see Notice 2005-31, 2005-1 CB 830).

The IRS has posted Publication 600, State and Local General Sales Taxes, to its website, www.IRS.gov. Publication 600 was updated to reflect the extension of the deduction and includes the state and local sales tax tables, a worksheet, and instructions for figuring the deduction. The actual deduction amount will depend on the taxpayer's income and the number of exemptions.

▶ **Effective date.** The provision applies to tax years beginning after December 31, 2007 (Division C, Act Sec. 201(b) of the Emergency Economic Stabilization Act of 2008 (P.L. 110-343)).

Law source: Law at ¶5220. Committee Reports at ¶10,330.

— Division C, Act Sec. 201(a) of the Emergency Economic Stabilization Act of 2008 (P.L. 110-343), amending Code Sec. 164(b)(5)(I);

— Division C, Act Sec. 201(b) providing the effective date.

Reporter references: For further information, consult the following CCH reporters.

— Standard Federal Tax Reporter, ¶9502.0385

— Tax Research Consultant, INDIV: 45,106.05

— Federal Tax Guide, ¶4265 and ¶6541

¶245 Deduction for Qualified Tuition and Related Expenses

SUMMARY OF NEW LAW

The deduction for qualified tuition and related expenses is extended for two years, through December 31, 2009.

BACKGROUND

One of the education tax breaks included in the Economic Growth and Tax Relief Reconciliation Act of 2001 (P.L. 107-16) was an above-the-line deduction for qualified tuition and related expenses (Code Sec. 222). The provision was added to provide taxpayers with a greater choice of available education tax benefits (S. Rep. No. 107-30). As originally enacted, the deduction did not apply to tax years beginning after December 31, 2005 (Code Sec. 222(e)). Pursuant to the Tax Relief and Health Care Act of 2006 (P.L. 109-432), the deduction was extended for two years, so that it is not available for tax years beginning after December 31, 2007 (Division A, Act Sec. 101(a), P.L. 109-432).

BACKGROUND

The term "qualified tuition and related expenses" is defined in Code Sec. 25A(f) (Code Sec. 222(d)). These expenses include tuition and fees required for the enrollment or attendance of the taxpayer, the taxpayer's spouse, or dependent at an eligible institution of higher education. Expenses connected to meals, lodging, insurance, transportation, and similar living expenses are not eligible for the deduction. The deduction is not available for expenses paid for elementary or secondary education. The expenses must be incurred in connection with enrollment during the tax year, or with an academic term beginning during the tax year or during the first three months of the following tax year (Code Sec. 222(d)(3)(B)).

Taxpayers cannot use their education expenses to claim a double tax benefit. If an expense is deductible under any other provision, it will not be deductible under Code Sec. 222. No deduction is allowed for qualified tuition and related expenses if the taxpayer or any other person takes a Hope Scholarship Credit or Lifetime Learning Credit with respect to the student (Code Sec. 222(c)(2)(A)). For purposes of the deduction, the taxpayer must reduce the total amount of qualified tuition and related expenses by the amount that is taken into account for purposes of: (1) excluded distributions from a qualified tuition plan (Code Sec. 529(c)(1), (2)) excluded distributions from a Coverdell Education Savings Account (Code Sec. 530(d)(2)), and (3) excluded interest on U.S. savings bonds to pay for higher education (Code Sec. 135). However, qualified expenses are not reduced by any portion of a distribution from a qualified tuition plan that represents a return of contributions to the plan (Code Sec. 222(c)(2)(B)).

The amount of the deduction allowed depends on the taxpayer's adjusted gross income (AGI). Taxpayers whose AGI does not exceed $65,000 ($130,000 for joint filers) for 2007 may deduct a maximum of $4,000 (Code Sec. 222(b)(2)(B)(i)). Taxpayers with AGI of more than $65,000 ($130,000 for joint filers) but less than $80,000 ($160,000 for joint filers) may deduct a maximum of $2,000 (Code Sec. 222(b)(2)(B)(ii)). These amounts are not adjusted for inflation and married individuals filing separately may not claim the deduction (Code Sec. 222(d)(4)). No deduction is allowed to any individual with respect to whom a personal exemption deduction may be claimed by another taxpayer for the tax year (Code Sec. 222(c)(3)).

NEW LAW EXPLAINED

Tuition deduction extended.—The deduction for qualified tuition and related expenses is extended for two years. The deduction will not apply to tax years beginning after December 31, 2009 (Code Sec. 222(e), as amended by the Emergency Economic Stabilization Act of 2008 (P.L. 110-343)).

> **Compliance Pointer:** The taxpayer must include the name and taxpayer identification number (TIN) of the student for whom the expenses were paid on the taxpayer's return in order to claim the deduction (Code Sec. 222(d)(2)). As an above-the-line deduction, it can even be taken by taxpayers who do not itemize deductions.

¶245

NEW LAW EXPLAINED

> **Planning Note:** Taxpayers may not claim the deduction for qualified tuition and related expenses and a Hope Scholarship or Lifetime Learning Credit for the same student in the same year (Code Sec. 222(c)(2)(A)).

The maximum deduction is $4,000 for taxpayers whose AGI does not exceed $65,000 ($130,000 for joint filers) and $2,000 for taxpayers whose AGI does not exceed $80,000 ($160,000 for joint filers) (Code Sec. 222(b)(2)(B)(i)). Taxpayers with AGI exceeding $80,000 ($160,000 for joint filers) cannot take the deduction (Code Sec. 222(b)(2)(B)(ii)).

Effective date. The provision applies to tax years beginning after December 31, 2007 (Division C, Act Sec. 202(b) of the Emergency Economic Stabilization Act of 2008 (P.L. 110-343)).

Law source: Law at ¶5285. Committee Report at ¶10,340.

— Division C, Act Sec. 202(a) of the Emergency Economic Stabilization Act of 2008 (P.L. 110-343), amending Code Sec. 222(e);

— Division C, Act Sec. 202(b), providing the effective date.

Reporter references: For further information, consult the following CCH reporters.

— Standard Federal Tax Reporter, ¶12,772.01

— Tax Research Consultant, INDIV: 60,064 and FILEIND: 9,086

— Federal Tax Guide, ¶6434

¶250 Above-the-Line Deduction for Certain Expenses of School Teachers

SUMMARY OF NEW LAW

The deduction for eligible educator expenses has been extended through December 31, 2009.

BACKGROUND

For tax years 2002 through 2007, eligible educators have been allowed an above-the-line deduction of up to $250 (annually) for unreimbursed expenses paid or incurred for books, supplies (other than nonathletic supplies for health or physical education courses), computer equipment (including related software and services), and other equipment, including supplementary materials used by the eligible educator in the classroom (Code Sec. 62(a)(2)(D)). For purposes of this deduction, an "eligible educator" is an individual who is a kindergarten through grade 12 teacher, instructor, counselor, principal, or aide working in a school for at least 900 hours during the school year; a "school" is any school that provides elementary or secondary educa-

BACKGROUND

tion (kindergarten through grade 12), as determined under state law (Code Sec. 62(d)(1)).

The deduction for eligible educator classroom expenses was enacted as part of the Job Creation and Worker Assistance Act of 2002 (P.L. 107-147). It applied to classroom expenses paid in 2002 and 2003 (Code Sec. 62(a)(2)(D)). This above-the-line deduction for eligible educator expenses was extended by the Working Families Tax Relief Act of 2004 (P.L. 108-311) to apply also to tax years 2004 and 2005. The deduction applied only to the extent that the expenses exceeded the amount excludable from income for the year under Code Secs. 135 (education savings bonds), 529(c)(1) (qualified tuition programs), and 530(d)(2) (Coverdell education savings accounts). The deduction for eligible educator classroom expenses was extended for two years by the Tax Relief and Health Care Act of 2006 (P.L. 109-432). The above-the-line deduction for eligible educators was scheduled to expire for tax years beginning after December 31, 2007.

NEW LAW EXPLAINED

Eligible educator expense deduction extended.—The deduction for eligible educator expenses, allowing eligible educators an above-the-line deduction of up to $250 for educational expenses, has been extended to apply to tax years beginning in 2008 and 2009 (Code Sec. 62(a)(2)(D), as amended by the Emergency Economic Stabilization Act of 2008 (P.L. 110-343)).

> **Practical Analysis:** Michelle Ward, J.D., Senior Consultant on the Estate Planning Team of Virchow Krause & Co., Appleton, Wisconsin, observes that Code Sec. 62(a)(2)(D) allows elementary and secondary school teachers a deduction from gross income for expenses, not in excess of $250, that the teacher paid for books, supplies (other than nonathletic supplies for courses of instruction in health or physical education), computer equipment and other equipment, and supplementary materials used by the teacher in the classroom. This deduction is currently only available for the 2002–2007 tax years. Division C, Act Sec. 203 of the Emergency Economic Stabilization Act of 2008 (P.L. 110-343), however, expands the eligible tax years to include 2008 and 2009. This change would apply to tax years beginning after December 31, 2007.

Comment: It is unclear whether an otherwise eligible educator who has not worked 900 hours in a school during the school year (September to June) would be eligible for the deduction if that educator met the 900 hour requirement through additional teaching during July and August, as part of a summer school or year-round program ("The Tax Deduction for Classroom Expenses of Elementary and Secondary School Teachers, Updated May 23, 2008," Congressional Research Service Report for Congress).

Effective date. The provision applies to tax years beginning after December 31, 2007 (Division C, Act Sec. 203(b) of the Emergency Economic Stabilization Act of 2008 (P.L. 110-343)).

¶250

NEW LAW EXPLAINED

Law source: Law at ¶5180. Committee Report at ¶10,350.

— Division C, Act Sec. 203(a) of the Emergency Economic Stabilization Act of 2008 (P.L. 110-343), amending Code Sec. 62(a)(2)(D);

— Division C, Act Sec. 203(b), providing the effective date.

Reporter references: For further information, consult the following CCH reporters.

— Standard Federal Tax Reporter, ¶6005.029

— Tax Research Consultant, INDIV: 36,364

— Federal Tax Guide, ¶6430

QUALIFYING CHILDREN

¶255 Refundable Child Tax Credit

SUMMARY OF NEW LAW

For the 2008 tax year, if the total amount of a taxpayer's allowable child tax credit exceeds the taxpayer's total tax liability (regular and alternative minimum), the taxpayer is eligible for a refundable child credit equal to 15 percent of the taxpayer's earned income in excess of $8,500, up to the per child credit amount.

BACKGROUND

Taxpayers who have dependent children under age 17 at the close of a calendar year are eligible for a child tax credit (CTC) in the amount of $1,000 per child through 2010 (Code Sec. 24). The CTC is subject to income phase-out rules and is limited to *qualifying* children (Code Sec. 24(b)(1), (b)(2), and (c)). The CTC is generally a nonrefundable credit that may be offset against both the taxpayer's regular and alternative minimum tax liabilities (Code Secs. 24(b)(3) and 26(a)(2)).

The CTC does have a refundable component when the total amount of the CTC exceeds the taxpayer's total tax liability minus nonrefundable credits previously taken. The CTC is refundable to the extent of 15 percent of the taxpayer's earned income in excess of $10,000, as adjusted for inflation, up to the per child credit amount, if the taxpayer has a total tax liability of less than his or her allowable CTC (Code Sec. 24(d)(1)). The $10,000 amount is subject to cost-of-living adjustments and the inflation adjusted base amount of earned income is $11,750 in 2007 (Code Sec. 24(d)(3); Rev. Proc. 2006-53, I.R.B. 2006-48,996). For 2008, the inflation adjusted base amount of earned income is $12,050 (Rev. Proc. 2007-66, I.R.B. 2007-45,970). Taxpayers with earned income of less than $12,050 in 2008 are not eligible for the refundable CTC.

The 15 percent of earned income refundable CTC is subject to a sunset provision and will not apply for tax years beginning after December 31, 2010. Furthermore, taxpay-

BACKGROUND

ers with three or more children may calculate the refundable portion of the credit using the excess of their social security taxes over their earned income credit (additional credit for families with three or more children), instead of the 15 percent method, if it results in a greater refundable credit (Code Sec. 24(d)(1)).

The refundable credit amount will reduce the nonrefundable credit otherwise allowable (*i.e.*, converting some or all of the nonrefundable credit into a refundable credit), and the refundable credit is not taken into account in applying the tax liability limitation on nonrefundable personal credits (Code Sec. 24(d)(1)). These rules apply regardless of whether the refundable credit is computed under the 15 percent of earned income method or the additional credit for families with three or more children method.

NEW LAW EXPLAINED

Refundable child tax credit increased for 2008 by reducing the threshold income amount—In 2008, the child tax credit (CTC) is refundable to the extent of 15 percent of the taxpayer's earned income in excess of $8,500, up to the per child credit amount, if the taxpayer has a total tax liability (regular and alternative minimum) of less than his or her allowable CTC minus nonrefundable credits previously taken (Code Sec. 24(d)(4), as added by the Emergency Economic Stabilization Act of 2008 (P.L. 110-343)).

> **Comment:** Division C, Act Sec. 501(b) of the Emergency Economic Act of 2008 states that the amendment applies to tax years beginning after December 31, 2007, but Code Sec. 24(d)(4), as added by the Emergency Economic Act of 2008, clearly restricts the special rule to tax years beginning in 2008 only.

In 2008, the threshold requirements for the 15 percent of earned income refundable component of the CTC are:

(1) a total tax liability (regular plus alternative minimum), minus nonrefundable credits previously taken, of less than the taxpayer's allowable CTC ($1,000 per qualifying child); and

(2) earned income in excess of $8,500.

> **Example:** In 2008, Sue and Jim Warren have two children and earned income of $25,000. They have no other income and no alternative minimum tax liability. They are entitled to no nonrefundable personal credits other than the CTC. Since they file jointly, they are entitled to a standard deduction of $10,900. They are also entitled to a personal exemption of $3,500 for each family member, or $14,000. Their taxable income is $100 and their tax is $10. Their nonrefundable CTC is equal to $2,000 ($1,000 per child). However, the nonrefundable credit is limited to the amount of tax liability, or $10.
>
> The refundable credit is equal to the lesser of either the unclaimed portion of the nonrefundable credit amount, $1,990 ($2,000 − $10), or 15 percent of the

NEW LAW EXPLAINED

Warrens' earned income that exceeds $8,500, $2,475 (($25,000 − $8,500) × .15). Therefore, the total refundable credit amount is $1,990. The Warrens get the full benefit of the CTC ($10 nonrefundable and $1,990 refundable).

Without the amendment reducing the threshold amount of earned income in 2008, the inflation adjusted amount of earned income would have been $12,050. This would have given the Warrens a refundable CTC of $1,942.50 (($25,000 − $12,050) × .15) and a nonrefundable credit of $10 (tax liability). Their total CTC would have been $1,952.50, $47.50 less than the full $2,000.

Example: In 2008, Jane Allen has two children and earned income of $10,000. She has no other income and no alternative minimum tax liability. Jane is not entitled to any nonrefundable personal credits except the CTC. She files as head of household and, therefore, is entitled to a standard deduction of $8,000. She is also entitled to a personal exemption of $3,500 for each family member, or $10,500. Jane has no taxable income and no tax liability. Her nonrefundable CTC is equal to $2,000 ($1,000 per child). However, the nonrefundable credit is limited to the amount of tax liability, or zero.

The refundable credit is equal to the lesser of either the unclaimed portion of the nonrefundable credit amount, $2,000, or 15 percent of Jane's earned income that exceeds $8,500, $225 (($10,000 − $8,500) × .15). Jane's total refundable credit is $225. Jane receives $1,775 ($2,000 − $225) less than the full $2,000 CTC; however, if the threshold amount had not been reduced for 2008, Jane would have received no CTC (($10,000 − $12,050) × .15).

Comment: The effect of reducing the earned income threshold for computing the refundable CTC is an increase in the amount of the refundable CTC for more taxpayers. However, 15 percent of $3,550 (the difference between $12,050 and $8,500) is only $532.50; therefore, the maximum refundable CTC increase in 2008 will not exceed $532.50 for any taxpayer.

▶ **Effective date.** The amendment applies to tax years beginning after December 31, 2007 (Division C, Act Sec. 501(b) of the Emergency Economic Stabilization Act of 2008 (P.L. 110-343)).

Law source: Law at ¶5010. Committee Report at ¶10,640.

— Division C, Act Sec. 501(a) of the Emergency Economic Stabilization Act of 2008 (P.L. 110-343), adding Code Sec. 24(d)(4);

— Division C, Act Sec. 501(b), providing the effective date.

Reporter references: For further information, consult the following CCH reporters.

— Standard Federal Tax Reporter, ¶3770.01, ¶3770.03 and ¶3770.035

— Tax Research Consultant, INDIV: 57,450, INDIV: 57,454.05 and INDIV: 57,454.10

— Federal Tax Guide, ¶2222

¶260 "Qualifying Child" Tests, Tiebreaker Rules and Child Credit Requirements

SUMMARY OF NEW LAW

The definition of a "qualifying child" is modified with respect to age and joint returns, the tiebreaker rules are clarified, and the child tax credit is tied to the child's dependency exemption.

BACKGROUND

A taxpayer who has a qualifying child may be able to claim several tax benefits:

- A taxpayer who maintains a home for a qualifying child may be able to file returns as a head of household (Code Sec. 2).

- A taxpayer who incurs employment-related expenses and has a qualifying child under the age of 13 may be able to claim the child and dependent care credit (Code Sec. 21).

- A taxpayer may be able to claim a child tax credit for each qualifying child under the age of 17 (Code Sec. 24).

- A taxpayer with a qualifying child is more likely to qualify for the earned income credit, and the amount of the credit is larger (Code Sec. 32).

- Each qualifying child may entitle the taxpayer to a dependency exemption (Code Sec. 151).

A qualifying child generally must satisfy these four tests:

(1) Relationship test. Qualifying children must be the taxpayer's children, siblings stepsiblings, or their descendants (Code Sec. 152(c)(1)(A) and (c)(2)). Children include the taxpayer's natural children, stepchildren, legally adopted children, children who are lawfully placed in the taxpayer's household for legal adoption, and eligible foster children (that is, children placed with the taxpayer by an authorized placement agency or court order) (Code Sec. 152(f)(1)). Brothers and sisters include half-brothers and half-sisters (Code Sec. 152(f)(4)).

(2) Abode test. A qualifying child must have the same principal place of abode as the taxpayer for more than one-half of the taxpayer's tax year (Code Sec. 152(c)(1)(B)).

(3) Age test. As of the close of the calendar year in which the taxpayer's tax year begins, a qualifying child must be (i) under 19 years old; (ii) a student under 24 years old; or (iii) permanently and totally disabled (Code Sec. 152(c)(1)(C) and (c)(3)).

(4) Support test. A qualifying child must not have provided more than one-half of his or her own support during the calendar year in which the taxpayer's tax year begins (Code Sec. 152(c)(1)(D)).

BACKGROUND

The tax benefits that incorporate this definition of "qualifying child" also impose additional tests. For instance, a qualifying child who files a joint return with a spouse cannot qualify as a taxpayer's dependent (Code Sec. 152(b)(2)). In addition, a qualifying child who is not a citizen or national of the United States cannot be a dependent unless he or she is a resident of the U.S., Canada or Mexico; or is an adopted child of a taxpayer who is a U.S. citizen or national and who shares the child's abode (Code Sec. 152(b)(3)).

Special tiebreaker rules apply when a single individual is a qualifying child for multiple taxpayers. If only one of the taxpayers is the child's parent, the child is a qualifying child for that parent. If two of the taxpayers are the child's parents and they do not file a joint return, the child is a qualifying child for the parent with whom the child resided for the longest period during the year; if the child spent equal amounts of time residing with each parent, the child is a qualifying child for the parent with the highest adjusted gross income. If none of the taxpayers is the child's parent, the child is a qualifying child for the taxpayer with the highest adjusted gross income (Code Sec. 152(c)(4)).

NEW LAW EXPLAINED

Definition of "qualifying child" modified; child credit and tiebreaker rules clarified.—The definition of a qualifying child is changed with respect to age and joint returns, the tiebreaker rules that apply when multiple taxpayers can claim the same qualifying child are clarified, and the child credit is tied to the child's dependency exemption.

Qualifying child. Two new elements are added to the definition of "qualifying-child." First, the age test is expanded to require that a qualifying child must be younger than the taxpayer (Code Sec. 152(c)(3)(A), as amended by the Fostering Connection to Success and Increasing Adoptions Act of 2008 (P.L. 110-351)). For instance, a taxpayer's older brother or sister cannot be the taxpayer's qualifying child.

Second, a new test is added with respect to joint returns. A qualifying child cannot file a joint return with a spouse for any tax year beginning during the calendar year in which the taxpayer's tax year begins. This test does not apply if the qualifying child files a joint return only to obtain a refund (Code Sec. 152(c)(1)(E), as added by the Foster Care Act). This often happens, for instance, when a taxpayer is entitled to a refund of taxes withheld from wages.

> **Comment:** Current law already prohibits a dependent from filing a joint return (Code Sec. 152(b)(2)). Thus, this change does not affect the dependency exemption, but it can affect other tax benefits that incorporate the definition of "qualifying child."

Tiebreaker rules. Two clarifications are added to the tiebreaker rules that apply when a single individual is a qualifying child for more than one taxpayer. First, the law clarifies that the tie-breaker rules apply whenever two or more taxpayers *can* claim the individual as a qualifying child, regardless of whether they actually do so (Code Sec. 152(c)(4)(A), as amended by the Foster Care Act). Second, if the parents can claim

NEW LAW EXPLAINED

an individual as a qualifying child, but neither parent does so, another taxpayer may claim the individual as a qualifying child only if that taxpayer's adjusted gross income (AGI) is higher than the highest AGI of any of the individual's parents (Code Sec. 152(c)(4)(C), as added by the Foster Care Act).

Example: Jenny is the biological child of Craig and Lisa, who are not married. She satisfies the qualifying-child requirements for both of them. Lisa's AGI is higher than Craig's AGI. Craig cannot claim Jenny as a qualifying child on his return, even if Lisa does not claim Jenny as a qualifying child on her return.

Jenny also satisfies the qualifying-child requirements for Nelson, an unrelated person. He can claim her as a qualifying child on his return only if neither of her parents claims her, and Nelson's AGI is higher than both of her parent's AGI. For instance, if Lisa's AGI is also higher than Nelson's AGI, Nelson cannot claim Jenny as a qualifying child on his return, even if Lisa and Craig do not claim her on their returns.

Child credit. Finally, a qualifying child for purposes of the child tax credit must also be the taxpayer's dependent (Code Sec. 24(a), as amended by the Foster Care Act).

> **Comment:** This restores the pre-2005 rule, under which the child credit was explicitly tied to the child's dependency exemption (Code Sec. 24(c)(1), prior to amendment by the Working Families Tax Relief Act of 2004 (P.L. 108-311)).

▶ **Effective date.** The provision applies to tax years beginning after December 31, 2008 (Act Sec. 501(d) of the Fostering Connection to Success and Increasing Adoptions Act of 2008 (P.L. 110-351)).

Law source: Law at ¶5010 and ¶5212.

— Act Sec. 501(a) of the Fostering Connection to Success and Increasing Adoptions Act of 2008 (P.L. 110-351), amending Code Sec. 152(c)(3)(A);

— Act Sec. 501(b), adding Code Sec. 152(c)(1)(E);

— Act Sec. 501(c)(1), amending Code Sec. 24(a);

— Act Sec. 501(c)(2), adding Code Sec. 152(c)(4)(C) and amending Code Sec. 152(c)(4)(A);

— Act Sec. 501(d), providing the effective date.

Reporter references: For further information, consult the following CCH reporters.

— Standard Federal Tax Reporter, ¶8250.023 and ¶3770.023

— Tax Research Consultant, FILEIND: 6,158 and INDIV: 57,452

— Federal Tax Guide, ¶6110 and ¶2222

Business Deductions

3

DEPRECIATION

EXPENSING

OTHER DEDUCTIONS

DEPRECIATION

¶305 15-Year MACRS Recovery Period for Qualified Leasehold Improvements

SUMMARY OF NEW LAW

The 15-year MACRS recovery period for qualified leasehold improvement property is extended to apply to property placed in service in 2008 and 2009.

BACKGROUND

The American Jobs Creation Act of 2004 (P.L. 108-357) created a 15-year recovery period under the Modified Adjusted Cost Recovery System (MACRS) for qualified leasehold improvement property placed in service after October 22, 2004, and before January 1, 2006, using the straight-line method and the half-year convention (unless the mid-quarter convention applies) (Code Sec. 168(e)(3)(E)(iv)). The Tax Relief and Health Care Act of 2006 (P.L. 109-432) extended the 15-year recovery period to apply to qualified leasehold improvement property placed in service before January 1, 2008. If the MACRS alternative depreciation system (ADS) is elected or otherwise applies, the recovery period is 39 years and depreciation is computed using the straight-line method and half-year or mid-quarter convention (Code Sec. 168(g)(3)(B)).

Leasehold improvement. But for this provision, a leasehold improvement is generally considered a structural component of a building and depreciated over 39 years using the straight-line method beginning in the month the improvement was placed in service. To be eligible for the 15-year recovery period, a"qualified leasehold improvement property" is any improvement to an interior portion of *nonresidential real property* if the following requirements are satisfied:

- the improvement is made under, or pursuant to, a lease by the lessee, lessor or any sublessee of the interior portion;
- the improvement is section 1250 property (i.e., a structural component and not section 1245 personal property that is eligible for a shortened recovery period under the cost segregation rules);
- the lease is not between related persons;
- the interior portion of the building is to be occupied exclusively by the lessee or any sublessee of that interior portion; and
- the improvement is placed in service more than three years after the date the building was first placed in service by any person (Code Sec. 168(k)(3); Reg. § 1.168(k)-1(c)).

Expenditures for the following are not qualified leasehold improvement property:

- the enlargement (as defined in Reg. § 1.48-12(c)(10)) of the building;
- elevators and escalators;

BACKGROUND

- structural components (as defined in Reg. § 1.48-1(e)(2)) that benefit a common area; and

- internal structural framework (as defined in Reg. § 1.48-12(b)(3)(i)(D)).

NEW LAW EXPLAINED

Extension of 15-year MACRS recovery period for qualified leasehold improvement property.—The 15-year MACRS recovery period for qualified leasehold improvement property is extended two years to apply to qualified leasehold improvement property placed in service before January 1, 2010 (Code Sec. 168(e)(3)(E)(iv), as amended by the Emergency Economic Stabilization Act of 2008 (P.L. 110-343)).

Practical Analysis: James Sowell, J.D., LL.M., Principal in KPMG's Washington National Tax Office, notes that Division C, Act Sec. 305(a) of the Emergency Economic Stabilization Act of 2008 (P.L. 110-343) not only extends the provisions granting 15-year depreciation for qualified leasehold improvements and qualified restaurant improvements for two years, but it also expands the scope of these provisions.

Planning Note: The 15-year recovery period is not elective. However, a taxpayer could effectively elect out by making an ADS election and depreciating the property using the straight-line method. An ADS election, however, would apply to all MACRS 15-year property placed in service by the taxpayer during the tax year, not just qualified leasehold improvement property.

Practical Analysis: Vincent O'Brien, President of Vincent J. O'Brien, CPA, PC, Lynbrook, New York, observes that practitioners must carefully note the interplay between the Emergency Economic Stabilization Act of 2008 (P.L. 110-343) and the Economic Stimulus Act of 2008 (P.L. 110-185), which was enacted on February 13, 2008.

Leasehold Improvements. The cost-recovery rules for qualified leasehold improvements were affected by both laws. Leasehold improvements acquired and placed in service after December 31, 2007, and before January 1, 2009, are eligible for 50-percent bonus depreciation. The remaining half of the cost of the improvement is eligible for the shorter 15-year recovery period, instead of the normal 39-year recovery period that would otherwise apply to such property.

Comment: Fiscal-year taxpayers that have already filed a return using a 39-year recovery period for qualified leasehold improvement property placed in service during 2008 should file an amended return to correct the depreciation period. Note, however, the IRS also allows a taxpayer that has filed only one incorrect return to file Form 3115 and claim a section 481 adjustment. See Section 4 of Rev. Proc. 2007-16, I.R.B. 2004-3.

NEW LAW EXPLAINED

Comment: Bonus depreciation on qualified leasehold improvement property is generally available for property acquired after December 31, 2007, and placed in service before January 1, 2009 (Code Sec. 168(k)(2)(A) and (k)(3)). This placed-in-service deadline was not extended by the new law.

> **Practical Analysis:** Robert S. Winters, Shareholder, Buchanan Ingersoll and Rooney and former Chief Tax Counsel, Committee on Ways and Means, House of Representatives, and Donald B. Reynolds, Jr., J.D., Shareholder, Buchanan Ingersoll and Rooney, note that Division C, Act Sec. 305(a) of the Emergency Economic Stabilization Act of 2008 (P.L. 110-343) includes a significant expansion of depreciation benefits for leasehold and restaurant improvements. Not only does the bill extend the availability of 15-year straight-line depreciation for these improvements for property placed in service through 2009, it also offers this favorable cost recovery method to two additional types of real property in 2009: new restaurant construction and retail space.

▶ **Effective date.** This provision applies to property placed in service after December 31, 2007 (Division C, Act Sec. 305(a)(2) of the Emergency Economic Stabilization Act of 2008 (P.L. 110-343)).

Law source: Law at ¶5230. Committee Report at ¶10,450.

— Division C, Act Sec. 305(a)(1) of the Emergency Economic Stabilization Act of 2008 (P.L. 110-343), amending Code Sec. 168(e)(3)(E)(iv);

— Division C, Act Sec. 305(a)(2), providing the effective date.

Reporter references: For further information, consult the following CCH reporters.

— Standard Federal Tax Reporter ¶11,279.0312

— Tax Research Consultant, DEPR: 3,156.25

— Federal Tax Guide, ¶9110

¶310 15-Year MACRS Recovery Period for Restaurant Improvements and Buildings

SUMMARY OF NEW LAW

The 15-year recovery period for improvements to a restaurant building is extended to apply to improvements placed in service in 2008 and 2009. A 15-year recovery period now applies to restaurant buildings placed in service in 2009.

¶310

BACKGROUND

The American Jobs Creation Act of 2004 (P.L. 108-357) created a new category of 15-year property under the Modified Adjusted Cost Recovery System (MACRS) called "qualified restaurant property." This category applies to property placed in service after October 22, 2004 and before January 1, 2008 (Code Sec. 168(e)(3)(E)(v)). The straight-line method applies to such property (Code Sec. 168(b)(3)(H)). If the MACRS alternative depreciation system (ADS) is elected or otherwise applies, the recovery period is 39 years and the straight-line method applies (Code Sec. 168(g)(3)(B)). Whether or not ADS is elected, the applicable convention is the half-year convention, unless the mid-quarter convention applies.

Qualified restaurant property is any section 1250 property which is an improvement to a building if the improvement is placed in service more than three years after the date the building was first placed in service and more than 50 percent of the building's square footage is devoted to preparation of and seating for on-premises consumption of prepared meals (Code Sec. 168(e)(7)). The three-year period is measured from the date that the building was originally placed in service, whether or not it was originally placed in service by the taxpayer. For example, improvements to a restaurant building that is at least three years old at the time the taxpayer buys the building may qualify.

Prior to enactment of this provision, a section 1250 improvement to a restaurant building would be depreciated over 39 years beginning in the month that it was placed in service using the mid-month convention. An improvement to a restaurant that is section 1245 property (personal property) may be depreciated as MACRS five-year property (Asset Class 57.0) under the MACRS cost segregation rules.

The provision only applies to improvements to a restaurant building. Improvements that are not part of or attached to the restaurant building, for example, a detached sign supported on a concrete foundation, sidewalk, or depreciable landscaping, would generally constitute separately depreciable land improvements which also have a 15-year recovery period but may be depreciated using the 150-percent declining balance method. Other unattached improvements may qualify for a shorter recovery period if not considered a land improvement

NEW LAW EXPLAINED

15-year recovery period for restaurant improvements extended provided for restaurant buildings.—The 15-year MACRS recovery period for qualified restaurant property that is an improvement to a restaurant is extended to apply to property placed in service before January 1, 2010 (Code Sec. 168(e)(3)(E)(v), as amended by Emergency Economic Stabilization Act of 2008 (P.L. 110-343)).

> **Planning Note:** The 15-year recovery period is not elective. However, a taxpayer could effectively elect out by making an ADS election and depreciating the property using the straight-line method. An ADS election, however, would apply to all MACRS 15-year property placed in service by the taxpayer during the tax year, not just qualified leasehold improvement property.

¶310

NEW LAW EXPLAINED

Comment: Fiscal-year taxpayers that filed a return using a 39-year recovery period for qualified restaurant property placed in service during 2008 should file an amended return to correct the depreciation period. Note, however, the IRS also allows a taxpayer that has filed only one incorrect return to file Form 3115 and claim a section 481 adjustment. See Section 4 of Rev. Proc. 2007-16, I.R.B. 2004-3.

Practical Analysis: Vincent O'Brien, President of Vincent J. O'Brien, CPA, PC, Lynbrook, New York, notes that restaurant improvements are ineligible for bonus depreciation under the Economic Stimulus Act of 2008 (P.L. 110-185). However, such improvements are eligible for the shorter 15-year recovery period.

The new law also expands the definition of qualified restaurant property to include a building placed in service after December 31, 2008, and before January 1, 2010, if more than 50 percent of the building's square footage is devoted to preparation of, and seating for on-premises consumption of, prepared meals (Code Sec. 168(e)(7)(A), as amended by the Emergency Economic Act of 2008). Such a building is depreciated similarly to an improvement to a restaurant building. Thus, the building is depreciated over 15 years (39 years under the MACRS alternative depreciation system (ADS)) using the straight-line method and the half-year or mid-quarter convention.

Practical Analysis: Robert S. Winters, Shareholder, Buchanan Ingersoll and Rooney and former Chief Tax Counsel, Committee on Ways and Means, House of Representatives, and Donald B. Reynolds, Jr., J.D., Shareholder, Buchanan Ingersoll and Rooney, observe that in Division C, Act Sec. 305(b) of the Emergency Economic Stabilization Act of 2008 (P.L. 110-343), restaurant property comprising either 1250 property or building improvements qualifies for the benefit if more than half of the building square footage is devoted to the preparation and seating for on-site consumption of meals. Buildings placed in service during 2009 are eligible. Regarding improvements made in 2009, there is no requirement that they be made over three years from the time the building is placed in service. Property on which the benefit is taken is ineligible for bonus depreciation.

Comment: Under prior law, an improvement to a restaurant building could only qualify for a 15-year recovery period if the building was at least three years old at the time the improvement was made (Code Sec. 168(e)(7), prior to amendment by the Emergency Economic Act of 2008, which is effective for property placed in service before 2009). The new law eliminates this rule but only with respect to improvements placed in service in 2009 (Code Sec. 168(e)(7)), as amended by the Emergency Economic Act of 2008, which pursuant to Act Sec. 305(b)(2) of the Emergency Economic Act of 2008, is effective for property placed in service after 2008).

Comment: The provision allowing a 15-year recovery period for restaurant buildings applies to a building, if such a building is placed in service after

NEW LAW EXPLAINED

December 31, 2008 and before January 1, 2010 (Code Sec. 168(e)(7)(A)(i), as amended by the Economic Emergency Act of 2008). Thus, even though the amended Code does not refer to a building first placed in service after December 31, 2008 and before January 1, 2010, Congress interprets the provision to only apply to new construction placed in service in 2009. The amended heading of Code Sec. 168(e)(7) specifically refers to "new construction." In addition, a Senate Finance Committee summary of the provision refers to "new restaurants." The provision, however, does not contain a binding contract rule which would prevent a taxpayer who places a new restaurant building in service in 2009 from qualifying for the 15-year recovery period even if the taxpayer entered into a binding contract for its construction before 2009. Nor is the provision inapplicable if construction began before 2009 so long as the building is placed in service in 2009.

Comment: The provision for restaurant buildings is non-elective but a taxpayer could effectively elect out by making an ADS election to depreciate the property over 39 years using the half-year or mid-quarter convention.

Practical Analysis: James Sowell, J.D., LL.M., Principal in KPMG's Washington National Tax Office, indicates that Division C, Act Sec. 305(b) of the Emergency Economic Stabilization Act of 2008 (P.L. 110-343) eliminates the "qualified restaurant improvement" requirement that the improvement must be placed in service more than three years after the building was first placed in service. In addition, this provision now can apply, not just to improvements to a restaurant, but to an entirely new building that is placed in service during the 2009 calendar year.

Bonus depreciation denied. The 50-percent bonus depreciation deduction allowed under Code Sec. 168(k) may not be claimed on any qualified restaurant property (Code Sec. 168(e)(7)(B), as amended by the Emergency Economic Act of 2008).

Comment: The Code Sec. 168(k) bonus allowance is generally available for property acquired after December 31, 2007, and placed in service before January 1, 2009. It only applies to MACRS property with a regular recovery period of 20 years or less. Thus, but for this prohibition, 15-year restaurant improvements placed in service in 2008 could qualify for the allowance. Note that the bonus depreciation placed-in-service deadline was not extended by the new law.

▶ **Effective date.** The provision extending the placed-in service deadline for qualified restaurant property that is an improvement or a building applies to property placed in service after December 31, 2007 (Division C, Act Sec. 305(a)(2) of the Emergency Economic Stabilization Act of 2008 (P.L. 110-343)). The provision expanding the definition of qualified restaurant property to include a building applies to property placed in service after December 31, 2008 (Division C, Act Sec. 305(b)(2), of the Emergency Economic Act of 2008).

Law source: Law at ¶5230. Committee Reports at ¶10,450.

— Division C, Act Sec. 305(a)(1) of the Emergency Economic Stabilization Act of 2008 (P.L. 110-343), amending Code Sec. 168(e)(3)(E)(v);

— Division C, Act Sec. 305(b)(1), amending Code Sec. 168(e)(7);

— Division C, Act Sec. 305(a)(2) and (b)(2), providing the effective dates.

NEW LAW EXPLAINED

Reporter references: For further information, consult the following CCH reporters.

— Standard Federal Tax Reporter, ¶11,279.0311

— Tax Research Consultant, DEPR: 3,156.25

— Federal Tax Guide, ¶9110

¶315   15-Year MACRS Recovery Period Qualified Retail Improvement Property

SUMMARY OF NEW LAW

A qualified interior improvement to a building used for a retail business is depreciated under MACRS over 15 years using the straight-line method if the improvement is placed in service during the 2009 calendar year and the building is at least three years old when the improvement is placed in service.

BACKGROUND

Additions and improvements to a building are generally depreciated in the same manner that the building would be depreciated if the building was placed in service when the addition or improvement was placed in service (Code Sec. 168(i)(6)).

> **Example:** Hunt owns a building used for business and replaces certain of the interior walls in the building in June 2008. Since the building would be depreciated as 39-year nonresidential real property if it was placed in service in 2008, the walls (an addition or improvement to the building) are depreciated as 39-year nonresidential real property that is placed in service in June 2008.

There are two major exceptions to the general rule for additions and improvements. First, the American Jobs Creation Act of 2004 (P.L. 108-357) created a new category of 15-year MACRS property referred to as "qualified leasehold improvement property" (Code Sec. 168(e)(3)(E)(iv), as added by P.L. 108-357). In general, qualified leasehold improvement property is a section 1250 improvement (i.e., an improvement that is a structural component rather than section 1245 personal property) made by a lessor or lessee pursuant to or under a lease to the interior portion of nonresidential real property after October 22, 2004 and before January 1, 2010. See ¶ 305 for details.

The Jobs Act also created another category of 15-year property referred to as "qualified restaurant property." Qualified restaurant property is any section 1250 improvement to a building that qualifies as a restaurant and is placed in service after October 22, 2004 and before January 1, 2010 (Code Sec. 168(e)(7)). See ¶ 310 for details.

NEW LAW EXPLAINED

Qualified retail improvement property placed in service in 2009 treated as MACRS 15-year property. A new category of MACRS property—"qualified retail improvement property"—is created (Code Sec. 168(e)(3)(E)(ix) and Code Sec. 168(e)(9), as added by the Emergency Economic Stabilization Act of 2008 (P.L. 110-343)). This property is treated as MACRS 15-year property and, accordingly, has a 15-year recovery period. A 39-year MACRS alternative depreciation system (ADS) recovery period applies if ADS is elected or required. The straight-line method must be used to depreciate qualified retail improvement property (Code Sec. 168(b)(3)(I)), as added by the Emergency Economic Act of 2008). The half-year convention applies unless the mid-quarter convention is applicable because the taxpayer placed more than 40 percent of the total basis of its depreciable property (other than residential rental and nonresidential real property) in service in the last quarter of its tax year.

> **Practical Analysis:** James Sowell, J.D., LL.M., Principal in KPMG's Washington National Tax Office, notes that in Division C, Act Sec. 305(c) of the Emergency Economic Stabilization Act of 2008 (P.L. 110-343) a new classification of 15-year property is added for qualified retail improvement property placed in service during the 2009 calendar year. This provision essentially extends the benefits provided for qualified leasehold improvements to retail properties that are owner-occupied.

Comment: But for this provision, qualified retail improvement property would be treated as nonresidential real property and depreciated over 39 years using the mid-month convention.

Comment: Although a 15-year recovery period applies, qualified retail improvement property does not lose its status as section 1250 property. Therefore, it does not qualify for the Code Sec. 179 expense allowance, which is limited to section 1245 property (Code Sec. 179(d)(1)). In addition, it remains subject to the Code Sec. 1250 recapture rules. Consequently, no depreciation recapture is required upon a disposition since the straight-line method is used.

Comment: The mid-month convention only applies to nonresidential real property and residential rental property (Code Sec. 168(d)(2)). Qualified retail improvement property is not considered MACRS nonresidential real property because it is specifically categorized as MACRS 15-year property. Thus, it is depreciated using the half-year convention unless the mid-quarter convention applies because the taxpayer placed more than 40 percent of the total basis of its depreciable property other than residential rental and nonresidential real property in service in the last quarter of the tax year.

Comment: MACRS 15-year property is generally depreciated using the 150 percent declining balance method (Code Sec. 168(b)(2)(A)). The new law, however, requires a taxpayer to use the straight-line method to depreciate qualified retail improvement property (Code Sec. 168(b)(3)(I), as added by the Emergency Economic Act of 2008).

NEW LAW EXPLAINED

Comment: This provision is not elective. However, if a taxpayer elects to depreciate all types of 15-year MACRS property that it places in service during the tax year using the MACRS alternative depreciation system (ADS), it may depreciate its qualified retail improvement property using the straight-line method, a 39-year recovery period, and the half-year or mid-quarter convention. In effect, the ADS election operates as an election out of the provision.

Qualified retail improvement property defined. The following requirements must be met in order to meet the definition of a qualified retail improvement (Code Sec. 168(e)(8)(A) and (E), as added by the Emergency Economic Act of 2008):

• the property must be an improvement to an interior portion of a building that is nonresidential real property;

• the interior portion of the building must be open to the general public and used in the retail trade or business of selling tangible personal property to the general public;

• the improvement must be placed in service more than three years after the building was first placed in service; and

• the improvement must be placed in service after December 31, 2008, and before January 1, 2010 (i.e., it must be placed in service during the 2009 calendar year).

The following improvements are specifically disqualified from the definition of qualified retail improvement property (Code Sec. 168(e)(8)(D), as added by the Emergency Economic Act of 2008):

• elevators and escalators

• internal structural framework of a building

• structural components that benefit a common area

• improvements relating to the enlargement of a building

Comment: These types of improvements are also excluded from the definition of a qualified leasehold improvement which is eligible for a 15-year recovery period (Code Sec. 168(k)(3)(B)). Thus, the definition of these terms provided in Reg. §1.168(k)-1(c)(3) for purposes of the qualified leasehold improvement provision should apply equally to qualified retail improvement property.

Practical Analysis: Robert S. Winters, Shareholder, Buchanan Ingersoll and Rooney and former Chief Tax Counsel, Committee on Ways and Means, House of Representatives, and Donald B. Reynolds, Jr., J.D., Shareholder, Buchanan Ingersoll and Rooney, state that in Division C, Act Sec. 305(c) of the Emergency Economic Stabilization Act of 2008 (P.L. 110-343), the retail space benefit is available for 2009 "qualified retail improvements" to the interior of nonresidential real property. These improvements must be to space open to the general public and used in the retail business of selling tangible personal property to the public. The statute excludes certain improvements from eligibility: Building enlargements, elevators, escalators, structural components benefiting a common area and a building's internal

NEW LAW EXPLAINED

> structural framework are ineligible. Further, improvements must be made over three years after the building is placed in service to qualify. If improvements are made by a building's owner who sells the building, the improvements lose their eligibility for 15-year straight-line depreciation in the hands of the buyer. As is the case for restaurants, retail improvements benefiting from the new provision are ineligible for bonus depreciation.

Internal structural framework. Internal structural framework is defined to include all load-bearing internal walls and any other internal structural supports, including the columns, girders, beams, trusses, spandrels, and all other members that are essential to the stability of the building (Reg. § 1.48-12 (b) (3) (i) (d) (iii); Reg. § 1.168 (k)-1 (c) (3) (v)).

Common area. A common area means any portion of a building that is equally available to all users of the building on the same basis for uses that are incidental to the primary use of the building. For example, stairways, hallways, lobbies, common seating areas, interior and exterior pedestrian walkways and pedestrian bridges, loading docks and areas, and rest rooms generally are treated as common areas if they are used by different lessees of a building (Reg. § 1.168 (k)-1 (c) (3) (ii)).

Enlargement. A building is enlarged to the extent that the total volume of the building is increased. An increase in floor space resulting from interior remodelling is not considered an enlargement. The total volume of a building is generally equal to the product of the floor area of the base of the building and the height from the underside of the lowest floor (including the basement) to the average height of the finished roof (as it exists or existed). For this purpose, floor area is measured from the exterior faces of external walls (other than shared walls that are external walls) and from the centerline of shared walls that are external walls (Reg. § 1.168 (k)-1 (c) (3) (iv); Reg. § 1.48-12 (c) (10)).

> **Comment:** An exterior improvement such as a new roof is not qualified retail improvement property. Furthermore, an interior improvement will only qualify if the portion of the building to which the improvement is made is open to public (but is not a common area) and used in a retail trade or business of selling tangible property to the public. Thus, for example, improvements made to an inventory storage area that is not open to the general public would not qualify.

> **Comment:** Presumably, qualified retail improvement property must be section 1250 property (i.e., a structural component) even though this requirements is not specifically stated. Improvements to retail property that are section 1245 property should, therefore, continue to be eligible for a shortened recovery period under the cost segregation rules. Note that the definition in Code Sec. 168(k)(3) of a qualified leasehold improvement also does not specifically limit that provision to section 1250 property. Reg. § 1.168(k)-1(c), however, does impose this requirement.

Bonus depreciation denied. The 50-percent bonus depreciation deduction allowed by Code Sec. 168(k) may not be claimed on qualified retail improvement property (Code Sec. 168(e)(8)(D), as added by the Emergency Economic Act of 2008).

NEW LAW EXPLAINED

Improvements made by owner. Qualified retail improvement property retains its status only so long as the improvement is held by the owner that made the improvement (Code Sec. 168(e)(8)(B), as added by the Emergency Economic Act of 2008).

> **Example:** John Johnston owns a retail established and places a qualified retail improvement in service in 2009. Johnson sells the building with the improvement to Fred Jackson in 2010. Jackson may not separately depreciate the improvement as 15-year qualified retail improvement property.

ADS recovery period. The MACRS alternative depreciation system (ADS) recovery period for qualified retail improvement property is 39 years if ADS is elected or required (Code Sec. 168(g)(3)(b), as amended by the Emergency Economic Act of 2008). The half-year or mid-quarter convention applies even if ADS is used to depreciate the property over 39 years.

> **Comment:** Qualified retail improvement property must be placed in service after December 31, 2008, and before January 1, 2010. Thus, if a taxpayer began construction of an improvement on or before December 31, 2008, the improvement may still qualify provided it is placed in service during 2009.

Alternative minimum tax. The straight-line depreciation deduction claimed on qualified retail improvement property is allowed in full for alternative minimum tax (AMT) purposes (Code Sec. 56(a)(1)(A)).

▶ **Effective date.** The provision applies to property placed in service after December 31, 2008 (Division C, Act Sec. 305(c)(5) of the Emergency Economic Stabilization Act of 2008 (P.L. 110-343)).

Law source: Law at ¶5230.

— Division C, Act Sec. 305(c)(1) of the Emergency Economic Stabilization Act of 2008 (P.L. 110-343), adding Code Sec. 168(e)(3)(E)(ix);

— Division C, Act Sec. 305(c)(2), adding Code Sec. 168(e)(8);

— Division C, Act Sec. 305(c)(3), adding Code Sec. 168(b)(3)(I);

— Division C, Act Sec. 305(c)(4), amending Code Sec. 168(g)(3)(B);

— Division C, Act Sec. 305(c)(5), providing the effective date.

Reporter references: For further information, consult the following CCH reporters.

— Standard Federal Tax Reporter, ¶11,279.05

— Tax Research Consultant, DEPR: 6052

— Federal Tax Guide, ¶9110

¶315

¶320 Certain Farming Business Machinery and Equipment Treated as Five-Year Property

SUMMARY OF NEW LAW

Machinery or equipment (other than a grain bin, cotton ginning asset, fence or land improvement) which is used in a farming business, where the original use of the machinery or equipment commences with the taxpayer in 2009, is treated as five-year property for purposes of claiming Modified Accelerated Cost Recovery System (MACRS) depreciation under the General Depreciation System (GDS).

BACKGROUND

Property, such as machinery or equipment, with a determinable useful life of more than a year that is used in a business or held for the production of income and is placed in service after December 31, 1986, is depreciated under the Modified Accelerated Cost Recovery System (MACRS) over the property's recovery period. MACRS consists of two ways of computing depreciation: the more commonly used General Depreciation System (GDS) and the Alternative Depreciation System (ADS), which generally provides for slower cost recovery over a longer period of time than GDS.

Property that is used in a farming business is depreciated under GDS (unless ADS is required or is elected by the taxpayer) using the 150-percent declining-balance method. The term "farming business" means the trade or business of farming, which also includes the trade or business of operating a nursery or sod farm and the raising or harvesting of trees bearing fruit, nuts, or other crops, or ornamental trees. The "trade or business of farming" involves the cultivation of land or the raising or harvesting of any agricultural or horticultural commodity (Code Sec. 263A(e)(4); Treas. Reg. §1.264A-4(a)(4)). Farm machinery and equipment generally has a seven-year recovery period under GDS (Code Sec. 168; Rev. Proc. 87-57, 1987-2 CB 687).

Taxpayers are required to use ADS for the following property:

- All property used predominately in a farming business and placed in service in any tax year during which an election not to apply the uniform capitalization rules (Code Sec. 263A) to certain farming costs is in effect.

- Listed property (as defined in Code Sec. 280F(d)(4)) used 50 percent or less for business.

- Any tax-exempt use property (as defined in Code Sec. 470(c)(2)).

- Any tax-exempt bond-financed property.

- Any imported property covered by an executive order of the President of the United States described in Code Sec. 168(g)(6).

- Any tangible property used predominately outside the United States during the year.

Farm machinery and equipment generally has a recovery period of 10 years under ADS and is depreciated using the straight-line method (Code Sec. 168(g)).

NEW LAW EXPLAINED

Certain farming business machinery and equipment treated as five-year property.—Under the new provision, any machinery or equipment (other than a grain bin, cotton ginning asset, fence, or land improvement), the original use of which begins with the taxpayer in 2009, and that is placed in service by the taxpayer in a farming business in 2009, has a recovery period of five years under GDS (Code Sec. 168(e)(3)(B)(vii), as added by Division C, Sec. 505(a) of the Emergency Economic Stabilization Act of 2008 (P.L. 110-343)). Such property has a recovery period of 10 years under ADS (Code Sec. 168(g)(3)(B), as amended by Division C, Sec. 505(b) of the Emergency Economic Act of 2008).

▶ **Effective date.** The provision applies to property placed in service after December 31, 2008 (Act Sec. 505(c) of the Emergency Economic Stabilization Act of 2008 (P.L. 110-343)).

Law source: Law at ¶5230.

— Division C, Act Sec. 505(a) of the Emergency Economic Stabilization Act of 2008 (P.L. 110-343), adding new Code Sec. 168(e)(3)(B)(vii);

— Division C, Act Sec. 505(b), amending Code Sec. 168(g)(3)(B);

— Division C, Act Sec. 505(c), providing the effective date.

Reporter references: For further information, consult the following CCH reporters.

— Standard Federal Tax Reporter, ¶11,017.021

— Tax Research Consultant, FARM: 9,078

— Federal Tax Guide, ¶25,377

¶325 Seven-Year Depreciation Period for Motorsports Facilities

SUMMARY OF NEW LAW

The 7-year MACRS recovery period for motorsports entertainment complexes and related ancillary and support facilities is extended to property placed in service in 2008 and 2009.

BACKGROUND

Under the modified accelerated cost recovery system (MACRS), most types of property associated with theme parks and/or amusement parks are depreciated over a 7-year period (Code Sec. 168(e)(1)). For depreciation purposes, Rev. Proc. 87-56, 1987-2 CB 674, as clarified and modified by Rev. Proc. 88-22, 1988-1 CB 785, provides that theme parks and amusement parks fall within Asset Class 80.0 and have a class life of 12.5 years. Historically, racing track facilities were treated by the IRS the same as theme or amusement parks and, thus, were depreciated over a 7-year period. The

BACKGROUND

American Jobs Creation Act of 2004 (P.L. 108-357) codified this treatment by adding motorsports entertainment complexes (and their related ancillary and support facilities) to the list of "7-year property" types (Code Sec. 168(e)(3)(C)(ii)).

Motorsports entertainment complex. A "motorsports entertainment complex" is a racing track facility that is permanently situated on land, hosts at least one racing event for cars of any type, trucks, or motorcycles during the 36-month period following the first day of the month in which it is placed in service, and is open to the public for an admission fee (Code Sec. 168(i)(15)(A)). If owned by the taxpayer who owns the complex and provided for the benefit of the complex's patrons, the term also includes:

- ancillary facilities and land improvements in support of the complex's activities, including parking lots, sidewalks, waterways, bridges, fences, and landscaping;

- support facilities, including food and beverage retailing, souvenir vending, and other nonlodging accommodations; and

- appurtenances associated with the facilities and related attractions and amusements, including ticket booths, race track surfaces, suites and hospitality facilities, grandstands and viewing structures, props, walls, facilities that support entertainment services delivery, other special purpose structures, facades, shop interiors, and buildings (Code Sec. 168(i)(15)(B)).

"Motorsports entertainment complex" does *not* include any transportation equipment, administrative services assets, warehouses, administrative buildings, hotels, or motels (Code Sec. 168(i)(15)(C)). In addition, motorsports facilities placed in service after October 22, 2004, are *not* treated as theme and amusement facilities classified as Asset Class 80.0 in Rev. Proc. 87-56 (Act Sec. 704(c)(2) of the 2004 Jobs Act).

NEW LAW EXPLAINED

7-year depreciation period for motorsports entertainment complexes extended.—The 7-year cost recovery period for a motorsports entertainment complex and related ancillary and support facilities placed in service after October 22, 2004, has been extended for two years to apply to motorsports entertainment complex property placed in service before January 1, 2010 (Code Sec. 168(i)(15)(D), as amended by the Emergency Economic Stabilization Act of 2008 (P.L. 110-343)).

▶ **Effective date.** The provision applies to property placed in service after December 31, 2007 (Division C, Act Sec. 317(b) of the Emergency Economic Stabilization Act of 2008 (P.L. 110-343)).

Law source: Law at ¶5230. Committee Reports at ¶10,550.

— Division C, Act Sec. 317(a) of the Emergency Economic Stabilization Act of 2008 (P.L. 110-343), amending Code Sec. 168(i)(15)(D);

— Division C, Act Sec. 317(b), providing the effective date.

Reporter references: For further information, consult the following CCH reporters.

— Standard Federal Tax Reporter, ¶11,279.01 and ¶11,279.0313

NEW LAW EXPLAINED

— Tax Research Consultant, DEPR: 3,156.152

— Federal Tax Guide, ¶9110

¶330 Additional Depreciation Allowance for Biomass Ethanol Plant Property

SUMMARY OF NEW LAW

Taxpayers are allowed to immediately write off 50 percent of the cost of facilities that produce cellulosic biofuel in addition to cellulosic ethanol if such facilities are placed in service after October 3, 2008, and before January 1, 2013. Regular MACRS depreciation deductions are computed on the adjusted basis of the property after reduction by the 50 percent allowance (Code Sec. 168(l)(1)(B)). The deduction is claimed in full for purposes of determining alternative minimum tax liability. In addition, all MACRS depreciation deductions claimed on the QCBEPP are allowed in full in computing AMT (i.e., no depreciation adjustment is required) (Code Sec. 168(l)(6)).

BACKGROUND

Code Sec. 168(l) allows a 50-percent first year additional depreciation allowance for qualified cellulosic biomass ethanol plant property (QCBEPP) acquired and placed in service after December 20, 2006 and before January 1, 2013.

QCBEPP defined. To qualify as QCBEPP:

- the property must be depreciable and used in the United States solely to produce cellulosic biomass ethanol;

- the taxpayer must acquire the property by purchase, within the meaning of Code Sec. 179(d), after December 20, 2006;

- no written binding contract for the purchase of the property may be in effect on or before December 20, 2006;

- the original use of the property must commence with the taxpayer after December 20, 2006;

- the property must be placed in service by the taxpayer before January 1, 2013 (Code Sec. 168(l)(2)).

For this purpose, cellulosic biomass ethanol means ethanol produced by hydrolysis of any lignocellulosic or hemicellulosic matter that is available on a renewable or recurring basis (Code Sec. 168(l)(3)). Lignocellulosic or hemicellulosic matter that is available on a renewable or recurring basis includes, but is not limited to, bagasse (from sugar cane), corn stalks, and switchgrass (Joint Committee on Taxation, Technical Explanation of the Tax Relief and Health Care Act of 2006 (P.L. 109-432) (JCX-50-06)).

¶330

BACKGROUND

Property manufactured, constructed or produced by or for a taxpayer. Property manufactured, constructed or produced by the taxpayer for the taxpayer's own use may qualify as QCBEPP if the taxpayer begins the manufacture, construction or production of the property after December 20, 2006, and the property is placed in service before January 1, 2013. Property manufactured, constructed or produced for the taxpayer by another person under a contract entered into prior to the manufacture, construction or production of the property is considered manufactured, constructed or produced by the taxpayer.

Tax-exempt bond-financed property excluded. Property financed with tax-exempt bonds cannot qualify as QCBEPP and, therefore, does not qualify for the additional deduction (Code Sec. 168(l)(4)(C)).

Mandatory ADS property excluded. Property required to be depreciated under the MACRS alternative depreciation system (ADS) does not qualify as QCBEPP. The deduction is not denied if a taxpayer merely elects to depreciate the QCBEPP using ADS (Code Sec. 168(l)(4)(B)).

Election out. A taxpayer may elect not to claim the deduction with respect to any class of property for any tax year. The election out applies to all property in the class for which the election out is made and which is placed in service during the tax year (Code Sec. 168(l)(4)(D)).

Recapture when property loses QCBEPP status. Recapture of the deduction is required in a tax year in which QCBEPP ceases to be a QCBEPP. The recapture amount is computed in a similar manner to the recapture of the Code Sec. 179 deduction when section 179 property ceases to be used more than 50 percent in the active conduct of a taxpayer's trade or business during any year of the section 179 property's MACRS recovery period (Code Sec. 168(l)(7)).

Coordination with Code Sec. 179C election to expense refineries. The 50-percent deduction for QCBEPP does not apply to any QCBEPP with respect to which the taxpayer claims the 50-percent deduction allowed by Code Sec. 179C for qualified refinery property.

NEW LAW EXPLAINED

Expansion of additional depreciation allowance for biomass ethanol plant property to include cellulosic biofuel.—The additional depreciation allowance that may be claimed on the adjusted basis of qualified cellulosic biomass ethanol plant property (QCBEPP) has been expanded to include cellulosic biofuel, which is defined as any liquid fuel produced from any lignocellulosic or hemicellulosic matter that is available on a renewable or recurring basis (Code Sec. 168(l) (3), as amended by the Emergency Economic Stabilization Act of 2008 (P.L. 110-343)).

> **Comment:** Cellulosic biofuel is a renewable fuel derived from natural, plant waste products such as rice straw, sugarcane stalks (bagasse), switchgrass and wood chips. With current fossil fuel prices at high levels, biofuels are proving to be a viable way to reduce greenhouse gas emissions where costs are low and the

NEW LAW EXPLAINED

conversion technology is mature (Next-Generation Cellulosic Ethanol Factsheet, www.verenium.com).

▶ **Effective date.** The provision applies to property placed in service after October 3, 2008, the date of enactment, in tax years ending after October 3, 2008 (Division B, Act Sec. 201(c) of the Emergency Economic Stabilization Act of 2008 (P.L. 110-343)).

Law source: Law at ¶5230. Committee Reports at ¶10,140.

— Division B, Act Sec. 201(a) of the Emergency Economic Stabilization Act of 2008 (P.L. 110-343), amending Code Sec. 168(l)(3);

— Division B, Act Sec. 201(b), amending the headings in Code Sec. 168(l);

— Division B, Act Sec. 201(c), providing the effective date.

Reporter references: For further information, consult the following CCH reporters.

— Standard Federal Tax Reporter, ¶11,279.0585

— Tax Research Consultant, TRC: DEPR: 3,750

— Federal Tax Guide, ¶9131

¶335 MACRS Recovery Periods for Qualified Indian Reservation Property

SUMMARY OF NEW LAW

The Modified Accelerated Cost Recovery System (MACRS) recovery periods that apply to qualified Indian reservation property have been extended for two years through December 31, 2009.

BACKGROUND

Special Modified Accelerated Cost Recovery System (MACRS) recovery periods that permit faster write-offs are provided for "qualified Indian reservation property" that is placed in service on or after January 1, 1994, and before January 1, 2008 (Code Sec. 168(j)). The regular tax depreciation deduction claimed on qualified Indian reservation property is allowed for alternative minimum tax (AMT) purposes (Code Sec. 168(j)(3)). Although the recovery periods are shortened for Indian reservation property, no change is made to the depreciation method or convention that would otherwise apply.

The following chart shows the shortened recovery periods.

Property Class	Recovery Period
3-year property	2 years
5-year property	3 years

BACKGROUND

Property Class	Recovery Period
7-year property	4 years
10-year property	6 years
15-year property	9 years
20-year property	12 years
Nonresidential real property	22 years

Comment: The recovery period for MACRS 27.5-year residential rental property used on an Indian reservation is not shortened.

Qualified Indian reservation property is MACRS 3-, 5-, 7-, 10-, 15-, and 20-year property and nonresidential real property that is:

- used predominantly in the active conduct of a trade or business within an Indian reservation;

- not used or located outside an Indian reservation on a regular basis;

- not acquired (directly or indirectly) from a related person (as defined by Code Sec. 465(b)(3)(C)); and

- not used for certain gaming purposes.

NEW LAW EXPLAINED

MACRS recovery periods for qualified Indian reservation property extended.— The accelerated Modified Accelerated Cost Recovery System (MACRS) recovery periods that apply to qualified Indian reservation property have been extended for two years and apply to qualified Indian reservation property placed in service before January 1, 2010 (Code Sec. 168(j)(8), as amended by the Emergency Economic Stabilization Act of 2008 (P.L. 110-343)).

Practical Analysis: John A. Sikora, J.D., Partner in the Milwaukee and Delafield offices of Weiss Berzowski Brady LLP, observes that Code Sec. 168(j) allows shorter depreciation recovery periods for certain assets used by the taxpayer predominantly in the active conduct of a trade or business within an Indian reservation (as defined in Code Sec. 108(j)(6)). The assets generally cannot be used or located outside the reservation on a regular basis (unless constituting "qualified infrastructure property," as defined in the statute, located outside the Indian reservation if the purpose of such property is to connect with qualified infrastructure property within the Indian reservation; the statute states that the term includes items such as roads, power lines, water systems, railroad spurs and communications facilities), cannot have been acquired from a related person and cannot have been placed in service for purposes of conducting or housing certain gaming. Code Sec. 168(j)(8)previously stated that the provision did not apply to property placed in service after December 31, 2007. Division C, Act Sec. 315 of the Emergency Economic Stabilization Act of 2008 (P.L. 110-343) states that the provision shall be retroactively extended so that it is effective

NEW LAW EXPLAINED

> for property placed in service after December 31, 2007, and on or before December 31, 2009.

▶ **Effective date.** The provision applies to property placed in service after December 31, 2007 (Division C, Act Sec. 315(b) of the Emergency Economic Stabilization Act of 2008 (P.L. 110-343)).

Law source: Law at ¶5230. Committee Report at ¶10,530.

— Division C, Act Sec. 315(a) of the Emergency Economic Stabilization Act of 2008 (P.L. 110-343), amending Code Sec. 168(j)(8);

— Division C, Act Sec. 315(b), providing the effective date.

Reporter references: For further information, consult the following CCH reporters.

— Standard Federal Tax Reporter, ¶11,279.031

— Tax Research Consultant, DEPR: 3,156.55

— Federal Tax Guide, ¶9110

EXPENSING

¶340 Deduction for Environmental Remediation Costs

SUMMARY OF NEW LAW

The election to deduct environmental remediation costs is extended for two years to cover expenditures paid or incurred in 2008 and 2009.

BACKGROUND

For both regular and alternative minimum tax (AMT) purposes, a taxpayer may elect to deduct certain environmental cleanup costs in the tax year paid or incurred, rather than capitalize them. However, the election can only be made if the costs are incurred in connection with the abatement or control of hazardous substances at a "qualified contaminated site" (a so-called "brownfield") (Code Sec. 198(b)). Deductions for environmental remediation expenditures are subject to recapture as ordinary income upon a sale or other disposition of the property (Code Sec. 198(e)).

A "qualified contaminated site," or "brownfield," is any urban or rural property that is held for use in a trade or business, for the production of income, or as inventory, and which is certified by the appropriate State environmental agency as an area at or on which there has been a release, threat of release, or disposal of a hazardous substance. However, sites that are identified on the national priorities list under the Comprehensive Environmental Response, Compensation, and Liability Act of 1980 (CERCLA) cannot qualify as targeted areas.

BACKGROUND

Hazardous substances are defined by reference to sections 101(14) and 102 of CER-CLA, subject to additional exclusions applicable to asbestos and similar substances within buildings, certain naturally occurring substances, and certain other substances released into drinking water supplies due to deterioration through ordinary use. The term "hazardous substance" also includes any petroleum product, as defined in Code Sec. 4612(a)(3), which includes crude oil, crude oil condensates, and natural gasoline.

The election to deduct environmental cleanup costs generally applies to qualifying expenditures paid or incurred before January 1, 2008 (Code Sec. 198(h)).

NEW LAW EXPLAINED

Election to deduct environmental remediation costs extended.—The election to deduct environmental remediation costs is extended for two years to cover qualifying expenditures paid or incurred before January 1, 2010 (Code Sec. 198(h), as amended by the Emergency Economic Stabilization Act of 2008 (P.L. 110-343)). The general tax law principle regarding expensing versus capitalization of expenditures continues to apply to environmental remediation efforts not specifically covered under Code Sec. 198. Thus, depending upon the specific situation, these costs may need to be capitalized.

> **Election:** The procedures for making the election under Code Sec. 198 are detailed in Rev. Proc. 98-47, 1998-2 CB 319. In general, the election must be made on or before the due date (including extensions) for filing the income tax return for the tax year in which the expenses are paid or incurred.

▶ **Effective date.** The amendment made by this provision applies to expenditures paid or incurred after December 31, 2007 (Division C, Act Sec. 318(b) of the Emergency Economic Stabilization Act of 2008 (P.L. 110-343)).

Law source: Law at ¶5270. Committee Report at ¶10,560.

— Division C, Act Sec. 318(a) of the Emergency Economic Stabilization Act of 2008 (P.L. 110-343), amending Code Sec. 198(h);

— Division C, Act Sec. 318(b), providing the effective date.

Reporter references: For further information, consult the following CCH reporters.

— Standard Federal Tax Reporter, ¶12,465.01

— Tax Research Consultant, BUSEXP: 18,756

— Federal Tax Guide, ¶7402

¶345 Expensing of Film and Television Productions

SUMMARY OF NEW LAW

The expensing election related to film and television productions is extended for one year to 2009 and the election may be made, in part, to productions with aggregate costs over the dollar production limits.

BACKGROUND

A taxpayer may elect to deduct the production costs of a qualifying film or television production that commences after October 22, 2004, and before January 1, 2009 (Code Sec. 181). The owner of the production makes the election and claims the deduction. The election is usually made in the first tax year that production costs are paid or incurred. The production costs are then deducted in each tax year that such costs are paid or incurred.

To qualify for the election, the aggregate production cost may not exceed $15 million ($20 million for films produced in certain low-income or distressed communities). In addition, 75 percent of the compensation paid with respect to the production must be for services performed in the United States. The deduction is recaptured if the production ceases to be a qualifying production either before or after it is placed in service.

NEW LAW EXPLAINED

Expensing election related to film and television productions extended; dollar limitation modified.—The election to expense qualifying film or television productions has been extended to qualified film and television productions commencing prior to January 1, 2010 (Code Sec. 181(f), as amended by the Emergency Economic Stabilization Act of 2008 (P.L. 110-343)).

Practical Analysis: Robert B. Teuber, J.D., Attorney in the Milwaukee office of Weiss Berzowski Brady LLP, observes that the changes made by Division C, Act Sec. 502 of the Emergency Economic Stabilization Act of 2008 (P.L. 110-343) to Code Sec. 181 not only extend the election to expense certain costs of qualified film and television productions through 2009, but also significantly expand its availability to taxpayers. The changes modify the dollar limitations imposed on taxpayers seeking to expense costs of such productions.

Prior to the change, Code Sec. 181(a)(2)(A) generally limited the election to expense these costs to qualified productions for which the aggregate cost equaled $15 million or less. The dollar limitations will now provide that the election to expense these costs applies to the first $15 million expended for any and all qualified productions. This means that the election no longer applies only to "small" productions. Now all qualified film and television productions have this option.

Practical Analysis: Kip Dellinger, CPA, Senior Tax Partner at Kallman And Co. LLP in Los Angeles, notes that the film and television industry was treated well under Division C, Act Sec. 502 of the Emergency Economic Stabilization Act of 2008 (P.L. 110-343)—likely because film and television products remain one of the United States' principal export properties in a time when our trade deficits are significant.

In addition to extending the allowable Code Sec. 181 deduction for production costs of "qualified" film and television productions commencing on before December 31,

NEW LAW EXPLAINED

2009 (the provision was to expire December 31, 2008), the Emergency Economic Act of 2008 liberally expanded the available deduction (see Division C, Act Sec. 502(b)).

As originally enacted, Code Sec. 181 allowed a deduction for production costs (otherwise required to be capitalized) for qualified film or television (by episode or program) when the aggregate cost of the show did not exceed $15 million, or under a special rule, $20 million if the film or program was produced in a low income or distressed community. A film or program with costs in excess of the limitations did not qualify for any deduction under Code Sec. 181. Costs included participations and residuals; consequently, a successful production might be disqualified due to its success because the payments to participants resulted in aggregate costs exceeding the allowable amounts. In practice, taxpayers often did not make the election to apply Code Sec. 181 because of this possibility.

The Emergency Economic Act of 2008, which amended Code Sec. 181 to permit a deduction of $15 million of aggregate production costs (or the higher $20 million special threshold) for any production regardless of the eventual total aggregate production costs, will greatly expand the application of Code Sec. 181. The election may be made for "big budget" as well as smaller budget pictures and successful television series will be permitted $15 million of deduction per episode (up to 44 episodes). It may also result in tax-planning "arrangements" that create entities that generate special allocations of production costs to take advantage of the liberalized provisions (e.g., the initial development cost incurred before "production deal" is entered into with a studio or broadcast entity).

The modification of Code Sec. 199 to provide that the methods and means of distributing a qualified film shall not affect the availability of the permitted deduction will also widely expand the availability of the production deduction (see Division C, Act Sec. 502(c)). Based on the manner in which the film was exhibited through various media (*e.g.*, television broadcast or over the internet), the regulations had placed limitations on which gross receipts were characterized as gross domestic production receipts that qualified for the deduction. Under the modified provisions, a far broader category of receipts will qualify for the production deduction. The largest immediate beneficiary though may be network television with respect to the shows they produce.

The Emergency Economic Act of 2008 also clarifies that the definitional term "qualified film" included costs to include any copyrights, trademarks and other intangibles with respect to the film; the regulations to Code Sec. 199 had provided that a qualified film only meant the master copy of the film or other film copy that the holder was licensed to make. This provision is also likely to widen the scope of film production activities that qualify for the deduction.

Finally, the modified provision with respect to partnership and S corporations also expands the applicability of Code Sec. 199. It is also favorable to the larger film production operations in the United States. One part of the modified provision will effectively permit distributors to qualify their respective interests in a qualified film as production activities where previously neither could meet the test in the regulations that it produced the film itself. This provision will also allow for domestic production deductions for a distributor, or studio and independent producer in a variety of

NEW LAW EXPLAINED

arrangements that are common in the film and television industry. It is likely that many major film productions in 2009 and 2010 will be structured to take advantage of the favorable modifications to Code Sec. 199. Some complex existing arrangements that endeavor to qualify under the existing regulations may be revised because the new rules will provide for more simple structures to qualify for the deduction.

Compliance Pointer: The election must be made by the due date (including extensions) for filing the taxpayer's return for the tax year in which costs of the film or television production are first paid or incurred. A six-month extension from the due date of the return (excluding extensions) is available if the taxpayer filed a timely original return for the tax year the election should have been made (Reg. § 301.9100-2).

Comment: For purposes of recapture under Code Sec. 1245, any deduction allowed under section 181 is treated as if it were a deduction allowable for amortization.

Caution: Once the election is made, it may not be revoked without IRS consent (Code Sec. 181(c)(2)). However, the IRS will grant its consent if the owner attaches a revocation statement to its return and recaptures the expensed amount.

The dollar limitation has also been modified so that the first $15 million ($20 million for productions in low income communities or distressed area or isolated area of distress) of an otherwise qualified film or television production may be treated as an expense in cases where the aggregate cost of the production exceeds the dollar limitation (Code Sec. 181(a)(2)(A), as amended by the Emergency Economic Stabilization Act of 2008). The cost of the production in excess of the dollar limitation is capitalized and recovered under the taxpayer's method of accounting for the recovery of such property.

▶ **Effective date.** The provision applies to qualified film and television productions commencing after December 31, 2007 (Division C, Act Sec. 502(e)(1) of the Emergency Economic Stabilization Act of 2008 (P.L. 110-343)).

Law source: Law at ¶5265. Committee Reports at ¶10,650 and ¶10,660.

— Division C, Act Sec. 502(a) of the Emergency Economic Stabilization Act of 2008 (P.L. 110-343), amending Code Sec. 181(f);

— Division C, Act Sec. 502(b), amending Code Sec. 181(a)(2)(A);

— Division C, Act Sec. 502(e)(1), providing the effective date.

Reporter references: For further information, consult the following CCH reporters.

— Standard Federal Tax Reporter, ¶12,146.023

— Tax Research Consultant, DEPR: 12,300

— Federal Tax Guide, ¶9325

¶350 Expensing of Qualified Refinery Property

SUMMARY OF NEW LAW

The placed-in-service and construction requirements for the Code Sec. 179C election to expense 50 percent of the cost of eligible qualified refinery property have been extended by two years to property placed-in-service in 2013 and 2014. In addition, the expensing deduction is also available with respect to refineries processing liquid fuel directly from shale or tar sands, for property placed in service after October 3, 2008.

BACKGROUND

Code Sec. 179C, which was added by the Energy Tax Incentives Act of 2005 (P.L. 109-58), allows a taxpayer to make an election to expense 50 percent of the cost of eligible qualified refinery property placed in service by the taxpayer (Code Sec. 179C(a) and (f)). A taxpayer who makes a Code Sec. 179C election to expense 50 percent of the cost of qualified refinery property may still recover the remaining 50 percent of such qualifying expenditures under Code Sec. 168 and Code Sec. 179B, if applicable.

Qualified refinery property is any portion of a qualified refinery ("property") which meets certain placed in service requirements and also meets certain construction and written binding contract requirements. In addition, other requirements regarding original use, production capacity, and compliance with environmental laws must be met. The property must be placed in service by the taxpayer after August 8, 2005, and before January 1, 2012, and there can be no written binding contract for the construction of the property in effect on or before June 14, 2005 (Code Sec. 179C(c)(1)(B) and (E)). Also:

- the construction of the property must be subject to a written binding construction contract entered into before January 1, 2008;

- the property must be placed in service before January 1, 2008; or

- in the case of self-constructed property, the construction of the property must begin after June 14, 2005, and before January 1, 2008 (Code Sec. 179C(c)(1)(F)).

For purposes of the Code Sec. 179C election, a "qualified refinery" means any refinery located in the United States that is designed to serve the primary purpose of processing liquid fuel from crude oil or qualified fuels (as defined in Code Sec. 45K(c)) (Code Sec. 179C(d)). Qualified fuels include oil produced from shale and tar sands; gas produced from geopressured brine, Devonian shale, coal seams, or a tight formation or biomass; and liquid, gaseous, or solid synthetic fuels produced from coal (including lignite), including such fuels when used as feedstocks (see Code Sec. 45K(c)).

No deduction is allowed for any qualified refinery property, however, which is built solely to comply with consent decrees or projects mandated by federal, state, or local governments, or if the primary purpose of the property is for use as a topping plant,

BACKGROUND

asphalt plant, lube oil facility, crude or product terminal, or blending facility (Code Sec. 179C(f)).

For qualified refinery property other than a qualified refinery which is separate from an existing refinery (e.g., expansion of an existing refinery), production capacity requirements apply. These requirements are met if the property enables the existing qualified refinery to (1) increase total volume output, determined without regard to asphalt or lube oil, by five percent or more on an average daily basis, or (2) process qualified fuels at a rate which is equal to or greater than 25 percent of the total throughput of the qualified refinery on an average daily basis (Code Sec. 179C(c)(1)(C) and (e)).

Temporary and proposed regulations have been issued and providing guidance with respect to the election to expense qualified refinery property (T.D. 9412, I.R.B. 2008-37, 687). The temporary regulations restate many of the statutory elements of the expense election, including the definition of eligible property, the description of a qualified refinery, compliance with applicable environmental laws, and the written binding contract requirement. They generally interpret the statute in a manner consistent with existing statutory and regulatory principles, and recognize that taxpayers have had to address issues related to the expense election for prior tax years in the absence of regulations.

NEW LAW EXPLAINED

Election to expense certain refineries modified, extended.—Placed-in-service and construction requirements for the Code Sec. 179C election to expense 50 percent of the cost of eligible qualified refinery property have been extended by two years, Code Sec. 179C(c)(1), as amended by the Emergency Economic Stabilization Act of 2008 (P.L. 110-343)).

Qualified refinery property is now any portion of a qualified refinery ("property") placed in service by the taxpayer after August 8, 2005, and before January 1, 2014 (rather than January 1, 2012), which meets all other requirements (Code Sec. 179C(c)(1)(B), as amended by the Emergency Economic Act of 2008). With respect to construction and written binding contract requirements, one of the following three requirements must be met:

- the construction of the property is subject to a written binding construction contract entered into before January 1, 2010 (rather than January 1, 2008);

- the property was placed in service before January 1, 2010 (rather than January 1, 2008); or

- in the case of self-constructed property, the construction of the property began after June 14, 2005, and before January 1, 2010 (rather than January 1, 2008) (Code Sec. 179C(c)(1)(F), as amended by the Emergency Economic Act of 2008).

> **Comment:** The two-year extension applies to property placed in service after October 3, 2008. Consequently, property placed in service on or after January 1,

NEW LAW EXPLAINED

2008, but on or before October 3, 2008, must still meet either requirement (1) or (3) under prior law (see discussion above), in addition to all other requirements.

The definition of a "qualified refinery" for purposes of the Code Sec. 179C election has also been modified and now includes a refinery located in the United States that is designed to serve the primary purpose of processing liquid fuel from crude oil or qualified fuels (as defined in Code Sec. 45K(c)), *or directly from shale or tar sands* (Code Sec. 179C(d), as amended by the Emergency Economic Act of 2008). Accordingly, for qualified refinery property other than a qualified refinery which is separate from an existing refinery (e.g., expansion of an existing refinery), production capacity requirements are met if the property enables the existing qualified refinery to (1) increase total volume output, determined without regard to asphalt or lube oil, by five percent or more on an average daily basis, or (2) process shale, tar sands, or qualified fuels at a rate which is equal to or greater than 25 percent of the total throughput of the qualified refinery on an average daily basis (Code Sec. 179C(e), as amended by the Emergency Economic Act of 2008).

▶ **Effective date.** The provision applies to property placed in service after October 3, 2008, the date of enactment, Division B, Act Sec. 209(c) of the Emergency Economic Stabilization Act of 2008 (P.L. 110-343).

Law source: Law at ¶5250.

— Division B, Act Sec. 209(a)(1) of the Emergency Economic Stabilization Act of 2008 (P.L. 110-343), amending Code Sec. 179C(c)(1);

— Division B, Act Sec. 209(a)(2), amending Code Sec. 179C(c)(1)(F);

— Division B, Act Sec. 209(b), amending Code Sec. 179C(d) and (e)(2);

— Division B, Act Sec. 209(c), providing the effective date.

Reporter references: For further information, consult the following CCH reporters.

— Standard Federal Tax Reporter, ¶12,137E.01

— Tax Research Consultant, BUSEXP: 18,900

— Federal Tax Guide, ¶8380

¶355 Suspension of Taxable Income Limit on Percentage Depletion for Oil and Gas Produced from Marginal Properties

SUMMARY OF NEW LAW

The suspension of the percentage depletion limitation for oil and gas produced from marginal properties is extended to include tax years beginning in 2009.

BACKGROUND

Code Sec. 613A imposes substantial limitations on the allowance for percentage depletion of oil and gas wells. Code Sec. 613A(c) allows percentage depletion only with respect to up to 1,000 barrels of average daily production of domestic crude oil or the equivalent amount of natural gas (six million cubic feet) to independent producers and royalty owners. For producers of both oil and natural gas, this limitation applies on a combined basis. This deduction is limited to 65-percent of the taxpayer's taxable income for the year (Code Sec. 613A(d)). Amounts disallowed under this provision are treated as a deduction in the succeeding tax year subject, again, to the 65-percent limitation.

The percentage depletion allowance for producers and royalty owners of oil and natural gas produced from marginal wells cannot exceed 100-percent of the taxpayer's net income from the property (computed without allowances for depletion and the Code Sec. 199 domestic production deduction) (Code Sec. 613(a)). This 100-percent net income limitation requires percentage depletion to be calculated on a property-by-property basis. The 100-percent of net income limitation on percentage depletion applies independently of the 65-percent taxable income limitation. The 100-percent of net income limitation was suspended for tax years beginning after December 31, 1997, and before January 1, 2008.

NEW LAW EXPLAINED

Extension of suspension of taxable income limit with respect to marginal production.—The temporary suspension of the taxable income limit on the percentage depletion allowance for oil and gas produced from marginal wells has been extended to include tax years beginning after December 31, 2008, and before January 1, 2010. Thus, the limitation on the amount of a percentage depletion deduction to 100 percent of the net income from an oil or gas producing property does not apply to domestic oil and gas produced from marginal properties during tax years beginning in 2009, but applies for tax years beginning in 2008 (Code Sec. 613A(c)(6)(H), as amended by the Emergency Economic Stabilization Act of 2008 (P.L. 110-343)).

> **Comment:** Marginal production means domestic crude oil or natural gas that is produced from a property that is a stripper well property for the calendar year in which the tax year begins or a property in which substantially all of the production during such calendar year is heavy oil (Code Sec. 613A(c)(6)(D)).

▶ **Effective date.** No specific effective date is provided by the Act. The provision is, therefore, considered effective on October 3, 2008, the date of enactment.

Law source: Law at ¶5315.

— Division B, Act Sec. 210 of the Emergency Economic Stabilization Act of 2008 (P.L. 110-343), amending Code Sec. 613A(c)(6)(H).

Reporter references: For further information, consult the following CCH reporters.

— Standard Federal Tax Reporter, ¶23.988.044

— Tax Research Consultant, FARM: 15,218

— Federal Tax Guide, ¶9645

¶360 Expensing Advanced Mine Safety Equipment

SUMMARY OF NEW LAW

The election to expense 50 percent of the cost of advanced mine safety equipment is extended for one year, for property placed in service in 2009.

BACKGROUND

In order to encourage mining companies to invest in safety equipment that goes above and beyond current safety requirements, the Tax Relief and Heath Care Act of 2006 (P.L. 109-432) provided that a taxpayer may elect to immediately expense 50 percent of the cost of qualified mine safety equipment including:

- communications technology enabling miners to remain in constant contact with an individual who is not in the mine;

- electronic tracking devices that enable an individual above ground to locate miners in the mine at all times;

- self-contained self-rescue emergency breathing apparatuses carried by miners;

- additional oxygen supplies stored in the mine; and

- comprehensive atmospheric monitoring equipment to measure levels of carbon monoxide, methane, and oxygen in the mine and which can detect smoke (Code Sec. 179E).

The election is made on the taxpayer's tax return and must specify the equipment to which the election applies. The election may only be revoked with IRS consent (Code Sec. 179E(b)(2)). The amount expensed is not capitalized and the election applies to new property placed in service after December 20, 2006, and before January 1, 2009 (Code Sec. 179E(c)).

NEW LAW EXPLAINED

Election to expense advanced mine safety equipment extended one year.—The election to expense 50 percent of the cost of advanced mine safety equipment is extended for one year to new property placed in service before January 1, 2010 (Code Sec. 179E(g), as amended by Division C, Act Sec. 311 of the Emergency Economic Stabilization Act of 2008 (P.L. 110-343)).

▶ **Effective date.** No specific effective date is provided by the Act. The provision is, therefore, considered effective on October 3, 2008, the date of enactment.

Law source: Law at ¶5260.

— Division C, Act Sec. 311 of the Emergency Economic Stabilization Act of 2008 (P.L. 110-343), amending Code Sec. 179E(g).

NEW LAW EXPLAINED

Reporter references: For further information, consult the following CCH reporters.

— Standard Federal Tax Reporter, ¶12,126.01

— Tax Research Consultant, BUSEXP: 19,000

— Federal Tax Guide, ¶25,299

OTHER DEDUCTIONS

¶365 Tax Incentives for Investment in the District of Columbia

SUMMARY OF NEW LAW

The District of Columbia enterprise zone provisions and the D.C. homebuyer credit are extended for two years to apply in 2008 and 2009.

BACKGROUND

Parts of the District of Columbia are treated as an empowerment zone, called the District of Columbia Enterprise Zone (the "DC Zone") (Code Sec. 1400). The designation of the area as the DC Zone is scheduled to end on December 31, 2007 (Code Sec. 1400(f)).

As with other empowerment zones, special tax incentives are provided for the DC Zone in order to attract businesses to the area. The DC Zone receives special tax-exempt financing incentives that apply to bonds issued from January 1, 1998, through December 31, 2007 (Code Sec. 1400A). Generally, the limit on the amount of bonds that can be allocated to a particular DC Zone business is $15 million and the bonds may be issued only while the DC Zone designation is in effect. This is higher than the $3 million that can be allocated to a particular enterprise zone business in an empowerment zone or enterprise community (Code Secs. 1400A and 1394(c)).

Another tax break for DC Zone businesses is an exclusion from income for qualified capital gain from the sale or exchange of a DC Zone asset held for more than five years (Code Sec. 1400B). The DC Zone assets, including DC Zone business stock, DC Zone partnership interests and DC Zone business property, must be acquired before January 1, 2006, and the gain cannot be attributable to periods before January 1, 1998, or after December 31, 2012 (Code Sec. 1400B(e)(2)).

First-time homebuyers of a principal residence in the District of Columbia are allowed a credit of up to $5,000 of the purchase price of the residence. The maximum amount of the credit is $2,500 for each married taxpayer filing a separate return (Code Sec. 1400C(a) and (e)(1)(A)). The credit phases out for individual taxpayers with adjusted gross income (AGI) between $70,000 and $90,000 ($110,000 and $130,000 for joint filers) (Code Sec. 1400C(b)). A first-time homebuyer means any individual who

¶365

BACKGROUND

did not have a present ownership interest in a principal residence in the District of Columbia in the one-year period ending on the date of the purchase of the residence to which the credit applies (Code Sec. 1400C(c)).

To qualify for the credit, the residence must have been purchased after August 4, 1997, and before January 1, 2008 (Code Sec. 1400C(i)). If the DC residence is newly constructed by the taxpayer, the date that the taxpayer first occupies the residence is treated as the purchase date (Code Sec. 1400C(e)(2)(B)).

NEW LAW EXPLAINED

D.C. enterprise zone and homebuyer credit provisions extended.—The designation of the applicable DC area as the DC Enterprise Zone for two years through December 31, 2009 (Code Sec. 1400(f), as amended by the Emergency Economic Stabilization Act of 2008 (P.L. 110-343)). The DC Zone tax-exempt bond financing incentives have also been extended to apply to bonds issued from January 1, 1998, through December 31, 2009 (Code Sec. 1400A(b), as amended by the Emergency Economic Act of 2008).

With respect to the zero-percent capital gains rate provisions of Code Sec. 1400B, the provision:

- extends the DC Zone business stock acquisition date from January 1, 2008, to January 1, 2010 (Code Sec. 1400B(b), as amended by the Emergency Economic Act of 2008);

- extends the ending date of the period to which "qualified capital gains" may be attributable from December 31, 2012 to December 31, 2014 (Code Sec. 1400B(e)(2), as amended by the Emergency Economic Act of 2008); and

- extends the ending date of the period during which qualified capital gains from the sales and exchanges of interests in partnerships and S corporations that are DC businesses may be determined from December 31, 2012, to December 31, 2014 (Code Sec. 1400B(g)(2), as amended by the Emergency Economic Act of 2008).

The termination of the first-time homebuyer credit for DC is extended from January 1, 2008, to January 1, 2010 (Code Sec. 1400C(i), as amended by the Emergency Economic Act of 2008).

> **Compliance Tip:** Taxpayers eligible for the District of Columbia first-time homebuyer credit must file Form 8859, District of Columbia First-Time Homebuyer Credit, with their Form 1040 to claim the credit.

▶ **Effective date.** The amendments made by this section are generally effective after December 31, 2007, except that the conforming amendments of Division C, Act Sec. 322(c)(2) are effective on October 3, 2008 (Division C, Act Sec. 322(a)(2), 322(b)(2), 322(c)(3), and 322(d)(2) of the Emergency Economic Stabilization Act of 2008 (P.L. 110-343)).

Law source: Law at ¶5370, ¶5375, ¶5380, ¶5385, and ¶5390. Committee Report at ¶10,590.

— Division C, Act Sec. 322(a)(1) of the Emergency Economic Stabilization Act of 2008 (P.L. 110-343), amending Code Sec. 1400(f);

NEW LAW EXPLAINED

— Division C, Act Sec. 322(b)(1), amending Code Sec. 1400A(b);

— Division C, Act Sec. 322(c), amending Code Secs. 1400B(b), (e)(2), (g)(2) and 1400F(d);

— Division C, Act Sec. 322(d)(1), amending Code Sec. 1400C(i);

— Division C, Act Sec. 322(a)(2), (b)(2), (c)(3) and (d)(2), providing the effective dates.

Reporter references: For further information, consult the following CCH reporters.

— Standard Federal Tax Reporter, ¶32,423.01, ¶32,425.01 and ¶32,429.01

— Tax Research Consultant, BUSEXP: 57,056.30

— Federal Tax Guide, ¶2226 and ¶8590

¶368 Code Sec. 199 Deduction for Film and Television Production

SUMMARY OF NEW LAW

The manufacturing deduction rules with respect to film and television production are modified.

BACKGROUND

Generally, a deduction may be claimed equal to an applicable percentage of the lesser of a taxpayer's qualified production activities income (QPAI) or taxable income (adjusted gross income in the case of an individual, estate or trust) (Code Sec. 199). The applicable percentage is, 6 percent for tax years beginning in 2008 through 2009, and 9 percent for years beginning after 2009.

A taxpayer's QPAI is its domestic production gross receipts (DPGR) attributable to the actual conduct of a trade or business by the taxpayer during the tax year, less the costs of goods sold allocable to those receipts, and other expenses, losses, or deductions properly allocable to those receipts. DPGR are the gross receipts of the taxpayer derived from:

- the lease, license, sale, exchange of other disposition of any:

  (1) qualifying production property (i.e., tangible personal property) manufactured, produced, grown or extracted by the taxpayer in whole or in significant part within the United States;

  (2) qualified film produced by the taxpayer within the United States; or

  (3) electricity, natural gas, or potable water produced by the taxpayer in the United States;

- the construction of real property that is performed by the taxpayer in the United States in the ordinary course of an taxpayer's construction trade or business; and

BACKGROUND

- architectural or engineering services that are performed by the taxpayer in the ordinary course of its architectural or engineering trade or business in the United States with respect to the construction of real property that is located in the United States.

The domestic production activities deduction cannot exceed more than 50 percent of the W-2 wages paid by the taxpayer to its employees for the calendar year ending during the tax year and properly allocable to the taxpayer's DPGR (those W-2 wages deducted in calculating QPAI). For this purpose, "wages" includes any amount paid by the taxpayer to its employees for services performed and which are subject to federal income tax withholding. Generally, no withholding is required on wages paid for services performed outside the United States, including wages paid to a bona fide resident of Puerto Rico for services performed in Puerto Rico.

With respect to the domestic production activities of a partnership or S corporation, the deduction under Code Sec. 199 is determined at the partner or shareholder level (Code Sec. 199(d)(1)(A)(i)). In performing the calculation, each partner or shareholder generally will take into account such person's allocable share of the components of the calculation (including DPGR; the cost of goods sold allocable to such receipts; and other expenses, losses, or deductions allocable to such receipts) from the partnership or S corporation as well as any items relating to the partner or shareholder's own qualified production activities, if any (Code Sec. 199(d)(1)(A)(ii)). Each partner or shareholder is treated as having W-2 wages for the tax year allocable to DPGR in an amount equal to such person's allocable share of the W-2 wages of the partnership or S corporation for the tax year allocable to DPGR (Code Sec. 199(d)(1)(A)(iii)).

Regulations provide that, generally, an owner of a pass-through entity is not treated as conducting the qualified production activities of the of the pass-through entity, and vice versa (Temporary Reg. § 1.199-5T(g)).

NEW LAW EXPLAINED

Manufacturing deduction rules with respect to film and television production are modified.—The new provision provides that a qualified film for purposes of the Code Sec. 199 deduction includes any copyrights, trademarks, and other intangibles with respect to a qualified film produced by the taxpayer(Code Sec. 199(c)(6), as amended by the Emergency Economic Stabilization Act of 2008). The Code Sec. 199 deduction for qualified films is not affected by the methods and means of distributing the film. For example, the distribution of a qualified film via the internet (whether the film is viewed online or downloaded or whether or not there is a fee charged) is now considered to be a disposition of the film for purposes of determining domestic production gross receipts (DPGR).

> **Comment:** Likewise, the distribution of a qualified film through an open air (free of charge) broadcast is considered a disposition of the film for these purposes.

W-2 wage limitation. The new provision also modifies the W-2 wage limitation by defining the term "W-2 wages" for qualified films to include any compensation for services performed in the United States by actors, production personnel, directors,

NEW LAW EXPLAINED

and producers (Code Sec. 199(b)(2), as amended by the Emergency Economic Act of 2008).

> **Comment:** Thus, compensation is no longer restricted to W-2 wages for the limitation of qualified films.

Pass-through entities. The application of Code Sec. 199 to partnerships and S corporations has also modified. First, each partner with at least a 20-percent capital interest or shareholder with at least a 20-percent ownership interest, either directly or indirectly, in such entity is treated as having engaged directly in any film produced by the partnership or S corporation (Code Sec. 199(d)(1)(iv)(I), as amended by the Emergency Economic Act of 2008).

> **Example:** Studio A and Studio B form a partnership in which each is a 50-percent partner to produce a qualified film. Studio A has the rights to distribute the film domestically and Studio B has the rights to distribute the film outside the United States. Under the new provision, the production activities of the partnership are attributed to each partner, and thus each partner's revenue from the distribution of the qualified film is not treated as non-DPGR solely because neither Studio A nor Studio B produced the qualified film itself.

Additionally, a partnership or S corporation is treated as having engaged directly in any film produced by any partner with at least a 20-percent capital interest or shareholder with at least a 20-percent ownership interest, either directly or indirectly, in the partnership or S corporation (Code Sec. 199(d)(1)(iv)(II), as amended by the Emergency Economic Act of 2008).

> **Example:** Studio A and Studio B form a partnership in which each is a 50-percent partner to distribute a qualified film. Studio A produced the film and contributes it to the partnership and Studio B contributes distribution services to the partnership. The production activities of Studio A are attributed to the partnership, and thus the partnership's revenue from the distribution of the qualified film is not treated as non-DPGR solely because the partnership did not produce the qualified film.

> **Comment:** Thus, Temporary Reg. § 1.199-5T(g), which provides that an owner of a pass-through entity is not treated as conducting the qualified production activities of the of the pass-through entity, and vice versa, does not apply to this situation.

▶ **Effective date.** The provision applies to tax years beginning after December 31, 2007 (Division C, Act Sec. 502(e)(2) of the Emergency Economic Stabilization Act of 2008 (P.L. 110-343)).

Law source: Law at ¶5280. Committee Reports at ¶10,670.

— Division C, Act Sec. 502(c)(1), of the Emergency Economic Stabilization Act of 2008 (P.L. 110-343), adding Code Sec. 199(b)(2)(D);

NEW LAW EXPLAINED

— Division C, Act Sec. 502(c)(2), amending Code Sec. 199(c)(6);

— Division C, Act Sec. 502(c)(3), amending Code Sec. 199(d)(1)(A);

— Division C, Act Sec. 502(d), amending Code Sec. 181(d)(3)(A);

— Division C, Act Sec. 502(e)(2), providing the effective date.

Reporter references: For further information, consult the following CCH reporters.

— Standard Federal Tax Reporter, ¶12,476.025

— Tax Research Consultant, BUSEXP: 6,152

— Federal Tax Guide, ¶13,720A

¶370 Code Sec. 199 Deduction for Production Activities in Puerto Rico

SUMMARY OF NEW LAW

The special rule which allows Puerto Rico to be considered part of the United States in determining domestic production gross receipts under Code Sec. 199 is extended two years to apply with respect to the tax years of a taxpayer beginning before January 1, 2010.

BACKGROUND

Generally, a deduction may be claimed equal to an applicable percentage of the lesser of a taxpayer's qualified production activities income (QPAI) or taxable income (adjusted gross income in the case of an individual, estate or trust) (Code Sec. 199). The applicable percentage is 6 percent for tax years beginning in 2008 through 2009, and 9 percent for years beginning after 2009.

A taxpayer's QPAI is its domestic production gross receipts (DPGR) attributable to the actual conduct of a trade or business by the taxpayer during the tax year, less the costs of goods sold allocable to those receipts, and other expenses, losses, or deductions properly allocable to those receipts. DPGR are the gross receipts of the taxpayer derived from:

- the lease, license, sale, exchange of other disposition of any:

   (1) qualifying production property (i.e., tangible personal property) manufactured, produced, grown or extracted by the taxpayer in whole or in significant part within the United States;

   (2) qualified film produced by the taxpayer within the United States; or

   (3) electricity, natural gas, or potable water produced by the taxpayer in the United States;

BACKGROUND

- the construction of real property that is performed by the taxpayer in the United States in the ordinary course of an taxpayer's construction trade or business; and

- architectural or engineering services that are performed by the taxpayer in the ordinary course of its architectural or engineering trade or business in the United States with respect to the construction of real property that is located in the United States.

The domestic production activities deduction cannot exceed more than 50 percent of the W-2 wages paid by the taxpayer to its employees for the calendar year ending during the tax year and properly allocable to the taxpayer's DPGR (those W-2 wages deducted in calculating QPAI). For this purpose, "wages" includes any amount paid by the taxpayer to its employees for services performed and which are subject to federal income tax withholding. Generally, no withholding is required on wages paid for services performed outside the United States, including wages paid to a bona fide resident of Puerto Rico for services performed in Puerto Rico.

Special rule for Puerto Rico. For purposes of the domestic production activities deduction, the term "United States" only includes the 50 States and the District of Columbia, as well as U.S. territorial waters. It does not include U.S. possessions or territories. However, if a taxpayer has gross receipts from sources within the Commonwealth of Puerto Rico, then Puerto Rico will be considered part of the United States if *all* of those receipts are subject to the U.S. Federal income tax (Code Sec. 199(d)(8)). Thus, if a taxpayer has gross receipts from qualified production activities within Puerto Rico and those receipts are subject to U.S. income tax, then such receipts will be considered DPGR. In such circumstances, wages paid by the taxpayer to a bona fide resident of Puerto Rico for services performed in Puerto Rico will be considered "wages" for purposes of calculating the 50-percent W-2 wage limitation. The treatment of Puerto Rico as part of the United States will only apply with respect to the first two tax years of a taxpayer beginning after December 31, 2005, and before January 1, 2008.

NEW LAW EXPLAINED

Code Sec. 199 deduction for production activities in Puerto Rico extended.— The special rule which permits Puerto Rico to be deemed part of the United States for purposes of the domestic production activities deduction under Code Sec. 199 is extended for two years. Thus, a taxpayer with gross receipts from qualified production activities within Puerto Rico which are subject to U.S. Federal income taxes may treat those receipts as domestic production gross receipts with respect to the first four tax years beginning after December 31, 2005, and before January 1, 2010 (Code Sec. 199(d)(8)(C), as amended by the Emergency Economic Stabilization Act of 2008 (P.L. 110-343)).

> **Comment:** For calendar-year taxpayers, this means that the rule will apply for tax years 2006 through 2009. For fiscal-year taxpayers, it means that the rule will apply for any tax year beginning in 2006 through 2009.

NEW LAW EXPLAINED

▶ **Effective date.** The provision applies to tax years beginning after December 31, 2007 (Section C, Act Sec. 312(b) of the Emergency Economic Stabilization Act of 2008 (P.L. 110-343)).

Law source: Law at ¶5280. Committee Report at ¶10,500.

— Section C, Act Sec. 312(a) of the Emergency Economic Stabilization Act of 2008 (P.L. 110-343)), amending Code Sec. 199(d)(8)(C);

— Section C, Act Sec. 312(b), providing the effective date.

Reporter references: For further information, consult the following CCH reporters.

— Standard Federal Tax Reporter, ¶12,476.0245

— Tax Research Consultant, BUSEXP: 6,054.05 and BUSEXP: 6,150

— Federal Tax Guide, ¶8315, ¶8320 and ¶8325

¶375 Limitation of Code Sec. 199 Deduction for Oil Related Production

SUMMARY OF NEW LAW

The manufacturing deduction for taxpayers having oil related qualified production activities income for tax years beginning after 2009 must be reduced by three percent of the least of: (1) the taxpayer's oil related qualified production activities income for the tax year; (2) the taxpayer's qualified production activities income for the tax year; or (3) taxable income (determined without regard to the manufacturing deduction).

BACKGROUND

Generally, a deduction may be claimed equal to an applicable percentage of the lesser of a taxpayer's qualified production activities income (QPAI) or taxable income (adjusted gross income in the case of an individual, estate or trust) (Code Sec. 199). The applicable percentage is 6 percent for tax years beginning in 2008 through 2009, and 9 percent for years beginning after 2009.

A taxpayer's QPAI is its domestic production gross receipts (DPGR) attributable to the actual conduct of a trade or business by the taxpayer during the tax year, less the costs of goods sold allocable to those receipts, and other expenses, losses, or deductions properly allocable to those receipts. DPGR are the gross receipts of the taxpayer derived from:

• the lease, license, sale, exchange of other disposition of any:

(1) qualifying production property (i.e., tangible personal property) manufactured, produced, grown or extracted by the taxpayer in whole or in significant part within the United States;

(2) qualified film produced by the taxpayer within the United States; or

BACKGROUND

    (3) electricity, natural gas, or potable water produced by the taxpayer in the United States;

- the construction of real property that is performed by the taxpayer in the United States in the ordinary course of an taxpayer's construction trade or business; and

- architectural or engineering services that are performed by the taxpayer in the ordinary course of its architectural or engineering trade or business in the United States with respect to the construction of real property that is located in the United States.

The domestic production activities deduction cannot exceed more than 50 percent of the W-2 wages paid by the taxpayer to its employees for the calendar year ending during the tax year and properly allocable to the taxpayer's DPGR (those W-2 wages deducted in calculating QPAI). For this purpose, "wages" includes any amount paid by the taxpayer to its employees for services performed and which are subject to federal income tax withholding. Generally, no withholding is required on wages paid for services performed outside the United States, including wages paid to a bona fide resident of Puerto Rico for services performed in Puerto Rico.

NEW LAW EXPLAINED

Manufacturing deduction limited.—A taxpayer having oil related qualified production activities income for any tax year beginning after 2009, must reduce the deduction allowable under Code Sec. 199 by 3 percent of the least of:

- the taxpayer's oil related qualified production activities income for the tax year;

- the taxpayer's qualified production activities income for the tax year; or

- taxable income (determined without regard to the Code Sec. 199 deduction) (Code Sec. 199(d)(9)(A), as added by the Emergency Economic Stabilization Act of 2008 (P.L. 110-343)).

If the taxpayer entitled to the deduction under Code Sec. 199 is an individual, then modified adjusted gross income (AGI) is substituted for taxable income (Code Sec. 199(d)(2), as amended by the Emergency Economic Act of 2008).

Oil related qualified production activities income. For purposes of this provision, the term "oil related qualified production activities income" is the qualified production activities income of the taxpayer that is attributable to the production, refining, processing, transportation or distribution of oil, gas or any of their primary products (Code Sec. 199(d)(9)(B), as added by the Emergency Economic Act of 2008).

For this purpose, the term "primary product" has the same meaning as when used in Code Sec. 927(a)(2)(C), as in effect before its repeal (Code Sec. 199(d)(9)(C), as added by the Emergency Economic Act of 2008). The regulations under Code Sec. 927 define the term "primary product from oil" as crude oil and all products derived from the destructive distillation of crude oil, including volatile products, light oils such as motor fuel and kerosene, distillates such as naphtha lubricating oils, greases and waxes and residues such as fuel oils (Temporary Reg. § 1.927(a)-1T(g)(2)(i)). In addition, a prod-

¶375

NEW LAW EXPLAINED

uct or commodity derived from shale oil which would be a primary product from oil if derived from crude oil is considered a primary product from oil (Temporary Reg. § 1.927(a)-1T(g)(2)(i)).

The term "primary product from gas" is defined as all gas and associated hydrocarbon components from gas wells or oil wells, whether recovered at the lease or upon further processing, including natural gas, condensates, liquefied petroleum gases such as ethane, propane and butane and liquid products such as natural gasoline (Temporary Reg. § 1.927(a)-1T(g)(2)(ii)). These primary products and processes are not intended to represent either the only primary products from oil or gas or the only processes from which primary products may be derived under existing and future technologies (Temporary Reg. § 1.927(a)-1T(g)(2)(iii)).

> **Comment:** Examples of nonprimary products include, but are not limited to, petrochemicals, medicinal products, insecticides and alcohols (Temporary Reg. § 1.927(a)-1T(g)(2)(iv)).

▶ **Effective date.** The provision applies to tax years beginning after December 31, 2008 (Division B, Act Sec. 401(c) of the Emergency Economic Stabilization Act of 2008 (P.L. 110-343)).

Law source: Law at ¶5280. Committee Reports at ¶10,260.

— Division B, Act Sec. 401(a) of the Emergency Economic Stabilization Act of 2008 (P.L. 110-343), redesignating Code Sec. 199(d)(9) as Code Sec. 199(d)(10) and adding new Code Sec. 199(d)(9);

— Division B, Act Sec. 401(b), amending Code Sec. 199(d)(2);

— Division B, Act Sec. 401(c), providing the effective date.

Reporter references: For further information, consult the following CCH reporters.

— Standard Federal Tax Reporter, ¶12,476.0125

— Tax Research Consultant, BUSEXP: 6,052

— Federal Tax Guide, ¶8305

¶380 Executive Compensation Limits for Financial Institutions Participating in the Troubled Asset Relief Program

SUMMARY OF NEW LAW

Certain financial institutions that sell troubled assets to the Treasury Department by means of a *public auction* are restricted for a period of time from deducting more than $500,000 for executive compensation. In addition, they are subject to the golden parachute rules for payments triggered by severance during this period, and the firm is prohibited from contracting for new golden parachute payments. A firm that sells troubled assets *directly* to the government must exclude incentives for executive officers to take unnecessary risks; recover bonuses to senior executives based on

SUMMARY OF NEW LAW

materially inaccurate information; and not make any golden parachute payments to senior executives while the government holds an equity or debt position in the firm.

BACKGROUND

There are three limits in the Internal Revenue Code to executive compensation: (1) a publicly held corporation cannot deduct applicable employee remuneration it pays to a covered employee to the extent it exceeds $1 million per tax year (Code Sec. 162(m)); (2) a corporation cannot deduct excess parachute payments paid to a disqualified individual that were triggered by a change of ownership or control (Code Sec. 280G); and (3) such excess payments are subject to a 20-percent excise tax payable by the recipient (Code Sec 4999).

$1 million deduction limit. Covered employees for purposes of the $1 million compensation deduction limitation include the principal executive officer (or anyone who acts in that capacity), and the three highest compensated officers other than the principal executive officer, whose total compensation must be reported to shareholders under the Securities Exchange Act of 1934 (Notice 2007-49, 2007-25 I.R.B. 1429). The determination of who are covered employees is made as of the close of the tax year (Code Sec. 162(m)(3)). The amount of an employee's compensation taken into account for purposes of the $1 million deduction limitation (known as "applicable employee remuneration") generally is the total compensation otherwise allowable as a deduction, with the important exceptions of commissions and performance-based pay. Stock options can qualify as performance-based pay (Code Sec. 162(m)(4)). The $1 million threshold is reduced by excess golden parachute payments for which the employer's deduction is disallowed (Code Sec. 162(m)(4)(F)).

Golden parachutes. A corporation cannot deduct excess parachute payments (Code Sec. 280G), and such excess payment are subject to a 20-percent excise tax (Code Sec. 4999). A parachute payment is any payment in the nature of compensation paid to a disqualified individual that either is contingent upon a change in ownership of the corporation and equals or exceeds a safe harbor, or is made under an agreement that violates securities laws or regulations. There is a safe harbor for payments the aggregate present value of which does not exceed three times the individual's base amount (Code Sec. 280G(b)(2)(A)(ii)). The base amount is the individual's annualized includible compensation for the base period (Code Sec. 280G(b)(3)). The base period is the most recent five tax years ending before the date on which the change in ownership or control occurs (Code Sec. 280G(d)(2)).

In general, excess parachute payments are any parachute payments in excess of the base amount allocated to the payment (Code Sec. 280G(b)(1)). The amount treated as an excess parachute payment is reduced by the portion of the payment that the taxpayer establishes by clear and convincing evidence is reasonable compensation for personal services actually rendered before the change in control (Code Sec. 280G(b)(4)). Small corporations are not subject to these rules (Code Sec. 280G(b)(5)).

¶380

Executive compensation limits apply to financial institutions that sell troubled assets to the Treasury.—The Emergency Economic Stabilization of 2008 (P.L. 110-343)) imposes a number of restrictions on executive compensation for financial institutions that sell troubled assets to the Treasury through the Troubled Asset Relief Program (TARP). Different rules may apply depending on whether the Treasury purchases these assets directly or through a public auction.

Limits when sales are made directly to the Treasury. If a firm sells troubled assets directly to the Treasury, and the government takes a "meaningful" equity or debt position in the firm as a result, the firm is required to follow certain standards that limit executive compensation. The standards are effective for the duration of the period that the government holds the equity or debt position (Division A, Act Sec. 111(b)(1) of the Emergency Economic Act of 2008). The standards include:

- Limits on compensation that exclude incentives for senior executive officers to take unnecessary and excessive risks that threaten the value of the firm during the period that the Treasury holds an equity or debt position in the firm;

- Provision for the recovery by the firm of any bonus or incentive compensation paid to a senior executive officer based on statements of earnings, gains, or other criteria that are later proven to be materially inaccurate (otherwise known as a "clawback" provision); and

- Prohibition on any golden parachute payment to senior executive officers during the period that the Secretary holds an equity or debt position in the firm (Division A, Sec. 111(b)(2) of the Emergency Economic Act of 2008).

For these purposes, a senior executive officer is an individual who is one of the top five highly paid executives of a public company whose compensation is required to be disclosed pursuant to the Securities Exchange Act of 1934, and non-public company counterparts (Division A, Act Sec. 111(b)(3) of the Emergency Economic Act of 2008).

Comment: If a firm only sells troubled assets *directly* to the Treasury, and does not sell any assets by way of a public auction, it is only subject to these standards and not to the Internal Revenue Code-based $500,000 deduction limit and excess parachute payment rules. However, if it also sells through a public auction, and its combined sales exceed $300 million (including the value of directly purchased assets), it is subject to both the standards and the Code-based limits. If the firm sells only through a public auction, and its sales exceed $300 million, it is only subject to the Code-based limits. If its sales are only through an auction, and they do not exceed $300 million, the firm is not subject to any of these limits or standards.

Comment: The TARP program requires the Treasury to obtain an equity or debt interest in any financial institution from which it purchases troubled assets, with the terms to be set by the Treasury. The Treasury is authorized to set a *de minimis* exception of up to $100 million in purchases from a financial institution. (Division A, Act Sec. 113(d) of the Emergency Economic Act of 2008). This rule applies whether or not the purchases are direct or through an auction.

NEW LAW EXPLAINED

Comment: There does not seem to be any enforcement mechanism with respect to the standards (including the clawback provision), but the prospect of a large-scale TARP rescue coupled with equity ownership in the firm does give the Treasury considerable leverage in determining how a firm is to meet the standards.

Practical Analysis: Arthur H. Kroll, J.D., CEO of KST Consulting in Hartsdale, New York, comments that the language of Division A, Act Sec. 302 of the Emergency Economic Stabilization Act of 2008 (P.L. 110-343) limiting the deduction for executive compensation is extremely vague. It appears that it would be extremely difficult for the governing body—organized under the Emergency Economic Act of 2008—to overturn an executive compensation decision that was decided by a truly independent board or committee, either under reorganization or some other terminating event. However, it is quite important that this provision was included in this Act because it may be an indication that Congress wants to consider regulating this area at least regarding severance benefits that are paid to an executive or CEO who leaves the business. The amount of benefits has been a matter of great contention by unions, institutional investors and state pension fund boards. This is especially true as CEO's of financial institutions were terminated because the institution needed to be rescued.

The second area that Congress is likely to focus on is requiring corporations to give shareholders an advisory vote on total executive compensation. Although the executive compensation provision lacks meaningful detail it does provide an indication that Congress would like to conduct a complete review in this area. Thus the passage of Division A, Act Sec. 302 may be the beginning of further legislation on executive compensation.

Limits when financial institutions sell troubled assets through a public auction. Executive compensation limits are imposed on a firm that sells troubled assets through a TARP managed public auction to the Treasury, and the purchases by that firm exceed $300 million (including direct purchases). These executive compensation limits include:

- $500,000 limit on the deductibility of executive compensation, including commissions and incentive pay (Code Sec. 162(m)(5), as added by the Emergency Economic Act of 2008);

- Expansion of the golden parachute rules (including the excise tax) to cover payments to executives by financial institutions that participate in TARP managed public auctions (Code Sec. 280G(e), as added by the Emergency Economic Act of 2008); and

- A prohibition against the firm entering into a new employment contract with a senior executive officer that provides a golden parachute in the event of an involuntary termination, bankruptcy filing, insolvency, or receivership (Division A, Act Sec. 111(c) of the Emergency Economic Act of 2008). This prohibition applies only to arrangements entered into during the period during which the authorities for TARP are in effect (the "TARP authorities period").

NEW LAW EXPLAINED

> **Comment:** The TARP authorities period begins on October 3, 2008, and terminates December 31, 2009, unless extended. The maximum extension is two years after October 3, 2008 (Division A, Act Secs. 101(a) and 120, of the Emergency Economic Act of 2008).

$500,000 limit on executive compensation deduction. An applicable employer's deduction for executive remuneration for any applicable taxable year attributable to services performed by a covered executive during that tax year is limited to $500,000 (Code Sec. 162(m)(5)(A)(i), as added by the Emergency Economic Act of 2008).

> **Comment:** This rule largely tracks the current $1 million deduction limit, although tailored to this situation. The most significant difference is that the big hole in the $1 million dollar limit for incentive pay and commissions is plugged for TARP purposes. Also, the employer need not be a publicly traded corporation, and can include partnerships if the partnership is an employer from which a troubled asset is acquired (Joint Committee on Taxation, Technical Explanation of of Division A of H.R. 1424, the "Emergency Economic Stabilization Act of 2008" (JCX-79-08)).

Practical Analysis: Robert S. Winters, Shareholder, Buchanan Ingersoll and Rooney and former Chief Tax Counsel, Committee on Ways and Means, House of Representatives, and Janine H. Bosley, J.D., Shareholder, Buchanan Ingersoll and Rooney, note that Division A, Act Sec. 302 of the Emergency Economic Stabilization Act of 2008 (P.L. 110-343) imposes limits on an "applicable employer's" ability to deduct compensation paid to a "covered executive" during any "applicable year."

Any employer with assets exceeding $300 million in aggregate value that is acquired by the Federal Government through the operation of the Emergency Economic Act of 2008 is considered to be an "applicable employer" under Division A, Act Sec. 302. Applicable employers will lose the ability to deduct compensation in excess of $500,000 per applicable year paid to "covered executives." An "applicable year" is a year during which the Troubled Assets Relief Program is in effect. A "covered executive" is defined under Division A, Act Sec. 302 as the chief executive officer, chief financial officer or any one of the three highest-paid employees of an applicable employer. Once an employee has been classified as a covered executive, that employee retains the covered executive status throughout the applicable year.

The definition of compensation under Division A, Act Sec. 302 of the Emergency Economic Act of 2008 is broader than that of Code Sec. 162(m) and applies to corporations, partnerships and other entities. Compensation under Division A, Act Sec. 302 of the Emergency Economic Act includes commissions, performance-based compensation and compensation covered by binding contracts. Deferred compensation based on services provided during an applicable year is also subject to the new limit. For example, if a covered executive is paid $400,000 during an applicable year and is covered by a deferred compensation program providing $300,000 in a later year, the employer can deduct only $500,000 of compensation during the deduction year. The limit does not, however, apply to nonqualified deferred compensation based on services that were not performed in an applicable year.

NEW LAW EXPLAINED

The $500,000 deduction limit provision contains a number of key definitions that are also used in the provision extending golden parachute rules to financial institutions that use TARP. These definitions include "applicable employers," "applicable taxable year," and "covered executive."

Applicable employers. An applicable employer is any employer from which one or more troubled assets are acquired under TARP if the aggregate amount of the assets so acquired for all tax years (including assets acquired through a direct purchase by the government) exceeds $300 million (Code Sec. 162(m)(5)(B)(i), as added by the Emergency Economic Act of 2008). Employers that purchase troubled assets solely through direct purchases are not included (Code Sec. 162(m)(5)(B)(ii), as added by the Emergency Economic Act of 2008).

> **Example 1:** The Barney Smith firm sells $250 million in troubled assets to the government through an auction system managed by the Treasury Department, and $100 million to the government in direct purchases. Because the firm sold through an auction, and because it sold over $300 million in troubled assets to the government, it is an applicable employer.

> **Example 2:** Assume the same facts as in Example 1, except the Treasury buys all $350 million worth of troubled in direct purchases. Because there is no sale by public auction, Barney Smith is not an applicable employer (Joint Committee on Taxation, Technical Explanation of Division A of H.R. 1424, the "Emergency Economic Stabilization Act of 2008" (JCX-79-08)).

> **Comment:** Setting a purchase price for troubled assets is one of the trickiest tasks for the Treasury Department in implementing TARP.

A modified version of the aggregation rules of Code Sec. 414(b) and (c) apply in determining whether an employer is an applicable employer. The rules are applied disregarding the rules for brother-sister controlled groups and combined groups in Code Sec. 1563(a)(2) and (3). Accordingly, this aggregation rule only applies to parent-subsidiary controlled groups (Code Sec. 162(m)(5)(B)(iii), as added by the Emergency Economic Act of 2008). Under the aggregation rules, all corporations in the same controlled group are treated as a single employer for purposes of identifying the covered executives, and all compensation from all members of the controlled group are taken into account for purposes of applying the $500,000 deduction limit. Further, all sales of assets under TARP from all members of the controlled group are considered in determining whether such sales exceed $300 million (Joint Committee on Taxation, Technical Explanation of Division A of H.R. 1424, the "Emergency Economic Stabilization Act of 2008" (JCX-79-08).

Applicable taxable year. An "applicable taxable year" with respect to an applicable employer is the first tax year that includes any portion of the TARP authorities period if the aggregate amount of troubled assets acquired from the employer under that authority during the tax year (when added to the aggregate amount so acquired for

NEW LAW EXPLAINED

all preceding tax years) exceeds $300 million. Any subsequent tax year that includes any portion of the authorities period is also an applicable taxable year (Code Sec. 162(m)(5)(C), as added by the Emergency Economic Act of 2008).

> **Example 3:** The Springfield National Bank sells $200 million in troubled assets through public auction to the Treasury during its 2008 tax year, and $120 million in troubled assets during its 2009 tax year. Thus, 2009 is an applicable taxable year for the Bank, but 2008 is not.

A carryover is allowed for compensation that relates to services that a covered executive performs during an applicable taxable year but which is not deductible until a later year ("deferred deduction executive remuneration"), such as nonqualified deferred compensation. Any unused portion of the $500,000 limit for the applicable taxable year is carried forward until the year in which the compensation is otherwise deductible, and the remaining unused limit is then applied to the compensation (Code Sec. 162(m)(5)(A)(ii) and (F), as added by the Emergency Economic Act of 2008).

> **Example 4:** Silas Potter, a covered executive, is paid $400,000 in cash salary by an applicable employer in 2008, which for this employer is an applicable taxable year. He also earns $100,000 in nonqualified deferred compensation (along with the right to future earnings credits) payable in 2020. The $100,000 grows to $300,000 by 2020. The full $400,000 in cash salary is deductible under the $500,000 limit in 2008. In 2020, the applicable employer's deduction will be limited to $100,000 (the lesser of the $300,000 in deductible compensation before considering the special limitation, and $500,000 less $400,000, which represents the unused portion of the $500,000 limit from 2008) (Joint Committee on Taxation, Technical Explanation of Division A of H.R. 1424, the "Emergency Economic Stabilization Act of 2008" (JCX-79-08)).

Deferred deduction executive remuneration that is otherwise properly deductible in an applicable taxable year but which is attributable to services performed in a prior applicable taxable year is subject to this carryover rule. A new $500,000 deduction limit will apply if the subsequent year is an applicable taxable year.

> **Example 5:** Assume the same facts as in Example 4, except the nonqualified deferred compensation is deferred until 2009, and 2009 is an applicable taxable year. The employer's deduction for the nonqualified deferred compensation for 2009 would be limited to $100,000. The limit that would apply under the provision for executive remuneration that is in a form other than deferred deduction executive remuneration and which is otherwise deductible for 2009 is $500,000. Thus, if the covered executive is paid $500,000 in cash compensation for 2009, all $500,000 of that cash compensation would be deductible in 2009 in addition to the $100,000 of deferred compensation (Joint Committee on

NEW LAW EXPLAINED

> Taxation, Technical Explanation of Division A of H.R. 1424, the "Emergency Economic Stabilization Act of 2008" (JCX-79-08)).

Covered executives. Covered executives include the chief executive officer (CEO) and the chief financial officer (CFO) of an applicable employer (or an individual acting in that capacity), at any time during a portion of the tax year that includes the TARP authorities period. It also includes any employee who is one of the three highest compensated officers of the applicable employer for the applicable taxable year (other than the CEO and CFO), by only taking into account employees employed during any portion of the tax year that includes the TARP authorities period.

The three highest compensated employees are determined on the basis of the shareholder disclosure rules for compensation under the Securities Exchange Act of 1934 (without regard to whether those rules apply to the employer), and by only taking into account employees employed during the portion of the tax year during which TARP is authorized (Code Sec. 162(m)(5)(D)(i) and (ii), as added by the Emergency Economic Act of 2008). If an employee is a covered executive with respect to an applicable employer for any applicable taxable year, the employee remains a covered executive with respect to such employer for all subsequent applicable taxable years, and for all subsequent tax years in which deferred deduction executive remuneration for services performed in all such applicable taxable years would be deductible (Code Sec. 162(m)(5)(D)(iii), as added by the Emergency Economic Act of 2008).

Executive remuneration. Executive remuneration generally incorporates the present law definition of applicable employee remuneration under the $1 million deduction limit, although the exceptions for commissions and performance-based compensation do not apply. The $500,000 limit only applies to executive remuneration attributable to services performed by a covered executive during an applicable taxable year (Code Sec. 162(m)(5)(E), as added by the Emergency Economic Act of 2008).

> **Example 6:** Henry Fabersham, a covered executive, is paid $500,000 in cash salary by an applicable employer in 2008, which for this employer is an applicable taxable year. He is also paid $300,000 in nonqualified deferred compensation attributable to services performed in 2006. Such payment is not treated as executive remuneration for purposes of the new $500,000 limit, and the employer may deduct all $800,000 of the compensation (Joint Committee on Taxation, Technical Explanation of Division A of H.R. 1424, the "Emergency Economic Stabilization Act of 2008" (JCX-79-08)).

Coordination with parachute payments. As under the $1 million deduction limit, the $500,000 deduction limit is reduced (but not below zero) by any disallowed parachute payments (including parachute payments under the expanded definition for TARP purposes) paid during the TARP authorities period, and any payment of the excise tax under Code Sec. 4985 for stock compensation of insiders in expatriated corporations (Code Sec. 162(m)(5)(G), as added by the Emergency Economic Act of 2008).

NEW LAW EXPLAINED

Regulations. The IRS is authorized to prescribe guidance, rules, or regulations regarding the $500,000 deduction limit, including the extent to which the limit applies in the case of any acquisition, merger, or reorganization of an applicable employer (Code Sec. 162(m)(5)(H), as added by the Emergency Economic Act of 2008).

Expansion of golden parachutes rules. The golden parachute rules, with certain modifications, apply in the event of a severance from employment by a covered executive of an applicable employer during the TARP authorities period. The golden parachute rules are modified to fit the TARP situation as follows:

- A covered executive is treated as a disqualified individual;

- An applicable severance from employment by a covered executive will be treated as a change in ownership or control; and

- Any payment made during an applicable taxable year of the employer on account of such applicable severance from employment is counted as payment contingent on a change in ownership or control (Code Sec. 280G(e)(1), as added by the Emergency Economic Act of 2008).

> **Comment:** The terms "covered executive," "applicable taxable year," and "applicable employer" have the same meaning as those under Code Sec. 162(m)(5) regarding the $500,000 deduction limit (Code Sec. 280(e)(2)(A), as added by the Emergency Economic Act of 2008).

A parachute payment includes any payments in the nature of compensation to a covered executive made during an applicable taxable year on account of an "applicable severance" from employment during the TARP authorities period if the aggregate present value of such payments equals or exceeds an amount equal to three times the covered executive's base amount (Code Sec. 280G(e)(1)(B), as added by the Emergency Economic Act of 2008). An applicable severance from employment is any severance from employment of a covered executive by reason of an involuntary termination of the executive by the employer, or in connection with a bankruptcy, liquidation, or receivership of the employer (Code Sec. 280G(e)(2)(B), as added by the Emergency Economic Act of 2008).

> **Comment:** There is no exception for small corporations under the modified TARP rules, and an employer cannot avoid the parachute limits by showing the compensation was reasonable (Code Sec. 280G(e)(1)(D), as added by the Emergency Economic Act of 2008).

In identifying payments contingent on severance, the general Code Sec. 280G rules would apply. A payment is on account of the employee's severance from employment if the payment would not have been made at that time if the severance from employment had not occurred. Such payments might include amounts payable on severance or separation from service, amounts that vest or are no longer subject to a substantial risk of forfeiture on account of such a separation, and amounts that are accelerated on account of severance from employment (Joint Committee on Taxation, Technical Explanation of Division A of H.R. 1424, the "Emergency Economic Stabilization Act of 2008" (JCX-79-08)).

NEW LAW EXPLAINED

A parachute payment during an applicable taxable year paid on account of a covered executive's applicable severance from employment is nondeductible on the part of the employer, and the covered executive is subject to the 20-percent excise tax (Code Sec. 4999), to the extent of the amount of the payment that is equal to the excess over the employee's base amount that is allocable to such payment.

> **Example 7:** A covered executive's annualized includible compensation is $1 million and the covered executive's only parachute payment under the provision is a lump-sum payment of $5 million. The covered executive's base amount is $1 million and the excess parachute payment is $4 million (Joint Committee on Taxation, Technical Explanation of Division A of H.R. 1424, the "Emergency Economic Stabilization Act of 2008" (JCX-79-08)).

The TARP golden parachute rules do not apply in the case of a payment that is treated as a parachute payment under the general Code Sec. 280G rules (Code Sec. 280G(e)(2)(C)(i), as added by the Emergency Economic Act of 2008). The IRS is authorized to issue regulations to implement the expanded parachute rules, including their application to payments some of which are parachute payments under the general Code Sec. 280G rules and others of which are parachute payments on account of the TARP parachute rules. Authority is also granted for regulations concerning these rules in the context of an acquisition, merger, or reorganization of an applicable employer. Additionally, regulations are authorized to prevent the avoidance of the expanded golden parachute rules by mischaracterizing a severance from employment, and to prevent avoidance through the acceleration, delay, or other modification of payment dates with respect to existing compensation arrangements (Code Sec. 280G(e)(2)(C)(ii), as added by the Emergency Economic Act of 2008).

> **Comment:** One criticism of the executive compensation limits is that executives will likely not take advantage of TARP unless their firms are on the brink of collapse. A mitigating feature of the legislation is that firms with smaller holdings or in less dire straights will be able to sell up to $300 million in troubled assets without any executive compensation limits so long as they stick to sales through public auctions. It remains to be seen when or if such auctions can be arranged.

▶ **Effective date.** The provision applies to tax years ending on or after October 3, 2008, the date of enactment, except that the modifications to Code Sec. 280G are effective for payments with respect to severances occurring during the TARP authorities period (Division A, Act Sec. 302(c) of the Emergency Economic Stabilization Emergency Economic Act of 2008 (P.L. 110-343)).

Law source: Law at ¶5215, ¶5290 and ¶7042. Committee Reports at ¶10,020.

— Division A, Act Sec. 302(a) of the Emergency Economic Stabilization Act of 2008 (P.L. 110-343), adding Code Sec. 162(m)(5);

— Division A, Act Sec. 302(b), redesignating Code Sec. 280G(e) as (f), and adding new Code Sec. 280G(e);

— Division A, Act Sec. 302(c), providing the effective date.

NEW LAW EXPLAINED

Reporter references: For further information, consult the following CCH reporters.
— Standard Federal Tax Reporter, ¶8636.0252 and ¶15,152.01
— Tax Research Consultant, COMPEN: 21,400 and COMPEN: 30,050
— Federal Tax Guide, ¶7423 and ¶12,036

Business Credits and Other Special Rules

4

TAX CREDITS

¶405 Research Credit for Increasing Research Activities

SUMMARY OF NEW LAW

The research credit is extended for two years, through December 31, 2009. In addition, for tax years beginning after December 31, 2008, the election to use the alternative incremental method to calculate the research credit can no longer be made. The percentage used in computing the credit under the alternative simplified method is increased to 14 percent. Finally, a technical correction clarifying the computation for determining the credit amount in the year of termination has been made.

BACKGROUND

In order to encourage businesses to increase their spending on research and development of new technologies, products, and services, a research credit is available under Code Sec. 41. The credit applies to incremental increases in qualified research expenses paid or incurred by a business, to increases in basic research payments made by a business to universities and certain other qualified organizations, and to payments made or incurred by a business to an energy research consortium. The credit applies to amounts paid or incurred (1) before July 1, 1995, and (2) after June 30, 1996, and before December 31, 2007 (Code Sec. 41(h)(1)). Expenditures made after June 30, 1995, and before July 1, 1996, are not eligible for the credit.

General rule. Under the general rule, the amount of the credit is equal to the sum of:

(1) 20 percent of the excess of a company's qualified research expenses for the tax year over its base amount;

(2) 20 percent of the excess of its qualified research payments made during the tax year over the average annual payments made during a base period; and

(3) 20 percent of all payments made during the tax year to an energy research consortium (Code Sec. 41(a)).

The base amount is computed by multiplying the taxpayer's fixed-base percentage by the taxpayer's average gross receipts for the four preceding tax years (Code Sec. 41(c)(1)). A taxpayer's fixed-base percentage is the ratio that its total qualified research expenditures for 1984 through 1988 bears to its total gross receipts for that period (subject to a maximum ratio of .16). Start-up companies are assigned a fixed-base percentage of three-percent (Code Sec. 41(c)(3)).

Qualified research expenses include expenses incurred with respect to in-house research, contract research, and basic research conducted by certain entities. There are basically four categories of expenses to which the credit applies, the first three of

BACKGROUND

which refer to in-house research activities: (1) wages for employees involved in the research activity, (2) costs of supplies used in research, (3) payments to others for the use of computer time in qualified research (except if the taxpayer, or a person with whom the taxpayer must aggregate expenditures in computing the credit, receives or accrues any amount from another person for computer use), and (4) 65 percent of costs of contracting with another party to conduct research on the taxpayer's behalf (75 percent of costs paid to a qualified research consortium and 100 percent of costs paid for energy research to eligible small businesses, universities, and federal laboratories) (Code Sec. 41(b)(1) through (3)).

Alternative incremental research credit. Taxpayers can elect to claim an alternative incremental research credit, which allows a business to calculate the research credit at reduced rates based upon the amount of research expenses over a lower base (fixed-base percentages). Once the election is made, it applies to all succeeding tax years unless revoked with the consent of the IRS. Under this method, the credit is equal to the sum of:

(1) 3 percent of that portion of the qualified research expenses that exceed one percent, but not more than 1.5 percent, of the average annual gross receipts for the four preceding tax years;

(2) 4 percent of that portion of the qualified research expenses that exceed 1.5 percent, but not more than two percent, of the average annual gross receipts for the four preceding tax years; and

(3) 5 percent of that portion of the qualified research expenses that exceed two percent of the average annual gross receipts for the four preceding tax years (Code Sec. 41(c)(4)).

Alternative simplified credit. A third method that taxpayers may elect to use to calculate the research credit amount is the alternative simplified method, which was added by the Tax Relief and Health Care Act of 2006 (P.L. 109-432). Under this method, a taxpayer can claim a credit equal to 12 percent of the amount by which the qualified research expenses exceed 50 percent of the average qualified research expenses for the three preceding tax years. In the event that a taxpayer had no qualified research expenses for any of the preceding three years, the credit amount equals six percent of the qualified research expenses for the current tax year. As with the alternative incremental method, once the election is made to use the alternative simplified method for calculating the amount of the research credit it remains in effect for all succeeding tax years unless revoked with consent of the IRS (Code Sec. 41(c)(5)).

> **Comment:** When it was first enacted in 1981, the research credit was to terminate after four and one-half years. However, it has been subject to several extensions over the years and was even allowed to expire at one point without the extension being made retroactive to the prior termination date. The latest extension was in 2006, for a period of two years. Manufacturing associations continue to lobby to make the credit permanent so that they can rely on the tax incentive to make long-term plans for research projects.

NEW LAW EXPLAINED

Research credit extended and modified.—The credit for increasing research activities (the research credit) termination date has been extended for two years or through December 31, 2009 (Code Sec. 41(h)(1)(B), as amended by the Emergency Economic Stabilization Act of 2008 (P.L. 110-343)). The orphan drug credit whose credit amount calculation is linked to the research credit, will continue to be effective for periods after December 31, 2009 (Code Sec. 45C(b)(1), as amended by the Emergency Economic Act of 2008).

Practical Analysis: Charles C. Hwang, J.D., Partner, Alex E. Sadler, J.D., Partner, and Jennifer A. Ray, J.D., Associate in the tax group of Crowell & Moring LLP in Washington, D.C., observes that Division C, Act Sec. 301 of the Emergency Economic Stabilization Act of 2008 (P.L. 110-343) extends the research tax credit to December 31, 2009, with modifications. For tax years beginning after December 31, 2008, taxpayers will no longer be able to elect the alternative incremental credit. That election generally allowed taxpayers to take a research credit equal to certain percentages of qualified research expenses over a threshold amount that is computed without regard to qualified research expenses in a base period. In addition, Code Sec. 41 is revised to increase the alternative simplified credit for tax years ending on or after January 1, 2009. Currently, a taxpayer can elect to take an alternative simplified credit equal to 12 percent of the excess of (i) the qualified research expenses for the tax year over (ii) 50 percent of the average qualified research expenses for the three preceding tax years. The revision increases the alternative simplified credit from 12 percent to 14 percent of such amount. Finally, there is a technical correction to the method of computing a credit for a tax year in which Code Sec. 41 does not apply for the entire year. In that case, for purposes of computing the regular credit, the taxpayer's average annual gross receipts for the four years preceding the credit year are pro-rated based on the number of days in the tax year to which Code Sec. 41 applies. A similar calculation is made for purposes of the alternative simplified credit.

These amendments to Code Sec. 41 apply to tax years beginning after December 31, 2007, and the extension applies to amounts paid or incurred after December 31, 2007.

Termination of the election for the alternative incremental credit. The election to use the alternative incremental method of calculating the research credit will no longer apply for tax years beginning after December 31, 2008 (Code Sec. 41(h)(2), as redesignated and added by the Emergency Economic Act of 2008).

Comment: Practitioners with clients currently claiming the research credit using the alternative incremental method under Code Sec. 41(c)(4) will need to decide whether to use the basic method under Code Sec. 41(c)(1) or elect to use the alternative simplified method under Code Sec. 41(c)(5). This determination should be made before the first corporate estimated tax payment is due in order to avoid possible underpayment penalties.

¶405

NEW LAW EXPLAINED

Modification of the alternative simplified method. For taxpayers that have elected to use the alternative simplified method, as well as those who may make this election beginning with the 2009 tax year, the credit amount is increased to equal 14 percent of the qualified research expenses for the tax year that exceed 50 percent of the average qualified research expenses for the prior three tax years (Code Sec. 41(c)(5), as amended by the Emergency Economic Act of 2008)). The percentage will remain at 12 percent for tax years ending before January 1, 2009 (Division C, Act Sec. 301(c) of the Emergency Economic Act of 2008)).

Technical correction for computing credit amounts in the year of termination. Under Code Sec. 41(h)(3) (formerly Code Sec. 41(h)(2) prior to redesignation by the Emergency Economic Act of 2008) the language used was unclear on how to prorate the credit amount in the year of the credit's termination. The Emergency Economic Act of 2008 amends Code Sec. 41(h)(3) by establishing specific ratios to prorate the credit amount depending on the method used by the taxpayer. For taxpayers using the basic method under Code Sec. 41(c)(1) in the year of termination, if such year contains fewer days than the total number of days in the taxpayer's tax year, the average annual gross receipts for the preceding four tax years will bear the same ratio to such amount determined without regard to the short year as the number of days in the short termination year bears to the total number of days in the taxpayer's tax year (Code Sec. 41(h)(3)(A), as amended by the Emergency Economic Act of 2008)). Similarly, for the alternative simplified method under Code Sec. 41(c)(5), the average qualified research expenses for the preceding three tax years is an amount that bears the same ratio to such average qualified research expenses as the number of days in the short year of termination bears to the total number of days in that taxpayer's tax year (Code Sec. 41(h)(3)(B), as amended by the Emergency Economic Act of 2008)).

▶ **Effective date.** The amendments made by this provision, with the exception of the extension of the credit termination date, apply to taxable years beginning after December 31, 2007 (Division C, Act Sec. 301(e)(1) of the Emergency Economic Stabilization Act of 2008 (P.L. 110-343)). The extension of the credit termination date applies to amounts paid or incurred after December 31, 2007 (Division C, Act Sec. 301(e)(2) of the Emergency Economic Act of 2008).

Law source: Law at ¶5070 and ¶5085. Committee Report at ¶10,410.

— Division C, Act Sec. 301(a)(1) of the Emergency Economic Stabilization Act of 2008 (P.L. 110-343), amending Code Sec. 41(h)(1)(B);

— Division C, Act Sec. 301(a)(2), amending Code Sec. 45C(b)(1)(D);

— Division C, Act Sec. 301(b), redesignating Code Sec. 41(h)(2) as (3) and adding new Code Sec. 41(h)(2);

— Division C, Act Sec. 301(c), amending Code Sec. 41(c)(5)(A);

— Division C, Act Sec. 301(d), amending Code Sec. 41(h)(3);

— Division C, Act Sec. 301(e), providing the effective date.

Reporter references: For further information, consult the following CCH reporters.

— Standard Federal Tax Reporter, ¶4362.01

— Tax Research Consultant, BUSEXP: 54,150

— Federal Tax Guide, ¶2450

¶410 New Markets Tax Credit

SUMMARY OF NEW LAW

The new markets tax credit is extended through 2009, permitting up to $3.5 billion in qualified equity investments for that calendar year.

BACKGROUND

The Internal Revenue Code offers a few incentives for taxpayers to invest in, or make loans to, small businesses located in low-income communities. One such incentive, the new markets tax credit (Code Sec. 45D), provides a credit for qualified equity investments made to acquire stock in a corporation, or a capital interest in a partnership, that is a qualified community development entity (CDE). The credit allowable to the investor is (1) a five-percent credit for the first three years from the date that the equity interest was purchased from the CDE, and (2) a six-percent credit for each of the following four years (Code Sec. 45D(a)(2)). The credit is determined by applying the applicable percentage (five or six) to the amount paid to the CDE for the investment at its original issue (Code Sec. 45D(a)(1)). The credit is subject to recapture in certain circumstances (Code Sec. 45D(g)).

There is a national limitation with respect to the new markets tax credit. The maximum annual amount of qualified equity investments is capped at $2 billion for calendar years 2004 and 2005. In 2006, 2007, and 2008, the cap is $3.5 billion (Code Sec. 45D(f)(1)). The Secretary of the Treasury is authorized to allocate the amounts among qualified CDEs, giving preference (in part) to any entity with a record of successfully providing capital or technical assistance to disadvantaged businesses or communities (Code Sec. 45D(f)(2)).

A qualified CDE includes any domestic corporation or partnership: (1) whose primary mission is serving or providing investment capital for low-income communities or persons; (2) that maintains accountability to the residents of low-income communities by their representation on any governing board of or any advisory board to the CDE; and (3) that is certified by the Secretary of the Treasury as being a qualified CDE (Code Sec. 45D(c)). A qualified equity investment means stock (other than nonqualified preferred stock) in a corporation or a capital interest in a partnership that is acquired directly from a CDE for cash. Substantially all of the investment proceeds must be used by the CDE to make qualified low-income community investments, as defined in Code Sec. 45D(d) (Code Sec. 45D(b)(1)).

One category of qualified low-income community investments is any capital or equity investment in (or loan to) any qualified active low-income community business (Code Sec. 45D(d)(1)(A)). For purposes of Code Sec. 45D, the term "low-income community" means any population census tract with either (1) a poverty rate of at least 20 percent or (2) median family income that does not exceed 80 percent of metropolitan area median family income (or in the case of a non-metropolitan census tract, does not exceed 80 percent of statewide median family income) (Code Sec.

BACKGROUND

45D(e)(1)). A modification is made for census tracts within high migration rural counties (Code Sec. 45D(e)(5)).

New markets tax credit extended.—The Code Sec. 45D new markets tax credit is extended through 2009 (Code Sec. 45D(f)(1)(D), as amended by the Emergency Economic Stabilization Act of 2008 (P.L. 110-343)). As a result, up to $3.5 billion in qualified equity investments may be allocated among qualified community development entities (CDEs) for that calendar year.

▶ **Effective date.** No specific effective date is provided by the Act. The provision is, therefore, considered effective on October 3, 2008.

Law source: Law at ¶5090. Committee Report at ¶10,420.

— Division C, Act Sec. 302 of the Emergency Economic Stabilization Act of 2008 (P.L. 110-343), amending Code Sec. 45D(f)(1)(D).

Reporter references: For further information, consult the following CCH reporters.

— Standard Federal Tax Reporter, ¶4490.01

— Tax Research Consultant, BUSEXP: 54,900

— Federal Tax Guide, ¶2490

¶415 Railroad Track Maintenance Credit

SUMMARY OF NEW LAW

The railroad track maintenance credit has been extended two years to apply to expenditures paid or incurred before 2010. Further, if the credit is determined after 2007, it can be used to offset alternative minimum tax liability.

BACKGROUND

The American Jobs Creation Act of 2004 (P.L. 108-357) added the railroad track maintenance credit as part of the general business credit to assist small and mid-sized railroads in upgrading their tracks and related infrastructure, and in maintaining those railroads as a viable alternative to shipping freight via over-the-road trucking. The credit is equal to 50 percent of any qualified railroad track maintenance expenditures paid or incurred by an eligible taxpayer during the tax year (Code Sec. 45G(a)). Eligible taxpayers include any Class II or Class III railroad, and any person who transports property using the rail facilities of a Class II or Class III railroad or who furnishes railroad-related property or services to such a railroad, but only regarding miles of track assigned to that person by the railroad (Code Sec. 45G(c)). Railroads are classified as Class II or Class III by the Surface Transportation Board of the Depart-

BACKGROUND

ment of Transportation (Code Sec. 45G(e)(1)). Special rules apply if an eligible taxpayer is a member of a controlled group of corporations (Code Sec. 45G(e)(2)).

Qualified railroad track maintenance expenditures include gross expenditures (whether or not otherwise chargeable to capital account) for maintaining railroad track (including roadbed, bridges, and related track structures) owned or leased as of January 1, 2005, by a Class II or Class III railroad. Qualified expenditures are determined regardless of any consideration for such expenditures (e.g., discounted shipping rates, the increment in a markup of track materials prices, debt forgiveness) given to a track assignee by the Class II or Class III railroad that made the track assignment (Code Sec. 45G(d)). Further, the taxpayer's basis in the track is reduced by the allowable credit (Code Sec. 45G(e)(3)).

Limitations. The credit is limited to $3,500 multiplied by the sum of (1) the number of miles of railroad track owned or leased by an eligible taxpayer as of the close of its tax year, and (2) the number of miles of track assigned to the eligible taxpayer by a Class II or Class III railroad that owns or leases the track at the close of the tax year. Each mile of track may be taken into account only once, either by the owner or the assignee. The assignment of a mile of track by a Class II or Class III railroad can only be made once in a tax year, and is treated as made at the close of the assignment tax year. The railroad cannot take the credit for any assigned mile, and the assignment must be taken into account for the assignee's tax year that includes the effective date of the assignment (Code Sec. 45G(b)).

> **Compliance Pointer:** The credit is claimed on Form 8900, Qualified Railroad Track Maintenance Credit. The credit is available for qualified expenditures paid or incurred during tax years beginning after December 31, 2004, and before January 1, 2008 (Code Sec. 45G(f)).

Credits against AMT. Individuals and corporations may be liable for the alternative minimum tax (AMT). The AMT is the excess of the taxpayer's tentative minimum tax over his regular tax, and is payable in addition to the regular tax. Tentative minimum tax is based on a taxpayer's alternative minimum taxable income (AMTI), which is the taxpayer's regular taxable income modified or redetermined to take into account certain preferences and adjustments (Code Sec. 55). Generally, the only tax credit that may directly offset the AMT by reducing the tentative minimum tax is the AMT foreign tax credit (Code Secs. 27 and 901). Also, for purposes of computing AMT, the regular tax against which the tentative minimum tax is compared may not be offset by any tax credit except the foreign tax credit, the U.S. possessions tax credit (Code Sec. 936), and the Puerto Rico economic activity credit (Code Secs. 30A). There is no AMT if the regular tax exceeds the tentative minimum tax.

In computing the regular tax liability, the general business credit under Code Sec. 38 has a limitation based on the amount of tax liability. Business tax credits generally may not exceed the excess of the taxpayer's net income tax over the tentative minimum tax (or, if greater, 25 percent of the regular tax liability in excess of $25,000) (Code Sec. 38(c)(1)). Net income tax is the sum of the regular tax liability and the alternative minimum tax, reduced by the sum of the nonrefundable personal credits (Code Secs. 21-25D), the foreign tax credit (Code Sec. 27), the alternative motor vehicle credit (Code Sec. 30B), and the credit for the installation of alternative fueling

BACKGROUND

stations (Code Sec. 30C). Net regular tax liability is the regular tax liability reduced by the sum of all those credits.

Certain specified credits—namely, the alcohol fuels credit (Code Sec. 40), the low-income housing credit (Code Sec. 42), the credit for electricity from renewable sources (Code Sec. 45), the FICA tip credit (Code Sec. 45B), the rehabilitation credit (Code Sec. 47), and the work opportunity tax credit (Code Sec. 51)—may be used against both regular and AMT liability (Code Sec. 38(c)(4)(B)). This is accomplished by modifying the general business credit limitation rules and related general business credit carry-over rules (Code Secs. 38 and 39) used to compute the taxpayer's regular tax liability. In particular, in the case of the specified credits, the tentative minimum tax is treated as being zero (Code Sec. 38(c)(4)(A)(ii)(I)).

The railroad track maintenance credit is one of the components of the general business credit, and thus is subject to the general business credit limitation. However, the credit is not one of the "specified credits" that can be used against both regular tax and AMT liability.

NEW LAW EXPLAINED

Railroad track maintenance credit extended, may offset AMT.—The railroad track maintenance credit has been extended for two years, to apply to qualified railroad track maintenance expenditures paid or incurred before January 1, 2010 (Code Sec. 45G(f), as amended by the Emergency Economic Stabilization Act of 2008 (P.L. 110-343)). Additionally, the railroad track maintenance credit has been added to the list of specified credits under Code Sec. 38(c)(4)(B) and, therefore, can be used to offset both regular tax and alternative minimum tax (AMT) liability (Code Sec. 38(c)(4)(B)(v), as added by the Emergency Economic Act of 2008). As a result, applying the general business credit tax liability limitation under Code Sec. 38(c)(1) to the railroad track maintenance credit, the tentative minimum tax is treated as zero.

> **Comment:** The IRS has released final regulations that provide detailed rules for claiming the railroad track maintenance credit. The final regulations generally apply to tax years ending on or after September 7, 2006, but a taxpayer may choose to apply them to any tax year beginning after December 31, 2004, and before September 7, 2006 (T.D. 9365, adding Reg. § 1.45G-1).

▶ **Effective date.** The amendment extending the railroad track maintenance credit applies to expenditures paid or incurred during tax years beginning after December 31, 2007 (Division C, Act Sec. 316(c)(1) of the Emergency Economic Stabilization Act of 2008 (P.L. 110-343)). The amendment allowing the credit against the alternative minimum tax applies to credits determined under Code Sec. 45G in tax years beginning after December 31, 2007, and to carrybacks of such credits (Division C, Act Sec. 316(c)(2) of the Emergency Economic Act of 2008).

Law source: Law at ¶5055 and ¶5095. Committee Report at ¶10,540.

— Division C, Act Sec. 316(a) of the Emergency Economic Stabilization Act of 2008 (P.L. 110-343), amending Code Sec. 45G(f);

NEW LAW EXPLAINED

— Division C, Act Sec. 316(b), redesignating Code Sec. 38(c)(4)(B)(v), (vi) and (vii) as Code Sec. 38(c)(4)(B)(vi), (vii) and (viii), and adding new Code Sec. 38(c)(4)(B)(v);

— Division C, Act Sec. 316(c), providing the effective dates.

Reporter references: For further information, consult the following CCH reporters.

— Standard Federal Tax Reporter, ¶4251.025 and ¶4496.01

— Tax Research Consultant, BUSEXP: 54,056.30 and BUSEXP: 55,050

— Federal Tax Guide, ¶2618 and ¶2628

¶420 Mine Rescue Team Training Tax Credit

SUMMARY OF NEW LAW

The mine rescue training team credit has been extended through December 31, 2009.

BACKGROUND

In response to a number of tragic mine accidents, the Tax Relief and Health Care Act of 2006 (P.L. 109-432) provided a tax credit to encourage not only additional mine safety training, but also the establishment of local mine rescue teams. Eligible employers may take a credit for mine rescue team training expenses.

The credit amount is equal to the lesser of:

(1) 20 percent of the training program costs paid or incurred during the tax year for each qualified mine rescue team employee, including wages paid while attending the training program; or

(2) $10,000 (Code Sec. 45N(a)).

An eligible employer is any taxpayer that employs individuals as miners in underground mines located in the United States (Code Sec. 45N(c)). A qualified mine rescue team employee is a full-time employee who is a miner eligible for more than six months of the tax year to serve as a mine rescue team member because he or she has either:

(1) completed, at minimum, an initial 20-hour instruction course as approved by the Mine Safety and Health Administration's Office of Educational Policy and Development; or

(2) received at least 40 hours of refresher training (Code Sec. 45N(b)).

Wages are defined as all compensation including noncash benefits under Code Sec. 3306(b), but without regard to any dollar limitation stated in that section (Code Sec. 45N(d)).

The mine rescue team training credit will not apply to tax years beginning after December 31, 2008.

¶420

NEW LAW EXPLAINED

Mine rescue training team credit extended.—The mine rescue team training credit is extended for one year. The credit now terminates for tax years beginning after December 31, 2009 (Code Sec. 45N(e), as amended by the Emergency Economic Stabilization Act of 2008 (P.L. 110-343)).

▶ **Effective date.** No specific effective date is provided by the Act. The provision is, therefore, considered effective on October 3, 2008.

Law source: Law at ¶5115.

— Division C, Act Sec. 310 of the Emergency Economic Stabilization Act of 2008 (P.L. 110-343), amending Code Sec. 45N(e).

Reporter references: For further information, consult the following CCH reporters.

— Standard Federal Tax Reporter, ¶4251.01

— Tax Research Consultant, BUSEXP: 55,450

— Federal Tax Guide, ¶2622

¶425 Indian Employment Tax Credit

SUMMARY OF NEW LAW

The Indian employment tax credit is extended for two years through December 31, 2009.

BACKGROUND

The Omnibus Budget Reconciliation Act of 1993 (P.L. 103-66) provided tax incentives to stimulate economic development and encourage investment on Indian reservations. A nonrefundable income tax credit is allowed for the first $20,000 of qualified wages and health insurance costs paid or incurred for qualified employees who work on an Indian reservation (Code Sec. 45A).

The credit is equal to 20 percent of the employer's costs for a qualified employee's wages and health insurance that exceed the amount the employer paid or incurred for such costs during the tax year. Employees are qualified employees if they or their spouses are enrolled members of an Indian tribe, who work within an Indian reservation, and whose principal place of abode while employed is on or near the reservation where they are working. Employees whose total wages exceed $30,000 per year (as adjusted for inflation) during the tax year are not qualified employees.

> **Practice Tip:** An employee is not a qualified employee if the total amount of wages paid or incurred by the employer to the employee (whether or not for services within an Indian reservation) exceeds $40,000 for 2007 (Form 8845, Indian Employment Credit (Dec. 2006)).

BACKGROUND

Originally scheduled to expire in 2003, the credit has been extended three times. The credit was most recently extended through December 31, 2007, by the Tax Relief and Health Care Act of 2006 (P.L. 109-432).

NEW LAW EXPLAINED

Indian employment tax credit extended.—The Indian employment tax credit is extended for two years through December 31, 2009 (Code Sec. 45A(f), as amended by the Emergency Economic Stabilization Act of 2008 (P.L. 110-343)).

> **Compliance Pointer:** Employers should use Form 8845, Indian Employment Credit, to compute the credit. Form 8845 is to be attached to the employer's tax return.

▶ **Effective date.** The amendment made by this section applies to tax years beginning after December 31, 2007 (Division C, Act Sec. 314(b) of the Emergency Economic Stabilization Act of 2008 (P.L. 110-343)).

Law source: Law at ¶5080. Committee Report at ¶10,520.

— Division C, Act Sec. 314(a) of the Emergency Economic Stabilization Act of 2008 (P.L. 110-343), amending Code Sec. 45A(f);

— Division C, Act Sec. 314(b), providing the effective date.

Reporter references: For further information, consult the following CCH reporters.

— Standard Federal Tax Reporter, ¶4440.01

— Tax Research Consultant, BUSEXP: 54,700

— Federal Tax Guide, ¶2775

¶430 American Samoa Economic Development Credit

SUMMARY OF NEW LAW

The temporary credit for qualifying possessions corporations operating in American Samoa has been extended and is now available for four tax years.

BACKGROUND

Certain domestic corporations with a substantial portion of business operations in U.S. possessions are eligible for a possession tax credit under Code Sec. 936. This credit offsets the U.S. tax imposed on taxable non-U.S.-source income from: (1) the active conduct of a trade or business within a U.S. possession; (2) the sale or exchange of substantially all of the assets used by the taxpayer in such a trade or business; or (3) qualified possessions investment. For purposes of the credit, the possessions include, among other places, American Samoa. U.S. corporations with activities in Puerto Rico are eligible for the Code Sec. 30A economic activity credit, which is

BACKGROUND

calculated under the rules set forth in Code Sec. 936. The Code Sec. 936 credit expired for tax years beginning after December 31, 2005, with some exceptions (Code Sec. 936(j)).

In order to qualify for the possession tax credit, a U.S. corporation must satisfy two gross income tests (Code Sec. 936(a)(2)). First, 80 percent or more of its gross income for the three-year period immediately preceding the close of the tax year must be from sources within a U.S. possession. Second, 75 percent or more of the corporation's gross income during the same period must be from the active conduct of a trade or business within a U.S. possession. The general rules for determining the source of the income apply. The possession tax credit is available only to a corporation that qualifies as an existing credit claimant. A determination as to whether that corporation is an existing credit claimant is made separately for each possession.

Existing credit claimant. An existing credit claimant is a corporation that was actively conducting a trade or business within a possession on October 13, 1995, and elected the benefits of the possession tax credit in an election in effect for its tax year that included October 13, 1995 (Code Sec. 936(j)(9)). Although a corporation can also qualify as an existing credit claimant if it acquires all of an existing credit claimant's trade or business, status as an existing claimant is lost if a substantial new line of business is added (Code Sec. 936(j)(9)(B)).

Economic activity-based limitation. The possession tax credit is computed separately for each possession with respect to which the corporation is an existing credit claimant. For tax years beginning after December 13, 1993, the credit is subject to either an economic activity-based limit or an income-based limit (Code Sec. 936(a)(4)). Under the economic activity-based limit, the amount of the credit for the tax year may not exceed an amount equal to the sum of:

(1) 60 percent of the possession corporation's "qualified possession wages" and "allocable employee fringe benefit expenses";

(2) 15 percent of the depreciation deductions allowable for the tax year under Code Sec. 167 with respect to short-life qualified tangible property (three-year or five-year property to which Code Sec. 168 applies);

(3) 40 percent of the depreciation deductions allowable for the tax year under Code Sec. 167 with respect to medium-life qualified tangible property (seven-year or 10-year property to which Code Sec. 168 applies);

(4) 65 percent of the depreciation deductions allowable for the tax year under Code Sec. 167 with respect to long-life qualified tangible property (property that is not described in (2) or (3) above and to which Code Sec. 168 applies); and

(5) in certain cases, a portion of the taxpayer's possession income taxes (Code Sec. 30A(d)).

Income based limitation/reduced credit election. As an alternative to the economic activity limitation, a possession corporation may elect to apply a limit equal to the applicable percentage of the credit that would otherwise be allowed with respect to possession business income; currently, that applicable percentage is 40 percent (Code Sec. 936(a)(4)(B)(ii)).

BACKGROUND

Repeal and transition rules. The Code Sec. 936 possession tax credit is not available to new claimants for any tax year beginning after 1995. The credit is phased out for existing credit claimants over a period that includes tax years beginning before 2008 (Act Sec. 119 of the Tax Relief and Health Care Act of 2006 (P.L. 109-432)). The amount of the credit available during the phase-out period is generally reduced according to special limitation rules. The special limitation rules do not apply, however, to existing credit claimants for income from activities in Guam, American Samoa, and the Northern Mariana Islands.

American Samoa economic development credit. A U.S. corporation that was an existing credit claimant with respect to American Samoa, and that elected the application of Code Sec. 936 for its last tax year beginning before January 1, 2006, is allowed a credit for two years. The credit applies to the first two tax years of a qualifying corporation that begin after December 31, 2005, and before January 1, 2008 (Act Sec. 119(d) of P.L. 109-432)

This temporary credit is not part of the Code, but is computed based on the rules in Code Sec. 936 and the economic-based limitation rules described above; any term used in the provision that is also used in Code Sec. 30A or 936 has the same meaning given to such term by Code Sec. 30A or 936 (Act Sec. 119(c) of P.L. 109-432).

Accordingly, the amount of the credit is equal to the sum of the amounts used in computing the corporation's economic activity-based limitation with respect to American Samoa, except that no credit is allowed for the amount of any American Samoa income taxes. Thus, the amount of the credit for any qualifying corporation equals the sum of:

(1) 60 percent of the corporation's qualified American Samoa wages and allocable employee fringe benefit expenses; plus

(2) the sum of the following depreciation allowances:

   (a) 15 percent of the corporation's depreciation allowances with respect to short-life qualified American Samoa tangible property (three-year or five-year property to which Code Sec. 168 applies), plus

   (b) 40 percent of the corporation's depreciation allowances with respect to medium-life qualified American Samoa tangible property (seven-year or 10-year property to which Code Sec. 168 applies), plus

   (c) 65 percent of the corporation's depreciation allowances with respect to long-life qualified American Samoa tangible property (property that is not described in (a) or (b) above and to which Code Sec. 168 applies).

Foreign tax credit allowed. The rule in Code Sec. 936(c) that denies a credit or deduction for any possessions or foreign tax paid with respect to taxable income taken into account in computing the Code Sec. 936 credit does not apply with respect to this temporary credit (Act Sec. 119(b)(3) of P.L. 109-432).

¶430

NEW LAW EXPLAINED

Economic development credit for American Samoa extended.—The economic development credit for a U.S. corporation that is an existing credit claimant with respect to American Samoa, and that elected the application of Code Sec. 936 for its last tax year beginning before January 1, 2006, has been extended for two more tax years. Thus, when the new extension is combined with the temporary credit that was previously allowed (Act Sec. 119(d) of the Tax Relief and Health Care Act of 2006 (P.L. 109-432)), the credit now applies to the first four tax years of a qualifying corporation that begin after December 31, 2005, and before January 1, 2010 (Division C, Act Sec. 309(a) of the Emergency Economic Stabilization Act of 2008 (P.L. 110-343)).

> **Comment:** Extension of the economic development credit has identified as critical to the economy of American Samoa. In American Samoa Governor Togiola Tulafono's testimony before the U.S. Senate on February 28, 2008, he stated that "it is important to encourage investment in American Samoa. With the expiration of the possession tax credit, the American Samoa economic development credit is an appropriate temporary provision while Congress considers long-term tax policy toward the U.S. possessions." He pointed out that "the Territory's income primarily comes from two fish canning operations and from the Federal Government's operational and capital grants." He further emphasized that "the growth of the fish canning industry has boosted employment and spurred development in the territory" but that "such a heavy reliance on two canneries is not economically sound" (Office of the Governor Press Release, American Samoa Government, February 28, 2008).

▶ **Effective date.** The extension is effective for tax years beginning after December 31, 2007 (Division C, Act Sec. 309(b) of the Emergency Economic Stabilization Act of 2008 (P.L. 110-343)).

Law source: Law at ¶7153. Committee Report at ¶10,490.

— Division C, Act Sec. 309(a) of the Emergency Economic Stabilization Act of 2008 (P.L. 110-343), amending section 119(d) of the Tax Relief and Health Care Act of 2006 (P.L. 109-432);

— Division C, Act Sec. 309(b), providing the effective date.

Reporter references: For further information, consult the following CCH reporters.

— Standard Federal Tax Reporter, ¶4059.01, ¶28,394.01 and ¶28,394.032

— Tax Research Consultant, INTL: 27,070.20

— Federal Tax Guide, ¶17,425

¶430

CHARITABLE CONTRIBUTIONS

¶435 Basis Adjustment to Stock of S Corporation Making Charitable Contributions

SUMMARY OF NEW LAW

The provision providing that the amount of a shareholder's basis reduction in the stock of an S corporation by reason of a charitable contribution made by the corporation equals the shareholder's pro rata share of the adjusted basis of the contributed property is extended to apply to tax years beginning before January 1, 2009.

BACKGROUND

Under prior law, if an S corporation contributed money or other property to a charity, each shareholder would take into account the shareholder's pro rata share of the contribution in determining its own income tax liability. The shareholder's basis in the stock of the S corporation was reduced by the amount of the charitable contribution, which was generally the fair market value of the contributed property, that flows through to the shareholder.

The Pension Protection Act of 2006 (P.L. 109-280) modified this rule by providing that the amount of the reduction of a shareholder's basis in the stock of an S corporation by reason of the S corporation's charitable contribution is equal to the shareholder's pro rata share of the adjusted basis of the contributed property. This provision applies to contributions made in tax years beginning after December 31, 2005, and before January 1, 2008. The prior law rule would apply to tax years beginning after December 31, 2007.

NEW LAW EXPLAINED

Modified basis reduction in stock of S corporation making charitable property donation extended.—The rule providing that the amount of the reduction of a shareholder's basis in the stock of an S corporation by reason of the corporation's charitable contribution is equal to the shareholder's pro rata share of the adjusted basis of the contributed property is extended. The modified basis reduction rule now applies to tax years beginning before January 1, 2009 (Code Sec. 1367(a)(2), as amended by the Emergency Economic Stabilization Act of 2008 (P.L. 110-343)).

> **Comment:** This provision has the effect of preserving the intended benefit of the fair market value deduction for the contributed appreciated property without causing the shareholders to recognize gain or a reduced loss that is attributable to the appreciation upon a subsequent sale of the stock.

¶435

NEW LAW EXPLAINED

▶ **Effective date.** The amendment made by this provision applies to contributions made in tax years beginning after December 31, 2007 (Division C, Act Sec. 307(b) of the Emergency Economic Stabilization Act of 2008 (P.L. 110-343)).

Law source: Law at ¶5360. Committee Reports at ¶10,470.

— Division C, Act Sec. 307(a) of the Emergency Economic Stabilization Act of 2008 (P.L. 110-343), amending Code Sec. 1367(a)(2);

— Division C, Act Sec. 307(b) , providing the effective date.

Reporter references: For further information, consult the following CCH reporters.

— Standard Federal Tax Reporter, ¶32,101.01

— Tax Research Consultant, SCORP: 410.05

— Federal Tax Guide, ¶13,210

¶440 Deduction for Charitable Contributions of Computers

SUMMARY OF NEW LAW

The enhanced corporate deduction for charitable contributions of computers is extended for two years and is now scheduled to expire for contributions made during any tax year beginning after December 31, 2009.

BACKGROUND

Generally, corporations may claim a deduction for charitable contributions limited to 10 percent of the corporation's taxable income (Code Sec. 170(b)(2)(A)). For this purpose, taxable income must be computed without regard to certain deductions and losses, namely: (1) the deduction for charitable contributions, (2) the deductions for certain dividends received and for dividends paid on certain preferred stock of public utilities, (3) any net operating loss carryback, (4) the deduction for income attributable to domestic production activities, and (5) any capital loss carryback (Code Sec. 170(b)(2)(C)). For charitable contributions of inventory or property, the deduction is typically limited to the corporation's basis in the property up to 10 percent of the corporation's taxable income (Code Sec. 170(e)).

Certain corporate contributions, however, qualify for preferential treatment. C corporations that make qualified contributions of computer technology and equipment ("qualified computer contributions") may claim an enhanced deduction equal to the corporation's basis in the donated property plus one-half of the ordinary income that would have been realized if the property had been sold. However, the enhanced deduction may not exceed twice the corporation's basis in the property (Code Sec. 170(e)(6)(A)).

BACKGROUND

Qualified computer contributions. Qualified donations of computer technology and equipment include contributions of computer software, computer or peripheral equipment, and fiber optic cable related to computer use that are to be used within the United States for educational purposes (Code Sec. 170(e)(6)(F)). An eligible donee includes:

(1) an educational organization that normally maintains a regular faculty and curriculum and has regularly enrolled students in attendance at the place where its educational activities are regularly conducted;

(2) a tax-exempt entity that is organized primarily for purposes of supporting elementary and secondary education;

(3) a private foundation that, within 30 days after receipt of the contribution, contributes the property to an eligible donee described in (1) or (2) above, and notifies the donor of the contribution (Code Sec. 170(e)(6)(B) and (C)); or

(4) a public library, as defined in the Library Services and Technology Act (20 U.S.C. §9122(2)(A)) (Code Sec. 170(e)(6)(B)(i)(III)).

In addition, the contribution must be made not later than three years after the corporation acquired the property or, if the corporation constructed or assembled the property, not later than the date construction or assembly of the property is substantially completed (Code Sec. 170(e)(6)(B)(ii)).

The enhanced charitable deduction for contributions of computer technology and/or equipment to schools or public libraries does not apply to contributions made during any tax year beginning after December 31, 2007.

NEW LAW EXPLAINED

Enhanced deduction for charitable contributions of computers extended.—The enhanced charitable deduction for corporate contributions of computer technology and/or equipment is extended for two years. The deduction is now set to expire for contributions made during any tax year beginning after December 31, 2009 (Code Sec. 170(e)(6)(G), as amended by the Emergency Economic Stabilization Act of 2008 (P.L. 110-343)).

▶ **Effective date.** This provision is effective for contributions made during tax years beginning after December 31, 2007 (Act Sec. 321(b) of the Emergency Economic Stabilization Act of 2008 (P.L. 110-343)).

Law source: Law at ¶5235. Committee Report at ¶10,580.

— Division C, Act Sec. 321(a) of the Emergency Economic Stabilization Act of 2008 (P.L. 110-343)), amending Code Sec. 170(e)(6)(G);

— Division C, Act Sec. 321(b), providing the effective date.

Reporter references: For further information, consult the following CCH reporters.

— Standard Federal Tax Reporter, ¶11,680.037

— Tax Research Consultant, CCORP: 9,358

— Federal Tax Guide, ¶6591

¶440

¶445 Charitable Contributions of Food Inventory

SUMMARY OF NEW LAW

The enhanced deduction for charitable donations of food inventory by noncorporate taxpayers that are engaged in a trade or business is extended two years and is now set to expire for contributions made after December 31, 2009. In addition, the 10-percent limitation is temporarily eliminated for food contributions by certain farmers and ranchers.

BACKGROUND

Generally, the amount of the deduction for gifts of property to charity is measured by the fair market value of the property on the date of contribution. However, for both individuals and corporations, the amount of the deduction for a charitable contribution of ordinary income property, such as inventory, is usually limited to the donor's basis in the donated property (Code Sec. 170(e)). Under an exception to this general rule, many C corporations can claim an enhanced deduction for inventory that is contributed to a qualified charity or private operating foundation for use in the care of the ill, the needy or infants. The amount of the enhanced deduction equals the lesser of (1) the donated item's basis plus one-half of the item's unrealized appreciation, or (2) two times the donated item's basis.

A corporation's charitable contribution deduction for a year is limited to 10 percent of the corporation's taxable income, computed with certain adjustments (Code Sec. 170(b)(2)). A corporation can carry over charitable contributions that exceed 10 percent of its taxable income for a five-year period (Code Sec. 170(d)(2)).

In response to the hurricane disasters along the Gulf coast in 2005, Congress, under the Katrina Emergency Tax Relief Act of 2005 (P.L. 109-73), temporarily modified the rules relating to charitable contributions in several ways. Under one provision, noncorporate, as well as corporate, taxpayers could claim an enhanced deduction for donations of food inventory during a temporary period (Code Sec. 170(e)(3)(C)). The food inventory had to consist of items fit for human consumption and had to be contributed to a qualified charity or private operating foundation for use in the care of the ill, the needy or infants.

Any taxpayer engaged in one or more trades or businesses that made qualified donations of food inventories on or after August 28, 2005, and before January 1, 2006, was eligible to claim the enhanced deduction for such donations (Code Sec. 170(e)(3)(C)(i) and (iv)). It did not matter whether the trade or business was conducted in corporate form. Thus, partnerships, S corporations and sole proprietorships could claim the enhanced deduction for donations of food inventory during the temporary period.

The amount of the enhanced deduction for donated food inventory equaled the lesser of (1) the donated item's basis plus one-half of the item's appreciation, or (2) two times the donated item's basis. For food items, the amount of appreciation was the

BACKGROUND

amount of gain that would be realized if the donated food item was sold at fair market value on the date of the gift (Announcement 2005-84, 2005-2 CB 1064).

For a taxpayer other than a C corporation, the total deduction for donations of food inventory during the tax year was limited to a maximum of 10 percent of the taxpayer's net income from those trades or businesses making such donations (Code Sec. 170(e)(3)(C)(ii)). Therefore, if a taxpayer owned three businesses and only one made a qualified contribution of food inventory, the taxpayer's deduction for such donation was limited to a maximum of 10 percent of his or her income from the business making the donation, not 10 percent of his or her total income (Joint Committee on Taxation, Technical Explanation of the Katrina Emergency Tax Relief Act of 2005 (JCX-69-05)).

Donated food inventories had to consist of "apparently wholesome food" (Code Sec. 170(e)(3)(C)(i)(II)). "Apparently wholesome food" was defined as food intended for human consumption that meets all quality and labeling standards imposed by federal, state, and local laws and regulations even though the food may not be readily marketable due to appearance, age, freshness, grade, size, surplus, or other conditions (Section 22(b)(2) of the Bill Emerson Good Samaritan Food Donation Act (42 U.S.C. 1791(b)(2)); Code Sec. 170(e)(3)(C)(iii)).

Pension Protection Act of 2006. In 2006, the Pension Protection Act of 2006 (P.L. 109-280) extended for two years the enhanced deduction for charitable donations of food inventory by noncorporate taxpayers that are engaged in a trade or business. Following that extension, the enhanced deduction then expired for contributions made after December 31, 2007.

NEW LAW EXPLAINED

Enhanced charitable deduction for food donations extended.—The enhanced deduction for charitable donations of food inventory by any taxpayer engaged in a trade or business, whether or not a C corporation, is extended for another two years. Thus, taxpayers may claim the enhanced deduction for food inventory donations contributed on or after August 28, 2005, and on or before December 31, 2009 (Code Sec. 170(e)(3)(C)(iv), as amended by the Emergency Economic Stabilization Act of 2008 (P.L. 110-343)).

> **Comment:** The Joint Committee on Taxation, Technical Explanation of H.R. 7060, the "Renewable Energy and Job Creation Tax Act of 2008" (JCX-75-08), emphasized that for taxpayers other than C corporations, the total deduction for contributions of food inventory is limited to a maximum of 10 percent of the taxpayer's net income from all sole proprietorships, S corporations, partnerships or other non-C corporations making such donations. That rule continues under the new two-year extension. However, see below for a special rule temporarily eliminating the 10-percent limitation for food contributions by certain farmers and ranchers.
>
> The Joint Committee Report pointed out that the 10-percent limitation has no effect on the operation of otherwise applicable percentage limitations. Thus, if 10

¶445

NEW LAW EXPLAINED

percent of a sole proprietor's net income from the business exceeded 50 percent of the proprietor's contribution base (adjusted gross income computed without regard to charitable contributions and net operating loss carrybacks), the available deduction for the tax year, with respect to contributions of food inventory to public charities, would be 50 percent of the proprietor's contribution base. Under the law, such contributions may be carried over if they exceed the 50-percent limitation. However, contributions of food inventory by the sole proprietor that exceed the 10-percent limitation but not the 50-percent limitation could not be carried over.

Temporary elimination of percentage limitation for farmers and ranchers. The 10-percent limitation applicable to qualified donations of food inventory under Code Sec. 170(e)(3)(C) is suspended for contributions made by qualified farmers and ranchers on or after October 3, 2008, but before January 1, 2009 (Code Sec. 170(b)(3), as added by the Emergency Economic Act of 2008). Instead, contributions are to be treated as if they were qualified conservation contributions under Code Sec. 170(b)(1)(E) (individuals) or Code Sec. 170(b)(2)(B) (corporations), whichever is applicable. A qualified farmer or rancher, as defined under Code Sec. 170(b)(1)(E)(v), means a taxpayer whose gross income from the trade or business of farming is greater than 50 percent of the taxpayer's gross income for the tax year.

▶ **Effective date.** The provision extending the enhanced deduction for donated food inventory is effective for contributions made after December 31, 2007 (Division C, Act Sec. 323(a)(2) of the Emergency Economic Stabilization Act of 2008 (P.L. 110-343)). The provision temporarily suspending the percentage limitation for qualified farmers and ranchers is effective for tax years ending after October 3, 2008, the date of enactment. (Division C, Act Sec. 323(b)(2) of the Emergency Economic Act of 2008).

Law source: Law at ¶5235. Committee Report at ¶10,600.

— Division C, Act Sec. 323(a)(1) of the Emergency Economic Stabilization Act of 2008 (P.L. 110-343), amending Code Sec. 170(e)(3)(C)(iv);

— Division C, Act Sec. 323(b)(1), adding Code Sec. 170(b)(3);

— Division C, Act Sec. 323(a)(2) and (b)(2), providing the effective dates.

Reporter references: For further information, consult the following CCH reporters.

— Standard Federal Tax Reporter, ¶11,620.059, ¶11,660.027, ¶11,670.033, ¶11,680.031 and ¶11,680.033

— Tax Research Consultant, INDIV: 51,152.15, INDIV: 51,256.20, CCORP: 9,354 and CCORP: 9,350

— Federal Tax Guide, ¶6589 and ¶6631

¶450 Charitable Contributions of Book Inventory to Public Schools

SUMMARY OF NEW LAW

The enhanced deduction for corporate donations of book inventory to public schools is extended for another two years and is now set to expire for contributions made after December 31, 2009.

BACKGROUND

Generally, the amount of the deduction for gifts of property to charity is measured by the fair market value of the property on the date of contribution. However, for both individuals and corporations, the amount of the deduction for a charitable contribution of ordinary income property, such as inventory, is usually limited to the donor's basis in the donated property (Code Sec. 170(e)). Under an exception to this general rule, many C corporations can claim an enhanced deduction for inventory that is contributed to a qualified charity or private operating foundation for use in the care of the ill, the needy or infants. The amount of the enhanced deduction equals the lesser of (1) the donated item's basis plus one-half of the item's appreciation, or (2) two times the donated item's basis. A second exception allows a C corporation to claim a similar enhanced deduction for certain ordinary income property that is donated to a college, university, or tax-exempt scientific organization for use in research (Code Sec. 170(e)(4)).

In response to the hurricane disasters along the Gulf coast in 2005, Congress, under the Katrina Emergency Tax Relief Act of 2005 (P.L. 109-73), temporarily modified the rules relating to charitable contributions in several ways. One provision essentially took the present-law enhanced deduction for donations of inventory to a qualified charity or private operating foundation and extended it to qualified donations of book inventory to public schools (Code Sec. 170(e)(3)(D)). The enhanced deduction generally increased the deductible amount from the donated inventory item's basis to the lesser of (1) the donated inventory item's basis plus one-half of the item's appreciation, or (2) two times the donated inventory item's basis.

Any corporation (other than an S corporation) that made a qualified book contribution on or after August 28, 2005, and before January 1, 2006, was eligible for the enhanced deduction for such donation (Code Sec. 170(e)(3)(D)(iv)). A qualified book contribution meant a charitable contribution of books to a public school that provided elementary or secondary education (kindergarten through grade 12) and maintained a regular faculty and curriculum with a regularly enrolled student body (Code Sec. 170(e)(3)(D)(ii)). In addition, the donee educational institution was required to certify in writing that:

(1) the books were suitable in terms of currency, content and quality for use in the school's educational programs, and

(2) the school would actually use the books in its educational programs (Code Sec. 170(e)(3)(D)(iii)).

¶450

BACKGROUND

Pension Protection Act of 2006. In 2006, the Pension Protection Act of 2006 (P.L. 109-280) extended for two years the enhanced deduction for charitable donations of book inventory to public schools. Following that extension, the enhanced deduction then expired for contributions made after December 31, 2007.

NEW LAW EXPLAINED

Enhanced charitable deduction for book donations to public schools extended.—The enhanced deduction for corporate donations of book inventory to public schools (i.e., qualified book contributions) is extended for another two years. Thus, C corporations may claim a charitable deduction for book inventory donations contributed on or after August 28, 2005, and on or before December 31, 2009 (Code Sec. 170(e)(3)(D)(iv), as amended by the Emergency Economic Stabilization Act of 2008 (P.L. 110-343)).

▶ **Effective date.** This provision is effective for contributions made after December 31, 2007 (Division C, Act Sec. 324(c) of the Emergency Economic Stabilization Act of 2008 (P.L. 110-343)).

Law source: Law at ¶5235. Committee Report at ¶10,610.

— Division C, Act Sec. 324(a) of the Emergency Economic Stabilization Act of 2008 (P.L. 110-343), amending Code Sec. 170(e)(3)(D)(iv);

— Division C, Act Sec. 324(c), providing the effective date.

Reporter references: For further information, consult the following CCH reporters.

— Standard Federal Tax Reporter, 2008FED ¶11,620.059, ¶11,660.027 and ¶11,680.031

— Tax Research Consultant, CCORP: 9,354

— Federal Tax Guide, 2008FTG ¶6589

EMPLOYEE COMPENSATION

¶455 Nonqualified Deferred Compensation from Certain Tax Indifferent Parties

SUMMARY OF NEW LAW

Compensation from nonqualified deferred compensation plans maintained by foreign corporations will generally be taxable when it is not subject to substantial risk of forfeiture. Compensation is not treated as deferred for this purpose, if the service provider receives payment 12 months or less after the end of the year that the compensation vests.

BACKGROUND

The determination of when amounts deferred under a nonqualified deferred compensation arrangement are includible in gross income of the person earning the compensation depends on the facts and circumstances of the arrangement. A variety of tax principles and Code provisions may be relevant in making this determination, including the requirements of Code Sec. 409A. Generally, the timing of income inclusion of nonqualified deferred compensation depends on whether the arrangement is unfunded or funded.

Congress enacted Code Sec. 409A because it was concerned that many nonqualified deferred compensation arrangements had developed that allowed improper deferral of income. Executives often used arrangements that allowed deferral of income, but also provided security of future payment and control over amounts deferred. Under Code Sec. 409A, all amounts deferred by a service provider under a nonqualified deferred compensation plan for all tax years are includible in gross income of the service provider to the extent such amounts are not subject to a substantial risk of forfeiture and not previously included in income, unless certain requirements are satisfied.

Code Sec. 409A requires current income inclusion in the case of certain offshore funding of nonqualified deferred compensation. In the case of assets set aside (directly or indirectly) in a trust (or other arrangement determined by the Secretary of the Treasury) for purposes of paying nonqualified deferred compensation, such assets are treated as property transferred in connection with the performance of services under Code Sec. 83 (whether or not the assets are available to satisfy the claims of general creditors): (1) at the time set aside, if the assets are located outside of the United States, or (2) at the time transferred, if such assets are subsequently transferred outside of the United States (Code Sec. 409A(b)(1)). Any subsequent increases in the value of, or any earnings with respect to, the assets are treated as additional transfers of property.

Interest at the underpayment rate plus one percentage point is imposed on the underpayments of tax that would have occurred had the amounts set aside been includible in income for the tax year in which first deferred or, if later, the first tax year not subject to a substantial risk of forfeiture. The amount required to be included in income also is subject to an additional 20-percent tax (Code Sec. 409A(a)(1)(B)). The special funding rule does not apply to assets located in a foreign jurisdiction if substantially all of the services to which the nonqualified deferred compensation relates are performed in the foreign jurisdiction (Code Sec. 409A(b)(1)). The Secretary of the Treasury has authority to exempt arrangements from the provision if the arrangements do not result in an improper deferral of U.S. tax and will not result in assets being effectively beyond the reach of creditors (Code Sec. 409A(e)(3)).

NEW LAW EXPLAINED

Offshore nondeferred compensation plans subject to new rules.—In general, any compensation which is deferred under a nonqualified deferred compensation plan of a nonqualified entity is includible in gross income when there is no substantial risk of

NEW LAW EXPLAINED

forfeiture of the rights to the compensation (Code Sec. 457A(a), as added by the Emergency Economic Stabilization Act of 2008 (P.L. 110-343)). If the amount of any compensation is not determinable at the time that such compensation is otherwise includible in gross income, then, in addition to income inclusion when the amount is determinable, the tax imposed for the year in which such compensation is includible in income must be increased. Such increase is equal to the sum of: (1) 20 percent of the amount of such compensation, and (2) interest at the underpayment rate under Code Sec. 6621 plus one percentage point is imposed on the underpayments that would have occurred had the compensation been includible in income for the tax year when first deferred, or if later, the first tax year when the deferred compensation is not subject to a substantial risk of forfeiture. The amount required to be included in income is also subject to an additional 20-percent tax. (Code Sec. 457A(c), as added by the Emergency Economic Act of 2008).

> **Comment:** These rules apply in addition to the requirements of Code 409A or any other tax law provisions with respect to nonqualified deferred compensation. The term, "service provider" has the same meaning as in the underlying regulations except that whether a person is a service provider is determined without regard to the person's method of accounting (Joint Committee on Taxation, Technical Explanation of H.R. 7060, the "Renewable Energy and Job Creation Tax Act of 2008" (JCX-75-08)).

Practical Analysis: Pamela D. Perdue, Of Counsel with Summers, Compton, Wells & Hamburg in St. Louis, Missouri, notes that while Division A, Act Sec. 302 of the Emergency Economic Stabilization Act of 2008 (P.L. 110-343) includes the well-discussed limitations on executive compensation where the federal government directly purchases troubled assets, another extremely significant provision has not been so well discussed. Division C, Act Sec. 801 of the Emergency Economic Act of 2008 may result in the current inclusion in income of some deferred compensation where the deferred compensation is paid from an offshore corporation or a corporation located in a low- or no-tax jurisdiction. Specifically, the provision requires the inclusion in income of any compensation that is deferred under a nonqualified deferred compensation plan when there is no substantial risk of forfeiture. The thinking is that the deferral that is possible in a typical deferred compensation arrangement is made possible by the offsetting deferral of the deduction to the corporation. However, when deferred compensation is paid by an "indifferent tax party," the federal Treasury loses because there is no offsetting deduction that can be deferred."

Nonqualified entity. A nonqualified entity is any foreign corporation unless substantially all of its income is effectively connected with the conduct of a U.S. trade or business or is subject to a comprehensive foreign income tax. A partnership (either foreign or domestic) is a nonqualified entity unless substantially all of its income is allocated to: (1) U.S. persons with respect to whom such income is not subject to a comprehensive foreign income tax, and (2) organizations that are exempt from U.S. income tax (Code Sec. 457A(b), as added by the Emergency Economic Act of 2008).

NEW LAW EXPLAINED

Comprehensive foreign income tax. Comprehensive foreign income tax is the income tax of a foreign country if (1) the person is eligible for the benefits of a comprehensive income tax treaty between the foreign country and the United States, or (2) such person demonstrates to the satisfaction of the Secretary of the Treasury that the foreign country has a comprehensive income tax (Code Sec. 457A(d)(2), as added by the Emergency Economic Act of 2008).

Substantial risk of forfeiture. The rights of a person to compensation will be treated as subject to a substantial risk of forfeiture only if the person's rights to the compensation are conditioned upon the future performance of substantial services by any individual. To the extent provided in regulations prescribed by the Secretary, if compensation is determined solely by reference to the amount of gain recognized on the disposition of an investment asset, the compensation will be treated as subject to substantial risk of forfeiture until the date of such disposition (Code Sec. 457A(d)(1), as added by the Emergency Economic Act of 2008). An investment asset is any single asset (other than an investment fund or similar activity):

- acquired directly by an investment fund or similar entity;
- with respect to which the entity does not (nor does any person related to the entity) participate in the active management of the activities of such asset (or if the asset is an interest in an entity, in the active management of the activities of the entity), and
- substantially all of any gain on the disposition of which (other than the deferred compensation) is allocated to investors in the entity.

   Comment: The rule only applies if the compensation is determined solely by reference to the gain upon the disposition of an investment asset. Thus, for example, the rule does not apply in the case of an arrangement under which the amount of the compensation is reduced for losses on the disposition of any other asset. With respect to any gain attributable to the period before the asset is treated as no longer subject to a substantial risk of forfeiture, it is intended that Treasury regulations will limit the application of this rule to gain attributable to the period that the service provider is performing services. (Joint Committee on Taxation, Technical Explanation of H.R. 7060, the "Renewable Energy and Job Creation Tax Act of 2008" (JCX-75-08)).

Nonqualified deferred compensation. The term nonqualified deferred compensation plan for these purposes is defined in the same manner as for purposes of Code Sec. 409A, and includes any earnings with respect to previously deferred amounts. The term does not include any plan that provides a right to compensation based on the appreciation in value of a specified number of equity units of the service recipient. Under Code Sec. 409A(d), a nonqualified deferred compensation plan generally includes any plan that provides for the deferral of compensation other than a qualified employer plan or any bona fide vacation leave, sick leave, compensatory time, disability pay, or death benefit plan. A qualified employer plan means a qualified retirement plan, tax-deferred annuity, simplified employee pension (SEP), and SIMPLE 401(k). A qualified governmental excess benefit arrangement (Code Sec. 415(m)) and an eligible deferred compensation plan (Code Sec. 457(b)) are qualified employer plans. Compensation is not treated as deferred for purposes of this provi-

¶455

NEW LAW EXPLAINED

sion if the service provider receives payment of the compensation not later than 12 months after the end of the first tax year of the service recipient during which the right to the payment of such compensation is no longer subject to a substantial risk of forfeiture (Code Sec. 457A(d)(3), as added by the Emergency Economic Act of 2008).

In the case of a foreign corporation with income that is taxable under Code Sec. 882 as effectively connected with a U.S. trade or business, the provision does not apply to compensation which, had the compensation been paid in cash on the date that it ceased to be subject to a substantial risk of forfeiture, would have been deductible by the foreign corporation against such income (Code Sec. 457A(d)(4), as added by the Emergency Economic Act of 2008).

Practical Analysis: Charles C. Hwang, J.D., Partner, Alex E. Sadler, J.D., Partner, and Jennifer A. Ray, J.D., Associate in the tax group of Crowell & Moring LLP in Washington, D.C., observes that Division C, Act Sec. 801 of the Emergency Economic Stabilization Act of 2008 (P.L. 110-343) creates new Code Sec. 457A, which requires a service provider (including an employee or independent contractor) to include in gross income any compensation deferred (and earnings thereon) under a nonqualified deferred compensation plan of a nonqualified entity at the time that the compensation is no longer subject to a substantial risk of forfeiture. Thus, Code Sec. 457A creates an immediate inclusion rule similar to existing Code Secs. 457(f) and 409A.

Nonqualified Deferred Compensation Plan. Code Sec. 457A provides that nonqualified deferred compensation plan generally has the same meaning as under Code Sec. 409A(d). Under Code Sec. 409A(d), a nonqualified deferred compensation plan is any plan (or arrangement) that provides for the deferral of compensation, other than certain retirement plans, certain plans established by governments and non-profit entities, and *bona fide* vacation leave sick leave, compensatory time, disability pay or death benefit plans. However, under Code Sec. 457A, nonqualified deferred compensation plan also includes any plan that provides a right to compensation based on the appreciation in value of a specified number of the employer's equity units.

Nonqualified Entity. Nonqualified entity is broadly defined. Any foreign corporation is a nonqualified entity, unless substantially all of the corporation's income is effectively connected with a U.S. trade or business or is subject to a comprehensive foreign income tax. Any partnership is also a nonqualified entity, unless substantially all of its income is allocated to persons other than (i) foreign persons with respect to whom such income is not subject to a comprehensive foreign income tax, and (ii) tax-exempt organizations. Income is subject to a comprehensive foreign income tax if the recipient is eligible for the benefits of a comprehensive income tax treaty between the United States and the foreign country, or if the recipient demonstrates to the satisfaction of the Secretary that the foreign country has a comprehensive income tax.

Substantial Risk of Forfeiture. As in Code Secs. 409A and 457(f), a right to compensation is subject to a substantial risk of forfeiture if such right is conditioned upon the

NEW LAW EXPLAINED

future performance of substantial services by any individual. Note that this definition is different from the Code Sec. 83 definition of substantial risk of forfeiture.

Additional Tax. If the amount of compensation is not determinable at the time that it would otherwise be included in income under Code Sec. 457A, the amount will be included in income as soon as it is determinable, and will be subject to an additional 20-percent tax and interest at that time.

Exceptions. There are several exceptions from the immediate inclusion rule. First, to the extent provided in regulations, compensation determined solely by reference to the amount of gain recognized on the disposition of an investment asset is treated as subject to a substantial risk of forfeiture until the date of such disposition. Investment asset is defined narrowly and includes any single asset (but not an investment fund or similar entity) acquired directly by an investment fund or similar entity, if such entity does not participate in the active management of the asset, and if substantially all of the gain on the disposition of the asset is allocated to investors in the entity. This exception is intended to exclude many "carried interest" arrangements from Code Sec. 457A. Next, compensation is not subject to Code Sec. 457A if the employee receives the compensation within 12 months after the end of the employer's tax year during which the right to the payment is no longer subject to a substantial risk of forfeiture. Finally, there is an exception for certain compensation paid by a foreign corporation that has income effectively connected to the conduct of a U.S. trade or business. This exception applies only when the compensation would have been deductible by the foreign corporation against its effectively connected income if the compensation had been paid in cash on the date it ceased to be subject to a substantial risk of forfeiture.

Effective Date. Generally, Code Sec. 457A applies to deferred amounts attributable to services performed after December 31, 2008. Any deferred amounts attributable to services performed before January 1, 2009 and not includible in gross income in a tax year beginning before 2018 will be includible in gross income in the last tax year beginning before 2018 or, if later, the tax year in which there the amounts are no longer subject to a substantial risk of forfeiture. In other words, existing deferrals must be included in income no later than the last tax year beginning before 2018 if such deferred amounts cease to be subject to a substantial risk of forfeiture by that year.

Regulations and Guidance. The Secretary has authority to prescribe regulations to carry out the purposes of Code Sec. 457A. The Secretary is required to issue guidance within 120 days of the date the Act is enacted to provide a limited period of time during which a nonqualified deferred compensation arrangement attributable to services performed on or before December 31, 2008, may be amended to conform to the Code Sec. 457A distribution requirements without violating Code Sec. 409A(a). Such guidance will also permit the amendment of certain back-to-back agreements to conform to Code Sec. 457A. Finally, any amendment permitted by such guidance will not constitute a material modification of the arrangement pursuant to Code Sec. 409A.

¶455

NEW LAW EXPLAINED

Application of rules. The treatment of earnings and the aggregation rules under Code Sec. 409A(5)) and (6) apply (Code Sec. 457A(d)(5), as added by the Emergency Economic Act of 2008).

Regulations. The Secretary will prescribe any necessary and appropriate regulations, including regulations disregarding a substantial risk of forfeiture in cases where necessary (Code Sec. 457A(e), as added by the Emergency Economic Act of 2008).

▶ **Effective date.** The provision generally applies to amounts deferred which are attributable to services performed after December 31, 2008 (Division C, Act Sec. 801(d)(1) of the Emergency Economic Stabilization Act of 2008 (P.L. 110-343)).

Applicable to existing deferrals, in the case of any amount deferred to which the amendments do not apply solely by reason of the fact that the amount is attributable to services performed before January 1, 2009, to the extent such amount is not includible in gross income in a tax year beginning before 2018, the amounts will be includible in gross income in the later of: (A) the last tax year beginning before 2018, or (B) the tax year in which there is no substantial risk of forfeiture of the rights to such compensation (determined in the same manner as determined for purposes of Code Sec. 457A as added by this section) (Division C, Act Sec. 801(d)(2) of the Emergency Economic Act of 2008).

For accelerated payments, no later than 120 days after October 3, 2008, the Secretary will issue guidance providing a limited period of time during which a nonqualified deferred compensation arrangement attributable to services performed on or before December 31, 2008, may, without violating the requirements of Code Sec. 409A(a), be amended to conform the date of distribution to the date the amounts are required to be included in income (Division C, Act Sec. 801(d)(3) of the Emergency Economic Act of 2008).

Applicable to certain back-to-back arrangements, if the taxpayer is also a service recipient and maintains one or more nonqualified deferred compensation arrangements for its service providers under which any amount is attributable to services performed on or before December 31, 2008, the guidance issued on accelerated payments will permit such arrangements to be amended to conform the dates of distribution under the arrangement to the date amounts are required to be included in the income of the taxpayer (Division C, Act Sec. 801(d)(4) of the Emergency Economic Act of 2008).

Any amendment to a nonqualified deferred compensation arrangement made pursuant to the above rules for accelerated payments and back-to-back arrangements will not be treated as a material modification of the arrangement for purposes of Code Sec. 409A (Division C, Act Sec. 801(d)(5) of the Emergency Economic Act of 2008 (P.L. 110-343)).

Law source: Law at ¶5035 and ¶5305. Committee Reports at ¶10,750.

— Division C, Act Sec. 801(a) of the Emergency Economic Stabilization Act of 2008 (P.L. 110-343), adding Code Sec. 457A;

— Division C, Act Sec. 801(b), amending Code Sec. 26(b)(2);

— Division C, Act Sec. 801(d), providing the effective date.

Reporter references: For further information, consult the following CCH reporters.

— Standard Federal Tax Reporter, ¶21,401

— Tax Research Consultant, COMPEN: 15,000

— Federal Tax Guide, ¶11,735

¶460 Temporary 0.2 Percent FUTA Surtax

SUMMARY OF NEW LAW

The temporary FUTA surtax of 0.2 percent of taxable wages is extended through December 31, 2009.

BACKGROUND

The Federal Unemployment Tax Act (FUTA) imposes a payroll tax of 6.2 percent on the first $7,000 paid by a covered employer to each employee per calendar year (Code Sec. 3301(1)). Employers in states with federally approved unemployment insurance programs may credit up to 5.4 percentage points against the 6.2 percent gross rate (Code Sec. 3302), making the net effective federal unemployment tax rate equal to 0.8 percent. This rate is made up of two components: a permanent tax rate of 0.6 percent, and a temporary surtax rate of 0.2 percent. Congress last extended the temporary surtax through 2008, in the Energy Independence and Security Act of 2007 (P.L. 110-140). The FUTA tax is scheduled to decrease to 6.0 percent in 2009 and thereafter (Code Sec. 3301(2)).

> **Comment:** The revenue generated by the FUTA tax for the federal government finances administration of the federal unemployment system, half of the federal-state extended benefits program, and a federal account for state loans. State governments use the revenue turned over to them (represented by the 5.4 percent credit) to finance their regular state programs and their half of the federal-state extended benefits program.

Employers are subject to FUTA if, during the previous or current year, they have paid wages of $1,500 or more in any calendar quarter, or have had one or more employees at any time in each of 20 calendar weeks (Code Sec. 3306(a)(1)). Certain agricultural, domestic, and state and local employers are also subject to FUTA tax. The term "wages" generally means all remuneration for services performed by employees for their employers, including the cash value of all remuneration paid in any medium other than cash, unless specifically excepted by law (Code Sec. 3306(b)). Only employers are subject to the FUTA tax. Since no employee contributions are required, withholding from employee wages is not involved.

NEW LAW EXPLAINED

Temporary 0.2 percent FUTA surtax extended.—The imposition of the 0.2 percent temporary Federal Unemployment Tax Act (FUTA) surtax has been extended one year (Code Sec. 3301(1), as amended by the Emergency Economic Stabilization Act of 2008 (P.L. 110-343)). Thus, the FUTA tax rate of 6.2 percent applies through December 31, 2009, and will decrease to 6.0 percent for calendar years beginning in 2010 and after (Code Sec. 3301(2), as amended by the Emergency Economic Act of 2008).

¶460

NEW LAW EXPLAINED

Practical Analysis: Robert B. Teuber, J.D., Attorney in the Milwaukee office of Weiss Berzowski Brady LLP, observes that Division B, Act Sec. 404 of the Emergency Economic Stabilization Act of 2008 (P.L. 110-343) extends the FUTA surcharge of 0.2 percent through the calendar year 2009. The initial surcharge, passed by Congress in 1976, has been extended on numerous occasions and in 1997, was extended for an additional 10 years. In late 2007, as the surcharge was set to expire, it was again extended through 2008. The new act serves to extend the surcharge for an additional year. However, based on the history of the surcharge, practitioners should watch for yet another extension before the close of 2009.

Compliance Tip: Employers must report their FUTA tax liability annually on Form 940, Employer's Annual Federal Unemployment (FUTA) Tax Return. If the amount of an employer's FUTA tax liability for any calendar quarter exceeds $500, then the taxes must be deposited electronically through the Electronic Federal Tax Payment System (EFTPS) or at an authorized financial institution using Form 8109, Federal Tax Coupon. However, an employer is required to deposit its FUTA taxes through EFTPS in 2008, if its total payment of all employment taxes, excise taxes, and income taxes in 2006 exceeded $200,000, or it was required to use EFTPS in 2007 or an earlier year.

▶ **Effective date.** This provision applies to wages paid after December 31, 2008 (Division B, Act Sec. 404(b), Emergency Economic Stabilization Act of 2008 (P.L. 110-343)).

Law source: Law at ¶5405. Committee Reports at ¶10,290.

— Division B, Act Sec. 404(a) of the Emergency Economic Stabilization Act of 2008 (P.L. 110-343), amending Code Sec. 3301;

— Division B, Act Sec. 404(b), providing the effective date.

Reporter references: For further information, consult the following CCH reporters.

— Tax Research Consultant, PAYROLL: 9,102.

— Federal Tax Guide, ¶18,230.

— Payroll Management Guide, ¶1390.

SPECIAL BUSINESS ENTITIES

¶465 Publicly Traded Partnership Income Treatment of Alternative Fuels

SUMMARY OF NEW LAW

Certain income and gains related to the marketing of industrial source carbon dioxide and the transportation or storage of certain alcohol, biodiesel and alternative fuels are treated as qualifying income for publicly traded partnerships.

BACKGROUND

A publicly traded partnership (PTP) is treated as a corporation for federal income tax purposes unless 90 percent of its gross income is qualifying income. Qualifying income included interest, dividends, real property rents, gains from the disposition of real property, income and gains derived from the exploration, development, mining or production, processing, refining, transportation (including pipelines transporting gas, oil, or products thereof), or the marketing of any mineral or natural resource (including fertilizer, geothermal energy and timber) (Code Sec. 7704(d)(1)).

Oil and gas products beyond those produced at petroleum refineries and field processing units are not included in minerals and natural resources. Qualified passive-type income from transportation of natural resources products is similarly limited. Income from transportation of oil and gas to a bulk distribution center (whether by pipeline, truck, barge, or rail) is qualifying income. However, except for pipeline transport, the transportation of oil or gas to a place from which it is dispensed or sold to retail customers is not qualifying income.

NEW LAW EXPLAINED

PTPs can treat income related to alternative fuels as qualifying income.—Qualifying income for purposes of the publicly traded partnership (PTP) rules has been expanded to include income and gains derived from the marketing of industrial source carbon dioxide or the transportation or storage of certain fuels. Thus, qualifying income from alternative fuels now includes income derived from the exploration, development, mining or production, processing, refining, transportation (including pipelines transporting gas, oil, or products thereof), or the marketing of any mineral or natural resource (including fertilizer, geothermal energy, timber or industrial source carbon dioxide, as well as income derived from the transportation or storage of certain alcohol fuels and mixtures, biodiesel fuels and mixtures and alternative fuels and mixtures (Code Sec. 7704(d)(1)(E), as amended by the Emergency Economic Stabilization Act of 2008 (P.L. 110-343)).

> **Comment:** The Joint Committee on Taxation, Technical Explanation of H.R. 7060, the "Renewable Energy and Job Creation Tax Act of 2008" (JCX-75-08) states that income derived from the transportation or storage of the following fuels will be considered qualifying income for purposes of the PTP rules:
>
> (1) any fuel described in Code Sec. 6426(b), (c),(d) or (e), namely, alcohol fuel mixtures, biodiesel mixtures, alternative fuels (which include liquefied petroleum gas, P Series Fuels, compressed or liquefied natural gas, liquefied hydrogen, liquid fuel derived from coal through the Fischer-Tropsch process, and liquid fuel derived from biomass), and alternative fuel mixtures;
>
> (2) neat alcohol other than alcohol derived from petroleum, natural gas, or coal, or having a proof of less than 190 (as defined in Code Sec. 6426(b)(4)(A)); and
>
> (3) neat biodiesel (as defined in Code Sec. 40A(d)(1)).

¶465

NEW LAW EXPLAINED

Therefore, a PTP generating at least 90 percent of its income from these activities and from other types of qualifying income will be treated as a partnership for federal tax purposes.

> **Practical Analysis:** Charles R. Goulding, J.D., CPA, MBA, President and founder of Energy Tax Savers Inc., notes that it is believed that Division B, Act Sec. 116 of the Emergency Economic Stabilization Act of 2008 (P.L. 110-343) may be designed to platform a cap and trade system. Under cap and trade systems, companies that reduce their carbon emissions can sell their carbon credits to companies that did exceed them. The issue is whether the provision applies to businesses that generate their income from selling credits.

▶ **Effective date.** The amendments made by these provisions take effect on October 3, 2008, the date of enactment, in tax years ending after that date (Division B, Act Secs. 116(b) and 208(b) of the Emergency Economic Stabilization Act of 2008 (P.L. 110-343)).

Law source: Law at ¶5495. Committee Report at ¶10,120.

— Division B, Act Sec. 116(a) of the Emergency Economic Stabilization Act of 2008 (P.L. 110-343), amending Code Sec. 7704(d)(1)(E);

— Division B, Act Sec. 208(a), amending Code Sec. 7704(d)(1)(E).

— Division B, Act Secs. 116(b) and 208(b), providing the effective dates.

Reporter references: For further information, consult the following CCH reporters.

— Standard Federal Tax Reporter, ¶43,182.03

— Tax Research Consultant, PART: 3,254

— Federal Tax Guide, ¶14,010

¶470 Tax Treatment of Regulated Investment Company Dividends Paid to Foreign Persons

SUMMARY OF NEW LAW

The exemption from the 30-percent tax, collected through withholding, on regulated investment company (RIC) dividends, designated as either an interest-related or short-term capital gain dividends, is extended for two years.

BACKGROUND

A regulated investment company (RIC), commonly known as a mutual fund, is a domestic corporation or common trust fund that invests in stocks and securities. RICs must satisfy a number of complex tests relating to income, assets, and other matters (Code Secs. 851 and 852). A RIC passes through the character of its long-term capital

BACKGROUND

gains to its shareholders, by designating a dividend paid as a capital gain dividend to the extent that the RIC has net capital gains available. Shareholders treat these gains as long-term capital gains (Code Sec. 852(b)(3)).

Generally, U.S. source income received by a nonresident alien or foreign corporation that is not "effectively connected with a U.S. trade or business" is subject to a flat 30-percent tax, collected through withholding (or, if applicable, a lower treaty tax rate) (Code Secs. 871(a) and 881). U.S. source net income that is "effectively connected" to a trade or business is subject to the regular graduated tax rates (Code Secs. 871(b) and 882).

The following items received by a nonresident alien or foreign corporation are exempt from the 30-percent tax:

(1) interest from certain bank deposits (Code Secs. 871(i)(2)(A) and 881(d));

(2) original issue discount obligations that mature within 183 days or less from the original issue date (Code Sec. 871(g)); and

(3) interest paid on portfolio obligations (Code Secs. 871(h) and 881(c)).

Foreign persons are generally not subject to tax on gain realized when they dispose of stock or securities issued by a U.S. entity, unless the gain is effectively connected with the conduct of a U.S. trade or business. This exception does not apply, however, in the case of a nonresident alien who is present in the United States for more than 183 aggregated days in a tax year (Code Sec. 871(a)(2)). A RIC may elect to withhold tax on a distribution, representing a capital gain dividend, to a foreign person (Reg. § 1.1441-3(c)(2)(i)(D)).

Interest-related dividend. For dividends with respect to tax years of RICs beginning after December 31, 2004, but before January 1, 2008, a RIC can designate all or a portion of a dividend paid to a nonresident alien or foreign corporation as an interest-related dividend. The RIC must designate the dividend as an interest-dividend by written notice mailed to its shareholders no later than 60 days after the close of its tax year. As a result of the designation, and with some exceptions, the dividend is exempt from the 30-percent tax, collected through withholding. The provision applies to amounts that would be exempt if paid to a nonresident alien or foreign corporation directly (Code Secs. 871(k)(1)(C), 881(e)(1), 1441(c)(12) and 1442(a)). An interest-related dividend is limited to the RIC's qualified net interest income. Qualified interest income is the sum of the RIC's U.S. source income with respect to:

(1) bank deposit interest;

(2) short-term original issue discount that is currently exempt from tax under Code Sec. 871;

(3) any interest (including amounts recognized as ordinary income in respect of original issue discount, market discount, or acquisition discount, and any other such amounts that may be prescribed by regulations) on an obligation that is in registered form (unless the interest was earned on an obligation issued by a corporation or partnership in which the RIC is a 10-percent shareholder or is contingent interest not treated as portfolio interest under Code Sec. 871(h)(4)); and

(4) any interest-related dividend from another RIC (Code Sec. 871(k)(1)(E)).

BACKGROUND

If the exemption is inapplicable because the interest is on certain debt of the recipient or any corporation or partnership for which the recipient is a 10-percent shareholder, the RIC remains exempt from its withholding obligation unless it knows the dividend is subject to the exception (Code Secs. 871(k)(1)(B)(i) and 1441(c)(12)(B)). A similar rule applies in the case of dividends received by controlled foreign corporations where the interest is attributable to a related person (Code Secs. 881(e)(1)(B)(ii) and 1442(a)).

Short-term capital gain dividend. For dividends with respect to tax years of a RIC beginning after December 31, 2004, but before January 1, 2008, a RIC can designate all or a portion of a dividend paid to a nonresident alien or foreign corporation as a short-term capital gain dividend. The RIC must designate the dividend as a short-term capital gains dividend by written notice mailed to its shareholders no later than 60 days after the close of its tax year. As a result of the designation, the short-term capital gain dividend is exempt from the 30-percent tax, collected through withholding (Code Secs. 871(k)(2)(C), 881(e)(1)(C), 1441(c)(12) and 1442(a)). This exemption does not apply when the nonresident alien is present in the United States for 183 days or more during the tax year (Code Sec. 871(k)(2)(B)). If the exemption is inapplicable, the RIC, nevertheless, remains exempt from its withholding obligation, unless it knows that the dividend recipient has been present in the United States for such period (Code Sec. 1441(c)(12)(B)).

The amount designated as a short-term capital gain dividend cannot exceed the qualified short-term capital gain for the tax year. The amount qualified to be designated as a short-term capital gain dividend for the RIC's tax year is equal to the excess of the RIC's net short-term capital gain over its net long-term capital losses. Short-term capital gain includes short-term capital gain dividends from another RIC. Net short-term capital gain is determined without regard to any net capital loss or net short-term capital loss attributable to transactions occurring after October 31 of the tax year. The loss is treated as arising on the first day of the next tax year. To the extent provided in regulations, this rule will apply for purposes of computing the RIC's taxable income (Code Sec. 871(k)(2)(D)).

NEW LAW EXPLAINED

Favorable tax treatment of RIC dividends paid to foreign persons extended.—The provision that allows a regulated investment company (RIC) to designate dividends paid to nonresident aliens or foreign corporations as interest-related dividends or short-term capital gains dividends is extended for two years. Dividends that are so designated are generally exempt from the 30-percent tax, collected through withholding. Specifically, interest-related dividends and short-term capital gain dividends do not include dividends with respect to any tax year of a RIC beginning after December 31, 2009 (Code Sec. 871(k)(1)(C) and (2)(C), as amended by the Emergency Economic Stabilization Act of 2008 (P.L. 110-343)).

▶ **Effective date.** The amendments made by this provision apply to dividends with respect to tax years of regulated investment companies (RICs) beginning after December 31, 2007

NEW LAW EXPLAINED

(Division C, Act Sec. 206(c) of the Emergency Economic Stabilization Act of 2008 (P.L. 110-343)).

Law source: Law at ¶5320. Committee Reports at ¶10,380.

— Division C, Act Sec. 206(a) of the Emergency Economic Stabilization Act of 2008 (P.L. 110-343), amending Code Sec. 871(k)(1)(C);

— Division C, Act Sec. 206(b), amending Code Sec. 871(k)(2)(C);

— Division C, Act Sec. 206(c), providing the effective date.

Reporter references: For further information, consult the following CCH reporters.

— Standard Federal Tax Reporter, ¶27,343.0444, ¶27,484.0255

— Tax Research Consultant, EXPAT: 15,150

— Federal Tax Guide, ¶17,120

¶475 Estate Tax Treatment of Stock in Regulated Investment Companies

SUMMARY OF NEW LAW

The favorable estate tax treatment that excludes from the estate a portion of the stock in a regulated investment company (RIC) owned by a decedent who was a nonresident, non-U.S. citizen, is extended for two years.

BACKGROUND

The value of the gross estate of a nonresident decedent who was not a citizen of the United States includes only the portion of the gross estate located in the United States (Code Sec. 2103). A portion of stock in a regulated investment company (RIC), commonly known as a mutual fund, that is owned by a nonresident, non-U.S. citizen, is treated as property located outside of the United States and is not includible in the estate of the person for federal estate tax purposes (Code Sec. 2105(d)(1)). The exempt amount is the proportion of the RIC's assets that were "qualifying assets" in relation to the total assets of the RIC. Qualifying assets are assets that, if owned directly by the decedent, would have been:

(1) bank deposits that are exempt from income tax;

(2) portfolio debt obligations;

(3) certain original issue discount obligations;

(4) debt obligations of a U.S. corporation that are treated as giving rise to foreign source income; and

(5) other property not within the United States (Code Sec. 2105(d)(2)).

The favorable estate tax treatment applies to estates of decedents dying after December 31, 2004, and before January 1, 2008.

Favorable estate tax treatment of RIC stock extended.—The favorable estate tax treatment afforded a portion of stock in a regulated investment company (RIC) that is owned by a nonresident, non-U.S. citizen, is extended for two years. Specifically, stock of a RIC is not deemed property located within the United States in the proportion that the assets held by the RIC are debt obligations, deposits, or other property that would be treated as situated outside the United States if held directly by the estate. With the two-year extension, the provision now applies to the estates of nonresident, non-U.S. citizens, dying after December 31, 2004, and before January 1, 2010 (Code Sec. 2105(d)(3), as amended by the Emergency Economic Stabilization Act of 2008 (P.L. 110-343)).

▶ **Effective date.** This provision applies to the estates of decedents dying after December 31, 2007 (Division C, Act Sec. 207(b) of the Emergency Economic Stabilization Act of 2008 (P.L. 110-343)).

Law source: Law at ¶5400. Committee Reports at ¶10,390.

— Division C, Act Sec. 207(a) of the Emergency Economic Stabilization Act of 2008 (P.L. 110-343), amending Code Sec. 2105(d)(3);

— Division C, Act Sec. 207(b), providing the effective date.

Reporter references: For further information, consult the following CCH reporters.

— Tax Research Consultant, ESTGIFT: 60,150

— Federal Tax Guide, ¶20,390

— Federal Estate and Gift Tax Reporter, ¶7975.11

¶480 Tax Treatment of Certain Payments to Controlling Exempt Organizations

SUMMARY OF NEW LAW

The application of special rules that permit the exclusion of certain qualifying payments by a controlled entity to a tax-exempt organization from that tax-exempt organization's unrelated business income is extended through December 31, 2009. Also, the application of the 20-percent valuation misstatement penalty is extended.

BACKGROUND

A tax-exempt organization is taxed on its unrelated business taxable income (UBTI), which is generally the organization's gross income from an unrelated trade or business, less the deductions related to that trade or business. An unrelated trade or business is a trade or business that is regularly carried on by the exempt organization, but that is not substantially related to the performance of its exempt activities (Code Sec. 512).

BACKGROUND

Specified payments. UBTI includes specified payments that the organization receives or accrues from a controlled entity, to the extent they either reduce the controlled entity's net unrelated income or increase its net unrelated loss. Specified payments are interest, annuities, royalties or rents, but not dividends (Code Sec. 512(b)(13)(A) and (C)). For a controlled entity that is also tax-exempt, net unrelated income is the entity's UBTI. For a controlled entity that is taxable, net unrelated income is the portion of the entity's taxable income that would be UBTI if the entity were a tax-exempt organization with the same exempt purposes as the controlling organization. Net unrelated loss is determined under similar rules (Code Sec. 513(b)(13)(B)).

Control. An exempt organization controls another entity if it owns more than 50 percent of a corporation's stock (by vote or by value), more than 50 percent of a partnership's profits interests or capital interests, or more than 50 percent of the beneficial interests in any other entity (Code Sec. 513(b)(13)(D)).

Excess qualifying specified payments. Two special rules apply to specified payments received or accrued after December 31, 2005, and before January 1, 2008 (Code Sec. 512(b)(13)(E)(iv)):

(1) Only the excess amount of qualifying specified payments are included in the controlling organization's UBTI (Code Sec. 512(b)(13)(E)(i)).

- A *qualifying* specified payment is one made in connection with a binding written contract that is in effect on August 17, 2006 (including a renewal of the contract under substantially similar terms).

- A qualifying specified payment is *excess* to the extent it exceeds an amount that would meet the anti-abuse requirements of Code Sec. 482 (that is, to the extent it exceeds an amount that would be paid in an arm's-length transaction between unrelated parties) (Code Sec. 512(b)(13)(E)(iii)).

(2) A valuation misstatement *penalty* applies to excess qualifying specified payments that are included in UBTI. Any federal income tax imposed on the controlling organization (including tax on UBTI) is increased by an amount equal to 20 percent of the excess payment, determined with (or, if larger, without) regard to return amendments or supplements (Code Sec. 512(b)(13)(E)(ii)).

Application of the special rules expired on December 31, 2007.

NEW LAW EXPLAINED

Rules for payments to controlling exempt organizations extended.—The application of special rules that permit the exclusion of certain qualifying payments by a controlled entity to a tax-exempt organization from that tax-exempt organization's unrelated business income is extended through December 31, 2009 (Code Sec. 512(b)(13)(E)(iv), as amended by the Emergency Economic Stabilization Act of 2008 (P.L. 110-343)). Accordingly, payments of rent, royalties, annuities, or interest income by a controlled organization to a controlling organization pursuant to a binding written contract in effect on August 17, 2006 (or renewal of such a contract on substantially similar terms), may be includible in the unrelated business taxable income (UBTI) of

¶480

NEW LAW EXPLAINED

the controlling organization only to the extent the payment exceeds the amount of the payment determined under the principles of Code Sec. 482 (*i.e.*, at arm's length).

In addition, the application of the 20-percent valuation misstatement penalty is extended. Thus, any excess payment amount is subject to a 20-percent penalty on the larger of such excess determined without regard to any amendment or supplement to a return of tax, or such excess determined with regard to all such amendments and supplements (Code Sec. 512(b)(13)(E)(ii)).

▶ **Effective date.** The extension of the special rules for excess qualifying specified payments is effective for payments received or accrued after December 31, 2007 (Division C, Act Sec. 306(b) of the Emergency Economic Stabilization Act of 2008 (P.L. 110-343)).

Law source: Law at ¶5310. Committee Report at ¶10,460.

— Division C, Act Sec. 306(a) of the Emergency Economic Stabilization Act of 2008 (P.L. 110-343), amending Code Sec. 512(b)(13)(E)(iv);

— Division C, Act Sec. 306(b), providing the effective date.

Reporter references: For further information, consult the following CCH reporters.

— Standard Federal Tax Reporter, 2008FED ¶22,837.053

— Tax Research Consultant EXEMPT: 15,304

— Federal Tax Guide, 2008FTG ¶16,320

¶485 Gain or Loss from Sale or Exchange of Fannie Mae or Freddie Mac Preferred Stock

SUMMARY OF NEW LAW

Certain financial institutions will receive ordinary income or loss treatment on the sale or exchange of preferred stock in the Federal National Mortgage Association ("Fannie Mae") or the Federal Home Loan Mortgage Corporation ("Freddie Mac").

BACKGROUND

Certain financial institutions do not treat the sale or exchange of indebtedness (a bond or note, for example) as a capital asset transaction (Code Sec. 582(c)). Any resulting gain or loss receives ordinary rather than capital treatment for federal income tax purposes. However, preferred stock of the Federal National Mortgage Association ("Fannie Mae") or the Federal Home Loan Mortgage Corporation ("Freddie Mac") is not indebtedness under the federal tax rules. Therefore, a transaction in Fannie Mae or Freddie Mac preferred stock receives treatment as capital gain or loss. A capital loss would be allowed only to the extent of capital gains. In a tax year when there is no capital gain, the loss cannot be used except under the capital loss carryforward and carryback rules. This tax treatment applies to banks, savings

BACKGROUND

institutions, small business investment companies, and business development corporations, as those categories are defined in the Internal Revenue Code.

NEW LAW EXPLAINED

Ordinary income or loss on Fannie Mae or Freddie Mac preferred stock.— Certain financial institutions will be able to take ordinary gain or loss on the sale or exchange of the preferred stock of the Federal National Mortgage Association ("Fannie Mae") or the Federal Home Loan Mortgage Corporation ("Freddie Mac") (Division A, Act Sec. 301(a) of the Emergency Economic Stabilization Act of 2008 (P.L. 110-343)). Several limitations and special rules have been enacted for the application of this tax treatment. The new law applies to financial institutions, as that term is defined in Code Sec. 582(c)(2). This means banks, savings institutions, small business investment companies, and business development corporations. The rule is also extended to depository institution holding companies as they are defined in the Federal Deposit Insurance Act (12 U.S.C. 1813(w)(1)). Collectively, these institutions are referred to as applicable financial institutions (Division A, Act Sec. 301(c)(1) of the Emergency Economic Act of 2008).

The preferred stock covered by the new law (applicable preferred stock) must be held by the applicable financial institution on September 6, 2008. In the alternative, the stock could be sold or exchanged by the applicable financial institution on or after January 1, 2008, and before September 7, 2008. When there is a sale or exchange on or after January 1, 2008 and before September 7, 2008, the transferor must be an applicable financial institution at the time of the sale or exchange for the new law to apply. When there is a sale or exchange after September 6, 2008, the transferor must be an applicable financial institution at all times during the period beginning on September 6, 2008, and ending on the date of the sale or exchange for the new law to apply (Division A, Act Sec. 301(b) and (c)(2) of the Emergency Economic Act of 2008).

The Secretary of the Treasury has been granted authority to extend the application of the new law to two specified situations where the applicable preferred stock was not held on September 6, 2008 (Division A, Act Sec. 301(d) of the Emergency Economic Act of 2008). First, the new law may be extended to a sale or exchange by an applicable financial institution, occurring after September 6, 2008, where the applicable preferred stock was not held on September 6, 2008 but was acquired in a carryover basis transaction from an applicable financial institution holding the stock on September 6, 2008. This situation could occur in a section 368 transaction where one applicable financial institution acquires the assets of another applicable financial institution including applicable preferred stock (Division A, Act Sec. 301(d)(1) of the Emergency Economic Act of 2008).

Second, the Secretary of the Treasury may extend the new law to a situation where the applicable financial institution is a partner in a partnership that either (a) held the applicable preferred stock on September 6, 2008, and later sold or exchanged the stock, or (b) sold or exchanged the applicable preferred stock on or after January 1, 2008, and

NEW LAW EXPLAINED

before September 7, 2008 (Division A, Act Sec. 301(d)(2) of the Emergency Economic Act of 2008).

The Secretary of the Treasury is also authorized to issue guidance, rules, or regulations to carry out this rule (Division A, Act Sec. 301(e) of the Emergency Economic Act of 2008).

▶ **Effective date.** The provision applies to sales or exchanges occurring after December 31, 2007 in tax years ending after that date (Division A, Act Sec. 301(f) of the Emergency Economic Stabilization Act of 2008 (P.L. 110-343)).

Law source: Law at ¶7132. Committee Reports at ¶10,010.

— Division A, Act Sec. 301(a) - (e), of the Emergency Economic Stabilization Act of 2008 (P.L. 110-343);

— Division A, Act Sec. 301(f), providing the effective date.

Reporter references: For further information, consult the following CCH reporters.

— Standard Federal Tax Reporter, ¶23,611.021

— Tax Research Consultant, SALES: 15,212

— Federal Tax Guide, ¶5540, and ¶16,465

Energy Conservation

5

INDIVIDUAL TAX CREDITS

¶505 Residential Energy Property Credit

SUMMARY OF NEW LAW

The residential energy property credit has been reinstated for qualified energy property placed in service only in 2009. The credit is expanded to include stoves using renewable plant-derived fuel to heat a taxpayer's residence or the water for the residence (qualified biomass fuel property) and asphalt roofs with cooling granules. A natural gas, propane, or oil water heater placed in service in 2009 must either have an energy factor of at least 0.80, or a thermal efficiency of at least 90 percent. The term energy-efficient building property no longer includes geothermal heat pump property since geothermal heat pump property qualifies for the residential alternative energy credit (Code Sec. 25D) as to property placed in service during tax years 2008 through 2016.

BACKGROUND

A tax credit of up to $500 is available to individuals for nonbusiness energy property, such as residential exterior doors and windows, metal roofs, insulation, heat pumps, furnaces, central air conditioners and water heaters (Code Sec. 25C). The credit is equal to (1) residential energy-efficient building property expenditures for heat pumps, air conditioners and water heaters, plus (2) 10 percent of the cost of qualified energy efficiency improvements (building envelope components) installed during the year at the taxpayer's principal residence in the United States. The residential energy property credit is limited to a maximum of $500 for all tax years and no more than $200 of the credit can be based on expenditures for windows (Code Sec. 25C(b)). The residential energy property credit applies to qualified energy efficiency improvements and qualified energy-efficient building property placed in service in 2006 and 2007 (Code Sec. 25C(g)).

NEW LAW EXPLAINED

Residential energy property credit reinstated, expanded and clarified.—The Emergency Economic Stabilization Act of 2008 (P.L. 110-343) made several changes to the residential energy property credit that applies to residential energy property such as exterior doors and windows, insulation, heat pumps, furnaces, central air conditioners and water heaters. These changes include reinstatement of the credit for tax year 2009 only, expansion of the credit to include certain stoves that use renewable plant-derived fuel and asphalt roofs with cooling granules, clarification of the efficiency standards applicable to water heaters, and removal of geothermal heat pump property as qualified energy-efficient building property for purposes of this credit.

¶505

NEW LAW EXPLAINED

Reinstatement of residential energy property credit. The residential energy property credit has been reinstated for property placed in service in tax year 2009 (Code Sec. 25C(g), as amended by the Emergency Economic Stabilization Act of 2008 (P.L. 110-343)).

> **Caution Note:** There is no residential energy property credit applicable to residential energy-efficient building property expenditures or qualified energy efficiency improvements installed at a taxpayer's principal U.S. residence in 2008. The credit expired as to property placed in service after December 31, 2007. It was not extended, but rather, reinstated after one year of no applicability.

Qualified biomass fuel property. For expenditures made in 2009, the term energy-efficient building property includes a stove that has a thermal efficiency rating of at least 75 percent, and that uses the burning of biomass fuel to heat a taxpayer's U.S. residence, or to heat water for the residence (Code Sec. 25C(d)(3)(E), as added and redesignated by the Emergency Economic Act of 2008). Any plant-derived fuel available on a renewable or recurring basis, including agricultural crops and trees, wood and wood waste and residues (including wood pellets), plants (including aquatic plants), grasses, residues, and fibers is biomass fuel (Code Sec. 25C(d)(6), as added by the Emergency Economic Act of 2008).

Asphalt roofs with cooling granules. For property placed in service after October 3, 2008, the term building envelope component is expanded to include an asphalt roof with appropriate cooling granules that meets the Energy Star program requirements (Code Sec. 25C(c)(1) and 25C(c)(2)(D), as amended by the Emergency Economic Act of 2008; Division B, Act Sec. 302(f)(2) of the Emergency Economic Act of 2008). Ten percent of the cost of the qualifying roof may qualify for the residential energy property credit if all other credit requirements are satisfied.

> **Comment:** In 2006 and 2007, the only type of roof that qualified as an envelope component for purposes of this credit was a metal roof with appropriate pigmented coating to reduce heat gain.

> **Caution Note:** Although the residential energy property credit was reinstated only for 2009 (Code Sec. 25C(g), as amended by the Emergency Economic Act of 2008), the effective date language as to asphalt roofs (Division B, Act Sec. 302(f)(2)) does clearly say "placed in service after the date of enactment of this Act", which is October 3, 2008.

> **Planning Note:** For taxpayers wishing to take advantage of the residential energy property credit by installing an asphalt roof with the appropriate cooling granules on their principal U.S. residence, the safest course of action is to have the roof installed in 2009. Placing the roof in service in 2009 avoids any potential dispute as to the application of the residential energy property credit.

Efficiency standard for water heaters. A natural gas, propane, or oil water heater placed in service in 2009 must either have an energy factor of at least 0.80, or a thermal efficiency of at least 90 percent (Code Sec. 25C(d)(3)(D), as amended and redesignated by the Emergency Economic Act of 2008).

Geothermal heat pump property. Since geothermal heat pump property qualifies for the residential alternative energy credit as to property placed in service during tax years 2008 through 2016 pursuant to Code Sec. 25D(a)(5), as added by the Emergency

NEW LAW EXPLAINED

Economic Act of 2008, the term energy-efficient building property no longer includes geothermal heat pump property for expenditures made in 2009 (Code Sec. 25C(d)(3)(C), as stricken by, and Code Sec. 25C(g), as amended by the Emergency Economic Act of 2008). See ¶510 for a discussion of the application of the residential alternative energy credit to geothermal heat pump property. Furthermore, the performance and quality requirements and standards applicable to air conditioners and heat pumps have been modified to reference only electric, not geothermal, heat pumps (Code Sec. 25C(d)(2)(C), as amended by the Emergency Economic Act of 2008).

> **Comment:** The effective date language in Division B, Act Sec. 302(f)(1), applicable to the Code Sec. 25C amendments, states that the amendments apply to expenditures made after December 31, 2008. This does raise some ambiguity since the effective date language for the amendments to Code Sec. 25D (Division B, Act Sec. 106(f)(1)), including those adding geothermal heat pump property, say that they apply to "taxable years beginning after December 31, 2007."

> **Planning Point:** Taxpayers who are interested in installing a geothermal heat pump at their U.S. residence might be wise to wait until on or after January 1, 2009, when the residential energy property credit ($300 maximum credit for geothermal pump) clearly no longer applies to geothermal heat pump property. If the pump is placed in service in 2009 through 2016, 30 percent of the cost, up to a maximum of $2,000, will qualify for the residential alternative energy credit if all other credit requirements are satisfied.

▶ **Effective date.** The amendments generally apply to expenditures made after December 31, 2008 (Division B, Act Sec. 302(f)(1) of the Emergency Economic Stabilization Act of 2008 (P.L. 110-343)). The amendment expanding the credit to include asphalt roofs with cooling granules applies to property placed in service after October 3, 2008, the date of enactment (Division B, Act Sec. 302(f)(2) of the Emergency Economic Act of 2008).

Law source: Law at ¶5025. Committee Reports at ¶10,210.

— Division B, Act Sec. 302(a) of the Emergency Economic Stabilization Act of 2008 (P.L. 110-343), amending Code Sec. 25C(g);

— Division B, Act Sec. 302(b), adding Code Sec. 25C(d)(3)(F) and Code Sec. 25C(d)(6);

— Division B, Act Sec. 302(c), amending Code Sec. 25C(d)(3)(E);

— Division B, Act Sec. 302(d), amending Code Sec. 25C(d)(3) and Code Sec. 25C(d)(2)(C);

— Division B, Act Sec. 302(e), amending Code Sec. 25C(c)(1) and Code Sec. 25C(c)(2)(D);

— Division B, Act Sec. 302(f), providing the effective date.

Reporter references: For further information, consult the following CCH reporters.

— Standard Federal Tax Reporter, ¶3843.01, ¶3843.025, ¶3843.03 and ¶3843.06

— Tax Research Consultant, INDIV: 57,800, INDIV: 57,804, INDIV: 57,806 and INDIV: 57,810

— Federal Tax Guide, ¶2235

¶505

¶510 Residential Alternative Energy Credit

SUMMARY OF NEW LAW

The residential alternative energy credit has been extended for eight years, through 2016. The credit has also been expanded to include expenditures for qualified small wind energy property and qualified geothermal heat pump property placed in service in 2008 through 2016. The $2,000 maximum annual credit limit for qualified solar electric property expenditures is eliminated after 2008. The residential alternative energy credit may be offset against regular tax and AMT liabilities in 2008.

BACKGROUND

A nonrefundable tax credit is available to help individual taxpayers pay for specific residential alternative energy equipment installed on or in connection with a dwelling unit located in the United States that is used as a residence by the taxpayer (Code Sec. 25D). Note that fuel cell property must be installed in connection with the taxpayer's *principal* U.S. residence (Code Sec. 25D(d)(3)). The residential alternative energy credit is 30 percent of the following expenditures made by the taxpayer during the tax year:

(1) a qualified solar electric property expenditure (including, but not limited to, a photovoltaic property expenditure);

(2) a qualified solar water heating property expenditure; and

(3) a qualified fuel cell property expenditure (Code Sec. 25D(a)).

The maximum credit for any tax year is $2,000 for each category of solar equipment, and $500 for each half kilowatt of capacity of fuel cell property installed during the year (Code Sec. 25D(b)).

> **Comment:** The Tax Relief and Health Care Act of 2006 (P.L. 109-432) clarified that all property that uses solar energy to generate electricity for use in a taxpayer's U.S. dwelling is qualified solar electric property for purposes of the residential alternative energy credit, not just photovoltaic property (Code Sec. 25D(d)(2)). According to the U.S. Department of Energy, a viable alternative to photovoltaic technology for converting solar energy to electricity is Concentrating Solar Power (CSP). CSP plants generate electric power by using mirrors to concentrate the sun's energy and convert it into steam, which is then channeled through a conventional turbine generator. Within the United States, over 350 megawatts of CSP capacity exist and these plants have been operating reliably for more than 15 years. Smaller systems with home-sized capacity are under development (www.eere.energy.gov/solar).

Cooperative and condominium dwellers can claim the credit by splitting the cost of installing equipment with other unit owners. In the case of a residence occupied by two or more taxpayers, the maximum amount of expenditures that may be used in calculating the credit is $6,667 per tax year for each category of solar equipment, and $1,667 per tax year for each half kilowatt of capacity of fuel cell property (Code Sec.

BACKGROUND

25D(e)(4)(A)). Eligible equipment must be placed in service during 2006, 2007 or 2008 (Code Sec. 25D(g)).

The residential alternative energy credit may be offset against regular tax and alternative minimum tax liabilities in 2006 through 2007 (Code Sec. 26(a)(2)). In 2008, the credit may not exceed the excess, if any, of the regular tax over the tentative minimum tax for the tax year, reduced by the sum of the nonrefundable personal credits (Code Secs. 21, 22, 25A, 25C) other than the adoption, child tax and saver's credits (Code Sec. 26(a)(1)).

NEW LAW EXPLAINED

Residential alternative energy credit extended and expanded.—The Emergency Economic Stabilization Act of 2008 (P.L. 110-343) made several changes to the residential alternative energy credit. These changes include extension of the credit for eight years, expansion of the credit by removal of the credit cap for solar electric investments and inclusion of small wind investment property and geothermal heat pump expenditures, and offset of the credit against alternative minimum tax (AMT).

Extension of residential alternative energy credit. For tax years beginning after December 31, 2007, the residential alternative energy credit applies to expenditures for qualified:

(1) solar electric property,

(2) solar water heating property,

(3) fuel cell property,

(4) small wind energy property, and

(5) geothermal heat pump property

The property must be placed in service on or before December 31, 2016 (Code Sec. 25D(a)(4) and (5), as added by, and Code Sec. 25D(g), as amended by the Emergency Economic Act of 2008).

> **Planning Point:** The residential alternative energy credit applies for eight additional years, through 2016. In addition, for tax years 2008 through 2016, the credit also applies to expenditures made for qualified small wind energy property and qualified geothermal heat pump property (see the discussions, below, on the new types of qualified property). Time is now on the side of the taxpayer in planning alternative energy residential expenditures, as well as investigating what state and regional utility company rebates, tax credits, or buy-down programs may be available. However, taxpayers must be aware that any expenditures made with funds obtained from subsidized energy financing are ineligible for this energy credit (Code Sec. 25D(d)(9)). Despite this prohibition, having more time to plan expenditures that qualify for the credit and taking advantage of subsidized energy financing may result in more residential alternative energy equipment being installed on or in connection with U.S. dwellings.

Solar electric property credit cap removed. For tax years beginning after December 31, 2008, the $2,000 maximum annual residential alternative energy credit limit for

NEW LAW EXPLAINED

qualified solar electric property expenditures has been eliminated (Code Sec. 25D(b)(1), as amended by the Emergency Economic Act of 2008).

Comment: For tax years 2009 through 2016, 30 percent of qualified solar electric property expenditures made during a tax year qualify for the residential alternative energy credit. There is no annual maximum credit amount applicable to expenditures made in 2009 through 2016 for qualified solar electric property.

Caution: The $2,000 maximum annual residential alternative energy credit limit for qualified solar electric property expenditures applies through tax year 2008.

Qualified small wind energy property. An expenditure for property that uses a wind turbine to generate electricity for use in connection with a dwelling unit located in the U.S. and used as a residence by the taxpayer is a qualified small wind energy property expenditure (Code Sec. 25D(d)(4), as added by the Emergency Economic Act of 2008). Thirty percent of such expenditures made in a tax year qualify for the residential alternative energy credit for property placed in service during tax years 2008 through 2016 (Code Sec. 25D(a)(4), as added by the Emergency Economic Act of 2008). There is a credit maximum of $500 for each half kilowatt of electric capacity generated by a wind turbine, not to exceed $4,000 annually (Code Sec. 25D(b)(1)(C), as added and redesignated by the Emergency Economic Act of 2008).

Caution: Qualified small wind energy property expenditures cannot generate a double benefit. For purposes of the renewable electricity production credit under Code Sec. 45, *wind facility*, as defined at Code Sec. 45(d)(1), doesn't include qualified small wind energy property expenditures that are taken into account in determining the residential alternative energy credit under Code Sec. 25D (Code Sec. 45(d)(1), as amended by the Emergency Economic Act of 2008).

In the case of a residence occupied by two or more taxpayers, the maximum amount of wind energy property expenditures that may be used by all such individuals in calculating the credit is $1,667 per tax year for each half kilowatt of capacity of wind turbines, not to exceed $13,333 annually (Code Sec. 25D(e)(4)(A)(iii), as added and redesignated by the Emergency Economic Act of 2008).

Practical Analysis: Charles R. Goulding, J.D., CPA, MBA, President and founder of Energy Tax Savers Inc., observes that in Division B, Act Sec. 106(b) of the Emergency Economic Stabilization Act of 2008 (P.L. 110-343), the removal of the $2,000 cap on the 30-percent residential solar P.V. tax credit is a major change that we believe is going stimulate a tremendous increase in solar residential projects for individual residences and qualifying condo and coop projects. A 30-percent credit coupled with local utility rebates and the increasing ability to sell the extra electricity or so-called nega watts into the electric grid is going to greatly increase economic payback.

In Division B, Act Sec. 106(d) of the Emergency Economic Act, the $2,000 geothermal heat pump tax credit will be very beneficial for those residences where the geological conditions for geothermal technology is suitable. Note that the $6,667 expenditure cap is consistent since 30 percent of $6,667 is $2,000.

NEW LAW EXPLAINED

Qualified geothermal heat pump property. Equipment that uses the ground or ground water as a thermal energy source to heat a U.S. residential dwelling unit, or as a thermal energy sink to cool the unit, and meets the Energy Star program requirements in effect at the time the expenditure is made, is qualified geothermal heat pump property (Code Sec. 25D(d)(5)(B), as added by the Emergency Economic Act of 2008). An expenditure for qualified geothermal heat pump property installed on or in connection with a dwelling unit located in the U.S. and used as a residence by the taxpayer is a qualified geothermal heat pump property expenditure (Code Sec. 25D(d)(5)(A), as added by the Emergency Economic Act of 2008). Thirty percent of such expenditures made in a tax year qualify for the residential alternative energy credit for property placed in service during tax years 2008 through 2016 (Code Sec. 25D(a)(5), as added by the Emergency Economic Act of 2008). There is an annual maximum credit of $2,000 for geothermal heat pump property (Code Sec. 25D(b)(1)(D), as added and redesignated by the Emergency Economic Act of 2008).

In the case of a residence occupied by two or more taxpayers, the maximum amount of geothermal heat pump property expenditures that may be used by all such individuals in calculating the credit is $6,667 per tax year (Code Sec. 25D(e)(4)(A)(iv), as added and redesignated by the Emergency Economic Act of 2008).

Offset of credit against AMT. The residential alternative energy credit may be offset against regular tax and AMT liabilities in 2008 (Code Sec. 26(a)(2), as amended by the Emergency Economic Act of 2008). See ¶ 210 for further discussion. For tax years in which Code Sec. 26(a)(2) does not apply (after 2008), the residential alternative energy credit can be offset against the excess of both regular tax and AMT liabilities over the sum of the credits for dependent care, the elderly and disabled, adoption, child tax, home mortgage interest, education expenses, saver's, and nonbusiness energy property (Code Sec. 25D(c)(1), as amended by the Emergency Economic Act of 2008).

Carryforward. When the residential alternative energy credit can be offset against both regular tax and AMT (through 2008), if this credit exceeds both tax liabilities reduced by all other nonrefundable credits except this energy credit, the excess is carried forward to the next tax year and added to any residential alternative energy credit for that tax year (Code Sec. 25D(c)(2)(A), as amended by the Emergency Economic Act of 2008). When the offset against both regular tax and AMT does not apply (after 2008), if the energy credit exceeds the excess of both regular tax and AMT liabilities over the sum of the credits for dependent care, the elderly and disabled, adoption, child tax, home mortgage interest, education expenses, saver's, and nonbusiness energy property, the excess can be carried to the next tax year and added to any residential energy credit for that tax year (Code Sec. 25D(c)(2)(B), as amended by the Emergency Economic Act of 2008).

▶ **Effective date.** The amendments generally apply to tax years beginning after December 31, 2007 (Division B, Act Sec. 106(f)(1) of the Emergency Economic Stabilization Act of 2008 (P.L. 110-343)). The amendment removing the credit cap on qualified solar electric property expenditures applies to tax years beginning after December 31, 2008 (Division B, Act Sec. 106(f)(2) of the Emergency Economic Act of 2008).

NEW LAW EXPLAINED

Law source: Law at ¶5005, ¶5010, ¶5020, ¶5030, ¶5035 and ¶5075. Committee Reports at ¶10,060.

— Division B, Act Sec. 106(a) of the Emergency Economic Stabilization Act of 2008 (P.L. 110-343), amending Code Sec. 25D(g);

— Division B, Act Sec. 106(b), amending Code Sec. 25D(b)(1) and Code Sec. 25D(e)(4)(A);

— Division B, Act Sec. 106(c)(1), adding Code Sec. 25D(a)(4);

— Division B, Act Sec. 106(c)(2), adding Code Sec. 25D(b)(1)(D);

— Division B, Act Sec. 106(c)(3)(A), adding Code Sec. 25D(d)(4);

— Division B, Act Sec. 106(c)(3)(B), amending Code Sec. 45(d)(1);

— Division B, Act Sec. 106(c)(4), adding Code Sec. 25D(e)(4)(A)(iv);

— Division B, Act Sec. 106(d), adding Code Sec. 25D(a)(5), Code Sec. 25D(b)(1)(E), Code Sec. 25D(d)(5) and Code Sec. 25D(e)(4)(A)(v);

— Division B, Act Sec. 106(e), amending Code Sec. 23(b)(4)(B), Code Sec. 24(b)(3)(B), Code Sec. 25B(g)(2), Code Sec. 25D(c) and Code Sec. 26(a)(1);

— Division B, Act Sec. 106(f), providing the effective date.

Reporter references: For further information, consult the following CCH reporters.

— Standard Federal Tax Reporter, ¶3847.01, ¶3847.02, ¶3847.021,¶3847.03, ¶3847.06 and ¶3847.07

— Tax Research Consultant, INDIV: 57,850, INDIV: 57,852 and INDIV: 57,854

— Federal Tax Guide, ¶2240

¶515 Plug-in Electric Drive Motor Vehicle Credit

SUMMARY OF NEW LAW

A new credit against tax, is available for tax years beginning after December 31, 2008, for new qualified plug-in electric drive motor vehicles. The amount of the credit is $2,500, plus $417 for each kilowatt hour of traction battery capacity in excess of four kilowatt hours.

BACKGROUND

Prior to passage of the Energy Tax Incentives Act of 2005 (P.L. 109-58), the only tax incentives to encourage development of alternative fuels for motor vehicles were the credit for qualified electric vehicles and the deduction for the cost of clean-fuel vehicles and related property (Code Secs. 30 and 179A). The Energy Act of 2005 changed the landscape for developing alternative fuels by creating the alternative motor vehicle credit and the alternative fuel vehicle refueling property credit (Code Secs. 30B and 30C). The alternative motor vehicle credit has four components:

BACKGROUND

(1) the qualified motor vehicle credit (Code Sec. 30B(b)),

(2) the advanced lean burn technology motor vehicle credit (Code Sec. 30B(c)),

(3) the qualified hybrid motor vehicle credit (Code Sec. 30B(d)), and

(4) the qualified alternative fuel motor vehicle credit (Code Sec. 30B(e)).

Each component deals with a different type of alternative fuel currently being developed or already available in the marketplace. The fuel type drives the credit calculation which is generally based on a combination of the increase in miles per gallon over a base year, vehicle weight, and lifetime energy conservation. For vehicles used in business, the Code Sec. 38 tax liability limitations apply, while personal use vehicles are governed by the tax liability rules under Code Sec. 26. The alternative motor vehicle credit is phased out over a 12 month period beginning with the second quarter after the quarter in which the manufacturer sells its 60,000th advanced lean burn technology or qualified hybrid vehicle.

> **Comment:** The following manufacturers produced very successful hybrid motor vehicles that no longer qualify for any credit under the hybrid component of the alternative motor vehicle credit:
>
> - Toyota Motor Corporation (Toyota and Lexus models), for vehicles sold after September 30, 2007, and
> - Honda, for vehicles sold after December 31, 2008.

Currently, no American manufacturer is close to phase out of the alternative motor vehicle credit prior to its termination date.

The alternative fuel vehicle refueling property credit encourages the installation of refueling property for use by the alternative motor vehicles. For commercial installations, the credit amount limit is $30,000 while the individual credit limit is $1,000.

NEW LAW EXPLAINED

New plug-in electric drive motor vehicle credit.—A new credit against tax applies for qualified plug-in electric drive motor vehicles placed in service in 2009 through 2014. The credit is equal to the applicable amount for each new qualified plug-in electric drive motor vehicle placed in service by the taxpayer during the tax year (Code Sec. 30D(a), as added by the Emergency Economic Stabilization Act of 2008 (P.L. 110-343)). The applicable amount is the sum of $2,500, plus an additional $417 for each kilowatt hour of traction battery capacity in excess of four kilowatt hours (Code Sec. 30D(a)(2), as added by the Emergency Economic Act of 2008).

> **Practical Analysis:** Charles R. Goulding, J.D., CPA, MBA, President and founder of Energy Tax Savers Inc., notes that various car manufacturers are racing to bring electric cars to the market. Existing manufacturers include Chrysler, which is developing multiple electric models, and GM, which recently unveiled the Chevrolet Volt, an electric model it plans to start producing in 2010.

¶515

NEW LAW EXPLAINED

> New entrants include Tesla motors and Fisher Automotive. Tesla, who has developed an electric sports car, says it plans to build a $250 million dollar facility in San Jose, California. Tesla has raised more than $100 million and Fisher has raised $5 million of venture capital.

Comment: Generally, the plug-in electric vehicle credit rules are very similar to the rules that apply to the Code Sec. 30B alternative motor vehicle credit. There are credit limits based on vehicle weight, a credit phaseout, specific requirements applicable to the vehicle, as well as special rules for basis reduction and to prevent a double tax benefit.

Comment: This new credit may be claimed by both business and individual taxpayers. The use of placed-in-service language may again cause some confusion for individual taxpayers. When the alternative motor vehicle credit was established, the issue arose as to what date the IRS would consider the placed-in-service date for individuals. Although no pronouncement was every made, the language used in other official announcements led practitioners to conclude that the date of purchase was the placed-in-service date for individuals. It seems that the same placed-in-service date would apply for the new credit.

New qualified plug-in electric drive motor vehicle. In order for a motor vehicle to qualify as a new plug-in electric drive vehicle, the vehicle must be made by a manufacturer, acquired for use or lease, but not resale, the original use must begin with the taxpayer, and the motor vehicle must have:

(1) a traction battery (high power battery for electric vehicle traction) propulsion source with at least four kilowatt hours of capacity;

(2) an offboard source of energy to recharge the battery;

(3) a certificate of conformity under the Clean Air Act, and meet or exceed the equivalent qualifying California low emission vehicle standard (section 243(e)(2) of the Clean Air Act) for that make and model year, in the case of a passenger vehicle or light truck with a gross vehicle weight rating of not more than 8,500 pounds, and

    (a) if the vehicle weight rating is 6,000 pounds or less, meet the Bin 5 Tier II emission standard established in the regulations prescribed by the Administrator of the Environmental Protection Agency (section 202(i) of the Clean Air Act) for that make and model year, and

    (b) if the vehicle weight rating is more than 6,000 but not more than 8,500 pounds, meet the Bin 8 Tier II emission standards established in the regulations prescribed by the Administrator of the Environmental Protection Agency (section 202(i) of the Clean Air Act) for that make and model year (Code Sec. 30D(c), as added by the Emergency Economic Act of 2008).

The term motor vehicle means any vehicle that has at least four wheels and is manufactured primarily for use on public streets, roads, and highways (Code Secs. 30D(e)(1), as added by the Emergency Economic Act of 2008 and 30(c)(2)). The terms passenger automobile, light truck and manufacturer are given the same meanings

NEW LAW EXPLAINED

given such terms in regulations prescribed by the Administrator of the Environmental Protection Agency for purposes of the administration of title II of the Clean Air Act (Code Sec. 30D(e)(2), as added by the Emergency Economic Act of 2008). A traction battery capacity is measured in kilowatt hours from 100 percent state of charge to a zero percent state of charge (Code Sec. 30D(e)(3), as added by Emergency Economic Act of 2008). A motor vehicle will not be eligible for the new qualified plug-in electric drive motor vehicle credit unless it is in compliance with the applicable provisions of the Clean Air Act (or equivalent State law) for the applicable make and model year, and the motor vehicle safety provisions of sections 30101 through 30169 of title 49 of the United States Code (Code Sec. 30D(e)(10), as added by the Emergency Economic Act of 2008).

Limitations on credit amount. The plug-in electric drive motor vehicle credit amount is limited based on the weight of the vehicle and the number of vehicles sold. The maximum credit amount that may be claimed for a new qualified plug-in electric drive motor vehicle is:

- $7,500 for a vehicle with a gross vehicle weight rating of not more than 10,000 pounds;
- $10,000 for a vehicle with a gross vehicle weight rating of more than 10,000 pounds but not more than 14,000 pounds;
- $12,5000 for a vehicle with a gross vehicle weight rating of more than 14,000 pounds but not more than 26,000 pounds; and
- $15,000 for a vehicle with a gross vehicle weight rating of more than 26,000 pounds (Code Sec. 30D(b)(1), as added by the Emergency Economic Act of 2008).

The limitation based on vehicles sold operates in much the same way as the phaseout of the alternative motor vehicle credit for hybrid vehicles. When 250,000 new qualified plug-in electric drive motor vehicles have been sold for use in the United States, the phaseout will be triggered. The phaseout period begins with the second calendar quarter following the calendar quarter in which the 250,000th unit is sold. For the first two quarters of the phaseout period, the credit is cut to 50 percent of the full credit amount. The credit is cut to 25 percent for the third and fourth quarters of the phaseout period. Thereafter, there is no credit allowed (Code Sec. 30D(b)(2), as added by the Emergency Economic Act of 2008).

> **Example:** General Motors sells its 250,000th Volt, a certified qualified plug-in electric drive motor vehicle, during the first quarter of 2010. The full credit amount will continue to be available until June 30, 2010. The credit for qualified vehicles sold between July 1, 2010 and December 31, 2010, will only be 50 percent of the full credit amount. The credit between January 1, 2011 and June 30, 2011, will be 25 percent of the full credit amount. No credit is allowed for qualified vehicles sold after June 30, 2011.

Business versus personal use. If the plug-in electric drive motor vehicle is used in a trade or business and, is therefore, subject to depreciation, the credit allowed for the business use portion is treated as part of the general business credit and that portion is not

NEW LAW EXPLAINED

allowed to calculate the new qualified plug-in electric drive vehicle credit (Code Secs. 30D(d)(1) and 38(b)(35), as added by the Emergency Economic Act of 2008). If the plug-in electric drive motor vehicle is considered personal property the credit will be treated as if it is part of the nonrefundable personal credits under subpart A of the Internal Revenue Code (Code Sec. 30D(d)(2), as added by the Emergency Economic Act of 2008). This treatment allows the credit to be claimed against both a taxpayer's regular tax and minimum tax liabilities in years that Code Sec. 26(a)(2) applies. In the years that Code Sec. 26(a)(2) does not apply, the claimed credit amount for the qualified plug-in electric drive motor vehicle credit cannot exceed the excess of the sum of the regular tax liability (defined in Code Sec. 26(b)) plus the minimum tax liability over the sum of the nonrefundable personal credits less this credit, the child tax credit, the residential energy efficient property credit and the foreign tax credit (Code Sec. 30D(d)(2)(B), as added by the Emergency Economic Act of 2008).

> **Comment:** This is a significant difference from the alternative motor vehicle credit under Code Sec. 30B. Currently, the credit amount of the alternative motor vehicle credit is limited to the excess of the regular tax liability over the alternative minimum tax liability.

Property used by tax-exempt entity. Similar to the alternative motor vehicle credit, if the plug-in electric drive motor vehicle will be used by a tax-exempt organization or governmental unit, the seller of the vehicle may claim the credit provided the seller clearly discloses in writing to the entity the amount of any credit allowable with respect to the vehicle (Code Sec. 30D(6), as added by the Emergency Economic Act of 2008).

Basis. The basis of a new qualified plug-in electric drive motor vehicle will be reduced by the amount of any credit claimed (Code Sec. 30D(e)(4), as added by the Emergency Economic Act of 2008).

Disqualified property. No new qualified plug-in electric drive motor vehicle credit is allowed for property used predominately outside of the United States or for any portion of the cost of such vehicle taken into account as a deduction for clean-fuel vehicles under Code Sec. 179 (Code Sec. 30D(e)(7), as added by the Emergency Economic Act of 2008). Furthermore, a new qualified plug-in electric drive motor vehicle that is used to claim the plug-in electric drive motor vehicle credit may not be used to claim an alternative motor vehicle credit (Code Sec. 30B(d)(3)(D), as added by the Emergency Economic Act of 2008).

> **Comment:** Without the disqualification discussed, above, a qualified plug-in electric drive motor vehicle could potentially qualify as a hybrid motor vehicle under the alternative motor vehicle credit.

In addition, any other deduction or credit that a qualified plug-in electric drive motor vehicle may qualify for will be reduced by the amount of credit claimed under this plug-in electric drive motor vehicle credit (Code Sec. 30D(e)(5), as added by the Emergency Economic Act of 2008).

Termination. The credit does not apply to the purchase of new qualified plug-in electric drive motor vehicles after December 31, 2014 (Code Sec. 30D(g), as added by the Emergency Economic Act of 2008).

¶515

NEW LAW EXPLAINED

Election. Taxpayers can elect not to claim the new qualified plug-in electric drive motor vehicle credit (Code Sec. 30D(e)(9), as added by the Emergency Economic Act of 2008).

> **Comment:** The language used to allow a taxpayer to elect out of claiming this credit indicates an affirmative action. Practitioners should attach a statement to the return for the tax year a new qualified plug-in electric drive motor vehicle is placed in service until the IRS issues guidance on this election.

Conforming amendments. The general tax liability limitation on the amount of nonrefundable personal tax credits that may be claimed has led Congress to create special tax liability limitation rules for specific credits to insure that taxpayers receive the benefits of these tax credits. To insure that the tax benefits will continue for certain credits in view of the special tax liability limitation on the credit for qualified plug-in electric drive motor vehicles, the following credits were amended: the child tax credit, the mortgage interest certificate credit, the retirement saving contribution credit, and the first-time District of Columbia homebuyer credit (Code Sec. 24(b)(3)(B), Code Sec. 25(e)(1)(C)(ii), Code Sec. 25B(g)(2), Code Sec. 26(a)(1) and Code Sec. 1400C(d)(2), as amended by the Emergency Economic Act of 2008).

> **Caution:** The conforming amendment to the child tax credit is subject to a sunset provision under section 901 of the Economic Growth and Tax Relief Reconciliation Act of 2001 (P.L. 107-16) (Division B, Act Sec. 205(f) of the Emergency Economic Act of 2008).

Regulations. The Secretary of the Treasury is to issue regulations providing for the recapture of the new qualified plug-in electric drive motor vehicle credit benefit in the event the property ceases to be eligible property (Code Sec. 30D(e)(8), as added by the Emergency Economic Act of 2008). The Secretary of the Treasury is also authorized to act in conjunction with the Secretary of Transportation and the Administrator of the Environmental Protection Agency to provide regulations detailing the motor vehicle requirements that must be met for this credit (Code Sec. 30D(f), as added by the Emergency Economic Act of 2008).

▶ **Effective date.** The amendments made by this section apply to tax years beginning after December 31, 2008 (Division B, Act Sec. 205(e) of the Emergency Economic Stabilization Act of 2008 (P.L. 110-343)).

Law source: Law at ¶5010, ¶5015, ¶5020, ¶5035, ¶5040, ¶5050, ¶5055, ¶5350, ¶5385 and ¶5465. Committee Reports at ¶10,170.

— Division B, Act Sec. 205(a) of the Emergency Economic Stabilization Act of 2008, adding Code Sec. 30D;

— Division B, Act Sec. 205(b), adding Code Sec. 30B(d)(3)(D);

— Division B, Act Sec. 205(c), adding Code Sec. 38(b)(35);

— Division B, Act Sec. 205(d)(1), amending Code Secs. 24(b)(3)(B), 25(e)(1)(C)(ii), 25B(g)(2), 26(a)(1) and 1400C(d)(2);

— Division B, Act Sec. 205(d)(2), adding Code Sec. 1016(a)(37);

— Division B, Act Sec. 205(d)(3), amending Code Sec. 6501(m);

— Division B, Act Sec. 205(e), providing the effective date.

¶515

NEW LAW EXPLAINED

Reporter references: For further information, consult the following CCH reporters.

— Standard Federal Tax Reporter, ¶4059E.01

— Tax Research Consultant, INDIV: 57,702 and BUSEXP: 54,000

— Federal Tax Guide, ¶2290

¶520 Alternative Fuel Vehicle Refueling Property Credit

SUMMARY OF NEW LAW

The alternative fuel vehicle refueling property credit is extended through December 31, 2010 and, for purposes of the credit, the definition of a clean-burning fuel is modified to include electricity.

BACKGROUND

A credit for the installation of alternative fuel vehicle refueling property used in a trade or business or installed at the taxpayer's residence, applies to property placed in service after December 31, 2005 (Code Sec. 30C). To qualify, the property must be depreciable, except if the refueling property is installed on residential property. The property must also be used for the storage or dispensing of a clean-burning fuel at the location where the fuel is delivered into the vehicle.

For purposes of the alternative fuel vehicle refueling property credit, the alternative fuel must either consist of (1) 85 percent by volume of ethanol, natural gas, compressed natural gas, liquefied natural gas, liquefied petroleum gas or hydrogen, or (2) any mixture of biodiesel, diesel fuel and/or kerosene or at least 20 percent by volume of biodiesel without regard to kerosene (Code Sec. 30C(1)).

The credit is equal to 30 percent of the cost of the property placed in service at each location by the taxpayer during the tax year. However, the credit is limited to $30,000 for depreciable property (such as a commercial or retail refueling station) and $1,000 for any other property (such as refueling property installed at a residence) (Code Sec. 30C(b)).

The alternative fuel vehicle refueling property credit does not apply to property placed in service after December 31, 2009 (or December 31, 2014 for hydrogen refueling property) (Code Sec. 30C(g)).

NEW LAW EXPLAINED

Alternative fuel vehicle refueling property credit extended and modified.—The alternative fuel vehicle refueling property credit is extended to apply to refueling property (other than property relating to hydrogen) placed in service through Decem-

NEW LAW EXPLAINED

ber 31, 2010 (Code Sec. 30C (g) (2), as amended by the Emergency Economic Stabilization Act of 2008 (P.L. 110-343)).

> **Caution:** The extension of the alternative fuel vehicle refueling property credit does not apply to property relating to refueling hydrogen. The alternative fuel vehicle refueling property credit continues to apply to refueling hydrogen property placed in service through December 31, 2014.

> **Compliance Tip:** The alternative fuel vehicle refueling property credit is claimed on Form 8911, Alternative Fuel Vehicle Refueling Property Credit.

Clean-burning fuel modified. The definition of a clean-burning fuel for purposes of the credit is modified to include electricity (Code Sec. 30C(c)(2)(C), as added by the Emergency Economic Act). As a result, the alternative fuel vehicle refueling property credit applies to property installed for the recharging of an electronically propelled vehicle placed in service before January 1, 2011.

▶ **Effective date.** The provision applies to property placed in service after October 3, 2008 in tax years ending after October 3, 2008 (Division B, Act Sec. 207(c) of the Emergency Economic Stabilization Act of 2008 (P.L. 110-343)).

Law source: Law at ¶5045. Committee Reports at ¶10,190.

— Division B, Act Sec. 207(a) of the Emergency Economic Stabilization Act of 2008, amending Code Sec. 30C(g)(2);

— Division B, Act Sec. 207(b), adding Code Sec. 30C(c)(2)(C);

— Division B, Act Sec. 207(c), providing the effective date.

Reporter references: For further information, consult the following CCH reporters.

— Standard Federal Tax Reporter, ¶4059K.05 and ¶4059K.021

— Tax Research Consultant, INDIV: 57,750 and INDIV: 57,754

— Federal Tax Guide, ¶2296

BUSINESS TAX CREDITS

¶525 Renewable Electricity Production Credit

SUMMARY OF NEW LAW

The placed in service date for the renewable electricity production credit is extended through December 31, 2009, in the case of wind and refined coal, and through December 31, 2010, in the case of other sources. The credit is also extended to facilities that generate electricity from marine renewables. Some definitions are updated, and the rules for the refined coal credit are modified.

BACKGROUND

An income tax credit is allowed for the production of electricity from qualified energy resources at qualified facilities (Code Sec. 45). Qualified energy resources include wind, closed-loop biomass, open-loop biomass, geothermal energy, solar energy, small irrigation power, municipal solid waste, and qualified hydropower production (Code Sec. 45(c)). Qualified facilities are generally facilities that generate electricity using qualified energy resources. To be eligible for the credit, electricity produced from qualified energy resources at qualified facilities must be sold by the taxpayer to an unrelated person. The base amount of the electricity production credit is 1.5 cents per kilowatt-hour (indexed annually for inflation) of electricity produced (Code Sec. 45(a)). The credit rate is reduced by one-half for electricity produced from open-loop biomass, small irrigation power, landfill gas, trash combustion and qualified hydropower facilities (Code Sec. 45(b)). The base amount of the credit is 2.1 cents per kilowatt-hour for 2008, and the reduced amount is one cent per hour (Notice 2008-48 I.R.B. 2008-21, 1008).

A taxpayer may generally claim a credit during the 10-year period commencing with the date the qualified facility is placed in service (Code Sec. 45(a)(2)(A)(ii)). The credit is reduced for grants, tax-exempt bonds, subsidized energy financing, and other credits. The amount of credit a taxpayer may claim is phased out as the market price of electricity exceeds certain threshold levels. No reduction applies to the credit for 2008 (Notice 2008-48 I.R.B. 2008-21, 1008).

In order to be eligible for the credit, the electricity must be produced at qualified facilities, which are defined as follows (Code Sec. 45(d)):

- A wind energy facility is a facility that uses wind to produce electricity. To be a qualified facility, a wind energy facility must be placed in service after December 31, 1993, and before January 1, 2009.

- A closed-loop biomass facility is a facility that uses any organic material from a plant which is planted exclusively for the purpose of being used at a qualifying facility to produce electricity. To be a qualified facility, a closed-loop biomass facility must be placed in service after December 31, 1992, and before January 1, 2009.

- A geothermal facility is a facility that uses geothermal energy to produce electricity. Geothermal energy is energy derived from a geothermal deposit that is a geothermal reservoir consisting of natural heat that is stored in rocks or in an aqueous liquid or vapor (whether or not under pressure). To be a qualified facility, a geothermal facility must be placed in service after October 22, 2004, and before January 1, 2009.

- A solar facility is a facility that uses solar energy to produce electricity. To be a qualified facility, a solar facility must be placed in service after October 22, 2004, and before January 1, 2006.

- A small irrigation power facility is a facility that generates electric power through an irrigation system canal or ditch without any dam or impoundment of water. The installed capacity of a qualified facility must be at least 150 kilowatts but less than five megawatts. To be a qualified facility, a small irrigation facility must be originally placed in service after October 22, 2004, and before January 1, 2009.

BACKGROUND

- A landfill gas facility is a facility that uses landfill gas to produce electricity. Landfill gas is defined as methane gas derived from the biodegradation of municipal solid waste. To be a qualified facility, a landfill gas facility must be placed in service after October 22, 2004, and before January 1, 2009.

- Trash combustion facilities are facilities that burn municipal solid waste (garbage) to produce steam to drive a turbine for the production of electricity. To be a qualified facility, a trash combustion facility must be placed in service after October 22, 2004, and before January 1, 2009. A qualified trash combustion facility includes a new unit, placed in service after October 22, 2004, that increases electricity production capacity at an existing trash combustion facility.

- A qualifying hydropower facility is (1) a facility that produced hydroelectric power (a hydroelectric dam) prior to August 8, 2005, at which efficiency improvements or additions to capacity have been made after such date and before January 1, 2009, that enable the taxpayer to produce incremental hydropower or (2) a facility placed in service before August 8, 2005, that did not produce hydroelectric power (a nonhydroelectric dam) on such date, and to which turbines or other electricity generating equipment have been added after such date and before January 1, 2009.

NEW LAW EXPLAINED

Renewable electricity credit extended and modified.—The placed in service date for purposes of the renewable electricity production tax credit in the case of qualified wind and refined coal production facilities is extended through December 31, 2009. The placed in service date is extended through December 31, 2010, in the case of facilities producing electricity from closed-loop biomass, open-loop biomass, geothermal or solar energy, small irrigation power, municipal solid waste, and from qualified hydropower (Code Sec. 45(d), as amended by the Emergency Economic Stabilization Act of 2008 (P.L. 110-343)).

Key Rates and Figures: The renewable electricity production credit for calendar year 2008 is 2.1 cents per kilowatt hour on sales of electricity produced from wind energy, closed-loop biomass, geothermal energy and solar energy, and 1.0 cent per kilowatt hour on sales of electricity produced from open-loop biomass, small irrigation power, landfill gas, trash combustion and qualified hydropower facilities (Notice 2008-48, I.R.B. 2008-21, 1008).

Marine renewables. Marine and hydrokinetic renewable energy is added as a qualified energy resource, and marine and hydrokinetic renewable energy facilities are added as qualified facilities. Marine and hydrokinetic renewable energy is energy derived from (1) waves, tides, and currents in oceans, estuaries, and tidal areas; (2) free flowing water in rivers, lakes, and streams; (3) free flowing water in an irrigation system, canal, or other man-made channel, including projects that utilize nonmechanical structures to accelerate the flow of water for electric power production purposes; or (4) differentials in ocean temperature (ocean thermal energy conversion). The term does not include energy derived from any source that uses a dam, diversionary structure (except for irrigation systems, canals, and other man-made channels), or

¶525

NEW LAW EXPLAINED

impoundment for electric power production (Code Sec. 45(c)(10), as added by Emergency Economic Act of 2008). A qualified marine and hydrokinetic renewable energy facility is any facility owned by the taxpayer and originally placed in service on or after October 3, 2008, and before January 1, 2012, that produces electric power from marine and hydrokinetic renewable energy and that has a nameplate capacity rating of at least 150 kilowatts (Code Sec. 45(d)(11), as added by Emergency Economic Act of 2008). Small irrigation power facilities, which were a separate category of qualified facilities, are subsumed into this new category for marine and hydrokinetic renewable energy facilities (Code Sec. 45(d)(5), as amended by the Emergency Economic Act of 2008). Electricity from marine renewables qualifies for the reduced amount of the base credit (Code Sec. 45(b)(4)(A), as amended by the Emergency Economic Act of 2008).

Hydropower production. For purposes of qualified hydropower production, the definition of nonhydroelectric dam is modified. Under the new definition, the nonhydroelectric dam must have been operated for flood control, navigation, or water supply purposes. The project can enlarge the diversion structure or bypass channel, or impound additional water from the natural stream channel. However, the project must be operated so that the water surface elevation at any given location and time be the same as would occur in absence of the project, subject to any license requirements aimed at improving the environmental quality of the affected waterway. The hydroelectric project installed on the nonhydroelectric dam must still be licensed by the Federal Energy Regulatory Commission and meet all other applicable environmental, licensing, and regulatory requirements, including applicable fish passage requirements (Code Sec. 45(c)(8), as amended by the Emergency Economic Act of 2008).

Open-loop and closed-loop biomass facilities. The definition of open-loop and closed-loop facilities is modified to include new power generation units placed in service at existing qualified facilities, but only to the extent of the increased amount of electricity produced at those facilities by reason of the new units (Code Sec. 45(d)(3), as amended by the Emergency Economic Act of 2008).

> **Compliance Tip:** The renewable electricity production credit is computed on Form 8835, Renewable Electricity Production Credit

Trash combustion facility modification. The definition of qualified trash combustion facility is clarified to permit facilities that use municipal solid waste as part of an electricity generation process to qualify for the electricity production credit, whether or not the facilities utilize a process that involves burning the waste (Code Sec. 45(d)(7), as amended by the Emergency Economic Act of 2008).

Modification of refined coal. The qualified reduction emission reductions standard for the refined coal credit is increased from 20 to 40 percent of the emissions of either sulfur dioxide or mercury released when burning the refined coal. The market value test is also eliminated (Code Sec. 45(c)(7)(A)(i) and (B), as amended by the Emergency Economic Act of 2008).

Steel industry fuel. Steel industry fuel is added to the definition of refined coal for purposes of the credit (Code Sec. 45(c)(7)(A), as amended by the Emergency Economic Act of 2008). Steel industry fuel is fuel that is (1) produced through a process

NEW LAW EXPLAINED

of liquefying coal waste sludge and distributing it on coal, and (2) used as a feedstock for the manufacture of coke. Coal waste sludge is the tar decanter sludge and related byproducts of the coking process, including such materials that have been stored in ground, in tanks and in lagoons that have been treated as hazardous wastes under applicable federal environmental rules absent liquefaction and processing with coal into a feedstock for the manufacture of coke (Code Sec. 45(c)(7)(C), as added the Emergency Economic Act of 2008).

Several modifications apply to the credit for steel industry fuel. First, the credit is increased by an amount equal to $2 (as adjusted for inflation) per barrel of oil equivalent (5,800,000 BTUs) instead of $4.375 per ton of qualified refined coal. Also, the normal 10-year credit period for refined coal is replaced. The new credit period begins on the later of (1) the date the facility is originally placed in service, or (2) the placed-in-service date of modifications to an existing facility that allow it to produce steel industry fuel, on October 1, 2008. The credit period ends on the later of (1) December 1, 2009, or (2) one year after the date the facility or modifications were placed in service. Finally, there is no phase out of this credit amount (Code Sec. 45(e)(8)(D)(ii), as added the Emergency Economic Act of 2008).

> **Comment:** There appears to be a clerical error in the amendments related to the inflation adjustment for the steel industry fuel credit. As discussed above, Code Sec. 45(e)(8)(D)(ii)(I) provides that the credit is increased by an amount equal to $2 per barrel of oil equivalent. However, the amendment to Code Sec. 45(b)(2), which adjusts this increase for inflation, refers to a $3 amount, rather than a $2 amount.

The credit for steel industry fuel is also coordinated with other provisions. Steel industry fuel is exempt from the rule that eliminates the refined coal credit when production from the facility was eligible for the nonconventional fuel source credit for any tax year under Code Sec. 45K (Code Sec. 45(e)(9)(B)(ii) as added by the Emergency Economic Act of 2008). However, the steel industry fuel credit is not allowed if the taxpayer is allowed the nonconventional fuel credit for the same fuel (Code Sec. 45K(g)(2)(E), as added by the Emergency Economic Act of 2008).

▶ **Effective date.** The extension of the electricity production credit applies to property originally placed in service after December 31, 2008. The amendments relating to the modification of refined coal as a qualified energy resource apply to coal produced and sold from facilities placed in service after December 31, 2008. The amendments concerning trash facility clarification apply to electricity produced and sold after October 3, 2008, the date of enactment. The amendments concerning the expansion of biomass facilities apply to property placed in service after October 3, 2008 (Division B, Act Sec. 101(f) of the Emergency Economic Stabilization Act of 2008 (P.L. 110-343)). The addition of marine and hydrokinetic renewable energy as a qualified energy resource applies to electricity produced and sold after October 3, 2008, in tax years ending after October 3, 2008 (Division B, Act Sec.102(f) of the Emergency Economic Act of 2008). The amendments to the refined coal production facilities provision apply to fuel produced and sold after September 30, 2008 (Division B, Act Sec. 108(e) of the Emergency Economic Act of 2008).

¶525

NEW LAW EXPLAINED

Law source: Law at ¶5075. Committee Reports at ¶10,040.

— Division B, Act Sec.101(a) of the Emergency Economic Stabilization Act of 2008 , amending Code Sec. 45(d);

— Division B, Act Sec. 101(b), amending Code Sec. 45(c)(7)(A)(i) and Code Sec. 45(c)(7)(B);

— Division B, Act Sec. 101(c), amending Code Sec. 45(d)(7);

— Division B, Act Sec. 101(d), amending Code Sec. 45(d)(2) and Code Sec. 45(d)(3);

— Division B, Act Sec. 101(e)(1), amending Code Sec. 45(c)(8)(C);

— Division B, Act Sec. 102(a), amending Code Sec. 45(c)(1);

— Division B, Act Sec. 102(b), adding Code Sec. 45(c)(10);

— Division B, Act Sec. 102(c), adding Code Sec. 45(d)(11);

— Division B, Act Sec. 102(d), amending Code Sec. 45(b)(4)(A);

— Division B, Act Sec. 108(a), amending Code Sec. 45(c)(7)(A) and adding Code Sec. 45(c)(7)(C);

— Division B, Act Sec. 108(b), adding Code Sec. 45(e)(8)(D) and amending Code Sec. 45(b)(2);

— Division B, Act Sec. 108(c), amending Code Sec. 45(d)(8);

— Division B, Act Sec. 108(d), amending Code Sec. 45(e)(9)(B) and adding Code Sec. 45K(g)(2)(E);

— Division B, Act Secs. 101(f), 102(f) and 108(e), providing the effective date.

Reporter references: For further information, consult the following CCH reporters.

— Standard Federal Tax Reporter, ¶4415.03

— Tax Research Consultant, BUSEXP: 54,550

— Federal Tax Guide, ¶2575

¶530 Energy Investment Credit

SUMMARY OF NEW LAW

The 30-percent investment tax credit for solar energy property and qualified fuel cell property and the 10-percent investment tax credit for microturbines are extended through 2016. A new 10-percent tax credit applies to combined heat and power systems and geothermal heat pumps. A new 30-percent tax credit applies to small wind energy property. Public utility property also becomes eligible for the credit. The $500 per half kilowatt of capacity cap for qualified fuel cells is increased to $1,500 per half kilowatt of capacity. These credits may be used to offset the alternative minimum tax.

BACKGROUND

The nonrefundable business energy credit is 10 percent of the taxpayer's basis in stationery microturbine property and other energy property placed in service during the tax year. A 30-percent credit applies for (1) qualified fuel cell property, (2) equipment that uses solar energy to generate electricity to heat or cool a structure (including provide hot water) or provide solar process heat, and (3) equipment that illuminates the inside of a structure using fiber-optic distributed sunlight (Code Sec. 48(a)). Qualified fuel cell property and microturbine property do not include any property for periods after December 31, 2008 (Code Sec. 48(c)(1)(E) and (c)(2)(E)). Furthermore, the 30 percent credit for property that uses solar energy to generate electricity to heat or cool a structure (including provide hot water) or provide solar process heat or that illuminates the inside of a structure using fiber-optic distributed sunlight applies only for periods beginning before January 1, 2009. For periods beginning on or after January 1, 2009, the credit for property that uses solar energy to generate electricity to heat or cool a structure (including provide hot water) or provide solar process heat, is reduced from 30 percent to 10 percent (Code Sec. 48(a)(2)(A)(i)(II) and (3)(A)(i)). The 30-percent credit for property that uses solar energy to illuminate the inside of a structure using fiber-optic distributed sunlight applies only for periods beginning before January 1, 2009 (Code Sec. 48(a)(2)(A)(i)(III), (3)(A)(ii)). In general, public utility property is not eligible for the credit (Code Sec. 48(a)(3)). The credit for qualified fuel cell property may not exceed $500 for each 0.5 kilowatt of capacity (Code Sec. 48(c)(1)(D)). The energy credit under Code Sec. 48 is one component of the general business tax credit, and as such is subject to the alternative minimum tax (Code Sec. 38(b)(1)).

NEW LAW EXPLAINED

Energy credit extended and expanded.—The expiring provisions of the energy credit are extended for eight years, through December 31, 2016 (Code Sec. 48(a)(2)(A)(i)(II), Code Sec. 48(a)(3)(A)(ii), Code Sec. 48(c)(1)(D)) and Code Sec. 48(c)(2)(D), as amended by the Emergency Economic Stabilization Act of 2008 (P.L. 110-343)). The $500 per half kilowatt of capacity credit cap with respect to fuel cell property is increased to $1,500 per half kilowatt of capacity (Code Sec. 48(c)(1)(B), as amended by the Emergency Economic Act of 2008). In addition, the restrictions on public utility property being eligible for the credit are repealed (Code Sec. 48(a)(3), as amended by the Emergency Economic Act of 2008). The provision makes the energy credit allowable against the alternative minimum tax (Code Sec. 38(c)(4)(B)(v), as added by the Emergency Economic Act of 2008).

Combined heat and power property eligible for credit. Combined heat and power system property is eligible for the 10-percent energy credit through December 31, 2016 (Code Sec. 48(a)(3)(v), as added by the Emergency Economic Act of 2008).

Combined heat and power system (CHPS) property is property: (1) that uses the same energy source for the simultaneous or sequential generation of electrical power, mechanical shaft power, or both, in combination with the generation of steam or other forms of useful thermal energy (including heating and cooling applications); (2) that

NEW LAW EXPLAINED

produces at least 20 percent of its total useful energy in the form of thermal energy that is not used to produce electrical or mechanical power (or a combination thereof), and produces at least 20 percent of its total useful energy in the form of electrical or mechanical power (or a combination thereof); and (3) the energy efficiency percentage of which exceeds 60 percent (Code Sec. 48(c)(3)(A), as added by the Emergency Economic Act of 2008). CHPS property does not include property used to transport the energy source to the generating facility or to distribute energy produced by the facility (Code Sec. 48(c)(3)(C)(iii), as added by the Emergency Economic Act of 2008).

> **Practical Analysis:** Charles R. Goulding, J.D., CPA, MBA, President and founder of Energy Tax Savers Inc., observes that Division B, Act Sec. 103 of the Emergency Economic Stabilization Act of 2008 (P.L. 110-343) now includes Combined Heat and Power or CHP systems. CHP systems are commonly called cogeneration systems whereby heat and electricity is generated in an integrated system. These systems currently account for approximately seven percent of U.S. electricity generation capacity. Because a CHP system captures the heat that would otherwise be rejected in the traditional generation of power, the total efficiency of these systems is much greater than from separate systems. CHP systems generate a fraction of the nitrogen oxides that conventional systems do. As result of the potential energy efficiency and the greenhouse gas reduction both the U.S. Department of Energy and the Environmental Protection Agency have the achievable goal of doubling the number of these CHP systems in the United States.

The energy efficiency percentage of a system is a fraction, the numerator of which is the total useful electrical, thermal, and mechanical power produced by the system at normal operating rates, and expected to be consumed in its normal application, and the denominator of which is the lower heating value of the fuel sources for the system. The energy efficiency percentage is determined on a Btu basis (Code Sec. 48(c)(3)(C), as added by the Emergency Economic Act of 2008).

The otherwise allowable credit with respect to CHPS property is reduced to the extent the property has an electrical capacity or mechanical capacity in excess of any applicable limits. Property in excess of the applicable limit (15 megawatts or a mechanical energy capacity of more than 20,000 horsepower or an equivalent combination of electrical and mechanical energy capacities) is permitted to claim a fraction of the otherwise allowable credit. The fraction is equal to the applicable limit divided by the capacity of the property. For example, a 45 megawatt property would be eligible to claim 15/45ths, or one third, of the otherwise allowable credit. No credit is allowed if the system has a capacity of more than 50 megawatts or 67,000 horsepower (Code Sec. 48(c)(3)(B), as added by the Emergency Economic Act of 2008).

Systems whose fuel source is at least 90 percent open-loop biomass and that would qualify for the credit but for the failure to meet the efficiency standard are eligible for a credit that is reduced in proportion to the degree to which the system fails to meet the efficiency standard. For example, a system that would otherwise be required to meet the 60-percent efficiency standard, but which only achieves 30-percent efficiency, would

NEW LAW EXPLAINED

be permitted a credit equal to one-half of the otherwise allowable credit (i.e., a five-percent credit) (Code Sec. 48(c)(3)(D), as added by the Emergency Economic Act of 2008).

Practical Analysis: Glenn Graff, J.D., Partner in the firm of Applegate & Thorne-Thomsen, PC, Chicago, Illinois, states that unlike some of the other tax credits that were extended only through 2009 by the Emergency Economic Stabilization Act of 2008 (P.L. 110-343), Division B, Act Sec. 103(a) of the Act extends the energy credit under Code Sec. 48 for solar energy property through the end of 2016. Previously investment in qualifying solar energy property was being impacted by the impending reduction of the credit from 30 to 10 percent at the end of 2008. The extension of the credit through 2016 should provide a stable investment atmosphere for taxpayers looking to acquire solar energy property.

Division B, Act Sec. 103(b) of the Emergency Economic Act of 2008, allowing the energy credit to apply against the alternative minimum tax, should broaden the appeal of the credit. Previously some investors were reluctant to invest in energy credit property because they were either subject to the alternative minimum tax or feared that they might become subject to it at the time the credits were generated. This should especially help in situations where the energy credits are syndicated through investment partnerships as more investors may be interested in the credits and that could help lead to a slightly higher price for the credit.

Combined heat and power systems, also known as "cogeneration systems," result in a very efficient use of power. Systems that create only power generally results in waste heat, which is not put to use. In a cogeneration system, the excess heat is used to produce heat or cooling and results in a much more efficient use of the energy created. The expansion of the energy credit in Division B, Act Sec. 103(b) of the Emergency Economic Act of 2008 to include combined heat and cooling systems should help incentivize taxpayers to invest in such facilities and make more efficient use of fossil fuels.

Energy credit expanded to include qualified small wind energy property. A new 30 percent credit is available for qualified small wind energy property expenses made by the taxpayer during the tax year (Code Secs. 48(a)(2)(A)(i)(IV) and (3)(A)(vi), as added by the Emergency Economic Act of 2008). The credit is limited to $4,000 for the tax year and is allowed for property placed in service prior to January 1, 2017 (Code Sec. 48(c)(4), as added by the Emergency Economic Act of 2008).

Qualified small wind energy property is property that uses a qualifying small wind turbine (one with a nameplate capacity of not more than 100 kilowatts) to generate electricity (Code Sec. 48(c)(4), as added by the Emergency Economic Act of 2008).

Energy credit allowed for geothermal heat pump systems. A 10-percent credit for geothermal heat pump systems is allowed for periods ending before January 1, 2017. Such systems include any equipment that uses the ground or ground water as a thermal energy source to heat a structure (Code Sec. 48(a)(3)(A)(vii), as added by the Emergency Economic Act of 2008).

¶530

NEW LAW EXPLAINED

▶ **Effective date.** The provision relating to the extension of the energy credit is effective on October 3, 2008, the date of enactment (Division B, Act Sec. 103(f)(1) of the Emergency Economic Stabilization Act of 2008 (P.L. 110-343)).

The provision relating to the allowance of the energy credit against the alternative minimum tax applies to credits determined under Code Sec. 46 in tax years beginning after October 3, 2008, and to carrybacks of such credits (Division B, Act Sec. 103(f)(2) of the Emergency Economic Act of 2008).

The provision relating to public utility property apply to periods after February 13, 2008, in taxable years ending after such date, under rules similar to those in Code Sec. 48(m), as in effect on the day before the enactment of the Revenue Reconciliation Act of 1990 (Division B, Act Sec. 103(f)(4) of the Emergency Economic Act of 2008).

The (1) combined heat and power and fuel cell property provisions, (2) the credit for small wind property, and (3) the credit for geothermal heat pump systems, apply to periods after October 3, 2008, in tax years ending after such date, under rules similar to those in Code Sec. 48(m), as in effect on the day before the enactment of the Revenue Reconciliation Act of 1990 (Division B, Act Secs. 103(f)(3), 104(e) and 105(b) of the Emergency Economic Act of 2008).

Law source: Law at ¶5055 and ¶5125. Committee Reports at ¶10,050.

— Division B, Act Sec. 103(a)(1) of the Emergency Economic Stabilization Act of 2008 (P.L. 110-343), amending Code Sec. 48;

— Division B, Act Secs. 103(a)(2) and (3) and 104(c), amending Code Sec. 48(c);

— Division B, Act Sec. 103(b)(1) and (2), amending Code Sec. 38(c)(4);

— Division B, Act Sec. 103(c), (d), and (e), amending Code Sec. 48;

— Division B, Act Secs. 104(a), (b), and (d) and 105(a), amending Code Sec. 48(a);

— Division B, Act Sec. 105(a), amending Code Sec. 48(a)(3)(A).

— Division B, Act Secs. 103(f), 104(e) and 105(b), providing the effective dates.

Reporter references: For further information, consult the following CCH reporters.

— Standard Federal Tax Reporter, ¶4671.01

— Tax Research Consultant, BUSEXP: 51,100

— Federal Tax Guide, ¶2725

¶535 Credit for New Energy-Efficient Homes

SUMMARY OF NEW LAW

The credit available to contractors for the construction or manufacture of a new energy efficient homes is extended through December 31, 2009.

BACKGROUND

As part of the general business credit, a contractor may claim a tax credit of $1,000 or $2,000 for the construction or manufacture of qualified new energy-efficient home (Code Secs. 38(b)(23) and 45L(a)). Substantial construction of a qualified new energy efficient home must be completed after August 8, 2005, and the home must be acquired from an eligible contractor during 2006, 2007, or 2008 by a person for use as a residence during the tax year. The home must also be located in the United States and meet the applicable energy-savings requirements.

The applicable amount of the credit depends on the energy savings achieved by the home. The maximum credit is $2,000 for homes and manufactured homes that meet more rigorous energy requirements. Manufactured homes that meet a less demanding test can qualify for a $1,000 credit. A qualified new energy efficient home must also receive a written certification that describes its energy-saving features. The taxpayer's basis in property is reduced by the amount of any new energy efficient home credit allowed with respect to that property.

The homebuilder's credit is a part of the general business credit (Code Sec. 38(b)(23)). Expenditures taken into account under the rehabilitation and energy components of the investment tax credit are not taken into account under the energy-efficient home credit. The credit generally can be carried back for one year, and carried forward for 20 years, but it cannot be carried back to a tax year ending before 2006 (Code Sec. 39). Any portion of the new energy efficient home credit that remains unused at the end of the carryover period may be deducted (Code Sec. 196(c)(13)). The credit does not apply to any home acquired after December 31, 2008 (Code Sec. 45L(g)).

NEW LAW EXPLAINED

Credit for new energy-efficient homes extended.—The credit available to contractors for the construction or manufacture of new energy efficient homes is extended for one year. Accordingly, the credit expires for energy efficient homes acquired after December 31, 2009 (Code Sec. 45L(g), as amended by the Emergency Economic Stabilization Act of 2008 (P.L. 110-343)).

▶ **Effective date.** No specific effective date is provided by the Act. The provision is, therefore, considered effective on October 3, 2008, the date of enactment.

Law source: Law at ¶5105.

— Division B, Act Sec. 304 of the Emergency Economic Stabilization Act of 2008 (P.L. 110-343), amending Code Sec. 45L(g).

Reporter references: For further information, consult the following CCH reporters.

— Standard Federal Tax Reporter, ¶4500L.01 and ¶4500L.021

— Tax Research Consultant, BUSEXP: 55,352

— Federal Tax Guide, ¶2604

¶535

¶540 Energy Efficient Appliance Production Credit

SUMMARY OF NEW LAW

The credit allowed for the manufacture of energy efficient dishwashers, clothes washers, and refrigerators is extended through 2010. Additionally, the standards that the manufactured appliances must meet for application of the credit are modified.

BACKGROUND

The general business credit (under Code Sec. 38) is a limited nonrefundable credit against income tax that is claimed after all other nonrefundable credits (except the Code Sec. 53 credit for prior year alternative minimum tax). The general business credit for a tax year is the sum of: (1) the business credit carryforwards to such year; (2) the amount of the current year business credits; and (3) the business credit carrybacks for such year (Code Sec. 38(a)). The list of specific credits frequently changes from year to year as individual credits are added or expire. For credits arising in tax years beginning after 1997, any unused general business credit generally may be carried back one year and carried forward 20 years (Code Sec. 39).

The Energy Tax Incentives Act of 2005 (P.L. 109-58) added a new credit for the manufacture of energy-efficient appliances, applicable to appliances produced after December 31, 2005. This credit applies only to energy-efficient dishwashers, clothes washers and refrigerators. The credit is a part of the general business credit and is used to determine a taxpayer's current year business credit (Code Sec. 38(b)(24)). The total amount of credit available for a tax year is equal to the sum of the credit amount separately calculated for each type of qualified energy-efficient appliance produced by the taxpayer during the calendar year ending with or within that tax year. The credit amount for each type of qualified appliance is determined by multiplying the eligible production for that type of appliance by the type's applicable amount (Code Sec. 45M(a)(2)).

Practical Analysis: Charles R. Goulding, J.D., CPA, MBA, President and founder of Energy Tax Savers Inc., observes that Division B, Act Sec. 305 of the Emergency Economic Stabilization Act of 2008 (P.L. 110-343) provides appliance manufacturers with per-unit tax credits for qualifying energy efficient appliances. It is our view that appliance manufacturers might expect future tax guidance regarding qualifying appliances in terms of actual specifications necessary to qualify for these credits.

Because of the current severe housing downturn affecting the durable goods sector, these incentives for manufacturers of dishwashers, clothes washers and refrigerators will not have the impact they would have had during normal times.

Dishwashers. In order for a manufactured dishwasher to meet the required standard for application of this credit, the dishwasher must be manufactured during calendar year 2006 or 2007 and meet the requirements of the Federal energy conservation standards (Energy Star program) as in effect for dishwashers in 2007 (Code Sec. 45M(b)(1)(A)).

BACKGROUND

For this purpose, a "dishwasher" means a residential dishwasher that is subject to the Department of Energy conservation standards (Code Sec. 45M(f)(2)). The applicable amount for qualified dishwashers is the energy savings amount, which is equal to the lesser of $100 or the product of $3 and 100 multiplied by the energy savings percentage. The energy savings percentage is the ratio of: (1) the energy factor (EF) established by the Department of Energy for compliance with the Energy Star program for dishwashers in 2007, minus the EF required by the Energy Star program for dishwashers in 2005; to (2) the EF required by the Energy Star program for dishwashers in 2007 (Code Sec. 45M(b)(2)).

Clothes washers. In order for a manufactured clothes washer to meet the required standard for application of the energy-efficient appliance credit, the clothes washer must be manufactured during calendar year 2006 or 2007 and meet the requirements of the Energy Star program as in effect for clothes washers in 2007 (Code Sec. 45M(b)(1)(B)). The clothes washer must be a residential clothes washer, and this includes residential style coin-operated washers (Code Sec. 45M(f)(3)). The applicable amount for qualified clothes washers in determining the credit is $100 (Code Sec. 45M(b)(1)(B)).

Refrigerators. In order for a manufactured refrigerator to meet the required standard for application of the energy-efficient appliance credit, the refrigerator must have an interior volume of at least 16.5 cubic feet and be equipped with automatic defrost for the refrigerator and freezer compartments (Code Sec. 45M(f)(4)). For purposes of calculating the energy-efficient appliance credit, refrigerators may fall into one of three types, each with a different applicable amount:

- If a refrigerator is manufactured during calendar year 2006 and consumes at least 15 percent—but not more than 20 percent—less kilowatt hours per year than the conservation standards for refrigerators promulgated by the Department of Energy that took effect on July 1, 2001, then the applicable amount for purposes of calculating the credit is $75 (Code Sec. 45M(b)(1)(C)(i)).

- If a refrigerator is manufactured during calendar years 2006 or 2007 and consumes at least 20 percent—but not more than 25 percent—less kilowatt hours per year than the 2001 energy conservation standards, then the applicable amount is $125 (Code Sec. 45M(b)(1)(C)(ii)).

- If a refrigerator is manufactured during calendar year 2006 or 2007 and consumes at least 25 percent less kilowatt hours per year than the 2001 energy conservation standards, then the applicable amount is $175 (Code Sec. 45M(b)(1)(C)(iii)).

Eligible production. The eligible production amount for a particular type of energy-efficient appliance is determined by subtracting the average number of qualified appliances described above that the taxpayer produced during the preceding three-calendar-year period from the number of appliances of the same type that the taxpayer produced during the applicable calendar year. For this purpose, only qualified appliances produced in the United States apply (Code Sec. 45M(c)(1)).

A special rule applies to calculating eligible production for refrigerators. For this type of appliance, eligible production is determined by subtracting 110 percent of the average

BACKGROUND

number of qualified refrigerators that the taxpayer produced during the preceding three-calendar-year period from the number of qualified refrigerators that the taxpayer produced during the applicable calendar year. Again, only qualified refrigerators produced in the United States apply (Code Sec. 45M(c)(2)).

Limitations. The maximum amount of the credit allowable to a taxpayer is capped at $75 million per tax year for all qualifying appliances manufactured during that year (Code Sec. 45M(e)(1)). In each subsequent year, the cap is reduced by the amount (if any) of the credit used in any prior tax year. Of that $75 million (or reduced) cap, no more than $20 million of credit amount in a single tax year may result from the manufacture of refrigerators to which the $75 applicable amount applies (i.e., refrigerators that are at least 15 percent but no more than 20 percent below 2001 energy conservation standards) (Code Sec. 45M(e)(2)).

In addition to the $75 million cap on the credit allowed, the overall credit amount claimed for a particular tax year may not exceed two percent of the taxpayer's average annual gross receipts for the preceding three tax years (Code Sec. 45M(e)(3)). For this purpose, the aggregation rules under Code Sec. 448(c)(2) and (3) for determining a taxpayer's eligibility to use the cash method of accounting apply in determining the taxpayer's gross receipts. For example, all persons will be treated as a single employer under the controlled group rules. In addition, all persons treated as a single employer under the controlled group rules of Code Sec. 52 are treated as a single manufacturer for purposes of the credit.

NEW LAW EXPLAINED

Energy-efficient appliance credit extended and modified.—The credit allowed for the manufacture of energy-efficient dishwashers, clothes washers and refrigerators is extended through 2010. Additionally, the standards required for manufacturers to qualify for the energy-efficient appliance credit have been substantially modified for years after 2007, and the applicable amounts have also changed. (Code Sec. 45M, as amended by Division B, Act Sec. 305 of the Emergency Economic Stabilization Act of 2008 (P.L. 110-343)). Code Sec. 45M as originally enacted continues to apply for years appliances produced in 2006 and 2007, and this modified version applies to appliances produced in years 2008, 2009 and 2010 (Code Sec. 45M, as amended by the Emergency Economic Act of 2008).

> **Caution:** The credit is allowed only to *manufacturers* of energy-efficient appliances. Consumers are not eligible for the credit.

Dishwashers. In order for manufactured dishwashers to meet the required standard for application of this credit, the dishwashers must meet one of two standards:

- to qualify for the $45 applicable amount, the dishwasher must be manufactured during calendar year 2008 or 2009 and use no more than 324 kilowatt hours of electricity per year and 5.8 gallons of water per wash cycle (Code Sec. 45M(b)(1)(A), as amended by the Emergency Economic Act of 2008); or

NEW LAW EXPLAINED

- to qualify for the $75 applicable amount, the dishwasher must be manufactured during calendar years 2008, 2009, or 2010, and must use no more than 307 kilowatt hours per year and 5.0 gallons per cycle (increased to 5.5 gallons per cycle for dishwashers designed for greater than 12 place settings) (Code Sec. 45M(b)(1)(B), as amended by the Emergency Economic Act of 2008).

"Gallons per cycle" means the amount of water in gallons required to complete a normal cycle of the applicable dishwasher (Code Sec. 45M(b)(9), as added by the Emergency Economic Act of 2008).

Clothes washers. In order for manufactured clothes washers to meet the required standard for application of this credit, the clothes washers must meet one of four graduated standards:

- to qualify for the $75 applicable amount, the residential top-loading clothes washer must be manufactured during calendar year 2008 and (1) meet or exceed a 1.72 modified energy factor, and (2) not exceed an 8.0 water consumption factor (Code Sec. 45M(b)(2)(A), as amended by the Emergency Economic Act of 2008);

- to qualify for the $125 applicable amount, the residential top-loading clothes washer must be manufactured during calendar year 2008 or 2009 and (1) meet or exceed a 1.8 modified energy factor, and (2) not exceed a 7.5 water consumption factor (Code Sec. 45M(b)(2)(B), as amended by the Emergency Economic Act of 2008);

- to qualify for the $150 applicable amount, the residential or commercial clothes washer must be manufactured during calendar year 2008, 2009, or 2010 and (1) meet or exceed a 2.0 modified energy factor, and (2) not exceed a 6.0 water consumption factor (Code Sec. 45M(b)(2)(C), as amended by the Emergency Economic Act of 2008); or

- to qualify for the $250 applicable amount, the residential or commercial clothes washer must be manufactured during calendar year 2008, 2009, or 2010 and (1) meet or exceed a 2.2 modified energy factor, and (2) not exceed a 4.5 water consumption factor (Code Sec. 45M(b)(2)(D), as amended by the Emergency Economic Act of 2008).

The "modified energy factor" is established by the Department of Energy for compliance with the Federal energy conservation standard (Code Sec. 45M(f)(6), as redesignated and amended by the Emergency Economic Act of 2008). The "water consumption factor" is the quotient of the total weighted per-cycle water consumption divided by the cubic foot (or cubic liter) capacity of the clothes washer (Code Sec. 45M(f)(10), as added by the Emergency Economic Act of 2008).

Refrigerators. In order for manufactured refrigerators to meet the required standard for application of this credit, the refrigerators also must meet one of four graduated standards:

- to qualify for the $50 applicable amount, the refrigerator must be manufactured during calendar year 2008 and consume at least 20 percent but not more than 22.9 percent less kilowatt hours per year than the 2001 energy conservation standards (Code Sec. 45M(b)(3)(A), as amended by the Emergency Economic Act of 2008);

¶540

NEW LAW EXPLAINED

- to qualify for the $75 applicable amount, the refrigerator must be manufactured during calendar year 2008 or 2009 and consume at least 23 percent but no more than 24.9 percent less kilowatt hours per year than the 2001 energy conservation standards (Code Sec. 45M(b)(2)(B), as amended by the Emergency Economic Act of 2008);

- to qualify for the $100 applicable amount, the refrigerator must be manufactured during calendar year 2008, 2009 or 2010 and consume at least 25 percent but not more than 29.9 percent less kilowatt hours per year than the 2001 energy conservation standards (Code Sec. 45M(b)(2)(C), as amended by the Emergency Economic Act of 2008); or

- to qualify for the $200 applicable amount, the refrigerator must be manufactured during calendar year 2008, 2009, or 2010 and consume at least 30 percent less kilowatt hours per year than the 2001 energy conservation standards (Code Sec. 45M(b)(2)(D), as amended by the Emergency Economic Act of 2008).

Eligible production. The eligible production amount for a particular type of energy efficient appliance is determined by subtracting the average number of qualified appliances described above that the taxpayer produced during the base period from the number of appliances of the same type that the taxpayer produced during the applicable calendar year. Only qualified appliances produced in the United States apply. The base period has been reduced for 2008, 2009, and 2010 from the preceding three year period (for 2006 and 2007) to the preceding two year period (Code Sec. 45M(c)(1)(B), redesignated Code Sec. 45M(c)(2), as amended by the Emergency Economic Act of 2008).

> **Caution:** The special rule applicable for calculating the eligible production for refrigerators using 110 percent of the average number of qualified refrigerators produced during the base period has been eliminated for appliances produced after December 31, 2007 (Code Sec. 45M(c)(2), prior to removal by the Emergency Economic Act of 2008). Apparently, this was done to ensure that all energy-efficient appliances received similar treatment under this provision of the Code.

Credit amount limitations. The maximum amount of the credit allowable to a taxpayer is capped at $75 million per tax year for all qualifying appliances manufactured during that year (Code Sec. 45M(e)(1), as amended by the Emergency Economic Act of 2008)). In each subsequent year the cap is reduced by the amount (if any) of the credit used in any prior tax year. The limitation that no more than $20 million of credit amount in a single tax year may result from the manufacture of refrigerators to which the lowest applicable amount applied has been eliminated for appliances manufactured after December 31, 2007 (Code Sec. 45M(e)(2), prior to removal by the Emergency Economic Act of 2008). Instead, refrigerators and clothes washers to which the highest applicable amount applies ($200 for refrigerators and $250 for clothes washers) are not taken into account for purposes of the $75 million yearly cap (Code Sec. 45M(e)(2), as amended by the Emergency Economic Act of 2008).

▶ **Effective date.** The amendments made by this section will apply to appliances produced after December 31, 2007 (Division B, Act Sec. 305(f) of the Emergency Economic Stabilization Act of 2008 (P.L. 110-343).

NEW LAW EXPLAINED

Law source: Law at ¶5110. Committee Reports at ¶10,230.

— Division B, Act Sec. 305(a) of the Emergency Economic Stabilization Act of 2008 (P.L. 110-343), amending Code Sec. 45M(b);

— Division B, Act Sec. 305(b), amending Code Sec. 45M(c);

— Division B, Act Sec. 305(c), amending Code Sec. 45M(d);

— Division B, Act Sec. 305(d), amending Code Sec. 45M(e)(1) and (2);

— Division B, Act Sec. 305(e)(1), amending Code Sec. 45M(f)(1);

— Division B, Act Sec. 305(e)(2), amending Code Sec. 45M(f)(3);

— Division B, Act Sec. 305(e)(3), redesignating Code Sec. 45M(f)(4), (5), (6) and (7) as Code Sec. 45M(f)(5), (6), (7), (8), respectively, and adding new Code Sec. 45M(f)(4);

— Division B, Act Sec. 305(e)(4), amending Code Sec. 45M(f)(6), as redesignated;

— Division B, Act Sec. 305(e)(5), adding Code Sec. 45M(f)(9) and (10);

— Division B, Act Sec. 305(f), providing the effective date.

Reporter references: For further information, consult the following CCH reporters.

— Standard Federal Tax Reporter, ¶4500R.01

— Tax Research Consultant, BUSEXP: 55,400

— Federal Tax Guide, ¶2606

¶545 Advanced Coal Project Investment Credit

SUMMARY OF NEW LAW

The advanced coal project investment credit is increased to 30 percent and the IRS is authorized to allocate an additional $1.25 billion in credits to qualified projects that separate and sequester at least 65 percent of total carbon dioxide emissions.

BACKGROUND

The Energy Tax Incentives Act of 2005 (P.L. 109-58) added the qualifying advanced coal project credit (Code Sec. 48A) under the investment credit provisions of Code Sec. 46. The credit is available only to taxpayers who have applied for and received certification that their project satisfies the relevant requirements. The IRS and Energy Department jointly established programs to evaluate applications for such certifications using a competitive bidding process.

This investment tax credit is available for power generation projects that use integrated gasification combined cycle (IGCC) or other advanced coal-based electricity generating technologies. The credit amount is (1) 20 percent of the qualified investment for the tax year for IGCC projects, and (2) 15 percent of the qualified investment for projects using other advanced coal-based generation technologies (Code Sec. 48A(a)(1)).

BACKGROUND

Under the program, taxpayers seeking subsidies for their advanced coal projects will file applications for certification. Up to $1,300,000,000 in credits will be allocated to taxpayers whose applications for certification are approved. The IRS is authorized to allocate a maximum of $800,000,000 in credits for IGCC projects, and a maximum of $500,000,000 in credits for projects using other advanced coal-based generation technologies (Code Sec. 48A(d)(3)).

A project is a qualifying advanced coal project that may obtain certification if the IRS determines that: (1) the project uses an advanced coal-based generation technology to power a new electric generation unit or to refit or repower an existing electric generation unit (including an existing natural gas-fired combined cycle unit); (2) the fuel input for the project, when completed, will be at least 75-percent coal; (3) the electric generation unit or units at the project site will have a total nameplate generating capacity of at least 400 megawatts; (4) a majority of the output of the project is reasonably expected to be acquired or utilized; (5) the applicant/taxpayer provides evidence of ownership or control of a site of sufficient size to allow the proposed project to be constructed and to operate on a long term basis; and (6) the project will be located in the United States (Code Sec. 48A(e)(1)).

The IRS was instructed to give high priority to projects that included (1) greenhouse gas capture capability, (2) increased by-product utilization, and (3) other benefits (Code Sec. 48A(e)(3)(B)).

Taxpayers are eligible to apply for the credits during a three-year period beginning on the date the IRS established the program (Code Sec. 48A(d)(2)(A)).

NEW LAW EXPLAINED

Advanced coal project investment credit modified.—The modified amount of credits that may be allocated under the advanced coal project investment credit is increased from $1.3 billion to $2.55 billion (Code Sec. 48A(d)(3)(A), as amended by the Emergency Economic Stabilization Act of 2008 (P.L. 110-343)).

This additional allocation of $1.25 billion is authorized for advanced coal-based generation technology projects (Code Sec. 48A(d)((3)(B)(iii), as added by the Emergency Economic Act of 2008). The period for submitting an application for an allocation from the amount is the three-year period beginning at the earlier of the termination of the current certification program or a date prescribed by the IRS (Code Sec. 48A(d)(2)(A)(ii) as added by the Emergency Economic Act of 2008).

> **Comment:** The IRS established the certification program on February 21, 2006 (Notice 2006-24, I.R.B. 2006-11, 595.). By the original terms of the advanced coal project program, applicants would no longer be able to submit certification requests after February 21, 2009 (Code Sec. 48A(d)(2)(A), prior to amendment by the Emergency Economic Act of 2008). Unlike the Energy Tax Incentives Act of 2005 (P.L. 109-58), which required the IRS to establish the advanced coal project credit certification program within 180 days of the passage of the Energy Act, this legislation allows the IRS some flexibility in establishing the new program.

¶545

NEW LAW EXPLAINED

The amount of the new credit rate for advanced coal projects that qualify during the new three-year application period is increased to 30 percent of the qualified investment for the tax year (Code Sec. 48A(a)(3), as added by the Emergency Economic Act of 2008).

For any advanced coal project to receive certification during the new certification period, the project must include equipment that separates and sequesters at least 65 percent of the projects's total carbon dioxide emissions (Code Sec. 48A(d)(2)(A)(ii), as added by the Emergency Economic Act of 2008). This percentage increases to 70 percent if the credits are later reallocated by the IRS (Code Sec. 48A(e)(1)(G), as added by the Emergency Economic Act of 2008).

The IRS is required to give highest priority to projects that demonstrate the greatest separation and sequestration percentage of total carbon dioxide emissions (Code Sec. 48A(e)(3)(C), as added by the Emergency Economic Act of 2008). In addition, applicants who have a research partnerships with an eligible educational institution (as defined in Code Sec. 529(e)(5)) are also to receive high priority (Code Sec. 48A(e)(3)(B)(iii), as added by the Emergency Economic Act of 2008).

> **Comment:** The Heartland, Habitat, Harvest, and Horticulture Act of 2008 modified Code Sec. 48A by directing the IRS, with some exceptions, to modify the terms of any competitive certification award and any associated closing agreement where the modification was consistent with the objectives of the advanced coal project credit, was requested by the recipient of the certification award, and involved "moving the project to improve the potential to capture and sequester carbon dioxide emissions. . ."(Code Sec. 48A(h)).

The IRS is required to recapture the benefit of any allocated credit if the project fails to attain or maintain the carbon dioxide separation and sequestration requirements (Code Sec. 48A(i), as added by the Emergency Economic Act of 2008). In addition, the IRS is required to disclose which projects receive credit allocations, including the taxpayer's identity and credit amount (Code Sec. 48A(d)(5), as added by the Emergency Economic Act of 2008).

▶ **Effective date.** No specific effective date is provided by the Act, the provision is, therefore, considered effective on October 3, 2008, the date of enactment. The increased credit rate and the carbon dioxide separation and sequestration rules are effective with respect to these additional credits. (Act Sec. 111(e)(1) of the Emergency Economic Stabilization Act of 2008 (P.L. 110-343)). The disclosure of allocations provision applies to certifications made after October 3, 2008 (Act Sec. 111(e)(2) of the Emergency Economic Act of 2008).

Law source: Law at ¶5130. Committee Reports at ¶10,080.

— Division B, Act Sec. 111(a) of the Emergency Economic Stabilization Act of 2008 (P.L. 110-343), adding Code Sec. 48A(a)(3);

— Division B, Act Sec. 111(b), amending Code Sec. 48A(d)(3)(A);

— Division B, Act Sec. 111(c)(1) amending Code Sec. 48A(d)(3)(B);

— Division B, Act Sec. 111(c)(2), amending Code Sec. 48A(d)(2)(A);

— Division B, Act Sec. 111(c)(3), adding Code Sec. 48A(e)(1)(G), Code Sec. 48A(e)(3)(C) and Code Sec. 48A(i);

NEW LAW EXPLAINED

— Division B, Act Sec. 111(c)(4), adding Code Sec. 48A(e)(3)(B)(iii);

— Division B, Act Sec. 111(d), adding Code Sec. 48A(d)(5);

— Division B, Act Sec. 111(e), providing the effective date.

Reporter references: For further information, consult the following CCH reporters.

— Standard Federal Tax Reporter, ¶4675.029

— Tax Research Consultant, BUSEXP: 51,704

— Federal Tax Guide, ¶2608

¶550 Coal Gasification Investment Credit

SUMMARY OF NEW LAW

The gasification project credit is increased to 30 percent and the IRS is authorized to allocate an additional $250 million in credits to qualified projects that separate and sequester at least 75 percent of total carbon dioxide emissions.

BACKGROUND

The Energy Tax Incentives Act of 2005 (P.L. 109-58) added the coal gasification project credit (Code Sec. 48B) under the investment credit provisions of Code Sec. 46. The credit is available only to taxpayers who have applied for and received certification that their project satisfies the relevant criteria. The IRS and Energy Department jointly established programs to evaluate applications for these certifications using a competitive bidding process. Up to $350,000,000 in credits were allocated to taxpayers whose applications for certification were approved (Code Sec. 48B(d)(1)). In general, the qualifying gasification project credit for any tax year is equal to 20 percent of the qualified investment for the tax year (Code Sec. 48B(a)).

The qualified investment for any tax year is the basis of eligible property placed in service by the taxpayer during the tax year that is part of the qualifying gasification project. Eligible property is limited to property for which depreciation or amortization is available and (1) the construction, reconstruction, or erection which is completed by the taxpayer, or (2) which is acquired by the taxpayer, if the original use of the property commences with the taxpayer (Code Sec. 48B(b)(1)). The basis of property, for purposes of calculating the qualified investment, is reduced to the extent the property was financed by tax-exempt private activity bonds or subsidized energy financing (Code Sec. 48B(b)(2)).

A qualifying gasification project is a project that (1) employs gasification technology, (2) will be carried out by an eligible entity, and (3) any portion of the qualified investment of which is certified under the qualifying gasification program as eligible for a credit under Code Sec. 48B. The qualified investment in a particular project cannot exceed $650,000,000 (Code Sec. 48B(c)(1)). Since the credit is equal to 20

BACKGROUND

percent of the qualified investment, the maximum credit for any single project is $130,000,000.

NEW LAW EXPLAINED

Gasification project credit modified.—The IRS is authorized to allocate an additional $250 million in qualifying gasification project credits for projects that include equipment that separates and sequesters at least 75 percent of the project's total carbon dioxide emissions (Code Sec. 48B(d)(1), as amended by the Emergency Economic Stabilization Act of 2008 (P.L. 110-343)). The gasification project credit rate is increased to 30 percent (Code Sec. 48B(a), as amended by the Emergency Economic Act of 2008).

The IRS is required to recapture the benefit of any allocated credit if the project fails to attain or maintain the 75-percent separation and sequestration requirements (Code Sec. 48B(f), as added by the Emergency Economic Act of 2008).

The list of entities that are eligible for the gasification project credit has been expanded to include a domestic project which employs gasification applications related to transportation grade liquid fuels (Code Sec. 48B(c)(7)(H), as added by the Emergency Economic Act of 2008).

The IRS is required to give highest priority to projects that demonstrate the greatest separation and sequestration percentage of total carbon dioxide emissions and to give high priority to applicants who have a research partnership with an eligible educational institution (as defined in Code Sec. 529(e)(5)) (Code Sec. 48B(d)(4), as added by the Emergency Economic Act of 2008).

Under an amendment to the advanced coal project investment credit (Code Sec. 48A) (see ¶ 545), the IRS is required to disclose which projects receive gasification project credit allocations, including the taxpayer's identity and credit amount (Code Sec. 48(A)(d)(5), as added by the Emergency Economic Act of 2008).

> **Practical Analysis:** Charles R. Goulding, J.D., CPA, MBA, President and founder of Energy Tax Savers Inc., observes that Division B, Act Sec. 112 of the Emergency Economic Stabilization Act of 2008 (P.L. 110-343) is meant to encourage cleaner coal technology. Liquefied coal-based jet fuels have been added to the fuels eligible for the 50-cents-a-gallon credit. This is important because military jets are predicted to be the first significant users of the fuel made from liquefied coal.

▶ **Effective date.** The provisions apply to credits allocated or reallocated after October 3, 2008, for qualifying gasification projects which include equipment that separates and sequesters at least 75 percent of the project's total carbon dioxide emissions (Act Sec. 112(f) of the Emergency Economic Stabilization Act of 2008 (P.L. 110-343)).

Law source: Law at ¶5135. Committee Reports at ¶10,090.

— Division B, Act Sec. 112(a) of the Emergency Economic Stabilization Act of 2008 (P.L. 110-343), amending Code Sec. 48B(a);

¶550

NEW LAW EXPLAINED

— Division B, Act Sec. 112(b), amending Code Sec. 48B(d)(1);

— Division B, Act Sec. 112(c), adding Code Sec. 48B(f);

— Division B, Act Sec. 112(d), adding Code Sec. 48B(d)(4);

— Division B, Act Sec. 112(e), adding Code Sec. 48B(c)(7)(H);

— Division B, Act Sec. 112(f), providing the effective date.

Reporter references: For further information, consult the following CCH reporters.

— Standard Federal Tax Reporter, ¶4680.029 and ¶4680.045

— Tax Research Consultant, BUSEXP: 51,754 and BUSEXP: 51,758

— Federal Tax Guide, ¶2610

¶555 Carbon Dioxide Capture Credit

SUMMARY OF NEW LAW

A tax credit of $10 per metric ton is provided for carbon dioxide that is captured and transported from an industrial source for use in enhanced oil recovery. The credit is $20 per metric ton in the case of carbon dioxide captured and transported from an industrial source for permanent storage in a geologic formation.

BACKGROUND

The general business credit (Code Sec. 38) is a limited nonrefundable credit against income tax that is claimed after all other nonrefundable credits. The general business tax credit includes many credits, including the investment credit, work opportunity credit, alcohol fuels credit, enhanced oil recovery credit, renewable electricity production credit, and marginal oil and gas well production credit. Present law does not provide a credit for carbon dioxide sequestration.

Carbon dioxide sequestration technology helps to capture, purify and store carbon dioxide in order to reduce greenhouse gas emissions.

NEW LAW EXPLAINED

New carbon dioxide sequestration tax credit.—The Emergency Economic Stabilization Act of 2008 (P.L. 110-343) establishes a credit for the capture and transport of carbon dioxide from an industrial source for use in enhanced oil recovery or for permanent storage in a geologic formation (Code Sec. 45Q, as added by the Emergency Economic Act of 2008 (P.L. 110-343)).

The credit is $20 per metric ton of qualified carbon dioxide that is captured by the taxpayer at a qualified facility and disposed of in secure geological storage, and $10 per metric ton of qualified carbon dioxide that is captured by the taxpayer at a qualified

NEW LAW EXPLAINED

facility and used as a tertiary injectant in a qualified enhanced oil or natural gas recovery project (Code Sec. 45Q(a), as added by the Emergency Economic Act of 2008).

The credit is attributable to the person that captures and physically or contractually ensures the disposal, or the use as a tertiary injectant, of the qualified carbon dioxide, except to the extent provided by regulations (Code Sec. 45Q(d)(5), as added by the Emergency Economic Act of 2008).

Pursuant to regulations, the credit will be recaptured with respect to any qualified carbon dioxide that ceases to be captured, disposed or, or used as a tertiary injectant in accordance with the credit requirements (Code Sec. 45Q(d)(6), as added by the Emergency Economic Act of 2008).

The $10 and $20 credit amounts will be adjusted for inflation in tax years beginning after 2009. The adjusted amount will be equal to the product of the original credit amount and the inflation adjustment factor for the calendar year determined under Code Sec. 43(b)(3)(B) for that calendar year, determined by substituting "2008" for "1990" (Code Sec. 46Q(d)(7), as added by the Emergency Economic Act of 2008).

The credit will apply with respect to qualified carbon dioxide before the end of the calendar year in which the IRS, in consultation with the Environmental Protection Agency, certifies that 75 million metric tons of qualified carbon dioxide have been captured or disposed of or used as a tertiary injectant (Code Sec. 45Q(e), as added by the Emergency Economic Act of 2008).

Qualified carbon dioxide is carbon dioxide captured from an industrial source that would otherwise be released into the atmosphere as industrial emission of greenhouse gas and that is measured at the source of capture and verified at the point of disposal or injection. Qualified carbon dioxide includes the initial deposit of captured carbon dioxide used as a tertiary injectant, but does not include carbon dioxide that is re-captured, recycled, and re-injected as part of the enhanced oil and natural gas recovery process (Code Sec. 45Q(b), as added by the Emergency Economic Act of 2008).

> **Practical Analysis:** Charles R. Goulding, J.D., CPA, MBA, President and founder of Energy Tax Savers Inc., notes that the concept behind Division B, Act Sec. 115 of the Emergency Economic Stabilization Act of 2008 (P.L. 110-343) is to collect carbon dioxide from sources such as power plants and store in the deep ocean and in deep geological formations. This is developing technology.

Only carbon dioxide captured and disposed of or used within the United States or its possessions (including the continental shelf areas as defined in Code Sec. 638) is taken into account in computing the credit (Code Sec. 45Q(d)(1), as added by the Emergency Economic Act of 2008).

A qualified facility is any industrial facility: (1) that is owned by the taxpayer, (2) at which carbon capture equipment is placed in service, and (3) that captures at least 500,000 metric tons of carbon dioxide during the tax year (Code Sec. 45Q(c), as added by the Emergency Economic Act of 2008).

¶555

NEW LAW EXPLAINED

Secure geological storage will include storage at deep saline formations and unminable coal seems under conditions to be determined by regulations established by the IRS in consultation with the Environmental Protection Agency (Code Sec. 45Q(d)(2), added by the Emergency Economic Act of 2008).

The term tertiary injectant has the same meaning as when used in Code Sec. 193(b)(1), that is, any injectant (other than a recoverable hydrocarbon injectant) that is used as part of a tertiary recovery method. A tertiary recovery method is: (1) any method described in subparagraphs (1) through (9) of Section 212.78(c) of the June 1979 energy regulations (as defined by Code Sec. 4996(b)(8)(C) as in effect before its repeal) or (2) any other method to provide tertiary enhanced recovery that is approved by the IRS (Code Sec. 45Q(d)(3), as added by the Emergency Economic Act of 2008).

The term qualified enhanced oil or natural gas recovery project is any project: (1) that involves the application (in accordance with sound engineering principles) of one or more tertiary recovery methods (as defined in Code Sec. 193(b)(3)) that can reasonably be expected to result in more than an insignificant increase in the amount of crude oil or natural gas that will ultimately be recovered), (2) that is located in the United States (including the continental shelf areas within the meaning of Code Sec. 638(1)); and (3) with respect to which the first injection of liquids, gases, or other matter commences after December 31, 1990 (Code Sec. 45Q(d)(4), added by the Emergency Economic Act of 2008).

▶ **Effective date.** The provision shall apply to carbon dioxide recaptured after October 3, 2008, the date of enactment (Act Sec. 115(d) of the Emergency Economic Stabilization Act of 2008 (P.L. 110-343)).

Law source: Law at ¶5055 and ¶5120.

— Division B, Act Sec. 115(a) of the Emergency Economic Stabilization Act of 2008 (P.L. 110-343), adding Code Sec. 45Q;

— Division B, Act Sec. 115(b), amending Code Sec. 38(b);

— Division B, Act Sec. 115(d), providing the effective date.

Reporter references: For further information, consult the following CCH reporters.

— Standard Federal Tax Reporter, ¶4251.01

— Tax Research Consultant, BUSEXP: 54,000

— Federal Tax Guide, ¶2625

DEDUCTIONS

¶560 Energy Efficient Commercial Buildings Deduction

SUMMARY OF NEW LAW

The deduction for costs associated with energy efficient commercial building property is extended for five years.

BACKGROUND

A taxpayer may deduct the cost of certain energy efficiency improvements installed on or in a depreciable building located in the United States, effective for improvements placed in service after December 31, 2005, and before January 1, 2009 (Code Sec. 179D). The deduction applies to "energy efficient commercial building property," which is defined as depreciable property that is installed as part of a building's (1) interior lighting systems, (2) heating, cooling, ventilation, and hot water systems, or (3) envelope, and is part of a certified plan to reduce the total annual energy and power costs of these systems by at least 50 percent in comparison to a reference building that meets specified minimum standards. The deduction is limited to the product of $1.80 and the total square footage of the building, reduced by the aggregate amount deducted in any prior tax year.

A taxpayer may also claim a partial deduction for the costs of property that meet energy savings targets set by the IRS in Notice 2006-52, I.R.B. 2006-26, 1175. The deduction is determined by substituting $.60 for $1.80.

Generally, the deduction is claimed by the building's owner. However, in the case of a public building, the person primarily responsible for designing the property may claim the deduction. The deduction reduces the depreciable basis of the building and is treated as a depreciation deduction for Code Sec. 1245 recapture purposes (Code Sec. 1245(a)(3)(C)).

The Department of Energy will create and maintain a list of the software that must be used to calculate power consumption and energy costs for purposes of certifying the required energy savings necessary to claim the deduction. This list will be available to the public at http://www.eere.energy.gov/buildings/info/tax_credit_2006.html (Notice 2006-52, I.R.B. 2006-26, 1175.). The certification need not be attached to the taxpayer's return but must be retained as part of the taxpayer's books and records.

NEW LAW EXPLAINED

Energy efficient commercial buildings deduction extended.—The deduction for energy-efficient commercial building property is extended for five years. The deduction is available for qualified property placed into service after December 31, 2005, and

NEW LAW EXPLAINED

before January 1, 2014 (Code Sec. 179D(h), as amended by the Emergency Economic Stabilization Act of 2008 (P.L. 110-343)).

Practical Analysis: Charles R. Goulding, J.D., CPA, MBA, President and founder of Energy Tax Savers Inc., states that the Division B, Act Sec. 303 of the Emergency Economic Stabilization Act of 2008 (P.L. 110-343) extension of the existing commercial building tax deduction comes at very opportune time. This is the tax provision that allows for immediate tax deductions up to $0.60 per square foot for energy-efficient investments in three categories: lighting, HVAC and the building envelope. Facilities departments analyzing energy reducing building investments are in the process of setting their 2009 budgets. They can use the certainty of five years of additional tax incentives to enhance economic payback and get more energy-reducing projects approved.

The lighting industry in particular has made tremendous investments in the last three years in processes to help customers understand and utilize EPAct. These investments can now be leveraged to use the lighting commercial business deduction to drive huge amounts of energy-efficient lighting into the market place. It is anticipated that a substantial amount of highly energy-efficient LED (Light Emitting Diode) lighting will increasingly become available in the market. This lighting is still relatively expensive so the immediate tax deduction will be helpful.

The building envelope industry obtained a reduction in the required energy cost savings from 16.67 percent to 10 percent, which is enabling more projects to qualify for multiple EPAct tax deductions. The large increase in LEED buildings is enabling more and more buildings to qualify for multiple commercial building deductions.

▶ **Effective date.** No specific effective date is provided by the Act. The provision is, therefore, considered effective on, October 3, 2008, the date of enactment.

Law source: Law at ¶5255. Committee Reports at ¶10,220.

— Division B, Act Sec. 303 of the Emergency Economic Stabilization Act of 2008 (P.L. 110-343), amending Code Sec. 179D(h).

Reporter references: For further information, consult the following CCH reporters.

— Standard Federal Tax Reporter, ¶12,138D.01

— Tax Research Consultant, BUSEXP: 18,950

— Federal Tax Guide, ¶8365

¶565 Special Depreciation Allowance for Certain Reuse and Recycling Property

SUMMARY OF NEW LAW

A 50-percent additional depreciation allowance may be claimed on the adjusted basis of qualified reuse and recycling property acquired and placed in service after August 31, 2008.

BACKGROUND

The cost of depreciable property placed in service after 1986 is generally recovered using the Modified Accelerated Cost Recovery System (MACRS). Each type of property is assigned to a property class in accordance with the property class table issued by the IRS in Rev. Proc. 87-56, 1987-2 CB 674. The property classes for personal property are: three-year property, five-year property, seven-year property, 10-year property, 15-year property, and 20-year property. The depreciation periods are three years for three-year property, five years for five-year property, seven years for seven-year property, 10 years for 10-year property, etc. Longer recovery periods apply if the MACRS alternative depreciation system (ADS) is used. In the case of 3-, 5-, 7-, and 10-year property, the applicable depreciation method is the 200-percent declining balance method. The 150-percent declining balance method applies to 15- and 20-year property. The half-year or mid-quarter convention applies to personal property. Under these conventions, an asset is considered placed in service or disposed of on the midpoint of the year or quarter, respectively, in which it is placed in service or disposed of.

Subject to certain limitations, a taxpayer may claim a current deduction under Code Sec. 179 for the cost of tangible personal property acquired for use in the active conduct of a trade or business. For 2008, the maximum deduction is $250,000. The basis of any property expensed under Code Sec. 179 is reduced for purposes of computing depreciation.

Taxpayers who place qualifying property in service in the 2008 calendar year may claim 50-percent additional depreciation allowance (bonus depreciation) on such property (Code Sec. 168(k)). Generally, to be eligible to claim bonus depreciation, property must be: eligible for MACRS, with a depreciation period of 20 years or less; water utility property; off-the-shelf computer software; or qualified leasehold property. The property generally must be purchased and placed in service during 2008. In other words, the original use of the property must begin with the taxpayer and must occur after December 31, 2007, and before January 1, 2009. There cannot be a binding written contract before January 1, 2008, to acquire the property. Property qualifies only if it is acquired under a binding written contract entered into during 2008. In the case of self-constructed property, the taxpayer must begin the manufacture, construction or production of qualifying property for its own use during 2008. Bonus depreciation is claimed for both regular tax and alternative minimum tax (AMT) liability unless the taxpayer makes an election out of bonus depreciation.

BACKGROUND

Congress had previously, from time to time, enacted bonus depreciation provisions that allow taxpayers additional depreciation on depreciable property, typically 30 to 50 percent of a property's basis, in the year the property is placed in service. For example, after the terrorist attacks of September 11, 2001, Congress enacted the Job Creation and Worker Assistance Act of 2002 (P.L. 107-147), which created a 30-percent additional first-year depreciation allowance for qualifying modified accelerated cost recovery system (MACRS) property, later increased to 50 percent by the Jobs and Growth Tax Relief Reconciliation Act of 2003 (P.L. 108-27) (former Code Sec. 168(k)). Congress enacted a similar provision after Hurricane Katrina struck New Orleans, which applied to certain property placed in service in the areas affected by that storm (Code Sec. 1400N(d), as added by the Gulf Opportunity Zone Act of 2005 (P.L. 109-135)). Property placed in service in areas of Kansas affected by a series of storms and tornadoes in May 2007 is also eligible for bonus depreciation (Act Sec. 15345(a)(1) and (d)(1) of the Heartland, Habitat, Harvest, and Horticulture Act of 2008 (P.L. 110-246)). Congress has also provided for a 50-percent additional depreciation allowance for qualified cellulosic biomass ethanol plant property acquired and placed in service after December 20, 2006 and before January 1, 2013 (Code Sec. 168(l), as added by the Tax Relief and Health Care Act of 2006 (P.L. 109-432)).

NEW LAW EXPLAINED

Special depreciation allowance for qualified reuse and recycling property—A 50-percent additional depreciation allowance (bonus depreciation) may be claimed on the adjusted basis of qualified reuse and recycling property acquired and placed in service after August 31, 2008. The additional depreciation is claimed in the tax year the property is placed in service. The original use of the property must begin with the taxpayer after August 31, 2008 (i.e., the property must be new) (Code Sec. 168(m), as added by the Emergency Economic Stabilization Act of 2008 (P.L. 110-343)). Regular MACRS depreciation deductions are computed on the adjusted basis of the property beginning in the tax year the property is placed in service after reduction by the 50-percent allowance (Code Sec. 168(m)(1)(B), as added by Emergency Economic Act of 2008).

> **Comment:** Since this bonus depreciation deduction is computed on the adjusted basis of the property, it would be computed after the original basis is reduced by any Code Sec. 179 allowance that is claimed. This is the same rule that applies when computing the bonus depreciation allowance under Code Sec. 168(k).

> **Comment:** For purposes of Code Sec. 168(m), the term "recycle" or "recycling" means the process by which worn or superfluous materials are processed into materials for use in manufacturing consumer and commercial products, including packaging (Code Sec. 168(m)(3)(C), as added by the Emergency Economic Act of 2008).

No AMT adjustment required. The bonus deduction is claimed in full for purposes of determining alternative minimum tax liability. In addition, all MACRS depreciation deductions claimed on the qualified reuse and recycling property are allowed in full

NEW LAW EXPLAINED

in computing AMT (i.e., no depreciation adjustment is required) (Code Sec. 168(m)(2)(D), as added by the Emergency Economic Act of 2008).

Qualified reuse and recycling property defined. "Qualified reuse and recycling property" is reuse and recycling property that meets certain conditions. "Reuse and recycling property" is machinery and equipment (not including buildings, real estate, rolling stock or equipment used to transport reuse and recyclable materials) that is used exclusively to collect, distribute, or recycle qualified reuse and recyclable materials. Machinery and equipment include appurtenances such as software necessary to operate the equipment. "Qualified reuse and recyclable materials" are scrap plastic, glass, textiles, rubber, packaging, and metal, as well as recovered fiber and electronic scrap (Code Sec. 168(m)(3), as added by the Emergency Economic Act of 2008).

> **Comment:** For purposes of this depreciation allowance, "electronic scrap" includes cathode ray tubes, flat panel screens or similar video display devices with screen sizes greater than 4 inches when measured diagonally, as well as central processing units (Code Sec. 168(m)(2)(A)(ii), as added by the Emergency Economic Act of 2008).

In order to be considered "qualified reuse and recycling property," the property must have a "useful life" of at least five years and the original use of the property must begin with the taxpayer after August 31, 2008. In addition, the property must either be acquired by purchase by the taxpayer after August 31, 2008 (but only if there is not written binding contract for the acquisition in effect before September 1, 2008), or acquired by the taxpayer pursuant to a written binding contract which was entered into after August 31, 2008 (Code Sec. 168(m)(2)(A), as added by the Emergency Economic Act of 2008).

> **Comment:** "Purchase" for this purpose has the meaning given to such term in Code Sec. 179(d)(2), which defines the term as any acquisition of property, but excludes acquisitions from related parties, transfers of property from a decedent in which the acquiror takes a stepped-up basis in the property under Code Sec. 1014(a), or transfers in which the acquiror takes a substituted basis in the property, such as like-kind exchanges qualifying under Code Sec. 1031. In addition, property acquired by purchase will only be considered qualified reuse and recycling property if no written, binding contract for the acquisition was in effect before September 1, 2008 (Code Sec. 168(m)(2)(A)(i), as added by the Emergency Economic Act of 2008).

> **Comment:** The requirement of an acquisition by purchase is not imposed on acquisitions pursuant to a written binding contract entered into after August 31, 2008 (Code Sec. 168(m)(2)(A)(iv), as added by the Emergency Economic Act of 2008). Presumably, it was not the intent of Congress to eliminate the purchase requirement simply because the reuse or recycling property was acquired pursuant to a contract entered into after August 31, 2008. For example, as enacted, it appears that a taxpayer could enter into a post-August 31, 2008 contract for an acquisition from a related person and qualify for the deduction even though such an acquisition is not considered a purchase under Code Sec. 179(d)(2). A technical correction may be required.

NEW LAW EXPLAINED

Comment: Qualified reuse and recyling property must have a *useful life* of at least five years (Code Sec. 168(m)(2)(A)(ii), as added by the Emergency Economic Act of 2008). The term useful life is not defined. It appears in the context of this provision to refer to actual economic useful life to the taxpayer rather than the length of the assigned MACRS recovery period. The only MACRS recovery period which is less than five years is three years (i.e., three-year property). MACRS 3-year property does not include any type of property that would be considered qualified reuse or recycling property. Similar considerations prevent the term from being defined by reference to an asset's class life as set forth in Rev. Proc. 87-56, 1987-2 CB 674.

Self-constructed property. The special depreciation allowance may be claimed on qualified reuse and recycling property the taxpayer manufactures, constructs, or produces for its own use, if the taxpayer begins manufacturing, constructing, or producing the property after August 31, 2008 (Code Sec. 168(m)(2)(C), as added by the Emergency Economic Act of 2008).

Exceptions. A taxpayer cannot "double dip" and claim the special qualified reuse and recycling property depreciation allowance for any property for which it may claim bonus depreciation under Code Sec. 168(k). Thus, if bonus depreciation is available under either this new provision or Code Sec. 168(k) it must be claimed under Code Sec. 168(k). In addition, a taxpayer cannot take the special depreciation allowance on property which it is required to depreciate under the MACRS alternative depreciation system (ADS). However, if a taxpayer is not required to depreciate property under ADS, but elects to do so under Code Sec. 168(g)(7), the taxpayer may still claim the special depreciation allowance (Code Sec. 168(m)(2)(B), as added by the Emergency Economic Act of 2008).

Election out. A taxpayer may elect not to claim the deduction with respect to any MACRS assigned class of property for any tax year. The election out applies to all qualified reuse and recycling property in the particular MACRS property class (e.g., 5-, 7-, 10-, or 15-year property) for which the election out is made and which is placed in service during the tax year for which the election is made (Code Sec. 168(m)(2)(B)(iii), as added by the Emergency Economic Act of 2008).

▶ **Effective date.** This provision applies to property placed in service after August 31, 2008 (Act Sec. 308(b) of the Emergency Economic Stabilization Act of 2008 (P.L. 110-343)).

Law source: Law at ¶5230.

— Act Sec. 308(a) of the Emergency Economic Stabilization Act of 2008, adding Code Sec. 168(m);

— Act Sec. 308(b), providing the effective date.

Reporter references: For further information, consult the following CCH reporters.

— Standard Federal Tax Reporter, ¶11,279.058

— Tax Research Consultant, DEPR: 3,600

— Federal Tax Guide, ¶9131

¶570 Accelerated Depreciation for Smart Electric Meters and Smart Grid Systems

SUMMARY OF NEW LAW

A 10-year recovery period and 150-percent declining balance method is provided for any qualified smart electric meter and any qualified smart electric grid system.

BACKGROUND

Tangible property generally is depreciated under the modified accelerated cost recovery system ("MACRS"). MACRS determines depreciation by applying specific recovery periods, placed-in-service conventions, and depreciation methods to the cost of various types of depreciable property. Assets used in the transmission and distribution of electricity for sale and related land improvements, are assigned a class life of 30 years and a recovery period of 20 years (Asset Class 49.14 of Rev. Proc. 87-56, 1987-2 CB 674). The applicable depreciation method for 20-year property is the 150 percent declining balance method (Code Sec. 168(b)(2)).

NEW LAW EXPLAINED

Accelerated depreciation for qualified smart electric meters and qualified smart grid systems.—The Emergency Economic Stabilization Act of 2008 (P.L. 110-343) provides accelerated depreciation for qualified smart electric meters and qualified smart electric grid systems. Taxpayers can recover the cost of such equipment over a 10-year period instead of 20 years (Code Sec. 168(e)(3)(D), as amended by Emergency Economic Act of 2008). The 150-percent declining balance method continues as the applicable depreciation method (Code Sec. 168(b)(2), as amended by Emergency Economic Act of 2008).

A qualified smart electric meter is any time-based meter and related communication equipment placed in service by a taxpayer who is a supplier of electric energy or a provider of electric energy services, and which is capable of being used by the taxpayer as part of a system that:

(1) Measures and records electricity usage data on a time-differentiated basis in at least 24 separate time segments per day;

(2) Provides for the exchange of information between the supplier or provider and the customer's smart electric meter in support of time-based rates or other forms of demand response;

(3) Provides data to such supplier or provider so that the supplier or provider can provide energy usage information to customers electronically; and

(4) Provides net metering (Code Sec. 168(i)(18), as amended by Emergency Economic Act of 2008; Joint Committee on Taxation, Technical Explanation of H.R. 7060, the "Renewable Energy and Job Creation Tax Act of 2008" (JCX-75-08)).

NEW LAW EXPLAINED

Comment: No definition of net metering appears to be provided. However, previous versions of the provision have defined the term as the ability of the meter to provide a credit to the customer for providing electricity to the supplier or provider.

Practical Analysis: Charles R. Goulding, J.D., CPA, MBA, President and founder of Energy Tax Savers Inc., states that Division B, Act Sec. 306 of the Emergency Economic Stabilization Act of 2008 (P.L. 110-343) incentivizes smart meters that can measure and record on at least 24 separate time periods. Select utilities in the United States have begun to implement large-scale smart meter and smart grid systems. Many utilities utilize time of day pricing where nighttime electric rates may be substantially lower than daytime rates. Initial results indicate that when end users view electric uses on real-time basis, they adjust their behavior by curtailing energy use and shifting high electric cost activities to lower cost time periods.

Often high peak electric use occurs on the hottest days of the summer, creating what the utilities call demand events that potentially can cause system wide interruptions. With the required two-way communication capability included in this new tax provision, the utilities will have the ability to adjust customer demand and protect the integrity of the grid. The ultimate goal is to have a nationwide two-way smart grid that connects all electricity users.

A qualified smart electric grid system is any smart grid property used as part of a system for electric distribution grid communications, monitoring, and management placed in service by a taxpayer who is a supplier of electric energy or a provider of electric energy services. Smart grid property includes electronics and related equipment that is capable of:

(1) Sensing, collecting, and monitoring data of or from all portions of a utility's electric distribution grid;

(2) Providing real-time, two-way communications to monitor to manage such grid; and

(3) Providing real-time analysis of an event prediction based upon collected data that can be used to improve electric distribution system reliability, quality, and performance (Code Sec. 168(i)(19), as amended by Emergency Economic Act of 2008).

Property that would otherwise have a class life of less than 10 years does not qualify as a qualified smart electric meter or a qualified smart electric grid system (Code Sec. 168(i)(18)(A)(ii) and (19)(A)(ii)).

Comment: MACRS property with a class life of less than 16 years but 10 or more years is classified as seven-year property. If the class life is less than 10 years but more than 4 years it is classified as five-year property. Property with a class life of 4 years or less is considered three-year property (Code Sec. 168(e)(1)). The rule that property with a class life of less than 10 years does not qualify as a smart meter or smart electric grid system means that the new provision does not change the depreciation period of property that would otherwise qualify as

NEW LAW EXPLAINED

3-year or 5-year property. On the other hand, seven-year property is depreciated as 10-year property under this provision because seven-year property has a class life of 10 years or more but less then 16 years. It is unclear why Congress would want to apply a longer recovery period to seven-year property insofar as the provision is intended to provide an energy incentive. Nevertheless, as indicated in the Background section, most property that qualifies as a smart electric meter or a smart electric grid is assigned a class life of 30 years, and therefore would be treated as MACRS 20-year property but for this new provision.

Comment: The unenrolled version of the bill (H.R. 1424) provided that property with a class life of less than 16 years did not qualify as a qualified smart electric meter or a qualified smart electric grid system. If the final version of the bill had been so enacted, then 7-year property that otherwise qualifies as a smart electric meter or a smart electric grid would have continued to be depreciated as MACRS seven-year property.

▶ **Effective date.** This provision is effective for property placed in service after October 3, 2008, the date of enactment (Division B, Act Sec. 306 Emergency Economic Stabilization Act of 2008 (P.L. 110-343)).

Law source: Law at ¶5230. Committee Reports at ¶10,240.

— Division B, Act Sec. 306(a) of the Emergency Economic Stabilization Act of 2008 (P.L. 110-343), amending Code Sec. 168(e)(3)(D);

— Division B, Act Sec. 306(b), amending Code Sec. 168(i);

— Division B, Act Sec. 306(c), redesignating Code Sec. 168(b)(2)(C) as (D), and adding new Code Sec. 168(b)(2)(C);

— Division B, Act Sec. 306(d), providing the effective date.

Reporter references: For further information, consult the following CCH reporters.

— Standard Federal Tax Reporter, ¶11,279.023

— Tax Research Consultant, DEPR: 3,156.30

— Federal Tax Guide, ¶9110

STUDY

¶575 Carbon Audit of the Internal Revenue Code

SUMMARY OF NEW LAW

The National Academy of Sciences is to undertake a comprehensive review of the Internal Revenue Code to identify tax provisions having the largest effects on carbon and other greenhouse gas emissions, and to estimate and report the magnitude of those effects.

¶575

BACKGROUND

The National Academy of Sciences serves to investigate, examine, experiment and report on a subject of science whenever called upon to do so by a department of the government.

NEW LAW EXPLAINED

Carbon audit of the tax code.—The Secretary of the Treasury is directed to enter into an agreement with the National Academy of Sciences to undertake a comprehensive review of the Internal Revenue Code of 1986 to identify the types of and specific tax provisions that have the largest effects on carbon and other greenhouse gas emissions and to estimate the magnitude of those effects. To carry this out, $1,500,000 for the period of fiscal years 2009 and 2010 is authorized to be appropriated. The National Academy of Sciences is directed to submit to Congress, no later than October 4, 2010, a report containing the results of this study.

Practical Analysis: Charles R. Goulding, J.D., CPA, MBA, President and founder of Energy Tax Savers Inc., states that Division B, Act Sec. 117 of the Emergency Economic Stabilization Act of 2008 (P.L. 110-343) is a fascinating development since it in essence requires the Internal Revenue Code to have its carbon and greenhouse gas footprint analyzed by the National Academy of Sciences (NAS). This project will require a high level of interdiscplinary tax, green chemistry and dynamic computer modeling skills since the Internal Revenue Code is so pervasive and impacts so many carbon- and greenhouse gas–creating activities. It is well recognized that some of the leading carbon creating activities include cement kilns, coal-based utility electrify production, agricultural activities, auto and transportation activities, and buildings including data centers, all of which are impacted by specific Internal Revenue Code provisions. This project will require dynamic modeling and estimating because many of the tax provisions currently enacted with this statute themselves are going have a meaningful impact on current carbon emissions levels in the United States.

Act Sec. 15322 of the Heartland, Habitat, Harvest and Horticulture Act of 2008 already obligates the NAS to complete a comprehensive study in consultation with the Secretary of Agriculture, the Secretary of Energy and the EPA for biofuels including the impact of current biofuels tax credits. Since both studies require tax code impact analysis and are both being handled by the National Science Foundation, presumably the findings will be consistent.

This NAS analysis could potentially have major impact on the Internal Revenue Code, particularly in the capitalization area since the tax code generally requires unfavorable capitalization of betterments, whereas many of the carbon reducing investments require capital equipment upgrades.

It may also be relevant to consider how the current and future tax code should treat current and developing carbon and green house cap and trading activities.

NEW LAW EXPLAINED

▶ **Effective date.** No effective date is provided by the Act. The provision is therefore, considered effective on October 3, 2008, the date of enactment.

Law source: Law at ¶7144. Committee Reports at ¶10,130.

— Division B, Act Sec. 117 of the Emergency Economic Stabilization Act of 2008 (P.L. 110-343).

Reporter references: For further information, consult the following CCH reporters.

— Standard Federal Tax Reporter, ¶43,251

— Tax Research Consultant, IRS: 3,252

— Federal Tax Guide, ¶22,709

Disaster Relief

6

LOSSES AND OTHER DEDUCTIONS

REPORTING

TAX CREDITS AND BONDS

TEMPORARY RELIEF PROVISIONS

LOSSES AND OTHER DEDUCTIONS

¶605 Casualty Losses Attributable to Federally Declared Disasters

SUMMARY OF NEW LAW

Personal casualty losses attributable to a federally declared disaster occurring in 2008 and 2009 are deductible without regard to whether the losses exceed 10 percent of a taxpayer's adjusted gross income (AGI). The deduction for any casualty attributable to a federally declared disaster occurring in 2009 is limited to the amount of the loss that exceeds $500. Additionally, for tax years beginning after December 31, 2007, the standard deduction is increased by the amount of any disaster loss amount.

BACKGROUND

Taxpayers may generally deduct losses that are sustained during the tax year and not compensated for by insurance or otherwise (Code Sec. 165). For individual taxpayers, deductible losses must fall within one of three categories:

- losses incurred in a trade or business;

- losses incurred in transactions entered into for profit but not connected with a trade or business; and

- losses incurred as the result of fire, storm, shipwreck or other casualty, or from theft (Code Sec. 165(c)).

Personal casualty or theft losses are deductible only to the extent to which they exceed $100 per casualty or theft (Code Sec. 165(h)(1)). Further, personal casualty or theft losses for a tax year are deductible only if they exceed personal casualty gains, and only to the extent of the sum of the amount of personal casualty gains plus the amount by which the excess of personal casualty losses over gains is greater than 10 percent of the taxpayer's adjusted gross income (AGI) (Code Sec. 165(h)(2)).

Special relief is provided for taxpayers who sustain losses attributable to a disaster occurring in an area that is later determined by the President of the United States to warrant assistance by the federal government under the Robert T. Stafford Disaster Relief and Emergency Assistance Act. Under this provision, a taxpayer may elect to deduct a loss on his or her return for the immediately preceding tax year (Code Sec. 165(i)). For example, a calendar-year taxpayer who suffers a disaster loss any time during 2008 may elect to deduct it on his or her 2007 return, or the taxpayer may wait and deduct it on his or her 2008 return in the regular manner. In either case, however, the taxpayer is still subject to the $100 and 10 percent of AGI limits.

The deduction for casualty losses is an itemized deduction. Individuals who elect the standard deduction may not claim a deduction for casualty losses incurred during the tax year.

NEW LAW EXPLAINED

Losses attributable to federally declared disasters fully deductible, included in standard deduction.—The 10 percent of AGI limitation applicable to personal casualty loss deductions is waived for personal casualty losses that are "net disaster losses" (Code Sec. 165(h)(3)(A), as added by the Emergency Economic Stabilization Act of 2008 (P.L. 110-343)). For this purpose, a "net disaster loss" means the excess of the personal casualty losses attributable to a federally declared disaster occurring after 2007 before 2010, and occurring in a disaster area, over personal casualty gains (Code Sec. 165(h)(3)(B), as added by the Emergency Economic Act of 2008). A federally declared disaster is any disaster subsequently determined by the President of the United States to warrant assistance by the federal government under the Robert T. Stafford Disaster Relief and Emergency Assistance Act. A disaster area means the area so determined to warrant such assistance (Code Sec. 165(h)(3)(C), as added by the Emergency Economic Act of 2008).

> **Comment:** The definition of a "federally declared disaster" and "disaster area" as added by the new law in Code Sec. 165(h)(3)(C) has replaced the term "Presidentially declared disaster" used in other parts of the Code. A "Presidentially declared disaster" was defined as any disaster which, with respect to the area in which the property is located, resulted in a subsequent determination by the President that such area warrants assistance by the Federal Government under the Robert T. Stafford Disaster Relief and Emergency Assistance Act (Code Sec. 1033(h), prior to amendment by the Emergency Economic Act of 2008). Thus, the new and old definitions are practically identical. However, the terms "federally declared disaster" and "disaster area" will now be used not only for determining casualty losses under Code Sec. 165(h)(3) described above, but will also be used for other purposes including:
>
> - the special rule for property compulsorily or involuntarily converted as a result of a disaster under Code Sec. 1033(h);
> - the exclusion of "qualified disaster relief payments" from gross income under Code Sec. 139;
> - the three-year carryback period for net operating losses (NOLs) of farmers and small businesses under Code Sec. 172(b)(1)(F)(ii); and
> - the IRS' authority to postpone any deadline imposed under federal tax laws for up to one year for taxpayers affected by a disaster under Code Sec. 7508A.

The 10 percent of AGI limitation continues to apply to casualty or theft losses that are not net disaster losses. Net disaster losses are deductible without regard to whether a taxpayer's aggregate net casualty losses exceed 10 percent of the taxpayer's AGI (Code Sec. 165(h)(3)(A)(i), as added by the Emergency Economic Act of 2008). For purposes of applying the limitation to other casualty or theft losses, net disaster loses are disregarded (Code Sec. 165(h)(3)(A)(ii), as added by the Emergency Economic Act of 2008).

The $100 limitation applicable to each casualty or theft is also temporarily increased to $500 for tax years beginning in 2009. The limitation amount for tax years beginning

NEW LAW EXPLAINED

after 2009, however, will return to $100 (Code Sec. 165(h)(1), as added by the Emergency Economic Act of 2008).

> **Example:** Sam, an individual taxpayer with AGI of $75,000, has the following personal casualty items during the 2009 tax year: $5,000 personal casualty gain, $15,000 allowable personal casualty loss attributable to a federally declared disaster of $15,000 ($15,500 less application of the $500 limitation per casualty under Code Sec. 165(h)(1), as amended by the Emergency Economic Act of 2008), and an allowable personal casualty loss of $8,000 ($8,500 less application of the $500 limitation per casualty). The deductible net disaster loss is $10,000 ($15,000 allowable disaster casualty loss less the $5,000 personal casualty gain). The deductible non-disaster casualty loss is $500 ($8,000 non-disaster casualty loss less $7,500 (10 percent of AGI limitation). Sam's deductible net personal casualty loss for the taxable year is $10,500 (the sum of the net disaster loss and the excess of the other casualty losses over the 10-percent limitation).

For tax years beginning after 2007, the amount of the standard deduction claimed by a taxpayer is increased by the amount of his or her disaster loss deduction (Code Sec. 63(c)(1)(D), as added by the Emergency Economic Act of 2008). For this purpose, the term "disaster loss deduction" is defined as the net disaster loss under new Code Sec. 165(h)(3)(B) (Code Sec. 63(c)(8), as added by the Emergency Economic Act of 2008). Unlike the basic standard deduction, for purposes of calculating alternative minimum taxable (AMT) income under Code Sec. 56, the portion of the standard deduction amount attributable to the disaster loss deduction is allowed as a deduction (Code Sec. 56(b)(1)(E), as amended by the Emergency Economic Act of 2008).

Midwest disaster area exclusion. The waiver of AGI limitations for losses in federally declared disasters and the increase in the standard deduction by the disaster loss deduction amount do not apply to any disaster with respect to which the President has declared a major disaster on or after May 20, 2008, and before August 1, 2008, under section 401 of the Robert T. Stafford Disaster Relief and Emergency Assistance Act by reason of severe storms, tornados or flooding occurring in Arkansas, Illinois, Indiana, Iowa, Kansas, Michigan, Minnesota, Missouri, Nebraska or Wisconsin (Division C, Act Sec. 712 of the Emergency Economic Act of 2008, referencing Division C, Act Sec. 702(c)[b](1)(A)). See ¶ 655.

▶ **Effective date.** The provisions relating to the waiver of adjusted gross income limitations for losses in federally declared disasters and the increase in the standard deduction by the disaster loss deduction amount apply to disasters declared in tax years beginning after December 31, 2007. The provision relating to the increase in the limitation on individual losses per casualty applies for tax years beginning after December 31, 2008 (Division C, Act Sec. 706(d) of the Emergency Economic Stabilization Act of 2008 (P.L. 110-343)).

Law source: Law at ¶5175, ¶5185, ¶5200, ¶5225, ¶5240, ¶5355 and ¶5480. Committee Reports at ¶10,710.

¶605

NEW LAW EXPLAINED

— Division C, Act Sec. 706(a)(1) of the Emergency Economic Stabilization Act of 2008 (P.L. 110-343), redesignating Code Sec. 165(h)(3) and (4) as (h)(4) and (5), respectively, and adding new Code Sec. 165(h)(3);

— Division C, Act Sec. 706(a)(2)(A)-(C) amending Code Sec. 165(h)(4)(B), (i)(1) and (i)(4);

— Division C, Act Sec. 706(a)(2)(D) amending Code Sec. 139(c)(2), 172(b)(1)(F)(ii), 1033(h), and 7508A;

— Division C, Act Sec. 706(b), adding Code Sec. 63(c)(1)(D) and (c)(8) and amending Code Sec. 56(b)(1)(E);

— Division C, Act Sec. 706(c), amending Code Sec. 165(h)(1);

— Division C, Act Sec. 706(d), providing the effective dates.

Reporter references: For further information, consult the following CCH reporters.

— Standard Federal Tax Reporter, ¶6023.023, ¶10,005.01, and ¶10,201.03

— Tax Research Consultant, FILEIND: 12,100 and INDIV: 54,200

— Federal Tax Guide, ¶6020 and ¶6320

¶610 Net Operating Losses Attributable to Federally Declared Disasters

SUMMARY OF NEW LAW

A special five-year carryback period for net operating losses (NOLs) has been created for qualified disaster losses.

BACKGROUND

A net operating loss (NOL) occurs when a taxpayer's deductible business expenses (including employee business expenses), flow-through losses from a partnership or S corporation, and casualty and theft losses (whether personal, business, or investment-related) exceed the taxpayer's gross income from all sources. In general, a NOL may be carried back and deducted against taxable income in the two tax years before the NOL year, and then carried forward and applied against taxable income for up to 20 years after the NOL year.

Special rules apply to certain taxpayers or in certain circumstances. For example, electric utilities may elect a five-year carryback period for certain taxable years and subject to certain limitations, and businesses with NOLs resulting from specified liability losses may carry back such losses for 10 years. Real estate investment trusts (REITs), on the other hand, are not allowed to carry NOLs back, but may only carry them forward. A three-year carryback applies when the NOLs arise from the casualty or theft losses of individuals, or when they may be attributed to Presidentially-declared disaster areas for small business owners or farmers. A five-year carryback applies to farmers generally (irrespective of whether or not the NOL occurred within

BACKGROUND

a disaster area), and to NOLs in the Gulf Opportunity Zone arising after August 28, 2005, and before January 1, 2009, or the Kansas disaster area arising after May 5, 2007, and before January 1, 2010.

NEW LAW EXPLAINED

NOLs attributable to Federally declared disasters.—A special five-year carryback period for net operating losses (NOLs) has been created for qualified disaster losses (Code Sec. 172(b)(1)(J), as added by the Emergency Economic Stabilization Act of 2008 (P.L. 110-343)). The amount of the NOL that qualifies for this five-year carryback is limited to the taxpayer's overall NOL for the tax year in which the NOL occurs. Remaining NOLs (if any) will be subject to the general two-year carryback period, and will also be subject to rules similar to those applicable to specified liability losses (Code Sec. 172(j)(2), as added by the Emergency Economic Act of 2008). This includes ordering rules similar to those for specified liability losses that are carried back (Joint Committee on Taxation, Technical Explanation of H.R. 7006, the "Disaster Relief Act of 2008" (JCX-73-08), September 24, 2008).

> **Planning Note:** Taxpayers may elect to not have this five-year carryback period apply to NOLs generated by qualified disaster losses. If such an election is made, a different carryback period, such as the normal two-year period would usually apply, unless the taxpayer elected out of that carryback period as well. Once the election out of the five-year carryback period is made for a tax year, it will generally be irrevocable for that tax year (Code Sec. 172(j)(3), as added by the Emergency Economic Act of 2008).

"Qualified disaster losses" are defined for this purpose as the lesser of:

- the sum of Code Sec. 165 losses occurring within a disaster area and attributable to a Federally-declared disaster occurring after December 31, 2007, and before January 1, 2010, plus the deduction for qualified disaster expenses allowable for the tax year under Code Sec. 198A(a) (or which would have been allowed if not otherwise treated as an expense); or

- the NOL for that tax year (Code Sec. 172(j)(1), as added by the Emergency Economic Act of 2008).

A qualified disaster loss may not include any amounts with respect to any property used in connection with any private or commercial golf course, country club, massage parlor, hot tub facility, suntan facility, or any store the principal business of which is the sale of alcoholic beverages for consumption off premises; or any gambling or animal racing property, as described in Code Sec. 1400N(p)(3) (Code Sec. 172(j)(4), as added by the Emergency Economic Act of 2008).

Alternative tax. A taxpayer electing the five-year carryback under this provision will not be subject to the general rule limiting a taxpayer's NOL deduction to 90 percent of alternative minimum taxable income (AMTI) (Code Sec. 56(d)(3), as added by the Emergency Economic Act of 2008). Instead, the taxpayer may offset up to 100 percent of AMTI with such NOL carryback.

¶610

NEW LAW EXPLAINED

Midwestern disaster area exclusion. Specifically excluded from "qualified disaster losses" for this purpose are any losses arising in any disaster area with respect to which the President has declared a major disaster on or after May 20, 2008, and before August 1, 2008, under section 401 of the Robert T. Stafford Disaster Relief and Emergency Assistance Act by reason of severe storms, tornados or flooding occurring in Arkansas, Illinois, Indiana, Iowa, Kansas, Michigan, Minnesota, Missouri, Nebraska or Wisconsin (Division C, Act Sec. 712 of the Emergency Economic Act of 2008, referencing Division C, Act Sec. 702(c)[b](1)(A)). See ¶655.

▶ **Effective date.** This provision applies for net operating losses arising in tax years beginning after December 31, 2007, in connection with disasters declared after such date. (Division C, Act Sec. 708(e) of the Emergency Economic Stabilization Act of 2008 (P.L. 110-343)).

Law source: Law at ¶5175 and ¶5240. Committee Reports at ¶10,730.

— Division C, Act Sec. 708(a) of the Emergency Economic Stabilization Act of 2008 (P.L. 110-343), adding Code Sec. 172(b)(1)(J);

— Division C, Act Sec. 708(b), redesignating Code Sec. 172(j) and (k) as (k) and (l), respectively, and adding a new Code Sec. 172(j);

— Division C, Act Sec. 708(c), adding Code Sec. 56(d)(3);

— Division C, Act Sec. 708(d), amending Code Sec. 172(b)(1)(F) and (i)(1);

— Division C, Act Sec. 708(e), providing the effective date.

Reporter references: For further information, consult the following CCH reporters.

— Standard Federal Tax Reporter, ¶12,014.01, ¶12,014.05 and ¶32,487.038

— Tax Research Consultant, BUSEXP: 45,154.05 and BUSEXP: 57,304.45

— Federal Tax Guide, ¶6325 and ¶9132

¶615 Expensing of Qualified Disaster Costs

SUMMARY OF NEW LAW

A taxpayer can elect to expense qualified disaster expenses after 2007, rather than capitalizing them.

BACKGROUND

The tax treatment of costs arising from disaster damage to business property can depend on several factors. Many recovery costs can qualify as deductible business expenses (Code Sec. 162), including costs for incidental repairs and maintenance of property that do not materially add to the value of the property or appreciably prolong its life (Reg. §§1.162-4 and 1.263(a)-1(b)). However, expenses paid or incurred to add to the value or substantially prolong the useful life of property, or to adapt it to a new or different use, generally must be capitalized (Code Sec. 263(a)(1)). The IRS has stated that the treatment of costs to restore uninsured property damage

BACKGROUND

caused by a natural disaster depends on the facts and circumstances of the particular case, regardless of whether the costs were incurred due to a casualty. However, proposed regulations would require capitalization of all costs to restore property after a casualty, to the extent the taxpayer deducted a Code Sec. 165 casualty loss with respect to that property (Proposed Reg. § 1.263(a)-3(f)(3)(iv)).

Environmental cleanup costs. Two special rules can apply to costs arising from environmental damage. First, qualified environmental remediation (QER) expenditures are currently deductible if they are (a) otherwise chargeable to a capital account; and (b) paid or incurred in connection with the abatement or control of hazardous substances at a qualified contaminated site. QER costs generally do not include expenses for the acquisition of depreciable property used in connection with the abatement or control of hazardous substances at a qualified contaminated site, but depreciation deductions allowable for such property are treated as QER expenditures (Code Sec. 198(b)). QER deductions are treated as depreciation deductions, and the underlying property is treated as section 1245 property. Thus, the QER deductions must be recaptured if the taxpayer sells or otherwise disposes of the underlying property.

Under the second special rule, QER expenses paid or incurred on or after August 28, 2005, and before January 1, 2008, to abate contamination at qualified contaminated sites located in the Gulf Opportunity Zone can also be expensed. For this purpose, hazardous substances include petroleum products (Code Sec. 1400N(g)).

Demolition and debris removal costs. The cost of demolishing a structure is generally capitalized and included in the taxpayer's basis in the land on which the structure is located (Code Sec. 280B). The treatment of debris removal costs depends on their nature; that is, whether they are repair-type costs that are deductible as ordinary and necessary business expenses, or more in the nature of replacement-type costs that must be capitalized. However, taxpayers can deduct 50 percent of their demolition and debris removal expenses that would otherwise be capital costs if: (1) the underlying property is held for business use, for the production of income, or as inventory; and (2) the costs are paid or incurred (a) on or after August 28, 2005, and before January 1, 2008, in the Gulf Opportunity Zone; or (b) on or after May 4, 2007, and before January 1, 2009, in the Kansas disaster area (Code Sec. 1400N(f); Act Sec. 15345(a)(3) and (d)(3) of the Heartland, Habitat, Harvest, and Horticulture Act of 2008 (P.L. 110-246)).

Mining and solid waste disposal costs. Taxpayers can elect to adopt a uniform method for deducting qualified reclamation and closing costs associated with certain mining and solid waste disposal properties in advance of economic performance. In general, qualified reclamation and closing costs include expenses incurred under the Surface Mining Control and Reclamation Act of 1977, the Solid Waste Disposal Act, or any other similar federal, state, or, in the case of waste disposal sites, local law. The deduction of qualified reclamation costs for any tax year is equal to the current reclamation costs allocable to a property disturbed during that year. Current reclamation costs are the qualified costs that would be paid if the reclamation activities were performed currently. The deduction for qualified closing costs for any tax year is equal to the current closing costs allocable to the production from a property during

BACKGROUND

such tax year. Current closing costs are the qualifying costs that would be paid if the closing activities were performed currently (Code Sec. 468).

Section 1245 property. Property generally qualifies as Section 1245 property if it is used in a trade or business or held for investment, and it is (or is treated as) subject to depreciation. Section 1245 property does not include most real property (land and buildings). Capital gain realized on the disposition of section 1245 property generally must be recaptured as ordinary income. The amount of gain that must be recaptured as ordinary income is the lesser of the total gain realized, or the total of the depreciation, cost recovery or other amortization deductions allowed or allowable with respect to the property (Code Sec. 1245(a)).

NEW LAW EXPLAINED

Qualified disaster costs can be expensed.—Taxpayers may elect to deduct their qualified disaster expenses when they are paid or incurred, rather than charging them to a capital account. The election is available for amounts paid or incurred after December 31, 2007, in connection with a disaster declared after that date (Code Sec. 198A, as added by the Emergency Economic Stabilization Act of 2008 (P.L. 110-343)).

Qualified disaster expenses include any expenditure that is:

- paid or incurred in connection with a trade, business or business-related property;
- otherwise chargeable to a capital account; and
- made for (a) the abatement or control of hazardous substances that were released on account of a federally declared disaster; (b) the removal of debris from, or the demolition of structures on, business-related real property that is damaged or destroyed as a result of a federally declared disaster; or (c) the repair of business-related property damaged as a result of a federally declared disaster. (Code Sec. 198A(b), as added by the Emergency Economic Act of 2008).

> **Caution:** Although the qualified disaster expense rules do not have a termination date, they apply only to disasters that occur before 2010.

For this purpose, business-related property is property that (a) is held by the taxpayer for use in a trade or business or for the production of income, or (b) qualifies as section 1221(a)(1) property in the hands of the taxpayer (that is, inventoriable stock in trade or property held primarily for sale to customers in the ordinary course of the taxpayer's trade or business) (Code Sec. 198A(c)(1), as added by the Emergency Economic Act of 2008).

A federally declared disaster is any disaster subsequently determined by the President of the United States to warrant assistance by the federal government under the Robert T. Stafford Disaster Relief and Emergency Assistance Act (see 42 U.S.C. §5121 et seq.) (Code Sec. 198A(c)(2), as added by the Emergency Economic Act of 2008; see Code Sec. 165(h)(3)(C)(i)).

Recapture. When, but for these rules, a disaster expense would have been capitalized as part of the affected property, the deduction under the new disaster expense rule is treated as a depreciation deduction; thus, it must be recaptured as ordinary income if

NEW LAW EXPLAINED

the taxpayer realizes capital gain on a subsequent disposition of the property. For this purpose, any property that is not section 1245 property is treated as section 1245 property (Code Sec. 198A(d), as added by the Emergency Economic Act of 2008).

Coordination. Qualified disaster expenses that are expensed and deducted under these rules are not subject to Code Sec. 198 (which allows a deduction for qualified environmental remediation expenses), Code Sec. 280B (which capitalizes most demolition expenses) and Code Sec. 468 (which allows a deduction for qualified reclamation and closing costs related to certain mining and solid waste disposal properties) (Code Sec. 198A(e), as added by the Emergency Economic Act of 2008). These new expensing rules also do not apply to any disaster with respect to which the President has declared a major disaster on or after May 2008, and before August 1, 2008, because of severe storms, tornadoes or flooding in Arkansas, Illinois, Indiana, Iowa, Kansas, Michigan, Minnesota, Missouri, Nebraska or Wisconsin; or to expenditures and losses resulting from those disasters (Division C, Act Sec. 712 of the Emergency Economic Act of 2008, referencing Division C, Act Sec. 702(c)[b](i)(A)). See ¶ 655.

> **Comment:** The election to expense qualified environmental expenses was scheduled to terminate at the end of 2007, but has been extended through 2009 (see ¶ 340).

Regulations. The Treasury Secretary is authorized to prescribe regulations that are necessary or appropriate to carry out the purposes of the deduction (Code Sec. 198A(f), as added by the Emergency Economic Act of 2008).

▶ **Effective date.** The provision applies to amounts paid or incurred after December 31, 2007, in connection with a disaster declared after that date (Division C, Act Sec. 707(c) of the Emergency Economic Stabilization Act of 2008 (P.L. 110-343)).

Law source: Law at ¶ 5275. Committee Reports at ¶ 10,720.

— Division C, Act Sec. 707(a) of the Emergency Economic Stabilization Act of 2008 (P.L. 110-343), adding new Code Sec. 198A;

— Division C, Act Sec. 707(c), providing the effective date.

Reporter references: For further information, consult the following CCH reporters.

— Standard Federal Tax Reporter, 12,465 and 32,487

— Tax Research Consultant, BUSEXP: 57,300

— Federal Tax Guide, ¶ 7402

¶ 620 Special Depreciation Allowance for Qualified Disaster Assistance Property

SUMMARY OF NEW LAW

An additional 50-percent depreciation allowance can be claimed for real and personal business property that is purchased to rehabilitate or replace similar property that is destroyed or condemned as a result of a presidentially declared disaster. The provi-

SUMMARY OF NEW LAW

sion applies to property placed in service after December 31, 2007, with respect to disasters declared after that date and occurring before January 1, 2010.

BACKGROUND

Bonus depreciation is available for qualifying property that is: (1) placed in service before January 1, 2005, or (2) acquired after December 31, 2007, and placed in service before January 1, 2009 (Code Sec. 168(k)). The placed-in-service date is extended to January 1, 2010, for certain property with a long production period, including certain commercial and noncommerical aircraft. Qualifying property includes:

- new computer software as defined in, and depreciated under Code Sec. 167(f)(1) (that is, off-the-shelf software with a three-year depreciation period);

- new MACRS property with a recovery period of 20 years or less;

- new water utility property that is depreciated under MACRS; and

- qualified leasehold improvement property depreciated under MACRS (Code Sec. 168(k)(2)).

Bonus depreciation does not apply to most property that is subject to the alternative depreciation system (ADS); qualified New York Liberty Zone leasehold improvement property (see Code Sec. 1400L(c)(2)); and, if the taxpayer elects out of bonus depreciation with respect to any class of property for any tax year, all property in that class placed in service during that tax year (Code Sec. 168(k)(2)(D)). Bonus deprecation also is not available if the property user or a related party had a pre-2008 contract to acquire or produce the property. Special placed-in-service dates can apply to self-constructed property, sale-leaseback property and syndication property (Code Sec. 168(k)(2)(E)).

The amount of the bonus depreciation is equal to 50 percent of the adjusted basis of the property. The cost of the property is reduced by the amount of any Code Sec. 179 expense allowance claimed on the property. For purposes of computing subsequent depreciation deductions, the basis of the property is reduced by the amount of the bonus depreciation and any Code Sec. 179 allowance. Cumulative depreciation is limited to the asset's basis, regardless of whether the additional first-year bonus depreciation is claimed (Code Sec. 168(k)(1); Reg. § 1.168(k)-1(d)).

GO Zone and Kansas disaster area. These general bonus depreciation rules are extended to, and slightly modified for Gulf Opportunity (GO) Zone property acquired on or after August 28, 2005, and placed in service on or before December 31, 2007 (December 31, 2008, in the case of nonresidential real property and residential rental property) (Code Sec. 1400N(d)). Bonus depreciation in the GO Zone does not apply to any property used in connection with any private or commercial golf course, country club, massage parlor, hot tub facility or suntan facility; any store whose principal business is the sale of alcoholic beverages for consumption off premises; or any gambling or animal racing property (Code Sec. 1400N(p)(3)). These bonus depreciation rules are, in turn, extended to Recovery Assistance property placed in service in the Kansas disaster area after May 4, 2007, and before January 1, 2009 (January 1, 2010

BACKGROUND

in certain cases) (Act Sec. 15345 of the Heartland, Habitat, Harvest and Horticulture Act of 2008 (P.L. 110-246)).

NEW LAW EXPLAINED

Additional first-year depreciation allowed for qualified disaster assistance property.—An additional depreciation allowance (bonus depreciation) is permitted for the tax year in which qualified disaster assistance property is placed in service (Code Sec. 168(n), as added by the Emergency Economic Stabilization Act of 2008 (P.L. 110-343)). The additional first-year depreciation deduction is equal to 50 percent of the adjusted basis of the qualified disaster assistance property. The adjusted basis of the property is reduced by the amount of the additional deduction before computing the amount otherwise allowable as a depreciation deduction for the tax year in which the property is placed in service and for any subsequent tax year (Code Sec. 168(n)(1), as added by the Emergency Economic Act of 2008).

> **Comment:** Since the bonus allowance is computed on the property's adjusted basis, the basis of the property is first reduced by any Code Sec. 179 allowance claimed. For a special provision that increases the Code Sec. 179 allowance on disaster assistance property, see ¶625.

Qualified disaster assistance property must meet all of the following tests:

- The property must be described in Code Sec. 168(k)(2)(A)(i) (i.e., MACRS recovery property with an recovery period of 20 years or less, computer software that is depreciable over three years, water utility property, or qualified leasehold improvement property) or be nonresidential real property or residential rental property.

- Substantially all of the use of the property must be in a disaster area with respect to a federally declared disaster occurring before January 1, 2010, and in the active conduct of the taxpayer's trade or business in that disaster area.

- The property must rehabilitate property damaged, or replace property destroyed or condemned, as a result of the disaster. Property is treated as replacing property destroyed or condemned if, as part of an integrated plan, it replaces property that is included in a continuous area that includes real property destroyed or condemned. The property must also be similar in nature to, and located in the same county as, the property being rehabilitated or replaced.

- The original use of the property in the disaster area must commence with an eligible taxpayer on or after the applicable disaster date.

- The property must be acquired by the eligible taxpayer by purchase on or after the applicable disaster date, but only if no written binding contract for the acquisition was in effect before that date. A purchase is defined by reference to the definition in Code Sec. 179(d); therefore, it cannot be a transaction between related parties or members of the same controlled group, and the transferee's basis in the property cannot be determined by reference to the transferor's basis.

¶620

NEW LAW EXPLAINED

• The property must be placed in service by the eligible taxpayer on or before the date that is the last day of the third calendar year following the applicable disaster date (or the fourth calendar year in the case of nonresidential real property and residential rental property) (Code Sec. 168(n)(2)(A), as added by the Emergency Economic Act of 2008).

> **Comment:** The property need not be new. Used property that is acquired outside of the disaster area may qualify, as long as its first original use in the disaster area is by an eligible taxpayer.

An eligible taxpayer is a taxpayer who has suffered an economic loss attributable to a federally declared disaster (Code Sec. 168(n)(3)(D), as added by the Emergency Economic Act of 2008). A federally declared disaster is any disaster subsequently determined by the President of the United States to warrant assistance by the federal government under the Robert T. Stafford Disaster Relief and Emergency Assistance Act (see 42 U.S.C. § 5121 et seq.) (Code Sec. 168(n)(3)(B), as added by the Emergency Economic Act of 2008). The disaster area is the area determined to warrant disaster assistance (Code Sec. 168(n)(3)(C), as added by the Emergency Economic Act of 2008). The applicable disaster date is the date the federally declared disaster occurs (Code Sec. 168(n)(3)(A), as added by the Emergency Economic Act of 2008).

Practical Analysis: Glenn Graff, J.D., Partner in the firm of Applegate & Thorne-Thomsen, PC, Chicago, Illinois, notes that in Division C, Act Sec. 710 of the Emergency Economic Stabilization Act of 2008 (P.L. 110-343) the allowance of 50-percent "bonus depreciation" for disaster assistance property will provide a significant incentive for taxpayers to rebuild property damaged by federally declared disasters occurring after December 31, 2007, and before January 1, 2010. By requiring the replacement property be placed in service within three years of the end of the calendar year of the disaster (four years in the case of nonresidential real property and residential rental property), Congress is incentivizing taxpayers to proceed quickly with reconstruction work. Taxpayers should pay careful attention to the placement in service deadlines. Experience in the GO Zone has shown that unexpected delays can result in difficulties meeting the Congressionally imposed deadlines. This is especially true for projects with complicated financing such as buildings using the Low-Income Housing Tax Credit under Code Sec. 42. Another interesting note is that Congress has been proactive in having bonus depreciation for federal disaster areas apply to disaster areas that do not exist yet, but that are declared before January 1, 2010. Congress has not previously authorized bonus depreciation under Code Sec. 168 or GO Zone type depreciation under Code Sec. 1400N for disasters that had not occurred as of the time the legislation passed. It is noteworthy that the 50-percent bonus depreciation applies to nonresidential real property and residential rental property, i.e., buildings. Bonus depreciation under Code Sec. 168 was not previously available for buildings because of the Code Sec. 168(k)(2)(A)(i)(I) requirement that the property have a recovery period of less than 20 years. However, the allowance of bonus depreciation on buildings is consistent with the bonus depreciation made available in the GO Zone under Code Sec. 1400N(d). This approach seems to represent a distinction by Congress that bonus depreciation

NEW LAW EXPLAINED

granted in response to local disasters should include buildings but general grants of bonus depreciation as a national economic stimulus should not include buildings. It is also noteworthy that the new bonus depreciation provision is limited to property that "rehabilitates property damaged, or replaces property destroyed or condemned, as a result of such federally declared disaster." The 50-percent depreciation for GO Zone property under "Code Sec. 1400N(d)" was not limited to rehabilitation or replacement costs, but also included new property located in the GO Zone.

Exceptions. Qualified disaster assistance property does not include:

- any property that is eligible for bonus depreciation under Code Sec. 168(k) (without regard to any election under Code Sec. 168(k)(4) to forgo bonus depreciation in favor of an accelerated research or AMT credit), cellulosic biomass ethanol plant property (Code Sec. 168(l)), and qualified refuse and recycling property (Code Sec. 168(m));

- property that qualifies for bonus depreciation under the special rules for the Gulf Opportunity (GO) Zone (Code Sec. 1400N(d));

- any property used in connection with any private or commercial golf course, country club, massage parlor, hot tub facility, or suntan facility; any store whose principal business is the sale of alcoholic beverages for consumption off premises; or any gambling or animal racing property (i.e., property described in Code Sec. 1400N(p)(3));

- property that must be depreciated under the MACRS alternative depreciation system (ADS) (not including property for which an ADS election is made);

- property financed by tax-exempt bonds;

- qualified revitalization buildings for which the taxpayer has elected the Code Sec. 1400I commercial revitalization deduction; and

- if the taxpayer elects out of this bonus depreciation with respect to any class of property for any tax year, all property in that class placed in service during that tax year (Code Sec. 168(n)(2)(B), as added by the Emergency Economic Act of 2008).

Special rules. Bonus depreciation for qualified disaster assistance property applies to the taxpayer's self-constructed property if the taxpayer begins manufacturing, constructing, or producing the property after the applicable disaster date. Sale-leaseback property that a taxpayer places in service after the applicable disaster date, and then sells and leases back within three months, is treated as originally placed in service no earlier than the date on which the property is used under the taxpayer's leaseback. If property is originally placed in service after the applicable disaster date by a lessor, then is sold by the lessor or any subsequent purchaser within three months after being placed in service, and the user of the property after the last sale during that three-month period remains the same as when the property was originally placed in service, the property is treated as originally placed in service no earlier than the date of the last sale. Finally, property is not qualified disaster assistance property if the user or a related party has a pre-2008 contract to acquire or produce it (Code Sec. 168(n)(2)(B), as added by the Emergency Economic Act of 2008; see Code Sec. 168(k)(2)(E)).

¶620

NEW LAW EXPLAINED

AMT. As with regular Code Sec. 168(k) bonus depreciation, the additional depreciation allowance for qualified disaster assistance property may be claimed for alternative minimum tax purposes in the tax year that qualifying property is placed in service. No AMT adjustment is required. Furthermore, no AMT adjustment is required on any regular depreciation deductions claimed on the property over its entire recovery period (Code Sec. 168(n)(2)(D), as added by the Emergency Economic Act of 2008; see Code Sec. 168(k)(2)(G) and Reg. § 1.168(k)-1(d)).

Recapture. The tax benefits of the bonus depreciation must be recaptured as ordinary income in a tax year in which the qualified disaster assistance property ceases to be qualified disaster assistance property (Code Sec. 168(n)(2)(B), as added by the Emergency Economic Act of 2008; see Code Sec. 179(d)(10)).

▶ **Effective date.** The provision applies to property placed in service after December 31, 2007, with respect to disasters declared after such date (Division C, Act Sec. 710(b) of the Emergency Economic Stabilization Act of 2008 (P.L. 110-343)).

Law source: Law at ¶5230.

— Division C, Act Sec. 710(a) of the Emergency Economic Stabilization Act of 2008 (P.L. 110-343), adding new Code Sec. 168(n);

— Division C, Act Sec. 710(b), providing the effective date.

Reporter references: For further information, consult the following CCH reporters.

— Standard Federal Tax Reporter, ¶11,279.058

— Tax Research Consultant, DEPR: 3,600

— Federal Tax Guide, ¶9131 and ¶9132

¶625 Increased Expensing for Qualified Disaster Assistance Property

SUMMARY OF NEW LAW

The maximum Code Sec. 179 expense allowance and investment limitation amount are both increased for qualified section 179 disaster assistance property placed in service after 2007.

BACKGROUND

Taxpayers, other than estates, trusts, and certain noncorporate lessors, can elect to claim a Code Sec. 179 expense deduction for the cost of qualifying property acquired by purchase (Code Sec. 179). The Code Sec. 179 expense deduction is taken in lieu of depreciation deductions for the property. Since the Code Sec. 179 deduction is taken in the year the property is placed in service, it allows taxpayers to recover their

BACKGROUND

investment in the property more quickly than they would have by taking depreciation deductions over time.

For tax years beginning in 2008, the maximum Code Sec. 179 expense deduction is $250,000 (Code Sec. 179(b)(1); Code Sec. 179(b)(7)(A), as added by the Economic Stimulus Act of 2008 (P.L. 110-185)). This amount is lowered if the cost of qualifying property that is placed in service during the tax year exceeds the investment limitation, which is $800,000 for 2008 (Code Sec. 179(b)(2); Code Sec. 179(b)(7)(B), as added by the Economic Stimulus Act of 2008 (P.L. 110-185)).

Qualifying property that is eligible for Section 179 expensing, must satisfy the following conditions.

- The property must be tangible property subject to the MACRS depreciation rules, or off-the-shelf computer software placed in service in tax years that begin during 2003 through 2010.

- The property must be Section 1245 property (generally, tangible personal property, tangible property other than most buildings, real property if its adjusted basis reflects amortization adjustments, single-purpose agricultural or horticultural structures, storage facilities (other than buildings) used for distributing petroleum and petroleum products, and railroad grading and tunnel bores).

- The property must be acquired by purchase for use in the active conduct of the taxpayer's trade or business. Property is not acquired by purchase if it is transferred between related persons or members of the same controlled group, or if the transferee receives a carryover of stepped-up basis in the property (Code Sec. 179(d)).

Modifications. Prior tax acts have increased the maximum Code Sec. 179 expense allowance and the investment limitation amount for property placed in service in certain targeted areas, such as empowerment zones, renewal communities, the New York Liberty Zone, the Gulf Opportunity Zone, or the Kansas disaster area. For example, the otherwise allowable Code Sec. 179 expense deduction for property placed in service in the Kansas disaster area is increased by the lesser of $100,000 or the cost of such property placed in service during the tax year. Similarly, the investment limitation for property placed in service in the Kansas disaster area is increased by the lesser of $600,000 or the cost of such property placed in service during the tax year (Act Sec. 15345 of the the Heartland, Habitat, Harvest, and Horticulture Act of 2008 (P.L. 110-246).

Recapture. Tax benefits derived from section 179 expensing must be recaptured in the tax year in which the property is no longer predominantly used in the active conduct of a trade or business prior to the end of the property's recovery period. Recapture means the taxpayer must include as ordinary income the tax benefit derived from section 179 expensing from the time the property was placed in service to the time the property is no longer used predominantly in a trade or business (Code Sec. 179(d)(10); Reg. § 1.179-1(e)).

Empowerment zones and renewal communities. Communities that meet eligibility criteria concerning population, size, poverty and distress can be designated as empowerment zones or renewal communities (Code Sec. 1400E). Several tax benefits are available

BACKGROUND

for qualified zone property in empowerment zones and qualified renewal property in renewal communities. Qualified zone property is any depreciable tangible property that was acquired or renovated by the taxpayer after the date on which the empowerment zone designation took effect, if the original use of the property in the zone began with the taxpayer, and substantially all of its use is in the taxpayer's active conduct of a qualified trade or business in the zone (Code Sec. 1397D). Qualified renewal property is depreciable property that qualifies as section 179 property acquired by purchase by the taxpayer after December 31, 2001, and before January 1, 2010, if its original use in the renewal community began with the taxpayer and substantially all of its use is in the taxpayer's active conduct of a qualified business in the renewal community (Code Sec. 1400J(b)).

NEW LAW EXPLAINED

First-year expensing increased for disaster property.—The maximum allowable Code Sec. 179 expense deduction and the investment limitation are both increased for qualified section 179 disaster assistance property placed in service after December 31, 2007, with respect to disasters declared after December 31, 2007 (Act Sec. 711(b) of the Emergency Economic Stabilization Act of 2008 (P.L. 110-343)).

- The Code Sec. 179 expense deduction ($250,000 for 2008) is increased by the lesser of $100,000 or the cost of qualified section 179 disaster assistance property placed in service during the tax year (Code Sec. 179(e)(1)(A), as added by the Emergency Economic Act of 2008).

- The amount of the investment limitation ($800,000 for 2008) is increased by the lesser of $600,000 or the cost of qualified section 179 disaster assistance property placed in service during the tax year (Code Sec. 179(e)(1)(B), as added by the Emergency Economic Act of 2008).

    Comment: These increases mean that for qualified Section 179 disaster assistance property placed in service during 2008, the maximum allowable Code Sec. 179 expense deduction is $350,000, and the investment limitation is $1,400,000.

Eligible property. Qualified Section 179 disaster assistance property is Section 179 property that is qualified disaster assistance property (Code Sec. 179(e)(2), as added by the Emergency Economic Act of 2008). Qualified disaster assistance property is defined in Code Sec. 168(n)(2) (as added by the Emergency Economic Act of 2008). For the detailed definition of qualified disaster assistance property, see ¶620.

Recapture. If any qualified Section 179 disaster assistance property ceases to be qualified Section 179 disaster assistance property, then recapture of the tax benefit received is required under the normal recapture rules (Code Sec. 179(e)(4), as added by the Emergency Economic Act of 2008; see Code Sec. 179(d)(10)). Thus, in the year that property ceases to be qualified Section 179 disaster assistance property, the taxpayer must generally include in income the amount of tax benefit derived from the Code Sec. 179 deduction claimed in the year that the property was placed in service.

NEW LAW EXPLAINED

Limitations. Qualified Section 179 disaster assistance property cannot be treated as qualified zone property for purposes of the empowerment zone rules in Code Sec. 1397A, or as qualified renewal property for purposes of the renewal community rules in Code Sec. 1400J, unless the taxpayer elects not to take qualified section 179 disaster assistance property into account for purposes of the increased expensing amount and investment limitation (Code Sec. 179(e)(3), as added by the Emergency Economic Act of 2008).

▶ **Effective date.** The provision applies to property placed in service after December 31, 2007, with respect to disasters declared after such date (Division C, Act Sec. 711(b) of the Emergency Economic Stabilization Act of 2008 (P.L. 110-343)).

Law source: Law at ¶5245.

— Division C, Act Sec. 711(a) of the Emergency Economic Stabilization Act of 2008 (P.L. 110-343), adding new Code Sec. 179(e);

— Division C, Act Sec. 711(b), providing the effective date.

Reporter references: For further information, consult the following CCH reporters.

— Standard Federal Tax Reporter, ¶12,126.01, ¶12,126.03 and ¶12,126.04

— Tax Research Consultant, DEPR: 12,100

— Federal Tax Guide, ¶9130

REPORTING

¶630 Reporting Requirements Relating to Disaster Relief Charitable Contributions

SUMMARY OF NEW LAW

The annual information reporting requirements for tax exempt entities has been expanded to cover information regarding disaster relief activities and certain charitable contributions.

BACKGROUND

The fact that an organization is exempt from income tax does not mean that it need not file an annual return. As a general rule, all exempt organizations under Code Sec. 501(a) must file an annual information return reporting items of gross income, receipts, disbursements and other information required by the IRS (Code Sec. 6033(a)). A charitable organization under Code Sec. 501(c)(3) must include on its annual return the organization's gross income, expenses, disbursements for exempt purposes, fund balances, balance sheet, total contributions, the names and addresses of persons contributing $5,000 or more during the tax year (or substantial contributors, in the case of private foundations), and the names, addresses and compensation

BACKGROUND

of its officers, directors, trustees and foundation managers (Code Sec. 6033(b)). In addition, Code Sec. 501(c)(3) charitable organizations must report information regarding direct or indirect transfers, transactions and relationships with other Code Sec. 501(c) organizations (other than Code Sec. 501(c)(3) organizations) and political organizations described in Code Sec. 527, including political campaign committees and political action committees. A Code Sec. 501(c)(3) organization is also required to report annually on its Form 990 the amounts of certain excise taxes paid by the organization, its managers, or a disqualified person, as well as any reimbursements paid to an organization manager with respect to the taxes. An exempt organization is also required to provide such other information as the Secretary of the Treasury and the IRS require in order to carry out the internal revenue laws.

NEW LAW EXPLAINED

Tax exempt entity reporting requirements expanded.—The Secretary of the Treasury may require that the annual information return filed by a Code Sec. 501(c)(3) charitable organization include information regarding the disaster relief activities conducted by the charity (Code Sec. 6033(b)(14), as added by the Emergency Economic Stabilization Act of 2008 (P.L. 110-343)). This includes the use of "qualified contributions" made by individuals to the charity which are not subject to the 50-percent contribution base deduction limitation for charitable contributions and the limitation on overall itemized deductions, as well as "qualified contributions" made by corporations to the charity which are not subject to the 10-percent of taxable income deduction limitation (Code Sec. 1400S(a), as amended by the Emergency Economic Act of 2008).

> **Comment:** For this purpose, a "qualified contribution" is any charitable contribution made in cash by an individual or corporation from August 28, 2005, through December 31, 2005, to any "50-percent" charitable organization (other than a Code Sec. 509(a)(3) "supporting" organization) and for which the donor has elected qualified contribution treatment. It also includes any charitable contribution made in cash before 2009 to a "50-percent" charitable organization for relief efforts for victims of the storms that hit the Midwest of the United States in the summer of 2008 (see ¶ 655).

▶ **Effective date.** The provision applies to returns the due date for which (determined without regard to any extensions) occurs after December 31, 2008 (Division C, Act Sec. 703(b) of the Emergency Economic Stabilization Act of 2008 (P.L. 110-343).

Law source: Law at ¶ 5430.

— Division C, Act Sec. 703(a) of the Emergency Economic Stabilization Act of 2008 (P.L. 110-343), redesignating Code Sec. 6033(b)(14) as Code Sec. 6033(b)(15), and adding Code Sec. 6033(b)(14).

— Division C, Act Sec. 703(b), providing the effective date.

Reporter references: For further information, consult the following CCH reporters.

— Standard Federal Tax Reporter, ¶ 35,425.021

— Tax Research Consultant, EXEMPT: 12,252

— Federal Tax Guide, ¶ 16,010 and ¶ 22,085

TAX CREDITS AND BONDS

¶635 Work Opportunity Tax Credit for Hurricane Katrina Employees

SUMMARY OF NEW LAW

The hiring period for eligibility for the Work Opportunity Tax Credit applicable to Hurricane Katrina employees is extended to four years or until August 25, 2009.

BACKGROUND

The Work Opportunity Tax Credit (WOTC) was designed to provide an incentive to hire persons from certain disadvantaged groups that have a particularly high unemployment rate (Code Sec. 51). For targeted employees, employers may generally claim a credit equal to 40 percent of the first $6,000 of qualified wages paid (*i.e.*, a $2,400 credit) during an employee's first year of employment, provided the employee performs at least 400 hours of service. If an employee works less than 400 hours, but at least 120 hours, the credit is reduced to 25 percent. No credit is available for employees who work fewer than 120 hours.

The credit applies to the wages of the following groups:

- families receiving cash welfare benefits for at least nine months;
- veterans who are members of families receiving assistance or food stamps;
- high-risk youth, age 18 through 24 on their hiring date, who live in an empowerment zone, or enterprise or renewal community;
- vocational rehabilitation referrals certified to have a physical or mental disability;
- qualified summer youth employees, age 16 or 17 on their hiring date, who live in an empowerment zone, or enterprise or renewal community, perform services during a 90-day period between May 1 and September 15, and who have not previously worked for the employer;
- ex-felons hired not more than one year after the later of their conviction or release from prison, who are members of low-income families;
- individuals, age 18 to 24, who are in families that have been receiving food stamps for six months;
- Supplemental Security Income (SSI) beneficiaries; and
- designated community residents, age 18 through 39 on their hiring date, who live in an empowerment zone, an enterprise or renewal community, or a rural renewal county.

Following the devastating Hurricane Katrina, a new target group, "Hurricane Katrina employees," was created for the WOTC by section 201(a) of the Katrina Emergency

BACKGROUND

Tax Relief Act of 2005 (P.L. 109-73). It applied to those qualifying employees hired during a two-year period, beginning on August 28, 2005, for a position, the principal place of employment of which is located in the core disaster area.

A "Hurricane Katrina employee" is an individual whose principal residence was in the core disaster area on August 28, 2005, and:

- who was hired during a two-year period beginning August 25, 2005, for a position where the principal place of employment is in a core disaster area; or

- who was displaced from the residence because of Hurricane Katrina and who was hired from August 28, 2005, to December 31, 2005 (Act Sec. 201(b) of the Katrina Emergency Tax Relief Act of 2005 (P.L. 109-73)).

The core disaster area is the portion of the Hurricane Katrina disaster area determined by the President to warrant individual or individual and public assistance from the government under the Robert T. Stafford Disaster Relief and Emergency Assistance Act (Act Sec. 2 of the Katrina Relief Act).

NEW LAW EXPLAINED

Extension of the qualifying hiring period for Hurricane Katrina employees.—The eligible hiring period for employers to claim the work opportunity tax credit for hiring eligible "Hurricane Katrina employees" has been extended an additional two years or until August 25, 2009 (Division C, Act Sec. 319(a) of the Emergency Economic Stabilization Act of 2008 (P.L. 110-343) amending Act Sec. 201(b)(1) of the Katrina Emergency Tax Relief Act of 2005 (P.L. 109-73).

▶ **Effective date.** The provision applies to individuals hired after August 27, 2007 (Division C, Act Sec. 319(b) of the Emergency Economic Stabilization Act of 2008 (P.L. 110-343)).

Law source: Law at ¶7156. Committee Report at ¶10,570.

— Divison C, Act Sec. 319(a) of the Emergency Economic Stabilization Act of 2008 (P.L. 110-343), amending Act Sec. 201(b)(1) of the Katrina Emergency Tax Relief Act of 2005 (P.L. 109-73);

— Division C, Act Sec. 319(b), providing the effective date.

Reporter references: For further information, consult the following CCH reporters.

— Standard Federal Tax Reporter, ¶4803.031

— Tax Research Consultant, BUSEXP: 54,258.45

— Federal Tax Guide, ¶2800

¶640 GO Zone Rehabilitation Credit for Qualifying Expenditures

SUMMARY OF NEW LAW

The increased percentages of 13 and 26 percent for claiming the rehabilitation credit on qualified rehabilitated buildings and certified historic structures in the Gulf Opportunity (GO) Zone has been extended for one year or until December 31, 2009.

BACKGROUND

In general, a two-tier tax credit, the rehabilitation credit, is available to be claimed for qualified rehabilitation expenditures. First, a 20-percent credit is available on qualified rehabilitation expenditures for certified historic structures. A certified historic structure is any building (and its structural components) that is listed in the National Register of Historic Places or located in a registered historic district and certified by the Secretary of the Interior as being of historic significance (Code Sec. 47(c)(3); Reg. § 1.48-12(d)(1)-(3)).

The pre-1936 building must meet certain requirements (Code Sec. 47(c)(1)):

- Qualified rehabilitation expenditures during a 24-month period exceed the greater of the adjusted basis of the building or $5,000;

- The building was placed in service before the beginning of the rehabilitation;

- Except for certified historic structures, the rehabilitation meets certain requirements on retention of external walls and internal structural framework; and

- Depreciation or amortization is allowable with respect to the building.

For purposes of the credit, a qualified rehabilitation expenditures include amounts paid or incurred by a taxpayer that are chargeable to a capital account for real property that is depreciable under, and made in connection with, the rehabilitation of a qualified rehabilitated building. Rehabilitation includes renovation, restoration, or construction of a building but not enlargement or new construction (Code Sec. 47(c)(2)).

Straight-line depreciation or the alternative depreciation system must be used in order for rehabilitation expenditures to be treated as qualified. Qualified rehabilitation expenditures do not include the costs of acquiring or enlarging an existing building. Nor do they include any expenditures allocable to any portion of a rehabilitated building that is, or may reasonably be expected to be, a tax-exempt use of property. The credits are also not allowable unless the rehabilitation expenditures exceed the adjusted basis of the building, and not merely the allocable adjusted basis of the part of the building that was rehabilitated (Code Sec. 47(c)(2)(B)). The rehabilitation tax credit is allowed in the year the qualified rehabilitated building is placed in service (Code Sec. 47(b)(1)).

Disaster relief. Following the large-scale destruction caused by Hurricanes Katrina, Rita and Wilma, the rehabilitation tax credit percentages under Code Sec. 47 were

BACKGROUND

increased with respect to qualifying buildings and structures located in the Gulf Opportunity Zone (Code Sec. 1400N(h), as added by the Gulf Opportunity Zone Act of 2005 (P.L. 109-135)). For certified historic structures located in the Gulf Opportunity Zone ("GO Zone"), the rehabilitation tax credit increased from 20 percent to 26 percent; for qualified rehabilitated buildings, the rehabilitation tax credit increased from 10 percent to 13 percent. The increased credit applied to qualified rehabilitation expenditures that are paid or incurred on or after August 28, 2005, and ending on December 31, 2008 (Code Sec. 1400N(h)).

NEW LAW EXPLAINED

Increased rehabilitation credit extended for GO Zone structures.—The 13 and 26 percent rehabilitation tax credit for qualified expenditures on, respectively, qualifying rehabilitated buildings and certified historic structures in the Gulf Opportunity (GO) Zone has been extended for one year or until December 31, 2009 (Code Sec. 1400N(h), as amended by Division C, Act Sec. 320(a) of the Emergency Economic Stabilization Act of 2008 (P.L. 110-343)).

Practical Analysis: Glenn Graff, J.D., Partner in the firm of Applegate & Thorne-Thomsen, PC, Chicago, Illinois, observes that the Gulf Opportunity Zone Act of 2005 increased the tax credit for the qualified rehabilitations in the Gulf Opportunity Zone as follows: (i) for certified historic structures, the credit was increased form 20 to 26 percent; (ii) for other buildings, the credit was increased from 10 to 13 percent. Code Sec. 47(c)(3) defines "Certified Historic Structures" as those that are on the National Register or are in a registered historic district and are certified by the Secretary of the Interior as being of historic significant to the district. As originally enacted, the increased credit was only available for qualified rehabilitation expenditures paid or incurred during the period beginning on August 28, 2005, and ending on December 31, 2008. Division C, Act Sec. 320 of the Emergency Economic Stabilization Act of 2008 (P.L. 110-343) allows the increased credit to apply to qualified rehabilitation expenditures incurred through December 31, 2009. This extension should help many projects in the GO Zone that have struggled to achieve completion prior to the end of 2008.

Compliance Tip: The rehabilitation credit may be claimed on Form 3468, Investment Credit.

▶ **Effective date.** The provision applies to expenditures paid or incurred after October 3, 2008, the date of enactment (Division C, Act Sec. 320(b) of the Emergency Economic Stabilization Act of 2008 (P.L. 110-343)).

Law source: Law at ¶5395.

— Division C, Act Sec. 320(a) of the Emergency Economic Stabilization Act of 2008 (P.L. 110-343), amending Code Sec. 1400N(h);

— Division C, Act Sec. 320(b), providing the effective date.

NEW LAW EXPLAINED

Reporter references: For further information, consult the following CCH reporters.

— Standard Federal Tax Reporter,¶4650.038 and ¶4650.07

— Tax Research Consultant, BUSEXP: 51,150 and REAL: 3,056.05

— Federal Tax Guide, ¶2700

¶645 Mortgage Revenue Bond Requirements Following Federally Declared Disaster

SUMMARY OF NEW LAW

At the election of the taxpayer, first-time homebuyer and purchase price limitation requirements for mortgage revenue bonds are waived for a principal residence destroyed in a federally declared disaster area.

BACKGROUND

Under present law, gross income does not include interest on state or local bonds (Code Sec. 103). State and local bonds are classified generally as either governmental bonds or private activity bonds. The exclusion from income for state and local bonds does not apply to private activity bonds, unless the bonds are issued for certain permitted purposes (qualified private activity bonds) (Code Secs. 103(b)(1) and 141).

The definition of a qualified private activity bond includes a qualified mortgage bond (Code Sec. 143). Qualified mortgage bonds are issued to make mortgage loans to qualified mortgagors for the purchase, improvement, or rehabilitation of owner-occupied residences. Rehabilitation loans are eligible for such financing if:

- the mortgagor receiving the financing is the first resident after the completion of the rehabilitation;

- at least 20 years have elapsed between the first use of the residence and the start of the physical work of the rehabilitation;

- certain percentages of internal and external walls are retained after the rehabilitation; and

- rehabilitation expenditures equal at least 25 percent of the taxpayer's adjusted basis in the residence after such rehabilitation (Code Sec. 143(k)(5)).

The Internal Revenue Code imposes several limitations on qualified mortgage bonds, including purchase price limitations for a home financed with bond proceeds and income limitations for homebuyers. In general, the purchase price limitation is met if the acquisition cost of each residence financed does not exceed 90 percent of the average area purchase applicable to the residence (i.e., the average single-family residence purchase price purchased during the one-year period in the statistical area in which the residence is located) (Code Sec. 143(e)).

BACKGROUND

The requirements for qualified mortgage revenue bonds generally do not apply to loans made to finance homes in economically distressed areas and Presidentially declared disaster areas. A residence is located in a disaster area if the area is determined by the president to warrant assistance from the federal government under the Disaster Relief and Emergency Assistance Act, as in effect on August 5, 1997. Financing must be provided within two years after the date the disaster is declared (Code Sec. 143(k)(11)).

NEW LAW EXPLAINED

Special rules for residences destroyed in federally declared disasters.—The provision replaces, at the election of the taxpayer, the temporary present-law provision for residences located in federally declared disaster areas with:

* a waiver of the first-time homebuyer requirement; and

* the purchase price limitation otherwise applicable to targeted area residences (i.e., the purchase price limitation is met if the acquisition cost of each residence financed does not exceed 110 percent of the average area purchase applicable to the residence).

The provision applies for the two-year period beginning on the date of the disaster, when the principal residence of a taxpayer is: rendered unsafe for use by reason of a federally declared disaster, or demolished or relocated by reason of an order of the government of a state or political subdivision thereof on account of a federally declared disaster (Code Sec. 143(k)(12)[13](A), as added by the Emergency Economic Stabilization Act of 2008 (P.L. 110-343).

Also, the provision expands the definition of rehabilitation loans to include the cost of repair or reconstruction of a taxpayer's principal residence for damage from a federally declared disaster occurring before January 1, 2010 (Code Sec. 143(k)(12)[13](B)(i), as added by the Emergency Economic Act of 2008). Such rehabilitation loans are limited to the lesser of $150,000 or the cost of repair or reconstruction (Code Sec. 143(k)(12)[13](B)(ii), as added by the Emergency Economic Act of 2008)).

For purposes of the provision, the term "federally declared disaster" means any disaster subsequently determined by the President to warrant assistance by the federal government under the Robert T. Stafford Disaster Relief and Emergency Assistance Act (Code Sec. 165(h)(3)(C)(i) (Code Sec. 143(k)(12)[13](C), as added by the Emergency Economic Act of 2008)).

An election cannot be revoked except with the consent of the IRS (Code Sec. 143(k)(12)[13](D), as added by the Emergency Economic Act of 2008). In addition, a taxpayer who makes the election is denied a double benefit (under Code Sec. 143(k)(12)[13] and Code Sec. 143(k)(11)) with respect to the purchase or financing of any residence by the taxpayer.

▶ **Effective date.** The provision applies to disasters occurring after December 31, 2007 (Division C, Act Sec. 709(b) of the Emergency Economic Stabilization Act of 2008 (P.L. 110-343)).

¶645

NEW LAW EXPLAINED

Law source: Law at ¶5210. Committee Reports at ¶10,740.

— Division C, Act Sec. 709(a) of the Emergency Economic Stabilization Act of 2008 (P.L. 110-343), adding Code Sec. 143(k)(12) [13];

— Division C, Act Sec. 709(b), providing the effective date.

Reporter references: For further information, consult the following CCH reporters.

— Standard Federal Tax Reporter, ¶7786.066

— Tax Research Consultant, INDIV: 54,300

— Federal Tax Guide, ¶4787

TEMPORARY RELIEF PROVISIONS

¶650 Tax Relief for Hurricane Ike Area

SUMMARY OF NEW LAW

The tax-exempt bond rules and the increase in the low income housing cap currently available in the Gulf Opportunity Zone are extended to areas hit by Hurricane Ike in 2008.

BACKGROUND

Under present law, gross income does not include interest on state or local bonds (Code Sec. 103). State and local bonds are classified generally as either governmental bonds or private activity bonds if they are issued for certain permitted purposes (qualified private activity bonds) (Code Secs. 103(b)(1) and 141). State and local governments in the Gulf Opportunity Zone (GO Zone) are allowed to issue tax-exempt private activity bonds after December 21, 2005, and before January 1, 2011, for rebuilding Gulf Coast infrastructure and residential property (Code Sec. 1400N(a)). The maximum aggregate face amount of qualified GO Zone bonds that can be issued by each of the affected states cannot exceed $2,500 multiplied by the portion of the state population which is in the GO Zone (based on census figures released before August 28, 2005).

A GO Zone bond may be treated as a qualified mortgage bond if it meets the Code Sec. 143 requirements for a qualified mortgage issue, with some modifications, and the residences that are financed with the bond are owner-occupied and located in the GO Zone. Normally, the proceeds of qualified mortgage bonds are available only for first-time homebuyers for the purchase of an owner-occupied, single-family residence. This first-time homebuyer restriction means that the bond proceeds cannot be used to help individuals who had an ownership interest in their principal residence within the three years prior to executing their mortgage. However, there is an existing exception to the first-time homebuyer restriction for qualified home im-

BACKGROUND

provement and rehabilitation loans and financing for residences in certain targeted areas. The GO Zone was designated as such a targeted area and any residence in the GO Zone as a targeted area residence.

A GO Zone bond may also be treated as an exempt facility bond if it is part of a bond issue where 95 percent or more of the net proceeds of the bond issue are used for qualified project costs. Qualified project costs include the costs of:

- any qualified residential rental project (Code Sec. 142(d)) located in the GO Zone;
- acquisition, construction, reconstruction, and renovation of nonresidential real property (including buildings and their structural components and fixed improvements associated with such property) located in the GO Zone; and
- acquisition, construction, reconstruction, and renovation of public utility property (Code Sec. 168(i)(10)) located in the GO Zone.

Low-income housing credit. The general business credit includes the low-income housing credit which may be claimed over a 10-year period for the cost of rental housing occupied by tenants having incomes below specified levels (Code Sec. 38(b)(5)). The amount of the credit is based on an applicable percentage of the qualified basis of the qualified low-income building. The credit can be claimed for any tax year, but generally only to the extent that the owner of a qualified low-income building receives a housing credit allocation from a state or local housing credit agency (Code Sec. 42(h)). The aggregate amount of housing credit allocations that may be made in any calendar year by all housing credit agencies within a state is limited by a state housing credit ceiling. The state housing credit ceiling is the sum of:

- the unused state housing credit ceiling for the preceding calendar year,
- the greater of $2.00 (for 2008) multiplied by the state population or $2,325,000 (for 2008) (Rev. Proc. 2007-66, I.R.B. 2007-45),
- the amount of housing credit ceiling returned in the calendar year, and
- the amount of unused credit carryover assigned to the state by the IRS.

For calendar years 2006, 2007, and 2008, the population component of the state housing credit ceiling was modified to allow for increased ceilings for the housing in the GO Zone. The increase is the lesser of: (1) the aggregate housing credit dollar amount allocated by the state housing credit agency to buildings located in the GO Zone for such calendar year; or (2) an amount equal to $18 multiplied by the portion of the state population located in the GO Zone according to the population census estimate released before August 28, 2005 (Code Sec. 1400N(c)(1)(A) and (B)).

NEW LAW EXPLAINED

Gulf coast tax benefits extended to region hit by Hurricane Ike.—Subject to certain modifications, the provision extends the liberalized tax-exempt bond rules found in Code Sec. 1400N(a) and the low income housing credit of Code Sec. 1400N(c) to the "Hurricane Ike disaster area" (Division C, Act Sec. 704 of the Emergency Economic Stabilization Act of 2008 (P.L. 110-343)). This is an area in Texas or Louisiana with respect to which a major disaster has been declared by the President on September 13,

NEW LAW EXPLAINED

2008, under section 401 of the Robert T. Stafford Disaster Relief and Emergency Assistance Act by reason of Hurricane Ike; and determined by the President to warrant individual or individual and public assistance from the federal government with respect to damages attributable to Hurricane Ike (Division C, Act Sec. 704(c) of the Emergency Economic Act of 2008).

Tax-exempt bonds. The existing rules of Code Sec. 1400N(a) are amended as follows for the Hurricane Ike disaster area (Division C, Act. Sec. 704(a) of the Emergency Economic Act of 2008):

- bonds may be issued after October 3, 2008 and before January 1, 2013;
- "qualified project costs" only include: (1) projects involving a private business (as defined in Code Sec. 141(b)(6)) that suffered losses in Hurricane Ike or projects replacing businesses that suffered losses; and (2) projects relating to public utility property damaged by Hurricane Ike;
- "qualified mortgage issues" mean issuances where at least 95 percent of the net proceeds (as defined in Code Sec. 150(a)(3)) provide financing for mortgagors whose primary residences were damaged by Hurricane Ike;
- use of bond proceeds remain at the discretion of state bond commissions or the relevant governor but now must be allocated on a most needed basis; and
- the maximum aggregate amount of a qualifying bond is limited to $2,000 multiplied by the population of either the Texas counties of Brazoria, Chambers, Galveston, Jefferson and Orange, or the Louisiana parishes of Calcasieu and Cameron, as determined by the most recent census released before September 13, 2008.

Low income housing credit. The increase to the Code Sec. 38(b)(5) low income housing credit found in Code Sec. 1400N(c) is modified and extended to the Hurricane Ike disaster area as follows. The aggregate increase is the lesser of the aggregate housing credit dollar amount allocated by the state housing credit agency to buildings located in the Hurricane Ike disaster area for the relevant year, or an amount equal to $16 multiplied by the population of either the Texas counties of Brazoria, Chambers, Galveston, Jefferson and Orange, or the Louisiana parishes of Calcasieu and Cameron, as determined by the most recent census released before September 13, 2008. The increase is only available in 2008, 2009 and 2010. Finally, the increase is determined without applying the additional rules of Code Secs. 1400N(c)(2) through (6) (Div. C, Act. Sec. 704(b) of the Emergency Economic Act of 2008).

> **Practical Analysis:** Glenn Graff, J.D., Partner in the firm of Applegate & Thorne-Thomsen, PC, Chicago, Illinois, observes that for 2008, 2009 and 2010, Division C, Act Sec. 704(b) of the Emergency Economic Stabilization Act of 2008 (P.L. 110-3430) provides an additional $16.00 per capital of low-income housing tax credits for each person in a Hurricane Ike disaster area. Because 2008 tax credits must be allocated by the end of December 31, 2008, state tax credit agencies will need to work quickly to allocate the 2008 credits. Also, unlike the additional credits that were previously

NEW LAW EXPLAINED

allocated for the Gulf Opportunity Zone, the Rita Zone and the Katrina Zone, carryover allocations of the additional credits for Hurricane Ike disaster areas will need to meet the requirements of Code Sec. 42(h)(1)(E). This section requires that 10 percent of project costs be incurred within a year of the carryover allocation and that the project buildings must be placed in service by the end of the second calendar year following the year of the carryover allocation.

▶ **Effective date.** No specific effective date is provided by the Act. The provision is, therefore, considered effective on October 3, 2008, the date of enactment.

Law source: Law at ¶7183.

— Division C, Act Sec. 704 of the Emergency Economic Stabilization Act of 2008 (P.L. 110-343).

Reporter references: For further information, consult the following CCH reporters.

— Standard Federal Tax Reporter, ¶32,487.021 and ¶32,487.041

— Tax Research Consultant, BUSEXP: 57,302.05 and BUSEXP: 57,306.05

¶655   Relief for Midwestern Disaster Area

SUMMARY OF NEW LAW

Many of the tax benefits extended to the victims of the Katrina, Wilma and Rita hurricanes are modified and available for victims of the storms that hit the Midwestern United States in the summer of 2008.

BACKGROUND

In the aftermath of the series of hurricanes that hit the Gulf region in 2005, Congress passed the Katrina Emergency Tax Relief Act of 2005 (P.L. 109-73) and the Gulf Opportunity Zone Act of 2005 (P.L. 109-135). These acts provided a variety of tax relief provisions for victims of those hurricanes. These provisions include the following: suspending certain limitations on deductions for personal casualty losses under Code Sec. 165; extending the replacement period for nonrecognition of gain under Code Sec. 1033; providing an employee retention credit for affected employers; allowing additional first-year depreciation for certain property; increasing the amount that may be expensed under Code Sec. 179; allowing certain demolition and clean up costs to be expensed; altering the carryback period for net operating losses that result from public utility property disaster losses; extending the carryback period for net operating losses; liberalizing the representation requirements for owners of residential real property financed by private activity bonds; providing tax beneficial rules for distributions to disaster victims from qualified retirement plans; and,

BACKGROUND

allowing certain retirement plan amendments made in light of the disaster to be retroactive.

NEW LAW EXPLAINED

Disaster relief extended to Midwestern disaster area.—The Emergency Economic Stabilization Act of 2008 (P.L. 110-343) provides tax relief to the victims of storms that hit the Midwestern United States in the summer of 2008. The area designated for tax relief is the "Midwestern disaster area," which is, generally:

- an area with respect to which a major disaster has been declared by the President under section 401 of the Robert T. Stafford Disaster Relief and Emergency Assistance Act (P.L. 100-707) by reason of severe storms, tornadoes or flooding on or after May 20, 2008, and before August 1, 2008, in any of the following states: Arkansas, Illinois, Indiana, Iowa, Kansas, Michigan, Minnesota, Missouri, Nebraska and Wisconsin; and

- determined by the President to warrant individual or individual and public assistance from the federal government under the Act with respect to damages attributable to storms, tornadoes or flooding (Act Sec. 702(b)(1) of the Emergency Economic Act of 2008).

> **Caution:** The second prong of the definition for Midwestern disaster area relating to individual and public assistance does not apply in certain instances noted below (Act Sec. 702(b)(2) of the Emergency Economic Act of 2008).

In general, the provision provides for the application of certain provisions of Code Secs. 1400N, 1400O, 1400P, 1400Q, 1400R, 1400S, and 1400T for the benefit of taxpayers within the Midwestern disaster area. In addition, certain sections of the Katrina Emergency Tax Relief Act of 2005 (P.L. 109-73) are made applicable to survivors of the Midwestern storms (Act Sec. 702(a) of the Emergency Economic Act of 2008). In applying these provisions to the Midwestern disaster area, the term "applicable disaster date," means the date on which the relevant storms occurred (Act Sec. 702(c)(3) of the Emergency Economic Act of 2008).

> **Comment:** The Emergency Economic Act of 2008 does not actually amend provisions of the Internal Revenue Code. Rather, it provides rules for the selective extension, and modified application, of the current provisions to victims of the recent floods in the Midwest.

Tax Exempt Bond Financing. Subject to certain modifications, the liberalized tax exempt bond rules found in Code Sec. 1400N(a) (see ¶650) have been amended as follows for the Midwestern disaster area (Division C, Act Sec. 702(a)(1)(A) and (d)(1) of the Emergency Economic Act of 2008):

- bonds may be issued after October 3, 2008, and before January 1, 2013;

- "qualified project costs" only include: (1) projects involving a private business (as defined in Code Sec. 141(b)(6)) that suffered losses attributable to the storms, or projects replacing businesses that suffered losses; and (2) projects relating to public utility property damaged by the relevant storms;

NEW LAW EXPLAINED

- "qualified mortgage issues" means issuances where at least 95 percent of the net proceeds (as defined in Code Sec. 150(a)(3)) provide financing for mortgagors whose primary residences were damaged by the applicable storms;

- use of bond proceeds remain at the discretion of state bond commissions or the relevant governor but now must be allocated on a most needed basis; and

- the maximum aggregate amount of a qualifying bond is limited to $1,000 multiplied by the census of the relevant state before the earliest date in which the state became part of the Midwestern Disaster Area.

Low income housing credit. The increase to the Code Sec. 38(b)(5) low income housing credit found in Code Sec. 1400N(c) is modified and extended to the Midwestern disaster area (see also ¶650). The aggregate increase is the lesser of the aggregate housing credit dollar amount allocated by the state housing credit agency to buildings located in the Midwestern disaster area for the relevant year, or an amount equal to $8 multiplied by the portion of the state population located in the Midwestern disaster area according to the most recent census estimate released before the earliest applicable disaster date. The increase is only available in 2008, 2009 and 2010. Finally, the increase is determined without applying the additional rules of Code Sec. 1400N(c)(2) through (6) (Division C, Act Sec. 702(a)(1)(A) and (d)(2) of the Emergency Economic Act of 2008).

> **Practical Analysis:** Glenn Graff, J.D., Partner in the firm of Applegate & Thorne-Thomsen, PC, Chicago, Illinois, observes that for 2008, 2009 and 2010, Division C, Act Sec. 702(d) of the Emergency Economic Stabilization Act of 2008 (P.L. 110-343) provides an additional $8.00 per capital of low-income housing tax credits for each person in a Midwestern disaster area. Because 2008 tax credits must be allocated by the end of December 31, 2008, state tax credit agencies will need to work quickly to allocate the 2008 credits. Also, unlike the additional credits that were previously allocated for the Gulf Opportunity Zone, the Rita Zone and the Katrina Zone, carryover allocations of the additional credits for Midwestern disaster areas will need to meet the requirements of Code Sec. 42(h)(1)(E). This section requires that 10 percent of project costs be incurred within a year of the carryover allocation and that the project buildings must be placed in service by the end of the second calendar year following the year of the carryover allocation.

Expensing for certain demolition and clean-up costs. Under current law, the cost of debris removal is generally capitalized. The new law applies a modified version of Code Sec. 1400N(f) to the Midwestern disaster area, which permits a 50-percent deduction for a "qualified Disaster Recovery Assistance clean-up cost" paid or incurred during the period beginning on the applicable disaster date, and ending on December 31, 2010. A "qualified Disaster Recovery Assistance clean-up cost" is an amount paid or incurred for the removal of debris from, or the demolition of structures on, real property located in the Midwestern disaster area to the extent that the amount would otherwise be capitalized. In order to qualify, the property must be held for use in a trade or business,

NEW LAW EXPLAINED

for the production of income, or as inventory (Division C, Act Sec. 702(a)(1)(A) and (d)(3) of the Emergency Economic Act of 2008).

Extension of expensing for environmental remediation costs. The extension provided in Code Sec. 1400N(g) of the expiration date of the environmental remediation expenditure deduction under Code Sec. 198, is extended to December 31, 2010, in the case of qualified environmental remediation expenditures paid or incurred in connection with a qualified contaminated site located in the Midwestern disaster area. In order to be treated as a qualified contaminated site, the release (or threat of release) or disposal of a hazardous substance at the site must be attributable to the applicable storms. In addition, expenditures paid or incurred for the clean-up of petroleum products in the Midwestern disaster area may qualify for the deduction (Division C, Act Sec. 702(a)(1)(A) and (d)(4) of the Emergency Economic Act of 2008).

Increase in rehabilitation credit. Code Sec. 1400N(h) increased the credit allowed under Code Sec. 47 from 20 to 26 percent for any certified historic structure, and from 10 to 13 percent for qualified rehabilitated buildings, located in the areas affected by the 2005 Gulf hurricanes (see ¶ 640). The new law extends this increase for qualified rehabilitation expenditures made on or after the applicable disaster date, and before January 1, 2012. To qualify, the expenditure must be made on building or structures damaged or destroyed by the Midwestern storms that otherwise qualify under Code Sec. 47 (Division C, Act Sec. 702(a)(1)(A) and (d)(5) of the Emergency Economic Act of 2008).

Net operating losses (NOLs) attributable to storm losses. A modified version of Code Sec. 1400N(k) applies to the Midwestern disaster area which, in general, allows taxpayers to use a five-year carryback period for NOLs. The amount of eligible NOLs is limited to the aggregate amount of the following deductions: (1) "qualified Disaster Recovery Assistance losses"; (2) certain moving expenses; (3) certain temporary housing expenses; (4) depreciation deductions with respect to qualified Recovery Assistance property for the tax year the property is placed in service; and (5) deductions for certain repair expenses resulting from the relevant storms. The provision applies for losses paid or incurred after the applicable disaster date, and before January 1, 2011. However, an irrevocable election not to apply the five-year carryback under the provision may be made with respect to any tax year (Division C, Act Sec. 702(a)(1)(A) and (d)(6) of the Emergency Economic Act of 2008).

- *Qualified Disaster Recovery Assistance losses.* The amount of "qualified Disaster Recovery Assistance loss" which may be included in the eligible NOL is the amount of the taxpayer's casualty losses with respect to: (1) property used in a trade or business, and (2) capital assets held for more than one year in connection with either a trade or business or a transaction entered into for profit. In addition, the property must be located in the Midwestern disaster area, must be deductible under Code Sec. 165 and the loss must be attributable to the applicable Midwestern storms. The amount of any casualty loss does not include any insurance compensation, and the total loss that may be included in the eligible NOL is reduced by any gain recognized from involuntary conversions of property located in the Midwestern disaster area caused by the storms or tornadoes. To the extent that a casualty loss is included in the

¶655

NEW LAW EXPLAINED

eligible NOL and is carried back under the provision, the taxpayer cannot also treat the loss as having occurred in the prior tax year under Code Sec. 165(i).

- *Moving expenses.* Moving expenses of an employer may be included in the eligible NOL if the amount is paid or incurred after the applicable disaster date, and before January 1, 2011, with respect to an employee who: (1) lived in the Midwestern disaster area before the applicable disaster date, (2) was displaced from his or her home either temporarily or permanently as a result of the Midwestern storms, and (3) is employed in the Midwestern disaster area by the taxpayer after the expense is paid or incurred. The former residence and the new residence may be the same if the employee initially vacated the residence as a result of the relevant storms. The individual with respect to whom the moving expenses are incurred does not have to be an employee of the taxpayer at the time the expenses were incurred. Thus, assuming the other requirements are met, a taxpayer who pays the moving expenses of a prospective employee and subsequently employs the individual in the Midwestern disaster area may include those expenses in the eligible NOL.

Comment: Moving expenses are defined under Code Sec. 217(b) to include only the reasonable expenses of moving household goods and personal effects, and travelling from the former residence to the new residence. However, as noted, the new law has modified this definition so that the former residence and the new residence can be the same residence if it was initially vacated due to the storms.

- *Temporary housing expenses.* Employer deductions for expenses incurred to temporarily house employees who are employed in the Midwestern disaster area may be included in the eligible NOL. While the temporary housing does not need to be located in the Midwestern disaster area, the employee's principal place of employment with the taxpayer must be in the Midwestern disaster area.

- *Depreciation of Disaster Recovery Assistance property.* Eligible NOLs include depreciation deductions (or amortization deductions in lieu of depreciation) with respect to qualified Disaster Recovery Assistance property placed in service during the tax year. The special carryback period applies to the entire allowable depreciation deduction for such property for the tax year in which it is placed in service.

- *Repair expenses.* Eligible NOLs include deductions for repair expenses (including the cost of removing debris) with respect to damage caused by the Midwestern storms. In order to qualify, the amount must be paid or incurred after the applicable disaster date, and before January 1, 2011, and the property must be located in the Midwestern disaster area.

- *Other rules.* The amount of the NOL to which the five-year carryback period applies is limited to the amount of the corporation's overall NOL for the tax year. Any remaining portion of the taxpayer's NOL is subject to the general two-year carryback period. Ordering rules similar to those for specified liability losses apply to losses carried back under the provision. In addition, the general rule which limits a taxpayer's NOL deduction to 90 percent of AMTI does not apply to any NOL to which the five-year carryback period applies under the provision. Instead, a taxpayer may apply such NOL carrybacks to offset up to 100 percent of AMTI.

NEW LAW EXPLAINED

- *Gambling and other property ineligible for five-year carryback.* The five-year carryback of NOLs generally allowed for qualified Midwestern disaster area property under Code Sec. 1400N(k) does not include property used in connection with: private or commercial golf courses, country clubs, massage parlors, hot tub or suntan facilities, stores whose principal business is the sale of alcoholic beverages for consumption off premises, or gambling or animal racing property (Code Sec. 1400N(p)(3)(A)). A *de minimis* rule applies to exclude from gambling and animal racing property any real property if the portion dedicated to gambling or animal racing is less than 100 square feet (Code Sec. 1400N(p)(3)(B)(ii)).

Midwestern tax credit bonds. States located in the Midwestern disaster area are authorized to issue Midwestern tax credit bonds during 2009, which can be used, in effect, to extend the maturity of existing obligations by two years at lower interest costs (Code Sec. 1400N(l)). The maximum aggregate face amount of bonds that may be designated by the governor of a state is not to exceed: (1) $100 million in the case of any state with an aggregate population located in Midwestern disaster areas within the state of at least 2 million, and (2) $50 million in the case of any state with an aggregate population located in Midwestern disaster areas within the state of at least 1 million but less than 2 million. States with an aggregate population located in Midwestern disaster areas within the state of less 1 million are not authorized to issue Midwestern tax credit bonds under these new provisions.

A taxpayer holding a Midwestern tax credit bond on one or more credit allowance dates during a tax year is allowed a credit equivalent to the interest that the bond would otherwise pay (Code Sec. 1400N(l)(1)). Credit allowance dates are March 15, June 15, September 15, December 15, and the last day the bond is outstanding. The credit with respect to each credit allowance date is generally equal to 25 percent of the annual credit for the bond, though a pro rata reduction applies for the quarters in which the bond is issued, redeemed or matures. The annual credit is equal to the face amount of the bond multiplied by a credit rate determined by the IRS. The credit rate is the rate that the IRS estimates will allow the issuance of bonds with a specified maturity at face value and without interest cost to the state (Code Sec. 1400N(l)(2)). The amount of the credit allowed to the taxpayer must be included in gross income and treated as interest income (Code Sec. 1400N(l)(6)).

> **Caution Note:** Although items of income generally increase the basis of a partner or S corporation shareholder in their interest, that basis is not increased by the amount of any credit included in income by the holder of a Midwestern tax credit bond (Code Sec. 1400N(l)(7)(B)(ii)).

The credit is not refundable (Code Sec. 1400N(l)(3)). In the case of a person who receives a passthrough of the credit from a partnership, trust, S corporation or other entity, the credit cannot exceed the tax attributable to the portion of the person's income attributable to the passthrough entity (Code Sec. 1400N(l)(7)(B)(i)). The rules for this limitation are to be similar to the rules under Code Sec. 41(g) that limit the passthrough of the research credit. Furthermore, although tax credit bonds are not tax-exempt bonds, issuers are subject to certain of the rules developed for tax-exempt bonds including the arbitrage requirements of Code Sec. 148 and information reporting requirements of Code Sec. 149(e). A bond is a Midwestern tax credit bond if it

NEW LAW EXPLAINED

satisfies the following requirements (Division C, Act Sec. 702(a)(1)(A) and (d)(7) of the Emergency Economic Act of 2008):

- the bond is issued by a state in the Midwestern disaster area;
- 95 percent or more of the bond proceeds are to be used to pay off qualified bonds issued by the state or a political subdivision, or to make a loan to a political subdivision that will use the funds to pay off its own qualified bonds;
- the governor of the issuing state designates the bond as a Midwestern tax credit bond;
- the bond is a general obligation of the state and is issued in registered form;
- the maturity of the bond does not exceed two years; and
- the "state matching requirement" is met (the state matching requirement will be satisfied if the issuing state pledges to match the face amount of the bonds with other funds to be used for the same payoffs and loans, and all such payoffs and loans are made equally from the bond proceeds and the pledged funds; individual payments will be deemed to be made equally from bond proceeds and pledged funds if the total payments for each one-year period after the date of issuance are made equally from bond proceeds and pledged funds).

Proceeds of a Midwestern tax credit bonds must be used to pay off "qualified bonds." These include any obligation of a state or political subdivision that was outstanding on earliest applicable disaster date for the Midwestern disaster areas within the state, except:

- any private activity bond;
- any bond for which there is an outstanding refunded or refunding bond; and
- any bond issued as part of an issue any portion of the proceeds of which was used (or is to be used) to provide certain prohibited property (any private or commercial golf course, country club, massage parlor, hot tub facility, suntan facility, racetrack or other gambling facility, or liquor store) (Code Sec. 1400N(l)(5)).

Qualified rental project requirements. Subject to certain requirements, Code Sec. 141 qualified private activity bonds may be issued to finance a "qualified residential rental project." Operators of a qualified residential rental project must annually certify that such project meets the requirements for qualification, including meeting the income limitations for renters. The Emergency Economic Act of 2008 extends the application of Code Sec. 1400N(n) to the Midwestern disaster area to provide that operators of a qualified residential rental project may rely on the representations of prospective tenants displaced by reason of the relevant storms for purposes of determining whether such individuals satisfy the income limitations for qualified residential rental projects. This rule only applies if the individual's tenancy begins during the six-month period beginning on the date when such individual was displaced (Division C, Act Sec. 702(a)(1)(A) of the Emergency Economic Act of 2008).

Education credits extended to students in Midwestern disaster area.. For tax years 2008 and 2009, the provisions of Code Sec. 1400O apply to expand the nonrefundable Hope and Lifetime Learning Credits under Code Sec. 25A for students attending an eligible

NEW LAW EXPLAINED

institution in the Midwestern disaster areas (Division C, Act Sec. 702(a)(1)(B) and (d)(8) of the Emergency Economic Act of 2008).

Housing tax benefits. The Emergency Economic Act of 2008 extends the housing benefits of Code Sec. 1400P to victims of the Midwestern storms. Under the applicable version of Code Sec. 1400P, qualified employees in the Midwestern disaster area may exclude the value of in-kind lodging provided to them and their families by or on behalf of a qualified employer. The amount of the exclusion cannot exceed $600 for any month lodging is provided. In addition, qualified employers are entitled to a temporary credit of 30 percent of the value of employer provided lodging excluded from the income of the employer's qualified employees. The credit is limited to a six-month period beginning on the applicable disaster date (Division C, Act Sec. 702(a)(1)(C) and (d)(9) of the Emergency Economic Act of 2008).

Special rules for the use of retirement funds. Many victims of the Midwestern storms are able to use the rules of Code Sec. 1400Q to access retirement funds without triggering the standard early withdrawal penalties (Division C, Act Sec. 702(a)(1)(D) and (d)(10) of the Emergency Economic Act of 2008). For purposes of applying Code Sec. 1400Q, the Midwestern disaster area is not defined as determined by the President to warrant individual or individual and public assistance (Division C, Act Sec. 702(b)(2)(A) of the Emergency Economic Act of 2008).

- *Tax favored withdrawals.* Under the provision, an exception to the 10-percent early withdrawal penalty of Code Sec. 72(t) applies to "qualified Disaster Recovery Assistance distributions" from a qualified retirement or annuity plan, a Code Sec. 403(b) annuity, or an IRA. In addition, income attributable to a "qualified Disaster Recovery Assistance distribution" may be included in income ratably over three years, and may be recontributed to an eligible retirement plan within three years without being included in the distributee's income. "Qualified Disaster Recovery Assistance distributions" include distributions made on or after the applicable disaster date, and before January 1, 2010, to an individual whose principal place of abode on the applicable disaster date, is in the Midwestern disaster area and who has sustained an economic loss by reason of the relevant storms. Such distributions are limited to $100,000 and are subject to the income tax withholding rules applicable to distributions other than eligible rollover distributions. Thus, the 20-percent mandatory withholding does not apply (Code Sec. 1400Q(a)).

- *Recontributions of withdrawals for home purchases.* A "qualified storm damage distribution" from certain retirement plans may be recontributed to such plans in certain circumstances. A "qualified storm damage distribution" is a distribution that is received from a Code Sec. 401(k) plan, Code Sec. 403(b) annuity, an IRA, and certain hardship distributions from qualified plans that are received after the date which is six months before the applicable disaster date, and before the date which is the day after the applicable disaster date, where the distribution was to be used to purchase or construct a principal residence in the Midwestern disaster area. The recontribution of the distribution may be made without tax or penalty if it is recontributed between the applicable disaster date, and March 3, 2009 (Code Sec. 1400Q(b)).

NEW LAW EXPLAINED

- *Loans from qualified plans to individuals sustaining an economic loss.* A modified version of Code Sec. 1400Q(c) provides an exception to the income inclusion rule for loans from a qualified employer plan if the loan is to an individual whose principal place of abode on the applicable disaster date, is located in the Midwestern disaster area and who has sustained an economic loss by reason of the relevant storms. The exception only applies to the extent that the loan (when added to the outstanding balance of all other loans to the participant from all plans maintained by the employer) does not exceed the lesser of: (1) $100,000 reduced by the excess of the highest outstanding balance of loans from such plans during the one-year period ending on the day before the date the loan is made over the outstanding balance of loans from the plan on the date the loan is made, or (2) the greater of $10,000 or the participant's accrued benefit under the plan.

- *Plan amendments.* A modified version of Code Sec. 1400Q(d) that permits certain plan amendments made pursuant to Code Sec. 1400Q, or regulations issued thereunder, to be retroactively effective. In order for this treatment to apply, the plan amendment generally must be made on or before the last day of the first plan year beginning on or after January 1, 2010, or such later date as provided by the IRS.

Employee retention credit. An employee retention credit is allowed for certain employers in the Midwestern disaster area by applying a modified Code Sec. 1400R(a) (Division C, Act Sec. 702(a)(1)(E) and (d)(11) of the Emergency Economic Act of 2008). The modified Code Sec. 1400R(a) grants eligible employers in the Midwestern disaster area a 40-percent credit for qualified wages paid to eligible employees. The amount of qualified wages which may be taken into account with respect to any eligible employee may not exceed $6,000. The credit is part of the current year business credit under Code Sec. 38(b) and therefore is subject to the tax liability limitations of Code Sec. 38(c). Rules similar to Code Secs. 51(i)(1) and 52 apply to the credit. For purposes of the provision:

- An eligible employer is any employer that conducted an active trade or business in the Midwestern disaster area which, as a result of damage sustained by reason of the tornadoes and storms, became inoperable on any day from the applicable disaster date, and before January 1, 2009. In addition, an eligible employer is one that employed an average of not more than 200 employees on business days during the tax year before the applicable disaster date.

- Eligible employees are employees of an eligible employer whose principal place of employment on the applicable disaster date was with the eligible employer in the Midwestern disaster area.

- Qualified wages are wages (as defined in Code Sec. 51(c)(1), but without regard to Code Sec. 3306(b)(2)(B)) paid or incurred by an eligible employer with respect to an eligible employee on any day after the applicable disaster date, and before January 1, 2009, during the period: (1) beginning on the date on which the trade or business first became inoperable at the principal place of employment of the employee immediately before the Midwestern disaster area storms, and (2) ending on the date on which such trade or business has resumed significant operations at such principal place of employment. Qualified wages include wages paid without

NEW LAW EXPLAINED

regard to whether the employee performs no services, performs services at a different place of employment than such principal place of employment, or performs services at such principal place of employment before significant operations have resumed.

Personal casualty losses. The deduction for personal casualty or theft losses arising in the Midwestern disaster area and attributable to the relevant storms on or after the applicable disaster date is not subject to the $100 reduction per loss occurrence, nor to the 10 percent of adjusted gross income reduction, under Code Sec. 165(h) (Division C, Act Sec. 702(a)(1)(F) and (d)(13) of the Emergency Economic Act of 2008). Thus, the losses are fully deductible (see ¶605). For purposes of applying this rule, the Midwestern disaster area is not defined as determined by the President to warrant individual or individual and public assistance (Division C, Act Sec. 702(b)(2)(A) of the Emergency Economic Act of 2008).

Charitable contributions. Taxpayers are allowed to elect to temporarily suspend for all "qualified contributions" by individuals (1) the 50-percent contribution base limitation, and (2) the limitation on overall itemized deductions. Similarly, corporations may suspend the 10-percent of taxable income limitation. "Qualified contributions" are:

- charitable contributions, as defined by Code Sec. 170(c),
- made in cash for relief efforts in the Midwestern disaster area,
- to a Code Sec. 170(b)(1)(A) organization, and
- paid during the period beginning on the earliest applicable disaster date, and ending on December 31, 2008.

Furthermore, the taxpayer must obtain a contemporaneous writing, as required under Code Sec. 170(f)(8)(A), from the recipient stating that the contributions will be used for the intended relief efforts. The term "qualified contributions" specifically excludes contributions to donor advised funds (Code Sec. 4966(d)(2)) or to an organization that avoids private foundation status under Code Sec. 509(a)(3). In the case of a partnership or S corporation, the election should be made separately by each partner or shareholder (Division C, Act Sec. 702(a)(1)(F) and (d)(12) of the Emergency Economic Act of 2008).

Special rule for determining earned income. A modified version of Code Sec. 1400S(d) to permit individuals whose principal place of abode was in the Midwestern disaster to elect to calculate their refundable child tax credit and earned income credit for a tax year that includes the applicable disaster date, by using their earned income from the preceding tax year (Division C, Act Sec. 702(a)(1)(F) and (d)(14) of the Emergency Economic Act of 2008). For purposes of applying Code Sec. 1400S(d), the Midwestern disaster area is not defined as determined by the President to warrant individual or individual and public assistance (Division C, Act Sec. 702(b)(2)(A) of the Emergency Economic Act of 2008).

Dependency status. For tax years beginning in 2008 or 2009, the IRS may adjust the application of the tax laws to ensure that taxpayers do not lose any deduction or credit or experience a change of filing status due to temporary relocations caused by

¶655

NEW LAW EXPLAINED

the storms that struck the Midwestern disaster areas (Division C, Act Sec. 702(a)(1)(F) and (d)(15) of the Emergency Economic Act of 2008).

Mortgage revenue bonds. The Emergency Economic Act of 2008 states that the mortgage revenue bond restriction modifications of Code Sec. 1400T apply to the Midwestern disaster area. The legislation provides no specific modifications to Code Sec. 1400T other than applying it to the Midwestern disaster area. Thus, the first-time homebuyer requirement for owner-occupied residences in the disaster areas that normally apply under Code Sec. 143 and the purchase price and family income requirements are relaxed for owner-occupied residences in these areas. The loan limit for qualified home improvement loans made with mortgage revenue bonds is $150,000 for owner-occupied residences in the disaster areas. The provision is effective for qualified disasters occurring after December 31, 2007, and before January 1, 2010 (Division C, Act Sec. 702(a)(1)(G) of the Emergency Economic Act of 2008).

Additional exemption for housing displaced individuals For tax years 2008 and 2009, an individual can claim an additional exemption for providing housing free of charge to Midwestern displaced individuals. The additional exemption is $500 for housing each displaced individual up to a maximum of $2,000 per taxpayer over the two applicable tax years. The additional exemption is not allowed if the taxpayer receives any rent or other amount from any source for housing a displaced individual. The taxpayer must include the displaced individual's taxpayer identification number on his or her tax return for the tax year in which the additional exemption is claimed (Division C, Act Sec. 702(a)(2) and (e)(1) of the Emergency Economic Act of 2008). For purposes of applying this rule, the Midwestern disaster area is not defined as determined by the President to warrant individual or individual and public assistance (Division C, Act Sec. 702(b)(2)(B) of the Emergency Economic Act of 2008).

Standard mileage rate increased. The statutory standard mileage rate for charity work related to the Midwestern disaster area is raised to 70 percent of the standard business mileage rate for the period beginning on the applicable disaster date, and ending on December 31, 2008. This rate is rounded up to the next highest cent (Division C, Act Sec. 702(a)(2) and (e)(2) of the Emergency Economic Act of 2008).

Mileage reimbursements excluded from gross income. Rather than taking a deduction, a volunteer who is reimbursed by a Code Sec. 170(c) organization for the costs of using a passenger automobile to provide relief related to the Midwestern disaster area may exclude those costs from his or her gross income up to an amount that does not exceed the standard mileage rate prescribed for business use. This provision applies to services contributed during the period beginning on the applicable disaster date, and ending on December 31, 2008 (Division C, Act Sec. 702(a)(2) and (e)(3) of the Emergency Economic Act of 2008).

Cancellation of indebtedness income. The Emergency Economic Act of 2008 excludes from gross income certain discharged indebtedness of storm victims whose principal residence on the applicable disaster date was located in the Midwestern disaster area, and applies to discharge of debt on or after the applicable disaster date, and before January 1, 2010. The exclusion applies only to debt that is not incurred in connection with a trade or business, and does not apply to any indebtedness to the extent it is secured by real property located outside the Midwestern disaster area. The amount of

NEW LAW EXPLAINED

discharged debt excluded from income under this provision is treated in the same manner as the amount excluded under Code Sec. 108(a) (Division C, Act Sec. 702(a)(2) and (e)(4) of the Emergency Economic Act of 2008). For purposes of applying this rule, the Midwestern disaster area is not defined as determined by the President to warrant individual or individual and public assistance (Division C, Act Sec. 702(b)(2)(B) of the Emergency Economic Act of 2008).

Replacement period for converted property in Midwestern disaster area extended. The replacement period for property in the Midwestern disaster area that is compulsorily or involuntarily converted on or after the applicable disaster date due to the relevant storms is extended from two years to five years (Division C, Act Sec. 702(a)(2) and (e)(5) of the Emergency Economic Act of 2008). For purposes of applying this rule, the Midwestern disaster area is not defined as determined by the President to warrant individual or individual and public assistance (Division C, Act Sec. 702(b)(2)(B) of the Emergency Economic Act of 2008).

▶ **Effective date.** No specific effective date is provided by the Act. The provision is, therefore, considered effective on October 3, 2008, the date of enactment.

Law source: Law at ¶7180.

— Division C, Act Sec. 702 of the Emergency Economic Stabilization Act of 2008 (P.L. 110-343).

Reporter references: For further information, consult the following CCH reporters.

— Standard Federal Tax Reporter, ¶4251.01, ¶7707.01, ¶10,005.041, ¶11,279.01, ¶12,014.021, ¶14,901.01, ¶32,487.037, and ¶32,507.01

— Tax Research Consultant, DEPR: 6,152, DEPR: 3,000, BUSEXP: 54,000, BUSEXP: 54,052, BUSEXP: 57,300, BUSEXP: 57,304, BUSEXP: 45,150, INDIV: 39,054, SALES: 6,352.15, SALES: 51,100

— Federal Tax Guide, ¶4095, ¶6325, ¶8620, ¶9100, ¶9130, ¶9132, ¶9910 and ¶10,830

Tax Practice and Procedure

7

TAX ADMINISTRATION

TAX ADMINISTRATION

¶705 Tax Return Preparer Penalty on Understatement of Taxpayer's Liability

SUMMARY OF NEW LAW

The definition of "unreasonable position" is revised, and the standards for imposition of the tax return preparer penalty are modified.

BACKGROUND

The Small Business and Work Opportunity Tax Act of 2007 (P.L. 110-28) expanded the scope of return preparer penalties to include all tax return preparers for returns prepared after May 25, 2007 (Code Sec. 6694). The phrase "tax return preparer" covers preparers of not only income tax returns but also estate and gift tax, employment tax, excise tax, and exempt organization returns.

Under the Small Business Tax Act an "unreasonable position" penalty applies to tax return preparers if the preparer knew (or reasonably should have known) of the position, did not have a reasonable belief that the position would more likely than not be sustained on its merits, and either did not disclose the position as provided in Code Sec. 6662(d)(2)(B)(ii) or did not have a reasonable basis for the position. The more likely than not standard adopted by the Small Business Tax Act replaced the previous realistic possibility standard.

Interim guidance concerning application of the more likely than not standard was subsequently provided (Notice 2008-13, IRB 2008-3, 282). The interim guidance explains that a tax return preparer may rely in good faith without verification upon information furnished by the taxpayer, as well as information furnished by another advisor, tax return preparer or other third party. Thus, a tax return preparer is not required to independently verify or review the items reported on tax returns, schedules or other third party documents to determine if the items meet the standard, but the preparer may not ignore the implications of information furnished to or actually known to the preparer. The tax return preparer must make reasonable inquiries if the information furnished by another tax return preparer or a third party appears to be incorrect or incomplete.

For disclosed positions, Code Sec. 6694(a) requires that there be a reasonable basis for the tax treatment of the position. One way to disclose a position is to use Form 8275, Disclosure Statement, which is attached to the taxpayer's return. The interim guidance also permits a tax return preparer to advise the taxpayer of the difference between the penalty standards applicable to the taxpayer and the penalty standards applicable to the preparer along with contemporaneously documenting that the advice was provided (Notice 2008-13, IRB 2008-3, 282).

Proposed regulations were subsequently issued addressing the return preparer penalty standards, and providing that a tax return preparer may reasonably believe that a position would more likely than not be sustained on its merits if, after analyzing the pertinent facts and authorities and, in reliance upon that analysis, the tax return preparer reasonably concludes in good faith that the position has a greater than 50-percent likelihood of being sustained on its merits (Prop. Reg. §1.6694-2(b)(1), NPRM REG-129243-07).

The amount of the return preparer penalty for the understatement of a tax liability is the greater of $1,000 or 50 percent of the income derived (or to be derived) by the preparer with respect to the return or refund claim (Code Sec. 6694(a)(1)). The return preparer penalty for an understatement of a tax liability due to willful or reckless conduct is the greater of $5,000 or 50 percent of the income derived (or to be derived) by the preparer with respect to the return or refund claim (Code Sec. 6694(b)(1)).

NEW LAW EXPLAINED

Penalty on understatement of taxpayer's liability by tax return preparer modified.—For tax returns prepared after May 25, 2007, the definition of "unreasonable position" is revised, and the standards for imposition of the tax return preparer penalty are modified. The definition of unreasonable position is divided into three categories—a general category, a disclosed positions category, and a tax shelters and reportable transactions category—each with its own standard to determine whether such position is an unreasonable position (Code Sec. 6694(a)(2), as amended by the Emergency Economic Stabilization Act of 2008 (P.L. 110-343)).

Practical Analysis: Kip Dellinger, CPA, Senior Tax Partner at Kallman And Co. LLP in Los Angeles, notes that "substantial authority" is the nondisclosure standard retroactive to May 26, 2007 replacing the requirement that a preparer was required to have a reasonable belief that a tax position would "more likely than not"(MLTN) be sustained on its merits if challenged by the IRS. Substantial authority for a tax position is analogous to the exception to the accuracy-related penalty for taxpayers under Code Sec. 6662.

Now, Division C, Act Sec. 506 of the Emergency Economic Stabilization Act of 2008 (P.L. 110-343) requires that the MLTN confidence threshold apply in determining the tax preparer penalty to a reportable transaction under Code Sec. 6662A, or if a significant purpose of an entity, plan or arrangement is the avoidance of income tax described as a tax shelter in Code Sec. 6662(d)(2)(C)(ii). The tax shelter language is identical to the language that—when imported into Circular 230 in June 2005—caused practitioners to "brand" all types of written communications to client with language that the contents of the communication does not protect the taxpayer against penalties imposed by the IRS. Therefore, it appears that if tax practitioners were concerned about the application of Circular 230, they will need to evaluate tax positions for significant purpose potential. Consequently, some of the time and subjective evaluation saved from lowering the confidence threshold to substantial authority will be lost to the time incurred and subjective evaluation involved in vetting for "significant purpose."

In reality, there is little change for "nondisclosure" or disclosure under the tax preparer regulations proposed in June of 2008 except that the practitioner no longer needs to have or document a conversation with the client when substantial authority exists but the practitioner cannot reach MLTN. However, the practitioner very well may have to document why the tax position does not have as a "significant purpose" the avoidance of a Federal tax (other than where the statute and Congress intended the tax treatment to apply).

Nonsigning preparers advising a taxpayer are really not affected by this change, although when advising a tax professional, they have a duty under the regulations to advise a tax preparer when a confidence threshold requirement is not met.

Interestingly, the "significant purpose—MLTN" exception for tax shelters applies only to the tax treatment of an item for income tax purposes, while Code Sec. 6694 encompasses the preparation of all Federal tax returns. Thus, for estate and gift tax returns (as well as other non–income tax returns), the required confidence threshold

NEW LAW EXPLAINED

> appears to be substantial authority regardless of whether a significant purpose of an entity, plan or arrangement is the avoidance of Federal tax. Estate and gift tax return preparers (and nonsigning advisers) may find this particularly comforting with respect to certain tax planning techniques, e.g., family limited partnerships.

For undisclosed positions, which fall into the general category, the penalty applies unless there is or was substantial authority for the position (Code Sec. 6694(a)(2)(A), as amended by the Emergency Economic Act of 2008).

Practical Analysis: Charles P. Rettig, J.D., LL.M., Principal with Hochman, Salkin, Rettig, Toscher & Perez, P.C. in Beverly Hills, California, Member of the IRS Advisory Council (IRSAC - SB/SE Subgroup) and the Advisory Board for the California Franchise Tax Board, observes that effective May 25, 2007, the Small Business and Work Opportunity Act of 2007 (SBWOA) (P.L. 110-28) amended Code Sec. 6694 to: (1) broaden the scope of the tax return preparer penalties to include preparers of returns other than income tax returns, (2) revise the standards of conduct tax return preparers must satisfy regarding uncertain "tax positions" to avoid imposition of the Code Sec. 6694 penalty, and (3) change the computation for the applicable monetary penalties for: (i) understatements due to unreasonable positions under Code Sec. 6694(a) from $250 to the greater of $1,000 or 50 percent of the income derived or to be derived by the return preparer from the preparation of the return or claim, and (ii) understatements due to a willful attempt to understate the tax liability or a reckless disregard or intentional disregard of rules and regulations under Code Sec. 6694(b) from $1,000 to the greater of $5,000 or 50 percent of the income derived or to be derived by the return preparer from the preparation of the return or claim.

Most practitioners quickly became familiar with the "standards" to be satisfied to avoid application of the Code Sec. 6694 penalty for undisclosed and for disclosed positions. For undisclosed positions, SBWOA amended Code Sec. 6694(a) to replace the "realistic possibility of success" standard with a requirement that the preparer knew (or reasonably should have known) of the position and had a "reasonable belief" that the tax treatment of the position would "more likely than not" be sustained on its merits. "More likely than not" has been the standard under various corresponding state regulations for years. For disclosed positions, SBWOA amended Code Sec. 6694(a) to replace the "non-frivolous" standard with the requirement that the preparer knew (or reasonably should have known) of the position and had a "reasonable basis" for the tax treatment of the position.

Code Sec. 6694, as amended by SBWOA, created a disparity in the penalty standards applicable to preparers as compared to taxpayers, holding preparers to a "more likely than not" (greater than 50 percent likelihood of being sustained on the merits if challenged), while taxpayers only needed the lesser substantial authority standard for a return position in order to avoid an accuracy-related penalty. Division C, Act Sec. 506 of the Emergency Economic Stabilization Act of 2008 (P.L. 110-343) brings the standards for preparers into alignment with the standards for taxpayers.

NEW LAW EXPLAINED

Treasury and the IRS issued Code Sec. 6694 Proposed Regulations in June 2008 incorporating the more likely than not standard with an intention to issue Final Regulations before the end of 2008. Much of the information set forth in the Proposed Regulations will continue to apply.

Revised Code Sec. 6694(a)(3) retained the good faith reasonable cause exception to imposition of the penalty. A preparer is not considered to have relied in good faith if: (i) the advice is unreasonable on its face; (ii) the preparer knew or should have known that the third party advisor was not aware of all relevant facts; or (iii) the preparer knew or should have known (given the nature of the tax return preparer's practice), at the time the tax return or claim for refund was prepared, that the advice was no longer reliable due to developments in the law since the time the advice was given (Proposed Reg. § 1.6694-2(d)(5)).

The reasonable cause exception to the Code Sec. 6694(a) penalty requires a review of all applicable facts and circumstances with reference to the nature of the error, the frequency and materiality of the errors, the preparer's normal office practice, reliance on another preparer's advice, and reliance on generally accepted administrative or industry practice. The most relevant Code Sec. 6694(a) penalty issue remains the reasonableness of the preparers belief in the reported position, not the likelihood it will prevail.

In the "tax trenches" it is almost virtually impossible to distinguish between "more likely than not" and "substantial authority" when facing a government agent who just reversed some "position" for which the preparer had primary responsibility.

Although the preparer does not have to examine or verify supporting information, they should make sure to inquire as to whether such data has been satisfactorily maintained. Encourage the client to maintain proper information supporting the information reflected on the return. "Best practices" likely require documentation of any tax related research (including authorities both for and against the tax position), the reasoning behind the conclusion, and relevant authorities supporting the conclusion.

The judgment for most positions set forth within the return belongs to the preparer, not the client. The Code Sec. 6694 preparer penalty and possible Circular 230 violations apply to the preparer, not the client! When in doubt, recommend disclosure. When really in doubt, do not prepare the return or provide the advice.

Comment: This is a reduced standard from the more likely than not standard under prior law and conforms the tax return preparer penalty standard for positions falling within the general category to the Code Sec. 6662(d)(2)(B)(i) taxpayer standard for imposition of the accuracy-related penalty (Joint Committee on Taxation, Technical Explanation of H.R. 7060, the "Renewable Energy and Job Creation Tax Act of 2008" (JCX-75-08)). By reducing the standard from more likely than not to substantial authority, and conforming the tax return preparer standard to the taxpayer standard, much of the content of the proposed regulations appears no longer to be relevant.

The preparer standard for disclosed positions is the reasonable basis standard (Code Sec. 6694(a)(2)(B), as amended by the Emergency Economic Act of 2008). For tax shelters and reportable transactions to which Code Sec. 6662A applies (listed transac-

NEW LAW EXPLAINED

tions and reportable transactions with significant avoidance or evasion purposes) a tax return preparer continues to be required to have a reasonable belief that such transaction would more likely than not be sustained on the merits (Code Sec. 6694(a)(2)(C), as amended by the Emergency Economic Act of 2008). This standard applies to returns prepared for tax years ending after October 3, 2008.

Practical Analysis: Michael Schlesinger, J.D., LL.M., Partner at Schlesinger & Sussman of New York, New York, observes that while Congress has removed a major conflict between tax preparers and clients, it remains to be seen what the IRS will do in the area of preparer penalties. Under prior law, two cases stand out, both involving the deduction of business expenses. In *J.J. Schneider*, DC-IN, 2003-1 USTC ¶50,352, a preparer was held liable for violating Code Sec. 6694's predecessor. In *S.P. Wilfong*, CA-7, 93-1 USTC ¶50,232, 991 F2d 359, after a jury trial, the reverse. *Wilfong* is even more telling because the preparer was able to beat the preparer penalty rap even though he corrected a major error from a prior year on the current return rather than amend the prior year's return.

Practical Analysis: Charles C. Hwang, J.D., Partner, Alex E. Sadler, J.D., Partner, and Jennifer A. Ray, J.D., Associate in the tax group of Crowell & Moring LLP in Washington, D.C., notes that Division C, Act Sec. 506 of the Emergency Economic Stabilization Act of 2008 (P.L. 110-343) amends the standard for tax return preparer penalties in Code Sec. 6694(a). Under revised Code Sec. 6694(a), the penalty applies to understatements of liability on a return or claim of refund if the understatement results from an unreasonable position and the tax return preparer knew (or reasonably should have known) of the position. Generally, a position is unreasonable for this purpose unless there is or was substantial authority for the position. However, only a "reasonable basis" is required if the position is disclosed as provided in Code Sec. 6662(d)(2)(B)(ii)(I) and is not a tax shelter or reportable transaction. On the other hand, if the position is with respect to a tax shelter (as defined in Code Sec. 6662(d)(2)(C)(ii)) or reportable transaction to which Code Sec. 6662A applies, the position is unreasonable unless it is reasonable to believe that the position would more likely that not be sustained on its merits. There is an exception from the penalty where it is shown that there is reasonable cause for the understatement and the tax return preparer acted in good faith. For positions other than with respect to tax shelters or reportable transactions, these standards will apply to returns prepared after May 25, 2007. For positions with respect to tax shelters or reportable transactions, the standards will apply for tax years ending after the date the Emergency Economic Act of 2008 is enacted.

The penalty amount is the greater of $1,000 or 50 percent of the income derived or to be derived by the tax return preparer with respect to the return or claim for refund.

Prior to this revision, Code Sec. 6694(a) imposed a "more likely than not" accuracy standard for a position taken on a return to be considered reasonable. However, only a "reasonable basis" was required if the position was disclosed as provided in Code Sec. 6662(d)(2)(B)(ii)(I). The previous standard was the result of an amendment by

NEW LAW EXPLAINED

> the Small Business and Work Opportunity Tax Act of 2007 (P.L. 110-28), which was effective for returns prepared after May 25, 2007. Prior to the 2007 statutory change, the penalty applied to understatements unless there was a "realistic probability" of being sustained on the merits.

Comment: As under prior law, the tax return preparer is not liable for the penalty if it shown that there is reasonable cause for the understatement and the tax return preparer acted in good faith.

▶ **Effective date.** The amendment applies to returns prepared after May 25, 2007, unless the position is with respect to a tax shelter, listed transaction, or reportable transaction with significant avoidance or evasion purposes, in which case the amendment applies to returns prepared for tax years ending after October 3, 2008, the date of enactment (Division C, Act Sec. 506(b) of the Emergency Economic Stabilization Act of 2008 (P.L. 110-343)).

Law source: Law at ¶5470. Committee Reports at ¶10,690.

— Division C, Act Sec. 506(a) of the Emergency Economic Stabilization Act of 2008 (P.L. 110-343), amending Code Sec. 6694(a);

— Division C, Act Sec. 506(b), providing the effective date.

Reporter references: For further information, consult the following CCH reporters.

— Standard Federal Tax Reporter, ¶36,956C.01

— Tax Research Consultant, IRS: 6,000

— Federal Tax Guide, ¶24,210

— Federal Estate and Gift Tax Reporter, ¶21,855.01

¶710 Refund Offsets for Unemployment Compensation Debts

SUMMARY OF NEW LAW

Any state that is owed a past-due debt for erroneous payment of unemployment compensation due to fraud may notify the Secretary of the Treasury of the debt to be collected. If certain requirements are met, the IRS is required to reduce the amount of any overpayment of federal taxes payable to a taxpayer by the amount of the unemployment compensation debts, and pay the amount by which the overpayment is reduced to the state.

BACKGROUND

Within the applicable period of limitations, the IRS may credit any overpayment of tax, including interest on such overpayment, against any outstanding liability for any tax, interest, additional amount, addition to tax, or assessable penalty, owed by the person making the overpayment. Any remaining balance will be refunded to the

BACKGROUND

person making the overpayment (Code Sec. 6402; Reg. § 301.6402-1). However, in addition to the IRS's discretion to claim the overpayment in satisfaction of outstanding tax liabilities, a taxpayer's refund is subject to offset to collect the any of the following, listed in order of priority:

- past-due child support;
- debts owed to federal agencies; and
- past due, legally enforceable state income tax debts.

The Secretary of the Treasury is authorized to disclose information regarding the collection of past-due child support, debts owed to other federal agencies and past due, legally enforceable state income tax debts to the agency seeking an offset. Disclosure is limited to information directly connected to the offset (Code Sec. 6103(l)(10)). As a condition of receiving such information, recipients are required to:

- establish and maintain records of disclosure requests made by or of it, and any disclosures pursuant to those requests;
- establish and maintain a secure area for storing returns and return information;
- restrict access to returns or return information only to authorized persons;
- provide other safeguards to the confidentiality of the returns or return information that the Secretary sets forth in regulations;
- provide the Secretary with a report describing the procedures used to ensure the confidentiality of returns and return information; and
- upon completion of use of returns or return information, send the data, along with any copies made, back to the Secretary or otherwise make the data undisclosable (Code Sec. 6103(p)(4)).

The refund offset program is administered by the Financial Management Service (FMS), the Treasury agency that ordinarily handles all government collections and disbursements of funds. FMS has issued its own regulations governing the refund offset process (FMS Regs. § 285.1, § 285.2, § 285.3 and § 285.8).

NEW LAW EXPLAINED

Refund offsets to collect unemployment compensation debts resulting from fraud.—Upon receiving notice from a State that a named person owes a covered unemployment compensation debt to that State, the Secretary of the Treasury is required to offset any overpayment of federal taxes by that person by the amount of the covered employment compensation debt, and pay the amount of the offset to the State (Code Sec. 6402(f)(1), as added by the SSI Extension for Elderly and Disabled Refugees Act (P.L. 110-328)). A covered unemployment compensation debt is defined as:

- a past-due debt for erroneous payment of unemployment compensation due to fraud which has become final under the law of a State certified by the Secretary of Labor pursuant to Code Sec. 3304 and which remains uncollected for not more than 10 years;

NEW LAW EXPLAINED

- contributions due to the unemployment fund of a State for which the state has determined the person to be liable due to fraud and which remain uncollected for not more than 10 years; and

- any penalties and interest assessed on such debt (Code Sec. 6402(f)(5), as added by the SSI Extension Act).

Upon offset, the IRS must notify the State of the taxpayer's name, taxpayer identification number, address and the amount collected. The IRS must also notify the taxpayer that his or her overpayment has been reduced by an amount necessary to satisfy a covered unemployment compensation debt. If the offset is made pursuant to a joint return, the notice must include information related to the rights of a spouse of a person subject to such an offset (Code Sec. 6402(f)(1), as added by the SSI Extension Act).

The offset for covered unemployment compensation debt applies after the offsets provided in present law for federal tax liabilities, past-due child support, past-due, and legally enforceable debts owed to a federal agency, and before any overpayment is applied to future federal tax liability. If a State or states notify the IRS that a person owes more than one debt that is subject to offset as covered unemployment compensation debt under the new Code Sec. 6402(f)(1) or past-due, legally enforceable state income tax obligations under Code Sec. 6402(e), any overpayment by that person shall be applied against such debts in the order in which they were accrued (Code Sec. 6402(f)(2), as added by the SSI Extension Act).

Offsets to collect covered unemployment compensation debts are only permitted against residents of the state seeking the offset. An offset of an overpayment will only be allowed if the taxpayer who makes the overpayment has shown on the federal return for the year of the overpayment an address within the state seeking the offset (Code Sec. 6402(f)(3), as added by the SSI Extension Act).

Notification Requirements. Prior to pursuing a refund offset to collect a covered unemployment compensation debt, a state is required to notify by certified mail the person owing the debt that the state proposes to take action to collect the covered unemployment compensation debt by offset. The state must provide the person at least 60 days to present evidence that all or part of the liability is not legally enforceable or due to fraud. The state must consider any evidence presented and determine that an amount of the debt is legally enforceable and due to fraud. Further, the state must also satisfy any other conditions that the Secretary may prescribe to ensure that the state's determination is valid and that the state has made reasonable efforts to obtain payment of the debt (Code Sec. 6402(f)(4), as added by the SSI Extension Act).

The IRS is authorized to issue regulations regarding the time and manner in which states submit notices of covered unemployment compensation debt, and the necessary information that must be contained in or accompany the notices. The regulations may specify a minimum amount of debt for which the offset procedure may be used to collect. The regulations may require states to pay a fee to reimburse the IRS for the cost of providing the offset procedure. Further, the regulations may require states to submit notices of covered unemployment compensation debt through and in accordance with procedures established by the Secretary of Labor, and may impose a fee payable to the Secretary of Labor to reimburse the Secretary of Labor for the costs of applying the

NEW LAW EXPLAINED

offset procedure (Code Sec. 6402(f)(6), as added by the SSI Extension Act). States are authorized to deduct from amounts collected through the offset for covered unemployment compensation debt in order to pay any fees imposed under the regulations that may be issued. Further, the amount of any penalties and interest collected through the offset may be transferred to the state fund to which the amounts would have been paid if the person owing the debt had paid the amounts directly to the state (Code Sec. 3304(a)(4)(G), as added by the SSI Extension Act).

Erroneous payments to states. If a state receives notification from the IRS that the IRS has made an erroneous payment to the state under the offset program, the state must repay that amount in accordance with regulations that the IRS may prescribe. The repayment must be made without regard to whether any other amounts payable to the state under the offset program have been paid (Code Sec. 6402(f)(7), as added by the SSI Extension Act).

Information disclosure to states. As is the case with past-due child support, debts due to other federal agencies, and state income tax debts, the IRS may disclose information regarding its collection of covered unemployment compensation debts to the state seeking an offset. The IRS is also authorized to disclose return information to the Department of Labor for purposes of facilitating the exchange of data in connection with requests by states for offsets of covered unemployment compensation debts. Disclosure is limited to information directly connected to the offset (Code Sec. 6103(l)(10), as amended by the SSI Extension Act). Recipients of such information are required to meet the existing rules regarding safeguards for disclosed information (Code Sec. 6103(p)(4), as amended by the SSI Extension Act).

Termination. The new provision shall not apply to refunds payable after the date which is 10 years after September 30, 2008 (Code Sec. 6402(f)(8), as added by the SSI Extension Act).

▶ **Effective date.** The provision applies to refunds payable under Code Sec. 6402 on or after September 30, 2008, the date of enactment (Act Sec. 3(e) of the SSI Extension for Elderly and Disabled Refugees Act (P.L. 110-328)).

Law source: Law at ¶5407, ¶5450 and ¶5452.

— Act Sec. 3(a) of the SSI Extension for Elderly and Disabled Refugees Act (P.L. 110-328), redesignating Code Sec. 6402(f) through (k) as Code Sec. 6402(g) through (l), respectively, and adding new Code Sec. 6402(f);

— Act Sec. 3(b), amending Code Sec. 6103(a)(3), (l)(10) and (p)(4);

— Act Sec. 3(c) and (d), amending Code Secs. 3304(a)(4) and 6402(a), (d)(2), (e)(3), (g) and (i);

— Act Sec. 3(e), providing the effective date.

Reporter references: For further information, consult the following CCH reporters.

— Standard Federal Tax Reporter, ¶38,530.01

— Tax Research Consultant, IRS: 33,304 and IRS: 9,254

— Federal Tax Guide, ¶22,430

¶715 IRS Disclosure of Return Information Relating to Terrorist Activities

SUMMARY OF NEW LAW

The IRS has permanent authority to disclose return information to federal law enforcement or intelligence agencies to apprise the agencies of terrorist activities and when requests for return information by such agencies relate to investigating or analyzing terrorist activities.

BACKGROUND

A taxpayer's return and return information is generally considered confidential and cannot be disclosed by the IRS, federal employees, or other persons who have access to the information (Code Sec. 6103). However, there are a number of statutory exceptions to this nondisclosure rule that permit a taxpayer's return and return information to be disclosed, such as situations involving court orders, emergencies, violations of federal criminal law, or administrative proceedings (Code Sec. 6103(i)).

One such exception permits the disclosure of returns and return information that may be related to terrorist incidents, threats, or activities or analyzing intelligence concerning such activities (Code Sec. 6103(i)(3)(C) and (i)(7)). A "terrorist incident, threat, or activity" can involve either an act of domestic terrorism or international terrorism as defined in Code Sec. 6103(b)(11) and 18 U.S.C. §§ 2331(1) and 2331(5). Disclosure may be made to the extent necessary to apprise the head of the federal law enforcement agency responsible for investigating such terrorist incident, threat or activity. The head of this agency may disclose the return information to officers and employees of the agency to the extent necessary to investigate and respond (Code Sec. 6103(i)(3)(C)(i)). Disclosure may also be made to the Department of Justice for use in preparing an application for an *ex parte* court order for disclosure, if there is reasonable cause to believe that the return and return information are relevant to a matter relating to such terrorist incident, threat or activity and the return or return information is sought for use in a federal investigation, analysis or proceeding involving terrorism (Code Sec. 6103(i)(3)(C)(ii)).

To the extent the federal law enforcement agency can show that it is involved in a response and investigation of a terrorist incident, threat or activity and can articulate the specific reason why disclosure may be relevant to a terrorist incident, threat or activity, the IRS, upon written request, may disclose return information to officers and employees of the federal law enforcement agency. The head of the federal law enforcement agency may disclose return information to officers and employees of any state or local law enforcement agency, but only if such agency is part of a team with the federal law enforcement agency (Code Sec. 6103(i)(7)(A)(ii)). The IRS's ability to disclose tax return information that may be related to terrorist activities is authorized through December 31, 2007.

NEW LAW EXPLAINED

Permanent authority to disclose return information when related to terrorist activities.—The IRS's authority to disclose certain tax return information is made permanent in cases where federal law enforcement or intelligence agencies request that return information be disclosed in order to investigate or analyze terrorist activities (Code Sec. 6103(i)(7), as amended by the Emergency Economic Stabilization Act of 2008 (P.L. 110-343)) or to apprise a federal law enforcement agency of terrorist activities (Code Sec. 6103(i)(3)(C), as amended by the Emergency Economic Act of 2008).

▶ **Effective date.** The provision is effective for disclosures after October 3, 2008, the date of enactment (Division C, Act Sec. 402(c) of the Emergency Economic Stabilization Act of 2008 (P.L. 110-343)).

Law source: Law at ¶5450. Committee Reports at ¶10,630.

— Division C, Act Sec. 402(a) of the Emergency Economic Stabilization Act of 2008 (P.L. 110-343), striking Code Sec. 6103(i)(3)(C)(iv);

— Division C, Act Sec. 402(b), striking Code Sec. 6103(i)(7)(E);

— Division C, Act Sec. 402(c), providing the effective date.

Reporter references: For further information, consult the following CCH reporters.

— Standard Federal Tax Reporter, ¶36,894.026 and ¶36,894.0272

— Tax Research Consultant, IRS: 9208

— Federal Tax Guide, ¶22,221

— Federal Estate and Gift Tax Reporter, ¶20,435.05

¶718 IRS Disclosure of Prisoner Return Information

SUMMARY OF NEW LAW

Effective January 1, 2009, disclosure of return information to the head of the Federal Bureau of Prisons, regarding incarcerated individuals that may have filed, or facilitated the filing, of false returns, may be made to the extent necessary to permit effective tax administration.

BACKGROUND

Disclosure of returns and return information is generally prohibited under the Internal Revenue Code except to the extent authorized (Code Sec. 6103). However, disclosure of returns or return information may be made for tax administration purposes as provided in Code Sec. 6103(k). Permitted disclosures under Code Sec. 6103(k) for tax administration purposes include those which meet the applicable requirements regarding competent authorities under tax conventions (Code Sec. 6103(k)(4)), state agencies regulating return preparers (Code Sec. 6103(k)(5)), investigative purposes (Code Sec. 6103(k)(6)), offers-in compromise (Code Sec. 6103(k)(1)), levies and outstanding liens (Code Sec. 6103(k)(2) and (8)), administration of Code Sec. 6311 (Code Sec. 6103(k)(9)), correcting misstatements of fact (Code Sec.

BACKGROUND

6103(k)(3)), and excise tax registration information (Code Sec. 6103(k)(7)). Also, under Code Sec. 6103(n), returns and return information may be disclosed, pursuant to regulations, to the extent necessary in connection with the processing, storage, transmission, and reproduction of such returns and return information, the programming, maintenance, repair, testing, and procurement of equipment, and the providing of other services, for purposes of tax administration. Procedures and recordkeeping provisions with respect to the disclosure of return information are provided in Code Sec. 6103(p).

NEW LAW EXPLAINED

Disclosure of prisoner return information to Federal Bureau of Prisons permitted for tax administration purposes.—Beginning on January 1, 2009, the IRS may disclose to the head of the Federal Bureau of Prisons return information with respect to individuals incarcerated in Federal prison whom it has determined may have filed, or facilitated the filing of, a false return, to the extent that it determines that the disclosure is necessary to permit effective Federal tax administration (Code Sec. 6103(k)(10)(A)), as added by the Inmate Tax Fraud Prevention Act of 2008 (H.R. 7082)). However, no disclosure may be made after December 31, 2011 (Code Sec. 6103(k)(10)(D), as added by the Inmate Tax Fraud Act).

Notwithstanding Code Sec. 6103(n), the head of the Federal Bureau of Prisons may not disclose any information it obtains from this disclosure to any person other than an officer or employee of the Federal Bureau of Prisons (Code Sec. 6103(k)(10)(B), as added by the Inmate Tax Fraud Act). Also, any return information received, pursuant to this permitted disclosure, can be used only for purposes of, and to the extent necessary in, taking administrative action to prevent the filing of false and fraudulent returns, including administrative actions to address possible violations of administrative rules and regulations of the prison facility (Code Sec. 6103(k)(10)(C), as added by the Inmate Tax Fraud Act).

> **Comment:** The IRS detects over 18,000 cases of tax return fraud by prison inmates each year. However, under prior law, it could not inform prison authorities when inmates had committed fraud.

Also, as a condition for receiving the return information, the agency must comply with the procedure and recordkeeping safeguards under Code Sec. 6103(p) (Code Sec. 6103(p)(4), as amended by the Inmate Tax Fraud Act).

Written report required. The Treasury Inspector General for Tax Administration must submit a written report to Congress on the implementation of this permitted disclosure, no later than December 31, 2010 (Code Sec. 7803(d), as amended by the Inmate Tax Fraud Act).

Annual reports required. The Secretary of Treasury must annually submit to Congress, and make publicly available, a report on the filing of false and fraudulent returns by individuals incarcerated in Federal and State prisons. This report must include statistics on the number of false and fraudulent returns associated with each Federal and State prison (Act Sec. 2(e) of the Inmate Tax Fraud Act).

NEW LAW EXPLAINED

▶ **Effective date.** The provision applies to disclosures made after December 31, 2008 (Act Sec. 2(d) of the Inmate Tax Fraud Prevention Act of 2008 (H.R. 7082).

Law source: Law at ¶5450 and ¶5497.

— Act Sec. 2(a) of the Inmate Tax Fraud Prevention Act of 2008 (H.R. 7082), adding Code Sec. 6103(k)(10);

— Act Sec. 2(b), amending Code Sec. 6103(p)(4);

— Act Sec. 2(c), amending Code Sec. 7803(d)(3);

— Act Sec. 2(d), providing the effective date.

Reporter references: For further information, consult the following CCH reporters.

— Standard Federal Tax Reporter, ¶36,894.0276

— Tax Research Consultant, IRS: 9,000

— Federal Tax Guide, ¶22,221

— Federal Estate and Gift Tax Reporter, ¶20,430

¶720 IRS Authority to Use Proceeds from Undercover Operations

SUMMARY OF NEW LAW

The IRS has permanent authority to use the funds received from an undercover operation to pay for additional expenses of further operations.

BACKGROUND

In general, the use of government funds is restricted by requiring receipts to be deposited in the general fund of the U.S. Treasury and by requiring expenses to be paid out of appropriated funds. However, funds appropriated by the IRS for undercover investigations to detect and prosecute criminal violations of the internal revenue laws may be used to: (1) purchase or lease property or (2) establish, acquire or operate a corporation or business entity as part of an undercover operation (Code Sec. 7608(c)(1)(A)). Proceeds obtained from the undercover operation may be used to offset expenses incurred in the operation (Code Sec. 7608(c)(1)(C)).

The exemption was originally enacted as part of the Anti-Drug Abuse Act of 1988 (P.L. 100-690). Although the provision was allowed to lapse after December 31, 1989, it was reinstated in 1996 and has been regularly extended. The most recent extension granted the IRS authority to use the proceeds from undercover operations through December 31, 2007 (Tax Relief and Health Care Act of 2006 (P.L. 109-432)).

NEW LAW EXPLAINED

Permanent authority to use proceeds of undercover operations.—The IRS authority to use proceeds obtained from an undercover operation to pay additional expenses incurred in conducting such operations has been made permanent (Code Sec. 7608(c), as amended by the Emergency Economic Stabilization Act of 2008 (P.L. 110-343)). Without such authority, the IRS may be hindered in conducting undercover operations by having to deposit all income from the investigative operations into the general fund of the U.S. Treasury and to pay all expenses out of appropriated funds.

> **Practical Analysis:** Charles P. Rettig, J.D., LL.M., Principal with Hochman, Salkin, Rettig, Toscher & Perez, P.C. in Beverly Hills, California, Member of the IRS Advisory Council (IRSAC - SB/SE Subgroup) and the Advisory Board for the California Franchise Tax Board, notes that Code Sec. 7608(c) provides the authority of the IRS to utilize proceeds received from an undercover operation to offset necessary and reasonable expenses incurred in the operation. Without this authority, IRS undercover operations could be jeopardized if all receipts were required to be deposited into the general fund of the United States Treasury as miscellaneous receipts. Code Sec. 7608(c)(3) merely requires the deposit of such proceeds at such time as they are no longer necessary for the undercover operation. Division C, Act Sec. 401 of the Emergency Economic Stabilization Act of 2008 (P.L. 110-343) amends Code Sec. 7608(c) by indefinitely extending the authority of the IRS to utilize such proceeds to offset the necessary and reasonable expenses incurred in the operation that generated the proceeds. Practitioners should be reminded that the IRS conducts undercover operations for the purpose of determining whether the criminal provisions of the Code may have been violated.

▶ **Effective date.** The provision is effective for undercover operations conducted after October 3, 2008, the date of enactment (Division C, Act. Sec. 401(b) of the Emergency Economic Stabilization Act of 2008 (P.L. 110-343)).

Law source: Law at ¶5485. Committee Reports at ¶10,620.

— Division C, Act Sec. 401(a) of the Emergency Economic Stabilization Act of 2008 (P.L. 110-343), striking Code Sec. 7608(c)(6).

— Division C, Act Sec. 401(b), providing the effective date.

Reporter references: For further information, consult the following CCH reporters.

— Standard Federal Tax Reporter, ¶42,885.03

— Tax Research Consultant, IRS: 63,170

BROKER REPORTING

¶725 Broker Reporting of Customer's Basis in Securities Transactions

SUMMARY OF NEW LAW

Starting in 2011, brokers required to file information returns on covered securities transactions must report the customer's adjusted basis in the security and whether any gain or loss is long- or short-term. The broker must generally determine adjusted basis under the "first-in, first-out method" unless the taxpayer adequately identifies the stock sold. The broker also must furnish a written statement to the customer by February 15 of the year following the calendar year when the return must be made. Other provisions affect broker reporting on sales by S corporations, short sales, and options transactions.

BACKGROUND

A broker must file an information return for each person for whom the broker has sold stocks, bonds, most commodities, regulated futures contracts, forward contracts, debt instruments, or other property or services (Code Sec. 6045(a), Reg. §1.6045-1). The broker generally must report the name, address and taxpayer identification number of the customer, the property sold, the Committee on Uniform Security Identification Procedures (CUSIP) number of the security sold (if known), gross proceeds, sale date, and such other information as may be required by Form 1099, in the form, manner and number of copies required by Form 1099. If required to make the return described above in a calendar year, the broker must also furnish a written statement to each customer named in the return by January 31 of the following year (Code Sec. 6045(b)).

> **Compliance Tip:** The information is reported on Form 1099-B, Proceeds From Broker and Barter Exchange Transactions, or an acceptable substitute statement.

Options excluded. The broker reporting requirements do not cover certain options transactions. Under the requirements, a "security" includes a share of stock in a domestic or foreign corporation or a debt obligation, but does not include options or executory contracts that require delivery of these types of securities (Reg. §1.6045-1(a)(3)(vi)). Further, a "sale" does not include grants or purchases of options, exercises of call options, or enterings into contracts that require delivery of personal property or an interest therein (Reg. §1.6045-1(a)(9)).

Short sales. If a broker lends a customer's securities for use in a short sale or similar transaction and receives on the customer's behalf a payment in lieu of a dividend or tax-exempt interest (or other item as prescribed by regulation) during the period the short sale is open, the broker must send the customer a written notice identifying the nature of the substitute payment (Code Sec. 6045(d)). The statement must be furnished after April 30th of such calendar year (but never before the final substitute

BACKGROUND

payment for the calendar year is made), and on or before January 31 of the following calendar year (Reg. § 1.6045-2(d)).

Determining basis. While a broker is not required to report a customer's basis on securities transactions, the taxpayer customer still must determine his adjusted basis to calculate gain or loss for federal tax purposes (Code Sec. 1001). In most situations, the original basis of property is its cost to the taxpayer (Code Sec. 1012). The original basis is generally adjusted upward to reflect income, gain inclusions and capital outlays regarding the property, and downward to reflect depreciation, amortization, and returns on capital (Code Sec. 1016).

If a taxpayer buys and sells securities from lots on different dates and at different prices and cannot adequately identify the shares sold, the basis of the securities sold is the basis of the securities acquired first. In other words, the taxpayer must apply the "first-in, first-out" (FIFO) rule. However, FIFO does not apply if the taxpayer can adequately identify the lot from which the securities are sold or transferred (Reg. § 1.1012-1(c)(1)).

An adequate identification is made if the taxpayer shows that certificates representing shares of stock from a lot which was purchased or acquired on a certain date or for a certain price were delivered to the taxpayer's transferee (Reg. § 1.1012-1(c)(1)). When a single stock certificate represents stock from different lots and a part of the stock is being sold, adequate identification is made if the taxpayer specifies the particular stock to be sold by identifying its purchase date, purchase price, or both, and if written confirmation is received from the broker within a reasonable time. If part of the stock represented by a single certificate is sold directly to the purchaser and not through a broker, adequate identification is made if the taxpayer maintains a written record of the particular stock he intended to sell. If shares are held by a broker or other agent, adequate identification is made if, at the time of sale, the taxpayer specifies to the broker or other agent the specific stock to be sold and written confirmation is received from the broker or other agent within a reasonable time. The stock sold should be identified by purchase date, purchase price, or both (Reg. § 1.1012-1(c)(2) and (3)).

Wash sales and basis. Under the wash sale rules, a taxpayer who realizes a loss upon a sale or other disposition of stock or securities may not take a deduction for the loss. In general, these rules apply if, within a period beginning 30 days before the date of the sale or disposition and ending 30 days after that date, the taxpayer has acquired (or entered a contract or option to acquire) substantially identical stock or securities (Code Sec. 1091(a); Reg. § 1.1091-1). The disallowed loss is added to the cost of the new stock or securities. The basis adjustment postpones the loss deduction until the new stock or securities are sold or disposed (Code Sec. 1091(d); Reg. § 1.1091-2).

NEW LAW EXPLAINED

Broker reporting of customer's basis in securities transactions.—Starting in 2011, every broker required to file an information return under Code Sec. 6045(a) (Form 1099-B, Proceeds from Broker and Barter Exchange Transactions) to report the gross proceeds from the sale of a covered security must also include the customer's adjusted

NEW LAW EXPLAINED

basis in the security, and whether any gain or loss regarding the security is long-term or short-term (Code Sec. 6045(g), as added by the Emergency Economic Stabilization Act of 2008 (P.L. 110-343)).

Adjusted basis. Generally, a broker must determine a customer's adjusted basis in a covered security according to the "first-in first-out" (FIFO) method, unless the customer notifies the broker by making an adequate identification of the stock sold or transferred (under the specific identification rules). However, for any stock for which an average basis method is allowed under Code Sec. 1012 (i.e., stock in a mutual fund, or stock acquired in connection with a dividend reinvestment plan; see ¶ 730), the customer's adjusted basis is determined according to the broker's default method, unless the customer notifies the broker that he elects another acceptable method under Code Sec. 1012 regarding the account in which the stock is held (Code Sec. 6045(g)(2)(B)(i), as added by the Emergency Economic Act of 2008). The notification is made separately for each account in which average cost method stock is held, and once made, the notification applies to all stock in that account (Joint Committee on Taxation, Technical Explanation of H.R. 7060, the "Renewable Energy and Job Creation Tax Act of 2008" (JCX-75-08)).

> **Comment:** As a result of the new rule, a broker's basis computation method used for stock held in one account with that broker might differ from the method used for stock held in another account with that broker (Joint Committee on Taxation, Technical Explanation of H.R. 7060, the "Renewable Energy and Job Creation Tax Act of 2008" (JCX-75-08)).

Wash sale exception. Unless the Treasury Secretary provides otherwise, the customer's adjusted basis in a covered security is determined without regard to the wash sale rules of Code Sec. 1091. The exception does not apply if the acquisition and sale transactions resulting in a wash sale occur in the same account and are in identical securities (Code Sec. 6045(g)(2)(B)(ii), as added by the Emergency Economic Act of 2008). Securities are "identical" for this purpose only if they have the same Committee on Uniform Security Identification Procedures (CUSIP) number (Joint Committee on Taxation, Technical Explanation of H.R. 7060, the "Renewable Energy and Job Creation Tax Act of 2008" (JCX-75-08)).

Covered security. A "covered security" is any specified security acquired on or after the applicable date that was: (1) acquired through a transaction in the account in which such security is held; or (2) transferred to such account from an account in which the security was a covered security, but only if the broker received a basis statement under Code Sec. 6045A (see ¶ 735) with respect to the transfer (Code Sec. 6045(g)(3)(A), as added by the Emergency Economic Act of 2008). Under this rule, securities acquired by gift or inheritance are not covered securities (Joint Committee on Taxation, Technical Explanation of H.R. 7060, the "Renewable Energy and Job Creation Tax Act of 2008" (JCX-75-08)).

A "specified security" is:

- a share of stock in a corporation;

- a note, bond, debenture or other evidence of indebtedness;

NEW LAW EXPLAINED

- any commodity, or contract or derivative regarding the commodity, if the Treasury Secretary determines that adjusted basis reporting is appropriate; and

- any other financial instrument for which the Secretary determines that adjusted basis reporting is appropriate (Code Sec. 6045(g)(3)(B), as added by the Emergency Economic Act of 2008).

The "applicable date" on or after which a specified security must be acquired to be treated as a covered security is:

- January 1, 2011, for corporate stock, generally,

- January 1, 2012, for stock for which an average basis method is permitted (see ¶730), and

- January 1, 2013 (or a later date if determined by the Secretary) for other types of specified securities (Code Sec. 6045(g)(3)(C), as added by the Emergency Economic Act of 2008).

S corporations. For a sale of a covered security acquired by an S corporation (other than a financial institution) after December 31, 2011, the S corporation is treated in the same manner as a partnership for broker reporting purposes (Code Sec. 6045(g)(4), as added by the Emergency Economic Act of 2008). Therefore, brokers generally will be required to report gross proceeds and basis information to customers that are S corporations (Joint Committee on Taxation, Technical Explanation of H.R. 7060, the "Renewable Energy and Job Creation Tax Act of 2008" (JCX-75-08)).

Short sales. For a short sale, gross proceeds and basis reporting under Code Sec. 6045 generally is required in the year in which the short sale is *closed* rather than the year in which the short sale is entered into (Code Sec. 6045(g)(5), as added by the Emergency Economic Act of 2008). The broker must furnish the required written statement for the short sale to the customer on or before February 15 of the year following the calendar year in which the payment was made (Code Sec. 6045(d), as amended by the Emergency Economic Act of 2008).

Options. The regulatory exception from Code Sec. 6045(a) reporting for certain options has been eliminated (Code Sec. 6045(h), as added by the Emergency Economic Act of 2008; Joint Committee on Taxation, Technical Explanation of H.R. 7060, the "Renewable Energy and Job Creation Tax Act of 2008" (JCX-75-08)). If a covered security is acquired by or delivered to satisfy the exercise of an option, and the option was granted or acquired in the same account as the covered security, the amount of the premium received or paid for the option is treated as an adjustment to the gross proceeds from the later sale of the covered security or as an adjustment to the customer's adjusted basis in that security. Gross proceeds and basis reporting also generally is required when there is a lapse or closing transaction (as defined in Code Sec. 1234(b)(2)(A)) with respect to an option on a specified security. These options reporting rules apply only to options granted or acquired on or after January 1, 2013.

Extended period for sending customer statements. The deadline for the broker to furnish a written statement of gross proceeds and basis information to the customer is extended to February 15 of the year following the calendar year for which the return was required (Code Sec. 6045(b), as amended by the Emergency Economic Act of 2008). As noted above, the deadline for furnishing the short sale statement to the

NEW LAW EXPLAINED

customer is also extended from January 31 to February 15 (Code Sec. 6045(d), as amended by the Emergency Economic Act of 2008).

For consolidated reporting statements (as defined in regulations) regarding any customer, any statement otherwise required to be furnished on or before January 31 of a calendar year regarding any item reportable to the taxpayer must instead be furnished on or before February 15 of such calendar year if furnished along with the consolidated reporting statement (Code Sec. 6045(b), as amended by the Emergency Economic Act of 2008). A "consolidated reporting statement" refers to annual account information statements containing tax-related information that brokerage firms customarily provide to customers. The February 15 deadline is intended to apply in the same manner to statements furnished for any taxable and retirement account(s) held by a customer with a mutual fund or other broker (Joint Committee on Taxation, Technical Explanation of H.R. 7060, the "Renewable Energy and Job Creation Tax Act of 2008" (JCX-75-08)).

> **Comment:** Members of Congress have introduced numerous proposals requiring broker basis reporting on securities sales as one way to reduce the tax gap, which is currently estimated at $345 billion. (The "tax gap" is the estimated difference between the taxes that should have been paid and what was actually paid in a specific year.) In a report studying ways to reduce taxpayer misreporting of capital gains in securities transactions, the Government Accountability Office (GAO) identified several challenges that broker reporting requirements may pose, and suggested ways to mitigate those challenges (Government Accountability Office Report to the Senate Finance Committee, "Capital Gains Tax Gap: Requiring Brokers to Report Securities Cost Basis Would Improve Compliance if Related Challenges Are Addressed" (GAO-06-603)):

- *Brokers may face increased costs from having to implement systems to track and report basis.* The GAO recognized that some brokers already have systems to track basis, but said that brokers could leverage existing systems and the IRS could provide an effective date that would allow brokers to develop systems.

- *Brokers may not be able to determine basis in some transactions due to complex tax laws.* The GAO said that to mitigate these costs the tax laws could be simplified or the IRS could develop consistent reporting rules.

- *Brokers may not know the basis of securities purchased though other brokers.* The GAO said that brokers may be able to use an existing system to transfer basis information when taxpayers move their holdings.

- *Brokers may not know the basis for securities purchased through companies that directly issue stock.* The GAO suggested such companies could track and report basis and use the basis transfer system.

- *Brokers may not know the basis of older securities.* The GAO suggested that basis be tracked prospectively for securities purchased after a set date.

- *Brokers that do not know the basis may rely on taxpayers to provide basis without verifying it, which could lead to the same reporting problems.* The GAO believed prospective reporting will lead to fewer instances of not knowing the basis at

NEW LAW EXPLAINED

all, and brokers also could indicate on the return that the information was provided by the taxpayer.

- *Brokers may have difficulties obtaining adjusted basis information on a timely basis.* The GAO said that the companies, securities industries and the IRS would have to develop a system to obtain timely information.

Comment: For discussion of determining the basis of securities using the average basis method, see ¶730. For the new information reporting requirement for securities transfers to brokers, see ¶735. The new return requirements affecting basis of specified securities are analyzed at ¶740.

▶ **Effective date.** Generally, the provisions takes effect on January 1, 2011. However, the provision that extends the period for statements to be sent to customers applies to statements required to be furnished after December 31, 2008 (Division B, Act Sec. 403(e) of the Emergency Economic Stabilization Act of 2008 (P.L. 110-343)).

Law source: Law at ¶5435. Committee Reports at ¶10,280.

— Division B, Act Sec. 403(a)(1) of the Emergency Economic Stabilization Act of 2008 (P.L. 110-343), adding Code Sec. 6045(g);

— Division B, Act Sec. 403(a)(2), adding Code Sec. 6045(h);

— Division B, Act Sec. 403(a)(3), amending Code Sec. 6045(b) and (d);

— Division B, Act Sec. 403(e), providing the effective date.

Reporter references: For further information, consult the following CCH reporters.

— Standard Federal Tax Reporter, ¶35,930.01 and ¶35,930.026

— Tax Research Consultant, FILEBUS: 9,252

— Federal Tax Guide, ¶22,115

¶730 Determination of Basis for Certain Securities

SUMMARY OF NEW LAW

The determination of the basis of securities is to be done on an account by account basis using existing conventions prescribed by IRS regulations. There are special rules for mutual funds and dividend reinvestment plans.

BACKGROUND

In general, the basis of property is the cost of the property (Code Sec. 1012). For stocks and bonds, the basis is computed using a first-in, first-out method (FIFO), unless there is a specific identification of the share or bond (Reg. §1.1012-1(c)(1)). There is a different rule for shares in a regulated investment company (i.e., a mutual fund). An average cost method can be used for shares in a regulated investment company (Reg. §1.1012-1(e)).

NEW LAW EXPLAINED

Determining the customer's basis in certain securities.—In conjunction with new rules requiring a broker to report a customer's basis in certain securities transactions (see ¶ 725), the Emergency Economic Stabilization Act of 2008 (P.L. 110-343) has modified the general cost basis provision to specifically address the basis of stock held in certain accounts and dividend reinvestment plans (Code Sec. 1012(c) and (d), as added by the Emergency Economic Act of 2008).

Determinations by account. In the case of a sale, exchange or other disposition on or after the applicable date, the reported basis in a specified security is determined under the conventions prescribed in the existing regulations and applied to each separate account, on an account-by-account basis (Code Sec. 1012(c)(1), as added by the Emergency Economic Act of 2008). In general, the basis to be reported is computed using a first-in, first-out (FIFO) method, the specific identification method, or the average basis convention (Reg. § 1.1012-1; Joint Committee on Taxation, Technical Explanation of H.R. 7060, the "Renewable Energy and Job Creation Tax Act of 2008" (JCX-75-08).

> **Comment:** The terms "specified security" and "applicable date" are defined in new Code Sec. 6045(g). Generally, a specified security is stock, note and other debt, certain commodity contracts and derivatives, and other securities deemed appropriate by the Secretary. The applicable date is January 1, 2012, for "average basis" stock, January 1, 2011, for other stock, and January 1, 2013, for other specified securities. See ¶ 725 for details.

Stock in a mutual fund, and certain stock acquired in connection with a dividend reinvestment plan (see below), acquired before January 1, 2012 is generally treated as a separate account from stock acquired after that date (Code Sec. 1012(c)(2)(A), as added by the Emergency Economic Act of 2008). However, the fund may elect, on a stockholder by stockholder basis, to treat all the shares of the affected shareholder(s) as "covered securities" (see ¶725) held in a single account, regardless of when acquired (Code Sec. 1012(c)(2)(B), as added by the Emergency Economic Act of 2008; Joint Committee on Taxation, Technical Explanation of H.R. 7060, the "Renewable Energy and Job Creation Tax Act of 2008" (JCX-75-08)). A broker who is a nominee holder may make a similar election (Code Sec. 1012(c)(3), as added by the Emergency Economic Act of 2008).

> **Comment:** Stock in a mutual fund acquired before January 1, 2012, can be reported using any acceptable method, that is, (FIFO), average cost, or specific identification. Stock in a mutual fund acquired on or after January 1, 2012 is reported using the broker's default method of determining basis unless the customer notifies the broker of an election for another acceptable method. See ¶725 for details.

Dividend, reinvestment plans. There is a special rule for stock acquired after December 31, 2010 in connection with a dividend reinvestment plan. The basis of that stock is determined using one of the methods permissible for stock in an open-end fund. If the stock is later transferred to another account, the basis in the other account is a cost basis equal to the basis in the dividend reinvestment plan immediately before the transfer as adjusted for fees and charges on the transfer. The rules discussed above

NEW LAW EXPLAINED

regarding separate accounts and the election for treatment as a single account also apply for a dividend reinvestment plan (Code Sec. 1012(d), as added by the Emergency Economic Act of 2008).

A dividend reinvestment plan is any arrangement under which dividends on stock are reinvested in identical stock. Stock is treated as acquired in connection with the plan if the stock is acquired pursuant to the plan or the dividends paid on such stock are subject to the plan (Code Sec. 1012(d)(4), as added by the Emergency Economic Act of 2008).

▶ **Effective date.** The provision takes effect on January 1, 2011 (Division B, Act Sec. 403(e) of the Emergency Economic Stabilization Act of 2008 (P.L. 110-343)).

Law source: Law at ¶5345. Committee Reports at ¶10,280.

— Division B, Act Sec. 403(b)(1) and (2) of the Emergency Economic Stabilization Act of 2008 (P.L. 110-343), redesignating Code Sec. 1012 as Code Sec. 1012(a) and (b);

— Division B, Act Sec. 403(b)(3), adding Code Sec. 1012(c) and (d);

— Division B, Act Sec. 403(e), providing the effective date.

Reporter references: For further information, consult the following CCH reporters.

— Standard Federal Tax Reporter, ¶29,335.01

— Tax Research Consultant, SALES: 6,050, SALES: 6,068, SALES: 6,212.35, SALES: 6,212.45, SALES: 45,406.15 and FILEBUS: 9,250

— Federal Tax Guide, ¶5,130, ¶22,115

¶735 Broker-to-Broker Information Reporting

SUMMARY OF NEW LAW

Every broker (and any other person specified in regulations) that transfers to a broker a security that is a "covered security" in the hands of the transferor broker (or other person) is required to furnish to the transferee broker a written statement that permits the transferee broker to satisfy the basis and holding-period reporting requirements under new Code Sec. 6045(g). That provision requires a broker to report, with respect to the sale of a covered security, the customer's adjusted basis in the security and whether any gain or loss on the sale is long-term or short-term.

BACKGROUND

Information reporting is imposed on participants in various tax-related transactions. Code Sec. 6045(a) requires that every person doing business as a broker must file an information return with the IRS showing the name and address of each customer for whom he makes a sale, as well as gross proceeds and certain other information required by the forms and regulations (including the customer's taxpayer identification number, Committee on Uniform Security Identification Procedures (CUSIP) number of any security sold and sale date) (Reg. §1.6045-1(d)(2)). A "broker" is

BACKGROUND

defined, under Code Sec. 6045(c)(1), as a dealer, a barter exchange, or any other person who, for consideration, regularly acts as a middleman of property or services. Under an alternative definition (Reg. § 1.6045-1(a)(1)), a broker is a person who, in the ordinary course of a trade or business during the calendar year, stands ready to effect sales to be made by others.

Code Sec. 6045(b) requires that brokers furnish every customer information statements ("payee statements") containing the name, address and phone number of the information contact of the broker, along with the same gross proceeds information included in the information returns filed with the IRS. These payee statements must be provided to the customer by January 31 of the year following the calendar year for which the information return must be filed.

A penalty applies for a failure to timely file a correct information return (Code Sec. 6721). The penalty ranges from $15 to $50 per return, depending upon how late the return is filed. The maximum penalty is $250,000 per calendar year ($100,000 for persons with gross receipts of not more than $5 million). Any failure to furnish a required payee statement is subject to a flat penalty of $50, up to a maximum penalty of $100,000 for a calendar year (Code Sec. 6722). These penalty amounts are increased, and the limitations on the maximum penalty do not apply, when the failure to file a correct information return or to furnish a payee statement is due to intentional disregard of the filing requirements. These penalties do not apply when the failure to file or provide correct information is due to reasonable cause and not willful neglect. Information returns and payee statements subject to these penalties are described, respectively, in Code Sec. 6724(d)(1) and (2).

NEW LAW EXPLAINED

Broker-to-broker information reporting required for covered securities transfers.—Any broker (as defined in Code Sec. 6045(c)(1)), as well as any other person specified in regulations, that transfers to a broker a security that is a "covered security" (as defined in new Code Sec. 6045(g)(3)) (see ¶ 725) when held by the transferor broker (or other person) is required to provide to the transferee broker a written statement that permits the transferee broker to satisfy the basis and holding-period reporting requirements under new Code Sec. 6045(g) (Code Sec. 6045A, as added by the Emergency Economic Stabilization Act of 2008 (P.L. 110-343). (Code Sec. 6045(g) requires a broker to report, with respect to the sale of a covered security, the customer's adjusted basis in the security and whether any gain or loss on the sale is long-term or short-term (see ¶ 725)) The IRS may provide regulations that set forth the content of the written statement and the manner in which it must be furnished.

> **Comment:** According to the Joint Committee on Taxation, Technical Explanation of H.R. 7060, the "Renewable Energy and Job Creation Tax Act of 2008" (JCX-75-08), it is intended that the IRS will allow the broker-to-broker reporting requirement to be met electronically rather than by paper.

The written statement must be furnished no later than 15 days after the date of the transfer, except as provided otherwise by the IRS (Code Sec. 6045A(c), as added by the Emergency Economic Act of 2008). Failure to provide correct payee statements to

NEW LAW EXPLAINED

brokers with respect to the transfer of covered securities is subject to current law penalties for failure to furnish correct payee statements (Code Sec. 6724(d)(2), as amended by the Emergency Economic Act of 2008).

▶ **Effective date.** The provision takes effect on January 1, 2011 (Division B, Act Sec. 403(e) of the Emergency Economic Stabilization Act of 2008 (P.L. 110-343)).

Law source: Law at ¶5440 and ¶5475. Committee Reports at ¶10,280.

— Division B, Act Sec. 403(c)(1) of the Emergency Economic Stabilization Act of 2008 (P.L. 110-343), adding Code Sec. 6045A;

— Division B, Act Sec. 403(c)(2), amending Code Sec. 6724(d)(2);

— Division B, Act Sec. 403(e), providing the effective date.

Reporter references: For further information, consult the following CCH reporters.

— Standard Federal Tax Reporter, ¶35,930.01, ¶40,240.01, ¶40,285.03

— Tax Research Consultant, FILEBUS: 9,250, PENALTY: 3,204

— Federal Tax Guide, ¶22,115, ¶22,573

¶740 Returns Relating to Adjustments to Basis of Specified Securities

SUMMARY OF NEW LAW

Beginning January 1, 2011, the issuer of a specified security is required to file an information return describing any organizational action which affects the basis of the security and the quantitative effect on the basis of the security resulting from such action. A person required to file a return under the new provision is also required to furnish a written statement to the holder of the specified security or their nominee, detailing the contents of the informational return.

BACKGROUND

Participants in certain transactions are required to meet information reporting requirements, under which information is reported to the IRS and furnished to taxpayers. For example, a person engaged in a trade or business is generally required to file information returns for each calendar year for payments of $600 or more made in the course of the payor's trade or business (Code Sec. 6041(a)). Brokers are not required to report a customer's basis in securities. However, taxpayers must determine their adjusted basis to calculate gain or loss for federal tax purposes (Code Sec. 1001).

A penalty applies for failing to timely file an information return or including incorrect or incomplete information on an information return. The amount of the penalty ranges from $15 to $50 for each return with respect to which such a failure occurs, depending upon how late the return is filed, up to a maximum total penalty of $250,000 for all failures during a calendar year (Code Sec. 6721). Similarly, failures

BACKGROUND

to furnish correct information statements to recipients of payments for which information reporting is required is subject to a penalty of $50 for each statement, up to a maximum penalty of $100,000 for all failures during a calendar year (Code Sec. 6722). The information returns and payee statements that are subject to these penalties are described in Code Sec. 6724(d)(1) and (2), respectively.

NEW LAW EXPLAINED

Information reporting relating to actions affecting basis of specified securities.— An issuer of a specified security is required to file an information return describing any organizational action which affects the basis of the specified security, the quantitative effect of the organizational action on the basis of that specified security, and any other information the Secretary of the Treasury may prescribe. (Code Sec. 6045B(a), as added by the Emergency Economic Stabilization Act of 2008 (P.L. 110-343)). The return must be filed by the earlier of 45 days after the organizational action or January 15 of the year following the calendar year during which the organizational action took place (Code Sec. 6045B(b), as added by the Emergency Economic Act of 2008). However, no return is required with respect to a specified security regarding organizational actions which occur before the applicable date (as defined below) with respect to that security (Code Sec. 6045B(d), as added by the Emergency Economic Act of 2008).

> **Comment:** Examples of organizational actions that would affect the basis of a specified security include a stock split or a merger or acquisition (Joint Committee on Taxation, Technical Explanation of H.R. 7060, the "Renewable Energy and Job Creation Tax Act of 2008" (JCX-75-08)).

For purposes of the new reporting requirement, a "specified security" is:

- any share of stock in a corporation;
- any note, bond, debenture, or other evidence of indebtedness;
- any commodity, or contract or derivative with respect to such commodity, if the Secretary determines that adjusted basis reporting is appropriate; and
- any other financial instrument with respect to which the Secretary determines that adjusted basis reporting is appropriate (6045(g)(3)(B) and Code Secs. 6045B(d), as added by the Emergency Economic Act of 2008).

The "applicable date" on or after which organizational actions must be reported with respect to a specified security is:

- January 1, 2011, for corporate stock, generally;
- January 1, 2012, for stock for which use of the average basis method is permitted under Code Sec. 1012 (see ¶730); and
- January 1, 2013 (or a later date if determined by the Secretary) for any other specified security (Code Secs. 6045B(d) and 6045(g)(3)(C), as added by the Emergency Economic Act of 2008).

A person required to file a return under the new provision is also required to furnish the holder of the specified security or their nominee with a written statement showing the name, address and phone number of the information contact of the

NEW LAW EXPLAINED

person required to make the return; the information required to be shown on the return with respect to such security; and any other information required by the Secretary. The statement must be furnished on or before January 15 of the year following the year during which the organizational action affecting the basis of the security took place (Code Sec. 6045B(c), as added by the Emergency Economic Act of 2008).

> **Comment:** According to a House Ways and Means Committee report on an earlier bill, it is believed that there may be significant underreporting of capital gain income as a result of misreporting of basis. This provision, in conjunction with other new rules regarding broker reporting of basis (see ¶725, ¶730 and ¶735), is intended to facilitate accurate reporting of tax basis (House Ways and Means Committee Report on HR 3996, the Temporary Tax Relief Act of 2007 (November 7, 2007)).

The Secretary of the Treasury may waive the return filing and information statement requirements if the person required to file the return makes publicly available, in the form and manner specified by the Secretary, the name, address, phone number and email address of the information contact of that person, and the description of the organizational action affecting the basis of the specified security, the quantitative effect of the organizational action on the basis of that specified security, and such other information as the Secretary may prescribe (Code Sec. 6045B(e), as added by the Emergency Economic Act of 2008).

Failure to file correct information returns in connection with organizational actions is subject to the existing penalties for failure to file correct information returns (Code Sec. 6724(d)(1)(B)(iv), as added by the Emergency Economic Act of 2008). Similarly, the present-law penalties for failure to furnish correct payee statements apply to a failure to furnish correct statements to holders or nominees or to provide required publicly-available information in lieu of returns and written statements (Code Sec. 6724(d)(2)(J), as added by the Emergency Economic Act of 2008).

▶ **Effective date.** The provision takes effect on January 1, 2011 (Division B, Act Sec. 403(e) of the Emergency Economic Stabilization Act of 2008 (P.L. 110-343)).

Law source: Law at ¶5445 and ¶5475. Committee Reports at ¶10,280.

— Division B, Act Sec. 403(d)(1) of the Emergency Economic Stabilization Act of 2008 (P.L. 110-343), adding Code Sec. 6045B;

— Division B, Act Sec. 403(d)(2), amending Code Sec. 6724(d)(1) and (d)(2);

— Division B, Act Sec. 403(e), providing the effective date.

Reporter references: For further information, consult the following CCH reporters.

— Standard Federal Tax Reporter, ¶35,930.01, ¶40,240.01 and ¶40,285.03

— Tax Research Consultant, FILEBUS: 9,250 and PENALTY: 3,204

— Federal Tax Guide, ¶22,571 and ¶22,573

ACCOUNTING

¶745 SEC Authority to Suspend Mark-to-Market Accounting

SUMMARY OF NEW LAW

The Securities and Exchange Commission (SEC) is given the authority to suspend the application of Statement of Financial Accounting Standards No. 157, Fair Value Measurements (FAS 157) for any issuer of securities or for any class or category of transaction. The SEC, in consultation with the Board of Governors of the Federal Reserve System and the Secretary of the Treasury, also must conduct a study on mark-to-market accounting standards as provided in FAS 157 and submit a report to Congress on its findings.

BACKGROUND

In September 2006, the Financial Accounting Standards Board (FASB) issued Statement of Financial Accounting Standards No. 157, Fair Value Measurements (FAS 157), effective for financial statements issued for fiscal years beginning after November 15, 2007, and interim periods within those fiscal years. FAS 157 defines fair value and provides a framework for determining the fair value of an asset or liability. It also requires expanded disclosures about the use of fair value, the inputs used to measure fair value, and the effect of fair value measurements on earnings and/or changes in net assets. By providing detailed standards, FAS 157 was intended to improve consistency and comparability in fair value measurements.

> **Comment:** The FASB is an independent organization, separate from the federal government and professional organizations such as the American Institute of Certified Public Accountants (AICPA), that develops and issues financial accounting and reporting rules for U.S. companies. A single set of accounting standards makes consistent reporting of financial information possible and allows investors and other interested parties to compare companies more easily. Although the Securities and Exchange Commission (SEC) has the authority to issue financial reporting rules for public companies under the Securities Exchange Act of 1934, it has left this task for the most part to the FASB and its predecessors.

During 2008, at the height of the sub-prime mortgage and housing market crisis, financial institutions holding mortgage-backed securities found that the securities had lost almost all of their value and could not be sold. Under the mark-to-market accounting rules, financial institutions were forced to value these securities at a fraction of their original cost. Doing so had an incredible negative impact on their balance sheets, making such institutions unattractive to lenders and investors and forcing some into bankruptcy or out of business entirely.

Perhaps in an attempt to keep Congress from making changes to the mark-to-market accounting rules to support these failing financial institutions, the SEC and the FASB

BACKGROUND

issued a joint statement on September 30, 2008, to clarify sections of FAS 157. The clarifications were intended to provide immediate help for preparers, auditors, investors, and other users of financial information, while the FASB staff prepared additional interpretive guidance on fair value measurement. In general, the clarifications acknowledged that the determination of fair value requires use of estimates and reasonable judgment calls when there is no market or an inactive market or there is the presence of distressed or disorderly transactions. In such cases, disclosure of the grounds for the fair value determinations is necessary to maintain transparency in reporting.

Mark-to-market rules are also a part of tax accounting. The Internal Revenue Code contains several sections governing mark-to-market accounting. The most notable of these is Code Sec. 475, which requires dealers in securities to mark securities in inventory to fair market value and allows dealers in commodities and traders in securities or commodities to elect to mark such securities or commodities to market value.

NEW LAW EXPLAINED

SEC granted authority to suspend mark-to-market accounting rules.—The Emergency Economic Stabilization Act of 2008 (P.L. 110-343) gives the Securities and Exchange Commission (SEC) the authority to suspend the application of the mark-to-market financial accounting rules, as provided in Statement of Financial Accounting Standards No. 157, Fair Value Measurements (FAS 157), through issuance of a rule, regulation or order. The suspension could be applied to any issuer of securities or with respect to any class or category of transaction, if the SEC determines that it is necessary or appropriate in the public interest and is consistent with the protection of investors (Division A, Act Sec. 132(a) of the Emergency Economic Act of 2008 (P.L. 110-343)). An issuer for this purpose is generally any person who issues or proposes to issue any security (section 3(a)(8) of the Securities Exchange Act of 1934; 15 U.S.C. 78c(a)(8)).

> **Caution:** Since the suspension of the mark-to-market rules can be applied to any issuer and no criteria was provided on how issuers should be selected, the SEC can pick and choose the issuers to which the suspension would apply. Thus, different valuation and reporting standards can be applied to similarly situated issuers, making comparisons of companies' financial health very difficult.

The new authority of the SEC to suspend the mark-to-market accounting rules does not restrict or limit any existing authority of the SEC under the securities laws as in effect on October 3, 2008 (Division A, Act Sec. 132(b) of the Emergency Economic Act of 2008 (P.L. 110-343)).

> **Comment:** The SEC is not required to suspend the mark-to-market accounting rules. It could choose not to exert its authority to do so. However, given the pressure from failing financial institutions, this appears unlikely.

> **Comment:** The provision does not have a termination date. Thus, it is a permanent grant of authority to the SEC within the limits of administrative jurisdiction.

¶745

NEW LAW EXPLAINED

Study on Mark-to-Market Accounting. The SEC, in consultation with the Board of Governors of the Federal Reserve System and the Secretary of the Treasury, must conduct a study on the mark-to-market accounting standards provided in FAS 157, as such standards apply to financial institutions, including depository institutions (Division A, Act Sec. 133(a) of the Emergency Economic Act of 2008 (P.L. 110-343)). At a minimum, the study must consider:

- the effects of such accounting standards on a financial institution's balance sheet;
- the impacts of such accounting on bank failures in 2008;
- the impact of such standards on the quality of financial information available to investors;
- the process used by the FASB in developing accounting standards;
- the advisability and feasibility of modifications to such standards; and
- alternative accounting standards to those provided in FAS 157.

The SEC must submit a report of its study to Congress before the end of the 90-day period beginning on October 3, 2008. The report must contain the findings and determinations of the SEC, including any administrative and legislative recommendations as the SEC deems appropriate (Division A, Act Sec. 133(b) of the Emergency Economic Act of 2008 (P.L. 110-343)).

> **Comment:** The study on mark-to-market accounting does not require input from the private sector or accounting organizations. Thus, the SEC can make recommendations on further changes without considering possible opposing viewpoints.

▶ **Effective date.** No specific effective date is provided by the Act. The provision is, therefore, considered effective on October 3, 2008, the date of enactment.

Law source: Law at ¶7105 and ¶7108.

— Division A, Act Secs. 132 and 133 of the Emergency Economic Stabilization Act of 2008 (P.L. 110-343).

Reporter references: For further information, consult the following CCH reporters.

— Standard Federal Tax Reporter, ¶22,268.01
— Tax Research Consultant, SALES: 45,350
— Federal Tax Guide, ¶15,635

¶750 Tax Treatment of Exxon Valdez Settlement or Judgment Amounts

SUMMARY OF NEW LAW

Fishermen and other individuals who receive any settlement or judgment-related income in connection with the civil action for damages from the 1989 Exxon Valdez oil spill may use three-year income averaging for reporting such amounts for federal income tax purposes. These individuals may also use the settlement or judgment-

SUMMARY OF NEW LAW

related income to make contributions to eligible retirement plans without having it treated as taxable.

BACKGROUND

Individuals engaged in a farming or commercial fishing business may elect to compute their tax by averaging their business income over three years (Code Sec. 1301(a)). The three-year averaging option is designed to even out the wide variations in a farmer's or fisherman's tax liabilities that may occur from year to year due to weather and other uncontrollable factors that impact their farming or fishing income.

The Exxon Valdez oil tanker that struck a reef on March 24, 1989, spilled millions of gallons of oil into Prince William Sound off the coast of Alaska. The oil spill caused significant environmental damage that impacted the recreational sport fishing, tourism and commercial fishing industries. During the lengthy litigation that followed, Exxon Mobil was at one point found liable for $2.5 billion in punitive damages. In June 2008, the U.S. Supreme Court cut the $2.5 billion punitive damages award to approximately $500 million.

NEW LAW EXPLAINED

Treatment of settlement income from Exxon Valdez litigation.—Qualified taxpayers who receive settlement or judgment-related income from the litigation surrounding the 1989 Exxon Valdez oil spill can use three-year income averaging for reporting such amounts or can contribute such amounts to eligible retirement plans without having the income treated as taxable. First, individuals receiving such settlement or judgment-related amounts are treated as engaged in a fishing business and, thus, eligible to use income averaging under Code Sec. 1301. Such treatment applies to any qualified taxpayer who receives any qualified settlement income in any tax year. The taxpayer shall be treated as engaged in a fishing business (determined without regard to the commercial nature of the business), and the qualified settlement income shall be treated as income attributable to a fishing business for the tax year (Division C, Act Sec. 504(a) of the Emergency Economic Stabilization Act of 2008 (P.L. 110-343)).

A "qualified taxpayer" is any individual who is a plaintiff in the civil action *In re Exxon Valdez*, No. 89-095-CV (HRH) (Consolidated) (D. Alaska). It also includes any individual who is a beneficiary of the estate of such a plaintiff who acquired the right to receive qualified settlement income from that plaintiff and was the spouse or an immediate relative of that plaintiff (Division C, Act Sec. 504(d) of the Emergency Economic Act of 2008).

The term "qualified settlement income" means any taxable interest and punitive damage awards that are received, whether as lump sums or periodic payments, in connection with the civil action *In re Exxon Valdez*, No. 89-095-CV (HRH) (Consolidated) (D. Alaska). Such amounts may be received pre- or post-judgment and may be related to either a settlement or judgment (Division C, Act Sec. 504(e) of the Emergency Economic Act of 2008).

¶750

NEW LAW EXPLAINED

Contributions of amounts received to retirement accounts. Instead of using income averaging for reporting qualified settlement income, taxpayers can contribute such amounts, subject to limitations, to an eligible retirement plan without having the amounts included in income.

> **Comment:** In general, qualifying taxpayers can treat up to $100,000 of qualified settlement income as a rollover distribution that can be contributed to a retirement plan.

Specifically, any qualified taxpayer who receives qualified settlement income during the tax year may, at any time before the end of the tax year in which the income was received, make one or more contributions to an eligible retirement plan (see Code Sec. 402(c)(8)(B)) of which such qualified taxpayer is a beneficiary. The aggregate amount of such contributions is limited to the lesser of $100,000 (reduced by the amount of qualified settlement income contributed to an eligible retirement plan in prior tax years), or the amount of qualified settlement income received by the individual during the tax year (Division C, Act Sec. 504(b)(1) of the Emergency Economic Act of 2008). A contribution to an eligible retirement plan is deemed to be made by a qualified taxpayer on the last day of the tax year in which such income is received if the contribution is made on account of such tax year and is made not later than the time prescribed by law for filing the return for such tax year (not including extensions) (Division C, Act Sec. 504(b)(2) of the Emergency Economic Act of 2008).

If a contribution is made to an eligible retirement plan with respect to qualified settlement income, then to the extent of such contribution, the qualified settlement income shall not be included in the taxpayer's taxable income. Further, for purposes of Code Sec. 72, such contribution shall not be considered to be investment in the contract. This rule does not apply if the contribution is made to a Roth IRA or to a Roth 401(k).

To the extent of the amount of the contribution, the qualified taxpayer shall be treated as having received the qualified settlement income: (1) in the case of a contribution to an individual retirement plan (as defined under Code Sec. 7701(a)(37)), in a distribution described in Code Sec. 408(d)(3), and (2) in the case of any other eligible retirement plan, in an eligible rollover distribution (as defined under Code Sec. 402(f)(2). The taxpayer is also treated as having transferred the amount to the eligible retirement plan in a direct trustee-to-trustee transfer within 60 days of the distribution. The limitation on rollover contributions in Code Sec. 408(d)(3)(B) shall not apply with respect to amounts treated as a rollover, and the limitation on rollover contributions to a Roth IRA in Code Sec. 408A(c)(3)(B) shall not apply with respect to amounts contributed to a Roth IRA or a designated Roth contribution to an applicable retirement plan (within the meaning of Code Sec. 402A) (Division C, Act Sec. 504(c) of the Emergency Economic Act of 2008).

Special rule for Roth IRAs and Roth 401(k)s. If a contribution is made with respect to qualified settlement income to a Roth IRA or as a designated Roth contribution to an applicable retirement plan, then the qualified settlement income shall be included in taxable income. Further, for purposes of Code Sec. 72, such contribution shall be considered to be investment in the contract (Division C, Act Sec. 504(b)(4) of the Emergency Economic Act of 2008).

¶750

NEW LAW EXPLAINED

Treatment of qualified settlement income for employment tax purposes. No portion of qualified settlement income received by a qualified taxpayer shall be treated as self-employment income for self-employment tax (SECA) purposes. Also, no portion of qualified settlement income received by a qualified taxpayer shall be treated as wages for Social Security tax (FICA) purposes (Division C, Act Sec. 504(c) of the Emergency Economic Act of 2008).

▶ **Effective date.** No specific effective date is provided by the Act. The provision is, therefore, considered effective on October 3, 2008, the date of enactment.

Law source: Law at ¶7162.

— Division C, Act Sec. 504 of the Emergency Economic Stabilization Act of 2008 (P.L. 110-343).

Reporter references: For further information, consult the following CCH reporters.

— Standard Federal Tax Reporter, ¶31,791.023

— Tax Research Consultant, FARM: 3,302 and FILEIND: 15,054.30

— Federal Tax Guide, ¶25,337

¶755 Gain on Sales or Dispositions to Implement FERC or State Electric Restructuring Policy

SUMMARY OF NEW LAW

The special gain recognition rule for qualifying electric transmission transactions that implement Federal Energy Regulatory Commission (FERC) or state electric restructuring policy is extended two years for qualified electric utilities to sales or dispositions prior to January 1, 2010.

BACKGROUND

A special gain recognition rule applies to sales or dispositions of qualifying electric transmission property that are made to implement Federal Energy Regulatory Commission (FERC) or state electric restructuring policy (Code Sec. 451(i)). A taxpayer can elect to recognize qualified gain from a qualifying electric transmission transaction over an eight-year period to the extent that the amount realized from the sale is used to purchase exempt utility property within the applicable period (Code Sec. 451(i)(1)(B)). Qualified gain is immediately recognized beginning in the tax year of the transaction to the extent the amount realized from the transaction exceeds:

- the cost of *exempt utility property* that is purchased by the taxpayer during the four-year period beginning on the date of the transaction reduced, but not below zero, by

- any portion of the cost previously taken into account under these rules (Code Sec. 451(i)(1)(A)).

BACKGROUND

Exempt utility property is property used in the trade or business of generating, transmitting, distributing, or selling electricity, or producing, transmitting, distributing, or selling natural gas (Code Sec. 451(i)(5)).

Qualified gain is:

- any ordinary income derived from a qualifying electric transmission transaction that would be required to be recognized under Code Secs. 1245 or 1250, and
- any income from a transaction in excess of the amount, above, which is required to be included in gross income for the tax year (Code Sec. 451(i)(2)).

Qualifying electric transmission transaction. A qualifying electric transmission transaction is any sale or other disposition to an independent transmission company of: (1) property used in the trade or business of providing electric transmission services; or (2) an ownership interest in a corporation or partnership whose principal trade or business consists of providing such services. The sale or disposition must be made before January 1, 2008 (Code Sec. 451(i)(3)).

An independent transmission company is:

(1) an independent transmission provider approved by the FERC;

(2) a person: (a) who the FERC determines is not a "market participant," and (b) whose transmission facilities to which the election applies are under the *operational control* of a FERC-approved independent transmission provider within a specified time frame; or

(3) in the case of facilities subject to the jurisdiction of the Public Utility Commission of Texas, a person approved by that commission as consistent with Texas state law regarding an independent transmission organization, or a political subdivision or affiliate whose transmission facilities are under the operational control of that person (Code Sec. 451(i)(4)).

In the case of item (2) above, the transmission facilities must be under the control of the independent transmission provider before the close of the period specified in the FERC authorization of the transaction (Code Sec. 451(i)(4)(B)(ii)). In any event, control must be exercised no later than December 31, 2007 (Code Sec. 451(i)(4)(B)(ii)).

NEW LAW EXPLAINED

Tax deferral extended for qualified electric utilities.—Deferral treatment for sales or other dispositions of electric transmission property to independent transmission companies has been extended two years to transactions occurring before January 1, 2010, for sales or dispositions by qualified electric utilities (Code Sec. 451(i)(3), as amended by the Emergency Economic Stabilization Act of 2008 (P.L. 110-343)).

A qualified electric utility is a person that, as of the date of the qualifying electric transmission transaction, is vertically integrated. Vertically integrated means that it is both:

- a transmitting utility (as defined in section 3(23) of the Federal Power Act (16 U.S.C. § 796(23)) with respect to the transmission facilities to which the deferral election applies, and

NEW LAW EXPLAINED

- an electric utility (as defined in section (3)(22) of the Federal Power Act (16 U.S.C. § 796(22)) (Code Sec. 451(i)(6), as added by the Emergency Economic Act of 2008).

In determining whether a sale or disposition is a qualifying electric transmission transaction, the period for transfer of operational control to an independent transmission provider authorized by FERC has been extended from December 31, 2007, to the date which is four years after the close of the tax year in which the transaction occurs (Code Sec. 451(i)(4)(B)(ii), as amended by the Emergency Economic Act of 2008).

The term "exempt utility property" does not include any property that is located outside the United States (Code Sec. 451(i)(5), as amended by the Emergency Economic Act of 2008).

▶ **Effective date.** The provision extending the deferral two years for qualified electric utilities applies to transactions after December 31, 2007 (Division B, Act Sec. 109(d)(1) of the Emergency Economic Stabilization Act of 2008 (P.L. 110-343)). The provision related to the period for transfer of operational control applies to transactions occurring after October 22, 2004, in tax years ending after such date (Division B, Act Sec. 109(d)(2) of the Emergency Economic Act of 2008; Act Sec. 909 of the American Jobs Creation Act of 2004 (P.L. 108-357)). The exception to the definition of exempt utility property for property located outside the United States applies to transactions after October 3, 2008, the date of enactment (Division B, Act Sec. 109(d)(3) of the Emergency Economic Act of 2008).

Law source: Law at ¶5300. Committee Report at ¶10,070.

— Division B, Act Sec. 109(a) of the Emergency Economic Stabilization Act of 2008 (P.L. 110-343), amending Code Sec. 451(i)(3), redesignating (i)(6) through (i)(10) as (i)(7) through (i)(11), respectively, and adding a new (i)(6);

— Division B, Act Sec. 109(b), amending Code Sec. 451(i)(4)(B)(ii);

— Division B, Act Sec. 109(c), adding Code Sec. 451(i)(5)(C);

— Division B, Act Sec. 109(d), providing the effective date.

Reporter references: For further information, consult the following CCH reporters.

— Standard Federal Tax Reporter, ¶21,030.022 and ¶21,030.06

— Tax Research Consultant, SALES: 21,056

— Federal Tax Guide, ¶15,350

Bonds, Excise Taxes and Other Provisions

8

TAX-EXEMPT BONDS

EXCISE TAXES

FOREIGN TAXATION

HEALTH BENEFITS

TAX-EXEMPT BONDS

¶805 Clean Renewable Energy Bonds

SUMMARY OF NEW LAW

The deadline for issuing clean renewable energy bonds under Code Sec. 54 is extended for one year, to the end of 2009. A new category of tax credit bonds, new clean renewable energy bonds, is authorized under new Code Sec. 54C. A national limitation of $800 million on the new bonds will be allocated by the IRS among non-profit electricity generating companies seeking to finance capital investments in clean renewable energy facilities.

BACKGROUND

Increasing awareness of the political and environmental dangers of dependence on nonrenewable energy sources has led to efforts to encourage the development of clean, renewable energy sources. State regulators are increasingly adopting renewable portfolio standards, which require all electricity suppliers to provide a certain amount of electricity generated from renewable sources.

The federal government has provided incentives for the development of renewable energy sources and technologies through a number of programs. For-profit energy companies may claim a tax credit for the production of electricity from certain renewable sources under Code Sec. 45. Non-profit electricity producers can obtain incentives under the Department of Energy's Renewable Energy Production Incentive program and by issuing tax credit bonds known as clean renewable energy bonds (CREBs) under Code Sec. 54. Incentives provided under both of these programs are subject to dollar limits. In contrast, the production credit is not subject to any such limitation. Despite these programs, according to the American Public Power Association, "renewable resources (exclusive of hydropower) still account for less than two percent of the nation's overall generating portfolio."

Clean renewable energy bonds. The Energy Tax Incentives Act of 2005 (P.L. 109-58) authorized the issuance of up to $800 million of CREBs during 2006 and 2007 to finance capital expenditures by tax-exempt electricity producers to increase their capacity to produce electricity from clean renewable sources (Code Sec. 54). Governmental bodies, cooperative electricity companies, and cooperative lenders owned by cooperative electricity companies are eligible to issue such bonds. The bonds provide a federal subsidy to allow nonprofit electricity providers to compete more evenly with for-profit companies that can take advantage of the existing tax credit under Code Sec. 45. The $800 million national limit was to be allocated among qualified projects at the discretion of the IRS, except that not more than $500 million could be allocated to governmental projects (Code Sec. 54(f), as added by the Energy Act).

An additional $400 million of CREBs, raising the national limitation on the amount of bonds to $1.2 billion, was authorized under the Tax Relief and Health Care Act of 2006 (Code Sec. 54(f)(1), as amended by the Tax Relief and Health Care Act of 2006

BACKGROUND

(P.L. 109-432)). At the same time, the maximum amount of CREBs that could be allocated to finance qualified projects by qualified governmental bodies was increased by $250 million, raising that limitation to $750 million (Code Sec. 54(f)(2)). The authority to issue CREBs was also extended through December 31, 2008 (Code Sec. 54(m)).

Tax credit bonds generally. Tax credit bonds are not interest-bearing obligations. Instead, a taxpayer holding a tax credit bond on one or more allowance dates during a tax year is allowed a credit against federal income tax equivalent to the interest that the bond would otherwise pay. In effect, the existence of the credit allows the issuer to borrow interest free. The bondholder must include the amount of the credit in his or her gross income and treat it as interest income.

The Code provisions authorizing the issuance of tax credit bonds for various purposes include *mechanical* provisions, relating to the credit and the application of tax-exempt bond rules, and *substantive* provisions, which vary depending on what the bond proceeds are to be used to finance. Prior to 2008, tax credit bond provisions for clean renewable energy tax bonds and for qualified zone academy bonds had been added to the Code separately, each with their own substantive provisions and each with similar but not identical mechanical provisions. The Heartland, Habitat, Harvest, and Horticulture Act of 2008 (P.L. 110-246) added a new Subpart I to Part IV of the Code (regarding credits against tax) where common mechanical provisions for such bonds were placed, in new Code Section 54A, with room for substantive provisions relating to the various types of tax credit bonds to follow in succeeding Code Sections. However, the existing provisions for CREBs and qualified zone academy bonds were not moved into the new Subpart.

The common mechanical requirements for tax credit bonds include requirements that the proceeds of the bonds be spent for specified purposes within three years, that the issuer meet certain reporting and arbitrage requirements generally applicable to tax-exempt bonds, that the maturity of the bonds not exceed a maximum term to be set each month by the IRS, and that any applicable conflict-of-interest rules are satisfied (Code Sec. 54A(d)).

NEW LAW EXPLAINED

Authorization of clean renewable energy bonds extended and refreshed.—The authorization for non-profit electricity producers to issue clean renewable energy bonds under Code Sec. 54 (CREBs) has been extended for an additional year, through the end of 2009 (Code Sec. 54(m), as amended by the Emergency Economic Stabilization Act of 2008 (P.L. 110-343)). There is no provision for any additional dollar amount of CREBs to be issued. Instead, the Emergency Economic Act of 2008 authorizes the issuance of $800 million worth of a similar but new category of tax credit bonds called "new clean renewable energy bonds" (New CREBS) (Code Sec. 54C, as added by the Emergency Economic Act of 2008). These tax credit bonds provide a federal subsidy to allow nonprofit electricity producers, including cooperatives and government-owned utilities, to compete more evenly with for-profit companies that can take advantage of the production tax credit under Code Sec. 45.

NEW LAW EXPLAINED

Holders of tax credit bonds are generally entitled to an annual tax credit calculated by multiplying the outstanding face amount of the bonds held by the applicable credit rate, which is set by the IRS. The credit rate is set so that the bonds can be issued at face value with no interest. For New CREBs, however, the annual tax credit is limited to 70 percent of the face amount times the applicable credit rate (Code Sec. 54C(b), as added by the Emergency Economic Act of 2008).

> **Comment:** As a result of the reduced credit amount, New CREBs will presumably have to be issued at a discount.

New CREBS. A New CREB is a bond issued as part of an issue if:

- 100 percent of the available project proceeds of the issue are to be used for capital expenditures incurred by governmental bodies, public power providers, or cooperative electric companies for one or more qualified renewable energy facilities;
- the bond is issued by a qualified issuer; and
- the issuer designates the bond as a New CREB (Code Sec. 54C(a), as added by the Emergency Economic Act of 2008).

The $800 million national limit for New CREBs is to be allocated among qualified projects at the discretion of the IRS, except that not more than $33\frac{1}{3}$ percent each of the $800 million can be allocated to qualified projects of governmental bodies, public power providers, and cooperative electric companies (Code Sec. 54C(c)(2), as added by the Emergency Economic Act of 2008). Each issuer can designate an amount of its eligible bonds not exceeding the limitation amount allocated to it as New CREBs (Code Sec. 54C(c)(1), as added by the Emergency Economic Act of 2008).

The portion allocated to projects of public power providers is to be allocated to all eligible projects on a pro rata basis; the IRS has discretion to determine the method of allocation for amounts allocated to projects of governmental bodies and cooperative electric companies (Code Sec. 54C(c)(3), as added by the Emergency Economic Act of 2008).

> **Comment:** For clean renewable energy bonds, a portion of the national limit was reserved for government projects, with the rest available to public power companies and cooperatives. The IRS had allocated the limitation to the smallest qualified projects first (Notice 2007-26, I.R.B. 2007-14, 870). The public power sector believed it was shortchanged under that method and successfully lobbied for separate allocations.

Qualified renewable energy facilities. Qualified renewable energy facilities are those facilities producing electrical power that are owned by a public power provider, a governmental body or a cooperative electric company and that qualify under the renewable electricity production credit (Code Sec. 45) as:

- wind facilities;
- closed-loop biomass facilities;
- open-loop biomass facilities;
- geothermal or solar energy facilities;
- small irrigation power facilities;

NEW LAW EXPLAINED

- landfill gas facilities;

- trash combustion facilities; or

- qualified hydropower facilities (Code Sec. 54C(d)(1), as added by the Emergency Economic Act of 2008).

Definitions. The following definitions apply:

- Qualified issuers are public power providers, cooperative electric companies, governmental bodies, clean renewable energy bond lenders, and not-for-profit electric utilities that have received a loan or loan guarantee under the Rural Electrification Act (Code Sec. 54C(d)(6), as added by the Emergency Economic Act of 2008).

- A public power provider is a state or any political subdivision of a state, or any state or local agency, authority, or instrumentality, or a corporation that is wholly owned, directly or indirectly, by any one or more of the foregoing, competent to carry on the business of developing, transmitting, utilizing, or distributing power that is required or authorized under federal, state, or local law or under long-term contracts to provide electric service to end-users or to a distribution utility (Code Sec. 54C(d)(2), as added by the Emergency Economic Act of 2008, referring to definitions in 16 U.S.C. § 824q(a)).

- A cooperative electric company means a mutual or cooperative electric company described in Code Secs. 501(c)(12) or 1381(a)(2)(C) (Code Sec. 54C(d)(4), as added by the Emergency Economic Act of 2008).

- A governmental body means any state or Indian tribal government or any political subdivision of either (Code Sec. 54C(d)(3), as added by the Emergency Economic Act of 2008).

- A clean renewable energy bond lender is a lender that is a cooperative owned by, or having outstanding loans to, 100 or more cooperative electric companies and in existence on February 1, 2002.

- A clean renewable energy lender includes any affiliated entity controlled by the lender (Code Sec. 54C(d)(5), as added by the Emergency Economic Act of 2008).

Interaction with Code Sec. 54A. The provisions of Code Sec. 54A, which provide mechanical rules for multiple types of tax credit bonds, apply to New CREBs (Code Sec. 54A(d)(1), (d)(2)(C), as amended by the Emergency Economic Act of 2008).

▶ **Effective date.** The provisions apply to obligations issued after October 3, 2008 (Division B, Act Sec. 107(d) of the Emergency Economic Stabilization Act of 2008 (P.L. 110-343)).

Law source: Law at ¶5145, ¶5150 and ¶5155.

— Division B, Act Sec. 107(a) of the Emergency Economic Stabilization Act of 2008 (P.L. 110-343), adding Code Sec. 54C;

— Division B, Act Sec. 107(b), amending Code Sec. 54A(d);

— Division B, Act Sec. 107(c), amending Code Sec. 54(m);

— Division B, Act Sec. 107(d), providing the effective date.

¶**805**

NEW LAW EXPLAINED

Reporter references: For further information, consult the following CCH reporters.

— Standard Federal Tax Reporter, ¶4888.01

— Tax Research Consultant, BUSEXP: 54,558

— Federal Tax Guide, ¶2612

¶810 Qualified Energy Conservation Bonds

SUMMARY OF NEW LAW

A new category of tax credit bonds, qualified energy conservation bonds, is authorized. A national limitation of $800 million on the amount of new bonds authorized will be allocated by the IRS to the states and large local communities in proportion to their populations. The bond proceeds must be used for qualified conservation purposes.

BACKGROUND

The Code has long contained provisions making the interest on qualifying state and local bonds exempt from federal income tax, which provides an indirect federal subsidy for state and local government operations and activities (Code Sec. 103). Tax-exempt bonds are subject to a number of restrictions intended to insure that their proceeds are indeed used for public purposes (Code Secs. 141-150). Notably, bonds issued by a state or local government to finance private activity, as opposed to general government operations, are subject to a volume cap and must satisfy a number of requirements including maturity limitations, public approval requirements, and use restrictions. All tax-exempt bonds are subject to arbitrage restrictions and registration requirements.

Tax credit bonds generally. A new method of subsidizing state and local governments was introduced with the authorization of tax credit bonds, first exemplified in the form of qualified zone academy bonds, in the Taxpayer Relief Act of 1997 (P.L. 105-34). Tax credit bonds are not interest-bearing obligations. Instead, a taxpayer holding a tax credit bond on one or more allowance dates during a tax year is allowed a credit against federal income tax equivalent to the interest that the bond would otherwise pay. The bondholder must include the amount of the credit in his or her gross income and treat it as interest income. In effect, the federal government pays the interest, allowing the issuer to borrow interest free. In return, the issuer must follow certain requirements with regard to the form of the bonds and the use of the proceeds.

The Code provisions authorizing the issuance of tax credit bonds for various financing purposes include *mechanical* provisions, relating to the credit and the application of tax-exempt bond rules, and *substantive* provisions, which vary depending on what the bond proceeds are to be used to finance. Prior to 2008, tax credit bonds for clean

BACKGROUND

renewable energy purposes and for qualified zone academy purposes had been added to the Code separately, each with their own separate substantive and mechanical provisions. The Heartland, Habitat, Harvest, and Horticulture Act of 2008 (P.L. 110-246) added a new Subpart I to Part IV of the Code (regarding credits against tax), placing common mechanical provisions for tax credit bonds in new Code Sec. 54A, with room for substantive provisions relating to various types of tax credit bonds to follow in succeeding Code Sections.

The common mechanical requirements for tax credit bonds include requirements that:

- the available project proceeds of the bonds be spent for the specified purposes within three years;

- the issuer meet certain reporting and arbitrage requirements generally applicable to tax-exempt bonds;

- the maturity of the bonds not exceed a maximum term to be set each month by the IRS; and

- any applicable conflict-of-interest rules are satisfied (Code Sec. 54A(d)).

NEW LAW EXPLAINED

Qualified energy conservation bonds authorized.—The Emergency Economic Stabilization Act of 2008 (P.L. 110-343) authorizes the issuance of $800 million worth of a new type of tax credit bond called "qualified energy conservation bonds" (Code Sec. 54D, as added by the Emergency Economic Act of 2008). These tax credit bonds provide a federal subsidy to assist state and local governments in financing the expenses of a laundry list of energy conservation projects, including capital expenditures, research expenditures, expenses for mass commuting facilities, demonstration projects, and public education campaigns.

Holders of tax credit bonds are generally entitled to an annual tax credit calculated by multiplying the outstanding face amount of the bonds held by the applicable credit rate, which is set by the IRS. The credit rate is set so that the bonds can be issued at face value with no interest. For qualified energy conservation bonds, however, the annual tax credit is limited to 70 percent of the face amount times the applicable credit rate (Code Sec. 54D(b), as added by the Emergency Economic Act of 2008).

> **Comment:** As a result of the reduced credit amount, qualified energy conservation bonds will presumably have to be issued at a discount.

Qualified energy conservation bonds. A qualified energy conservation bond is a bond issued as part of an issue if:

- 100 percent of the available project proceeds of the issue are to be used for one or more qualified conservation purposes;

- the bond is issued by a state or local government; and

- the issuer designates the bond as a qualified energy conservation bond (Code Sec. 54D(a), as added by the Emergency Economic Act of 2008).

NEW LAW EXPLAINED

The $800 million national limit for qualified energy conservation bonds is to be allocated among the states in proportion to their populations (Code Sec. 54D(e)(1), as added by the Emergency Economic Act of 2008). Any municipality or county with a population of 100,000 or more, known as a large local government, will get a direct allocation from its state's allocation, in an amount that bears the same ratio to the state's allocation as the locality's population bears to the state population. A large local government may choose to reallocate its direct allocation to its state (Code Sec. 54D(e)(2), as added by the Emergency Economic Act of 2008). Each state and each large local government must then allocate its own allocation to issuers within the state (Code Sec. 54D(e)(3), as added by the Emergency Economic Act of 2008).

Although each issuer can designate an amount of its eligible bonds not exceeding the limitation amount allocated to it as qualified energy conservation bonds, each state and each large local government must ensure that no less than 70 percent of its allocation is used to designate bonds that are not private activity bonds (Code Sec. 54D(c), 54D(e)(3), as added by the Emergency Economic Act of 2008). For purposes of the allocation, an Indian tribal government will be treated as located within a state to the extent that its population resides within the state, so that an Indian tribal government that straddles state lines will receive a direct allocation from each state's allocated limitation (Code Sec. 54D(h)(1), as added by the Emergency Economic Act of 2008).

Indian tribal governments are generally treated as large local governments for energy conservation bond purposes even if their population is not 100,000 or more (Code Sec. 54D(h), as added by the Emergency Economic Act of 2008). Thus, they are entitled to their own direct allocations based on their proportion their population bears to the state's population. However, a bond issued by an Indian tribal government will be treated as a qualified energy conservation bond only if the available project proceeds of its issue are used for purposes for which the tribal government could issue tax-exempt bonds (Code Sec. 54D(h)(2), as added by the Emergency Economic Act of 2008).

The population of any location for a calendar year is determined by reference to the most recent census estimate of the location's population that is issued before the beginning of the year in question (Code Sec. 54D(g)(1), as added by the Emergency Economic Act of 2008). If a municipality is a large local government (that is, it has 100,000 or more residents), that municipality's population is not counted in determining the population of its county (Code Sec. 54D(g)(2), as added by the Emergency Economic Act of 2008).

Qualified conservation purposes. In order to be a qualified energy conservation bond, a bond must be part of an issue for which 100 percent of the available project proceeds are to be used for one or more qualified conservation purposes (Code Sec. 54D(a)(1), as added by the Emergency Economic Act of 2008). Qualified conservation purposes include:

(1) Capital expenditures incurred for purposes of: (a) reducing energy consumption in publicly owned buildings by at least 20 percent; (b) implementing green community programs; (c) rural development involving the production of electricity from renewable energy resources; or (d) any qualified facility for purposes

NEW LAW EXPLAINED

of the renewable electricity production credit under Code Sec. 45 (excluding refined coal production facilities and Indian coal production facilities, without taking into account the placed in service date restrictions in Code Sec. 45);

(2) Expenditures with respect to research facilities and research grants to support research in: (a) development of cellulosic ethanol and other nonfossil fuels; (b) technologies for the capture and sequestration of carbon dioxide produced from the use of fossil fuels; (c) increasing the efficiency of existing technologies for producing nonfossil fuels; (d) auto battery technologies and other technologies to reduce fossil fuel consumption in transportation; or (e) technologies to reduce energy use in buildings;

(3) Mass commuting facilities and related facilities that reduce the consumption of energy, including expenditures to reduce pollution from vehicles used for mass commuting;

(4) Demonstration projects designed to promote the commercialization of: (a) green building technology; (b) the conversion of agricultural waste for use in the production of fuel or otherwise; (c) advanced battery manufacturing technologies; (d) technologies to reduce peak use of electricity; or (e) technologies for the capture and sequestration of carbon dioxide emitted from burning fossil fuels to produce electricity; and

(5) Public education campaigns to promote energy efficiency (Code Sec. 54D(f)(1), as added by the Emergency Economic Act of 2008).

If the bond in question is a private activity bond, any expenditure that is not a capital expenditure is not a qualified conservation purpose (Code Sec. 54D(f)(2), as added by the Emergency Economic Act of 2008).

Interaction with Code Sec. 54A. The provisions of Code Sec. 54A, which provide mechanical rules for multiple types of tax credit bonds, apply to qualified energy conservation bonds (Code Sec. 54A(d)(1), (d)(2)(C), as amended by the Emergency Economic Act of 2008).

▶ **Effective date.** The provisions apply to obligations issued after October 3, 2008 (Division B, Act Sec. 301(c) of the Emergency Economic Stabilization Act of 2008 (P.L. 110-343)).

Law source: Law at ¶5150 and ¶5160.

— Division B, Act Sec. 301(a) of the Emergency Economic Stabilization Act of 2008 (P.L. 110-343), adding Code Sec. 54D;

— Division B, Act Sec. 301(b), amending Code Sec. 54A(d);

— Division B, Act Sec. 301(c), providing the effective date.

Reporter references: For further information, consult the following CCH reporters.

— Standard Federal Tax Reporter, ¶4888.01

— Tax Research Consultant, BUSEXP: 54,550

— Federal Tax Guide, ¶2101

¶815 Qualified Zone Academy Bonds

SUMMARY OF NEW LAW

State and local governments are authorized to issue qualified zone academy bonds in 2008 and 2009. The provisions governing these bonds are moved to new Code Sec. 54E and are now coordinated with the general rules governing tax credit bonds.

BACKGROUND

The Code has long contained provisions making the interest on qualifying state and local bonds exempt from federal income tax, which provides an indirect federal subsidy for state and local government operations and activities (Code Sec. 103). Tax-exempt bonds are subject to a number of restrictions intended to insure that their proceeds are indeed used for public purposes (Code Secs. 141-150). Notably, bonds issued by a state or local government to finance private activity, as opposed to general government operations, are subject to a volume cap and must satisfy a number of requirements including maturity limitations, public approval requirements, and use restrictions. All tax-exempt bonds are subject to arbitrage restrictions and registration requirements.

Tax credit bonds generally. A new method of subsidizing state and local governments was introduced with the authorization of tax credit bonds, first exemplified in the form of qualified zone academy bonds (QZABs), in the Taxpayer Relief Act of 1997 (P.L. 105-34). Tax credit bonds are not interest-bearing obligations. Instead, a taxpayer holding a tax credit bond on one or more allowance dates during a tax year is allowed a credit against federal income tax equivalent to the interest that the bond would otherwise pay. The bondholder must include the amount of the credit in his or her gross income and treat it as interest income. In effect, the federal government pays the interest, allowing the issuer to borrow interest free. In return, the issuer must follow certain requirements with regard to the form of the bonds and the use of the proceeds.

The Code provisions authorizing the issuance of tax credit bonds for various financing purposes include *mechanical* provisions, relating to the credit and the application of tax-exempt bond rules, and *substantive* provisions, which vary depending on what the bond proceeds are to be used to finance. Prior to 2008, tax credit bonds for clean renewable energy purposes and for qualified zone academy purposes had been added to the Code separately, each with their own separate substantive and mechanical provisions. The Heartland, Habitat, Harvest, and Horticulture Act of 2008 (P.L. 110-246) added a new Subpart I to Part IV of the Code (regarding credits against tax), placing common mechanical provisions for tax credit bonds in new Code Sec. 54A, with room for substantive provisions relating to various types of tax credit bonds to follow in succeeding Code Sections, beginning with qualified forestry conservation bonds in Code Sec. 54B. However, the existing provisions for clean renewable energy bonds and QZABs were not moved into the new Subpart.

BACKGROUND

The common mechanical requirements for tax credit bonds include requirements that (1) the available project proceeds of the bonds be spent for the specified purposes within three years; (2) the issuer meet certain reporting and arbitrage requirements generally applicable to tax-exempt bonds; (3) the maturity of the bonds not exceed a maximum term to be set each month by the IRS; and (4) any applicable conflict-of-interest rules are satisfied (Code Sec. 54A(d)).

QZABs. Under Code Sec. 1397E, $400 million in QZABs were authorized to be issued by state or local governments in each year from 1998 to 2007. The national limit is allocated among the states in proportion to their respective populations of individuals living below the poverty line. Each state then allocates its credit authority to qualified zone academies within its borders. The credit for holders of QZABs is only available to banks, insurance companies, and corporations engaged in the business of lending money.

To be a QZAB, at least 95 percent of the proceeds of a bond must be used within five years to provide certain assistance to a qualified zone academy, and commitments must have been obtained for private sector contributions of property or services equal to at least 10 percent of the bond proceeds. A school is a qualified zone academy if it is a pre-college public school that operates a special academic program in cooperation with businesses to enhance the academic curriculum and increase graduation and employment rates and either it is located in an empowerment zone or enterprise community designated under the Code, or it is reasonably expected that at least 35 percent of the students at the school will be eligible for free or reduced-cost lunches under the National School Lunch Act.

The Tax Relief and Health Care Act of 2006 (P.L. 109-432) imposed the arbitrage requirements generally applicable to tax-exempt bonds on QZABs, and also added the applicable spending requirements. As noted above, the Heartland, Habitat, Harvest, and Horticulture Act of 2008 (P.L. 110-246) did not coordinate the existing provisions relating to QZABs with its new general framework for tax credit bonds generally.

NEW LAW EXPLAINED

Authorization of qualified zone academy bonds extended and modified.—The Emergency Economic Stabilization Act of 2008 (P.L. 110-343) has extended the authority of state and local governments to issue qualified zone academy bonds (QZABs) for two additional years, through 2009 (Code Sec. 54E, as added by the Emergency Economic Act of 2008). The Act authorizes the issuance of up to $400 million of such bonds in 2008 and in 2009. For QZABs issued on or before October 3, 2008, the provisions of Code Sec. 1397E continue to apply (Code Sec. 1397E(m), as added by the Emergency Economic Act of 2008). For bonds issued after October 3, 2008, new provisions that are coordinated with the general framework governing tax credit bonds apply. The substantive rules of new Code Sec. 54E are mostly identical to those in Code Sec. 1397E. The mechanical provisions in Code Secs. 54A and 1397E have more differences.

NEW LAW EXPLAINED

Comment: The use of QZABs require coordination among the state education agency, the state or local government issuer, the local education agency, the academy, and the contributing businesses.

Under the new provisions, a QZAB is a bond issued as part of an issue if:

- 100 percent of the available project proceeds of the issue are to be used for a qualified purpose with respect to a qualified zone academy established by an eligible local education agency;

- the bond is issued by the state or a local government within the jurisdiction of which the academy is located; and

- the issuer designates the bond as a QZAB, certifies that it has written assurances of the required private contributions with respect to the academy, and certifies that it has the written approval of the eligible local education agency for the bond issuance (Code Sec. 54E(a), as added by the Emergency Economic Act of 2008).

Requirement (1) differs from the rules under Code Sec. 1397E. Under those rules, a bond can be qualified if "95 percent or more of the proceeds of the issue" are to be used for the requisite purposes, rather than "100 percent of the available project proceeds of the issue." Available project proceeds are the proceeds from the sale of the issue, less the issuance costs paid from the proceeds (not to exceed two percent of the proceeds), plus any investment income on the net proceeds (Code Sec. 54A(e)(4)).

Allocation of the limit. The $400 million annual limit for QZABs for 2008 and 2009 is to be allocated among the states on the basis of their respective populations of individuals below the poverty line. Each state's education agency then allocates its state's portion of the national limit to qualified zone academies in its jurisdiction (Code Sec. 54E(c), as added by the Emergency Economic Act of 2008). Each bond issuer can designate an amount of its eligible bonds as QZABs with respect to each academy not exceeding the limitation amount allocated to the academy by the state education agency (Code Sec. 54E(c)(3), as added by the Emergency Economic Act of 2008).

If the designated QZABs issued during a calendar year for academies within a state do not use up the state's allocation for the year, the excess is carried over to increase the state's allocated limit for the next year. Any carryforward can be carried only to the first two years following the unused limitation year. Carryforwards are treated as used on a first-in, first-out basis. The same carryforward rules apply under Code Sec. 1397E and the new provisions in Code Sec. 54E. Any carryforwards remaining from the time period subject to Code Sec. 1397E will continue to be available on the same basis under the new provisions (Code Sec. 54E(c)(4), as added by the Emergency Economic Act of 2008).

Qualified purposes. The qualified purposes for which the proceeds of QZABs must be used under the new provisions are identical to those under existing law. A qualified purpose, with respect to any particular qualified academy includes:

- rehabilitating or repairing the public school facility in which the academy is established;

- providing equipment for use at the academy;

- developing course materials for use in the academy; and

NEW LAW EXPLAINED

- training teachers and other school personnel in the academy (Code Sec. 54E(d)(3), as added by the Emergency Economic Act of 2008).

Qualified zone academies. The definition of a qualified zone academy under the new provisions is identical to the existing rule. A qualified zone academy is a public school (or academic program within a public school) established by and operated under the supervision of an eligible local education agency (generally the local public school board) to provide education or training below the post-secondary level if:

- the school or program is designed in cooperation with business to enhance the academic curriculum, increase graduation and employment rates, and better prepare students for the rigors of college and the increasingly complex workforce;

- students in the school or program will be subject to the same academic standards and assessments as other students educated by the local education agency;

- the comprehensive education plan of the school or program is approved by the local education agency; and

- (a) the public school is located in empowerment zone or enterprise community; or (b) there is a reasonable expectation, at the date of issuance of the bonds, that at least 35 percent of the students in the school or program will be eligible for free or reduced-cost school lunches (Code Sec. 54E(d)(1), as added by the Emergency Economic Act of 2008).

Private business contribution requirement. The private business contribution requirement under the new provisions is identical to the existing rule. The local education agency that established the academy must have written commitments from private entities to make qualified contributions having a present value, as of the date the bonds are issued, of not less than 10 percent of the proceeds of the issue (Code Sec. 54E(b), as added by the Emergency Economic Act of 2008). Qualified contributions include:

- equipment for use in the academy;

- technical assistance in developing curriculum or training teachers in order to promote appropriate market-driven technology in the classroom;

- services of employees as volunteer mentors;

- internships, field trips, or other educational opportunities outside the academy for students; or

- any other property or service specified by the local education agency (Code Sec. 54E(d)(4), as added by the Emergency Economic Act of 2008).

Interaction with Code Sec. 54A. The provisions of Code Sec. 54A, which provide mechanical rules for multiple types of tax credit bonds, apply to QZABs issued after October 3, 2008 (Code Sec. 54A(d)(1), (d)(2)(C), as amended by the Emergency Economic Act of 2008). Although many of the mechanical rules are the same under both regimes, certain differences between old QZABs and new QZABs should be noted. In particular:

- the restriction of the credit for holders of QZABs to banks, insurance companies and corporate lenders does not apply to new bonds;

NEW LAW EXPLAINED

- the credit on new bonds is allowed ratably on four credit allowance dates during each year, rather than on a single date;

- the credit on new bonds is explicitly treated by bondholders as interest income;

- proceeds of new bonds must be spent within three years of the date of issuance, instead of five years;

- new bonds are not subject to the old expenditures rule requiring that the issuer expect at the date of the issue that the qualified purposes will be completed with due diligence and the proceeds from the bonds will be spent with due diligence is eliminated;

- new bonds are subject to relaxed arbitrage requirements;

- the issuer of new bonds must certify its satisfaction of all applicable state and local conflict-of-interest requirements and any similar requirements imposed by IRS regulation; and

- the old rule that shareholders of an S corporation holding a QZAB must take their pro rata share of the credit into account but may not adjust their basis in their stock is restated and its application expanded by requiring that an allocation of the credit to S corporation shareholders (or partners in a partnership holding a QZAB) be treated as a distribution.

▶ **Effective date.** The provisions apply to obligations issued after October 3, 2008 (Division C, Act Sec. 313(c) of the Emergency Economic Stabilization Act of 2008 (P.L. 110-343)).

Law source: Law at ¶5150, ¶5165, and ¶5365. Committee Reports at ¶10,510.

— Division C, Act Sec. 313(a) of the Emergency Economic Stabilization Act of 2008 P.L. 110-343, adding Code Sec. 54E;

— Division C, Act Sec. 313(b)(1) and (2), amending Code Sec. 54A(d);

— Division C, Act Sec. 313(b)(3), adding Code Sec. 1397E(m);

— Division C, Act Sec. 313(c), providing the effective date.

Reporter references: For further information, consult the following CCH reporters.

— Standard Federal Tax Reporter, ¶32,407.01

— Tax Research Consultant, BUSEXP: 57,150

— Federal Tax Guide, ¶2224

¶820 Qualified Green Building and Sustainable Design Project Bonds

SUMMARY OF NEW LAW

The authority to issue qualified green building and sustainable design project bonds is extended through September 30, 2012, and the special treatment for current refunding bonds is extended to bonds issued before October 1, 2012.

BACKGROUND

State or local governments may provide tax-exempt financing for private activities by issuing private activity bonds (Code Secs. 103 and 141). Interest on these bonds is tax-exempt if they are classified as exempt facility bonds. To qualify as an exempt facility bond, at least 95 percent of the net proceeds of the bond must be used to finance a qualified exempt facility (Code Sec. 142(a)). The American Jobs Creation Act of 2004 (2004 Jobs Act (P.L. 108-357)) added green building and sustainable design projects to the list of facilities that can be financed by exempt facility bonds under Code Sec. 142(a)(14). A qualified green bond is any bond issued as part of an issue that finances a project designated as a qualified green building and sustainable design project by the Secretary of the Treasury, after consultation with the Administrator of the Environmental Protection Agency (EPA).

A qualified green building and sustainable design project must meet several criteria relating to design features, location, government support, size, employment, energy use, emissions and use of tax benefits (Code Sec. 142(l)(1) and (4)(A)(i)-(iv)):

- at least 75 percent of the square footage of the commercial buildings that are part of the project is registered for the U.S. Green Building Council's Leadership in Energy and Environmental Design (LEED) certification and is reasonably expected at the time of designation to meet such certification;
- the project includes a brownfield site;
- the project receives at least $5 million in specific state or local resources; and
- the project includes at least one million square feet of building or at least 20 acres of land.

Bond volume limitations. Qualified green bonds are not subject to the state bond volume limitations. However, the Secretary may not allocate authority to issue qualified green building and sustainable design project bonds in an aggregate face amount exceeding $2 billion (Code Sec. 142(l)(7)(B)).

Treatment of current refunding bonds. Qualified green bonds may be currently refunded if certain conditions are met, but they cannot be advance refunded. The bond volume limitations and the termination of the exempt facility bond designation does not apply to any bond or series of bonds issued to refund a qualified green bond issued before October 1, 2009, if:

- the average maturity date of the issue of which the refunding bond is a part is no later than the average maturity date of the bonds to be refunded;
- the amount of the refunding bond does not exceed the outstanding amount of the refunded bond; and
- the net proceeds of the refunding bond are used to redeem the refunded bond no later than 90 days after the issuance date of the refunding bond (Code Sec. 142(l)(9)).

Accountability. Issuers must maintain an interest-bearing reserve account on behalf of each project, in an amount equal to one percent of the net proceeds of any qualified green bond issued for the project. Within five years after the issuance date, the Secretary of the Treasury is to consult with the EPA Administrator to determine

BACKGROUND

whether the project has substantially complied with the requirements described in the project application for designation, including certification. If the project is found to have substantially complied with those requirements, the funds in the reserve account, including interest, will be released to the project. If substantial compliance is lacking, the funds in the reserve account, including interest, will be forfeited to the U.S. Treasury (Act Sec. 701(d) of the 2004 Jobs Act).

Termination. The authority to issue qualified green bonds terminates after September 30, 2009 (Code Sec. 142(l)(8)).

NEW LAW EXPLAINED

Authority to Issue Qualified Green Bonds Extended.—The authority for issuing qualified green building and sustainable design project bonds has been extended to September 30, 2012 (Code Sec. 142(l)(8), as amended by the Emergency Economic Stabilization Act of 2008 (P.L. 110-343)). Further, the $2 billion limitation and the deadline for issuance of green building and sustainable design project bonds will not apply to current refunding bonds issued prior to October 1, 2012, if the requirements under Code Sec. 142(l)(9)(A)-(C) are met (Code Sec. 142(l)(9), as amended by the Emergency Economic Act of 2008).

Accountability. The Emergency Economic Act of 2008 also clarifies that the date for determining whether amounts in a reserve account may be released to a green building and sustainable design project is five years after the date of issuance of the last bond issue issued with respect to the project (Act Sec. 701(d) of the American Jobs Creation Act of 2004 (P.L. 108-357), as amended by the Emergency Economic Act of 2008).

▶ **Effective date.** No specific effective date is provided by the Act. The provision is, therefore, considered effective on October 3, 2008, the date of enactment.

Law source: Law at ¶5205 and ¶7147. Committee Reports at ¶10,250.

— Division B, Act Sec. 307(a) of the Emergency Economic Stabilization Act of 2008 (P.L. 110-343), amending Code Sec. 142(l)(8);

— Division B, Act Sec. 307(b), amending Code Sec. 142(l)(9);

— Division B, Act Sec. 307(c), amending Act Sec. 701(d) of the American Jobs Creation Act of 2004 (P.L. 108-357).

Reporter references: For further information, consult the following CCH reporters.

— Standard Federal Tax Reporter, ¶4888.01, ¶7752.0575

— Tax Research Consultant, SALES: 51,202

— Federal Tax Guide, ¶4784

EXCISE TAXES

¶825 Biodiesel, Renewable Diesel and Alternative Fuel Credits

SUMMARY OF NEW LAW

The per-gallon incentives for biodiesel, agri-biodiesel, renewable diesel, and alternative fuels have been extended through December 31, 2009. The incentives for biodiesel have increased to $1 per gallon to match the agri-biodiesel incentives. Also, the definition of renewable diesel has been modified. Congress has clarified that the per-gallon incentives are only for U.S. production and use. Finally, starting on October 1, 2009, for liquid fuel derived from coal to qualify for the per-gallon alternative fuel incentives, it must be produced at a facility that sequesters its carbon dioxide emissions.

BACKGROUND

For biodiesel, agri-biodiesel, and renewable diesel fuels, the Internal Revenue Code provides an income tax credit for both straight fuels and fuel mixtures (Code Sec. 40A), an excise tax credit for fuel mixtures (Code Sec. 6426(c)) and a payment provision for fuel mixtures (Code Sec. 6427(e)). For this purpose, renewable diesel is generally treated as biodiesel (Code Sec. 40A(f)(1)). The rules are coordinated so that taxpayers may not receive a double benefit for a single gallon of fuel (Code Secs. 40A(c), 6426(g) and 6427(e)(3)).

"Biodiesel" generally refers to a fuel mixture made from vegetable oils or animal fats combined with diesel. The Code provides a more technical definition (Code Sec. 40A(d)).

"Agri-biodiesel" means biodiesel derived solely from virgin oils, including esters derived from virgin vegetable oils from corn, soybeans, sunflower seeds, cottonseeds, canola, crambe, rapeseeds, safflowers, flaxseeds, rice bran, and mustard seeds, and from animal fats.

"Renewable diesel" means diesel fuel derived from biomass using a thermal depolymerization process that meets the registration requirements for fuels and fuel additives established by the Environmental Protection Agency under section 211 of the Clean Air Act and the requirements of the American Society of Testing and Materials (ASTM) D975 or D396.

The amount of the biodiesel mixture income tax credit, excise tax credit, or payment is 50 cents for each gallon of biodiesel used to produce a qualified biodiesel mixture (Code Secs. 40A(b)(1)(A) and 6426(c)(2)(A)). The income tax credit for straight biodiesel is also 50 cents per gallon (Code Sec. 40A(b)(2)(A)).

The amount of the agri-biodiesel mixture income tax credit, excise tax credit, or payment is $1 (Code Secs. 40A(b)(3) and 6426(c)(2)(B)).

BACKGROUND

The amount of the renewable diesel mixture and straight renewable diesel income tax credit, excise tax credit, or payment is $1 per gallon (Code Sec. 40A(f)(2)(A); Notice 2007-37, I.R.B. 2007-17, 1002). Fuel coproduced from biomass and petroleum feedstocks may qualify as a renewable diesel mixture. But only the portion attributable to biomass qualifies as renewable diesel used in the production of a renewable diesel mixture (Notice 2007-37, I.R.B. 2007-17, 1002).

There is also a small agri-biodiesel producer credit of 10 cents per gallon for up to 15 million gallons of agri-biodiesel fuel produced and sold by the producer during the tax year (Code Sec. 40A(b)(5))

The income tax credits, excise tax credits, and payment provisions for biodiesel, agri-biodiesel and renewable diesel are scheduled to expire after 2008 (Code Secs. 40A(g), 6426(c)(6), 6427(e)(5)(B)).

Although the cellulosic biofuel credit is allowed only for fuel produced and used as fuel in the United States or in a U.S. possession (Code Sec. 40(d)(6)), the Code does not fix any geographic limitations concerning where fuel must be produced, used, or sold with respect to the per-gallon incentives for alcohol fuels (including ethanol), biodiesel, agri-biodiesel, renewable diesel, and certain alternative fuels (Joint Committee on Taxation, Technical Explanation of H.R. 7060, the "Renewable Energy and Job Creation Tax Act of 2008" (JCX-75-08)).

The alternative fuel tax credit is a credit against the excise tax imposed under Code Sec. 4041 on the retail sale or use of alternative fuels. The alternative fuel credit is 50 cents per gallon of alternative fuel sold by the taxpayer for use as fuel in a motor vehicle or motorboat, or so used by the taxpayer. Alternative fuels include liquefied petroleum gas, compressed or liquefied natural gas, liquefied hydrogen, any liquid derived from coal (including peat) through the Fischer-Tropsch process, liquid fuels derived from biomass, and P series fuels (as defining by the Secretary of Energy) (Code Sec. 6426(d)).

The alternative fuel *mixture* credit is a credit against the excise tax on certain removals, entries, and sales imposed under Code Sec. 4081. The alternative fuel mixture credit is 50 cents per gallon of alternative fuel used by the taxpayer in producing any alternative fuel mixture for sale or use in a trade or business of the taxpayer (Code Sec. 6426(e)).

Both the alternative fuel credit and the alternative fuel mixture credit, along with the related payment provision under Code Sec. 6427(e), are scheduled to terminate with respect to any sale or use for any period after September 30, 2009. For liquefied hydrogen, however, the credits are in effect until after September 30, 2014 (Code Sec. 6426(d)(4) and (e)(3), and Code Sec. 6427(e)(5)(C)).

NEW LAW EXPLAINED

Incentives extended; biodiesel credit to increase; definition of renewable diesel modified.—The income tax credits, excise tax credits, and payment provisions for biodiesel, agri-biodiesel, and renewable diesel have been extended through December

NEW LAW EXPLAINED

31, 2009 (Code Secs. 40A(g), 6426(c)(6) and 6427(e)(5)(B), as amended by the Emergency Economic Stabilization Act of 2008 (P.L. 110-343)).

The income tax credits, excise tax credit, and payment provisions for biodiesel have been increased from 50 cents to $1 per gallon so that the incentive for biodiesel now matches the $1 per gallon credit for agri-biodiesel (Code Secs. 40A(b)(1)(A), 40A(b)(2)(A) and 6426(c)(2), as amended by the Emergency Economic Act of 2008). Also, the definition of agri-biodiesel now includes biodiesel derived from camelina (Code Sec. 40A(d)(2), as amended by the Emergency Economic Act of 2008).

The Emergency Economic Act of 2008 has made several important changes affecting the definition of renewable diesel fuel. First, renewable diesel no longer has to meet the definition of "diesel fuel"—being "liquid fuel" derived from biomass is sufficient. Second, renewable diesel no longer has to be derived using a thermal depolymerization process (Code Sec. 40A(f)(3), as amended by the Emergency Economic Act of 2008). Third, failing to meet the requirements of the American Society of Testing and Materials (ASTM) D975 and D396 will no longer automatically disqualify a liquid fuel as renewable diesel. Rather, the provision permits the IRS to identify other standards equivalent to the ASTM standards for renewable diesel (Code Sec. 40A(f)(3)(B), as amended by the Emergency Economic Act of 2008).

In addition, renewable diesel now also includes biomass fuel that meets a Department of Defense military specification for jet fuel or an ASTM for aviation turbine fuel. Such fuel would be termed "renewable jet fuel." In connection with this, for purposes of the renewable diesel mixture credit, kerosene is treated as diesel fuel when in a mixture with renewable jet fuel (Code Sec. 40A(f)(4), as added by the Emergency Economic Act of 2008; Joint Committee on Taxation, Technical Explanation of H.R. 7060, the "Renewable Energy and Job Creation Tax Act of 2008" (JCX-75-08)).

Finally, the Emergency Economic Act of 2008 overrides the IRS' position in Notice 2007-37, 1002 allowing fuel coproduced from biomass and petroleum feedstocks to qualify as a renewable diesel mixture. Instead, under the Emergency Economic Act of 2008, renewable diesel does not include any fuel derived from coprocessing biomass with a non-biomass feedstock (Code Sec. 40A(f)(3), as amended by the Emergency Economic Act of 2008).

Incentives for U.S. production. No fuel that is produced outside of the United States or its possessions for use as fuel outside of the United States is eligible for the per-gallon tax incentives relating to alcohol, biodiesel, renewable diesel, and alternative fuel (Code Secs. 40(d)(7), 40A(d)(5), 6426(i) and 6427(e)(5), as added by the Emergency Economic Act of 2008; Joint Committee on Taxation, Technical Explanation of H.R. 7060, the "Renewable Energy and Job Creation Tax Act of 2008" (JCX-75-08)).

> **Comment:** The Joint Committee on Taxation lists the following as examples of situations in which fuel is ineligible for incentives:
>
> (1) biodiesel, which is not in a mixture, that is both produced and used outside the United States;

NEW LAW EXPLAINED

(2) foreign-produced biodiesel that is used to make a qualified mixture outside of the United States for foreign use; and

(3) foreign-produced biodiesel that is used to make a qualified mixture in the United States that is then exported for foreign use (Joint Committee on Taxation, Technical Explanation of H.R. 7060, the "Renewable Energy and Job Creation Tax Act of 2008" (JCX-75-08)).

Alternative fuel credits extended. The alternative fuel credit and the alternative fuel mixture credit, along with the related payment provision under Code Sec. 6427(e), are extended to December 31, 2009 (Code Sec. 6426(d)(5), as redesignated and amended by the Emergency Economic Act of 2008, and Code Secs. 6426(e)(3) and 6427(e)(5)(C), as amended by the Emergency Economic Act of 2008). However, the expiration date for liquefied hydrogen incentives remains September 30, 2014.

In addition, compressed or liquefied gas derived from biomass, as defined in Code Sec. 45K(c)(3), has been added to the list of alternative fuels that may qualify for the per-gallon incentives under Code Sec. 6426(d) and (e) (Code Sec. 6426(d)(2)(F), as added by the Emergency Economic Act of 2008). Finally, the uses of alternative fuel that may give rise to an alternative fuel credit now includes use as a fuel in aviation, in addition to use as a fuel in a motor vehicle or motorboat (Code Sec. 6426(d)(1), as amended by the Emergency Economic Act of 2008).

Carbon capture. Beginning on October 1, 2009, for liquid fuel derived from coal through the Fischer-Tropsch process to qualify for the per-gallon alternative fuel incentives, it must be produced at a facility that separates and sequesters at least 50 percent of its carbon dioxide emissions. Then, starting on December 31, 2009, this requirement increases to 75 percent of carbon dioxide emissions (Code Sec. 6426(d)(4), as added by the Emergency Economic Act of 2008; the Energy Improvement and Extension Act of 2008, Senate Finance Committee Summary, September 17, 2008).

▶ **Effective date.** The amendments concerning credits for biodiesel and renewable diesel apply to fuel produced, and sold or used, after December 31, 2008 (Division B, Act Sec. 202(g)(1) of the Emergency Economic Stabilization Act of 2008 (P.L. 110-343)). The amendment concerning the coproduction of renewable diesel with petroleum feedstock applies to fuel produced, and sold or used, after October 3, 2008, the date of enactment (Division B, Act Sec. 202(g)(2) of the Emergency Economic Act of 2008). The amendments concerning incentives for U.S. production applies to claims for credit or payment made on or after May 15, 2008 (Division B, Act Sec. 203(d) of the Emergency Economic Act of 2008). The amendments concerning the extension and modification of the alternative fuel credit applies to fuel sold or used after October 3, 2008 (Division B, Act Sec. 204(d) of the Emergency Economic Act of 2008).

Law source: Law at ¶5060, ¶5065, ¶5455 and ¶5460. Committee Reports at ¶10,150 and ¶10,160.

— Division B, Act Sec. 202(a) of the Emergency Economic Stabilization Act of 2008, amending Code Secs. 40A(g), 6426(c)(6), and 6427(e)(5)(B);

— Division B, Act Sec. 202(b), amending Code Sec. 40A(b) and (f)(2) and Code Sec. 6426(c)(2);

¶825

NEW LAW EXPLAINED

— Division B, Act Sec. 202(c), (d) and (e), amending Code Sec. 40A(f)(3) and adding Code Sec. 40A(f)(4);

— Division B, Act Sec. 202(f), amending Code Sec. 40A(d)(2);

— Division B, Act Sec. 203(a), (b) and (c)(1), adding Code Secs. 40(d)(7), 40A(d)(5) and 6426(i), respectively;

— Division B, Act Sec. 203(c)(2), redesignating Code Sec. 6427(e)(5) as (6) and adding new Code Sec. 6427(e)(5);

— Division B, Act Sec. 204(a), amending Code Sec. 6426(d)(4) and (e)(3) and Code Sec. 6427(e)(5)(C);

— Division B, Act Sec. 204(b)(1), amending and redesignating Code Sec. 6426(d)(2)(F) as (G), and adding new Code Sec. 6426(d)(2)(F);

— Division B, Act Sec. 204(b)(2), amending Code Sec. 6426(d)(1);

— Division B, Act Sec. 204(c)(1), redesignating Code Sec. 6426(d)(4) as (5) and adding new Code Sec. 6426(d)(4);

— Division B, Act Sec. 204(c)(2), amending Code Sec. 6426(d)(2);

— Division B, Act Secs. 202(g), 203(d) and 204(d), providing the effective dates.

Reporter references: For further information, consult the following CCH reporters.

— Standard Federal Tax Reporter, ¶4320.01

— Tax Research Consultant, EXCISE: 24,374 and BUSEXP: 55,100

— Federal Tax Guide, ¶2616

— Federal Excise Tax Reporter, ¶2325 and ¶49,250

¶830 Cover Over of Tax on Rum

SUMMARY OF NEW LAW

The $13.25 per proof gallon cover over amount for rum brought into the United States is extended through December 31, 2009.

BACKGROUND

A $13.50 per proof gallon excise tax is imposed on all distilled spirits produced in, or imported into, the United States (Code Sec. 5001(a)(1)). A proof gallon is a liquid gallon consisting of 50-percent alcohol. This excise tax does not apply to distilled spirits that are exported from the United States, including those exported to U.S. possessions, such as Puerto Rico and the Virgin Islands.

Puerto Rico and the Virgin Islands receive a payment ("cover over") limited to the amount of $10.50 per proof gallon of the excise tax imposed on rum brought into the United States (Code Sec. 7652(f)). The payment is made with respect to all rum entering the United States on which tax is paid, not just on rum originating from the

BACKGROUND

two U.S. possessions. The cover over payment limit was temporarily set at $13.25 per proof gallon for the period July 1, 1999, through December 31, 2005. The Tax Relief and Health Care Act of 2006 (P.L. 109-432) extended the $13.25 per proof gallon cover over through December 31, 2007.

Tax amounts from rum produced in Puerto Rico are covered over to Puerto Rico while tax amounts from rum produced in the Virgin Islands are covered over to the Virgin Islands. Tax amounts from rum produced in neither Puerto Rico nor the Virgin Islands are divided and covered over to the two possessions under a formula. All amounts covered over are subject to the dollar limitation.

NEW LAW EXPLAINED

Increased cover over limit extended.—The $13.25 per proof gallon cover over amount to Puerto Rico and the Virgin Islands for rum brought into the United States is extended for two more years, through December 31, 2009 (Code Sec. 7652(f)(1), as amended by the Emergency Economic Stabilization Act of 2008 (P.L. 110-343). Beginning on January 1, 2010, the cover over amount reverts to $10.50 per proof gallon.

▶ **Effective date.** The provision applies to distilled spirits brought into the United States after December 31, 2007 (Division C, Act Sec. 308(b) of the Emergency Economic Stabilization Act of 2008 (P.L. 110-343)).

Law source: Law at ¶5490. Committee Report at ¶10,480.

— Division C, Act Sec. 308(a) of the Emergency Economic Stabilization Act of 2008 (P.L. 110-343), amending Code Sec. 7652(f)(1);

— Division C, Act Sec. 308(b), providing the effective date.

Reporter references: For further information, consult the following CCH reporters.

— Standard Federal Tax Reporter, ¶42,968F.01

— Federal Tax Guide, ¶21,740

— Federal Excise Tax Reporter, ¶58,275.01

¶835 Aviation Excise Taxes

SUMMARY OF NEW LAW

Excise taxes on aviation fuel taxes, airline passenger tickets, and air cargo have been extended through March 31, 2009.

BACKGROUND

The Airport and Airway Trust Fund of the federal government provides funding for capital improvements to the U.S. airport and airway system, as well as supporting the Federal Aviation Administration (FAA) (Code Sec. 9502). The fund is financed

BACKGROUND

through various excises taxes. For example, a 19.3 cents per gallon excise tax is imposed on aviation gasoline when it is removed from a terminal facility (Code Sec. 4081(a)(2)(A)(ii)). An excise tax of 7.5 percent is imposed on the amount a person pays for "taxable transportation" by air, as well as a flat rate per each flight segment regardless of whether sleeping or seating accommodations are provided (Code Sec. 4261). Different rates apply for the transportation of persons depending on whether the travel is within the continental United States, Alaska or Hawaii, or is for international travel. Finally, an excise tax of 6.25 percent is imposed on the amount paid within or outside the United States for the "taxable transportation" of property by air (Code Sec. 4271). The tax is paid by the person making payment for the taxable transportation, but only if such payment is made to a person engaged in the business of transporting property by air for hire. All of these excise taxes are scheduled to expire after September 30, 2008.

NEW LAW EXPLAINED

Airport and Airway Trust Fund excise taxes extended.—The Airport and Airway Trust Fund excise taxes are extended through March 31, 2009 (Code Secs. 4081(d)(2), 4261(j)(1)(A), and 4271(d)(1)(A), as amended by the Federal Aviation Administration Extension Act of 2008, Part II (P.L. 110-330)). The expenditure authority of the Airport and Airway Trust Fund has also been extended through March 31, 2009 (Code Sec. 9502(d)(1) and (e)(2), as amended by the FAA Extension Act, Part II).

▶ **Effective date.** The amendments made by this section will take effect on October 1, 2008 (Act Secs. 2(c) and 3(c) of the Federal Aviation Administration Extension Act of 2008, Part II (P.L. 110-330))

Law source: Law at ¶5412, ¶5422, ¶5424, and ¶5499.

— Act Sec. 2(a) of the Federal Aviation Administration Extension Act of 2008 (P.L. 110-330), amending Code Sec. 4081(d)(2);

— Act Sec. 2(b), amending Code Secs. 4261(j)(1)(A)(ii) and 4271(d)(1)(A)(ii);

— Act Sec. 3(a), amending Code Sec. 9502(d)(1) and (e)(2);

— Act Secs. 2(c) and 3(c), providing the effective dates.

Reporter references: For further information, consult the following CCH reporters.

— Tax Research Consultant, EXCISE: 6,114.05, EXCISE: 9,102.05, and EXCISE: 9,106.05.

— Federal Tax Guide, ¶21,050, ¶21,140, and ¶21,145.

— Federal Excise Tax Reporter, ¶8919.01, ¶19,305.014, and ¶20,115.03.

¶840 Tax Exemption for Children's Wooden Arrows

SUMMARY OF NEW LAW

Shafts used in wooden arrows designed for use by children are now exempt from the Code Sec. 4161(b)(2) excise tax.

BACKGROUND

A 43-cent per shaft excise tax applies to all arrow shafts (Code Sec. 4161(b)(2)). This tax is adjusted annually for inflation (Code Sec. 4161(b)(2)(B)). The tax applies to shafts (whether sold separately or incorporated as part of a finished or unfinished product) that:

(1) measures 18 inches or more in overall length or

(2) to shorter shafts that are suitable for use with a bow with a peak draw weight of 30 pounds or more.

The tax is imposed at the time of sale by the manufacturer, producer, or importer of the shaft.

NEW LAW EXPLAINED

Children's wooden arrows exempted.—Wooden arrows designed for use by children are exempt from the 43-cent per shaft excise tax. Specifically, the excise tax on shafts does not apply to any shaft made of all natural woods with no laminations or artificial means of enhancing the spine of the shaft. Additionally, the shaft must be of a type used in the manufacture of an arrow which after its assembly measures 5/16 of an inch or less in diameter and not be suitable for use with a bow with a peak draw weight of 30 pounds or more (Code Sec. 4161(b)(2)(B), as added by the Emergency Economic Stabilization Act of 2008 (P.L. 110-343).

▶ **Effective date.** The exemption from tax for shafts used in wooden arrows designed for use by children applies to shafts first sold after October 3, 2008 (Division C, Act Sec. 503(b) of the Emergency Economic Stabilization Act of 2008).

Law source: Law at ¶5420. Committee Reports at ¶10,680.

— Division C, Act Sec. 503(a) of the Emergency Economic Stabilization Act of 2008 (P.L. 110-343), adding Code Sec. 4161(b)(2)(B);

— Division C, Act Sec. 503(b) , providing the effective date.

Reporter references: For further information, consult the following CCH reporters.

— CCH Tax Research Consultant, EXCISE: 6,156.05

— Federal Excise Tax Reporter, ¶13,105.01

¶845 Exemptions from Heavy Truck and Trailer Tax

SUMMARY OF NEW LAW

The cost of idling reduction devices and the installation of advanced insulation are exempt from the heavy truck and trailer retail excise tax.

BACKGROUND

A 12-percent excise tax is imposed on the sale price of the first retail sale of (1) truck bodies and chassis suitable for use with a vehicle having a gross vehicle weight of over 33,000 pounds, (2) truck trailer and semitrailer bodies and chassis suitable for use with a vehicle having a gross vehicle weight over 26,000 pounds, and (3) tractors of the kind chiefly used for highway transportation in combination with a trailer or semitrailer (Code Sec. 4051(a), Temporary Reg. § 145.4051-1(a)). The tax does not apply to certain articles. For example, camper coaches, feed, seed and fertilizer equipment, house trailers, ambulances, hearses, concrete mixers, trash containers and rail trailers and rail vans are exempted from the tax (Code Sec. 4053).

NEW LAW EXPLAINED

Idling reduction units and advance insulation.—The cost of qualifying idling reduction devices such as auxiliary power units (APUs), which are designed to eliminate the need for truck engine idling (e.g., to provide heating, air conditioning, or electricity) at vehicle rest stops or other temporary parking locations are now exempted from the 12-percent excise tax on heavy trucks and trailers (Code Sec. 4053(9), as added by the Emergency Economic Stabilization Act of 2008 (P.L. 110-343)). A qualifying idling reduction device is defined as any device or system of devices that is:

- designed to provide to a vehicle those services (such as heat, air conditioning, or electricity), which would otherwise require the operation of the main drive engine while the vehicle is temporarily parked or remains stationary, by using one or more devices affixed to a tractor, and

- determined by the Administrator of the Environmental Protection Agency, in consultation with the Secretary of Energy and the Secretary of Transportation, to reduce idling of such vehicle at a motor vehicle rest stop or other location where the vehicles are temporarily parked or remain stationary.

The installation of advanced insulation, which can reduce the need for energy consumption by transportation vehicles carrying refrigerated cargo, is also exempted from the heavy truck and trailer excise tax (Code Sec. 4053(10), as added by the Emergency Economic Act of 2008). "Advanced insulation" is insulation that has an R value of not less than R35 per inch.

NEW LAW EXPLAINED

Both exemptions apply regardless of whether the device or insulation is factory installed or later added as an accessory (Joint Committee on Taxation, Technical Explanation of H.R. 7060, the "Renewable Energy and Job Creation Tax Act of 2008" (JCX-75-08)).

> **Comment:** Both exemptions are aimed at reducing carbon emissions in the transportation sector.

▶ **Effective date.** The provisions apply to sales or installations after October 3, 2008, the date of enactment (Division B, Act Sec. 206(b) of the Emergency Economic Stabilization Act of 2008 (P.L. 110-343)).

Law source: Law at ¶5410. Committee Reports at ¶10,180.

— Division B, Act Sec. 206(a) of the Emergency Economic Stabilization Act of 2008 (P.L. 110-343), adding Code Sec. 4053(9) and (10);

— Division B, Act Sec. 206(b), providing the effective date.

Reporter references: For further information, consult the following CCH reporters.

— Tax Research Consultant, EXCISE: 3,160

— Federal Excise Tax Reporter, ¶6775.01

¶850 Coal Tax Rates and Refund System

SUMMARY OF NEW LAW

The current rates for the excise tax on coal taken from U.S. mines are extended until the earlier of December 31, 2018, or the first December 31 after 2007 as of which the Black Lung Disability Trust Fund has repaid, with interest, all amounts borrowed from the General Fund of the Treasury. In addition, a new procedure has been established under which certain coal producers and exporters can claim a refund of excise taxes paid on exported coal, such claims to be approved or disapproved and paid by the Secretary of the Treasury.

BACKGROUND

A manufacturers excise tax is imposed on sales of coal taken from U.S. mines (Code Sec. 4121). The producer that sold or used the coal is liable for the excise tax. The tax collected is placed into the Black Lung Disability Trust Fund (Trust Fund), which finances black lung benefits to qualified miners. Specifically, the Trust Fund is used to pay compensation and medical and survivor benefits to eligible miners and their survivors, and to cover administrative costs. The Trust Fund can borrow from the General Fund of the Treasury if excise tax receipts on sales of coal do not provide sufficient funding. Currently, the Trust Fund is running a deficit because previous spending was financed with interest-bearing advances from the General Fund (Joint Committee on Taxation, Technical Explanation of H.R. 7060, the "Renewable Energy and Job Creation Tax Act of 2008" (JCX-75-08)).

BACKGROUND

Coal from underground mines is taxed at the rate of $1.10 per ton sold, and coal from surface mines is taxed at the rate of 55 cents per ton sold. (The tax is capped, however, at 4.4 percent of the producer's selling price.) These temporary rates are scheduled to go down the earlier of January 1, 2014, or the first January 1 after 1981 as of which there is no fund balance of repayable advances made to the Trust Fund.

Thus, after December 31, 2013, or the date on which the Trust Fund has repaid, with interest, all amounts borrowed from the General Fund, reduced rates of excise tax apply. The reduced tax rate for coal from underground mines is 50 cents per ton sold; for coal from surface mines, the reduced tax rate is 25 cents per ton sold. Also, the tax cap is scheduled to go down to two percent of the producer's selling price.

Exported coal. In 1999, a U.S. District Court in Virginia ruled that the excise tax on coal violated the Article I, Section 9, Clause 5, constitutional prohibition against taxing exports (*Ranger Fuel Corp.*, 99-1 USTC ¶70,109). Therefore, excise tax imposed on exported coal is subject to a claim for refund. But the claimant must satisfy various requirements contained in the Internal Revenue Code, IRS guidance, and case law.

In *Clintwood Elkhorn Mining Co.* (2008-1 USTC ¶70,275), the Supreme Court ruled that taxpayers seeking a refund of excise taxes on exported coal must proceed under the rules imposed by the Code. Specifically, under Code Sec. 7422(a), no suit for the recovery of tax may be maintained until a refund claim has been filed with the IRS. And, under Code Sec. 6511(a), such a refund claim must be filed within three years from when the return was filed or two years from when the tax was paid, whichever is later.

Also, a civil action for refund cannot be filed before six months passes from the date the claim was filed (unless the IRS disallowed the claim during that time). Nor may a civil action be filed after two years from the date that the notice of claim disallowance was mailed (Code Sec. 6532(a)). Finally, the claimant must establish that it actually bore the tax, as opposed, for example, to the purchaser or the ultimate vendor (Code Sec. 6416(a)(1)). The tax may be refunded to the exporter or shipper if the actual taxpayer waives its claim (Code Sec 6416(c)).

The IRS issued guidance for making nontaxable sales of coal for export and for obtaining a credit or refund when the tax has been paid on coal for export (Notice 2000-28). The guidance requires a coal producer or exporter to provide various information. Part of this information includes statements establishing that the claimant actually bore the tax, that the claimant has evidence that the coal was in the stream of export when sold by the producer, and that the coal was actually exported. Exporters must provide a statement that the actual taxpayer waived the right to a refund claim as well as providing proof of exportation (Joint Committee on Taxation, Technical Explanation of H.R. 7060, the "Renewable Energy and Job Creation Tax Act of 2008" (JCX-75-08)).

NEW LAW EXPLAINED

Current rates on coal extended; new procedure created to refund taxes on exported coal.—The current rates for the excise tax on coal are extended until the

NEW LAW EXPLAINED

earlier of December 31, 2018, or the first December 31 after 2007 as of which the Black Lung Disability Trust Fund (Trust Fund) has repaid, with interest, all amounts borrowed from the General Fund of the Treasury (Code Sec. 4121(e)(2), as amended by the Emergency Economic Stabilization Act of 2008 (P.L. 110-343). Thus, coal from underground mines will continue to be taxed at the rate of $1.10 per ton sold, and coal from surface mines will continue to be taxed at the rate of 55 cents per ton sold. The cap on the coal excise tax of 4.4 percent of the producer's selling price is similarly extended.

> **Comment:** The provision is intended to bring the Black Lung Disability Trust Fund out of debt.

Thus, beginning on the earlier of December 31, 2018, or the date on which the Trust Fund has repaid, with interest, all amounts borrowed from the General Fund, reduced rates of excise tax will apply. The reduced tax rate for coal from underground mines is 50 cents per ton sold; for coal from surface mines, the reduced tax rate is 25 cents per ton sold; and the tax cap will be two percent of the producer's selling price.

In addition, the Black Lung Disability Trust Fund debt has been restructured (Act Sec. 113(b), Emergency Economic Act of 2008 (P.L. 110-343)). This restructuring includes refinancing the outstanding principal of repayable advances and unpaid interest on those advances, a one time appropriation to the Trust Fund sufficient to repay the General Fund of the Treasury, and a provision that establishes the consequences if the Trust Fund prepays any obligation issued to the Treasury prior it its maturity.

Refunds of tax on exported coal. The Emergency Economic Act of 2008 establishes a new procedure under which certain coal producers and exporters can claim a refund of excise taxes paid on exported coal, with such claims to be approved or disapproved and paid by the Secretary of the Treasury. Specifically, a coal producer (or related party) that exported coal to a foreign country or shipped it to a possession of the United States may qualify for a payment from the IRS equal to the tax it paid under Code Sec. 4121. In order to obtain the refund, the producer must have filed an excise tax return between October 1, 1990, and October 3, 2008. Also, the producer must file a claim for refund with the IRS no later than November 1, 2008 (Act Sec. 114(a)(1)(A), Emergency Economic Act of 2008 (P.L. 110-343)). However, the producer's export or shipment of the coal at issue cannot have been through an exporter that has filed a valid and timely claim for refund under the new procedure (Joint Committee on Taxation, Technical Explanation of H.R. 7060, the "Renewable Energy and Job Creation Tax Act of 2008" (JCX-75-08)).

If a coal producer or any party related to the coal producer receives a favorable court judgment relating to the constitutionality of any tax paid under Code Sec. 4121 on exported coal, the producer will be deemed to have established the export of coal to a foreign country or a shipment to a U.S. possession. However, any payment by the IRS will be reduced by the amount of the judgment (Act Sec. 114(a)(1)(B), Emergency Economic Act of 2008 (P.L. 110-343)).

If the above requirements are met, an exporter that exported coal to a foreign country or shipped it to a possession of the United States may qualify for a payment by the Treasury equal to $0.825 per ton of coal exported or shipped. (Act Sec. 114(a)(2),

NEW LAW EXPLAINED

Emergency Economic Act of 2008 (P.L. 110-343)). The IRS must decide whether to approve a claim within 180 days after it is filed, and must pay the claim not later than 180 days after making its determination (Act Sec. 114(e), Emergency Economic Act of 2008 (P.L. 110-343)). Any refund paid under the new procedure will be paid with interest from the date of overpayment using the overpayment rate and method under Code Sec. 6621 (Act Sec. 114(f), Emergency Economic Act of 2008 (P.L. 110-343)).

Limitation. No refund under the system established by Emergency Economic Act of 2008 will be paid on exported coal if a credit or refund of the tax paid has been made by the IRS to any person, or if a settlement with the Federal Government has been made and accepted by the coal producer or the coal exporter. This limitation, however, does not include a settlement or stipulation that contemplates a judgment from which any party has filed an appeal or has a right to file an appeal (Act Sec. 114(b), Emergency Economic Act of 2008 (P.L. 110-343)).

Finally, a payment to a producer under the new refund procedure is not to exceed the Code Sec. 4121 tax imposed on exported coal, and a payment to an exporter is not to exceed $0.825 per ton of exported coal (Act Sec. 114(g), Emergency Economic Act of 2008 (P.L. 110-343)).

▶ **Effective date.** No specific effective date is provided by the Act. The provision is, therefore, considered effective on October 3, 2008, the date of enactment.

Law source: Law at ¶5415, ¶7138 and ¶7141. Committee Reports at ¶10,100 and ¶10,110.

— Division B, Act Sec. 113(a) of the Emergency Economic Stabilization Act of 2008 (P.L. 110-343), amending Code Sec. 4121(e)(2);

— Division B, Act Sec. 113(b);

— Division B, Act Sec. 114.

Reporter references: For further information, consult the following CCH reporters.

— Tax Research Consultant, EXCISE: 6,512.10 and EXCISE: 6,152.30

— Federal Tax Guide, ¶21,085

— Federal Excise Tax Reporter, ¶11,815

¶855 Oil Spill Liability Trust Fund Tax

SUMMARY OF NEW LAW

The Oil Spill Liability Trust Fund Tax has been extended through December 31, 2017, and increased to 8 cents-per-barrel for crude oil receive or petroleum products entering the United States through 2016 and 9 cents-per-barrel for crude oil receive or petroleum products entering the United States in 2017.

BACKGROUND

The Oil Spill Liability Trust Fund ("Oil Spill Fund") was established by the Omnibus Budget Reconciliation Act of 1986 (P.L. 99-509) primarily to pay for removal and related costs associated with oil spills. The Oil Spill Fund is financed in part by a five-cent-per-barrel tax ("oil spill tax") on domestic crude oil received at a U.S. refinery; on imported petroleum products that enter into the United States for consumption, use, or warehousing; and on domestic crude oil used in or exported from the United States not yet subjected to the tax before its use or exportation (Code Sec. 4611(a) and (b)). The oil spill tax is imposed on the operator of a U.S. refinery receiving the domestic crude oil, on the person importing the petroleum products, and on the person using or exporting the crude oil (Code Sec. 4611(d)).

Effective July 1, 1994, the oil spill tax was suspended because the Treasury Department estimated that the Oil Spill Fund would have an unobligated balance of over $1 billion at the end of the second calendar quarter of 1993 (IRS Announcement 93-90, I.R.B. 1993-23). The tax was, however, reapplied effective July 1, 1994, until December 31, 1994, when it expired by operation of law (IRS Announcement 97-74, I.R.B. 1994-22). The oil spill tax was subsequently reinstated on April 1, 2006, pursuant to the Energy Tax Incentives Act of 2005 (P.L. 109-58). The oil spill tax does not apply for any calendar quarter if the unobligated balance of the Oil Spill Trust Fund exceeds $2.7 billion for the preceding calendar quarter (Code Sec. 4611(f)). Thereafter, the oil spill tax will be reinstated 30 days after the last day of any calendar quarter for which the IRS estimates that, as of the close of that quarter, the unobligated balance of the Oil Spill Fund is less than $2 billion. The oil spill tax will cease to apply after December 31, 2014, regardless of the Oil Spill Fund balance.

NEW LAW EXPLAINED

Increase and extension of Oil Spill Liability Trust Fund Tax.—The oil spill tax is extended for three years and increased from five cents-per-barrel to:

- 8 cents-per-barrel for crude oil received or petroleum products entering into the United States before January 1, 2017; and

- 9 cents-per-barrel for crude oil received or petroleum products entering into the United States after December 31, 2016.

The oil spill tax rate of 9 cents-per-barrel will apply for only one year (Code Sec. 4611(c)(2)(B), as amended by the Emergency Economic Stabilization Act of 2008 (P.L. 110-343)). The oil spill tax will no longer apply after December 31, 2017 (Code Sec. 4611(f), as amended by the Emergency Economic Act of 2008). The requirement that the oil spill tax be suspended when the unobligated balance exceeds $2.7 million is repealed.

▶ **Effective date.** The extension and increase in the oil spill tax is effective on or after the first day of the first calendar quarter beginning more than 60 days after October 3, 2008, the date of enactment (Division B, Act Sec. 405(a)(2) of the Emergency Economic Stabilization Act of 2008 (P.L. 110-343)). The repeal of the requirement that the tax be suspended when the unobligated balance exceeds $2.7 million is effective on October 3, 2008, the date of enactment (Division B, Act Sec. 405(b)(3) of the Emergency Economic Act of 2008).

NEW LAW EXPLAINED

Law source: Law at ¶5425. Committee Reports at ¶10,300.

— Division B, Act Sec. 405(a)(1) of the Emergency Economic Stabilization Act of 2008 (P.L. 110-343), amending Code Sec. 4611(c)(2)(B);

— Division B, Act Sec. 405(b)(1), amending Code Sec. 4611(f);

— Division B, Act Secs. 405(a)(2) and 405(b)(3), providing the effective date.

Reporter references: For further information, consult the following CCH reporters.

— Tax Research Consultant, EXCISE: 21,104

— Excise Tax Reporter, ¶31,630.31

FOREIGN TAXATION

¶860 Subpart F Exceptions for Insurance Income

SUMMARY OF NEW LAW

The temporary exceptions from subpart F income for certain insurance and insurance investment income are extended through 2009.

BACKGROUND

Under the subpart F rules, certain income earned by a controlled foreign corporation (CFC) may be currently taxed to U.S. shareholders, even though the earnings are not distributed to the shareholders (Code Secs. 951-965). For this purpose, a CFC is a foreign corporation with at least 50 percent of its stock owned (by vote or value) by 10-percent U.S. shareholders (Code Sec. 957). A U.S. shareholder is a shareholder that owns at least 10 percent of the voting stock of a foreign corporation (Code Sec. 951(b)).

A CFC's subpart F income that is currently taxed to its U.S. shareholders is made up of the following three categories of income: (1) insurance income (Code Sec. 953); (2) foreign base company income (Code Sec. 954); and (3) income related to international boycotts and other violations of public policy (Code Sec. 952(a)(3)-(5)).

A CFC's subpart F insurance income is the corporation's income that is attributable to issuing or reinsuring an insurance or annuity contract. The income must be the type of income that would be taxed (with some modifications) under the rules of sub-chapter L, if the income were earned by a U.S. insurance company (Code Sec. 953(a)).

Foreign base company income is made up of several categories of income, one of which is foreign personal holding company income (FPHCI). FPHCI is generally passive type income, such as dividend, interest, rent and royalty income (Code Sec. 954(c)).

BACKGROUND

Temporary exception for insurance income. Under a temporary exception, the "exempt insurance income" of a qualifying insurance company or a qualifying insurance company branch is not considered subpart F income. In general, exempt insurance income is income from an insurance or annuity contract issued or reinsured by a qualifying insurance company or a qualifying insurance company branch in connection with risks located outside of the United States (Code Sec. 953(a) and (e)). However, the qualifying insurance company or branch must separately meet a minimum home country requirement -- more than 30 percent of net premiums on exempt contracts must cover home country risks with respect to unrelated persons. Additionally, exempt income will not include income from covering home country risks if, as a result of an arrangement, another company receives a substantially equal amount of consideration for covering non-home country risks.

If risks from both the home country and non-home country are covered under the contract, the income is not exempt unless the qualifying insurance company or branch conduct substantial activities in its home country with respect to the insurance business. Additionally, substantially all of the activities necessary to give rise to the contract must be performed in the home country (Code Sec. 953(e)(2)(C)).

The definition of a "qualifying insurance company" is intended to make sure that the exception applies to income from active insurance operations. Thus, a qualifying insurance company is a CFC that meets the following requirements (Code Sec. 953(e)(3) and (6)):

- it is regulated in its home country (i.e., country where the CFC is created or organized) as an insurance or reinsurance company and is allowed by the applicable insurance regulatory body to sell insurance, reinsurance or annuity contracts to unrelated persons;

- more than 50 percent of the aggregate net written premiums on the contracts of the CFC and each qualifying insurance company branch are from covering home country risks with respect to unrelated persons; and

- the CFC is engaged in the insurance business and would be taxed under subchapter L, if it were a U.S. company.

A "qualifying insurance company branch" is, in general, a separate and clearly identified qualified business unit of the CFC (under Code Sec. 989) that is a qualifying insurance company. The branch must maintain its own books and records, and must be allowed to sell insurance by the applicable insurance regulatory body in its home country (i.e., the country where the unit has its principal office) (Code Sec. 953(e)(4)).

Temporary exception for insurance investment income. Under a temporary exception, subpart F FPHIC does not include qualified insurance income of a qualifying insurance company (Code Sec. 954(i)).

Qualified insurance incomes may also include income received from an unrelated party and derived from investments made of the qualified insurance company's assets allocable to exempt contracts in an amount equal to: one-third of the premiums earned during the tax year on the property, casualty or health insurance contracts;

BACKGROUND

and 10 percent of the loss reserves for life insurance or annuity contracts (Code Sec. 954(i)(2)(B)).

Qualified insurance income is income received from an unrelated person derived from the investments made by the qualifying insurance company or qualifying insurance company branch of its reserves that are allocable to exempt contracts; or 80 percent of its unearned premiums from exempt contracts (Code Sec. 954(i)(2)(A)).

> **Comment:** An exempt contract is defined the same way for both the subpart F insurance company exception, see above, and this exception. Thus, the amounts invested are allocable to the insuring or reinsuring of risks in the home country and other risks outside of the United States, if certain requirements are met (Code Sec. 954(i)(6)).

Application of temporary exceptions. The temporary exceptions from subpart F for insurance income apply to tax years of a foreign corporation beginning after December 31, 1998, and before January 1, 2009, and to tax years of U.S. shareholders with and within which such tax years of foreign corporations end (Code Sec. 953(e)(10)).

NEW LAW EXPLAINED

Temporary exceptions from subpart F income for insurance income extended one year.—The temporary exception from subpart F insurance income for "exempt insurance income" of a qualifying insurance company or a qualifying insurance company branch is extended for one year, through 2009 (Code Sec. 953(e) (10), as amended by the Emergency Economic Stabilization Act of 2008 (P.L. 110-343)). The temporary exception from foreign personal holding company income for "qualified insurance income" of a qualifying insurance company or a qualifying insurance company branch is also extended for one year, through 2009 (Code Sec. 953(e)(10), as amended by the Emergency Economic Act of 2008). The temporary exceptions apply to tax years of a foreign corporation beginning after December 31, 1998, and before January 1, 2010, and to tax years of U.S. shareholders with or within which any such tax years of the foreign corporation ends.

> **Practical Analysis:** Paul C. Lau, CPA, CMA, CFM, and Sandy Soltis, CPA, CFP, Partners at Blackman Kallick Bartelstein, LLP in Chicago, note that Subpart F income is income that is currently taxable to a U.S. shareholder (defined as a shareholder with 10 percent or more voting right) of a controlled foreign corporation (CFC) even though the income is not repatriated. Subpart F income is generally passive income (*e.g.*, dividends, interest, rents, royalties) and income earned outside its country of incorporation by a CFC from certain transactions involving related parties.
>
> Without special exceptions, offshore income earned by CFCs of financial institutions, securities dealers and insurance companies can be Subpart F income subject to current U.S. taxation. Since 1999, "active financing income" has been temporarily exempted from current U.S. taxation. "Active financing income" is certain income

NEW LAW EXPLAINED

from active banking, financing or similar business (e.g., security dealer) and insurance business.

The exemption was to expire for tax years beginning after 2008. Division C, Act Sec. 303 of the Emergency Economic Stabilization Act of 2008 (P.L. 110-343) provides a one-year extension, which allows the exemption to apply to tax years of CFCs beginning before 2010 and tax years of U.S. shareholders with or within which such tax years of such CFCs end.

For tax years beyond the extension, Code Sec. 953(a), which defines subpart F insurance income, is applied as if the tax year of the foreign corporation began in 1998 (Code Sec. 953(e)(10), as amended by the Emergency Economic Act of 2008). Consequently, only income attributable to insuring or reinsuring home country risks is excluded from subpart F insurance income. However, that income from issuing home country risks could be subpart F income if, as a result of an arrangement, another corporation receives a substantially equal amount for insuring non-home country risks (Code Sec. 953(a), prior to amendment by the Tax and Trade Relief Extension Act of 1998 (P.L. 105-277)).

Comment: Prior to the Tax Reform Act of 1986 (P.L. 99-514), exceptions from subpart F were provided for income earned in the active conduct of a banking, financing or similar business, or from certain investments made by insurance companies. The exceptions were eliminated and the income was subject to tax on a current basis under the general subpart F rules. Since 1997, Congress has enacted six temporary exceptions from the subpart F rules.

Comment: See ¶863 for a discussion of the temporary exceptions from subpart F income for income earned in the active conduct of a banking, financing or similar business.

▶ **Effective date.** No specific effective date is provided by the Act. The provision is, therefore, considered effective on October 3, 2008, the date of enactment.

Law source: Law at ¶5335. Committee Reports at ¶10,430.

— Division C, Act Sec. 303(a) of the Emergency Economic Stabilization Act of 2008 (P.L. 110-343), amending Code Sec. 953(e)(10).

Reporter references: For further information, consult the following CCH reporters.

— Standard Federal Tax Reporter, ¶28,518.066

— Tax Research Consultant, INTLOUT: 9,102, INTLOUT: 9,102.05 and INTLOUT: 9,106.30

— Federal Tax Guide, ¶17,445

¶863 Subpart F Exceptions for Active Financing Income

SUMMARY OF NEW LAW

The exceptions from subpart F income for so-called active financing income have been extended through 2009.

BACKGROUND

Under the subpart F rules, certain income earned by a controlled foreign corporation (CFC) may be currently taxed to U.S. shareholders, even though the earnings are not distributed to the shareholders (Code Secs. 951-965). For this purpose, a CFC is a foreign corporation with at least 50 percent of its stock owned (by vote or value) by 10-percent U.S. shareholders (Code Sec. 957). A U.S. shareholder is a shareholder that owns at least 10 percent of the voting stock of a foreign corporation (Code Sec. 951(b)).

A CFC's subpart F income that is currently taxed to its U.S. shareholders is made up of the following three categories of income: (1) insurance income (Code Sec. 953); (2) foreign base company income (Code Sec. 954); and (3) income related to international boycotts and other violations of public policy (Code Sec. 952(a)(3)-(5)).

Foreign base company income is made up of several categories of income, including Foreign base company services income and foreign personal holding company income (FPHCI). Foreign base company services income is income from the performance of services outside of the CFC's home country, for, or on behalf of, a related person (Code Sec. 954(e)). FPHCI is generally passive type income, such as dividend, interest, rent and royalty income (Code Sec. 954(c)). FPHCI also includes the excess of gains over losses on the sale of non-inventory property (Code Sec. 954(c)(1)(B)). A regular dealer exception applies to gains from this type of property, if the gain is derived from a transaction entered into in the ordinary course of a dealer's trade or business, including a bona fide hedging transaction. However, dealers must treat interest, dividends, and equivalent amounts as FPHCI (Code Sec. 954(c)(2)(C)).

Temporary exceptions from subpart F income for active financing income. Income derived in the active conduct of a banking, finance or similar business, or in an insurance business (see ¶860) (so-called active financing income) is temporarily excepted from subpart F income. The temporary exceptions apply to tax years of a foreign corporation beginning after December 31, 1998, and before January 1, 2009, and to tax years of U.S. shareholders with or within which any such tax year of the foreign corporation ends (Code Sec. 954(h)(9)).

Under the exceptions, FPHCI does not include the active financing income of a CFC or its qualified business unit (QBU) (as defined under Code Sec. 989(a)). For the exception to apply, the CFC must be predominately engaged in the active conduct of a banking, financing or similar business and must conduct substantial activity with respect to that business. Further, the income must be earned by the CFC or its

BACKGROUND

qualified business unit (QBU) in the active conduct of the business (Code Sec. 954(h)(2) and (3)). Only income earned in transactions with customers located outside of the United States where substantially all of the activities of the transaction are conducted in the corporation's or QBU's home country (i.e., where the CFC is created or organized or where the QBU has its principal office) is excepted. For cross-border transactions, the corporation or QBU must conduct substantial activities with respect to the business in the home country. The income must also be treated as earned by the corporation or QBU in its home country (Code Sec. 954(h)(3) and (5)(B)).

FPHCI also does not temporarily include income with respect to a securities dealer's interest, dividends and equivalent amounts from transactions, including hedging transactions, entered into in the ordinary course of the dealer's trade or business as a securities dealer. The income must be attributable to the dealer's activities in the country where the dealer is created or organized (or where the QBU of the dealer has its principal office and conducts substantial business activity) (Code Sec. 954(c)(2)(C)(ii)).

Finally, income that falls within the following temporary exceptions is not considered foreign base company services income (Code Sec. 954(e)(2)):

- the temporary exception from subpart F insurance income under Code Sec. 953(e), see ¶860;

- the temporary exception from FPHCI for insurance investment income under Code Sec. 954(i), see ¶860;

- the temporary exception from FPHCI for securities dealers under Code Sec. 954(c)(2)(C)(ii), see above; and

- the temporary exception from FPHCI for income derived in the active conduct of a banking, financing or similar business, see above.

NEW LAW EXPLAINED

Temporary exceptions from subpart F active financing income extended one year.—The exceptions from subpart F income for so-called active financing income, are extended for one year, through 2009 (Code Sec. 954(h)(9), as amended by the Emergency Economic Stabilization Act of 2008 (P.L. 110-343)). The extension applies to the temporary exceptions from foreign personal holding company income for:

- income derived in the active conduct of a banking, financing or similar business under Code Sec. 954(h), and

- income derived in the ordinary course of a security dealer's trade or business under Code Sec. 954(c)(2)(C)(ii).

The extension also applies to the temporary exception from foreign base company services income for income that falls within the other temporary exceptions for active financing income (Code Sec. 954(e)(2)).

Comment: Prior to the Tax Reform Act of 1986 (P.L. 99-514), exceptions from subpart F were provided for income earned in the active conduct of a banking,

NEW LAW EXPLAINED

financing or similar business, or from certain investments made by insurance companies. The exceptions were eliminated and the income was subject to tax on a current basis under the general subpart F rules. Since 1997, Congress has enacted six temporary exceptions from the subpart F rules.

The temporary exceptions apply to tax years of foreign corporations beginning after December 31, 1998, and before January 1, 2010, and to tax years of U.S. shareholders with or within which any such tax year of the foreign corporation ends.

Comment: See ¶860 for a discussion of the extension of the temporary exceptions from subpart F insurance income under Code Sec. 953(e) and from foreign personal holding company income for insurance investment income under Code Sec. 954(i).

▶ **Effective date.** No specific effective date is provided by the Act. The provision is, therefore, considered effective on October 3, 2008, the date of enactment.

Law source: Law at ¶5340. Committee Reports at ¶10,430.

— Division C, Act Sec. 303(b) of the Emergency Economic Stabilization Act of 2008 (P.L. 110-343), amending Code Sec. 954(h)(9).

Reporter references: For further information, consult the following CCH reporters.

— Standard Federal Tax Reporter, ¶28,543.0662

— Tax Research Consultant, INTLOUT: 9,106, INTLOUT: 9,106.30 and INTLOUT: 9,110

— Federal Tax Guide, ¶17,445

¶865 Look-Through Rule for Related Controlled Foreign Corporation Payments

SUMMARY OF NEW LAW

Look-through treatment for related controlled foreign corporation payments is extended through 2009.

BACKGROUND

Under the subpart F rules, certain income earned by a controlled foreign corporation (CFC) may be currently taxed to U.S. shareholders, even though the earnings are not distributed to the shareholders (Code Secs. 951-965). For this purpose, a CFC is a foreign corporation with at least 50 percent of its stock owned (by vote or value) by 10-percent U.S. shareholders (Code Sec. 957). A U.S. shareholder is a shareholder that owns at least 10 percent of the voting stock of a foreign corporation (Code Sec. 951(b)).

One of the main categories of subpart F income is foreign base company income. Foreign base company income is made up of several subcategories of income, one of

BACKGROUND

which is foreign personal holding company income (FPHCI). FPHCI generally includes dividends, interest, rents, royalties and annuities.

Amounts may be excluded from FPHCI, and, therefore, escape current taxation, under a look-through rule that applies to dividend, interest, rent and royalty payments received by a CFC from a related CFC (Code Sec. 954(c)(6)). To be eligible for the look-through rule, the payment must not be attributable to either subpart F income or income that is effectively connected to a U.S. trade or business. The look-though rule will not apply to the extent that an interest, rent or royalty payment either creates or increases a deficit under Code Sec. 952(c) that reduces subpart F income of either the payor or another CFC (Code Sec. 954(c)(6)(B)).

Prior to the addition of the look-through exception, an exception from FPHCI applied for payments received from a related corporation only where a same-country requirement was met. Under the same-country exception, in the case of dividends and interest, the related corporation must be created or organized under the law of the same country where the CFC was created or organized. In the case of rents and royalties, the exception applies only where property is used in the same country where the CFC is created or organized (Code Sec. 954(c)(3)).

The look-through exception applies to tax years of a foreign corporation beginning after December 31, 2005, and before January 1, 2009, and to tax years of U.S. shareholders with or within which such tax years of foreign corporations end (Code Sec. 954(c)(6)(C)).

NEW LAW EXPLAINED

Look-through treatment for related CFCs extended one year.—The look-through rule that applies to dividend, interest, rent and royalty payments received by a controlled foreign corporation from a related corporation is extended for one year. The look-through rule applies to tax years of a foreign corporation beginning after December 31, 2005, and before January 1, 2010, and to tax years of U.S. shareholders with or within which such tax years of foreign corporations end (Code Sec. 954(c)(6)(C), as amended by the Emergency Economic Stabilization Act of 2008 (P.L. 110-343)).

Practical Analysis: Paul C. Lau, CPA, CMA, CFM, and Sandy Soltis, CPA, CFP, Partners at Blackman Kallick Bartelstein, LLP in Chicago, observe that for tax years beginning before 2006, dividends, interest, rents and royalties received by one CFC from a related CFC were currently taxable as Subpart F income unless the payments qualified for the "same country exception" under Code Sec. 954(c)(3). In many instances, taxpayers were able to avoid the Subpart F income characterization by making the "check-the-box" election to treat certain foreign entities as disregarded entities for U.S. tax purposes. For example, a dividend from a second tier CFC to a first-tier CFC would be Subpart F income before 2006. However, if the second-tier CFC were a disregarded entity, the dividend would not be Subpart F income.

NEW LAW EXPLAINED

Code Sec. 954(c)(6) provides look-through treatment for payments between related CFCs for tax years beginning after December 31, 2005, and before January 1, 2009. Under the look-through rules, dividends, interest, rents and royalties received by one CFC from a related CFC generally would not be Subpart F income to the extent attributable to non–Subpart F income (or income that was not effectively connected with the conduct of a U.S. trade or business) of the payer. A related CFC is a CFC that controls or is controlled by the other CFC, or a CFC that is controlled by the same person or persons that control the other CFC.

This temporary provision allows U.S. companies greater flexibility to move non–Subpart F income among CFCs as business needs may require. U.S. companies would not need to apply the check-the-box provision to move non–Subpart F income among the CFCs.

Division C, Act Sec. 304 of the Emergency Economic Stabilization Act of 2008 (P.L. 110-343) extends the look-through rule for one year. Thus, it would apply to payments between related CFCs for tax years beginning before January 1, 2010, and tax years of U.S. shareholders with or within which such tax years of CFCs end.

▶ **Effective date.** The provision applies to tax years of foreign corporations beginning after December 31, 2007, and to tax years of U.S. shareholders with or within which such tax years of foreign corporations end (Division C, Act Sec. 304(b) of the Emergency Economic Stabilization Act of 2008 (P.L. 110-343)).

Law source: Law at ¶5340. Committee Reports at ¶10,440.

— Division C, Act Sec. 304(a) of the Emergency Economic Stabilization Act of 2008 (P.L. 110-343), amending Code Sec. 954(c)(6)(C);

— Division C, Act Sec. 304(b), providing the effective date.

Reporter references: For further information, consult the following CCH reporters.

— Standard Federal Tax Reporter, ¶28,543.0252

— Tax Research Consultant, INTLOUT: 9,106.105

— Federal Tax Guide, ¶17,445

¶870 Look-Through Rule for FIRPTA Distributions

SUMMARY OF NEW LAW

The term qualified investment entity will continue to include regulated investment companies (RICs) that are U.S. real property holding companies (USRPHCs) through December 31, 2009.

BACKGROUND

Under the Foreign Investment in Real Property Tax Act (FIRPTA), as codified in Code Sec. 897, any gain realized by a nonresident alien or a foreign corporation from a disposition of a U.S. real property interest, including a disposition of an interest in a U.S. real property holding corporation (USRPHC), is treated as income effectively connected with the conduct of a U.S. trade or business. As a result, the foreign distributees are taxed on the net gain in the same manner as a U.S. citizen or domestic corporation and are required to report the gain on a U.S. tax return (Code Sec. 897(a)(1)).

A U.S. real property interest includes real property located in the U.S. or the Virgin Islands (Code Sec. 897(c)(1)(A)(i)) and any interest (*e.g.*, stock) in a domestic corporation, unless the corporation was not a USRPHC during the five-year period ending on the date of disposition or, if shorter, during the period the taxpayer held the interest (Code Sec. 897(c)(1)(A)(ii)). A corporation is a USRPHC if the fair market value (FMV) of all of its U.S. real property interests equals or exceeds 50 percent of the total FMV of its real property interests within and outside the U.S. and any other assets used or held for use in a trade or business (Code Sec. 897(c)(2)). However, if any class of stock of a corporation is regularly traded on an established securities market, such class of stock is not treated as a U.S. real property interest in the case of a person who owns five percent or less of such class of stock during the five-year period ending on the date of disposition of the interest or during the period the taxpayer held the interest, if shorter (Code Sec. 897(c)(3)).

Look-through rule. Special rules apply to interests in qualified investment entities. A qualified investment entity includes any real estate investment trust (REIT), and any regulated investment company (RIC) (mutual fund) that is a USRPHC or would be a USRPHC if the exceptions for regularly traded stock (Code Sec. 897(c)(3)) and domestically controlled entities (Code Sec. 897(h)(2)) did not apply to the mutual fund's interest in any REIT or other mutual fund (Code Sec. 897(h)(4)(A)(i)).

Generally, under the look-through rule, any distribution by a qualified investment entity to a nonresident alien individual, a foreign corporation, or other qualified investment entity that is attributable to gain from a sale or exchange of a U.S. real property interest by the qualified investment entity is treated as gain recognized by the nonresident alien individual, foreign corporation, or other qualified investment entity from the sale or exchange of a U.S. real property interest (Code Sec. 897(h)(1) and (h)(4)(A)(i)(II)). The distributions are, therefore, subject to income taxation as effectively connected income under Code Secs. 897(a)(1) and 882(a)(1). The look-through rule doesn't apply to distributions involving regularly traded stock or entities that are domestically controlled.

Regularly traded stock exception. The look-through rule does not apply to distributions from a REIT or from a mutual fund that is a USRPHC to a nonresident alien individual or a foreign corporation based on any class of their stock that is regularly traded on an established securities market as long as the distributee did not own more than five percent of such class of stock during the one-year period ending on the date of distribution (Code Sec. 897(h)(1)). These distributions are recharacterized as dividends and are subject to the 30 percent, or a lower treaty rate, withholding (Code Secs. 852(b)(3)(E) and 871(k)(2)(E)).

¶870

BACKGROUND

Domestically controlled entity exception. If less than 50 percent in value of the stock of a mutual fund or REIT is held directly or indirectly by foreign persons at all times during the shorter of:

- the period beginning on June 19, 1980, and ending on the date of the disposition or distribution,

- the 5-year period ending on the date of the disposition or distribution, or

- the period during which the qualified investment entity was in existence (Code Sec. 897(h)(4)(D)),

then an interest in the mutual fund or REIT is not treated as a U.S. real property interest because the mutual fund or REIT is domestically controlled (Code Sec. 897(h)(4)(B) and (h)(2)).

Wash sale transactions. A nonresident alien, foreign corporation, or qualified investment entity that disposes of an interest in a domestically controlled qualified investment entity within 30 days prior to a distribution of FIRPTA income by that entity and acquires a substantially identical interest in the entity within a 61 day period, must pay FIRPTA tax on an amount equal to the amount of the distribution that was not taxed because of the disposition (Code Sec. 897(h)(5)(A)).

Withholding on qualified investment entity distributions. A REIT or mutual fund that is a USRPHC is required to withhold 35 percent from any distribution to a nonresident alien individual or a foreign corporation that is treated as gain realized from the sale or exchange of a U.S. real property interest (Code Sec. 1445(e)(6)). The withholding percent may be reduced to 15 percent by regulations (20 percent in tax years beginning after 2010).

Modification of RIC termination date. A mutual fund that is a USRPHC is no longer treated as a qualified investment entity after December 31, 2007, except with respect to distributions it makes to a nonresident alien or foreign corporation that is attributable to a distribution the mutual fund that is a USRPHC received from a REIT, whether before or after December 31, 2007, for purposes of applying the look-through, wash sale and general withholding rules (Code Sec. 897(h)(4)(A)(ii)).

NEW LAW EXPLAINED

Qualified investment entity definition includes RICs through 2009.—The term qualified investment entity, as used in Code Sec. 897, continues to include regulated investment companies (RICs) (mutual funds) that are U.S. real property holding companies (USRPHCs) through December 31, 2009, for all situations in which the inclusion would otherwise expire at the end of 2007 (Code Sec. 897(h)(4)(A)(ii), as amended by the Emergency Economic Stabilization Act of 2008 (P.L. 110-343)).

> **Comment:** For purposes of applying the look-through, wash sale and general withholding rules, a mutual fund that is a USRPHC will continue to be treated as a qualified investment entity even after 2009 with respect to any distribution it makes to a nonresident alien individual or a foreign corporation attributable to a distribution it received from a REIT.

NEW LAW EXPLAINED

Practical Analysis: Paul C. Lau, CPA, CMA, CFM, and Sandy Soltis, CPA, CFP, Partners at Blackman Kallick Bartelstein, LLP in Chicago, observe that foreign persons usually are not taxed on U.S. source capital gains unless such gains are effectively connected to a U.S. trade or business. Code Sec. 897(a), however, treats any gain from a disposition of a U.S. real property interest (USRPI) as income effectively connected to a U.S. trade or business. Under Code Secs. 882(a)(1) and 871(b)(1), the gain is subject to U.S. income tax at the same rates as a U.S. person. In addition, Code Sec. 1445 generally requires a 10-percent withholding tax on the amount realized on the disposition of the USRPI.

A USRPI is any interest (other than an interest solely as a creditor) in real property located in the U.S. or the U.S. Virgin islands. A USRPI is broadly defined and includes an interest in a domestic corporation if the corporation is a U.S. real property holding company (USRPHC). A USRPHC is a corporation that holds USRPIs with a total fair market value at least equal to 50 percent of the fair market value of the total of its worldwide real property interests and other assets used (or held for use) in a trade or business at anytime during a five-year look-back period.

Under the so-called five-percent publicly traded exception of Code Sec. 897(c)(3), a USRPI does not include stock that is publicly traded, provided the foreign seller did not hold more than five percent of the stock during the five-year period ending on the date of disposition.

Another exception is the "domestically controlled qualified investment entity (DCQIE) exception" under Code Sec. 897(h)(2). An interest in a DCQIE, regardless of its size, is not a USRPI. A disposition of such an interest is generally not subject to U.S. tax unless the disposition falls within the applicable wash sale rules under Code Sec. 897(h)(5). The applicable wash sale rules generally apply when a foreign person sells the DCQIE interest before a taxable dividend distribution and acquires a substantially similar interest (or an option to acquire such interest) during the 30 days before or after the ex-dividend date. A taxable dividend distribution is a distribution that is taxable to the extent attributable to gain from the sales or exchanges of USRPIs by the DCQIE. This wash sale rule does not apply if the disposed interest is publicly traded on a U.S. exchange and the foreign seller did not hold more than five percent of such class of interest during the one-year period before the dividend distribution.

A DCQIE is a qualified investment entity (QIC) that has less than 50 percent (in value) of its stock held directly or indirectly by foreign persons during the five-year period ending on the date that an interest is disposed of. A QIE includes (1) a real estate investment trust (REIT), and (2) a regulated investment company (RIC) that is a USRPHC or that would be a USRPHC if its holdings in publicly traded USRPHCs were treated as USRPIs (collectively RIC/USRPHCs). However, the inclusion of a RIC/USRPHC as an QIE expired on January 1, 2008, except that a RIC/USRPHC is still treated as an QIE for the purposes of (1) the applicable wash sale rules; and (2) the taxation of distributions by the RIC/USRPHC that are attributable to distributions from lower tier REITs.

Division C, Act Sec. 208 of the Emergency Economic Stabilization Act of 2008 (P.L. 110-343) extends the inclusion of a RIC/USRPHC as a QIE through December 31,

NEW LAW EXPLAINED

> 2009. The extension is welcome, as it avoids the burden of treating a RIC /USRPHC differently for different purposes and the filing of U.S. tax returns by foreign investors on certain dispositions of RIC/USRPHC interests.

Generally, the continuing inclusion of a mutual fund that is a USRPHCs in the term qualified investment entity is effective on January 1, 2008; however, no withholding is required with regard to any payment made on or before October 3, 2008, by a mutual fund that is a USRPHC (Division C, Act Sec. 208(b) of the Emergency Economic Act of 2008).

Comment: Although the term qualified investment entity continuously includes RIC USRPHCs, no withholding is required on payments made by RIC USRPHCs on or after January 1, 2008, and on or before October 3, 2008, the date of enactment.

▶ **Effective date.** The provision applies on January 1, 2008 (Division C, Act Sec. 208(b) of the Emergency Economic Stabilization Act of 2008 (P.L. 110-343)).

Law source: Law at ¶5325. Committee Report at ¶10,400.

— Division C, Act Sec. 208(a) of the Emergency Economic Stabilization Act of 2008 (P.L. 110-343), amending Code Sec. 897(h)(4)(A)(ii);

— Division C, Act Sec. 208(b), providing the effective date.

Reporter references: For further information, consult the following CCH reporters.

— Standard Federal Tax Reporter, ¶27,711.033, ¶32,792.01 and ¶32,792.04

— Tax Research Consultant, INTLIN: 6,068, INTLIN: 6,112, RIC: 3,250 and RIC: 3,258

— Federal Tax Guide, ¶17,115 and ¶18,635

¶875 Foreign Tax Credit Treatment of FOGEI and FORI

SUMMARY OF NEW LAW

The separate foreign tax credit limitations for foreign oil and gas extraction income (FOGEI) and foreign oil related income (FORI) have been eliminated; FOGEI and FORI are now combined into one foreign oil basket to which the existing FOGEI limitation applies.

BACKGROUND

U.S. taxpayers are allowed to reduce their U.S. tax liability on foreign-source income by the amount of foreign taxes paid or accrued on that income. The amount of credit that may be claimed is subject to an overall limitation under Code Sec. 904. This limitation operates so that the amount of foreign tax credit claimed by a taxpayer for the tax year cannot exceed the amount of U.S. tax imposed on its foreign-source

BACKGROUND

income. The limitation is calculated by multiplying the taxpayer's pre-credit U.S. tax liability for the tax year by the ratio that the taxpayer's foreign-source taxable income has to its worldwide taxable income for the year.

A taxpayer is required to compute its foreign tax credit limitation separately for various categories of income, generally known as "separate limitation categories" or "baskets" (Code Sec. 904(d)). For tax years beginning after December 31, 2006, there are generally two foreign tax credit baskets—a passive category income basket and a general category income basket. Where foreign taxes paid or accrued for any tax year are more than the amount allowed, then the taxpayer winds up with an excess credit. This excess may be carried back one year and then carried forward to the 10 succeeding tax years (Code Secs. 904(c) and 907(f)(1)).

In addition to the foreign tax credit limitation that applies to all foreign tax credits, a special limitation is placed on foreign income taxes on foreign oil and gas extraction income (FOGEI) (Code Sec. 907(a)). FOGEI is foreign-source taxable income derived from the extraction of minerals from oil or gas wells and the sale or exchange of assets used in extracting minerals from oil or gas wells. Foreign oil-related income (FORI) encompasses income from activities downstream from the well, including foreign-source taxable income derived from processing minerals extracted from oil and gas wells into their primary products and related activities.

The regulations provide that gross income from extraction is determined by reference to the fair market value of the minerals in the immediate vicinity of the well, although they do not provide specific methods for determining the fair market value. Rather, the regulations provide that all the facts and circumstances in the particular case must be considered, including those pertaining to the independent market value, if any, in the immediate vicinity of the well, the fair market value at the port of the foreign country, and the relationships between the taxpayer and the foreign government (Reg. § 1.907(c)-1(b)(2) and Reg. § 1.907(c)-1(b)(6)).

In 2004, the IRS issued a Large and Mid-Size Business Field Directive to their personnel for evaluating taxpayer methods of determining FOGEI and FORI under Code Sec. 907. The memorandum sets forth the background to Code Sec. 907 and discusses both the residual method (rate of return) and the proportionate profits method of determining FOGEI and FORI when there is no ascertainable market price for oil and gas in the immediate vicinity of the well. It also discusses classification of assets for both FOGEI and FORI assets, and provides definitions for various relevant terms for FOGEI and FORI. (*Field Directive on IRC § 907 Evaluating Taxpayer Methods of Determining Foreign Oil and Gas Extraction Income (FOGEI) and Foreign Oil Related Income (FORI)*, October 12, 2004).

Oil companies frequently pay both a royalty for and taxes to a foreign country on oil and gas extracted from that country, which are often hard to distinguish. Because the tax credit is more valuable to the taxpayer than the deduction for royalties paid, tax rates on the oil and gas income tended to be high and constituted a large percentage of the payments to foreign countries. In addition to providing a direct benefit for oil and gas income, high-taxed extraction income was used to shelter other foreign-source income from U.S. tax (Joint Committee on Taxation, Explanation of the Revenue Provisions of the Tax Equity and Fiscal Responsibility Act of 1982 (P.L.

¶875

BACKGROUND

97-248), (JCS-38-82)). To address these concerns, a limit is placed on the amount of the foreign tax credit that may be claimed for oil and gas extraction taxes on FOGEI. For corporations, the credit for foreign oil and gas extraction taxes is limited to the product of the corporation's FOGEI for the tax year multiplied by the highest applicable U.S. corporate tax rate. For individuals, the credit is limited to the taxpayer's effective tax rate which is the ratio of the taxpayer's entire tax liability (calculated before application of the foreign tax credit for income taxes), over the individual's entire taxable income (Code Sec. 907(a)).

Reduction of creditable FORI taxes. Taxes on FORI are not creditable to the extent that the foreign law imposing the tax is structured, or in fact operates, so that the amount imposed on FORI will generally be materially greater than the amount of tax imposed on income that is neither FORI nor FOGEI. Foreign law imposing a tax on FORI will be considered either to be structured or to operate in the stated manner if under the facts and circumstances there has been a shifting of tax from a tax on FOGEI to a tax on FORI (Code Sec. 907(b)).

Recapture of foreign oil and gas extraction losses. Taxpayers who have overall foreign oil extraction losses, incurred in a tax year beginning after 1982, that reduce nonextraction income for the year must recapture the loss in a later year in which they have FOGEI (Code Sec. 907(c)(4)). This provision operates only for the purpose of determining FOGEI and is independent of the overall foreign loss recapture rules under Code Sec. 904(f). The recapture is accomplished by recharacterizing a portion of the extraction income earned in subsequent tax years as foreign nonextraction income until the prior loss is wiped out. A "foreign oil extraction loss" is the amount by which foreign source gross income from extraction is exceeded by the sum of the deductions properly apportioned or allocated to such income. Net operating losses, foreign expropriation losses, and casualty and theft losses are disregarded in computing the amount of the loss. A "foreign expropriation loss" is defined in Code Sec. 172(h), as in effect the day before the enactment of the Revenue Reconciliation Act of 1990 (Code Sec. 907(c)(4)(B)(iii)(I)).

Carrybacks and carryovers of disallowed credit. FOGEI taxes not taken into account under Code Sec. 907(a), for purposes of the foreign tax credit, because they exceed the tax year's limitation level—called the "unused FOGEI tax"—may nevertheless be carried back or carried forward to other tax years. Unused FOGEI tax from a year of origin may be deemed paid or accrued in any preceding or succeeding tax year to the extent of the lesser of the (1) excess extraction limitation or (2) excess general Code Sec. 904 limitation for the carryback or carryover year. The unused FOGEI tax is carried to tax years in the following order: the first preceding tax year, then to the first, second, third, fourth, fifth, sixth, seventh, eighth, ninth and tenth succeeding tax years. The amount deemed paid cannot be used as a deduction but must be used for a tax credit (Code Sec. 904(f)).

Excess extraction limitation. This is the amount by which the year's Code Sec. 907(a) extraction limitation exceeds the sum of the FOGEI taxes paid or accrued and the FOGEI taxes deemed paid or accrued in that year as a result of a carryback or carryover of unused FOGEI taxes (Reg. § 1.907(f)-1(d)).

BACKGROUND

Excess general Code Sec. 904 limitation. This is the amount by which the tax year's general limitation, under Code Sec. 904, exceeds the sum of (1) the general limitation taxes paid or accrued (or deemed paid under Code Sec. 902 or Code Sec. 960) in such tax year to all foreign countries and U.S. possessions, (2) the general limitation taxes deemed paid or accrued in such tax year under Code Sec. 904(c) that are attributable to tax years preceding the unused credit year (year of origin), and (3) the FOGEI taxes deemed paid or accrued in that year because of a carryover or carryback of unused FOGEI taxes (Reg. § 1.907(f)-1(e)).

NEW LAW EXPLAINED

FOGEI and FORI combined for foreign tax credit limitation purposes.—The scope of the foreign oil and gas extraction income (FOGEI) rules is expanded to apply to "combined foreign oil and gas income." Accordingly, amounts claimed as foreign oil and gas taxes paid or accrued (or deemed to have been paid) during the tax year are creditable subject to a limitation that takes both FOGEI and FORI into account. In the case of a corporation, the credit for foreign oil and gas taxes is limited to the product of its combined foreign oil and gas income for the tax year, multiplied by the highest applicable U.S. corporate tax rate. For an individual, the credit is limited to the taxpayer's effective tax rate, which is the ratio of the taxpayer's entire tax liability (calculated before the application of the foreign tax credit for income taxes), over the individual's entire taxable income (Code Sec. 907(a) and (b), as amended by the Emergency Economic Stabilization Act of 2008 (P.L. 110-343)).

Terms defined. "Combined foreign oil and gas income" is the sum of foreign oil and gas extraction income (FOGEI) and foreign oil related income (FORI). "Foreign oil and gas taxes" is the sum of: (1) oil and gas extraction taxes, and (2) any income, war profits, and excess profits taxes paid or accrued (or deemed paid or accrued under Code Secs. 902 or 960) during the tax year with respect to FORI, determined without regard to the loss recapture rules of Code Sec. 907(c)(4) or losses that would otherwise be taken into account under Code Sec. 901 (Code Sec. 907(b), as amended by the Emergency Economic Act of 2008).

Recapture of foreign oil and gas losses. In general, the combined foreign oil and gas income of a taxpayer is reduced first by "pre-2009 foreign oil extraction losses," and then by "post-2008 foreign oil and gas losses." The aggregate amount of these reductions is treated as foreign-source income and not combined foreign oil and gas income (Code Sec. 907(c)(4)(A), as amended by the Emergency Economic Act of 2008).

Pre-2009 foreign oil extraction losses. The reduction for pre-2009 foreign oil extraction losses is equal to the lesser of:

(1) the taxpayer's FOGEI for the tax year, or

(2) the excess of the aggregate amount of foreign oil extraction losses for preceding tax years beginning after December 31, 1982 and before January 1, 2009, over the aggregate amount that was recharacterized under this provision (as in effect before and after October 3, 2008, the date of enactment of the Emergency Economic Act of 2008) for

¶875

NEW LAW EXPLAINED

preceding tax years beginning after December 31, 1982 (Code Sec. 907(c)(4)(B), as amended by the Emergency Economic Act of 2008).

Foreign oil extraction losses are determined as in effect on the day before October 3, 2008, the date of enactment of the Emergency Economic Act of 2008 (Code Sec. 904(c)(4)((D)(iv), as amended by the Emergency Economic Act of 2008).

Post-2008 foreign oil and gas losses. The reduction for post-2008 foreign oil and gas losses is equal to the lesser of:

(1) the taxpayer's combined foreign oil and gas income for the tax year without regard to the recapture provision, reduced by an amount equal to the aggregate reduction under Code Sec. 907(c)(4)(A), or

(2) the excess of the aggregate amount of foreign oil and gas losses for preceding tax years beginning after December 31, 2008, over the aggregate amount that was recharacterized under this recapture provision for preceding tax years beginning after December 31, 2008 (Code Sec. 907(c)(4)(C), as amended by the Emergency Economic Act of 2008).

Foreign oil and gas loss defined. The term "foreign oil and gas loss" is the amount by which the taxpayer's foreign source gross income, taken into account in determining combined foreign oil and gas income for the year, is exceeded by the sum of the deductions properly apportioned or allocated to such income. Net operating losses, foreign expropriation losses, and casualty and theft losses (not compensated by insurance) are disregarded in computing the amount of the loss. A "foreign expropriation loss" is defined in Code Sec. 172(h) as in effect the day before the date of enactment of the Revenue Reconciliation Act of 1990 (P.L. 101-508). (Code Sec. 907(c)(4)(D), as amended by the Emergency Economic Act of 2008).

Carryback and carryover of disallowed credits. As under present law for oil and gas extraction taxes, excess foreign oil and gas taxes may be carried back to the immediately preceding tax year and carried forward 10 tax years. The amount deemed paid cannot be used as a deduction but must be used for a tax credit (Code Sec. 907(f)(1), as amended by the Emergency Economic Act of 2008).

Transition rules for pre-2009 and 2009 disallowed credits. Pre-2009 credits carried forward to post-2008 years will continue to be governed by present law for purposes of determining the amount of carryforward credits eligible to be claimed in a post-2008 year. However, for purposes of determining whether excess credits generated in 2009 can be carried back to offset 2008 tax liability, the new rules will be treated as being in effect for any preceding year beginning before January 1, 2009, for purposes of determining how much of the unused credits may be deemed paid or accrued in that carryback year (Code Sec. 907(f)(4), as added by the Emergency Economic Act of 2008).

> **Comment:** The effect of this provision is that it tightens the rules for oil and gas companies to pay taxes on overseas income. It eliminates the distinction between foreign oil and gas extraction income (FOGEI) and foreign oil-related income (FORI) from transportation and refining and applies the FOGEI foreign tax credit

NEW LAW EXPLAINED

limitation to income from oil and gas production and sales. The provision takes effect in 2009 and is expected to raise $2.2 billion over 10 years.

▶ **Effective date.** The provision applies to tax years beginning after December 31, 2008 (Division B, Act Sec. 402(e) of the Emergency Economic Stabilization Act of 2008 (P.L. 110-343)).

Law source: Law at ¶5330 and ¶5465. Committee Reports at ¶10,270.

— Division B, Act Sec. 402(a) of the Emergency Economic Stabilization Act of 2008 (P.L. 110-343), amending Code Sec. 907(a) and (b);

— Division B, Act Sec. 402(b), amending Code Sec. 907(c)(4);

— Division B, Act Sec. 402(c), amending Code Sec. 907(f);

— Division B, Act Sec. 402(d), amending Code Sec. 6501(i);

— Division B, Act Sec. 402(e), providing the effective date.

Reporter references: For further information, consult the following CCH reporters.

— Standard Federal Tax Reporter, ¶27,963.01

— Tax Research Consultant, INTLOUT: 6,350

— Federal Tax Guide, ¶17,260

HEALTH BENEFITS

¶880 Parity in Mental Health and Substance Use Disorder Benefits

SUMMARY OF NEW LAW

The mental health parity requirements under the Code, ERISA and the Public Health Service Act have been made permanent. In addition, the financial requirements and treatment limitations for mental health and substance use disorder benefits are required to be in parity with medical and surgical benefits in case of a group health plan that offer both benefits.

BACKGROUND

According to National Mental Health Association, every year, about 54 million Americans suffer from clearly diagnosable mental or substance abuse disorders. A major part of this problem is that private health insurers generally provide less coverage for mental illnesses and substance abuse than for other medical conditions. According to a 2002 Kaiser Family Foundation study, while 98 percent of workers with employer-sponsored health insurance had coverage for mental health care, 74 percent of those workers were subject to annual outpatient visit limits, and 64 percent were subject to annual inpatient daily limits.

BACKGROUND

The Mental Health Parity Act of 1996 (P.L. 104-204) was enacted to require employers with group health plans to apply aggregate lifetime limits and annual limits to mental health benefits in parity with medical and surgical benefits limits. The mental parity provisions were incorporated into the Internal Revenue Code, as Code Sec. 9812, by the Taxpayer Relief Act of 1997 (P.L. 105-34). These provisions were also included in the Employee Retirement Income Security Act (ERISA) and the Public Health Service Act. Employers whose group health plans fail to comply with the mental health parity rules are subject to the Code Sec. 4980D penalty of $100 per day per affected individual.

The mental health coverage parity rules do not require a group health plan to provide any mental health benefits (Code Sec. 9812(b)(1); Temporary Reg. § 54.9812-1T(d)(3)(i)). If a group health plan does provide mental health benefits, the parity rules are not construed to affect the terms and conditions relating to the amount, duration, or scope of mental health benefits under the plan, including cost sharing, limits on numbers of visits or days of coverage, and requirements relating to medical necessity, except as specifically provided by the rules regarding parity in the imposition of aggregate lifetime limits and annual limits for mental health benefits (Code Sec. 9812(b)(2); Temporary Reg. § 54.9812-1T(d)(3)(ii)).

The mental health coverage parity rules do not apply to any group health plan for any plan year of a small employer (Code Sec. 4980D(d)(2); Temporary Reg. § 54.9812-1T(e)(1)). A small employer is an employer who employed an average of at least two but not more than 50 employees on business days during the preceding calendar year and who employs at least two employees on the first day of the plan year. Further, the mental health coverage parity rules also do not apply with respect to a group health plan if the application of the parity rules results in an increase in the cost under the plan of at least 1 percent (Code Sec. 9812(c)).

The mental health coverage parity rules do not apply to group health plans for plan years beginning before January 1, 1998, or to benefits for services furnished on or after September 30, 2001, and before January 10, 2002. The rules also do not apply to benefits for services furnished on or after January 1, 2008, but before June 17, 2008, and to services furnished after December 31, 2008 (Code Sec. 9812(f)).

NEW LAW EXPLAINED

Mental health parity and substance addiction coverage enhanced.—The mental health parity requirements under the Code, ERISA and the Public Health Service Act have been made permanent (Act Sec. 512(a), (b)(5), and (c)(5) of the Emergency Economic Stabilization Act of 2008 (P.L. 110-343)). The new law adds financial requirements and treatment limitations to the existing mental health parity provisions and expressly adds substance use disorder to the coverage of the parity provisions (Code Secs. 9812(a)(3), section 712(a)(3) of Employment Retirement Income Security Act of 1974 (ERISA), section 2705(a)(3) of the Public Health Service Act (PHSA), as added by Emergency Economic Act of 2008).

NEW LAW EXPLAINED

Mental health benefits for these purposes means benefits with respect to services for mental health conditions as defined under the terms of the plan and in accordance with federal and state law (Code Sec. 9812(e)(4), Section 712(e)(4) of ERISA, Section 2705(e)(4) of PHSA, as amended by Emergency Economic Stabilization Act of 2008). The new law eliminates the express exclusion of treatment of substance abuse or chemical dependency from the term "mental health benefits." Substance use disorder benefits means benefits with respect to services for substance use disorders as defined under the terms of the plan and in accordance with federal and state law (Code Sec. 9812(e)(5), Section 712(e)(5) of ERISA, Section 2705(e)(5) of PHSA, as amended by Emergency Economic Stabilization Act of 2008).

The new law requires group plans that provide both medical and surgical benefits and mental health or substance use disorder to apply the financial requirements and treatment limitations for both benefits equally. Financial requirements and treatment limitations for mental health or substance addiction should not be more restrictive than the predominant financial requirements applied to other health benefits and there should be no separate cost sharing requirements or treatment limitations applicable only to mental health or substance addiction benefits. A financial requirement or treatment limit is considered "predominant" if it is the most common of such type of limit or requirement.

> **Comment:** Mental Health America (www.nmha.org) hailed the passing of this new law as "a great civil rights victory" that will broadly outlaw health insurance discrimination against Americans with mental health and substance-use conditions in employer-sponsored health plans.

> **Practical Analysis:** Pamela D. Perdue, Of Counsel with Summers, Compton, Wells & Hamburg in St. Louis, Missouri, observes that plans subject to Division C, Act Sec. 512 of the Emergency Economic Stabilization Act of 2008 (P.L. 110-343) (the "mental health parity provision") will now have to make sure that financial requirements for mental health treatment, such as co-payments for office visits, deductibles and treatment limitations, are not less generous than those applied to substantially all medical and surgical benefits. This will result in a significant change since most plans currently impose some differences which may include differences such as lower limits per treatment days for in-patient treatment than for other hospital stays, or higher co-payments for office visits or different rules for out-of-network coverage. These will have to change under the new law.

A beneficiary financial requirement includes, with respect to the group health plan, deductibles, copayments, coinsurance, and out-of-pocket expenses, but excludes the existing aggregate lifetime limit and an annual limit under the Internal Revenue Code, ERISA and PHSA. A treatment limitation includes limits on the frequency of treatment, number of visits, days of coverage, or other similar limits on the scope or duration of treatment (Code Sec. 9812(a)(3)(B), Section 712(a)(3)(B) of ERISA, Section 2705(a)(3)(B) of PHSA, as added by Emergency Economic Stabilization Act of 2008). In addition, if a plan offers out-of-network benefits for medical or surgical care, it must also

NEW LAW EXPLAINED

offer out-of-network coverage for mental health and addiction treatment and provide services at parity (Code Sec. 9812(a)(5), Section 712(a)(5) of ERISA, Sec. 2705(a)(5) of PHSA, as added by Emergency Economic Stabilization Act of 2008).

The new law requires that the criteria for medical necessity determinations made under a plan as well as any denial of reimbursement or payment of services with respect to mental health or substance addiction benefits be made available to a current or potential participant, beneficiary, or contracting provider upon request (Code Sec. 9812(a)(4), Section 712(a)(4) of ERISA, Section 2705(a)(4) of PHSA, as added by Emergency Economic Stabilization Act of 2008).

Small employer exemption. The parity for financial requirements and treatment limitations will not apply to any group health plan of a small employer. For this purpose, a small employer is an employer who employed an average of at least two but not more than 50 employees on business days during the preceding calendar year Code Sec. 9812(c)(1), Section 712(c)(1) of ERISA, Section 2705(c)(1) of PHSA, as amended by Emergency Economic Stabilization Act of 2008). A small employer also includes an employer who employed on average at least one employee during such period in the case of an employer residing in a State that permits small groups health plans for a single individual.

Increased cost exemption. If the application of the mental health and substance-related disorder parity requirements results in an increase for the plan year involved of the actual total costs of coverage by an amount that exceeds one percent (two percent in the case of the first plan year to which the provision applies) of the actual total plan costs, then the requirements do not apply to the plan during the following plan year (Code Sec. 9812(c)(2), Section 712(c)(2) of ERISA, Section 2705(c)(2) of PHSA, as amended by Emergency Economic Stabilization Act of 2008). This exception applies to the plan for one plan year. If a plan seeks use of the exemption, the determination whether the exemption applies must be made after the plan has complied with the rules for the first six months of the plan year involved. Determinations as to increases in actual costs under a plan for purposes of this exemption must be made by a qualified and licensed actuary who is a member in good standing of the American Academy of Actuaries. The determination must be certified by the actuary and made available to the general public.

A plan that qualifies for a cost exemption and elects to implement the exemption shall promptly notify the appropriate Secretary (of the Treasury, Labor or Health and Human Services), the appropriate state agencies, and the participants and beneficiaries (Code Sec. 9812(c)(2)(E), Section 712(c)(2)(E) of ERISA, Section 2705(c)(2)(E) of PHSA, as amended by Emergency Economic Stabilization Act of 2008).

GAO study and report. The Comptroller General of the United States will conduct a study that analyzes the specific coverage rates, patterns and trends in coverage and exclusion of specific mental health and substance use disorder diagnoses by health plans and health insurance (Division C, Act Sec. 512(h) of the Emergency Economic Stabilization Act of 2008). A report on the result of the study will be submitted to Congress not later than October 3, 2011, and two years after the submission of the first report.

NEW LAW EXPLAINED

▶ **Effective date.** The provisions apply generally with respect to group health plans for plan years beginning after October 3, 2009, regardless of whether regulations have been issued to carry out such provisions by such effective date. However, the provisions making the mental health parity requirements permanent apply on January 1, 2009 (Division C, Act Sec. 512(e)(1) of the Emergency Economic Stabilization Act of 2008 (P.L. 110-343)). In the case of a group health plan maintained pursuant to one or more collective bargaining agreements (CBA) ratified before October 3, 2008, these provisions will not apply to plan years beginning before the later of the date on which the last of the CBA relating to the plan terminate, determined without regard to any extension agreed to after October 3, 2008, or January 1, 2009 (Division C, Act Sec. 512(e)(2) of the Emergency Economic Act of 2008).

Law source: Law at ¶5500 and ¶7168.

— Division C, Act Sec. 512(a) of the Emergency Economic Stabilization Act of 2008 (P.L. 110-343), amending Section 712 of Employment Retirement Income Security Act of 1974;

— Division C, Act Sec. 512(b), amending Section 2705 of Public Health Service Act;

— Division C, Act Sec. 512(c), amending Code Sec. 9812;

— Division C, Act Sec. 512(e), providing the effective date.

Reporter references: For further information, consult the following CCH reporters.

— Standard Federal Tax Reporter, ¶44,088.021

— Tax Research Consultant, COMPEN: 45,224.15

— Federal Tax Guide, ¶21,475

¶885 Health Insurance Coverage for Dependent Students on Medically Necessary Leave

SUMMARY OF NEW LAW

Group health insurance plans must continue coverage, up to one year, for full-time post secondary students that suffer a serious illness requiring a medical leave that causes them to lose full-time student status.

BACKGROUND

Health insurance contracts define who can be considered a dependent for purposes of a family health insurance policy. Often, though not always, the terms of the contract provide that a dependent includes college-age students who are enrolled as full-time students.

Some states have laws allowing dependents to retain health insurance coverage under their parents' policy for a period of time while reducing their course load below full-time status because of serious illness. Several other states have enacted laws defining dependents by an age requirement, for example between age 18 and 23, regardless of student status. State law can govern individually-offered health insur-

BACKGROUND

ance (not through employment) and employment-based coverage if it is coverage through an insurance product offered by companies in the business of selling insurance. However, state laws regulating the business of insurance do not apply to employer self-insured plans. According to the Department of Labor, more than half of all employees are covered by employment based self-insured plans.

The issue of continuity of health insurance coverage for students who become seriously ill was highlighted by the case of a full-time college student in New Hampshire who was diagnosed with colon cancer in 2003. The student's physician recommended a reduced course load while the student had 14 rounds of chemotherapy. The student, Michelle Morse, was forced to remain in school as a full-time student, however, because taking a reduced course load would have resulted in the loss of health insurance coverage as a dependent on her parents' health insurance plan. Morse succumbed to her illness in 2005. The American Cancer Society estimates that approximately 2,400 college-age students are diagnosed with cancer each year and could be in a similar position to the New Hampshire student (Conference Committee Report on H.R. 2851).

NEW LAW EXPLAINED

Health insurance coverage extended to students on medical leave from school.— A group health plan must continue coverage for a full-time post-secondary student beneficiary under the plan for up to one year from the date the student loses full-time student status because of a medically necessary leave of absence, unless the coverage would otherwise terminate earlier under the terms of the plan (Code Sec. 9813(b)(1), ERISA Sec. 714(b)(1) and Sec. 2707(b)(1) of the Public Health Service Act, as added by Michelle's Law (H.R. 2851). This rule applies to plan years beginning on or after October 9, 2009 for medically necessary leaves during those plan years (Act. Sec. 2(d) of Michelle's Law).

> **Comment:** "Financially dependent individuals seeking an education should not lose their health insurance just when they need it the most—they did not choose this battle, the battle chose them," stated the National Health Council. The National Education Association added, "This vital legislation would expand access to health insurance for college students. Michelle was forced to maintain a full college course load while undergoing debilitating cancer treatment, or risk losing her health insurance. Students like Michelle, who are working hard to improve their lives, shouldn't have to choose between their studies and their health."

The full-time post-secondary student is required to have full-time student status until the first day of the leave, be enrolled in the plan on the first day of the leave, and be a dependent child of a participant or beneficiary under the plan (Code Sec. 9813(b)(2), ERISA Sec. 714(b)(2) and Sec. 2707(b)(2) of the Public Health Service Act, as added by Michelle's Law). School semester breaks do not disqualify the student from maintaining full-time status until the leave begins (Code Sec. 9813(c) and ERISA Sec. 714(c), as added by Michelle's Law). A leave of absence of a dependent child from a post-secondary educational institution, or a change in enrollment status, that is medically

NEW LAW EXPLAINED

necessary as a result of illness or injury that cause the child to lose full-time student status is a medically necessary leave of absence (Code Sec. 9813(a), ERISA Sec. 714(a) and Sec. 2707(a) of the Public Health Service Act, as added by Michelle's Law).

Certification. The dependent child's physician must certify to the plan or issuer the nature of the child's illness and that the leave is medically necessary (Code Sec. 9813(b)(3), ERISA Sec. 714(b)(3) and Sec. 2707(b)(3) of the Public Health Service Act, as added by Michelle's Law). For purposes of administrative or judicial proceedings, the certification creates a rebuttal presumption that the dependent child is suffering from a severe illness or injury and that a leave of absence is medically necessary (Code Sec. 9813(f) and ERISA Sec. 714(f), as added by Michelle's Law).

A group health plan, and a health insurance issuer providing health insurance coverage in conjunction with a group health plan, must include an understandable description of the applicable terms for continued coverage during medically necessary leaves of absence as part of the notice describing the certification requirement (Sec. 2707(c) of the Public Health Service Act, as added by Michelle's Law).

Benefits. The dependent child is entitled to the same health benefits while on leave that he was entitled to as a full-time student (Code Sec. 9813(d), ERISA Sec. 714(d) and Sec. 2707(d) of the Public Health Service Act, as added by Michelle's Law). The dependent child is also entitled to benefits under any successor plan if the plan sponsor changes group health plans after the child's leave has commenced (Code Sec. 9813(e), ERISA Sec. 714(e) and Sec. 2707(e) of the Public Health Service Act, as added by Michelle's Law).

These provisions apply to health insurance coverage offered by a health insurance issuer in the individual market just as they apply to a health insurance issuer in regard to a group health plan in the small or large group market (Sec. 2753 of the Public Health Service Act, as added by Michelle's Law).

▶ **Effective date.** The provisions apply to plan years beginning on or after October 9, 2009, and to medically necessary leaves of absence beginning during such plan years (Act. Sec. 2(d) of Michelle's Law (P.L. 110-381)).

Law source: Law at ¶5505. Committee Reports at ¶15,010.

— Act Sec. 2(a) of Michelle's Law (H.R. 2851), adding ERISA Sec. 714;

— Act Sec. 2(b)(1), adding Sec. 2707 of the Public Health Service Act;

— Act Sec. 2(b)(2), adding Sec. 2753 of the Public Health Service Act;

— Act Sec. 2(c), adding Code Sec. 9813;

— Act Sec. 2(d), providing the effective date.

Reporter references: For further information, consult the following CCH reporters.

— Standard Federal Tax Reporter, ¶44,089G

— Tax Research Consultant, COMPEN: 42,218

¶885

Code Sections Added, Amended Or Repealed

[¶5001]

INTRODUCTION.

The Internal Revenue Code provisions amended by the Emergency Economic Stabilization Act of 2008 (P.L. 110-343), the Federal Administration Extension Act of 2008, Part II (P.L. 110-330), the SSI Extension for Elderly and Disabled Refugees Act (P.L. 110-328), the Fostering Connections to Success and Increasing Adoptions Act of 2008 (P.L. 110-351), the Inmate Tax Fraud Prevention Act of 2008 (H.R. 7082), and Michelle's Law (P.L. 110-381), are shown in the following paragraphs. Deleted Code material or the text of the Code Section prior to amendment appears in the amendment notes following each amended Code provision. *Any changed or added material is set out in italics.*

[¶5005] CODE SEC. 23. ADOPTION EXPENSES.

* * *

(b) LIMITATIONS.—

* * *

(4) LIMITATION BASED ON AMOUNT OF TAX.—In the case of a taxable year to which section 26(a)(2) does not apply, the credit allowed under subsection (a) for any taxable year shall not exceed the excess of—

(A) the sum of the regular tax liability (as defined in section 26(b)) plus the tax imposed by section 55, over

»»→ Caution: *Code Sec. 23(b)(4)(B), below, was amended by P.L. 110-343. For sunset provision, see P.L. 110-343, §106(f)(3), in the amendment notes.*

(B) the sum of the credits allowable under this subpart (other than this section *and section 25D*) and section 27 for the taxable year.

* * *

[CCH Explanation at ¶510. Committee Reports at ¶10,060.]

Amendments

• **2008, Energy Improvement and Extension Act of 2008 (P.L. 110-343)**

P.L. 110-343, Division B, §106(e)(2)(A):

Amended Code Sec. 23(b)(4)(B) by inserting "and section 25D" after "this section". Effective for tax years beginning after 12-31-2007.

P.L. 110-343, Division B, §106(f)(3), provides:

(3) APPLICATION OF EGTRRA SUNSET.—The amendments made by subparagraphs (A) and (B) of subsection (e)(2) shall be subject to title IX of the Economic Growth and Tax Relief Reconciliation Act of 2001 in the same manner as the provisions of such Act to which such amendments relate.

[¶5010] CODE SEC. 24. CHILD TAX CREDIT.

»»→ Caution: *Code Sec. 24(a), below, as amended by P.L. 110-351, applies to tax years beginning after December 31, 2008.*

(a) ALLOWANCE OF CREDIT.—There shall be allowed as a credit against the tax imposed by this chapter for the taxable year with respect to each qualifying child of the taxpayer *for which the taxpayer is allowed a deduction under section 151* an amount equal to $1,000.

[CCH Explanation at ¶ 260.]

Amendments

• **2008, Fostering Connections to Success and Increasing Adoptions Act of 2008 (P.L. 110-351)**

P.L. 110-351, § 501(c)(1):

Amended Code Sec. 24(a) by inserting "for which the taxpayer is allowed a deduction under section 151" after "of the taxpayer". **Effective** for tax years beginning after 12-31-2008.

(b) LIMITATIONS.—

* * *

(3) LIMITATION BASED ON AMOUNT OF TAX.—In the case of a taxable year to which section 26(a)(2) does not apply, the credit allowed under subsection (a) for any taxable year shall not exceed the excess of—

(A) the sum of the regular tax liability (as defined in section 26(b)) plus the tax imposed by section 55, over

≫→ *Caution: Code Sec. 24(b)(3)(B), as amended by P.L. 110-343, Div. B, §106(e)(2)(B), but prior to amendment by P.L. 110-343, Div. B, §205(d)(1)(A), applies to tax years beginning on or before December 31, 2008.*

(B) the sum of the credits allowable under this subpart (other than this section and sections 23, *25B, and 25D*) and section 27 for the taxable year.

≫→ *Caution: Code Sec. 24(b)(3)(B), below, as amended by P.L. 110-343, Div. B, §§106(e)(2)(B) and 205(d)(1)(A), applies to tax years beginning after December 31, 2008. For sunset provisions, see P.L. 110-343, §§106(f)(3) and 205(f) in the amendment notes.*

(B) the sum of the credits allowable under this subpart (other than this section and sections 23, *25B, 25D, and 30D*) and section 27 for the taxable year.

* * *

[CCH Explanations at ¶ 510 and ¶ 515. Committee Reports at ¶ 10,060 and ¶ 10,170.]

Amendments

• **2008, Energy Improvement and Extension Act of 2008 (P.L. 110-343)**

P.L. 110-343, Division B, § 106(e)(2)(B):

Amended Code Sec. 24(b)(3)(B) by striking "and 25B" and inserting ", 25B, and 25D". **Effective** for tax years beginning after 12-31-2007.

P.L. 110-343, Division B, § 106(f)(3), provides:

(3) APPLICATION OF EGTRRA SUNSET.—The amendments made by subparagraphs (A) and (B) of subsection (e)(2) shall be subject to title IX of the Economic Growth and Tax Relief Reconciliation Act of 2001 in the same manner as the provisions of such Act to which such amendments relate.

P.L. 110-343, Division B, § 205(d)(1)(A):

Amended Code Sec. 24(b)(3)(B), as amended by Act Sec. 106, by striking "and 25D" and inserting "25D, and 30D". **Effective** for tax years beginning after 12-31-2008.

P.L. 110-343, Division B, § 205(f), provides:

(f) APPLICATION OF EGTRRA SUNSET.—The amendment made by subsection (d)(1)(A) shall be subject to title IX of the Economic Growth and Tax Relief Reconciliation Act of 2001 in the same manner as the provision of such Act to which such amendment relates.

(d) PORTION OF CREDIT REFUNDABLE.—

* * *

(4) SPECIAL RULE FOR 2008.—*Notwithstanding paragraph (3), in the case of any taxable year beginning in 2008, the dollar amount in effect for such taxable year under paragraph (1)(B)(i) shall be $8,500.*

* * *

* * *

[CCH Explanation at ¶ 255. Committee Reports at ¶ 10,640.]

Amendments

• **2008, Tax Extenders and Alternative Minimum Tax Relief Act of 2008 (P.L. 110-343)**

P.L. 110-343, Division C, § 501(a):

Amended Code Sec. 24(d) by adding at the end a new paragraph (4). **Effective** for tax years beginning after 12-31-2007.

[¶ 5015] CODE SEC. 25. INTEREST ON CERTAIN HOME MORTGAGES.

* * *

(e) SPECIAL RULES AND DEFINITIONS.—For purposes of this section—

    (1) CARRYFORWARD OF UNUSED CREDIT.—

* * *

        (C) APPLICABLE TAX LIMIT.—For purposes of this paragraph, the term "applicable tax limit" means—

* * *

           (ii) in the case of a taxable year to which section 26(a)(2) does not apply, the limitation imposed by section 26(a)(1) for the taxable year reduced by the sum of the credits allowable under this subpart (other than this section and sections 23, 24, 25B, 25D, *30D* and 1400C).

* * *

[CCH Explanation at ¶ 515. Committee Reports at ¶ 10,170.]

Amendments

• **2008, Energy Improvement and Extension Act of 2008 (P.L. 110-343)**

P.L. 110-343, Division B, § 205(d)(1)(B):

Amended Code Sec. 25(e)(1)(C)(ii) by inserting "30D," after "25D,". **Effective** for tax years beginning after 12-31-2008.

[¶ 5020] CODE SEC. 25B. ELECTIVE DEFERRALS AND IRA CONTRIBUTIONS BY CERTAIN INDIVIDUALS.

* * *

(g) LIMITATION BASED ON AMOUNT OF TAX.—In the case of a taxable year to which section 26(a)(2) does not apply, the credit allowed under subsection (a) for the taxable year shall not exceed the excess of—

    (1) the sum of the regular tax liability (as defined in section 26(b)) plus the tax imposed by section 55, over

    (2) the sum of the credits allowable under this subpart (other than this section and *sections 23, 25D, and 30D*) and section 27 for the taxable year.

[CCH Explanations at ¶ 510 and ¶ 515. Committee Reports at ¶ 10,060 and ¶ 10,170.]

Amendments

• **2008, Energy Improvement and Extension Act of 2008 (P.L. 110-343)**

P.L. 110-343, Division B, § 106(e)(2)(C):

Amended Code Sec. 25B(g)(2) by striking "section 23" and inserting "sections 23 and 25D". **Effective** for tax years beginning after 12-31-2007.

P.L. 110-343, Division B, § 205(d)(1)(C):

Amended Code Sec. 25B(g)(2), as amended by Act Sec. 106, by striking "and 25D" and inserting ", 25D, and 30D". **Effective** for tax years beginning after 12-31-2008.

[¶5025] CODE SEC. 25C. NONBUSINESS ENERGY PROPERTY.

* * *

(c) QUALIFIED ENERGY EFFICIENCY IMPROVEMENTS.—For purposes of this section—

(1) IN GENERAL.—The term "qualified energy efficiency improvements" means any energy efficient building envelope component which meets the prescriptive criteria for such component established by the 2000 International Energy Conservation Code, as such Code (including supplements) is in effect on the date of the enactment of this section (or, in the case of a metal roof with appropriate pigmented coatings, *or an asphalt roof with appropriate cooling granules,* which meet the Energy Star program requirements), if—

(A) such component is installed in or on a dwelling unit located in the United States and owned and used by the taxpayer as the taxpayer's principal residence (within the meaning of section 121),

(B) the original use of such component commences with the taxpayer, and

(C) such component reasonably can be expected to remain in use for at least 5 years.

(2) BUILDING ENVELOPE COMPONENT.—The term "building envelope component" means—

* * *

(D) any metal roof *or asphalt roof* installed on a dwelling unit, but only if such roof has appropriate pigmented coatings *or cooling granules* which are specifically and primarily designed to reduce the heat gain of such dwelling unit.

* * *

[CCH Explanation at ¶505. Committee Reports at ¶10,210.]

Amendments

• **2008, Energy Improvement and Extension Act of 2008 (P.L. 110-343)**

P.L. 110-343, Division B, §302(e)(1):

Amended Code Sec. 25C(c)(1) by inserting ", or an asphalt roof with appropriate cooling granules," before "which meet the Energy Star program requirements". **Effective** for property placed in service after 10-3-2008.

P.L. 110-343, Division B, §302(e)(2)(A)-(B):

Amended Code Sec. 25C(c)(2)(D) by inserting "or asphalt roof" after "metal roof", and by inserting "or cooling granules" after "pigmented coatings". **Effective** for property placed in service after 10-3-2008.

(d) RESIDENTIAL ENERGY PROPERTY EXPENDITURES.—For purposes of this section—

* * *

(2) QUALIFIED ENERGY PROPERTY.—

* * *

⫸→ Caution: *Code Sec. 25C(d)(2)(C), below, as amended by P.L. 110-343, applies to expenditures made after December 31, 2008.*

(C) *REQUIREMENTS AND STANDARDS FOR AIR CONDITIONERS AND HEAT PUMPS.—The standards and requirements prescribed by the Secretary under subparagraph (B) with respect to the energy efficiency ratio (EER) for central air conditioners and electric heat pumps—*

(i) *shall require measurements to be based on published data which is tested by manufacturers at 95 degrees Fahrenheit, and*

(ii) *may be based on the certified data of the Air Conditioning and Refrigeration Institute that are prepared in partnership with the Consortium for Energy Efficiency.*

(3) ENERGY-EFFICIENT BUILDING PROPERTY.—The term "energy-efficient building property" means—

* * *

⫸→ Caution: *Code Sec. 25C(d)(3)(C), below, was stricken by P.L. 110-343, applicable to expenditures made after December 31, 2008.*

(C) a geothermal heat pump which—

(i) in the case of a closed loop product, has an energy efficiency ratio (EER) of at least 14.1 and a heating coefficient of performance (COP) of at least 3.3,

(ii) in the case of an open loop product, has an energy efficiency ratio (EER) of at least 16.2 and a heating coefficient of performance (COP) of at least 3.6, and

(iii) in the case of a direct expansion (DX) product, has an energy efficiency ratio (EER) of at least 15 and a heating coefficient of performance (COP) of at least 3.5,

»»→ Caution: *Former Code Sec. 25C(d)(3)(D) was redesignated as Code Sec. 25C(d)(3)(C), below, by P.L. 110-343, applicable to expenditures made after December 31, 2008.*

(C) a central air conditioner which achieves the highest efficiency tier established by the Consortium for Energy Efficiency, as in effect on January 1, 2006,

»»→ Caution: *Former Code Sec. 25C(d)(3)(E) was redesignated as Code Sec. 25C(d)(3)(D), below, and further amended by P.L. 110-343, applicable to expenditures made after December 31, 2008.*

(D) a natural gas, propane, or oil water heater which has an energy factor of at least 0.80 or a thermal efficiency of at least 90 percent, and

»»→ Caution: *Former Code Sec. 25C(d)(3)(F) was added and then redesignated as Code Sec. 25C(d)(3)(E), below, by P.L. 110-343, applicable to expenditures made after December 31, 2008.*

(E) a stove which uses the burning of biomass fuel to heat a dwelling unit located in the United States and used as a residence by the taxpayer, or to heat water for use in such a dwelling unit, and which has a thermal efficiency rating of at least 75 percent.

* * *

»»→ Caution: *Code Sec. 25C(d)(6), below, as added by P.L. 110-343, applies to expenditures made after December 31, 2008.*

(6) BIOMASS FUEL.—The term "biomass fuel" means any plant-derived fuel available on a renewable or recurring basis, including agricultural crops and trees, wood and wood waste and residues (including wood pellets), plants (including aquatic plants), grasses, residues, and fibers.

* * *

[CCH Explanation at ¶505. Committee Reports at ¶10,210.]

Amendments

• **2008, Energy Improvement and Extension Act of 2008 (P.L. 110-343)**

P.L. 110-343, Division B, §302(b)(1)(A)-(C):

Amended Code Sec. 25C(d)(3) by striking "and" at the end of subparagraph (D), by striking the period at the end of subparagraph (E) and inserting ", and", and by adding at the end a new subparagraph (F). **Effective** for expenditures made after 12-31-2008.

P.L. 110-343, Division B, §302(b)(2):

Amended Code Sec. 25C(d) by adding at the end a new paragraph (6). **Effective** for expenditures made after 12-31-2008.

P.L. 110-343, Division B, §302(c):

Amended Code Sec. 25C(d)(3)(E) by inserting "or a thermal efficiency of at least 90 percent" after "0.80". **Effective** for expenditures made after 12-31-2008.

P.L. 110-343, Division B, §302(d)(1):

Amended Code Sec. 25C(d)(3), as amended by Act Sec. 302(b)-(c), by striking subparagraph (C) and by redesignating subparagraphs (D), (E), and (F) as subparagraphs (C), (D), and (E), respectively. **Effective** for expenditures made after 12-31-2008. Prior to being stricken, Code Sec. 25C(d)(3)(C) read as follows:

(C) a geothermal heat pump which—

(i) in the case of a closed loop product, has an energy efficiency ratio (EER) of at least 14.1 and a heating coefficient of performance (COP) of at least 3.3,

(ii) in the case of an open loop product, has an energy efficiency ratio (EER) of at least 16.2 and a heating coefficient of performance (COP) of at least 3.6, and

(iii) in the case of a direct expansion (DX) product, has an energy efficiency ratio (EER) of at least 15 and a heating coefficient of performance (COP) of at least 3.5,

P.L. 110-343, Division B, §302(d)(2):

Amended Code Sec. 25C(d)(2)(C). **Effective** for expenditures made after 12-31-2008. Prior to amendment, Code Sec. 25C(d)(2)(C) read as follows:

(C) REQUIREMENTS FOR STANDARDS.—The standards and requirements prescribed by the Secretary under subparagraph (B)—

(i) in the case of the energy efficiency ratio (EER) for central air conditioners and electric heat pumps—

(I) shall require measurements to be based on published data which is tested by manufacturers at 95 degrees Fahrenheit, and

(II) may be based on the certified data of the Air Conditioning and Refrigeration Institute that are prepared in partnership with the Consortium for Energy Efficiency, and

(ii) in the case of geothermal heat pumps—

(I) shall be based on testing under the conditions of ARI/ISO Standard 13256-1 for Water Source Heat Pumps or ARI 870 for Direct Expansion GeoExchange Heat Pumps (DX), as appropriate, and

(II) shall include evidence that water heating services have been provided through a desuperheater or integrated water heating system connected to the storage water heater tank.

>>→ *Caution: Code Sec. 25C(g), below, as amended by P.L. 110-343, applies to expenditures made after December 31, 2008.*

(g) TERMINATION.—This section shall not apply with respect to any property *placed in service*—

(1) *after December 31, 2007, and before January 1, 2009, or*

(2) *after December 31, 2009.*

[CCH Explanation at ¶ 505. Committee Reports at ¶ 10,210.]

Amendments

• **2008, Energy Improvement and Extension Act of 2008 (P.L. 110-343)**

P.L. 110-343, Division B, § 302(a):

Amended Code Sec. 25C(g) by striking "placed in service after December 31, 2007" and inserting "placed in service—"

and new paragraphs (1) and (2). **Effective** for expenditures made after 12-31-2008.

[¶ 5030] CODE SEC. 25D. RESIDENTIAL ENERGY EFFICIENT PROPERTY.

(a) ALLOWANCE OF CREDIT.—In the case of an individual, there shall be allowed as a credit against the tax imposed by this chapter for the taxable year an amount equal to the sum of—

(1) 30 percent of the qualified solar electric property expenditures made by the taxpayer during such year,

(2) 30 percent of the qualified solar water heating property expenditures made by the taxpayer during such year,

(3) 30 percent of the qualified fuel cell property expenditures made by the taxpayer during such year,

(4) *30 percent of the qualified small wind energy property expenditures made by the taxpayer during such year, and*

(5) *30 percent of the qualified geothermal heat pump property expenditures made by the taxpayer during such year.*

[CCH Explanation at ¶ 510. Committee Reports at ¶ 10,060.]

Amendments

• **2008, Energy Improvement and Extension Act of 2008 (P.L. 110-343)**

P.L. 110-343, Division B, § 106(c)(1):

Amended Code Sec. 25D(a) by striking "and" at the end of paragraph (2), by striking the period at the end of paragraph (3) and inserting ", and", and by adding at the end a new paragraph (4). **Effective** for tax years beginning after 12-31-2007.

P.L. 110-343, Division B, § 106(d)(1):

Amended Code Sec. 25D(a), as amended by Act Sec. 106(c), by striking "and" at the end of paragraph (3), by striking the period at the end of paragraph (4) and inserting ", and", and by adding at the end a new paragraph (5). **Effective** for tax years beginning after 12-31-2007.

(b) LIMITATIONS.—

(1) MAXIMUM CREDIT.—The credit allowed under subsection (a) (determined without regard to subsection (c)) for any taxable year shall not exceed—

>>→ *Caution: Code Sec. 25D(b)(1)(A), below, was stricken by P.L. 110-343, applicable to tax years beginning after December 31, 2008.*

(A) $2,000 with respect to any qualified solar electric property expenditures,

>>→ *Caution: Former Code Sec. 25D(b)(1)(B)-(E), was redesignated as Code Sec. 25D(b)(1)(A)-(D), below, by P.L. 110-343, applicable to tax years beginning after December 31, 2008.*

(A) *$2,000 with respect to any qualified solar water heating property expenditures,*

(B) *$500 with respect to each half kilowatt of capacity of qualified fuel cell property (as defined in section 48(c)(1)) for which qualified fuel cell property expenditures are made,*

(C) *$500 with respect to each half kilowatt of capacity (not to exceed $4,000) of wind turbines for which qualified small wind energy property expenditures are made, and*

(D) *$2,000 with respect to any qualified geothermal heat pump property expenditures.*

* * *

[CCH Explanation at ¶510. Committee Reports at ¶10,060.]

Amendments

• **2008, Energy Improvement and Extension Act of 2008 (P.L. 110-343)**

P.L. 110-343, Division B, §106(b)(1)(A)-(B):

Amended Code Sec. 25D(b)(1), as amended by Act Sec. 106(c)-(d), by striking subparagraph (A), and by redesignating subparagraphs (B) through (E) as subparagraphs (A) through (D), respectively. **Effective** for tax years beginning after 12-31-2008. Prior to being stricken, Code Sec. 25D(b)(1)(A) read as follows:

(A) $2,000 with respect to any qualified solar electric property expenditures,

P.L. 110-343, Division B, §106(c)(2):

Amended Code Sec. 25D(b)(1) by striking "and" at the end of subparagraph (B), by striking the period at the end of subparagraph (C) and inserting ", and", and by adding at the end a new subparagraph (D). **Effective** for tax years beginning after 12-31-2007.

P.L. 110-343, Division B, §106(d)(2):

Amended Code Sec. 25D(b)(1), as amended by Act Sec. 106(c), by striking "and" at the end of subparagraph (C), by striking the period at the end of subparagraph (D) and inserting ", and", and by adding at the end a new subparagraph (E). **Effective** for tax years beginning after 12-31-2007.

(c) LIMITATION BASED ON AMOUNT OF TAX; CARRYFORWARD OF UNUSED CREDIT.—

(1) LIMITATION BASED ON AMOUNT OF TAX.—In the case of a taxable year to which section 26(a)(2) does not apply, the credit allowed under subsection (a) for the taxable year shall not exceed the excess of—

(A) the sum of the regular tax liability (as defined in section 26(b)) plus the tax imposed by section 55, over

(B) the sum of the credits allowable under this subpart (other than this section) and section 27 for the taxable year.

(2) CARRYFORWARD OF UNUSED CREDIT.—

(A) RULE FOR YEARS IN WHICH ALL PERSONAL CREDITS ALLOWED AGAINST REGULAR AND ALTERNATIVE MINIMUM TAX.—In the case of a taxable year to which section 26(a)(2) applies, if the credit allowable under subsection (a) exceeds the limitation imposed by section 26(a)(2) for such taxable year reduced by the sum of the credits allowable under this subpart (other than this section), such excess shall be carried to the succeeding taxable year and added to the credit allowable under subsection (a) for such succeeding taxable year.

(B) RULE FOR OTHER YEARS.—In the case of a taxable year to which section 26(a)(2) does not apply, if the credit allowable under subsection (a) exceeds the limitation imposed by paragraph (1) for such taxable year, such excess shall be carried to the succeeding taxable year and added to the credit allowable under subsection (a) for such succeeding taxable year.

[CCH Explanation at ¶510. Committee Reports at ¶10,060.]

Amendments

• **2008, Energy Improvement and Extension Act of 2008 (P.L. 110-343)**

P.L. 110-343, Division B, §106(e)(1):

Amended Code Sec. 25D(c). **Effective** for tax years beginning after 12-31-2007. Prior to amendment, Code Sec. 25D(c) read as follows:

(c) CARRYFORWARD OF UNUSED CREDIT.—

(1) RULE FOR YEARS IN WHICH ALL PERSONAL CREDITS ALLOWED AGAINST REGULAR AND ALTERNATIVE MINIMUM TAX.—In the case of a taxable year to which section 26(a)(2) applies, if the credit allowable under subsection (a) exceeds the limitation

imposed by section 26(a)(2) for such taxable year reduced by the sum of the credits allowable under this subpart (other than this section), such excess shall be carried to the succeeding taxable year and added to the credit allowable under subsection (a) for such succeeding taxable year.

(2) RULE FOR OTHER YEARS.—In the case of a taxable year to which section 26(a)(2) does not apply, if the credit allowable under subsection (a) exceeds the limitation imposed by section 26(a)(1) for such taxable year reduced by the sum of the credits allowable under this subpart (other than this section and sections 23, 24, and 25B), such excess shall be carried to the succeeding taxable year and added to the credit allowable under subsection (a) for such succeeding taxable year.

(d) DEFINITIONS.—For purposes of this section—

* * *

(4) QUALIFIED SMALL WIND ENERGY PROPERTY EXPENDITURE.—The term "qualified small wind energy property expenditure" means an expenditure for property which uses a wind turbine to generate electricity for use in connection with a dwelling unit located in the United States and used as a residence by the taxpayer.

(5) *QUALIFIED GEOTHERMAL HEAT PUMP PROPERTY EXPENDITURE.—*

(A) *IN GENERAL.—The term "qualified geothermal heat pump property expenditure" means an expenditure for qualified geothermal heat pump property installed on or in connection with a dwelling unit located in the United States and used as a residence by the taxpayer.*

(B) *QUALIFIED GEOTHERMAL HEAT PUMP PROPERTY.—The term "qualified geothermal heat pump property" means any equipment which—*

(i) *uses the ground or ground water as a thermal energy source to heat the dwelling unit referred to in subparagraph (A) or as a thermal energy sink to cool such dwelling unit, and*

(ii) *meets the requirements of the Energy Star program which are in effect at the time that the expenditure for such equipment is made.*

[CCH Explanation at ¶ 510. Committee Reports at ¶ 10,060.]

Amendments

• 2008, Energy Improvement and Extension Act of 2008 (P.L. 110-343)

P.L. 110-343, Division B, § 106(c)(3)(A):

Amended Code Sec. 25D(d) by adding at the end a new paragraph (4). **Effective** for tax years beginning after 12-31-2007.

P.L. 110-343, Division B, § 106(d)(3):

Amended Code Sec. 25D(d), as amended by Act Sec. 106(c), by adding at the end a new paragraph (5). **Effective** for tax years beginning after 12-31-2007.

(e) *SPECIAL RULES.—*For purposes of this section—

* * *

(4) *DOLLAR AMOUNTS IN CASE OF JOINT OCCUPANCY.—*In the case of any dwelling unit which is jointly occupied and used during any calendar year as a residence by two or more individuals the following rules shall apply:

(A) *MAXIMUM EXPENDITURES.—*The maximum amount of expenditures which may be taken into account under subsection (a) by all such individuals with respect to such dwelling unit during such calendar year shall be—

➤➤➤ *Caution: Former Code Sec. 25D(e)(4)(A)(i), below, was stricken by P.L. 110-343, applicable to tax years beginning after December 31, 2008.*

(i) $6,667 in the case of any qualified solar electric property expenditures,

➤➤➤ *Caution: Former Code Sec. 25D(e)(4)(A)(ii)-(v), below, was redesignated as Code Sec. 25D(e)(4)(A)(i)-(iv), respectively, by P.L. 110-343, applicable to tax years beginning after December 31, 2008.*

(i) *$6,667 in the case of any qualified solar water heating property expenditures,*

(ii) *$1,667 in the case of each half kilowatt of capacity of qualified fuel cell property (as defined in section 48(c)(1)) for which qualified fuel cell property expenditures are made,*

(iii) *$1,667 in the case of each half kilowatt of capacity (not to exceed $13,333) of wind turbines for which qualified small wind energy property expenditures are made, and*

(iv) *$6,667 in the case of any qualified geothermal heat pump property expenditures.*

* * *

[CCH Explanation at ¶ 510. Committee Reports at ¶ 10,060.]

Amendments

• 2008, Energy Improvement and Extension Act of 2008 (P.L. 110-343)

P.L. 110-343, Division B, § 106(b)(2)(A)-(B):

Amended Code Sec. 25D(e)(4)(A), as amended by Act Sec. 106(c)-(d), by striking clause (i), and by redesignating clauses (ii) through (v) as clauses (i) through (iv), respectively. **Effective** for tax years beginning after 12-31-2008.

Prior to being stricken, Code Sec. 25D(e)(4)(A)(i) read as follows:

(i) $6,667 in the case of any qualified solar electric property expenditures,

P.L. 110-343, Division B, § 106(c)(4):

Amended Code Sec. 25D(e)(4)(A) by striking "and" at the end of clause (ii), by striking the period at the end of clause (iii) and inserting ", and", and by adding at the end a new clause (iv). **Effective** for tax years beginning after 12-31-2007.

P.L. 110-343, Division B, §106(d)(4):

Amended Code Sec. 25D(e)(4)(A), as amended by Act Sec. 106(c), is amended by striking "and" at the end of clause

(iii), by striking the period at the end of clause (iv) and inserting ", and", and by adding at the end a new clause (v). **Effective** for tax years beginning after 12-31-2007.

(g) TERMINATION.—The credit allowed under this section shall not apply to property placed in service after *December 31, 2016*.

[CCH Explanation at ¶510. Committee Reports at ¶10,060.]

Amendments

• **2008, Energy Improvement and Extension Act of 2008 (P.L. 110-343)**

P.L. 110-343, Division B, §106(a):

Amended Code Sec. 25D(g) by striking "December 31, 2008" and inserting "December 31, 2016". **Effective** for tax years beginning after 12-31-2007.

[¶5035] CODE SEC. 26. LIMITATION BASED ON TAX LIABILITY; DEFINITION OF TAX LIABILITY.

(a) LIMITATION BASED ON AMOUNT OF TAX.—

(1) IN GENERAL.—The aggregate amount of credits allowed by this subpart (other than sections 23, 24, *25B, 25D, and 30D*) for the taxable year shall not exceed the excess (if any) of—

(A) the taxpayer's regular tax liability for the taxable year, over

(B) the tentative minimum tax for the taxable year (determined without regard to the alternative minimum tax foreign tax credit).

For purposes of subparagraph (B), the taxpayer's tentative minimum tax for any taxable year beginning during 1999 shall be treated as being zero.

(2) SPECIAL RULE FOR TAXABLE YEARS 2000 THROUGH *2008*.—For purposes of any taxable year beginning during 2000, 2001, 2002, 2003, 2004, 2005, 2006, *2007, or 2008*, the aggregate amount of credits allowed by this subpart for the taxable year shall not exceed the sum of—

(A) the taxpayer's regular tax liability for the taxable year reduced by the foreign tax credit allowable under section 27(a), and

(B) the tax imposed by section 55(a) for the taxable year.

[CCH Explanations at ¶210, ¶510 and ¶515. Committee Reports at ¶10,060, ¶10,170 and ¶10,310.]

Amendments

• **2008, Energy Improvement and Extension Act of 2008 (P.L. 110-343)**

P.L. 110-343, Division B, §106(e)(2)(D):

Amended Code Sec. 26(a)(1) by striking "and 25B" and inserting "25B, and 25D". **Effective** for tax years beginning after 12-31-2007.

P.L. 110-343, Division B, §205(d)(1)(D):

Amended Code Sec. 26(a)(1), as amended by Act Sec. 106, by striking "and 25D" and inserting "25D, and 30D". **Effective** for tax years beginning after 12-31-2008.

• **2008, Tax Extenders and Alternative Minimum Tax Relief Act of 2008 (P.L. 110-343)**

P.L. 110-343, Division C, §101(a)(1)-(2):

Amended Code Sec. 26(a)(2) by striking "or 2007" and inserting "2007, or 2008", and by striking "2007" in the heading thereof and inserting "2008". **Effective** for tax years beginning after 12-31-2007.

(b) REGULAR TAX LIABILITY.—For purposes of this part—

* * *

(2) EXCEPTION FOR CERTAIN TAXES.—For purposes of paragraph (1), any tax imposed by any of the following provisions shall not be treated as tax imposed by this chapter:

* * *

(V) subsections (a)(1)(B)(i) and (b)(4)(A) of section 409A (relating to interest and additional tax with respect to certain deferred compensation),

(W) section 36(f) (relating to recapture of homebuyer credit), *and*

»»→ Caution: *Code Sec. 26(b)(2)(X), as added by P.L. 110-343, applies generally to amounts deferred which are attributable to services performed after December 31, 2008.*

(X) *section 457A(c)(1)(B) (relating to determinability of amounts of compensation).*

[CCH Explanation at ¶ 455. Committee Reports at ¶ 10,750.]

Amendments

• **2008, Tax Extenders and Alternative Minimum Tax Relief Act of 2008 (P.L. 110-343)**

P.L. 110-343, Division C, § 801(b):

Amended Code Sec. 26(b)(2), as amended by the Housing Assistance Tax Act of 2008 (P.L. 110-289), by striking "and" at the end of subparagraph (V), by striking the period at the end of subparagraph (W) and inserting ", and", and by adding at the end a new subparagraph (X). **Effective** generally for amounts deferred which are attributable to services performed after 12-31-2008. For a special rule, see Act Sec. 801(d)(2), below.

P.L. 110-343, Division C, § 801(d)(2), provides:

(2) Application to existing deferrals.—In the case of any amount deferred to which the amendments made by this section do not apply solely by reason of the fact that the amount is attributable to services performed before January 1, 2009, to the extent such amount is not includible in gross income in a taxable year beginning before 2018, such amounts shall be includible in gross income in the later of—

(A) the last taxable year beginning before 2018, or

(B) the taxable year in which there is no substantial risk of forfeiture of the rights to such compensation (determined in the same manner as determined for purposes of section 457A of the Internal Revenue Code of 1986, as added by this section).

[¶ 5040] CODE SEC. 30B. ALTERNATIVE MOTOR VEHICLE CREDIT.

* * *

(d) New Qualified Hybrid Motor Vehicle Credit.—

* * *

(3) New qualified hybrid motor vehicle.—For purposes of this subsection—

* * *

»»→ Caution: *Code Sec. 30B(d)(3)(D), below, as added by P.L. 110-343, applies to tax years beginning after December 31, 2008.*

(D) Exclusion of plug-in vehicles.—*Any vehicle with respect to which a credit is allowable under section 30D (determined without regard to subsection (d) thereof) shall not be taken into account under this section.*

* * *

[CCH Explanation at ¶ 515. Committee Reports at ¶ 10,170.]

Amendments

• **2008, Energy Improvement and Extension Act of 2008 (P.L. 110-343)**

P.L. 110-343, Division B, § 205(b):

Amended Code Sec. 30B(d)(3) by adding at the end a new subparagraph (D). **Effective** for tax years beginning after 12-31-2008.

[¶ 5045] CODE SEC. 30C. ALTERNATIVE FUEL VEHICLE REFUELING PROPERTY CREDIT.

* * *

(c) Qualified Alternative Fuel Vehicle Refueling Property.—For purposes of this section, the term "qualified alternative fuel vehicle refueling property" has the same meaning as the term "qualified clean-fuel vehicle refueling property" would have under section 179A if—

* * *

(2) only the following were treated as clean-burning fuels for purposes of section 179A(d):

* * *

(C) Electricity.

* * *

[CCH Explanation at ¶ 520. Committee Reports at ¶ 10,190.]

Amendments

• **2008, Energy Improvement and Extension Act of 2008 (P.L. 110-343)**

P.L. 110-343, Division B, § 207(b):

Amended Code Sec. 30C(c)(2) by adding at the end a new subparagraph (C). **Effective** for property placed in service after 10-3-2008, in tax years ending after such date.

(g) TERMINATION.—This section shall not apply to any property placed in service—

(1) in the case of property relating to hydrogen, after December 31, 2014, and

(2) in the case of any other property, after *December 31, 2010.*

[CCH Explanation at ¶ 520. Committee Reports at ¶ 10,190.]

Amendments

• **2008, Energy Improvement and Extension Act of 2008 (P.L. 110-343)**

P.L. 110-343, Division B, § 207(a):

Amended Code Sec. 30C(g)(2) by striking "December 31, 2009" and inserting "December 31, 2010". **Effective** for property placed in service after 10-3-2008, in tax years ending after such date.

»»→ Caution: *Code Sec. 30D, below, as added by P.L. 110-343, applies to tax years beginning after December 31, 2008.*

[¶ 5050] *CODE SEC. 30D. NEW QUALIFIED PLUG-IN ELECTRIC DRIVE MOTOR VEHICLES.*

(a) ALLOWANCE OF CREDIT.—

(1) IN GENERAL.—There shall be allowed as a credit against the tax imposed by this chapter for the taxable year an amount equal to the applicable amount with respect to each new qualified plug-in electric drive motor vehicle placed in service by the taxpayer during the taxable year.

(2) APPLICABLE AMOUNT.—For purposes of paragraph (1), the applicable amount is sum of—

(A) $2,500, plus

(B) $417 for each kilowatt hour of traction battery capacity in excess of 4 kilowatt hours.

(b) LIMITATIONS.—

(1) LIMITATION BASED ON WEIGHT.—The amount of the credit allowed under subsection (a) by reason of subsection (a)(2) shall not exceed—

(A) $7,500, in the case of any new qualified plug-in electric drive motor vehicle with a gross vehicle weight rating of not more than 10,000 pounds,

(B) $10,000, in the case of any new qualified plug-in electric drive motor vehicle with a gross vehicle weight rating of more than 10,000 pounds but not more than 14,000 pounds,

(C) $12,500, in the case of any new qualified plug-in electric drive motor vehicle with a gross vehicle weight rating of more than 14,000 pounds but not more than 26,000 pounds, and

(D) $15,000, in the case of any new qualified plug-in electric drive motor vehicle with a gross vehicle weight rating of more than 26,000 pounds.

(2) LIMITATION ON NUMBER OF PASSENGER VEHICLES AND LIGHT TRUCKS ELIGIBLE FOR CREDIT.—

(A) IN GENERAL.—In the case of a new qualified plug-in electric drive motor vehicle sold during the phaseout period, only the applicable percentage of the credit otherwise allowable under subsection (a) shall be allowed.

(B) PHASEOUT PERIOD.—For purposes of this subsection, the phaseout period is the period beginning with the second calendar quarter following the calendar quarter which includes the first date on which the total number of such new qualified plug-in electric drive motor vehicles sold for use in the United States after December 31, 2008, is at least 250,000.

(C) APPLICABLE PERCENTAGE.—For purposes of subparagraph (A), the applicable percentage is—

(i) 50 percent for the first 2 calendar quarters of the phaseout period,

(ii) 25 percent for the 3d and 4th calendar quarters of the phaseout period, and

(iii) 0 percent for each calendar quarter thereafter.

(D) CONTROLLED GROUPS.—Rules similar to the rules of section 30B(f)(4) shall apply for purposes of this subsection.

(c) NEW QUALIFIED PLUG-IN ELECTRIC DRIVE MOTOR VEHICLE.—For purposes of this section, the term "new qualified plug-in electric drive motor vehicle" means a motor vehicle—

(1) which draws propulsion using a traction battery with at least 4 kilowatt hours of capacity,

(2) which uses an offboard source of energy to recharge such battery,

(3) which, in the case of a passenger vehicle or light truck which has a gross vehicle weight rating of not more than 8,500 pounds, has received a certificate of conformity under the Clean Air Act and meets or exceeds the equivalent qualifying California low emission vehicle standard under section 243(e)(2) of the Clean Air Act for that make and model year, and

(A) in the case of a vehicle having a gross vehicle weight rating of 6,000 pounds or less, the Bin 5 Tier II emission standard established in regulations prescribed by the Administrator of the Environmental Protection Agency under section 202(i) of the Clean Air Act for that make and model year vehicle, and

(B) in the case of a vehicle having a gross vehicle weight rating of more than 6,000 pounds but not more than 8,500 pounds, the Bin 8 Tier II emission standard which is so established,

(4) the original use of which commences with the taxpayer,

(5) which is acquired for use or lease by the taxpayer and not for resale, and

(6) which is made by a manufacturer.

(d) APPLICATION WITH OTHER CREDITS.—

(1) BUSINESS CREDIT TREATED AS PART OF GENERAL BUSINESS CREDIT.—So much of the credit which would be allowed under subsection (a) for any taxable year (determined without regard to this subsection) that is attributable to property of a character subject to an allowance for depreciation shall be treated as a credit listed in section 38(b) for such taxable year (and not allowed under subsection (a)).

(2) PERSONAL CREDIT.—

(A) IN GENERAL.—For purposes of this title, the credit allowed under subsection (a) for any taxable year (determined after application of paragraph (1)) shall be treated as a credit allowable under subpart A for such taxable year.

(B) LIMITATION BASED ON AMOUNT OF TAX.—In the case of a taxable year to which section 26(a)(2) does not apply, the credit allowed under subsection (a) for any taxable year (determined after application of paragraph (1)) shall not exceed the excess of—

(i) the sum of the regular tax liability (as defined in section 26(b)) plus the tax imposed by section 55, over

(ii) the sum of the credits allowable under subpart A (other than this section and sections 23 and 25D) and section 27 for the taxable year.

(e) OTHER DEFINITIONS AND SPECIAL RULES.—For purposes of this section—

(1) MOTOR VEHICLE.—The term "motor vehicle" has the meaning given such term by section 30(c)(2).

(2) OTHER TERMS.—The terms "passenger automobile", "light truck", and "manufacturer" have the meanings given such terms in regulations prescribed by the Administrator of the Environmental Protection Agency for purposes of the administration of title II of the Clean Air Act (42 U.S.C. 7521 et seq.).

(3) TRACTION BATTERY CAPACITY.—Traction battery capacity shall be measured in kilowatt hours from a 100 percent state of charge to a zero percent state of charge.

(4) REDUCTION IN BASIS.—For purposes of this subtitle, the basis of any property for which a credit is allowable under subsection (a) shall be reduced by the amount of such credit so allowed.

(5) NO DOUBLE BENEFIT.—The amount of any deduction or other credit allowable under this chapter for a new qualified plug-in electric drive motor vehicle shall be reduced by the amount of credit allowed under subsection (a) for such vehicle for the taxable year.

(6) PROPERTY USED BY TAX-EXEMPT ENTITY.—In the case of a vehicle the use of which is described in paragraph (3) or (4) of section 50(b) and which is not subject to a lease, the person who sold such vehicle to the person or entity using such vehicle shall be treated as the taxpayer that placed such vehicle in service, but only if such person clearly discloses to such person or entity in a document the amount of any credit allowable under subsection (a) with respect to such vehicle (determined without regard to subsection (b)(2)).

(7) PROPERTY USED OUTSIDE UNITED STATES, ETC., NOT QUALIFIED.—No credit shall be allowable under subsection (a) with respect to any property referred to in section 50(b)(1) or with respect to the portion of the cost of any property taken into account under section 179.

(8) RECAPTURE.—The Secretary shall, by regulations, provide for recapturing the benefit of any credit allowable under subsection (a) with respect to any property which ceases to be property eligible for such credit (including recapture in the case of a lease period of less than the economic life of a vehicle).

(9) ELECTION TO NOT TAKE CREDIT.—No credit shall be allowed under subsection (a) for any vehicle if the taxpayer elects not to have this section apply to such vehicle.

(10) INTERACTION WITH AIR QUALITY AND MOTOR VEHICLE SAFETY STANDARDS.—Unless otherwise provided in this section, a motor vehicle shall not be considered eligible for a credit under this section unless such vehicle is in compliance with—

(A) the applicable provisions of the Clean Air Act for the applicable make and model year of the vehicle (or applicable air quality provisions of State law in the case of a State which has adopted such provision under a waiver under section 209(b) of the Clean Air Act), and

(B) the motor vehicle safety provisions of sections 30101 through 30169 of title 49, United States Code.

(f) REGULATIONS.—

(1) IN GENERAL.—Except as provided in paragraph (2), the Secretary shall promulgate such regulations as necessary to carry out the provisions of this section.

(2) COORDINATION IN PRESCRIPTION OF CERTAIN REGULATIONS.—The Secretary of the Treasury, in coordination with the Secretary of Transportation and the Administrator of the Environmental Protection Agency, shall prescribe such regulations as necessary to determine whether a motor vehicle meets the requirements to be eligible for a credit under this section.

(g) TERMINATION.—This section shall not apply to property purchased after December 31, 2014.

[CCH Explanation at ¶515. Committee Reports at ¶10,170.]

Amendments

• **2008, Energy Improvement and Extension Act of 2008 (P.L. 110-343)**

P.L. 110-343, Division B, §205(a):

Amended subpart B of part IV of subchapter A of chapter 1 by adding at the end a new Code Sec. 30D. **Effective** for tax years beginning after 12-31-2008.

[¶5055] CODE SEC. 38.   GENERAL BUSINESS CREDIT.

* * *

(b) CURRENT YEAR BUSINESS CREDIT.—For purposes of this subpart, the amount of the current year business credit is the sum of the following credits determined for the taxable year:

* * *

(32) in the case of an eligible agricultural business (as defined in section 45O(e)), the agricultural chemicals security credit determined under section 45O(a),

(33) the differential wage payment credit determined under section 45P(a),

(34) *the carbon dioxide sequestration credit determined under section 45Q(a)[,] plus*

≫→ *Caution: Code Sec 38(b)(35), below, as added by P.L. 110-343, is effective for tax years beginning after December 31, 2008.*

(35) *the portion of the new qualified plug-in electric drive motor vehicle credit to which section 30D(d)(1) applies.*

[CCH Explanations at ¶515 and ¶555. Committee Reports at ¶10,170.]

Amendments

• **2008, Energy Improvement and Extension Act of 2008 (P.L. 110-343)**

P.L. 110-343, Division B, §115(b):

Amended Code Sec. 38(b) by striking "plus" at the end of paragraph (32), by striking the period at the end of paragraph (33) and inserting "plus", and by adding at the end a new paragraph (34). **Effective** for carbon dioxide captured after 10-3-2008.

P.L. 110-343, Division B, §205(c):

Amended Code Sec. 38(b), as amended by this Act, by striking "plus" at the end of paragraph (33), by striking the period at the end of paragraph (34) and inserting "[,] plus", and by adding at the end a new paragraph (35). **Effective** for tax years beginning after 12-31-2008.

(c) LIMITATION BASED ON AMOUNT OF TAX.—

* * *

(4) SPECIAL RULES FOR SPECIFIED CREDITS.—

* * *

(B) SPECIFIED CREDITS.—For purposes of this subsection, the term "specified credits" means—

* * *

(v) *the credit determined under section 45G,*

(vi) *the credit determined under section 46 to the extent that such credit is attributable to the energy credit determined under section 48,*

(vii) the credit determined under *section 46 to the extent that such credit is attributable to the rehabilitation credit under section 47, but only with respect to* qualified rehabilitation expenditures properly taken into account for periods after December 31, 2007, and

(viii) *the credit determined under section 51.*

* * *

[CCH Explanations at ¶415 and ¶530. Committee Reports at ¶10,050 and ¶10,540.]

Amendments

• **2008, Energy Improvement and Extension Act of 2008 (P.L. 110-343)**

P.L. 110-343, Division B, §103(b)(1):

Amended Code Sec. 38(c)(4)(B), as amended by the Housing Assistance Tax Act of 2008 (P.L. 110-289), by redesignating clause (vi) [clauses (v) and (vi)] as clause[s] (vi) and (vii), respectively, and by inserting after clause (iv) a new clause (v). **Effective** for credits determined under Code Sec. 46 in tax years beginning after 10-3-2008 and to carrybacks of such credits.

P.L. 110-343, Division B, §103(b)(2):

Amended Code Sec. 38(c)(4)(B)(vi), as redesignated by Act Sec. 103(b)(1), by striking "section 47 to the extent attributable to" and inserting "section 46 to the extent that such credit is attributable to the rehabilitation credit under section 47, but only with respect to". **Effective** for credits determined under Code Sec. 46 in tax years beginning after 10-3-2008 and to carrybacks of such credits.

• **2008, Tax Extenders and Alternative Minimum Tax Relief Act of 2008 (P.L. 110-343)**

P.L. 110-343, Division C, §316(b)(1)-(2):

Amended Code Sec. 38(c)(4)(B), as amended by this Act, by redesignating clauses (v), (vi), and (vii) as clauses (vi), (vii), and (viii), respectively, and by inserting after clause (iv) a new clause (v). **Effective** for credits determined under Code Sec. 45G in tax years beginning after 12-31-2007, and to carrybacks of such credits.

[¶5060] CODE SEC. 40. ALCOHOL, etc., USED AS FUEL.

* * *

(d) DEFINITIONS AND SPECIAL RULES.—For purposes of this section—

* * *

(7) LIMITATION TO ALCOHOL WITH CONNECTION TO THE UNITED STATES.—*No credit shall be determined under this section with respect to any alcohol which is produced outside the United States for use as a fuel outside the United States. For purposes of this paragraph, the term "United States" includes any possession of the United States.*

* * *

[CCH Explanation at ¶825. Committee Reports at ¶10,160.]

Amendments

• **2008, Energy Improvement and Extension Act of 2008 (P.L. 110-343)**

P.L. 110-343, Division B, §203(a):

Amended Code Sec. 40(d) by adding at the end a new paragraph (7). **Effective** for claims for credit or payment made on or after 5-15-2008.

[¶5065] CODE SEC. 40A. BIODIESEL AND RENEWABLE DIESEL USED AS FUEL.

* * *

(b) DEFINITION OF BIODIESEL MIXTURE CREDIT, BIODIESEL CREDIT, AND SMALL AGRI-BIODIESEL PRODUCER CREDIT.—For purposes of this section—

(1) BIODIESEL MIXTURE CREDIT.—

* * *

≫→ Caution: *Code Sec. 40A(b)(1)(A), below, as amended by P.L. 110-343, applies to fuel produced, and sold or used, after December 31, 2008.*

(A) IN GENERAL.—The biodiesel mixture credit of any taxpayer for any taxable year is $1.00 for each gallon of biodiesel used by the taxpayer in the production of a qualified biodiesel mixture.

* * *

(2) BIODIESEL CREDIT.—

* * *

⋙→ *Caution: Code Sec. 40A(b)(2)(A), below, as amended by P.L. 110-343, applies to fuel produced, and sold or used, after December 31, 2008.*

(A) IN GENERAL.—The biodiesel credit of any taxpayer for any taxable year is $1.00 for each gallon of biodiesel which is not in a mixture with diesel fuel and which during the taxable year—

(i) is used by the taxpayer as a fuel in a trade or business, or

(ii) is sold by the taxpayer at retail to a person and placed in the fuel tank of such person's vehicle.

* * *

⋙→ *Caution: Code Sec. 40A(b)(3), below, was stricken by P.L. 110-343, applicable to fuel produced, and sold or used, after December 31, 2008.*

(3) CREDIT FOR AGRI-BIODIESEL.—In the case of any biodiesel which is agri-biodiesel, paragraphs (1)(A) and (2)(A) shall be applied by substituting "$1.00" for "50 cents".

⋙→ *Caution: Former Code Sec. 40A(b)(4)-(5) was redesignated as Code Sec. 40A(b)(3)-(4), below, by P.L. 110-343, applicable to fuel produced , and sold or used, after December 31, 2008.*

(3) CERTIFICATION FOR BIODIESEL.—No credit shall be allowed under paragraph (1) or (2) of subsection (a) unless the taxpayer obtains a certification (in such form and manner as prescribed by the Secretary) from the producer or importer of the biodiesel which identifies the product produced and the percentage of biodiesel and agri-biodiesel in the product.

(4) SMALL AGRI-BIODIESEL PRODUCER CREDIT.—

* * *

[CCH Explanation at ¶ 825. Committee Reports at ¶ 10,150.]

Amendments

• **2008, Energy Improvement and Extension Act of 2008 (P.L. 110-343)**

P.L. 110-343, Division B, § 202(b)(1):

Amended Code Sec. 40A(b)(1)(A) and (2)(A) by striking "50 cents" and inserting "$1.00". **Effective** for fuel produced, and sold or used, after 12-31-2008.

P.L. 110-343, Division B, § 202(b)(3)(A):

Amended Code Sec. 40A(b) by striking paragraph (3) and by redesignating paragraphs (4) and (5) as paragraphs (3)

and (4), respectively. **Effective** for fuel produced, and sold or used, after 12-31-2008. Prior to being stricken, Code Sec. 40A(b)(3) read as follows:

(3) CREDIT FOR AGRI-BIODIESEL.—In the case of any biodiesel which is agri-biodiesel, paragraphs (1)(A) and (2)(A) shall be applied by substituting "$1.00" for "50 cents".

(d) DEFINITIONS AND SPECIAL RULES.—For purposes of this section—

* * *

⋙→ *Caution: Code Sec. 40A(d)(2), below, as amended by P.L. 110-343, applies to fuel produced, and sold or used, after December 31, 2008.*

(2) AGRI-BIODIESEL.—The term "agri-biodiesel" means biodiesel derived solely from virgin oils, including esters derived from virgin vegetable oils from corn, soybeans, sunflower seeds, cottonseeds, canola, crambe, rapeseeds, safflowers, flaxseeds, rice bran, *mustard seeds, and camelina*, and from animal fats.

(3) MIXTURE OR BIODIESEL NOT USED AS A FUEL, ETC.—

* * *

(C) PRODUCER CREDIT.—If—

* * *

≫→ *Caution: Code Sec. 40A(d)(3)(C)(ii), below, as amended by P.L. 110-343, applies to fuel produced, and sold or used, after December 31, 2008.*

(ii) any person does not use such fuel for a purpose described in *subsection (b)(4)(B)*, then there is hereby imposed on such person a tax equal to 10 cents a gallon for each gallon of such agri-biodiesel.

* * *

(5) LIMITATION TO BIODIESEL WITH CONNECTION TO THE UNITED STATES.—*No credit shall be determined under this section with respect to any biodiesel which is produced outside the United States for use as a fuel outside the United States. For purposes of this paragraph, the term "United States" includes any possession of the United States.*

[CCH Explanation at ¶ 825. Committee Reports at ¶ 10,150 and ¶ 10,160.]

Amendments

• **2008, Energy Improvement and Extension Act of 2008 (P.L. 110-343)**

P.L. 110-343, Division B, § 202(b)(3)(D):

Amended Code Sec. 40A(d)(3)(C)(ii) by striking "subsection (b)(5)(B)" and inserting "subsection (b)(4)(B)". **Effective** for fuel produced, and sold or used, after 12-31-2008.

P.L. 110-343, Division B, § 202(f):

Amended Code Sec. 40A(d)(2) by striking "and mustard seeds" and inserting "mustard seeds, and camelina". **Effective** for fuel produced, and sold or used, after 12-31-2008.

P.L. 110-343, Division B, § 203(b):

Amended Code Sec. 40A(d) by adding at the end a new paragraph (5). **Effective** for claims for credit or payment made on or after 5-15-2008.

(e) DEFINITIONS AND SPECIAL RULES FOR SMALL AGRI-BIODIESEL PRODUCER CREDIT.—For purposes of this section—

* * *

≫→ *Caution: Code Sec. 40A(e)(2)-(3), below, as amended by P.L. 110-343, applies to fuel produced, and sold or used, after December 31, 2008.*

(2) AGGREGATION RULE.—For purposes of the 15,000,000 gallon limitation under *subsection (b)(4)(C)* and the 60,000,000 gallon limitation under paragraph (1), all members of the same controlled group of corporations (within the meaning of section 267(f)) and all persons under common control (within the meaning of section 52(b) but determined by treating an interest of more than 50 percent as a controlling interest) shall be treated as 1 person.

(3) PARTNERSHIP, S CORPORATION, AND OTHER PASS-THRU ENTITIES.—In the case of a partnership, trust, S corporation, or other pass-thru entity, the limitations contained in *subsection (b)(4)(C)* and paragraph (1) shall be applied at the entity level and at the partner or similar level.

* * *

[CCH Explanation at ¶ 825. Committee Reports at ¶ 10,150.]

Amendments

• **2008, Energy Improvement and Extension Act of 2008 (P.L. 110-343)**

P.L. 110-343, Division B, § 202(b)(3)(C):

Amended Code Sec. 40A(e)(2) and (3) by striking "subsection (b)(5)(C)" and inserting "subsection (b)(4)(C)". **Effective** for fuel produced, and sold or used, after 12-31-2008.

(f) RENEWABLE DIESEL.—For purposes of this title—

* * *

⋙→ *Caution: Code Sec. 40A(f)(2), below, as amended by P.L. 110-343, applies to fuel produced, and sold or used, after December 31, 2008.*

(2) EXCEPTION.—*Subsection (b)(4) shall not apply with respect to renewable diesel.*

⋙→ *Caution: Code Sec. 40A(f)(3), below, as amended by P.L. 110-343, Div. B, §202(d)(1)-(2), but prior to amendment by P.L. 110-343, Div. B, §202(c)(1)-(3), applies to fuel produced, and sold or used, on or before December 31, 2008.*

(3) RENEWABLE DIESEL DEFINED.—The term "renewable diesel" means diesel fuel derived from biomass using a thermal depolymerization process which meets—

(A) the registration requirements for fuels and fuel additives established by the Environmental Protection Agency under section 211 of the Clean Air Act (42 U.S.C. 7545), and

(B) the requirements of the American Society of Testing and Materials D975 or D396.

Such term shall not include any liquid with respect to which a credit may be determined under section 40. *Such term does not include any fuel derived from coprocessing biomass with a feedstock which is not biomass. For purposes of this paragraph, the term "biomass" has the meaning given such term by section 45K(c)(3).*

⋙→ *Caution: Code Sec. 40A(f)(3), below, as amended by P.L. 110-343, Div. B, §§202(c)(1)-(3) and 202(d)(1)-(2), applies to fuel produced, and sold or used, after December 31, 2008.*

(3) RENEWABLE DIESEL DEFINED.—The term "renewable diesel" means *liquid fuel* derived from biomass which meets—

(A) the registration requirements for fuels and fuel additives established by the Environmental Protection Agency under section 211 of the Clean Air Act (42 U.S.C. 7545), and

(B) the requirements of the American Society of Testing and Materials D975 or D396, *or other equivalent standard approved by the Secretary.*

Such term shall not include any liquid with respect to which a credit may be determined under section 40. *Such term does not include any fuel derived from coprocessing biomass with a feedstock which is not biomass. For purposes of this paragraph, the term "biomass" has the meaning given such term by section 45K(c)(3).*

⋙→ *Caution: Code Sec. 40A(f)(4), as added by P.L. 110-343, applies to fuel produced, and sold or used, after December 31, 2008.*

(4) CERTAIN AVIATION FUEL.—

(A) IN GENERAL.—*Except as provided in the last 3 sentences of paragraph (3), the term "renewable diesel" shall include fuel derived from biomass which meets the requirements of a Department of Defense specification for military jet fuel or an American Society of Testing and Materials specification for aviation turbine fuel.*

(B) APPLICATION OF MIXTURE CREDITS.—*In the case of fuel which is treated as renewable diesel solely by reason of subparagraph (A), subsection (b)(1) and section 6426(c) shall be applied with respect to such fuel by treating kerosene as though it were diesel fuel.*

[CCH Explanation at ¶825. Committee Reports at ¶10,150.]

Amendments

• **2008, Energy Improvement and Extension Act of 2008 (P.L. 110-343)**

P.L. 110-343, Division B, §202(b)(3)(B):

Amended Code Sec. 40A(f)(2). **Effective** for fuel produced, and sold or used, after 12-31-2008. Prior to amendment, Code Sec. 40A(f)(2) read as follows:

(2) EXCEPTIONS.—

(A) RATE OF CREDIT.—Subsections (b)(1)(A) and (b)(2)(A) shall be applied with respect to renewable diesel by substituting "$1.00" for "50 cents".

(B) NONAPPLICATION OF CERTAIN CREDITS.—Subsections (b)(3) and (b)(5) shall not apply with respect to renewable diesel.

P.L. 110-343, Division B, §202(c)(1)-(3):

Amended Code Sec. 40A(f)(3) by striking "diesel fuel" and inserting "liquid fuel", by striking "using a thermal depolymerization process" before "which meets—", and by inserting ", or other equivalent standard approved by the Secretary" after "D396". **Effective** for fuel produced, and sold or used, after 12-31-2008.

P.L. 110-343, Division B, § 202(d)(1):

Amended Code Sec. 40A(f)(3) by adding at the end two new sentences. **Effective** for fuel produced, and sold or used, after 10-3-2008.

P.L. 110-343, Division B, § 202(d)(2):

Amended Code Sec. 40A(f)(3) by striking "(as defined in section 45K(c)(3))" after "derived from biomass". **Effective** for fuel produced, and sold or used, after 10-3-2008.

P.L. 110-343, Division B, § 202(e):

Amended Code Sec. 40A(f) by adding at the end a new paragraph (4). **Effective** for fuel produced, and sold or used, after 12-31-2008.

(g) TERMINATION.—This section shall not apply to any sale or use after *December 31, 2009.*

[CCH Explanation at ¶ 825. Committee Reports at ¶ 10,150.]

• **2008, Energy Improvement and Extension Act of 2008 (P.L. 110-343)**

P.L. 110-343, Division B, § 202(a):

Amended Code Sec. 40A(g) by striking "December 31, 2008" and inserting "December 31, 2009". **Effective** for fuel produced, and sold or used, after 12-31-2008.

[¶ 5070] CODE SEC. 41. CREDIT FOR INCREASING RESEARCH ACTIVITIES.

* * *

(c) BASE AMOUNT.—

* * *

(5) ELECTION OF ALTERNATIVE SIMPLIFIED CREDIT.—

(A) IN GENERAL.—At the election of the taxpayer, the credit determined under subsection (a)(1) shall be equal to *14 percent (12 percent in the case of taxable years ending before January 1, 2009)* of so much of the qualified research expenses for the taxable year as exceeds 50 percent of the average qualified research expenses for the 3 taxable years preceding the taxable year for which the credit is being determined.

* * *

[CCH Explanation at ¶ 405. Committee Reports at ¶ 10,410.]

Amendments

• **2008, Tax Extenders and Alternative Minimum Tax Relief Act of 2008 (P.L. 110-343)**

P.L. 110-343, Division C, § 301(c):

Amended Code Sec. 41(c)(5)(A) by striking "12 percent" and inserting "14 percent (12 percent in the case of taxable

years ending before January 1, 2009)". **Effective** for tax years beginning after 12-31-2007.

(h) TERMINATION.—

(1) IN GENERAL.—This section shall not apply to any amount paid or incurred—

* * *

(B) after *December 31, 2009.*

(2) TERMINATION OF ALTERNATIVE INCREMENTAL CREDIT.—*No election under subsection (c)(4) shall apply to taxable years beginning after December 31, 2008.*

(2)[(3)] COMPUTATION FOR TAXABLE YEAR IN WHICH CREDIT TERMINATES.—*In the case of any taxable year with respect to which this section applies to a number of days which is less than the total number of days in such taxable year—*

(A) the amount determined under subsection (c)(1)(B) with respect to such taxable year shall be the amount which bears the same ratio to such amount (determined without regard to this paragraph) as the number of days in such taxable year to which this section applies bears to the total number of days in such taxable year, and

(B) for purposes of subsection (c)(5), the average qualified research expenses for the preceding 3 taxable years shall be the amount which bears the same ratio to such average qualified research

expenses (determined without regard to this paragraph) as the number of days in such taxable year to which this section applies bears to the total number of days in such taxable year.

[CCH Explanation at ¶405. Committee Reports at ¶10,410.]

Amendments

• **2008, Tax Extenders and Alternative Minimum Tax Relief Act of 2008 (P.L. 110-343)**

P.L. 110-343, Division C, §301(a)(1):

Amended Code Sec. 41(h)(1)(B) by striking "December 31, 2007" and inserting "December 31, 2009". **Effective** for amounts paid or incurred after 12-31-2007.

P.L. 110-343, Division C, §301(b):

Amended Code Sec. 41(h) by redesignating paragraph (2) as paragraph (3), and by inserting after paragraph (1) a new paragraph (2). **Effective** for tax years beginning after 12-31-2007.

P.L. 110-343, Division C, §301(d):

Amended Code Sec. 41(h)(3) [as redesignated]. **Effective** for tax years beginning after 12-31-2007. Prior to amendment, Code Sec. 41(h)(3) read as follows:

(3) COMPUTATION OF BASE AMOUNT.—In the case of any taxable year with respect to which this section applies to a number of days which is less than the total number of days in such taxable year, the base amount with respect to such taxable year shall be the amount which bears the same ratio to the base amount for such year (determined without regard to this paragraph) as the number of days in such taxable year to which this section applies bears to the total number of days in such taxable year.

[¶5075] CODE SEC. 45. ELECTRICITY PRODUCED FROM CERTAIN RENEWABLE RESOURCES, etc. [sic]

* * *

(b) LIMITATIONS AND ADJUSTMENTS.—

* * *

(2) CREDIT AND PHASEOUT ADJUSTMENT BASED ON INFLATION.—The 1.5 cent amount in subsection (a), the 8 cent amount in paragraph (1), the $4.375 amount in subsection (e)(8)(A), *the $3 amount in subsection (e)(8)(D)(ii)(I),* and in subsection (e)(8)(B)(i) the reference price of fuel used as a feedstock (within the meaning of subsection (c)(7)(A)) in 2002 shall each be adjusted by multiplying such amount by the inflation adjustment factor for the calendar year in which the sale occurs. If any amount as increased under the preceding sentence is not a multiple of 0.1 cent, such amount shall be rounded to the nearest multiple of 0.1 cent.

* * *

(4) CREDIT RATE AND PERIOD FOR ELECTRICITY PRODUCED AND SOLD FROM CERTAIN FACILITIES.—

(A) CREDIT RATE.—In the case of electricity produced and sold in any calendar year after 2003 at any qualified facility described in paragraph (3), (5), (6), (7), *(9), or (11)* of subsection (d), the amount in effect under subsection (a)(1) for such calendar year (determined before the application of the last sentence of paragraph (2) of this subsection) shall be reduced by one-half.

* * *

[CCH Explanation at ¶525.]

Amendments

• **2008, Energy Improvement and Extension Act of 2008 (P.L. 110-343)**

P.L. 110-343, Division B, §102(d):

Amended Code Sec. 45(b)(4)(A) by striking "or (9)" and inserting "(9), or (11)". **Effective** for electricity produced and sold after 10-3-2008, in tax years ending after such date.

P.L. 110-343, Division B, §108(b)(2):

Amended Code Sec. 45(b)(2) by inserting "the $3 amount in subsection (e)(8)(D)(ii)(I)," after "subsection (e)(8)(A),". **Effective** for fuel produced or sold after 9-30-2008.

(c) RESOURCES.—For purposes of this section:

(1) IN GENERAL.—The term "qualified energy resources" means—

* * *

(G) municipal solid waste,

(H) qualified hydropower production, *and*

(I) *marine and hydrokinetic renewable energy.*

* * *

(7) REFINED COAL.—

(A) IN GENERAL.—*The term "refined coal" means a fuel—*

(i) *which—*

(I) *is a liquid, gaseous, or solid fuel produced from coal (including lignite) or high carbon fly ash, including such fuel used as a feedstock,*

(II) *is sold by the taxpayer with the reasonable expectation that it will be used for purpose of producing steam, and*

(III) *is certified by the taxpayer as resulting (when used in the production of steam) in a qualified emission reduction.*

≫→ **Caution: Code Sec. 45(c)(7)(A)(i)(IV), below, as added by P.L. 110-343, Div. B, §108(a)(1), was stricken by P.L. 110-343, Div. B, §101(b)(1)(A), applicable to coal produced and sold from facilities placed in service after December 31, 2008.**

(IV) *is produced in such a manner as to result in an increase of at least 50 percent in the market value of the refined coal (excluding any increase caused by materials combined or added during the production process), as compared to the value of the feedstock coal, or*

(ii) *which is steel industry fuel.*

* * *

≫→ **Caution: Code Sec. 45(c)(7)(B), below, as amended by P.L. 110-343, applies to coal produced and sold from facilities placed in service after December 31, 2008.**

(B) QUALIFIED EMISSION REDUCTION.—The term "qualified emission reduction" means a reduction of at least 20 percent of the emissions of nitrogen oxide and *at least 40 percent of the emissions of* either sulfur dioxide or mercury released when burning the refined coal (excluding any dilution caused by materials combined or added during the production process), as compared to the emissions released when burning the feedstock coal or comparable coal predominantly available in the marketplace as of January 1, 2003.

(C) STEEL INDUSTRY FUEL.—

(i) IN GENERAL.—*The term "steel industry fuel" means a fuel which—*

(I) *is produced through a process of liquifying coal waste sludge and distributing it on coal, and*

(II) *is used as a feedstock for the manufacture of coke.*

(ii) COAL WASTE SLUDGE.—*The term "coal waste sludge"' means the tar decanter sludge and related byproducts of the coking process, including such materials that have been stored in ground, in tanks and in lagoons, that have been treated as hazardous wastes under applicable Federal environmental rules absent liquefaction and processing with coal into a feedstock for the manufacture of coke.*

(8) QUALIFIED HYDROPOWER PRODUCTION.—

* * *

≫→ **Caution: Code Sec. 45(c)(8)(C), below, as amended by P.L. 110-343, applies to property originally placed in service after December 31, 2008.**

(C) NONHYDROELECTRIC DAM.—*For purposes of subparagraph (A), a facility is described in this subparagraph if—*

(i) *the hydroelectric project installed on the nonhydroelectric dam is licensed by the Federal Energy Regulatory Commission and meets all other applicable environmental, licensing, and regulatory requirements,*

(ii) *the nonhydroelectric dam was placed in service before the date of the enactment of this paragraph and operated for flood control, navigation, or water supply purposes and did not produce hydroelectric power on the date of the enactment of this paragraph, and*

(iii) *the hydroelectric project is operated so that the water surface elevation at any given location and time that would have occurred in the absence of the hydroelectric project is maintained, subject to any license requirements imposed under applicable law that change the water surface elevation for the purpose of improving environmental quality of the affected waterway.*

The Secretary, in consultation with the Federal Energy Regulatory Commission, shall certify if a hydroelectric project licensed at a nonhydroelectric dam meets the criteria in clause (iii). Nothing in this section shall affect the standards under which the Federal Energy Regulatory Commission issues licenses for and regulates hydropower projects under part I of the Federal Power Act.

* * *

(10) MARINE AND HYDROKINETIC RENEWABLE ENERGY.—

(A) IN GENERAL.—The term "marine and hydrokinetic renewable energy" means energy derived from—

(i) *waves, tides, and currents in oceans, estuaries, and tidal areas,*

(ii) *free flowing water in rivers, lakes, and streams,*

(iii) *free flowing water in an irrigation system, canal, or other man-made channel, including projects that utilize nonmechanical structures to accelerate the flow of water for electric power production purposes, or*

(iv) *differentials in ocean temperature (ocean thermal energy conversion).*

(B) EXCEPTIONS.—Such term shall not include any energy which is derived from any source which utilizes a dam, diversionary structure (except as provided in subparagraph (A)(iii)), or impoundment for electric power production purposes.

[CCH Explanation at ¶ 525. Committee Reports at ¶ 10,040.]

Amendments

• 2008, Energy Improvement and Extension Act of 2008 (P.L. 110-343)

P.L. 110-343, Division B, § 101(b)(1)(A)-(C):

Amended Code Sec. 45(c)(7)(A)(i), as amended by Act Sec. 108, by striking subclause (IV), by adding "and" at the end of subclause (II), and by striking ", and" at the end of subclause (III) and inserting a period. **Effective** for coal produced and sold from facilities placed in service after 12-31-2008. Prior to being stricken, Code Sec. 45(c)(7)(A)(i)(IV) read as follows:

(IV) is produced in such a manner as to result in an increase of at least 50 percent in the market value of the refined coal (excluding any increase caused by materials combined or added during the production process), as compared to the value of the feedstock coal, or

P.L. 110-343, Division B, § 101(b)(2):

Amended Code Sec. 45(c)(7)(B) by inserting "at least 40 percent of the emissions of" after "nitrogen oxide and". **Effective** for coal produced and sold from facilities placed in service after 12-31-2008.

P.L. 110-343, Division B, § 101(e):

Amended Code Sec. 45(c)(8)(C). **Effective** for property originally placed in service after 12-31-2008. Prior to amendment, Code Sec. 45(c)(8)(C) read as follows:

(C) NONHYDROELECTRIC DAM.—For purposes of subparagraph (A), a facility is described in this subparagraph if—

(i) the facility is licensed by the Federal Energy Regulatory Commission and meets all other applicable environmental, licensing, and regulatory requirements,

(ii) the facility was placed in service before the date of the enactment of this paragraph and did not produce hydroelectric power on the date of the enactment of this paragraph, and

(iii) turbines or other generating devices are to be added to the facility after such date to produce hydroelectric power, but only if there is not any enlargement of the diversion structure, or construction or enlargement of a bypass channel, or the impoundment or any withholding of any additional water from the natural stream channel.

P.L. 110-343, Division B, § 102(a):

Amended Code Sec. 45(c)(1) by striking "and" at the end of subparagraph (G), by striking the period at the end of subparagraph (H) and inserting ", and", and by adding at the end a new subparagraph (I). **Effective** for electricity produced and sold after 10-3-2008, in tax years ending after such date.

P.L. 110-343, Division B, § 102(b):

Amended Code Sec. 45(c) by adding at the end a new paragraph (10). **Effective** for electricity produced and sold after 10-3-2008, in tax years ending after such date.

P.L. 110-343, Division B, § 108(a)(1):

Amended Code Sec. 45(c)(7)(A), as amended by this Act. **Effective** for fuel produced and sold after 9-30-2008. Prior to amendment, Code Sec. 45(c)(7)(A) read as follows:

(A) IN GENERAL.—The term "refined coal" means a fuel which—

(i) is a liquid, gaseous, or solid fuel produced from coal (including lignite) or high carbon fly ash, including such fuel used as a feedstock,

(ii) is sold by the taxpayer with the reasonable expectation that it will be used for purpose of producing steam,

(iii) is certified by the taxpayer as resulting (when used in the production of steam) in a qualified emission reduction, and

(iv) is produced in such a manner as to result in an increase of at least 50 percent in the market value of the refined coal (excluding any increase caused by materials combined or added during the production process), as compared to the value of the feedstock coal.

P.L. 110-343, Division B, §108(a)(2):

Amended Code Sec. 45(c)(7) by adding at the end a new subparagraph (C). **Effective** for fuel produced and sold after 9-30-2008.

(d) QUALIFIED FACILITIES.—For purposes of this section:

(1) WIND FACILITY.—In the case of a facility using wind to produce electricity, the term "qualified facility" means any facility owned by the taxpayer which is originally placed in service after December 31, 1993, and before *January 1, 2010. Such term shall not include any facility with respect to which any qualified small wind energy property expenditure (as defined in subsection (d)(4) of section 25D) is taken into account in determining the credit under such section.*

(2) CLOSED-LOOP BIOMASS FACILITY.—

(A) IN GENERAL.—In the case of a facility using closed-loop biomass to produce electricity, the term "qualified facility" means any facility—

(i) owned by the taxpayer which is originally placed in service after December 31, 1992, and before *January 1, 2011,* or

(ii) owned by the taxpayer which before *January 1, 2011,* is originally placed in service and modified to use closed-loop biomass to co-fire with coal, with other biomass, or with both, but only if the modification is approved under the Biomass Power for Rural Development Programs or is part of a pilot project of the Commodity Credit Corporation as described in 65 Fed. Reg. 63052.

(B) EXPANSION OF FACILITY.—Such term shall include a new unit placed in service after the date of the enactment of this subparagraph in connection with a facility described in subparagraph (A)(i), but only to the extent of the increased amount of electricity produced at the facility by reason of such new unit.

(C) SPECIAL RULES.—In the case of a qualified facility described in subparagraph (A)(ii)—

(i) the 10-year period referred to in subsection (a) shall be treated as beginning no earlier than the date of the enactment of this clause, and

(ii) if the owner of such facility is not the producer of the electricity, the person eligible for the credit allowable under subsection (a) shall be the lessee or the operator of such facility.

(3) OPEN-LOOP BIOMASS FACILITIES.—

(A) IN GENERAL.—In the case of a facility using open-loop biomass to produce electricity, the term "qualified facility" means any facility owned by the taxpayer which—

(i) in the case of a facility using agricultural livestock waste nutrients—

(I) is originally placed in service after the date of the enactment of this subclause and before *January 1, 2011,* and

* * *

(ii) in the case of any other facility, is originally placed in service before *January 1, 2011.*

(B) EXPANSION OF FACILITY.—Such term shall include a new unit placed in service after the date of the enactment of this subparagraph in connection with a facility described in subparagraph (A), but only to the extent of the increased amount of electricity produced at the facility by reason of such new unit.

(C) CREDIT ELIGIBILITY.—In the case of any facility described in subparagraph (A), if the owner of such facility is not the producer of the electricity, the person eligible for the credit allowable under subsection (a) shall be the lessee or the operator of such facility.

(4) GEOTHERMAL OR SOLAR ENERGY FACILITY.—In the case of a facility using geothermal or solar energy to produce electricity, the term "qualified facility" means any facility owned by the

taxpayer which is originally placed in service after the date of the enactment of this paragraph and before *January 1, 2011* (January 1, 2006, in the case of a facility using solar energy). Such term shall not include any property described in section 48(a)(3) the basis of which is taken into account by the taxpayer for purposes of determining the energy credit under section 48.

(5) SMALL IRRIGATION POWER FACILITY.—In the case of a facility using small irrigation power to produce electricity, the term "qualified facility" means any facility owned by the taxpayer which is originally placed in service after the date of the enactment of this paragraph and before *January 1, 2011.*

(6) LANDFILL GAS FACILITIES.—In the case of a facility producing electricity from gas derived from the biodegradation of municipal solid waste, the term "qualified facility" means any facility owned by the taxpayer which is originally placed in service after the date of the enactment of this paragraph and before *January 1, 2011.*

(7) TRASH FACILITIES.—In the case of a *facility (other than a facility described in paragraph (6)) which uses* municipal solid waste to produce electricity, the term "qualified facility" means any facility owned by the taxpayer which is originally placed in service after the date of the enactment of this paragraph and before *January 1, 2011.* Such term shall include a new unit placed in service in connection with a facility placed in service on or before the date of the enactment of this paragraph, but only to the extent of the increased amount of electricity produced at the facility by reason of such new unit.

(8) REFINED COAL PRODUCTION FACILITY.—In the case of a facility that produces refined coal, the term "refined coal production facility" means—

(A) with respect to a facility producing steel industry fuel, any facility (or any modification to a facility) which is placed in service before January 1, 2010, and

(B) with respect to any other facility producing refined coal, any facility placed in service after the date of the enactment of the American Jobs Creation Act of 2004 and before January 1, 2010.

(9) QUALIFIED HYDROPOWER FACILITY.—In the case of a facility producing qualified hydroelectric production described in subsection (c)(8), the term "qualified facility" means—

(A) in the case of any facility producing incremental hydropower production, such facility but only to the extent of its incremental hydropower production attributable to efficiency improvements or additions to capacity described in subsection (c)(8)(B) placed in service after the date of the enactment of this paragraph and before *January 1, 2011,* and

(B) any other facility placed in service after the date of the enactment of this paragraph and before *January 1, 2011.*

* * *

(11) MARINE AND HYDROKINETIC RENEWABLE ENERGY FACILITIES.—In the case of a facility producing electricity from marine and hydrokinetic renewable energy, the term "qualified facility" means any facility owned by the taxpayer—

(A) which has a nameplate capacity rating of at least 150 kilowatts, and

(B) which is originally placed in service on or after the date of the enactment of this paragraph and before January 1, 2012.

[CCH Explanations at ¶510 and ¶525. Committee Reports at ¶10,040 and ¶10,060.]

Amendments

• 2008, Energy Improvement and Extension Act of 2008 (P.L. 110-343)

P.L. 110-343, Division B, §101(a)(1):

Amended Code Sec. 45(d)(1) and (8) by striking "January 1, 2009" and inserting "January 1, 2010". **Effective** for property originally placed in service after 12-31-2008.

P.L. 110-343, Division B, §101(a)(2)(A)-(G):

Amended Code Sec. 45(d) by striking "January 1, 2009" and inserting "January 1, 2011" in clauses (i) and (ii) of

paragraph (2)(A), clauses (i)(I) and (ii) of paragraph (3)(A), paragraphs (4), (5), (6), and (7), and subparagraphs (A) and (B) of paragraph (9). **Effective** for property originally placed in service after 12-31-2008.

P.L. 110-343, Division B, §101(c)(1)-(2):

Amended Code Sec. 45(d)(7) by striking "facility which burns" and inserting "facility (other than a facility described in paragraph (6)) which uses", and by striking "COMBUSTION" following "TRASH" in the heading. **Effective** for electricity produced and sold after 10-3-2008.

P.L. 110-343, Division B, § 101(d)(1):

Amended Code Sec. 45(d)(3) by redesignating subparagraph (B) as subparagraph (C) and by inserting after subparagraph (A) a new subparagraph (B). **Effective** for property placed in service after 10-3-2008.

P.L. 110-343, Division B, § 101(d)(2):

Amended Code Sec. 45(d)(2) by redesignating subparagraph (B) as subparagraph (C) and inserting after subparagraph (A) a new subparagraph (B). **Effective** for property placed in service after 10-3-2008.

P.L. 110-343, Division B, § 102(c):

Amended Code Sec. 45(d) by adding at the end a new paragraph (11). **Effective** for electricity produced and sold after 10-3-2008, in tax years ending after such date.

P.L. 110-343, Division B, § 102(e):

Amended Code Sec. 45(d)(5), as amended by Act Sec. 101, by striking "January 1, 2012" and inserting "the date of the enactment of paragraph (11)". **Effective** for electricity produced and sold after 10-3-2008, in tax years ending after such date. [This amendment cannot be made because the text "January 1, 2012" does not exist. —CCH.]

P.L. 110-343, Division B, § 106(c)(3)(B):

Amended Code Sec. 45(d)(1) by adding at the end a new sentence. **Effective** for tax years beginning after 12-31-2007.

P.L. 110-343, Division B, § 108(c):

Amended Code Sec. 45(d)(8), as amended by this Act. **Effective** for fuel produced and sold after 9-30-2008. Prior to amendment, Code Sec. 45(d)(8) read as follows:

(8) REFINED COAL PRODUCTION FACILITY.—In the case of a facility that produces refined coal, the term "refined coal production facility" means a facility which is placed in service after the date of the enactment of this paragraph and before January 1, 2010.

(e) DEFINITIONS AND SPECIAL RULES.—For purposes of this section—

* * *

(8) REFINED COAL PRODUCTION FACILITIES.—

* * *

(D) SPECIAL RULE FOR STEEL INDUSTRY FUEL.—

(i) IN GENERAL.—*In the case of a taxpayer who produces steel industry fuel—*

(I) *this paragraph shall be applied separately with respect to steel industry fuel and other refined coal, and*

(II) *in applying this paragraph to steel industry fuel, the modifications in clause (ii) shall apply.*

(ii) MODIFICATIONS.—

(I) CREDIT AMOUNT.—*Subparagraph (A) shall be applied by substituting*

"*$2 per barrel-of-oil equivalent" for "$4.375 per ton".*

(II) CREDIT PERIOD.—*In lieu of the 10-year period referred to in clauses (i) and (ii)(II) of subparagraph (A), the credit period shall be the period beginning on the later of the date such facility was originally placed in service, the date the modifications described in clause (iii) were placed in service, or October 1, 2008, and ending on the later of December 31, 2009, or the date which is 1 year after the date such facility or the modifications described in clause (iii) were placed in service.*

(III) NO PHASEOUT.—*Subparagraph (B) shall not apply.*

(iii) MODIFICATIONS.—*The modifications described in this clause are modifications to an existing facility which allow such facility to produce steel industry fuel.*

(iv) BARREL-OF-OIL EQUIVALENT.—*For purposes of this subparagraph, a barrel-of-oil equivalent is the amount of steel industry fuel that has a Btu content of 5,800,000 Btus.*

(9) COORDINATION WITH CREDIT FOR PRODUCING FUEL FROM A NONCONVENTIONAL SOURCE.—

* * *

(B) REFINED COAL FACILITIES.—

(i) IN GENERAL.—*The term* "refined coal production facility" shall not include any facility the production from which is allowed as a credit under section 45K for the taxable year or any prior taxable year (or under section 29, as in effect on the day before the date of enactment of the Energy Tax Incentives Act of 2005, for any prior taxable year).

(ii) EXCEPTION FOR STEEL INDUSTRY COAL.—*In the case of a facility producing steel industry fuel, clause (i) shall not apply to so much of the refined coal produced at such facility as is steel industry fuel.*

* * *

[CCH Explanation at ¶ 525.]

Amendments

• **2008, Energy Improvement and Extension Act of 2008 (P.L. 110-343)**

P.L. 110-343, Division B, § 108(b)(1):

Amended Code Sec. 45(e)(8) by adding at the end a new subparagraph (D). **Effective** for fuel produced and sold after 9-30-2008.

P.L. 110-343, Division B, § 108(d)(1)(A)-(B):

Amended Code Sec. 45(e)(9)(B) by striking "The term" and inserting

"(i) IN GENERAL.—The term"

and by adding at the end a new clause (ii). **Effective** for fuel produced and sold after 9-30-2008.

[¶ 5080] CODE SEC. 45A. INDIAN EMPLOYMENT CREDIT.

* * *

(f) TERMINATION.—This section shall not apply to taxable years beginning after *December 31, 2009.*

[CCH Explanation at ¶ 425. Committee Reports at ¶ 10,520.]

Amendments

• **2008, Tax Extenders and Alternative Minimum Tax Relief Act of 2008 (P.L. 110-343)**

P.L. 110-343, Division C, § 314(a):

Amended Code Sec. 45A(f) by striking "December 31, 2007" and inserting "December 31, 2009". **Effective** for tax years beginning after 12-31-2007.

[¶ 5085] CODE SEC. 45C. CLINICAL TESTING EXPENSES FOR CERTAIN DRUGS FOR RARE DISEASES OR CONDITIONS.

* * *

(b) QUALIFIED CLINICAL TESTING EXPENSES.—For purposes of this section—

(1) QUALIFIED CLINICAL TESTING EXPENSES.—

* * *

(D) SPECIAL RULE.—For purposes of this paragraph, section 41 shall be deemed to remain in effect for periods after June 30, 1995, and before July 1, 1996, and periods *after December 31, 2009.*

* * *

[CCH Explanation at ¶ 405. Committee Reports at ¶ 10,410.]

Amendments

• **2008, Tax Extenders and Alternative Minimum Tax Relief Act of 2008 (P.L. 110-343)**

P.L. 110-343, Division C, § 301(a)(2):

Amended Code Sec. 45C(b)(1)(D) by striking "after December 31, 2007" and inserting "after December 31, 2009". **Effective** for amounts paid or incurred after 12-31-2007.

[¶ 5090] CODE SEC. 45D. NEW MARKETS TAX CREDIT.

* * *

(f) NATIONAL LIMITATION ON AMOUNT OF INVESTMENTS DESIGNATED.—

(1) IN GENERAL.—There is a new markets tax credit limitation for each calendar year. Such limitation is—

* * *

(D) $3,500,000,000 for 2006, 2007, *2008, and 2009.*

* * *

[CCH Explanation at ¶410. Committee Reports at ¶10,420.]

Amendments

• 2008, Tax Extenders and Alternative Minimum Tax Relief Act of 2008 (P.L. 110-343)

P.L. 110-343, Division C, §302:

Amended Code Sec. 45D(f)(1)(D) by striking "and 2008" and inserting "2008, and 2009". **Effective** 10-3-2008.

[¶5095] CODE SEC. 45G. RAILROAD TRACK MAINTENANCE CREDIT.

* * *

(f) APPLICATION OF SECTION.—This section shall apply to qualified railroad track maintenance expenditures paid or incurred during taxable years beginning after December 31, 2004, and before *January 1, 2010.*

[CCH Explanation at ¶415. Committee Reports at ¶10,540.]

Amendments

• 2008, Tax Extenders and Alternative Minimum Tax Relief Act of 2008 (P.L. 110-343)

P.L. 110-343, Division C, §316(a):

Amended Code Sec. 45G(f) by striking "January 1, 2008" and inserting "January 1, 2010". **Effective** for expenditures paid or incurred during tax years beginning after 12-31-2007.

[¶5100] CODE SEC. 45K. CREDIT FOR PRODUCING FUEL FROM A NONCONVENTIONAL SOURCE.

* * *

(g) EXTENSION FOR FACILITIES PRODUCING COKE OR COKE GAS.—Notwithstanding subsection (e)—

* * *

(2) SPECIAL RULES.—In determining the amount of credit allowable under this section solely by reason of this subsection—

* * *

(E) *COORDINATION WITH SECTION 45.—No credit shall be allowed with respect to any qualified fuel which is steel industry fuel (as defined in section 45(c)(7)) if a credit is allowed to the taxpayer for such fuel under section 45.*

[CCH Explanation at ¶525.]

Amendments

• 2008, Energy Improvement and Extension Act of 2008 (P.L. 110-343)

P.L. 110-343, Division B, §108(d)(2):

Amended Code Sec. 45K(g)(2) by adding at the end a new subparagraph (E). **Effective** for fuel produced or sold after 9-30-2008.

[¶5105] CODE SEC. 45L. NEW ENERGY EFFICIENT HOME CREDIT.

* * *

(g) TERMINATION.—This section shall not apply to any qualified new energy efficient home acquired after *December 31, 2009.*

[CCH Explanation at ¶535.]

Amendments

• 2008, Energy Improvement and Extension Act of 2008 (P.L. 110-343)

P.L. 110-343, Division B, §304:

Amended Code Sec. 45L(g) by striking "December 31, 2008" and inserting "December 31, 2009". **Effective** 10-3-2008.

[¶5110] CODE SEC. 45M. ENERGY EFFICIENT APPLIANCE CREDIT.

* * *

(b) *APPLICABLE AMOUNT.—For purposes of subsection (a)—*

(1) *DISHWASHERS.—The applicable amount is—*

(A) *$45 in the case of a dishwasher which is manufactured in calendar year 2008 or 2009 and which uses no more than 324 kilowatt hours per year and 5.8 gallons per cycle, and*

(B) *$75 in the case of a dishwasher which is manufactured in calendar year 2008, 2009, or 2010 and which uses no more than 307 kilowatt hours per year and 5.0 gallons per cycle (5.5 gallons per cycle for dishwashers designed for greater than 12 place settings).*

(2) *CLOTHES WASHERS.—The applicable amount is—*

(A) *$75 in the case of a residential top-loading clothes washer manufactured in calendar year 2008 which meets or exceeds a 1.72 modified energy factor and does not exceed a 8.0 water consumption factor,*

(B) *$125 in the case of a residential top-loading clothes washer manufactured in calendar year 2008 or 2009 which meets or exceeds a 1.8 modified energy factor and does not exceed a 7.5 water consumption factor,*

(C) *$150 in the case of a residential or commercial clothes washer manufactured in calendar year 2008, 2009, or 2010 which meets or exceeds 2.0 modified energy factor and does not exceed a 6.0 water consumption factor, and*

(D) *$250 in the case of a residential or commercial clothes washer manufactured in calendar year 2008, 2009, or 2010 which meets or exceeds 2.2 modified energy factor and does not exceed a 4.5 water consumption factor.*

(3) *REFRIGERATORS.—The applicable amount is—*

(A) *$50 in the case of a refrigerator which is manufactured in calendar year 2008, and consumes at least 20 percent but not more than 22.9 percent less kilowatt hours per year than the 2001 energy conservation standards,*

(B) *$75 in the case of a refrigerator which is manufactured in calendar year 2008 or 2009, and consumes at least 23 percent but no more than 24.9 percent less kilowatt hours per year than the 2001 energy conservation standards,*

(C) *$100 in the case of a refrigerator which is manufactured in calendar year 2008, 2009, or 2010, and consumes at least 25 percent but not more than 29.9 percent less kilowatt hours per year than the 2001 energy conservation standards, and*

(D) *$200 in the case of a refrigerator manufactured in calendar year 2008, 2009, or 2010 and which consumes at least 30 percent less energy than the 2001 energy conservation standards.*

[CCH Explanation at ¶540. Committee Reports at ¶10,230.]

Amendments

• 2008, Energy Improvement and Extension Act of 2008 (P.L. 110-343)

P.L. 110-343, Division B, §305(a):

Amended Code Sec. 45M(b). **Effective** for appliances produced after 12-31-2007. Prior to amendment, Code Sec. 45M(b) read as follows:

(b) APPLICABLE AMOUNT.—

(1) IN GENERAL.—For purposes of subsection (a)—

(A) DISHWASHERS.—The applicable amount is the energy savings amount in the case of a dishwasher which—

(i) is manufactured in calendar year 2006 or 2007, and

(ii) meets the requirements of the Energy Star program which are in effect for dishwashers in 2007.

(B) CLOTHES WASHERS.—The applicable amount is $100 in the case of a clothes washer which—

(i) is manufactured in calendar year 2006 or 2007, and

(ii) meets the requirements of the Energy Star program which are in effect for clothes washers in 2007.

(C) REFRIGERATORS.—

(i) 15 PERCENT SAVINGS.—The applicable amount is $75 in the case of a refrigerator which—

(I) is manufactured in calendar year 2006, and

(II) consumes at least 15 percent but not more than 20 percent less kilowatt hours per year than the 2001 energy conservation standards.

(ii) 20 PERCENT SAVINGS.—The applicable amount is $125 in the case of a refrigerator which—

(I) is manufactured in calendar year 2006 or 2007, and

(II) consumes at least 20 percent but not more than 25 percent less kilowatt hours per year than the 2001 energy conservation standards.

(iii) 25 PERCENT SAVINGS.—The applicable amount is $175 in the case of a refrigerator which—

(I) is manufactured in calendar year 2006 or 2007, and

(II) consumes at least 25 percent less kilowatt hours per year than the 2001 energy conservation standards.

(2) ENERGY SAVINGS AMOUNT.—For purposes of paragraph (1)(A)—

(A) IN GENERAL.—The energy savings amount is the lesser of—

(i) the product of—

(I) $3, and

(II) 100 multiplied by the energy savings percentage, or

(ii) $100.

(B) ENERGY SAVINGS PERCENTAGE.—For purposes of subparagraph (A), the energy savings percentage is the ratio of—

(i) the EF required by the Energy Star program for dishwashers in 2007 minus the EF required by the Energy Star program for dishwashers in 2005, to

(ii) the EF required by the Energy Star program for dishwashers in 2007.

(c) ELIGIBLE PRODUCTION.—*The eligible* production in a calendar year with respect to each type of energy efficient appliance is the excess of—

(1) the number of appliances of such type which are produced by the taxpayer in the United States during such calendar year, over

(2) the average number of appliances of such type which were produced by the taxpayer (or any predecessor) in the United States during the preceding *2-calendar year* period.

[CCH Explanation at ¶ 540. Committee Reports at ¶ 10,230.]

Amendments

● **2008, Energy Improvement and Extension Act of 2008 (P.L. 110-343)**

P.L. 110-343, Division B, § 305(b)(1)(A)-(D):

Amended Code Sec. 45M(c) by striking paragraph (2), by striking "(1) IN GENERAL" and all that follows through "the eligible" and inserting "The eligible", by moving the text of such subsection in line with the subsection heading, and by redesignating subparagraphs (A) and (B) as paragraphs (1) and (2), respectively, and by moving such paragraphs 2 ems to the left. **Effective** for appliances produced after 12-31-2007. Prior to amendment, Code Sec. 45M(c) read as follows:

(c) ELIGIBLE PRODUCTION.—

(1) IN GENERAL.—Except as provided in paragraphs [sic](2), the eligible production in a calendar year with respect to each type of energy efficient appliance is the excess of—

(A) the number of appliances of such type which are produced by the taxpayer in the United States during such calendar year, over

(B) the average number of appliances of such type which were produced by the taxpayer (or any predecessor) in the United States during the preceding 3-calendar year period.

(2) SPECIAL RULE FOR REFRIGERATORS.—The eligible production in a calendar year with respect to each type of refrigerator described in subsection (b)(1)(C) is the excess of—

(A) the number of appliances of such type which are produced by the taxpayer in the United States during such calendar year, over

(B) 110 percent of the average number of appliances of such type which were produced by the taxpayer (or any predecessor) in the United States during the preceding 3-calendar year period.

P.L. 110-343, Division B, § 305(b)(2):

Amended Code Sec. 45M(c)(2), as amended by Act Sec. 305(b)(1), by striking "3-calendar year" and inserting "2-calendar year". **Effective** for appliances produced after 12-31-2007.

(d) TYPES OF ENERGY EFFICIENT APPLIANCE.—*For purposes of this section, the types of energy efficient appliances are—*

(1) dishwashers described in subsection (b)(1),

(2) clothes washers described in subsection (b)(2), and

(3) refrigerators described in subsection (b)(3).

[CCH Explanation at ¶ 540. Committee Reports at ¶ 10,230.]

Amendments

• **2008, Energy Improvement and Extension Act of 2008 (P.L. 110-343)**

P.L. 110-343, Division B, § 305(c):

Amended Code Sec. 45M(d). **Effective** for appliances produced after 12-31-2007. Prior to amendment, Code Sec. 45M(d) read as follows:

(d) TYPES OF ENERGY EFFICIENT APPLIANCE.—For purposes of this section, the types of energy efficient appliances are—

(1) dishwashers described in subsection (b)(1)(A),

(2) clothes washers described in subsection (b)(1)(B),

(3) refrigerators described in subsection (b)(1)(C)(i),

(4) refrigerators described in subsection (b)(1)(C)(ii), and

(5) refrigerators described in subsection (b)(1)(C)(iii).

(e) LIMITATIONS.—

(1) AGGREGATE CREDIT AMOUNT ALLOWED.—The aggregate amount of credit allowed under subsection (a) with respect to a taxpayer for any taxable year shall not exceed $75,000,000 reduced by the amount of the credit allowed under subsection (a) to the taxpayer (or any predecessor) for all prior taxable years beginning after December 31, 2007.

(2) AMOUNT ALLOWED FOR CERTAIN REFRIGERATORS AND CLOTHES WASHERS.—Refrigerators described in subsection (b)(3)(D) and clothes washers described in subsection (b)(2)(D) shall not be taken into account under paragraph (1).

* * *

[CCH Explanation at ¶ 540. Committee Reports at ¶ 10,230.]

Amendments

• **2008, Energy Improvement and Extension Act of 2008 (P.L. 110-343)**

P.L. 110-343, Division B, § 305(d)(1):

Amended Code Sec. 45M(e)(1). **Effective** for appliances produced after 12-31-2007. Prior to amendment, Code Sec. 45M(e)(1) read as follows:

(1) AGGREGATE CREDIT AMOUNT ALLOWED.—The aggregate amount of credit allowed under subsection (a) with respect to a taxpayer for any taxable year shall not exceed $75,000,000 reduced by the amount of the credit allowed under subsection (a) to the taxpayer (or any predecessor) for all prior taxable years.

P.L. 110-343, Division B, § 305(d)(2):

Amended Code Sec. 45M(e)(2). **Effective** for appliances produced after 12-31-2007. Prior to amendment, Code Sec. 45M(e)(2) read as follows:

(2) AMOUNT ALLOWED FOR 15 PERCENT SAVINGS REFRIGERATORS.—In the case of refrigerators described in subsection (b)(1)(C)(i), the aggregate amount of the credit allowed under subsection (a) with respect to a taxpayer for any taxable year shall not exceed $20,000,000.

(f) DEFINITIONS.—For purposes of this section—

(1) QUALIFIED ENERGY EFFICIENT APPLIANCE.—The term "qualified energy efficient appliance" means—

(A) any dishwasher described in subsection (b)(1),

(B) any clothes washer described in subsection (b)(2), and

(C) any refrigerator described in subsection (b)(3).

* * *

(3) CLOTHES WASHER.—The term "clothes washer" means a residential model clothes washer, including a *commercial* residential style coin operated washer.

(4) TOP-LOADING CLOTHES WASHER.—The term "top-loading clothes washer" means a clothes washer which has the clothes container compartment access located on the top of the machine and which operates on a vertical axis.

(5) REFRIGERATOR.—The term "refrigerator" means a residential model automatic defrost refrigerator-freezer which has an internal volume of at least 16.5 cubic feet.

(6) MODIFIED ENERGY FACTOR.—The term "modified energy factor" means the modified energy factor established by the Department of Energy for compliance with the Federal energy conservation standard.

(7) PRODUCED.—The term "produced" includes manufactured.

(8) 2001 ENERGY CONSERVATION STANDARD.—The term "2001 energy conservation standard" means the energy conservation standards promulgated by the Department of Energy and effective July 1, 2001.

(9) GALLONS PER CYCLE.—The term "gallons per cycle" means, with respect to a dishwasher, the amount of water, expressed in gallons, required to complete a normal cycle of a dishwasher.

(10) WATER CONSUMPTION FACTOR.—The term "water consumption factor" means, with respect to a clothes washer, the quotient of the total weighted per-cycle water consumption divided by the cubic foot (or liter) capacity of the clothes washer.

* * *

[CCH Explanation at ¶540. Committee Reports at ¶10,230.]

Amendments

• **2008, Energy Improvement and Extension Act of 2008 (P.L. 110-343)**

P.L. 110-343, Division B, §305(e)(1):

Amended Code Sec. 45M(f)(1). **Effective** for appliances produced after 12-31-2007. Prior to amendment, Code Sec. 45M(f)(1) read as follows:

(1) QUALIFIED ENERGY EFFICIENT APPLIANCE.—The term "qualified energy efficient appliance" means—

(A) any dishwasher described in subsection (b)(1)(A),

(B) any clothes washer described in subsection (b)(1)(B), and

(C) any refrigerator described in subsection (b)(1)(C).

P.L. 110-343, Division B, §305(e)(2):

Amended Code Sec. 45M(f)(3) by inserting "commercial" before "residential" the second place it appears. **Effective** for appliances produced after 12-31-2007.

P.L. 110-343, Division B, §305(e)(3):

Amended Code Sec. 45M(f) by redesignating paragraphs (4), (5), (6), and (7) as paragraphs (5), (6), (7), and (8), respectively, and by inserting after paragraph (3) a new paragraph (4). **Effective** for appliances produced after 12-31-2007.

P.L. 110-343, Division B, §305(e)(4):

Amended Code Sec. 45M(f)(6), as redesignated by Act Sec. 305(e)(3). **Effective** for appliances produced after 12-31-2007. Prior to amendment, Code Sec. 45M(f)(6) read as follows:

(6) EF.—The term "EF" means the energy factor established by the Department of Energy for compliance with the Federal energy conservation standards.

P.L. 110-343, Division B, §305(e)(5):

Amended Code Sec. 45M(f), as amended by Act Sec. 305(e)(3), by adding at the end new paragraphs (9)-(10). **Effective** for appliances produced after 12-31-2007.

[¶5115] CODE SEC. 45N. MINE RESCUE TEAM TRAINING CREDIT.

* * *

(e) TERMINATION.—This section shall not apply to taxable years beginning after *December 31, 2009.*

[CCH Explanation at ¶420.]

Amendments

• **2008, Tax Extenders and Alternative Minimum Tax Relief Act of 2008 (P.L. 110-343)**

P.L. 110-343, Division C, §310:

Amended Code Sec. 45N(e) by striking "December 31, 2008" and inserting "December 31, 2009". **Effective** 10-3-2008.

[¶5120] *CODE SEC. 45Q. CREDIT FOR CARBON DIOXIDE SEQUESTRATION.*

(a) GENERAL RULE.—For purposes of section 38, the carbon dioxide sequestration credit for any taxable year is an amount equal to the sum of—

(1) $20 per metric ton of qualified carbon dioxide which is—

(A) captured by the taxpayer at a qualified facility, and

(B) disposed of by the taxpayer in secure geological storage, and

(2) $10 per metric ton of qualified carbon dioxide which is—

(A) captured by the taxpayer at a qualified facility, and

(B) used by the taxpayer as a tertiary injectant in a qualified enhanced oil or natural gas recovery project.

(b) QUALIFIED CARBON DIOXIDE.—For purposes of this section—

(1) IN GENERAL.—The term "qualified carbon dioxide" means carbon dioxide captured from an industrial source which—

    (A) would otherwise be released into the atmosphere as industrial emission of greenhouse gas, and

    (B) is measured at the source of capture and verified at the point of disposal or injection.

(2) RECYCLED CARBON DIOXIDE.—The term "qualified carbon dioxide" includes the initial deposit of captured carbon dioxide used as a tertiary injectant. Such term does not include carbon dioxide that is re-captured, recycled, and re-injected as part of the enhanced oil and natural gas recovery process.

(c) QUALIFIED FACILITY.—For purposes of this section, the term "qualified facility" means any industrial facility—

    (1) which is owned by the taxpayer,

    (2) at which carbon capture equipment is placed in service, and

    (3) which captures not less than 500,000 metric tons of carbon dioxide during the taxable year.

(d) SPECIAL RULES AND OTHER DEFINITIONS.—For purposes of this section—

    (1) ONLY CARBON DIOXIDE CAPTURED AND DISPOSED OF OR USED WITHIN THE UNITED STATES TAKEN INTO ACCOUNT.—The credit under this section shall apply only with respect to qualified carbon dioxide the capture and disposal or use of which is within—

        (A) the United States (within the meaning of section 638(1)), or

        (B) a possession of the United States (within the meaning of section 638(2)).

    (2) SECURE GEOLOGICAL STORAGE.—The Secretary, in consultation with the Administrator of the Environmental Protection Agency, shall establish regulations for determining adequate security measures for the geological storage of carbon dioxide under subsection (a)(1)(B) such that the carbon dioxide does not escape into the atmosphere. Such term shall include storage at deep saline formations and unminable coal seems under such conditions as the Secretary may determine under such regulations.

    (3) TERTIARY INJECTANT.—The term "tertiary injectant" has the same meaning as when used within section 193(b)(1).

    (4) QUALIFIED ENHANCED OIL OR NATURAL GAS RECOVERY PROJECT.—The term "qualified enhanced oil or natural gas recovery project" has the meaning given the term "qualified enhanced oil recovery project" by section 43(c)(2), by substituting "crude oil or natural gas" for "crude oil" in subparagraph (A)(i) thereof.

    (5) CREDIT ATTRIBUTABLE TO TAXPAYER.—Any credit under this section shall be attributable to the person that captures and physically or contractually ensures the disposal of or the use as a tertiary injectant of the qualified carbon dioxide, except to the extent provided in regulations prescribed by the Secretary.

    (6) RECAPTURE.—The Secretary shall, by regulations, provide for recapturing the benefit of any credit allowable under subsection (a) with respect to any qualified carbon dioxide which ceases to be captured, disposed of, or used as a tertiary injectant in a manner consistent with the requirements of this section.

    (7) INFLATION ADJUSTMENT.—In the case of any taxable year beginning in a calendar year after 2009, there shall be substituted for each dollar amount contained in subsection (a) an amount equal to the product of—

        (A) such dollar amount, multiplied by

        (B) the inflation adjustment factor for such calendar year determined under section 43(b)(3)(B) for such calendar year, determined by substituting "2008" for "1990".

(e) APPLICATION OF SECTION.—The credit under this section shall apply with respect to qualified carbon dioxide before the end of the calendar year in which the Secretary, in consultation with the Administrator of the Environmental Protection Agency, certifies that 75,000,000 metric tons of qualified carbon dioxide have been captured and disposed of or used as a tertiary injectant.

[CCH Explanation at ¶ 555.]

Amendments

● **2008, Energy Improvement and Extension Act of 2008 (P.L. 110-343)**

P.L. 110-343, Division B, § 115(a):

Amended subpart D of part IV of subchapter A of chapter 1 by adding a the end a new Code Sec. 45Q. **Effective** for carbon dioxide captured after 10-3-2008.

[¶ 5125] CODE SEC. 48. ENERGY CREDIT.

(a) ENERGY CREDIT.—

(1) IN GENERAL.—For purposes of section 46, except as provided in *paragraphs (1)(B), (2)(B), (3)(B), and (4)(B)* of subsection (c), the energy credit for any taxable year is the energy percentage of the basis of each energy property placed in service during such taxable year.

(2) ENERGY PERCENTAGE.—

(A) IN GENERAL.—The energy percentage is—

(i) 30 percent in the case of—

* * *

(II) energy property described in paragraph (3)(A)(i) but only with respect to periods ending before *January 1, 2017,*

* * *

(IV) *qualified small wind energy property, and*

* * *

(3) ENERGY PROPERTY.—For purposes of this subpart, the term "energy property" means any property—

(A) which is—

(i) equipment which uses solar energy to generate electricity, to heat or cool (or provide hot water for use in) a structure, or to provide solar process heat, excepting property used to generate energy for the purposes of heating a swimming pool,

(ii) equipment which uses solar energy to illuminate the inside of a structure using fiber-optic distributed sunlight but only with respect to periods ending before *January 1, 2017,*

(iii) equipment used to produce, distribute, or use energy derived from a geothermal deposit (within the meaning of section 613(e)(2)), but only, in the case of electricity generated by geothermal power, up to (but not including) the electrical transmission stage,

(iv) qualified fuel cell property or qualified microturbine property,

(v) *combined heat and power system property,*

(vi) *qualified small wind energy property, or*

(vii) *equipment which uses the ground or ground water as a thermal energy source to heat a structure or as a thermal energy sink to cool a structure, but only with respect to periods ending before January 1, 2017,*

(B)(i) the construction, reconstruction, or erection of which is completed by the taxpayer, or

(ii) which is acquired by the taxpayer if the original use of such property commences with the taxpayer,

(C) with respect to which depreciation (or amortization in lieu of depreciation) is allowable, and

(D) which meets the performance and quality standards (if any) which—

(i) have been prescribed by the Secretary by regulations (after consultation with the Secretary of Energy), and

(ii) are in effect at the time of the acquisition of the property.

Such term shall not include any property which is part of a facility the production from which is allowed as a credit under section 45 for the taxable year or any prior taxable year.

* * *

[CCH Explanation at ¶530. Committee Reports at ¶10,050.]

Amendments

• **2008, Energy Improvement and Extension Act of 2008 (P.L. 110-343)**

P.L. 110-343, Division B, §103(a)(1):

Amended Code Sec. 48(a)(2)(A)(i)(II) and (3)(A)(ii) by striking "January 1, 2009" and inserting "January 1, 2017". **Effective** 10-3-2008.

P.L. 110-343, Division B, §103(c)(1):

Amended Code Sec. 48(a)(3)(A) by striking "or" at the end of clause (iii), by inserting "or" at the end of clause (iv), and by adding at the end a new clause (v). **Effective** for periods after 10-3-2008, in tax years ending after such date, under rules similar to the rules of Code Sec. 48(m) (as in effect on the day before the date of the enactment of the Revenue Reconciliation Act of 1990 (P.L. 101-508)).

P.L. 110-343, Division B, §103(c)(3):

Amended Code Sec. 48(a)(1) by striking "paragraphs (1)(B) and (2)(B)" and inserting "paragraphs (1)(B), (2)(B), and (3)(B)". **Effective** for periods after 10-3-2008, in tax years ending after such date, under rules similar to the rules of Code Sec. 48(m) (as in effect on the day before the date of the enactment of the Revenue Reconciliation Act of 1990 (P.L. 101-508)).

P.L. 110-343, Division B, §103(e)(1):

Amended Code Sec. 48(a)(3) by striking the second sentence thereof. **Effective** for periods after 2-13-2008, in tax years ending after such date, under rules similar to the rules of Code Sec. 48(m) (as in effect on the day before the date of the enactment of the Revenue Reconciliation Act of 1990 (P.L. 101-508)). Prior to being stricken, the second sentence of Code Sec. 48(a)(3) read as follows:

The term "energy property" shall not include any property which is public utility property (as defined in section 46(f)(5) as in effect on the day before the date of the enactment of the Revenue Reconciliation Act of 1990).

P.L. 110-343, Division B, §104(a):

Amended Code Sec. 48(a)(3)(A), as amended by Act Sec. 103, by striking "or" at the end of clause (iv), by adding "or" at the end of clause (v), and by inserting after clause (v) a new clause (vi). **Effective** for periods after 10-3-2008, in tax years ending after such date, under rules similar to the rules of Code Sec. 48(m) (as in effect on the day before the date of the enactment of the Revenue Reconciliation Act of 1990 (P.L. 101-508)).

P.L. 110-343, Division B, §104(b):

Amended Code Sec. 48(a)(2)(A)(i) by striking "and" at the end of subclause (II) and by inserting "or" a new subclause (IV). **Effective** for periods after 10-3-2008, in tax years ending after such date, under rules similar to the rules of Code Sec. 48(m) (as in effect on the day before the date of the enactment of the Revenue Reconciliation Act of 1990 (P.L. 101-508)).

P.L. 110-343, Division B, §104(d):

Amended Code Sec. 48(a)(1), as amended by Act Sec. 103, by striking "paragraphs (1)(B), (2)(B), and (3)(B)" and inserting "paragraphs (1)(B), (2)(B), (3)(B), and (4)(B)". **Effective** for periods after 10-3-2008, in tax years ending after such date, under rules similar to the rules of Code Sec. 48(m) (as in effect on the day before the date of the enactment of the Revenue Reconciliation Act of 1990 (P.L. 101-508)).

P.L. 110-343, Division B, §105(a):

Amended Code Sec. 48(a)(3)(A), as amended by this Act, by striking "or" at the end of clause (v), by inserting "or" at the end of clause (vi), and by adding at the end a new clause (vii). **Effective** for periods after 10-3-2008, in tax years ending after such date, under rules similar to the rules of Code Sec. 48(m) (as in effect on the day before the date of the enactment of the Revenue Reconciliation Act of 1990 (P.L. 101-508)).

(c) DEFINITIONS.—For purposes of this section—

(1) QUALIFIED FUEL CELL PROPERTY.—

(A) IN GENERAL.—The term "qualified fuel cell property" means a fuel cell power plant which—

(i) has a nameplate capacity of at least 0.5 kilowatt of electricity using an electrochemical process, and

(ii) has an electricity-only generation efficiency greater than 30 percent.

(B) LIMITATION.—In the case of qualified fuel cell property placed in service during the taxable year, the credit otherwise determined under subsection (a) for such year with respect to such property shall not exceed an amount equal to *$1,500* for each 0.5 kilowatt of capacity of such property.

(C) FUEL CELL POWER PLANT.—The term "fuel cell power plant" means an integrated system comprised of a fuel cell stack assembly and associated balance of plant components which converts a fuel into electricity using electrochemical means.

(D) TERMINATION.—The term "qualified fuel cell property" shall not include any property for any period after *December 31, 2016.*

(2) QUALIFIED MICROTURBINE PROPERTY.—

(A) IN GENERAL.—The term "qualified microturbine property" means a stationary microturbine power plant which—

(i) has a nameplate capacity of less than 2,000 kilowatts, and

(ii) has an electricity-only generation efficiency of not less than 26 percent at International Standard Organization conditions.

(B) LIMITATION.—In the case of qualified microturbine property placed in service during the taxable year, the credit otherwise determined under subsection (a) for such year with respect to such property shall not exceed an amount equal [to] $200 for each kilowatt of capacity of such property.

(C) STATIONARY MICROTURBINE POWER PLANT.—The term "stationary microturbine power plant" means an integrated system comprised of a gas turbine engine, a combustor, a recuperator or regenerator, a generator or alternator, and associated balance of plant components which converts a fuel into electricity and thermal energy. Such term also includes all secondary components located between the existing infrastructure for fuel delivery and the existing infrastructure for power distribution, including equipment and controls for meeting relevant power standards, such as voltage, frequency, and power factors.

(D) TERMINATION.—The term "qualified microturbine property" shall not include any property for any period after *December 31, 2016.*

(3) COMBINED HEAT AND POWER SYSTEM PROPERTY.—

(A) COMBINED HEAT AND POWER SYSTEM PROPERTY.—The term "combined heat and power system property" means property comprising a system—

(i) which uses the same energy source for the simultaneous or sequential generation of electrical power, mechanical shaft power, or both, in combination with the generation of steam or other forms of useful thermal energy (including heating and cooling applications),

(ii) which produces—

(I) at least 20 percent of its total useful energy in the form of thermal energy which is not used to produce electrical or mechanical power (or combination thereof), and

(II) at least 20 percent of its total useful energy in the form of electrical or mechanical power (or combination thereof),

(iii) the energy efficiency percentage of which exceeds 60 percent, and

(iv) which is placed in service before January 1, 2017.

(B) LIMITATION.—

(i) IN GENERAL.—In the case of combined heat and power system property with an electrical capacity in excess of the applicable capacity placed in service during the taxable year, the credit under subsection (a)(1) (determined without regard to this paragraph) for such year shall be equal to the amount which bears the same ratio to such credit as the applicable capacity bears to the capacity of such property.

(ii) APPLICABLE CAPACITY.—For purposes of clause (i), the term "applicable capacity" means 15 megawatts or a mechanical energy capacity of more than 20,000 horsepower or an equivalent combination of electrical and mechanical energy capacities.

(iii) MAXIMUM CAPACITY.—The term "combined heat and power system property" shall not include any property comprising a system if such system has a capacity in excess of 50 megawatts or a mechanical energy capacity in excess of 67,000 horsepower or an equivalent combination of electrical and mechanical energy capacities.

(C) SPECIAL RULES.—

(i) ENERGY EFFICIENCY PERCENTAGE.—*For purposes of this paragraph, the energy efficiency percentage of a system is the fraction—*

(I) *the numerator of which is the total useful electrical, thermal, and mechanical power produced by the system at normal operating rates, and expected to be consumed in its normal application, and*

(II) *the denominator of which is the lower heating value of the fuel sources for the system.*

(ii) DETERMINATIONS MADE ON BTU BASIS.—*The energy efficiency percentage and the percentages under subparagraph (A)(ii) shall be determined on a Btu basis.*

(iii) INPUT AND OUTPUT PROPERTY NOT INCLUDED.—*The term "combined heat and power system property" does not include property used to transport the energy source to the facility or to distribute energy produced by the facility.*

(D) SYSTEMS USING BIOMASS.—*If a system is designed to use biomass (within the meaning of paragraphs (2) and (3) of section 45(c) without regard to the last sentence of paragraph (3)(A)) for at least 90 percent of the energy source—*

(i) *subparagraph (A)(iii) shall not apply, but*

(ii) *the amount of credit determined under subsection (a) with respect to such system shall not exceed the amount which bears the same ratio to such amount of credit (determined without regard to this subparagraph) as the energy efficiency percentage of such system bears to 60 percent.*

(4) QUALIFIED SMALL WIND ENERGY PROPERTY.—

(A) IN GENERAL.—*The term "qualified small wind energy property" means property which uses a qualifying small wind turbine to generate electricity.*

(B) LIMITATION.—*In the case of qualified small wind energy property placed in service during the taxable year, the credit otherwise determined under subsection (a)(1) for such year with respect to all such property of the taxpayer shall not exceed $4,000.*

(C) QUALIFYING SMALL WIND TURBINE.—*The term "qualifying small wind turbine" means a wind turbine which has a nameplate capacity of not more than 100 kilowatts.*

(D) TERMINATION.—*The term "qualified small wind energy property" shall not include any property for any period after December 31, 2016.*

[CCH Explanation at ¶ 530. Committee Reports at ¶ 10,050.]

Amendments

• **2008, Energy Improvement and Extension Act of 2008 (P.L. 110-343)**

P.L. 110-343, Division B, § 103(a)(2):

Amended Code Sec. 48(c)(1)(E) by striking "December 31, 2008" and inserting "December 31, 2016". **Effective** 10-3-2008.

P.L. 110-343, Division B, § 103(a)(3):

Amended Code Sec. 48(c)(2)(E) by striking "December 31, 2008" and inserting "December 31, 2016". **Effective** 10-3-2008.

P.L. 110-343, Division B, § 103(c)(2)(A)-(B):

Amended Code Sec. 48(c) by striking "QUALIFIED FUEL CELL PROPERTY; QUALIFIED MICROTURBINE PROPERTY" in the heading and inserting "DEFINITIONS", and by adding at the end a new paragraph (3). **Effective** for periods after 10-3-2008, in tax years ending after such date, under rules similar to the rules of Code Sec. 48(m) (as in effect on the day before the date of the enactment of the Revenue Reconciliation Act of 1990 (P.L. 101-508)).

P.L. 110-343, Division B, § 103(d):

Amended Code Sec. 48(c)(1)(B) by striking "$500" and inserting "$1,500". **Effective** for periods after 10-3-2008, in tax years ending after such date, under rules similar to the rules of Code Sec. 48(m) (as in effect on the day before the date of the enactment of the Revenue Reconciliation Act of 1990 (P.L. 101-508)).

P.L. 110-343, Division B, § 103(e)(2)(A):

Amended Code Sec. 48(c)(1) by striking subparagraph (D) and redesignating subparagraph (E) as subparagraph (D). **Effective** for periods after 2-13-2008, in tax years ending after such date, under rules similar to the rules of Code Sec. 48(m) (as in effect on the day before the date of the enactment of the Revenue Reconciliation Act of 1990 (P.L. 101-508)). Prior to being stricken, Code Sec. 48(c)(1)(D) read as follows:

(D) SPECIAL RULE.—The first sentence of the matter in subsection (a)(3) which follows subparagraph (D) thereof shall not apply to qualified fuel cell property which is used predominantly in the trade or business of the furnishing or sale of telephone service, telegraph service by means of domestic telegraph operations, or other telegraph services (other than international telegraph services).

P.L. 110-343, Division B, §103(e)(2)(B):

Amended Code Sec. 48(c)(2) by striking subparagraph (D) and redesignating subparagraph (E) as subparagraph (D). **Effective** for periods after 2-13-2008, in tax years ending after such date, under rules similar to the rules of Code Sec. 48(m) (as in effect on the day before the date of the enactment of the Revenue Reconciliation Act of 1990 (P.L. 101-508)). Prior to being stricken, Code Sec. 48(c)(2)(D) read as follows:

(D) SPECIAL RULE.—The first sentence of the matter in subsection (a)(3) which follows subparagraph (D) thereof shall

not apply to qualified microturbine property which is used predominantly in the trade or business of the furnishing or sale of telephone service, telegraph service by means of domestic telegraph operations, or other telegraph services (other than international telegraph services).

P.L. 110-343, Division B, §104(c):

Amended Code Sec. 48(c), as amended by Act Sec. 103, by adding at the end a new paragraph (4). **Effective** for periods after 10-3-2008, in tax years ending after such date, under rules similar to the rules of Code Sec. 48(m) (as in effect on the day before the date of the enactment of the Revenue Reconciliation Act of 1990 (P.L. 101-508)).

[¶5130] CODE SEC. 48A. QUALIFYING ADVANCED COAL PROJECT CREDIT.

(a) IN GENERAL.—For purposes of section 46, the qualifying advanced coal project credit for any taxable year is an amount equal to—

(1) 20 percent of the qualified investment for such taxable year in the case of projects described in subsection (d)(3)(B)(i),

(2) 15 percent of the qualified investment for such taxable year in the case of projects described in subsection (d)(3)(B)(ii), *and*

(3) *30 percent of the qualified investment for such taxable year in the case of projects described in clause (iii) of subsection (d)(3)(B).*

* * *

[CCH Explanation at ¶545. Committee Reports at ¶10,080.]

Amendments

• **2008, Energy Improvement and Extension Act of 2008 (P.L. 110-343)**

P.L. 110-343, Division B, §111(a):

Amended Code Sec. 48A(a) by striking "and" at the end of paragraph (1), by striking the period at the end of para-

graph (2) and inserting ", and", and by adding at the end a new paragraph (3). **Effective** for credits the application for which is submitted during the period described in Code Sec. 48A(d)(2)(A)(ii) and which are allocated or reallocated after 10-3-2008.

(d) QUALIFYING ADVANCED COAL PROJECT PROGRAM.—

* * *

(2) CERTIFICATION.—

(A) APPLICATION PERIOD.—*Each applicant for certification under this paragraph shall submit an application meeting the requirements of subparagraph (B). An applicant may only submit an application—*

(i) *for an allocation from the dollar amount specified in clause (i) or (ii) of paragraph (3)(B) during the 3-year period beginning on the date the Secretary establishes the program under paragraph (1), and*

(ii) *for an allocation from the dollar amount specified in paragraph (3)(B)(iii) during the 3-year period beginning at the earlier of the termination of the period described in clause (i) or the date prescribed by the Secretary.*

* * *

(3) AGGREGATE CREDITS.—

(A) IN GENERAL.—The aggregate credits allowed under subsection (a) for projects certified by the Secretary under paragraph (2) may not exceed $2,550,000,000.

(B) PARTICULAR PROJECTS.—*Of the dollar amount in subparagraph (A), the Secretary is authorized to certify—*

(i) *$800,000,000 for integrated gasification combined cycle projects the application for which is submitted during the period described in paragraph (2)(A)(i),*

(ii) $500,000,000 for projects which use other advanced coal-based generation technologies the application for which is submitted during the period described in paragraph (2)(A)(i), and

(iii) $1,250,000,000 for advanced coal-based generation technology projects the application for which is submitted during the period described in paragraph (2)(A)(ii).

* * *

(5) DISCLOSURE OF ALLOCATIONS.—The Secretary shall, upon making a certification under this subsection or section 48B(d), publicly disclose the identity of the applicant and the amount of the credit certified with respect to such applicant.

[CCH Explanation at ¶ 545. Committee Reports at ¶ 10,080.]

Amendments

• 2008, Energy Improvement and Extension Act of 2008 (P.L. 110-343)

P.L. 110-343, Division B, § 111(b):

Amended Code Sec. 48A(d)(3)(A) by striking "$1,300,000,000" and inserting "$2,550,000,000". **Effective** for credits the application for which is submitted during the period described in Code Sec. 48A(d)(2)(A)(ii) and which are allocated or reallocated after 10-3-2008.

P.L. 110-343, Division B, § 111(c)(1):

Amended Code Sec. 48A(d)(3)(B). **Effective** for credits the application for which is submitted during the period described in Code Sec. 48A(d)(2)(A)(ii) and which are allocated or reallocated after 10-3-2008. Prior to amendment, Code Sec. 48A(d)(3)(B) read as follows:

(B) PARTICULAR PROJECTS.—Of the dollar amount in subparagraph (A), the Secretary is authorized to certify—

(i) $800,000,000 for integrated gasification combined cycle projects, and

(ii) $500,000,000 for projects which use other advanced coal-based generation technologies.

P.L. 110-343, Division B, § 111(c)(2):

Amended Code Sec. 48A(d)(2)(A). **Effective** for credits the application for which is submitted during the period described in Code Sec. 48A(d)(2)(A)(ii) and which are allocated or reallocated after 10-3-2008. Prior to amendment, Code Sec. 48A(d)(2)(A) read as follows:

(A) APPLICATION PERIOD.—Each applicant for certification under this paragraph shall submit an application meeting the requirements of subparagraph (B). An applicant may only submit an application during the 3-year period beginning on the date the Secretary establishes the program under paragraph (1).

P.L. 110-343, Division B, § 111(d):

Amended Code Sec. 48A(d) by adding at the end a new paragraph (5). **Effective** for certifications made after 10-3-2008.

(e) QUALIFYING ADVANCED COAL PROJECTS.—

(1) REQUIREMENTS.—For purposes of subsection (c)(1), a project shall be considered a qualifying advanced coal project that the Secretary may certify under subsection (d)(2) if the Secretary determines that, at a minimum—

* * *

(E) the applicant provides evidence of ownership or control of a site of sufficient size to allow the proposed project to be constructed and to operate on a long-term basis;

(F) the project will be located in the United States; *and*

(G) in the case of any project the application for which is submitted during the period described in subsection (d)(2)(A)(ii), the project includes equipment which separates and sequesters at least 65 percent (70 percent in the case of an application for reallocated credits under subsection (d)(4)) of such project's total carbon dioxide emissions.

* * *

(3) PRIORITY FOR CERTAIN PROJECTS.—In determining which qualifying advanced coal projects to certify under subsection (d)(2), the Secretary shall—

(A) certify capacity, in accordance with the procedures set forth in subsection (d), in relatively equal amounts to—

(i) projects using bituminous coal as a primary feedstock,

(ii) projects using subbituminous coal as a primary feedstock, and

(iii) projects using lignite as a primary feedstock,

(B) give high priority to projects which include, as determined by the Secretary—

(i) greenhouse gas capture capability,

(ii) increased by-product utilization,

(iii) applicant participants who have a research partnership with an eligible educational institution (as defined in section 529(e)(5)), and

(iv) other benefits, *and*

(C) give highest priority to projects with the greatest separation and sequestration percentage of total carbon dioxide emissions.

* * *

[CCH Explanation at ¶545. Committee Reports at ¶10,080.]

Amendments

• **2008, Energy Improvement and Extension Act of 2008 (P.L. 110-343)**

P.L. 110-343, Division B, §111(c)(3)(A):

Amended Code Sec. 48A(e)(1) by striking "and" at the end of subparagraph (E), by striking the period at the end of subparagraph (F) and inserting "; and", and by adding at the end a new subparagraph (G). **Effective** for credits the application for which is submitted during the period described in Code Sec. 48A(d)(2)(A)(ii) and which are allocated or reallocated after 10-3-2008.

P.L. 110-343, Division B, §111(c)(3)(B):

Amended Code Sec. 48A(e)(3) by striking "and" at the end of subparagraph (A)(iii), by striking the period at the end of subparagraph (B)(iii) and inserting ", and", and by adding at the end a new subparagraph (C). **Effective** for credits the application for which is submitted during the period described in Code Sec. 48A(d)(2)(A)(ii) and which are allocated or reallocated after 10-3-2008.

P.L. 110-343, Division B, §111(c)(4)(A)-(C):

Amended Code Sec. 48A(e)(3)(B), as amended by Act Sec. 111(c)(3)(B), by striking "and" at the end of clause (ii), by redesignating clause (iii) as clause (iv), and by inserting after clause (ii) a new clause (iii). **Effective** for credits the application for which is submitted during the period described in Code Sec. 48A(d)(2)(A)(ii) and which are allocated or reallocated after 10-3-2008.

P.L. 110-343, Division B, §111(c)(5):

Amended Code Sec. 48A(e)(3) by striking "INTEGRATED GASIFICATION COMBINED CYCLE" in the heading and inserting "CERTAIN". **Effective** as if included in the amendment made by §1307(b) of the Energy Tax Incentives Act of 2005 [**effective** for periods after 8-8-2005, under rules similar to the rules of Code Sec. 48(m) (as in effect on the day before the date of the enactment of the Energy Tax Incentives Act of 2005 (P.L. 110-508).—CCH].

(i) RECAPTURE OF CREDIT FOR FAILURE TO SEQUESTER.—The Secretary shall provide for recapturing the benefit of any credit allowable under subsection (a) with respect to any project which fails to attain or maintain the separation and sequestration requirements of subsection (e)(1)(G).

[CCH Explanation at ¶545. Committee Reports at ¶10,080.]

Amendments

• **2008, Energy Improvement and Extension Act of 2008 (P.L. 110-343)**

P.L. 110-343, Division B, §111(c)(3)(C):

Amended Code Sec. 48A by adding at the end a new subsection (i). **Effective** for credits the application for which

is submitted during the period described in Code Sec. 48A(d)(2)(A)(ii) and which are allocated or reallocated after 10-3-2008.

[¶5135] CODE SEC. 48B. QUALIFYING GASIFICATION PROJECT CREDIT.

(a) IN GENERAL.—For purposes of section 46, the qualifying gasification project credit for any taxable year is an amount equal to 20 percent *(30 percent in the case of credits allocated under subsection (d)(1)(B))* of the qualified investment for such taxable year.

* * *

[CCH Explanation at ¶550. Committee Reports at ¶10,090.]

Amendments

• **2008, Energy Improvement and Extension Act of 2008 (P.L. 110-343)**

P.L. 110-343, Division B, §112(a):

Amended Code Sec. 48B(a) by inserting "(30 percent in the case of credits allocated under subsection (d)(1)(B))"

after "20 percent". **Effective** for credits described in Code Sec. 48B(d)(1)(B) which are allocated or reallocated after 10-3-2008.

(c) DEFINITIONS.—For purposes of this section—

* * *

(7) ELIGIBLE ENTITY.—The term "eligible entity" means any person whose application for certification is principally intended for use in a domestic project which employs domestic gasification applications related to—

* * *

(F) forest products,

(G) agriculture, including feedlots and dairy operations, *and*

(H) *transportation grade liquid fuels.*

* * *

[CCH Explanation at ¶ 550. Committee Reports at ¶ 10,090.]

Amendments

• 2008, Energy Improvement and Extension Act of 2008 (P.L. 110-343)

P.L. 110-343, Division B, § 112(e):

Amended Code Sec. 48B(c)(7) by striking "and" at the end of subparagraph (F), by striking the period at the end of subparagraph (G) and inserting ", and", and by adding at the end a new subparagraph (H). **Effective** for credits described in Code Sec. 48B(d)(1)(B) which are allocated or reallocated after 10-3-2008.

(d) QUALIFYING GASIFICATION PROJECT PROGRAM.—

(1) IN GENERAL.—Not later than 180 days after the date of the enactment of this section, the Secretary, in consultation with the Secretary of Energy, shall establish a qualifying gasification project program to consider and award certifications for qualified investment eligible for credits under this section to qualifying gasification project sponsors under this section. The total amounts of credit that may be allocated under the program *shall not exceed—*

(A) *$350,000,000, plus*

(B) *$250,000,000 for qualifying gasification projects that include equipment which separates and sequesters at least 75 percent of such project's total carbon dioxide emissions.*

* * *

(4) SELECTION PRIORITIES.—*In determining which qualifying gasification projects to certify under this section, the Secretary shall—*

(A) *give highest priority to projects with the greatest separation and sequestration percentage of total carbon dioxide emissions, and*

(B) *give high priority to applicant participants who have a research partnership with an eligible educational institution (as defined in section 529(e)(5)).*

* * *

[CCH Explanation at ¶ 550. Committee Reports at ¶ 10,090.]

Amendments

• 2008, Energy Improvement and Extension Act of 2008 (P.L. 110-343)

P.L. 110-343, Division B, § 112(b):

Amended Code Sec. 48B(d)(1) by striking "shall not exceed $350,000,000" and all that follows and inserting "shall not exceed—"and new subparagraphs (A)-(B). **Effective** for credits described in Code Sec. 48B(d)(1)(B) which are allocated or reallocated after 10-3-2008. Prior to amendment, Code Sec. 48B(d)(1) read as follows:

(1) IN GENERAL.—Not later than 180 days after the date of the enactment of this section, the Secretary, in consultation with the Secretary of Energy, shall establish a qualifying gasification project program to consider and award certifications for qualified investment eligible for credits under this section to qualifying gasification project sponsors under this section. The total amounts of credit that may be allocated under the program shall not exceed $350,000,000 under rules similar to the rules of section 48A(d)(4).

P.L. 110-343, Division B, § 112(d):

Amended Code Sec. 48B(d) by adding at the end a new paragraph (4). **Effective** for credits described in Code Sec. 48B(d)(1)(B) which are allocated or reallocated after 10-3-2008.

(f) RECAPTURE OF CREDIT FOR FAILURE TO SEQUESTER.—*The Secretary shall provide for recapturing the benefit of any credit allowable under subsection (a) with respect to any project which fails to attain or maintain the separation and sequestration requirements for such project under subsection (d)(1).*

[CCH Explanation at ¶ 550. Committee Reports at ¶ 10,090.]

Amendments

• **2008, Energy Improvement and Extension Act of 2008 (P.L. 110-343)**

P.L. 110-343, Division B, § 112(c):

Amended Code Sec. 48B by adding at the end a new subsection (f). **Effective** for credits described in Code Sec.

48B(d)(1)(B) which are allocated or reallocated after 10-3-2008.

[¶ 5140] CODE SEC. 53. CREDIT FOR PRIOR YEAR MINIMUM TAX LIABILITY.

* * *

(e) SPECIAL RULE FOR INDIVIDUALS WITH LONG-TERM UNUSED CREDITS.—

* * *

(2) AMT REFUNDABLE CREDIT AMOUNT.—*For purposes of paragraph (1), the term "AMT refundable credit amount" means, with respect to any taxable year, the amount (not in excess of the long-term unused minimum tax credit for such taxable year) equal to the greater of—*

(A) *50 percent of the long-term unused minimum tax credit for such taxable year, or*

(B) *the amount (if any) of the AMT refundable credit amount determined under this paragraph for the taxpayer's preceding taxable year (determined without regard to subsection (f)(2)).*

* * *

[CCH Explanation at ¶ 215. Committee Reports at ¶ 10,320.]

Amendments

• **2008, Tax Extenders and Alternative Minimum Tax Relief Act of 2008 (P.L. 110-343)**

P.L. 110-343, Division C, § 103(a):

Amended Code Sec. 53(e)(2). **Effective** for tax years beginning after 12-31-2007. Prior to amendment, Code Sec. 53(e)(2) read as follows:

(2) AMT REFUNDABLE CREDIT AMOUNT.—For purposes of paragraph (1)—

(A) IN GENERAL.—The term "AMT refundable credit amount" means, with respect to any taxable year, the amount (not in excess of the long-term unused minimum tax credit for such taxable year) equal to the greater of—

(i) $5,000,

(ii) 20 percent of the long-term unused minimum tax credit for such taxable year, or

(iii) the amount (if any) of the AMT refundable credit amount determined under this paragraph for the taxpayer's preceding taxable year (as determined before any reduction under subparagraph (B)).

(B) PHASEOUT OF AMT REFUNDABLE CREDIT AMOUNT.—

(i) IN GENERAL.—In the case of an individual whose adjusted gross income for any taxable year exceeds the threshold amount (within the meaning of section 151(d)(3)(C)), the AMT refundable credit amount determined under subparagraph (A) for such taxable year shall be reduced by the applicable percentage (within the meaning of section 151(d)(3)(B)).

(ii) ADJUSTED GROSS INCOME.—For purposes of clause (i), adjusted gross income shall be determined without regard to sections 911, 931, and 933.

(f) TREATMENT OF CERTAIN UNDERPAYMENTS, INTEREST, AND PENALTIES ATTRIBUTABLE TO THE TREATMENT OF INCENTIVE STOCK OPTIONS.—

(1) ABATEMENT.—*Any underpayment of tax outstanding on the date of the enactment of this subsection which is attributable to the application of section 56(b)(3) for any taxable year ending before January 1, 2008, and any interest or penalty with respect to such underpayment which is outstanding on such date of enactment, is hereby abated. The amount determined under subsection (b)(1) shall not include any tax abated under the preceding sentence.*

(2) INCREASE IN CREDIT FOR CERTAIN INTEREST AND PENALTIES ALREADY PAID.—*The AMT refundable credit amount, and the minimum tax credit determined under subsection (b), for the taxpayer's first 2 taxable years beginning after December 31, 2007, shall each be increased by 50 percent of the aggregate amount of the interest and penalties which were paid by the taxpayer before the date of the enactment of this subsection and which would (but for such payment) have been abated under paragraph (1).*

[CCH Explanation at ¶ 215. Committee Reports at ¶ 10,320.]

Amendments

• **2008, Tax Extenders and Alternative Minimum Tax Relief Act of 2008 (P.L. 110-343)**

P.L. 110-343, Division C, § 103(b):

Amended Code Sec. 53 by adding at the end a new subsection (f). **Effective**, generally, for tax years beginning

after 12-31-2007. Division C, Act Sec. 103(c)(2) provides that Code Sec. 53(f)(1) is effective 10-3-2008.

[¶ 5145] CODE SEC. 54. CREDIT TO HOLDERS OF CLEAN RENEWABLE ENERGY BONDS.

* * *

(m) TERMINATION.—This section shall not apply with respect to any bond issued after *December 31, 2009.*

[CCH Explanation at ¶ 805.]

Amendments

• **2008, Energy Improvement and Extension Act of 2008 (P.L. 110-343)**

P.L. 110-343, Division B, § 107(c):

Amended Code Sec. 54(m) by striking "December 31, 2008" and inserting "December 31, 2009". **Effective** for obligations issued after 10-3-2008.

[¶ 5150] CODE SEC. 54A. CREDIT TO HOLDERS OF QUALIFIED TAX CREDIT BONDS.

* * *

(d) QUALIFIED TAX CREDIT BOND.—For purposes of this section—

    (1) QUALIFIED TAX CREDIT BOND.—The term "qualified tax credit bond" means—

        (A) a qualified forestry conservation bond,

        (B) a new clean renewable energy bond,

        (C) a qualified energy conservation bond, or

        (D) a qualified zone academy bond,

which is part of an issue that meets requirements of paragraphs (2), (3), (4), (5), and (6).

    (2) SPECIAL RULES RELATING TO EXPENDITURES.—

* * *

        (C) QUALIFIED PURPOSE.—For purposes of this paragraph, the term "qualified purpose" means—

            (i) in the case of a qualified forestry conservation bond, a purpose specified in section 54B(e),

            (ii) in the case of a new clean renewable energy bond, a purpose specified in section 54C(a)(1),

            (iii) in the case of a qualified energy conservation bond, a purpose specified in section 54D(a)(1), and

            (iv) in the case of a qualified zone academy bond, a purpose specified in section 54E(a)(1).

* * *

[CCH Explanations at ¶805, ¶810 and ¶815.]

Amendments

• **2008, Energy Improvement and Extension Act of 2008 (P.L. 110-343)**

P.L. 110-343, Division B, §107(b)(1):

Amended Code Sec. 54A(d)(1). **Effective** for obligations issued after 10-3-2008. Prior to amendment, Code Sec. 54A(d)(1) read as follows:

(1) QUALIFIED TAX CREDIT BOND.—The term "qualified tax credit bond" means a qualified forestry conservation bond which is part of an issue that meets the requirements of paragraphs (2), (3), (4), (5), and (6).

P.L. 110-343, Division B, §107(b)(2):

Amended Code Sec. 54A(d)(2)(C). **Effective** for obligations issued after 10-3-2008. Prior to amendment, Code Sec. 54A(d)(2)(C) read as follows:

(C) QUALIFIED PURPOSE.—For purposes of this paragraph, the term "qualified purpose" means a purpose specified in section 54B(e).

P.L. 110-343, Division B, §301(b)(1):

Amended Code Sec. 54A(d)(1), as amended by this Act. **Effective** for obligations issued after 10-3-2008. Prior to amendment, Code Sec. 54A(d)(1) read as follows:

(1) QUALIFIED TAX CREDIT BOND.—The term "qualified tax credit bond" means—

(A) a qualified forestry conservation bond, or

(B) a new clean renewable energy bond,

which is part of an issue that meets requirements of paragraphs (2), (3), (4), (5), and (6).

P.L. 110-343, Division B, §301(b)(2):

Amended Code Sec. 54A(d)(2)(C), as amended by this Act. **Effective** for obligations issued after 10-3-2008. Prior to amendment, Code Sec. 54A(d)(2)(C) read as follows:

(C) QUALIFIED PURPOSE.—For purposes of this paragraph, the term "qualified purpose" means—

(i) in the case of a qualified forestry conservation bond, a purpose specified in section 54B(e), and

(ii) in the case of a new clean renewable energy bond, a purpose specified in section 54C(a)(1).

• **2008, Tax Extenders and Alternative Minimum Tax Relief Act of 2008 (P.L. 110-343)**

P.L. 110-343, Division C, §313(b)(1):

Amended Code Sec. 54A(d)(1), as amended by this Act, by striking "or" at the end of subparagraph (B), by inserting "or" at the end of subparagraph (C), and by inserting after subparagraph (C) a new subparagraph (D). **Effective** for obligations issued after 10-3-2008.

P.L. 110-343, Division C, §313(b)(2):

Amended Code Sec. 54A(d)(2)(C), as amended by this Act, by striking "and" at the end of clause (ii), by striking the period at the end of clause (iii) and inserting ", and", and by adding at the end a new clause (iv). **Effective** for obligations issued after 10-3-2008.

[¶5155] *CODE SEC. 54C. NEW CLEAN RENEWABLE ENERGY BONDS.*

(a) NEW CLEAN RENEWABLE ENERGY BOND.—For purposes of this subpart, the term "new clean renewable energy bond" means any bond issued as part of an issue if—

(1) 100 percent of the available project proceeds of such issue are to be used for capital expenditures incurred by governmental bodies, public power providers, or cooperative electric companies for one or more qualified renewable energy facilities,

(2) the bond is issued by a qualified issuer, and

(3) the issuer designates such bond for purposes of this section.

(b) REDUCED CREDIT AMOUNT.—The annual credit determined under section 54A(b) with respect to any new clean renewable energy bond shall be 70 percent of the amount so determined without regard to this subsection.

(c) LIMITATION ON AMOUNT OF BONDS DESIGNATED.—

(1) IN GENERAL.—The maximum aggregate face amount of bonds which may be designated under subsection (a) by any issuer shall not exceed the limitation amount allocated under this subsection to such issuer.

(2) NATIONAL LIMITATION ON AMOUNT OF BONDS DESIGNATED.—There is a national new clean renewable energy bond limitation of $800,000,000 which shall be allocated by the Secretary as provided in paragraph (3), except that—

(A) not more than 33 ⅓ percent thereof may be allocated to qualified projects of public power providers,

(B) not more than 33 ⅓ percent thereof may be allocated to qualified projects of governmental bodies, and

(C) not more than 33 ⅓ percent thereof may be allocated to qualified projects of cooperative electric companies.

(3) *METHOD OF ALLOCATION.—*

(A) *ALLOCATION AMONG PUBLIC POWER PROVIDERS.—After the Secretary determines the qualified projects of public power providers which are appropriate for receiving an allocation of the national new clean renewable energy bond limitation, the Secretary shall, to the maximum extent practicable, make allocations among such projects in such manner that the amount allocated to each such project bears the same ratio to the cost of such project as the limitation under paragraph (2)(A) bears to the cost of all such projects.*

(B) *ALLOCATION AMONG GOVERNMENTAL BODIES AND COOPERATIVE ELECTRIC COMPANIES.—The Secretary shall make allocations of the amount of the national new clean renewable energy bond limitation described in paragraphs (2)(B) and (2)(C) among qualified projects of governmental bodies and cooperative electric companies, respectively, in such manner as the Secretary determines appropriate.*

(d) *DEFINITIONS.—For purposes of this section—*

(1) *QUALIFIED RENEWABLE ENERGY FACILITY.—The term "qualified renewable energy facility" means a qualified facility (as determined under section 45(d) without regard to paragraphs (8) and (10) thereof and to any placed in service date) owned by a public power provider, a governmental body, or a cooperative electric company.*

(2) *PUBLIC POWER PROVIDER.—The term "public power provider" means a State utility with a service obligation, as such terms are defined in section 217 of the Federal Power Act (as in effect on the date of the enactment of this paragraph).*

(3) *GOVERNMENTAL BODY.—The term "governmental body" means any State or Indian tribal government, or any political subdivision thereof.*

(4) *COOPERATIVE ELECTRIC COMPANY.—The term "cooperative electric company" means a mutual or cooperative electric company described in section 501(c)(12) or section 1381(a)(2)(C).*

(5) *CLEAN RENEWABLE ENERGY BOND LENDER.—The term "clean renewable energy bond lender" means a lender which is a cooperative which is owned by, or has outstanding loans to, 100 or more cooperative electric companies and is in existence on February 1, 2002, and shall include any affiliated entity which is controlled by such lender.*

(6) *QUALIFIED ISSUER.—The term "qualified issuer" means a public power provider, a cooperative electric company, a governmental body, a clean renewable energy bond lender, or a not-for-profit electric utility which has received a loan or loan guarantee under the Rural Electrification Act.*

[CCH Explanation at ¶ 805.]
Amendments
• 2008, Energy Improvement and Extension Act of 2008 (P.L. 110-343)

P.L. 110-343, Division B, §107(a):

Amended subpart I of part IV of subchapter A of chapter 1 by adding at the end a new Code Sec. 54C. **Effective** for obligations issued after 10-3-2008.

[¶ 5160] *CODE SEC. 54D. QUALIFIED ENERGY CONSERVATION BONDS.*

(a) *QUALIFIED ENERGY CONSERVATION BOND.—For purposes of this subchapter, the term "qualified energy conservation bond" means any bond issued as part of an issue if—*

(1) *100 percent of the available project proceeds of such issue are to be used for one or more qualified conservation purposes,*

(2) *the bond is issued by a State or local government, and*

(3) *the issuer designates such bond for purposes of this section.*

(b) *REDUCED CREDIT AMOUNT.—The annual credit determined under section 54A(b) with respect to any qualified energy conservation bond shall be 70 percent of the amount so determined without regard to this subsection.*

(c) LIMITATION ON AMOUNT OF BONDS DESIGNATED.—*The maximum aggregate face amount of bonds which may be designated under subsection (a) by any issuer shall not exceed the limitation amount allocated to such issuer under subsection (e).*

(d) NATIONAL LIMITATION ON AMOUNT OF BONDS DESIGNATED.—*There is a national qualified energy conservation bond limitation of $800,000,000.*

(e) ALLOCATIONS.—

(1) IN GENERAL.—*The limitation applicable under subsection (d) shall be allocated by the Secretary among the States in proportion to the population of the States.*

(2) ALLOCATIONS TO LARGEST LOCAL GOVERNMENTS.—

(A) IN GENERAL.—*In the case of any State in which there is a large local government, each such local government shall be allocated a portion of such State's allocation which bears the same ratio to the State's allocation (determined without regard to this subparagraph) as the population of such large local government bears to the population of such State.*

(B) ALLOCATION OF UNUSED LIMITATION TO STATE.—*The amount allocated under this subsection to a large local government may be reallocated by such local government to the State in which such local government is located.*

(C) LARGE LOCAL GOVERNMENT.—*For purposes of this section, the term "large local government" means any municipality or county if such municipality or county has a population of 100,000 or more.*

(3) ALLOCATION TO ISSUERS; RESTRICTION ON PRIVATE ACTIVITY BONDS.—*Any allocation under this subsection to a State or large local government shall be allocated by such State or large local government to issuers within the State in a manner that results in not less than 70 percent of the allocation to such State or large local government being used to designate bonds which are not private activity bonds.*

(f) QUALIFIED CONSERVATION PURPOSE.—*For purposes of this section—*

(1) IN GENERAL.—*The term "qualified conservation purpose" means any of the following:*

(A) *Capital expenditures incurred for purposes of—*

(i) *reducing energy consumption in publicly-owned buildings by at least 20 percent,*

(ii) *implementing green community programs,*

(iii) *rural development involving the production of electricity from renewable energy resources, or*

(iv) *any qualified facility (as determined under section 45(d) without regard to paragraphs (8) and (10) thereof and without regard to any placed in service date).*

(B) *Expenditures with respect to research facilities, and research grants, to support research in—*

(i) *development of cellulosic ethanol or other nonfossil fuels,*

(ii) *technologies for the capture and sequestration of carbon dioxide produced through the use of fossil fuels,*

(iii) *increasing the efficiency of existing technologies for producing nonfossil fuels,*

(iv) *automobile battery technologies and other technologies to reduce fossil fuel consumption in transportation, or*

(v) *technologies to reduce energy use in buildings.*

(C) *Mass commuting facilities and related facilities that reduce the consumption of energy, including expenditures to reduce pollution from vehicles used for mass commuting.*

(D) *Demonstration projects designed to promote the commercialization of—*

(i) *green building technology,*

(ii) *conversion of agricultural waste for use in the production of fuel or otherwise,*

(iii) *advanced battery manufacturing technologies,*

(iv) *technologies to reduce peak use of electricity, or*

(v) *technologies for the capture and sequestration of carbon dioxide emitted from combusting fossil fuels in order to produce electricity.*

(E) *Public education campaigns to promote energy efficiency.*

(2) SPECIAL RULES FOR PRIVATE ACTIVITY BONDS.—*For purposes of this section, in the case of any private activity bond, the term "qualified conservation purposes" shall not include any expenditure which is not a capital expenditure.*

(g) POPULATION.—

(1) IN GENERAL.—*The population of any State or local government shall be determined for purposes of this section as provided in section 146(j) for the calendar year which includes the date of the enactment of this section.*

(2) SPECIAL RULE FOR COUNTIES.—*In determining the population of any county for purposes of this section, any population of such county which is taken into account in determining the population of any municipality which is a large local government shall not be taken into account in determining the population of such county.*

(h) APPLICATION TO INDIAN TRIBAL GOVERNMENTS.—*An Indian tribal government shall be treated for purposes of this section in the same manner as a large local government, except that—*

(1) *an Indian tribal government shall be treated for purposes of subsection (e) as located within a State to the extent of so much of the population of such government as resides within such State, and*

(2) *any bond issued by an Indian tribal government shall be treated as a qualified energy conservation bond only if issued as part of an issue the available project proceeds of which are used for purposes for which such Indian tribal government could issue bonds to which section 103(a) applies.*

[CCH Explanation at ¶ 810.]

Amendments

• **2008, Energy Improvement and Extension Act of 2008 (P.L. 110-343)**

P.L. 110-343, Division B, § 301(a):

Amended subpart I of part IV of subchapter A of chapter 1, as amended by Act Sec. 107, by adding at the end a new

Code Sec. 54D. **Effective** for obligations issued after 10-3-2008.

[¶ 5165]   *CODE SEC. 54E.   QUALIFIED ZONE ACADEMY BONDS.*

(a) QUALIFIED ZONE ACADEMY BONDS.—*For purposes of this subchapter, the term "qualified zone academy bond" means any bond issued as part of an issue if—*

(1) *100 percent of the available project proceeds of such issue are to be used for a qualified purpose with respect to a qualified zone academy established by an eligible local education agency,*

(2) *the bond is issued by a State or local government within the jurisdiction of which such academy is located, and*

(3) *the issuer—*

(A) *designates such bond for purposes of this section,*

(B) *certifies that it has written assurances that the private business contribution requirement of subsection (b) will be met with respect to such academy, and*

(C) *certifies that it has the written approval of the eligible local education agency for such bond issuance.*

(b) PRIVATE BUSINESS CONTRIBUTION REQUIREMENT.—*For purposes of subsection (a), the private business contribution requirement of this subsection is met with respect to any issue if the eligible local education agency that established the qualified zone academy has written commitments from private entities to make qualified contributions having a present value (as of the date of issuance of the issue) of not less than 10 percent of the proceeds of the issue.*

(c) LIMITATION ON AMOUNT OF BONDS DESIGNATED.—

(1) NATIONAL LIMITATION.—*There is a national zone academy bond limitation for each calendar year. Such limitation is $400,000,000 for 2008 and 2009, and, except as provided in paragraph (4), zero thereafter.*

(2) ALLOCATION OF LIMITATION.—*The national zone academy bond limitation for a calendar year shall be allocated by the Secretary among the States on the basis of their respective populations of individuals below the poverty line (as defined by the Office of Management and Budget). The limitation amount allocated to a State under the preceding sentence shall be allocated by the State education agency to qualified zone academies within such State.*

(3) DESIGNATION SUBJECT TO LIMITATION AMOUNT.—*The maximum aggregate face amount of bonds issued during any calendar year which may be designated under subsection (a) with respect to any qualified zone academy shall not exceed the limitation amount allocated to such academy under paragraph (2) for such calendar year.*

(4) CARRYOVER OF UNUSED LIMITATION.—

(A) IN GENERAL.—*If for any calendar year—*

(i) the limitation amount for any State, exceeds

(ii) the amount of bonds issued during such year which are designated under subsection (a) with respect to qualified zone academies within such State,

the limitation amount for such State for the following calendar year shall be increased by the amount of such excess.

(B) LIMITATION ON CARRYOVER.—*Any carryforward of a limitation amount may be carried only to the first 2 years following the unused limitation year. For purposes of the preceding sentence, a limitation amount shall be treated as used on a first-in first-out basis.*

(C) COORDINATION WITH SECTION 1397E.—*Any carryover determined under section 1397E(e)(4) (relating to carryover of unused limitation) with respect to any State to calendar year 2008 or 2009 shall be treated for purposes of this section as a carryover with respect to such State for such calendar year under subparagraph (A), and the limitation of subparagraph (B) shall apply to such carryover taking into account the calendar years to which such carryover relates.*

(d) DEFINITIONS.—*For purposes of this section—*

(1) QUALIFIED ZONE ACADEMY.—*The term "qualified zone academy" means any public school (or academic program within a public school) which is established by and operated under the supervision of an eligible local education agency to provide education or training below the postsecondary level if—*

(A) such public school or program (as the case may be) is designed in cooperation with business to enhance the academic curriculum, increase graduation and employment rates, and better prepare students for the rigors of college and the increasingly complex workforce,

(B) students in such public school or program (as the case may be) will be subject to the same academic standards and assessments as other students educated by the eligible local education agency,

(C) the comprehensive education plan of such public school or program is approved by the eligible local education agency, and

(D)(i) such public school is located in an empowerment zone or enterprise community (including any such zone or community designated after the date of the enactment of this section), or

(ii) there is a reasonable expectation (as of the date of issuance of the bonds) that at least 35 percent of the students attending such school or participating in such program (as the case may be) will be eligible for free or reduced-cost lunches under the school lunch program established under the National School Lunch Act.

(2) ELIGIBLE LOCAL EDUCATION AGENCY.—*For purposes of this section, the term "eligible local education agency" means any local educational agency as defined in section 9101 of the Elementary and Secondary Education Act of 1965.*

(3) QUALIFIED PURPOSE.—The term "qualified purpose" means, with respect to any qualified zone academy—

(A) rehabilitating or repairing the public school facility in which the academy is established,

(B) providing equipment for use at such academy,

(C) developing course materials for education to be provided at such academy, and

(D) training teachers and other school personnel in such academy.

(4) QUALIFIED CONTRIBUTIONS.—The term "qualified contribution" means any contribution (of a type and quality acceptable to the eligible local education agency) of—

(A) equipment for use in the qualified zone academy (including state-of-the-art technology and vocational equipment),

(B) technical assistance in developing curriculum or in training teachers in order to promote appropriate market driven technology in the classroom,

(C) services of employees as volunteer mentors,

(D) internships, field trips, or other educational opportunities outside the academy for students, or

(E) any other property or service specified by the eligible local education agency.

[CCH Explanation at ¶ 815.]

Amendments

• **2008, Tax Extenders and Alternative Minimum Tax Relief Act of 2008 (P.L. 110-343)**

P.L. 110-343, Division C, § 313(a):

Amended subpart I of part IV of subchapter A of chapter 1 by adding at the end a new Code Sec. 54E. **Effective** for obligations issued after 10-3-2008.

[¶ 5170] CODE SEC. 55. ALTERNATIVE MINIMUM TAX IMPOSED.

* * *

(d) EXEMPTION AMOUNT.—For purposes of this section—

(1) EXEMPTION AMOUNT FOR TAXPAYERS OTHER THAN CORPORATIONS.—In the case of a taxpayer other than a corporation, the term "exemption amount" means—

(A) $45,000 in the case of (*$69,950 in the case of taxable years beginning in 2008*)—

(i) a joint return, or

(ii) a surviving spouse,

(B) $33,750 in the case of an individual who (*$46,200 in the case of taxable years beginning in 2008*)—

(i) is not a married individual, and

(ii) is not a surviving spouse,

* * *

[CCH Explanation at ¶ 205.]

Amendments

• **2008, Tax Extenders and Alternative Minimum Tax Relief Act of 2008 (P.L. 110-343)**

P.L. 110-343, Division C, § 102(a)(1)-(2):

Amended Code Sec. 55(d)(1) by striking "($66,250 in the case of taxable years beginning in 2007)" in subparagraph (A) and inserting "($69,950 in the case of taxable years beginning in 2008)", and by striking "($44,350 in the case of taxable years beginning in 2007)" in subparagraph (B) and inserting "($46,200 in the case of taxable years beginning in 2008)". **Effective** for tax years beginning after 12-31-2007.

[¶ 5175] CODE SEC. 56. ADJUSTMENTS IN COMPUTING ALTERNATIVE MINIMUM TAXABLE INCOME.

* * *

(b) ADJUSTMENTS APPLICABLE TO INDIVIDUALS.—In determining the amount of the alternative minimum taxable income of any taxpayer (other than a corporation), the following treatment shall apply (in lieu of the treatment applicable for purposes of computing the regular tax):

(1) LIMITATION ON DEDUCTIONS.—

* * *

(E) STANDARD DEDUCTION AND DEDUCTION FOR PERSONAL EXEMPTIONS NOT ALLOWED.—The standard deduction under section 63(c), the deduction for personal exemptions under section 151, and the deduction under section 642(b) shall not be allowed. *The preceding sentence shall not apply to so much of the standard deduction as is determined under section 63(c)(1)(D).*

* * *

[CCH Explanation at ¶ 605. Committee Reports at ¶ 10,710.]
Amendments
• 2008, Tax Extenders and Alternative Minimum Tax Relief Act of 2008 (P.L. 110-343)

P.L. 110-343, Division C, § 706(b)(3):
Amended Code Sec. 56(b)(1)(E) by adding at the end a new sentence. **Effective** for disasters declared in tax years beginning after 12-31-2007.

(d) ALTERNATIVE TAX NET OPERATING LOSS DEDUCTION DEFINED.—

* * *

(3) NET OPERATING LOSS ATTRIBUTABLE TO FEDERALLY DECLARED DISASTERS.—*In the case of a taxpayer which has a qualified disaster loss (as defined by section 172(b)(1)(J)) for the taxable year, paragraph (1) shall be applied by increasing the amount determined under subparagraph (A)(ii)(I) thereof by the sum of the carrybacks and carryovers of such loss.*

* * *

[CCH Explanation at ¶ 610. Committee Reports at ¶ 10,730.]
Amendments
• 2008, Tax Extenders and Alternative Minimum Tax Relief Act of 2008 (P.L. 110-343)

P.L. 110-343, Division C, § 708(c):
Amended Code Sec. 56(d) by adding at the end a new paragraph (3). **Effective** for losses arising in tax years begin-ning after 12-31-2007, in connection with disasters declared after such date.

[¶ 5180] CODE SEC. 62. ADJUSTED GROSS INCOME DEFINED.

(a) GENERAL RULE.—For purposes of this subtitle, the term "adjusted gross income" means, in the case of an individual, gross income minus the following deductions:

* * *

(2) CERTAIN TRADE AND BUSINESS DEDUCTIONS OF EMPLOYEES.—

* * *

(D) CERTAIN EXPENSES OF ELEMENTARY AND SECONDARY SCHOOL TEACHERS.—In the case of taxable years beginning during 2002, 2003, 2004, 2005, 2006, *2007, 2008, or 2009,* the deductions allowed by section 162 which consist of expenses, not in excess of $250, paid or incurred by an eligible educator in connection with books, supplies (other than nonathletic supplies for courses of instruction in health or physical education), computer equipment (including related software and services) and other equipment, and supplementary materials used by the eligible educator in the classroom.

* * *

[CCH Explanation at ¶250. Committee Reports at ¶10,350.]

Amendments

• **2008, Tax Extenders and Alternative Minimum Tax Relief Act of 2008 (P.L. 110-343)**

P.L. 110-343, Division C, §203(a):

Amended Code Sec. 62(a)(2)(D) by striking "or 2007" and inserting "2007, 2008, or 2009". **Effective** for tax years beginning after 12-31-2007.

[¶5185] CODE SEC. 63. TAXABLE INCOME DEFINED.

* * *

(c) STANDARD DEDUCTION.—For purposes of this subtitle—

(1) IN GENERAL.—Except as otherwise provided in this subsection, the term "standard deduction" means the sum of—

(A) the basic standard deduction,

(B) the additional standard deduction,

(C) in the case of any taxable year beginning in 2008 *or 2009*, the real property tax deduction, *and*

(D) the disaster loss deduction.

* * *

(8) DISASTER LOSS DEDUCTION.—For the purposes of paragraph (1), the term "disaster loss deduction" means the net disaster loss (as defined in section 165(h)(3)(B)).

* * *

[CCH Explanations at ¶235 and ¶605. Committee Reports at ¶10,350 and ¶10,710.]

Amendments

• **2008, Tax Extenders and Alternative Minimum Tax Relief Act of 2008 (P.L. 110-343)**

P.L. 110-343, Division C, §204(a):

Amended Code Sec. 63(c)(1)(C), as added by the Housing Assistance Tax Act of 2008 (P.L. 110-289), by inserting "or 2009" after "2008". **Effective** for tax years beginning after 12-31-2008.

P.L. 110-343, Division C, §706(b)(1):

Amended Code Sec. 63(c)(1), as amended by the Housing Assistance Tax Act of 2008 (P.L. 110-289), by striking "and"

at the end of subparagraph (B), by striking the period at the end of subparagraph (C) and inserting ", and", and by adding at the end a new subparagraph (D). **Effective** for disasters declared in tax years beginning after 12-31-2007.

P.L. 110-343, Division C, §706(b)(2):

Amended Code Sec. 63(c), as amended by the Housing Assistance Tax Act of 2008 (P.L. 110-289), by adding at the end a new paragraph (8). **Effective** for disasters declared in tax years beginning after 12-31-2007.

[¶5190] CODE SEC. 108. INCOME FROM DISCHARGE OF INDEBTEDNESS.

(a) EXCLUSION FROM GROSS INCOME.—

(1) IN GENERAL.—Gross income does not include any amount which (but for this subsection) would be includible in gross income by reason of the discharge (in whole or in part) of indebtedness of the taxpayer if—

* * *

⟫⟫→ *Caution: Code Sec. 108(a)(1)(E), as amended by P.L. 110-343, applies to discharges of indebtedness occurring on or after January 1, 2010.*

(E) the indebtedness discharged is qualified principal residence indebtedness which is discharged before *January 1, 2013.*

* * *

[CCH Explanation at ¶ 220. Committee Reports at ¶ 10,030.]

Amendments

• **2008, Emergency Economic Stabilization Act of 2008 (P.L. 110-343)**

P.L. 110-343, Division A, § 303(a):

Amended Code Sec. 108(a)(1)(E) by striking "January 1, 2010" and inserting "January 1, 2013". **Effective** for discharges of indebtedness occurring on or after 1-1-2010.

[¶ 5195] CODE SEC. 132. CERTAIN FRINGE BENEFITS.

* * *

(f) QUALIFIED TRANSPORTATION FRINGE.—

(1) IN GENERAL.— For purposes of this section, the term "qualified transportation fringe" means any of the following provided by an employer to an employee:

* * *

➤➤➤ *Caution: Code Sec. 132(f)(1)(D), as added by P.L. 110-343, applies to tax years beginning after December 31, 2008.*

(D) *Any qualified bicycle commuting reimbursement.*

(2) LIMITATION ON EXCLUSION.— The amount of the fringe benefits which are provided by an employer to any employee and which may be excluded from gross income under subsection (a)(5) shall not exceed—

(A) $100 per month in the case of the aggregate of the benefits described in subparagraphs (A) and (B) of paragraph (1),

(B) $175 per month in the case of qualified parking, *and*

➤➤➤ *Caution: Code Sec. 132(f)(2)(C), as added by P.L. 110-343, applies to tax years beginning after December 31, 2008.*

(C) *the applicable annual limitation in the case of any qualified bicycle commuting reimbursement.*

* * *

➤➤➤ *Caution: Code Sec. 132(f)(4), as amended by P.L. 110-343, applies to tax years beginning after December 31, 2008.*

(4) NO CONSTRUCTIVE RECEIPT.— No amount shall be included in the gross income of an employee solely because the employee may choose between any qualified transportation fringe *(other than a qualified bicycle commuting reimbursement)* and compensation which would otherwise be includible in gross income of such employee.

(5) DEFINITIONS.— For purposes of this subsection—

* * *

➤➤➤ *Caution: Code Sec. 132(f)(5)(F), as added by P.L. 110-343, applies to tax years beginning after December 31, 2008.*

(F) DEFINITIONS RELATED TO BICYCLE COMMUTING REIMBURSEMENT.—

(i) QUALIFIED BICYCLE COMMUTING REIMBURSEMENT.—*The term "qualified bicycle commuting reimbursement" means, with respect to any calendar year, any employer reimbursement during the 15-month period beginning with the first day of such calendar year for reasonable expenses incurred by the employee during such calendar year for the purchase of a bicycle and bicycle improvements, repair, and storage, if such bicycle is regularly used for travel between the employee's residence and place of employment.*

(ii) APPLICABLE ANNUAL LIMITATION.—*The term "applicable annual limitation" means, with respect to any employee for any calendar year, the product of $20 multiplied by the number of qualified bicycle commuting months during such year.*

(iii) QUALIFIED BICYCLE COMMUTING MONTH.—*The term "qualified bicycle commuting month" means, with respect to any employee, any month during which such employee—*

(I) regularly uses the bicycle for a substantial portion of the travel between the employee's residence and place of employment, and

(II) does not receive any benefit described in subparagraph (A), (B), or (C) of paragraph (1).

* * *

[CCH Explanation at ¶ 230. Committee Reports at ¶ 10,200.]

Amendments

• **2008, Energy Improvement and Extension Act of 2008 (P.L. 110-343)**

P.L. 110-343, Division B, § 211(a):

Amended Code Sec. 132(f)(1) by adding at the end a new subparagraph (D). **Effective** for tax years beginning after 12-31-2008.

P.L. 110-343, Division B, § 211(b):

Amended Code Sec. 132(f)(2) by striking "and" at the end of subparagraph (A), by striking the period at the end of subparagraph (B) and inserting ", and", and by adding at

the end a new subparagraph (C). **Effective** for tax years beginning after 12-31-2008.

P.L. 110-343, Division B, § 211(c):

Amended Code Sec. 132(f)(5) by adding at the end a new subparagraph (F). **Effective** for tax years beginning after 12-31-2008.

P.L. 110-343, Division B, § 211(d):

Amended Code Sec. 132(f)(4) by inserting "(other than a qualified bicycle commuting reimbursement)" after "qualified transportation fringe". **Effective** for tax years beginning after 12-31-2008.

[¶ 5200] CODE SEC. 139. DISASTER RELIEF PAYMENTS.

* * *

(c) QUALIFIED DISASTER DEFINED.—For purposes of this section, the term "qualified disaster" means—

* * *

(2) federally declared disaster (as defined by section 165(h)(3)(C)(i)),

* * *

[CCH Explanation at ¶ 605. Committee Reports at ¶ 10,710.]

Amendments

• **2008, Tax Extenders and Alternative Minimum Tax Relief Act of 2008 (P.L. 110-343)**

P.L. 110-343, Division C, § 706(a)(2)(D)(iv):

Amended Code Sec. 139(c)(2). **Effective** for disasters declared in tax years beginning after 12-31-2007. Prior to amendment, Code Sec. 139(c)(2) read as follows:

(2) a Presidentially declared disaster (as defined in section 1033(h)(3)),

[¶ 5205] CODE SEC. 142. EXEMPT FACILITY BOND.

* * *

(l) QUALIFIED GREEN BUILDING AND SUSTAINABLE DESIGN PROJECTS.—

* * *

(8) TERMINATION.—Subsection (a)(14) shall not apply with respect to any bond issued after September 30, 2012.

(9) TREATMENT OF CURRENT REFUNDING BONDS.—Paragraphs (7)(B) and (8) shall not apply to any bond (or series of bonds) issued to refund a bond issued under subsection (a)(14) before October 1, 2012, if—

(A) the average maturity date of the issue of which the refunding bond is a part is not later than the average maturity date of the bonds to be refunded by such issue,

(B) the amount of the refunding bond does not exceed the outstanding amount of the refunded bond, and

(C) the net proceeds of the refunding bond are used to redeem the refunded bond not later than 90 days after the date of the issuance of the refunding bond.

For purposes of subparagraph (A), average maturity shall be determined in accordance with section 147(b)(2)(A).

* * *

[CCH Explanation at ¶820. Committee Reports at ¶10,250.]

Amendments

• **2008, Energy Improvement and Extension Act of 2008 (P.L. 110-343)**

P.L. 110-343, Division B, §307(a):

Amended Code Sec. 142(l)(8) by striking "September 30, 2009" and inserting "September 30, 2012". **Effective** 10-3-2008.

P.L. 110-343, Division B, §307(b):

Amended Code Sec. 142(l)(9) by striking "October 1, 2009" and inserting "October 1, 2012". **Effective** 10-3-2008.

[¶5210] CODE SEC. 143. MORTGAGE REVENUE BONDS: QUALIFIED MORTGAGE BOND AND QUALIFIED VETERANS' MORTGAGE BOND.

* * *

(k) OTHER DEFINITIONS AND SPECIAL RULES.—For purposes of this section—

* * *

(12)[13] SPECIAL RULES FOR RESIDENCES DESTROYED IN FEDERALLY DECLARED DISASTERS.—

(A) PRINCIPAL RESIDENCE DESTROYED.—At the election of the taxpayer, if the principal residence (within the meaning of section 121) of such taxpayer is—

(i) rendered unsafe for use as a residence by reason of a federally declared disaster occurring before January 1, 2010, or

(ii) demolished or relocated by reason of an order of the government of a State or political subdivision thereof on account of a federally declared disaster occurring before such date,

then, for the 2-year period beginning on the date of the disaster declaration, subsection (d)(1) shall not apply with respect to such taxpayer and subsection (e) shall be applied by substituting "110" for "90" in paragraph (1) thereof.

(B) PRINCIPAL RESIDENCE DAMAGED.—

(i) IN GENERAL.—At the election of the taxpayer, if the principal residence (within the meaning of section 121) of such taxpayer was damaged as the result of a federally declared disaster occurring before January 1, 2010, any owner-financing provided in connection with the repair or reconstruction of such residence shall be treated as a qualified rehabilitation loan.

(ii) LIMITATION.—The aggregate owner-financing to which clause (i) applies shall not exceed the lesser of—

(I) the cost of such repair or reconstruction, or

(II) $150,000.

(C) FEDERALLY DECLARED DISASTER.—For purposes of this paragraph, the term "federally declared disaster" has the meaning given such term by section 165(h)(3)(C)(i).

(D) ELECTION; DENIAL OF DOUBLE BENEFIT.—

(i) ELECTION.—An election under this paragraph may not be revoked except with the consent of the Secretary.

(ii) DENIAL OF DOUBLE BENEFIT.—If a taxpayer elects the application of this paragraph, paragraph (11) shall not apply with respect to the purchase or financing of any residence by such taxpayer.

* * *

[CCH Explanation at ¶ 645. Committee Reports at ¶ 10,740.]

Amendments

• 2008, Tax Extenders and Alternative Minimum Tax Relief Act of 2008 (P.L. 110-343)

P.L. 110-343, Division C, §709(a):

Amended Code Sec. 143(k) by adding at the end a new paragraph (12)[13]. **Effective** for disasters occurring after 12-31-2007.

[¶ 5212] CODE SEC. 152. DEPENDENT DEFINED.

* * *

(c) QUALIFYING CHILD.—For purposes of this section—

(1) IN GENERAL.—The term "qualifying child" means, with respect to any taxpayer for any taxable year, an individual—

(A) who bears a relationship to the taxpayer described in paragraph (2),

(B) who has the same principal place of abode as the taxpayer for more than one-half of such taxable year,

(C) who meets the age requirements of paragraph (3),

(D) who has not provided over one-half of such individual's own support for the calendar year in which the taxable year of the taxpayer begins, *and*

⋙➔ *Caution: Code Sec. 152(c)(1)(E), below, as added by P.L. 110-351, applies to tax years beginning after December 31, 2008.*

(E) *who has not filed a joint return (other than only for a claim of refund) with the individual's spouse under section 6013 for the taxable year beginning in the calendar year in which the taxable year of the taxpayer begins.*

* * *

(3) AGE REQUIREMENTS.—

⋙➔ *Caution: Code Sec. 152(c)(3)(A), below, as amended by P.L. 110-351, applies to tax years beginning after December 31, 2008.*

(A) IN GENERAL.—For purposes of paragraph (1)(C), an individual meets the requirements of this paragraph if such individual *is younger than the taxpayer claiming such individual as a qualifying child and—*

(i) has not attained the age of 19 as of the close of the calendar year in which the taxable year of the taxpayer begins, or

(ii) is a student who has not attained the age of 24 as of the close of such calendar year.

* * *

⋙➔ *Caution: The heading for Code Sec. 152(c)(4), below, as amended by P.L. 110-351, applies to tax years beginning after December 31, 2008.*

(4) SPECIAL RULE RELATING TO 2 OR MORE *WHO CAN CLAIM THE SAME* QUALIFYING CHILD.—

⋙➔ *Caution: Code Sec. 152(c)(4)(A), below, as amended by P.L. 110-351, applies to tax years beginning after December 31, 2008.*

(A) IN GENERAL.—*Except as provided in subparagraphs (B) and (C), if (but for this paragraph) an individual may be claimed as a qualifying child by 2 or more taxpayers* for a taxable year beginning in the same calendar year, such individual shall be treated as the qualifying child of the taxpayer who is—

(i) a parent of the individual, or

(ii) if clause (i) does not apply, the taxpayer with the highest adjusted gross income for such taxable year.

* * *

≫→ *Caution: Code Sec. 152(c)(4)(C), below, as added by P.L. 110-351, applies to tax years beginning after December 31, 2008.*

(C) No PARENT CLAIMING QUALIFYING CHILD.—If the parents of an individual may claim such individual as a qualifying child but no parent so claims the individual, such individual may be claimed as the qualifying child of another taxpayer but only if the adjusted gross income of such taxpayer is higher than the highest adjusted gross income of any parent of the individual.

* * *

Amendments

● **2008, Fostering Connections to Success and Increasing Adoptions Act of 2008 (P.L. 110-351)**

P.L. 110-351, § 501(a):

Amended Code Sec. 152(c)(3)(A) by inserting "is younger than the taxpayer claiming such individual as a qualifying child and" after "such individual". **Effective** for tax years beginning after 12-31-2008.

P.L. 110-351, § 501(b):

Amended Code Sec. 152(c)(1) by striking "and" at the end of subparagraph (C), by striking the period at the end of subparagraph (D) and inserting ", and", and by adding at the end a new subparagraph (E). **Effective** for tax years beginning after 12-31-2008.

P.L. 110-351, § 501(c)(2)(A):

Amended Code Sec. 152(c)(4) by adding at the end a new subparagraph (C). **Effective** for tax years beginning after 12-31-2008.

P.L. 110-351, § 501(c)(2)(B)(i):

Amended Code Sec. 152(c)(4)(A) by striking "Except" through "2 or more taxpayers" and inserting "Except as provided in subparagraphs (B) and (C), if (but for this paragraph) an individual may be claimed as a qualifying child by 2 or more taxpayers". **Effective** for tax years beginning after 12-31-2008. Prior to being stricken, the text "Except" through "2 or more taxpayers" read as follows:

Except as provided in subparagraph (B), if (but for this paragraph) an individual may be and is claimed as a qualifying child by 2 or more taxpayers

P.L. 110-351, § 501(c)(2)(B)(ii):

Amended the heading for Code Sec. 152(c)(4) by striking "CLAIMING" and inserting "WHO CAN CLAIM THE SAME". **Effective** for tax years beginning after 12-31-2008.

[¶ 5215] CODE SEC. 162. TRADE OR BUSINESS EXPENSES.

* * *

(m) CERTAIN EXCESSIVE EMPLOYEE REMUNERATION.—

* * *

(5) SPECIAL RULE FOR APPLICATION TO EMPLOYERS PARTICIPATING IN THE TROUBLED ASSETS RELIEF PROGRAM.—

(A) IN GENERAL.—In the case of an applicable employer, no deduction shall be allowed under this chapter—

(i) in the case of executive remuneration for any applicable taxable year which is attributable to services performed by a covered executive during such applicable taxable year, to the extent that the amount of such remuneration exceeds $500,000, or

(ii) in the case of deferred deduction executive remuneration for any taxable year for services performed during any applicable taxable year by a covered executive, to the extent that the amount of such remuneration exceeds $500,000 reduced (but not below zero) by the sum of—

(I) the executive remuneration for such applicable taxable year, plus

(II) the portion of the deferred deduction executive remuneration for such services which was taken into account under this clause in a preceding taxable year.

(B) APPLICABLE EMPLOYER.—For purposes of this paragraph—

(i) IN GENERAL.—Except as provided in clause (ii), the term "applicable employer" means any employer from whom 1 or more troubled assets are acquired under a program established by the Secretary under section 101(a) of the Emergency Economic Stabilization Act of 2008 if the aggregate amount of the assets so acquired for all taxable years exceeds $300,000,000.

(ii) DISREGARD OF CERTAIN ASSETS SOLD THROUGH DIRECT PURCHASE.—If the only sales of troubled assets by an employer under the program described in clause (i) are through 1 or more direct purchases (within the meaning of section 113(c) of the Emergency Economic Stabilization

Act of 2008), such assets shall not be taken into account under clause (i) in determining whether the employer is an applicable employer for purposes of this paragraph.

(iii) AGGREGATION RULES.—Two or more persons who are treated as a single employer under subsection (b) or (c) of section 414 shall be treated as a single employer, except that in applying section 1563(a) for purposes of either such subsection, paragraphs (2) and (3) thereof shall be disregarded.

(C) APPLICABLE TAXABLE YEAR.—For purposes of this paragraph, the term "applicable taxable year" means, with respect to any employer—

(i) the first taxable year of the employer—

(I) which includes any portion of the period during which the authorities under section 101(a) of the Emergency Economic Stabilization Act of 2008 are in effect (determined under section 120 thereof), and

(II) in which the aggregate amount of troubled assets acquired from the employer during the taxable year pursuant to such authorities (other than assets to which subparagraph (B)(ii) applies), when added to the aggregate amount so acquired for all preceding taxable years, exceeds $300,000,000, and

(ii) any subsequent taxable year which includes any portion of such period.

(D) COVERED EXECUTIVE.—For purposes of this paragraph—

(i) IN GENERAL.—The term "covered executive" means, with respect to any applicable taxable year, any employee—

(I) who, at any time during the portion of the taxable year during which the authorities under section 101(a) of the Emergency Economic Stabilization Act of 2008 are in effect (determined under section 120 thereof), is the chief executive officer of the applicable employer or the chief financial officer of the applicable employer, or an individual acting in either such capacity, or

(II) who is described in clause (ii).

(ii) HIGHEST COMPENSATED EMPLOYEES.—An employee is described in this clause if the employee is 1 of the 3 highest compensated officers of the applicable employer for the taxable year (other than an individual described in clause (i)(I)), determined—

(I) on the basis of the shareholder disclosure rules for compensation under the Securities Exchange Act of 1934 (without regard to whether those rules apply to the employer), and

(II) by only taking into account employees employed during the portion of the taxable year described in clause (i)(I).

(iii) EMPLOYEE REMAINS COVERED EXECUTIVE.—If an employee is a covered executive with respect to an applicable employer for any applicable taxable year, such employee shall be treated as a covered executive with respect to such employer for all subsequent applicable taxable years and for all subsequent taxable years in which deferred deduction executive remuneration with respect to services performed in all such applicable taxable years would (but for this paragraph) be deductible.

(E) EXECUTIVE REMUNERATION.—For purposes of this paragraph, the term "executive remuneration" means the applicable employee remuneration of the covered executive, as determined under paragraph (4) without regard to subparagraphs (B), (C), and (D) thereof. Such term shall not include any deferred deduction executive remuneration with respect to services performed in a prior applicable taxable year.

(F) DEFERRED DEDUCTION EXECUTIVE REMUNERATION.—For purposes of this paragraph, the term "deferred deduction executive remuneration" means remuneration which would be executive remuneration for services performed in an applicable taxable year but for the fact that the deduction under this chapter (determined without regard to this paragraph) for such remuneration is allowable in a subsequent taxable year.

(G) COORDINATION.—*Rules similar to the rules of subparagraphs (F) and (G) of paragraph (4) shall apply for purposes of this paragraph.*

(H) REGULATORY AUTHORITY.—*The Secretary may prescribe such guidance, rules, or regulations as are necessary to carry out the purposes of this paragraph and the Emergency Economic Stabilization Act of 2008, including the extent to which this paragraph applies in the case of any acquisition, merger, or reorganization of an applicable employer.*

* * *

[CCH Explanation at ¶380. Committee Reports at ¶10,020.]

Amendments

• **2008, Emergency Economic Stabilization Act of 2008 (P.L. 110-343)**

P.L. 110-343, Division A, §302(a):

Amended Code Sec. 162(m) by adding at the end a new paragraph (5). **Effective** for tax years ending on or after 10-3-2008.

[¶5220] CODE SEC. 164. TAXES.

* * *

(b) DEFINITIONS AND SPECIAL RULES.—For purposes of this section—

* * *

(5) GENERAL SALES TAXES.—For purposes of subsection (a)—

* * *

(I) APPLICATION OF PARAGRAPH.—This paragraph shall apply to taxable years beginning after December 31, 2003, and before *January 1, 2010.*

* * *

[CCH Explanation at ¶240. Committee Reports at ¶10,330.]

Amendments

• **2008, Tax Extenders and Alternative Minimum Tax Relief Act of 2008 (P.L. 110-343)**

P.L. 110-343, Division C, §201(a):

Amended Code Sec. 164(b)(5)(I) by striking "January 1, 2008" and inserting "January 1, 2010". **Effective** for tax years beginning after 12-31-2007.

[¶5225] CODE SEC. 165. LOSSES.

* * *

(h) TREATMENT OF CASUALTY GAINS AND LOSSES.—

* * *

⋙→ Caution: *Code Sec. 165(h)(1), below, as amended by P.L. 110-343, applies to tax years beginning after December 31, 2008.*

(1) $100 LIMITATION PER CASUALTY.—Any loss of an individual described in subsection (c)(3) shall be allowed only to the extent that the amount of the loss to such individual arising from each casualty, or from each theft, exceeds *$500 ($100 for taxable years beginning after December 31, 2009).*

* * *

(3) SPECIAL RULE FOR LOSSES IN FEDERALLY DECLARED DISASTERS.—

(A) IN GENERAL.—*If an individual has a net disaster loss for any taxable year, the amount determined under paragraph (2)(A)(ii) shall be the sum of—*

(i) *such net disaster loss, and*

(ii) *so much of the excess referred to in the matter preceding clause (i) of paragraph (2)(A) (reduced by the amount in clause (i) of this subparagraph) as exceeds 10 percent of the adjusted gross income of the individual.*

(B) NET DISASTER LOSS.—*For purposes of subparagraph (A), the term "net disaster loss" means the excess of—*

(i) *the personal casualty losses—*

(I) *attributable to a federally declared disaster occurring before January 1, 2010, and*

(II) *occurring in a disaster area, over*

(ii) *personal casualty gains.*

(C) FEDERALLY DECLARED DISASTER.—*For purposes of this paragraph—*

(i) FEDERALLY DECLARED DISASTER.—*The term "federally declared disaster" means any disaster subsequently determined by the President of the United States to warrant assistance by the Federal Government under the Robert T. Stafford Disaster Relief and Emergency Assistance Act.*

(ii) DISASTER AREA.—*The term "disaster area" means the area so determined to warrant such assistance.*

(4) DEFINITIONS OF PERSONAL CASUALTY GAIN AND PERSONAL CASUALTY LOSS.—For purposes of this subsection—

(A) PERSONAL CASUALTY GAIN.—The term "personal casualty gain" means the recognized gain from any involuntary conversion of property, which is described in subsection (c)(3) arising from fire, storm, shipwreck, or other casualty, or from theft.

(B) PERSONAL CASUALTY LOSS.—The term "personal casualty loss" means any loss described in subsection (c)(3). For purposes of *paragraphs (2) and (3)*, the amount of any personal casualty loss shall be determined after the application of paragraph (1).

(5) SPECIAL RULES.—

* * *

[CCH Explanation at ¶605. Committee Reports at ¶10,710.]

Amendments

• **2008, Tax Extenders and Alternative Minimum Tax Relief Act of 2008 (P.L. 110-343)**

P.L. 110-343, Division C, §706(a)(1):

Amended Code Sec. 165(h) by redesignating paragraphs (3) and (4) as paragraphs (4) and (5), respectively, and by inserting after paragraph (2) a new paragraph (3). **Effective** for disasters declared in tax years beginning after 12-31-2007.

P.L. 110-343, Division C, §706(a)(2)(A):

Amended Code Sec. 165(h)(4)(B) (as so redesignated) by striking "paragraph (2)" and inserting "paragraphs (2) and

(3)". **Effective** for disasters declared in tax years beginning after 12-31-2007.

P.L. 110-343, Division C, §706(c):

Amended Code Sec. 165(h)(1) by striking "$100" and inserting "$500 ($100 for taxable years beginning after December 31, 2009)". **Effective** for tax years beginning after 12-31-2008.

(i) DISASTER LOSSES.—

(1) ELECTION TO TAKE DEDUCTION FOR PRECEDING YEAR.—Notwithstanding the provisions of subsection (a), any *loss occurring in a disaster area (as defined by clause (ii) of subsection (h)(3)(C)) and attributable to a federally declared disaster (as defined by clause (i) of such subsection)* may, at the election of the taxpayer, be taken into account for the taxable year immediately preceding the taxable year in which the disaster occurred.

* * *

(4) USE OF DISASTER LOAN APPRAISALS TO ESTABLISH AMOUNT OF LOSS.—Nothing in this title shall be construed to prohibit the Secretary from prescribing regulations or other guidance under

which an appraisal for the purpose of obtaining a loan of Federal funds or a loan guarantee from the Federal Government as a result of a *federally declared disaster (as defined by subsection (h)(3)(C)(i)[)]* may be used to establish the amount of any loss described in paragraph (1) or (2).

* * *

[CCH Explanation at ¶605. Committee Reports at ¶10,710.]

Amendments

• **2008, Tax Extenders and Alternative Minimum Tax Relief Act of 2008 (P.L. 110-343)**

P.L. 110-343, Division C, §706(a)(2)(B):

Amended Code Sec. 165(i)(1) by striking "loss" and all that follows through "Act" and inserting "loss occurring in a disaster area (as defined by clause (ii) of subsection (h)(3)(C)) and attributable to a federally declared disaster (as defined by clause (i) of such subsection)". **Effective** for disasters declared in tax years beginning after 12-31-2007. Prior to being stricken, "loss" and all that follows through "Act" read as follows:

loss attributable to a disaster occurring in an area subsequently determined by the President of the United States to warrant assistance by the Federal Government under the Robert T. Stafford Disaster Relief and Emergency Assistance Act

P.L. 110-343, Division C, §706(a)(2)(C):

Amended Code Sec. 165(i)(4) by striking "Presidentially declared disaster (as defined by section 1033(h)(3))" and inserting "federally declared disaster (as defined by subsection (h)(3)(C)(i)[)]". **Effective** for disasters declared in tax years beginning after 12-31-2007.

[¶5230] CODE SEC. 168. ACCELERATED COST RECOVERY SYSTEM.

* * *

(b) APPLICABLE DEPRECIATION METHOD.—For purposes of this section—

* * *

(2) 150 PERCENT DECLINING BALANCE METHOD IN CERTAIN CASES.—Paragraph (1) shall be applied by substituting "150 percent" for "200 percent" in the case of—

* * *

(B) any property used in a farming business (within the meaning of section 263A(e)(4)),

(C) *any property (other than property described in paragraph (3)) which is a qualified smart electric meter or qualified smart electric grid system, or*

(D) any property (other than property described in paragraph (3)) with respect to which the taxpayer elects under paragraph (5) to have the provisions of this paragraph apply.

(3) PROPERTY TO WHICH STRAIGHT LINE METHOD APPLIES.—The applicable depreciation method shall be the straight line method in the case of the following property:

* * *

⇥ *Caution: Code Sec. 168(b)(3)(I), below, as added by P.L. 110-343, applies to property placed in service after December 31, 2008.*

(I) *Qualified retail improvement property described in subsection (e)(8).*

* * *

[CCH Explanations at ¶315 and ¶570. Committee Reports at ¶10,240 and ¶10,450.]

Amendments

• **2008, Tax Extenders and Alternative Minimum Tax Relief Act of 2008 (P.L. 110-343)**

P.L. 110-343, Division C, §305(c)(3):

Amended Code Sec. 168(b)(3) by adding at the end a new subparagraph (I). **Effective** for property placed in service after 12-31-2008.

P.L. 110-343, Division B, §306(c):

Amended Code Sec. 168(b)(2) by striking "or" at the end of subparagraph (B), redesignating subparagraph (C) as subparagraph (D), and by inserting after subparagraph (B) a new subparagraph (C). **Effective** for property placed in service after 10-3-2008.

(e) CLASSIFICATION OF PROPERTY.—For purposes of this section—

* * *

(3) CLASSIFICATION OF CERTAIN PROPERTY.—

* * *

(B) 5-YEAR PROPERTY.—The term "5-year property" includes—

* * *

(v) any section 1245 property used in connection with research and experimentation,

(vi) any property which—

* * *

(III) is described in section 48(l)(3)(A)(ix) (as in effect on the day before the date of the enactment of the Revenue Reconciliation Act of 1990), *and*

»»→ *Caution: Code Sec. 168(e)(3)(B)(vii), below, as added by P.L. 110-343, applies to property placed in service after December 31, 2008.*

(vii) any machinery or equipment (other than any grain bin, cotton ginning asset, fence, or other land improvement) which is used in a farming business (as defined in section 263A(e)(4)), the original use of which commences with the taxpayer after December 31, 2008, and which is placed in service before January 1, 2010.

* * *

(D) 10-YEAR PROPERTY.—The term "10-year property" includes—

(i) any single purpose agricultural or horticultural structure (within the meaning of subsection (i)(13)),

(ii) any tree or vine bearing fruit or nuts,

(iii) any qualified smart electric meter, and

(iv) any qualified smart electric grid system.

(E) 15-YEAR PROPERTY.—The term "15-year property" includes—

* * *

(iv) any qualified leasehold improvement property placed in service before *January 1, 2010,*

(v) any qualified restaurant property placed in service before *January 1, 2010,*

* * *

(vii) any section 1245 property (as defined in section 1245(a)(3)) used in the transmission at 69 or more kilovolts of electricity for sale and the original use of which commences with the taxpayer after April 11, 2005,

(viii) any natural gas distribution line the original use of which commences with the taxpayer after April 11, 2005, and which is placed in service before January 1, 2011, *and*

»»→ *Caution: Code Sec. 168(e)(3)(E)(ix), below, as added by P.L. 110-343, applies to property placed in service after December 31, 2008.*

(ix) any qualified retail improvement property placed in service after December 31, 2008, and before January 1, 2010.

* * *

»»→ *Caution: Code Sec. 168(e)(7), below, as amended by P.L. 110-343, applies to property placed in service after December 31, 2008.*

(7) QUALIFIED RESTAURANT PROPERTY.—

(A) IN GENERAL.—The term "qualified restaurant property" means any section 1250 property which is—

(i) a building, if such building is placed in service after December 31, 2008, and before January 1, 2010, or

(ii) an improvement to a building,

if more than 50 percent of the building's square footage is devoted to preparation of, and seating for on-premises consumption of, prepared meals.

(B) EXCLUSION FROM BONUS DEPRECIATION.—*Property described in this paragraph shall not be considered qualified property for purposes of subsection (k).*

≫→ Caution: Code Sec. 168(e)(8), below, as added by P.L. 110-343, applies to property placed in service after December 31, 2008.

(8) QUALIFIED RETAIL IMPROVEMENT PROPERTY.—

(A) IN GENERAL.—*The term "qualified retail improvement property" means any improvement to an interior portion of a building which is nonresidential real property if—*

(i) such portion is open to the general public and is used in the retail trade or business of selling tangible personal property to the general public, and

(ii) such improvement is placed in service more than 3 years after the date the building was first placed in service.

(B) IMPROVEMENTS MADE BY OWNER.—*In the case of an improvement made by the owner of such improvement, such improvement shall be qualified retail improvement property (if at all) only so long as such improvement is held by such owner. Rules similar to the rules under paragraph (6)(B) shall apply for purposes of the preceding sentence.*

(C) CERTAIN IMPROVEMENTS NOT INCLUDED.—*Such term shall not include any improvement for which the expenditure is attributable to—*

(i) the enlargement of the building,

(ii) any elevator or escalator,

(iii) any structural component benefitting a common area, or

(iv) the internal structural framework of the building.

(D) EXCLUSION FROM BONUS DEPRECIATION.—*Property described in this paragraph shall not be considered qualified property for purposes of subsection (k).*

(E) TERMINATION.—*Such term shall not include any improvement placed in service after December 31, 2009.*

* * *

[CCH Explanation at ¶570. Committee Reports at ¶10,240.]

Amendments

• **2008, Energy Improvement and Extension Act of 2008 (P.L. 110-343)**

P.L. 110-343, Division B, §306(a):

Amended Code Sec. 168(e)(3)(D) by striking "and" at the end of clause (i), by striking the period at the end of clause (ii) and inserting a comma, and by inserting after clause (ii) new clauses (iii)-(iv). **Effective** for property placed in service after 10-3-2008.

• **2008, Tax Extenders and Alternative Minimum Tax Relief Act of 2008 (P.L. 110-343)**

P.L. 110-343, Division C, §305(a)(1):

Amended Code Sec. 168(e)(3)(E)(iv) and (v) by striking "January 1, 2008" and inserting "January 1, 2010". **Effective** for property placed in service after 12-31-2007.

P.L. 110-343, Division C, §305(b)(1):

Amended Code Sec. 168(e)(7). **Effective** for property placed in service after 12-31-2008. Prior to amendment, Code Sec. 168(e)(7) read as follows:

(7) QUALIFIED RESTAURANT PROPERTY.—The term "qualified restaurant property" means any section 1250 property which is an improvement to a building if—

(A) such improvement is placed in service more than 3 years after the date such building was first placed in service, and

(B) more than 50 percent of the building's square footage is devoted to preparation of, and seating for on-premises consumption of, prepared meals.

P.L. 110-343, Division C, §305(c)(1):

Amended Code Sec. 168(e)(3)(E) by striking "and" at the end of clause (vii), by striking the period at the end of clause (viii) and inserting ", and", and by adding at the end a new clause (ix). **Effective** for property placed in service after 12-31-2008.

P.L. 110-343, Division C, §305(c)(2):

Amended Code Sec. 168(e) by adding at the end a new paragraph (8). **Effective** for property placed in service after 12-31-2008.

P.L. 110-343, Division C, §505(a):

Amended Code Sec. 168(e)(3)(B) by striking "and" at the end of clause (v), by striking the period at the end of clause (vi)(III) and inserting ", and", and by inserting after clause (vi) a new clause (vii). **Effective** for property placed in service after 12-31-2008.

(g) ALTERNATIVE DEPRECIATION SYSTEM FOR CERTAIN PROPERTY.—

* * *

(3) SPECIAL RULES FOR DETERMINING CLASS LIFE.—

* * *

➤➤➤ *Caution: The table in Code Sec. 168(g)(3)(B), below, as amended by P.L. 110-343, applies to property place in service after December 31, 2008.*

(B) SPECIAL RULE FOR CERTAIN PROPERTY ASSIGNED TO CLASSES.—For purposes of paragraph (2), in the case of property described in any of the following subparagraphs of subsection (e)(3), the class life shall be determined as follows:

If property is described in subparagraph:	The class life is:
(A)(iii)	4
(B)(ii)	5
(B)(iii)	9.5
(B)(vii)	10
(C)(i)	10
(C)(iii)	22
(C)(iv)	14
(D)(i)	15
(D)(ii)	20
(E)(i)	24
(E)(ii)	24
(E)(iii)	20
(E)(iv)	39
(E)(v)	39
(E)(vi)	20
(E)(vii)	30
(E)(viii)	35
(E)(ix)	39
(F)	25

* * *

[CCH Explanations at ¶315 and ¶320. Committee Reports at ¶10,450.]

Amendments

• 2008, Tax Extenders and Alternative Minimum Tax Relief Act of 2008 (P.L. 110-343)

P.L. 110-343, Division C, §305(c)(4):

Amended the table contained in Code Sec. 168(g)(3)(B) by inserting after the item relating to subparagraph (E)(viii) a new item. **Effective** for property placed in service after 12-31-2008.

P.L. 110-343, Division C, §505(b):

Amended the table contained in Code Sec. 168(g)(3)(B) by inserting after the item relating to subparagraph (B)(iii) a new item. **Effective** for property placed in service after 12-31-2008.

(i) DEFINITIONS AND SPECIAL RULES.—For purposes of this section—

* * *

(15) MOTORSPORTS ENTERTAINMENT COMPLEX.—

* * *

(D) TERMINATION.—Such term shall not include any property placed in service after December 31, 2009.

* * *

(18) QUALIFIED SMART ELECTRIC METERS.—

(A) IN GENERAL.—The term *"qualified smart electric meter"* means any smart electric meter which—

(i) is placed in service by a taxpayer who is a supplier of electric energy or a provider of electric energy services, and

(ii) *does not have a class life (determined without regard to subsection (e)) of less than 10 years.*

(B) SMART ELECTRIC METER.—*For purposes of subparagraph (A), the term "smart electric meter" means any time-based meter and related communication equipment which is capable of being used by the taxpayer as part of a system that—*

(i) *measures and records electricity usage data on a time-differentiated basis in at least 24 separate time segments per day,*

(ii) *provides for the exchange of information between supplier or provider and the customer's electric meter in support of time-based rates or other forms of demand response,*

(iii) *provides data to such supplier or provider so that the supplier or provider can provide energy usage information to customers electronically, and*

(iv) *provides net metering.*

(19) QUALIFIED SMART ELECTRIC GRID SYSTEMS.—

(A) IN GENERAL.—*The term "qualified smart electric grid system" means any smart grid property which—*

(i) *is used as part of a system for electric distribution grid communications, monitoring, and management placed in service by a taxpayer who is a supplier of electric energy or a provider of electric energy services, and*

(ii) *does not have a class life (determined without regard to subsection (e)) of less than 10 years.*

(B) SMART GRID PROPERTY.—*For the purposes of subparagraph (A), the term "smart grid property" means electronics and related equipment that is capable of—*

(i) *sensing, collecting, and monitoring data of or from all portions of a utility's electric distribution grid,*

(ii) *providing real-time, two-way communications to monitor or manage such grid, and*

(iii) *providing real time analysis of and event prediction based upon collected data that can be used to improve electric distribution system reliability, quality, and performance.*

[CCH Explanation at ¶570. Committee Reports at ¶10,240.]

Amendments

• **2008, Energy Improvement and Extension Act of 2008 (P.L. 110-343)**

P.L. 110-343, Division B, §306(b):

Amended Code Sec. 168(i) by inserting at the end new paragraph[s] (18)-(19). **Effective** for property placed in service after 10-3-2008.

• **2008, Tax Extenders and Alternative Minimum Tax Relief Act of 2008 (P.L. 110-343)**

P.L. 110-343, Division C, §317(a):

Amended Code Sec. 168(i)(15)(D) by striking "December 31, 2007" and inserting "December 31, 2009". **Effective** for property placed in service after 12-31-2007.

(j) PROPERTY ON INDIAN RESERVATIONS.—

* * *

(8) TERMINATION.—This subsection shall not apply to property placed in service after *December 31, 2009.*

* * *

[CCH Explanation at ¶335. Committee Reports at ¶10,530.]

Amendments

• **2008, Tax Extenders and Alternative Minimum Tax Relief Act of 2008 (P.L. 110-343)**

P.L. 110-343, Division C, §315(a):

Amended Code Sec. 168(j)(8) by striking "December 31, 2007" and inserting "December 31, 2009". **Effective** for property placed in service after 12-31-2007.

(l) SPECIAL ALLOWANCE FOR *CELLULOSIC BIOFUEL* PLANT PROPERTY.—

(1) ADDITIONAL ALLOWANCE.—In the case of any qualified *cellulosic biofuel* plant property—

(A) the depreciation deduction provided by section 167(a) for the taxable year in which such property is placed in service shall include an allowance equal to 50 percent of the adjusted basis of such property, and

(B) the adjusted basis of such property shall be reduced by the amount of such deduction before computing the amount otherwise allowable as a depreciation deduction under this chapter for such taxable year and any subsequent taxable year.

(2) QUALIFIED *CELLULOSIC BIOFUEL* PLANT PROPERTY.—The term "qualified *cellulosic biofuel* plant property" means property of a character subject to the allowance for depreciation—

(A) which is used in the United States solely to produce *cellulosic biofuel,*

(B) the original use of which commences with the taxpayer after the date of the enactment of this subsection,

(C) which is acquired by the taxpayer by purchase (as defined in section 179(d)) after the date of the enactment of this subsection, but only if no written binding contract for the acquisition was in effect on or before the date of the enactment of this subsection, and

(D) which is placed in service by the taxpayer before January 1, 2013.

(3) CELLULOSIC BIOFUEL.—The term "cellulosic biofuel" means any liquid fuel which is produced from any lignocellulosic or hemicellulosic matter that is available on a renewable or recurring basis.

* * *

(5) SPECIAL RULES.—For purposes of this subsection, rules similar to the rules of subparagraph (E) of section 168(k)(2) shall apply, except that such subparagraph shall be applied—

(A) by substituting "the date of the enactment of subsection (l)" for "December 31, 2007" each place it appears therein,

(B) by substituting "January 1, 2013" for "January 1, 2009" in clause (i) thereof, and

(C) by substituting "qualified *cellulosic biofuel* plant property" for "qualified property" in clause (iv) thereof.

* * *

(7) RECAPTURE.—For purposes of this subsection, rules similar to the rules under section 179(d)(10) shall apply with respect to any qualified *cellulosic biofuel* plant property which ceases to be qualified *cellulosic biofuel* plant property.

(8) DENIAL OF DOUBLE BENEFIT.—Paragraph (1) shall not apply to any qualified *cellulosic biofuel* plant property with respect to which an election has been made under section 179C (relating to election to expense certain refineries).

[CCH Explanation at ¶330. Committee Reports at ¶10,140.]

Amendments

• **2008, Energy Improvement and Extension Act of 2008 (P.L. 110-343)**

P.L. 110-343, Division B, §201(a):

Amended Code Sec. 168(l)(3). **Effective** for property placed in service after 10-3-2008, in tax years ending after such date. Prior to amendment, Code Sec. 168(l)(3) read as follows:

(3) CELLULOSIC BIOMASS ETHANOL.—For purposes of this subsection, the term "cellulosic biomass ethanol" means ethanol produced by hydrolysis of any lignocellulosic or hemicellulosic matter that is available on a renewable or recurring basis.

P.L. 110-343, Division B, §201(b)(1)-(3):

Amended Code Sec. 168(l) by striking "cellulosic biomass ethanol" each place it appears and inserting "cellulosic biofuel", by striking "CELLULOSIC BIOMASS ETHANOL" in the heading of such subsection and inserting "CELLULOSIC BIOFUEL", and by striking CELLULOSIC BIOMASS ETHANOL in the heading of paragraph (2) thereof and inserting CELLULOSIC BIOFUEL. **Effective** for property placed in service after 10-3-2008, in tax years ending after such date.

(m) SPECIAL ALLOWANCE FOR CERTAIN REUSE AND RECYCLING PROPERTY.—

(1) IN GENERAL.—In the case of any qualified reuse and recycling property—

(A) the depreciation deduction provided by section 167(a) for the taxable year in which such property is placed in service shall include an allowance equal to 50 percent of the adjusted basis of the qualified reuse and recycling property, and

(B) the adjusted basis of the qualified reuse and recycling property shall be reduced by the amount of such deduction before computing the amount otherwise allowable as a depreciation deduction under this chapter for such taxable year and any subsequent taxable year.

(2) QUALIFIED REUSE AND RECYCLING PROPERTY.—For purposes of this subsection—

(A) IN GENERAL.—The term "qualified reuse and recycling property" means any reuse and recycling property—

(i) to which this section applies,

(ii) which has a useful life of at least 5 years,

(iii) the original use of which commences with the taxpayer after August 31, 2008, and

(iv) which is—

(I) acquired by purchase (as defined in section 179(d)(2)) by the taxpayer after August 31, 2008, but only if no written binding contract for the acquisition was in effect before September 1, 2008, or

(II) acquired by the taxpayer pursuant to a written binding contract which was entered into after August 31, 2008.

(B) EXCEPTIONS.—

(i) BONUS DEPRECIATION PROPERTY UNDER SUBSECTION (k).—The term "qualified reuse and recycling property" shall not include any property to which section 168(k) applies.

(ii) ALTERNATIVE DEPRECIATION PROPERTY.—The term "qualified reuse and recycling property" shall not include any property to which the alternative depreciation system under subsection (g) applies, determined without regard to paragraph (7) of subsection (g) (relating to election to have system apply).

(iii) ELECTION OUT.—If a taxpayer makes an election under this clause with respect to any class of property for any taxable year, this subsection shall not apply to all property in such class placed in service during such taxable year.

(C) SPECIAL RULE FOR SELF-CONSTRUCTED PROPERTY.—In the case of a taxpayer manufacturing, constructing, or producing property for the taxpayer's own use, the requirements of clause (iv) of subparagraph (A) shall be treated as met if the taxpayer begins manufacturing, constructing, or producing the property after August 31, 2008.

(D) DEDUCTION ALLOWED IN COMPUTING MINIMUM TAX.—For purposes of determining alternative minimum taxable income under section 55, the deduction under subsection (a) for qualified reuse and recycling property shall be determined under this section without regard to any adjustment under section 56.

(3) DEFINITIONS.—For purposes of this subsection—

(A) REUSE AND RECYCLING PROPERTY.—

(i) IN GENERAL.—The term "reuse and recycling property" means any machinery and equipment (not including buildings or real estate), along with all appurtenances thereto, including software necessary to operate such equipment, which is used exclusively to collect, distribute, or recycle qualified reuse and recyclable materials.

(ii) EXCLUSION.—Such term does not include rolling stock or other equipment used to transport reuse and recyclable materials.

(B) QUALIFIED REUSE AND RECYCLABLE MATERIALS.—

(i) IN GENERAL.—The term "qualified reuse and recyclable materials" means scrap plastic, scrap glass, scrap textiles, scrap rubber, scrap packaging, recovered fiber, scrap ferrous and nonferrous metals, or electronic scrap generated by an individual or business.

Code Sec. 168(m)(3)(B)(i)   ¶5230

(ii) ELECTRONIC SCRAP.—*For purposes of clause (i), the term "electronic scrap" means—*

(I) *any cathode ray tube, flat panel screen, or similar video display device with a screen size greater than 4 inches measured diagonally, or*

(II) *any central processing unit.*

(C) RECYCLING OR RECYCLE.—*The term "recycling" or "recycle" means that process (including sorting) by which worn or superfluous materials are manufactured or processed into specification grade commodities that are suitable for use as a replacement or substitute for virgin materials in manufacturing tangible consumer and commercial products, including packaging.*

[CCH Explanation at ¶ 565.]
Amendments
• **2008, Energy Improvement and Extension Act of 2008 (P.L. 110-343)**

P.L. 110-343, Division B, § 308(a):

Amended Code Sec. 168 by adding at the end a new subsection (m). **Effective** for property placed in service after 8-31-2008.

(n) SPECIAL ALLOWANCE FOR QUALIFIED DISASTER ASSISTANCE PROPERTY.—

(1) IN GENERAL.—*In the case of any qualified disaster assistance property—*

(A) *the depreciation deduction provided by section 167(a) for the taxable year in which such property is placed in service shall include an allowance equal to 50 percent of the adjusted basis of the qualified disaster assistance property, and*

(B) *the adjusted basis of the qualified disaster assistance property shall be reduced by the amount of such deduction before computing the amount otherwise allowable as a depreciation deduction under this chapter for such taxable year and any subsequent taxable year.*

(2) QUALIFIED DISASTER ASSISTANCE PROPERTY.—*For purposes of this subsection—*

(A) IN GENERAL.—*The term "qualified disaster assistance property" means any property—*

(i)(I) *which is described in subsection (k)(2)(A)(i), or*

(II) *which is nonresidential real property or residential rental property,*

(ii) *substantially all of the use of which is—*

(I) *in a disaster area with respect to a federally declared disaster occurring before January 1, 2010, and*

(II) *in the active conduct of a trade or business by the taxpayer in such disaster area,*

(iii) *which—*

(I) *rehabilitates property damaged, or replaces property destroyed or condemned, as a result of such federally declared disaster, except that, for purposes of this clause, property shall be treated as replacing property destroyed or condemned if, as part of an integrated plan, such property replaces property which is included in a continuous area which includes real property destroyed or condemned, and*

(II) *is similar in nature to, and located in the same county as, the property being rehabilitated or replaced,*

(iv) *the original use of which in such disaster area commences with an eligible taxpayer on or after the applicable disaster date,*

(v) *which is acquired by such eligible taxpayer by purchase (as defined in section 179(d)) on or after the applicable disaster date, but only if no written binding contract for the acquisition was in effect before such date, and*

(vi) *which is placed in service by such eligible taxpayer on or before the date which is the last day of the third calendar year following the applicable disaster date (the fourth calendar year in the case of nonresidential real property and residential rental property).*

(B) EXCEPTIONS.—

(i) OTHER BONUS DEPRECIATION PROPERTY.—The term "qualified disaster assistance property" shall not include—

(I) any property to which subsection (k) (determined without regard to paragraph (4)), (l), or (m) applies,

(II) any property to which section 1400N(d) applies, and

(III) any property described in section 1400N(p)(3).

(ii) ALTERNATIVE DEPRECIATION PROPERTY.—The term "qualified disaster assistance property" shall not include any property to which the alternative depreciation system under subsection (g) applies, determined without regard to paragraph (7) of subsection (g) (relating to election to have system apply).

(iii) TAX-EXEMPT BOND FINANCED PROPERTY.—Such term shall not include any property any portion of which is financed with the proceeds of any obligation the interest on which is exempt from tax under section 103.

(iv) QUALIFIED REVITALIZATION BUILDINGS.—Such term shall not include any qualified revitalization building with respect to which the taxpayer has elected the application of paragraph (1) or (2) of section 1400I(a).

(v) ELECTION OUT.—If a taxpayer makes an election under this clause with respect to any class of property for any taxable year, this subsection shall not apply to all property in such class placed in service during such taxable year.

(C) SPECIAL RULES.—For purposes of this subsection, rules similar to the rules of subparagraph (E) of subsection (k)(2) shall apply, except that such subparagraph shall be applied—

(i) by substituting "the applicable disaster date" for "December 31, 2007" each place it appears therein,

(ii) without regard to "and before January 1, 2009" in clause (i) thereof, and

(iii) by substituting "qualified disaster assistance property" for "qualified property" in clause (iv) thereof.

(D) ALLOWANCE AGAINST ALTERNATIVE MINIMUM TAX.—For purposes of this subsection, rules similar to the rules of subsection (k)(2)(G) shall apply.

(3) OTHER DEFINITIONS.—For purposes of this subsection—

(A) APPLICABLE DISASTER DATE.—The term "applicable disaster date" means, with respect to any federally declared disaster, the date on which such federally declared disaster occurs.

(B) FEDERALLY DECLARED DISASTER.—The term "federally declared disaster" has the meaning given such term under section 165(h)(3)(C)(i).

(C) DISASTER AREA.—The term "disaster area" has the meaning given such term under section 165(h)(3)(C)(ii).

(D) ELIGIBLE TAXPAYER.—The term "eligible taxpayer" means a taxpayer who has suffered an economic loss attributable to a federally declared disaster.

(4) RECAPTURE.—For purposes of this subsection, rules similar to the rules under section 179(d)(10) shall apply with respect to any qualified disaster assistance property which ceases to be qualified disaster assistance property.

[CCH Explanation at ¶ 620.]

Amendments

• **2008, Tax Extenders and Alternative Minimum Tax Relief Act of 2008 (P.L. 110-343)**

P.L. 110-343, Division C, § 710(a):

Amended Code Sec. 168, as amended by this Act, by adding at the end a new subsection (n). **Effective** for prop-

erty placed in service after 12-31-2007, with respect [to] disasters declared after such date.

[¶ 5235] CODE SEC. 170. CHARITABLE, ETC., CONTRIBUTIONS AND GIFTS.

* * *

(b) PERCENTAGE LIMITATIONS.—

* * *

(3) TEMPORARY SUSPENSION OF LIMITATIONS ON CHARITABLE CONTRIBUTIONS.—In the case of a qualified farmer or rancher (as defined in paragraph (1)(E)(v)), any charitable contribution of food—

(A) to which subsection (e)(3)(C) applies (without regard to clause (ii) thereof), and

(B) which is made during the period beginning on the date of the enactment of this paragraph and before January 1, 2009,

shall be treated for purposes of paragraph (1)(E) or (2)(B), whichever is applicable, as if it were a qualified conservation contribution which is made by a qualified farmer or rancher and which otherwise meets the requirements of such paragraph.

* * *

[CCH Explanation at ¶ 445. Committee Reports at ¶ 10,600.]

Amendments

• **2008, Tax Extenders and Alternative Minimum Tax Relief Act of 2008 (P.L. 110-343)**

P.L. 110-343, Division C, § 323(b)(1):

Amended Code Sec. 170(b) by adding a new paragraph (3). **Effective** for tax years ending after 10-3-2008.

(e) CERTAIN CONTRIBUTIONS OF ORDINARY INCOME AND CAPITAL GAIN PROPERTY.—

* * *

(3) SPECIAL RULE FOR CERTAIN CONTRIBUTIONS OF INVENTORY AND OTHER PROPERTY.—

* * *

(C) SPECIAL RULE FOR CONTRIBUTIONS OF FOOD INVENTORY.—

* * *

(iv) TERMINATION.—This subparagraph shall not apply to contributions made after *December 31, 2009.*

(D) SPECIAL RULE FOR CONTRIBUTIONS OF BOOK INVENTORY TO PUBLIC SCHOOLS.—

* * *

(iii) CERTIFICATION BY DONEE.—Subparagraph (A) shall not apply to any contribution *of books* unless (in addition to the certifications required by subparagraph (A) (as modified by this subparagraph))), the donee certifies in writing that—

(I) the books are suitable, in terms of currency, content, and quantity, for use in the donee's educational programs, and

(II) the donee will use the books in its educational programs.

(iv) TERMINATION.—This subparagraph shall not apply to contributions made after *December 31, 2009.*

* * *

(6) SPECIAL RULE FOR CONTRIBUTIONS OF COMPUTER TECHNOLOGY AND EQUIPMENT FOR EDUCATIONAL PURPOSES.—

* * *

(G) TERMINATION.—This paragraph shall not apply to any contribution made during any taxable year beginning after *December 31, 2009*.

* * *

[CCH Explanations at ¶440, ¶445 and ¶450. Committee Reports at ¶10,580, ¶10,600 and ¶10,610.]

Amendments

• **2008, Tax Extenders and Alternative Minimum Tax Relief Act of 2008 (P.L. 110-343)**

P.L. 110-343, Division C, §321(a):

Amended Code Sec. 170(e)(6)(G) by striking "December 31, 2007" and inserting "December 31, 2009". **Effective** for contributions made during tax years beginning after 12-31-2007.

P.L. 110-343, Division C, §323(a)(1):

Amended Code Sec. 170(e)(3)(C)(iv) by striking "December 31, 2007" and inserting "December 31, 2009". **Effective** for contributions made after 12-31-2007.

P.L. 110-343, Division C, §324(a):

Amended Code Sec. 170(e)(3)(D)(iv) by striking "December 31, 2007" and inserting "December 31, 2009". **Effective** for contributions made after 12-31-2007.

P.L. 110-343, Division C, §324(b):

Amended Code Sec. 170(e)(3)(D)(iii) by inserting "of books" after "to any contribution". **Effective** for contributions made after 12-31-2007.

[¶5240] CODE SEC. 172. NET OPERATING LOSS DEDUCTION.

* * *

(b) NET OPERATING LOSS CARRYBACKS AND CARRYOVERS.—

(1) YEARS TO WHICH LOSS MAY BE CARRIED.—

* * *

(F) RETENTION OF 3-YEAR CARRYBACK IN CERTAIN CASES.—

* * *

(ii) ELIGIBLE LOSS.—For purposes of clause (i), the term "eligible loss" means—

(I) in the case of an individual, losses of property arising from fire, storm, shipwreck, or other casualty, or from theft,

(II) in the case of a taxpayer which is a small business, net operating losses attributable to *federally declared disasters (as defined by subsection (h)(3)(C)(i))*, and

(III) in the case of a taxpayer engaged in the trade or business of farming (as defined in section 263A(e)(4)), net operating losses attributable to such *federally declared disasters*.

Such term shall not include any farming loss (as defined in subsection (i)) *or qualified disaster loss (as defined in subsection (j))*.

* * *

(J) *CERTAIN LOSSES ATTRIBUTABLE FEDERALLY DECLARED DISASTERS.—In the case of a taxpayer who has a qualified disaster loss (as defined in subsection (j)), such loss shall be a net operating loss carryback to each of the 5 taxable years preceding the taxable year of such loss.*

* * *

[CCH Explanations at ¶ 605 and ¶ 610. Committee Reports at ¶ 10,710 and ¶ 10,730.]

Amendments

• **2008, Tax Extenders and Alternative Minimum Tax Relief Act of 2008 (P.L. 110-343)**

P.L. 110-343, Division C, § 706(a)(2)(D)(v):

Amended Code Sec. 172(b)(1)(F)(ii)(II) by striking "Presidentially declared disasters (as defined in section 1033(h)(3))" and inserting "federally declared disasters (as defined by subsection (h)(3)(C)(i))". **Effective** for disasters declared in tax years beginning after 12-31-2007.

P.L. 110-343, Division C, § 706(a)(2)(D)(vi):

Amended Code Sec. 172(b)(1)(F)(ii)(III) by striking "Presidentially declared disasters" and inserting "federally declared disasters". **Effective** for disasters declared in tax years beginning after 12-31-2007.

P.L. 110-343, Division C, § 708(a):

Amended Code Sec. 172(b)(1) by adding at the end a new subparagraph (J). **Effective** for losses arising in tax years beginning after 12-31-2007, in connection with disasters declared after such date.

P.L. 110-343, Division C, § 708(d)(1):

Amended Code Sec. 172(b)(1)(F)(ii) by inserting "or qualified disaster loss (as defined in subsection (j))" before the period at the end of the last sentence. **Effective** for losses arising in tax years beginning after 12-31-2007, in connection with disasters declared after such date.

(i) RULES RELATING TO FARMING LOSSES.—For purposes of this section—

(1) IN GENERAL.—The term "farming loss" means the lesser of—

(A) the amount which would be the net operating loss for the taxable year if only income and deductions attributable to farming businesses (as defined in section 263A(e)(4)) are taken into account, or

(B) the amount of the net operating loss for such taxable year.

Such term shall not include any qualified disaster loss (as defined in subsection (j)).

* * *

[CCH Explanation at ¶ 610. Committee Reports at ¶ 10,730.]

Amendments

• **2008, Tax Extenders and Alternative Minimum Tax Relief Act of 2008 (P.L. 110-343)**

P.L. 110-343, Division C, § 708(d)(2):

Amended Code Sec. 172(i)(1) by adding at the end a new flush sentence. **Effective** for losses arising in tax years beginning after 12-31-2007, in connection with disasters declared after such date.

(j) RULES RELATING TO QUALIFIED DISASTER LOSSES.—*For purposes of this section—*

(1) IN GENERAL.—*The term "qualified disaster loss" means the lesser of—*

(A) the sum of—

(i) the losses allowable under section 165 for the taxable year—

(I) attributable to a federally declared disaster (as defined in section 165(h)(3)(C)(i)) occurring before January 1, 2010, and

(II) occurring in a disaster area (as defined in section 165(h)(3)(C)(ii)), and

(ii) the deduction for the taxable year for qualified disaster expenses which is allowable under section 198A(a) or which would be so allowable if not otherwise treated as an expense, or

(B) the net operating loss for such taxable year.

(2) COORDINATION WITH SUBSECTION (b)(2).—*For purposes of applying subsection (b)(2), a qualified disaster loss for any taxable year shall be treated in a manner similar to the manner in which a specified liability loss is treated.*

(3) ELECTION.—*Any taxpayer entitled to a 5-year carryback under subsection (b)(1)(J) from any loss year may elect to have the carryback period with respect to such loss year determined without regard to subsection (b)(1)(J). Such election shall be made in such manner as may be prescribed by the Secretary and shall be made by the due date (including extensions of time) for filing the taxpayer's return for the taxable year of the net operating loss. Such election, once made for any taxable year, shall be irrevocable for such taxable year.*

(4) EXCLUSION.—The term "qualified disaster loss" shall not include any loss with respect to any property described in section 1400N(p)(3).

[CCH Explanation at ¶ 610. Committee Reports at ¶ 10,730.]

<table>
<tr><td>

Amendments

• **2008, Tax Extenders and Alternative Minimum Tax Relief Act of 2008 (P.L. 110-343)**

P.L. 110-343, Division C, § 708(b):

Amended Code Sec. 172 by redesignating subsections (j) and (k) as subsections (k) and (l), respectively, and by

</td><td>

inserting after subsection (i) a new subsection (j). **Effective** for losses arising in tax years beginning after 12-31-2007, in connection with disasters declared after such date.

</td></tr>
</table>

(k) ELECTION TO DISREGARD 5-YEAR CARRYBACK FOR CERTAIN NET OPERATING LOSSES.—Any taxpayer entitled to a 5-year carryback under subsection (b)(1)(H) from any loss year may elect to have the carryback period with respect to such loss year determined without regard to subsection (b)(1)(H). Such election shall be made in such manner as may be prescribed by the Secretary and shall be made by the due date (including extensions of time) for filing the taxpayer's return for the taxable year of the net operating loss. Such election, once made for any taxable year, shall be irrevocable for such taxable year.

[CCH Explanation at ¶ 610. Committee Reports at ¶ 10,730.]

<table>
<tr><td>

Amendments

• **2008, Tax Extenders and Alternative Minimum Tax Relief Act of 2008 (P.L. 110-343)**

P.L. 110-343, Division C, § 708(b):

Amended Code Sec. 172 by redesignating subsections (j) as subsection (k). **Effective** for losses arising in tax years

</td><td>

beginning after 12-31-2007, in connection with disasters declared after such date.

</td></tr>
</table>

(l) CROSS REFERENCES.—

(1) For treatment of net operating loss carryovers in certain corporate acquisitions, see section 381.

(2) For special limitation on net operating loss carryovers in case of a corporate change of ownership, see section 382.

[CCH Explanation at ¶ 610. Committee Reports at ¶ 10,730.]

<table>
<tr><td>

Amendments

• **2008, Tax Extenders and Alternative Minimum Tax Relief Act of 2008 (P.L. 110-343)**

P.L. 110-343, Division C, § 708(b):

Amended Code Sec. 172 by redesignating subsection (k) as subsection (l). **Effective** for losses arising in tax years

</td><td>

beginning after 12-31-2007, in connection with disasters declared after such date.

</td></tr>
</table>

[¶ 5245] CODE SEC. 179. ELECTION TO EXPENSE CERTAIN DEPRECIABLE BUSINESS ASSETS.

* * *

(e) SPECIAL RULES FOR QUALIFIED DISASTER ASSISTANCE PROPERTY.—

(1) IN GENERAL.—For purposes of this section—

(A) the dollar amount in effect under subsection (b)(1) for the taxable year shall be increased by the lesser of—

(i) $100,000, or

(ii) the cost of qualified section 179 disaster assistance property placed in service during the taxable year, and

(B) the dollar amount in effect under subsection (b)(2) for the taxable year shall be increased by the lesser of—

(i) $600,000, or

(ii) *the cost of qualified section 179 disaster assistance property placed in service during the taxable year.*

(2) QUALIFIED SECTION 179 DISASTER ASSISTANCE PROPERTY.—*For purposes of this subsection, the term "qualified section 179 disaster assistance property" means section 179 property (as defined in subsection (d)) which is qualified disaster assistance property (as defined in section 168(n)(2)).*

(3) COORDINATION WITH EMPOWERMENT ZONES AND RENEWAL COMMUNITIES.—*For purposes of sections 1397A and 1400J, qualified section 179 disaster assistance property shall not be treated as qualified zone property or qualified renewal property, unless the taxpayer elects not to take such qualified section 179 disaster assistance property into account for purposes of this subsection.*

(4) RECAPTURE.—*For purposes of this subsection, rules similar to the rules under subsection (d)(10) shall apply with respect to any qualified section 179 disaster assistance property which ceases to be qualified section 179 disaster assistance property.*

[CCH Explanation at ¶ 625.]

Amendments

• **2008, Tax Extenders and Alternative Minimum Tax Relief Act of 2008 (P.L. 110-343)**

P.L. 110-343, Division C, § 711(a):

Amended Code Sec. 179 by adding at the end a new subsection (e). **Effective** for property placed in service after 12-31-2007, with respect [to] disasters declared after such date.

[¶ 5250] CODE SEC. 179C. ELECTION TO EXPENSE CERTAIN REFINERIES.

* * *

(c) QUALIFIED REFINERY PROPERTY.—

(1) IN GENERAL.—The term "qualified refinery property" means any portion of a qualified refinery—

* * *

(B) which is placed in service by the taxpayer after the date of the enactment of this section and before *January 1, 2014,*

* * *

(F)(i) the construction of which is subject to a written binding construction contract entered into before *January 1, 2010,*

(ii) which is placed in service before *January 1, 2010,* or

(iii) in the case of self-constructed property, the construction of which began after June 14, 2005, and before *January 1, 2010.*

* * *

[CCH Explanation at ¶ 350.]

Amendments

• **2008, Energy Improvement and Extension Act of 2008 (P.L. 110-343)**

P.L. 110-343, Division B, § 209(a)(1)-(2):

Amended Code Sec. 179C(c)(1) by striking "January 1, 2012" in subparagraph (B) and inserting "January 1, 2014",

and by striking "January 1, 2008" each place it appears in subparagraph (F) and inserting "January 1, 2010". **Effective** for property placed in service after 10-3-2008.

(d) QUALIFIED REFINERY.—For purposes of this section, the term "qualified refinery" means any refinery located in the United States which is designed to serve the primary purpose of processing liquid fuel from crude oil or qualified fuels (as defined in section 45K(c)), *or directly from shale or tar sands.*

[CCH Explanation at ¶350.]

Amendments

• 2008, Energy Improvement and Extension Act of 2008 (P.L. 110-343)

P.L. 110-343, Division B, §209(b)(1):

Amended Code Sec. 179C(d) by inserting ", or directly from shale or tar sands" after "(as defined in section 45K(c))". **Effective** for property placed in service after 10-3-2008.

(e) PRODUCTION CAPACITY.—The requirements of this subsection are met if the portion of the qualified refinery—

* * *

(2) enables the existing qualified refinery to process *shale, tar sands, or* qualified fuels (as defined in section 45K(c)) at a rate which is equal to or greater than 25 percent of the total throughput of such qualified refinery on an average daily basis.

* * *

[CCH Explanation at ¶350.]

Amendments

• 2008, Energy Improvement and Extension Act of 2008 (P.L. 110-343)

P.L. 110-343, Division B, §209(b)(2):

Amended Code Sec. 179C(e)(2) by inserting "shale, tar sands, or" before "qualified fuels". **Effective** for property placed in service after 10-3-2008.

[¶5255] CODE SEC. 179D. ENERGY EFFICIENT COMMERCIAL BUILDINGS DEDUCTION.

* * *

(h) TERMINATION.—This section shall not apply with respect to property placed in service after *December 31, 2013.*

[CCH Explanation at ¶560. Committee Reports at ¶10,220.]

Amendments

• 2008, Energy Improvement and Extension Act of 2008 (P.L. 110-343)

P.L. 110-343, Division B, §303:

Amended Code Sec. 179D(h) by striking "December 31, 2008" and inserting "December 31, 2013". **Effective** 10-3-2008.

[¶5260] CODE SEC. 179E. ELECTION TO EXPENSE ADVANCED MINE SAFETY EQUIPMENT.

* * *

(g) TERMINATION.—This section shall not apply to property placed in service after *December 31, 2009.*

[CCH Explanation at ¶360.]

Amendments

• 2008, Tax Extenders and Alternative Minimum Tax Relief Act of 2008 (P.L. 110-343)

P.L. 110-343, Division C, §311:

Amended Code Sec. 179E(g) by striking "December 31, 2008" and inserting "December 31, 2009". **Effective** 10-3-2008.

[¶5265] CODE SEC. 181. TREATMENT OF CERTAIN QUALIFIED FILM AND TELEVISION PRODUCTIONS.

(a) ELECTION TO TREAT COSTS AS EXPENSES.—

* * *

(2) DOLLAR LIMITATION.—

(A) IN GENERAL.—*Paragraph (1) shall not apply to so much of the aggregate cost of any qualified film or television production as exceeds $15,000,000.*

* * *

[CCH Explanation at ¶345. Committee Reports at ¶10,650 and ¶10,660.]

Amendments

• **2008, Tax Extenders and Alternative Minimum Tax Relief Act of 2008 (P.L. 110-343)**

P.L. 110-343, Division C, §502(b):

Amended Code Sec. 181(a)(2)(A). **Effective** for qualified film and television productions commencing after

12-31-2007. Prior to amendment, Code Sec. 181(a)(2)(A) read as follows:

(A) IN GENERAL.—Paragraph (1) shall not apply to any qualified film or television production the aggregate cost of which exceeds $15,000,000.

(d) QUALIFIED FILM OR TELEVISION PRODUCTION.—For purposes of this section—

* * *

(3) QUALIFIED COMPENSATION.—For purposes of paragraph (1)—

(A) IN GENERAL.—The term "qualified compensation" means compensation for services performed in the United States by *actors, production personnel, directors, and producers.*

* * *

[CCH Explanation at ¶345. Committee Reports at ¶10,650 and ¶10,660.]

Amendments

• **2008, Tax Extenders and Alternative Minimum Tax Relief Act of 2008 (P.L. 110-343)**

P.L. 110-343, Division C, §502(d):

Amended Code Sec. 181(d)(3)(A) by striking "actors" and all that follows and inserting "actors, production personnel,

directors, and producers.". **Effective** for qualified film and television productions commencing after 12-31-2007. Prior to amendment, Code Sec. 181(d)(3)(A) read as follows:

(A) IN GENERAL.—The term "qualified compensation" means compensation for services performed in the United States by actors, directors, producers, and other relevant production personnel.

(f) TERMINATION.—This section shall not apply to qualified film and television productions commencing after *December 31, 2009.*

[CCH Explanation at ¶345. Committee Reports at ¶10,650 and ¶10,660.]

Amendments

• **2008, Tax Extenders and Alternative Minimum Tax Relief Act of 2008 (P.L. 110-343)**

P.L. 110-343, Division C, §502(a):

Amended Code Sec. 181(f) by striking "December 31, 2008" and inserting "December 31, 2009". **Effective** for qual-

ified film and television productions commencing after 12-31-2007.

[¶5270] CODE SEC. 198. EXPENSING OF ENVIRONMENTAL REMEDIATION COSTS.

* * *

(h) TERMINATION.—This section shall not apply to expenditures paid or incurred after *December 31, 2009.*

[CCH Explanation at ¶340. Committee Reports at ¶10,560.]

Amendments

• 2008, Tax Extenders and Alternative Minimum Tax Relief Act of 2008 (P.L. 110-343)

P.L. 110-343, Division C, §318(a):

Amended Code Sec. 198(h) by striking "December 31, 2007" and inserting "December 31, 2009". **Effective** for expenditures paid or incurred after 12-31-2007.

[¶5275] CODE SEC. 198A. EXPENSING OF QUALIFIED DISASTER EXPENSES.

(a) IN GENERAL.—*A taxpayer may elect to treat any qualified disaster expenses which are paid or incurred by the taxpayer as an expense which is not chargeable to capital account. Any expense which is so treated shall be allowed as a deduction for the taxable year in which it is paid or incurred.*

(b) QUALIFIED DISASTER EXPENSE.—*For purposes of this section, the term "qualified disaster expense" means any expenditure—*

(1) *which is paid or incurred in connection with a trade or business or with business-related property,*

(2) *which is—*

(A) *for the abatement or control of hazardous substances that were released on account of a federally declared disaster occurring before January 1, 2010,*

(B) *for the removal of debris from, or the demolition of structures on, real property which is business-related property damaged or destroyed as a result of a federally declared disaster occurring before such date, or*

(C) *for the repair of business-related property damaged as a result of a federally declared disaster occurring before such date, and*

(3) *which is otherwise chargeable to capital account.*

(c) OTHER DEFINITIONS.—*For purposes of this section—*

(1) BUSINESS-RELATED PROPERTY.—*The term "business-related property" means property—*

(A) *held by the taxpayer for use in a trade or business or for the production of income, or*

(B) *described in section 1221(a)(1) in the hands of the taxpayer.*

(2) FEDERALLY DECLARED DISASTER.—*The term "federally declared disaster" has the meaning given such term by section 165(h)(3)(C)(i).*

(d) DEDUCTION RECAPTURED AS ORDINARY INCOME ON SALE, ETC.—*Solely for purposes of section 1245, in the case of property to which a qualified disaster expense would have been capitalized but for this section—*

(1) *the deduction allowed by this section for such expense shall be treated as a deduction for depreciation, and*

(2) *such property (if not otherwise section 1245 property) shall be treated as section 1245 property solely for purposes of applying section 1245 to such deduction.*

(e) COORDINATION WITH OTHER PROVISIONS.—*Sections 198, 280B, and 468 shall not apply to amounts which are treated as expenses under this section.*

(f) REGULATIONS.—*The Secretary shall prescribe such regulations as may be necessary or appropriate to carry out the purposes of this section.*

[CCH Explanation at ¶615. Committee Reports at ¶10,720.]

Amendments

• 2008, Tax Extenders and Alternative Minimum Tax Relief Act of 2008 (P.L. 110-343)

P.L. 110-343, Division C, §707(a):

Amended part VI of subchapter B of chapter 1 by inserting after Code Sec. 198 a new Code Sec. 198A. **Effective** for amounts paid or incurred after 12-31-2007 in connection with disaster declared after such date.

[¶ 5280] CODE SEC. 199. INCOME ATTRIBUTABLE TO DOMESTIC PRODUCTION ACTIVITIES.

* * *

(b) DEDUCTION LIMITED TO WAGES PAID.—

* * *

(2) W-2 WAGES.—For purposes of this section—

* * *

(D) SPECIAL RULE FOR QUALIFIED FILM.—*In the case of a qualified film, such term shall include compensation for services performed in the United States by actors, production personnel, directors, and producers.*

* * *

[CCH Explanation at ¶ 368. Committee Reports at ¶ 10,670.]
Amendments
• **2008, Tax Extenders and Alternative Minimum Tax Relief Act of 2008 (P.L. 110-343)**

P.L. 110-343, Division C, § 502(c)(1):

Amended Code Sec. 199(b)(2) by adding at the end a new subparagraph (D). **Effective** for tax years beginning after 12-31-2007.

(c) QUALIFIED PRODUCTION ACTIVITIES INCOME.—For purposes of this section—

* * *

(6) QUALIFIED FILM.—The term "qualified film" means any property described in section 168(f)(3) if not less than 50 percent of the total compensation relating to the production of such property is compensation for services performed in the United States by actors, production personnel, directors, and producers. Such term does not include property with respect to which records are required to be maintained under section 2257 of title 18, United States Code. *A qualified film shall include any copyrights, trademarks, or other intangibles with respect to such film. The methods and means of distributing a qualified film shall not affect the availability of the deduction under this section.*

* * *

[CCH Explanation at ¶ 368. Committee Reports at ¶ 10,670.]
Amendments
• **2008, Tax Extenders and Alternative Minimum Tax Relief Act of 2008 (P.L. 110-343)**

P.L. 110-343, Division C, § 502(c)(2):

Amended Code Sec. 199(c)(6) by adding at the end two new sentences. **Effective** for tax years beginning after 12-31-2007.

(d) DEFINITIONS AND SPECIAL RULES.—

(1) APPLICATION OF SECTION TO PASS-THRU ENTITIES.—

(A) PARTNERSHIPS AND S CORPORATIONS.—In the case of a partnership or S corporation—

* * *

(ii) each partner or shareholder shall take into account such person's allocable share of each item described in subparagraph (A) or (B) of subsection (c)(1) (determined without regard to whether the items described in such subparagraph (A) exceed the items described in such subparagraph (B)),

(iii) each partner or shareholder shall be treated for purposes of subsection (b) as having W-2 wages for the taxable year in an amount equal to such person's allocable share of the W-2 wages of the partnership or S corporation for the taxable year (as determined under regulations prescribed by the Secretary), *and*

(iv) in the case of each partner of a partnership, or shareholder of an S corporation, who owns (directly or indirectly) at least 20 percent of the capital interests in such partnership or of the stock of such S corporation—

(I) such partner or shareholder shall be treated as having engaged directly in any film produced by such partnership or S corporation, and

(II) such partnership or S corporation shall be treated as having engaged directly in any film produced by such partner or shareholder.

* * *

>>>→ *Caution: Code Sec. 199(d)(2), below, as amended by P.L. 110-343, applies to tax years beginning after December 31, 2008.*

(2) APPLICATION TO INDIVIDUALS.—In the case of an individual, *subsections (a)(1)(B) and (d)(9)(A)(iii)* shall be applied by substituting "adjusted gross income" for "taxable income". For purposes of the preceding sentence, adjusted gross income shall be determined—

(A) after application of sections 86, 135, 137, 219, 221, 222, and 469, and

(B) without regard to this section.

* * *

(8) TREATMENT OF ACTIVITIES IN PUERTO RICO.—

* * *

(C) TERMINATION.—This paragraph shall apply only with respect to the *first 4 taxable years* of the taxpayer beginning after December 31, 2005, and before *January 1, 2010.*

>>>→ *Caution: Code Sec. 199(d)(9), below, as added by P.L. 110-343, applies to tax years beginning after December 31, 2008.*

(9) SPECIAL RULE FOR TAXPAYERS WITH OIL RELATED QUALIFIED PRODUCTION ACTIVITIES INCOME.—

(A) IN GENERAL.—If a taxpayer has oil related qualified production activities income for any taxable year beginning after 2009, the amount otherwise allowable as a deduction under subsection (a) shall be reduced by 3 percent of the least of—

(i) the oil related qualified production activities income of the taxpayer for the taxable year,

(ii) the qualified production activities income of the taxpayer for the taxable year, or

(iii) taxable income (determined without regard to this section).

(B) OIL RELATED QUALIFIED PRODUCTION ACTIVITIES INCOME.—For purposes of this paragraph, the term "oil related qualified production activities income" means for any taxable year the qualified production activities income which is attributable to the production, refining, processing, transportation, or distribution of oil, gas, or any primary product thereof during such taxable year.

(C) PRIMARY PRODUCT.—For purposes of this paragraph, the term "primary product'" has the same meaning as when used in section 927(a)(2)(C), as in effect before its repeal.

(10) REGULATIONS.—The Secretary shall prescribe such regulations as are necessary to carry out the purposes of this section, including regulations which prevent more than 1 taxpayer from being allowed a deduction under this section with respect to any activity described in subsection (c)(4)(A)(i).

[CCH Explanations at ¶ 368, ¶ 370 and ¶ 375. Committee Reports at ¶ 10,260, ¶ 10,500 and ¶ 10,670.]

Amendments

• 2008, Energy Improvement and Extension Act of 2008 (P.L. 110-343)

P.L. 110-343, Division B, § 401(a):

Amended Code Sec. 199(d) by redesignating paragraph (9) as paragraph (10) and by inserting after paragraph (8) a new paragraph (9). **Effective** for tax years beginning after 12-31-2008.

P.L. 110-343, Division B, § 401(b):

Amended Code Sec. 199(d)(2) by striking "subsection (a)(1)(B)" and inserting "subsections (a)(1)(B) and (d)(9)(A)(iii)". **Effective** for tax years beginning after 12-31-2008.

• 2008, Tax Extenders and Alternative Minimum Tax Relief Act of 2008 (P.L. 110-343)

P.L. 110-343, Division C, § 312(a)(1)-(2):

Amended Code Sec. 199(d)(8)(C) by striking "first 2 taxable years" and inserting "first 4 taxable years", and by striking "January 1, 2008" and inserting "January 1, 2010". **Effective** for tax years beginning after 12-31-2007.

P.L. 110-343, Division C, § 502(c)(3):

Amended Code Sec. 199(d)(1)(A) by striking "and" at the end of clause (ii), by striking the period at the end of clause (iii) and inserting ", and", and by adding at the end a new clause (iv). **Effective** for tax years beginning after 12-31-2007.

[¶ 5285] CODE SEC. 222. QUALIFIED TUITION AND RELATED EXPENSES.

* * *

(e) TERMINATION.—This section shall not apply to taxable years beginning after *December 31, 2009.*

[CCH Explanation at ¶ 245. Committee Reports at ¶ 10,340.]

Amendments

• 2008, Tax Extenders and Alternative Minimum Tax Relief Act of 2008 (P.L. 110-343)

P.L. 110-343, Division C, § 202(a):

Amended Code Sec. 222(e) by striking "December 31, 2007" and inserting "December 31, 2009". **Effective** for tax years beginning after 12-31-2007.

[¶ 5290] CODE SEC. 280G. GOLDEN PARACHUTE PAYMENTS.

* * *

(e) SPECIAL RULE FOR APPLICATION TO EMPLOYERS PARTICIPATING IN THE TROUBLED ASSETS RELIEF PROGRAM.—

(1) IN GENERAL.—*In the case of the severance from employment of a covered executive of an applicable employer during the period during which the authorities under section 101(a) of the Emergency Economic Stabilization Act of 2008 are in effect (determined under section 120 of such Act), this section shall be applied to payments to such executive with the following modifications:*

(A) *Any reference to a disqualified individual (other than in subsection (c)) shall be treated as a reference to a covered executive.*

(B) *Any reference to a change described in subsection (b)(2)(A)(i) shall be treated as a reference to an applicable severance from employment of a covered executive, and any reference to a payment contingent on such a change shall be treated as a reference to any payment made during an applicable taxable year of the employer on account of such applicable severance from employment.*

(C) *Any reference to a corporation shall be treated as a reference to an applicable employer.*

(D) *The provisions of subsections (b)(2)(C), (b)(4), (b)(5), and (d)(5) shall not apply.*

(2) DEFINITIONS AND SPECIAL RULES.—*For purposes of this subsection:*

(A) DEFINITIONS.—*Any term used in this subsection which is also used in section 162(m)(5) shall have the meaning given such term by such section.*

(B) APPLICABLE SEVERANCE FROM EMPLOYMENT.—*The term "applicable severance from employment" means any severance from employment of a covered executive—*

(i) *by reason of an involuntary termination of the executive by the employer, or*

(ii) *in connection with any bankruptcy, liquidation, or receivership of the employer.*

(C) COORDINATION AND OTHER RULES.—

(i) IN GENERAL.—*If a payment which is treated as a parachute payment by reason of this subsection is also a parachute payment determined without regard to this subsection, this subsection shall not apply to such payment.*

(ii) REGULATORY AUTHORITY.—*The Secretary may prescribe such guidance, rules, or regulations as are necessary—*

(I) *to carry out the purposes of this subsection and the Emergency Economic Stabilization Act of 2008, including the extent to which this subsection applies in the case of any acquisition, merger, or reorganization of an applicable employer,*

(II) *to apply this section and section 4999 in cases where one or more payments with respect to any individual are treated as parachute payments by reason of this subsection, and other payments with respect to such individual are treated as parachute payments under this section without regard to this subsection, and*

(III) *to prevent the avoidance of the application of this section through the mischaracterization of a severance from employment as other than an applicable severance from employment.*

[CCH Explanation at ¶380. Committee Reports at ¶10,020.]

Amendments

• **2008, Emergency Economic Stabilization Act of 2008 (P.L. 110-343)**

P.L. 110-343, Division A, §302(b)(1)-(2):

Amended Code Sec. 280G by redesignating subsection (e) as subsection (f), and by inserting after subsection (d) a new

subsection (e). **Effective** for payments with respect to severances occurring during the period during which the authorities under section 101(a) of this Act are in effect (determined under section 120 of this Act).

(f) REGULATIONS.—The Secretary shall prescribe such regulations as may be necessary or appropriate to carry out the purposes of this section (including regulations for the application of this section in the case of related corporations and in the case of personal service corporations).

[CCH Explanation at ¶380. Committee Reports at ¶10,020.]

Amendments

• **2008, Emergency Economic Stabilization Act of 2008 (P.L. 110-343)**

P.L. 110-343, Division A, §302(b)(1)-(2):

Amended Code Sec. 280G by redesignating subsection (e) as subsection (f). **Effective** for payments with respect to

severances occurring during the period during which the authorities under section 101(a) of this Act are in effect (determined under section 120 of this Act).

[¶5295] CODE SEC. 408. INDIVIDUAL RETIREMENT ACCOUNTS.

* * *

(d) TAX TREATMENT OF DISTRIBUTIONS.—

* * *

(8) DISTRIBUTIONS FOR CHARITABLE PURPOSES.—

* * *

(F) TERMINATION.—This paragraph shall not apply to distributions made in taxable years beginning after *December 31, 2009.*

* * *

[CCH Explanation at ¶ 225. Committee Reports at ¶ 10,370.]

Amendments

• **2008, Tax Extenders and Alternative Minimum Tax Relief Act of 2008 (P.L. 110-343)**

P.L. 110-343, Division C, § 205(a):

Amended Code Sec. 408(d)(8)(F) by striking "December 31, 2007" and inserting "December 31, 2009". **Effective** for distributions made in tax years beginning after 12-31-2007.

[¶ 5300] CODE SEC. 451. GENERAL RULE FOR TAXABLE YEAR OF INCLUSION.

* * *

(i) Special Rule for Sales or Dispositions To Implement Federal Energy Regulatory Commission or State Electric Restructuring Policy.—

* * *

(3) Qualifying electric transmission transaction.—For purposes of this subsection, the term "qualifying electric transmission transaction" means any sale or other disposition before January 1, 2008 *(before January 1, 2010, in the case of a qualified electric utility)*, of—

(A) property used in the trade or business of providing electric transmission services, or

(B) any stock or partnership interest in a corporation or partnership, as the case may be, whose principal trade or business consists of providing electric transmission services,

but only if such sale or disposition is to an independent transmission company.

(4) Independent transmission company.—For purposes of this subsection, the term "independent transmission company" means—

* * *

(B) a person—

* * *

(ii) whose transmission facilities to which the election under this subsection applies are under the operational control of a Federal Energy Regulatory Commission-approved independent transmission provider before the close of the period specified in such authorization, but not later than *the date which is 4 years after the close of the taxable year in which the transaction occurs,* or

* * *

(5) Exempt utility property.—For purposes of this subsection:

* * *

(C) Exception for property located outside the United States.—*The term "exempt utility property" shall not include any property which is located outside the United States.*

(6) Qualified Electric Utility.—*For purposes of this subsection, the term "qualified electric utility" means a person that, as of the date of the qualifying electric transmission transaction, is vertically integrated, in that it is both—*

(A) *a transmitting utility (as defined in section 3(23) of the Federal Power Act (16 U.S.C. 796(23))) with respect to the transmission facilities to which the election under this subsection applies, and*

(B) *an electric utility (as defined in section 3(22) of the Federal Power Act (16 U.S.C. 796(22))).*

(7) Special rule for consolidated groups.—In the case of a corporation which is a member of an affiliated group filing a consolidated return, any exempt utility property purchased by another member of such group shall be treated as purchased by such corporation for purposes of applying paragraph (1)(A).

(8) TIME FOR ASSESSMENT OF DEFICIENCIES.—If the taxpayer has made the election under paragraph (1) and any gain is recognized by such taxpayer as provided in paragraph (1)(B), then—

(A) the statutory period for the assessment of any deficiency, for any taxable year in which any part of the gain on the transaction is realized, attributable to such gain shall not expire prior to the expiration of 3 years from the date the Secretary is notified by the taxpayer (in such manner as the Secretary may by regulations prescribe) of the purchase of exempt utility property or of an intention not to purchase such property, and

(B) such deficiency may be assessed before the expiration of such 3-year period notwithstanding any law or rule of law which would otherwise prevent such assessment.

(9) PURCHASE.—For purposes of this subsection, the taxpayer shall be considered to have purchased any property if the unadjusted basis of such property is its cost within the meaning of section 1012.

(10) ELECTION.—An election under paragraph (1) shall be made at such time and in such manner as the Secretary may require and, once made, shall be irrevocable.

(11) NONAPPLICATION OF INSTALLMENT SALES TREATMENT.—Section 453 shall not apply to any qualifying electric transmission transaction with respect to which an election to apply this subsection is made.

[CCH Explanation at ¶755. Committee Reports at ¶10,070.]

Amendments

• **2008, Energy Improvement and Extension Act of 2008 (P.L. 110-343)**

P.L. 110-343, Division B, §109(a)(1):

Amended Code Sec. 451(i)(3) by inserting "(before January 1, 2010, in the case of a qualified electric utility)" after "January 1, 2008". **Effective** for transactions after 12-31-2007.

P.L. 110-343, Division B, §109(a)(2):

Amended Code Sec. 451(i) by redesignating paragraphs (6) through (10) as paragraphs (7) through (11), respectively, and by inserting after paragraph (5) a new paragraph (6). **Effective** for transactions after 12-31-2007.

P.L. 110-343, Division B, §109(b):

Amended Code Sec. 451(i)(4)(B)(ii) by striking "December 31, 2007" and inserting "the date which is 4 years after the close of the taxable year in which the transaction occurs". **Effective** as if included in Act Sec. 909 of the American Jobs Creation Act of 2004 [**effective** for transactions occurring after 10-22-2004, in tax years ending after such date.—CCH].

P.L. 110-343, Division B, §109(c):

Amended Code Sec. 451(i)(5) by adding at the end a new subparagraph (C). **Effective** for transactions after 10-3-2008.

»»→ Caution: *Code Sec. 457A, below, as added by P.L. 110-343, applies generally to amounts deferred which are attributable to services performed after December 31, 2008.*

[¶5305] *CODE SEC. 457A. NONQUALIFIED DEFERRED COMPENSATION FROM CERTAIN TAX INDIFFERENT PARTIES.*

(a) IN GENERAL.—*Any compensation which is deferred under a nonqualified deferred compensation plan of a nonqualified entity shall be includible in gross income when there is no substantial risk of forfeiture of the rights to such compensation.*

(b) NONQUALIFIED ENTITY.—*For purposes of this section, the term "nonqualified entity" means—*

(1) any foreign corporation unless substantially all of its income is—

(A) effectively connected with the conduct of a trade or business in the United States, or

(B) subject to a comprehensive foreign income tax, and

(2) any partnership unless substantially all of its income is allocated to persons other than—

(A) foreign persons with respect to whom such income is not subject to a comprehensive foreign income tax, and

(B) organizations which are exempt from tax under this title.

(c) DETERMINABILITY OF AMOUNTS OF COMPENSATION.—

(1) IN GENERAL.—*If the amount of any compensation is not determinable at the time that such compensation is otherwise includible in gross income under subsection (a)—*

(A) such amount shall be so includible in gross income when determinable, and

(B) the tax imposed under this chapter for the taxable year in which such compensation is includible in gross income shall be increased by the sum of—

(i) the amount of interest determined under paragraph (2), and

(ii) an amount equal to 20 percent of the amount of such compensation.

(2) INTEREST.—For purposes of paragraph (1)(B)(i), the interest determined under this paragraph for any taxable year is the amount of interest at the underpayment rate under section 6621 plus 1 percentage point on the underpayments that would have occurred had the deferred compensation been includible in gross income for the taxable year in which first deferred or, if later, the first taxable year in which such deferred compensation is not subject to a substantial risk of forfeiture.

(d) OTHER DEFINITIONS AND SPECIAL RULES.—For purposes of this section—

(1) SUBSTANTIAL RISK OF FORFEITURE.—

(A) IN GENERAL.—The rights of a person to compensation shall be treated as subject to a substantial risk of forfeiture only if such person's rights to such compensation are conditioned upon the future performance of substantial services by any individual.

(B) EXCEPTION FOR COMPENSATION BASED ON GAIN RECOGNIZED ON AN INVESTMENT ASSET.—

(i) IN GENERAL.—To the extent provided in regulations prescribed by the Secretary, if compensation is determined solely by reference to the amount of gain recognized on the disposition of an investment asset, such compensation shall be treated as subject to a substantial risk of forfeiture until the date of such disposition.

(ii) INVESTMENT ASSET.—For purposes of clause (i), the term "investment asset" means any single asset (other than an investment fund or similar entity)—

(I) acquired directly by an investment fund or similar entity,

(II) with respect to which such entity does not (nor does any person related to such entity) participate in the active management of such asset (or if such asset is an interest in an entity, in the active management of the activities of such entity), and

(III) substantially all of any gain on the disposition of which (other than such deferred compensation) is allocated to investors in such entity.

(iii) COORDINATION WITH SPECIAL RULE.—Paragraph (3)(B) shall not apply to any compensation to which clause (i) applies.

(2) COMPREHENSIVE FOREIGN INCOME TAX.—The term "comprehensive foreign income tax" means, with respect to any foreign person, the income tax of a foreign country if—

(A) such person is eligible for the benefits of a comprehensive income tax treaty between such foreign country and the United States, or

(B) such person demonstrates to the satisfaction of the Secretary that such foreign country has a comprehensive income tax.

(3) NONQUALIFIED DEFERRED COMPENSATION PLAN.—

(A) IN GENERAL.—The term "nonqualified deferred compensation plan" has the meaning given such term under section 409A(d), except that such term shall include any plan that provides a right to compensation based on the appreciation in value of a specified number of equity units of the service recipient.

(B) EXCEPTION.—Compensation shall not be treated as deferred for purposes of this section if the service provider receives payment of such compensation not later than 12 months after the end of the taxable year of the service recipient during which the right to the payment of such compensation is no longer subject to a substantial risk of forfeiture.

(4) EXCEPTION FOR CERTAIN COMPENSATION WITH RESPECT TO EFFECTIVELY CONNECTED INCOME.—In the case a foreign corporation with income which is taxable under section 882, this section shall not apply to compensation which, had such compensation had been paid in cash on the date that such compensation

ceased to be subject to a substantial risk of forfeiture, would have been deductible by such foreign corporation against such income.

(5) APPLICATION OF RULES.—Rules similar to the rules of paragraphs (5) and (6) of section 409A(d) shall apply.

(e) REGULATIONS.—The Secretary shall prescribe such regulations as may be necessary or appropriate to carry out the purposes of this section, including regulations disregarding a substantial risk of forfeiture in cases where necessary to carry out the purposes of this section.

[CCH Explanation at ¶455. Committee Reports at ¶10,750.]

Amendments

• **2008, Tax Extenders and Alternative Minimum Tax Relief Act of 2008 (P.L. 110-343)**

P.L. 110-343, Division C, §801(a):

Amended subpart B of part II of subchapter E of chapter 1 by inserting after Code Sec. 457 a new Code Sec. 457A. **Effective** generally for amounts deferred which are attributable to services performed after 12-31-2008. For a special rule, see Act Sec. 801(d)(2), below.

P.L. 110-343, Division C, §801(d)(2)-(5), provides:

(2) APPLICATION TO EXISTING DEFERRALS.—In the case of any amount deferred to which the amendments made by this section do not apply solely by reason of the fact that the amount is attributable to services performed before January 1, 2009, to the extent such amount is not includible in gross income in a taxable year beginning before 2018, such amounts shall be includible in gross income in the later of—

(A) the last taxable year beginning before 2018, or

(B) the taxable year in which there is no substantial risk of forfeiture of the rights to such compensation (determined in the same manner as determined for purposes of section 457A of the Internal Revenue Code of 1986, as added by this section).

(3) ACCELERATED PAYMENTS.—No later than 120 days after the date of the enactment of this Act, the Secretary shall issue guidance providing a limited period of time during which a nonqualified deferred compensation arrangement attributable to services performed on or before December 31, 2008, may, without violating the requirements of section 409A(a) of the Internal Revenue Code of 1986, be amended to conform the date of distribution to the date the amounts are required to be included in income.

(4) CERTAIN BACK-TO-BACK ARRANGEMENTS.—If the taxpayer is also a service recipient and maintains one or more nonqualified deferred compensation arrangements for its service providers under which any amount is attributable to services performed on or before December 31, 2008, the guidance issued under paragraph (4) shall permit such arrangements to be amended to conform the dates of distribution under such arrangement to the date amounts are required to be included in the income of such taxpayer under this subsection.

(5) ACCELERATED PAYMENT NOT TREATED AS MATERIAL MODIFICATION.—Any amendment to a nonqualified deferred compensation arrangement made pursuant to paragraph (4) or (5) shall not be treated as a material modification of the arrangement for purposes of section 409A of the Internal Revenue Code of 1986.

[¶5310] CODE SEC. 512. UNRELATED BUSINESS TAXABLE INCOME.

* * *

(b) MODIFICATIONS.—The modifications referred to in subsection (a) are the following:

* * *

(13) SPECIAL RULES FOR CERTAIN AMOUNTS RECEIVED FROM CONTROLLED ENTITIES.—

* * *

(E) PARAGRAPH TO APPLY ONLY TO CERTAIN EXCESS PAYMENTS.—

* * *

(iv) TERMINATION.—This subparagraph shall not apply to payments received or accrued after *December 31, 2009.*

* * *

[CCH Explanation at ¶480. Committee Reports at ¶10,460.]

Amendments

• **2008, Tax Extenders and Alternative Minimum Tax Relief Act of 2008 (P.L. 110-343)**

P.L. 110-343, Division C, §306(a):

Amended Code Sec. 512(b)(13)(E)(iv) by striking "December 31, 2007" and inserting "December 31, 2009". **Effective** for payments received or accrued after 12-31-2007.

[¶5315] CODE SEC. 613A. LIMITATIONS ON PERCENTAGE DEPLETION IN CASE OF OIL AND GAS WELLS.

* * *

(c) EXEMPTION FOR INDEPENDENT PRODUCERS AND ROYALTY OWNERS.—

* * *

(6) OIL AND NATURAL GAS PRODUCED FROM MARGINAL PROPERTIES.—

* * *

(H) TEMPORARY SUSPENSION OF TAXABLE INCOME LIMIT WITH RESPECT TO MARGINAL PRODUCTION.—The second sentence of subsection (a) of section 613 shall not apply to so much of the allowance for depletion as is determined under subparagraph (A) *for any taxable year—*

(i) *beginning after December 31, 1997, and before January 1, 2008, or*

(ii) *beginning after December 31, 2008, and before January 1, 2010.*

* * *

[CCH Explanation at ¶355.]

Amendments

• **2008, Energy Improvement and Extension Act of 2008 (P.L. 110-343)**

P.L. 110-343, Division B, §210:

Amended Code Sec. 613A(c)(6)(H) by striking "for any taxable year" and all that follows and inserting "for any taxable year—" and new clauses (i)-(ii). **Effective** 10-3-2008.

Prior to amendment, Code Sec. 613A(c)(6)(H) read as follows:

(H) TEMPORARY SUSPENSION OF TAXABLE INCOME LIMIT WITH RESPECT TO MARGINAL PRODUCTION.—The second sentence of subsection (a) of section 613 shall not apply to so much of the allowance for depletion as is determined under subparagraph (A) for any taxable year beginning after December 31, 1997, and before January 1, 2008.

[¶5320] CODE SEC. 871. TAX ON NONRESIDENT ALIEN INDIVIDUALS.

* * *

(k) EXEMPTION FOR CERTAIN DIVIDENDS OF REGULATED INVESTMENT COMPANIES.—

(1) INTEREST-RELATED DIVIDENDS.—

* * *

(C) INTEREST-RELATED DIVIDEND.—For purposes of this paragraph, the term "interest-related dividend" means any dividend (or part thereof) which is designated by the regulated investment company as an interest-related dividend in a written notice mailed to its shareholders not later than 60 days after the close of its taxable year. If the aggregate amount so designated with respect to a taxable year of the company (including amounts so designated with respect to dividends paid after the close of the taxable year described in section 855) is greater than the qualified net interest income of the company for such taxable year, the portion of each distribution which shall be an interest-related dividend shall be only that portion of the amounts so designated which such qualified net interest income bears to the aggregate amount so designated. Such term shall not include any dividend with respect to any taxable year of the company beginning after *December 31, 2009.*

* * *

(2) SHORT-TERM CAPITAL GAIN DIVIDENDS.—

* * *

(C) SHORT-TERM CAPITAL GAIN DIVIDEND.—For purposes of this paragraph, the term "short-term capital gain dividend" means any dividend (or part thereof) which is designated by the regulated investment company as a short-term capital gain dividend in a written notice mailed to its shareholders not later than 60 days after the close of its taxable year. If the aggregate amount so designated with respect to a taxable year of the company (including amounts so designated with respect to dividends paid after the close of the taxable year described in section 855) is greater than the qualified short-term gain of the company for such taxable year, the portion of each distribution which shall be a short-term capital gain dividend shall be only that portion of the amounts so designated which such qualified short-term gain bears to the aggregate amount so designated. Such term shall not include any dividend with respect to any taxable year of the company beginning after *December 31, 2009.*

* * *

[CCH Explanation at ¶470. Committee Reports at ¶10,380.]

Amendments

• **2008, Tax Extenders and Alternative Minimum Tax Relief Act of 2008 (P.L. 110-343)**

P.L. 110-343, Division C, §206(a):

Amended Code Sec. 871(k)(1)(C) by striking "December 31, 2007" and inserting "December 31, 2009". **Effective** for dividends with respect to tax years of regulated investment companies beginning after 12-31-2007.

P.L. 110-343, Division C, §206(b):

Amended Code Sec. 871(k)(2)(C) by striking "December 31, 2007" and inserting "December 31, 2009". **Effective** for dividends with respect to tax years of regulated investment companies beginning after 12-31-2007.

[¶5325] CODE SEC. 897. DISPOSITION OF INVESTMENT IN UNITED STATES REAL PROPERTY.

* * *

(h) SPECIAL RULES FOR CERTAIN INVESTMENT ENTITIES.—For purposes of this section—

* * *

(4) DEFINITIONS.—

(A) QUALIFIED INVESTMENT ENTITY.—

* * *

(ii) TERMINATION.—Clause (i)(II) shall not apply after *December 31, 2009.* Notwithstanding the preceding sentence, an entity described in clause (i)(II) shall be treated as a qualified investment entity for purposes of applying paragraphs (1) and (5) and section 1445 with respect to any distribution by the entity to a nonresident alien individual or a foreign corporation which is attributable directly or indirectly to a distribution to the entity from a real estate investment trust.

* * *

[CCH Explanation at ¶870. Committee Reports at ¶10,400.]

Amendments

• **2008, Tax Extenders and Alternative Minimum Tax Relief Act of 2008 (P.L. 110-343)**

P.L. 110-343, Division C, §208(a):

Amended Code Sec. 897(h)(4)(A)(ii) by striking "December 31, 2007" and inserting "December 31, 2009". **Effective** 1-1-2008.

[¶5330] CODE SEC. 907. SPECIAL RULES IN CASE OF FOREIGN OIL AND GAS INCOME.

⮞⮞➔ *Caution: Code Sec. 907(a), below, as amended by P.L. 110-343, applies to tax years beginning after December 31, 2008.*

(a) REDUCTION IN AMOUNT ALLOWED AS FOREIGN TAX UNDER SECTION 901.—*In applying section 901, the amount of any foreign oil and gas taxes paid or accrued (or deemed to have been paid) during the taxable year which would (but for this subsection) be taken into account for purposes of section 901 shall be reduced by the amount (if any) by which the amount of such taxes exceeds the product of—*

(1) the amount of the combined foreign oil and gas income for the taxable year,

(2) multiplied by—

(A) in the case of a corporation, the percentage which is equal to the highest rate of tax specified under section 11(b), or

(B) in the case of an individual, a fraction the numerator of which is the tax against which the credit under section 901(a) is taken and the denominator of which is the taxpayer's entire taxable income.

[CCH Explanation at ¶ 875. Committee Reports at ¶ 10,270.]

Amendments

• **2008, Energy Improvement and Extension Act of 2008 (P.L. 110-343)**

P.L. 110-343, Division B, § 402(a):

Amended Code Sec. 907(a). **Effective** for tax years beginning after 12-31-2008. Prior to amendment, Code Sec. 907(a) read as follows:

(a) REDUCTION IN AMOUNT ALLOWED AS FOREIGN TAX UNDER SECTION 901.—In applying section 901, the amount of any oil and gas extraction taxes paid or accrued (or deemed to have been paid) during the taxable year which would (but for this subsection) be taken into account for purposes of sec-

tion 901 shall be reduced by the amount (if any) by which the amount of such taxes exceeds the product of—

(1) the amount of the foreign oil and gas extraction income for the taxable year,

(2) multiplied by—

(A) in the case of a corporation, the percentage which is equal to the highest rate of tax specified under section 11(b), or

(B) in the case of an individual, a fraction the numerator of which is the tax against which the credit under section 901(a) is taken and the denominator of which is the taxpayer's entire taxable income.

>>>→ *Caution: Code Sec. 907(b), below, as amended by P.L. 110-343, applies to tax years beginning after December 31, 2008.*

(b) COMBINED FOREIGN OIL AND GAS INCOME; FOREIGN OIL AND GAS TAXES.—For purposes of this section—

(1) COMBINED FOREIGN OIL AND GAS INCOME.—The term "combined foreign oil and gas income" means, with respect to any taxable year, the sum of—

(A) foreign oil and gas extraction income, and

(B) foreign oil related income.

(2) FOREIGN OIL AND GAS TAXES.—The term "foreign oil and gas taxes" means, with respect to any taxable year, the sum of—

(A) oil and gas extraction taxes, and

(B) any income, war profits, and excess profits taxes paid or accrued (or deemed to have been paid or accrued under section 902 or 960) during the taxable year with respect to foreign oil related income (determined without regard to subsection (c)(4)) or loss which would be taken into account for purposes of section 901 without regard to this section.

[CCH Explanation at ¶ 875. Committee Reports at ¶ 10,270.]

Amendments

• **2008, Energy Improvement and Extension Act of 2008 (P.L. 110-343)**

P.L. 110-343, Division B, § 402(a):

Amended Code Sec. 907(b). **Effective** for tax years beginning after 12-31-2008. Prior to amendment, Code Sec. 907(b) read as follows:

(b) FOREIGN TAXES ON FOREIGN OIL RELATED INCOME.—For purposes of this subtitle, in the case of taxes paid or accrued to any foreign country with respect to foreign oil related

income, the term "income, war profits, and excess profits taxes" shall not include any amount paid or accrued after December 31, 1982, to the extent that the Secretary determines that the foreign law imposing such amount of tax is structured, or in fact operates, so that the amount of tax imposed with respect to foreign oil related income will generally be materially greater, over a reasonable period of time, than the amount generally imposed on income that is neither foreign oil related income nor foreign oil and gas extraction income. In computing the amount not treated as tax under this subsection, such amount shall be treated as a deduction under the foreign law.

(c) FOREIGN INCOME DEFINITIONS AND SPECIAL RULES.—For purposes of this section—

* * *

>>>→ *Caution: Code Sec. 907(c)(4), below, as amended by P.L. 110-343, applies to tax years beginning after December 31, 2008.*

(4) RECAPTURE OF FOREIGN OIL AND GAS LOSSES BY RECHARACTERIZING LATER COMBINED FOREIGN OIL AND GAS INCOME.—

(A) IN GENERAL.—The combined foreign oil and gas income of a taxpayer for a taxable year (determined without regard to this paragraph) shall be reduced—

(i) first by the amount determined under subparagraph (B), and

(ii) then by the amount determined under subparagraph (C).

The aggregate amount of such reductions shall be treated as income (from sources without the United States) which is not combined foreign oil and gas income.

(B) REDUCTION FOR PRE-2009 FOREIGN OIL EXTRACTION LOSSES.—The reduction under this paragraph shall be equal to the lesser of—

(i) the foreign oil and gas extraction income of the taxpayer for the taxable year (determined without regard to this paragraph), or

(ii) the excess of—

(I) the aggregate amount of foreign oil extraction losses for preceding taxable years beginning after December 31, 1982, and before January 1, 2009, over

(II) so much of such aggregate amount as was recharacterized under this paragraph (as in effect before and after the date of the enactment of the Energy Improvement and Extension Act of 2008) for preceding taxable years beginning after December 31, 1982.

(C) REDUCTION FOR POST-2008 FOREIGN OIL AND GAS LOSSES.—The reduction under this paragraph shall be equal to the lesser of—

(i) the combined foreign oil and gas income of the taxpayer for the taxable year (determined without regard to this paragraph), reduced by an amount equal to the reduction under subparagraph (A) for the taxable year, or

(ii) the excess of—

(I) the aggregate amount of foreign oil and gas losses for preceding taxable years beginning after December 31, 2008, over

(II) so much of such aggregate amount as was recharacterized under this paragraph for preceding taxable years beginning after December 31, 2008.

(D) FOREIGN OIL AND GAS LOSS DEFINED.—

(i) IN GENERAL.—For purposes of this paragraph, the term "foreign oil and gas loss" means the amount by which—

(I) the gross income for the taxable year from sources without the United States and its possessions (whether or not the taxpayer chooses the benefits of this subpart for such taxable year) taken into account in determining the combined foreign oil and gas income for such year, is exceeded by

(II) the sum of the deductions properly apportioned or allocated thereto.

(ii) NET OPERATING LOSS DEDUCTION NOT TAKEN INTO ACCOUNT.—For purposes of clause (i), the net operating loss deduction allowable for the taxable year under section 172(a) shall not be taken into account.

(iii) EXPROPRIATION AND CASUALTY LOSSES NOT TAKEN INTO ACCOUNT.—For purposes of clause (i), there shall not be taken into account—

(I) any foreign expropriation loss (as defined in section 172(h) (as in effect on the day before the date of the enactment of the Revenue Reconciliation Act of 1990)) for the taxable year, or

(II) any loss for the taxable year which arises from fire, storm, shipwreck, or other casualty, or from theft,

to the extent such loss is not compensated for by insurance or otherwise.

(iv) FOREIGN OIL EXTRACTION LOSS.—For purposes of subparagraph (B)(ii)(I), foreign oil extraction losses shall be determined under this paragraph as in effect on the day before the date of the enactment of the Energy Improvement and Extension Act of 2008.

* * *

Code Sec. 907(c)(4)(D)(iv)   ¶5330

[CCH Explanation at ¶875. Committee Reports at ¶10,270.]

Amendments

● **2008, Energy Improvement and Extension Act of 2008 (P.L. 110-343)**

P.L. 110-343, Division B, §402(b):

Amended Code Sec. 907(c)(4). **Effective** for tax years beginning after 12-31-2008. Prior to amendment, Code Sec. 907(c)(4) read as follows:

(4) RECAPTURE OF FOREIGN OIL AND GAS EXTRACTION LOSSES BY RECHARACTERIZING LATER EXTRACTION INCOME.—

(A) IN GENERAL.—That portion of the income of the taxpayer for the taxable year which (but for this paragraph) would be treated as foreign oil and gas extraction income shall be treated as income (from sources without the United States) which is not foreign oil and gas extraction income to the extent of the excess of—

(i) the aggregate amount of foreign oil extraction losses for preceding taxable years beginning after December 31, 1982, over

(ii) so much of such aggregate amount as was recharacterized under this subparagraph for preceding taxable years beginning after December 31, 1982.

(B) FOREIGN OIL EXTRACTION LOSS DEFINED.—

(i) IN GENERAL.—For purposes of this paragraph, the term "foreign oil extraction loss" means the amount by which—

(I) the gross income for the taxable year from sources without the United States and its possessions (whether or not the taxpayer chooses the benefits of this subpart for such taxable year) taken into account in determining the foreign oil and gas extraction income for such year, is exceeded by

(II) the sum of the deductions properly apportioned or allocated thereto.

(ii) NET OPERATING LOSS DEDUCTION NOT TAKEN INTO ACCOUNT.—For purposes of clause (i), the net operating loss deduction allowable for the taxable year under section 172(a) shall not be taken into account.

(iii) EXPROPRIATION AND CASUALTY LOSSES NOT TAKEN INTO ACCOUNT.—For purposes of clause (i), there shall not be taken into account—

(I) any foreign expropriation loss (as defined in section 172(h) (as in effect on the day before the date of the enactment of the Revenue Reconciliation Act of 1990)) for the taxable year, or

(II) any loss for the taxable year which arises from fire, storm, shipwreck, or other casualty, or from theft,

to the extent such loss is not compensated for by insurance or otherwise.

»»→ Caution: Code Sec. 907(f), below, as amended by P.L. 110-343, applies to tax years beginning after December 31, 2008.

(f) CARRYBACK AND CARRYOVER OF DISALLOWED CREDITS.—

(1) IN GENERAL.—If the amount of the *foreign oil and gas taxes* paid or accrued during any taxable year exceeds the limitation provided by subsection (a) for such taxable year (hereinafter in this subsection referred to as the "unused credit year"), such excess shall be deemed to be *foreign oil and gas taxes* paid or accrued in the first preceding taxable year, and in any of the first 10 succeeding taxable year, in that order and to the extent not deemed tax paid or accrued in a prior taxable year by reason of the limitation imposed by paragraph (2). Such amount deemed paid or accrued in any taxable year may be availed of only as a tax credit and not as a deduction and only if the taxpayer for such year chooses to have the benefits of this subpart as to taxes paid or accrued for that year to foreign countries or possessions.

(2) LIMITATION.—The amount of the unused *foreign oil and gas taxes* which under paragraph (1) may be deemed paid or accrued in any preceding or succeeding taxable year shall not exceed the lesser of—

(A) the amount by which the limitation provided by subsection (a) for such taxable year exceeds the sum of—

(i) the *foreign oil and gas taxes* paid or accrued during such taxable year, plus

(ii) the amounts of the *foreign oil and gas taxes* which by reason of this subsection are deemed paid or accrued in such taxable year and are attributable to taxable years preceding the unused credit year; or

(B) the amount by which the limitation provided by section 904 for such taxable year exceeds the sum of—

(i) the taxes paid or accrued (or deemed to have been paid under section 902 or 960) to all foreign countries and possessions of the United States during such taxable year,

(ii) the amount of such taxes which were deemed paid or accrued in such taxable year under section 904(c) and which are attributable to taxable years preceding the unused credit year, plus

(iii) the amount of the *foreign oil and gas taxes* which by reason of this subsection are deemed paid or accrued in such taxable year and are attributable to taxable years preceding the unused credit year.

* * *

(4) TRANSITION RULES FOR PRE-2009 AND 2009 DISALLOWED CREDITS.—

(A) PRE-2009 CREDITS.—In the case of any unused credit year beginning before January 1, 2009, this subsection shall be applied to any unused oil and gas extraction taxes carried from such unused credit year to a year beginning after December 31, 2008—

(i) by substituting "oil and gas extraction taxes" for "foreign oil and gas taxes" each place it appears in paragraphs (1), (2), and (3), and

(ii) by computing, for purposes of paragraph (2)(A), the limitation under subparagraph (A) for the year to which such taxes are carried by substituting "foreign oil and gas extraction income" for "foreign oil and gas income" in subsection (a).

(B) 2009 CREDITS.—In the case of any unused credit year beginning in 2009, the amendments made to this subsection by the Energy Improvement and Extension Act of 2008 shall be treated as being in effect for any preceding year beginning before January 1, 2009, solely for purposes of determining how much of the unused foreign oil and gas taxes for such unused credit year may be deemed paid or accrued in such preceding year.

[CCH Explanation at ¶ 875. Committee Reports at ¶ 10,270.]

Amendments

• **2008, Energy Improvement and Extension Act of 2008 (P.L. 110-343)**

P.L. 110-343, Division B, § 402(c)(1)-(2):

Amended Code Sec. 907(f) by striking "oil and gas extraction taxes" each places it appears and inserting "foreign oil and gas taxes", and by adding at the end a new paragraph (4). **Effective** for tax years beginning after 12-31-2008.

[¶ 5335] CODE SEC. 953. INSURANCE INCOME.

* * *

(e) EXEMPT INSURANCE INCOME.—For purposes of this section—

* * *

(10) APPLICATION.—This subsection and section 954(i) shall apply only to taxable years of a foreign corporation beginning after December 31, 1998, and before *January 1, 2010,* and to taxable years of United States shareholders with or within which any such taxable year of such foreign corporation ends. If this subsection does not apply to a taxable year of a foreign corporation beginning after *December 31, 2009* (and taxable years of United States shareholders ending with or within such taxable year), then, notwithstanding the preceding sentence, subsection (a) shall be applied to such taxable years in the same manner as it would if the taxable year of the foreign corporation began in 1998.

* * *

[CCH Explanation at ¶ 860. Committee Reports at ¶ 10,430.]

Amendments

• **2008, Tax Extenders and Alternative Minimum Tax Relief Act of 2008 (P.L. 110-343)**

P.L. 110-343, Division C, § 303(a)(1)-(2):

Amended Code Sec. 953(e)(10) by striking "January 1, 2009" and inserting "January 1, 2010", and by striking "December 31, 2008" and inserting "December 31, 2009". **Effective** 10-3-2008.

[¶ 5340] CODE SEC. 954. FOREIGN BASE COMPANY INCOME.

* * *

(c) FOREIGN PERSONAL HOLDING COMPANY INCOME.—

* * *

(6) LOOK-THRU RULE FOR RELATED CONTROLLED FOREIGN CORPORATIONS.—

* * *

(C) APPLICATION.—Subparagraph (A) shall apply to taxable years of foreign corporations beginning after December 31, 2005, and before *January 1, 2010*, and to taxable years of United States shareholders with or within which such taxable years of foreign corporations end.

* * *

[CCH Explanation at ¶ 865. Committee Reports at ¶ 10,440.]

Amendments

• **2008, Tax Extenders and Alternative Minimum Tax Relief Act of 2008 (P.L. 110-343)**

P.L. 110-343, Division C, § 304(a):

Amended Code Sec. 954(c)(6)(C) by striking "January 1, 2009" and inserting "January 1, 2010". **Effective** for tax years of foreign corporations beginning after 12-31-2007, and for tax years of United States shareholders with or within which such tax years of foreign corporations end.

(h) SPECIAL RULE FOR INCOME DERIVED IN THE ACTIVE CONDUCT OF BANKING, FINANCING, OR SIMILAR BUSINESSES.—

* * *

(9) APPLICATION.—This subsection, subsection (c)(2)(C)(ii), and the last sentence of subsection (e)(2) shall apply only to taxable years of a foreign corporation beginning after December 31, 1998, and before *January 1, 2010*, and to taxable years of United States shareholders with or within which any such taxable year of such foreign corporation ends.

* * *

[CCH Explanation at ¶ 860. Committee Reports at ¶ 10,430.]

Amendments

• **2008, Tax Extenders and Alternative Minimum Tax Relief Act of 2008 (P.L. 110-343)**

P.L. 110-343, Division C, § 303(b):

Amended Code Sec. 954(h)(9) by striking "January 1, 2009" and inserting "January 1, 2010". **Effective** 10-3-2008.

»»➔ *Caution: Code Sec. 1012, below, as amended by P.L. 110-343, is effective January 1, 2011.*

[¶ 5345] *CODE SEC. 1012.* BASIS OF PROPERTY—COST.

(a) IN GENERAL.—*The basis of property* shall be the cost of such property, except as otherwise provided in this subchapter and subchapters C (relating to corporate distributions and adjustments), K (relating to partners and partnerships), and P (relating to capital gains and losses).

(b) SPECIAL RULE FOR APPORTIONED REAL ESTATE TAXES.—*The cost of real property* shall not include any amount in respect of real property taxes which are treated under section 164(d) as imposed on the taxpayer.

(c) DETERMINATIONS BY ACCOUNT.—

(1) IN GENERAL.—*In the case of the sale, exchange, or other disposition of a specified security on or after the applicable date, the conventions prescribed by regulations under this section shall be applied on an account by account basis.*

(2) APPLICATION TO CERTAIN FUNDS.—

(A) IN GENERAL.—*Except as provided in subparagraph (B), any stock for which an average basis method is permissible under section 1012 which is acquired before January 1, 2012, shall be treated as a separate account from any such stock acquired on or after such date.*

(B) ELECTION FUND FOR TREATMENT AS SINGLE ACCOUNT.—*If a fund described in subparagraph (A) elects to have this subparagraph apply with respect to one or more of its stockholders—*

(i) *subparagraph (A) shall not apply with respect to any stock in such fund held by such stockholders, and*

(ii) *all stock in such fund which is held by such stockholders shall be treated as covered securities described in section 6045(g)(3) without regard to the date of the acquisition of such stock.*

A rule similar to the rule of the preceding sentence shall apply with respect to a broker holding such stock as a nominee.

(3) DEFINITIONS.—*For purposes of this section, the terms "specified security" and "applicable date" shall have the meaning given such terms in section 6045(g).*

(d) AVERAGE BASIS FOR STOCK ACQUIRED PURSUANT TO A DIVIDEND REINVESTMENT PLAN.—

(1) IN GENERAL.—*In the case of any stock acquired after December 31, 2010, in connection with a dividend reinvestment plan, the basis of such stock while held as part of such plan shall be determined using one of the methods which may be used for determining the basis of stock in an open-end fund.*

(2) TREATMENT AFTER TRANSFER.—*In the case of the transfer to another account of stock to which paragraph (1) applies, such stock shall have a cost basis in such other account equal to its basis in the dividend reinvestment plan immediately before such transfer (properly adjusted for any fees or other charges taken into account in connection with such transfer).*

(3) SEPARATE ACCOUNTS; ELECTION FOR TREATMENT AS SINGLE ACCOUNT.—*Rules similar to the rules of subsection (c)(2) shall apply for purposes of this subsection.*

(4) DIVIDEND REINVESTMENT PLAN.—*For purposes of this subsection—*

(A) IN GENERAL.—*The term "dividend reinvestment plan" means any arrangement under which dividends on any stock are reinvested in stock identical to the stock with respect to which the dividends are paid.*

(B) INITIAL STOCK ACQUISITION TREATED AS ACQUIRED IN CONNECTION WITH PLAN.—*Stock shall be treated as acquired in connection with a dividend reinvestment plan if such stock is acquired pursuant to such plan or if the dividends paid on such stock are subject to such plan.*

[CCH Explanation at ¶730. Committee Reports at ¶10,280.]

Amendments

• **2008, Energy Improvement and Extension Act of 2008 (P.L. 110-343)**

P.L. 110-343, Division B, §403(b)(1)-(3):

Amended Code Sec. 1012 by striking "The basis of property" and inserting "(a) IN GENERAL.—The basis of property", by striking "The cost of real property" and inserting "(b) SPECIAL RULE FOR APPORTIONED REAL ESTATE TAXES.—The cost of real property", and by adding at the end new subsections (c)-(d). **Effective** 1-1-2011. Prior to amendment, Code Sec. 1012 read as follows:

SEC. 1012. BASIS OF PROPERTY—COST.

The basis of property shall be the cost of such property, except as otherwise provided in this subchapter and subchapters C (relating to corporate distributions and adjustments), K (relating to partners and partnerships), and P (relating to capital gains and losses). The cost of real property shall not include any amount in respect of real property taxes which are treated under section 164(d) as imposed on the taxpayer.

[¶5350] CODE SEC. 1016. ADJUSTMENTS TO BASIS.

* * *

(a) GENERAL RULE.—Proper adjustment in respect of the property shall in all cases be made—

* * *

(35) to the extent provided in section 30B(h)(4),

(36) to the extent provided in section 30C(e)(1), *and*

⋙→ *Caution: Code Sec. 1016(a)(37), below, as added by P.L. 110-343, applies to tax years beginning after December 31, 2008.*

(37) *to the extent provided in section 30D(e)(4).*

* * *

[CCH Explanation at ¶515. Committee Reports at ¶10,170.]

Amendments

• **2008, Energy Improvement and Extension Act of 2008 (P.L. 110-343)**

P.L. 110-343, Division B, §205(d)(2):

Amended Code Sec. 1016(a) by striking "and" at the end of paragraph (35), by striking the period at the end of paragraph (36) and inserting ", and", and by adding at the end a new paragraph (37). **Effective** for tax years beginning after 12-31-2008.

[¶5355] CODE SEC. 1033. INVOLUNTARY CONVERSIONS.

* * *

(h) SPECIAL RULES FOR PROPERTY DAMAGED BY FEDERALLY DECLARED DISASTERS.—

(1) PRINCIPAL RESIDENCES.—*If the taxpayer's principal residence or any of its contents is located in a disaster area and is compulsorily or involuntarily converted as a result of a federally declared disaster—*

(A) TREATMENT OF INSURANCE PROCEEDS.—

* * *

(2) TRADE OR BUSINESS AND INVESTMENT PROPERTY.—If a taxpayer's property held for productive use in a trade or business or for *investment located in a disaster area and compulsorily or involuntarily converted as a result of a federally declared disaster*, tangible property of a type held for productive use in a trade or business shall be treated for purposes of subsection (a) as property similar or related in service or use to the property so converted.

(3) FEDERALLY DECLARED DISASTER; DISASTER AREA.—*The terms "federally declared disaster" and "disaster area" shall have the respective meaning given such terms by section 165(h)(3)(C).*

* * *

[CCH Explanation at ¶605. Committee Reports at ¶10,710.]

Amendments

• **2008, Heartland Disaster Tax Relief Act of 2008 (P.L. 110-343)**

P.L. 110-343, Division C, §706(a)(2)(D)(i):

Amended so much of Code Sec. 1033(h) as precedes subparagraph (1)(A). **Effective** for disasters declared in tax years beginning after 12-31-2007. Prior to amendment, so much of Code Sec. 1033(h) as precedes subparagraph (1)(A) read as follows:

(h) SPECIAL RULES FOR PROPERTY DAMAGED BY PRESIDENTIALLY DECLARED DISASTERS.—

(1) PRINCIPAL RESIDENCES.—If the taxpayer's principal residence or any of its contents is compulsorily or involuntarily converted as a result of a Presidentially declared disaster—

P.L. 110-343, Division C, §706(a)(2)(D)(ii):

Amended Code Sec. 1033(h)(2) by striking "investment" and all that follows through "disaster" and inserting "in-

vestment located in a disaster area and compulsorily or involuntarily converted as a result of a federally declared disaster". **Effective** for disasters declared in tax years beginning after 12-31-2007. Prior to being stricken, "investment" and all that follows through "disaster" read as follows:

investment is compulsorily or involuntarily converted as a result of a Presidentially declared disaster

P.L. 110-343, Division C, §706(a)(2)(D)(iii):

Amended Code Sec. 1033(h)(3). **Effective** for disasters declared in tax years beginning after 12-31-2007. Prior to amendment, Code Sec. 1033(h)(3) read as follows:

(3) PRESIDENTIALLY DECLARED DISASTER.—For purposes of this subsection, the term "Presidentially declared disaster" means any disaster which, with respect to the area in which the property is located, resulted in a subsequent determination by the President that such area warrants assistance by the Federal Government under the Robert T. Stafford Disaster Relief and Emergency Assistance Act.

[¶5360] CODE SEC. 1367. ADJUSTMENTS TO BASIS OF STOCK OF SHAREHOLDERS, ETC.

(a) GENERAL RULE.—

* * *

(2) DECREASES IN BASIS.—The basis of each shareholder's stock in an S corporation shall be decreased for any period (but not below zero) by the sum of the following items determined with respect to the shareholder for such period:

(A) distributions by the corporation which were not includible in the income of the shareholder by reason of section 1368,

(B) the items of loss and deduction described in subparagraph (A) of section 1366(a)(1),

(C) any nonseparately computed loss determined under subparagraph (B) of section 1366(a)(1),

(D) any expense of the corporation not deductible in computing its taxable income and not properly chargeable to capital account, and

(E) the amount of the shareholder's deduction for depletion for any oil and gas property held by the S corporation to the extent such deduction does not exceed the proportionate share of the adjusted basis of such property allocated to such shareholder under section 613A(c)(11)(B).

The decrease under subparagraph (B) by reason of a charitable contribution (as defined in section 170(c)) of property shall be the amount equal to the shareholder's pro rata share of the adjusted basis of such property. The preceding sentence shall not apply to contributions made in taxable years beginning after *December 31, 2009.*

* * *

[CCH Explanation at ¶435. Committee Reports at ¶10,470.]

Amendments

• **2008, Tax Extenders and Alternative Minimum Tax Relief Act of 2008 (P.L. 110-343)**

P.L. 110-343, Division C, §307(a):

Amended the last sentence of Code Sec. 1367(a)(2) by striking "December 31, 2007" and inserting "December 31,

2009". **Effective** for contributions made in tax years beginning after 12-31-2007.

[¶5365] CODE SEC. 1397E. CREDIT TO HOLDERS OF QUALIFIED ZONE ACADEMY BONDS.

* * *

(m) TERMINATION.—This section shall not apply to any obligation issued after the date of the enactment of the Tax Extenders and Alternative Minimum Tax Relief Act of 2008.

[CCH Explanation at ¶815. Committee Reports at ¶10,510.]

Amendments

• **2008, Tax Extenders and Alternative Minimum Tax Relief Act of 2008 (P.L. 110-343)**

P.L. 110-343, Division C, §313(b)(3):

Amended Code Sec. 1397E by adding at the end a new subsection (m). **Effective** for obligations issued after 10-3-2008.

[¶5370] CODE SEC. 1400. ESTABLISHMENT OF DC ZONE.

* * *

(f) TIME FOR WHICH DESIGNATION APPLICABLE.—

(1) IN GENERAL.—The designation made by subsection (a) shall apply for the period beginning on January 1, 1998, and ending on December 31, *2009.*

(2) COORDINATION WITH DC ENTERPRISE COMMUNITY DESIGNATED UNDER SUBCHAPTER U.—The designation under subchapter U of the census tracts referred to in subsection (b)(1) as an enterprise community shall terminate on December 31, *2009.*

[CCH Explanation at ¶365. Committee Reports at ¶10,590.]

Amendments

• **2008, Tax Extenders and Alternative Minimum Tax Relief Act of 2008 (P.L. 110-343)**

P.L. 110-343, Division C, §322(a)(1):

Amended Code Sec. 1400(f) by striking "2007" both places it appears and inserting "2009". **Effective** for periods beginning after 12-31-2007.

[¶5375] CODE SEC. 1400A. TAX-EXEMPT ECONOMIC DEVELOPMENT BONDS.

* * *

(b) PERIOD OF APPLICABILITY.—This section shall apply to bonds issued during the period beginning on January 1, 1998, and ending on December 31, *2009.*

[CCH Explanation at ¶365. Committee Reports at ¶10,590.]

Amendments

• **2008, Tax Extenders and Alternative Minimum Tax Relief Act of 2008 (P.L. 110-343)**

P.L. 110-343, Division C, §322(b)(1):

Amended Code Sec. 1400A(b) by striking "2007" and inserting "2009". **Effective** for bonds issued after 12-31-2007.

[¶5380] CODE SEC. 1400B. ZERO PERCENT CAPITAL GAINS RATE.

* * *

(b) DC ZONE ASSET.—For purposes of this section—

* * *

(2) DC ZONE BUSINESS STOCK.—

(A) IN GENERAL.—The term "DC Zone business stock" means any stock in a domestic corporation which is originally issued after December 31, 1997, if—

(i) such stock is acquired by the taxpayer, before January 1, *2010,* at its original issue (directly or through an underwriter) solely in exchange for cash,

* * *

(3) DC ZONE PARTNERSHIP INTEREST.—The term "DC Zone partnership interest" means any capital or profits interest in a domestic partnership which is originally issued after December 31, 1997, if—

(A) such interest is acquired by the taxpayer, before January 1, *2010,* from the partnership solely in exchange for cash,

* * *

(4) DC ZONE BUSINESS PROPERTY.—

(A) IN GENERAL.—The term "DC Zone business property" means tangible property if—

(i) such property was acquired by the taxpayer by purchase (as defined in section 179(d)(2)) after December 31, 1997, and before January 1, *2010,*

* * *

(B) SPECIAL RULE FOR BUILDINGS WHICH ARE SUBSTANTIALLY IMPROVED.—

(i) IN GENERAL.—The requirements of clauses (i) and (ii) of subparagraph (A) shall be treated as met with respect to—

(I) property which is substantially improved by the taxpayer before January 1, *2010,* and

* * *

[CCH Explanation at ¶365. Committee Reports at ¶10,590.]

Amendments

• **2008, Tax Extenders and Alternative Minimum Tax Relief Act of 2008 (P.L. 110-343)**

P.L. 110-343, Division C, §322(c)(1):

Amended Code Sec. 1400B(b) by striking "2008" each place it appears and inserting "2010". **Effective** for acquisitions after 12-31-2007.

(e) OTHER DEFINITIONS AND SPECIAL RULES.—For purposes of this section—

* * *

(2) GAIN BEFORE 1998 OR AFTER *2014* NOT QUALIFIED.—The term "qualified capital gain" shall not include any gain attributable to periods before January 1, 1998, or after December 31, *2014*.

* * *

[CCH Explanation at ¶365. Committee Reports at ¶10,590.]

Amendments

• **2008, Tax Extenders and Alternative Minimum Tax Relief Act of 2008 (P.L. 110-343)**

P.L. 110-343, Division C, §322(c)(2)(A)(i)-(ii):

Amended Code Sec. 1400B(e)(2) by striking "2012" and inserting "2014", and by striking "2012" in the heading thereof and inserting "2014". **Effective** 10-3-2008.

(g) SALES AND EXCHANGES OF INTERESTS IN PARTNERSHIPS AND S CORPORATIONS WHICH ARE DC ZONE BUSINESSES.—In the case of the sale or exchange of an interest in a partnership, or of stock in an S corporation, which was a DC Zone business during substantially all of the period the taxpayer held such interest or stock, the amount of qualified capital gain shall be determined without regard to—

* * *

(2) any gain attributable to periods before January 1, 1998, or after December 31, *2014*.

[CCH Explanation at ¶365. Committee Reports at ¶10,590.]

Amendments

• **2008, Tax Extenders and Alternative Minimum Tax Relief Act of 2008 (P.L. 110-343)**

P.L. 110-343, Division C, §322(c)(2)(B):

Amended Code Sec. 1400B(g)(2) by striking "2012" and inserting "2014". **Effective** 10-3-2008.

[¶5385] CODE SEC. 1400C. FIRST-TIME HOMEBUYER CREDIT FOR DISTRICT OF COLUMBIA.

* * *

(d) CARRYFORWARD OF UNUSED CREDIT.—

* * *

(2) RULE FOR OTHER YEARS.—In the case of a taxable year to which section 26(a)(2) does not apply, if the credit allowable under subsection (a) exceeds the limitation imposed by section 26(a)(1) for such taxable year reduced by the sum of the credits allowable under subpart A of part IV of subchapter A (other than this section and sections 23, 24, 25B *25D, and 30D*), such excess shall be carried to the succeeding taxable year and added to the credit allowable under subsection (a) for such taxable year.

* * *

[CCH Explanation at ¶515. Committee Reports at ¶10,170.]
Amendments
• **2008, Energy Improvement and Extension Act of 2008 (P.L. 110-343)**

P.L. 110-343, Division B, §205(d)(1)(E):

Amended Code Sec. 1400C(d)(2) by striking "and 25D" and inserting "25D, and 30D". **Effective** for tax years beginning after 12-31-2008.

(i) APPLICATION OF SECTION.—This section shall apply to property purchased after August 4, 1997, and before January 1, *2010.*

[CCH Explanation at ¶365. Committee Reports at ¶10,590.]
Amendments
• **2008, Tax Extenders and Alternative Minimum Tax Relief Act of 2008 (P.L. 110-343)**

P.L. 110-343, Division C, §322(d)(1):

Amended Code Sec. 1400C(i) by striking "2008" and inserting "2010". **Effective** for property purchased after 12-31-2007.

[¶5390] CODE SEC. 1400F. RENEWAL COMMUNITY CAPITAL GAIN.

* * *

(d) CERTAIN RULES TO APPLY.—For purposes of this section, rules similar to the rules of paragraphs (5), (6), and (7) of subsection (b), and subsections (f) and (g), of section 1400B shall apply; except that for such purposes section 1400B(g)(2) shall be applied by substituting "January 1, 2002" for "January 1, 1998" and "December 31, 2014" for "December 31, *2014*" [sic].

* * *

[CCH Explanation at ¶365. Committee Reports at ¶10,590.]
Amendments
• **2008, Tax Extenders and Alternative Minimum Tax Relief Act of 2008 (P.L. 110-343)**

P.L. 110-343, Division C, §322(c)(2)(C):

Amended Code Sec. 1400F(d) by striking "2012" and inserting "2014". **Effective** 10-3-2008.

[¶5395] CODE SEC. 1400N. TAX BENEFITS FOR GULF OPPORTUNITY ZONE.

* * *

(h) INCREASE IN REHABILITATION CREDIT.—In the case of qualified rehabilitation expenditures (as defined in section 47(c)) paid or incurred during the period beginning on August 28, 2005, and ending on *December 31, 2009,* with respect to any qualified rehabilitated building or certified historic structure (as defined in section 47(c)) located in the Gulf Opportunity Zone, subsection (a) of section 47 (relating to rehabilitation credit) shall be applied—

(1) by substituting "13 percent" for "10 percent" in paragraph (1) thereof, and

(2) by substituting "26 percent" for "20 percent" in paragraph (2) thereof.

[CCH Explanation at ¶640.]
Amendments
• **2008, Tax Extenders and Alternative Minimum Tax Relief Act of 2008 (P.L. 110-343)**

P.L. 110-343, Division C, §320(a):

Amended Code Sec. 1400N(h) by striking "December 31, 2008" and inserting "December 31, 2009". **Effective** for expenditures paid or incurred after 10-3-2008.

[¶ 5400] CODE SEC. 2105. PROPERTY WITHOUT THE UNITED STATES.

* * *

(d) STOCK IN A RIC.—

* * *

(3) TERMINATION.—This subsection shall not apply to estates of decedents dying after *December 31, 2009*.

[CCH Explanation at ¶ 475. Committee Reports at ¶ 10,390.]
Amendments
• **2008, Tax Extenders and Alternative Minimum Tax Relief Act of 2008 (P.L. 110-343)**

P.L. 110-343, Division C, § 207(a):

Amended Code Sec. 2105(d)(3) by striking "December 31, 2007" and inserting "December 31, 2009". **Effective** for decedents dying after 12-31-2007.

[¶ 5405] CODE SEC. 3301. RATE OF TAX.

There is hereby imposed on every employer (as defined in section 3306(a)) for each calendar year an excise tax, with respect to having individuals in his employ, equal to—

(1) 6.2 percent in the case of calendar years 1988 *through 2009*; or

(2) 6.0 percent in the case of *calendar year 2010* and each calendar year thereafter;

of the total wages (as defined in section 3306(b)) paid by him during the calendar year with respect to employment (as defined in section 3306(c)).

[CCH Explanation at ¶ 460. Committee Reports at ¶ 10,290.]
Amendments
• **2008, Energy Improvement and Extension Act of 2008 (P.L. 110-343)**

P.L. 110-343, Division B, § 404(a)(1)-(2):

Amended Code Sec. 3301 by striking "through 2008" in paragraph (1) and inserting "through 2009", and by striking "calendar year 2009" in paragraph (2) and inserting "calendar year 2010". **Effective** for wages paid after 12-31-2008.

[¶ 5407] CODE SEC. 3304. APPROVAL OF STATE LAWS.

(a) REQUIREMENTS.—The Secretary of Labor shall approve any State law submitted to him, within 30 days of such submission, which he finds provides that—

* * *

(4) all money withdrawn from the unemployment fund of the State shall be used solely in the payment of unemployment compensation, exclusive of expenses of administration, and for refunds of sums erroneously paid into such fund and refunds paid in accordance with the provisions of section 3305(b); except that—

* * *

(E) amounts may be withdrawn for the payment of short-time compensation under a plan approved by the Secretary of Labor;

(F) amounts may be withdrawn for the payment of allowances under a self-employed assistance program (as defined in section 3306(t)); *and*

(G) *with respect to amounts of covered unemployment compensation debt (as defined in section 6402(f)(4)) collected under section 6402(f)(4)—*

(i) *amounts may be deducted to pay any fees authorized under such section; and*

(ii) *the penalties and interest described in section 6402(f)(4)(B) may be transferred to the appropriate State fund into which the State would have deposited such amounts had the person owing the debt paid such amounts directly to the State;*

* * *

* * *

[CCH Explanation at ¶710.]

Amendments

• **2008, SSI Extension for Elderly and Disabled Refugees Act (P.L. 110-328)**

P.L. 110-328, §3(c)(1)-(3):

Amended Code Sec. 3304(a)(4) in subparagraph (E), by striking "and" after the semicolon; in subparagraph (F), by inserting "and" after the semicolon; and by adding at the end a new subparagraph (G). **Effective** for refunds payable under Code Sec. 6402 on or after 9-30-2008.

[¶5410] CODE SEC. 4053. EXEMPTIONS.

No tax shall be imposed by section 4051 on any of the following articles:

* * *

(9) IDLING REDUCTION DEVICE.—Any device or system of devices which—

(A) is designed to provide to a vehicle those services (such as heat, air conditioning, or electricity) that would otherwise require the operation of the main drive engine while the vehicle is temporarily parked or remains stationary using one or more devices affixed to a tractor, and

(B) is determined by the Administrator of the Environmental Protection Agency, in consultation with the Secretary of Energy and the Secretary of Transportation, to reduce idling of such vehicle at a motor vehicle rest stop or other location where such vehicles are temporarily parked or remain stationary.

(10) ADVANCED INSULATION.—Any insulation that has an R value of not less than R35 per inch.

[CCH Explanation at ¶845. Committee Reports at ¶10,180.]

Amendments

• **2008, Energy Improvement and Extension Act of 2008 (P.L. 110-343)**

P.L. 110-343, Division B, §206(a):

Amended Code Sec. 4053 by adding at the end new paragraphs (9)-(10). **Effective** for sales or installations after 10-3-2008.

[¶5412] CODE SEC. 4081. IMPOSITION OF TAX.

* * *

(d) TERMINATION.—

* * *

(2) AVIATION FUELS.—The rates of tax specified in subsections (a)(2)(A)(ii) and (a)(2)(C)(ii) shall be 4.3 cents per gallon—

(A) after December 31, 1996, and before the date which is 7 days after the date of the enactment of the Airport and Airway Trust Fund Tax Reinstatement Act of 1997, and

(B) after *March 31, 2009.*

* * *

[CCH Explanation at ¶835.]

Amendments

• **2008, Federal Aviation Administration Extension Act of 2008, Part II (P.L. 110-330)**

P.L. 110-330, §2(a):

Amended Code Sec. 4081(d)(2)(B) by striking "September 30, 2008" and inserting "March 31, 2009". **Effective** 10-1-2008.

[¶ 5415] CODE SEC. 4121. IMPOSITION OF TAX.

* * *

(e) Reduction in Amount of Tax.—

* * *

(2) Temporary increase termination date.—For purposes of paragraph (1), the temporary increase termination date is the earlier of—

(A) *December 31, 2018* or

(B) the first *December 31 after 2007* as of which there is—

(i) no balance of repayable advances made to the Black Lung Disability Trust Fund, and

(ii) no unpaid interest on such advances.

[CCH Explanation at ¶ 850. Committee Reports at ¶ 10,100.]

Amendments

• **2008, Energy Improvement and Extension Act of 2008 (P.L. 110-343)**

P.L. 110-343, Division B, § 113(a)(1)-(2):

Amended Code Sec. 4121(e)(2) by striking "January 1, 2014" in subparagraph (A) and inserting "December 31,

2018", and by striking "January 1 after 1981" in subparagraph (B) and inserting "December 31 after 2007". **Effective** 10-3-2008.

[¶ 5420] CODE SEC. 4161. IMPOSITION OF TAX.

* * *

(b) Bows and Arrows, Etc.—

* * *

(2) Arrows.—

* * *

(B) Exemption for certain wooden arrow shafts.—Subparagraph (A) shall not apply to any shaft consisting of all natural wood with no laminations or artificial means of enhancing the spine of such shaft (whether sold separately or incorporated as part of a finished or unfinished product) of a type used in the manufacture of any arrow which after its assembly—

(i) measures 5/16 of an inch or less in diameter, and

(ii) is not suitable for use with a bow described in paragraph (1)(A).

(C) Adjustment for inflation.—

* * *

[CCH Explanation at ¶ 840. Committee Reports at ¶ 10,680.]

Amendments

• **2008, Tax Extenders and Alternative Minimum Tax Relief Act of 2008 (P.L. 110-343)**

P.L. 110-343, Division C, § 503(a):

Amended Code Sec. 4161(b)(2) by redesignating subparagraph (B) as subparagraph (C) and by inserting after sub-

paragraph (A) a new subparagraph (B). **Effective** for shafts first sold after 10-3-2008.

[¶ 5422] CODE SEC. 4261. IMPOSITION OF TAX.

* * *

(j) Application of Taxes.—

(1) In general.—The taxes imposed by this section shall apply to—

(A) transportation beginning during the period—

(i) beginning on the 7th day after the date of the enactment of the Airport and Airway Trust Fund Tax Reinstatement Act of 1997, and

(ii) ending on *March 31, 2009,* and

(B) amounts paid during such period for transportation beginning after such period.

* * *

[CCH Explanation at ¶ 835.]
Amendments
• 2008, Federal Aviation Administration Extension Act of 2008, Part II (P.L. 110-330)

P.L. 110-330, §2(b)(1):

Amended Code Sec. 4261(j)(1)(A)(ii) by striking "September 30, 2008" and inserting "March 31, 2009". **Effective** 10-1-2008.

[¶ 5424] CODE SEC. 4271. IMPOSITION OF TAX.
* * *

(d) APPLICATION OF TAX.—

(1) IN GENERAL.—The tax imposed by subsection (a) shall apply to—

(A) transportation beginning during the period—

(i) beginning on the 7th day after the date of the enactment of the Airport and Airway Trust Fund Tax Reinstatement Act of 1997, and

(ii) ending on *March 31, 2009,* and

(B) amounts paid during such period for transportation beginning after such period.

* * *

[CCH Explanation at ¶ 835.]
Amendments
• 2008, Federal Aviation Administration Extension Act of 2008, Part II (P.L. 110-330)

P.L. 110-330, §2(b)(2):

Amended Code Sec. 4271(d)(1)(A)(ii) by striking "September 30, 2008" and inserting "March 31, 2009". **Effective** 10-1-2008.

[¶ 5425] CODE SEC. 4611. IMPOSITION OF TAX.
* * *

(c) RATE OF TAX.—

* * *

(2) RATES.—For purposes of paragraph (1)—

* * *

⧽⧽⧽→ *Caution: Code Sec. 4611(c)(2)(B), as amended by P.L. 110-343, applies on and after the the first day of the first calendar quarter beginning more than 60 days after October 3, 2008.*

(B) *the Oil Spill Liability Trust Fund financing rate is—*

(i) *in the case of crude oil received or petroleum products entered before January 1, 2017, 8 cents a barrel, and*

(ii) *in the case of crude oil received or petroleum products entered after December 31, 2016, 9 cents a barrel.*

* * *

[CCH Explanation at ¶ 855. Committee Reports at ¶ 10,300.]

Amendments

• 2008, Energy Improvement and Extension Act of 2008 (P.L. 110-343)

P.L. 110-343, Division B, § 405(a)(1):

Amended Code Sec. 4611(c)(2)(B) by striking "is 5 cents a barrel." and inserting "is—" and new clauses (i)-(ii). **Effec-**tive on and after the first day of the first calendar quarter beginning more than 60 days after 10-3-2008.

(f) APPLICATION OF OIL SPILL LIABILITY TRUST FUND FINANCING RATE.—

(1) IN GENERAL.—Except as provided in *paragraph (2)*, the Oil Spill Liability Trust Fund financing rate under subsection (c) shall apply on and after April 1, 2006, or if later, the date which is 30 days after the last day of any calendar quarter for which the Secretary estimates that, as of the close of that quarter, the unobligated balance in the Oil Spill Liability Trust Fund is less than $2,000,000,000.

(2) TERMINATION.—*The Oil Spill Liability Trust Fund financing rate shall not apply after December 31, 2017.*

[CCH Explanation at ¶ 855. Committee Reports at ¶ 10,300.]

Amendments

• 2008, Energy Improvement and Extension Act of 2008 (P.L. 110-343)

P.L. 110-343, Division B, § 405(b)(1):

Amended Code Sec. 4611(f) by striking paragraphs (2) and (3) and inserting a new paragraph (2). **Effective** 10-3-2008. Prior to being stricken, Code Sec. 4611(f)(2)-(3) read as follows:

(2) FUND BALANCE.—The Oil Spill Liability Trust Fund financing rate shall not apply during a calendar quarter if the Secretary estimates that, as of the close of the preceding calendar quarter, the unobligated balance in the Oil Spill Liability Trust Fund exceeds $2,700,000,000.

(3) TERMINATION.—The Oil Spill Liability Trust Fund financing rate shall not apply after December 31, 2014.

P.L. 110-343, Division B, § 405(b)(2):

Amended Code Sec. 4611(f)(1) by striking "paragraphs (2) and (3)" and inserting "paragraph (2)". **Effective** 10-3-2008.

[¶ 5430] CODE SEC. 6033. RETURNS BY EXEMPT ORGANIZATIONS.

* * *

(b) CERTAIN ORGANIZATIONS DESCRIBED IN SECTION 501(c)(3).—Every organization described in section 501(c)(3) which is subject to the requirements of subsection (a) shall furnish annually information, at such time and in such manner as the Secretary may by forms or regulations prescribe, setting forth—

* * *

(13) such information with respect to disqualified persons as the Secretary may prescribe,

⋙➤ *Caution: Code Sec. 6033(b)(14), below, as added by P.L. 110-343, applies to returns the due date for which (determined without regard to any extension) occurs after December 31, 2008.*

(14) *such information as the Secretary may require with respect to disaster relief activities, including the amount and use of qualified contributions to which section 1400S(a) applies, and*

(15) such other information for purposes of carrying out the internal revenue laws as the Secretary may require.

* * *

[CCH Explanation at ¶ 630.]

Amendments

• 2008, Heartland Disaster Tax Relief Act of 2008 (P.L. 110-343)

P.L. 110-343, Division C, § 703(a):

Amended Code Sec. 6033(b) by striking "and" at the end of paragraph (13), by redesignating paragraph (14) as para-graph (15), and by adding after paragraph (13) a new paragraph (14). **Effective** for returns the due date for which (determined without regard to any extension) occurs after 12-31-2008.

[¶5435] CODE SEC. 6045. RETURNS OF BROKERS.

* * *

(b) STATEMENTS TO BE FURNISHED TO CUSTOMERS.—Every person required to make a return under subsection (a) shall furnish to each customer whose name is required to be set forth in such return a written statement showing—

(1) the name, address and phone number of the information contact of the person required to make such return, and

(2) the information required to be shown on such return with respect to such customer.

⟫→ *Caution: The flush text of Code Sec. 6045(b), below, as amended by P.L. 110-343, applies to statements required to be furnished after December 31, 2008.*

The written statement required under the preceding sentence shall be furnished to the customer on or before *February 15 of the year following the calendar year for which the return under subsection (a) was required to be made. In the case of a consolidated reporting statement (as defined in regulations) with respect to any customer, any statement which would otherwise be required to be furnished on or before January 31 of a calendar year with respect to any item reportable to the taxpayer shall instead be required to be furnished on or before February 15 of such calendar year if furnished with such consolidated reporting statement.*

* * *

[CCH Explanation at ¶725. Committee Reports at ¶10,280.]

Amendments

• 2008, Energy Improvement and Extension Act of 2008 (P.L. 110-343)

P.L. 110-343, Division B, §403(a)(3)(A):

Amended Code Sec. 6045(b) by striking "January 31" and inserting "February 15". **Effective** for statements required to be furnished after 12-31-2008.

P.L. 110-343, Division B, §403(a)(3)(C):

Amended Code Sec. 6045(b) by adding at the end a new sentence. **Effective** for statements required to be furnished after 12-31-2008.

(d) STATEMENTS REQUIRED IN CASE OF CERTAIN SUBSTITUTE PAYMENTS.—If any broker—

(1) transfers securities of a customer for use in a short sale or similar transaction, and

(2) receives (on behalf of the customer) a payment in lieu of—

(A) a dividend,

(B) tax-exempt interest, or

(C) such other items as the Secretary may prescribe by regulations,

⟫→ *Caution: The flush text of Code Sec. 6045(d), below, as amended by P.L. 110-343, applies to statements required to be furnished after December 31, 2008.*

during the period such short sale or similar transaction is open, the broker shall furnish such customer a written statement (in the manner as the Secretary shall prescribe by regulations) identifying such payment as being in lieu of the dividend, tax-exempt interest, or such other item. *The written statement required under the preceding sentence shall be furnished on or before February 15 of the year following the calendar year in which the payment was made.* The Secretary may prescribe regulations which require the broker to make a return which includes the information contained in such written statement.

* * *

[CCH Explanation at ¶725. Committee Reports at ¶10,280.]

Amendments

• 2008, Energy Improvement and Extension Act of 2008 (P.L. 110-343)

P.L. 110-343, Division B, §403(a)(3)(B)(i)-(ii):

Amended Code Sec. 6045(d) by striking "at such time and" before "in the manner", and by inserting after "other

item." a new sentence. **Effective** for statements required to be furnished after 12-31-2008.

»»→ *Caution: Code Sec. 6045(g), below, as added by P.L. 110-343, is effective January 1, 2011.*

(g) ADDITIONAL INFORMATION REQUIRED IN THE CASE OF SECURITIES TRANSACTIONS, ETC.—

(1) IN GENERAL.—*If a broker is otherwise required to make a return under subsection (a) with respect to the gross proceeds of the sale of a covered security, the broker shall include in such return the information described in paragraph (2).*

(2) ADDITIONAL INFORMATION REQUIRED.—

(A) IN GENERAL.—*The information required under paragraph (1) to be shown on a return with respect to a covered security of a customer shall include the customer's adjusted basis in such security and whether any gain or loss with respect to such security is long-term or short-term (within the meaning of section 1222).*

(B) DETERMINATION OF ADJUSTED BASIS.—*For purposes of subparagraph (A)—*

(i) IN GENERAL.—*The customer's adjusted basis shall be determined—*

(I) *in the case of any security (other than any stock for which an average basis method is permissible under section 1012), in accordance with the first-in first-out method unless the customer notifies the broker by means of making an adequate identification of the stock sold or transferred, and*

(II) *in the case of any stock for which an average basis method is permissible under section 1012, in accordance with the broker's default method unless the customer notifies the broker that he elects another acceptable method under section 1012 with respect to the account in which such stock is held.*

(ii) EXCEPTION FOR WASH SALES.—*Except as otherwise provided by the Secretary, the customer's adjusted basis shall be determined without regard to section 1091 (relating to loss from wash sales of stock or securities) unless the transactions occur in the same account with respect to identical securities.*

(3) COVERED SECURITY.—*For purposes of this subsection—*

(A) IN GENERAL.—*The term "covered security" means any specified security acquired on or after the applicable date if such security—*

(i) *was acquired through a transaction in the account in which such security is held, or*

(ii) *was transferred to such account from an account in which such security was a covered security, but only if the broker received a statement under section 6045A with respect to the transfer.*

(B) SPECIFIED SECURITY.—*The term "specified security" means—*

(i) *any share of stock in a corporation,*

(ii) *any note, bond, debenture, or other evidence of indebtedness,*

(iii) *any commodity, or contract or derivative with respect to such commodity, if the Secretary determines that adjusted basis reporting is appropriate for purposes of this subsection, and*

(iv) *any other financial instrument with respect to which the Secretary determines that adjusted basis reporting is appropriate for purposes of this subsection.*

(C) APPLICABLE DATE.—*The term "applicable date" means—*

(i) *January 1, 2011, in the case of any specified security which is stock in a corporation (other than any stock described in clause (ii)),*

(ii) *January 1, 2012, in the case of any stock for which an average basis method is permissible under section 1012, and*

(iii) *January 1, 2013, or such later date determined by the Secretary in the case of any other specified security.*

(4) TREATMENT OF S CORPORATIONS.—*In the case of the sale of a covered security acquired by an S corporation (other than a financial institution) after December 31, 2011, such S corporation shall be treated in the same manner as a partnership for purposes of this section.*

(5) SPECIAL RULES FOR SHORT SALES.—*In the case of a short sale, reporting under this section shall be made for the year in which such sale is closed.*

[CCH Explanation at ¶725. Committee Reports at ¶10,280.]
Amendments
• 2008, Energy Improvement and Extension Act of 2008 (P.L. 110-343)

P.L. 110-343, Division B, §403(a)(1):

Amended Code Sec. 6045 by adding at the end a new subsection (g). **Effective** 1-1-2011.

≫→ *Caution: Code Sec. 6045(h), below, as added by P.L. 110-343, is effective January 1, 2011.*

(h) APPLICATION TO OPTIONS ON SECURITIES.—

(1) EXERCISE OF OPTION.—*For purposes of this section, if a covered security is acquired or disposed of pursuant to the exercise of an option that was granted or acquired in the same account as the covered security, the amount received with respect to the grant or paid with respect to the acquisition of such option shall be treated as an adjustment to gross proceeds or as an adjustment to basis, as the case may be.*

(2) LAPSE OR CLOSING TRANSACTION.—*In the case of the lapse (or closing transaction (as defined in section 1234(b)(2)(A))) of an option on a specified security or the exercise of a cash-settled option on a specified security, reporting under subsections (a) and (g) with respect to such option shall be made for the calendar year which includes the date of such lapse, closing transaction, or exercise.*

(3) PROSPECTIVE APPLICATION.—*Paragraphs (1) and (2) shall not apply to any option which is granted or acquired before January 1, 2013.*

(4) DEFINITIONS.—*For purposes of this subsection, the terms "covered security" and "specified security" shall have the meanings given such terms in subsection (g)(3).*

[CCH Explanation at ¶725. Committee Reports at ¶10,280.]
Amendments
• 2008, Energy Improvement and Extension Act of 2008 (P.L. 110-343)

P.L. 110-343, Division B, §403(a)(2):

Amended Code Sec. 6045, as amended by Act Sec. 403(a), by adding at the end a new subsection (h). **Effective** 1-1-2011.

≫→ *Caution: Code Sec. 6045A, below, as added by P.L. 110-343, is effective January 1, 2011.*

[¶5440] CODE SEC. 6045A. INFORMATION REQUIRED IN CONNECTION WITH TRANSFERS OF COVERED SECURITIES TO BROKERS.

(a) FURNISHING OF INFORMATION.—*Every applicable person which transfers to a broker (as defined in section 6045(c)(1)) a security which is a covered security (as defined in section 6045(g)(3)) in the hands of such applicable person shall furnish to such broker a written statement in such manner and setting forth such information as the Secretary may by regulations prescribe for purposes of enabling such broker to meet the requirements of section 6045(g).*

(b) APPLICABLE PERSON.—*For purposes of subsection (a), the term "applicable person" means—*

(1) *any broker (as defined in section 6045(c)(1)), and*

(2) *any other person as provided by the Secretary in regulations.*

(c) TIME FOR FURNISHING STATEMENT.—*Except as otherwise provided by the Secretary, any statement required by subsection (a) shall be furnished not later than 15 days after the date of the transfer described in such subsection.*

[CCH Explanation at ¶735. Committee Reports at ¶10,280.]

Amendments
• **2008, Energy Improvement and Extension Act of 2008 (P.L. 110-343)**

P.L. 110-343, Division B, §403(c)(1):

Amended subpart B of part III of subchapter A of chapter 61 by inserting after Code Sec. 6045 a new Code Sec. 6045A. **Effective** 1-1-2011.

⧉→ *Caution: Code Sec. 6045B, below, as added by P.L. 110-343, is effective January 1, 2011.*

[¶5445] *CODE SEC. 6045B. RETURNS RELATING TO ACTIONS AFFECTING BASIS OF SPECIFIED SECURITIES.*

(a) IN GENERAL.—According to the forms or regulations prescribed by the Secretary, any issuer of a specified security shall make a return setting forth—

(1) a description of any organizational action which affects the basis of such specified security of such issuer,

(2) the quantitative effect on the basis of such specified security resulting from such action, and

(3) such other information as the Secretary may prescribe.

(b) TIME FOR FILING RETURN.—Any return required by subsection (a) shall be filed not later than the earlier of—

(1) 45 days after the date of the action described in subsection (a), or

(2) January 15 of the year following the calendar year during which such action occurred.

(c) STATEMENTS TO BE FURNISHED TO HOLDERS OF SPECIFIED SECURITIES OR THEIR NOMINEES.—According to the forms or regulations prescribed by the Secretary, every person required to make a return under subsection (a) with respect to a specified security shall furnish to the nominee with respect to the specified security (or certificate holder if there is no nominee) a written statement showing—

(1) the name, address, and phone number of the information contact of the person required to make such return,

(2) the information required to be shown on such return with respect to such security, and

(3) such other information as the Secretary may prescribe.

The written statement required under the preceding sentence shall be furnished to the holder on or before January 15 of the year following the calendar year during which the action described in subsection (a) occurred.

(d) SPECIFIED SECURITY.—For purposes of this section, the term "specified security" has the meaning given such term by section 6045(g)(3)(B). No return shall be required under this section with respect to actions described in subsection (a) with respect to a specified security which occur before the applicable date (as defined in section 6045(g)(3)(C)) with respect to such security.

(e) PUBLIC REPORTING IN LIEU OF RETURN.—The Secretary may waive the requirements under subsections (a) and (c) with respect to a specified security, if the person required to make the return under subsection (a) makes publicly available, in such form and manner as the Secretary determines necessary to carry out the purposes of this section—

(1) the name, address, phone number, and email address of the information contact of such person, and

(2) the information described in paragraphs (1), (2), and (3) of subsection (a).

[CCH Explanation at ¶ 740. Committee Reports at ¶ 10,280.]

Amendments

• 2008, Energy Improvement and Extension Act of 2008 (P.L. 110-343)

P.L. 110-343, Division B, § 403(d)(1):

Amended subpart B of part III of subchapter A of chapter 61, as amended by Act Sec. 403(b), by inserting after Code Sec. 6045A a new Code Sec. 6045B. **Effective** 1-1-2011.

[¶ 5450] CODE SEC. 6103. CONFIDENTIALITY AND DISCLOSURE OF RETURNS AND RETURN INFORMATION.

(a) GENERAL RULE.—Returns and return information shall be confidential, and except as authorized by this title—

* * *

(3) no other person (or officer or employee thereof) who has or had access to returns or return information under subsection (e)(1)(D)(iii), paragraph (6), *(10)*, (12), (16), (19), or (20) of subsection (l), paragraph (2) or (4)(B) of subsection (m), or subsection (n),

shall disclose any return or return information obtained by him in any manner in connection with his service as such an officer or an employee or otherwise or under the provisions of this section. For purposes of this subsection, the term "officer or employee" includes a former officer or employee.

Amendments

• 2008, SSI Extension for Elderly and Disabled Refugees Act (P.L. 110-328)

P.L. 110-328, § 3(b)(1):

Amended Code Sec. 6103(a)(3) by inserting "(10)," after "(6),". **Effective** for refunds payable under Code Sec. 6402 on or after 9-30-2008.

(i) DISCLOSURE TO FEDERAL OFFICERS OR EMPLOYEES FOR ADMINISTRATION OF FEDERAL LAWS NOT RELATING TO TAX ADMINISTRATION.—

* * *

(3) DISCLOSURE OF RETURN INFORMATION TO APPRISE APPROPRIATE OFFICIALS OF CRIMINAL OR TERRORIST ACTIVITIES OR EMERGENCY CIRCUMSTANCES.—

* * *

(C) TERRORIST ACTIVITIES, ETC.—

* * *

(iv) *[Stricken.]*

* * *

(7) DISCLOSURE UPON REQUEST OF INFORMATION RELATING TO TERRORIST ACTIVITIES, ETC.—

* * *

(E) *[Stricken.]*

* * *

[CCH Explanation at ¶ 715. Committee Reports at ¶ 10,630.]

Amendments

• 2008, Tax Extenders and Alternative Minimum Tax Relief Act of 2008 (P.L. 110-343)

P.L. 110-343, Division C, § 402(a):

Amended Code Sec. 6103(i)(3)(C) by striking clause (iv). **Effective** for disclosures after 10-3-2008. Prior to being stricken, Code Sec. 6103(i)(3)(C)(iv) read as follows:

(iv) TERMINATION.—No disclosure may be made under this subparagraph after December 31, 2007.

P.L. 110-343, Division C, § 402(b):

Amended Code Sec. 6103(i)(7) by striking paragraph (E). **Effective** for disclosures after 10-3-2008. Prior to being stricken, Code Sec. 6103(i)(7)(E) read as follows:

(E) TERMINATION.—No disclosure may be made under this paragraph after December 31, 2007.

(k) DISCLOSURE OF CERTAIN RETURNS AND RETURN INFORMATION FOR TAX ADMINISTRATION PURPOSES.—

* * *

≫→ *Caution: Code Sec. 6103(k)(10), below, as added by H.R. 7082, applies to disclosures made after December 31, 2008.*

(10) DISCLOSURE OF CERTAIN RETURN INFORMATION OF PRISONERS TO FEDERAL BUREAU OF PRISONS.—

(A) IN GENERAL.—*Under such procedures as the Secretary may prescribe, the Secretary may disclose to the head of the Federal Bureau of Prisons any return information with respect to individuals incarcerated in Federal prison whom the Secretary has determined may have filed or facilitated the filing of a false return to the extent that the Secretary determines that such disclosure is necessary to permit effective Federal tax administration.*

(B) RESTRICTION ON REDISCLOSURE.—*Notwithstanding subsection (n), the head of the Federal Bureau of Prisons may not disclose any information obtained under subparagraph (A) to any person other than an officer or employee of such Bureau.*

(C) RESTRICTION ON USE OF DISCLOSED INFORMATION.—*Return information received under this paragraph shall be used only for purposes of and to the extent necessary in taking administrative action to prevent the filing of false and fraudulent returns, including administrative actions to address possible violations of administrative rules and regulations of the prison facility.*

(D) TERMINATION.—*No disclosure may be made under this paragraph after December 31, 2011.*

[CCH Explanation at ¶718.]

Amendments

• **2008, Inmate Tax Fraud Prevention Act of 2008 (H.R. 7082)**

H.R. 7082, §2(a):

Amended Code Sec. 6103(k) by adding at the end a new paragraph (10). **Effective** for disclosures made after 12-31-2008.

H.R. 7082, §2(e), provides:

(e) ANNUAL REPORTS.—The Secretary of the Treasury shall annually submit to Congress and make publicly available a report on the filing of false and fraudulent returns by individuals incarcerated in Federal and State prisons. Such report shall include statistics on the number of false and fraudulent returns associated with each Federal and State prison.

(l) DISCLOSURE OF RETURNS AND RETURN INFORMATION FOR PURPOSES OTHER THAN TAX ADMINISTRATION.—

* * *

(10) DISCLOSURE OF CERTAIN INFORMATION TO AGENCIES REQUESTING A REDUCTION UNDER SUBSECTION (c), (d), (e), OR (f) OF SECTION 6402.—

(A) RETURN INFORMATION FROM INTERNAL REVENUE SERVICE.—The Secretary may, upon receiving a written request, disclose to officers and employees of any agency seeking a reduction under subsection *(c), (d), (e)* or *(f)* of section 6402, *to officers and employees of the Department of Labor for purposes of facilitating the exchange of data in connection with a request made under subsection (f)(5) of section 6402,* and to officers and employees of the Department of the Treasury in connection with such reduction—

(i) taxpayer identity information with respect to the taxpayer against whom such a reduction was made or not made and with respect to any other person filing a joint return with such taxpayer,

(ii) the fact that a reduction has been made or has not been made under such subsection with respect to such taxpayer,

(iii) the amount of such reduction,

(iv) whether such taxpayer filed a joint return, and

(v) the fact that a payment was made (and the amount of the payment) to the spouse of the taxpayer on the basis of a joint return.

(B)(i) RESTRICTION ON USE OF DISCLOSED INFORMATION.—Any officers and employees of an agency receiving return information under subparagraph (A) shall use such information only for the purposes of, and to the extent necessary in, establishing appropriate agency records, locating any person with respect to whom a reduction under subsection *(c), (d), (e), or (f)* of section 6402 is sought for purposes of collecting the debt with respect to which the reduction is sought, or in the defense of any litigation or administrative procedure ensuing from a reduction made under subsection *(c), (d), (e), or (f)* of section 6402.

(ii) Notwithstanding clause (i), return information disclosed to officers and employees of the Department of Labor may be accessed by agents who maintain and provide technological support to the Department of Labor's Interstate Connection Network (ICON) solely for the purpose of providing such maintenance and support.

* * *

[CCH Explanation at ¶ 710.]

Amendments

• 2008, SSI Extension for Elderly and Disabled Refugees Act (P.L. 110-328)

P.L. 110-328, § 3(b)(2)(A)-(C):

Amended Code Sec. 6103(l)(10) by striking "(c), (d), or (e)" each place it appears in the heading and text and inserting "(c), (d), (e), or (f)", in subparagraph (A) by inserting ", to officers and employees of the Department of Labor for purposes of facilitating the exchange of data in connection with a request made under subsection (f)(5) of section 6402," after "section 6402", and in subparagraph (B) by inserting "(i)" after "(B)"; and by adding at the end a new clause (ii). **Effective** for refunds payable under Code Sec. 6402 on or after 9-30-2008.

(p) PROCEDURE AND RECORDKEEPING.—

* * *

Caution: Code Sec. 6103(p)(4), as amended by H.R. 7082, applies to disclosures made after December 31, 2008.

(4) SAFEGUARDS.—Any Federal agency described in subsection (h)(2), (h)(5), (i)(1), (2), (3), (5), or (7), (j)(1), (2), or (5), *(k)(8) or (10)*, (l)(1), (2), (3), (5), (10), (11), (13), (14), or (17) or (o)(1), the Government Accountability Office, the Congressional Budget Office, or any agency, body, or commission described in subsection (d), (i)(3)(B)(i) or 7(A)(ii), or (l)(6), (7), (8), (9), (12), (15), or (16), any appropriate State officer (as defined in section 6104(c)), or any other person described in subsection *(l)(10), (16)*, (18), (19), or (20) shall, as a condition for receiving returns or return information—

(A) establish and maintain, to the satisfaction of the Secretary, a permanent system of standardized records with respect to any request, the reason for such request, and the date of such request made by or of it and any disclosure of return or return information made by or to it;

(B) establish and maintain, to the satisfaction of the Secretary, a secure area or place in which such returns or return information shall be stored;

(C) restrict, to the satisfaction of the Secretary, access to the returns or return information only to persons whose duties or responsibilities require access and to whom disclosure may be made under the provisions of this title;

(D) provide such other safeguards which the Secretary determines (and which he prescribes in regulations) to be necessary or appropriate to protect the confidentiality of the returns or return information;

(E) furnish a report to the Secretary, at such time and containing such information as the Secretary may prescribe, which describes the procedures established and utilized by such agency, body, or commission, the Government Accountability Office, or the Congressional Budget Office for ensuring the confidentiality of returns and return information required by this paragraph; and

(F) upon completion of use of such returns or return information—

(i) in the case of an agency, body, or commission described in subsection (d), (i)(3)(B)(i), or (l)(6), (7), (8), (9), or (16), any appropriate State officer (as defined in section 6104(c)), or any other person described in subsection *(l)(10), (16)*, (18), (19), or (20) return to the Secretary such returns or return information (along with any copies made there-from) or make such returns or return information undisclosable in any manner and furnish a written report to the Secretary describing such manner,

(ii) in the case of an agency described in subsections (h)(2), (h)(5), (i)(1), (2), (3), (5) or (7), (j)(1), (2), or (5), *(k)(8) or (10)*, (l)(1), (2), (3), (5), (10), (11), (12), (13), (14), (15), or (17) or (o)(1), the Government Accountability Office, or the Congressional Budget Office, either—

(I) return to the Secretary such returns or return information (along with any copies made therefrom),

(II) otherwise make such returns or return information undisclosable, or

(III) to the extent not so returned or made undisclosable, ensure that the conditions of subparagraphs (A), (B), (C), (D), and (E) of this paragraph continue to be met with respect to such returns or return information, and

(iii) in the case of the Department of Health and Human Services for purposes of subsection (m)(6), destroy all such return information upon completion of its use in providing the notification for which the information was obtained, so as to make such information undisclosable;

except that the conditions of subparagraphs (A), (B), (C), (D), and (E) shall cease to apply with respect to any return or return information if, and to the extent that, such return or return information is disclosed in the course of any judicial or administrative proceeding and made a part of the public record thereof. If the Secretary determines that any such agency, body, or commission, including an agency, an appropriate State officer (as defined in section 6104(c)), or any other person described in subsection *(l)(10)*, (16), (18), (19), or (20), or the Government Accountability Office or the Congressional Budget Office, has failed to, or does not, meet the requirements of this paragraph, he may, after any proceedings for review established under paragraph (7), take such actions as are necessary to ensure such requirements are met, including refusing to disclose returns or return information to such agency, body, or commission, including an agency, an appropriate State officer (as defined in section 6104(c)), or any other person described in subsection *(l)(10)*, (16), (18), (19), or (20), or the Government Accountability Office or the Congressional Budget Office, until he determines that such requirements have been or will be met. In the case of any agency which receives any mailing address under paragraph (2), (4), (6), or (7) of subsection (m) and which discloses any such mailing address to any agent or which receives any information under paragraph (6)(A), *(10)*, (12)(B), or (16) of subsection (l) and which discloses any such information to any agent, or any person including an agent described in subsection *(l)(10) or (16)*, this paragraph shall apply to such agency and each such agent or other person (except that, in the case of an agent, or any person including an agent described in subsection *(l)(10) or (16)*, any report to the Secretary or other action with respect to the Secretary shall be made or taken through such agency). For purposes of applying this paragraph in any case to which subsection (m)(6) applies, the term "return information" includes related blood donor records (as defined in section 1141(h)(2) of the Social Security Act).

* * *

[CCH Explanation at ¶ 718.]

Amendments

- **2008, Inmate Tax Fraud Prevention Act of 2008 (H.R. 7082)**

H.R. 7082, § 2(b):

Amended Code Sec. 6103(p)(4) by striking "(k)(8)" both places it appears and inserting "(k)(8) or (10)". **Effective for** disclosures made after 12-31-2008.

- **2008, SSI Extension for Elderly and Disabled Refugees Act (P.L. 110-328)**

P.L. 110-328, § 3(b)(3)(A)-(C):

Amended Code Sec. 6103(p)(4) in the matter preceding subparagraph (A), by striking "(l)(16)," and inserting

"(l)(10), (16),"; in subparagraph (F)(i), by striking "(l)(16)," and inserting "(l)(10), (16),"; and in the matter following subparagraph (F)(iii), in each of the first two places it appears, by striking "(l)(16)," and inserting "(l)(10), (16),"; by inserting "(10)," after "paragraph (6)(A),"; and in each of the last two places it appears, by striking "(l)(16)" and inserting "(l)(10) or (16)". **Effective** for refunds payable under Code Sec. 6402 on or after 9-30-2008.

[¶ 5452] CODE SEC. 6402. AUTHORITY TO MAKE CREDITS OR REFUNDS.

(a) GENERAL RULE.—In the case of any overpayment, the Secretary, within the applicable period of limitations, may credit the amount of such overpayment, including any interest allowed thereon, against any liability in respect of an internal revenue tax on the part of the person who made the overpayment and shall, subject to subsections *(c), (d), (e), and (f)* refund any balance to such person.

* * *

[CCH Explanation at ¶710.]

Amendments

• 2008, SSI Extension for Elderly and Disabled Refugees Act (P.L. 110-328)

P.L. 110-328, §3(d)(1):

Amended Code Sec. 6402(a) by striking "(c), (d), and (e)," and inserting "(c), (d), (e), and (f)". **Effective** for refunds payable under Code Sec. 6402 on or after 9-30-2008.

(d) COLLECTION OF DEBTS OWED TO FEDERAL AGENCIES.—

* * *

(2) PRIORITIES FOR OFFSET.—Any overpayment by a person shall be reduced pursuant to this subsection after such overpayment is reduced pursuant to subsection (c) with respect to past-due support collected pursuant to an assignment under section 402(a)(26) of the Social Security Act *and before such overpayment is reduced pursuant to subsections (e) and (f)* and before such overpayment is credited to the future liability for tax of such person pursuant to subsection (b). If the Secretary receives notice from a Federal agency or agencies of more than one debt subject to paragraph (1) that is owed by a person to such agency or agencies, any overpayment by such person shall be applied against such debts in the order in which such debts accrued.

* * *

[CCH Explanation at ¶710.]

Amendments

• 2008, SSI Extension for Elderly and Disabled Refugees Act (P.L. 110-328)

P.L. 110-328, §3(d)(2):

Amended Code Sec. 6402(d)(2) by striking "and before such overpayment is reduced pursuant to subsection (e)" and inserting "and before such overpayment is reduced pursuant to subsections (e) and (f)". **Effective** for refunds payable under Code Sec. 6402 on or after 9-30-2008.

(e) COLLECTION OF PAST-DUE, LEGALLY ENFORCEABLE STATE INCOME TAX OBLIGATIONS.—

* * *

(3) PRIORITIES FOR OFFSET.—Any overpayment by a person shall be reduced pursuant to this subsection—

(A) after such overpayment is reduced pursuant to—

(i) subsection (a) with respect to any liability for any internal revenue tax on the part of the person who made the overpayment;

(ii) subsection (c) with respect to past-due support; and

(iii) subsection (d) with respect to any past-due, legally enforceable debt owed to a Federal agency; and

(B) before such overpayment is credited to the future liability for any Federal internal revenue tax of such person pursuant to subsection (b).

If the Secretary receives notice from one or more agencies of the State of more than one debt subject to paragraph (1) *or subsection (f)* that is owed by such person to such an agency, any overpayment by such person shall be applied against such debts in the order in which such debts accrued.

* * *

[CCH Explanation at ¶710.]

Amendments

• **2008, SSI Extension for Elderly and Disabled Refugees Act (P.L. 110-328)**

P.L. 110-328, §3(d)(3):

Amended the last sentence of Code Sec. 6402(e)(3) by inserting "or subsection (f)" after "paragraph (1)". **Effective** for refunds payable under Code Sec. 6402 on or after 9-30-2008.

(f) COLLECTION OF UNEMPLOYMENT COMPENSATION DEBTS RESULTING FROM FRAUD.—

(1) IN GENERAL.—Upon receiving notice from any State that a named person owes a covered unemployment compensation debt to such State, the Secretary shall, under such conditions as may be prescribed by the Secretary—

(A) reduce the amount of any overpayment payable to such person by the amount of such covered unemployment compensation debt;

(B) pay the amount by which such overpayment is reduced under subparagraph (A) to such State and notify such State of such person's name, taxpayer identification number, address, and the amount collected; and

(C) notify the person making such overpayment that the overpayment has been reduced by an amount necessary to satisfy a covered unemployment compensation debt.

If an offset is made pursuant to a joint return, the notice under subparagraph (C) shall include information related to the rights of a spouse of a person subject to such an offset.

(2) PRIORITIES FOR OFFSET.—Any overpayment by a person shall be reduced pursuant to this subsection—

(A) after such overpayment is reduced pursuant to—

(i) subsection (a) with respect to any liability for any internal revenue tax on the part of the person who made the overpayment;

(ii) subsection (c) with respect to past-due support; and

(iii) subsection (d) with respect to any past-due, legally enforceable debt owed to a Federal agency; and

(B) before such overpayment is credited to the future liability for any Federal internal revenue tax of such person pursuant to subsection (b).

If the Secretary receives notice from a State or States of more than one debt subject to paragraph (1) or subsection (e) that is owed by a person to such State or States, any overpayment by such person shall be applied against such debts in the order in which such debts accrued.

(3) OFFSET PERMITTED ONLY AGAINST RESIDENTS OF STATE SEEKING OFFSET.—Paragraph (1) shall apply to an overpayment by any person for a taxable year only if the address shown on the Federal return for such taxable year of the overpayment is an address within the State seeking the offset.

(4) NOTICE; CONSIDERATION OF EVIDENCE.—No State may take action under this subsection until such State—

(A) notifies by certified mail with return receipt the person owing the covered unemployment compensation debt that the State proposes to take action pursuant to this section;

(B) provides such person at least 60 days to present evidence that all or part of such liability is not legally enforceable or due to fraud;

(C) considers any evidence presented by such person and determines that an amount of such debt is legally enforceable and due to fraud; and

(D) satisfies such other conditions as the Secretary may prescribe to ensure that the determination made under subparagraph (C) is valid and that the State has made reasonable efforts to obtain payment of such covered unemployment compensation debt.

(5) COVERED UNEMPLOYMENT COMPENSATION DEBT.—For purposes of this subsection, the term "covered unemployment compensation debt" means—

(A) a past-due debt for erroneous payment of unemployment compensation due to fraud which has become final under the law of a State certified by the Secretary of Labor pursuant to section 3304 and which remains uncollected for not more than 10 years;

(B) contributions due to the unemployment fund of a State for which the State has determined the person to be liable due to fraud and which remain uncollected for not more than 10 years; and

(C) any penalties and interest assessed on such debt.

(6) REGULATIONS.—

(A) IN GENERAL.—The Secretary may issue regulations prescribing the time and manner in which States must submit notices of covered unemployment compensation debt and the necessary information that must be contained in or accompany such notices. The regulations may specify the minimum amount of debt to which the reduction procedure established by paragraph (1) may be applied.

(B) FEE PAYABLE TO SECRETARY.—The regulations may require States to pay a fee to the Secretary, which may be deducted from amounts collected, to reimburse the Secretary for the cost of applying such procedure. Any fee paid to the Secretary pursuant to the preceding sentence shall be used to reimburse appropriations which bore all or part of the cost of applying such procedure.

(C) SUBMISSION OF NOTICES THROUGH SECRETARY OF LABOR.—The regulations may include a requirement that States submit notices of covered unemployment compensation debt to the Secretary via the Secretary of Labor in accordance with procedures established by the Secretary of Labor. Such procedures may require States to pay a fee to the Secretary of Labor to reimburse the Secretary of Labor for the costs of applying this subsection. Any such fee shall be established in consultation with the Secretary of the Treasury. Any fee paid to the Secretary of Labor may be deducted from amounts collected and shall be used to reimburse the appropriation account which bore all or part of the cost of applying this subsection.

(7) ERRONEOUS PAYMENT TO STATE.—Any State receiving notice from the Secretary that an erroneous payment has been made to such State under paragraph (1) shall pay promptly to the Secretary, in accordance with such regulations as the Secretary may prescribe, an amount equal to the amount of such erroneous payment (without regard to whether any other amounts payable to such State under such paragraph have been paid to such State).

(8) TERMINATION.—This section shall not apply to refunds payable after the date which is 10 years after the date of the enactment of this subsection.

[CCH Explanation at ¶ 710.]

Amendments

• **2008, SSI Extension for Elderly and Disabled Refugees Act (P.L. 110-328)**

P.L. 110-328, § 3(a):

Amended Code Sec. 6402 by redesignating subsections (f) through (k) as subsections (g) through (l), respectively, and

by inserting after subsection (e) a new subsection (f). **Effective** for refunds payable under Code Sec. 6402 on or after 9-30-2008.

(g) REVIEW OF REDUCTIONS.—No court of the United States shall have jurisdiction to hear any action, whether legal or equitable, brought to restrain or review a reduction authorized by subsection *(c), (d), (e),* or *(f).* No such reduction shall be subject to review by the Secretary in an administrative proceeding. No action brought against the United States to recover the amount of any such reduction shall be considered to be a suit for refund of tax. This subsection does not preclude any legal, equitable, or administrative action against the Federal agency or State to which the amount of such reduction was paid or any such action against the Commissioner of Social Security which is otherwise available with respect to recoveries of overpayments of benefits under section 204 of the Social Security Act.

[CCH Explanation at ¶710.]

Amendments

• **2008, SSI Extension for Elderly and Disabled Refugees Act (P.L. 110-328)**

P.L. 110-328, §3(a):

Amended Code Sec. 6402 by redesignating subsection (f) as subsection (g). **Effective** for refunds payable under Code Sec. 6402 on or after 9-30-2008.

P.L. 110-328, §3(d)(4):

Amended Code Sec. 6402(g), as redesignated by Act Sec. 3(a), by striking "(c), (d), or (e)" and inserting "(c), (d), (e), or (f)". **Effective** for refunds payable under Code Sec. 6402 on or after 9-30-2008.

(h) FEDERAL AGENCY.—For purposes of this section, the term "Federal agency" means a department, agency, or instrumentality of the United States, and includes a Government corporation (as such term is defined in section 103 of title 5, United States Code).

[CCH Explanation at ¶710.]

Amendments

• **2008, SSI Extension for Elderly and Disabled Refugees Act (P.L. 110-328)**

P.L. 110-328, §3(a):

Amended Code Sec. 6402 by redesignating subsection (g) as subsection (h). **Effective** for refunds payable under Code Sec. 6402 on or after 9-30-2008.

(i) TREATMENT OF PAYMENTS TO STATES.—The Secretary may provide that, for purposes of determining interest, the payment of any amount withheld under *subsection (c), (e), or (f)* to a State shall be treated as a payment to the person or persons making the overpayment.

[CCH Explanation at ¶710.]

Amendments

• **2008, SSI Extension for Elderly and Disabled Refugees Act (P.L. 110-328)**

P.L. 110-328, §3(a):

Amended Code Sec. 6402 by redesignating subsection (h) as subsection (i). **Effective** for refunds payable under Code Sec. 6402 on or after 9-30-2008.

P.L. 110-328, §3(d)(5):

Amended Code Sec. 6402(i), as redesignated by Act Sec. 3(a), by striking "subsection (c) or (e)" and inserting "subsection (c), (e), or (f)". **Effective** for refunds payable under Code Sec. 6402 on or after 9-30-2008.

(j) CROSS REFERENCE.—

For procedures relating to agency notification of the Secretary, see section 3721 of title 31, United States Code.

[CCH Explanation at ¶710.]

Amendments

• **2008, SSI Extension for Elderly and Disabled Refugees Act (P.L. 110-328)**

P.L. 110-328, §3(a):

Amended Code Sec. 6402 by redesignating subsection (i) as subsection (j). **Effective** for refunds payable under Code Sec. 6402 on or after 9-30-2008.

(k) REFUNDS TO CERTAIN FIDUCIARIES OF INSOLVENT MEMBERS OF AFFILIATED GROUPS.—Notwithstanding any other provision of law, in the case of an insolvent corporation which is a member of an affiliated group of corporations filing a consolidated return for any taxable year and which is subject to a statutory or court-appointed fiduciary, the Secretary may by regulation provide that any refund for such taxable year may be paid on behalf of such insolvent corporation to such fiduciary to the extent that the Secretary determines that the refund is attributable to losses or credits of such insolvent corporation.

[CCH Explanation at ¶ 710.]

Amendments

• **2008, SSI Extension for Elderly and Disabled Refugees Act (P.L. 110-328)**

P.L. 110-328, § 3(a):

Amended Code Sec. 6402 by redesignating subsection (j) as subsection (k). **Effective** for refunds payable under Code Sec. 6402 on or after 9-30-2008.

(l) EXPLANATION OF REASON FOR REFUND DISALLOWANCE.—In the case of a disallowance of a claim for refund, the Secretary shall provide the taxpayer with an explanation for such disallowance.

[CCH Explanation at ¶ 710.]

Amendments

• **2008, SSI Extension for Elderly and Disabled Refugees Act (P.L. 110-328)**

P.L. 110-328, § 3(a):

Amended Code Sec. 6402 by redesignating subsection (k) as subsection (l). **Effective** for refunds payable under Code Sec. 6402 on or after 9-30-2008.

[¶ 5455] CODE SEC. 6426. CREDIT FOR ALCOHOL FUEL, BIODIESEL, AND ALTERNATIVE FUEL MIXTURES.

* * *

(c) BIODIESEL MIXTURE CREDIT.—

* * *

≫→ *Caution: Code Sec. 6426(c)(2), as amended by P.L. 110-343, applies to fuel produced, and sold or used, after December 31, 2008.*

(2) APPLICABLE AMOUNT.—*For purposes of this subsection, the applicable amount is $1.00.*

* * *

(6) TERMINATION.—This subsection shall not apply to any sale, use, or removal for any period after *December 31, 2009.*

[CCH Explanation at ¶ 825. Committee Reports at ¶ 10,150.]

Amendments

• **2008, Energy Improvement and Extension Act of 2008 (P.L. 110-343)**

P.L. 110-343, Division B, § 202(a):

Amended Code Sec. 6426(c)(6) by striking "December 31, 2008" and inserting "December 31, 2009". **Effective** for fuel produced, and sold or used, after 12-31-2008.

P.L. 110-343, Division B, § 202(b)(2):

Amended Code Sec. 6426(c)(2). **Effective** for fuel produced, and sold or used, after 12-31-2008. Prior to amendment, Code Sec. 6426(c)(2) read as follows:

(2) APPLICABLE AMOUNT.—For purposes of this subsection—

(A) IN GENERAL.—Except as provided in subparagraph (B), the applicable amount is 50 cents.

(B) AMOUNT FOR AGRI-BIODIESEL.—In the case of any biodiesel which is agri-biodiesel, the applicable amount is $1.00.

(d) ALTERNATIVE FUEL CREDIT.—

(1) IN GENERAL.—For purposes of this section, the alternative fuel credit is the product of 50 cents and the number of gallons of an alternative fuel or gasoline gallon equivalents of a nonliquid alternative fuel sold by the taxpayer for use as a fuel in a motor vehicle or motorboat, *sold by the taxpayer for use as a fuel in aviation,* or so used by the taxpayer.

(2) ALTERNATIVE FUEL.—For purposes of this section, the term "alternative fuel" means—

* * *

(E) any liquid fuel *which meets the requirements of paragraph (4) and which is* derived from coal (including peat) through the Fischer-Tropsch process,

(F) *compressed or liquefied gas derived from biomass (as defined in section 45K(c)(3)), and*

(G) liquid fuel derived from biomass (as defined in section 45K(c)(3)). Such term does not include ethanol, methanol, or biodiesel.

* * *

(4) CARBON CAPTURE REQUIREMENT.—

(A) IN GENERAL.—*The requirements of this paragraph are met if the fuel is certified, under such procedures as required by the Secretary, as having been derived from coal produced at a gasification facility which separates and sequesters not less than the applicable percentage of such facility's total carbon dioxide emissions.*

(B) APPLICABLE PERCENTAGE.—*For purposes of subparagraph (A), the applicable percentage is—*

(i) *50 percent in the case of fuel produced after September 30, 2009, and on or before December 30, 2009, and*

(ii) *75 percent in the case of fuel produced after December 30, 2009.*

(5) TERMINATION.—This subsection shall not apply to any sale or use for any period after *December 31, 2009* (September 30, 2014, in the case of any sale or use involving liquefied hydrogen).

[CCH Explanation at ¶ 825.]

Amendments

- **2008, Energy Improvement and Extension Act of 2008 (P.L. 110-343)**

P.L. 110-343, Division B, § 204(a)(1):

Amended Code Sec. 6426(d)(4) by striking "September 30, 2009" and inserting "December 31, 2009". **Effective** for fuel sold or used after 10-3-2008.

P.L. 110-343, Division B, § 204(b)(1):

Amended Code Sec. 6426(d)(2) by striking "and" at the end of subparagraph (E), by redesignating subparagraph (F) as subparagraph (G), and by inserting after subparagraph (E) a new subparagraph (F). **Effective** for fuel sold or used after 10-3-2008.

P.L. 110-343, Division B, § 204(b)(2):

Amended Code Sec. 6426(d)(1) by inserting "sold by the taxpayer for use as a fuel in aviation," after "motorboat,". **Effective** for fuel sold or used after 10-3-2008.

P.L. 110-343, Division B, § 204(c)(1):

Amended Code Sec. 6426(d), as amended by Act Sec. 204(a), by redesignating paragraph (4) as paragraph (5) and by inserting after paragraph (3) a new paragraph (4). **Effective** for fuel sold or used after 10-3-2008.

P.L. 110-343, Division B, § 204(c)(2):

Amended Code Sec. 6426(d)(2)(E) by inserting "which meets the requirements of paragraph (4) and which is" after "any liquid fuel". **Effective** for fuel sold or used after 10-3-2008.

(e) ALTERNATIVE FUEL MIXTURE CREDIT.—

* * *

(3) TERMINATION.—This subsection shall not apply to any sale or use for any period after *December 31, 2009* (September 30, 2014, in the case of any sale or use involving liquefied hydrogen).

* * *

[CCH Explanation at ¶ 825.]

Amendments

- **2008, Energy Improvement and Extension Act of 2008 (P.L. 110-343)**

P.L. 110-343, Division B, § 204(a)(2):

Amended Code Sec. 6426(e)(3) by striking "September 30, 2009" and inserting "December 31, 2009". **Effective** for fuel sold or used after 10-3-2008.

(i) LIMITATION TO FUELS WITH CONNECTION TO THE UNITED STATES.—

(1) ALCOHOL.—No credit shall be determined under this section with respect to any alcohol which is produced outside the United States for use as a fuel outside the United States.

(2) BIODIESEL AND ALTERNATIVE FUELS.—No credit shall be determined under this section with respect to any biodiesel or alternative fuel which is produced outside the United States for use as a fuel outside the United States.

For purposes of this subsection, the term "United States" includes any possession of the United States.

[CCH Explanation at ¶ 825. Committee Reports at ¶ 10,160.]

Amendments

• 2008, Energy Improvement and Extension Act of 2008 (P.L. 110-343)

P.L. 110-343, Division B, § 203(c)(1):

Amended Code Sec. 6426 by adding at the end a new subsection (i). **Effective** for claims for credit or payment made on or after 5-15-2008.

[¶ 5460] CODE SEC. 6427. FUELS NOT USED FOR TAXABLE PURPOSES.

* * *

(e) ALCOHOL, BIODIESEL, OR ALTERNATIVE FUEL.—Except as provided in subsection (k)—

* * *

(5) LIMITATION TO FUELS WITH CONNECTION TO THE UNITED STATES.—No amount shall be payable under paragraph (1) or (2) with respect to any mixture or alternative fuel if credit is not allowed with respect to such mixture or alternative fuel by reason of section 6426(i).

(6) TERMINATION.—This subsection shall not apply with respect to—

(A) any alcohol fuel mixture (as defined in section 6426(b)(3)) sold or used after December 31, 2010,

(B) any biodiesel mixture (as defined in section 6426(c)(3)) sold or used after *December 31, 2009,*

(C) except as provided in subparagraph (D), any alternative fuel or alternative fuel mixture (as defined in subsection (d)(2) or (e)(3) of section 6426) sold or used after *December 31, 2009,* and

(D) any alternative fuel or alternative fuel mixture (as so defined) involving liquefied hydrogen sold or used after September 30, 2014.

* * *

[CCH Explanation at ¶ 825. Committee Reports at ¶ 10,150 and ¶ 10,160.]

Amendments

• 2008, Energy Improvement and Extension Act of 2008 (P.L. 110-343)

P.L. 110-343, Division B, § 202(a):

Amended Code Sec. 6427(e)(5)(B) by striking "December 31, 2008" and inserting "December 31, 2009". **Effective** for fuel produced, and sold or used, after 12-31-2008.

P.L. 110-343, Division B, § 203(c)(2):

Amended Code Sec. 6427(e) by redesignating paragraph (5) as paragraph (6) and inserting after paragraph (4) a new

paragraph (5). **Effective** for claims for credit or payment made on or after 5-15-2008.

P.L. 110-343, Division B, § 204(a)(3):

Amended Code Sec. 6427(e)(5)(C) [prior to redesignation as Code Sec. 6427(e)(6)(C) by Act Sec. 203(c)(2)] by striking "September 30, 2009" and inserting "December 31, 2009". **Effective** for fuel sold or used after 10-3-2008.

[¶ 5465] CODE SEC. 6501. LIMITATIONS ON ASSESSMENT AND COLLECTION.

* * *

»»→ *Caution: Code Sec. 6501(i), below, as amended by P.L. 110-343, applies to tax years beginning after December 31, 2008.*

(i) FOREIGN TAX CARRYBACKS.—In the case of a deficiency attributable to the application to the taxpayer of a carryback under section 904(c) (relating to carryback and carryover of excess foreign taxes), or under section 907(f) (relating to carryback and carryover of disallowed *foreign oil and gas taxes*), such deficiency may be assessed at any time before the expiration of one year after the expiration of the period within which a deficiency may be assessed for the taxable year of the excess taxes described in section 904(c) or 907(f) which result in such carryback.

* * *

[CCH Explanation at ¶ 875. Committee Reports at ¶ 10,270.]
Amendments
• **2008, Energy Improvement and Extension Act of 2008 (P.L. 110-343)**

P.L. 110-343, Division B, § 402(d):

Amended Code Sec. 6501(i) by striking "oil and gas extraction taxes" and inserting "foreign oil and gas taxes". **Effective** for tax years beginning after 12-31-2008.

(m) DEFICIENCIES ATTRIBUTABLE TO ELECTION OF CERTAIN CREDITS.—The period for assessing a deficiency attributable to any election under section 30(d)(4), 30B(h)(9), 30C(e)(5) [30C(e)(4)], *30D(e)(9)*, 40(f), 43, 45B, 45C(d)(4), 45H(g), or 51(j) (or any revocation thereof) shall not expire before the date 1 year after the date on which the Secretary is notified of such election (or revocation).

* * *

[CCH Explanation at ¶ 515. Committee Reports at ¶ 10,170.]
Amendments
• **2008, Energy Improvement and Extension Act of 2008 (P.L. 110-343)**

P.L. 110-343, Division B, § 205(d)(3):

Amended Code Sec. 6501(m) by inserting "30D(e)(9)," after "30C(e)(5),". **Effective** for tax years beginning after 12-31-2008.

[¶ 5470] CODE SEC. 6694. UNDERSTATEMENT OF TAXPAYER'S LIABILITY BY TAX RETURN PREPARER.

(a) UNDERSTATEMENT DUE TO UNREASONABLE POSITIONS.—

(1) IN GENERAL.—If a tax return preparer—

(A) prepares any return or claim of refund with respect to which any part of an understatement of liability is due to a position described in paragraph (2), and

(B) knew (or reasonably should have known) of the position,

such tax return preparer shall pay a penalty with respect to each such return or claim in an amount equal to the greater of $1,000 or 50 percent of the income derived (or to be derived) by the tax return preparer with respect to the return or claim.

(2) UNREASONABLE POSITION.—

(A) IN GENERAL.—Except as otherwise provided in this paragraph, a position is described in this paragraph unless there is or was substantial authority for the position.

(B) DISCLOSED POSITIONS.—If the position was disclosed as provided in section 6662(d)(2)(B)(ii)(I) and is not a position to which subparagraph (C) applies, the position is described in this paragraph unless there is a reasonable basis for the position.

(C) TAX SHELTERS AND REPORTABLE TRANSACTIONS.—If the position is with respect to a tax shelter (as defined in section 6662(d)(2)(C)(ii)) or a reportable transaction to which section 6662A applies,

the position is described in this paragraph unless it is reasonable to believe that the position would more likely than not be sustained on its merits.

(3) REASONABLE CAUSE EXCEPTION.—*No penalty shall be imposed under this subsection if it is shown that there is reasonable cause for the understatement and the tax return preparer acted in good faith.*

* * *

[CCH Explanation at ¶705. Committee Reports at ¶10,690.]

Amendments

• 2008, Tax Extenders and Alternative Minimum Tax Relief Act of 2008 (P.L. 110-343)

P.L. 110-343, Division C, §506(a):

Amended Code Sec. 6694(a). For the **effective** date, see Act Sec. 506(b), below. Prior to amendment, Code Sec. 6694(a) read as follows:

(a) UNDERSTATEMENT DUE TO UNREASONABLE POSITIONS.—

(1) IN GENERAL.—Any tax return preparer who prepares any return or claim for refund with respect to which any part of an understatement of liability is due to a position described in paragraph (2) shall pay a penalty with respect to each such return or claim in an amount equal to the greater of—

(A) $1,000, or

(B) 50 percent of the income derived (or to be derived) by the tax return preparer with respect to the return or claim.

(2) UNREASONABLE POSITION.—A position is described in this paragraph if—

(A) the tax return preparer knew (or reasonably should have known) of the position,

(B) there was not a reasonable belief that the position would more likely than not be sustained on its merits, and

(C)(i) the position was not disclosed as provided in section 6662(d)(2)(B)(ii), or

(ii) there was no reasonable basis for the position.

(3) REASONABLE CAUSE EXCEPTION.—No penalty shall be imposed under this subsection if it is shown that there is reasonable cause for the understatement and the tax return preparer acted in good faith.

P.L. 110-343, Division C, §506(b), provides:

(b) EFFECTIVE DATE.—The amendment made by this section shall apply—

(1) in the case of a position other than a position described in subparagraph (C) of section 6694(a)(2) of the Internal Revenue Code of 1986 (as amended by this section), to returns prepared after May 25, 2007, and

(2) in the case of a position described in such subparagraph (C), to returns prepared for taxable years ending after the date of the enactment of this Act [10-3-2008.—CCH].

[¶5475] CODE SEC. 6724. WAIVER; DEFINITIONS AND SPECIAL RULES.

* * *

(d) DEFINITIONS.—For purposes of this part—

(1) INFORMATION RETURN.—The term "information return" means—

* * *

(B) any return required by—

* * *

»»→ Caution: *Code Sec. 6724(d)(1)(B)(iv), as added by P.L. 110-343, is effective January 1, 2011.*

(iv) section 6045B(a) (relating to returns relating to actions affecting basis of specified securities),

»»→ Caution: *Former Code Sec. 6724(d)(1)(B)(iv)-(xxii) was redesignated as Code Sec. 6724(d)(1)(B)(v)-(xxiii), respectively, by P.L. 110-343, effective January 1, 2011.*

(v) section 6050H(a) or (h)(1)(relating to mortgage interest received in trade or business from individuals),

(vi) section 6050I(a) or (g)(1) (relating to cash received in trade or business, etc.),

(vii) section 6050J(a) (relating to foreclosures and abandonments of security),

(viii) section 6050K(a) (relating to exchanges of certain partnership interests),

(ix) section 6050L(a) (relating to returns relating to certain dispositions of donated property),

(x) section 6050P (relating to returns relating to the cancellation of indebtedness by certain financial entities),

(xi) section 6050Q (relating to certain long-term care benefits),

(xii) section 6050S (relating to returns relating to payments for qualified tuition and related expenses), *(xiii)* section 6050T (relating to returns relating to credit for health insurance costs of eligible individuals),

(xiv) section 6052(a) (relating to reporting payment of wages in the form of group-life insurance),

(xv) section 6050V (relating to returns relating to applicable insurance contracts in which certain exempt organizations hold interests),

(xvi) section 6053(c)(1) (relating to reporting with respect to certain tips),

(xvii) subsection (b) or (e) of section 1060 (relating to reporting requirements of transferors and transferees in certain asset acquisitions),

(xviii) section 4101(d) (relating to information reporting with respect to fuels taxes),

(xix) subparagraph (C) of section 338(h)(10) (relating to information required to be furnished to the Secretary in case of elective recognition of gain or loss),

(xx) section 264(f)(5)(A)(iv) (relating to reporting with respect to certain life insurance and annuity contracts),

(xxi) section 6050U (relating to charges or payments for qualified long-term care insurance contracts under combined arrangements),

(xxii) section 6039(a) (relating to returns required with respect to certain options), or

(xxiii) section 6050W (relating to returns to payments made in settlement of payment card transactions), and

* * *

(2) PAYEE STATEMENT.—The term "payee statement" means any statement required to be furnished under—

* * *

»»➔ Caution: *Code Sec. 6724(d)(2)(I)-(J), below, as added by P.L. 110-343, are effective January 1, 2011.*

(I) section 6045A (relating to information required in connection with transfers of covered securities to brokers),

(J) subsections (c) and (e) of section 6045B (relating to returns relating to actions affecting basis of specified securities),

»»➔ Caution: *Former Code Sec. 6724(d)(2)(I)-(DD), below, were redesignated as Code Sec. 6724(d)(2)(K)-(FF), respectively, by P.L. 110-343, effective January 1, 2011.*

(K) section 6049(c) (relating to returns regarding payments of interest),

(L) section 6050A(b) (relating to reporting requirements of certain fishing boat operators),

(M) section 6050H(d) or (h)(2) (relating to returns relating to mortgage interest received in trade or business from individuals),

(N) section 6050I(e) or paragraph (4) or (5) of section 6050I(g) (relating to cash received in trade or business, etc.),

(O) section 6050J(e) (relating to returns relating to foreclosures and abandonments of security),

(P) section 6050K(b) (relating to returns relating to exchanges of certain partnership interests),

(Q) section 6050L(c) (relating to returns relating to certain dispositions of donated property),

(R) section 6050N(b) (relating to returns regarding payments of royalties),

(S) section 6050P(d) (relating to returns relating to the cancellation of indebtedness by certain financial entities),

(T) section 6050Q(b) (relating to certain long-term care benefits),

(U) section 6050R(c) (relating to returns relating to certain purchases of fish),

(V) section 6051 (relating to receipts for employees),

(W) section 6052(b) (relating to returns regarding payment of wages in the form of group-term life insurance),

(X) section 6053(b) or (c) (relating to reports of tips),

(Y) section 6048(b)(1)(B) (relating to foreign trust reporting requirements),

(Z) section 408(i) (relating to reports with respect to individual retirement plans) to any person other than the Secretary with respect to the amount of payments made to such person,

(AA) section 6047(d) (relating to reports by plan administrators) to any person other than the Secretary with respect to the amount of payments made to such person,

(BB) section 6050S(d) (relating to returns relating to qualified tuition and related expenses),

(CC) section 264(f)(5)(A)(iv) (relating to reporting with respect to certain life insurance and annuity contracts),

(DD) section 6050T (relating to returns relating to credit for health insurance costs of eligible individuals),

(EE) section 6050U (relating to charges or payments for qualified long-term care insurance contracts under combined arrangements), or

(FF) section 6050W(c) (relating to returns relating to payments made in settlement of payment card transactions).

* * *

[CCH Explanations at ¶735 and ¶740. Committee Reports at ¶10,280.]

Amendments

• 2008, Energy Improvement and Extension Act of 2008 (P.L. 110-343)

P.L. 110-343, Division B, §403(c)(2):

Amended Code Sec. 6724(d)(2), as amended by the Housing Assistance Tax Act of 2008 (P.L. 110-289), by redesignating subparagraphs (I) through (DD) as subparagraphs (J) through (EE), respectively, and by inserting after subparagraph (H) a new subparagraph (I). **Effective** 1-1-2011.

P.L. 110-343, Division B, §403(d)(2)(A):

Amended Code Sec. 6724(d)(1)(B), as amended by the Housing Assistance Tax Act of 2008 (P.L. 110-289), by redes-

ignating clause (iv) and each of the clauses which follow [clauses (v)-(xxii).—CCH] as clauses (v) through (xxiii), respectively, and by inserting after clause (iii) a new clause (iv). **Effective** 1-1-2011.

P.L. 110-343, Division B, §403(d)(2)(B):

Amended Code Sec. 6724(d)(2), as amended by the Housing Assistance Tax Act of 2008 (P.L. 110-289) and by Act Sec. 403(c)(2), by redesignating subparagraphs (J) through (EE) as subparagraphs (K) through (FF), respectively, and by inserting after subparagraph (I) a new subparagraph (J). **Effective** 1-1-2011.

[¶5480] CODE SEC. 7508A. AUTHORITY TO POSTPONE CERTAIN DEADLINES BY REASON OF PRESIDENTIALLY DECLARED DISASTER OR TERRORISTIC OR MILITARY ACTIONS.

(a) IN GENERAL.—In the case of a taxpayer determined by the Secretary to be affected by a *federally declared disaster (as defined by section 165(h)(3)(C)(i))* or a terroristic or military action (as defined in section 692(c)(2)), the Secretary may specify a period of up to 1 year that may be disregarded in determining, under the internal revenue laws, in respect of any tax liability of such taxpayer—

(1) whether any of the acts described in paragraph (1) of section 7508(a) were performed within the time prescribed therefor (determined without regard to extension under any other provision of this subtitle for periods after the date (determined by the Secretary) of such disaster or action),

(2) the amount of any interest, penalty, additional amount, or addition to the tax for periods after such date, and

(3) the amount of any credit or refund.

* * *

[CCH Explanation at ¶ 605. Committee Reports at ¶ 10,710.]

Amendments

• **2008, Heartland Disaster Tax Relief of 2008 (P.L. 110-343)**

P.L. 110-343, Division C, § 706(a)(2)(D)(vii):

Amended Code Sec. 7508A(a) by striking "Presidentially declared disaster (as defined in section 1033(h)(3))" and

inserting "federally declared disaster (as defined by section 165(h)(3)(C)(i))". **Effective** for disasters declared in tax years beginning after 12-31-2007.

[¶ 5485] CODE SEC. 7608. AUTHORITY OF INTERNAL REVENUE ENFORCEMENT OFFICERS.

* * *

(c) RULES RELATING TO UNDERCOVER OPERATIONS.—

* * *

(6) *[Stricken.]*

[CCH Explanation at ¶ 720. Committee Reports at ¶ 10,620.]

Amendments

• **2008, Tax Extenders and Alternative Minimum Tax Relief Act of 2008 (P.L. 110-343)**

P.L. 110-343, Division C, § 401(a):

Amended Code Sec. 7608(c) by striking paragraph (6). **Effective** for operations conducted after 10-3-2008. Prior to being stricken, Code Sec. 7608(c)(6) read as follows:

(6) APPLICATION OF SECTION.—The provisions of this subsection—

(A) shall apply after November 17, 1988, and before January 1, 1990, and

(B) shall apply after the date of the enactment of this paragraph and before January 1, 2008.

All amounts expended pursuant to this subsection during the period described in subparagraph (B) shall be recovered to the extent possible, and deposited in the Treasury of the United States as miscellaneous receipts, before January 1, 2008.

[¶ 5490] CODE SEC. 7652. SHIPMENTS TO THE UNITED STATES.

* * *

(f) LIMITATION ON COVER OVER OF TAX ON DISTILLED SPIRITS.—For purposes of this section, with respect to taxes imposed under section 5001 or this section on distilled spirits, the amount covered into the treasuries of Puerto Rico and the Virgin Islands shall not exceed the lesser of the rate of—

(1) $10.50 ($13.25 in the case of distilled spirits brought into the United States after June 30, 1999, and before *January 1, 2010*), or

(2) the tax imposed under section 5001(a)(1), on each proof gallon.

* * *

[CCH Explanation at ¶ 830. Committee Reports at ¶ 10,480.]

Amendments

• **2008, Tax Extenders and Alternative Minimum Tax Relief Act of 2008 (P.L. 110-343)**

P.L. 110-343, Division C, § 308(a):

Amended Code Sec. 7652(f)(1) by striking "January 1, 2008" and inserting "January 1, 2010". **Effective** for distilled spirits brought into the United States after 12-31-2007.

[¶ 5495] CODE SEC. 7704. CERTAIN PUBLICLY TRADED PARTNERSHIPS TREATED AS CORPORATIONS.

* * *

(d) QUALIFYING INCOME.—For purposes of this section—

(1) IN GENERAL.—Except as otherwise provided in this subsection, the term "qualifying income" means—

* * *

(E) income and gains derived from the exploration, development, mining or production, processing, refining, transportation (including pipelines transporting gas, oil, or products thereof), or the marketing of any mineral or natural resource (including fertilizer, geothermal energy, and timber), *industrial source carbon dioxide, or the transportation or storage of any fuel described in subsection (b), (c), (d), or (e) of section 6426, or any alcohol fuel defined in section 6426(b)(4)(A) or any biodiesel fuel as defined in section 40A(d)(1),*

* * *

[CCH Explanation at ¶ 465. Committee Reports at ¶ 10,120.]

Amendments

• **2008, Energy Improvement and Extension Act of 2008 (P.L. 110-343)**

P.L. 110-343, Division B, § 116(a):

Amended Code Sec. 7704(d)(1)(E) by inserting "or industrial source carbon dioxide" after "timber)". **Effective** 10-3-2008, in tax years ending after such date.

P.L. 110-343, Division B, § 208(a):

Amended Code Sec. 7704(d)(1)(E), as amended by this Act, by striking "or industrial source carbon dioxide" and

inserting ", industrial source carbon dioxide, or the transportation or storage of any fuel described in subsection (b), (c), (d), or (e) of section 6426, or any alcohol fuel defined in section 6426(b)(4)(A) or any biodiesel fuel as defined in section 40A(d)(1)" after "timber)". **Effective** 10-3-2008, in tax years ending after such date.

[¶ 5497] CODE SEC. 7803. COMMISSIONER OF INTERNAL REVENUE; OTHER OFFICIALS.

* * *

(d) ADDITIONAL DUTIES OF THE TREASURY INSPECTOR GENERAL FOR TAX ADMINISTRATION.—

* * *

(3) OTHER RESPONSIBILITIES.—The Treasury Inspector General for Tax Administration shall—

(A) conduct periodic audits of a statistically valid sample of the total number of determinations made by the Internal Revenue Service to deny written requests to disclose information to taxpayers on the basis of section 6103 of this title or section 552(b)(7) of title 5, United States Code;

(B) establish and maintain a toll-free telephone number for taxpayers to use to confidentially register complaints of misconduct by Internal Revenue Service employees and incorporate the telephone number in the statement required by section 6227 of the Omnibus Taxpayer Bill of Rights (Internal Revenue Service Publication No. 1); *and*

➤➤➤ *Caution: Code Sec. 7803(d)(3)(C), below, as added by H.R. 7082, applies to disclosures made after December 31, 2008.*

(C) *not later than December 31, 2010, submit a written report to Congress on the implementation of section 6103(k)(10),*

[CCH Explanation at ¶ 718.]

Amendments

• **2008, Inmate Tax Fraud Prevention Act of 2008 (H.R. 7082)**

H.R. 7082, § 2(c):

Amended Code Sec. 7803(d)(3) by striking "and" at the end of subparagraph (A), by striking the period at the end

of subparagraph (B) and inserting "; and", and by adding at the end a new subparagraph (C). **Effective** for disclosures made after 12-31-2008.

[¶ 5499] CODE SEC. 9502. AIRPORT AND AIRWAY TRUST FUND.

* * *

(d) EXPENDITURES FROM AIRPORT AND AIRWAY TRUST FUND.—

(1) AIRPORT AND AIRWAY PROGRAM.—Amounts in the Airport and Airway Trust Fund shall be available, as provided by appropriation Acts, for making expenditures before *April 1, 2009,* to meet those obligations of the United States—

(A) incurred under title I of the Airport and Airway Development Act of 1970 or of the Airport and Airway Development Act Amendments of 1976 or of the Aviation Safety and Noise Abatement Act of 1979 (as such Acts were in effect on the date of enactment of the Fiscal Year 1981 Airport Development Authorization Act) or under the Fiscal Year 1981 Airport Development Authorization Act or the provisions of the Airport and Airway Improvement Act of 1982 or the Airport and Airway Safety and Capacity Expansion Act of 1987 or the Federal Aviation Administration Research, Engineering, and Development Authorization Act of 1990 or the Aviation Safety and Capacity Expansion Act of 1990 or the Airport and Airway Safety, Capacity, Noise Improvement, and Intermodal Transportation Act of 1992 or the Airport Improvement Program Temporary Extension Act of 1994 or the Federal Aviation Administration Authorization Act of 1994 or the Federal Aviation Reauthorization Act of 1996 or the provisions of the Omnibus Consolidated and Emergency Supplemental Appropriations Act, 1999 providing for payments from the Airport and Airway Trust Fund or the Interim Federal Aviation Administration Authorization Act or section 6002 of the 1999 Emergency Supplemental Appropriations Act, Public Law 106-59, or the Wendell H. Ford Aviation Investment and Reform Act for the 21st Century or the Aviation and Transportation Security Act or the Vision 100—Century of Aviation Reauthorization Act or any joint resolution making continuing appropriations for the fiscal year 2008 or the Department of Transportation Appropriations Act, 2008 or the Airport and Airway Extension Act of 2008 or the Federal Aviation Administration Extension Act of 2008 *or the Federal Aviation Administration Extension Act of 2008, Part II;*

* * *

[CCH Explanation at ¶ 835.]

Amendments

• **2008, Federal Aviation Administration Extension Act of 2008, Part II (P.L. 110-330)**

P.L. 110-330, §3(a)(1)-(2):

Amended Code Sec. 9502(d)(1) by striking "October 1, 2008" and inserting "April 1, 2009", and by inserting "or the

Federal Aviation Administration Extension Act of 2008, Part II" before the semicolon at the end of subparagraph (A). **Effective** 10-1-2008.

(e) LIMITATION ON TRANSFERS TO TRUST FUND.—

* * *

(2) EXCEPTION FOR PRIOR OBLIGATIONS.—Paragraph (1) shall not apply to any expenditure to liquidate any contract entered into (or for any amount otherwise obligated) before *April 1, 2009,* in accordance with the provisions of this section.

[CCH Explanation at ¶ 835.]

Amendments

• **2008, Federal Aviation Administration Extension Act of 2008, Part II (P.L. 110-330)**

P.L. 110-330, §3(b):

Amended Code Sec. 9502(e)(2) by striking the date specified in such paragraph [October 1, 2008.—CCH] and inserting "April 1, 2009". **Effective** 10-1-2008.

[¶5500] CODE SEC. 9812. *PARITY IN MENTAL HEALTH AND SUBSTANCE USE DISORDER BENEFITS.*

⟫⟶ *Caution: Code Sec. 9812(a), below, as amended by P.L. 110-343, applies generally with respect to group health plans for plan years beginning after the date that is 1 year after October 3, 2008.*

(a) IN GENERAL.—

(1) AGGREGATE LIFETIME LIMITS.—In the case of a group health plan that provides both medical and surgical benefits and *mental health and substance use disorder benefits*—

(A) NO LIFETIME LIMIT.—If the plan does not include an aggregate lifetime limit on substantially all medical and surgical benefits, the plan may not impose any aggregate lifetime limit on *mental health or substance use disorder benefits*.

(B) LIFETIME LIMIT.—If the plan includes an aggregate lifetime limit on substantially all medical and surgical benefits (in this paragraph referred to as the "applicable lifetime limit"), the plan shall either—

(i) apply the applicable lifetime limit both to the medical and surgical benefits to which it otherwise would apply and to *mental health and substance use disorder benefits* and not distinguish in the application of such limit between such medical and surgical benefits and *mental health and substance use disorder benefits*; or

(ii) not include any aggregate lifetime limit on *mental health or substance use disorder benefits* that is less than the applicable lifetime limit.

(C) RULE IN CASE OF DIFFERENT LIMITS.—In the case of a plan that is not described in subparagraph (A) or (B) and that includes no or different aggregate lifetime limits on different categories of medical and surgical benefits, the Secretary shall establish rules under which subparagraph (B) is applied to such plan with respect to *mental health and substance use disorder benefits* by substituting for the applicable lifetime limit an average aggregate lifetime limit that is computed taking into account the weighted average of the aggregate lifetime limits applicable to such categories.

(2) ANNUAL LIMITS.—In the case of a group health plan that provides both medical and surgical benefits and *mental health or substance use disorder benefits*—

(A) NO ANNUAL LIMIT.—If the plan does not include an annual limit on substantially all medical and surgical benefits, the plan may not impose any annual limit on *mental health or substance use disorder benefits*.

(B) ANNUAL LIMIT.—If the plan includes an annual limit on substantially all medical and surgical benefits (in this paragraph referred to as the "applicable annual limit"), the plan shall either—

(i) apply the applicable annual limit both to medical and surgical benefits to which it otherwise would apply and to *mental health and substance use disorder benefits* and not distinguish in the application of such limit between such medical and surgical benefits and *mental health and substance use disorder benefits*; or

(ii) not include any annual limit on *mental health or substance use disorder benefits* that is less than the applicable annual limit.

(C) RULE IN CASE OF DIFFERENT LIMITS.—In the case of a plan that is not described in subparagraph (A) or (B) and that includes no or different annual limits on different categories of medical and surgical benefits, the Secretary shall establish rules under which subparagraph (B) is applied to such plan with respect to *mental health and substance use disorder benefits* by substituting for the applicable annual limit an average annual limit that is computed taking into account the weighted average of the annual limits applicable to such categories.

(3) FINANCIAL REQUIREMENTS AND TREATMENT LIMITATIONS.—

(A) IN GENERAL.—In the case of a group health plan that provides both medical and surgical benefits and mental health or substance use disorder benefits, such plan shall ensure that—

(i) the financial requirements applicable to such mental health or substance use disorder benefits are no more restrictive than the predominant financial requirements applied to substantially all medical and surgical benefits covered by the plan, and there are no separate cost sharing requirements that are applicable only with respect to mental health or substance use disorder benefits; and

(ii) the treatment limitations applicable to such mental health or substance use disorder benefits are no more restrictive than the predominant treatment limitations applied to substantially all medical and surgical benefits covered by the plan and there are no separate treatment

limitations that are applicable only with respect to mental health or substance use disorder benefits.

(B) DEFINITIONS.—In this paragraph:

(i) FINANCIAL REQUIREMENT.—The term "financial requirement" includes deductibles, copayments, coinsurance, and out-of-pocket expenses, but excludes an aggregate lifetime limit and an annual limit subject to paragraphs (1) and (2),

(ii) PREDOMINANT.—A financial requirement or treatment limit is considered to be predominant if it is the most common or frequent of such type of limit or requirement.

(iii) TREATMENT LIMITATION.—The term "treatment limitation" includes limits on the frequency of treatment, number of visits, days of coverage, or other similar limits on the scope or duration of treatment.

(4) AVAILABILITY OF PLAN INFORMATION.—The criteria for medical necessity determinations made under the plan with respect to mental health or substance use disorder benefits shall be made available by the plan administrator in accordance with regulations to any current or potential participant, beneficiary, or contracting provider upon request. The reason for any denial under the plan of reimbursement or payment for services with respect to mental health or substance use disorder benefits in the case of any participant or beneficiary shall, on request or as otherwise required, be made available by the plan administrator to the participant or beneficiary in accordance with regulations.

(5) OUT-OF-NETWORK PROVIDERS.—In the case of a plan that provides both medical and surgical benefits and mental health or substance use disorder benefits, if the plan provides coverage for medical or surgical benefits provided by out-of-network providers, the plan shall provide coverage for mental health or substance use disorder benefits provided by out-of-network providers in a manner that is consistent with the requirements of this section.

[CCH Explanation at ¶ 880.]

Amendments

• **2008, Paul Wellstone and Pete Domenici Mental Health Parity and Addiction Equity Act of 2008 (P.L. 110-343)**

P.L. 110-343, Division C, § 512(c)(1):

Amended Code Sec. 9812(a) by adding at the end new paragraphs (3)-(5). For the **effective** date and special rules, see Act Sec. 512(d)-(f), below.

P.L. 110-343, Division C, § 512(c)(6):

Amended Code Sec. 9812(a)(1)(B)(i), (1)(C), (2)(B)(i), and (2)(C) by striking "mental health benefits" and inserting "mental health and substance use disorder benefits" each place it appears. For the **effective** date and special rules, see Act Sec. 512(d)-(f), below.

H.R. 1424, Division C, § 512(c)(7):

Amended Code Sec. 9812 by striking "mental health benefits" and inserting "mental health or substance use disorder benefits" each place it appears (other than in any provision amended by Act Sec. 512(c)(6)). For the **effective** date and special rules, see Act Sec. 512(d)-(f), below.

P.L. 110-343, Division C, § 512(d)-(f), provides:

(d) REGULATIONS.—Not later than 1 year after the date of enactment of this Act, the Secretaries of Labor, Health and Human Services, and the Treasury shall issue regulations to carry out the amendments made by subsections (a), (b), and (c), respectively.

(e) EFFECTIVE DATE.—

(1) IN GENERAL.—The amendments made by this section shall apply with respect to group health plans for plan years beginning after the date that is 1 year after the date of enactment of this Act, regardless of whether regulations have been issued to carry out such amendments by such

effective date, except that the amendments made by subsections (a)(5), (b)(5), and (c)(5), relating to striking of certain sunset provisions, shall take effect on January 1, 2009.

(2) SPECIAL RULE FOR COLLECTIVE BARGAINING AGREEMENTS.— In the case of a group health plan maintained pursuant to one or more collective bargaining agreements between employee representatives and one or more employers ratified before the date of the enactment of this Act, the amendments made by this section shall not apply to plan years beginning before the later of—

(A) the date on which the last of the collective bargaining agreements relating to the plan terminates (determined without regard to any extension thereof agreed to after the date of the enactment of this Act), or

(B) January 1, 2009.

For purposes of subparagraph (A), any plan amendment made pursuant to a collective bargaining agreement relating to the plan which amends the plan solely to conform to any requirement added by this section shall not be treated as a termination of such collective bargaining agreement.

(f) ASSURING COORDINATION.—The Secretary of Health and Human Services, the Secretary of Labor, and the Secretary of the Treasury may ensure, through the execution or revision of an interagency memorandum of understanding among such Secretaries, that—

(1) regulations, rulings, and interpretations issued by such Secretaries relating to the same matter over which two or more such Secretaries have responsibility under this section (and the amendments made by this section) are administered so as to have the same effect at all times; and

(2) coordination of policies relating to enforcing the same requirements through such Secretaries in order to have a coordinated enforcement strategy that avoids duplication of enforcement efforts and assigns priorities in enforcement.

P.L. 110-343, Division C, § 512(g)(3)(A):

Amended the heading of Code Sec. 9812. **Effective** 10-3-2008. Prior to amendment, the heading of Code Sec. 9812 read as follows:

PARITY IN THE APPLICATION OF CERTAIN LIMITS TO MENTAL HEALTH BENEFITS.

⟫⟫→ Caution: *Code Sec. 9812(b), below, as amended by P.L. 110-343, applies generally with respect to group health plans for plan years beginning after the date that is 1 year after October 3, 2008.*

(b) CONSTRUCTION.—Nothing in this section shall be construed—

(1) as requiring a group health plan to provide any *mental health or substance use disorder benefits; or*

(2) *in the case of a group health plan that provides mental health or substance use disorder benefits, as affecting the terms and conditions of the plan relating to such benefits under the plan, except as provided in subsection (a).*

[CCH Explanation at ¶ 880.]
Amendments

• 2008, Paul Wellstone and Pete Domenici Mental Health Parity and Addiction Equity Act of 2008 (P.L. 110-343)

P.L. 110-343, Division C, § 512(c)(2):

Amended Code Sec. 9812(b)(2). For the **effective** date and special rules, see Act Sec. 512(d)-(f), in the amendment notes for Code Sec. 9812(a). Prior to amendment, Code Sec. 9812(b)(2) read as follows:

(2) in the case of a group health plan that provides mental health benefits, as affecting the terms and conditions (including cost sharing, limits on numbers of visits or days of

coverage, and requirements relating to medical necessity) relating to the amount, duration, or scope of mental health benefits under the plan, except as specifically provided in subsection (a) (in regard to parity in the imposition of aggregate lifetime limits and annual limits for mental health benefits).

H.R. 1424, Division C, § 512(c)(7):

Amended Code Sec. 9812 by striking "mental health benefits" and inserting "mental health or substance use disorder benefits" each place it appears (other than in any provision amended by Act Sec. 512(c)(6)). For the **effective** date and special rules, see Act Sec. 512(d)-(f), in the amendment notes for Code Sec. 9812(a).

⟫⟫→ Caution: *Code Sec. 9812(c), below, as amended by P.L. 110-343, applies generally with respect to group health plans for plan years beginning after the date that is 1 year after October 3, 2008.*

(c) EXEMPTIONS.—

(1) SMALL EMPLOYER EXEMPTION.—

(A) IN GENERAL.—*This section shall not apply to any group health plan for any plan year of a small employer.*

(B) SMALL EMPLOYER.—*For purposes of subparagraph (A), the term "small employer" means, with respect to a calendar year and a plan year, an employer who employed an average of at least 2 (or 1 in the case of an employer residing in a State that permits small groups to include a single individual) but not more than 50 employees on business days during the preceding calendar year. For purposes of the preceding sentence, all persons treated as a single employer under subsection (b), (c), (m), or (o) of section 414 shall be treated as 1 employer and rules similar to rules of subparagraphs (B) and (C) of section 4980D(d)(2) shall apply.*

(2) COST EXEMPTION.—

(A) IN GENERAL.—*With respect to a group health plan, if the application of this section to such plan results in an increase for the plan year involved of the actual total costs of coverage with respect to medical and surgical benefits and mental health and substance use disorder benefits under the plan (as determined and certified under subparagraph (C)) by an amount that exceeds the applicable percentage described in subparagraph (B) of the actual total plan costs, the provisions of this section shall not apply to such plan during the following plan year, and such exemption shall apply to the plan for 1 plan year. An employer may elect to continue to apply mental health and substance use disorder parity pursuant to this section with respect to the group health plan involved regardless of any increase in total costs.*

(B) APPLICABLE PERCENTAGE.—*With respect to a plan, the applicable percentage described in this subparagraph shall be—*

(i) *2 percent in the case of the first plan year in which this section is applied; and*

(ii) *1 percent in the case of each subsequent plan year.*

(C) DETERMINATIONS BY ACTUARIES.—*Determinations as to increases in actual costs under a plan for purposes of this section shall be made and certified by a qualified and licensed actuary who is a member in good standing of the American Academy of Actuaries. All such determinations shall be in a written report prepared by the actuary. The report, and all underlying documentation relied upon by the actuary, shall be maintained by the group health plan for a period of 6 years following the notification made under subparagraph (E).*

(D) 6-MONTH DETERMINATIONS.—*If a group health plan seeks an exemption under this paragraph, determinations under subparagraph (A) shall be made after such plan has complied with this section for the first 6 months of the plan year involved.*

(E) NOTIFICATION.—

(i) IN GENERAL.—*A group health plan that, based upon a certification described under subparagraph (C), qualifies for an exemption under this paragraph, and elects to implement the exemption, shall promptly notify the Secretary, the appropriate State agencies, and participants and beneficiaries in the plan of such election.*

(ii) REQUIREMENT.—*A notification to the Secretary under clause (i) shall include—*

(I) *a description of the number of covered lives under the plan involved at the time of the notification, and as applicable, at the time of any prior election of the cost-exemption under this paragraph by such plan;*

(II) *for both the plan year upon which a cost exemption is sought and the year prior, a description of the actual total costs of coverage with respect to medical and surgical benefits and mental health and substance use disorder benefits under the plan; and*

(III) *for both the plan year upon which a cost exemption is sought and the year prior, the actual total costs of coverage with respect to mental health and substance use disorder benefits under the plan.*

(iii) CONFIDENTIALITY.—*A notification to the Secretary under clause (i) shall be confidential. The Secretary shall make available, upon request and on not more than an annual basis, an anonymous itemization of such notifications, that includes—*

(I) *a breakdown of States by the size and type of employers submitting such notification; and*

(II) *a summary of the data received under clause (ii).*

(F) AUDITS BY APPROPRIATE AGENCIES.—*To determine compliance with this paragraph, the Secretary may audit the books and records of a group health plan relating to an exemption, including any actuarial reports prepared pursuant to subparagraph (C), during the 6 year period following the notification of such exemption under subparagraph (E). A State agency receiving a notification under subparagraph (E) may also conduct such an audit with respect to an exemption covered by such notification.*

* * *

[CCH Explanation at ¶ 880.]

Amendments

• **2008, Paul Wellstone and Pete Domenici Mental Health Parity and Addiction Equity Act of 2008 (P.L. 110-343)**

P.L. 110-343, Division C, § 512(c)(3)(A)-(B):

Amended Code Sec. 9812(c) by amending paragraph (1) and by striking paragraph (2) and inserting a new paragraph (2). For the **effective** date and special rules, see Act Sec. 512(d)-(f), in the amendment notes for Code Sec. 9812(a). Prior to amendment, Code Sec. 9812(c)(1) read as follows:

(1) SMALL EMPLOYER EXEMPTION.—This section shall not apply to any group health plan for any plan year of a small employer (as defined in section 4980D(d)(2)).

Prior to being stricken, Code Sec. 9812(c)(2) read as follows:

(2) INCREASED COST EXEMPTION.—This section shall not apply with respect to a group health plan if the application of this section to such plan results in an increase in the cost under the plan of at least 1 percent.

⇨ *Caution: Code Sec. 9812(e), below, as amended by P.L. 110-343, applies generally with respect to group health plans for plan years beginning after the date that is 1 year after October 3, 2008.*

(e) DEFINITIONS.—For purposes of this section:

* * *

(3) MEDICAL OR SURGICAL BENEFITS.—The term "medical or surgical benefits" means benefits with respect to medical or surgical services, as defined under the terms of the plan, but does not include *mental health or substance use disorder benefits.*

(4) MENTAL HEALTH BENEFITS.—*The term "mental health benefits" means benefits with respect to services for mental health conditions, as defined under the terms of the plan and in accordance with applicable Federal and State law.*

(5) SUBSTANCE USE DISORDER BENEFITS.—*The term "substance use disorder benefits" means benefits with respect to services for substance use disorders, as defined under the terms of the plan and in accordance with applicable Federal and State law.*

[CCH Explanation at ¶ 880.]

Amendments

• **2008, Paul Wellstone and Pete Domenici Mental Health Parity and Addiction Equity Act of 2008 (P.L. 110-343)**

P.L. 110-343, Division C, § 512(c)(4):

Amended Code Sec. 9812(e) by striking paragraph (4) and inserting new paragraphs (4)-(5). For the **effective** date and special rules, see Act Sec. 512(d)-(f), in the amendment notes for Code Sec. 9812(a). Prior to being stricken, Code Sec. 9812(e)(4) read as follows:

(4) MENTAL HEALTH BENEFITS.—The term "mental health benefits" means benefits with respect to mental health ser-

vices, as defined under the terms of the plan, but does not include benefits with respect to treatment of substance abuse or chemical dependency.

H.R. 1424, Division C, § 512(c)(7):

Amended Code Sec. 9812 by striking "mental health benefits" and inserting "mental health or substance use disorder benefits" each place it appears (other than in any provision amended by Act Sec. 512(c)(6)). For the **effective** date and special rules, see Act Sec. 512(d)-(f), in the amendment notes for Code Sec. 9812(a).

⇨ *Caution: Code Sec. 9812(f), below, was stricken by P.L. 110-343, effective January 1, 2009.*

(f) APPLICATION OF SECTION.—This section shall not apply to benefits for services furnished—

(1) on or after September 30, 2001, and before January 10, 2002,

(2) on or after January 1, 2004, and before the date of the enactment of the Working Families Tax Relief Act of 2004,

(3) on or after January 1, 2008, and before the date of the enactment of the Heroes Earnings Assistance and Relief Tax Act of 2008, and

(4) after December 31, 2008.

[CCH Explanation at ¶ 880.]

Amendments

• **2008, Paul Wellstone and Pete Domenici Mental Health Parity and Addiction Equity Act of 2008 (P.L. 110-343)**

P.L. 110-343, Division C, § 512(c)(5):

Amended Code Sec. 9812 by striking subsection (f). **Effective** 1-1-2009. For special rules, see Act Sec. 512(d)-(f), in the amendment notes for Code Sec. 9812(a). Prior to being stricken, Code Sec. 9812(f) read as follows:

(f) APPLICATION OF SECTION.—This section shall not apply to benefits for services furnished—

(1) on or after September 30, 2001, and before January 10, 2002,

(2) on or after January 1, 2004, and before the date of the enactment of the Working Families Tax Relief Act of 2004,

(3) on or after January 1, 2008, and before the date of the enactment of the Heroes Earnings Assistance and Relief Tax Act of 2008, and

(4) after December 31, 2008.

[¶ 5505] CODE SEC. 9813. COVERAGE OF DEPENDENT STUDENTS ON MEDICALLY NECESSARY LEAVE OF ABSENCE.

(a) MEDICALLY NECESSARY LEAVE OF ABSENCE.—*In this section, the term "medically necessary leave of absence" means, with respect to a dependent child described in subsection (b)(2) in connection with a group health plan, a leave of absence of such child from a postsecondary educational institution (including an* institution of higher education as defined in section 102 of the Higher Education Act of 1965), or any other change in enrollment of such child at such an institution, that—

(1) commences while such child is suffering from a serious illness or injury;

(2) is medically necessary; and

(3) causes such child to lose student status for purposes of coverage under the terms of the plan or coverage.

(b) REQUIREMENT TO CONTINUE COVERAGE.—

(1) IN GENERAL.—In the case of a dependent child described in paragraph (2), a group health plan shall not terminate coverage of such child under such plan due to a medically necessary leave of absence before the date that is the earlier of—

(A) the date that is 1 year after the first day of the medically necessary leave of absence; or

(B) the date on which such coverage would otherwise terminate under the terms of the plan.

(2) DEPENDENT CHILD DESCRIBED.—A dependent child described in this paragraph is, with respect to a group health plan, a beneficiary under the plan who—

(A) is a dependent child, under the terms of the plan, of a participant or beneficiary under the plan; and

(B) was enrolled in the plan, on the basis of being a student at a postsecondary educational institution (as described in subsection (a)), immediately before the first day of the medically necessary leave of absence involved.

(3) CERTIFICATION BY PHYSICIAN.—Paragraph (1) shall apply to a group health plan only if the plan, or the issuer of health insurance coverage offered in connection with the plan, has received written certification by a treating physician of the dependent child which states that the child is suffering from a serious illness or injury and that the leave of absence (or other change of enrollment) described in subsection (a) is medically necessary.

(c) NOTICE.—A group health plan shall include, with any notice regarding a requirement for certification of student status for coverage under the plan, a description of the terms of this section for continued coverage during medically necessary leaves of absence. Such description shall be in language which is understandable to the typical plan participant.

(d) NO CHANGE IN BENEFITS.—A dependent child whose benefits are continued under this section shall be entitled to the same benefits as if (during the medically necessary leave of absence) the child continued to be a covered student at the institution of higher education and was not on a medically necessary leave of absence.

(e) CONTINUED APPLICATION IN CASE OF CHANGED COVERAGE.—If—

(1) a dependent child of a participant or beneficiary is in a period of coverage under a group health plan, pursuant to a medically necessary leave of absence of the child described in subsection (b);

(2) the manner in which the participant or beneficiary is covered under the plan changes, whether through a change in health insurance coverage or health insurance issuer, a change between health insurance coverage and self-insured coverage, or otherwise; and

(3) the coverage as so changed continues to provide coverage of beneficiaries as dependent children, this section shall apply to coverage of the child under the changed coverage for the remainder of the period of the medically necessary leave of absence of the dependent child under the plan in the same manner as it would have applied if the changed coverage had been the previous coverage.

[CCH Explanation at ¶885. Committee Reports at ¶15,010.]

Amendments

• **2008, Michelle's Law (P.L. 110-381)**

P.L. 110-381, §2(c)(1):

Amended subchapter B of chapter 100 by inserting after Code Sec. 9812 a new Code Sec. 9813. **Effective** with respect to plan years beginning on or after the date that is one year after 10-9-2008 and to medically necessary leaves of absence beginning during such plan years.

Act Sections Not Amending Code Sections

EMERGENCY ECONOMIC STABILIZATION ACT OF 2008

DIVISION A—EMERGENCY ECONOMIC STABILIZATION

[¶7003] ACT SEC. 1. SHORT TITLE AND TABLE OF CONTENTS.

(a) SHORT TITLE.—This division may be cited as the "Emergency Economic Stabilization Act of 2008".

* * *

[¶7006] ACT SEC. 2. PURPOSES.

The purposes of this Act are—

(1) to immediately provide authority and facilities that the Secretary of the Treasury can use to restore liquidity and stability to the financial system of the United States; and

(2) to ensure that such authority and such facilities are used in a manner that—

(A) protects home values, college funds, retirement accounts, and life savings;

(B) preserves homeownership and promotes jobs and economic growth;

(C) maximizes overall returns to the taxpayers of the United States; and

(D) provides public accountability for the exercise of such authority.

[¶7009] ACT SEC. 3. DEFINITIONS.

For purposes of this Act, the following definitions shall apply:

(1) APPROPRIATE COMMITTEES OF CONGRESS.—The term "appropriate committees of Congress" means—

(A) the Committee on Banking, Housing, and Urban Affairs, the Committee on Finance, the Committee on the Budget, and the Committee on Appropriations of the Senate; and

(B) the Committee on Financial Services, the Committee on Ways and Means, the Committee on the Budget, and the Committee on Appropriations of the House of Representatives.

(2) BOARD.—The term "Board" means the Board of Governors of the Federal Reserve System.

(3) CONGRESSIONAL SUPPORT AGENCIES.—The term "congressional support agencies" means the Congressional Budget Office and the Joint Committee on Taxation.

(4) CORPORATION.—The term "Corporation" means the Federal Deposit Insurance Corporation.

(5) FINANCIAL INSTITUTION.—The term "financial institution" means any institution, including, but not limited to, any bank, savings association, credit union, security broker or dealer, or insurance company, established and regulated under the laws of the United States or any State, territory, or possession of the United States, the District of Columbia, Commonwealth of Puerto Rico, Commonwealth of Northern Mariana Islands, Guam, American Samoa, or the United States Virgin Islands, and having significant operations in the United States, but excluding any central bank of, or institution owned by, a foreign government.

(6) FUND.—The term "Fund" means the Troubled Assets Insurance Financing Fund established under section 102.

(7) SECRETARY.—The term "Secretary" means the Secretary of the Treasury.

(8) TARP.—The term "TARP" means the Troubled Asset Relief Program established under section 101.

(9) TROUBLED ASSETS.—The term "troubled assets" means—

(A) residential or commercial mortgages and any securities, obligations, or other instruments that are based on or related to such mortgages, that in each case was originated or issued on or before March 14, 2008, the purchase of which the Secretary determines promotes financial market stability; and

(B) any other financial instrument that the Secretary, after consultation with the Chairman of the Board of Governors of the Federal Reserve System, determines the purchase of which is necessary to promote financial market stability, but only upon transmittal of such determination, in writing, to the appropriate committees of Congress.

TITLE I—TROUBLED ASSETS RELIEF PROGRAM

[¶7012] ACT SEC. 101. PURCHASES OF TROUBLED ASSETS.

(a) OFFICES; AUTHORITY.—

(1) AUTHORITY.—The Secretary is authorized to establish the Troubled Asset Relief Program (or "TARP") to purchase, and to make and fund commitments to purchase, troubled assets from any financial institution, on such terms and conditions as are determined by the Secretary, and in accordance with this Act and the policies and procedures developed and published by the Secretary.

(2) COMMENCEMENT OF PROGRAM.—Establishment of the policies and procedures and other similar administrative requirements imposed on the Secretary by this Act are not intended to delay the commencement of the TARP.

(3) ESTABLISHMENT OF TREASURY OFFICE.—

(A) IN GENERAL.—The Secretary shall implement any program under paragraph (1) through an Office of Financial Stability, established for such purpose within the Office of Domestic Finance of the Department of the Treasury, which office shall be headed by an Assistant Secretary of the Treasury, appointed by the President, by and with the advice and consent of the Senate, except that an interim Assistant Secretary may be appointed by the Secretary.

(B) CLERICAL AMENDMENTS.—

(i) TITLE 5.—Section 5315 of title 5, United States Code, is amended in the item relating to Assistant Secretaries of the Treasury, by striking "(9)" and inserting "(10)".

(ii) TITLE 31.—Section 301(e) of title 31, United States Code, is amended by striking "9" and inserting "10".

(b) CONSULTATION.—In exercising the authority under this section, the Secretary shall consult with the Board, the Corporation, the Comptroller of the Currency, the Director of the Office of Thrift Supervision, the Chairman of the National Credit Union Administration Board, and the Secretary of Housing and Urban Development.

(c) NECESSARY ACTIONS.—The Secretary is authorized to take such actions as the Secretary deems necessary to carry out the authorities in this Act, including, without limitation, the following:

(1) The Secretary shall have direct hiring authority with respect to the appointment of employees to administer this Act.

(2) Entering into contracts, including contracts for services authorized by section 3109 of title 5, United States Code.

(3) Designating financial institutions as financial agents of the Federal Government, and such institutions shall perform all such reasonable duties related to this Act as financial agents of the Federal Government as may be required.

(4) In order to provide the Secretary with the flexibility to manage troubled assets in a manner designed to minimize cost to the taxpayers, establishing vehicles that are authorized, subject to supervision by the Secretary, to purchase, hold, and sell troubled assets and issue obligations.

(5) Issuing such regulations and other guidance as may be necessary or appropriate to define terms or carry out the authorities or purposes of this Act.

(d) PROGRAM GUIDELINES.—Before the earlier of the end of the 2-business-day period beginning on the date of the first purchase of troubled assets pursuant to the authority under this section or the end of the 45-day period beginning on the date of enactment of this Act, the Secretary shall publish program guidelines, including the following:

(1) Mechanisms for purchasing troubled assets.

(2) Methods for pricing and valuing troubled assets.

(3) Procedures for selecting asset managers.

(4) Criteria for identifying troubled assets for purchase.

(e) PREVENTING UNJUST ENRICHMENT.—In making purchases under the authority of this Act, the Secretary shall take such steps as may be necessary to prevent unjust enrichment of financial institutions participating in a program established under this section, including by preventing the sale of a troubled asset to the Secretary at a higher price than what the seller paid to purchase the asset. This subsection does not apply to troubled assets acquired in a merger or acquisition, or a purchase of assets from a financial institution in conservatorship or receivership, or that has initiated bankruptcy proceedings under title 11, United States Code.

[¶7015] ACT SEC. 102. INSURANCE OF TROUBLED ASSETS.

(a) AUTHORITY.—

(1) IN GENERAL.—If the Secretary establishes the program authorized under section 101, then the Secretary shall establish a program to guarantee troubled assets originated or issued prior to March 14, 2008, including mortgage-backed securities.

(2) GUARANTEES.—In establishing any program under this subsection, the Secretary may develop guarantees of troubled assets and the associated premiums for such guarantees. Such guarantees and premiums may be determined by category or class of the troubled assets to be guaranteed.

(3) EXTENT OF GUARANTEE.—Upon request of a financial institution, the Secretary may guarantee the timely payment of principal of, and interest on, troubled assets in amounts not to exceed 100 percent of such payments. Such guarantee may be on such terms and conditions as are determined by the Secretary, provided that such terms and conditions are consistent with the purposes of this Act.

(b) REPORTS.—Not later than 90 days after the date of enactment of this Act, the Secretary shall report to the appropriate committees of Congress on the program established under subsection (a).

(c) PREMIUMS.—

(1) IN GENERAL.—The Secretary shall collect premiums from any financial institution participating in the program established under subsection (a). Such premiums shall be in an amount that the Secretary determines necessary to meet the purposes of this Act and to provide sufficient reserves pursuant to paragraph (3).

(2) AUTHORITY TO BASE PREMIUMS ON PRODUCT RISK.—In establishing any premium under paragraph (1), the Secretary may provide for variations in such rates according to the credit risk associated with the particular troubled asset that is being guaranteed. The Secretary shall publish the methodology for setting the premium for a class of troubled assets together with an explanation of the appropriateness of the class of assets for participation in the program established under this section. The methodology shall ensure that the premium is consistent with paragraph (3).

(3) MINIMUM LEVEL.—The premiums referred to in paragraph (1) shall be set by the Secretary at a level necessary to create reserves sufficient to meet anticipated claims, based on an actuarial analysis, and to ensure that taxpayers are fully protected.

(4) ADJUSTMENT TO PURCHASE AUTHORITY.—The purchase authority limit in section 115 shall be reduced by an amount equal to the difference between the total of the outstanding guaranteed obligations and the balance in the Troubled Assets Insurance Financing Fund.

(d) TROUBLED ASSETS INSURANCE FINANCING FUND.—

(1) DEPOSITS.—The Secretary shall deposit fees collected under this section into the Fund established under paragraph (2).

(2) ESTABLISHMENT.—There is established a Troubled Assets Insurance Financing Fund that shall consist of the amounts collected pursuant to paragraph (1), and any balance in such fund shall be invested by the Secretary in United States Treasury securities, or kept in cash on hand or on deposit, as necessary.

(3) PAYMENTS FROM FUND.—The Secretary shall make payments from amounts deposited in the Fund to fulfill obligations of the guarantees provided to financial institutions under subsection (a).

[¶7018] ACT SEC. 103. CONSIDERATIONS.

In exercising the authorities granted in this Act, the Secretary shall take into consideration—

(1) protecting the interests of taxpayers by maximizing overall returns and minimizing the impact on the national debt;

(2) providing stability and preventing disruption to financial markets in order to limit the impact on the economy and protect American jobs, savings, and retirement security;

(3) the need to help families keep their homes and to stabilize communities;

(4) in determining whether to engage in a direct purchase from an individual financial institution, the long-term viability of the financial institution in determining whether the purchase represents the most efficient use of funds under this Act;

(5) ensuring that all financial institutions are eligible to participate in the program, without discrimination based on size, geography, form of organization, or the size, type, and number of assets eligible for purchase under this Act;

(6) providing financial assistance to financial institutions, including those serving low- and moderate-income populations and other underserved communities, and that have assets less than $1,000,000,000, that were well or adequately capitalized as of June 30, 2008, and that as a result of the devaluation of the preferred government-sponsored enterprises stock will drop one or more capital levels, in a manner sufficient to restore the financial institutions to at least an adequately capitalized level;

(7) the need to ensure stability for United States public instrumentalities, such as counties and cities, that may have suffered significant increased costs or losses in the current market turmoil;

(8) protecting the retirement security of Americans by purchasing troubled assets held by or on behalf of an eligible retirement plan described in clause (iii), (iv), (v), or (vi) of section 402(c)(8)(B) of the Internal Revenue Code of 1986, except that such authority shall not extend to any compensation arrangements subject to section 409A of such Code; and

(9) the utility of purchasing other real estate owned and instruments backed by mortgages on multifamily properties.

[¶7021] ACT SEC. 104. FINANCIAL STABILITY OVERSIGHT BOARD.

(a) ESTABLISHMENT.—There is established the Financial Stability Oversight Board, which shall be responsible for—

(1) reviewing the exercise of authority under a program developed in accordance with this Act, including—

(A) policies implemented by the Secretary and the Office of Financial Stability created under sections 101 and 102, including the appointment of financial agents, the designation of asset classes to be purchased, and plans for the structure of vehicles used to purchase troubled assets; and

(B) the effect of such actions in assisting American families in preserving home ownership, stabilizing financial markets, and protecting taxpayers;

(2) making recommendations, as appropriate, to the Secretary regarding use of the authority under this Act; and

(3) reporting any suspected fraud, misrepresentation, or malfeasance to the Special Inspector General for the Troubled Assets Relief Program or the Attorney General of the United States, consistent with section 535(b) of title 28, United States Code.

(b) MEMBERSHIP.—The Financial Stability Oversight Board shall be comprised of—

(1) the Chairman of the Board of Governors of the Federal Reserve System;

(2) the Secretary;

(3) the Director of the Federal Housing Finance Agency;

(4) the Chairman of the Securities Exchange Commission; and

(5) the Secretary of Housing and Urban Development.

(c) CHAIRPERSON.—The chairperson of the Financial Stability Oversight Board shall be elected by the members of the Board from among the members other than the Secretary.

(d) MEETINGS.—The Financial Stability Oversight Board shall meet 2 weeks after the first exercise of the purchase authority of the Secretary under this Act, and monthly thereafter.

(e) ADDITIONAL AUTHORITIES.—In addition to the responsibilities described in subsection (a), the Financial Stability Oversight Board shall have the authority to ensure that the policies implemented by the Secretary are—

(1) in accordance with the purposes of this Act;

(2) in the economic interests of the United States; and

(3) consistent with protecting taxpayers, in accordance with section 113(a).

(f) CREDIT REVIEW COMMITTEE.—The Financial Stability Oversight Board may appoint a credit review committee for the purpose of evaluating the exercise of the purchase authority provided under this Act and the assets acquired through the exercise of such authority, as the Financial Stability Oversight Board determines appropriate.

(g) REPORTS.—The Financial Stability Oversight Board shall report to the appropriate committees of Congress and the Congressional Oversight Panel established under section 125, not less frequently than quarterly, on the matters described under subsection (a)(1).

(h) TERMINATION.—The Financial Stability Oversight Board, and its authority under this section, shall terminate on the expiration of the 15-day period beginning upon the later of—

(1) the date that the last troubled asset acquired by the Secretary under section 101 has been sold or transferred out of the ownership or control of the Federal Government; or

(2) the date of expiration of the last insurance contract issued under section 102.

[¶7024] ACT SEC. 105. REPORTS.

(a) IN GENERAL.—Before the expiration of the 60-day period beginning on the date of the first exercise of the authority granted in section 101(a), or of the first exercise of the authority granted in section 102, whichever occurs first, and every 30-day period thereafter, the Secretary shall report to the appropriate committees of Congress, with respect to each such period—

(1) an overview of actions taken by the Secretary, including the considerations required by section 103 and the efforts under section 109;

(2) the actual obligation and expenditure of the funds provided for administrative expenses by section 118 during such period and the expected expenditure of such funds in the subsequent period; and

(3) a detailed financial statement with respect to the exercise of authority under this Act, including—

    (A) all agreements made or renewed;

    (B) all insurance contracts entered into pursuant to section 102;

    (C) all transactions occurring during such period, including the types of parties involved;

    (D) the nature of the assets purchased;

    (E) all projected costs and liabilities;

    (F) operating expenses, including compensation for financial agents;

    (G) the valuation or pricing method used for each transaction; and

    (H) a description of the vehicles established to exercise such authority.

(b) TRANCHE REPORTS TO CONGRESS.—

    (1) REPORTS.—The Secretary shall provide to the appropriate committees of Congress, at the times specified in paragraph (2), a written report, including—

        (A) a description of all of the transactions made during the reporting period;

        (B) a description of the pricing mechanism for the transactions;

        (C) a justification of the price paid for and other financial terms associated with the transactions;

        (D) a description of the impact of the exercise of such authority on the financial system, supported, to the extent possible, by specific data;

        (E) a description of challenges that remain in the financial system, including any benchmarks yet to be achieved; and

        (F) an estimate of additional actions under the authority provided under this Act that may be necessary to address such challenges.

    (2) TIMING.—The report required by this subsection shall be submitted not later than 7 days after the date on which commitments to purchase troubled assets under the authorities provided in this Act first reach an aggregate of $50,000,000,000 and not later than 7 days after each $50,000,000,000 interval of such commitments is reached thereafter.

(c) REGULATORY MODERNIZATION REPORT.—The Secretary shall review the current state of the financial markets and the regulatory system and submit a written report to the appropriate committees of Congress not later than April 30, 2009, analyzing the current state of the regulatory system and its effectiveness at overseeing the participants in the financial markets, including the over-the-counter swaps market and government-sponsored enterprises, and providing recommendations for improvement, including—

    (1) recommendations regarding—

        (A) whether any participants in the financial markets that are currently outside the regulatory system should become subject to the regulatory system; and

        (B) enhancement of the clearing and settlement of over-the-counter swaps; and

    (2) the rationale underlying such recommendations.

(d) SHARING OF INFORMATION.—Any report required under this section shall also be submitted to the Congressional Oversight Panel established under section 125.

(e) SUNSET.—The reporting requirements under this section shall terminate on the later of—

    (1) the date that the last troubled asset acquired by the Secretary under section 101 has been sold or transferred out of the ownership or control of the Federal Government; or

    (2) the date of expiration of the last insurance contract issued under section 102.

[¶7027] ACT SEC. 106. RIGHTS; MANAGEMENT; SALE OF TROUBLED ASSETS; REVENUES AND SALE PROCEEDS.

(a) EXERCISE OF RIGHTS.—The Secretary may, at any time, exercise any rights received in connection with troubled assets purchased under this Act.

(b) MANAGEMENT OF TROUBLED ASSETS.—The Secretary shall have authority to manage troubled assets purchased under this Act, including revenues and portfolio risks therefrom.

(c) SALE OF TROUBLED ASSETS.—The Secretary may, at any time, upon terms and conditions and at a price determined by the Secretary, sell, or enter into securities loans, repurchase transactions, or other financial transactions in regard to, any troubled asset purchased under this Act.

(d) TRANSFER TO TREASURY.—Revenues of, and proceeds from the sale of troubled assets purchased under this Act, or from the sale, exercise, or surrender of warrants or senior debt instruments acquired under section 113 shall be paid into the general fund of the Treasury for reduction of the public debt.

(e) APPLICATION OF SUNSET TO TROUBLED ASSETS.—The authority of the Secretary to hold any troubled asset purchased under this Act before the termination date in section 120, or to purchase or fund the purchase of a troubled asset under a commitment entered into before the termination date in section 120, is not subject to the provisions of section 120.

[¶7030] ACT SEC. 107. CONTRACTING PROCEDURES.

(a) STREAMLINED PROCESS.—For purposes of this Act, the Secretary may waive specific provisions of the Federal Acquisition Regulation upon a determination that urgent and compelling circumstances make compliance with such provisions contrary to the public interest. Any such determination, and the justification for such determination, shall be submitted to the Committees on Oversight and Government Reform and Financial Services of the House of Representatives and the Committees on Homeland Security and Governmental Affairs and Banking, Housing, and Urban Affairs of the Senate within 7 days.

(b) ADDITIONAL CONTRACTING REQUIREMENTS.—In any solicitation or contract where the Secretary has, pursuant to subsection (a), waived any provision of the Federal Acquisition Regulation pertaining to minority contracting, the Secretary shall develop and implement standards and procedures to ensure, to the maximum extent practicable, the inclusion and utilization of minorities (as such term is defined in section 1204(c) of the Financial Institutions Reform, Recovery, and Enforcement Act of 1989 (12 U.S.C. 1811 note)) and women, and minority- and women-owned businesses (as such terms are defined in section 21A(r)(4) of the Federal Home Loan Bank Act (12 U.S.C. 1441a(r)(4)), in that solicitation or contract, including contracts to asset managers, servicers, property managers, and other service providers or expert consultants.

(c) ELIGIBILITY OF FDIC.—Notwithstanding subsections (a) and (b), the Corporation—

(1) shall be eligible for, and shall be considered in, the selection of asset managers for residential mortgage loans and residential mortgage-backed securities; and

(2) shall be reimbursed by the Secretary for any services provided.

[¶7033] ACT SEC. 108. CONFLICTS OF INTEREST.

(a) STANDARDS REQUIRED.—The Secretary shall issue regulations or guidelines necessary to address and manage or to prohibit conflicts of interest that may arise in connection with the administration and execution of the authorities provided under this Act, including—

(1) conflicts arising in the selection or hiring of contractors or advisors, including asset managers;

(2) the purchase of troubled assets;

(3) the management of the troubled assets held;

(4) post-employment restrictions on employees; and

(5) any other potential conflict of interest, as the Secretary deems necessary or appropriate in the public interest.

(b) TIMING.—Regulations or guidelines required by this section shall be issued as soon as practicable after the date of enactment of this Act.

[¶7036] ACT SEC. 109. FORECLOSURE MITIGATION EFFORTS.

(a) RESIDENTIAL MORTGAGE LOAN SERVICING STANDARDS.—To the extent that the Secretary acquires mortgages, mortgage backed securities, and other assets secured by residential real estate, including multifamily housing, the Secretary shall implement a plan that seeks to maximize assistance for homeowners and use the authority of the Secretary to encourage the servicers of the underlying mortgages, considering net present value to the taxpayer, to take advantage of the HOPE for Homeowners Program under section 257 of the National Housing Act or other available programs to minimize foreclosures. In addition, the Secretary may use loan guarantees and credit enhancements to facilitate loan modifications to prevent avoidable foreclosures.

(b) COORDINATION.—The Secretary shall coordinate with the Corporation, the Board (with respect to any mortgage or mortgage-backed securities or pool of securities held, owned, or controlled by or on behalf of a Federal reserve bank, as provided in section 110(a)(1)(C)), the Federal Housing Finance Agency, the Secretary of Housing and Urban Development, and other Federal Government entities that hold troubled assets to attempt to identify opportunities for the acquisition of classes of troubled assets that will improve the ability of the Secretary to improve the loan modification and restructuring process and, where permissible, to permit bona fide tenants who are current on their rent to remain in their homes under the terms of the lease. In the case of a mortgage on a residential rental property, the plan required under this section shall include protecting Federal, State, and local rental subsidies and protections, and ensuring any modification takes into account the need for operating funds to maintain decent and safe conditions at the property.

(c) CONSENT TO REASONABLE LOAN MODIFICATION REQUESTS.—Upon any request arising under existing investment contracts, the Secretary shall consent, where appropriate, and considering net present value to the taxpayer, to reasonable requests for loss mitigation measures, including term extensions, rate reductions, principal write downs, increases in the proportion of loans within a trust or other structure allowed to be modified, or removal of other limitation on modifications.

[¶7039] ACT SEC. 110. ASSISTANCE TO HOMEOWNERS.

(a) DEFINITIONS.—As used in this section—

(1) the term "Federal property manager" means—

(A) the Federal Housing Finance Agency, in its capacity as conservator of the Federal National Mortgage Association and the Federal Home Loan Mortgage Corporation;

(B) the Corporation, with respect to residential mortgage loans and mortgage-backed securities held by any bridge depository institution pursuant to section 11(n) of the Federal Deposit Insurance Act; and

(C) the Board, with respect to any mortgage or mortgage-backed securities or pool of securities held, owned, or controlled by or on behalf of a Federal reserve bank, other than mortgages or securities held, owned, or controlled in connection with open market operations under section 14 of the Federal Reserve Act (12 U.S.C. 353), or as collateral for an advance or discount that is not in default;

(2) the term "consumer" has the same meaning as in section 103 of the Truth in Lending Act (15 U.S.C. 1602);

(3) the term "insured depository institution" has the same meaning as in section 3 of the Federal Deposit Insurance Act (12 U.S.C. 1813); and

(4) the term "servicer" has the same meaning as in section 6(i)(2) of the Real Estate Settlement Procedures Act of 1974 (12 U.S.C. 2605(i)(2)).

(b) HOMEOWNER ASSISTANCE BY AGENCIES-

(1) IN GENERAL.—To the extent that the Federal property manager holds, owns, or controls mortgages, mortgage backed securities, and other assets secured by residential real estate, including multifamily housing, the Federal property manager shall implement a plan that seeks to maximize assistance for homeowners and use its authority to encourage the servicers of the

underlying mortgages, and considering net present value to the taxpayer, to take advantage of the HOPE for Homeowners Program under section 257 of the National Housing Act or other available programs to minimize foreclosures.

(2) MODIFICATIONS.—In the case of a residential mortgage loan, modifications made under paragraph (1) may include—

(A) reduction in interest rates;

(B) reduction of loan principal; and

(C) other similar modifications.

(3) TENANT PROTECTIONS.—In the case of mortgages on residential rental properties, modifications made under paragraph (1) shall ensure—

(A) the continuation of any existing Federal, State, and local rental subsidies and protections; and

(B) that modifications take into account the need for operating funds to maintain decent and safe conditions at the property.

(4) TIMING.—Each Federal property manager shall develop and begin implementation of the plan required by this subsection not later than 60 days after the date of enactment of this Act.

(5) REPORTS TO CONGRESS.—Each Federal property manager shall, 60 days after the date of enactment of this Act and every 30 days thereafter, report to Congress specific information on the number and types of loan modifications made and the number of actual foreclosures occurring during the reporting period in accordance with this section.

(6) CONSULTATION.—In developing the plan required by this subsection, the Federal property managers shall consult with one another and, to the extent possible, utilize consistent approaches to implement the requirements of this subsection.

(c) ACTIONS WITH RESPECT TO SERVICERS.—In any case in which a Federal property manager is not the owner of a residential mortgage loan, but holds an interest in obligations or pools of obligations secured by residential mortgage loans, the Federal property manager shall—

(1) encourage implementation by the loan servicers of loan modifications developed under subsection (b); and

(2) assist in facilitating any such modifications, to the extent possible.

(d) LIMITATION.—The requirements of this section shall not supersede any other duty or requirement imposed on the Federal property managers under otherwise applicable law.

[¶7042] ACT SEC. 111. EXECUTIVE COMPENSATION AND CORPORATE GOVERNANCE.

(a) APPLICABILITY.—Any financial institution that sells troubled assets to the Secretary under this Act shall be subject to the executive compensation requirements of subsections (b) and (c) and the provisions under the Internal Revenue Code of 1986, as provided under the amendment by section 302, as applicable.

(b) DIRECT PURCHASES.—

(1) IN GENERAL.—Where the Secretary determines that the purposes of this Act are best met through direct purchases of troubled assets from an individual financial institution where no bidding process or market prices are available, and the Secretary receives a meaningful equity or debt position in the financial institution as a result of the transaction, the Secretary shall require that the financial institution meet appropriate standards for executive compensation and corporate governance. The standards required under this subsection shall be effective for the duration of the period that the Secretary holds an equity or debt position in the financial institution.

(2) CRITERIA.—The standards required under this subsection shall include—

(A) limits on compensation that exclude incentives for senior executive officers of a financial institution to take unnecessary and excessive risks that threaten the value of the financial institution during the period that the Secretary holds an equity or debt position in the financial institution;

(B) a provision for the recovery by the financial institution of any bonus or incentive compensation paid to a senior executive officer based on statements of earnings, gains, or other criteria that are later proven to be materially inaccurate; and

(C) a prohibition on the financial institution making any golden parachute payment to its senior executive officer during the period that the Secretary holds an equity or debt position in the financial institution.

(3) DEFINITION.—For purposes of this section, the term "senior executive officer" means an individual who is one of the top 5 highly paid executives of a public company, whose compensation is required to be disclosed pursuant to the Securities Exchange Act of 1934, and any regulations issued thereunder, and non-public company counterparts.

(c) AUCTION PURCHASES.—Where the Secretary determines that the purposes of this Act are best met through auction purchases of troubled assets, and only where such purchases per financial institution in the aggregate exceed $300,000,000 (including direct purchases), the Secretary shall prohibit, for such financial institution, any new employment contract with a senior executive officer that provides a golden parachute in the event of an involuntary termination, bankruptcy filing, insolvency, or receivership. The Secretary shall issue guidance to carry out this paragraph not later than 2 months after the date of enactment of this Act, and such guidance shall be effective upon issuance.

(d) SUNSET.—The provisions of subsection (c) shall apply only to arrangements entered into during the period during which the authorities under section 101(a) are in effect, as determined under section 120.

[¶7045] ACT SEC. 112. COORDINATION WITH FOREIGN AUTHORITIES AND CENTRAL BANKS.

The Secretary shall coordinate, as appropriate, with foreign financial authorities and central banks to work toward the establishment of similar programs by such authorities and central banks. To the extent that such foreign financial authorities or banks hold troubled assets as a result of extending financing to financial institutions that have failed or defaulted on such financing, such troubled assets qualify for purchase under section 101.

[¶7048] ACT SEC. 113. MINIMIZATION OF LONG-TERM COSTS AND MAXIMIZATION OF BENEFITS FOR TAXPAYERS.

(a) LONG-TERM COSTS AND BENEFITS.—

(1) MINIMIZING NEGATIVE IMPACT.—The Secretary shall use the authority under this Act in a manner that will minimize any potential long-term negative impact on the taxpayer, taking into account the direct outlays, potential long-term returns on assets purchased, and the overall economic benefits of the program, including economic benefits due to improvements in economic activity and the availability of credit, the impact on the savings and pensions of individuals, and reductions in losses to the Federal Government.

(2) AUTHORITY.—In carrying out paragraph (1), the Secretary shall—

(A) hold the assets to maturity or for resale for and until such time as the Secretary determines that the market is optimal for selling such assets, in order to maximize the value for taxpayers; and

(B) sell such assets at a price that the Secretary determines, based on available financial analysis, will maximize return on investment for the Federal Government.

(3) PRIVATE SECTOR PARTICIPATION.—The Secretary shall encourage the private sector to participate in purchases of troubled assets, and to invest in financial institutions, consistent with the provisions of this section.

(b) USE OF MARKET MECHANISMS.—In making purchases under this Act, the Secretary shall—

(1) make such purchases at the lowest price that the Secretary determines to be consistent with the purposes of this Act; and

(2) maximize the efficiency of the use of taxpayer resources by using market mechanisms, including auctions or reverse auctions, where appropriate.

(c) DIRECT PURCHASES.—If the Secretary determines that use of a market mechanism under subsection (b) is not feasible or appropriate, and the purposes of the Act are best met through direct purchases from an individual financial institution, the Secretary shall pursue additional measures to ensure that prices paid for assets are reasonable and reflect the underlying value of the asset.

(d) CONDITIONS ON PURCHASE AUTHORITY FOR WARRANTS AND DEBT INSTRUMENTS.—

(1) IN GENERAL.—The Secretary may not purchase, or make any commitment to purchase, any troubled asset under the authority of this Act, unless the Secretary receives from the financial institution from which such assets are to be purchased—

(A) in the case of a financial institution, the securities of which are traded on a national securities exchange, a warrant giving the right to the Secretary to receive nonvoting common stock or preferred stock in such financial institution, or voting stock with respect to which, the Secretary agrees not to exercise voting power, as the Secretary determines appropriate; or

(B) in the case of any financial institution other than one described in subparagraph (A), a warrant for common or preferred stock, or a senior debt instrument from such financial institution, as described in paragraph (2)(C).

(2) TERMS AND CONDITIONS.—The terms and conditions of any warrant or senior debt instrument required under paragraph (1) shall meet the following requirements:

(A) PURPOSES.—Such terms and conditions shall, at a minimum, be designed—

(i) to provide for reasonable participation by the Secretary, for the benefit of taxpayers, in equity appreciation in the case of a warrant or other equity security, or a reasonable interest rate premium, in the case of a debt instrument; and

(ii) to provide additional protection for the taxpayer against losses from sale of assets by the Secretary under this Act and the administrative expenses of the TARP.

(B) AUTHORITY TO SELL, EXERCISE, OR SURRENDER.—The Secretary may sell, exercise, or surrender a warrant or any senior debt instrument received under this subsection, based on the conditions established under subparagraph (A).

(C) CONVERSION.—The warrant shall provide that if, after the warrant is received by the Secretary under this subsection, the financial institution that issued the warrant is no longer listed or traded on a national securities exchange or securities association, as described in paragraph (1)(A), such warrants shall convert to senior debt, or contain appropriate protections for the Secretary to ensure that the Treasury is appropriately compensated for the value of the warrant, in an amount determined by the Secretary.

(D) PROTECTIONS.—Any warrant representing securities to be received by the Secretary under this subsection shall contain anti-dilution provisions of the type employed in capital market transactions, as determined by the Secretary. Such provisions shall protect the value of the securities from market transactions such as stock splits, stock distributions, dividends, and other distributions, mergers, and other forms of reorganization or recapitalization.

(E) EXERCISE PRICE.—The exercise price for any warrant issued pursuant to this subsection shall be set by the Secretary, in the interest of the taxpayers.

(F) SUFFICIENCY.—The financial institution shall guarantee to the Secretary that it has authorized shares of nonvoting stock available to fulfill its obligations under this subsection. Should the financial institution not have sufficient authorized shares, including preferred shares that may carry dividend rights equal to a multiple number of common shares, the Secretary may, to the extent necessary, accept a senior debt note in an amount, and on such terms as will compensate the Secretary with equivalent value, in the event that a sufficient shareholder vote to authorize the necessary additional shares cannot be obtained.

(3) EXCEPTIONS.—

(A) DE MINIMIS.—The Secretary shall establish de minimis exceptions to the requirements of this subsection, based on the size of the cumulative transactions of troubled assets purchased from any one financial institution for the duration of the program, at not more than $100,000,000.

(B) OTHER EXCEPTIONS.—The Secretary shall establish an exception to the requirements of this subsection and appropriate alternative requirements for any participating financial institution that is legally prohibited from issuing securities and debt instruments, so as not to allow circumvention of the requirements of this section.

[¶7051] ACT SEC. 114. MARKET TRANSPARENCY.

(a) PRICING.—To facilitate market transparency, the Secretary shall make available to the public, in electronic form, a description, amounts, and pricing of assets acquired under this Act, within 2 business days of purchase, trade, or other disposition.

(b) DISCLOSURE.—For each type of financial institutions that sells troubled assets to the Secretary under this Act, the Secretary shall determine whether the public disclosure required for such financial institutions with respect to off-balance sheet transactions, derivatives instruments, contingent liabilities, and similar sources of potential exposure is adequate to provide to the public sufficient information as to the true financial position of the institutions. If such disclosure is not adequate for that purpose, the Secretary shall make recommendations for additional disclosure requirements to the relevant regulators.

[¶7054] ACT SEC. 115. GRADUATED AUTHORIZATION TO PURCHASE.

(a) AUTHORITY.—The authority of the Secretary to purchase troubled assets under this Act shall be limited as follows:

(1) Effective upon the date of enactment of this Act, such authority shall be limited to $250,000,000,000 outstanding at any one time.

(2) If at any time, the President submits to the Congress a written certification that the Secretary needs to exercise the authority under this paragraph, effective upon such submission, such authority shall be limited to $350,000,000,000 outstanding at any one time.

(3) If, at any time after the certification in paragraph (2) has been made, the President transmits to the Congress a written report detailing the plan of the Secretary to exercise the authority under this paragraph, unless there is enacted, within 15 calendar days of such transmission, a joint resolution described in subsection (c), effective upon the expiration of such 15-day period, such authority shall be limited to $700,000,000,000 outstanding at any one time.

(b) AGGREGATION OF PURCHASE PRICES.—The amount of troubled assets purchased by the Secretary outstanding at any one time shall be determined for purposes of the dollar amount limitations under subsection (a) by aggregating the purchase prices of all troubled assets held.

(c) JOINT RESOLUTION OF DISAPPROVAL.—

(1) IN GENERAL.—Notwithstanding any other provision of this section, the Secretary may not exercise any authority to make purchases under this Act with regard to any amount in excess of $350,000,000,000 previously obligated, as described in this section if, within 15 calendar days after the date on which Congress receives a report of the plan of the Secretary described in subsection (a)(3), there is enacted into law a joint resolution disapproving the plan of the Secretary with respect to such additional amount.

(2) CONTENTS OF JOINT RESOLUTION.—For the purpose of this section, the term "joint resolution" means only a joint resolution—

(A) that is introduced not later than 3 calendar days after the date on which the report of the plan of the Secretary referred to in subsection (a)(3) is received by Congress;

(B) which does not have a preamble;

(C) the title of which is as follows: "Joint resolution relating to the disapproval of obligations under the Emergency Economic Stabilization Act of 2008"; and

(D) the matter after the resolving clause of which is as follows: "That Congress disapproves the obligation of any amount exceeding the amounts obligated as described in paragraphs (1) and (2) of section 115(a) of the Emergency Economic Stabilization Act of 2008.".

(d) Fast Track Consideration in House of Representatives.—

(1) Reconvening.—Upon receipt of a report under subsection (a)(3), the Speaker, if the House would otherwise be adjourned, shall notify the Members of the House that, pursuant to this section, the House shall convene not later than the second calendar day after receipt of such report;

(2) Reporting and discharge.—Any committee of the House of Representatives to which a joint resolution is referred shall report it to the House not later than 5 calendar days after the date of receipt of the report described in subsection (a)(3). If a committee fails to report the joint resolution within that period, the committee shall be discharged from further consideration of the joint resolution and the joint resolution shall be referred to the appropriate calendar.

(3) Proceeding to consideration.—After each committee authorized to consider a joint resolution reports it to the House or has been discharged from its consideration, it shall be in order, not later than the sixth day after Congress receives the report described in subsection (a)(3), to move to proceed to consider the joint resolution in the House. All points of order against the motion are waived. Such a motion shall not be in order after the House has disposed of a motion to proceed on the joint resolution. The previous question shall be considered as ordered on the motion to its adoption without intervening motion. The motion shall not be debatable. A motion to reconsider the vote by which the motion is disposed of shall not be in order.

(4) Consideration.—The joint resolution shall be considered as read. All points of order against the joint resolution and against its consideration are waived. The previous question shall be considered as ordered on the joint resolution to its passage without intervening motion except two hours of debate equally divided and controlled by the proponent and an opponent. A motion to reconsider the vote on passage of the joint resolution shall not be in order.

(e) Fast Track Consideration in Senate.—

(1) Reconvening.—Upon receipt of a report under subsection (a)(3), if the Senate has adjourned or recessed for more than 2 days, the majority leader of the Senate, after consultation with the minority leader of the Senate, shall notify the Members of the Senate that, pursuant to this section, the Senate shall convene not later than the second calendar day after receipt of such message.

(2) Placement on calendar.—Upon introduction in the Senate, the joint resolution shall be placed immediately on the calendar.

(3) Floor consideration

(A) In general.—Notwithstanding Rule XXII of the Standing Rules of the Senate, it is in order at any time during the period beginning on the 4th day after the date on which Congress receives a report of the plan of the Secretary described in subsection (a)(3) and ending on the 6th day after the date on which Congress receives a report of the plan of the Secretary described in subsection (a)(3) (even though a previous motion to the same effect has been disagreed to) to move to proceed to the consideration of the joint resolution, and all points of order against the joint resolution (and against consideration of the joint resolution) are waived. The motion to proceed is not debatable. The motion is not subject to a motion to postpone. A motion to reconsider the vote by which the motion is agreed to or disagreed to shall not be in order. If a motion to proceed to the consideration of the resolution is agreed to, the joint resolution shall remain the unfinished business until disposed of.

(B) Debate.—Debate on the joint resolution, and on all debatable motions and appeals in connection therewith, shall be limited to not more than 10 hours, which shall be divided equally between the majority and minority leaders or their designees. A motion further to limit debate is in order and not debatable. An amendment to, or a motion to postpone, or a motion to proceed to the consideration of other business, or a motion to recommit the joint resolution is not in order.

(C) Vote on passage.—The vote on passage shall occur immediately following the conclusion of the debate on a joint resolution, and a single quorum call at the conclusion of the debate if requested in accordance with the rules of the Senate.

(D) Rulings of the chair on procedure.—Appeals from the decisions of the Chair relating to the application of the rules of the Senate, as the case may be, to the procedure relating to a joint resolution shall be decided without debate.

(f) Rules Relating to Senate and House of Representatives.—

(1) Coordination with action by other house.—If, before the passage by one House of a joint resolution of that House, that House receives from the other House a joint resolution, then the following procedures shall apply:

(A) The joint resolution of the other House shall not be referred to a committee.

(B) With respect to a joint resolution of the House receiving the resolution—

(i) the procedure in that House shall be the same as if no joint resolution had been received from the other House; but

(ii) the vote on passage shall be on the joint resolution of the other House.

(2) Treatment of joint resolution of other house.—If one House fails to introduce or consider a joint resolution under this section, the joint resolution of the other House shall be entitled to expedited floor procedures under this section.

(3) Treatment of companion measures.—If, following passage of the joint resolution in the Senate, the Senate then receives the companion measure from the House of Representatives, the companion measure shall not be debatable.

(4) Consideration after passage.—

(A) In general.—If Congress passes a joint resolution, the period beginning on the date the President is presented with the joint resolution and ending on the date the President takes action with respect to the joint resolution shall be disregarded in computing the 15-calendar day period described in subsection (a)(3).

(B) Vetoes.—If the President vetoes the joint resolution—

(i) the period beginning on the date the President vetoes the joint resolution and ending on the date the Congress receives the veto message with respect to the joint resolution shall be disregarded in computing the 15-calendar day period described in subsection (a)(3), and

(ii) debate on a veto message in the Senate under this section shall be 1 hour equally divided between the majority and minority leaders or their designees.

(5) Rules of house of representatives and senate.—This subsection and subsections (c), (d), and (e) are enacted by Congress—

(A) as an exercise of the rulemaking power of the Senate and House of Representatives, respectively, and as such it is deemed a part of the rules of each House, respectively, but applicable only with respect to the procedure to be followed in that House in the case of a joint resolution, and it supersedes other rules only to the extent that it is inconsistent with such rules; and

(B) with full recognition of the constitutional right of either House to change the rules (so far as relating to the procedure of that House) at any time, in the same manner, and to the same extent as in the case of any other rule of that House.

[¶7057] ACT SEC. 116. OVERSIGHT AND AUDITS.

(a) COMPTROLLER GENERAL OVERSIGHT.—

(1) SCOPE OF OVERSIGHT.—The Comptroller General of the United States shall, upon establishment of the troubled assets relief program under this Act (in this section referred to as the "TARP"), commence ongoing oversight of the activities and performance of the TARP and of any agents and representatives of the TARP (as related to the agent or representative's activities on behalf of or under the authority of the TARP), including vehicles established by the Secretary under this Act. The subjects of such oversight shall include the following:

(A) The performance of the TARP in meeting the purposes of this Act, particularly those involving—

(i) foreclosure mitigation;

(ii) cost reduction;

(iii) whether it has provided stability or prevented disruption to the financial markets or the banking system; and

(iv) whether it has protected taxpayers.

(B) The financial condition and internal controls of the TARP, its representatives and agents.

(C) Characteristics of transactions and commitments entered into, including transaction type, frequency, size, prices paid, and all other relevant terms and conditions, and the timing, duration and terms of any future commitments to purchase assets.

(D) Characteristics and disposition of acquired assets, including type, acquisition price, current market value, sale prices and terms, and use of proceeds from sales.

(E) Efficiency of the operations of the TARP in the use of appropriated funds.

(F) Compliance with all applicable laws and regulations by the TARP, its agents and representatives.

(G) The efforts of the TARP to prevent, identify, and minimize conflicts of interest involving any agent or representative performing activities on behalf of or under the authority of the TARP.

(H) The efficacy of contracting procedures pursuant to section 107(b), including, as applicable, the efforts of the TARP in evaluating proposals for inclusion and contracting to the maximum extent possible of minorities (as such term is defined in 1204(c) of the Financial Institutions Reform, Recovery, and Enhancement Act of 1989 (12 U.S.C. 1811 note), women, and minority- and women-owned businesses, including ascertaining and reporting the total amount of fees paid and other value delivered by the TARP to all of its agents and representatives, and such amounts paid or delivered to such firms that are minority- and women-owned businesses (as such terms are defined in section 21A of the Federal Home Loan Bank Act (12 U.S.C. 1441a)).

(2) CONDUCT AND ADMINISTRATION OF OVERSIGHT.—

(A) GAO PRESENCE.—The Secretary shall provide the Comptroller General with appropriate space and facilities in the Department of the Treasury as necessary to facilitate oversight of the TARP until the termination date established in section 120.

(B) ACCESS TO RECORDS.—To the extent otherwise consistent with law, the Comptroller General shall have access, upon request, to any information, data, schedules, books, accounts, financial records, reports, files, electronic communications, or other papers, things, or property belonging to or in use by the TARP, or any vehicles established by the Secretary under this Act, and to the officers, directors, employees, independent public accountants, financial advisors, and other agents and representatives of the TARP (as related to the agent or representative's activities on behalf of or under the authority of the TARP) or any such vehicle at such reasonable time as the Comptroller General may request. The Comptroller General shall be afforded full facilities for verifying transactions with the balances or securities held by depositaries, fiscal agents, and custodians. The Comptroller General may make and retain copies of such books, accounts, and other records as the Comptroller General deems appropriate.

(C) REIMBURSEMENT OF COSTS.—The Treasury shall reimburse the Government Accountability Office for the full cost of any such oversight activities as billed therefor by the Comptroller General of the United States. Such reimbursements shall be credited to the appropriation account "Salaries and Expenses, Government Accountability Office" current when the payment is received and remain available until expended.

(3) REPORTING.—The Comptroller General shall submit reports of findings under this section, regularly and no less frequently than once every 60 days, to the appropriate committees of Congress, and the Special Inspector General for the Troubled Asset Relief Program established under this Act on the activities and performance of the TARP. The Comptroller may also submit special reports under this subsection as warranted by the findings of its oversight activities.

(b) COMPTROLLER GENERAL AUDITS.—

(1) ANNUAL AUDIT.—The TARP shall annually prepare and issue to the appropriate committees of Congress and the public audited financial statements prepared in accordance with generally accepted accounting principles, and the Comptroller General shall annually audit such statements in accordance with generally accepted auditing standards. The Treasury shall reimburse the Government Accountability Office for the full cost of any such audit as billed therefor by the Comptroller General. Such reimbursements shall be credited to the appropriation account "Salaries and Expenses, Government Accountability Office" current when the payment is received and remain available until expended. The financial statements prepared under this paragraph shall be on the fiscal year basis prescribed under section 1102 of title 31, United States Code.

(2) AUTHORITY.—The Comptroller General may audit the programs, activities, receipts, expenditures, and financial transactions of the TARP and any agents and representatives of the TARP (as related to the agent or representative's activities on behalf of or under the authority of the TARP), including vehicles established by the Secretary under this Act.

(3) CORRECTIVE RESPONSES TO AUDIT PROBLEMS.—The TARP shall—

(A) take action to address deficiencies identified by the Comptroller General or other auditor engaged by the TARP; or

(B) certify to appropriate committees of Congress that no action is necessary or appropriate.

(c) INTERNAL CONTROL.—

(1) ESTABLISHMENT.—The TARP shall establish and maintain an effective system of internal control, consistent with the standards prescribed under section 3512(c) of title 31, United States Code, that provides reasonable assurance of—

(A) the effectiveness and efficiency of operations, including the use of the resources of the TARP;

(B) the reliability of financial reporting, including financial statements and other reports for internal and external use; and

(C) compliance with applicable laws and regulations.

(2) REPORTING.—In conjunction with each annual financial statement issued under this section, the TARP shall—

(A) state the responsibility of management for establishing and maintaining adequate internal control over financial reporting; and

(B) state its assessment, as of the end of the most recent year covered by such financial statement of the TARP, of the effectiveness of the internal control over financial reporting.

(d) SHARING OF INFORMATION.—Any report or audit required under this section shall also be submitted to the Congressional Oversight Panel established under section 125.

(e) TERMINATION.—Any oversight, reporting, or audit requirement under this section shall terminate on the later of—

(1) the date that the last troubled asset acquired by the Secretary under section 101 has been sold or transferred out of the ownership or control of the Federal Government; or

(2) the date of expiration of the last insurance contract issued under section 102.

[¶7060] ACT SEC. 117. STUDY AND REPORT ON MARGIN AUTHORITY.

(a) STUDY.—The Comptroller General shall undertake a study to determine the extent to which leverage and sudden deleveraging of financial institutions was a factor behind the current financial crisis.

(b) CONTENT.—The study required by this section shall include—

(1) an analysis of the roles and responsibilities of the Board, the Securities and Exchange Commission, the Secretary, and other Federal banking agencies with respect to monitoring leverage and acting to curtail excessive leveraging;

(2) an analysis of the authority of the Board to regulate leverage, including by setting margin requirements, and what process the Board used to decide whether or not to use its authority;

(3) an analysis of any usage of the margin authority by the Board; and

(4) recommendations for the Board and appropriate committees of Congress with respect to the existing authority of the Board.

(c) REPORT.—Not later than June 1, 2009, the Comptroller General shall complete and submit a report on the study required by this section to the Committee on Banking, Housing, and Urban Affairs of the Senate and the Committee on Financial Services of the House of Representatives.

(d) SHARING OF INFORMATION.—Any reports required under this section shall also be submitted to the Congressional Oversight Panel established under section 125.

[¶7063] ACT SEC. 118. FUNDING.

For the purpose of the authorities granted in this Act, and for the costs of administering those authorities, the Secretary may use the proceeds of the sale of any securities issued under chapter 31 of title 31, United States Code, and the purposes for which securities may be issued under chapter 31 of title 31, United States Code, are extended to include actions authorized by this Act, including the payment of administrative expenses. Any funds expended or obligated by the Secretary for actions authorized by this Act, including the payment of administrative expenses, shall be deemed appropriated at the time of such expenditure or obligation.

[¶7066] ACT SEC. 119. JUDICIAL REVIEW AND RELATED MATTERS.

(a) JUDICIAL REVIEW.—

(1) STANDARD.—Actions by the Secretary pursuant to the authority of this Act shall be subject to chapter 7 of title 5, United States Code, including that such final actions shall be held unlawful and set aside if found to be arbitrary, capricious, an abuse of discretion, or not in accordance with law.

(2) LIMITATIONS ON EQUITABLE RELIEF.—

(A) INJUNCTION.—No injunction or other form of equitable relief shall be issued against the Secretary for actions pursuant to section 101, 102, 106, and 109, other than to remedy a violation of the Constitution.

(B) TEMPORARY RESTRAINING ORDER.—Any request for a temporary restraining order against the Secretary for actions pursuant to this Act shall be considered and granted or denied by the court within 3 days of the date of the request.

(C) PRELIMINARY INJUNCTION.—Any request for a preliminary injunction against the Secretary for actions pursuant to this Act shall be considered and granted or denied by the court on an expedited basis consistent with the provisions of rule 65(b)(3) of the Federal Rules of Civil Procedure, or any successor thereto.

(D) PERMANENT INJUNCTION.—Any request for a permanent injunction against the Secretary for actions pursuant to this Act shall be considered and granted or denied by the court on an expedited basis. Whenever possible, the court shall consolidate trial on the merits with any hearing on a request for a preliminary injunction, consistent with the provisions of rule 65(a)(2) of the Federal Rules of Civil Procedure, or any successor thereto.

(3) LIMITATION ON ACTIONS BY PARTICIPATING COMPANIES.—No action or claims may be brought against the Secretary by any person that divests its assets with respect to its participation in a program under this Act, except as provided in paragraph (1), other than as expressly provided in a written contract with the Secretary.

(4) STAYS.—Any injunction or other form of equitable relief issued against the Secretary for actions pursuant to section 101, 102, 106, and 109, shall be automatically stayed. The stay shall be lifted unless the Secretary seeks a stay from a higher court within 3 calendar days after the date on which the relief is issued.

(b) RELATED MATTERS.—

(1) TREATMENT OF HOMEOWNERS' RIGHTS.—The terms of any residential mortgage loan that is part of any purchase by the Secretary under this Act shall remain subject to all claims and defenses that would otherwise apply, notwithstanding the exercise of authority by the Secretary under this Act.

(2) SAVINGS CLAUSE.—Any exercise of the authority of the Secretary pursuant to this Act shall not impair the claims or defenses that would otherwise apply with respect to persons other than the Secretary. Except as established in any contract, a servicer of pooled residential mortgages owes any duty to determine whether the net present value of the payments on the loan, as modified, is likely to be greater than the anticipated net recovery that would result from foreclosure to all investors and holders of beneficial interests in such investment, but not to any individual or groups of investors or beneficial interest holders, and shall be deemed to act in the best interests of all such investors or holders of beneficial interests if the servicer agrees to or implements a modification or workout plan when the servicer takes reasonable loss mitigation actions, including partial payments.

[¶7069] ACT SEC. 120. TERMINATION OF AUTHORITY.

(a) TERMINATION.—The authorities provided under sections 101(a), excluding section 101(a)(3), and 102 shall terminate on December 31, 2009.

(b) EXTENSION UPON CERTIFICATION.—The Secretary, upon submission of a written certification to Congress, may extend the authority provided under this Act to expire not later than 2 years from the date of enactment of this Act. Such certification shall include a justification of why the extension is necessary to assist American families and stabilize financial markets, as well as the expected cost to the taxpayers for such an extension.

[¶7072] ACT SEC. 121. SPECIAL INSPECTOR GENERAL FOR THE TROUBLED ASSET RELIEF PROGRAM.

(a) OFFICE OF INSPECTOR GENERAL.—There is hereby established the Office of the Special Inspector General for the Troubled Asset Relief Program.

(b) APPOINTMENT OF INSPECTOR GENERAL; REMOVAL.—(1) The head of the Office of the Special Inspector General for the Troubled Asset Relief Program is the Special Inspector General for the Troubled Asset Relief Program (in this section referred to as the "Special Inspector General"), who shall be appointed by the President, by and with the advice and consent of the Senate.

(2) The appointment of the Special Inspector General shall be made on the basis of integrity and demonstrated ability in accounting, auditing, financial analysis, law, management analysis, public administration, or investigations.

(3) The nomination of an individual as Special Inspector General shall be made as soon as practicable after the establishment of any program under sections 101 and 102.

(4) The Special Inspector General shall be removable from office in accordance with the provisions of section 3(b) of the Inspector General Act of 1978 (5 U.S.C. App.).

(5) For purposes of section 7324 of title 5, United States Code, the Special Inspector General shall not be considered an employee who determines policies to be pursued by the United States in the nationwide administration of Federal law.

(6) The annual rate of basic pay of the Special Inspector General shall be the annual rate of basic pay for an Inspector General under section 3(e) of the Inspector General Act of 1978 (5 U.S.C. App.).

(c) DUTIES.—(1) It shall be the duty of the Special Inspector General to conduct, supervise, and coordinate audits and investigations of the purchase, management, and sale of assets by the Secretary of the Treasury under any program established by the Secretary under section 101, and the management by the Secretary of any program established under section 102, including by collecting and summarizing the following information:

(A) A description of the categories of troubled assets purchased or otherwise procured by the Secretary.

(B) A listing of the troubled assets purchased in each such category described under subparagraph (A).

(C) An explanation of the reasons the Secretary deemed it necessary to purchase each such troubled asset.

(D) A listing of each financial institution that such troubled assets were purchased from.

(E) A listing of and detailed biographical information on each person or entity hired to manage such troubled assets.

(F) A current estimate of the total amount of troubled assets purchased pursuant to any program established under section 101, the amount of troubled assets on the books of the Treasury, the amount of troubled assets sold, and the profit and loss incurred on each sale or disposition of each such troubled asset.

(G) A listing of the insurance contracts issued under section 102.

(2) The Special Inspector General shall establish, maintain, and oversee such systems, procedures, and controls as the Special Inspector General considers appropriate to discharge the duty under paragraph (1).

(3) In addition to the duties specified in paragraphs (1) and (2), the Inspector General shall also have the duties and responsibilities of inspectors general under the Inspector General Act of 1978.

(d) POWERS AND AUTHORITIES.—(1) In carrying out the duties specified in subsection (c), the Special Inspector General shall have the authorities provided in section 6 of the Inspector General Act of 1978.

(2) The Special Inspector General shall carry out the duties specified in subsection (c)(1) in accordance with section 4(b)(1) of the Inspector General Act of 1978.

(e) PERSONNEL, FACILITIES, AND OTHER RESOURCES.—(1) The Special Inspector General may select, appoint, and employ such officers and employees as may be necessary for carrying out the duties of the Special Inspector General, subject to the provisions of title 5, United States Code, governing appointments in the competitive service, and the provisions of chapter 51 and subchapter III of chapter 53 of such title, relating to classification and General Schedule pay rates.

(2) The Special Inspector General may obtain services as authorized by section 3109 of title 5, United States Code, at daily rates not to exceed the equivalent rate prescribed for grade GS-15 of the General Schedule by section 5332 of such title.

(3) The Special Inspector General may enter into contracts and other arrangements for audits, studies, analyses, and other services with public agencies and with private persons, and make such payments as may be necessary to carry out the duties of the Inspector General.

Act Sec. 121(e)(3)   ¶7072

(4)(A) Upon request of the Special Inspector General for information or assistance from any department, agency, or other entity of the Federal Government, the head of such entity shall, insofar as is practicable and not in contravention of any existing law, furnish such information or assistance to the Special Inspector General, or an authorized designee.

(B) Whenever information or assistance requested by the Special Inspector General is, in the judgment of the Special Inspector General, unreasonably refused or not provided, the Special Inspector General shall report the circumstances to the appropriate committees of Congress without delay.

(f) REPORTS.—(1) Not later than 60 days after the confirmation of the Special Inspector General, and every calendar quarter thereafter, the Special Inspector General shall submit to the appropriate committees of Congress a report summarizing the activities of the Special Inspector General during the 120-day period ending on the date of such report. Each report shall include, for the period covered by such report, a detailed statement of all purchases, obligations, expenditures, and revenues associated with any program established by the Secretary of the Treasury under sections 101 and 102, as well as the information collected under subsection (c)(1).

(2) Nothing in this subsection shall be construed to authorize the public disclosure of information that is—

(A) specifically prohibited from disclosure by any other provision of law;

(B) specifically required by Executive order to be protected from disclosure in the interest of national defense or national security or in the conduct of foreign affairs; or

(C) a part of an ongoing criminal investigation.

(3) Any reports required under this section shall also be submitted to the Congressional Oversight Panel established under section 125.

(g) FUNDING.—(1) Of the amounts made available to the Secretary of the Treasury under section 118, $50,000,000 shall be available to the Special Inspector General to carry out this section.

(2) The amount available under paragraph (1) shall remain available until expended.

(h) TERMINATION.—The Office of the Special Inspector General shall terminate on the later of—

(1) the date that the last troubled asset acquired by the Secretary under section 101 has been sold or transferred out of the ownership or control of the Federal Government; or

(2) the date of expiration of the last insurance contract issued under section 102.

[¶7075] ACT SEC. 122. INCREASE IN STATUTORY LIMIT ON THE PUBLIC DEBT.

Subsection (b) of section 3101 of title 31, United States Code, is amended by striking out the dollar limitation contained in such subsection and inserting "$11,315,000,000,000".

[¶7078] ACT SEC. 123. CREDIT REFORM.

(a) IN GENERAL.—Subject to subsection (b), the costs of purchases of troubled assets made under section 101(a) and guarantees of troubled assets under section 102, and any cash flows associated with the activities authorized in section 102 and subsections (a), (b), and (c) of section 106 shall be determined as provided under the Federal Credit Reform Act of 1990 (2 U.S.C. 661 et. seq.).

(b) COSTS.—For the purposes of section 502(5) of the Federal Credit Reform Act of 1990 (2 U.S.C. 661a(5))—

(1) the cost of troubled assets and guarantees of troubled assets shall be calculated by adjusting the discount rate in section 502(5)(E) (2 U.S.C. 661a(5)(E)) for market risks; and

(2) the cost of a modification of a troubled asset or guarantee of a troubled asset shall be the difference between the current estimate consistent with paragraph (1) under the terms of the troubled asset or guarantee of the troubled asset and the current estimate consistent with paragraph (1) under the terms of the troubled asset or guarantee of the troubled asset, as modified.

[¶7081] ACT SEC. 124. HOPE FOR HOMEOWNERS AMENDMENTS.

Section 257 of the National Housing Act (12 U.S.C. 1715z-23) is amended—

(1) in subsection (e)—

(A) in paragraph (1)(B), by inserting before "a ratio" the following: ", or thereafter is likely to have, due to the terms of the mortgage being reset,";

(B) in paragraph (2)(B), by inserting before the period at the end "(or such higher percentage as the Board determines, in the discretion of the Board)";

(C) in paragraph (4)(A)—

(i) in the first sentence, by inserting after "insured loan" the following: "and any payments made under this paragraph,"; and

(ii) by adding at the end the following: "Such actions may include making payments, which shall be accepted as payment in full of all indebtedness under the eligible mortgage, to any holder of an existing subordinate mortgage, in lieu of any future appreciation payments authorized under subparagraph (B)."; and

(2) in subsection (w), by inserting after "administrative costs" the following: "and payments pursuant to subsection (e)(4)(A)".

[¶7084] ACT SEC. 125. CONGRESSIONAL OVERSIGHT PANEL.

(a) ESTABLISHMENT.—There is hereby established the Congressional Oversight Panel (hereafter in this section referred to as the "Oversight Panel") as an establishment in the legislative branch.

(b) DUTIES.—The Oversight Panel shall review the current state of the financial markets and the regulatory system and submit the following reports to Congress:

(1) REGULAR REPORTS.—

(A) IN GENERAL.—Regular reports of the Oversight Panel shall include the following:

(i) The use by the Secretary of authority under this Act, including with respect to the use of contracting authority and administration of the program.

(ii) The impact of purchases made under the Act on the financial markets and financial institutions.

(iii) The extent to which the information made available on transactions under the program has contributed to market transparency.

(iv) The effectiveness of foreclosure mitigation efforts, and the effectiveness of the program from the standpoint of minimizing long-term costs to the taxpayers and maximizing the benefits for taxpayers.

(B) TIMING.—The reports required under this paragraph shall be submitted not later than 30 days after the first exercise by the Secretary of the authority under section 101(a) or 102, and every 30 days thereafter.

(2) SPECIAL REPORT ON REGULATORY REFORM.—The Oversight Panel shall submit a special report on regulatory reform not later than January 20, 2009, analyzing the current state of the regulatory system and its effectiveness at overseeing the participants in the financial system and protecting consumers, and providing recommendations for improvement, including recommendations regarding whether any participants in the financial markets that are currently outside the regulatory system should become subject to the regulatory system, the rationale underlying such recommendation, and whether there are any gaps in existing consumer protections.

(c) MEMBERSHIP.—

(1) IN GENERAL.—The Oversight Panel shall consist of 5 members, as follows:

(A) 1 member appointed by the Speaker of the House of Representatives.

(B) 1 member appointed by the minority leader of the House of Representatives.

(C) 1 member appointed by the majority leader of the Senate.

(D) 1 member appointed by the minority leader of the Senate.

(E) 1 member appointed by the Speaker of the House of Representatives and the majority leader of the Senate, after consultation with the minority leader of the Senate and the minority leader of the House of Representatives.

(2) PAY.—Each member of the Oversight Panel shall each be paid at a rate equal to the daily equivalent of the annual rate of basic pay for level I of the Executive Schedule for each day (including travel time) during which such member is engaged in the actual performance of duties vested in the Commission.

(3) PROHIBITION OF COMPENSATION OF FEDERAL EMPLOYEES.—Members of the Oversight Panel who are full-time officers or employees of the United States or Members of Congress may not receive additional pay, allowances, or benefits by reason of their service on the Oversight Panel.

(4) TRAVEL EXPENSES.—Each member shall receive travel expenses, including per diem in lieu of subsistence, in accordance with applicable provisions under subchapter I of chapter 57 of title 5, United States Code.

(5) QUORUM.—Four members of the Oversight Panel shall constitute a quorum but a lesser number may hold hearings.

(6) VACANCIES.—A vacancy on the Oversight Panel shall be filled in the manner in which the original appointment was made.

(7) MEETINGS.—The Oversight Panel shall meet at the call of the Chairperson or a majority of its members.

(d) STAFF.—

(1) IN GENERAL.—The Oversight Panel may appoint and fix the pay of any personnel as the Commission considers appropriate.

(2) EXPERTS AND CONSULTANTS.—The Oversight Panel may procure temporary and intermittent services under section 3109(b) of title 5, United States Code.

(3) STAFF OF AGENCIES.—Upon request of the Oversight Panel, the head of any Federal department or agency may detail, on a reimbursable basis, any of the personnel of that department or agency to the Oversight Panel to assist it in carrying out its duties under this Act.

(e) POWERS.—

(1) HEARINGS AND SESSIONS.—The Oversight Panel may, for the purpose of carrying out this section, hold hearings, sit and act at times and places, take testimony, and receive evidence as the Panel considers appropriate and may administer oaths or affirmations to witnesses appearing before it.

(2) POWERS OF MEMBERS AND AGENTS.—Any member or agent of the Oversight Panel may, if authorized by the Oversight Panel, take any action which the Oversight Panel is authorized to take by this section.

(3) OBTAINING OFFICIAL DATA.—The Oversight Panel may secure directly from any department or agency of the United States information necessary to enable it to carry out this section. Upon request of the Chairperson of the Oversight Panel, the head of that department or agency shall furnish that information to the Oversight Panel.

(4) REPORTS.—The Oversight Panel shall receive and consider all reports required to be submitted to the Oversight Panel under this Act.

(f) TERMINATION.—The Oversight Panel shall terminate 6 months after the termination date specified in section 120.

(g) FUNDING FOR EXPENSES.—

(1) AUTHORIZATION OF APPROPRIATIONS.—There is authorized to be appropriated to the Oversight Panel such sums as may be necessary for any fiscal year, half of which shall be derived

from the applicable account of the House of Representatives, and half of which shall be derived from the contingent fund of the Senate.

(2) REIMBURSEMENT OF AMOUNTS.—An amount equal to the expenses of the Oversight Panel shall be promptly transferred by the Secretary, from time to time upon the presentment of a statement of such expenses by the Chairperson of the Oversight Panel, from funds made available to the Secretary under this Act to the applicable fund of the House of Representatives and the contingent fund of the Senate, as appropriate, as reimbursement for amounts expended from such account and fund under paragraph (1).

[¶7087] ACT SEC. 126. FDIC AUTHORITY.

(a) IN GENERAL.—Section 18(a) of the Federal Deposit Insurance Act (12 U.S.C. 1828(a)) is amended by adding at the end the following new paragraph:

"(4) FALSE ADVERTISING, MISUSE OF FDIC NAMES, AND MISREPRESENTATION TO INDICATE INSURED STATUS.—

"(A) PROHIBITION ON FALSE ADVERTISING AND MISUSE OF FDIC NAMES.—No person may represent or imply that any deposit liability, obligation, certificate, or share is insured or guaranteed by the Corporation, if such deposit liability, obligation, certificate, or share is not insured or guaranteed by the Corporation—

"(i) by using the terms 'Federal Deposit', 'Federal Deposit Insurance', 'Federal Deposit Insurance Corporation', any combination of such terms, or the abbreviation 'FDIC' as part of the business name or firm name of any person, including any corporation, partnership, business trust, association, or other business entity; or

"(ii) by using such terms or any other terms, sign, or symbol as part of an advertisement, solicitation, or other document.

"(B) PROHIBITION ON MISREPRESENTATIONS OF INSURED STATUS.—No person may knowingly misrepresent—

"(i) that any deposit liability, obligation, certificate, or share is insured, under this Act, if such deposit liability, obligation, certificate, or share is not so insured; or

"(ii) the extent to which or the manner in which any deposit liability, obligation, certificate, or share is insured under this Act, if such deposit liability, obligation, certificate, or share is not so insured, to the extent or in the manner represented.

"(C) AUTHORITY OF THE APPROPRIATE FEDERAL BANKING AGENCY.—The appropriate Federal banking agency shall have enforcement authority in the case of a violation of this paragraph by any person for which the agency is the appropriate Federal banking agency, or any institution-affiliated party thereof.

"(D) CORPORATION AUTHORITY IF THE APPROPRIATE FEDERAL BANKING AGENCY FAILS TO FOLLOW RECOMMENDATION.—

"(i) RECOMMENDATION.—The Corporation may recommend in writing to the appropriate Federal banking agency that the agency take any enforcement action authorized under section 8 for purposes of enforcement of this paragraph with respect to any person for which the agency is the appropriate Federal banking agency or any institution-affiliated party thereof.

"(ii) AGENCY RESPONSE.—If the appropriate Federal banking agency does not, within 30 days of the date of receipt of a recommendation under clause (i), take the enforcement action with respect to this paragraph recommended by the Corporation or provide a plan acceptable to the Corporation for responding to the situation presented, the Corporation may take the recommended enforcement action against such person or institution-affiliated party.

"(E) ADDITIONAL AUTHORITY.—In addition to its authority under subparagraphs (C) and (D), for purposes of this paragraph, the Corporation shall have, in the same manner and to the same extent as with respect to a State nonmember insured bank—

"(i) jurisdiction over—

"(I) any person other than a person for which another agency is the appropriate Federal banking agency or any institution-affiliated party thereof; and

"(II) any person that aids or abets a violation of this paragraph by a person described in subclause (I); and

"(ii) for purposes of enforcing the requirements of this paragraph, the authority of the Corporation under—

"(I) section 10(c) to conduct investigations; and

"(II) subsections (b), (c), (d) and (i) of section 8 to conduct enforcement actions.

"(F) OTHER ACTIONS PRESERVED.—No provision of this paragraph shall be construed as barring any action otherwise available, under the laws of the United States or any State, to any Federal or State agency or individual.".

(b) ENFORCEMENT ORDERS.—Section 8(c) of the Federal Deposit Insurance Act (12 U.S.C. 1818(c)) is amended by adding at the end the following new paragraph:

"(4) FALSE ADVERTISING OR MISUSE OF NAMES TO INDICATE INSURED STATUS.—

"(A) TEMPORARY ORDER.—

"(i) IN GENERAL.—If a notice of charges served under subsection (b)(1) specifies on the basis of particular facts that any person engaged or is engaging in conduct described in section 18(a)(4), the Corporation or other appropriate Federal banking agency may issue a temporary order requiring—

"(I) the immediate cessation of any activity or practice described, which gave rise to the notice of charges; and

"(II) affirmative action to prevent any further, or to remedy any existing, violation.

"(ii) EFFECT OF ORDER.—Any temporary order issued under this subparagraph shall take effect upon service.

"(B) EFFECTIVE PERIOD OF TEMPORARY ORDER.—A temporary order issued under subparagraph (A) shall remain effective and enforceable, pending the completion of an administrative proceeding pursuant to subsection (b)(1) in connection with the notice of charges—

"(i) until such time as the Corporation or other appropriate Federal banking agency dismisses the charges specified in such notice; or

"(ii) if a cease-and-desist order is issued against such person, until the effective date of such order.

"(C) CIVIL MONEY PENALTIES.—Any violation of section 18(a)(4) shall be subject to civil money penalties, as set forth in subsection (i), except that for any person other than an insured depository institution or an institution-affiliated party that is found to have violated this paragraph, the Corporation or other appropriate Federal banking agency shall not be required to demonstrate any loss to an insured depository institution.".

(c) UNENFORCEABILITY OF CERTAIN AGREEMENTS.—Section 13(c) of the Federal Deposit Insurance Act (12 U.S.C. 1823(c)) is amended by adding at the end the following new paragraph:

"(11) UNENFORCEABILITY OF CERTAIN AGREEMENTS.—No provision contained in any existing or future standstill, confidentiality, or other agreement that, directly or indirectly—

"(A) affects, restricts, or limits the ability of any person to offer to acquire or acquire,

"(B) prohibits any person from offering to acquire or acquiring, or

"(C) prohibits any person from using any previously disclosed information in connection with any such offer to acquire or acquisition of,

all or part of any insured depository institution, including any liabilities, assets, or interest therein, in connection with any transaction in which the Corporation exercises its authority under section 11 or 13, shall be enforceable against or impose any liability on such person, as such enforcement or liability shall be contrary to public policy.".

(d) TECHNICAL AND CONFORMING AMENDMENTS.—Section 18 of the Federal Deposit Insurance Act (12 U.S.C. 1828) is amended—

(1) in subsection (a)(3)—

(A) by striking "this subsection" the first place that term appears and inserting "paragraph (1)"; and

(B) by striking "this subsection" the second place that term appears and inserting "paragraph (2)"; and

(2) in the heading for subsection (a), by striking "INSURANCE LOGO.—" and inserting "REPRESENTATIONS OF DEPOSIT INSURANCE.—".

[¶ 7090] ACT SEC. 127. COOPERATION WITH THE FBI.

Any Federal financial regulatory agency shall cooperate with the Federal Bureau of Investigation and other law enforcement agencies investigating fraud, misrepresentation, and malfeasance with respect to development, advertising, and sale of financial products.

[¶ 7093] ACT SEC. 128. ACCELERATION OF EFFECTIVE DATE.

Section 203 of the Financial Services Regulatory Relief Act of 2006 (12 U.S.C. 461 note) is amended by striking "October 1, 2011" and inserting "October 1, 2008".

[¶ 7096] ACT SEC. 129. DISCLOSURES ON EXERCISE OF LOAN AUTHORITY.

(a) IN GENERAL.—Not later than 7 days after the date on which the Board exercises its authority under the third paragraph of section 13 of the Federal Reserve Act (12 U.S.C. 343; relating to discounts for individuals, partnerships, and corporations) the Board shall provide to the Committee on Banking, Housing, and Urban Affairs of the Senate and the Committee on Financial Services of the House of Representatives a report which includes—

(1) the justification for exercising the authority; and

(2) the specific terms of the actions of the Board, including the size and duration of the lending, available information concerning the value of any collateral held with respect to such a loan, the recipient of warrants or any other potential equity in exchange for the loan, and any expected cost to the taxpayers for such exercise.

(b) PERIODIC UPDATES.—The Board shall provide updates to the Committees specified in subsection (a) not less frequently than once every 60 days while the subject loan is outstanding, including—

(1) the status of the loan;

(2) the value of the collateral held by the Federal reserve bank which initiated the loan; and

(3) the projected cost to the taxpayers of the loan.

(c) CONFIDENTIALITY.—The information submitted to the Congress under this section shall be kept confidential, upon the written request of the Chairman of the Board, in which case it shall be made available only to the Chairpersons and Ranking Members of the Committees described in subsection (a).

(d) APPLICABILITY.—The provisions of this section shall be in force for all uses of the authority provided under section 13 of the Federal Reserve Act occurring during the period beginning on March 1, 2008 and ending on the after the date of enactment of this Act, and reports described in subsection (a) shall be required beginning not later than 30 days after that date of enactment, with respect to any such exercise of authority.

(e) SHARING OF INFORMATION.—Any reports required under this section shall also be submitted to the Congressional Oversight Panel established under section 125.

[¶ 7099] ACT SEC. 130. TECHNICAL CORRECTIONS.

(a) IN GENERAL.—Section 128(b)(2) of the Truth in Lending Act (15 U.S.C. 1638(b)(2)), as amended by section 2502 of the Mortgage Disclosure Improvement Act of 2008 (Public Law 110-289), is amended—

(1) in subparagraph (A), by striking "In the case" and inserting "Except as provided in subparagraph (G), in the case"; and

(2) by amending subparagraph (G) to read as follows:

"(G)(i) In the case of an extension of credit relating to a plan described in section 101(53D) of title 11, United States Code—

"(I) the requirements of subparagraphs (A) through (E) shall not apply; and

"(II) a good faith estimate of the disclosures required under subsection (a) shall be made in accordance with regulations of the Board under section 121(c) before such credit is extended, or shall be delivered or placed in the mail not later than 3 business days after the date on which the creditor receives the written application of the consumer for such credit, whichever is earlier.

"(ii) If a disclosure statement furnished within 3 business days of the written application (as provided under clause (i)(II)) contains an annual percentage rate which is subsequently rendered inaccurate, within the meaning of section 107(c), the creditor shall furnish another disclosure statement at the time of settlement or consummation of the transaction.".

(b) EFFECTIVE DATE.—The amendments made by subsection (a) shall take effect as if included in the amendments made by section 2502 of the Mortgage Disclosure Improvement Act of 2008 (Public Law 110-289).

[¶7102] ACT SEC. 131. EXCHANGE STABILIZATION FUND REIMBURSEMENT.

(a) REIMBURSEMENT.—The Secretary shall reimburse the Exchange Stabilization Fund established under section 5302 of title 31, United States Code, for any funds that are used for the Treasury Money Market Funds Guaranty Program for the United States money market mutual fund industry, from funds under this Act.

(b) LIMITS ON USE OF EXCHANGE STABILIZATION FUND.—The Secretary is prohibited from using the Exchange Stabilization Fund for the establishment of any future guaranty programs for the United States money market mutual fund industry.

[¶7105] ACT SEC. 132. AUTHORITY TO SUSPEND MARK-TO-MARKET ACCOUNTING.

(a) AUTHORITY.—The Securities and Exchange Commission shall have the authority under the securities laws (as such term is defined in section 3(a)(47) of the Securities Exchange Act of 1934 (15 U.S.C. 78c(a)(47)) to suspend, by rule, regulation, or order, the application of Statement Number 157 of the Financial Accounting Standards Board for any issuer (as such term is defined in section 3(a)(8) of such Act) or with respect to any class or category of transaction if the Commission determines that is necessary or appropriate in the public interest and is consistent with the protection of investors.

(b) SAVINGS PROVISION.—Nothing in subsection (a) shall be construed to restrict or limit any authority of the Securities and Exchange Commission under securities laws as in effect on the date of enactment of this Act.

[¶7108] ACT SEC. 133. STUDY ON MARK-TO-MARKET ACCOUNTING.

(a) STUDY.—The Securities and Exchange Commission, in consultation with the Board and the Secretary, shall conduct a study on mark-to-market accounting standards as provided in Statement Number 157 of the Financial Accounting Standards Board, as such standards are applicable to financial institutions, including depository institutions. Such a study shall consider at a minimum—

(1) the effects of such accounting standards on a financial institution's balance sheet;

(2) the impacts of such accounting on bank failures in 2008;

(3) the impact of such standards on the quality of financial information available to investors;

(4) the process used by the Financial Accounting Standards Board in developing accounting standards;

(5) the advisability and feasibility of modifications to such standards; and

(6) alternative accounting standards to those provided in such Statement Number 157.

(b) REPORT.—The Securities and Exchange Commission shall submit to Congress a report of such study before the end of the 90-day period beginning on the date of the enactment of this Act containing the findings and determinations of the Commission, including such administrative and legislative recommendations as the Commission determines appropriate.

[¶7111] ACT SEC. 134. RECOUPMENT.

Upon the expiration of the 5-year period beginning upon the date of the enactment of this Act, the Director of the Office of Management and Budget, in consultation with the Director of the Congressional Budget Office, shall submit a report to the Congress on the net amount within the Troubled Asset Relief Program under this Act. In any case where there is a shortfall, the President shall submit a legislative proposal that recoups from the financial industry an amount equal to the shortfall in order to ensure that the Troubled Asset Relief Program does not add to the deficit or national debt.

[¶7114] ACT SEC. 135. PRESERVATION OF AUTHORITY.

With the exception of section 131, nothing in this Act may be construed to limit the authority of the Secretary or the Board under any other provision of law.

[¶7117] ACT SEC. 136. TEMPORARY INCREASE IN DEPOSIT AND SHARE INSURANCE COVERAGE.

(a) FEDERAL DEPOSIT INSURANCE ACT; TEMPORARY INCREASE IN DEPOSIT INSURANCE.—

(1) INCREASED AMOUNT.—Effective only during the period beginning on the date of enactment of this Act and ending on December 31, 2009, section 11(a)(1)(E) of the Federal Deposit Insurance Act (12 U.S.C. 1821(a)(1)(E)) shall apply with "$250,000" substituted for "$100,000".

(2) TEMPORARY INCREASE NOT TO BE CONSIDERED FOR SETTING ASSESSMENTS.—The temporary increase in the standard maximum deposit insurance amount made under paragraph (1) shall not be taken into account by the Board of Directors of the Corporation for purposes of setting assessments under section 7(b)(2) of the Federal Deposit Insurance Act (12 U.S.C. 1817(b)(2)).

(3) BORROWING LIMITS TEMPORARILY LIFTED.—During the period beginning on the date of enactment of this Act and ending on December 31, 2009, the Board of Directors of the Corporation may request from the Secretary, and the Secretary shall approve, a loan or loans in an amount or amounts necessary to carry out this subsection, without regard to the limitations on such borrowing under section 14(a) and 15(c) of the Federal Deposit Insurance Act (12 U.S.C. 1824(a), 1825(c)).

(b) FEDERAL CREDIT UNION ACT; TEMPORARY INCREASE IN SHARE INSURANCE.—

(1) INCREASED AMOUNT.—Effective only during the period beginning on the date of enactment of this Act and ending on December 31, 2009, section 207(k)(5) of the Federal Credit Union Act (12 U.S.C. 1787(k)(5)) shall apply with "$250,000" substituted for "$100,000".

(2) TEMPORARY INCREASE NOT TO BE CONSIDERED FOR SETTING INSURANCE PREMIUM CHARGES AND INSURANCE DEPOSIT ADJUSTMENTS.—The temporary increase in the standard maximum share insurance amount made under paragraph (1) shall not be taken into account by the National Credit Union Administration Board for purposes of setting insurance premium charges and share insurance deposit adjustments under section 202(c)(2) of the Federal Credit Union Act (12 U.S.C. 1782(c)(2)).

(3) BORROWING LIMITS TEMPORARILY LIFTED.—During the period beginning on the date of enactment of this Act and ending on December 31, 2009, the National Credit Union Administration Board may request from the Secretary, and the Secretary shall approve, a loan or loans in an amount or amounts necessary to carry out this subsection, without regard to the limitations on such borrowing under section 203(d)(1) of the Federal Credit Union Act (12 U.S.C. 1783(d)(1)).

(c) NOT FOR USE IN INFLATION ADJUSTMENTS.—The temporary increase in the standard maximum deposit insurance amount made under this section shall not be used to make any inflation adjustment under section 11(a)(1)(F) of the Federal Deposit Insurance Act (12 U.S.C. 1821(a)(1)(F)) for purposes of that Act or the Federal Credit Union Act.

TITLE II—BUDGET-RELATED PROVISIONS

[¶7120] ACT SEC. 201. INFORMATION FOR CONGRESSIONAL SUPPORT AGENCIES.

Upon request, and to the extent otherwise consistent with law, all information used by the Secretary in connection with activities authorized under this Act (including the records to which the Comptroller General is entitled under this Act) shall be made available to congressional support agencies (in accordance with their obligations to support the Congress as set out in their authorizing statutes) for the purposes of assisting the committees of Congress with conducting oversight, monitoring, and analysis of the activities authorized under this Act.

[¶7123] ACT SEC. 202. REPORTS BY THE OFFICE OF MANAGEMENT AND BUDGET AND THE CONGRESSIONAL BUDGET OFFICE.

(a) REPORTS BY THE OFFICE OF MANAGEMENT AND BUDGET.—Within 60 days of the first exercise of the authority granted in section 101(a), but in no case later than December 31, 2008, and semiannually thereafter, the Office of Management and Budget shall report to the President and the Congress—

(1) the estimate, notwithstanding section 502(5)(F) of the Federal Credit Reform Act of 1990 (2 U.S.C. 661a(5)(F)), as of the first business day that is at least 30 days prior to the issuance of the report, of the cost of the troubled assets, and guarantees of the troubled assets, determined in accordance with section 123;

(2) the information used to derive the estimate, including assets purchased or guaranteed, prices paid, revenues received, the impact on the deficit and debt, and a description of any outstanding commitments to purchase troubled assets; and

(3) a detailed analysis of how the estimate has changed from the previous report.

Beginning with the second report under subsection (a), the Office of Management and Budget shall explain the differences between the Congressional Budget Office estimates delivered in accordance with subsection (b) and prior Office of Management and Budget estimates.

(b) REPORTS BY THE CONGRESSIONAL BUDGET OFFICE.—Within 45 days of receipt by the Congress of each report from the Office of Management and Budget under subsection (a), the Congressional Budget Office shall report to the Congress the Congressional Budget Office's assessment of the report submitted by the Office of Management and Budget, including—

(1) the cost of the troubled assets and guarantees of the troubled assets,

(2) the information and valuation methods used to calculate such cost, and

(3) the impact on the deficit and the debt.

(c) FINANCIAL EXPERTISE.—In carrying out the duties in this subsection or performing analyses of activities under this Act, the Director of the Congressional Budget Office may employ personnel and procure the services of experts and consultants.

(d) AUTHORIZATION OF APPROPRIATIONS.—There are authorized to be appropriated such sums as may be necessary to produce reports required by this section.

[¶7126] ACT SEC. 203. ANALYSIS IN PRESIDENT'S BUDGET.

(a) IN GENERAL.—Section 1105(a) of title 31, United States Code, is amended by adding at the end the following new paragraph:

"(35) as supplementary materials, a separate analysis of the budgetary effects for all prior fiscal years, the current fiscal year, the fiscal year for which the budget is submitted, and ensuing fiscal years of the actions the Secretary of the Treasury has taken or plans to take using any authority provided in the Emergency Economic Stabilization Act of 2008, including—

"(A) an estimate of the current value of all assets purchased, sold, and guaranteed under the authority provided in the Emergency Economic Stabilization Act of 2008 using methodology required by the Federal Credit Reform Act of 1990 (2 U.S.C. 661 et seq.) and section 123 of the Emergency Economic Stabilization Act of 2008;

"(B) an estimate of the deficit, the debt held by the public, and the gross Federal debt using methodology required by the Federal Credit Reform Act of 1990 and section 123 of the Emergency Economic Stabilization Act of 2008;

"(C) an estimate of the current value of all assets purchased, sold, and guaranteed under the authority provided in the Emergency Economic Stabilization Act of 2008 calculated on a cash basis;

"(D) a revised estimate of the deficit, the debt held by the public, and the gross Federal debt, substituting the cash-based estimates in subparagraph (C) for the estimates calculated under subparagraph (A) pursuant to the Federal Credit Reform Act of 1990 and section 123 of the Emergency Economic Stabilization Act of 2008; and

"(E) the portion of the deficit which can be attributed to any action taken by the Secretary using authority provided by the Emergency Economic Stabilization Act of 2008 and the extent to which the change in the deficit since the most recent estimate is due to a reestimate using the methodology required by the Federal Credit Reform Act of 1990 and section 123 of the Emergency Economic Stabilization Act of 2008."

(b) CONSULTATION.—In implementing this section, the Director of Office of Management and Budget shall consult periodically, but at least annually, with the Committee on the Budget of the House of Representatives, the Committee on the Budget of the Senate, and the Director of the Congressional Budget Office.

(c) EFFECTIVE DATE.—This section and the amendment made by this section shall apply beginning with respect to the fiscal year 2010 budget submission of the President.

[¶7129] ACT SEC. 204. EMERGENCY TREATMENT.

All provisions of this Act are designated as an emergency requirement and necessary to meet emergency needs pursuant to section 204(a) of S. Con. Res 21 (110th Congress), the concurrent resolution on the budget for fiscal year 2008 and rescissions of any amounts provided in this Act shall not be counted for purposes of budget enforcement.

TITLE III—TAX PROVISIONS

[¶7131] ACT SEC. 301. GAIN OR LOSS FROM SALE OR EXCHANGE OF CERTAIN PREFERRED STOCK.

(a) IN GENERAL.—For purposes of the Internal Revenue Code of 1986, gain or loss from the sale or exchange of any applicable preferred stock by any applicable financial institution shall be treated as ordinary income or loss.

(b) APPLICABLE PREFERRED STOCK.—For purposes of this section, the term "applicable preferred stock" means any stock—

(1) which is preferred stock in—

(A) the Federal National Mortgage Association, established pursuant to the Federal National Mortgage Association Charter Act (12 U.S.C. 1716 et seq.), or

(B) the Federal Home Loan Mortgage Corporation, established pursuant to the Federal Home Loan Mortgage Corporation Act (12 U.S.C. 1451 et seq.), and

(2) which—

(A) was held by the applicable financial institution on September 6, 2008, or

(B) was sold or exchanged by the applicable financial institution on or after January 1, 2008, and before September 7, 2008.

(c) APPLICABLE FINANCIAL INSTITUTION.—For purposes of this section:

(1) IN GENERAL.—Except as provided in paragraph (2), the term "applicable financial institution" means—

(A) a financial institution referred to in section 582(c)(2) of the Internal Revenue Code of 1986, or

(B) a depository institution holding company (as defined in section 3(w)(1) of the Federal Deposit Insurance Act (12 U.S.C. 1813(w)(1))).

(2) SPECIAL RULES FOR CERTAIN SALES.—In the case of—

(A) a sale or exchange described in subsection (b)(2)(B), an entity shall be treated as an applicable financial institution only if it was an entity described in subparagraph (A) or (B) of paragraph (1) at the time of the sale or exchange, and

(B) a sale or exchange after September 6, 2008, of preferred stock described in subsection (b)(2)(A), an entity shall be treated as an applicable financial institution only if it was an entity described in subparagraph (A) or (B) of paragraph (1) at all times during the period beginning on September 6, 2008, and ending on the date of the sale or exchange of the preferred stock.

(d) SPECIAL RULE FOR CERTAIN PROPERTY NOT HELD ON SEPTEMBER 6, 2008.—The Secretary of the Treasury or the Secretary's delegate may extend the application of this section to all or a portion of the gain or loss from a sale or exchange in any case where—

(1) an applicable financial institution sells or exchanges applicable preferred stock after September 6, 2008, which the applicable financial institution did not hold on such date, but the basis of which in the hands of the applicable financial institution at the time of the sale or exchange is the same as the basis in the hands of the person which held such stock on such date, or

(2) the applicable financial institution is a partner in a partnership which—

(A) held such stock on September 6, 2008, and later sold or exchanged such stock, or

(B) sold or exchanged such stock during the period described in subsection (b)(2)(B).

(e) REGULATORY AUTHORITY.—The Secretary of the Treasury or the Secretary's delegate may prescribe such guidance, rules, or regulations as are necessary to carry out the purposes of this section.

(f) EFFECTIVE DATE.—This section shall apply to sales or exchanges occurring after December 31, 2007, in taxable years ending after such date.

* * *

[CCH Explanation at ¶485. Committee Reports at ¶10,030.]

DIVISION B—ENERGY IMPROVEMENT AND EXTENSION ACT OF 2008

[¶7135] ACT SEC. 1. SHORT TITLE, ETC.

(a) SHORT TITLE.—This division may be cited as the "Energy Improvement and Extension Act of 2008".

* * *

TITLE I—ENERGY PRODUCTION INCENTIVES
* * *

Subtitle B—Carbon Mitigation and Coal Provisions
* * *

[¶7138] ACT SEC. 113. TEMPORARY INCREASE IN COAL EXCISE TAX; FUNDING OF BLACK LUNG DISABILITY TRUST FUND.
* * *

(b) RESTRUCTURING OF TRUST FUND DEBT.—

(1) DEFINITIONS.—For purposes of this subsection—

(A) MARKET VALUE OF THE OUTSTANDING REPAYABLE ADVANCES, PLUS ACCRUED INTEREST.—The term "market value of the outstanding repayable advances, plus accrued interest" means the present value (determined by the Secretary of the Treasury as of the refinancing date and using the Treasury rate as the discount rate) of the stream of principal and interest payments derived assuming that each repayable advance that is outstanding on the refinancing date is due on the 30th anniversary of the end of the fiscal year in which the advance was made to the Trust Fund, and that all such principal and interest payments are made on September 30 of the applicable fiscal year.

(B) REFINANCING DATE.—The term "refinancing date" means the date occurring 2 days after the enactment of this Act.

(C) REPAYABLE ADVANCE.—The term "repayable advance" means an amount that has been appropriated to the Trust Fund in order to make benefit payments and other expenditures that are authorized under section 9501 of the Internal Revenue Code of 1986 and are required to be repaid when the Secretary of the Treasury determines that monies are available in the Trust Fund for such purpose.

(D) TREASURY RATE.—The term "Treasury rate" means a rate determined by the Secretary of the Treasury, taking into consideration current market yields on outstanding marketable obligations of the United States of comparable maturities.

(E) TREASURY 1-YEAR RATE.—The term "Treasury 1-year rate" means a rate determined by the Secretary of the Treasury, taking into consideration current market yields on outstanding marketable obligations of the United States with remaining periods to maturity of approximately 1 year, to have been in effect as of the close of business 1 business day prior to the date on which the Trust Fund issues obligations to the Secretary of the Treasury under paragraph (2)(B).

(2) REFINANCING OF OUTSTANDING PRINCIPAL OF REPAYABLE ADVANCES AND UNPAID INTEREST ON SUCH ADVANCES.—

(A) TRANSFER TO GENERAL FUND.— On the refinancing date, the Trust Fund shall repay the market value of the outstanding repayable advances, plus accrued interest, by transferring into the general fund of the Treasury the following sums:

(i) The proceeds from obligations that the Trust Fund shall issue to the Secretary of the Treasury in such amounts as the Secretaries of Labor and the Treasury shall determine and bearing interest at the Treasury rate, and that shall be in such forms and denominations and be subject to such other terms and conditions, including maturity, as the Secretary of the Treasury shall prescribe.

(ii) All, or that portion, of the appropriation made to the Trust Fund pursuant to paragraph (3) that is needed to cover the difference defined in that paragraph.

(B) REPAYMENT OF OBLIGATIONS.—In the event that the Trust Fund is unable to repay the obligations that it has issued to the Secretary of the Treasury under subparagraph (A)(i) and this subparagraph, or is unable to make benefit payments and other authorized expenditures, the Trust Fund shall issue obligations to the Secretary of the Treasury in such amounts as may be necessary to make such repayments, payments, and expenditures, with a maturity of 1 year, and bearing interest at the Treasury 1-year rate. These obligations shall be in such forms and denominations and be subject to such other terms and conditions as the Secretary of the Treasury shall prescribe.

(C) AUTHORITY TO ISSUE OBLIGATIONS.—The Trust Fund is authorized to issue obligations to the Secretary of the Treasury under subparagraphs (A)(i) and (B). The Secretary of the Treasury is authorized to purchase such obligations of the Trust Fund. For the purposes of making such purchases, the Secretary of the Treasury may use as a public debt transaction the proceeds from the sale of any securities issued under chapter 31 of title 31, United States Code, and the purposes for which securities may be issued under such chapter are extended to include any purchase of such Trust Fund obligations under this subparagraph.

(3) ONE-TIME APPROPRIATION.—There is hereby appropriated to the Trust Fund an amount sufficient to pay to the general fund of the Treasury the difference between—

(A) the market value of the outstanding repayable advances, plus accrued interest; and

(B) the proceeds from the obligations issued by the Trust Fund to the Secretary of the Treasury under paragraph (2)(A)(i).

(4) PREPAYMENT OF TRUST FUND OBLIGATIONS.—The Trust Fund is authorized to repay any obligation issued to the Secretary of the Treasury under subparagraphs (A)(i) and (B) of paragraph (2) prior to its maturity date by paying a prepayment price that would, if the obligation being prepaid (including all unpaid interest accrued thereon through the date of prepayment) were purchased by a third party and held to the maturity date of such obligation, produce a yield to the third-party purchaser for the period from the date of purchase to the maturity date of such obligation substantially equal to the Treasury yield on outstanding marketable obligations of the United States having a comparable maturity to this period.

[CCH Explanation at ¶ 850. Committee Reports at ¶ 10,100.]

[¶ 7141] ACT SEC. 114. SPECIAL RULES FOR REFUND OF THE COAL EXCISE TAX TO CERTAIN COAL PRODUCERS AND EXPORTERS.

(a) REFUND.—

(1) COAL PRODUCERS.—

(A) IN GENERAL.—Notwithstanding subsections (a)(1) and (c) of section 6416 and section 6511 of the Internal Revenue Code of 1986, if—

(i) a coal producer establishes that such coal producer, or a party related to such coal producer, exported coal produced by such coal producer to a foreign country or shipped coal produced by such coal producer to a possession of the United States, or caused such coal to be exported or shipped, the export or shipment of which was other than through an exporter who meets the requirements of paragraph (2),

(ii) such coal producer filed an excise tax return on or after October 1, 1990, and on or before the date of the enactment of this Act, and

(iii) such coal producer files a claim for refund with the Secretary not later than the close of the 30-day period beginning on the date of the enactment of this Act,

then the Secretary shall pay to such coal producer an amount equal to the tax paid under section 4121 of such Code on such coal exported or shipped by the coal producer or a party related to such coal producer, or caused by the coal producer or a party related to such coal producer to be exported or shipped.

(B) SPECIAL RULES FOR CERTAIN TAXPAYERS.—For purposes of this section—

(i) IN GENERAL.—If a coal producer or a party related to a coal producer has received a judgment described in clause (iii), such coal producer shall be deemed to have established the export of coal to a foreign country or shipment of coal to a possession of the United States under subparagraph (A)(i).

(ii) AMOUNT OF PAYMENT.—If a taxpayer described in clause (i) is entitled to a payment under subparagraph (A), the amount of such payment shall be reduced by any amount paid pursuant to the judgment described in clause (iii).

(a) JUDGMENT DESCRIBED.—A judgment is described in this subparagraph if such judgment—

(I) is made by a court of competent jurisdiction within the United States,

(II) relates to the constitutionality of any tax paid on exported coal under section 4121 of the Internal Revenue Code of 1986, and

(III) is in favor of the coal producer or the party related to the coal producer.

(2) EXPORTERS.—Notwithstanding subsections (a)(1) and (c) of section 6416 and section 6511 of the Internal Revenue Code of 1986, and a judgment described in paragraph (1)(B)(iii) of this subsection, if—

(A) an exporter establishes that such exporter exported coal to a foreign country or shipped coal to a possession of the United States, or caused such coal to be so exported or shipped,

(B) such exporter filed a tax return on or after October 1, 1990, and on or before the date of the enactment of this Act, and

(C) such exporter files a claim for refund with the Secretary not later than the close of the 30-day period beginning on the date of the enactment of this Act,

then the Secretary shall pay to such exporter an amount equal to $0.825 per ton of such coal exported by the exporter or caused to be exported or shipped, or caused to be exported or shipped, by the exporter.

(b) LIMITATIONS.—Subsection (a) shall not apply with respect to exported coal if a settlement with the Federal Government has been made with and accepted by, the coal producer, a party related to such coal producer, or the exporter, of such coal, as of the date that the claim is filed under this section with respect to such exported coal. For purposes of this subsection, the term "settlement with the Federal Government" shall not include any settlement or stipulation entered into as of the date of the enactment of this Act, the terms of which contemplate a judgment concerning which any party has reserved the right to file an appeal, or has filed an appeal.

(c) SUBSEQUENT REFUND PROHIBITED.—No refund shall be made under this section to the extent that a credit or refund of such tax on such exported or shipped coal has been paid to any person.

(d) DEFINITIONS.—For purposes of this section—

(1) COAL PRODUCER.—The term "coal producer" means the person in whom is vested ownership of the coal immediately after the coal is severed from the ground, without regard to the existence of any contractual arrangement for the sale or other disposition of the coal or the payment of any royalties between the producer and third parties. The term includes any person who extracts coal from coal waste refuse piles or from the silt waste product which results from the wet washing (or similar processing) of coal.

(2) EXPORTER.—The term "exporter" means a person, other than a coal producer, who does not have a contract, fee arrangement, or any other agreement with a producer or seller of such coal to export or ship such coal to a third party on behalf of the producer or seller of such coal and—

(A) is indicated in the shipper's export declaration or other documentation as the exporter of record, or

(B) actually exported such coal to a foreign country or shipped such coal to a possession of the United States, or caused such coal to be so exported or shipped.

(3) RELATED PARTY.—The term "a party related to such coal producer" means a person who—

(A) is related to such coal producer through any degree of common management, stock ownership, or voting control,

(B) is related (within the meaning of section 144(a)(3) of the Internal Revenue Code of 1986) to such coal producer, or

(C) has a contract, fee arrangement, or any other agreement with such coal producer to sell such coal to a third party on behalf of such coal producer.

(4) SECRETARY.—The term "Secretary" means the Secretary of Treasury or the Secretary's designee.

(e) TIMING OF REFUND.—With respect to any claim for refund filed pursuant to this section, the Secretary shall determine whether the requirements of this section are met not later than 180 days after such claim is filed. If the Secretary determines that the requirements of this section are met, the claim for refund shall be paid not later than 180 days after the Secretary makes such determination.

(f) INTEREST.—Any refund paid pursuant to this section shall be paid by the Secretary with interest from the date of overpayment determined by using the overpayment rate and method under section 6621 of the Internal Revenue Code of 1986.

(g) DENIAL OF DOUBLE BENEFIT.—The payment under subsection (a) with respect to any coal shall not exceed—

(1) in the case of a payment to a coal producer, the amount of tax paid under section 4121 of the Internal Revenue Code of 1986 with respect to such coal by such coal producer or a party related to such coal producer, and

(2) in the case of a payment to an exporter, an amount equal to $0.825 per ton with respect to such coal exported by the exporter or caused to be exported by the exporter.

(h) APPLICATION OF SECTION.—This section applies only to claims on coal exported or shipped on or after October 1, 1990, through the date of the enactment of this Act.

(i) STANDING NOT CONFERRED.—

(1) EXPORTERS.—With respect to exporters, this section shall not confer standing upon an exporter to commence, or intervene in, any judicial or administrative proceeding concerning a claim for refund by a coal producer of any Federal or State tax, fee, or royalty paid by the coal producer.

(2) COAL PRODUCERS.—With respect to coal producers, this section shall not confer standing upon a coal producer to commence, or intervene in, any judicial or administrative proceeding concerning a claim for refund by an exporter of any Federal or State tax, fee, or royalty paid by the producer and alleged to have been passed on to an exporter.

* * *

[CCH Explanation at ¶ 850. Committee Reports at ¶ 10,110.]

[¶ 7144] ACT SEC. 117. CARBON AUDIT OF THE TAX CODE.

(a) STUDY.—The Secretary of the Treasury shall enter into an agreement with the National Academy of Sciences to undertake a comprehensive review of the Internal Revenue Code of 1986 to identify the types of and specific tax provisions that have the largest effects on carbon and other greenhouse gas emissions and to estimate the magnitude of those effects.

(b) REPORT.—Not later than 2 years after the date of enactment of this Act, the National Academy of Sciences shall submit to Congress a report containing the results of study authorized under this section.

(c) AUTHORIZATION OF APPROPRIATIONS.—There is authorized to be appropriated to carry out this section $1,500,000 for the period of fiscal years 2009 and 2010.

* * *

[CCH Explanation at ¶ 575. Committee Reports at ¶ 10,130.]

TITLE III—ENERGY CONSERVATION AND EFFICIENCY PROVISIONS

* * *

[¶ 7147] ACT SEC. 307. QUALIFIED GREEN BUILDING AND SUSTAINABLE DESIGN PROJECTS.

* * *

(c) ACCOUNTABILITY.—The second sentence of section 701(d) of the American Jobs Creation Act of 2004 is amended by striking "issuance," and inserting "issuance of the last issue with respect to such project,".

• • *AMERICAN JOBS CREATION ACT OF 2004 ACT SEC. 701(d) AS AMENDED*————

ACT SEC. 701. BROWNFIELDS DEMONSTRATION PROGRAM FOR QUALIFIED GREEN BUILDING AND SUSTAINABLE DESIGN PROJECTS.

* * *

(d) ACCOUNTABILITY .—Each issuer shall maintain, on behalf of each project, an interest bearing reserve account equal to 1 percent of the net proceeds of any bond issued under this section for such project. Not later than 5 years after the date of *issuance of the last issue with respect to such project*, the Secretary of the Treasury, after consultation with the Administrator of the Environmental Protection Agency, shall determine whether the project financed with such bonds has substantially complied with the terms and conditions described in section 142(l)(4) of the Internal Revenue Code of 1986 (as added by this section). If the Secretary, after such consultation, certifies that the project has substantially complied with such terms and conditions and meets the commitments set forth in the application for such project described in section 142(l)(4) of such Code, amounts in the reserve account, including all interest, shall be released to the project. If the Secretary determines that the project has not substantially complied with such terms and conditions, amounts in the reserve account, including all interest, shall be paid to the United States Treasury.

* * *

[CCH Explanation at ¶ 820. Committee Reports at ¶ 10,250.]

DIVISION C—TAX EXTENDERS AND ALTERNATIVE MINIMUM TAX RELIEF

[¶ 7150] ACT SEC. 1. SHORT TITLE; AMENDMENT OF 1986 CODE; TABLE OF CONTENTS.

(a) SHORT TITLE.—This division may be cited as the "Tax Extenders and Alternative Minimum Tax Relief Act of 2008".

(b) AMENDMENT OF 1986 CODE.—Except as otherwise expressly provided, whenever in this division an amendment or repeal is expressed in terms of an amendment to, or repeal of, a section or other provision, the reference shall be considered to be made to a section or other provision of the Internal Revenue Code of 1986.

* * *

TITLE III—EXTENSION OF BUSINESS TAX PROVISIONS
* * *

[¶ 7153] ACT SEC. 309. EXTENSION OF ECONOMIC DEVELOPMENT CREDIT FOR AMERICAN SAMOA.

(a) IN GENERAL.—Subsection (d) of section 119 of division A of the Tax Relief and Health Care Act of 2006 is amended—

(1) by striking "first two taxable years" and inserting "first 4 taxable years", and

(2) by striking "January 1, 2008" and inserting "January 1, 2010".

• • *TAX RELIEF AND HEALTH CARE ACT OF 2006 ACT SEC. 119(d) AS AMENDED*————

ACT SEC. 119. AMERICAN SAMOA ECONOMIC DEVELOPMENT CREDIT.
* * *

• • *TAX RELIEF AND HEALTH CARE ACT OF 2006 ACT SEC. 119(d) AS AMENDED*——

(d) APPLICATION OF SECTION.—Notwithstanding section 30A(h) or section 936(j) of such Code, this section (and so much of section 30A and section 936 of such Code as relates to this section) shall apply to the *first 4 taxable years* of a corporation to which subsection (a) applies which begin after December 31, 2005, and before *January 1, 2010*.

(b) EFFECTIVE DATE.—The amendments made by this section shall apply to taxable years beginning after December 31, 2007.

* * *

[CCH Explanation at ¶430. Committee Reports at ¶10,490.]

[¶7156] ACT SEC. 319. EXTENSION OF WORK OPPORTUNITY TAX CREDIT FOR HURRICANE KATRINA EMPLOYEES.

(a) IN GENERAL.—Paragraph (1) of section 201(b) of the Katrina Emergency Tax Relief Act of 2005 is amended by striking "2-year" and inserting "4-year".

• • *KATRINA EMERGENCY TAX RELIEF ACT OF 2005 ACT SEC. 201(b)(1) AS AMENDED*——

ACT SEC. 201. WORK OPPORTUNITY TAX CREDIT FOR HURRICANE KATRINA EMPLOYEES.

* * *

(b) HURRICANE KATRINA EMPLOYEE .—For purposes of this section, the term "Hurricane Katrina employee" means—

(1) any individual who on August 28, 2005, had a principal place of abode in the core disaster area and who is hired during the *4-year* period beginning on such date for a position the principal place of employment of which is located in the core disaster area, and

* * *

(b) EFFECTIVE DATE.—The amendment made by subsection (a) shall apply to individuals hired after August 27, 2007.

* * *

[CCH Explanation at ¶635. Committee Reports at ¶10,570.]

[¶7159] ACT SEC. 325. EXTENSION AND MODIFICATION OF DUTY SUSPENSION ON WOOL PRODUCTS; WOOL RESEARCH FUND; WOOL DUTY REFUNDS.

(a) EXTENSION OF TEMPORARY DUTY REDUCTIONS.—Each of the following headings of the Harmonized Tariff Schedule of the United States is amended by striking the date in the effective period column and inserting "12/31/2014":

(1) Heading 9902.51.11 (relating to fabrics of worsted wool).

(2) Heading 9902.51.13 (relating to yarn of combed wool).

(3) Heading 9902.51.14 (relating to wool fiber, waste, garnetted stock, combed wool, or wool top).

(4) Heading 9902.51.15 (relating to fabrics of combed wool).

(5) Heading 9902.51.16 (relating to fabrics of combed wool).

(b) EXTENSION OF DUTY REFUNDS AND WOOL RESEARCH TRUST FUND.—

(1) IN GENERAL.—Section 4002(c) of the Wool Suit and Textile Trade Extension Act of 2004 (Public Law 108-429; 118 Stat. 2603) is amended—

(A) in paragraph (3)(C), by striking "2010" and inserting "2015"; and

(B) in paragraph (6)(A), by striking "through 2009" and inserting "through 2014".

(2) SUNSET.— Section 506(f) of the Trade and Development Act of 2000 (Public 106-200; 114 Stat. 303 (7 U.S.C. 7101 note)) is amended by striking "2010" and inserting "2015".

* * *

TITLE V—ADDITIONAL TAX RELIEF AND OTHER TAX PROVISIONS

Subtitle A—General Provisions
* * *

[¶7162] ACT SEC. 504. INCOME AVERAGING FOR AMOUNTS RECEIVED IN CONNECTION WITH THE EXXON VALDEZ LITIGATION.

(a) INCOME AVERAGING OF AMOUNTS RECEIVED FROM THE EXXON VALDEZ LITIGATION.—For purposes of section 1301 of the Internal Revenue Code of 1986—

(1) any qualified taxpayer who receives any qualified settlement income in any taxable year shall be treated as engaged in a fishing business (determined without regard to the commercial nature of the business), and

(2) such qualified settlement income shall be treated as income attributable to such a fishing business for such taxable year.

(b) CONTRIBUTIONS OF AMOUNTS RECEIVED TO RETIREMENT ACCOUNTS.—

(1) IN GENERAL.—Any qualified taxpayer who receives qualified settlement income during the taxable year may, at any time before the end of the taxable year in which such income was received, make one or more contributions to an eligible retirement plan of which such qualified taxpayer is a beneficiary in an aggregate amount not to exceed the lesser of—

(A) $100,000 (reduced by the amount of qualified settlement income contributed to an eligible retirement plan in prior taxable years pursuant to this subsection), or

(B) the amount of qualified settlement income received by the individual during the taxable year.

(2) TIME WHEN CONTRIBUTIONS DEEMED MADE.—For purposes of paragraph (1), a qualified taxpayer shall be deemed to have made a contribution to an eligible retirement plan on the last day of the taxable year in which such income is received if the contribution is made on account of such taxable year and is made not later than the time prescribed by law for filing the return for such taxable year (not including extensions thereof).

(3) TREATMENT OF CONTRIBUTIONS TO ELIGIBLE RETIREMENT PLANS.—For purposes of the Internal Revenue Code of 1986, if a contribution is made pursuant to paragraph (1) with respect to qualified settlement income, then—

(A) except as provided in paragraph (4)—

(i) to the extent of such contribution, the qualified settlement income shall not be included in taxable income, and

(ii) for purposes of section 72 of such Code, such contribution shall not be considered to be investment in the contract,

(B) the qualified taxpayer shall, to the extent of the amount of the contribution, be treated—

(i) as having received the qualified settlement income—

(I) in the case of a contribution to an individual retirement plan (as defined under section 7701(a)(37) of such Code), in a distribution described in section 408(d)(3) of such Code, and

(II) in the case of any other eligible retirement plan, in an eligible rollover distribution (as defined under section 402(f)(2) of such Code), and

(ii) as having transferred the amount to the eligible retirement plan in a direct trustee to trustee transfer within 60 days of the distribution,

(C) section 408(d)(3)(B) of the Internal Revenue Code of 1986 shall not apply with respect to amounts treated as a rollover under this paragraph, and

(D) section 408A(c)(3)(B) of the Internal Revenue Code of 1986 shall not apply with respect to amounts contributed to a Roth IRA (as defined under section 408A(b) of such Code) or a designated Roth contribution to an applicable retirement plan (within the meaning of section 402A of such Code) under this paragraph.

(4) SPECIAL RULE FOR ROTH IRAS AND ROTH 401(k)S.—For purposes of the Internal Revenue Code of 1986, if a contribution is made pursuant to paragraph (1) with respect to qualified settlement income to a Roth IRA (as defined under section 408A(b) of such Code) or as a designated Roth contribution to an applicable retirement plan (within the meaning of section 402A of such Code), then—

(A) the qualified settlement income shall be includible in taxable income, and

(B) for purposes of section 72 of such Code, such contribution shall be considered to be investment in the contract.

(5) ELIGIBLE RETIREMENT PLAN.—For purpose of this subsection, the term "eligible retirement plan" has the meaning given such term under section 402(c)(8)(B) of the Internal Revenue Code of 1986.

(c) TREATMENT OF QUALIFIED SETTLEMENT INCOME UNDER EMPLOYMENT TAXES.—

(1) SECA.—For purposes of chapter 2 of the Internal Revenue Code of 1986 and section 211 of the Social Security Act, no portion of qualified settlement income received by a qualified taxpayer shall be treated as self-employment income.

(2) FICA.—For purposes of chapter 21 of the Internal Revenue Code of 1986 and section 209 of the Social Security Act, no portion of qualified settlement income received by a qualified taxpayer shall be treated as wages.

(d) QUALIFIED TAXPAYER.—For purposes of this section, the term "qualified taxpayer" means—

(1) any individual who is a plaintiff in the civil action In re Exxon Valdez, No. 89-095-CV (HRH) (Consolidated) (D. Alaska); or

(2) any individual who is a beneficiary of the estate of such a plaintiff who—

(A) acquired the right to receive qualified settlement income from that plaintiff; and

(B) was the spouse or an immediate relative of that plaintiff.

(e) QUALIFIED SETTLEMENT INCOME.—For purposes of this section, the term "qualified settlement income" means any interest and punitive damage awards which are—

(1) otherwise includible in taxable income, and

(2) received (whether as lump sums or periodic payments) in connection with the civil action In re Exxon Valdez, No. 89-095-CV (HRH) (Consolidated) (D. Alaska) (whether pre- or post-judgment and whether related to a settlement or judgment).

* * *

[CCH Explanation at ¶ 750.]

Subtitle B—Paul Wellstone and Pete Domenici Mental Health Parity and Addiction Equity Act of 2008

[¶ 7165] ACT SEC. 511. SHORT TITLE.

This subtitle may be cited as the "Paul Wellstone and Pete Domenici Mental Health Parity and Addiction Equity Act of 2008".

[¶ 7168] ACT SEC. 512. MENTAL HEALTH PARITY.

(a) AMENDMENTS TO ERISA.—Section 712 of the Employee Retirement Income Security Act of 1974 (29 U.S.C. 1185a) is amended—

(1) in subsection (a), by adding at the end the following:

"(3) FINANCIAL REQUIREMENTS AND TREATMENT LIMITATIONS.—

"(A) IN GENERAL.—In the case of a group health plan (or health insurance coverage offered in connection with such a plan) that provides both medical and surgical benefits and mental health or substance use disorder benefits, such plan or coverage shall ensure that—

"(i) the financial requirements applicable to such mental health or substance use disorder benefits are no more restrictive than the predominant financial requirements applied to substantially all medical and surgical benefits covered by the plan (or coverage), and there are no separate cost sharing requirements that are applicable only with respect to mental health or substance use disorder benefits; and

"(ii) the treatment limitations applicable to such mental health or substance use disorder benefits are no more restrictive than the predominant treatment limitations applied to substantially all medical and surgical benefits covered by the plan (or coverage) and there are no separate treatment limitations that are applicable only with respect to mental health or substance use disorder benefits.

"(B) DEFINITIONS.—In this paragraph:

"(i) FINANCIAL REQUIREMENT.—The term 'financial requirement' includes deductibles, copayments, coinsurance, and out-of-pocket expenses, but excludes an aggregate lifetime limit and an annual limit subject to paragraphs (1) and (2),

"(ii) PREDOMINANT.—A financial requirement or treatment limit is considered to be predominant if it is the most common or frequent of such type of limit or requirement.

"(iii) TREATMENT LIMITATION.—The term 'treatment limitation' includes limits on the frequency of treatment, number of visits, days of coverage, or other similar limits on the scope or duration of treatment.

"(4) AVAILABILITY OF PLAN INFORMATION.—The criteria for medical necessity determinations made under the plan with respect to mental health or substance use disorder benefits (or the health insurance coverage offered in connection with the plan with respect to such benefits) shall be made available by the plan administrator (or the health insurance issuer offering such coverage) in accordance with regulations to any current or potential participant, beneficiary, or contracting provider upon request. The reason for any denial under the plan (or coverage) of reimbursement or payment for services with respect to mental health or substance use disorder benefits in the case of any participant or beneficiary shall, on request or as otherwise required, be made available by the plan administrator (or the health insurance issuer offering such coverage) to the participant or beneficiary in accordance with regulations.

"(5) OUT-OF-NETWORK PROVIDERS.—In the case of a plan or coverage that provides both medical and surgical benefits and mental health or substance use disorder benefits, if the plan or coverage provides coverage for medical or surgical benefits provided by out-of-network providers, the plan or coverage shall provide coverage for mental health or substance use disorder benefits provided by out-of-network providers in a manner that is consistent with the requirements of this section.";

(2) in subsection (b), by amending paragraph (2) to read as follows:

"(2) in the case of a group health plan (or health insurance coverage offered in connection with such a plan) that provides mental health or substance use disorder benefits, as affecting the terms and conditions of the plan or coverage relating to such benefits under the plan or coverage, except as provided in subsection (a).";

(3) in subsection (c)—

(A) in paragraph (1)(B)—

(i) by inserting "(or 1 in the case of an employer residing in a State that permits small groups to include a single individual)" after "at least 2" the first place that such appears; and

(ii) by striking "and who employs at least 2 employees on the first day of the plan year"; and

(B) by striking paragraph (2) and inserting the following:

"(2) COST EXEMPTION.—

"(A) IN GENERAL.—With respect to a group health plan (or health insurance coverage offered in connection with such a plan), if the application of this section to such plan (or coverage) results in an increase for the plan year involved of the actual total costs of coverage with respect to medical and surgical benefits and mental health and substance use disorder benefits under the plan (as determined and certified under subparagraph (C)) by an amount that exceeds the applicable percentage described in subparagraph (B) of the actual total plan costs, the provisions of this section shall not apply to such plan (or coverage) during the following plan year, and such exemption shall apply to the plan (or coverage) for 1 plan year. An employer may elect to continue to apply mental health and substance use disorder parity pursuant to this section with respect to the group health plan (or coverage) involved regardless of any increase in total costs.

"(B) APPLICABLE PERCENTAGE.—With respect to a plan (or coverage), the applicable percentage described in this subparagraph shall be—

"(i) 2 percent in the case of the first plan year in which this section is applied; and

"(ii) 1 percent in the case of each subsequent plan year.

"(C) DETERMINATIONS BY ACTUARIES.—Determinations as to increases in actual costs under a plan (or coverage) for purposes of this section shall be made and certified by a qualified and licensed actuary who is a member in good standing of the American Academy of Actuaries. All such determinations shall be in a written report prepared by the actuary. The report, and all underlying documentation relied upon by the actuary, shall be maintained by the group health plan or health insurance issuer for a period of 6 years following the notification made under subparagraph (E).

"(D) 6-MONTH DETERMINATIONS.—If a group health plan (or a health insurance issuer offering coverage in connection with a group health plan) seeks an exemption under this paragraph, determinations under subparagraph (A) shall be made after such plan (or coverage) has complied with this section for the first 6 months of the plan year involved.

"(E) NOTIFICATION.—

"(i) IN GENERAL.—A group health plan (or a health insurance issuer offering coverage in connection with a group health plan) that, based upon a certification described under subparagraph (C), qualifies for an exemption under this paragraph, and elects to implement the exemption, shall promptly notify the Secretary, the appropriate State agencies, and participants and beneficiaries in the plan of such election.

"(ii) REQUIREMENT.—A notification to the Secretary under clause (i) shall include—

"(I) a description of the number of covered lives under the plan (or coverage) involved at the time of the notification, and as applicable, at the time of any prior election of the cost-exemption under this paragraph by such plan (or coverage);

"(II) for both the plan year upon which a cost exemption is sought and the year prior, a description of the actual total costs of coverage with respect to medical and surgical benefits and mental health and substance use disorder benefits under the plan; and

"(III) for both the plan year upon which a cost exemption is sought and the year prior, the actual total costs of coverage with respect to mental health and substance use disorder benefits under the plan.

"(iii) CONFIDENTIALITY.—A notification to the Secretary under clause (i) shall be confidential. The Secretary shall make available, upon request and on not more than an annual basis, an anonymous itemization of such notifications, that includes—

"(I) a breakdown of States by the size and type of employers submitting such notification; and

"(II) a summary of the data received under clause (ii).

"(F) AUDITS BY APPROPRIATE AGENCIES.—To determine compliance with this paragraph, the Secretary may audit the books and records of a group health plan or health insurance issuer relating to an exemption, including any actuarial reports prepared pursuant to subparagraph (C), during the 6 year period following the notification of such exemption under subparagraph (E). A State agency receiving a notification under subparagraph (E) may also conduct such an audit with respect to an exemption covered by such notification.";

(4) in subsection (e), by striking paragraph (4) and inserting the following:

"(4) MENTAL HEALTH BENEFITS.—The term "mental health benefits" means benefits with respect to services for mental health conditions, as defined under the terms of the plan and in accordance with applicable Federal and State law.

"(5) SUBSTANCE USE DISORDER BENEFITS.—The term 'substance use disorder benefits' means benefits with respect to services for substance use disorders, as defined under the terms of the plan and in accordance with applicable Federal and State law."

(5) by striking subsection (f);

(6) by inserting after subsection (e) the following:

"(f) SECRETARY REPORT.—The Secretary shall, by January 1, 2012, and every two years thereafter, submit to the appropriate committees of Congress a report on compliance of group health plans (and health insurance coverage offered in connection with such plans) with the requirements of this section. Such report shall include the results of any surveys or audits on compliance of group health plans (and health insurance coverage offered in connection with such plans) with such requirements and an analysis of the reasons for any failures to comply.

"(g) NOTICE AND ASSISTANCE.—The Secretary, in cooperation with the Secretaries of Health and Human Services and Treasury, as appropriate, shall publish and widely disseminate guidance and information for group health plans, participants and beneficiaries, applicable State and local regulatory bodies, and the National Association of Insurance Commissioners concerning the requirements of this section and shall provide assistance concerning such requirements and the continued operation of applicable State law. Such guidance and information shall inform participants and beneficiaries of how they may obtain assistance under this section, including, where appropriate, assistance from State consumer and insurance agencies.";

(7) by striking "mental health benefits" and inserting "mental health and substance use disorder benefits" each place it appears in subsections (a)(1)(B)(i), (a)(1)(C), (a)(2)(B)(i), and (a)(2)(C); and

(8) by striking "mental health benefits" and inserting "mental health or substance use disorder benefits" each place it appears (other than in any provision amended by the previous paragraph).

(b) AMENDMENTS TO PUBLIC HEALTH SERVICE ACT.—Section 2705 of the Public Health Service Act (42 U.S.C. 300gg-5) is amended—

(1) in subsection (a), by adding at the end the following:

"(3) FINANCIAL REQUIREMENTS AND TREATMENT LIMITATIONS.—

"(A) IN GENERAL.—In the case of a group health plan (or health insurance coverage offered in connection with such a plan) that provides both medical and surgical benefits and mental health or substance use disorder benefits, such plan or coverage shall ensure that—

"(i) the financial requirements applicable to such mental health or substance use disorder benefits are no more restrictive than the predominant financial requirements applied to substantially all medical and surgical benefits covered by the plan (or coverage), and there are no separate cost sharing requirements that are applicable only with respect to mental health or substance use disorder benefits; and

"(ii) the treatment limitations applicable to such mental health or substance use disorder benefits are no more restrictive than the predominant treatment limitations applied to substantially all medical and surgical benefits covered by the plan (or coverage) and there are no separate treatment limitations that are applicable only with respect to mental health or substance use disorder benefits.

"(B) DEFINITIONS.—In this paragraph:

"(i) FINANCIAL REQUIREMENT.—The term 'financial requirement' includes deductibles, copayments, coinsurance, and out-of-pocket expenses, but excludes an aggregate lifetime limit and an annual limit subject to paragraphs (1) and (2).

"(ii) PREDOMINANT.—A financial requirement or treatment limit is considered to be predominant if it is the most common or frequent of such type of limit or requirement.

"(iii) TREATMENT LIMITATION.—The term 'treatment limitation' includes limits on the frequency of treatment, number of visits, days of coverage, or other similar limits on the scope or duration of treatment.

"(4) AVAILABILITY OF PLAN INFORMATION.—The criteria for medical necessity determinations made under the plan with respect to mental health or substance use disorder benefits (or the health insurance coverage offered in connection with the plan with respect to such benefits) shall be made available by the plan administrator (or the health insurance issuer offering such coverage) in accordance with regulations to any current or potential participant, beneficiary, or contracting provider upon request. The reason for any denial under the plan (or coverage) of reimbursement or payment for services with respect to mental health or substance use disorder benefits in the case of any participant or beneficiary shall, on request or as otherwise required, be made available by the plan administrator (or the health insurance issuer offering such coverage) to the participant or beneficiary in accordance with regulations.

"(5) OUT-OF-NETWORK PROVIDERS.—In the case of a plan or coverage that provides both medical and surgical benefits and mental health or substance use disorder benefits, if the plan or coverage provides coverage for medical or surgical benefits provided by out-of-network providers, the plan or coverage shall provide coverage for mental health or substance use disorder benefits provided by out-of-network providers in a manner that is consistent with the requirements of this section.";

(2) in subsection (b), by amending paragraph (2) to read as follows:

"(2) in the case of a group health plan (or health insurance coverage offered in connection with such a plan) that provides mental health or substance use disorder benefits, as affecting the terms and conditions of the plan or coverage relating to such benefits under the plan or coverage, except as provided in subsection (a).";

(3) in subsection (c)—

(A) in paragraph (1), by inserting before the period the following: "(as defined in section 2791(e)(4), except that for purposes of this paragraph such term shall include employers with 1 employee in the case of an employer residing in a State that permits small groups to include a single individual)"; and

(B) by striking paragraph (2) and inserting the following:

"(2) COST EXEMPTION.—

"(A) IN GENERAL.—With respect to a group health plan (or health insurance coverage offered in connection with such a plan), if the application of this section to such plan (or coverage) results in an increase for the plan year involved of the actual total costs of coverage with respect to medical and surgical benefits and mental health and substance use disorder benefits under the plan (as determined and certified under subparagraph (C)) by an amount that exceeds the applicable percentage described in subparagraph (B) of the actual total plan costs, the provisions of this section shall not apply to such plan (or coverage) during the following plan year, and such exemption shall apply to the plan (or coverage) for 1 plan year. An employer may elect to continue to apply mental health and substance use disorder parity pursuant to this section with respect to the group health plan (or coverage) involved regardless of any increase in total costs.

"(B) APPLICABLE PERCENTAGE.—With respect to a plan (or coverage), the applicable percentage described in this subparagraph shall be—

"(i) 2 percent in the case of the first plan year in which this section is applied; and

"(ii) 1 percent in the case of each subsequent plan year.

"(C) DETERMINATIONS BY ACTUARIES.—Determinations as to increases in actual costs under a plan (or coverage) for purposes of this section shall be made and certified by a qualified and licensed actuary who is a member in good standing of the American Academy of Actuaries. All such determinations shall be in a written report prepared by the actuary. The report, and all underlying documentation relied upon by the actuary, shall be maintained by the group health plan or health insurance issuer for a period of 6 years following the notification made under subparagraph (E).

"(D) 6-MONTH DETERMINATIONS.—If a group health plan (or a health insurance issuer offering coverage in connection with a group health plan) seeks an exemption under this paragraph, determinations under subparagraph (A) shall be made after such plan (or coverage) has complied with this section for the first 6 months of the plan year involved.

"(E) NOTIFICATION.—

"(i) IN GENERAL.—A group health plan (or a health insurance issuer offering coverage in connection with a group health plan) that, based upon a certification described under subparagraph (C), qualifies for an exemption under this paragraph, and elects to implement the exemption, shall promptly notify the Secretary, the appropriate State agencies, and participants and beneficiaries in the plan of such election.

"(ii) REQUIREMENT.—A notification to the Secretary under clause (i) shall include—

"(I) a description of the number of covered lives under the plan (or coverage) involved at the time of the notification, and as applicable, at the time of any prior election of the cost-exemption under this paragraph by such plan (or coverage);

"(II) for both the plan year upon which a cost exemption is sought and the year prior, a description of the actual total costs of coverage with respect to medical and surgical benefits and mental health and substance use disorder benefits under the plan; and

"(III) for both the plan year upon which a cost exemption is sought and the year prior, the actual total costs of coverage with respect to mental health and substance use disorder benefits under the plan.

"(iii) CONFIDENTIALITY.—A notification to the Secretary under clause (i) shall be confidential. The Secretary shall make available, upon request and on not more than an annual basis, an anonymous itemization of such notifications, that includes—

"(I) a breakdown of States by the size and type of employers submitting such notification; and

"(II) a summary of the data received under clause (ii).

"(F) AUDITS BY APPROPRIATE AGENCIES.—To determine compliance with this paragraph, the Secretary may audit the books and records of a group health plan or health insurance issuer relating to an exemption, including any actuarial reports prepared pursuant to subparagraph (C), during the 6 year period following the notification of such exemption under subparagraph (E). A State agency receiving a notification under subparagraph (E) may also conduct such an audit with respect to an exemption covered by such notification.";

(4) in subsection (e), by striking paragraph (4) and inserting the following:

"(4) MENTAL HEALTH BENEFITS.—The term "mental health benefits" means benefits with respect to services for mental health conditions, as defined under the terms of the plan and in accordance with applicable Federal and State law.

"(5) SUBSTANCE USE DISORDER BENEFITS.—The term 'substance use disorder benefits' means benefits with respect to services for substance use disorders, as defined under the terms of the plan and in accordance with applicable Federal and State law.";

(5) by striking subsection (f);

(6) by striking "mental health benefits" and inserting "mental health and substance use disorder benefits" each place it appears in subsections (a)(1)(B)(i), (a)(1)(C), (a)(2)(B)(i), and (a)(2)(C); and

(7) by striking "mental health benefits" and inserting "mental health or substance use disorder benefits" each place it appears (other than in any provision amended by the previous paragraph).

* * *

(d) REGULATIONS.—Not later than 1 year after the date of enactment of this Act, the Secretaries of Labor, Health and Human Services, and the Treasury shall issue regulations to carry out the amendments made by subsections (a), (b), and (c), respectively.

(e) EFFECTIVE DATE.—

(1) IN GENERAL.—The amendments made by this section shall apply with respect to group health plans for plan years beginning after the date that is 1 year after the date of enactment of this Act, regardless of whether regulations have been issued to carry out such amendments by such effective date, except that the amendments made by subsections (a)(5), (b)(5), and (c)(5), relating to striking of certain sunset provisions, shall take effect on January 1, 2009.

(2) SPECIAL RULE FOR COLLECTIVE BARGAINING AGREEMENTS.—In the case of a group health plan maintained pursuant to one or more collective bargaining agreements between employee representatives and one or more employers ratified before the date of the enactment of this Act, the amendments made by this section shall not apply to plan years beginning before the later of—

(A) the date on which the last of the collective bargaining agreements relating to the plan terminates (determined without regard to any extension thereof agreed to after the date of the enactment of this Act), or

(B) January 1, 2009.

For purposes of subparagraph (A), any plan amendment made pursuant to a collective bargaining agreement relating to the plan which amends the plan solely to conform to any requirement added by this section shall not be treated as a termination of such collective bargaining agreement.

(f) ASSURING COORDINATION.—The Secretary of Health and Human Services, the Secretary of Labor, and the Secretary of the Treasury may ensure, through the execution or revision of an interagency memorandum of understanding among such Secretaries, that—

(1) regulations, rulings, and interpretations issued by such Secretaries relating to the same matter over which two or more such Secretaries have responsibility under this section (and the amendments made by this section) are administered so as to have the same effect at all times; and

(2) coordination of policies relating to enforcing the same requirements through such Secretaries in order to have a coordinated enforcement strategy that avoids duplication of enforcement efforts and assigns priorities in enforcement.

(g) CONFORMING CLERICAL AMENDMENTS.—

(1) ERISA HEADING—

(A) IN GENERAL.—The heading of section 712 of the Employee Retirement Income Security Act of 1974 is amended to read as follows:

"SEC. 712. PARITY IN MENTAL HEALTH AND SUBSTANCE USE DISORDER BENEFITS.".

(B) CLERICAL AMENDMENT.—The table of contents in section 1 of such Act is amended by striking the item relating to section 712 and inserting the following new item:

"Sec. 712. Parity in mental health and substance use disorder benefits.".

(2) PHSA HEADING.—The heading of section 2705 of the Public Health Service Act is amended to read as follows:

"SEC. 2705. PARITY IN MENTAL HEALTH AND SUBSTANCE USE DISORDER BENEFITS.".

(h) GAO STUDY ON COVERAGE AND EXCLUSION OF MENTAL HEALTH AND SUBSTANCE USE DISORDER DIAGNOSES.—

* * *

(1) IN GENERAL.—The Comptroller General of the United States shall conduct a study that analyzes the specific rates, patterns, and trends in coverage and exclusion of specific mental health and substance use disorder diagnoses by health plans and health insurance. The study shall include an analysis of—

(A) specific coverage rates for all mental health conditions and substance use disorders;

(B) which diagnoses are most commonly covered or excluded;

(C) whether implementation of this Act has affected trends in coverage or exclusion of such diagnoses; and

(D) the impact of covering or excluding specific diagnoses on participants' and enrollees' health, their health care coverage, and the costs of delivering health care.

(2) REPORTS.—Not later than 3 years after the date of the enactment of this Act, and 2 years after the date of submission of the first report under this paragraph, the Comptroller General shall submit to Congress a report on the results of the study conducted under paragraph (1).

[CCH Explanation at ¶880.]

TITLE VI—OTHER PROVISIONS

[¶7171] ACT SEC. 601. SECURE RURAL SCHOOLS AND COMMUNITY SELF-DETERMINATION PROGRAM.

(a) REAUTHORIZATION OF THE SECURE RURAL SCHOOLS AND COMMUNITY SELF-DETERMINATION ACT OF 2000.—The Secure Rural Schools and Community Self-Determination Act of 2000 (16 U.S.C. 500 note; Public Law 106-393) is amended by striking sections 1 through 403 and inserting the following:

"SEC. 1. SHORT TITLE.

"This Act may be cited as the 'Secure Rural Schools and Community Self-Determination Act of 2000'.

"SEC. 2. PURPOSES.

"The purposes of this Act are—

"(1) to stabilize and transition payments to counties to provide funding for schools and roads that supplements other available funds;

"(2) to make additional investments in, and create additional employment opportunities through, projects that—

"(A)(i) improve the maintenance of existing infrastructure;

"(ii) implement stewardship objectives that enhance forest ecosystems; and

"(iii) restore and improve land health and water quality;

"(B) enjoy broad-based support; and

"(C) have objectives that may include—

"(i) road, trail, and infrastructure maintenance or obliteration;

"(ii) soil productivity improvement;

"(iii) improvements in forest ecosystem health;

"(iv) watershed restoration and maintenance;

"(v) the restoration, maintenance, and improvement of wildlife and fish habitat;

"(vi) the control of noxious and exotic weeds; and

"(vii) the reestablishment of native species; and

"(3) to improve cooperative relationships among—

"(A) the people that use and care for Federal land; and

"(B) the agencies that manage the Federal land.

"SEC. 3. DEFINITIONS.

"In this Act:

"(1) ADJUSTED SHARE.—The term "adjusted share" means the number equal to the quotient obtained by dividing—

"(A) the number equal to the quotient obtained by dividing—

"(i) the base share for the eligible county; by

"(ii) the income adjustment for the eligible county; by

"(B) the number equal to the sum of the quotients obtained under subparagraph (A) and paragraph (8)(A) for all eligible counties.

"(2) BASE SHARE.—The term "base share" means the number equal to the average of—

"(A) the quotient obtained by dividing—

"(i) the number of acres of Federal land described in paragraph (7)(A) in each eligible county; by

"(ii) the total number acres of Federal land in all eligible counties in all eligible States; and

"(B) the quotient obtained by dividing—

"(i) the amount equal to the average of the 3 highest 25-percent payments and safety net payments made to each eligible State for each eligible county during the eligibility period; by

"(ii) the amount equal to the sum of the amounts calculated under clause (i) and paragraph (9)(B)(i) for all eligible counties in all eligible States during the eligibility period.

"(3) COUNTY PAYMENT.—The term 'county payment' means the payment for an eligible county calculated under section 101(b).

"(4) ELIGIBLE COUNTY.—The term 'eligible county' means any county that—

"(A) contains Federal land (as defined in paragraph (7)); and

"(B) elects to receive a share of the State payment or the county payment under section 102(b).

"(5) ELIGIBILITY PERIOD.—The term 'eligibility period' means fiscal year 1986 through fiscal year 1999.

"(6) ELIGIBLE STATE.—The term 'eligible State' means a State or territory of the United States that received a 25-percent payment for 1 or more fiscal years of the eligibility period.

"(7) FEDERAL LAND.—The term 'Federal land' means—

"(A) land within the National Forest System, as defined in section 11(a) of the Forest and Rangeland Renewable Resources Planning Act of 1974 (16 U.S.C. 1609(a)) exclusive of the National Grasslands and land utilization projects designated as National Grasslands administered pursuant to the Act of July 22, 1937 (7 U.S.C. 1010-1012); and

"(B) such portions of the revested Oregon and California Railroad and reconveyed Coos Bay Wagon Road grant land as are or may hereafter come under the jurisdiction of the Department of the Interior, which have heretofore or may hereafter be classified as timberlands, and power-site land valuable for timber, that shall be managed, except as provided in the former section 3 of the Act of August 28, 1937 (50 Stat. 875; 43 U.S.C. 1181c), for permanent forest production.

"(8) 50-PERCENT ADJUSTED SHARE.—The term '50-percent adjusted share' means the number equal to the quotient obtained by dividing—

"(A) the number equal to the quotient obtained by dividing—

"(i) the 50-percent base share for the eligible county; by

"(ii) the income adjustment for the eligible county; by

"(B) the number equal to the sum of the quotients obtained under subparagraph (A) and paragraph (1)(A) for all eligible counties.

"(9) 50-PERCENT BASE SHARE.—The term '50-percent base share' means the number equal to the average of—

"(A) the quotient obtained by dividing—

"(i) the number of acres of Federal land described in paragraph (7)(B) in each eligible county; by

"(ii) the total number acres of Federal land in all eligible counties in all eligible States; and

"(B) the quotient obtained by dividing—

"(i) the amount equal to the average of the 3 highest 50-percent payments made to each eligible county during the eligibility period; by

"(ii) the amount equal to the sum of the amounts calculated under clause (i) and paragraph (2)(B)(i) for all eligible counties in all eligible States during the eligibility period.

"(10) 50-PERCENT PAYMENT.—The term '50-percent payment' means the payment that is the sum of the 50-percent share otherwise paid to a county pursuant to title II of the Act of August 28, 1937 (chapter 876; 50 Stat. 875; 43 U.S.C. 1181f), and the payment made to a county pursuant to the Act of May 24, 1939 (chapter 144; 53 Stat. 753; 43 U.S.C. 1181f-1 et seq.).

"(11) FULL FUNDING AMOUNT.—The term 'full funding amount' means—

"(A) $500,000,000 for fiscal year 2008; and

"(B) for fiscal year 2009 and each fiscal year thereafter, the amount that is equal to 90 percent of the full funding amount for the preceding fiscal year.

"(12) INCOME ADJUSTMENT.—The term 'income adjustment' means the square of the quotient obtained by dividing—

"(A) the per capita personal income for each eligible county; by

"(B) the median per capita personal income of all eligible counties.

"(13) PER CAPITA PERSONAL INCOME.—The term 'per capita personal income' means the most recent per capita personal income data, as determined by the Bureau of Economic Analysis.

"(14) SAFETY NET PAYMENTS.—The term 'safety net payments' means the special payment amounts paid to States and counties required by section 13982 or 13983 of the Omnibus Budget Reconciliation Act of 1993 (Public Law 103-66; 16 U.S.C. 500 note; 43 U.S.C. 1181f note).

"(15) SECRETARY CONCERNED.—The term 'Secretary concerned' means—

"(A) the Secretary of Agriculture or the designee of the Secretary of Agriculture with respect to the Federal land described in paragraph (7)(A); and

"(B) the Secretary of the Interior or the designee of the Secretary of the Interior with respect to the Federal land described in paragraph (7)(B).

"(16) STATE PAYMENT.—The term 'State payment' means the payment for an eligible State calculated under section 101(a).

"(17) 25-PERCENT PAYMENT.—The term '25-percent payment' means the payment to States required by the sixth paragraph under the heading of 'FOREST SERVICE' in the Act of May 23, 1908 (35 Stat. 260; 16 U.S.C. 500), and section 13 of the Act of March 1, 1911 (36 Stat. 963; 16 U.S.C. 500).

"TITLE I—SECURE PAYMENTS FOR STATES AND COUNTIES CONTAINING FEDERAL LAND

"SEC. 101. SECURE PAYMENTS FOR STATES CONTAINING FEDERAL LAND.

"(a) STATE PAYMENT.—For each of fiscal years 2008 through 2011, the Secretary of Agriculture shall calculate for each eligible State an amount equal to the sum of the products obtained by multiplying—

"(1) the adjusted share for each eligible county within the eligible State; by

"(2) the full funding amount for the fiscal year.

"(b) COUNTY PAYMENT.—For each of fiscal years 2008 through 2011, the Secretary of the Interior shall calculate for each eligible county that received a 50-percent payment during the eligibility period an amount equal to the product obtained by multiplying—

"(1) the 50-percent adjusted share for the eligible county; by

"(2) the full funding amount for the fiscal year.

"SEC. 102. PAYMENTS TO STATES AND COUNTIES.

"(a) PAYMENT AMOUNTS—Except as provided in section 103, the Secretary of the Treasury shall pay to—

"(1) a State or territory of the United States an amount equal to the sum of the amounts elected under subsection (b) by each county within the State or territory for—

"(A) if the county is eligible for the 25-percent payment, the share of the 25-percent payment; or

"(B) the share of the State payment of the eligible county; and

"(2) a county an amount equal to the amount elected under subsection (b) by each county for—

"(A) if the county is eligible for the 50-percent payment, the 50-percent payment; or

"(B) the county payment for the eligible county.

"(b) ELECTION TO RECEIVE PAYMENT AMOUNT.—

"(1) ELECTION; SUBMISSION OF RESULTS.—

"(A) IN GENERAL.—The election to receive a share of the State payment, the county payment, a share of the State payment and the county payment, a share of the 25-percent payment, the 50-percent payment, or a share of the 25-percent payment and the 50-percent payment, as applicable, shall be made at the discretion of each affected county by August 1, 2008 (or as soon thereafter as the Secretary concerned determines is practicable), and August 1 of each second fiscal year thereafter, in accordance with paragraph (2), and transmitted to the Secretary concerned by the Governor of each eligible State.

"(B) FAILURE TO TRANSMIT.—If an election for an affected county is not transmitted to the Secretary concerned by the date specified under subparagraph (A), the affected county shall be considered to have elected to receive a share of the State payment, the county payment, or a share of the State payment and the county payment, as applicable.

"(2) DURATION OF ELECTION.—

"(A) IN GENERAL.—A county election to receive a share of the 25-percent payment or 50-percent payment, as applicable, shall be effective for 2 fiscal years.

"(B) FULL FUNDING AMOUNT.—If a county elects to receive a share of the State payment or the county payment, the election shall be effective for all subsequent fiscal years through fiscal year 2011.

"(3) SOURCE OF PAYMENT AMOUNTS.—The payment to an eligible State or eligible county under this section for a fiscal year shall be derived from—

"(A) any amounts that are appropriated to carry out this Act;

"(B) any revenues, fees, penalties, or miscellaneous receipts, exclusive of deposits to any relevant trust fund, special account, or permanent operating funds, received by the Federal Government from activities by the Bureau of Land Management or the Forest Service on the applicable Federal land; and

"(C) to the extent of any shortfall, out of any amounts in the Treasury of the United States not otherwise appropriated.

"(c) DISTRIBUTION AND EXPENDITURE OF PAYMENTS.—

"(1) DISTRIBUTION METHOD.—A State that receives a payment under subsection (a) for Federal land described in section 3(7)(A) shall distribute the appropriate payment amount among the appropriate counties in the State in accordance with—

"(A) the Act of May 23, 1908 (16 U.S.C. 500); and

"(B) section 13 of the Act of March 1, 1911 (36 Stat. 963; 16 U.S.C. 500).

"(2) EXPENDITURE PURPOSES.—Subject to subsection (d), payments received by a State under subsection (a) and distributed to counties in accordance with paragraph (1) shall be expended as required by the laws referred to in paragraph (1).

"(d) EXPENDITURE RULES FOR ELIGIBLE COUNTIES.—

"(1) ALLOCATIONS.—

"(A) USE OF PORTION IN SAME MANNER AS 25-PERCENT PAYMENT OR 50-PERCENT PAYMENT, AS APPLICABLE.—Except as provided in paragraph (3)(B), if an eligible county elects to receive its share of the State payment or the county payment, not less than 80 percent, but not more than 85 percent, of the funds shall be expended in the same manner in which the 25-percent payments or 50-percent payment, as applicable, are required to be expended.

"(B) ELECTION AS TO USE OF BALANCE.—Except as provided in subparagraph (C), an eligible county shall elect to do 1 or more of the following with the balance of any funds not expended pursuant to subparagraph (A):

"(i) Reserve any portion of the balance for projects in accordance with title II.

"(ii) Reserve not more than 7 percent of the total share for the eligible county of the State payment or the county payment for projects in accordance with title III.

"(iii) Return the portion of the balance not reserved under clauses (i) and (ii) to the Treasury of the United States.

"(C) COUNTIES WITH MODEST DISTRIBUTIONS.—In the case of each eligible county to which more than $100,000, but less than $350,000, is distributed for any fiscal year pursuant to either or both of paragraphs (1)(B) and (2)(B) of subsection (a), the eligible county, with respect to the balance of any funds not expended pursuant to subparagraph (A) for that fiscal year, shall—

"(i) reserve any portion of the balance for—

"(I) carrying out projects under title II;

"(II) carrying out projects under title III; or

"(III) a combination of the purposes described in subclauses (I) and (II); or

"(ii) return the portion of the balance not reserved under clause (i) to the Treasury of the United States.

"(2) DISTRIBUTION OF FUNDS.—

"(A) IN GENERAL.—Funds reserved by an eligible county under subparagraph (B)(i) or (C)(i) of paragraph (1) for carrying out projects under title II shall be deposited in a special account in the Treasury of the United States.

"(B) AVAILABILITY.—Amounts deposited under subparagraph (A) shall—

"(i) be available for expenditure by the Secretary concerned, without further appropriation; and

"(ii) remain available until expended in accordance with title II.

"(3) ELECTION.—

"(A) NOTIFICATION.—

"(i) IN GENERAL.—An eligible county shall notify the Secretary concerned of an election by the eligible county under this subsection not later than September 30, 2008 (or as soon thereafter as the Secretary concerned determines is practicable), and each September 30 thereafter for each succeeding fiscal year.

"(ii) FAILURE TO ELECT.—Except as provided in subparagraph (B), if the eligible county fails to make an election by the date specified in clause (i), the eligible county shall—

"(I) be considered to have elected to expend 85 percent of the funds in accordance with paragraph (1)(A); and

"(II) return the balance to the Treasury of the United States.

"(B) COUNTIES WITH MINOR DISTRIBUTIONS.—In the case of each eligible county to which less than $100,000 is distributed for any fiscal year pursuant to either or both of paragraphs (1)(B) and (2)(B) of subsection (a), the eligible county may elect to expend all the funds in the same manner in which the 25-percent payments or 50-percent payments, as applicable, are required to be expended.

"(e) TIME FOR PAYMENT.—The payments required under this section for a fiscal year shall be made as soon as practicable after the end of that fiscal year.

"SEC. 103. TRANSITION PAYMENTS TO STATES.

"(a) DEFINITIONS.—In this section:

"(1) ADJUSTED AMOUNT.—The term 'adjusted amount' means, with respect to a covered State—

"(A) for fiscal year 2008, 90 percent of—

"(i) the sum of the amounts paid for fiscal year 2006 under section 102(a)(2) (as in effect on September 29, 2006) for the eligible counties in the covered State that have elected under section 102(b) to receive a share of the State payment for fiscal year 2008; and

"(ii) the sum of the amounts paid for fiscal year 2006 under section 103(a)(2) (as in effect on September 29, 2006) for the eligible counties in the State of Oregon that have elected under section 102(b) to receive the county payment for fiscal year 2008;

"(B) for fiscal year 2009, 81 percent of—

"(i) the sum of the amounts paid for fiscal year 2006 under section 102(a)(2) (as in effect on September 29, 2006) for the eligible counties in the covered State that have elected under section 102(b) to receive a share of the State payment for fiscal year 2009; and

"(ii) the sum of the amounts paid for fiscal year 2006 under section 103(a)(2) (as in effect on September 29, 2006) for the eligible counties in the State of Oregon that have elected under section 102(b) to receive the county payment for fiscal year 2009; and

"(C) for fiscal year 2010, 73 percent of—

"(i) the sum of the amounts paid for fiscal year 2006 under section 102(a)(2) (as in effect on September 29, 2006) for the eligible counties in the covered State that have elected under section 102(b) to receive a share of the State payment for fiscal year 2010; and

"(ii) the sum of the amounts paid for fiscal year 2006 under section 103(a)(2) (as in effect on September 29, 2006) for the eligible counties in the State of Oregon that have elected under section 102(b) to receive the county payment for fiscal year 2010.

"(2) COVERED STATE.—The term 'covered State' means each of the States of California, Louisiana, Oregon, Pennsylvania, South Carolina, South Dakota, Texas, and Washington.

"(b) TRANSITION PAYMENTS.—For each of fiscal years 2008 through 2010, in lieu of the payment amounts that otherwise would have been made under paragraphs (1)(B) and (2)(B) of section 102(a), the Secretary of the Treasury shall pay the adjusted amount to each covered State and the eligible counties within the covered State, as applicable.

"(c) DISTRIBUTION OF ADJUSTED AMOUNT.—Except as provided in subsection (d), it is the intent of Congress that the method of distributing the payments under subsection (b) among the counties in the covered States for each of fiscal years 2008 through 2010 be in the same proportion that the payments were distributed to the eligible counties in fiscal year 2006.

"(d) DISTRIBUTION OF PAYMENTS IN CALIFORNIA.—The following payments shall be distributed among the eligible counties in the State of California in the same proportion that payments under section 102(a)(2) (as in effect on September 29, 2006) were distributed to the eligible counties for fiscal year 2006:

"(1) Payments to the State of California under subsection (b).

"(2) The shares of the eligible counties of the State payment for California under section 102 for fiscal year 2011.

"(e) TREATMENT OF PAYMENTS.—For purposes of this Act, any payment made under subsection (b) shall be considered to be a payment made under section 102(a).

"TITLE II—SPECIAL PROJECTS ON FEDERAL LAND

"SEC. 201. DEFINITIONS.

"In this title:

"(1) PARTICIPATING COUNTY.—The term 'participating county' means an eligible county that elects under section 102(d) to expend a portion of the Federal funds received under section 102 in accordance with this title.

"(2) PROJECT FUNDS.—The term 'project funds' means all funds an eligible county elects under section 102(d) to reserve for expenditure in accordance with this title.

"(3) RESOURCE ADVISORY COMMITTEE.—The term 'resource advisory committee' means—

"(A) an advisory committee established by the Secretary concerned under section 205; or

"(B) an advisory committee determined by the Secretary concerned to meet the requirements of section 205.

"(4) RESOURCE MANAGEMENT PLAN.—The term 'resource management plan' means—

"(A) a land use plan prepared by the Bureau of Land Management for units of the Federal land described in section 3(7)(B) pursuant to section 202 of the Federal Land Policy and Management Act of 1976 (43 U.S.C. 1712); or

"(B) a land and resource management plan prepared by the Forest Service for units of the National Forest System pursuant to section 6 of the Forest and Rangeland Renewable Resources Planning Act of 1974 (16 U.S.C. 1604).

"SEC. 202. GENERAL LIMITATION ON USE OF PROJECT FUNDS.

"(a) LIMITATION.—Project funds shall be expended solely on projects that meet the requirements of this title.

"(b) AUTHORIZED USES.—Project funds may be used by the Secretary concerned for the purpose of entering into and implementing cooperative agreements with willing Federal agencies, State and local governments, private and nonprofit entities, and landowners for protection, restoration, and enhancement of fish and wildlife habitat, and other resource objectives consistent with the purposes of this Act on Federal land and on non-Federal land where projects would benefit the resources on Federal land.

"SEC. 203. SUBMISSION OF PROJECT PROPOSALS.

"(a) SUBMISSION OF PROJECT PROPOSALS TO SECRETARY CONCERNED.—

"(1) PROJECTS FUNDED USING PROJECT FUNDS.—Not later than September 30 for fiscal year 2008 (or as soon thereafter as the Secretary concerned determines is practicable), and each September 30 thereafter for each succeeding fiscal year through fiscal year 2011, each resource advisory committee shall submit to the Secretary concerned a description of any projects that the resource advisory committee proposes the Secretary undertake using any project funds reserved by eligible counties in the area in which the resource advisory committee has geographic jurisdiction.

"(2) PROJECTS FUNDED USING OTHER FUNDS.—A resource advisory committee may submit to the Secretary concerned a description of any projects that the committee proposes the Secretary undertake using funds from State or local governments, or from the private sector, other than project funds and funds appropriated and otherwise available to do similar work.

"(3) JOINT PROJECTS.—Participating counties or other persons may propose to pool project funds or other funds, described in paragraph (2), and jointly propose a project or group of projects to a resource advisory committee established under section 205.

"(b) REQUIRED DESCRIPTION OF PROJECTS.—In submitting proposed projects to the Secretary concerned under subsection (a), a resource advisory committee shall include in the description of each proposed project the following information:

"(1) The purpose of the project and a description of how the project will meet the purposes of this title.

"(2) The anticipated duration of the project.

"(3) The anticipated cost of the project.

"(4) The proposed source of funding for the project, whether project funds or other funds.

"(5)(A) Expected outcomes, including how the project will meet or exceed desired ecological conditions, maintenance objectives, or stewardship objectives.

"(B) An estimate of the amount of any timber, forage, and other commodities and other economic activity, including jobs generated, if any, anticipated as part of the project.

"(6) A detailed monitoring plan, including funding needs and sources, that—

"(A) tracks and identifies the positive or negative impacts of the project, implementation, and provides for validation monitoring; and

"(B) includes an assessment of the following:

"(i) Whether or not the project met or exceeded desired ecological conditions; created local employment or training opportunities, including summer youth jobs programs such as the Youth Conservation Corps where appropriate.

"(ii) Whether the project improved the use of, or added value to, any products removed from land consistent with the purposes of this title.

"(7) An assessment that the project is to be in the public interest.

"(c) AUTHORIZED PROJECTS.—Projects proposed under subsection (a) shall be consistent with section 2.

"SEC. 204. EVALUATION AND APPROVAL OF PROJECTS BY SECRETARY CONCERNED.

"(a) CONDITIONS FOR APPROVAL OF PROPOSED PROJECT.—The Secretary concerned may make a decision to approve a project submitted by a resource advisory committee under section 203 only if the proposed project satisfies each of the following conditions:

"(1) The project complies with all applicable Federal laws (including regulations).

"(2) The project is consistent with the applicable resource management plan and with any watershed or subsequent plan developed pursuant to the resource management plan and approved by the Secretary concerned.

"(3) The project has been approved by the resource advisory committee in accordance with section 205, including the procedures issued under subsection (e) of that section.

"(4) A project description has been submitted by the resource advisory committee to the Secretary concerned in accordance with section 203.

"(5) The project will improve the maintenance of existing infrastructure, implement stewardship objectives that enhance forest ecosystems, and restore and improve land health and water quality.

"(b) ENVIRONMENTAL REVIEWS.—

"(1) REQUEST FOR PAYMENT BY COUNTY.—The Secretary concerned may request the resource advisory committee submitting a proposed project to agree to the use of project funds to pay for any environmental review, consultation, or compliance with applicable environmental laws required in connection with the project.

"(2) CONDUCT OF ENVIRONMENTAL REVIEW.—If a payment is requested under paragraph (1) and the resource advisory committee agrees to the expenditure of funds for this purpose, the Secretary concerned shall conduct environmental review, consultation, or other compliance responsibilities in accordance with Federal laws (including regulations).

"(3) EFFECT OF REFUSAL TO PAY.—

"(A) IN GENERAL.—If a resource advisory committee does not agree to the expenditure of funds under paragraph (1), the project shall be deemed withdrawn from further consideration by the Secretary concerned pursuant to this title.

"(B) EFFECT OF WITHDRAWAL.—A withdrawal under subparagraph (A) shall be deemed to be a rejection of the project for purposes of section 207(c).

"(c) DECISIONS OF SECRETARY CONCERNED.—

"(1) REJECTION OF PROJECTS.—

"(A) IN GENERAL.—A decision by the Secretary concerned to reject a proposed project shall be at the sole discretion of the Secretary concerned.

"(B) NO ADMINISTRATIVE APPEAL OR JUDICIAL REVIEW.—Notwithstanding any other provision of law, a decision by the Secretary concerned to reject a proposed project shall not be subject to administrative appeal or judicial review.

"(C) NOTICE OF REJECTION.—Not later than 30 days after the date on which the Secretary concerned makes the rejection decision, the Secretary concerned shall notify in writing the resource advisory committee that submitted the proposed project of the rejection and the reasons for rejection.

"(2) NOTICE OF PROJECT APPROVAL.—The Secretary concerned shall publish in the Federal Register notice of each project approved under subsection (a) if the notice would be required had the project originated with the Secretary.

"(d) SOURCE AND CONDUCT OF PROJECT.—Once the Secretary concerned accepts a project for review under section 203, the acceptance shall be deemed a Federal action for all purposes.

"(e) IMPLEMENTATION OF APPROVED PROJECTS.—

"(1) COOPERATION.—Notwithstanding chapter 63 of title 31, United States Code, using project funds the Secretary concerned may enter into contracts, grants, and cooperative agreements with States and local governments, private and nonprofit entities, and landowners and other persons to assist the Secretary in carrying out an approved project.

"(2) BEST VALUE CONTRACTING.—

"(A) IN GENERAL.—For any project involving a contract authorized by paragraph (1) the Secretary concerned may elect a source for performance of the contract on a best value basis.

"(B) FACTORS.—The Secretary concerned shall determine best value based on such factors as—

"(i) the technical demands and complexity of the work to be done;

"(ii)(I) the ecological objectives of the project; and

"(II) the sensitivity of the resources being treated;

"(iii) the past experience by the contractor with the type of work being done, using the type of equipment proposed for the project, and meeting or exceeding desired ecological conditions; and

"(iv) the commitment of the contractor to hiring highly qualified workers and local residents.

"(3) MERCHANTABLE TIMBER CONTRACTING PILOT PROGRAM.—

"(A) ESTABLISHMENT.—The Secretary concerned shall establish a pilot program to implement a certain percentage of approved projects involving the sale of merchantable timber using separate contracts for—

"(i) the harvesting or collection of merchantable timber; and

"(ii) the sale of the timber.

"(B) ANNUAL PERCENTAGES.—Under the pilot program, the Secretary concerned shall ensure that, on a nationwide basis, not less than the following percentage of all approved projects involving the sale of merchantable timber are implemented using separate contracts:

"(i) For fiscal year 2008, 35 percent.

"(ii) For fiscal year 2009, 45 percent.

"(iii) For each of fiscal years 2010 and 2011, 50 percent.

"(C) INCLUSION IN PILOT PROGRAM.—The decision whether to use separate contracts to implement a project involving the sale of merchantable timber shall be made by the Secretary concerned after the approval of the project under this title.

"(D) ASSISTANCE.—

"(i) IN GENERAL.—The Secretary concerned may use funds from any appropriated account available to the Secretary for the Federal land to assist in the administration of projects conducted under the pilot program.

"(ii) MAXIMUM AMOUNT OF ASSISTANCE.—The total amount obligated under this subparagraph may not exceed $1,000,000 for any fiscal year during which the pilot program is in effect.

"(E) REVIEW AND REPORT.—

"(i) INITIAL REPORT.—Not later than September 30, 2010, the Comptroller General shall submit to the Committees on Agriculture, Nutrition, and Forestry and Energy and Natural Resources of the Senate and the Committees on Agriculture and Natural Resources of the House of Representatives a report assessing the pilot program.

"(ii) ANNUAL REPORT.—The Secretary concerned shall submit to the Committees on Agriculture, Nutrition, and Forestry and Energy and Natural Resources of the Senate and the Committees on Agriculture and Natural Resources of the House of Representatives an annual report describing the results of the pilot program.

"(f) REQUIREMENTS FOR PROJECT FUNDS.—The Secretary shall ensure that at least 50 percent of all project funds be used for projects that are primarily dedicated—

"(1) to road maintenance, decommissioning, or obliteration; or

"(2) to restoration of streams and watersheds.

"SEC. 205. RESOURCE ADVISORY COMMITTEES.

"(a) ESTABLISHMENT AND PURPOSE OF RESOURCE ADVISORY COMMITTEES.—

"(1) ESTABLISHMENT.—The Secretary concerned shall establish and maintain resource advisory committees to perform the duties in subsection (b), except as provided in paragraph (4).

"(2) PURPOSE.—The purpose of a resource advisory committee shall be—

"(A) to improve collaborative relationships; and

"(B) to provide advice and recommendations to the land management agencies consistent with the purposes of this title.

"(3) ACCESS TO RESOURCE ADVISORY COMMITTEES.—To ensure that each unit of Federal land has access to a resource advisory committee, and that there is sufficient interest in participation on a committee to ensure that membership can be balanced in terms of the points of view represented and the functions to be performed, the Secretary concerned may, establish resource advisory committees for part of, or 1 or more, units of Federal land.

"(4) EXISTING ADVISORY COMMITTEES.—

"(A) IN GENERAL.—An advisory committee that meets the requirements of this section, a resource advisory committee established before September 29, 2006, or an advisory committee determined by the Secretary concerned before September 29, 2006, to meet the requirements of this section may be deemed by the Secretary concerned to be a resource advisory committee for the purposes of this title.

"(B) CHARTER.—A charter for a committee described in subparagraph (A) that was filed on or before September 29, 2006, shall be considered to be filed for purposes of this Act.

"(C) BUREAU OF LAND MANAGEMENT ADVISORY COMMITTEES.—The Secretary of the Interior may deem a resource advisory committee meeting the requirements of subpart 1784 of part 1780 of title 43, Code of Federal Regulations, as a resource advisory committee for the purposes of this title.

"(b) DUTIES.—A resource advisory committee shall—

"(1) review projects proposed under this title by participating counties and other persons;

"(2) propose projects and funding to the Secretary concerned under section 203;

"(3) provide early and continuous coordination with appropriate land management agency officials in recommending projects consistent with purposes of this Act under this title;

"(4) provide frequent opportunities for citizens, organizations, tribes, land management agencies, and other interested parties to participate openly and meaningfully, beginning at the early stages of the project development process under this title;

"(5)(A) monitor projects that have been approved under section 204; and

"(B) advise the designated Federal official on the progress of the monitoring efforts under subparagraph (A); and

"(6) make recommendations to the Secretary concerned for any appropriate changes or adjustments to the projects being monitored by the resource advisory committee.

"(c) APPOINTMENT BY THE SECRETARY.—

"(1) APPOINTMENT AND TERM.—

"(A) IN GENERAL.—The Secretary concerned, shall appoint the members of resource advisory committees for a term of 4 years beginning on the date of appointment.

"(B) REAPPOINTMENT.—The Secretary concerned may reappoint members to subsequent 4-year terms.

"(2) BASIC REQUIREMENTS.—The Secretary concerned shall ensure that each resource advisory committee established meets the requirements of subsection (d).

"(3) INITIAL APPOINTMENT.—Not later than 180 days after the date of the enactment of this Act, the Secretary concerned shall make initial appointments to the resource advisory committees.

"(4) VACANCIES.—The Secretary concerned shall make appointments to fill vacancies on any resource advisory committee as soon as practicable after the vacancy has occurred.

"(5) COMPENSATION.—Members of the resource advisory committees shall not receive any compensation.

"(d) COMPOSITION OF ADVISORY COMMITTEE.—

"(1) NUMBER.—Each resource advisory committee shall be comprised of 15 members.

"(2) COMMUNITY INTERESTS REPRESENTED.—Committee members shall be representative of the interests of the following 3 categories:

"(A) 5 persons that—

"(i) represent organized labor or non-timber forest product harvester groups;

"(ii) represent developed outdoor recreation, off highway vehicle users, or commercial recreation activities;

"(iii) represent—

"(I) energy and mineral development interests; or

"(II) commercial or recreational fishing interests;

"(iv) represent the commercial timber industry; or

"(v) hold Federal grazing or other land use permits, or represent nonindustrial private forest land owners, within the area for which the committee is organized.

"(B) 5 persons that represent—

"(i) nationally recognized environmental organizations;

"(ii) regionally or locally recognized environmental organizations;

"(iii) dispersed recreational activities;

"(iv) archaeological and historical interests; or

"(v) nationally or regionally recognized wild horse and burro interest groups, wildlife or hunting organizations, or watershed associations.

"(C) 5 persons that—

"(i) hold State elected office (or a designee);

"(ii) hold county or local elected office;

"(iii) represent American Indian tribes within or adjacent to the area for which the committee is organized;

"(iv) are school officials or teachers; or

"(v) represent the affected public at large.

"(3) BALANCED REPRESENTATION.—In appointing committee members from the 3 categories in paragraph (2), the Secretary concerned shall provide for balanced and broad representation from within each category.

"(4) GEOGRAPHIC DISTRIBUTION.—The members of a resource advisory committee shall reside within the State in which the committee has jurisdiction and, to extent practicable, the Secretary concerned shall ensure local representation in each category in paragraph (2).

"(5) CHAIRPERSON.—A majority on each resource advisory committee shall select the chairperson of the committee.

"(e) APPROVAL PROCEDURES.—

"(1) IN GENERAL.—Subject to paragraph (3), each resource advisory committee shall establish procedures for proposing projects to the Secretary concerned under this title.

"(2) QUORUM.—A quorum must be present to constitute an official meeting of the committee.

"(3) APPROVAL BY MAJORITY OF MEMBERS.—A project may be proposed by a resource advisory committee to the Secretary concerned under section 203(a), if the project has been approved by a majority of members of the committee from each of the 3 categories in subsection (d)(2).

"(f) OTHER COMMITTEE AUTHORITIES AND REQUIREMENTS.—

"(1) STAFF ASSISTANCE.—A resource advisory committee may submit to the Secretary concerned a request for periodic staff assistance from Federal employees under the jurisdiction of the Secretary.

"(2) MEETINGS.—All meetings of a resource advisory committee shall be announced at least 1 week in advance in a local newspaper of record and shall be open to the public.

"(3) RECORDS.—A resource advisory committee shall maintain records of the meetings of the committee and make the records available for public inspection.

"SEC. 206. USE OF PROJECT FUNDS.

"(a) AGREEMENT REGARDING SCHEDULE AND COST OF PROJECT.—

"(1) AGREEMENT BETWEEN PARTIES.—The Secretary concerned may carry out a project submitted by a resource advisory committee under section 203(a) using project funds or other funds described in section 203(a)(2), if, as soon as practicable after the issuance of a decision document for the project and the exhaustion of all administrative appeals and judicial review of the project decision, the Secretary concerned and the resource advisory committee enter into an agreement addressing, at a minimum, the following:

"(A) The schedule for completing the project.

"(B) The total cost of the project, including the level of agency overhead to be assessed against the project.

"(C) For a multiyear project, the estimated cost of the project for each of the fiscal years in which it will be carried out.

"(D) The remedies for failure of the Secretary concerned to comply with the terms of the agreement consistent with current Federal law.

"(2) LIMITED USE OF FEDERAL FUNDS.—The Secretary concerned may decide, at the sole discretion of the Secretary concerned, to cover the costs of a portion of an approved project using Federal funds appropriated or otherwise available to the Secretary for the same purposes as the project.

"(b) TRANSFER OF PROJECT FUNDS.—

"(1) INITIAL TRANSFER REQUIRED.—As soon as practicable after the agreement is reached under subsection (a) with regard to a project to be funded in whole or in part using project funds, or other funds described in section 203(a)(2), the Secretary concerned shall transfer to the applicable unit of National Forest System land or Bureau of Land Management District an amount of project funds equal to—

"(A) in the case of a project to be completed in a single fiscal year, the total amount specified in the agreement to be paid using project funds, or other funds described in section 203(a)(2); or

"(B) in the case of a multiyear project, the amount specified in the agreement to be paid using project funds, or other funds described in section 203(a)(2) for the first fiscal year.

"(2) CONDITION ON PROJECT COMMENCEMENT.—The unit of National Forest System land or Bureau of Land Management District concerned, shall not commence a project until the project funds, or other funds described in section 203(a)(2) required to be transferred under paragraph (1) for the project, have been made available by the Secretary concerned.

"(3) SUBSEQUENT TRANSFERS FOR MULTIYEAR PROJECTS.—

"(A) IN GENERAL.—For the second and subsequent fiscal years of a multiyear project to be funded in whole or in part using project funds, the unit of National Forest System land or Bureau of Land Management District concerned shall use the amount of project funds required to continue the project in that fiscal year according to the agreement entered into under subsection (a).

"(B) SUSPENSION OF WORK.—The Secretary concerned shall suspend work on the project if the project funds required by the agreement in the second and subsequent fiscal years are not available.

"SEC. 207. AVAILABILITY OF PROJECT FUNDS.

"(a) SUBMISSION OF PROPOSED PROJECTS TO OBLIGATE FUNDS.—By September 30, 2008 (or as soon thereafter as the Secretary concerned determines is practicable), and each September 30 thereafter for each succeeding fiscal year through fiscal year 2011, a resource advisory committee shall submit to the Secretary concerned pursuant to section 203(a)(1) a sufficient number of project proposals that, if approved, would result in the obligation of at least the full amount of the project funds reserved by the participating county in the preceding fiscal year.

"(b) USE OR TRANSFER OF UNOBLIGATED FUNDS.—Subject to section 208, if a resource advisory committee fails to comply with subsection (a) for a fiscal year, any project funds reserved by the participating county in the preceding fiscal year and remaining unobligated shall be available for use as part of the project submissions in the next fiscal year.

"(c) EFFECT OF REJECTION OF PROJECTS.—Subject to section 208, any project funds reserved by a participating county in the preceding fiscal year that are unobligated at the end of a fiscal year because the Secretary concerned has rejected one or more proposed projects shall be available for use as part of the project submissions in the next fiscal year.

"(d) EFFECT OF COURT ORDERS.—

"(1) IN GENERAL.—If an approved project under this Act is enjoined or prohibited by a Federal court, the Secretary concerned shall return the unobligated project funds related to the project to the participating county or counties that reserved the funds.

"(2) EXPENDITURE OF FUNDS.—The returned funds shall be available for the county to expend in the same manner as the funds reserved by the county under subparagraph (B) or (C)(i) of section 102(d)(1).

"SEC. 208. TERMINATION OF AUTHORITY.

"(a) IN GENERAL.—The authority to initiate projects under this title shall terminate on September 30, 2011.

"(b) DEPOSITS IN TREASURY.—Any project funds not obligated by September 30, 2012, shall be deposited in the Treasury of the United States.

"TITLE III—COUNTY FUNDS

"SEC. 301. DEFINITIONS.

"In this title:

"(1) COUNTY FUNDS.—The term 'county funds' means all funds an eligible county elects under section 102(d) to reserve for expenditure in accordance with this title.

"(2) PARTICIPATING COUNTY.—The term 'participating county' means an eligible county that elects under section 102(d) to expend a portion of the Federal funds received under section 102 in accordance with this title.

"SEC. 302. USE.

"(a) AUTHORIZED USES.—A participating county, including any applicable agencies of the participating county, shall use county funds, in accordance with this title, only—

"(1) to carry out activities under the Firewise Communities program to provide to homeowners in fire-sensitive ecosystems education on, and assistance with implementing, techniques in home siting, home construction, and home landscaping that can increase the protection of people and property from wildfires;

"(2) to reimburse the participating county for search and rescue and other emergency services, including firefighting, that are—

"(A) performed on Federal land after the date on which the use was approved under subsection (b);

"(B) paid for by the participating county; and

"(3) to develop community wildfire protection plans in coordination with the appropriate Secretary concerned.

"(b) PROPOSALS.—A participating county shall use county funds for a use described in subsection (a) only after a 45-day public comment period, at the beginning of which the participating county shall—

"(1) publish in any publications of local record a proposal that describes the proposed use of the county funds; and

"(2) submit the proposal to any resource advisory committee established under section 205 for the participating county.

"SEC. 303. CERTIFICATION.

"(a) IN GENERAL.—Not later than February 1 of the year after the year in which any county funds were expended by a participating county, the appropriate official of the participating county shall submit to the Secretary concerned a certification that the county funds expended in the applicable year have been used for the uses authorized under section 302(a), including a description of the amounts expended and the uses for which the amounts were expended.

"(b) REVIEW.—The Secretary concerned shall review the certifications submitted under subsection (a) as the Secretary concerned determines to be appropriate.

"SEC. 304. TERMINATION OF AUTHORITY.

"(a) IN GENERAL.—The authority to initiate projects under this title terminates on September 30, 2011.

"(b) AVAILABILITY.—Any county funds not obligated by September 30, 2012, shall be returned to the Treasury of the United States.

"TITLE IV—MISCELLANEOUS PROVISIONS

"SEC. 401. REGULATIONS.

"The Secretary of Agriculture and the Secretary of the Interior shall issue regulations to carry out the purposes of this Act.

"SEC. 402. AUTHORIZATION OF APPROPRIATIONS.

"There are authorized to be appropriated such sums as are necessary to carry out this Act for each of fiscal years 2008 through 2011.

"SEC. 403. TREATMENT OF FUNDS AND REVENUES.

"(a) RELATION TO OTHER APPROPRIATIONS.—Funds made available under section 402 and funds made available to a Secretary concerned under section 206 shall be in addition to any other annual appropriations for the Forest Service and the Bureau of Land Management.

"(b) DEPOSIT OF REVENUES AND OTHER FUNDS.—All revenues generated from projects pursuant to title II, including any interest accrued from the revenues, shall be deposited in the Treasury of the United States.".

(b) FOREST RECEIPT PAYMENTS TO ELIGIBLE STATES AND COUNTIES—

(1) ACT OF MAY 23, 1908.—The sixth paragraph under the heading "FOREST SERVICE" in the Act of May 23, 1908 (16 U.S.C. 500) is amended in the first sentence by striking "twenty-five percentum" and all that follows through "shall be paid" and inserting the following: "an amount equal to the annual average of 25 percent of all amounts received for the applicable fiscal year and each of the preceding 6 fiscal years from each national forest shall be paid".

(2) WEEKS LAW.—Section 13 of the Act of March 1, 1911 (commonly known as the "Weeks Law") (16 U.S.C. 500) is amended in the first sentence by striking "twenty-five percentum" and all that follows through "shall be paid" and inserting the following: "an amount equal to the annual average of 25 percent of all amounts received for the applicable fiscal year and each of the preceding 6 fiscal years from each national forest shall be paid".

(c) PAYMENTS IN LIEU OF TAXES—

(1) IN GENERAL.—Section 6906 of title 31, United States Code, is amended to read as follows:

"§ 6906. FUNDING

"For each of fiscal years 2008 through 2012—

"(1) each county or other eligible unit of local government shall be entitled to payment under this chapter; and

"(2) sums shall be made available to the Secretary of the Interior for obligation or expenditure in accordance with this chapter.".

(2) CONFORMING AMENDMENT.—The table of sections for chapter 69 of title 31, United States Code, is amended by striking the item relating to section 6906 and inserting the following:

"6906. FUNDING.".

(3) BUDGET SCOREKEEPING—

(A) IN GENERAL.—Notwithstanding the Budget Scorekeeping Guidelines and the accompanying list of programs and accounts set forth in the joint explanatory statement of the committee of conference accompanying Conference Report 105-217, the section in this title regarding Payments in Lieu of Taxes shall be treated in the baseline for purposes of section 257 of the Balanced Budget and Emergency Deficit Control Act of 1985 (as in effect prior to September 30, 2002), and by the Chairmen of the House and Senate Budget Committees, as appropriate, for purposes of budget enforcement in the House and Senate, and under the Congressional Budget Act of 1974 as if Payment in Lieu of Taxes (14-1114-0-1-806) were an account designated as Appropriated Entitlements and Mandatories for Fiscal Year 1997 in the joint explanatory statement of the committee of conference accompanying Conference Report 105-217.

(B) EFFECTIVE DATE.—This paragraph shall remain in effect for the fiscal years to which the entitlement in section 6906 of title 31, United States Code (as amended by paragraph (1)), applies.

[¶7174] ACT SEC. 602. TRANSFER TO ABANDONED MINE RECLAMATION FUND.

Subparagraph (C) of section 402(i)(1) of the Surface Mining Control and Reclamation Act of 1977 (30 U.S.C. 1232(i)(1)) is amended by striking "and $9,000,000 on October 1, 2009" and inserting "$9,000,000 on October 1, 2009, and $9,000,000 on October 1, 2010".

TITLE VII—DISASTER RELIEF

Subtitle A—Heartland and Hurricane Ike Disaster Relief

[¶7177] ACT SEC. 701. SHORT TITLE.

This subtitle may be cited as the "Heartland Disaster Tax Relief Act of 2008".

[¶7180] ACT SEC. 702. TEMPORARY TAX RELIEF FOR AREAS DAMAGED BY 2008 MIDWESTERN SEVERE STORMS, TORNADOS, AND FLOODING.

(a) IN GENERAL.—Subject to the modifications described in this section, the following provisions of or relating to the Internal Revenue Code of 1986 shall apply to any Midwestern disaster area in addition to the areas to which such provisions otherwise apply:

(1) GO ZONE BENEFITS.—

(A) Section 1400N (relating to tax benefits) other than subsections (b), (d), (e), (i), (j), (m), and (o) thereof.

(B) Section 1400O (relating to education tax benefits).

(C) Section 1400P (relating to housing tax benefits).

(D) Section 1400Q (relating to special rules for use of retirement funds).

(E) Section 1400R(a) (relating to employee retention credit for employers).

(F) Section 1400S (relating to additional tax relief) other than subsection (d) thereof.

(G) Section 1400T (relating to special rules for mortgage revenue bonds).

(2) OTHER BENEFITS INCLUDED IN KATRINA EMERGENCY TAX RELIEF ACT OF 2005.—Sections 302, 303, 304, 401, and 405 of the Katrina Emergency Tax Relief Act of 2005.

(b) MIDWESTERN DISASTER AREA.—

(1) IN GENERAL.—For purposes of this section and for applying the substitutions described in subsections (d) and (e), the term "Midwestern disaster area" means an area—

(A) with respect to which a major disaster has been declared by the President on or after May 20, 2008, and before August 1, 2008, under section 401 of the Robert T. Stafford Disaster Relief and Emergency Assistance Act by reason of severe storms, tornados, or flooding occurring in any of the States of Arkansas, Illinois, Indiana, Iowa, Kansas, Michigan, Minnesota, Missouri, Nebraska, and Wisconsin, and

(B) determined by the President to warrant individual or individual and public assistance from the Federal Government under such Act with respect to damages attributable to such severe storms, tornados, or flooding.

(2) CERTAIN BENEFITS AVAILABLE TO AREAS ELIGIBLE ONLY FOR PUBLIC ASSISTANCE.—For purposes of applying this section to benefits under the following provisions, paragraph (1) shall be applied without regard to subparagraph (B):

(A) Sections 1400Q, 1400S(b), and 1400S(d) of the Internal Revenue Code of 1986.

(B) Sections 302, 401, and 405 of the Katrina Emergency Tax Relief Act of 2005.

(c) REFERENCES.—

(1) AREA.—Any reference in such provisions to the Hurricane Katrina disaster area or the Gulf Opportunity Zone shall be treated as a reference to any Midwestern disaster area and any reference to the Hurricane Katrina disaster area or the Gulf Opportunity Zone within a State shall be treated as a reference to all Midwestern disaster areas within the State.

(2) ITEMS ATTRIBUTABLE TO DISASTER.—Any reference in such provisions to any loss, damage, or other item attributable to Hurricane Katrina shall be treated as a reference to any loss, damage, or other item attributable to the severe storms, tornados, or flooding giving rise to any Presidential declaration described in subsection (b)(1)(A).

(3) APPLICABLE DISASTER DATE.—For purposes of applying the substitutions described in subsections (d) and (e), the term "applicable disaster date" means, with respect to any Midwestern disaster area, the date on which the severe storms, tornados, or flooding giving rise to the Presidential declaration described in subsection (b)(1)(A) occurred.

(d) MODIFICATIONS TO 1986 CODE.—The following provisions of the Internal Revenue Code of 1986 shall be applied with the following modifications:

(1) TAX-EXEMPT BOND FINANCING.—Section 1400N(a)—

(A) by substituting "qualified Midwestern disaster area bond" for "qualified Gulf Opportunity Zone Bond" each place it appears, except that in determining whether a bond is a qualified Midwestern disaster area bond—

(i) paragraph (2)(A)(i) shall be applied by only treating costs as qualified project costs if—

(I) in the case of a project involving a private business use (as defined in section 141(b)(6)), either the person using the property suffered a loss in a trade or business attributable to the severe storms, tornados, or flooding giving rise to any Presidential declaration described in subsection (b)(1)(A) or is a person designated for purposes of this section by the Governor of the State in which the project is located as a person carrying on a trade or business replacing a trade or business with respect to which another person suffered such a loss, and

(II) in the case of a project relating to public utility property, the project involves repair or reconstruction of public utility property damaged by such severe storms, tornados, or flooding, and

(ii) paragraph (2)(A)(ii) shall be applied by treating an issue as a qualified mortgage issue only if 95 percent or more of the net proceeds (as defined in section 150(a)(3)) of the issue are to be used to provide financing for mortgagors who suffered damages to their principal residences attributable to such severe storms, tornados, or flooding.

(B) by substituting "any State in which a Midwestern disaster area is located" for "the State of Alabama, Louisiana, or Mississippi" in paragraph (2)(B),

(C) by substituting "designated for purposes of this section (on the basis of providing assistance to areas in the order in which such assistance is most needed)" for "designated for purposes of this section" in paragraph (2)(C),

(D) by substituting "January 1, 2013" for "January 1, 2011" in paragraph (2)(D),

(E) in paragraph (3)(A)—

(i) by substituting "$1,000" for "$2,500", and

(ii) by substituting "before the earliest applicable disaster date for Midwestern disaster areas within the State" for "before August 28, 2005",

(F) by substituting "qualified Midwestern disaster area repair or construction" for "qualified GO Zone repair or construction" each place it appears,

(G) by substituting "after the date of the enactment of the Heartland Disaster Tax Relief Act of 2008 and before January 1, 2013" for "after the date of the enactment of this paragraph and before January 1, 2011" in paragraph (7)(C), and

(H) by disregarding paragraph (8) thereof.

(2) LOW-INCOME HOUSING CREDIT.—Section 1400N(c)—

(A) only with respect to calendar years 2008, 2009, and 2010,

(B) by substituting "Disaster Recovery Assistance housing amount" for "Gulf Opportunity housing amount" each place it appears,

(C) in paragraph (1)(B)—

(i) by substituting "$8.00" for "$18.00", and

(ii) by substituting "before the earliest applicable disaster date for Midwestern disaster areas within the State" for "before August 28, 2005", and

(D) determined without regard to paragraphs (2), (3), (4), (5), and (6) thereof.

(3) EXPENSING FOR CERTAIN DEMOLITION AND CLEAN-UP COSTS.—Section 1400N(f)—

(A) by substituting "qualified Disaster Recovery Assistance clean-up cost" for "qualified Gulf Opportunity Zone clean-up cost" each place it appears,

(B) by substituting "beginning on the applicable disaster date and ending on December 31, 2010" for "beginning on August 28, 2005, and ending on December 31, 2007" in paragraph (2), and

(C) by treating costs as qualified Disaster Recovery Assistance clean-up costs only if the removal of debris or demolition of any structure was necessary due to damage attributable to the severe storms, tornados, or flooding giving rise to any Presidential declaration described in subsection (b)(1)(A).

(4) EXTENSION OF EXPENSING FOR ENVIRONMENTAL REMEDIATION COSTS.—Section 1400N(g)—

(A) by substituting "the applicable disaster date" for "August 28, 2005" each place it appears,

(B) by substituting "January 1, 2011" for "January 1, 2008" in paragraph (1),

(C) by substituting "December 31, 2010" for "December 31, 2007" in paragraph (1), and

(D) by treating a site as a qualified contaminated site only if the release (or threat of release) or disposal of a hazardous substance at the site was attributable to the severe storms, tornados, or flooding giving rise to any Presidential declaration described in subsection (b)(1)(A).

(5) INCREASE IN REHABILITATION CREDIT.—Section 1400N(h), as amended by this Act—

(A) by substituting "the applicable disaster date" for "August 28, 2005",

(B) by substituting "December 31, 2011" for "December 31, 2009" in paragraph (1), and

(C) by only applying such subsection to qualified rehabilitation expenditures with respect to any building or structure which was damaged or destroyed as a result of the severe storms, tornados, or flooding giving rise to any Presidential declaration described in subsection (b)(1)(A).

(6) TREATMENT OF NET OPERATING LOSSES ATTRIBUTABLE TO DISASTER LOSSES.—Section 1400N(k)—

(A) by substituting "qualified Disaster Recovery Assistance loss" for "qualified Gulf Opportunity Zone loss" each place it appears,

(B) by substituting "after the day before the applicable disaster date, and before January 1, 2011" for "after August 27, 2005, and before January 1, 2008" each place it appears,

(C) by substituting "the applicable disaster date" for "August 28, 2005" in paragraph (2)(B)(ii)(I),

(D) by substituting "qualified Disaster Recovery Assistance property" for "qualified Gulf Opportunity Zone property" in paragraph (2)(B)(iv), and

(E) by substituting "qualified Disaster Recovery Assistance casualty loss" for "qualified Gulf Opportunity Zone casualty loss" each place it appears.

(7) CREDIT TO HOLDERS OF TAX CREDIT BONDS.—Section 1400N(l)—

(A) by substituting "Midwestern tax credit bond" for "Gulf tax credit bond" each place it appears,

(B) by substituting "any State in which a Midwestern disaster area is located or any instrumentality of the State" for "the State of Alabama, Louisiana, or Mississippi" in paragraph (4)(A)(i),

(C) by substituting "after December 31, 2008 and before January 1, 2010" for "after December 31, 2005, and before January 1, 2007",

(D) by substituting "shall not exceed $100,000,000 for any State with an aggregate population located in all Midwestern disaster areas within the State of at least 2,000,000, $50,000,000 for any State with an aggregate population located in all Midwestern disaster areas within the State of at least 1,000,000 but less than 2,000,000, and zero for any other State. The population of a State within any area shall be determined on the basis of the most recent census estimate of resident population released by the Bureau of Census before the earliest applicable disaster date for Midwestern disaster areas within the State." for "shall not exceed" and all that follows in paragraph (4)(C), and

(E) by substituting "the earliest applicable disaster date for Midwestern disaster areas within the State" for "August 28, 2005" in paragraph (5)(A).

(8) EDUCATION TAX BENEFITS.—Section 1400O, by substituting "2008 or 2009" for "2005 or 2006".

(9) HOUSING TAX BENEFITS.—Section 1400P, by substituting "the applicable disaster date" for "August 28, 2005" in subsection (c)(1).

(10) SPECIAL RULES FOR USE OF RETIREMENT FUNDS.—Section 1400Q—

(A) by substituting "qualified Disaster Recovery Assistance distribution" for "qualified hurricane distribution" each place it appears,

(B) by substituting "on or after the applicable disaster date and before January 1, 2010" for "on or after August 25, 2005, and before January 1, 2007" in subsection (a)(4)(A)(i),

(C) by substituting "the applicable disaster date" for "August 28, 2005" in subsections (a)(4)(A)(i) and (c)(3)(B),

(D) by disregarding clauses (ii) and (iii) of subsection (a)(4)(A) thereof,

(E) by substituting "qualified storm damage distribution" for "qualified Katrina distribution" each place it appears,

(F) by substituting "after the date which is 6 months before the applicable disaster date and before the date which is the day after the applicable disaster date" for "after February 28, 2005, and before August 29, 2005" in subsection (b)(2)(B)(ii),

(G) by substituting "the Midwestern disaster area, but not so purchased or constructed on account of severe storms, tornados, or flooding giving rise to the designation of the area as a disaster area" for "the Hurricane Katrina disaster area, but not so purchased or constructed on account of Hurricane Katrina" in subsection (b)(2)(B)(iii),

(H) by substituting "beginning on the applicable disaster date and ending on the date which is 5 months after the date of the enactment of the Heartland Disaster Tax Relief Act of 2008" for "beginning on August 25, 2005, and ending on February 28, 2006" in subsection (b)(3)(A),

(I) by substituting "qualified storm damage individual" for "qualified Hurricane Katrina individual" each place it appears,

(J) by substituting "December 31, 2009" for "December 31, 2006" in subsection (c)(2)(A),

(K) by disregarding subparagraphs (C) and (D) of subsection (c)(3) thereof,

(L) by substituting "beginning on the date of the enactment of the Heartland Disaster Tax Relief Act of 2008 and ending on December 31, 2009" for "beginning on September 24, 2005, and ending on December 31, 2006" in subsection (c)(4)(A)(i),

(M) by substituting "the applicable disaster date" for "August 25, 2005" in subsection (c)(4)(A)(ii), and

(N) by substituting "January 1, 2010" for "January 1, 2007" in subsection (d)(2)(A)(ii).

(11) EMPLOYEE RETENTION CREDIT FOR EMPLOYERS AFFECTED BY SEVERE STORMS, TORNADOS, AND FLOODING.—Section 1400R(a)—

(A) by substituting "the applicable disaster date" for "August 28, 2005" each place it appears,

(B) by substituting "January 1, 2009" for "January 1, 2006" both places it appears, and

(C) only with respect to eligible employers who employed an average of not more than 200 employees on business days during the taxable year before the applicable disaster date.

(12) TEMPORARY SUSPENSION OF LIMITATIONS ON CHARITABLE CONTRIBUTIONS.—Section 1400S(a), by substituting the following paragraph for paragraph (4) thereof:

"(4) QUALIFIED CONTRIBUTIONS.—

"(A) IN GENERAL.—For purposes of this subsection, the term 'qualified contribution' means any charitable contribution (as defined in section 170(c)) if—

"(i) such contribution—

"(I) is paid during the period beginning on the earliest applicable disaster date for all States and ending on December 31, 2008, in cash to an organization described in section 170(b)(1)(A), and

"(II) is made for relief efforts in 1 or more Midwestern disaster areas,

"(ii) the taxpayer obtains from such organization contemporaneous written acknowledgment (within the meaning of section 170(f)(8)) that such contribution was used (or is to be used) for relief efforts in 1 or more Midwestern disaster areas, and

"(iii) the taxpayer has elected the application of this subsection with respect to such contribution.

"(B) EXCEPTION.—Such term shall not include a contribution by a donor if the contribution is—

"(i) to an organization described in section 509(a)(3), or

"(ii) for establishment of a new, or maintenance of an existing, donor advised fund (as defined in section 4966(d)(2)).

"(C) APPLICATION OF ELECTION TO PARTNERSHIPS AND S CORPORATIONS.—In the case of a partnership or S corporation, the election under subparagraph (A)(iii) shall be made separately by each partner or shareholder.".

(13) SUSPENSION OF CERTAIN LIMITATIONS ON PERSONAL CASUALTY LOSSES.—Section 1400S(b)(1), by substituting "the applicable disaster date" for "August 25, 2005".

(14) SPECIAL RULE FOR DETERMINING EARNED INCOME.—Section 1400S(d)—

(A) by treating an individual as a qualified individual if such individual's principal place of abode on the applicable disaster date was located in a Midwestern disaster area,

(B) by treating the applicable disaster date with respect to any such individual as the applicable date for purposes of such subsection, and

(C) by treating an area as described in paragraph (2)(B)(ii) thereof if the area is a Midwestern disaster area only by reason of subsection (b)(2) of this section (relating to areas eligible only for public assistance).

(15) ADJUSTMENTS REGARDING TAXPAYER AND DEPENDENCY STATUS.—Section 1400S(e), by substituting "2008 or 2009" for "2005 or 2006".

(e) MODIFICATIONS TO KATRINA EMERGENCY TAX RELIEF ACT OF 2005.—The following provisions of the Katrina Emergency Tax Relief Act of 2005 shall be applied with the following modifications:

(1) ADDITIONAL EXEMPTION FOR HOUSING DISPLACED INDIVIDUAL.—Section 302—

(A) by substituting "2008 or 2009" for "2005 or 2006" in subsection (a) thereof,

(B) by substituting "Midwestern displaced individual" for "Hurricane Katrina displaced individual" each place it appears, and

(C) by treating an area as a core disaster area for purposes of applying subsection (c) thereof if the area is a Midwestern disaster area without regard to subsection (b)(2) of this section (relating to areas eligible only for public assistance).

(2) INCREASE IN STANDARD MILEAGE RATE.—Section 303, by substituting "beginning on the applicable disaster date and ending on December 31, 2008" for "beginning on August 25, 2005, and ending on December 31, 2006".

(3) MILEAGE REIMBURSEMENTS FOR CHARITABLE VOLUNTEERS.—Section 304—

(A) by substituting "beginning on the applicable disaster date and ending on December 31, 2008" for "beginning on August 25, 2005, and ending on December 31, 2006" in subsection (a), and

(B) by substituting "the applicable disaster date" for "August 25, 2005" in subsection (a).

(4) EXCLUSION OF CERTAIN CANCELLATION OF INDEBTEDNESS INCOME.—Section 401—

(A) by treating an individual whose principal place of abode on the applicable disaster date was in a Midwestern disaster area (determined without regard to subsection (b)(2) of this section) as an individual described in subsection (b)(1) thereof, and by treating an individual whose principal place of abode on the applicable disaster date was in a Midwestern disaster area solely by reason of subsection (b)(2) of this section as an individual described in subsection (b)(2) thereof,

(B) by substituting "the applicable disaster date" for "August 28, 2005" both places it appears, and

(C) by substituting "January 1, 2010" for "January 1, 2007" in subsection (e).

(5) EXTENSION OF REPLACEMENT PERIOD FOR NONRECOGNITION OF GAIN.—Section 405, by substituting "on or after the applicable disaster date" for "on or after August 25, 2005".

[CCH Explanation at ¶ 655.]

* * *

[¶ 7183] ACT SEC. 704. TEMPORARY TAX-EXEMPT BOND FINANCING AND LOW-INCOME HOUSING TAX RELIEF FOR AREAS DAMAGED BY HURRICANE IKE.

(a) Tax-Exempt Bond Financing.—Section 1400N(a) of the Internal Revenue Code of 1986 shall apply to any Hurricane Ike disaster area in addition to any other area referenced in such section, but with the following modifications:

(1) By substituting "qualified Hurricane Ike disaster area bond" for "qualified Gulf Opportunity Zone Bond" each place it appears, except that in determining whether a bond is a qualified Hurricane Ike disaster area bond—

(A) paragraph (2)(A)(i) shall be applied by only treating costs as qualified project costs if—

(i) in the case of a project involving a private business use (as defined in section 141(b)(6)), either the person using the property suffered a loss in a trade or business attributable to Hurricane Ike or is a person designated for purposes of this section by the Governor of the State in which the project is located as a person carrying on a trade or business replacing a trade or business with respect to which another person suffered such a loss, and

(ii) in the case of a project relating to public utility property, the project involves repair or reconstruction of public utility property damaged by Hurricane Ike, and

(B) paragraph (2)(A)(ii) shall be applied by treating an issue as a qualified mortgage issue only if 95 percent or more of the net proceeds (as defined in section 150(a)(3)) of the issue are to be used to provide financing for mortgagors who suffered damages to their principal residences attributable to Hurricane Ike.

(2) By substituting "any State in which any Hurricane Ike disaster area is located" for "the State of Alabama, Louisiana, or Mississippi" in paragraph (2)(B).

(3) By substituting "designated for purposes of this section (on the basis of providing assistance to areas in the order in which such assistance is most needed)" for "designated for purposes of this section" in paragraph (2)(C).

(4) By substituting "January 1, 2013" for "January 1, 2011" in paragraph (2)(D).

(5) By substituting the following for subparagraph (A) of paragraph (3):

"(A) Aggregate amount designated.—The maximum aggregate face amount of bonds which may be designated under this subsection with respect to any State shall not exceed the product of $2,000 multiplied by the portion of the State population which is in—

"(i) in the case of Texas, the counties of Brazoria, Chambers, Galveston, Jefferson, and Orange, and

"(ii) in the case of Louisiana, the parishes of Calcasieu and Cameron,

(as determined on the basis of the most recent census estimate of resident population released by the Bureau of Census before September 13, 2008).".

(6) By substituting "qualified Hurricane Ike disaster area repair or construction" for "qualified GO Zone repair or construction" each place it appears.

(7) By substituting "after the date of the enactment of the Heartland Disaster Tax Relief Act of 2008 and before January 1, 2013" for "after the date of the enactment of this paragraph and before January 1, 2011" in paragraph (7)(C).

(8) By disregarding paragraph (8) thereof.

(9) By substituting "any Hurricane Ike disaster area" for "the Gulf Opportunity Zone" each place it appears.

(b) Low-Income Housing Credit.—Section 1400N(c) of the Internal Revenue Code of 1986 shall apply to any Hurricane Ike disaster area in addition to any other area referenced in such section, but with the following modifications:

(1) Only with respect to calendar years 2008, 2009, and 2010.

(2) By substituting "any Hurricane Ike disaster area" for "the Gulf Opportunity Zone" each place it appears.

(3) By substituting "Hurricane Ike Recovery Assistance housing amount" for "Gulf Opportunity housing amount" each place it appears.

(4) By substituting the following for subparagraph (B) of paragraph (1):

"(B) HURRICANE IKE HOUSING AMOUNT.—For purposes of subparagraph (A), the term 'Hurricane Ike housing amount' means, for any calendar year, the amount equal to the product of $16.00 multiplied by the portion of the State population which is in—

"(i) in the case of Texas, the counties of Brazoria, Chambers, Galveston, Jefferson, and Orange, and

"(ii) in the case of Louisiana, the parishes of Calcasieu and Cameron,

(as determined on the basis of the most recent census estimate of resident population released by the Bureau of Census before September 13, 2008).".

(5) Determined without regard to paragraphs (2), (3), (4), (5), and (6) thereof.

(c) HURRICANE IKE DISASTER AREA.—For purposes of this section and for applying the substitutions described in subsections (a) and (b), the term "Hurricane Ike disaster area" means an area in the State of Texas or Louisiana—

(1) with respect to which a major disaster has been declared by the President on September 13, 2008, under section 401 of the Robert T. Stafford Disaster Relief and Emergency Assistance Act by reason of Hurricane Ike, and

(2) determined by the President to warrant individual or individual and public assistance from the Federal Government under such Act with respect to damages attributable to Hurricane Ike.

[CCH Explanations at ¶650 and ¶655. Committee Reports at ¶10,700.]

Subtitle B—National Disaster Relief
* * *

[¶7186] ACT SEC. 712. COORDINATION WITH HEARTLAND DISASTER RELIEF.

The amendments made by this subtitle, other than the amendments made by sections 706(a)(2), 710, and 711, shall not apply to any disaster described in section 702(c)(1)(A), or to any expenditure or loss resulting from such disaster.

* * *

[CCH Explanations at ¶650 and ¶655.]

Committee Reports

Emergency Economic Stabilization Act of 2008

¶10,001 Introduction

The "Emergency Economic Stabilization Act of 2008" (P.L. 110-343) was passed by Congress and was signed into law on October 3, 2008. This Act was a combination of various pending bills, as reflected by the four technical explanations from the Joint Committee on Taxation which explain the act. These include the Joint Committee on Taxation, Technical Explanation of H.R. 7060, the "Renewable Energy and Job Creation Tax Act of 2008," as introduced in the House of Representatives on September 25, 2008 (JCX-75-08); the Joint Committee on Taxation, Technical Explanation of Title III (Tax Provisions) of Division A of H.R. 1424, the "Emergency Economic Stabilization Act of 2008," as introduced in the House of Representatives on March 9, 2007 (JCX-79-08); the Joint Committee on Taxation, Technical Explanation of H.R. 7006, the "Disaster Tax Relief Act of 2008," as introduced in the House of Representatives on September 23, 2008 (JCX-73-08); and the Joint Committee on Taxation, Technical Explanation of H.R. 7005, the "Alternative Minimum Tax Relief Act of 2008," as introduced in the House of Representatives on September 23, 2008 (JCX-71-08).

These technical explanations explain the intent of Congress regarding the provisions of the Act. There was no Conference Report issued for this Act. The Technical Explanations from the Joint Committee on Taxation are included in this section to aid the reader's understanding, but may not be cited as official House, Senate, or Conference Committee Reports accompanying the 2008 Emergency Economic Stabilization Act. At the end of each section, references are provided to the corresponding CCH explanations and Internal Revenue Code provisions. Subscribers to the electronic version can link from these references to the corresponding material. *The pertinent sections of the Technical Explanation appear beginning at ¶10,010. They are in order of Act Section as finally passed by Congress and signed by the President.*

Caution: The Technical Explanations were, in many cases, written before significant modifications were made to the Act as finally passed. The reader should be aware that the explanation given by the Joint Committee on Taxation may not correspond with the language of the law as enacted.

¶10,005 Background

The "Paul Wellstone Mental Health and Addiction Equity Act of 2007," H.R. 1424, was introduced in the House of Representatives on March 9, 2007. The bill was passed in the House of Representatives on March 5, 2008, by a vote of 268-148. The "Disaster Tax Relief Act of 2008," H.R. 7006, was introduced in the House of Representatives on September 23, 2008. On September 24, 2008 it was passed by the House and received in the Senate. The "Alternative Minimum Tax Relief Act of 2008," H.R. 7005, was introduced in the House on September 23, 2008. On September 24, 2008 it was passed by the House and received in the Senate. The "Renewable Energy and Job Creation Tax Act of 2008," H.R. 7060, was introduced in the House on September 25, 2008. On September 26, 2008 it was passed by the House and received in the Senate. The Senate took up H.R. 1424 and amended it, inserting provisions from all of the above bills into it, and retitling it the "Emergency Economic Stabilization Act of 2008." The Senate passed this bill on October 1, 2008, as amended, by a vote of 74-25. The House agreed to the Senate amendments on October 3, 2008, by a vote of 263-171. On that day, it was signed by the President.

References are to the following reports:

• Technical Explanation of H.R. 7060, the "Renewable Energy and Job Creation Tax Act of 2008," is referred to as Joint Committee on Taxation (J.C.T. REP. NO. JCX-75-08).

• Technical Explanation of Title III (Tax Provisions) of Division A of H.R. 1424, the "Emergency Economic Stabilization Act of 2008," is referred to as Joint Committee on Taxation (J.C.T. REP. NO. JCX-79-08).

• Technical Explanation of H.R. 7006, the "Disaster Tax Relief Act of 2008," is referred to as Joint Committee on Taxation (J.C.T. REP. NO. JCX-73-08).

• Technical Explanation of H.R. 7005, the "Alternative Minimum Tax Relief Act of 2008," is referred to as Joint Committee on Taxation (J.C.T. REP. NO. JCX-71-08).

[¶10,010]   Act Sec. A301. Treat gain or loss from sale or exchange of certain preferred stock by applicable financial institutions as ordinary income or loss

Joint Committee on Taxation (JCT REPT. No. JCX-79-08)

[Act Sec. A301]

Present Law

Under section 582(c)(1),[2] the sale or exchange of a bond, debenture, note, or certificate or other evidence of indebtedness by a financial institution described in section 582(c)(2) is not considered a sale or exchange of a capital asset. The financial institutions described in section 582(c)(2) are (i) any bank (including any corporation which would be a bank except for the fact that it is a foreign corporation), (ii) any financial institution referred to in section 591, which includes mutual savings banks, cooperative banks, domestic building and loan associations, and other savings institutions chartered and supervised as savings and loan or similar associations under Federal or State law, (iii) any small business investment company operating under the Small Business Investment Act of 1958, and (iv) any business development corporation, defined as a corporation which was created by or pursuant to an act of a State legislature for purposes of promoting, maintaining, and assisting the economy and industry within such State on a regional or statewide basis by making loans to be used in trades and businesses which would generally not be made by banks within such region or State in the ordinary course of their business (except on the basis of a partial participation) and which is operated primarily for such purposes. In the case of a foreign corporation, section 582(c)(1) applies only with respect to gains or losses that are effectively connected with the conduct of a banking business in the United States.

Preferred stock issued by the Federal National Mortgage Corporation ("Fannie Mae") or the Federal Home Loan Mortgage Corporation ("Freddie Mac") is not treated as indebtedness for Federal income tax purposes, and therefore is not treated as an asset to which section 582(c)(1) applies. Accordingly, a financial institution described in section 582(c)(2) that holds Fannie Mae or Freddie Mac preferred stock as a capital asset generally will recognize capital gain or loss upon the sale or taxable exchange of that stock. Section 1211 provides that, in the case of a corporation, losses from sales or exchanges of capital assets are allowed only to the extent of gains from such sales or exchanges.[3] Thus, in taxable years in which a corporation does not recognize gain from the sale of capital assets, its capital losses do not reduce its income.

Explanation of Provision

Under the provision, gain or loss recognized by an "applicable financial institution" from the sale or exchange of "applicable preferred stock" is treated as ordinary income or loss. An applicable financial institution is a financial institution

---

[2] Unless otherwise specified, all section references herein are to sections of the Internal Revenue Code of 1986, as amended.

[3] In general, corporations (other than S corporations) may carry capital losses back to each of the three taxable years preceding the loss year and forward to each of the five taxable years succeeding the loss year. Sec. 1212(a). In the case of an S corporation, net capital losses flow through to the corporation's shareholders. Banks hold a wide range of financial assets in the ordinary course of their banking business. For convenience, those assets often are described as "loans" or "investments," but both serve the same overall purpose (to earn a return on the bank's capital and borrowings consistent with prudent banking practices). A bank's investments are subject to the same regulatory capital adequacy supervision as are its loans, and a bank may acquire only certain types of financial assets as permitted investments. Banks determine how much of their assets to hold as loans or as investments based on the exercise of their commercial and financial judgment, taking into account such factors as return on the asset, relative liquidity, and diversification objectives. As a result, for Federal income tax purposes, gains and losses on a bank's investment portfolio ordinarily would be considered an integral part of the business operations of the bank, and ordinary losses that pass through to the shareholder of a bank that is an S corporation therefore could comprise part of such shareholder's net operating loss for the year attributable to that banking business.

Section 1366(d) provides that losses that flow through to an S corporation shareholder are limited to the sum of (i) the shareholder's adjusted basis in his S corporation stock and (ii) the shareholder's adjusted basis in any indebtedness of the S corporation to the shareholder; losses in excess of basis are suspended (and allowed to the extent of basis in subsequent years). An S corporation shareholder's ability to utilize any flow-through capital loss is subject to all limitations otherwise imposed by the Code on such shareholder. In general, under section 1211, an individual (including an individual S corporation shareholder) may deduct capital losses only against capital gains plus up to $3,000 of ordinary income; in addition, an individual may carry excess capital losses forward but not back..

referred to in section 582(c)(2) or a depository institution holding company (as defined in section 3(w)(1) of the Federal Deposit Insurance Act (12 U.S.C. 1813(w)(1)). Applicable preferred stock is preferred stock of Fannie Mae or Freddie Mac that was (i) held by the applicable financial institution on September 6, 2008, or (ii) was sold or exchanged by the applicable financial institution on or after January 1, 2008, and before September 7, 2008.[4]

In the case of a sale or exchange of applicable preferred stock on or after January 1, 2008, and before September 7, 2008, the provision applies only to taxpayers that were applicable financial institutions at the time of such sale or exchange. In the case of a sale or exchange of applicable preferred stock after September 6, 2008, by a taxpayer that held such preferred stock on September 6, 2008, the provision applies only where the taxpayer was an applicable financial institution at all times during the period beginning on September 6, 2008, and ending on the date of the sale or exchange of the applicable preferred stock. Thus, the provision is generally inapplicable to any Fannie Mae or Freddie Mac preferred stock held by a taxpayer that was not an applicable financial institution on September 6, 2008 (even if such taxpayer subsequently became an applicable financial institution).

The provision grants the Secretary authority to extend the provision to cases in which gain or loss is recognized on the sale or exchange of applicable preferred stock acquired in a carryover basis transaction by an applicable financial institution after September 6, 2008. For example, if after September 6, 2008, Bank A, an entity that was an applicable financial institution at all times during the period beginning on September 6, 2008, acquired assets of Bank T, an entity that also was an applicable financial institution at all times during the period beginning on September 6, 2008, in a transaction in which no gain or loss was recognized under section 368(a)(1), regulations could provide that Fannie Mae and Freddie Mac stock that was applicable preferred stock in the hands of Bank T will continue to be applicable preferred stock in the hands of Bank A.

In addition, the Secretary may, through regulations, extend the provision to cases in which the applicable financial institution is a partner in a partnership that (i) held preferred stock of Fannie Mae or Freddie Mac on September 6, 2008, and later sold or exchanged such stock, or (ii) sold or exchanged such preferred stock on or after January 1, 2008, and before September 7, 2008. It is intended that Treasury guidance will provide that loss (or gain) attributable to Fannie Mae or Freddie Mac preferred stock of a partnership is characterized as ordinary in the hands of a partner only if the partner is an applicable financial institution, and only if the institution would have been eligible for ordinary treatment under section 301 of the bill had the institution held the underlying preferred stock directly for the time period during which both (i) the partnership holds the preferred stock and (ii) the institution holds substantially the same partnership interest.

In particular, substantial amounts of the preferred stock of Fannie Mae and Freddie Mac are held through "pass-through trusts" analyzed as partnerships for Federal income tax purposes. Substantially all the assets of such a pass-through trust comprise Fannie Mae or Freddie Mac preferred stock, and the trust in turn passes through dividends received on such stock to its two outstanding classes of certificates (partnership interests): an auction-rate class, where the share of the underlying preferred stock dividend is determined by periodic auctions, and a residual class, which receives the remainder of any dividends received on the underlying stock. The bill's delegation of authority to the Secretary anticipates that regulations will promptly be issued confirming in general that losses recognized by such a trust on or after January 1, 2008, in respect of the preferred stock of Fannie Mae or Freddie Mac that it acquired before September 6, 2008, will be characterized as ordinary loss in the hands of a certificate holder that is an applicable financial institution and that would be eligible for the relief contemplated by this provision if the applicable financial institution had held the underlying preferred stock directly for the same period that it held the pass-through certificate. In light of the substantial amount of such pass-through certificates in the marketplace, and the importance of the prompt resolution of the character of any resulting losses allocated to certificate holders that are applicable financial institutions for purposes of their regulatory and investor financial statement filings, unnecessary disruptions to the marketplace could best be avoided if the Secretary were to exercise the

---

[4] On September 7, 2008, the Federal Housing Finance Agency ("FHFA") placed both Fannie Mae and Freddie Mac in a conservatorship. Also on September 7, 2008, FHFA and the Treasury Department entered into Preferred Stock Purchase Agreements, contractual agreements between the Treasury and the conserved entities. Under these agreements, the Treasury Department received senior preferred stock in the two companies and warrants to buy 79.9% of the common stock of such companies.

regulatory authority granted under the provision to address this case as soon as possible and, in any event, by October 31, 2008.

[Law at ¶ 7132. CCH Explanation at ¶ 485.]

Effective Date

This provision applies to sales or exchanges occurring after December 31, 2007, in taxable years ending after such date.

[¶10,020] Act Sec. A302. Special rules for tax treatment of executive compensation of employers participating in the troubled assets relief program

Joint Committee on Taxation (JCT REPT. NO. JCX-79-08)

[Code Secs. 162(m) and 280G]

Present Law

In general

An employer generally may deduct reasonable compensation for personal services as an ordinary and necessary business expense. Sections 162(m) and 280G provide explicit limitations on the deductibility of compensation expenses in the case of corporate employers.

Section 162(m)

In general

The otherwise allowable deduction for compensation paid or accrued with respect to a covered employee of a publicly held corporation[5] is limited to no more than $1 million per year.[6] The deduction limitation applies when the deduction would otherwise be taken. Thus, for example, in the case of compensation resulting from a transfer of property in connection with the performance of services, such compensation is taken into account in applying the deduction limitation for the year for which the compensation is deductible under section 83 (i.e., generally the year in which the employee's right to the property is no longer subject to a substantial risk of forfeiture).

Covered employees

Section 162(m) defines a covered employee as (1) the chief executive officer of the corporation (or an individual acting in such capacity) as of the close of the taxable year and (2) the four most highly compensated officers for the taxable year (other than the chief executive officer). Treasury regulations under section 162(m) provide that whether an employee is the chief executive officer or among the four most highly compensated officers should be determined pursuant to the executive compensation disclosure rules promulgated under the Securities Exchange Act of 1934 ("Exchange Act").

In 2006, the Securities and Exchange Commission amended certain rules relating to executive compensation, including which executive officers' compensation must be disclosed under the Exchange Act. Under the new rules, such officers consist of (1) the principal executive officer (or an individual acting in such capacity), (2) the principal financial officer (or an individual acting in such capacity), and (3) the three most highly compensated executive officers, other than the principal executive officer or financial officer.

In response to the Securities and Exchange Commission's new disclosure rules, the Internal Revenue Service issued updated guidance on identifying which employees are covered by section 162(m).[7] The new guidance provides that "covered employee" means any employee who is (1) the principal executive officer (or an individual acting in such capacity) defined in reference to the Exchange Act, or (2) among the three most highly compensated officers for the taxable year (other than the principal executive officer), again defined by reference to the Exchange Act. Thus, under current guidance, only four employees are covered under section 162(m) for any

---

[5] A corporation is treated as publicly held if it has a class of common equity securities that is required to be registered under section 12 of the Securities Exchange Act of 1934.

[6] Sec. 162(m). This deduction limitation applies for purposes of the regular income tax and the alternative minimum tax.

[7] Notice 2007-49, 2007-25 I.R.B. 1429.

taxable year. Under Treasury regulations, the requirement that the individual meet the criteria as of the last day of the taxable year applies to both the principal executive officer and the three highest compensated officers.[8]

Compensation subject to the deduction limitation

In general.—Unless specifically excluded, the deduction limitation applies to all remuneration for services, including cash and the cash value of all remuneration (including benefits) paid in a medium other than cash. If an individual is a covered employee for a taxable year, the deduction limitation applies to all compensation not explicitly excluded from the deduction limitation, regardless of whether the compensation is for services as a covered employee and regardless of when the compensation was earned. The $1 million cap is reduced by excess parachute payments (as defined in sec. 280G, discussed below) that are not deductible by the corporation.

Certain types of compensation are not subject to the deduction limit and are not taken into account in determining whether other compensation exceeds $1 million. The following types of compensation are not taken into account: (1) remuneration payable on a commission basis; (2) remuneration payable solely on account of the attainment of one or more performance goals if certain outside director and shareholder approval requirements are met ("performance-based compensation"); (3) payments to a tax-qualified retirement plan (including salary reduction contributions); (4) amounts that are excludable from the executive's gross income (such as employer-provided health benefits and miscellaneous fringe benefits (sec. 132)); and (5) any remuneration payable under a written binding contract which was in effect on February 17, 1993. In addition, remuneration does not include compensation for which a deduction is allowable after a covered employee ceases to be a covered employee. Thus, the deduction limitation often does not apply to deferred compensation that is otherwise subject to the deduction limitation (e.g., is not performance-based compensation) because the payment of compensation is deferred until after termination of employment.

Performance-based compensation.—Compensation qualifies for the exception for performance-based compensation only if (1) it is paid solely on account of the attainment of one or more performance goals, (2) the performance goals are established by a compensation committee consisting solely of two or more outside directors,[9] (3) the material terms under which the compensation is to be paid, including the performance goals, are disclosed to and approved by the shareholders in a separate vote prior to payment, and (4) prior to payment, the compensation committee certifies that the performance goals and any other material terms were in fact satisfied.

Compensation (other than stock options or other stock appreciation rights) is not treated as paid solely on account of the attainment of one or more performance goals unless the compensation is paid to the particular executive pursuant to a pre-established objective performance formula or standard that precludes discretion. Stock options or other stock appreciation rights generally are treated as meeting the exception for performance-based compensation, provided that the requirements for outside director and shareholder approval are met (without the need for certification that the performance standards have been met), because the amount of compensation attributable to the options or other rights received by the executive would be based solely on an increase in the corporation's stock price. Stock-based compensation is not treated as performance-based if it is dependent on factors other than corporate performance. For example, if a stock option is granted to an executive with an exercise price that is less than the current fair market value of the stock at the time of grant, then the executive would have the right to receive compensation on the exercise of the option even if the stock price decreases or stays the same. In contrast to options or other stock appreciation rights, grants of restricted stock are not inherently performance-based because the executive may receive compensation even if the stock price decreases or stays the same. Thus, a grant of restricted stock does not satisfy the definition of performance-based compensation unless the grant or vesting of the restricted stock is based upon the attainment of a performance goal and otherwise satisfies the standards for performance-based compensation.

---

[8] Treas. Reg. sec. 1.162-27(c)(2).

[9] A director is considered an outside director if he or she is not a current employee of the corporation (or related entities), is not a former employee of the corporation (or related entities) who is receiving compensation for prior services (other than benefits under a tax-qualified retirement plan), was not an officer of the corporation (or related entities) at any time, and is not currently receiving compensation for personal services in any capacity (e.g., for services as a consultant) other than as a director.

Section 280G

In general

In some cases, a compensation agreement for a corporate executive may provide for payments to be made if there is a change in control of the executive's employer, even if the executive does not lose his or her job as part of the change in control. Such payments are sometimes referred to as "golden parachute payments." The Code contains limits on the amount of certain types of such payments, referred to as "excess parachute payments." Excess parachute payments are not deductible by a corporation.[10] In addition, an excise tax is imposed on the recipient of any excess parachute payment equal to 20 percent of the amount of such payment.[11]

Definition of parachute payment

A "parachute payment" is any payment in the nature of compensation to (or for the benefit of) a disqualified individual which is contingent on a change in the ownership or effective control of a corporation or on a change in the ownership of a substantial portion of the assets of a corporation ("acquired corporation"), if the aggregate present value of all such payments made or to be made to the disqualified individual equals or exceeds three times the individual's "base amount."

The individual's base amount is the average annual compensation payable by the acquired corporation and includible in the individual's gross income over the five-taxable years of such individual preceding the individual's taxable year in which the change in ownership or control occurs.

The term parachute payment also includes any payment in the nature of compensation to a disqualified individual if the payment is made pursuant to an agreement which violates any generally enforced securities laws or regulations.

Certain amounts are not considered parachute payments, including payments under a qualified retirement plan, and payments that are reasonable compensation for services rendered on or after the date of the change in control. In addition, the term parachute payment does not include any payment to a disqualified individual with respect to a small business corporation or a corporation no stock of which was readily tradable, if certain shareholder approval requirements are satisfied.

Disqualified individual

A disqualified individual is any individual who is an employee, independent contractor, or other person specified in Treasury regulations who performs personal services for the corporation and who is an officer, shareholder, or highly compensated individual of the corporation. Personal service corporations and similar entities generally are treated as individuals for this purpose. A highly compensated individual is defined for this purpose as an employee (or a former employee) who is among the highest-paid one percent of individuals performing services for the corporation (or an affiliated corporation) or the 250 highest paid individuals who perform services for a corporation (or affiliated group).

Excess parachute payments

In general, excess parachute payments are any parachute payments in excess of the base amount allocated to the payment. The amount treated as an excess parachute payment is reduced by the portion of the payment that the taxpayer establishes by clear and convincing evidence is reasonable compensation for personal services actually rendered before the change in control.

Explanation of Provision

Section 162(m)

In general

Under the provision, the section 162(m) limit is reduced to $500,000 in the case of otherwise deductible compensation of a covered executive for any applicable taxable year of an applicable employer.

An applicable employer means any employer from which one or more troubled assets are acquired under the "troubled assets relief program" ("TARP") established by the bill if the aggregate amount of the assets so acquired for all taxable years (including assets acquired through a direct purchase by the Treasury Department, within the meaning of section 113(c) of Title I of the bill) exceeds $300,000,000. However, such term does not include any employer from which troubled assets are acquired by the Treasury Department solely through direct purchases (within the meaning of section 113(c) of Title I of the bill). For example, if a firm sells $250,000,000 in assets through an auction system managed by

---

[10] Sec. 280G.

[11] Sec. 4999.

the Treasury Department, and $100,000,000 to the Treasury Department in direct purchases, then the firm is an applicable employer. Conversely, if all $350,000,000 in sales take the form of direct purchases, then the firm would not be an applicable employer.

Unlike section 162(m), an applicable employer under this provision is not limited to publicly held corporations (or even limited to corporations). For example, an applicable employer could be a partnership if the partnership is an employer from which a troubled asset is acquired. The aggregation rules of Code section 414(b) and (c) apply in determining whether an employer is an applicable employer. However, these rules are applied disregarding the rules for brother-sister controlled groups and combined groups in sections 1563(a)(2) and (3). Thus, this aggregation rule only applies to parent-subsidiary controlled groups. A similar controlled group rule applies for trades and businesses under common control.

The result of this aggregation rule is that all corporations in the same controlled group are treated as a single employer for purposes of identifying the covered executives of that employer and all compensation from all members of the controlled group are taken into account for purposes of applying the $500,000 deduction limit. Further, all sales of assets under the TARP from all members of the controlled group are considered in determining whether such sales exceed $300,000,000.

An applicable taxable year with respect to an applicable employer means the first taxable year which includes any portion of the period during which the authorities for the TARP established under the bill are in effect (the "authorities period") if the aggregate amount of 10 troubled assets acquired from the employer under that authority during the taxable year (when added to the aggregate amount so acquired for all preceding taxable years) exceeds $300,000,000, and includes any subsequent taxable year which includes any portion of the authorities period.

A special rule applies in the case of compensation that relates to services that a covered executive performs during an applicable taxable year but that is not deductible until a later year ("deferred deduction executive remuneration"), such as nonqualified deferred compensation. Under the special rule, the unused portion (if any) of the $500,000 limit for the applicable tax year is carried forward until the year in which the compensation is otherwise deductible, and the remaining unused limit is then applied to the compensation.

For example, assume a covered executive is paid $400,000 in cash salary by an applicable employer in 2008 (assuming 2008 is an applicable taxable year) and the covered executive earns $100,000 in nonqualified deferred compensation (along with the right to future earnings credits) payable in 2020. Assume further that the $100,000 has grown to $300,000 in 2020. The full $400,000 in cash salary is deductible under the $500,000 limit in 2008. In 2020, the applicable employer's deduction with respect to the $300,000 will be limited to $100,000 (the lesser of the $300,000 in deductible compensation before considering the special limitation, and $500,000 less $400,000, which represents the unused portion of the $500,000 limit from 2008).

Deferred deduction executive remuneration that is properly deductible in an applicable taxable year (before application of the limitation under the provision) but is attributable to services performed in a prior applicable taxable year is subject to the special rule described above and is not double-counted. For example, assume the same facts as above, except that the nonqualified deferred compensation is deferred until 2009 and that 2009 is an applicable taxable year. The employer's deduction for the nonqualified deferred compensation for 2009 would be limited to $100,000 (as in the example above). The limit that would apply under the provision for executive remuneration that is in a form other than deferred deduction executive remuneration and that is otherwise deductible for 2009 is $500,000. For example, if the covered executive is paid $500,000 in cash compensation for 2009, all $500,000 of that cash compensation would be deductible in 2009 under the provision.

Covered executive

The term covered executive means any individual who is the chief executive officer or the chief financial officer of an applicable employer, or an individual acting in that capacity, at any time during a portion of the taxable year that includes the authorities period. It also includes any employee who is one of the three highest compensated officers of the applicable employer for the applicable taxable year (other than the chief executive officer or the chief financial officer and only taking into account employees employed during any portion of the taxable year that includes the authorities period).

The determination of the three highest compensated officers is made on the basis of the shareholder disclosure rules for compensation under the Exchange Act, except to the extent that the shareholder disclosure rules are inconsistent with the provision.[12] Such shareholder disclosure rules are applied without regard to whether those rules actually apply to the employer under the Exchange Act. If an employee is a covered executive with respect to an applicable employer for any applicable taxable year, the employee will be treated as a covered executive for all subsequent applicable taxable years (and will be treated as a covered executive for purposes of any subsequent taxable year for purposes of the special rule for deferred deduction executive remuneration).

Executive remuneration

The provision generally incorporates the present law definition of applicable employee remuneration. However, the present law exceptions for remuneration payable on commission and performance-based compensation do not apply for purposes of the new $500,000 limit. In addition, the new $500,000 limit only applies to executive remuneration which is attributable to services performed by a covered executive during an applicable taxable year. For example, assume the same facts as in the example above, except that the covered executive also receives in 2008 a payment of $300,000 in nonqualified deferred compensation that was attributable to services performed in 2006. Such payment is not treated as executive remuneration for purposes of the new $500,000 limit.

Other rules

The modification to section 162(m) provides the same coordination rules with disallowed parachute payment and stock compensation of insiders in expatriated corporations as exist under present law section 162(m). Thus, the $500,000 deduction limit under this section is reduced (but not below zero) by any parachute payments (including parachute payments under the expanded definition under this provision) paid during the authorities period and any payment of the excise tax under section 4985 for stock compensation of insiders in expatriated corporations.

The modification authorizes the Secretary of the Treasury to prescribe such guidance, rules, or regulations as are necessary to carry out the purposes of the $500,000 deduction limit, including the application of the limit in the case of any acquisition, merger, or reorganization of an applicable employer.

Section 280G

The provision also modifies section 280G by expanding the definition of parachute payment in the case of a covered executive of an applicable employer. For this purpose, the terms "covered executive," "applicable taxable year," and "applicable employer" have the same meaning as under the modifications to section 162(m) (described above).

Under the modification, a parachute payment means any payments in the nature of compensation to (or for the benefit of) a covered executive made during an applicable taxable year on account of an applicable severance from employment during the authorities period if the aggregate present value of such payments equals or exceeds an amount equal to three times the covered executive's base amount. An applicable severance from employment is any severance from employment of a covered executive (1) by reason of an involuntary termination of the executive by the employer or (2) in connection with a bankruptcy, liquidation, or receivership of the employer.

Whether a payment is on account of the employee's severance from employment is generally determined in the same manner as under present law. Thus, a payment is on account of the employee's severance from employment if the payment would not have been made at that time if the severance from employment had not occurred. Such payments include amounts that are payable upon severance from employment (or separation from service), vest or are no longer subject to a substantial risk of forfeiture on account of such a separation, or are accelerated on account of severance from employment.

---

[12] For example, the shareholder disclosure rules require the reporting of the compensation of the three most highly compensated executive officers (other than the principal executive officer and the principal financial officer) who were serving as executive officers at the end of the last completed fiscal year and up to two additional individuals from whom disclosure would have been provided but for the fact that the individual was not serving as an executive officer at the end of the last completed fiscal year. 17 C.F.R. sec. 229.402(a)(3)(iii), (iv). For purposes of the provision, the term "officer" is intended to mean those "executive officers" whose compensation is subject to reporting under the Exchange Act. Under the provision, however, an individual's status as one of the three most highly compensated officers takes into account only executive officers employed during the authorities period, regardless of whether the individual serves as an executive officer at year end. Additionally, the shareholder disclosure rules measure compensation for purposes of determining "high three" status by reference to total compensation for the last completed fiscal year, and compensation is measured without regard to whether the compensation is includible in an executive officer's gross income. It is intended that this broad measurement of compensation apply for purposes of the provision; however, the measurement period for purposes of the provision is the applicable taxable year for which "high three" status is being determined.

As under present law, the modified definition of parachute payment does not include amounts paid to a covered executive from certain tax qualified retirement plans.

A parachute payment during an applicable taxable year that is paid on account of a covered executive's applicable severance from employment is nondeductible on the part of the employer (and the covered executive is subject to the section 4999 excise tax) to the extent of the amount of the payment that is equal to the excess over the employee's base amount that is allocable to such payment. For example, assume that a covered executive's annualized includible compensation is $1 million and the covered executive's only parachute payment under the provision is a lump sum payment of $5 million. The covered executive's base amount is $1 million and the excess parachute payment is $4 million.

The modifications to section 280G do not apply in the case of a payment that is treated as a parachute payment under present law. The modifications further authorize the Secretary of Treasury to issue regulations to carry out the purposes of the provision, including the application of the provision in the case of a covered executive who receives payments some of which are treated as parachute payments under present law section 280G and others of which are treated as parachute payments on account of this provision, and the application of the provision in the event of any acquisition, merger, or reorganization of an applicable employer. The regulations shall also prevent the avoidance of the application of the provision through the mischaracterization of a severance from employment as other than an applicable severance from employment. It is intended that the regulations prevent the avoidance of the provision through the acceleration, delay, or other modification of payment dates with respect to existing compensation arrangements.

Effective Date

The provision is effective for taxable years ending on or after date of enactment, except that the modifications to section 280G are effective for payments with respect to severances occurring during the authorities period.

[Law at ¶ 5215 and ¶ 5290. CCH Explanation at ¶ 380.]

[¶10,030] Act Sec. A303. Exclude discharges of acquisition indebtedness on principal residences from gross income

Joint Committee on Taxation (JCT REPT. NO. JCX-79-08)

[Code Sec. 108]

Present Law

In general

Gross income includes income that is realized by a debtor from the discharge of indebtedness, subject to certain exceptions for debtors in Title 11 bankruptcy cases, insolvent debtors, certain student loans, certain farm indebtedness, and certain real property business indebtedness (secs. 61(a)(12) and 108).[13] In cases involving discharges of indebtedness that are excluded from gross income under the exceptions to the general rule, taxpayers generally reduce certain tax attributes, including basis in property, by the amount of the discharge of indebtedness.

The amount of discharge of indebtedness excluded from income by an insolvent debtor not in a Title 11 bankruptcy case cannot exceed the amount by which the debtor is insolvent. In the case of a discharge in bankruptcy or where the debtor is insolvent, any reduction in basis may not exceed the excess of the aggregate bases of properties held by the taxpayer immediately after the discharge over the aggregate of the liabilities of the taxpayer immediately after the discharge (sec. 1017).

For all taxpayers, the amount of discharge of indebtedness generally is equal to the difference between the adjusted issue price of the debt being cancelled and the amount used to satisfy the debt. These rules generally apply to the exchange of an old obligation for a new obligation, including a modification of indebtedness that is treated as an exchange (a debt-for-debt exchange).

Qualified principal residence indebtedness

An exclusion from gross income is provided for any discharge of indebtedness income by reason of a discharge (in whole or in part) of

---

[13] A debt cancellation which constitutes a gift or bequest is not treated as income to the donee debtor (sec. 102).

qualified principal residence indebtedness. Qualified principal residence indebtedness means acquisition indebtedness (within the meaning of section 163(h)(3)(B), except that the dollar limitation is $2,000,000) with respect to the taxpayer's principal residence. Acquisition indebtedness with respect to a principal residence generally means indebtedness which is incurred in the acquisition, construction, or substantial improvement of the principal residence of the individual and is secured by the residence. It also includes refinancing of such indebtedness to the extent the amount of the indebtedness resulting from such refinancing does not exceed the amount of the refinanced indebtedness. For these purposes, the term "principal residence" has the same meaning as under section 121 of the Code.

If, immediately before the discharge, only a portion of a discharged indebtedness is qualified principal residence indebtedness, the exclusion applies only to so much of the amount discharged as exceeds the portion of the debt which is not qualified principal residence indebtedness. Thus, assume that a principal residence is secured by an indebtedness of $1 million, of which $800,000 is qualified principal residence indebtedness. If the residence is sold for $700,000 and $300,000 debt is discharged, then only $100,000 of the amount discharged may be excluded from gross income under the qualified principal residence indebtedness exclusion.

The basis of the individual's principal residence is reduced by the amount excluded from income under the provision.

The qualified principal residence indebtedness exclusion does not apply to a taxpayer in a Title 11 case; instead the general exclusion rules apply. In the case of an insolvent taxpayer not in a Title 11 case, the qualified principal residence indebtedness exclusion applies unless the taxpayer elects to have the general exclusion rules apply instead.

The exclusion does not apply to the discharge of a loan if the discharge is on account of services performed for the lender or any other factor not directly related to a decline in the value of the residence or to the financial condition of the taxpayer.

The exclusion for qualified principal residence indebtedness is effective for discharges of indebtedness before January 1, 2010.

Explanation of Provision

The provision extends for three additional years the exclusion from gross income for discharges of qualified principal residence indebtedness.

Effective Date

The provision is effective for discharges of indebtedness on or after January 1, 2010, and before January 1, 2013.

[Law at ¶5190. CCH Explanation at ¶220.]

[¶10,040] Act Secs. B101 and B102. Extension and modification of the credit for the production of electricity from renewable resources

Joint Committee on Taxation (J.C.T. Rep. No. JCX-75-08)

[Code Sec. 45]

Present Law

In general

An income tax credit is allowed for the production of electricity from qualified energy resources at qualified facilities.[2] Qualified energy resources comprise wind, closed-loop biomass, open-loop biomass, geothermal energy, solar energy, small irrigation power, municipal solid waste, and qualified hydropower production.

Qualified facilities are, generally, facilities that generate electricity using qualified energy resources. To be eligible for the credit, electricity produced from qualified energy resources at qualified facilities must be sold by the taxpayer to an unrelated person.

Credit amounts and credit period

In general

The base amount of the electricity production credit is 1.5 cents per kilowatt-hour (indexed

---

[2] Sec. 45. In addition to the electricity production credit, section 45 also provides income tax credits for the production of Indian coal and refined coal at qualified facilities.

Unless otherwise stated, all section references are to the Internal Revenue Code of 1986, as amended (the "Code").

annually for inflation) of electricity produced. The amount of the credit was 2.1 cents per kilowatt-hour for 2008. A taxpayer may generally claim a credit during the 10-year period commencing with the date the qualified facility is placed in service. The credit is reduced for grants, tax-exempt bonds, subsidized energy financing, and other credits.

Credit phaseout

The amount of credit a taxpayer may claim is phased out as the market price of electricity exceeds certain threshold levels. The electricity production credit is reduced over a 3 cent phaseout range to the extent the annual average contract price per kilowatt-hour of electricity sold in the prior year from the same qualified energy resource exceeds 8 cents (adjusted for inflation; 11.8 cents for 2008).

Reduced credit periods and credit amounts

Generally, in the case of open-loop biomass facilities (including agricultural livestock waste nutrient facilities), geothermal energy facilities, solar energy facilities, small irrigation power facilities, landfill gas facilities, and trash combustion facilities placed in service before August 8, 2005, the 10-year credit period is reduced to five years commencing on the date the facility was originally placed in service. However, for qualified open-loop biomass facilities (other than a facility described in sec. 45(d)(3)(A)(i) that uses agricultural livestock waste nutrients) placed in service before October 22, 2004, the five-year period commences on January 1, 2005. In the case of a closed-loop biomass facility modified to co-fire with coal, to co-fire with other biomass, or to co-fire with coal and other biomass, the credit period begins no earlier than October 22, 2004.

In the case of open-loop biomass facilities (including agricultural livestock waste nutrient facilities), small irrigation power facilities, landfill gas facilities, trash combustion facilities, and qualified hydropower facilities the otherwise allowable credit amount is 0.75 cent per kilowatt-hour, indexed for inflation measured after 1992 (1 cent per kilowatt-hour for 2008).

Other limitations on credit claimants and credit amounts

In general, in order to claim the credit, a taxpayer must own the qualified facility and sell the electricity produced by the facility to an unrelated party. A lessee or operator may claim the credit in lieu of the owner of the qualifying facility in the case of qualifying open-loop biomass facilities and in the case of closed-loop biomass facilities modified to co-fire with coal, to co-fire with other biomass, or to co-fire with coal and other biomass. In the case of a poultry waste facility, the taxpayer may claim the credit as a lessee or operator of a facility owned by a governmental unit.

For all qualifying facilities, other than closed-loop biomass facilities modified to co-fire with coal, to co-fire with other biomass, or to co-fire with coal and other biomass, the amount of credit a taxpayer may claim is reduced by reason of grants, tax-exempt bonds, subsidized energy financing, and other credits, but the reduction cannot exceed 50 percent of the otherwise allowable credit. In the case of closed-loop biomass facilities modified to co-fire with coal, to co-fire with other biomass, or to co-fire with coal and other biomass, there is no reduction in credit by reason of grants, tax-exempt bonds, subsidized energy financing, and other credits.

The credit for electricity produced from renewable sources is a component of the general business credit.[3] Generally, the general business credit for any taxable year may not exceed the amount by which the taxpayer's net income tax exceeds the greater of the tentative minimum tax or so much of the net regular tax liability as exceeds $25,000. Excess credits may be carried back one year and forward up to 20 years.

A taxpayer's tentative minimum tax is treated as being zero for purposes of determining the tax liability limitation with respect to the section 45 credit for electricity produced from a facility (placed in service after October 22, 2004) during the first four years of production beginning on the date the facility is placed in service.

Qualified facilities

Wind energy facility

A wind energy facility is a facility that uses wind to produce electricity. To be a qualified facility, a wind energy facility must be placed in service after December 31, 1993, and before January 1, 2009.

Closed-loop biomass facility

A closed-loop biomass facility is a facility that uses any organic material from a plant which is planted exclusively for the purpose of being used at a qualifying facility to produce electricity. In addition, a facility can be a closed-loop biomass facility if it is a facility that is modified to use closed-loop biomass to co-fire

---

[3] Sec. 38(b)(8).

with coal, with other biomass, or with both coal and other biomass, but only if the modification is approved under the Biomass Power for Rural Development Programs or is part of a pilot project of the Commodity Credit Corporation.

To be a qualified facility, a closed-loop biomass facility must be placed in service after December 31, 1992, and before January 1, 2009. In the case of a facility using closed-loop biomass but also co-firing the closed-loop biomass with coal, other biomass, or coal and other biomass, a qualified facility must be originally placed in service and modified to co-fire the closed-loop biomass at any time before January 1, 2009.

Open-loop biomass (including agricultural livestock waste nutrients) facility

An open-loop biomass facility is a facility that uses open-loop biomass to produce electricity. For purposes of the credit, open-loop biomass is defined as (1) any agricultural livestock waste nutrients or (2) any solid, nonhazardous, cellulosic waste material or any lignin material that is segregated from other waste materials and which is derived from:

• forest-related resources, including mill and harvesting residues, precommercial thinnings, slash, and brush;

• solid wood waste materials, including waste pallets, crates, dunnage, manufacturing and construction wood wastes, and landscape or right-of-way tree trimmings; or

• agricultural sources, including orchard tree crops, vineyard, grain, legumes, sugar, and other crop by-products or residues.

Agricultural livestock waste nutrients are defined as agricultural livestock manure and litter, including bedding material for the disposition of manure. Wood waste materials do not qualify as open-loop biomass to the extent they are pressure treated, chemically treated, or painted. In addition, municipal solid waste, gas derived from the biodegradation of solid waste, and paper which is commonly recycled do not qualify as open-loop biomass. Open-loop biomass does not include closed-loop biomass or any biomass burned in conjunction with fossil fuel (co-firing) beyond such fossil fuel required for start up and flame stabilization.

In the case of an open-loop biomass facility that uses agricultural livestock waste nutrients, a qualified facility is one that was originally placed in service after October 22, 2004, and before January 1, 2009, and has a nameplate capacity rating which is not less than 150 kilowatts. In the case of any other open-loop biomass facility, a qualified facility is one that was

originally placed in service before January 1, 2009.

Geothermal facility

A geothermal facility is a facility that uses geothermal energy to produce electricity. Geothermal energy is energy derived from a geothermal deposit that is a geothermal reservoir consisting of natural heat that is stored in rocks or in an aqueous liquid or vapor (whether or not under pressure). To be a qualified facility, a geothermal facility must be placed in service after October 22, 2004, and before January 1, 2009.

Solar facility

A solar facility is a facility that uses solar energy to produce electricity. To be a qualified facility, a solar facility must be placed in service after October 22, 2004, and before January 1, 2006.

Small irrigation facility

A small irrigation power facility is a facility that generates electric power through an irrigation system canal or ditch without any dam or impoundment of water. The installed capacity of a qualified facility must be at least 150 kilowatts but less than five megawatts. To be a qualified facility, a small irrigation facility must be originally placed in service after October 22, 2004, and before January 1, 2009.

Landfill gas facility

A landfill gas facility is a facility that uses landfill gas to produce electricity. Landfill gas is defined as methane gas derived from the biodegradation of municipal solid waste. To be a qualified facility, a landfill gas facility must be placed in service after October 22, 2004, and before January 1, 2009.

Trash combustion facility

Trash combustion facilities are facilities that burn municipal solid waste (garbage) to produce steam to drive a turbine for the production of electricity. To be a qualified facility, a trash combustion facility must be placed in service after October 22, 2004, and before January 1, 2009. A qualified trash combustion facility includes a new unit, placed in service after October 22, 2004, that increases electricity production capacity at an existing trash combustion facility. A new unit generally would include a new burner/boiler and turbine. The new unit may share certain common equipment, such as trash handling equipment, with other pre-existing units at the same facility. Electricity produced at a new unit of an existing facility qualifies for the production credit only to the extent of the increased amount of electricity produced at the entire facility.

Hydropower facility

A qualifying hydropower facility is (1) a facility that produced hydroelectric power (a hydroelectric dam) prior to August 8, 2005, at which efficiency improvements or additions to capacity have been made after such date and before January 1, 2009, that enable the taxpayer to produce incremental hydropower or (2) a facility placed in service before August 8, 2005, that did not produce hydroelectric power (a nonhydroelectric dam) on such date, and to which turbines or other electricity generating equipment have been added after such date and before January 1, 2009.

At an existing hydroelectric facility, the taxpayer may claim credit only for the production of incremental hydroelectric power. Incremental hydroelectric power for any taxable year is equal to the percentage of average annual hydroelectric power produced at the facility attributable to the efficiency improvement or additions of capacity determined by using the same water flow information used to determine an historic average annual hydroelectric power production baseline for that facility. The Federal Energy Regulatory Commission will certify the baseline power production of the facility and the percentage increase due to the efficiency and capacity improvements.

At a nonhydroelectric dam, the facility must be licensed by the Federal Energy Regulatory Commission and meet all other applicable environmental, licensing, and regulatory requirements and the turbines or other generating devices must be added to the facility after August 8, 2005 and before January 1, 2009. In addition, there must not be any enlargement of the diversion structure, construction or enlargement of a bypass channel, or the impoundment or any withholding of additional water from the natural stream channel.

Summary of credit rate and credit period by facility type

Table 1.-Summary of Section 45 Credit for Electricity Produced from Certain Renewable Resources

Eligible electricity production activity	Credit amount for 2008 (cents per kilowatt-hour)	Credit period for facilities placed in service on or before August 8, 2005 (years from placed-in-service date)	Credit period for facilities placed in service after August 8, 2005 (years from placed-in-service date)
Wind	2.1	10	10
Closed-loop biomass	2.1	10[1]	10
Open-loop biomass (including agricultural livestock waste nutrient facilities)	1.0	5[2]	10
Geothermal	2.1	5	10
Solar (pre-2006 facilities only)	2.1	5	10
Small irrigation power	1.0	5	10
Municipal solid waste (including landfill gas facilities and trash combustion facilities)	1.0	5	10
Qualified hydropower	1.0	N/A	10

[1] In the case of certain co-firing closed-loop facilities, the credit period begins no earlier than October 22, 2004.

[2] For certain facilities placed in service before October 22, 2004, the five-year credit period commences on January 1, 2005.

Taxation of cooperatives and their patrons

For Federal income tax purposes, a cooperative generally computes its income as if it were a taxable corporation, with one exception: the cooperative may exclude from its taxable income distributions of patronage dividends. Generally, a cooperative that is subject to the cooperative tax rules of subchapter T of the Code[4] is permitted a deduction for patronage dividends paid only to the extent of net income that is derived from transactions with patrons who are members of the cooperative.[5] The availability of such deductions from taxable income has the effect of allowing the cooperative to be treated like a conduit with respect to profits derived from transactions with patrons who are members of the cooperative.

Eligible cooperatives may elect to pass any portion of the credit through to their patrons. An eligible cooperative is defined as a cooperative organization that is owned more than 50 percent by agricultural producers or entities owned by agricultural producers. The credit may be apportioned among patrons eligible to share in patronage dividends on the basis of the quantity or value of business done with or for such patrons for the taxable year. The election must be made on a timely filed return for the taxable year and, once made, is irrevocable for such taxable year.

Explanation of Provision

The provision extends and modifies the electricity production credit.

Extension of placed-in-service date for qualifying facilities

The provision extends for two years and nine months (through September 30, 2011) the period during which qualified facilities producing electricity from closed-loop biomass, open-loop biomass, geothermal energy, small irrigation power, municipal solid waste, and qualified hydropower may be placed in service for purposes of the electricity production credit. The provision extends for one year (through 2009) the placed-in-service period for qualified wind facilities.

Addition of marine and hydrokinetic renewable energy as a qualified resource

The provision adds marine and hydrokinetic renewable energy as a qualified energy resource and marine and hydrokinetic renewable energy facilities as qualified facilities. Marine and hydrokinetic renewable energy is defined as energy derived from (1) waves, tides, and currents in oceans, estuaries, and tidal areas; (2) free flowing water in rivers, lakes, and streams; (3) free flowing water in an irrigation system, canal, or other man-made channel, including projects that utilize nonmechanical structures to accelerate the flow of water for electric power production purposes; or (4) differentials in ocean temperature (ocean thermal energy conversion). The term does not include energy derived from any source that uses a dam, diversionary structure (except for irrigation systems, canals, and other man-made channels), or impoundment for electric power production. A qualified marine and hydrokinetic renewable energy facility is any facility owned by the taxpayer and placed in service after the date of enactment and before October 1, 2011, that produces electric power from marine and hydrokinetic renewable energy and that has a nameplate capacity rating of at least 150 kilowatts.

Under the provision, marine and hydrokinetic renewable energy facilities subsume small irrigation power facilities. The provision, therefore, terminates as a separate category of qualified facility small irrigation power facilities placed in service on or after the date of enactment. Such facilities qualify for the electricity production credit as marine and hydrokinetic renewable energy facilities.

Phaseout replaced by limitation based on investment in facility

The provision replaces the electricity production credit phaseout with an annual limit on the total credits that may be claimed with respect to any qualified facility placed in service after 2009 based on the investment in the facility. Under the limitation, the electricity production credit determined for any taxable year may not exceed the eligible basis of the facility multiplied by a limitation percentage (the "applicable percentage") determined by the Secretary for the month during which the facility is originally placed in service. The applicable percentage for any month is the percentage that yields over a 10-year period amounts of limitation that have a present value equal to 35 percent of the eligible basis of the facility. The discount rate for purposes of this calculation is the greater of 4.5 percent or 110 percent of the long-term Federal rate. The provision does not impose this limitation on the credit for electricity produced at qualified wind facilities. Whether it will apply in

---

[4] Secs. 1381-1383.

[5] Sec. 1382.

the future is a determination for another Congress.

Generally, the eligible basis of a facility is the basis of such facility at the time it is originally placed in service. In the case of a qualified geothermal facility, the eligible basis for purposes of the limitation includes intangible drilling and development costs described in section 263(c).

At the election of the taxpayer, all qualified facilities which are part of the same project and which are placed in service during the same calendar year may be treated as a single facility placed in service at either the mid-point of such year or the first day of the following calendar year.

Special rules apply for the first and last year of a facility's 10-year credit period to allocate the limitation across a taxpayer's taxable years. In addition, if a facility's production is less than the limitation amount for any taxable year, the limitation with respect to such facility for the next taxable year is increased by the amount of the unused limitation. Similarly, if the electricity production credit exceeds the limitation amount for any taxable year, but falls under the limit the following year, the credit for the following taxable year is increased, up to that year's limitation amount, by the amount of such excess, but not beyond the facility's 10-year credit eligibility period.

Clarification of the definition of trash combustion facility

The provision modifies the definition of qualified trash combustion facility to permit facilities that use municipal solid waste as part of an electricity generation process to qualify for the electricity production credit, whether or not such facilities utilize a process that involves burning the waste.

Modification of the definitions of open-loop biomass facility and closed-loop biomass facility to include new units added to existing qualified facilities

The definitions of qualified open-loop biomass facility and qualified closed-loop biomass facility are modified to include new power generation units placed in service at existing qualified facilities, but only to the extent of the increased amount of electricity produced at such facilities by reason of such new units.

Modification to definition of nonhydroelectric dam for purposes of qualified hydropower production

The provision modifies the definition of nonhydroelectric dam for purposes of qualified hydropower production. Under the new definition, the nonhydroelectric dam must have been operated for flood control, navigation, or water supply purposes.

The provision replaces the requirement that the project not enlarge the diversion structure or bypass channel, or impound additional water from the natural stream channel, with a requirement that the project be operated so that the water surface elevation at any given location and time be the same as would occur in absence of the project, subject to any license requirements aimed at improving the environmental quality of the affected waterway.

The hydroelectric project installed on the nonhydroelectric dam must still be licensed by the Federal Energy Regulatory Commission and meet all other applicable environmental, licensing, and regulatory requirements, including applicable fish passage requirements.

Effective Date

The extension of the electricity production credit is effective for facilities originally placed in service after 2008. The addition of marine and hydrokinetic renewable energy as a qualified energy resource is effective for electricity produced at qualified facilities and sold after the date of enactment in taxable years ending after such date. The repeal of the credit phaseout adjustment is effective for taxable years ending after 2008. The limitation based on investment is effective for facilities originally placed in service after 2009. The clarification of the definition of trash combustion facility is effective for electricity produced and sold after the date of enactment. The modifications to the definitions of open-loop biomass facility, closed-loop biomass facility, and nonhydroelectric dam are effective for property placed in service after the date of enactment.

[Law at ¶5075. CCH Explanation at ¶525.]

[¶10,050] Act Sec. B103. Extension and modification of energy credit

Joint Committee on Taxation (J.C.T. REP. NO. JCX-75-08)

[Code Sec. 48]

Present Law

In general

A nonrefundable, 10-percent business energy credit[6] is allowed for the cost of new property that is equipment that either (1) uses solar energy to generate electricity, to heat or cool a structure, or to provide solar process heat, or (2) is used to produce, distribute, or use energy derived from a geothermal deposit, but only, in the case of electricity generated by geothermal power, up to the electric transmission stage. Property used to generate energy for the purposes of heating a swimming pool is not eligible solar energy property.

The energy credit is a component of the general business credit[7] and as such is subject to the alternative minimum tax. An unused general business credit generally may be carried back one year and carried forward 20 years.[8] The taxpayer's basis in the property is reduced by one-half of the amount of the credit claimed. For projects whose construction time is expected to equal or exceed two years, the credit may be claimed as progress expenditures are made on the project, rather than during the year the property is placed in service. Similarly, the credit only applies to expenditures made after the effective date of the provision.

In general, property that is public utility property is not eligible for the credit. Public utility property is property that is used predominantly in the trade or business of the furnishing or sale of (1) electrical energy, water, or sewage disposal services, (2) gas through a local distribution system, or (3) telephone service, domestic telegraph services, or other communication services (other than international telegraph services), if the rates for such furnishing or sale have been established or approved by a State or political subdivision thereof, by an agency or instrumentality of the United States, or by a public service or public utility commission. This rule is waived in the case of telecommunication companies' purchases of fuel cell and microturbine property.

Special rules for solar energy property

The credit for solar energy property is increased to 30 percent in the case of periods after December 31, 2005 and prior to January 1, 2009. Additionally, equipment that uses fiber-optic distributed sunlight to illuminate the inside of a structure is solar energy property eligible for the 30-percent credit.

Fuel cells and microturbines

The business energy credit also applies for the purchase of qualified fuel cell power plants, but only for periods after December 31, 2005 and prior to January 1, 2009. The credit rate is 30 percent.

A qualified fuel cell power plant is an integrated system composed of a fuel cell stack assembly and associated balance of plant components that (1) converts a fuel into electricity using electrochemical means, and (2) has an electricity-only generation efficiency of greater than 30 percent and a capacity of at least on-half kilowatt. The credit may not exceed $500 for each 0.5 kilowatt of capacity.

The business energy credit also applies for the purchase of qualifying stationary microturbine power plants, but only for periods after December 31, 2005 and prior to January 1, 2009. The credit is limited to the lesser of 10 percent of the basis of the property or $200 for each kilowatt of capacity.

A qualified stationary microturbine power plant is an integrated system comprised of a gas turbine engine, a combustor, a recuperator or regenerator, a generator or alternator, and associated balance of plant components that converts a fuel into electricity and thermal energy. Such system also includes all secondary components located between the existing infrastructure for fuel delivery and the existing infrastructure for power distribution, including equipment and controls for meeting relevant power standards, such as voltage, frequency and power factors. Such system must have an electricity-only generation efficiency of not less that 26 percent at

---

[6] Sec. 48.

[7] Sec. 38(b)(1).

[8] Sec. 39.

International Standard Organization conditions and a capacity of less than 2,000 kilowatts.

Additionally, for purposes of the fuel cell and microturbine credits, and only in the case of telecommunications companies, the general present-law section 48 restriction that would otherwise prohibit telecommunication companies from claiming the new credit due to their status as public utilities is waived.

Explanation of Provision

The provision extends the otherwise expiring credits and credit rates for eight years, through December 31, 2016. The provision raises the $500 per half kilowatt of capacity credit cap with respect to fuel cells to $1500 per half kilowatt of capacity. Also, the restrictions on public utility property being eligible for the credit are repealed. The provision makes the energy credit allowable against the alternative minimum tax.

The provision makes combined heat and power ("CHP") property eligible for the 10-percent energy credit through December 31, 2016.

CHP property is property: (1) that uses the same energy source for the simultaneous or sequential generation of electrical power, mechanical shaft power, or both, in combination with the generation of steam or other forms of useful thermal energy (including heating and cooling applications); (2) that has an electrical capacity of not more than 50 megawatts or a mechanical energy capacity of no more than 67,000 horsepower or an equivalent combination of electrical and mechanical energy capacities; (3) that produces at least 20 percent of its total useful energy in the form of thermal energy that is not used to produce electrical or mechanical power, and produces at least 20 percent of its total useful energy in the form of electrical or mechanical power (or a combination thereof); and (4) the energy efficiency percentage of which exceeds 60 percent. CHP property does not include property used to transport the energy source to the generating facility or to distribute energy produced by the facility.

The otherwise allowable credit with respect to CHP property is reduced to the extent the property has an electrical capacity or mechanical capacity in excess of any applicable limits. Property in excess of the applicable limit (15 mega-watts or a mechanical energy capacity of more than 20,000 horsepower or an equivalent combination of electrical and mechanical energy capacities) is permitted to claim a fraction of the otherwise allowable credit. The fraction is equal to the applicable limit divided by the capacity of the property. For example, a 45 megawatt property would be eligible to claim 15/45ths, or one third, of the otherwise allowable credit. Again, no credit is allowed if the property exceeds the 50 megawatt or 67,000 horsepower limitations described above.

Additionally, the provision provides that systems whose fuel source is at least 90 percent open-loop biomass and that would qualify for the credit but for the failure to meet the efficiency standard are eligible for a credit that is reduced in proportion to the degree to which the system fails to meet the efficiency standard. For example, a system that would otherwise be required to meet the 60-percent efficiency standard, but which only achieves 30-percent efficiency, would be permitted a credit equal to one-half of the otherwise allowable credit (i.e., a 5-percent credit).

Effective Date

The provision is generally effective on the date of enactment.

The provision relating to combined heat and power property applies to periods after the date of enactment, in taxable years ending after such date, under rules similar to the rules of section 48(m) of the Code (as in effect on the day before the enactment of the Revenue Reconciliation Act of 1990).

The provision relating to the restrictions on public utility property applies to periods after February 13, 2008, in taxable years ending after such date, under rules similar to the rules of section 48(m) of the Code (as in effect on the day before the enactment of the Revenue Reconciliation Act of 1990).

The allowance of the credit against the alternative minimum tax is effective for credits determined in taxable years beginning after the date of enactment.

[Law at ¶5055 and ¶5125. CCH Explanation at ¶530.]

[¶10,060] Act Sec. B106. Credit for residential energy efficient property

Joint Committee on Taxation (J.C.T. REP. No. JCX-75-08)

[Code Sec. 25D]

Present Law

Code section 25D provides a personal tax credit for the purchase of qualified solar electric property and qualified solar water heating property that is used exclusively for purposes other than heating swimming pools and hot tubs. The credit is equal to 30 percent of qualifying expenditures, with a maximum credit for each of these systems of property of $2,000. Section 25D also provides a 30 percent credit for the purchase of qualified fuel cell power plants. The credit for any fuel cell may not exceed $500 for each 0.5 kilowatt of capacity.

Qualifying solar water heating property means an expenditure for property to heat water for use in a dwelling unit located in the United States and used as a residence if at least half of the energy used by such property for such purpose is derived from the sun. Qualified solar electric property is property that uses solar energy to generate electricity for use in a dwelling unit. A qualified fuel cell power plant is an integrated system comprised of a fuel cell stack assembly and associated balance of plant components that (1) converts a fuel into electricity using electrochemical means, (2) has an electricity-only generation efficiency of greater than 30 percent. The qualified fuel cell power plant must be installed on or in connection with a dwelling unit located in the United States and used by the taxpayer as a principal residence.

The credit is nonrefundable, and the depreciable basis of the property is reduced by the amount of the credit. Expenditures for labor costs allocable to onsite preparation, assembly, or original installation of property eligible for the credit are eligible expenditures.

Certain equipment safety requirements need to be met to qualify for the credit. Special proration rules apply in the case of jointly owned property, condominiums, and tenant-stockholders in cooperative housing corporations. If less than 80 percent of the property is used for nonbusiness purposes, only that portion of expenditures that is used for nonbusiness purposes is taken into account.

The credit applies to property placed in service prior to January 1, 2009.

Explanation of Provision

The provision extends the credit for eight years (through December 31, 2016) and allows the credit to be claimed against the alternative minimum tax. Additionally, the credit cap (currently $2,000) for solar electric property is eliminated.

The provision provides a new 30 percent credit for qualified small wind energy property expenses made by the taxpayer during the taxable year. The credit is limited to $500 with respect to each half kilowatt of capacity, not to exceed $4,000. The credit for qualified small wind energy property is allowed for expenditures after December 31, 2007, for property placed in service prior to January 1, 2017.

Qualified small wind energy property expenditures are expenditures for property that uses a wind turbine to generate electricity for use in a dwelling unit located in the U.S. and used as a residence by the taxpayer.

The provision also provides a 30 percent credit for qualified geothermal heat pump property expenditures, not to exceed $2,000. The term "qualified geothermal heat pump property expenditure" means an expenditure for qualified geothermal heat pump property installed on or in connection with a dwelling unit located in the United States and used as a residence by the taxpayer. Qualified geothermal heat pump property means any equipment which (1) uses the ground or ground water as a thermal energy source to heat the dwelling unit or as a thermal energy sink to cool such dwelling unit, and (2) meets the requirements of the Energy Star program which are in effect at the time that the expenditure for such equipment is made. The credit for qualified geothermal heat pump property is allowed for expenditures after December 31, 2007, for property placed in service prior to January 1, 2017.

Effective Date

Generally, the provision is effective for taxable years beginning after December 31, 2007, for property placed in service prior to January 1, 2017. The removal of the solar electric credit cap is effective for property placed in service after the date of enactment.

[Law at ¶ 5005, ¶ 5010, ¶ 5020, ¶ 5030, ¶ 5035 and ¶ 5075. CCH Explanation at ¶ 510.]

[¶10,070] Act Sec. B109. Special rule to implement FERC and State electric restructuring policy

Joint Committee on Taxation (J.C.T. Rep. No. JCX-75-08)

[Code Sec. 451(i)]

Present Law

Generally, a taxpayer selling property recognizes gain to the extent the sales price (and any other consideration received) exceeds the seller's basis in the property. The recognized gain is subject to current income tax unless the gain is deferred or not recognized under a special tax provision.

One such special tax provision permits taxpayers to elect to recognize gain from qualifying electric transmission transactions ratably over an eight-year period beginning in the year of sale if the amount realized from such sale is used to purchase exempt utility property within the applicable period[9] (the "reinvestment property"). If the amount realized exceeds the amount used to purchase reinvestment property, any realized gain is recognized to the extent of such excess in the year of the qualifying electric transmission transaction.

A qualifying electric transmission transaction is the sale or other disposition of property used by the taxpayer in the trade or business of providing electric transmission services, or an ownership interest in such an entity, to an independent transmission company prior to January 1, 2008. In general, an independent transmission company is defined as: (1) an independent transmission provider[10] approved by the FERC; (2) a person (i) who the FERC determines under section 203 of the Federal Power Act (or by declaratory order) is not a "market participant" and (ii) whose transmission facilities are placed under the operational control of a FERC-approved independent transmission provider before the close of the period specified in such authorization, but not later than December 31, 2007; or (3)

in the case of facilities subject to the jurisdiction of the Public Utility Commission of Texas, (i) a person which is approved by that Commission as consistent with Texas State law regarding an independent transmission organization, or (ii) a political subdivision, or affiliate thereof, whose transmission facilities are under the operational control of an organization described in (i).

Exempt utility property is defined as: (1) property used in the trade or business of generating, transmitting, distributing, or selling electricity or producing, transmitting, distributing, or selling natural gas, or (2) stock in a controlled corporation whose principal trade or business consists of the activities described in (1).

If a taxpayer is a member of an affiliated group of corporations filing a consolidated return, the reinvestment property may be purchased by any member of the affiliated group (in lieu of the taxpayer).

Explanation of Provision

The provision extends the treatment under the present-law deferral provision to sales or dispositions by a qualified electric utility prior to January 1, 2010. A qualified electric utility is defined as an electric utility, which as of the date of the qualifying electric transmission transaction, is vertically integrated in that it is both (1) a transmitting utility (as defined in the Federal Power Act)[11] with respect to the transmission facilities to which the election applies, and (2) an electric utility (as defined in the Federal Power Act).[12]

The definition of an independent transmission company is modified for taxpayers whose transmission facilities are placed under the operational control of a FERC-approved independent

---

[9] The applicable period for a taxpayer to reinvest the proceeds is four years after the close of the taxable year in which the qualifying electric transmission transaction occurs.

[10] For example, a regional transmission organization, an independent system operator, or an independent transmission company.

[11] Sec. 3(23), 16 U.S.C. 796, defines "transmitting utility" as any electric utility, qualifying cogeneration facility, quali-

fying small power production facility, or Federal power marketing agency which owns or operates electric power transmission facilities which are used for the sale of electric energy at wholesale.

[12] Sec. 3(22), 16 U.S.C. 796, defines "electric utility" as any person or State agency (including any municipality) which sells electric energy; such term includes the Tennessee Valley Authority, but does not include any Federal power marketing agency.

transmission provider, which under the provision must take place no later than four years after the close of the taxable year in which the transaction occurs.

The provision also changes the definition of exempt utility property to exclude property that is located outside the United States.

Effective Date

The extension provision applies to transactions after December 31, 2007. The change in the definition of an independent transmission company is effective as if included in section 909 of the American Jobs Creation Act of 2004. The exclusion for property located outside the United States applies to transactions after date of enactment.

[Law at ¶5300. CCH Explanation at ¶755.]

[¶10,080] Act Sec. B111. Expansion and modification of the advanced coal project credit

Joint Committee on Taxation (J.C.T. REP. NO. JCX-75-08)

[Code Sec. 48A]

Present Law

An investment tax credit is available for power generation projects that use integrated gasification combined cycle ("IGCC") or other advanced coal-based electricity generation technologies. The credit amount is 20 percent for investments in qualifying IGCC projects and 15 percent for investments in qualifying projects that use other advanced coal-based electricity generation technologies.

To qualify, an advanced coal project must be located in the United States and use an advanced coal-based generation technology to power a new electric generation unit or to retrofit or re-power an existing unit. Generally, an electric generation unit using an advanced coal-based technology must be designed to achieve a 99 percent reduction in sulfur dioxide and a 90 percent reduction in mercury, as well as to limit emissions of nitrous oxide and particulate matter.[13]

The fuel input for a qualifying project, when completed, must use at least 75 percent coal. The project, consisting of one or more electric generation units at one site, must have a nameplate generating capacity of at least 400 megawatts, and the taxpayer must provide evidence that a majority of the output of the project is reasonably expected to be acquired or utilized.

Credits are available only for projects certified by the Secretary of Treasury, in consultation with the Secretary of Energy. Certifications are issued using a competitive bidding process. The Secretary of Treasury must establish a certification program no later than 180 days after August 8, 2005,[14] and each project application must be submitted during the three-year period beginning on the date such certification program is established. An applicant for certification has two years from the date the Secretary accepts the application to provide the Secretary with evidence that the requirements for certification have been met. Upon certification, the applicant has five years from the date of issuance of the certification to place the project in service.

The Secretary of Treasury may allocate $800 million of credits to IGCC projects and $500 million to projects using other advanced coal-based electricity generation technologies. Qualified projects must be economically feasible and use the appropriate clean coal technologies. With respect to IGCC projects, credit-eligible investments include only investments in property associated with the gasification of coal, including any coal handling and gas separation equipment. Thus, investments in equipment that could operate by drawing fuel directly from a natural gas pipeline do not qualify for the credit.

In determining which projects to certify that use IGCC technology, the Secretary must allo-

---

[13] For advanced coal project certification applications submitted after October 2, 2006, an electric generation unit using advanced coal-based generation technology designed to use subbituminous coal can meet the performance requirement relating to the removal of sulfur dioxide if it is designed either to remove 99 percent of the sulfur dioxide or

to achieve an emission limit of 0.04 pounds of sulfur dioxide per million British thermal units on a 30-day average.

[14] The Secretary issued guidance establishing the certification program on February 21, 2006 (IRS Notice 2006-24).

cate power generation capacity in relatively equal amounts to projects that use bituminous coal, subbituminous coal, and lignite as primary feedstock. In addition, the Secretary must give high priority to projects which include greenhouse gas capture capability, increased by-product utilization, and other benefits.

Explanation of Provision

The provision increases to 30 percent the credit rate for IGCC and other advanced coal projects. In addition, the provision permits the Secretary to allocate an additional $950 million of credits to qualifying projects.

The provision modifies the definition of qualifying projects to require that projects include equipment which separates and sequesters at least 65 percent of the project's total carbon dioxide emissions. This percentage increases to 70 percent if the credits are later reallocated by the Secretary. The Secretary is required to recapture the benefit of any allocated credit if a project fails to attain or maintain these carbon dioxide separation and sequestration requirements.

In selecting projects, the provision requires the Secretary to give high priority to applicants who have a research partnership with an eligible educational institution. In addition, the Secretary must give the highest priority to projects with the greatest separation and sequestration percentage of total carbon dioxide emissions. The provision also requires that the Secretary disclose which projects receive credit allocations, including the identity of the taxpayer and the amount of the credit awarded.

Effective Date

The provision authorizing the Secretary to allocate additional credits is effective on the date of enactment. The increased credit rate along with the carbon dioxide sequestration and other rules are effective with respect to these additional credit allocations.

[Law at ¶ 5130. CCH Explanation at ¶ 545.]

[¶ 10,090] Act Sec. B112. Expansion and modification of the coal gasification investment credit

Joint Committee on Taxation (J.C.T. REP. No. JCX-75-08)

[Code Sec. 48B]

Present Law

A 20 percent investment tax credit is available for investments in certain qualifying coal gasification projects. Only property which is part of a qualifying gasification project and necessary for the gasification technology of such project is eligible for the gasification credit.

Qualified gasification projects convert coal, petroleum residue, biomass, or other materials recovered for their energy or feedstock value into a synthesis gas composed primarily of carbon monoxide and hydrogen for direct use or subsequent chemical or physical conversion. Qualified projects must be carried out by an eligible entity, defined as any person whose application for certification is principally intended for use in a domestic project which employs domestic gasification applications related to (1) chemicals, (2) fertilizers, (3) glass, (4) steel, (5) petroleum residues, (6) forest products, and (7) agriculture, including feedlots and dairy operations.

Credits are available only for projects certified by the Secretary of Treasury, in consultation with the Secretary of Energy. Certifications are issued using a competitive bidding process. The Secretary of Treasury must establish a certification program no later than 180 days after August 8, 2005,[15] and each project application must be submitted during the 3-year period beginning on the date such certification program is established. The Secretary of Treasury may not allocate more than $350 million in credits. In addition, the Secretary may certify a maximum of $650 million in qualified investment as eligible for credit with respect to any single project.

Explanation of Provision

The provision expands and modifies the coal gasification investment credit. The provision increases gasification project credit rate to 30 percent and permits the Secretary to allocate an additional $150 million of credits to qualified projects that separate and sequester at least 75 percent of total carbon dioxide emissions. The Secretary is required to recapture the benefit of

---

[15] The Secretary issued guidance establishing the certification program on February 21, 2006 (IRS Notice 2006-25).

any allocated credit if a project fails to attain or maintain these carbon dioxide separation and sequestration requirements.

In selecting projects, the provision requires the Secretary to give high priority to applicants who have a research partnership with an eligible educational institution. In addition, the Secretary must give the highest priority to projects with the greatest separation and sequestration percentage of total carbon dioxide emissions. The provision also requires that the Secretary disclose which projects receive credit allocations, including the identity of the taxpayer and the amount of the credit awarded.

Effective Date

The provision authorizing the Secretary to allocate additional credits is effective on the date of enactment. The increased credit rate along with the carbon dioxide sequestration and other rules are effective with respect to these additional credit allocations.

[Law at ¶5135. CCH Explanation at ¶550.]

[¶10,100] Act Sec. B113. Extend excise tax on coal at current rates

Joint Committee on Taxation (J.C.T. REP. No. JCX-75-08)

[Code Sec. 4121]

Present Law

A $1.10 per ton excise tax is imposed on coal sold by the producer from underground mines in the United States. The rate is 55 cents per ton on coal sold by the producer from surface mining operations. In either case, the tax cannot exceed 4.4 percent of the coal producer's selling price. No tax is imposed on lignite.

Gross receipts from the excise tax are dedicated to the Black Lung Disability Trust Fund to finance benefits under the Federal Black Lung Benefits Act. Currently, the Black Lung Disability Trust Fund is in a deficit position because previous spending was financed with interest-bearing advances from the General Fund.

The coal excise tax rates are scheduled to decline to 50 cents per ton for underground-mined coal and 25 cents per ton for surface-mined coal (and the cap is scheduled to decline to two percent of the selling price) for sales after January 1, 2014, or after any earlier January 1 on which there is no balance of repayable advances from the Black Lung Disability Trust Fund to the General Fund and no unpaid interest on such advances.

Explanation of Provision

The provision retains the excise tax on coal at the current rates until the earlier of the following dates: (1) January 1, 2019, and (2) the day after the first December 31 after 2007 on which the Black Lung Disability Trust Fund has repaid, with interest, all amounts borrowed from the General Fund. On and after that date, the reduced rates of $.50 per ton for coal from underground mines and $.25 per ton for coal from surface mines will apply and the tax per ton of coal will be capped at two percent of the amount for which it is sold by the producer.

Effective Date

The provision is effective on the date of enactment.

[Law at ¶5415 and ¶7138. CCH Explanation at ¶850.]

[¶10,110] Act Sec. B114. Temporary procedures for excise tax refunds on exported coal

Joint Committee on Taxation (J.C.T. REP. No. JCX-75-08)

[Act Sec. B114]

Present Law

In general

Excise tax is imposed on coal, except lignite, produced from mines located in the United

States.[16] The producer of the coal is liable for paying the tax to the IRS. Producers generally recover the tax from their purchasers.

The Export Clause of the U.S. Constitution provides that "no Tax or Duty shall be laid on Articles exported from any State."[17] Courts have determined that the Export Clause applies to excise tax on exported coal, and therefore such taxes are subject to a claim for refund.[18] The Supreme Court has ruled that taxpayers seeking a refund of such taxes must proceed under the rules of the Internal Revenue Code.[19]

Claims under the Code

In order to obtain a refund of taxes on exported coal, a claimant must satisfy the following requirements of the Code and case law:

1. A claim for refund must be filed within three years from the time the return was filed, or within two years from the time the tax was paid, whichever period expires later;[20]

2. The person must establish that the goods were in the stream of export when the excise tax was imposed;[21]

3. The claimant must establish that it has borne the tax. More specifically, the claimant must establish that the tax was neither included in the price of the article nor collected from the purchaser (or if so, that the claimant has repaid the amount of tax to the ultimate purchaser), that the claimant has repaid or agreed to repay the tax to the ultimate vendor or has obtained the written consent of such ultimate vendor to the allowance of the claim, or that the claimant has filed the written consent of the ultimate purchaser to the allowance of the claim;[22]

4. In the case of an exporter or shipper of an article exported to a foreign country or shipped to a possession, the amount of tax may be refunded to the exporter or shipper if the person who paid the tax waives its claim to such amount;[23] and

5. A civil action for refund must not be begun before the expiration of six months from the date of filing the claim (unless the claim has been disallowed during that time), nor after the expiration of two years from the date of mailing the notice of claim disallowance.[24]

In 2000, the Internal Revenue Service ("IRS") issued Notice 2000-28,[25] which summarizes the IRS position regarding claims for credits or refunds of excise taxes on exported coal and sets forth procedural rules relating to such claims. Under Notice 2000-28, a coal producer or exporter must provide the following information as part of its claim:

1. A statement by the person that paid the tax to the government that provides the quarter and the year for which the tax was reported on Form 720, the line number on such Form, the amount of tax paid on the coal, and the date of payment;

2. In the case of an exporter, a statement by the person that paid the tax to the government that such person has waived the right to claim a refund;

3. A statement that the claimant has evidence that the coal was in the stream of export when sold by the producer;

4. In the case of an exporter, proof of exportation;

5. In the case of a coal producer, a statement that the coal actually was exported; and

6. A statement that the claimant:

---

[16] Sec. 4121(a). Throughout the relevant period, the rate of tax on coal from underground mines has been $1.10 per ton and the rate of tax on coal from surface mines has been $0.55 per ton. These rates are subject to a limitation of 4.4 percent of the producer's sale price. Sec. 4121(b).

[17] U.S. Const., art. I, sec. 9, cl. 5.

[18] See Ranger Fuel Corp. v. United States, 33 F. Supp. 2d 466 (E.D. Va. 1998). The IRS subsequently provided guidance regarding how taxpayers may assure that exported coal would not be subject to excise tax. Notice 2000-28, 2000-1 C.B. 1116.

[19] United States v. Clintwood Elkhorn Mining Co., 128 S. Ct. 1511 (April 15, 2008). Prior to the Supreme Court's decision, some courts had allowed taxpayers to bring claims under the Tucker Act, 28 U.S.C. sec. 1491(a), which confers jurisdiction upon the Court of Federal Claims "to render judgment upon any claim against the United States founded either upon the Constitution, or any Act of Congress or any regu-

lation of an executive department . . . ." Lower courts had held that such a Tucker Act claim was subject to the Tucker Act's six-year statute of limitations and was not subject to the requirements of the Code. Venture Coal Sales Co. v. U.S., 93 AFTR 2d 2004-2495 (Fed. Cir. 2004); Cyprus Amax Coal Co. v. U.S., 205 F.3d 1369 (Fed. Cir. 2000). The Supreme Court held that the stricter Code rules apply to these refund claims.

[20] Sec. 6511(a).

[21] See Ranger Fuel Corp. v. United States, 33 F. Supp. 2d 466 (E.D. Va. 1998). See also United States v. International Business Machines Corp., 517 U.S. 843 (1996); Joy Oil, Ltd. v. State Tax Commission, 337 U.S. 286 (1949).

[22] Sec. 6416(a)(1).

[23] Sec. 6416(c).

[24] Sec. 6532(a).

[25] Notice 2000-28, 2001-1 C.B. 1116.

a. has neither included the tax in the price of the coal nor collected the amount of the tax from its buyer,

b. has repaid the amount of the tax to the ultimate purchaser of the coal, or

c. has obtained the written consent of the ultimate purchaser of the coal to the allowance of the claim.

If the IRS disallows the claim, the claimant may proceed in a Federal district court or the Court of Federal Claims under 28 U.S.C. sec. 1346(a)(1), which grants these courts concurrent jurisdiction over "[a]ny civil action against the United States for the recovery of any internal revenue tax alleged to have been erroneously or illegally assessed or collected . . . or any sum alleged to have been excessive or in any manner wrongfully collected under the internal-revenue laws."

With respect to claims under the Code allowed by the IRS or by a court, prejudgment interest is generally allowed.[26]

Explanation of Provision

The provision creates a new procedure under which certain coal producers and exporters may claim a refund of excise taxes imposed on coal exported from the United States. Coal producers or exporters that exported coal during the period beginning on or after October 1, 1990 and ending on or before the date of enactment of the provision, with respect to which a return was filed on or after October 1, 1990, and on or before the date of enactment, and that file a claim for refund not later than the close of the 30-day period beginning on the day of enactment, may obtain a refund from the Secretary of the Treasury of excise taxes paid on such exported coal and any interest accrued from the date of overpayment. Interest on such claims is computed under the Code.[27] The Secretary of the Treasury is required to determine whether to approve the claim within 180 days after such claim is filed, and to pay such claim not later than 180 days after making such determination.

In order to qualify for a refund under the provision, a coal producer must establish that it, or a party related to such coal producer, exported coal produced by such coal producer to a foreign country or shipped coal produced by such coal producer to a U.S. possession, the export or shipment of which was other than through an exporter that has filed a valid and timely claim for refund under the provision. An

exporter must establish that it exported coal to a foreign country, shipped coal to a U.S. possession, or caused such coal to be so exported or shipped. Refunds to producers are to be made in an amount equal to the tax paid on exported coal. Exporters are to receive a payment equal to $0.825 per ton of exported coal.

Special rules apply if a court has rendered a judgment. If a coal producer or a party related to a coal producer has received, from a court of competent jurisdiction in the United States, a judgment in favor of such coal producer (or party related to such coal producer) that relates to the constitutionality of Federal excise tax paid on exported coal, then such coal producer is deemed to have established the export of coal to a foreign country or shipment of coal to a possession of the United States. If such coal producer is entitled to a payment under this provision, the amount of such payment is reduced by any amount awarded under such court judgment. Subject to the rules below, a coal exporter may file a claim notwithstanding that a coal producer or a party related to a coal producer has received a court judgment relating to the same coal.

Under the provision, the term "coal producer" means the person that owns the coal immediately after the coal is severed from the ground, without regard to the existence of any contractual arrangement for the sale or other disposition of the coal or the payment of any royalties between the producer and third parties. The term also includes any person who extracts coal from coal waste refuse piles or from the silt waste product which results from the wet washing or similar processing of coal. The term "exporter" means a person, other than a coal producer, that does not have an agreement with a producer or seller of such coal to sell or export such coal to a third party on behalf of such producer or seller, and that is indicated as the exporter of record in the shipper's export declaration or other documentation, or actually exported such coal to a foreign country, shipped such coal to a U.S. possession, or caused such coal to be so exported or shipped. The term "a party related to such coal producer" means a person that is related to such coal producer through any degree of common management, stock ownership, or voting control, is related, within the meaning of section 144(a)(3), to such coal producer, or has a contract, fee arrangement, or any other agreement with such coal producer to sell such coal to a third party on behalf of such coal producer.

---

[26] See sec. 6611; 28 U.S.C. sec. 2411.

[27] See sec. 6621.

The provision does not apply with respect to excise tax on exported coal if a credit or refund of such tax has been allowed or made, or if a "settlement with the Federal Government" has been made with and accepted by the coal producer, a party related to such coal producer, or the exporter of such coal, as of the date that the claim is filed under the provision. The term "settlement with the Federal Government" does not include a settlement or stipulation entered into as of the date of enactment, if such settlement or stipulation contemplates a judgment with respect to which any party has filed an appeal or has reserved the right to file an appeal. In addition, the provision does not apply to the extent that a credit or refund of tax on exported coal has been paid to any person, regardless of whether such credit or refund occurs prior to, or after, the date of enactment.

The provision is not intended to create any inference than an exporter has standing to commence, or intervene in, any judicial or adminis-

trative proceeding concerning a claim for refund by a coal producer of any Federal or State tax, fee, or royalty paid by the coal producer. Similarly, the provision is not intended to create any inference that a coal producer has standing to commence, or intervene in, any judicial or administrative proceeding concerning a claim for refund by an exporter of any Federal or State tax, fee, or royalty paid by the producer and alleged to have been passed on to an exporter.

Effective Date

The provision applies to claims on coal exported on or after October 1, 1990 through the date of enactment, with respect to amounts of tax for which a return was filed on or after October 1, 1990, and on or before the date of enactment, and for which a claim for refund is filed not later than the close of the 30-day period beginning on the date of enactment.

[Law at ¶7141. CCH Explanation at ¶850.]

[¶10,120] Act Secs. B116 and B208. Certain income and gains relating to alcohol fuels and mixtures, biodiesel fuels and mixtures, and alternative fuels and mixtures treated as qualifying income for purposes of the exception from treatment of publicly traded partnerships as corporations

Joint Committee on Taxation (J.C.T. Rep. No. JCX-75-08)

[Code Sec. 7704]

Present Law

Partnerships in general

A partnership generally is not treated as a taxable entity (except for certain publicly traded partnerships), but rather, is treated as a pass-through entity. Income earned by a partnership, whether distributed or not, is taxed to the partners.[44] The character of partnership items passes through to the partners, as if the items were realized directly by the partners.[45] For example, a partner's share of the partnership's dividend income is generally treated as dividend income in the hands of the partner.

Publicly traded partnerships

Under present law, a publicly traded partnership generally is treated as a corporation for Federal tax purposes (sec. 7704(a)). For this purpose, a publicly traded partnership means any

partnership if interests in the partnership are traded on an established securities market, or interests in the partnership are readily tradable on a secondary market (or the substantial equivalent thereof).

An exception from corporate treatment is provided for certain publicly traded partnerships, 90 percent or more of whose gross income is qualifying income (sec. 7704(c)(2)). However, this exception does not apply to any partnership that would be described in section 851(a) if it were a domestic corporation, which includes a corporation registered under the Investment Company Act of 1940 as a management company or unit investment trust.

Qualifying income includes interest, dividends, and gains from the disposition of a capital asset (or of property described in section 1231(b)) that is held for the production of income that is qualifying income. Qualifying income also includes rents from real property, gains

---

[44] Section 701.   [45] Section 702.

from the sale or other disposition of real property, and income and gains from the exploration, development, mining or production, processing, refining, transportation (including pipelines transporting gas, oil, or products thereof), or the marketing of any mineral or natural resource (including fertilizer, geothermal energy, and timber). It also includes income and gains from commodities (not described in section 1221(a)(1)) or futures, options, or forward contracts with respect to such commodities (including foreign currency transactions of a commodity pool) in the case of partnership, a principal activity of which is the buying and selling of such commodities, futures, options or forward contracts.

Explanation of Provision

The provision provides that qualifying income of a publicly traded partnership includes income or gains from the transportation or storage of certain fuels. Specifically, the fuels are: (1) any fuel described in subsection (b), (c), (d) or (e) of section 6426, namely, alcohol fuel mixtures, biodiesel mixtures, alternative fuels (which include liquefied petroleum gas, P Series Fuels, compressed or liquefied natural gas, liquefied hydrogen, liquid fuel derived from coal through the Fischer-Tropsch process, and liquid fuel derived from biomass), and alternative fuel mixtures; (2) neat alcohol other than alcohol derived from petroleum, natural gas, or coal, or having a proof of less than 190 (as defined in section 6426(b)(4)(A)), and (3) neat biodiesel (as defined in section 40A(d)(1)).

Effective Date

The provision applies to taxable years beginning after the date of enactment.

[Law at ¶ 5495. CCH Explanation at ¶ 465.]

[¶ 10,130] Act Sec. B117. Carbon audit of provisions of the tax code

Joint Committee on Taxation (J.C.T. REP. No. JCX-75-08)

[Act Sec. B117]

Present Law

Present law does not require a review of the Code for provisions that affect carbon emissions and climate. The National Research Council is part of the National Academies. The National Academy of Sciences serves to investigate, examine, experiment and report upon any subject of science whenever called upon to do so by any department of the government. The National Research Council was organized by the National Academy of Sciences in 1916 and is its principal operating agency for conducting science policy and technical work.

Explanation of Provision

The provision directs the Secretary to request that the National Academy of Sciences undertake a comprehensive review of the Code to identify the types of and specific tax provisions that have the largest effects on carbon and other greenhouse gas emissions and to generally estimate the magnitude of those effects.[28] The report should identify the provisions of the Code that are most likely to have significant effects on carbon emissions and discuss the importance of controlling carbon and greenhouse gas emissions as part of a comprehensive national strategy for reducing U.S. contributions to global climate change.[29] The report will describe the processes by which the tax provisions affect emissions (both directly and indirectly), assess the relative influence of the identified provisions, and evaluate the potential for changes in the Code to reduce carbon emissions. The report also will identify other provisions of the Code that may have significant influence on other factors affecting climate change.

Within two years of the date of enactment, the National Academy of Sciences is to submit to Congress a report containing the results of the review. The provision authorizes the appropriation of $1,500,000 to carry out the review.

Effective Date

The provision is effective on the date of enactment.

[Law at ¶ 7144. CCH Explanation at ¶ 575.]

---

[28] A detailed quantitative analysis is not required. It is envisioned that the review will catalogue and provide a general analysis of the effect of each identified provision.

[29] "Greenhouse gas emissions" include, but are not limited to, methane, nitrous oxide, ozone, and fluorinated hydrocarbons.

[¶10,140] Act Sec. B201. Inclusion of cellulosic biofuel in bonus depreciation for biomass ethanol plant property

Joint Committee on Taxation (J.C.T. REP. NO. JCX-75-08)

[Code Sec. 168(l)]

Present Law

Section 168(l) allows an additional first-year depreciation deduction equal to 50 percent of the adjusted basis of qualified cellulosic biomass ethanol plant property. In order to qualify, the property generally must be placed in service before January 1, 2013.

Qualified cellulosic biomass ethanol plant property means property used in the U.S. solely to produce cellulosic biomass ethanol. For this purpose, cellulosic biomass ethanol means ethanol derived from any lignocellulosic or hemicellulosic matter that is available on a renewable or recurring basis. For example, lignocellulosic or hemicellulosic matter that is available on a renewable or recurring basis includes bagasse (from sugar cane), corn stalks, and switchgrass.

The additional first-year depreciation deduction is allowed for both regular tax and alternative minimum tax purposes for the taxable year in which the property is placed in service. The additional first-year depreciation deduction is subject to the general rules regarding whether an item is deductible under section 162 or subject to capitalization under section 263 or section 263A. The basis of the property and the depreciation allowances in the year of purchase and later years are appropriately adjusted to reflect the additional first-year depreciation deduction. In addition, there is no adjustment to the allowable amount of depreciation for purposes of computing a taxpayer's alternative minimum taxable income with respect to property to which the provision applies. A taxpayer is allowed to elect out of the additional first-year depreciation for any class of property for any taxable year.

In order for property to qualify for the additional first-year depreciation deduction, it must meet the following requirements. The original use of the property must commence with the taxpayer on or after December 20, 2006. The property must be acquired by purchase (as defined under section 179(d)) by the taxpayer after December 20, 2006, and placed in service before January 1, 2013. Property does not qualify if a binding written contract for the acquisition of such property was in effect on or before December 20, 2006.

Property that is manufactured, constructed, or produced by the taxpayer for use by the taxpayer qualifies if the taxpayer begins the manufacture, construction, or production of the property after December 20, 2006, and the property is placed in service before January 1, 2013 (and all other requirements are met). Property that is manufactured, constructed, or produced for the taxpayer by another person under a contract that is entered into prior to the manufacture, construction, or production of the property is considered to be manufactured, constructed, or produced by the taxpayer.

Property any portion of which is financed with the proceeds of a tax-exempt obligation under section 103 is not eligible for the additional first-year depreciation deduction. Recapture rules apply if the property ceases to be qualified cellulosic biomass ethanol plant property.

Property with respect to which the taxpayer has elected 50 percent expensing under section 179C is not eligible for the additional first-year depreciation deduction.

Explanation of Provision

The provision changes the definition of qualified property. Under the provision, qualified property includes cellulosic biofuel, which is defined as any liquid fuel which is produced from any lignocellulosic or hemicellulosic matter that is available on a renewable or recurring basis.

Effective Date

The provision is effective for property placed in service after the date of enactment, in taxable years ending after such date.

[Law at ¶5230. CCH Explanation at ¶330.]

[¶10,150] Act Secs. B202 and B204. Credits for biodiesel and renewable diesel

Joint Committee on Taxation (J.C.T. REP. NO. JCX-75-08)

[Code Secs. 40A, 6426 and 6427]

Present Law

Income tax credit

Overview

The Code provides an income tax credit for biodiesel fuels (the "biodiesel fuels credit").[30] The biodiesel fuels credit is the sum of three credits: (1) the biodiesel mixture credit, (2) the biodiesel credit, and (3) the small agri-biodiesel producer credit. The biodiesel fuels credit is treated as a general business credit. The amount of the biodiesel fuels credit is includable in gross income. The biodiesel fuels credit is coordinated to take into account benefits from the biodiesel excise tax credit and payment provisions discussed below. The credit does not apply to fuel sold or used after December 31, 2008.

Biodiesel is monoalkyl esters of long chain fatty acids derived from plant or animal matter that meet (1) the registration requirements established by the Environmental Protection Agency under section 211 of the Clean Air Act and (2) the requirements of the American Society of Testing and Materials ("ASTM") D6751. Agri-biodiesel is biodiesel derived solely from virgin oils including oils from corn, soybeans, sunflower seeds, cottonseeds, canola, crambe, rapeseeds, safflowers, flaxseeds, rice bran, mustard seeds, or animal fats.

Biodiesel may be taken into account for purposes of the credit only if the taxpayer obtains a certification (in such form and manner as prescribed by the Secretary) from the producer or importer of the biodiesel that identifies the product produced and the percentage of biodiesel and agri-biodiesel in the product.

Biodiesel mixture credit

The biodiesel mixture credit is 50 cents for each gallon of biodiesel (other than agri-biodiesel) used by the taxpayer in the production of a qualified biodiesel mixture. For agri-biodiesel, the credit is $1.00 per gallon. A qualified biodiesel mixture is a mixture of biodiesel and diesel fuel that is (1) sold by the taxpayer producing such mixture to any person for use as a fuel, or (2) is used as a fuel by the taxpayer

producing such mixture. The sale or use must be in the trade or business of the taxpayer and is to be taken into account for the taxable year in which such sale or use occurs. No credit is allowed with respect to any casual off-farm production of a qualified biodiesel mixture.

Biodiesel credit

The biodiesel credit is 50 cents for each gallon of biodiesel that is not in a mixture with diesel fuel (100 percent biodiesel or B-100) and which during the taxable year is (1) used by the taxpayer as a fuel in a trade or business or (2) sold by the taxpayer at retail to a person and placed in the fuel tank of such person's vehicle. For agri-biodiesel, the credit is $1.00 per gallon.

Small agri-biodiesel producer credit

The Code provides a small agri-biodiesel producer income tax credit, in addition to the biodiesel and biodiesel fuel mixture credits. The credit is a 10-cents-per-gallon credit for up to 15 million gallons of agri-biodiesel produced by small producers, defined generally as persons whose agri-biodiesel production capacity does not exceed 60 million gallons per year. The agri-biodiesel must (1) be sold by such producer to another person (a) for use by such other person in the production of a qualified biodiesel mixture in such person's trade or business (other than casual off-farm production), (b) for use by such other person as a fuel in a trade or business, or, (c) who sells such agri-biodiesel at retail to another person and places such agri-biodiesel in the fuel tank of such other person; or (2) used by the producer for any purpose described in (a), (b), or (c).

Biodiesel mixture excise tax credit

The Code also provides an excise tax credit for biodiesel mixtures.[31] The credit is 50 cents for each gallon of biodiesel used by the taxpayer in producing a biodiesel mixture for sale or use in a trade or business of the taxpayer. In the case of agri-biodiesel, the credit is $1.00 per gallon. A biodiesel mixture is a mixture of biodiesel and diesel fuel that (1) is sold by the taxpayer producing such mixture to any person for use as a fuel, or (2) is used as a fuel by the taxpayer producing such mixture. No credit is allowed

---

[30] Sec. 40A.

[31] Sec. 6426(c).

Act Sec. B202   ¶10,150

unless the taxpayer obtains a certification (in such form and manner as prescribed by the Secretary) from the producer of the biodiesel that identifies the product produced and the percentage of biodiesel and agri-biodiesel in the product.[32]

The credit is not available for any sale or use for any period after December 31, 2008. This excise tax credit is coordinated with the income tax credit for biodiesel such that credit for the same biodiesel cannot be claimed for both income and excise tax purposes.

Payments with respect to biodiesel fuel mixtures

If any person produces a biodiesel fuel mixture in such person's trade or business, the Secretary is to pay such person an amount equal to the biodiesel mixture credit.[33] To the extent the biodiesel fuel mixture credit exceeds the section 4081 liability of a person, the Secretary is to pay such person an amount equal to the biodiesel fuel mixture credit with respect to such mixture.[34] Thus, if the person has no section 4081 liability, the credit is refundable. The Secretary is not required to make payments with respect to biodiesel fuel mixtures sold or used after December 31, 2008.

Renewable diesel

"Renewable diesel" is diesel fuel that (1) is derived from biomass (as defined in section 45K(c)(3)) using a thermal depolymerization process; (2) meets the registration requirements for fuels and fuel additives established by the Environmental Protection Agency ("EPA") under section 211 of the Clean Air Act (42 U.S.C. sec. 7545); and (3) meets the requirements of the ASTM D975 or D396. ASTM D975 provides standards for diesel fuel suitable for use in diesel engines. ASTM D396 provides standards for fuel oil intended for use in fuel-oil burning equipment, such as furnaces.

For purposes of the Code, renewable diesel is generally treated the same as biodiesel. Like biodiesel, the incentive may be taken as an income tax credit, an excise tax credit, or as a payment from the Secretary.[35] The incentive for renewable diesel is $1.00 per gallon. There is no small producer credit for renewable diesel. The incentives for renewable diesel expire after December 31, 2008.

Pursuant to IRS Notice 2007-37, the Secretary provided that fuel produced as a result of

co-processing biomass and petroleum feedstock ("co-produced fuel") qualifies for the renewable diesel incentives to the extent of the fuel attributable to the biomass in the mixture. In co-produced fuel, the fuel attributable to the biomass does not exist as a distinct separate quantity prior to mixing.

Explanation of Provision

The provision extends an additional year (through December 31, 2009) the income tax credit, excise tax credit, and payment provisions for biodiesel (including agri-biodiesel) and renewable diesel. The provision provides that both biodiesel and agri-biodiesel are entitled to a credit of $1.00 per gallon.

The provision modifies the definition of renewable diesel. The provision eliminates the requirement that the fuel be made using a thermal depolymerization process. The provision also permits the Secretary to identify standards equivalent to ASTM D975 and ASTM D396 for renewable diesel. Thus, under the provision, renewable diesel is liquid fuel derived from biomass which meets (a) the registration requirements for fuels and fuel additives established by the EPA under section 211 of the Clean Air Act, and (b) the requirements of the ASTM D975, ASTM D396, or other equivalent standard approved by the Secretary. The provision also provides that renewable diesel includes biomass fuel that meets a Department of Defense military specification for jet fuel or an ASTM for aviation turbine fuel ("renewable jet fuel"). For purposes of the mixture credit, kerosene is treated as diesel fuel when in a mixture with renewable jet fuel.

The provision also overrides IRS Notice 2007-37 with respect to co-produced fuel, providing that renewable diesel does not include any fuel derived from co-processing biomass with a feedstock that is not biomass. The de minimis use of catalysts, such as hydrogen, is permitted under the provision.

Effective Date

The provision is generally effective for fuel produced, and sold or used, after December 31, 2008. The provision making co-produced fuel ineligible for the renewable diesel incentives is effective for fuel produced, and sold or used, after February 13, 2008.

[Law at ¶5065, ¶5455 and ¶5460. CCH Explanation at ¶825.]

---

[32] Sec. 6426(c)(4).
[33] Sec. 6427(e).

[34] Sec. 6427(e)(1) and sec. 6427(e)(3).
[35] Secs. 40A(f), 6426(c), and 6427(e).

[¶10,160] Act Sec. B203. Clarification that credits for fuel are designed to provide an incentive for United States production

Joint Committee on Taxation (J.C.T. REP. NO. JCX-75-08)

[Code Secs. 40, 40A, 6426 and 6427]

Present Law

The Code provides per-gallon incentives relating to the following qualified fuels: alcohol (including ethanol), biodiesel (including agri-biodiesel), renewable diesel, and certain alternative fuels.[36] The incentives may be taken as an income tax credit, excise tax credit or payment. The provisions are coordinated so that a gallon of qualified fuel is only taken into account once. If the qualified fuel is part of a qualified fuel mixture, the incentives apply only to the amount of qualified fuel in the mixture. The Code also provides an income tax credit for cellulosic biofuel. That credit is limited to fuel produced and sold in the United States. The cellulosic biofuel credit does not apply after December 31, 2012. Other than for cellulosic biofuel, the Code is silent as to the geographic limitations on where the fuel must be produced, used, or sold.

For alcohol, other than ethanol, the amount of the credit is 60 cents per gallon. For ethanol, the credit is 51 cents per gallon for calendar year 2008. An extra 10 cents per gallon available for small ethanol producers. The alcohol incentives generally are available through December 31, 2010.

The amount of the credit for biodiesel is 50 cents. For agri-biodiesel and renewable diesel, the credit amount is $1.00 per gallon. An extra 10 cents per gallon is available for small producers of agri-biodiesel. The biodiesel, agri-biodiesel and renewable diesel incentives do not apply after December 31, 2008.

The credit amount for alternative fuels is 50 cents per gallon. The incentives for alternative fuels expire do not apply after September 30, 2009 (after September 30, 2014, in the case of liquefied hydrogen).

Explanation of Provision

The provision provides that fuel that is produced outside the United States for use as a fuel outside the United States is ineligible for the per-gallon tax incentives relating to alcohol, biodiesel, renewable diesel, and alternative fuel. For example, fuel in the following situations is ineligible for incentives: (1) biodiesel, which is not in a mixture, that is both produced and used outside the United States, (2) foreign-produced biodiesel that is used to make a qualified mixture outside of the United States for foreign use, and (3) foreign-produced biodiesel that is used to make a qualified mixture in the United States that is then exported for foreign use.

Effective Date

The provision is effective for claims for credit or payment made on or after May 15, 2008.

[Law at ¶5060, ¶5065, ¶5455 and ¶5460. CCH Explanation at ¶825.]

[¶10,170] Act Sec. B205. Alternative motor vehicle credit and plug-in electric vehicle credit

Joint Committee on Taxation (J.C.T. REP. NO. JCX-75-08)

[Code Sec. 30B and New Code Sec. 30D]

Present Law

In general

A credit is available for each new qualified fuel cell vehicle, hybrid vehicle, advanced lean burn technology vehicle, and alternative fuel vehicle placed in service by the taxpayer during the taxable year.[37] In general, the credit amount varies depending upon the type of technology used, the weight class of the vehicle, the amount by which the vehicle exceeds certain fuel economy standards, and, for some vehicles, the estimated lifetime fuel savings. The credit generally is available for vehicles purchased after 2005. The credit terminates after 2009, 2010, or 2014, depending on the type of vehicle.

In general, the credit is allowed to the vehicle owner, including the lessor of a vehicle subject to a lease. If the use of the vehicle is

---

[36] See secs. 40, 40A, 6426, and 6427(e).

[37] Sec. 30B.

described in paragraphs (3) or (4) of section 50(b) (relating to use by tax-exempt organizations, governments, and foreign persons) and is not subject to a lease, the seller of the vehicle may claim the credit so long as the seller clearly discloses to the user in a document the amount that is allowable as a credit. A vehicle must be used predominantly in the United States to qualify for the credit.

Fuel cell vehicles

A qualified fuel cell vehicle is a motor vehicle that is propelled by power derived from one or more cells that convert chemical energy directly into electricity by combining oxygen with hydrogen fuel that is stored on board the vehicle and may or may not require reformation prior to use. A qualified fuel cell vehicle must be purchased before January 1, 2015. The amount of credit for the purchase of a fuel cell vehicle is determined by a base credit amount that depends upon the weight class of the vehicle and, in the case of automobiles or light trucks, an additional credit amount that depends upon the rated fuel economy of the vehicle compared to a base fuel economy. For these purposes the base fuel economy is the 2002 model year city fuel economy rating for vehicles of various weight classes.[38] Table 2, below, shows the base credit amounts.

Table 2.-Base Credit Amount for Fuel Cell Vehicles

Vehicle Gross Weight Rating (pounds)	Credit Amount
Vehicle ≤ 8,500	$8,000
8,500 < vehicle ≤ 14,000	$10,000
14,000 < vehicle ≤ 26,000	$20,000
26,000 < vehicle	$40,000

In the case of a fuel cell vehicle weighing less than 8,500 pounds and placed in service after December 31, 2009, the $8,000 amount in Table 2, above is reduced to $4,000.

Table 3, below, shows the additional credits for passenger automobiles or light trucks.

Table 3.-Credit for Qualified Fuel Cell Vehicles

Credit	If Fuel Economy of the Fuel Cell Vehicle Is:	
	at least	but less than
$1,000	150% of base fuel economy	175% of base fuel economy
$1,500	175% of base fuel economy	200% of base fuel economy
$2,000	200% of base fuel economy	225% of base fuel economy
$2,500	225% of base fuel economy	250% of base fuel economy
$3,000	250% of base fuel economy	275% of base fuel economy
$3,500	275% of base fuel economy	300% of base fuel economy
$4,000	300% of base fuel economy	

Hybrid vehicles and advanced lean burn technology vehicles

Qualified hybrid vehicle

A qualified hybrid vehicle is a motor vehicle that draws propulsion energy from on-board sources of stored energy that include both an internal combustion engine or heat engine using combustible fuel and a rechargeable energy storage system (e.g., batteries). A qualified hybrid vehicle must be placed in service before January 1, 2011 (January 1, 2010 in the case of a hybrid vehicle weighing more than 8,500 pounds).

Hybrid vehicles that are automobiles and light trucks

In the case of an automobile or light truck (vehicles weighing 8,500 pounds or less), the amount of credit for the purchase of a hybrid vehicle is the sum of two components: (1) a fuel economy credit amount that varies with the rated fuel economy of the vehicle compared to a 2002 model year standard and (2) a conservation credit based on the estimated lifetime fuel sav-

---

[38] See discussion surrounding Table 7, below.

ings of the qualified vehicle compared to a comparable 2002 model year vehicle that is powered solely by a gasoline or diesel internal combustion engine. A qualified hybrid automobile or light truck must have a maximum available power[39] from the rechargeable energy storage system of at least four percent. In addition, the vehicle must meet or exceed certain Environmental Protection Agency ("EPA") emissions standards. For a vehicle with a gross vehicle weight rating of 6,000 pounds or less the applicable emissions standards are the Bin 5 Tier II emissions standards. For a vehicle with a gross vehicle weight rating greater than 6,000 pounds and less than or equal to 8,500 pounds, the applicable emissions standards are the Bin 8 Tier II emissions standards.

Table 4, below, shows the fuel economy credit available to a hybrid passenger automobile or light truck whose fuel economy (on a gasoline gallon equivalent basis) exceeds that of a base fuel economy.

Table 4.-Fuel Economy Credit

Credit	If Fuel Economy of the Hybrid Vehicle Is:	
	at least	but less than
$400	125% of base fuel economy	150% of base fuel economy
$800	150% of base fuel economy	175% of base fuel economy
$1,200	175% of base fuel economy	200% of base fuel economy
$1,600	200% of base fuel economy	225% of base fuel economy
$2,000	225% of base fuel economy	250% of base fuel economy
$2,400	250% of base fuel economy	

Table 5, below, shows the conservation credit.

Table 5.-Conservation Credit

Estimated Lifetime Fuel Savings (gallons of gasoline)	Conservation Amount
At least 1,200 but less than 1,800	$250
At least 1,800 but less than 2,400	$500
At least 2,400 but less than 3,000	$750
At least 3,000	$1,000

Advanced lean burn technology vehicles

The amount of credit for the purchase of an advanced lean burn technology vehicle is the sum of two components: (1) a fuel economy credit amount that varies with the rated fuel economy of the vehicle compared to a 2002 model year standard as described in Table 4, above, and (2) a conservation credit based on the estimated lifetime fuel savings of a qualified vehicle compared to a comparable 2002 model year vehicle as described in Table 5, above. The amounts of the credits are determined after an adjustment is made to account for the different BTU content of gasoline and the fuel utilized by the lean burn technology vehicle.

A qualified advanced lean burn technology vehicle is a passenger automobile or a light truck that incorporates direct injection, achieves at least 125 percent of the 2002 model year city fuel economy, and for 2004 and later model vehicles meets or exceeds certain Environmental Protection Agency emissions standards. For a vehicle with a gross vehicle weight rating of 6,000 pounds or less the applicable emissions standards are the Bin 5 Tier II emissions standards. For a vehicle with a gross vehicle weight rating greater than 6,000 pounds and less than or equal to 8,500 pounds, the applicable emissions standards are the Bin 8 Tier II emissions standards. A qualified advanced lean burn technology vehicle must be placed in service before January 1, 2011.Limitation on number of qualified hybrid and advanced lean burn technology vehicles eligible for the credit

There is a limitation on the number of qualified hybrid vehicles and advanced lean burn technology vehicles sold by each manufacturer of such vehicles that are eligible for the credit. Taxpayers may claim the full amount of the allowable credit up to the end of the first calendar quarter after the quarter in which the manufac-

---

[39] For hybrid passenger vehicles and light trucks, the term "maximum available power" means the maximum power available from the rechargeable energy storage system, during a standard 10 second pulse power or equivalent test, divided by such maximum power and the SAE net power of the heat engine. Sec. 30B(d)(3)(C)(i).

turer records the 60,000th hybrid and advanced lean burn technology vehicle sale occurring after December 31, 2005. Taxpayers may claim one half of the otherwise allowable credit during the two calendar quarters subsequent to the first quarter after the manufacturer has recorded its 60,000th such sale. In the third and fourth calendar quarters subsequent to the first quarter after the manufacturer has recorded its 60,000th such sale, the taxpayer may claim one quarter of the otherwise allowable credit.

Thus, for example, summing the sales of qualified hybrid vehicles of all weight classes and all sales of qualified advanced lean burn technology vehicles, if a manufacturer records the sale of its 60,000th qualified vehicle in February of 2007, taxpayers purchasing such vehicles from the manufacturer may claim the full amount of the credit on their purchases of qualified vehicles through June 30, 2007. For the period July 1, 2007, through December 31, 2007, taxpayers may claim one half of the otherwise allowable credit on purchases of qualified vehicles of the manufacturer. For the period January 1, 2008, through June 30, 2008, taxpayers may claim one quarter of the otherwise allowable credit on the purchases of qualified vehicles of the manufacturer. After June 30, 2008, no credit may be claimed for purchases of hybrid vehicles or advanced lean burn technology vehicles sold by the manufacturer.

Hybrid vehicles that are medium and heavy trucks

In the case of a qualified hybrid vehicle weighing more than 8,500 pounds, the amount of credit is determined by the estimated increase in fuel economy and the incremental cost of the hybrid vehicle compared to a comparable vehicle powered solely by a gasoline or diesel internal combustion engine and that is comparable in weight, size, and use of the vehicle. For a vehicle that achieves a fuel economy increase of at least 30 percent but less than 40 percent, the credit is equal to 20 percent of the incremental cost of the hybrid vehicle. For a vehicle that achieves a fuel economy increase of at least 40 percent but less than 50 percent, the credit is equal to 30 percent

of the incremental cost of the hybrid vehicle. For a vehicle that achieves a fuel economy increase of 50 percent or more, the credit is equal to 40 percent of the incremental cost of the hybrid vehicle.

The credit is subject to certain maximum applicable incremental cost amounts. For a qualified hybrid vehicle weighing more than 8,500 pounds but not more than 14,000 pounds, the maximum allowable incremental cost amount is $7,500. For a qualified hybrid vehicle weighing more than 14,000 pounds but not more than 26,000 pounds, the maximum allowable incremental cost amount is $15,000. For a qualified hybrid vehicle weighing more than 26,000 pounds, the maximum allowable incremental cost amount is $30,000.

A qualified hybrid vehicle weighing more than 8,500 pounds but not more than 14,000 pounds must have a maximum available power from the rechargeable energy storage system of at least 10 percent. A qualified hybrid vehicle weighing more than 14,000 pounds must have a maximum available power from the rechargeable energy storage system of at least 15 percent.[40]

Alternative fuel vehicle

The credit for the purchase of a new alternative fuel vehicle is 50 percent of the incremental cost of such vehicle, plus an additional 30 percent if the vehicle meets certain emissions standards. The incremental cost of any new qualified alternative fuel vehicle is the excess of the manufacturer's suggested retail price for such vehicle over the price for a gasoline or diesel fuel vehicle of the same model. To be eligible for the credit, a qualified alternative fuel vehicle must be purchased before January 1, 2011.

The amount of the credit varies depending on the weight of the qualified vehicle. The credit is subject to certain maximum applicable incremental cost amounts. Table 6, below, shows the maximum permitted incremental cost for the purpose of calculating the credit for alternative fuel vehicles by vehicle weight class as well as the maximum credit amount for such vehicles.

---

[40] In the case of such heavy-duty hybrid motor vehicles, the percentage of maximum available power is computed by dividing the maximum power available from the rechargeable energy storage system during a standard 10-second pulse power test, divided by the vehicle's total traction power. A vehicle's total traction power is the sum of the peak power from the rechargeable energy storage system and the heat (e.g., internal combustion or diesel) engine's peak power. If the rechargeable energy storage system is the sole means by which the vehicle can be driven, then the total traction power is the peak power of the rechargeable energy storage system.

Table 6.-Maximum Allowable Incremental Cost for
Calculation of Alternative Fuel Vehicle Credit

Vehicle Gross Weight Rating (pounds)	Maximum Allowable Incremental Cost	Maximum Allowable Credit
Vehicle ≤ 8,500	$5,000	$4,000
8,500 < vehicle ≤ 14,000	$10,000	$8,000
14,000 < vehicle ≤ 26,000	$25,000	$20,000
26,000 < vehicle	$40,000	$32,000

Alternative fuels comprise compressed natural gas, liquefied natural gas, liquefied petroleum gas, hydrogen, and any liquid fuel that is at least 85 percent methanol. Qualified alternative fuel vehicles are vehicles that operate only on qualified alternative fuels and are incapable of operating on gasoline or diesel (except to the extent gasoline or diesel fuel is part of a qualified mixed fuel, described below).

Certain mixed fuel vehicles, that is vehicles that use a combination of an alternative fuel and a petroleum-based fuel, are eligible for a reduced credit. If the vehicle operates on a mixed fuel that is at least 75 percent alternative fuel, the vehicle is eligible for 70 percent of the otherwise allowable alternative fuel vehicle credit. If the vehicle operates on a mixed fuel that is at least 90 percent alternative fuel, the vehicle is eligible for 90 percent of the otherwise allowable alternative fuel vehicle credit.

Base fuel economy

The base fuel economy is the 2002 model year city fuel economy by vehicle type and vehicle inertia weight class. For this purpose, "vehicle inertia weight class" has the same meaning as when defined in regulations prescribed by the EPA for purposes of Title II of the Clean Air Act. Table 7, below, shows the 2002 model year city fuel economy for vehicles by type and by inertia weight class.

Table 7.-2002 Model Year City Fuel Economy

Vehicle Inertia Weight Class (pounds)	Passenger Automobile (miles per gallon)	Light Truck (miles per gallon)
1,500	45.2	39.4
1,750	45.2	39.4
2,000	39.6	35.2
2,250	35.2	31.8
2,500	31.7	29.0
2,750	28.8	26.8
3,000	26.4	24.9
3,500	22.6	21.8
4,000	19.8	19.4
4,500	17.6	17.6
5,000	15.9	16.1
5,500	14.4	14.8
6,000	13.2	13.7
6,500	12.2	12.8
7,000	11.3	12.1
8,500	11.3	12.1

Other rules

The portion of the credit attributable to vehicles of a character subject to an allowance for depreciation is treated as a portion of the general business credit; the remainder of the credit is allowable to the extent of the excess of the regular tax (reduced by certain other credits) over the alternative minimum tax for the taxable year.

Explanation of Provision

Treatment of alternative motor vehicle credit as a personal credit

The provision modifies the alternative motor vehicle credit by treating the nonbusiness portion of that credit as a personal credit. As a result, in the event Congress extends the provision allowing personal credits to offset the alternative minimum tax, the alternative motor vehicle credit will be allowable against the alternative minimum tax.

Plug-in electric drive motor vehicle credit

The provision allows a credit for each qualified plug-in electric drive motor vehicle placed in service. A qualified plug-in electric drive motor vehicle is a motor vehicle that meets certain emissions standards and is propelled to a significant extent by an electric motor that draws electricity from a battery that (1) has a capacity of at least four kilowatt-hours and (2) is capable of being recharged from an external source of electricity. Qualified vehicles must have a gross weight of less than 14,000 pounds. In addition, qualified vehicles weighing less than 8,500 pounds must be passenger automobiles or light trucks.

The base amount of the plug-in electric drive motor vehicle credit is $3,000. If the qualified vehicle draws propulsion from a battery with at least five kilowatt-hours of capacity, the credit amount is increased by $200, plus another $200 for each kilowatt-hour of battery capacity in excess of five kilowatt-hours, up to a maximum additional credit of $2,000.

In general, the credit is available to the vehicle owner, including the lessor of a vehicle subject to lease. If the qualified vehicle is used by certain tax-exempt organizations, governments, or foreign persons and is not subject to a lease, the seller of the vehicle may claim the credit so long as the seller clearly discloses to the user in a document the amount that is allowable as a credit. A vehicle must be used predominantly in the United States to qualify for the credit.

There is a limitation on the number of qualified plug-in electric drive motor vehicles sold by each manufacturer of such vehicles that are eligible for the credit. Taxpayers may claim the full amount of the allowable credit up to the end of the first calendar quarter after the quarter in which the manufacturer records the 60,000th plug-in electric drive motor vehicle sale. Taxpayers may claim one half of the otherwise allowable credit during the two calendar quarters subsequent to the first quarter after the manufacturer has recorded its 60,000th such sale. In the third and fourth calendar quarters subsequent to the first quarter after the manufacturer has recorded its 60,000th such sale, the taxpayer may claim one quarter of the otherwise allowable credit.

The basis of any qualified vehicle is reduced by the amount of the credit. To the extent a vehicle is eligible for credit as a qualified plug-in electric drive motor vehicle, it is not eligible for credit as a qualified hybrid vehicle under section 30B. The portion of the credit attributable to vehicles of a character subject to an allowance for depreciation is treated as part of the general business credit; the nonbusiness portion of the credit is allowable to the extent of the excess of the regular tax and the alternative minimum tax (reduced by certain other credits) for the taxable year.

Effective Date

The plug-in electric drive motor vehicle credit provision is effective for taxable years beginning after December 31, 2008. The provision treating the nonbusiness portion of the alternative motor vehicle credit as a personal credit is effective for taxable years beginning after December 31, 2007.

[Law at ¶5010, ¶5015, ¶5020, ¶5035, ¶5040, ¶5050, ¶5055, ¶5350, ¶5385, and ¶5465. CCH Explanation at ¶515.]

[¶10,180] Act Sec. B206. Exclusion from heavy vehicle excise tax for idling reduction units and advanced insulation

Joint Committee on Taxation (J.C.T. Rep. No. JCX-75-08)

[Code Sec. 4053]

Present Law

A 12 percent excise tax (the "heavy vehicle excise tax") is imposed on the first retail sale of automobile truck chassis and bodies, truck trailer and semitrailer chassis and bodies, and tractors of the kind chiefly used for highway transportation in combination with a trailer or semitrailer.[41] The heavy vehicle excise tax does not apply to automobile truck chassis and bodies suitable for use with a vehicle which has a gross vehicle weight of 33,000 pounds or less. The tax also does not apply to truck trailer and semi-trailer chassis and bodies suitable for use with a trailer or semitrailer which has a gross vehicle weight of 26,000 pounds or less, or to tractors having a gross vehicle weight of 19,500 pounds or less if such tractor in combination with a trailer or semitrailer has a gross combined weight of 33,000 pounds or less.

If the owner, lessee, or operator of a taxable article installs any part or accessory within six months after the date such vehicle was first placed in service, a 12 percent tax applies on the price of such part or accessory and its installation.

---

[41] Sec. 4051.

Explanation of Provision

The provision provides an exemption from the heavy vehicle excise tax for the cost of qualifying idling reduction devices. A qualifying idling reduction device means any device or system of devices that (1) is designed to provide to a vehicle those services (such as heat, air conditioning, or electricity), which would otherwise require the operation of the main drive engine while the vehicle is temporarily parked or remains stationary, by using one or more devices affixed to a tractor or truck, and (2) is certified by the Secretary of Energy, in consultation with the Administrator of the Environmental Protection Agency and the Secretary of Transportation, to reduce idling of such vehicle at a motor vehicle rest stop or other location where such vehicles are temporarily parked or remain stationary.

The provision also provides an exemption for the installation of "advanced insulation" in a commercial refrigerated truck or trailer that is subject to the heavy vehicle excise tax. Advanced insulation means insulation that has an R value of not less than R35 per inch.

Both exemptions apply regardless of whether the device or insulation is factory installed or later added as an accessory.

Effective Date

The provision is effective for retail sales or installations made after the date of enactment.

[Law at ¶5410. CCH Explanation at ¶845.]

[¶10,190] Act Sec. B207. Extension and modification of alternative fuel vehicle refueling property credit

Joint Committee on Taxation (J.C.T. REP. NO. JCX-75-08)

[Code Sec. 30C]

Present Law

Taxpayers may claim a 30-percent credit for the cost of installing qualified clean-fuel vehicle refueling property to be used in a trade or business of the taxpayer or installed at the principal residence of the taxpayer.[43] The credit may not exceed $30,000 per taxable year, per location, in the case of qualified refueling property used in a trade or business and $1,000 per taxable year per location in the case of qualified refueling property installed on property which is used as a principal residence.

Qualified refueling property is property (not including a building or its structural components) for the storage or dispensing of a clean-burning fuel into the fuel tank of a motor vehicle propelled by such fuel, but only if the storage or dispensing of the fuel is at the point where such fuel is delivered into the fuel tank of the motor vehicle. The use of such property must begin with the taxpayer.

Clean-burning fuels are any fuel at least 85 percent of the volume of which consists of ethanol, natural gas, compressed natural gas, liquefied natural gas, liquefied petroleum gas, or hydrogen. In addition, any mixture of biodiesel and diesel fuel, determined without regard to any use of kerosene and containing at least 20 percent biodiesel, qualifies as a clean fuel.

Credits for qualified refueling property used in a trade or business are part of the general business credit and may be carried back for one year and forward for 20 years. Credits for residential qualified refueling property cannot exceed for any taxable year the difference between the taxpayer's regular tax (reduced by certain other credits) and the taxpayer's tentative minimum tax. Generally, in the case of qualified refueling property sold to a tax-exempt entity, the taxpayer selling the property may claim the credit.

A taxpayer's basis in qualified refueling property is reduced by the amount of the credit. In addition, no credit is available for property used outside the United States or for which an election to expense has been made under section 179.

The credit is available for property placed in service after December 31, 2005, and (except in the case of hydrogen refueling property) before January 1, 2010. In the case of hydrogen refueling property, the property must be placed in service before January 1, 2015.

---

[43] Sec. 30C.

Explanation of Provision

The provision extends and modifies the credit for installing alternative fuel refueling property. The provision extends for one year (through 2010) the credit for installing alternative fuel refueling property, other than property relating to natural gas, compressed natural gas (CNG), liquefied natural gas (LNG), or hydrogen. The credit for property relating to natural gas, CNG, and LNG is extended through 2014 for depreciable property and through 2017 for nondepreciable property. (The provision does not extend the credit for property relating to hydrogen, which continues through 2014 under present law.)

The provision increases the credit amount to 50 percent of the cost of the qualified property. It also raises to $50,000 per taxable year, per location, the limit with respect to depreciable qualified property. With respect to qualified property that is not subject to depreciation, the limit is raised to $2,000 per taxable year.

Effective Date

The provision is effective for property placed in service after the date of enactment, in taxable years ending after such date.

[Law at ¶ 5045. CCH Explanation at ¶ 520.]

[¶ 10,200] Act Sec. B211. Extension of transportation fringe benefit to bicycle commuters

Joint Committee on Taxation (J.C.T. Rep. No. JCX-75-08)

[Code Sec. 132(f)]

Present Law

Qualified transportation fringe benefits provided by an employer are excluded from an employee's gross income.[42] Qualified transportation fringe benefits include parking, transit passes, and vanpool benefits. In addition, no amount is includible in income of an employee merely because the employer offers the employee a choice between cash and qualified transportation fringe benefits. Up to $220 (for 2008) per month of employer-provided parking is excludable from income. Up to $115 (for 2008) per month of employer-provided transit and vanpool benefits are excludable from gross income. These amounts are indexed annually for inflation, rounded to the nearest multiple of $5.

Under present law, qualified transportation fringe benefits include a cash reimbursement by an employer to an employee. However, in the case of transit passes, a cash reimbursement is considered a qualified transportation fringe benefit only if a voucher or similar item which may be exchanged only for a transit pass is not readily available for direct distribution by the employer to the employee.

Explanation of Provision

The provision adds a qualified bicycle commuting reimbursement fringe benefit as a qualified transportation fringe benefit. A qualified bicycle commuting reimbursement fringe benefit means, with respect to a calendar year, any employer reimbursement during the 15-month period beginning with the first day of such calendar year of an employee for reasonable expenses incurred by the employee during the calendar year for the purchase and repair of a bicycle, bicycle improvements, and bicycle storage, provided that the bicycle is regularly used for travel between the employee's residence and place of employment.

The maximum amount that can be excluded from an employee's gross income for a calendar year on account of a bicycle commuting reimbursement fringe benefit is the applicable annual limitation for the employee for that calendar year. The applicable annual limitation for an employee for a calendar year is equal to the product of $20 multiplied by the number of the employee's qualified bicycle commuting months for the year. The $20 amount is not indexed for inflation. A qualified bicycle commuting month means with respect to an employee any month for which the employee does not receive any other qualified transportation fringe benefit and during which the employee regularly uses a bicycle for a substantial portion of travel between the employee's residence and place of employment. Thus, no amount is credited towards an employee's applicable annual limitation for any month in which an employee's usage of a bicycle is infrequent or constitutes an insubstantial portion of the employee's commute.

---

[42] Sec. 132(f).

A bicycle commuting reimbursement fringe benefit cannot be funded by an elective salary contribution on the part of an employee.

Effective Date

The provision is effective for taxable years beginning after December 31, 2008.

[Law at ¶5195. CCH Explanation at ¶230.]

[¶10,210] Act Sec. B302. Extension and modification of energy efficient existing homes credit

Joint Committee on Taxation (J.C.T. REP. No. JCX-75-08)

[Code Sec. 25C]

Present Law

Code section 25C provides a 10-percent credit for the purchase of qualified energy efficiency improvements to existing homes. A qualified energy efficiency improvement is any energy efficiency building envelope component that meets or exceeds the prescriptive criteria for such a component established by the 2000 International Energy Conservation Code as supplemented and as in effect on August 8, 2005 (or, in the case of metal roofs with appropriate pigmented coatings, meets the Energy Star program requirements), and (1) that is installed in or on a dwelling located in the United States; (2) owned and used by the taxpayer as the taxpayer's principal residence; (3) the original use of which commences with the taxpayer; and (4) such component reasonably can be expected to remain in use for at least five years. The credit is nonrefundable.

Building envelope components are: (1) insulation materials or systems which are specifically and primarily designed to reduce the heat loss or gain for a dwelling; (2) exterior windows (including skylights) and doors; and (3) metal roofs with appropriate pigmented coatings which are specifically and primarily designed to reduce the heat loss or gain for a dwelling.

Additionally, code section 25C provides specified credits for the purchase of specific energy efficient property. The allowable credit for the purchase of certain property is (1) $50 for each advanced main air circulating fan, (2) $150 for each qualified natural gas, propane, or oil furnace or hot water boiler, and (3) $300 for each item of qualified energy efficient property.

An advanced main air circulating fan is a fan used in a natural gas, propane, or oil furnace originally placed in service by the taxpayer during the taxable year, and which has an annual electricity use of no more than two percent of the total annual energy use of the furnace (as determined in the standard Department of Energy test procedures).

A qualified natural gas, propane, or oil furnace or hot water boiler is a natural gas, propane, or oil furnace or hot water boiler with an annual fuel utilization efficiency rate of at least 95.

Qualified energy-efficient property is: (1) an electric heat pump water heater which yields an energy factor of at least 2.0 in the standard Department of Energy test procedure, (2) an electric heat pump which has a heating seasonal performance factor (HSPF) of at least 9, a seasonal energy efficiency ratio (SEER) of at least 15, and an energy efficiency ratio (EER) of at least 13, (3) a geothermal heat pump which (i) in the case of a closed loop product, has an energy efficiency ratio (EER) of at least 14.1 and a heating coefficient of performance (COP) of at least 3.3, (ii) in the case of an open loop product, has an energy efficiency ratio (EER) of at least 16.2 and a heating coefficient of performance (COP) of at least 3.6, and (iii) in the case of a direct expansion (DX) product, has an energy efficiency ratio (EER) of at least 15 and a heating coefficient of performance (COP) of at least 3.5, (4) a central air conditioner with energy efficiency of at least the highest efficiency tier established by the Consortium for Energy Efficiency as in effect on Jan. 1, 2006, and (5) a natural gas, propane, or oil water heater which has an energy factor of at least 0.80.

Under section 25C, the maximum credit for a taxpayer with respect to the same dwelling for all taxable years is $500, and no more than $200 of such credit may be attributable to expenditures on windows.

The taxpayer's basis in the property is reduced by the amount of the credit. Special rules apply in the case of condominiums and tenant-stockholders in cooperative housing corporations.

The credit applies to property placed in service prior to January 1, 2008.

Explanation of Provision

The 25C credit is expired for 2008. The provision reestablishes the credit for one year, for property placed in service after December 31, 2008 and before January 1, 2010. The provision also adds biomass fuel property to the list of qualified energy efficient building property eligible for a $300 credit. Biomass fuel property is a stove that burns biomass fuel to heat a dwelling unit located in the United States and used as a principal residence by the taxpayer, or to heat water for such dwelling unit, and that has a thermal efficiency rating of at least 75 percent. Biomass fuel is any plant-derived fuel available on a renewable or recurring basis, including agricultural crops and trees, wood and wood waste and residues (including wood pellets), plants (including aquatic plants, grasses, residues, and fibers.

The credit for geothermal heat pumps is eliminated to conform with the establishment of a residential geothermal heat pump credit under Code section 25D, as provided in section 104 of the bill.

Effective Date

The provision is effective for expenditures after December 31, 2008, for property placed in service after December 31, 2008 and prior to January 1, 2010.

[Law at ¶ 5025. CCH Explanation at ¶ 505.]

[¶ 10,220] Act Sec. B303. Energy efficient commercial buildings deduction

Joint Committee on Taxation (J.C.T. REP. NO. JCX-75-08)

[Code Sec. 179D]

Present Law

In general

Code section 179D provides a deduction equal to energy-efficient commercial building property expenditures made by the taxpayer. Energy-efficient commercial building property expenditures is defined as property (1) which is installed on or in any building located in the United States that is within the scope of Standard 90.1-2001 of the American Society of Heating, Refrigerating, and Air Conditioning Engineers and the Illuminating Engineering Society of North America ("ASHRAE/IESNA"), (2) which is installed as part of (i) the interior lighting systems, (ii) the heating, cooling, ventilation, and hot water systems, or (iii) the building envelope, and (3) which is certified as being installed as part of a plan designed to reduce the total annual energy and power costs with respect to the interior lighting systems, heating, cooling, ventilation, and hot water systems of the building by 50 percent or more in comparison to a reference building which meets the minimum requirements of Standard 90.1-2001 (as in effect on April 2, 2003). The deduction is limited to an amount equal to $1.80 per square foot of the property for which such expenditures are made. The deduction is allowed in the year in which the property is placed in service.

Certain certification requirements must be met in order to qualify for the deduction. The Secretary, in consultation with the Secretary of Energy, will promulgate regulations that describe methods of calculating and verifying energy and power costs using qualified computer software based on the provisions of the 2005 California Nonresidential Alternative Calculation Method Approval Manual or, in the case of residential property, the 2005 California Residential Alternative Calculation Method Approval Manual.

The Secretary shall prescribe procedures for the inspection and testing for compliance of buildings that are comparable, given the difference between commercial and residential buildings, to the requirements in the Mortgage Industry National Accreditation Procedures for Home Energy Rating Systems. Individuals qualified to determine compliance shall only be those recognized by one or more organizations certified by the Secretary for such purposes.

For energy-efficient commercial building property expenditures made by a public entity, such as public schools, the Secretary shall promulgate regulations that allow the deduction to be allocated to the person primarily responsible for designing the property in lieu of the public entity.

If a deduction is allowed under this section, the basis of the property shall be reduced by the amount of the deduction.

The deduction is effective for property placed in service after December 31, 2005 and prior to January 1, 2009.

Partial allowance of deduction

In the case of a building that does not meet the overall building requirement of a 50-percent energy savings, a partial deduction is allowed with respect to each separate building system that comprises energy efficient property and which is certified by a qualified professional as meeting or exceeding the applicable system-specific savings targets established by the Secretary of the Treasury. The applicable system-specific savings targets to be established by the Secretary are those that would result in a total annual energy savings with respect to the whole building of 50 percent, if each of the separate systems met the system specific target. The separate building systems are (1) the interior lighting system, (2) the heating, cooling, ventilation and hot water systems, and (3) the building envelope. The maximum allowable deduction is $0.60 per square foot for each separate system.

Interim rules for lighting systems

In the case of system-specific partial deductions, in general no deduction is allowed until the Secretary establishes system-specific targets.[46] However, in the case of lighting system retrofits, until such time as the Secretary issues final regulations, the system-specific energy savings target for the lighting system is deemed to be met by a reduction in Lighting Power Density of 40 percent (50 percent in the case of a warehouse) of the minimum requirements in Table 9.3.1.1 or Table 9.3.1.2 of ASHRAE/IESNA Standard 90.1-2001. Also, in the case of a lighting system that reduces lighting power density by 25 percent, a partial deduction of 30 cents per square foot is allowed. A pro-rated partial deduction is allowed in the case of a lighting system that reduces lighting power density between 25 percent and 40 percent. Certain lighting level and lighting control requirements must also be met in order to qualify for the partial lighting deductions under the interim rule.

Explanation of Provision

The provision extends the energy efficient commercial buildings deduction for five years, through December 31, 2013.

Effective Date

The provision is effective on the date of enactment.

[Law at ¶ 5255. CCH Explanation at ¶ 560.]

[¶ 10,230] Act Sec. B305. Extension and modification of energy efficient appliance credit

Joint Committee on Taxation (J.C.T. REP. NO. JCX-75-08)

[Code Sec. 45M]

Present Law

A credit is allowed for the eligible production of certain energy-efficient dishwashers, clothes washers, and refrigerators.

The credit for dishwashers applies to dishwashers produced in 2006 and 2007 that meet the Energy Star standards for 2007, and equals $32.31 per eligible dishwasher.[47]

The credit for clothes washers equals $100 for clothes washers manufactured in 2006-2007 that meet the requirements of the Energy Star program that are in effect for clothes washers in 2007.

The credit for refrigerators is based on energy savings and year of manufacture. The energy savings are determined relative to the energy conservation standards promulgated by the Department of Energy that took effect on July 1, 2001. Refrigerators that achieve a 15 to 20 percent energy saving and that are manufactured in 2006 receive a $75 credit. Refrigerators that achieve a 20 to 25 percent energy saving receive a (i) $125 credit if manufactured in 2006-2007. Refrigerators that achieve at least a 25 percent

---

[46] IRS Notice 2008-40 has set a target of a 10 percent reduction in total energy and power costs with respect to the building envelope, and 20 percent each with respect to the interior lighting system and the heating, cooling, ventilation and hot water systems.

[47] The credit amount equals $3 multiplied by 100 times the "energy savings percentage," but may not exceed $100 per dishwasher. The energy saving percentage is defined as the change in the energy factor (EF) required by the Energy Star program between 2007 and 2005 divided by the EF requirement for 2007. The EF required for the Energy Star program was 0.58 in 2005 and 0.65 in 2007, for a change of 0.07. The energy saving percentage is thus 0.07 / 0.65, which when multiplied by 100 times $3 equals $32.31 per refrigerator.

energy saving receive a (i) $175 credit if manufactured in 2006-2007.

Appliances eligible for the credit include only those produced in the United States and that exceed the average amount of U.S. production from the three prior calendar years for each category of appliance. In the case of refrigerators, eligible production is U.S. production that exceeds 110 percent of the average amount of U.S. production from the three prior calendar years.

A dishwasher is any a residential dishwasher subject to the energy conservation standards established by the Department of Energy. A refrigerator must be an automatic defrost refrigerator-freezer with an internal volume of at least 16.5 cubic feet to qualify for the credit. A clothes washer is any residential clothes washer, including a residential style coin operated washer, that satisfies the relevant efficiency standard.

The taxpayer may not claim credits in excess of $75 million for all taxable years, and may not claim credits in excess of $20 million with respect to clothes washers eligible for the $50 credit and refrigerators eligible for the $75 credit. A taxpayer may elect to increase the $20 million limitation described above to $25 million provided that the aggregate amount of credits with respect to such appliances, plus refrigerators eligible for the $100 and $125 credits, is limited to $50 million for all taxable years.

Additionally, the credit allowed in a taxable year for all appliances may not exceed two percent of the average annual gross receipts of the taxpayer for the three taxable years preceding the taxable year in which the credit is determined.

The credit is part of the general business credit.

Explanation of Provision

The provision extends and modifies the energy efficient appliance credit. The provision provides modified credits for eligible production as follows:

Dishwashers

1. $45 in the case of a dishwasher that is manufactured in calendar year 2008 or 2009 that uses no more than 324 kilowatt hours per year and 5.8 gallons per cycle, and

2. $75 in the case of a dishwasher that is manufactured in calendar year 2008, 2009, or 2010 and that uses no more than 307 kilowatt hours per year and 5.0 gallons per cycle (5.5 gallons per cycle for dishwashers designed for greater than 12 place settings).

Clothes washers

1. $75 in the case of a residential top-loading clothes washer manufactured in calendar year 2008 that meets or exceeds a 1.72 modified energy factor and does not exceed a 8.0 water consumption factor, and

2. $125 in the case of a residential top-loading clothes washer manufactured in calendar year 2008 or 2009 that meets or exceeds a 1.8 modified energy factor and does not exceed a 7.5 water consumption factor,

3. $150 in the case of a residential or commercial clothes washer manufactured in calendar year 2008, 2009 or 2010 that meets or exceeds a 2.0 modified energy factor and does not exceed a 6.0 water consumption factor, and

4. $250 in the case of a residential or commercial clothes washer manufactured in calendar year 2008, 2009, or 2010 that meets or exceeds a 2.2 modified energy factor and does not exceed a 4.5 water consumption factor.

Refrigerators

1. $50 in the case of a refrigerator manufactured in calendar year 2008 that consumes at least 20 percent but not more than 22.9 percent less kilowatt hours per year than the 2001 energy conservation standards,

2. $75 in the case of a refrigerator that is manufactured in calendar year 2008 or 2009 that consumes at least 23 percent but no more than 24.9 percent less kilowatt hours per year than the 2001 energy conservation standards,

3. $100 in the case of a refrigerator that is manufactured in calendar year 2008, 2009 or 2010 that consumes at least 25 percent but not more than 29.9 percent less kilowatt hours per year than the 2001 energy conservation standards, and

4. $200 in the case of a refrigerator manufactured in calendar year 2008, 2009 or 2010 that consumes at least 30 percent less energy than the 2001 energy conservation standards.

Appliances eligible for the credit include only those that exceed the average amount of production from the two prior calendar years for each category of appliance, rather than the present law three prior calendar years. Additionally, the special rule with respect to refrigerators is eliminated.

The aggregate credit amount allowed with respect to a taxpayer for all taxable years beginning after December 31, 2007 may not exceed $75 million, with the exception that the $200 refrigerator credit and the $250 clothes washer credit are not limited.

The term "modified energy factor" means the modified energy factor established by the Department of Energy for compliance with the Federal energy conservation standard.

The term "gallons per cycle" means, with respect to a dishwasher, the amount of water, expressed in gallons, required to complete a normal cycle of a dishwasher.

The term "water consumption factor" means, with respect to a clothes washer, the quotient of the total weighted per-cycle water consumption divided by the cubic foot (or liter) capacity of the clothes washer.

Effective Date

The provision applies to appliances produced after December 31, 2007.

[Law at ¶ 5110. CCH Explanation at ¶ 540.]

[¶ 10,240] Act Sec. B306. Accelerated recovery period for depreciation of smart meters and smart grid systems

Joint Committee on Taxation (J.C.T. REP. No. JCX-75-08)

[Code Sec. 168]

Present Law

A taxpayer generally must capitalize the cost of property used in a trade or business and recover such cost over time through annual deductions for depreciation or amortization. Tangible property generally is depreciated under the modified accelerated cost recovery system ("MACRS"), which determines depreciation by applying specific recovery periods, placed-in-service conventions, and depreciation methods to the cost of various types of depreciable property.[48] The class lives of assets placed in service after 1986 are generally set forth in Revenue Procedure 87-56.[49] Assets included in class 49.14, describing assets used in the transmission and distribution of electricity for sale and related land improvements, are assigned a class life of 30 years and a recovery period of 20 years.

Explanation of Provision

The provision provides a 10-year recovery period and 150 percent declining balance method for any qualified smart electric meter and any qualified smart electric grid system.[50] For purposes of the provision, a qualified smart electric meter means any time-based meter and related communication equipment which is placed in service by a taxpayer who is a supplier of electric energy or a provider of electric energy services and which is capable of being used by the taxpayer as part of a system that (1) mea-

sures and records electricity usage data on a time-differentiated basis in at least 24 separate time segments per day; (2) provides for the exchange of information between the supplier or provider and the customer's smart electric meter in support of time-based rates or other forms of demand response; and (3) provides data to such supplier or provider so that the supplier or provider can provide energy usage information to customers electronically; and (4) provides net metering.

For purposes of the provision, a qualified smart electric grid system means any smart grid property used as part of a system for electric distribution grid communications, monitoring, and management placed in service by a taxpayer who is a supplier of electric energy or a provider of electric energy services. Smart grid property includes electronics and related equipment that is capable of (1) sensing, collecting, and monitoring data of or from all portions of a utility's electric distribution grid; (2) providing real-time, two-way communications to monitor or manage such grid; and (3) providing real-time analysis of and event prediction based upon collected data that can be used to improve electric distribution system reliability, quality, and performance.

Effective Date

The provision is effective for property placed in service after the date of enactment.

[Law at ¶ 5230. CCH Explanation at ¶ 570.]

---

[48] Sec. 168.
[49] 1987-2 C.B. 674 (as clarified and modified by Rev. Proc. 88-22, 1988-1 C.B. 785).

[50] To the extent property otherwise qualified for a shorter recover period, such shorter recovery period shall apply.

[¶10,250] Act Sec. B307. Extension of issuance authority for qualified green building and sustainable design project bonds

Joint Committee on Taxation (J.C.T. Rep. No. JCX-75-08)

[Code Sec. 142]

Present Law

In general

Private activity bonds are bonds that nominally are issued by States or local governments, but the proceeds of which are used (directly or indirectly) by a private person and payment of which is derived from funds of such private person. The exclusion from income for State and local bonds does not apply to private activity bonds, unless the bonds are issued for certain permitted purposes ("qualified private activity bonds"). The definition of a qualified private activity bond includes exempt facility bonds.

In most cases, the aggregate volume of tax-exempt qualified private activity bonds, including most exempt facility bonds, is restricted by annual aggregate volume limits imposed on bonds issued by issuers within each State. For calendar year 2008, the State volume cap, which is indexed for inflation, equals $85 per resident of the State, or $262.09 million, if greater.

Qualified green building and sustainable design project bonds

The definition of exempt facility bond includes qualified green building and sustainable design project bonds ("qualified green bond"). A qualified green bond is defined as any bond issued as part of an issue that finances a project designated by the Secretary, after consultation with the Administrator of the Environmental Protection Agency (the "Administrator") as a green building and sustainable design project that meets the following eligibility requirements: (1) at least 75 percent of the square footage of the commercial buildings that are part of the project is registered for the U.S. Green Building Council's LEED[51] certification and is reasonably expected (at the time of designation) to meet such certification; (2) the project includes a brownfield site;[52] (3) the project receives at least $5 million dollars in specific State or local resources; and (4) the project includes at least one million square feet of building or at least 20 acres of land.

Qualified green bonds are not subject to the State bond volume limitations. Rather, there is a national limitation of $2 billion of qualified green bonds that the Secretary may allocate, in the aggregate, to qualified green building and sustainable design projects. Qualified green bonds may be currently refunded if certain conditions are met, but cannot be advance refunded. The authority to issue qualified green bonds terminates after September 30, 2009.

Under present law, each green building and sustainable design project must certify to the Secretary, no later than 30 days after the completion of the project, that the net benefit of the tax-exempt financing was used for the purposes described in the project application. Issuers are required to maintain, on behalf of each project, an interest bearing reserve account equal to one percent of the net proceeds of any qualified green bond issued for such project. Not later than five years after the date of issuance of bonds with respect to the project, the Secretary, after consultation with the Administrator, shall determine whether the project financed with the proceeds of qualified green bonds has substantially complied with the requirements and goals of the project. If the Secretary, after such consultation, certifies that the project has substantially complied with the requirements and goals, amounts in the reserve account, including all interest, shall be released to the project. If the Secretary determines that the project has not substantially complied with such requirements and goals, amounts in the reserve account, including all interest, shall be paid to the United States Treasury.

---

[51] The LEED ("Leadership in Energy and Environmental Design) Green Building Rating System is a voluntary, consensus-based national standard for developing high-performance sustainable buildings. Registration is the first step toward LEED certification. Actual certification requires that the applicant project satisfy a number of requirements. Commercial buildings, as defined by standard building codes are eligible for certification. Commercial occupancies include, but are not limited to, offices, retail and service establishments, institutional buildings (e.g. libraries, schools, museums, churches, etc.), hotels, and residential buildings of four or more habitable stories.

[52] For this purpose, a brownfield site is defined by section 101(39) of the Comprehensive Environmental Response, Compensation, and Liability Act of 1980 (42 U.S.C. sec. 9601), including a site described in subparagraph (D)(ii)(II)(aa) thereof (relating to a site that is contaminated by petroleum or a petroleum product excluded from the definition of 'hazardous substance' under section 101).

Explanation of Provision

The provision extends the authority to issue qualified green bonds through September 30, 2012.

The provision also clarifies that the date for determining whether amounts in a reserve account may be released to a green building and

sustainable design project is the date that is five years after the date of issuance of the last bond issue issued with respect to such project.

Effective Date

The provision applies on the date of enactment.

[Law at ¶ 5205. CCH Explanation at ¶ 820.]

[¶ 10,260] Act Sec. B401. Limitation of deduction for income attributable to domestic production of oil, gas, or primary products thereof

Joint Committee on Taxation (J.C.T. REP. NO. JCX-75-08)

[Code Sec. 199]

Present Law

In general

Section 199 of the Code provides a deduction equal to a portion of the taxpayer's qualified production activities income. For taxable years beginning after 2009, the deduction is nine percent of such income. For taxable years beginning in 2008 and 2009, the deduction is six percent of income. However, the deduction for a taxable year is limited to 50 percent of the wages properly allocable to domestic production gross receipts paid by the taxpayer during the calendar year that ends in such taxable year.[217]

Qualified production activities income

In general, "qualified production activities income" is equal to domestic production gross receipts (defined by section 199(c)(4)), reduced by the sum of: (1) the costs of goods sold that are allocable to such receipts; (2) other expenses, losses, or deductions which are properly allocable to such receipts.

Domestic production gross receipts

"Domestic production gross receipts" generally are gross receipts of a taxpayer that are derived from: (1) any sale, exchange or other disposition, or any lease, rental or license, of qualifying production property ("QPP") that was manufactured, produced, grown or ex-

tracted ("MPGE") by the taxpayer in whole or in significant part within the United States; (2) any sale, exchange or other disposition, or any lease, rental or license, of qualified film produced by the taxpayer; (3) any sale, exchange or other disposition of electricity, natural gas, or potable water produced by the taxpayer in the United States; (4) construction activities performed in the United States;[218] or (5) engineering or architectural services performed in the United States for construction projects located in the United States.

Congress granted Treasury broad authority to "prescribe such regulations as are necessary to carry out the purposes" of section 199.[219] In defining MPGE for purposes of section 199, Treasury described the following as MPGE activities: manufacturing, producing, growing, extracting, installing, developing, improving, and creating QPP; making QPP out of scrap, salvage, or junk material as well as from new or raw material by processing, manipulating, refining, or changing the form of an article, or by combining or assembling two or more articles; cultivating soil, raising livestock, fishing, and mining minerals.[220]

The regulations specifically cite an example of oil refining activities in describing the "in whole or in significant part" test in determining domestic production gross receipts. QPP is generally considered to be MPGE in significant part by the taxpayer within the United States if such activities are substantial in nature taking into

---

[217] For this purpose, "wages" include the sum of the amounts of wages as defined in section 3401(a) and elective deferrals that the taxpayer properly reports to the Social Security Administration with respect to the employment of employees of the taxpayer during the calendar year ending during the taxpayer's taxable year. Elective deferrals include elective deferrals as defined in section 402(g)(3), amounts deferred under section 457, and designated Roth contributions (as defined in section 402A).

[218] For this purpose, construction activities include activities that are directly related to the erection or substantial

renovation of residential and commercial buildings and infrastructure. Substantial renovation would include structural improvements, but not mere cosmetic changes, such as painting, that is not performed in connection with activities that otherwise constitute substantial renovation.

[219] Sec. 199(d)(9).

[220] Treas. Reg. sec. 1.199-3(e)(1).

account all of the facts and circumstances, including the relative value added by, and relative cost of, the taxpayer's MPGE activity within the United States, the nature of the QPP, and the nature of the MPGE activity that the taxpayer performs within the United States.[221] The following example is provided in the regulations to illustrate this "substantial in nature" standard:

> X purchases from Y, an unrelated person, unrefined oil extracted outside the United States. X refines the oil in the United States. The refining of the oil by X is an MPGE activity that is substantial in nature.[222]

Natural gas transmission or distribution

Domestic production gross receipts include gross receipts from the production in the United States of natural gas, but excludes gross receipts from the transmission or distribution of natural gas.[223] Production activities generally include all activities involved in extracting natural gas from the ground and processing the gas into pipeline quality gas. However, gross receipts of a taxpayer attributable to transmission of pipeline quality gas from a natural gas field (or from a natural gas processing plant) to a local distribution company's citygate (or to another customer) are not qualified domestic production gross receipts. Likewise, gas purchased by a local gas distribution company and distributed from the citygate to the local customers does not give rise to domestic production gross receipts.

Drilling oil or gas wells

The Treasury regulations provide that qualifying construction activities performed in the United States include activities relating to drilling an oil or gas well.[224] Under the regulations, activities the cost of which are intangible drilling and development costs within the meaning of Treas. Reg. sec. 1.612-4 are considered to be activities constituting construction for purposes of determining domestic production gross receipts.[225]

Qualifying in-kind partnerships

In general, an owner of a pass-thru entity is not treated as conducting the qualified production activities of the pass-thru entity, and vice versa. However, the Treasury regulations provide a special rule for "qualifying in-kind partnerships," which are defined as partnerships engaged solely in the extraction, refining, or processing of oil, natural gas, petrochemicals, or products derived from oil, natural gas, or petrochemicals in whole or in significant part within the United States, or the production or generation of electricity in the United States.[226] In the case of a qualifying in-kind partnership, each partner is treated as MPGE or producing the property MPGE or produced by the partnership that is distributed to that partner.[227] If a partner of a qualifying in-kind partnership derives gross receipts from the lease, rental, license, sale, exchange, or other disposition of the property that was MPGE or produced by the qualifying in-kind partnership, then, provided such partner is a partner of the qualifying in-kind partnership at the time the partner disposes of the property, the partner is treated as conducting the MPGE or production activities previously conducted by the qualifying in-kind partnership with respect to that property.[228]

Alternative minimum tax

The deduction for domestic production activities is allowed for purposes of computing alternative minimum taxable income (including adjusted current earnings). The deduction in computing alternative minimum taxable income is determined by reference to the lesser of the qualified production activities income (as determined for the regular tax) or the alternative minimum taxable income (in the case of an individual, adjusted gross income as determined for the regular tax) without regard to this deduction.

Explanation of Provision

The provision reduces the section 199 deduction for taxpayers with oil related qualified production activities income for any taxable year beginning after 2009 by three percent of the least of: (1) oil related qualified production activities income of the taxpayer for the taxable year; (2) qualified production activities income of the taxpayer for the taxable year; or (3) taxable income (determined without regard to the section 199 deduction). For purposes of this provision, the term "oil related qualified production activities income" means qualified production activities income for any taxable year which is attributable to the production, refining, processing, transpor-

---

[221] Treas. Reg. sec. 1.199-3(g)(2).

[222] Treas. Reg. sec. 1.199-3(g)(5), Example 1.

[223] H.R. Rep. No. 108-755 (conference report for the American Jobs Creation Act of 2004), footnote 28 at 272.

[224] Treas. Reg. sec. 1.199-3(m)(1)(i).

[225] Treas. Reg. sec. 1.199-3(m)(2)(iii).

[226] Treas. Reg. sec. 1.199-9(i)(2).

[227] Treas. Reg. sec. 1.199-9(i)(1).

[228] Id.

tation, or distribution of oil, gas, or any primary product thereof during such taxable year.

The term "primary product" has the same meaning as when used in section 927(a)(2)(C), as in effect before its repeal. The Treasury regulations define the term "primary product from oil" to mean crude oil and all products derived from the destructive distillation of crude oil, including volatile products, light oils such as motor fuel and kerosene, distillates such as naphtha, lubricating oils, greases and waxes, and residues such as fuel oil.[229] Additionally, a product or commodity derived from shale oil which would be a primary product from oil if derived from crude oil is considered a primary product from oil.[230] The term "primary product from gas" is defined as all gas and associated hydrocarbon components from gas wells or oil wells, whether recov-

ered at the lease or upon further processing, including natural gas, condensates, liquefied petroleum gases such as ethane, propane, and butane, and liquid products such as natural gasoline.[231] These primary products and processes are not intended to represent either the only primary products from oil or gas or the only processes from which primary products may be derived under existing and future technologies.[232] Examples of nonprimary products include, but are not limited to, petrochemicals, medicinal products, insecticides, and alcohols.[233]

Effective Date

The provision is effective for taxable years beginning after December 31, 2008.

[Law at ¶ 5280. CCH Explanation at ¶ 375.]

[¶ 10,270] Act Sec. B402. Eliminate the distinction between FOGEI and FORI and apply present-law FOGEI rules to all foreign income from the production and sale of oil and gas product

Joint Committee on Taxation (J.C.T. REP. NO. JCX-75-08)

[Code Sec. 907]

Present Law

In general

Foreign tax credit

The United States taxes its citizens and residents (including U.S. corporations) on their worldwide income. Because the countries in which income is earned also may assert their jurisdiction to tax the same income on the basis of source, foreign-source income earned by U.S. persons may be subject to double taxation. In order to mitigate this possibility, the United States generally provides a credit against U.S. tax liability for foreign income taxes paid or accrued.[234] In the case of foreign income taxes paid or accrued by a foreign subsidiary, a U.S. parent corporation is generally entitled to an indirect (also referred to as a deemed paid) credit for those taxes when it receives an actual or deemed distribution of the underlying earnings from the foreign subsidiary.[235]

Foreign tax credit limitations

The foreign tax credit generally is limited to the U.S. tax liability on a taxpayer's foreign-source income. This general limitation is intended to ensure that the credit serves its purpose of mitigating double taxation of foreign-source income without offsetting the U.S. tax on U.S.-source income.[236]

In addition, this limitation is calculated separately for various categories of income, generally referred to as "separate limitation categories." The total amount of the foreign tax credit used to offset the U.S. tax on income in each separate limitation category may not exceed the proportion of the taxpayer's U.S. tax which the taxpayer's foreign-source taxable income in that category bears to its worldwide taxable income in that category. The separate limitation rules are intended to reduce the extent to which excess foreign taxes paid in a high-tax foreign jurisdiction can be "cross-credited" against the

---

[229] Treas. Reg. sec. 1.927(a)-1T(g)(2)(i).
[230] Id.
[231] Treas. Reg. sec. 1.927(a)-1T(g)(2)(ii).
[232] Treas. Reg. sec. 1.927(a)-1T(g)(2)(iii).

[233] Treas. Reg. sec. 1.927(a)-1T(g)(2)(iv).
[234] Sec. 901.
[235] Secs. 902, 960.
[236] Sec. 904(a).

residual U.S. tax on low-taxed foreign-source income.[237]

Special limitation on credits for foreign extraction taxes and taxes on foreign oil related income

In addition to the foreign tax credit limitations that apply to all foreign tax credits, a special limitation is placed on foreign income taxes on foreign oil and gas extraction income ("FOGEI").[238] Under this special limitation, amounts claimed as taxes paid on FOGEI of a U.S. corporation qualify as creditable taxes (if they otherwise so qualify) only to the extent they do not exceed the product of the highest marginal U.S. tax rate on corporations (presently 35 percent) multiplied by such extraction income. Foreign taxes paid in excess of that amount on such income are, in general, neither creditable nor deductible. The amount of any such taxes paid or accrued (or deemed paid) in any taxable year which exceeds the FOGEI limitation may be carried back to the immediately preceding taxable year and carried forward 10 taxable years and credited (not deducted) to the extent that the taxpayer otherwise has excess FOGEI limitation for those years.[239]

A similar special limitation applies, in theory, to foreign taxes paid on foreign oil related income ("FORI") in certain cases where the foreign law imposing such amount of tax is structured, or in fact operates, so that the amount of tax imposed with respect to foreign oil related income will generally be "materially greater," over a "reasonable period of time," than the amount generally imposed on income that is neither FORI nor FOGEI.[240] Under the FORI rules, if this theoretical limitation were to apply, then the portion of the foreign taxes on FORI so disallowed would be recharacterized as a (non-creditable) deductible expense.[241]

As a general matter, the FOGEI and FORI rules of section 907 are informed by two related but distinct concerns. First, as described by the Staff of the Joint Committee on Taxation in 1982, the rules were designed to address the perceived problem of "disguised royalties" being improperly treated as creditable foreign taxes:

> When U.S. oil companies began operations in a number of major oil exporting countries, they paid only a royalty for the oil extracted since there was generally no applicable income tax in those countries. However, in part because of the benefit to the oil companies of imposing an income tax, as opposed to a royalty, those countries have adopted taxes applicable to extraction income and have labeled them income taxes. Moreover, because of this relative advantage to the oil companies of paying income taxes rather than royalties, many oil-producing nations in the post-World II era have tended to increase their revenues from oil extraction by increasing their taxes on U.S. oil companies.[242]

In addition, the section 907 rules have also been described as intended to prevent the crediting of high foreign taxes on FOGEI and FORI against the residual U.S. tax on other types of lower-taxed foreign source income.[243] Consistent with this concern, between 1975 and 1982 the foreign tax credit rules provided a separate limitation category (or "basket") under the general section 904 limitation for foreign oil income (broadly defined to include both FORI and FOGEI within the meaning of present law section 907); this separate basket for foreign oil income was eliminated when the present law FORI rules were added and other changes were made by the Tax Equity and Reform Act of 1982.[244]

Determination of FOGEI and FORI

In general

Determination of a taxpayer's FOGEI and FORI is highly specific to the taxpayer's relevant facts and circumstances. Under section 907(c)(1), FOGEI is defined as taxable income derived from sources outside the United States and its

---

[237] Sec. 904(d). For taxable years beginning prior to January 1, 2007, section 904(d) provides eight separate baskets as a general matter, and effectively many more in situations in which various special rules apply. The American Jobs Creation Act of 2004 reduced the number of baskets from nine to eight for taxable years beginning after December 31, 2002, and further reduced the number of baskets to two (i.e., "general" and "passive") for taxable years beginning after December 31, 2006. Pub. L. No. 108-357, sec. 404 (2004).

[238] Sec. 907(a).

[239] Sec. 907(f). These carryback and carryforward rules are similar to the general foreign tax credit carryback and carryforward rules of section 904(c).

[240] Sec. 907(b).

[241] Treas. Reg. sec. 1.907(a)-0(d).

[242] Joint Committee on Taxation, *Explanation of the Revenue Provisions of the Tax Equity and Fiscal Responsibility Act of 1982*, (JCS-38-82), December 31, 1982, sec. IV.A.7.a, footnote 63.

[243] H.R. Conf. Rep. No. 103-213, at 646 (1993).

[244] Pub. L. No. 97-248, sec. 211(c) (1982).

possessions from the extraction (by the taxpayer or any other person) of minerals from oil or gas wells located outside the United States and its possessions or from the sale or exchange of assets used by the taxpayer in the trade or business of extracting those minerals.[245] The regulations provide that "gross income from extraction is determined by reference to the fair market value of the minerals in the immediate vicinity of the well."[246]

The regulations do not provide specific methods for determining the fair market value of the extracted oil or gas in the immediate vicinity of the well, but simply provide that all the facts and circumstances that exist in the particular case must be considered, including (but not limited to) facts and circumstances pertaining to the independent market value (if any) in the immediate vicinity of the well, the fair market value at the port of the foreign county, and the relationships between the taxpayer and the foreign government.[247]

Section 907(c)(2) defines FORI to include taxable income from the processing of oil and gas into their primary products, from the transportation or distribution and sale of oil and gas and their primary products, from the disposition of assets used in these activities, and from the performance of any other related service.[248]

As a result of these separate rules governing FOGEI and FORI and the interaction between them, a taxpayer's determination of the amounts of FOGEI and FORI, as well as the allocation of foreign taxes to each class of income, can have a significant impact on the taxpayer's overall U.S. tax liability.

IRS field directive

An October 12, 2004, IRS field directive (the "2004 Field Directive") sets forth guidance to international examiners and specialists on the application of what it describes as the two most commonly used methods for determining FOGEI and FORI when there is no ascertainable market price for the oil and gas in the immediate vicinity of the well, namely the residual (rate of return) method and the proportionate profits method.[249]

Under the residual (rate of return) method, the taxpayer first calculates FORI by applying an assumed after-tax rate of return to the cost of its fixed "FORI assets." Then, because income from the production and sale of oil and gas product is equal to the sum of FORI and FOGEI, FOGEI is determined by subtracting FORI (as calculated) from the taxpayer's total foreign income from the production and sale of oil and gas product.

Under the proportionate profits method, the taxpayer allocates total income from the production and sale of the oil or gas product between FOGEI and FORI based on the relative costs of the FOGEI and FORI activities.

Under either method, the taxpayer must determine its total income from the production and sale of oil and gas product, and must distinguish between costs and assets classified as relating to FOGEI and those relating to FORI. Under the residual (rate of return) method, the taxpayer must also determine appropriate rates of return for FORI assets. The 2004 Field Directive sets forth examples of FOGEI assets[250] and FORI assets,[251] and further provides that assets that support both FOGEI and FORI may be allocated by any reasonable method.

Explanation of Provision

Under the provision, the scope of the present-law FOGEI rules is expanded to apply to all foreign income from production and other activity related to the sale of oil and gas product (i.e., the sum of FORI and FOGEI as classified under present law). Thus, amounts claimed as taxes paid on such amount of (combined) foreign oil and gas income are creditable in a given taxable year (if they otherwise so qualify) only to the extent they do not exceed the product of the

---

[245] Sec. 907(c)(1).

[246] Treas. Reg. sec. 1.907(c)-1(b)(2).

[247] Treas. Reg. sec. 1.907(c)-1(b)(6).

[248] Sec. 907(c)(1); Treas. Reg. sec. 1.907(c)-1(d).

[249] Memorandum for Industry Directors ("Field Directive on IRC §907 Evaluating Taxpayer Methods of Determining Foreign Oil and Gas Extraction Income (FOGEI) and Foreign Oil Related Income (FORI)"), October 12, 2004 (Tax Analysts Doc 2004-23010; 2004 TNT 233-8). By its terms, the 2004 Field Directive "is not an official pronouncement of the law or the Service's position and cannot be used, cited, or relied upon as such."

[250] Examples of FOGEI assets include wells, wellheads, and pumping equipment; slug catchers, separators, treaters,

emulsion breakers and stock tanks needed to obtain marketable crude (for oil production); primary separation and dehydration equipment needed to arrive at a gaseous stream in which hydrocarbons may be recovered (for gas production); lines interconnecting the above; the infrastructure-type equipment to provide for the operation of the above; and structures to physically support the above (such as offshore platforms).

[251] Examples of FORI assets include lines that carry natural gas beyond the primary separator and dehydration equipment and towards its sales point, and compressors needed to transport through these lines; lines that carry marketable crude oil from the premises, as well as pumps needed to transport crude oil through these lines; and assets used to process crude oil and natural gas.

highest marginal U.S. tax rate on corporations (in the case of corporations) multiplied by such combined foreign oil and gas income for such taxable year. As under the present-law FOGEI rules, excess foreign taxes may be carried back to the immediately preceding taxable year and carried forward 10 taxable years and credited (not deducted) to the extent that the taxpayer otherwise has excess limitation with regard to combined foreign oil and gas income in a carryover year. Under a transition rule, pre-2009 credits carried forward to post-2008 years will continue to governed by present law for purposes of determining the amount of carryforward credits eligible to be claimed in a post-2008 year; simi- larly, solely for purposes of determining whether excess credits generated in 2009 and carried back can be claimed to offset 2008 tax liability, the new rules will be deemed to apply in determining overall (combined FOGEI-FORI) limitation for the carryback year.

The provision repeals the present-law section 907(b) FORI limitation.

Effective Date

The provision is effective for taxable years beginning after December 31, 2008.

[Law at ¶ 5330 and ¶ 5465. CCH Explanation at ¶ 875.]

[¶ 10,280] Act Sec. B403. Broker reporting of customer's basis in securities transactions

Joint Committee on Taxation (J.C.T. Rᴇᴘ. Nᴏ. JCX-75-08)

[Code Sec. 6045 and New Code Secs. 6045A and 6045B]

Present Law

In general

Gain or loss generally is recognized for Federal income tax purposes on realization of that gain or loss (for example, through the sale of property giving rise to the gain or loss). The taxpayer's gain or loss on a disposition of property is the difference between the amount realized and the adjusted basis.[252]

To compute adjusted basis, a taxpayer must first determine the property's unadjusted or original basis and then make adjustments prescribed by the Code.[253] The original basis of property is its cost, except as otherwise prescribed by the Code (for example, in the case of property acquired by gift or bequest or in a tax-free exchange). Once determined, the taxpayer's original basis generally is adjusted downward to take account of depreciation or amortization, and generally is adjusted upward to reflect income and gain inclusions or capital outlays with respect to the property.

Basis computation rules

If a taxpayer has acquired stock in a corporation on different dates or at different prices and sells or transfers some of the shares of that stock, and the lot from which the stock is sold or transferred is not adequately identified, the shares deemed sold are the earliest acquired shares (the "first-in-first-out rule").[254] If a taxpayer makes an adequate identification of shares of stock that it sells, the shares of stock treated as sold are the shares that have been identified.[255] A taxpayer who owns shares in a regulated investment company ("RIC") generally is permitted to elect, in lieu of the specific identification or first-in-first-out methods, to determine the basis of RIC shares sold under one of two average-cost-basis methods described in Treasury regulations.[256]

Information reporting

Present law imposes information reporting requirements on participants in certain transactions. Under these requirements, information is generally reported to the IRS and furnished to taxpayers. These requirements are intended to assist taxpayers in preparing their income tax returns and to help the IRS determine whether taxpayers' tax returns are correct and complete. For example, every person engaged in a trade or business generally is required to file information returns for each calendar year for payments of $600 or more made in the course of the payor's trade or business.[257]

Section 6045(a) requires brokers to file with the IRS annual information returns showing the gross proceeds realized by customers from various sale transactions. The Secretary is authorized

---

[252] Sec. 1001.

[253] Sec. 1016.

[254] Treas. Reg. sec. 1.1012-1(c)(1).

[255] Treas. Reg. sec. 1.1012-1(c).

[256] Treas. Reg. sec. 1.1012-1(e).

[257] Sec. 6041(a).

to require brokers to report additional information related to customers.[258] Brokers are required to furnish to every customer information statements with the same gross proceeds information that is included in the returns filed with the IRS for that customer.[259] These information statements are required to be furnished by January 31 of the year following the calendar year for which the return under section 6045(a) is required to be filed.[260]

A person who is required to file information returns but who fails to do so by the due date for the returns, includes on the returns incorrect information, or files incomplete returns generally is subject to a penalty of $50 for each return with respect to which such a failure occurs, up to a maximum of $250,000 in any calendar year.[261] Similar penalties, with a $100,000 calendar year maximum, apply to failures to furnish correct information statements to recipients of payments for which information reporting is required.[262]

Present law does not require broker information reporting with respect to a customer's basis in property but does impose an obligation to keep records, as described below.

Basis recordkeeping requirements

Taxpayers are required to "keep such records . . . as the Secretary may from time to time prescribe."[263] Treasury regulations impose recordkeeping requirements on any person required to file information returns.[264]

Treasury regulations provide that donors and donees should keep records that are relevant in determining a donee's basis in property.[265] IRS Publication 552 states that a taxpayer should keep basis records for property until the period of limitations expires for the year in which the taxpayer disposes of the property.

Explanation of Provision

In general

Under the provision, every broker that is required to file a return under section 6045(a) reporting the gross proceeds from the sale of a covered security must include in the return (1) the customer's adjusted basis in the security and (2) whether any gain or loss with respect to the security is long-term or short-term (within the meaning of section 1222).

Covered securities

A covered security is any specified security acquired on or after an applicable date if the security was (1) acquired through a transaction in the account in which the security is held or (2) was transferred to that account from an account in which the security was a covered security, but only if the transferee broker received a statement under section 6045A (described below) with respect to the transfer. Under this rule, certain securities acquired by gift or inheritance are not covered securities.

A specified security is any share of stock in a corporation (including stock of a regulated investment company); any note, bond, debenture, or other evidence of indebtedness; any commodity or a contract or a derivative with respect to the commodity if the Secretary determines that adjusted basis reporting is appropriate; and any other financial instrument with respect to which the Secretary determines that adjusted basis reporting is appropriate.

For stock in a corporation (other than stock for which an average basis method is permissible under section 1012), the applicable date is January 1, 2011. For any stock for which an average basis method is permissible under section 1012, the applicable date is January 1, 2012. Consequently, the applicable date for certain stock acquired through a periodic stock investment plan (for which stock additional rules are described below) and for stock in a regulated investment company is January 1, 2012. A regulated investment company is permitted to elect to treat as a covered security any stock in the company acquired before January 1, 2012. This election is described below. For any specified security other than stock in a corporation or stock for which an average basis method is permitted, the applicable date is January 1, 2013, or a later date determined by the Secretary.

Computation of adjusted basis

The customer's adjusted basis required to be reported to the IRS is determined under the following rules. The adjusted basis of any security other than stock for which an average basis method is permissible under section 1012 is determined under the first-in, first-out method unless the customer notifies the broker by means of

---

[258] Sec. 6045(a).

[259] Sec. 6045(b).

[260] Id.

[261] Sec. 6721.

[262] Sec. 6722.

[263] Sec. 6001.

[264] Treas. Reg. sec. 1.6001-1(a).

[265] Treas. Reg. sec. 1.1015-1(g).

making an adequate identification (under the rules of section 1012 for specific identification) of the stock sold or transferred. The adjusted basis of stock for which an average basis method is permissible under section 1012 is determined in accordance with the broker's default method under section 1012 (that is, the first-in, first-out method, the average cost method, or the specific identification method) unless the customer notifies the broker that the customer elects another permitted method. This notification is made separately for each account in which stock for which the average cost method is permissible is held and, once made, applies to all stock held in that account. As a result of this rule, a broker's basis computation method used for stock held in one account with that broker may differ from the basis computation method used for stock held in another account with that broker.

For any sale, exchange, or other disposition of a specified security after the applicable date (defined previously), the provision modifies section 1012 so that the conventions prescribed by regulations under that section for determining adjusted basis (the first-in, first-out, specific identification, and average basis conventions) apply on an account-by-account basis. Under this rule, for example, if a customer holds shares of the same specified security in accounts with different brokers, each broker makes its adjusted basis determinations by reference only to the shares held in the account with that broker, and only shares in the account from which the sale is made may be identified as the shares sold. Unless the election described next applies, any stock for which an average basis method is permissible under section 1012 which is acquired before January 1, 2012 is treated as a separate account from any such stock acquired on or after that date. A consequence of this rule is that if adjusted basis is being determined using an average basis method, average basis is computed without regard to any stock acquired before January 1, 2012. A regulated investment company, however, may elect (at the time and in the form and manner prescribed by the Secretary), on a stockholder-by-stockholder basis, to treat as covered securities all stock in the company held by the stockholder without regard to when the stock was acquired. When this election applies, the average basis of a customer's regulated investment company stock is determined by taking into account shares of stock acquired before, on, and after January 1, 2012. A similar election is allowed for any broker holding stock in a regulated investment company as a nominee of the beneficial owner of the stock.

If stock is acquired on or after January 1, 2011 in connection with a periodic stock investment plan, the basis of that stock is determined under one of the basis computation methods permissible for stock in a regulated investment company. Accordingly, an average cost method may be used for determining the basis of stock acquired under a periodic stock investment plan. In determining basis under this rule, the account-by-account rules described previously, including the election available to regulated investment companies, apply. The special rule for stock acquired through a periodic stock investment plan, however, applies only while the stock is held as part of the plan. If stock to which this rule applies is transferred to another account, the stock will have a cost basis in that other account equal to its basis in the periodic stock investment plan immediately before the transfer (with any proper adjustment for charges incurred in connection with the transfer). After the transfer, however, the transferee broker may use the otherwise applicable convention (that is, the first-in, first-out method or the specific identification method) for determining which shares are sold when a sale is made of some but not all shares of a particular security. It is expected that when stock acquired through a periodic stock investment plan is transferred to another account, the broker executing the transfer will provide information necessary in applying an allowable convention for determining which shares are sold. Accordingly, the transferor broker will be expected to state that shares transferred have a long-term holding period or, for shares that have a short-term holding period, the dates on which the shares were acquired.

A periodic stock investment plan is any stock purchase plan and any dividend reinvestment plan. A stock purchase plan is any arrangement under which identical stock is periodically purchased pursuant to a written plan. A dividend reinvestment plan is any arrangement under which dividends on stock are reinvested in stock identical to the stock with respect to which the dividends are paid. Stock is treated as acquired in connection with a dividend reinvestment plan if the stock is acquired pursuant to the plan or if the dividends paid on the stock are subject to the plan.

Exception for wash sales

Unless the Secretary provides otherwise, a customer's adjusted basis in a covered security generally is determined without taking into account the effect on basis of the wash sale rules of section 1091. If, however, the acquisition and sale transactions resulting in a wash sale under section 1091 occur in the same account and are in identical securities, adjusted basis is determined by taking into account the effect of the wash sale rules. Securities are identical for this purpose only if they have the same Committee on Uniform Security Identification Procedures number.

Special rules for short sales

The provision provides that in the case of a short sale, gross proceeds and basis reporting under section 6045 generally is required in the year in which the short sale is closed (rather than, as under the present law rule for gross proceeds reporting, the year in which the short sale is entered into).

Reporting requirements for options

The provision generally eliminates the present-law regulatory exception from section 6045(a) reporting for certain options. If a covered security is acquired or disposed of by reason of the exercise of an option that was granted or acquired in the same account as the covered security, the amount of the premium received or paid with respect to the acquisition of the option is treated as an adjustment to the gross proceeds from the subsequent sale of the covered security or as an adjustment to the customer's adjusted basis in that security. Gross proceeds and basis reporting also is required when there is a lapse of, or a closing transaction with respect to, an option on a specified security or an exercise of a cash-settled option. Reporting is required for the calendar year that includes the date of the lapse, closing transaction, or exercise. For example, if a taxpayer acquires for $5 a cash settlement stock option with a strike price of $100 and settles the option when the stock trades at $120, a broker through which the acquisition and cash settlement are executed is required to report gross proceeds of $20 from the cash settlement and a basis in the option of $5. For purposes of the reporting requirement for closing transactions, a closing transaction includes a mark-to-market under section 1256. It is intended that a specified security for purposes of the reporting rules described in this paragraph includes a stock index such as the S&P 500. The reporting rules related to options transactions apply only to options granted or acquired on or after January 1, 2013.

Treatment of S corporations

The provision provides that for purposes of section 6045, an S corporation (other than a financial institution) is treated in the same manner as a partnership. This rule applies to any sale of a covered security acquired by an S corporation (other than a financial institution) after December 31, 2011. When this rule takes effect, brokers generally will be required to report gross proceeds and basis information to customers that are S corporations.

Time for providing statements to customers

The provision changes to February 15 the present-law January 31 deadline for furnishing certain information statements to customers. The statements to which the new February 15 deadline applies are (1) statements showing gross proceeds (under section 6045(b)) or substitute payments (under section 6045(d)) and (2) statements with respect to reportable items (including, but not limited to, interest, dividends, and royalties) that are furnished with consolidated reporting statements (as defined in regulations). The term "consolidated reporting statement" is intended to refer to annual account information statements that brokerage firms customarily provide to their customers and that include tax-related information. It is intended that the February 15 deadline for consolidated reporting statements apply in the same manner to statements furnished for any account or accounts, taxable and retirement, held by a customer with a mutual fund or other broker.

Broker-to-broker and issuer reporting

Every broker (as defined in section 6045(c)(1)), and any other person specified in Treasury regulations, that transfers to a broker (as defined in section 6045(c)(1)) a security that is a covered security when held by that broker or other person must, under new section 6045A, furnish to the transferee broker a written statement that allows the transferee broker to satisfy the provision's basis and holding period reporting requirements. The Secretary may provide regulations that prescribe the content of this statement and the manner in which it must be furnished. It is contemplated that the Secretary will permit this broker-to-broker reporting requirement to be satisfied electronically rather than by paper. Unless the Secretary provides otherwise, the statement required by this rule must be furnished not later than 15 days after the date of the transfer of the covered security.

Present law penalties for failure to furnish correct payee statements apply to failures to furnish correct statements in connection with the transfer of covered securities.

New section 6045B requires, according to forms or regulations prescribed by the Secretary, any issuer of a specified security to file a return setting forth a description of any organizational action (such as a stock split or a merger or acquisition) that affects the basis of the specified security, the quantitative effect on the basis of that specified security, and any other information required by the Secretary. This return must be filed within 45 days after the date of the organizational action or, if earlier, by January 15 of the year following the calendar year during which the action occurred. Every person required to file this return for a specified security also must furnish, according to forms or regulations prescribed by the Secretary, to the nominee with respect to that security (or to a certificate holder if there is no nominee) a written statement showing the name, address, and phone number of the information contact of the person required to file the return, the information required to be included on the return with respect to the security, and any other information required by the Secretary. This statement must be furnished to the nominee or certificate holder on or before January 15 of the year following the calendar year in which the organizational action took place. No return or information statement is required to be provided under new section 6045B for any action with respect to a specified security if the action occurs before the applicable date (as defined previously) for that security.

The Secretary may waive the return filing and information statement requirements if the person to which the requirements apply makes publicly available, in the form and manner determined by the Secretary, the name, address, phone number, and email address of the information contact of that person, and the information about the organizational action and its effect on basis otherwise required to be included in the return.

The present-law penalties for failure to file correct information returns apply to failures to file correct returns in connection with organizational actions. Similarly, the present-law penalties for failure to furnish correct payee statements apply to a failure under new section 6045B to furnish correct statements to nominees or holders or to provide required publicly-available information in lieu of returns and written statements.

Effective Date

The provision generally takes effect on January 1, 2011. The change to February 15 of the present-law January 31 deadline for furnishing certain information statements to customers applies to statements required to be furnished after December 31, 2008.

[Law at ¶ 5345, ¶ 5435, ¶ 5440, ¶ 5445 and ¶ 5475. CCH Explanation at ¶ 725, ¶ 730, ¶ 735 and ¶ 740.]

[¶ 10,290] Act Sec. B404. One-year extension of additional 0.2 Percent FUTA surtax

Joint Committee on Taxation (J.C.T. REP. NO. JCX-75-08)

[Code Sec. 3301]

Present Law

The Federal Unemployment Tax Act ("FUTA") imposes a 6.2 percent gross tax rate on the first $7,000 paid annually by covered employers to each employee. Employers in States with programs approved by the Federal Government and with no delinquent Federal loans may credit 5.4 percentage points against the 6.2 percent tax rate, making the minimum, net Federal unemployment tax rate 0.8 percent. Since all States have approved programs, 0.8 percent is the Federal tax rate that generally applies. This Federal revenue finances administration of the unemployment system, half of the Federal-State extended benefits program, and a Federal account for State loans. The States use the revenue turned back to them by the 5.4 percent credit to finance their regular State programs and half of the Federal-State extended benefits program.

In 1976, Congress passed a temporary surtax of 0.2 percent of taxable wages to be added to the permanent FUTA tax rate. Thus, the current 0.8 percent FUTA tax rate has two components: a permanent tax rate of 0.6 percent, and a temporary surtax rate of 0.2 percent. The temporary surtax subsequently has been extended through 2008.

Explanation of Provision

The Act extends the temporary surtax rate (for one year) through December 31, 2009.

Effective Date

The provision is effective for wages paid after December 31, 2008.

[Law at ¶ 5405. CCH Explanation at ¶ 460.]

[¶10,300] Act Sec. B405. Oil spill liability trust fund tax

Joint Committee on Taxation (J.C.T. REP. No. JCX-75-08)

[Code Sec. 4611]

Present Law

The Oil Spill Liability Trust Fund financing rate ("oil spill tax") was reinstated effective April 1, 2006.[266] The oil spill tax rate is five cents per barrel and generally applies to crude oil received at a U.S. refinery and to petroleum products entered into the United States for consumption, use, or warehousing.[267]

The oil spill tax also applies to certain uses and the exportation of domestic crude oil.[268] If any domestic crude oil is used in or exported from the United States, and before such use or exportation no oil spill tax was imposed on such crude oil, then the oil spill tax is imposed on such crude oil. The tax does not apply to any use of crude oil for extracting oil or natural gas on the premises where such crude oil was produced.

For crude oil received at a refinery, the operator of the U.S. refinery is liable for the tax. For imported petroleum products, the person entering the product for consumption, use, or warehousing is liable for the tax. For certain uses and exports, the person using or exporting the crude oil is liable for the tax. No tax is imposed with respect to any petroleum product if the person who would be liable for such tax establishes that a prior oil spill tax has been imposed with respect to such product.

The imposition of the tax is dependent in part on the balance of the Oil Spill Liability Trust Fund. The oil spill tax does not apply during a calendar quarter if the Secretary estimates that, as of the close of the preceding calendar quarter, the unobligated balance of the Oil Spill Liability Trust Fund exceeds $2.7 billion. If the Secretary estimates that the unobligated balance in the Oil Spill Liability Trust Fund is less than $2 billion at close of any calendar quarter, the oil spill tax will apply on the date that is 30 days from the last day of that quarter. The tax does not apply to any periods after December 31, 2014.

Explanation of Provision

The provision extends the oil spill tax through December 31, 2017. The provision increases the tax rate from five cents to eight cents per barrel for the first quarter that is more than 60 days after the date of enactment through December 31, 2016, and then increases the rate to nine cents per barrel for calendar year 2017. The tax does not apply after December 31, 2017. The provision also repeals the requirement that the tax be suspended when the unobligated balance exceeds $2.7 billion.

Effective Date

The provision increasing the tax rate is effective beginning the first quarter that is more than 60 days after the date of enactment. The remaining provisions are effective on the date of enactment.

[Law at ¶ 5425. CCH Explanation at ¶ 855.]

[¶10,310] Act Secs. C101 and C102. Extend alternative minimum tax relief for individuals

Joint Committee on Taxation (JCT REPT. No. JCX-71-08)

[Code Secs. 26 and 55]

Present Law

Present law imposes an alternative minimum tax ("AMT") on individuals. The AMT is the amount by which the tentative minimum tax exceeds the regular income tax. An individual's tentative minimum tax is the sum of (1) 26 percent of so much of the taxable excess as does not exceed $175,000 ($87,500 in the case of a married individual filing a separate return) and (2) 28 percent of the remaining taxable excess. The taxable excess is so much of the alternative minimum taxable income ("AMTI") as exceeds the

---

[266] Sec. 4611(f).

[267] The term "crude oil" includes crude oil condensates and natural gasoline. The term "petroleum product" includes crude oil.

[268] The term "domestic crude oil" means any crude oil produced from a well located in the United States.

exemption amount. The maximum tax rates on net capital gain and dividends used in computing the regular tax are used in computing the tentative minimum tax. AMTI is the individual's taxable income adjusted to take account of specified preferences and adjustments.

The present exemption amount is: (1) $66,250 ($45,000 in taxable years beginning after 2007) in the case of married individuals filing a joint return and surviving spouses; (2) $44,350 ($33,750 in taxable years beginning after 2007) in the case of other unmarried individuals; (3) $33,125 ($22,500 in taxable years beginning after 2007) in the case of married individuals filing separate returns; and (4) $22,500 in the case of an estate or trust. The exemption amount is phased out by an amount equal to 25 percent of the amount by which the individual's AMTI exceeds (1) $150,000 in the case of married individuals filing a joint return and surviving spouses, (2) $112,500 in the case of other unmarried individuals, and (3) $75,000 in the case of married individuals filing separate returns or an estate or a trust. These amounts are not indexed for inflation.

Present law provides for certain nonrefundable personal tax credits (i.e., the dependent care credit, the credit for the elderly and disabled, the adoption credit, the child credit[2], the credit for interest on certain home mortgages, the HOPE Scholarship and Lifetime Learning credits, the credit for savers, the credit for certain nonbusiness energy property, the credit for residential energy efficient property, and the D.C. first-time homebuyer credit).

For taxable years beginning before 2008, the nonrefundable personal credits are allowed to the extent of the full amount of the individual's regular tax and alternative minimum tax.

For taxable years beginning after 2007, the nonrefundable personal credits (other than the adoption credit, child credit and saver's credit) are allowed only to the extent that the individual's regular income tax liability exceeds the individual's tentative minimum tax, determined without regard to the minimum tax foreign tax credit. The adoption credit, child credit, and saver's credit are allowed to the full extent of the individual's regular tax and alternative minimum tax.[3]

Explanation of Provision

The provision provides that the individual AMT exemption amount for taxable years beginning in 2008 is (1) $69,950, in the case of married individuals filing a joint return and surviving spouses; (2) $46,200 in the case of other unmarried individuals; and (3) $34,975 in the case of married individuals filing separate returns.

For taxable years beginning in 2008, the bill allows individuals to offset their entire regular tax liability and alternative minimum tax liability by the nonrefundable personal credits.

Effective Date

The provision is effective for taxable years beginning in 2008.

[Law at ¶5035 and ¶5170. CCH Explanation at ¶205 and ¶210.]

[¶10,320] Act Sec. C103. Increase in AMT refundable credit amount for individuals with long-term unused credits for prior year minimum tax liability, etc.

Joint Committee on Taxation (JCT Rept. No. JCX-71-08)

[Code Sec. 53]

Present Law

In general

Present law imposes an alternative minimum tax on an individual taxpayer to the extent the taxpayer's tentative minimum tax liability exceeds his or her regular income tax liability. An individual's tentative minimum tax is the sum of (1) 26 percent of so much of the taxable excess as does not exceed $175,000 ($87,500 in the case of a married individual filing a separate return) and (2) 28 percent of the remaining taxable excess. The taxable excess is the amount by which the alternative minimum taxable income exceeds an exemption amount.

An individual's AMTI is the taxpayer's taxable income increased by certain preference items and adjusted by determining the tax treatment of certain items in a manner that negates the defer-

---

[2] The child credit may be refundable in whole or in part to a taxpayer.

[3] The rule applicable to the adoption credit and child credit is subject to the EGTRRA sunset.

ral of income resulting from the regular tax treatment of those items.

The individual AMT attributable to deferral adjustments generates a minimum tax credit that is allowable to the extent the regular tax (reduced by other nonrefundable credits) exceeds the tentative minimum tax in a future taxable year. Unused minimum tax credits are carried forward indefinitely.

AMT treatment of incentive stock options

One of the adjustments in computing AMTI is the tax treatment of the exercise of an incentive stock option. An incentive stock option is an option granted by a corporation in connection with an individual's employment, so long as the option meets certain specified requirements.[4]

Under the regular tax, the exercise of an incentive stock option is tax-free if the stock is not disposed of within one year of exercise of the option or within two years of the grant of the option.[5] When the stock is sold, the individual's long-term capital gain or loss is determined using the amount paid for the stock as the cost basis. If the holding period requirements are not satisfied, the individual generally takes into account at the exercise of the option an amount of ordinary income equal to the excess of the fair market value of the stock on the date of exercise over the amount paid for the stock. The cost basis of the stock is increased by the amount taken into account.[6]

Under the individual alternative minimum tax, the exercise of an incentive stock option is treated as the exercise of an option other than an incentive stock option. Under this treatment, generally the individual takes into account as ordinary income for purposes of computing AMTI the excess of the fair market value of the stock at the date of exercise over the amount paid for the stock.[7] When the stock is later sold, for purposes of computing capital gain or loss for purposes of AMTI, the adjusted basis of the stock includes the amount taken into account as AMTI.

The adjustment relating to incentive stock options is a deferral adjustment and therefore generates an AMT credit in the year the stock is sold.[8]

Allowance of long-term unused credits

Under present law, an individual's minimum tax credit allowable for any taxable year beginning after December 31, 2006, and beginning before January 1, 2013, is not less than the "AMT refundable credit amount." The "AMT refundable credit amount" is the amount (not in excess of the long-term unused minimum tax credit) equal to the greatest of (1) $5,000, (2) 20 percent of the long-term unused minimum tax credit for the taxable year, or (3) the amount (if any) of the AMT refundable credit amount for the preceding taxable year before any reduction by reason of the reduction for adjusted gross income described below. The long-term unused minimum tax credit for any taxable year means the portion of the minimum tax credit attributable to the adjusted net minimum tax for taxable years before the 3rd taxable year immediately preceding the taxable year (assuming the credits are used on a first-in, first-out basis).

In the case of an individual whose adjusted gross income for a taxable year exceeds the threshold amount (within the meaning of section 151(d)(3)(C)), the AMT refundable credit amount is reduced by the applicable percentage (within the meaning of section 151(d)(3)(B)). The additional credit allowable by reason of this provision is refundable.

Explanation of Provision

The provision generally allows the long-term unused minimum tax credit to be claimed over a two-year period (rather than five years) and eliminates the AGI phase-out.

The provision provides that any underpayment of tax outstanding on the date of enactment which is attributable to the application of the minimum tax adjustment for incentive stock options (including any interest or penalty relating thereto) is abated. No tax which is abated is taken into account in determining the minimum tax credit.

---

[4] Sec. 422.

[5] Sec. 421.

[6] If the stock is sold at a loss before the required holding periods are met, the amount taken into account may not exceed the amount realized on the sale over the adjusted basis of the stock. If the stock is sold after the taxable year in which the option was exercised but before the required holding periods are met, the required inclusion is made in the year the stock is sold.

[7] If the stock is sold in the same taxable year the option is exercised, no adjustment in computing AMTI is required.

[8] If the stock is sold for less than the amount paid for the stock, the loss may not be allowed in full in computing AMTI by reason of the $3,000 limit on the deductibility of net capital losses. Thus, the excess of the regular tax over the tentative minimum tax may not reflect the full amount of the loss.

The provision provides that the AMT refundable credit amount and the AMT credit for each of the first two taxable years beginning after December 31, 2007, are increased by one-half of the amount of any interest and penalty paid before the date of enactment on account of the application of the minimum adjustment for incentive stock options.

Effective Date

The provision generally applies to taxable years beginning after December 31, 2007.

The provision relating to the abatement of tax, interest, and penalties takes effect on date of enactment.

[Law at ¶ 5140. CCH Explanation at ¶ 215.]

[¶ 10,330] Act Sec. C201. Deduction of state and local general sales taxes

Joint Committee on Taxation (J.C.T. Rep. No. JCX-75-08)

[Code Sec. 164]

Present Law

For purposes of determining regular tax liability, an itemized deduction is permitted for certain State and local taxes paid, including individual income taxes, real property taxes, and personal property taxes. The itemized deduction is not permitted for purposes of determining a taxpayer's alternative minimum taxable income. For taxable years beginning in 2004 and 2005, at the election of the taxpayer, an itemized deduction may be taken for State and local general sales taxes in lieu of the itemized deduction provided under present law for State and local income taxes. As is the case for State and local income taxes, the itemized deduction for State and local general sales taxes is not permitted for purposes of determining a taxpayer's alternative minimum taxable income. Taxpayers have two options with respect to the determination of the sales tax deduction amount. Taxpayers may deduct the total amount of general State and local sales taxes paid by accumulating receipts showing general sales taxes paid. Alternatively, taxpayers may use tables created by the Secretary of the Treasury that show the allowable deduction. The tables are based on average consumption by taxpayers on a State-by-State basis taking into account number of dependents, modified adjusted gross income and rates of State and local general sales taxation. Taxpayers who live in more than one jurisdiction during the tax year are required to pro-rate the table amounts based on the time they live in each jurisdiction. Taxpayers who use the tables created by the Secretary may, in addition to the table amounts, deduct eligible general sales taxes paid with respect to the purchase of motor vehicles, boats and other items specified by the Secretary. Sales taxes for items that may be added to the tables are not reflected in the tables themselves.

The term "general sales tax" means a tax imposed at one rate with respect to the sale at retail of a broad range of classes of items. However, in the case of items of food, clothing, medical supplies, and motor vehicles, the fact that the tax does not apply with respect to some or all of such items is not taken into account in determining whether the tax applies with respect to a broad range of classes of items, and the fact that the rate of tax applicable with respect to some or all of such items is lower than the general rate of tax is not taken into account in determining whether the tax is imposed at one rate. Except in the case of a lower rate of tax applicable with respect to food, clothing, medical supplies, or motor vehicles, no deduction is allowed for any general sales tax imposed with respect to an item at a rate other than the general rate of tax. However, in the case of motor vehicles, if the rate of tax exceeds the general rate, such excess shall be disregarded and the general rate is treated as the rate of tax.

A compensating use tax with respect to an item is treated as a general sales tax, provided such tax is complementary to a general sales tax and a deduction for sales taxes is allowable with respect to items sold at retail in the taxing jurisdiction that are similar to such item.

Explanation of Provision

The present-law provision allowing taxpayers to elect to deduct State and local sales taxes in lieu of State and local income taxes is extended for two years (through December 31, 2009).

Effective Date

The provision applies to taxable years beginning after December 31, 2007.

[Law at ¶ 5220. CCH Explanation at ¶ 240.]

[¶10,340] Act Sec. C202. Above-the-line deduction for higher education expenses

Joint Committee on Taxation (J.C.T. REP. NO. JCX-75-08)

[Code Sec. 222]

Present Law

An individual is allowed an above-the-line deduction for qualified tuition and related expenses for higher education paid by the individual during the taxable year.[53] Qualified tuition and related expenses are defined in the same manner as for the Hope and Lifetime Learning credits, and includes tuition and fees required for the enrollment or attendance of the taxpayer, the taxpayer's spouse, or any dependent of the taxpayer with respect to whom the taxpayer may claim a personal exemption, at an eligible institution of higher education for courses of instruction of such individual at such institution.[54] The expenses must be in connection with enrollment at an institution of higher education during the taxable year, or with an academic period beginning during the taxable year or during the first three months of the next taxable year. The deduction is not available for tuition and related expenses paid for elementary or secondary education.

The maximum deduction is $4,000 for an individual whose adjusted gross income for the taxable year does not exceed $65,000 ($130,000 in the case of a joint return), or $2,000 for other individuals whose adjusted gross income does not exceed $80,000 ($160,000 in the case of a joint return). No deduction is allowed for an individual whose adjusted gross income exceeds the relevant adjusted gross income limitations, for a married individual who does not file a joint return, or for an individual with respect to whom a personal exemption deduction may be claimed by another taxpayer for the taxable year. The deduction is not available for taxable years beginning after December 31, 2007.

The amount of qualified tuition and related expenses must be reduced by certain scholarships, educational assistance allowances, and other amounts paid for the benefit of such individual,[55] and by the amount of such expenses taken into account for purposes of determining any exclusion from gross income of: (1) income from certain U.S. savings bonds used to pay higher education tuition and fees; and (2) income from a Coverdell education savings account.[56] Additionally, such expenses must be reduced by the earnings portion (but not the return of principal) of distributions from a qualified tuition program if an exclusion under section 529 is claimed with respect to expenses eligible for the qualified tuition deduction. No deduction is allowed for any expense for which a deduction is otherwise allowed or with respect to an individual for whom a Hope or Lifetime Learning credit is elected for such taxable year.

Explanation of Provision

The provision extends the qualified tuition deduction for two years so that it is generally available for taxable years beginning before January 1, 2010. However, the provision also modifies the qualified tuition deduction so that it is unavailable to any taxpayer for any taxable year beginning in 2008 or 2009 if the taxpayer would, in the absence of the alternative minimum tax, have a lower tax liability for that year if he or she elected the Hope or Lifetime Learning credit with respect to an eligible individual instead of the qualified tuition deduction.

Effective Date

The provision is effective for taxable years beginning after December 31, 2007.

[Law at ¶5285. CCH Explanation at ¶245.]

---

[53] Sec. 222.

[54] The deduction generally is not available for expenses with respect to a course or education involving sports, games, or hobbies, and is not available for student activity fees, athletic fees, insurance expenses, or other expenses unrelated to an individual's academic course of instruction.

[55] Secs. 222(d)(1) and 25A(g)(2).

[56] Sec. 222(c). These reductions are the same as those that apply to the Hope and Lifetime Learning credits.

[¶10,350] Act Sec. C203. Educator expense deduction

Joint Committee on Taxation (J.C.T. REP. No. JCX-75-08)

[Code Sec. 62(a)(2)(D)]

Present Law

In general, ordinary and necessary business expenses are deductible. However, unreimbursed employee business expenses generally are deductible only as an itemized deduction and only to the extent that the individual's total miscellaneous deductions (including employee business expenses) exceed two percent of adjusted gross income. An individual's otherwise allowable itemized deductions may be further limited by the overall limitation on itemized deductions, which reduces itemized deductions for taxpayers with adjusted gross income in excess of $159,950 (for 2008).[69] In addition, miscellaneous itemized deductions are not allowable under the alternative minimum tax.

Eligible educators are allowed an above-the-line deduction for certain expenses.[70] Specifically, for taxable years beginning after December 31, 2001, and prior to January 1, 2008, an above-the-line deduction is allowed for up to $250 annually of expenses paid or incurred by an eligible educator for books, supplies (other than nonathletic supplies for courses of instruction in health or physical education), computer equipment (including related software and services) and other equipment, and supplementary materials used by the eligible educator in the classroom. To be eligible for this deduction, the expenses must be otherwise deductible under section 162 as a trade or business expense. A deduction is allowed only to the extent the amount of expenses exceeds the amount excludable from income under section 135 (relating to education savings bonds), 529(c)(1) (relating to qualified tuition programs), and section 530(d)(2) (relating to Coverdell education savings accounts).

An eligible educator is a kindergarten through grade 12 teacher, instructor, counselor, principal, or aide in a school for at least 900 hours during a school year. A school means any school that provides elementary education or secondary education, as determined under State law.

The above-the-line deduction for eligible educators is not allowed for taxable years beginning after December 31, 2007.

Explanation of Provision

The provision extends the deduction for eligible educator expenses for two years so that it is available for taxable years beginning before January 1, 2010.

Effective Date

The provision is effective for expenses paid or incurred in taxable years beginning after December 31, 2007.

[Law at ¶5180. CCH Explanation at ¶250.]

[¶10,360] Act Sec. C204. Extension of the additional standard deduction for State and local real property taxes

Joint Committee on Taxation (J.C.T. REP. No. JCX-75-08)

[Code Sec. 63]

Present Law

In general

An individual taxpayer's taxable income is computed by reducing adjusted gross income either by a standard deduction or, if the taxpayer elects, by the taxpayer's itemized deductions. The deduction for certain taxes, including income taxes, real property taxes, and personal property taxes, generally is an itemized deduction.[77]

Additional standard deduction for State and local property taxes

An individual taxpayer's standard deduction for a taxable year beginning in 2008 is increased by the lesser of (1) the amount

---

[69] The adjusted gross income threshold is $79,975 in the case of a married individual filing a separate return (for 2008).

[70] Sec. 62(a)(2)(D).

[77] If the deduction for State and local taxes is attributable to business or rental income, the deduction is allowed in computing adjusted gross income and therefore is not an itemized deduction.

allowable[78] to the taxpayer as a deduction for State and local taxes described in section 164(a)(1) (relating to real property taxes), or (2) $500 ($1,000 in the case of a married individual filing jointly). The increased standard deduction is determined by taking into account real estate taxes for which a deduction is allowable to the taxpayer under section 164 and, in the case of a tenant-stockholder in a cooperative housing corporation, real estate taxes for which a deduction is allowable to the taxpayer under section 216. No taxes deductible in computing adjusted gross income are taken into account in computing the increased standard deduction.

Explanation of Provision

The provision extends the additional standard deduction for State and local real property taxes for one year.

Effective Date

The provision applies to taxable years beginning in 2009.

[Law at ¶5185. CCH Explanation at ¶235.]

[¶10,370] Act Sec. C205. Tax-free distributions from individual retirement plans for charitable purposes

Joint Committee on Taxation (J.C.T. Rep. No. JCX-75-08)

[Code Sec. 408]

Present Law

In general

If an amount withdrawn from a traditional individual retirement arrangement ("IRA") or a Roth IRA is donated to a charitable organization, the rules relating to the tax treatment of withdrawals from IRAs apply to the amount withdrawn and the charitable contribution is subject to the normally applicable limitations on deductibility of such contributions. An exception applies in the case of a qualified charitable distribution.

Charitable contributions

In computing taxable income, an individual taxpayer who itemizes deductions generally is allowed to deduct the amount of cash and up to the fair market value of property contributed to a charity described in section 501(c)(3), to certain veterans' organizations, fraternal societies, and cemetery companies,[57] or to a Federal, State, or local governmental entity for exclusively public purposes.[58] The deduction also is allowed for purposes of calculating alternative minimum taxable income.

The amount of the deduction allowable for a taxable year with respect to a charitable contribution of property may be reduced depending on the type of property contributed, the type of

charitable organization to which the property is contributed, and the income of the taxpayer.[59]

A taxpayer who takes the standard deduction (i.e., who does not itemize deductions) may not take a separate deduction for charitable contributions.[60]

A payment to a charity (regardless of whether it is termed a "contribution") in exchange for which the donor receives an economic benefit is not deductible, except to the extent that the donor can demonstrate, among other things, that the payment exceeds the fair market value of the benefit received from the charity. To facilitate distinguishing charitable contributions from purchases of goods or services from charities, present law provides that no charitable contribution deduction is allowed for a separate contribution of $250 or more unless the donor obtains a contemporaneous written acknowledgement of the contribution from the charity indicating whether the charity provided any good or service (and an estimate of the value of any such good or service) to the taxpayer in consideration for the contribution.[61] In addition, present law requires that any charity that receives a contribution exceeding $75 made partly as a gift and partly as consideration for goods or services furnished by the charity (a "quid pro quo" contribution) is required to inform the contributor in writing of an estimate of the value of the goods or services furnished by the charity

---

[78] In the case of an individual taxpayer who does not elect to itemize deductions, although no itemized deductions are allowed to the taxpayer, itemized deductions are nevertheless treated as "allowable." See section 63(e).

[57] Secs. 170(c)(3)-(5).

[58] Sec. 170(c)(1).

[59] Secs. 170(b) and (e).

[60] Sec. 170(a).

[61] Sec. 170(f)(8).

and that only the portion exceeding the value of the goods or services may be deductible as a charitable contribution.[62]

Under present law, total deductible contributions of an individual taxpayer to public charities, private operating foundations, and certain types of private nonoperating foundations may not exceed 50 percent of the taxpayer's contribution base, which is the taxpayer's adjusted gross income for a taxable year (disregarding any net operating loss carryback). To the extent a taxpayer has not exceeded the 50-percent limitation, (1) contributions of capital gain property to public charities generally may be deducted up to 30 percent of the taxpayer's contribution base, (2) contributions of cash to private foundations and certain other charitable organizations generally may be deducted up to 30 percent of the taxpayer's contribution base, and (3) contributions of capital gain property to private foundations and certain other charitable organizations generally may be deducted up to 20 percent of the taxpayer's contribution base.

Contributions by individuals in excess of the 50-percent, 30-percent, and 20-percent limits may be carried over and deducted over the next five taxable years, subject to the relevant percentage limitations on the deduction in each of those years.

In addition to the percentage limitations imposed specifically on charitable contributions, present law imposes a reduction on most itemized deductions, including charitable contribution deductions, for taxpayers with adjusted gross income in excess of a threshold amount, which is indexed annually for inflation. The threshold amount for 2008 is $159,950 ($79,975 for married individuals filing separate returns). For those deductions that are subject to the limit, the total amount of itemized deductions is reduced by three percent of adjusted gross income over the threshold amount, but not by more than 80 percent of itemized deductions subject to the limit. Beginning in 2006, the overall limitation on itemized deductions phases-out for all taxpayers. The overall limitation on itemized deductions was reduced by one-third in taxable years beginning in 2006 and 2007, and is reduced by two-thirds in taxable years beginning in 2008 and 2009. The overall limitation on itemized deductions is eliminated for taxable years beginning after December 31, 2009; however, this elimina-

tion of the limitation sunsets on December 31, 2010.

In general, a charitable deduction is not allowed for income, estate, or gift tax purposes if the donor transfers an interest in property to a charity (e.g., a remainder) while also either retaining an interest in that property (e.g., an income interest) or transferring an interest in that property to a noncharity for less than full and adequate consideration.[63] Exceptions to this general rule are provided for, among other interests, remainder interests in charitable remainder annuity trusts, charitable remainder unitrusts, and pooled income funds, and present interests in the form of a guaranteed annuity or a fixed percentage of the annual value of the property.[64] For such interests, a charitable deduction is allowed to the extent of the present value of the interest designated for a charitable organization.

IRA rules

Within limits, individuals may make deductible and nondeductible contributions to a traditional IRA. Amounts in a traditional IRA are includible in income when withdrawn (except to the extent the withdrawal represents a return of nondeductible contributions). Individuals also may make nondeductible contributions to a Roth IRA. Qualified withdrawals from a Roth IRA are excludable from gross income. Withdrawals from a Roth IRA that are not qualified withdrawals are includible in gross income to the extent attributable to earnings. Includible amounts withdrawn from a traditional IRA or a Roth IRA before attainment of age 59-1/2 are subject to an additional 10-percent early withdrawal tax, unless an exception applies. Under present law, minimum distributions are required to be made from tax-favored retirement arrangements, including IRAs. Minimum required distributions from a traditional IRA must generally begin by the April 1 of the calendar year following the year in which the IRA owner attains age 70-1/2.[65]

If an individual has made nondeductible contributions to a traditional IRA, a portion of each distribution from an IRA is nontaxable until the total amount of nondeductible contributions has been received. In general, the amount of a distribution that is nontaxable is determined by multiplying the amount of the distribution by the ratio of the remaining nondeductible contri-

---

[62] Sec. 6115.

[63] Secs. 170(f), 2055(e)(2), and 2522(c)(2).

[64] Sec. 170(f)(2).

[65] Minimum distribution rules also apply in the case of distributions after the death of a traditional or Roth IRA owner.

butions to the account balance. In making the calculation, all traditional IRAs of an individual are treated as a single IRA, all distributions during any taxable year are treated as a single distribution, and the value of the contract, income on the contract, and investment in the contract are computed as of the close of the calendar year.

In the case of a distribution from a Roth IRA that is not a qualified distribution, in determining the portion of the distribution attributable to earnings, contributions and distributions are deemed to be distributed in the following order: (1) regular Roth IRA contributions; (2) taxable conversion contributions;[66] (3) nontaxable conversion contributions; and (4) earnings. In determining the amount of taxable distributions from a Roth IRA, all Roth IRA distributions in the same taxable year are treated as a single distribution, all regular Roth IRA contributions for a year are treated as a single contribution, and all conversion contributions during the year are treated as a single contribution.

Distributions from an IRA (other than a Roth IRA) are generally subject to withholding unless the individual elects not to have withholding apply.[67] Elections not to have withholding apply are to be made in the time and manner prescribed by the Secretary.

Qualified charitable distributions

Present law provides an exclusion from gross income for otherwise taxable IRA distributions from a traditional or a Roth IRA in the case of qualified charitable distributions.[68] The exclusion may not exceed $100,000 per taxpayer per taxable year. Special rules apply in determining the amount of an IRA distribution that is otherwise taxable. The otherwise applicable rules regarding taxation of IRA distributions and the deduction of charitable contributions continue to apply to distributions from an IRA that are not qualified charitable distributions. Qualified charitable distributions are taken into account for purposes of the minimum distribution rules applicable to traditional IRAs to the same extent the distribution would have been taken into account under such rules had the distribution not been directly distributed under the qualified charitable distribution provision. An IRA does not fail to qualify as an IRA merely because qualified charitable distributions have been made from the IRA.

A qualified charitable distribution is any distribution from an IRA directly by the IRA trustee to an organization described in section 170(b)(1)(A) (other than an organization described in section 509(a)(3) or a donor advised fund (as defined in section 4966(d)(2)). Distributions are eligible for the exclusion only if made on or after the date the IRA owner attains age 70-1/2.

The exclusion applies only if a charitable contribution deduction for the entire distribution otherwise would be allowable (under present law), determined without regard to the generally applicable percentage limitations. Thus, for example, if the deductible amount is reduced because of a benefit received in exchange, or if a deduction is not allowable because the donor did not obtain sufficient substantiation, the exclusion is not available with respect to any part of the IRA distribution.

If the IRA owner has any IRA that includes nondeductible contributions, a special rule applies in determining the portion of a distribution that is includible in gross income (but for the qualified charitable distribution provision) and thus is eligible for qualified charitable distribution treatment. Under the special rule, the distribution is treated as consisting of income first, up to the aggregate amount that would be includible in gross income (but for the qualified charitable distribution provision) if the aggregate balance of all IRAs having the same owner were distributed during the same year. In determining the amount of subsequent IRA distributions includible in income, proper adjustments are to be made to reflect the amount treated as a qualified charitable distribution under the special rule.

Distributions that are excluded from gross income by reason of the qualified charitable distribution provision are not taken into account in determining the deduction for charitable contributions under section 170.

The exclusion for qualified charitable distributions applies to distributions made in taxable years beginning after December 31, 2005. Under present law, the exclusion does not apply to distributions made in taxable years beginning after December 31, 2007.

---

[66] Conversion contributions refer to conversions of amounts in a traditional IRA to a Roth IRA.

[67] Sec. 3405.

[68] The exclusion does not apply to distributions from employer-sponsored retirements plans, including SIMPLE IRAs and simplified employee pensions ("SEPs").

Explanation of Provision

The provision would extend the exclusion for qualified charitable distributions to distributions made in taxable years beginning after December 31, 2007, and before January 1, 2010.

Effective Date

The provision is effective for distributions made in taxable years beginning after December 31, 2007.

[Law at ¶ 5295. CCH Explanation at ¶ 225.]

[¶ 10,380] Act Sec. C206. Extension of special withholding tax rule for interest-related dividends paid by regulated investment companies

Joint Committee on Taxation (J.C.T. REP. NO. JCX-75-08)

[Code Sec. 871(k)]

Present Law

In general

Under present law, a regulated investment company ("RIC") that earns certain interest income that would not be subject to U.S. tax if earned by a foreign person directly may, to the extent of such income, designate a dividend it pays as derived from such interest income. A foreign person who is a shareholder in the RIC generally would treat such a dividend as exempt from gross-basis U.S. tax, as if the foreign person had earned the interest directly.

Interest-related dividends

Under present law, a RIC may, under certain circumstances, designate all or a portion of a dividend as an "interest-related dividend," by written notice mailed to its shareholders not later than 60 days after the close of its taxable year. In addition, an interest-related dividend received by a foreign person generally is exempt from U.S. gross-basis tax under sections 871(a), 881, 1441 and 1442.

However, this exemption does not apply to a dividend on shares of RIC stock if the withholding agent does not receive a statement, similar to that required under the portfolio interest rules, that the beneficial owner of the shares is not a U.S. person. The exemption does not apply to a dividend paid to any person within a foreign country (or dividends addressed to, or for the account of, persons within such foreign country) with respect to which the Treasury Secretary has determined, under the portfolio interest rules, that exchange of information is inadequate to prevent evasion of U.S. income tax by U.S. persons.

In addition, the exemption generally does not apply to dividends paid to a controlled foreign corporation to the extent such dividends are attributable to income received by the RIC on a debt obligation of a person with respect to which the recipient of the dividend (i.e., the controlled foreign corporation) is a related person. Nor does the exemption generally apply to dividends to the extent such dividends are attributable to income (other than short-term original issue discount or bank deposit interest) received by the RIC on indebtedness issued by the RIC-dividend recipient or by any corporation or partnership with respect to which the recipient of the RIC dividend is a 10-percent shareholder. However, in these two circumstances the RIC remains exempt from its withholding obligation unless the RIC knows that the dividend recipient is such a controlled foreign corporation or 10-percent shareholder. To the extent that an interest-related dividend received by a controlled foreign corporation is attributable to interest income of a RIC that would be portfolio interest if received by a foreign corporation, the dividend is treated as portfolio interest for purposes of the de minimis rules, the high-tax exception, and the same country exceptions of subpart F (see sec. 881(c)(5)(A)).

The aggregate amount designated as interest-related dividends for the RIC's taxable year (including dividends so designated that are paid after the close of the taxable year but treated as paid during that year as described in section 855) generally is limited to the qualified net interest income of the RIC for the taxable year. The qualified net interest income of the RIC equals the excess of: (1) the amount of qualified interest income of the RIC; over (2) the amount of expenses of the RIC properly allocable to such interest income.

Qualified interest income of the RIC is equal to the sum of its U.S.-source income with respect to: (1) bank deposit interest; (2) short term original issue discount that is currently exempt from the gross-basis tax under section 871; (3) any interest (including amounts recognized as ordinary income in respect of original issue discount, market discount, or acquisition discount under the provisions of sections 1271-1288, and such other amounts as regulations may provide) on an obligation which is in registered form, unless it is earned on an obligation issued by a corporation or partnership in which the RIC is a 10-percent shareholder or is contingent interest not treated as portfolio interest under section 871(h)(4); and (4) any interest-related dividend from another RIC.

If the amount designated as an interest-related dividend is greater than the qualified net interest income described above, the portion of the distribution so designated which constitutes an interest-related dividend will be only that proportion of the amount so designated as the amount of the qualified net interest income bears to the amount so designated.

This withholding tax rule for interest-related dividends received from a RIC does not apply to any taxable year of a RIC beginning after December 31, 2007.

Explanation of Provision

The provision extends the exemption from withholding tax of interest-related dividends received from a RIC to taxable years of a RIC beginning before January 1, 2010.

Effective Date

The provision applies to dividends with respect to taxable years of a RIC beginning after December 31, 2007.

[Law at ¶ 5320. CCH Explanation at ¶ 470.]

[¶ 10,390] Act Sec. C207. Extension of special rule for regulated investment company stock held in the estate of a nonresident non-citizen

Joint Committee on Taxation (J.C.T. REP. NO. JCX-75-08)

[Code Sec. 2105]

Present Law

The gross estate of a decedent who was a U.S. citizen or resident generally includes all property - real, personal, tangible, and intangible - wherever situated.[71] The gross estate of a nonresident non-citizen decedent, by contrast, generally includes only property that at the time of the decedent's death is situated within the United States.[72] Property within the United States generally includes debt obligations of U.S. persons, including the Federal government and State and local governments, but does not include either bank deposits or portfolio obligations the interest on which would be exempt from U.S. income tax under section 871.[73] Stock owned and held by a nonresident non-citizen generally is treated as property within the United States if the stock was issued by a domestic corporation.[74]

Treaties may reduce U.S. taxation of transfers of the estates of nonresident non-citizens. Under recent treaties, for example, U.S. tax generally may be eliminated except insofar as the property transferred includes U.S. real property or business property of a U.S. permanent establishment.

Although stock issued by a domestic corporation generally is treated as property within the United States, stock of a regulated investment company ("RIC") that was owned by a nonresident non-citizen is not deemed property within the United States in the proportion that, at the end of the quarter of the RIC's taxable year immediately before a decedent's date of death, the assets held by the RIC are debt obligations, deposits, or other property that would be treated as situated outside the United States if held directly by the estate (the "estate tax look-through rule for RIC stock").[75] This estate tax look-through rule for RIC stock does not apply to estates of decedents dying after December 31, 2007.

Explanation of Provision

The provision permits the estate tax look-through rule for RIC stock to apply to estates of decedents dying before January 1, 2010.

---

[71] Sec. 2031. The Economic Growth and Tax Relief Reconciliation Act of 2001 ("EGTRRA") repealed the estate tax for estates of decedents dying after December 31, 2009. EGTRRA, however, included a termination provision under which EGTRRA's rules, including estate tax repeal, do not apply to estates of decedents dying after December 31, 2010.

[72] Sec. 2103.

[73] Secs. 2104(c), 2105(b).

[74] Sec. 2104(a); Treas. Reg. sec. 20.2104-1(a)(5)).

[75] Sec. 2105(d).

Effective Date

[Law at ¶5400. CCH Explanation at ¶475.]

The provision applies to estates of decedents dying after December 31, 2007.

[¶10,400] Act Sec. C208. Extend RIC "qualified investment entity" treatment under FIRPTA

Joint Committee on Taxation (J.C.T. REP. NO. JCX-75-08)

[Code Sec. 897]

Present law

Special U.S. tax rules apply to capital gains of foreign persons that are attributable to dispositions of interests in U.S. real property. In general, a foreign person (a foreign corporation or a nonresident alien individual) is not generally taxed on U.S. source capital gains unless certain personal presence or effectively connected business requirements are met. However, under the Foreign Investment in Real Property Tax Act ("FIRPTA") provisions codified in section 897 of the Code, a foreign person who sells a U.S. real property interest (USRPI) is treated as if the gain from such a sale is effectively connected with a U.S. business, and is subject to tax at the same rates as a U.S. person. Withholding tax is also imposed under section 1445.

A USPRI, the sale of which is subject to FIRPTA tax, includes stock or a beneficial interest in any U.S. real property holding corporation (as defined), unless the stock is regularly traded on an established securities market and the selling foreign corporation or nonresident alien individual held no more than 5 percent of that stock within the 5-year period ending on date of disposition (or, if shorter, during the period in which the entity was in existence). There is an exception, however, for stock of a domestically controlled "qualified investment entity." However, if stock of a domestically controlled qualified investment entity is disposed of within the 30 days preceding a dividend distribution in an "applicable wash sale transaction," in which an amount that would have been a taxable distribution (as described below) is instead treated as nontaxable sales proceeds, but substantially similar stock is reacquired (or an option to obtain it is acquired) within a 61 day period, then the amount that would have been a taxable distribution continues to be taxed.

A distribution from a "qualified investment entity" that is attributable to the sale of a USRPI is subject to tax under FIRPTA unless the distribution is with respect to an interest that is regularly traded on an established securities market located in the United Sates and the recipient foreign corporation or nonresident alien individual held no more than 5 percent of that class of stock or beneficial interest within the 1-year period ending on the date of distribution. Special rules apply to situations involving tiers of qualified investment entities.

The term "qualified investment entity" includes a regulated investment company ("RIC") that meets certain requirements, although the inclusion of a RIC in that definition is scheduled to have expired, for certain purposes, on December 31, 2007.[76] The definition does not expire for purposes of taxing distributions from the RIC that are attributable directly or indirectly to a distribution to the entity from a real estate investment trust, nor for purposes of the applicable wash sale rules.

Explanation of Provision

The provision extends the inclusion of a regulated investment company ("RIC") within the definition of a "qualified investment entity" under section 897 of the Code through December 31, 2009, for those situations in which that that inclusion would otherwise expire at the end of 2007. However, such extension does not apply to the application of withholding requirements with respect to any payment made on or before date of enactment.

Effective Date

The provision takes effect on January 1, 2008.

[Law at ¶5325. CCH Explanation at ¶870.]

---

[76] Sec. 897(h).

[¶10,410] Act Sec. C301. Extend the research and experimentation tax credit

Joint Committee on Taxation (J.C.T. Rep. No. JCX-75-08)

[Code Sec. 41]

Present Law

General rule

A taxpayer may claim a research credit equal to 20 percent of the amount by which the taxpayer's qualified research expenses for a taxable year exceed its base amount for that year.[79] Thus, the research credit is generally available with respect to incremental increases in qualified research.

A 20-percent research tax credit is also available with respect to the excess of (1) 100 percent of corporate cash expenses (including grants or contributions) paid for basic research conducted by universities (and certain nonprofit scientific research organizations) over (2) the sum of (a) the greater of two minimum basic research floors plus (b) an amount reflecting any decrease in nonresearch giving to universities by the corporation as compared to such giving during a fixed-base period, as adjusted for inflation. This separate credit computation is commonly referred to as the university basic research credit.[80]

Finally, a research credit is available for a taxpayer's expenditures on research undertaken by an energy research consortium. This separate credit computation is commonly referred to as the energy research credit. Unlike the other research credits, the energy research credit applies to all qualified expenditures, not just those in excess of a base amount.

The research credit, including the university basic research credit and the energy research credit, has expired and does not apply to amounts paid or incurred after December 31, 2007.[81]

Computation of allowable credit

Except for energy research payments and certain university basic research payments made by corporations, the research tax credit applies only to the extent that the taxpayer's qualified research expenses for the current taxable year exceed its base amount. The base amount for the current year generally is computed by multiplying the taxpayer's fixed-base percentage by the average amount of the taxpayer's gross receipts for the four preceding years. If a taxpayer both incurred qualified research expenses and had gross receipts during each of at has been subsequently extended and modified numerous times. Most recently, the Tax Relief and Health Care Act of 2006 extended the research credit through December 31, 2007, modified the alternative incremental research credit, and added an election to claim an alternative simplified credit. least three years from 1984 through 1988, then its fixed-base percentage is the ratio that its total qualified research expenses for the 1984-1988 period bears to its total gross receipts for that period (subject to a maximum fixed-base percentage of 16 percent). All other taxpayers (so-called start-up firms) are assigned a fixed-base percentage of three percent.[82]

In computing the credit, a taxpayer's base amount cannot be less than 50 percent of its current-year qualified research expenses.

To prevent artificial increases in research expenditures by shifting expenditures among commonly controlled or otherwise related entities, a special aggregation rule provides that all members of the same controlled group of corporations are treated as a single taxpayer.[83] Under regulations prescribed by the Secretary, special

---

[79] Sec. 41.

[80] Sec. 41(e).

[81] The research tax credit was initially enacted in the Economic Recovery Tax Act of 1981. It has been subsequently extended and modified numerous times. Most recently, the Tax Relief and Health Care Act of 2006 extended the research credit through December 31, 2007, modified the alternative incremental research credit, and added an election to claim an alternative simplified credit.

[82] The Small Business Job Protection Act of 1996 expanded the definition of start-up firms under section 41(c)(3)(B)(i) to include any firm if the first taxable year in which such firm had both gross receipts and qualified research expenses began after 1983. A special rule (enacted in

1993) is designed to gradually recompute a start-up firm's fixed-base percentage based on its actual research experience. Under this special rule, a start-up firm is assigned a fixed-base percentage of three percent for each of its first five taxable years after 1993 in which it incurs qualified research expenses. A start-up firm's fixed-base percentage for its sixth through tenth taxable years after 1993 in which it incurs qualified research expenses is a phased-in ratio based on the firm's actual research experience. For all subsequent taxable years, the taxpayer's fixed-base percentage is its actual ratio of qualified research expenses to gross receipts for any five years selected by the taxpayer from its fifth through tenth taxable years after 1993. Sec. 41(c)(3)(B).

[83] Sec. 41(f)(1).

rules apply for computing the credit when a major portion of a trade or business (or unit thereof) changes hands, under which qualified research expenses and gross receipts for periods prior to the change of ownership of a trade or business are treated as transferred with the trade or business that gave rise to those expenses and receipts for purposes of recomputing a taxpayer's fixed-base percentage.[84]

Alternative incremental research credit regime

Taxpayers are allowed to elect an alternative incremental research credit regime.[85] If a taxpayer elects to be subject to this alternative regime, the taxpayer is assigned a three-tiered fixed-base percentage (that is lower than the fixed-base percentage otherwise applicable under present law) and the credit rate likewise is reduced.

Generally, for amounts paid or incurred prior to 2007, under the alternative incremental credit regime, a credit rate of 2.65 percent applies to the extent that a taxpayer's current-year research expenses exceed a base amount computed by using a fixed-base percentage of one percent (i.e., the base amount equals one percent of the taxpayer's average gross receipts for the four preceding years) but do not exceed a base amount computed by using a fixed-base percentage of 1.5 percent. A credit rate of 3.2 percent applies to the extent that a taxpayer's current-year research expenses exceed a base amount computed by using a fixed-base percentage of 1.5 percent but do not exceed a base amount computed by using a fixed-base percentage of two percent. A credit rate of 3.75 percent applies to the extent that a taxpayer's current-year research expenses exceed a base amount computed by using a fixed-base percentage of two percent. Generally, for amounts paid or incurred after 2006, the credit rates listed above are increased to three percent, four percent, and five percent, respectively.[86]

An election to be subject to this alternative incremental credit regime can be made for any taxable year beginning after June 30, 1996, and such an election applies to that taxable year and all subsequent years unless revoked with the consent of the Secretary of the Treasury.

Alternative simplified credit

Generally, for amounts paid or incurred after 2006, taxpayers may elect to claim an alternative simplified credit for qualified research expenses.[87] The alternative simplified research credit is equal to 12 percent of qualified research expenses that exceed 50 percent of the average qualified research expenses for the three preceding taxable years. The rate is reduced to six percent if a taxpayer has no qualified research expenses in any one of the three preceding taxable years.

An election to use the alternative simplified credit applies to all succeeding taxable years unless revoked with the consent of the Secretary. An election to use the alternative simplified credit may not be made for any taxable year for which an election to use the alternative incremental credit is in effect. A transition rule applies which permits a taxpayer to elect to use the alternative simplified credit in lieu of the alternative incremental credit if such election is made during the taxable year which includes January 1, 2007. The transition rule applies only to the taxable year which includes that date.

Eligible expenses

Qualified research expenses eligible for the research tax credit consist of: (1) in-house expenses of the taxpayer for wages and supplies attributable to qualified research; (2) certain time-sharing costs for computer use in qualified research; and (3) 65 percent of amounts paid or incurred by the taxpayer to certain other persons for qualified research conducted on the taxpayer's behalf (so-called contract research expenses).[88] Notwithstanding the limitation for contract research expenses, qualified research expenses include 100 percent of amounts paid or incurred by the taxpayer to an eligible small business, university, or Federal laboratory for qualified energy research.

To be eligible for the credit, the research does not only have to satisfy the requirements of present-law section 174 (described below) but also must be undertaken for the purpose of discovering information that is technological in nature, the application of which is intended to be useful in the development of a new or improved

---

[84] Sec. 41(f)(3).

[85] Sec. 41(c)(4).

[86] A special transition rule applies for fiscal year 2006-2007 taxpayers.

[87] A special transition rule applies for fiscal year 2006-2007 taxpayers.

[88] Under a special rule, 75 percent of amounts paid to a research consortium for qualified research are treated as qualified research expenses eligible for the research credit

(rather than 65 percent under the general rule under section 41(b)(3) governing contract research expenses) if (1) such research consortium is a tax-exempt organization that is described in section 501(c)(3) (other than a private foundation) or section 501(c)(6) and is organized and operated primarily to conduct scientific research, and (2) such qualified research is conducted by the consortium on behalf of the taxpayer and one or more persons not related to the taxpayer. Sec. 41(b)(3)(C).

business component of the taxpayer, and substantially all of the activities of which constitute elements of a process of experimentation for functional aspects, performance, reliability, or quality of a business component. Research does not qualify for the credit if substantially all of the activities relate to style, taste, cosmetic, or seasonal design factors.[89] In addition, research does not qualify for the credit: (1) if conducted after the beginning of commercial production of the business component; (2) if related to the adaptation of an existing business component to a particular customer's requirements; (3) if related to the duplication of an existing business component from a physical examination of the component itself or certain other information; or (4) if related to certain efficiency surveys, management function or technique, market research, market testing, or market development, routine data collection or routine quality control.[90] Research does not qualify for the credit if it is conducted outside the United States, Puerto Rico, or any U.S. possession.

Relation to deduction

Under section 174, taxpayers may elect to deduct currently the amount of certain research or experimental expenditures paid or incurred in connection with a trade or business, notwithstanding the general rule that business expenses to develop or create an asset that has a useful life extending beyond the current year must be capitalized.[91] However, deductions allowed to a taxpayer under section 174 (or any other section) are reduced by an amount equal to 100 percent of the taxpayer's research tax credit determined for the taxable year.[92] Taxpayers may alternatively elect to claim a reduced research tax credit amount under section 41 in lieu of reducing deductions otherwise allowed.[93]

Explanation of Provision

The provision extends the research credit for two years, through December 31, 2009. The provision also clarifies the computation of the alternative incremental research credit and the alternative simplified credit for the taxable year in which the credit terminates.

Effective Date

The provision is effective for amounts paid or incurred after December 31, 2007.

[Law at ¶5070 and ¶5085. CCH Explanation at ¶405.]

[¶10,420] Act Sec. C302. Extend the new markets tax credit

Joint Committee on Taxation (J.C.T. REP. NO. JCX-75-08)

[Code Sec. 45D]

Present Law

Section 45D provides a new markets tax credit for qualified equity investments made to acquire stock in a corporation, or a capital interest in a partnership, that is a qualified community development entity ("CDE").[95] The amount of the credit allowable to the investor (either the original purchaser or a subsequent holder) is (1) a five-percent credit for the year in which the equity interest is purchased from the CDE and for each of the following two years, and (2) a six-percent credit for each of the following four years. The credit is determined by applying the applicable percentage (five or six percent) to the amount paid to the CDE for the investment at its original issue, and is available for a taxable year to the taxpayer who holds the qualified equity investment on the date of the initial investment or on the respective anniversary date that occurs during the taxable year. The credit is recaptured if at any time during the seven-year period that begins on the date of the original issue of the investment the entity ceases to be a qualified CDE, the proceeds of the investment cease to be used as required, or the equity investment is redeemed.

A qualified CDE is any domestic corporation or partnership: (1) whose primary mission is serving or providing investment capital for low-income communities or low-income persons; (2) that maintains accountability to residents of low-income communities by their representation on any governing board of or any advisory board to the CDE; and (3) that is certified by the Secretary as being a qualified CDE. A qualified equity investment means stock (other than nonqualified preferred stock) in a corporation or a capital interest in a partnership that is acquired directly from a CDE for cash, and includes an investment

---

[89] Sec. 41(d)(3).

[90] Sec. 41(d)(4).

[91] Taxpayers may elect 10-year amortization of certain research expenditures allowable as a deduction under section 174(a). Secs. 174(f)(2) and 59(e).

[92] Sec. 280C(c).

[93] Sec. 280C(c)(3).

[95] Section 45D was added by section 121(a) of the Community Renewal Tax Relief Act of 2000, Pub. L. No. 106-554 (December 21, 2000).

of a subsequent purchaser if such investment was a qualified equity investment in the hands of the prior holder. Substantially all of the investment proceeds must be used by the CDE to make qualified low-income community investments. For this purpose, qualified low-income community investments include: (1) capital or equity investments in, or loans to, qualified active low-income community businesses; (2) certain financial counseling and other services to businesses and residents in low-income communities; (3) the purchase from another CDE of any loan made by such entity that is a qualified low-income community investment; or (4) an equity investment in, or loan to, another CDE.

A "low-income community" is a population census tract with either (1) a poverty rate of at least 20 percent or (2) median family income which does not exceed 80 percent of the greater of metropolitan area median family income or statewide median family income (for a non-metropolitan census tract, does not exceed 80 percent of statewide median family income). In the case of a population census tract located within a high migration rural county, low-income is defined by reference to 85 percent (rather than 80 percent) of statewide median family income. For this purpose, a high migration rural county is any county that, during the 20-year period ending with the year in which the most recent census was conducted, has a net out-migration of inhabitants from the county of at least 10 percent of the population of the county at the beginning of such period.

The Secretary has the authority to designate "targeted populations" as low-income communities for purposes of the new markets tax credit. For this purpose, a "targeted population" is defined by reference to section 103(20) of the Riegle Community Development and Regulatory Improvement Act of 1994 (12 U.S.C. 4702(20)) to mean individuals, or an identifiable group of individuals, including an Indian tribe, who (A) are low-income persons; or (B) otherwise lack adequate access to loans or equity investments. Under such Act, "low-income" means (1) for a targeted population within a metropolitan area, less than 80 percent of the area median family income; and (2) for a targeted population within a non-metropolitan area, less than the greater of 80 percent of the area median family income or 80 percent of the statewide non-metropolitan area median family income.[96] Under such Act, a targeted population is not required to be within any census tract. In addition, a population census tract with a population of less than 2,000 is treated as a low-income community for purposes of the credit if such tract is within an empowerment zone, the designation of which is in effect under section 1391, and is contiguous to one or more low-income communities.

A qualified active low-income community business is defined as a business that satisfies, with respect to a taxable year, the following requirements: (1) at least 50 percent of the total gross income of the business is derived from the active conduct of trade or business activities in any low-income community; (2) a substantial portion of the tangible property of such business is used in a low-income community; (3) a substantial portion of the services performed for such business by its employees is performed in a low-income community; and (4) less than five percent of the average of the aggregate unadjusted bases of the property of such business is attributable to certain financial property or to certain collectibles.

The maximum annual amount of qualified equity investments is capped at $2.0 billion per year for calendar years 2004 and 2005, and at $3.5 billion per year for calendar years 2006, 2007, and 2008.

Explanation of Provision

The provision extends the new markets tax credit for one year, through 2009, permitting up to $3.5 billion in qualified equity investments for that calendar year.

Effective Date

The provision is effective on the date of enactment.

[Law at ¶5090. CCH Explanation at ¶410.]

---

[96] 12 U.S.C. 4702(17) (defines "low-income" for purposes of 12 U.S.C. 4702(20)).

[¶10,430] Act Sec. C303. Subpart F exception for active financing income

Joint Committee on Taxation (J.C.T. REP. NO. JCX-75-08)

[Code Secs. 953 and 954]

Present Law

Under the subpart F rules,[163] 10-percent-or-greater U.S. shareholders of a controlled foreign corporation ("CFC") are subject to U.S. tax currently on certain income earned by the CFC, whether or not such income is distributed to the shareholders. The income subject to current inclusion under the subpart F rules includes, among other things, insurance income and foreign base company income. Foreign base company income includes, among other things, foreign personal holding company income and foreign base company services income (i.e., income derived from services performed for or on behalf of a related person outside the country in which the CFC is organized).

Foreign personal holding company income generally consists of the following: (1) dividends, interest, royalties, rents, and annuities; (2) net gains from the sale or exchange of (a) property that gives rise to the preceding types of income, (b) property that does not give rise to income, and (c) interests in trusts, partnerships, and REMICs; (3) net gains from commodities transactions; (4) net gains from certain foreign currency transactions; (5) income that is equivalent to interest; (6) income from notional principal contracts; (7) payments in lieu of dividends; and (8) amounts received under personal service contracts.

Insurance income subject to current inclusion under the subpart F rules includes any income of a CFC attributable to the issuing or reinsuring of any insurance or annuity contract in connection with risks located in a country other than the CFC's country of organization. Subpart F insurance income also includes income attributable to an insurance contract in connection with risks located within the CFC's country of organization, as the result of an arrangement under which another corporation receives a substantially equal amount of consideration for insurance of other country risks. Investment income of a CFC that is allocable to any insurance or annuity contract related to risks located outside the CFC's country of organization is taxable as subpart F insurance income.[164]

Temporary exceptions from foreign personal holding company income, foreign base company services income, and insurance income apply for subpart F purposes for certain income that is derived in the active conduct of a banking, financing, or similar business, as a securities dealer, or in the conduct of an insurance business (so-called "active financing income").[165]

With respect to income derived in the active conduct of a banking, financing, or similar business, a CFC is required to be predominantly engaged in such business and to conduct substantial activity with respect to such business in order to qualify for the active financing exceptions. In addition, certain nexus requirements apply, which provide that income derived by a CFC or a qualified business unit ("QBU") of a CFC from transactions with customers is eligible for the exceptions if, among other things, substantially all of the activities in connection with such transactions are conducted directly by the CFC or QBU in its home country, and such income is treated as earned by the CFC or QBU in its home country for purposes of such country's tax laws. Moreover, the exceptions apply to income derived from certain cross border transactions, provided that certain requirements are met. Additional exceptions from foreign personal holding company income apply for certain income derived by a securities dealer within the meaning of section 475 and for gain from the sale of active financing assets.

---

[163] Secs. 951-964.

[164] Prop. Treas. Reg. sec. 1.953-1(a).

[165] Temporary exceptions from the subpart F provisions for certain active financing income applied only for taxable years beginning in 1998 (Taxpayer Relief Act of 1997, Pub. L. No. 105-34). Those exceptions were modified and extended for one year, applicable only for taxable years beginning in 1999 (the Tax and Trade Relief Extension Act of 1998, Pub. L. No. 105-277). The Tax Relief Extension Act of 1999 (Pub. L. No. 106-170) clarified and extended the temporary exceptions for two years, applicable only for taxable years beginning after 1999 and before 2002. The Job Creation and Worker Assistance Act of 2002 (Pub. L. No. 107-147) modified and extended the temporary exceptions for five years, for taxable years beginning after 2001 and before 2007. The Tax Increase Prevention and Reconciliation Act of 2005 (Pub. L. No. 109-222) extended the temporary provisions for two years, for taxable years beginning after 2006 and before 2009.

In the case of a securities dealer, the temporary exception from foreign personal holding company income applies to certain income. The income covered by the exception is any interest or dividend (or certain equivalent amounts) from any transaction, including a hedging transaction or a transaction consisting of a deposit of collateral or margin, entered into in the ordinary course of the dealer's trade or business as a dealer in securities within the meaning of section 475. In the case of a QBU of the dealer, the income is required to be attributable to activities of the QBU in the country of incorporation, or to a QBU in the country in which the QBU both maintains its principal office and conducts substantial business activity. A coordination rule provides that this exception generally takes precedence over the exception for income of a banking, financing or similar business, in the case of a securities dealer.

In the case of insurance, a temporary exception from foreign personal holding company income applies for certain income of a qualifying insurance company with respect to risks located within the CFC's country of creation or organization. In the case of insurance, temporary exceptions from insurance income and from foreign personal holding company income also apply for certain income of a qualifying branch of a qualifying insurance company with respect to risks located within the home country of the branch, provided certain requirements are met under each of the exceptions. Further, additional temporary exceptions from insurance income and from foreign personal holding company income apply for certain income of certain CFCs or branches with respect to risks located in a country other than the United States, provided that the requirements for these exceptions are met. In

the case of a life insurance or annuity contract, reserves for such contracts are determined under rules specific to the temporary exceptions. Present law also permits a taxpayer in certain circumstances, subject to approval by the IRS through the ruling process or in published guidance, to establish that the reserve of a life insurance company for life insurance and annuity contracts is the amount taken into account in determining the foreign statement reserve for the contract (reduced by catastrophe, equalization, or deficiency reserve or any similar reserve). IRS approval is to be based on whether the method, the interest rate, the mortality and morbidity assumptions, and any other factors taken into account in determining foreign statement reserves (taken together or separately) provide an appropriate means of measuring income for Federal income tax purposes.

Explanation of Provision

The provision extends for one year (for taxable years beginning before 2010) the present-law temporary exceptions from subpart F foreign personal holding company income, foreign base company services income, and insurance income for certain income that is derived in the active conduct of a banking, financing, or similar business, or in the conduct of an insurance business.

Effective Date

The provision is effective for taxable years of foreign corporations beginning after December 31, 2008, and for taxable years of U.S. shareholders with or within which such taxable years of such foreign corporations end.

[Law at ¶5335 and ¶5340. CCH Explanation at ¶860 and ¶863.]

[¶10,440] Act Sec. C304. Look-through treatment of payments between related controlled foreign corporations under foreign personal holding company income rules

Joint Committee on Taxation (J.C.T. Rep. No. JCX-75-08)

[Code Sec. 954(c)(6)]

Present Law

In general

In general, the rules of subpart F (secs. 951-964) require U.S. shareholders with a 10-percent or greater interest in a controlled foreign corporation ("CFC") to include certain income of the CFC (referred to as "subpart F income") on a current basis for U.S. tax purposes, regardless of

whether the income is distributed to the shareholders.

Subpart F income includes foreign base company income. One category of foreign base company income is foreign personal holding company income. For subpart F purposes, foreign personal holding company income generally includes dividends, interest, rents, and royalties, among other types of income. There are several exceptions to these rules. For example, foreign personal holding company income does not include dividends and interest received by a CFC from a related corporation organized and operating in the same foreign country in which the CFC is organized, or rents and royalties received by a CFC from a related corporation for the use of property within the country in which the CFC is organized. Interest, rent, and royalty payments do not qualify for this exclusion to the extent that such payments reduce the subpart F income of the payor. In addition, subpart F income of a CFC does not include any item of income from sources within the United States which is effectively connected with the conduct by such CFC of a trade or business within the United States ("ECI") unless such item is exempt from taxation (or is subject to a reduced rate of tax) pursuant to a tax treaty.

The "look-through rule"[166]

Under the "look-through rule" (sec. 954(c)(6)), dividends, interest (including factoring income which is treated as equivalent to interest under section 954(c)(1)(E)), rents, and royalties received by one CFC from a related CFC are not treated as foreign personal holding company income to the extent attributable or properly allocable to income of the payor that is neither subpart F nor treated as ECI. For this purpose, a related CFC is a CFC that controls or is controlled by the other CFC, or a CFC that is controlled by the same person or persons that control the other CFC. Ownership of more than 50 percent of the CFC's stock (by vote or value) constitutes control for these purposes.

The Secretary is authorized to prescribe regulations that are necessary or appropriate to carry out the look-through rule, including such regulations as are appropriate to prevent the abuse of the purposes of such rule.

The look-through rule is effective for taxable years of foreign corporations beginning after December 31, 2005, but before January 1, 2009, and for taxable years of U.S. shareholders with or within which such taxable years of such foreign corporations end.

Explanation of Provision

The provision extends for one year the application of the look-through rule, to taxable years of foreign corporations beginning before January 1, 2010, and for taxable years of U.S. shareholders with or within which such taxable years of such foreign corporations end.

Effective Date

The provision is effective for taxable years of foreign corporations beginning after December 31, 2008 (but before January 1, 2010), and for taxable years of U.S. shareholders with or within which such taxable years of such foreign corporations end.

[Law at ¶5340. CCH Explanation at ¶865.]

[¶10,450] Act Sec. C305. Fifteen-year straight-line cost recovery for qualified leasehold improvements and qualified restaurant property

Joint Committee on Taxation (J.C.T. Rep. No. JCX-75-08)

[Code Sec. 168]

Present Law

In general

A taxpayer generally must capitalize the cost of property used in a trade or business and recover such cost over time through annual deductions for depreciation or amortization. Tangible property generally is depreciated under the modified accelerated cost recovery system ("MACRS"), which determines depreciation by applying specific recovery periods, placed-in-

service conventions, and depreciation methods to the cost of various types of depreciable property.[102] The cost of nonresidential real property is recovered using the straight-line method of depreciation and a recovery period of 39 years. Nonresidential real property is subject to the mid-month placed-in-service convention. Under the mid-month convention, the depreciation allowance for the first year property is placed in service is based on the number of months the property was in service, and property placed in service at any time during a month is treated as

---

[166] The look-through rule was enacted by the Tax Increase Prevention and Reconciliation Act of 2005, Pub. L. No. 109-222, sec. 103(b)(1) (2006).

[102] Sec. 168.

having been placed in service in the middle of the month.

Depreciation of leasehold improvements

Generally, depreciation allowances for improvements made on leased property are determined under MACRS, even if the MACRS recovery period assigned to the property is longer than the term of the lease. This rule applies regardless of whether the lessor or the lessee places the leasehold improvements in service. If a leasehold improvement constitutes an addition or improvement to nonresidential real property already placed in service, the improvement generally is depreciated using the straight-line method over a 39-year recovery period, beginning in the month the addition or improvement was placed in service. However, exceptions exist for certain qualified leasehold improvements and qualified restaurant property.

Qualified leasehold improvement property

Section 168(e)(3)(E)(iv) provides a statutory 15-year recovery period for qualified leasehold improvement property placed in service before January 1, 2008. Qualified leasehold improvement property is recovered using the straight-line method and a half-year convention. Leasehold improvements placed in service in 2008 and later will be subject to the general rules described above.

Qualified leasehold improvement property is any improvement to an interior portion of a building that is nonresidential real property, provided certain requirements are met. The improvement must be made under or pursuant to a lease either by the lessee (or sublessee), or by the lessor, of that portion of the building to be occupied exclusively by the lessee (or sublessee). The improvement must be placed in service more than three years after the date the building was first placed in service. Qualified leasehold improvement property does not include any improvement for which the expenditure is attributable to the enlargement of the building, any elevator or escalator, any structural component benefiting a common area, or the internal structural framework of the building.

If a lessor makes an improvement that qualifies as qualified leasehold improvement property, such improvement does not qualify as qualified leasehold improvement property to any subsequent owner of such improvement. An exception to the rule applies in the case of death and certain transfers of property that qualify for non-recognition treatment.

Qualified restaurant property

Section 168(e)(3)(E)(v) provides a statutory 15-year recovery period for qualified restaurant property placed in service before January 1, 2008. For purposes of the provision, qualified restaurant property means any improvement to a building if such improvement is placed in service more than three years after the date such building was first placed in service and more than 50 percent of the building's square footage is devoted to the preparation of, and seating for on-premises consumption of, prepared meals. Qualified restaurant property is recovered using the straight-line method and a half-year convention. Restaurant property placed in service in 2008 and later will be subject to the general rules described above.

Explanation of Provision

The present-law provisions for qualified leasehold improvement property and qualified restaurant property are extended for two years through December 31, 2009.

Effective Date

The provision applies to property placed in service after December 31, 2007.

[**Law at ¶5230. CCH Explanation at ¶305 and ¶310.**]

[¶10,460] Act Sec. C306. Modification of tax treatment of certain payments to controlling exempt organizations

Joint Committee on Taxation (J.C.T. REP. No. JCX-75-08)

[Code Sec. 512]

Present Law

In general, organizations exempt from Federal income tax are subject to the unrelated business income tax on income derived from a trade or business regularly carried on by the organization that is not substantially related to the performance of the organization's tax-exempt functions.[120] In general, interest, rents, royalties,

---

[120] Sec. 511.

and annuities are excluded from the unrelated business income of tax-exempt organizations.[121]

Section 512(b)(13) provides special rules regarding income derived by an exempt organization from a controlled subsidiary. In general, section 512(b)(13) treats otherwise excluded rent, royalty, annuity, and interest income as unrelated business income if such income is received from a taxable or tax-exempt subsidiary that is 50-percent controlled by the parent tax-exempt organization to the extent the payment reduces the net unrelated income (or increases any net unrelated loss) of the controlled entity (determined as if the entity were tax exempt). However, a special rule enacted as part of the Pension Protection Act of 2006 provides that, for payments made pursuant to a binding written contract in effect on August 17, 2006 (or renewal of such a contract on substantially similar terms), the general rule of section 512(b)(13) applies only to the portion of payments received or accrued (before January 1, 2008) in a taxable year that exceeds the amount of the payment that would have been paid or accrued if the amount of such payment had been determined under the principles of section 482 (i.e., at arm's length).[122] In addition, the special rule imposes a 20-percent penalty on the larger of such excess determined without regard to any amendment or supplement to a return of tax, or such excess determined with regard to all such amendments and supplements.

In the case of a stock subsidiary, "control" means ownership by vote or value of more than 50 percent of the stock. In the case of a partnership or other entity, "control" means ownership of more than 50 percent of the profits, capital, or beneficial interests. In addition, present law applies the constructive ownership rules of section 318 for purposes of section 512(b)(13). Thus, a parent exempt organization is deemed to control any subsidiary in which it holds more than 50 percent of the voting power or value, directly (as in the case of a first-tier subsidiary) or indirectly (as in the case of a second-tier subsidiary).

Explanation of Provision

The provision extends the special rule of the Pension Protection Act to payments received or accrued before January 1, 2010. Accordingly, under the provision, payments of rent, royalties, annuities, or interest income by a controlled organization to a controlling organization pursuant to a binding written contract in effect on August 17, 2006 (or renewal of such a contract on substantially similar terms), may be includible in the unrelated business taxable income of the controlling organization only to the extent the payment exceeds the amount of the payment determined under the principles of section 482 (i.e., at arm's length). Any such excess is subject to a 20-percent penalty on the larger of such excess determined without regard to any amendment or supplement to a return of tax, or such excess determined with regard to all such amendments and supplements.

Effective Date

The provision is effective for payments received or accrued after December 31, 2007.

[Law at ¶5310. CCH Explanation at ¶480.]

[¶10,470] Act Sec. C307. Basis adjustment to stock of S corporations making charitable contributions of property

Joint Committee on Taxation (J.C.T. Rep. No. JCX-75-08)

[Code Sec. 1367]

Present Law

Under present law, if an S corporation contributes money or other property to a charity, each shareholder takes into account the shareholder's pro rata share of the contribution in determining its own income tax liability.[159] A shareholder of an S corporation reduces the basis in the stock of the S corporation by the amount of the charitable contribution that flows through to the shareholder.[160]

In the case of contributions made in taxable years beginning after December 31, 2005, and before January 1, 2008, the amount of a shareholder's basis reduction in the stock of an S corporation by reason of a charitable contribution made by the corporation is equal to the shareholder's pro rata share of the adjusted basis

---

[121] Sec. 512(b).
[122] Sec. 512(b)(13)(E).

[159] Sec. 1366(a)(1)(A).
[160] Sec. 1367(a)(2)(B).

of the contributed property. For contributions made in taxable years beginning after December 31, 2007, the amount of the reduction is the shareholder's pro rata share of the fair market value of the contributed property.

Explanation of Provision

The bill extends the rule relating to the basis reduction on account of charitable contributions of property for two years to contributions made in taxable years beginning before January 1, 2010.

Effective Date

The provision applies to contributions made in taxable years beginning after December 31, 2007.

[Law at ¶ 5360. CCH Explanation at ¶ 435.]

[¶ 10,480] Act Sec. C308. Suspend limitation on rate of rum excise tax cover over to Puerto Rico and Virgin Islands

Joint Committee on Taxation (J.C.T. REP. No. JCX-75-08)

[Code Sec. 7652(f)]

Present Law

A $13.50 per proof gallon[180] excise tax is imposed on distilled spirits produced in or imported (or brought) into the United States.[181] The excise tax does not apply to distilled spirits that are exported from the United States, including exports to U.S. possessions (e.g., Puerto Rico and the Virgin Islands).[182]

The Code provides for cover over (payment) to Puerto Rico and the Virgin Islands of the excise tax imposed on rum imported (or brought) into the United States, without regard to the country of origin.[183] The amount of the cover over is limited under Code section 7652(f) to $10.50 per proof gallon ($13.25 per proof gallon during the period July 1, 1999 through December 31, 2007).

Tax amounts attributable to shipments to the United States of rum produced in Puerto Rico are covered over to Puerto Rico. Tax amounts attributable to shipments to the United States of rum produced in the Virgin Islands are covered over to the Virgin Islands. Tax amounts attributable to shipments to the United States of rum produced in neither Puerto Rico nor the Virgin Islands are divided and covered over to the two possessions under a formula.[184] Amounts covered over to Puerto Rico and the Virgin Islands are deposited into the treasuries of the two possessions for use as those possessions determine.[185] All of the amounts covered over are subject to the limitation.

Explanation of Provision

The provision suspends for two years the $10.50 per proof gallon limitation on the amount of excise taxes on rum covered over to Puerto Rico and the Virgin Islands. Under the provision, the cover over amount of $13.25 per proof gallon is extended for rum brought into the United States after December 31, 2007 and before January 1, 2010. After December 31, 2009, the cover over amount reverts to $10.50 per proof gallon.

Effective Date

The change in the cover over rate is effective for articles brought into the United States after December 31, 2007.

[Law at ¶ 5490. CCH Explanation at ¶ 830.]

---

[180] A proof gallon is a liquid gallon consisting of 50 percent alcohol. *See* sec. 5002(a)(10) and (11).

[181] Sec. 5001(a)(1).

[182] Secs. 5062(b), 7653(b) and (c).

[183] Secs. 7652(a)(3), (b)(3), and (e)(1). One percent of the amount of excise tax collected from imports into the United States of articles produced in the Virgin Islands is retained by the United States under section 7652(b)(3).

[184] Sec. 7652(e)(2).

[185] Secs. 7652(a)(3), (b)(3), and (e)(1).

[¶10,490] Act Sec. C309. Extension of economic development credit for American Samoa

Joint Committee on Taxation (J.C.T. REP. NO. JCX-75-08)

[Act Sec. C309]

Present and Prior Law

In general

For taxable years beginning before January 1, 2006, certain domestic corporations with business operations in the U.S. possessions were eligible for the possession tax credit.[140] This credit offset the U.S. tax imposed on certain income related to operations in the U.S. possessions.[141] For purposes of the credit, possessions included, among other places, American Samoa. Subject to certain limitations described below, the amount of the possession tax credit allowed to any domestic corporation equaled the portion of that corporation's U.S. tax that was attributable to the corporation's non-U.S. source taxable income from (1) the active conduct of a trade or business within a U.S. possession, (2) the sale or exchange of substantially all of the assets that were used in such a trade or business, or (3) certain possessions investment.[142] No deduction or foreign tax credit was allowed for any possessions or foreign tax paid or accrued with respect to taxable income that was taken into account in computing the credit under section 936.[143] The section 936 credit generally expired for taxable years beginning after December 31, 2005, but a special credit, described below, was allowed with respect to American Samoa.

To qualify for the possession tax credit for a taxable year, a domestic corporation was required to satisfy two conditions. First, the corporation was required to derive at least 80 percent of its gross income for the three-year period immediately preceding the close of the taxable year from sources within a possession. Second, the corporation was required to derive at least 75 percent of its gross income for that same period from the active conduct of a possession business.

The possession tax credit was available only to a corporation that qualified as an existing credit claimant. The determination of whether a corporation was an existing credit claimant was made separately for each possession. The possession tax credit was computed separately for each possession with respect to which the corporation was an existing credit claimant, and the credit was subject to either an economic activity-based limitation or an income-based limitation.

Qualification as existing credit claimant

A corporation was an existing credit claimant with respect to a possession if (1) the corporation was engaged in the active conduct of a trade or business within the possession on October 13, 1995, and (2) the corporation elected the benefits of the possession tax credit in an election in effect for its taxable year that included October 13, 1995.[144] A corporation that added a substantial new line of business (other than in a qualifying acquisition of all the assets of a trade or business of an existing credit claimant) ceased to be an existing credit claimant as of the close of the taxable year ending before the date on which that new line of business was added.

Economic activity-based limit

Under the economic activity-based limit, the amount of the credit determined under the rules described above was not permitted to exceed an amount equal to the sum of (1) 60 percent of the taxpayer's qualified possession wages and allocable employee fringe benefit expenses, (2) 15 percent of depreciation allowances with respect to short-life qualified tangible property, plus 40 percent of depreciation allowances with respect to medium-life qualified tangible property, plus 65 percent of depreciation allowances with respect to long-life qualified tangible property, and (3) in certain cases, a portion of the taxpayer's possession income taxes.

---

[140] Secs. 27(b), 936.

[141] Domestic corporations with activities in Puerto Rico are eligible for the section 30A economic activity credit. That credit is calculated under the rules set forth in section 936.

[142] Under phase-out rules described below, investment only in Guam, American Samoa, and the Northern Mariana Islands (and not in other possessions) now may give rise to income eligible for the section 936 credit.

[143] Sec. 936(c).

[144] A corporation will qualify as an existing credit claimant if it acquired all the assets of a trade or business of a corporation that (1) actively conducted that trade or business in a possession on October 13, 1995, and (2) had elected the benefits of the possession tax credit in an election in effect for the taxable year that included October 13, 1995.

Income-based limit

As an alternative to the economic activity-based limit, a taxpayer was permitted elect to apply a limit equal to the applicable percentage of the credit that otherwise would have been allowable with respect to possession business income; in taxable years beginning in 1998 and subsequent years, the applicable percentage was 40 percent.

Repeal and phase out

In 1996, the section 936 credit was repealed for new claimants for taxable years beginning after 1995 and was phased out for existing credit claimants over a period including taxable years beginning before 2006. The amount of the available credit during the phase-out period generally was reduced by special limitation rules. These phase-out period limitation rules did not apply to the credit available to existing credit claimants for income from activities in Guam, American Samoa, and the Northern Mariana Islands. As described previously, the section 936 credit generally was repealed for all possessions, including Guam, American Samoa, and the Northern Mariana Islands, for all taxable years beginning after 2005, but a modified credit was allowed for activities in American Samoa.

American Samoa economic development credit

A domestic corporation that was an existing credit claimant with respect to American Samoa and that elected the application of section 936 for its last taxable year beginning before January 1, 2006 is allowed a credit based on the economic activity-based limitation rules described above. The credit is not part of the Code but is computed based on the rules secs. 30A and 936. The credit is allowed for the first two taxable years of a corporation that begin after December 31, 2005, and before January 1, 2008.

The amount of the credit allowed to a qualifying domestic corporation under the provision is equal to the sum of the amounts used in computing the corporation's economic activity-based limitation (described previously) with respect to American Samoa, except that no credit is allowed for the amount of any American Samoa income taxes. Thus, for any qualifying corporation the amount of the credit equals the sum of (1) 60 percent of the corporation's qualified American Samoa wages and allocable employee fringe benefit expenses and (2) 15 percent of the corporation's depreciation allowances with respect to short-life qualified American Samoa tangible property, plus 40 percent of the corporation's depreciation allowances with respect to medium-life qualified American Samoa tangible property, plus 65 percent of the corporation's depreciation allowances with respect to long-life qualified American Samoa tangible property.

The section 936(c) rule denying a credit or deduction for any possessions or foreign tax paid with respect to taxable income taken into account in computing the credit under section 936 does not apply with respect to the credit allowed by the provision.

The credit is not available for taxable years beginning after December 31, 2007.

Explanation of Provision

The provision allows the American Samoa economic development credit to apply for the first four taxable years of a corporation that begin after December 31, 2005, and before January 1, 2010.

Effective Date

The provision is effective for taxable years beginning after December 31, 2007.

[Law at ¶7153. CCH Explanation at ¶430.]

[¶10,500] Act Sec. C312. Extension of deduction for income attributable to domestic production activities in Puerto Rico

Joint Committee on Taxation (J.C.T. REP. NO. JCX-75-08)

[Code Sec. 199]

Present Law

In general

Present law provides a deduction from taxable income (or, in the case of an individual, adjusted gross income) that is equal to a portion of the taxpayer's qualified production activities income. For taxable years beginning after 2009, the deduction is nine percent of that income. For taxable years beginning in 2005 and 2006, the deduction is three percent of qualified production activities income and for taxable years beginning in 2007, 2008, and 2009, the deduction is six percent of qualified production activities income. For taxpayers subject to the 35-percent corporate income tax rate, the nine-percent deduction effectively reduces the corporate income tax rate to just under 32 percent on qualified production activities income.

Qualified production activities income

In general, qualified production activities income is equal to domestic production gross receipts (defined by section 199(c)(4)), reduced by the sum of: (1) the costs of goods sold that are allocable to those receipts and (2) other expenses, losses, or deductions which are properly allocable to those receipts.

Domestic production gross receipts

Domestic production gross receipts generally are gross receipts of a taxpayer that are derived from (1) any sale, exchange, or other disposition, or any lease, rental, or license, of qualifying production property[113] that was manufactured, produced, grown or extracted by the taxpayer in whole or in significant part within the United States; (2) any sale, exchange, or other disposition, or any lease, rental, or license, of qualified film[114] produced by the taxpayer; (3) any lease, rental, license, sale, exchange, or other disposition of electricity, natural gas, or potable water produced by the taxpayer in the United States; (4) construction of real property performed in the United States by a taxpayer in the ordinary course of a construction trade or business; or (5) engineering or architectural services performed in the United States for the construction of real property located in the United States.

Wage limitation

For taxable years beginning after May 17, 2006, the amount of the deduction for a taxable year is limited to 50 percent of the wages paid by the taxpayer, and properly allocable to domestic production gross receipts, during the calendar year that ends in such taxable year.[115] Wages paid to bona fide residents of Puerto Rico generally are not included in the wage limitation amount.[116]

Rules for Puerto Rico

When used in the Code in a geographical sense, the term "United States" generally includes only the States and the District of Columbia.[117] A special rule for determining domestic production gross receipts, however, provides that in the case of any taxpayer with gross receipts from sources within the Commonwealth of Puerto Rico, the term "United States" includes the Commonwealth of Puerto Rico, but only if all of the taxpayer's gross receipts are taxable under the Federal income tax for individuals or corporations.[118] In computing the 50-percent wage limitation, that taxpayer is permitted to take into account wages paid to bona fide residents of Puerto Rico for services performed in Puerto Rico.[119]

The special rules for Puerto Rico apply only with respect to the first two taxable years of a taxpayer beginning after December 31, 2005 and before January 1, 2008.

Explanation of Provision

The provision allows the special domestic production activities rules for Puerto Rico to apply for the first four taxable years of a taxpayer beginning after December 31, 2005 and before January 1, 2010.

Effective Date

The provision is effective for taxable years beginning after December 31, 2007.

[Law at ¶5280. CCH Explanation at ¶370.]

---

[113] Qualifying production property generally includes any tangible personal property, computer software, and sound recordings.

[114] Qualified film includes any motion picture film or videotape (including live or delayed television programming, but not including certain sexually explicit productions) if 50 percent or more of the total compensation relating to the production of the film (including compensation in the form of residuals and participations) constitutes compensation for services performed in the United States by actors, production personnel, directors, and producers.

[115] For purposes of the provision, "wages" include the sum of the amounts of wages as defined in section 3401(a)

and elective deferrals that the taxpayer properly reports to the Social Security Administration with respect to the employment of employees of the taxpayer during the calendar year ending during the taxpayer's taxable year. For taxable years beginning before May 18, 2006, the limitation is based upon all wages paid by the taxpayer, rather than only wages properly allocable to domestic production gross receipts.

[116] Sec. 3401(a)(8)(C).

[117] Sec. 7701(a)(9).

[118] Sec. 199(d)(8)(A).

[119] Sec. 199(d)(8)(B).

[¶10,510] Act Sec. C313. Extend and modify qualified zone academy bonds

Joint Committee on Taxation (J.C.T. REP. No. JCX-75-08)

[New Code Sec. 54E]

Present Law

Tax-exempt bonds

Interest on State and local governmental bonds generally is excluded from gross income for Federal income tax purposes if the proceeds of the bonds are used to finance direct activities of these governmental units or if the bonds are repaid with revenues of the governmental units. Activities that can be financed with these tax-exempt bonds include the financing of public schools.[123] An issuer must file with the IRS certain information about the bonds issued by them in order for that bond issue to be tax-exempt.[124] Generally, this information return is required to be filed no later the 15th day of the second month after the close of the calendar quarter in which the bonds were issued.

The tax exemption for State and local bonds does not apply to any arbitrage bond.[125] An arbitrage bond is defined as any bond that is part of an issue if any proceeds of the issue are reasonably expected to be used (or intentionally are used) to acquire higher yielding investments or to replace funds that are used to acquire higher yielding investments.[126] In general, arbitrage profits may be earned only during specified periods (e.g., defined "temporary periods") before funds are needed for the purpose of the borrowing or on specified types of investments (e.g., "reasonably required reserve or replacement funds"). Subject to limited exceptions, investment profits that are earned during these periods or on such investments must be rebated to the Federal Government.

Qualified zone academy bonds

As an alternative to traditional tax-exempt bonds, States and local governments were given the authority to issue "qualified zone academy bonds."[127] A total of $400 million of qualified zone academy bonds is authorized to be issued annually in calendar years 1998 through 2007. The $400 million aggregate bond cap is allocated each year to the States according to their respective populations of individuals below the pov-

erty line. Each State, in turn, allocates the credit authority to qualified zone academies within such State.

Financial institutions that hold qualified zone academy bonds are entitled to a nonrefundable tax credit in an amount equal to a credit rate multiplied by the face amount of the bond. A taxpayer holding a qualified zone academy bond on the credit allowance date is entitled to a credit. The credit is includable in gross income (as if it were a taxable interest payment on the bond), and may be claimed against regular income tax and alternative minimum tax liability.

The Treasury Department sets the credit rate at a rate estimated to allow issuance of qualified zone academy bonds without discount and without interest cost to the issuer. The maximum term of the bond is determined by the Treasury Department, so that the present value of the obligation to repay the bond was 50 percent of the face value of the bond.

"Qualified zone academy bonds" are defined as any bond issued by a State or local government, provided that (1) at least 95 percent of the proceeds are used for the purpose of renovating, providing equipment to, developing course materials for use at, or training teachers and other school personnel in a "qualified zone academy" and (2) private entities have promised to contribute to the qualified zone academy certain equipment, technical assistance or training, employee services, or other property or services with a value equal to at least 10 percent of the bond proceeds.

A school is a "qualified zone academy" if (1) the school is a public school that provides education and training below the college level, (2) the school operates a special academic program in cooperation with businesses to enhance the academic curriculum and increase graduation and employment rates, and (3) either (a) the school is located in an empowerment zone or enterprise community designated under the Code, or (b) it is reasonably expected that at least 35 percent of the students at the school will be eligible for free or reduced-cost lunches under the school lunch

---

[123] Sec. 103.
[124] Sec. 149(e).
[125] Sec. 103(a) and (b)(2).

[126] Sec. 148.
[127] Sec. 1397E.

program established under the National School Lunch Act.

The Tax Relief and Health Care Act of 2006 ("TRHCA")[128] imposed the arbitrage requirements that generally apply to interest-bearing tax-exempt bonds to qualified zone academy bonds. In addition, an issuer of qualified zone academy bonds must reasonably expect to and actually spend 95 percent or more of the proceeds of such bonds on qualified zone academy property within the five-year period that begins on the date of issuance. To the extent less than 95 percent of the proceeds are used to finance qualified zone academy property during the five-year spending period, bonds will continue to qualify as qualified zone academy bonds if unspent proceeds are used within 90 days from the end of such five-year period to redeem any nonqualified bonds. The five-year spending period may be extended by the Secretary if the issuer establishes that the failure to meet the spending requirement is due to reasonable cause and the related purposes for issuing the bonds will continue to proceed with due diligence. Issuers of qualified zone academy bonds are required to report issuance to the IRS in a manner similar to the information returns required for tax-exempt bonds.

Explanation of Provision

The provision extends and modifies the present-law qualified zone academy bond program. The provision authorizes issuance of up to $400 million of qualified zone academy bonds annually through 2009.

For bonds issued after the date of enactment, the provision also modifies the spending and arbitrage rules that apply to qualified zone academy bonds. The provision modifies the spending rule by requiring 100 percent of available project proceeds to be spent on qualified zone academy property. In addition, the provision modifies the arbitrage rules by providing that available project proceeds invested during the five-year period beginning on the date of issue are not subject to the arbitrage restrictions (i.e., yield restriction and rebate requirements). The provision defines "available project proceeds" as proceeds from the sale of an issue of qualified zone academy bonds, less issuance costs (not to exceed two percent) and any investment earnings on such proceeds. Thus, available project proceeds invested during the five-year spending period may be invested at unrestricted yields, but the earnings on such investments must be spent on qualified zone academy property.

The provision provides that amounts invested in a reserve fund are not subject to the arbitrage restrictions to the extent: (1) such fund is funded at a rate not more rapid than equal annual installments; (2) such fund is funded in a manner reasonably expected to result in an amount not greater than an amount necessary to repay the issue; and (3) the yield on such fund is not greater than the average annual interest rate of tax-exempt obligations having a term of 10 years or more that are issued during the month the qualified zone academy bonds are issued.

Effective Date

The provision applies to bonds issued after the date of enactment.

[Law at ¶5165. CCH Explanation at ¶815.]

[¶10,520] Act Sec. C314. Indian employment tax credit

Joint Committee on Taxation (J.C.T. Rep. No. JCX-75-08)

[Code Sec. 45A]

Present Law

In general, a credit against income tax liability is allowed to employers for the first $20,000 of qualified wages and qualified employee health insurance costs paid or incurred by the employer with respect to certain employees (sec. 45A). The credit is equal to 20 percent of the excess of eligible employee qualified wages and health insurance costs during the current year over the amount of such wages and costs incurred by the employer during 1993. The credit is an incremental credit, such that an employer's current-year qualified wages and qualified employee health insurance costs (up to $20,000 per employee) are eligible for the credit only to the extent that the sum of such costs exceeds the sum of comparable costs paid during 1993. No deduction is allowed for the portion of the wages equal to the amount of the credit.

Qualified wages means wages paid or incurred by an employer for services performed by a qualified employee. A qualified employee means any employee who is an enrolled member

---

[128] Pub. L. No. 109-432 (2006).

of an Indian tribe or the spouse of an enrolled member of an Indian tribe, who performs substantially all of the services within an Indian reservation, and whose principal place of abode while performing such services is on or near the reservation in which the services are performed. An "Indian reservation" is a reservation as defined in section 3(d) of the Indian Financing Act of 1974 or section 4(1) of the Indian Child Welfare Act of 1978. For purposes of the preceding sentence, section 3(d) is applied by treating "former Indian reservations in Oklahoma" as including only lands that are (1) within the jurisdictional area of an Oklahoma Indian tribe as determined by the Secretary of the Interior, and (2) recognized by such Secretary as an area eligible for trust land status under 25 C.F.R. Part 151 (as in effect on August 5, 1997).

An employee is not treated as a qualified employee for any taxable year of the employer if the total amount of wages paid or incurred by the employer with respect to such employee during the taxable year exceeds an amount determined at an annual rate of $30,000 (which after adjustment for inflation is currently $40,000).[94] In addition, an employee will not be treated as a qualified employee under certain specific cir-cumstances, such as where the employee is related to the employer (in the case of an individual employer) or to one of the employer's shareholders, partners, or grantors. Similarly, an employee will not be treated as a qualified employee where the employee has more than a 5 percent ownership interest in the employer. Finally, an employee will not be considered a qualified employee to the extent the employee's services relate to gaming activities or are performed in a building housing such activities.

The Indian employment tax credit is not available for taxable years beginning after December 31, 2007.

Explanation of Provision

The provision extends for two years the present-law employment credit provision (through taxable years beginning on or before December 31, 2009).

Effective Date

The provision is effective for taxable years beginning after December 31, 2007.

[Law at ¶ 5080. CCH Explanation at ¶ 425.]

[¶ 10,530] Act Sec. C315. Accelerated depreciation for business property on Indian reservation

Joint Committee on Taxation (J.C.T. Rep. No. JCX-75-08)

[Code Sec. 168]

Present Law

With respect to certain property used in connection with the conduct of a trade or business within an Indian reservation, depreciation deductions under section 168(j) are determined using the following recovery periods:

3-year property	2 years
5-year property	3 years
7-year property	4 years
10-year property	6 years
15-year property	9 years
20-year property	12 years
Nonresidential real property	22 years

"Qualified Indian reservation property" eligible for accelerated depreciation includes property described in the table above which is: (1) used by the taxpayer predominantly in the active conduct of a trade or business within an Indian reservation; (2) not used or located outside the reservation on a regular basis; (3) not acquired (directly or indirectly) by the taxpayer from a person who is related to the taxpayer;[106] and (4) is not property placed in service for purposes of conducting gaming activities.[107] Certain "qualified infrastructure property" may be eligible for the accelerated depreciation even if located outside an Indian reservation, provided that the purpose of such property is to connect with qualified infrastructure property located within the reservation (e.g., roads, power lines, water systems, railroad spurs, and communications facilities).[108]

An "Indian reservation" means a reservation as defined in section 3(d) of the Indian Financing Act of 1974 or section 4(10) of the

---

[94] See Form 8845, Indian Employment Credit (Rev. December 2006).

[106] For these purposes, related persons is defined in Sec. 465(b)(3)(C).

[107] Sec. 168(j)(4)(A).

[108] Sec. 168(j)(4)(C).

Indian Child Welfare Act of 1978. For purposes of the preceding sentence, section 3(d) is applied by treating "former Indian reservations in Oklahoma" as including only lands that are (1) within the jurisdictional area of an Oklahoma Indian tribe as determined by the Secretary of the Interior, and (2) recognized by such Secretary as an area eligible for trust land status under 25 C.F.R. Part 151 (as in effect on August 5, 1997).

The depreciation deduction allowed for regular tax purposes is also allowed for purposes of the alternative minimum tax. The accelerated depreciation for Indian reservations is available with respect to property placed in service on or after January 1, 1994, and before January 1, 2008.

Explanation of Provision

The provision extends for two years the present-law incentive relating to depreciation of qualified Indian reservation property (to apply to property placed in service through December 31, 2009).

Effective Date

The provision applies to property placed in service after December 31, 2007.

[Law at ¶ 5230. CCH Explanation at ¶ 335.]

[¶ 10,540] Act Sec. C316. Railroad track maintenance

Joint Committee on Taxation (J.C.T. REP. NO. JCX-75-08)

[Code Sec. 45G]

Present Law

Present law provides a 50-percent business tax credit for qualified railroad track maintenance expenditures paid or incurred by an eligible taxpayer during the taxable year.[97] The credit is limited to the product of $3,500 times the number of miles of railroad track (1) owned or leased by an eligible taxpayer as of the close of its taxable year, and (2) assigned to the eligible taxpayer by a Class II or Class III railroad that owns or leases such track at the close of the taxable year.[98] Each mile of railroad track may be taken into account only once, either by the owner of such mile or by the owner's assignee, in computing the per-mile limitation. Under the provision, the credit is limited in respect of the total number of miles of track (1) owned or leased by the Class II or Class III railroad and (2) assigned to the Class II or Class III railroad for purposes of the credit.

Qualified railroad track maintenance expenditures are defined as gross expenditures (whether or not otherwise chargeable to capital account) for maintaining railroad track (including roadbed, bridges, and related track structures) owned or leased as of January 1, 2005, by a Class II or Class III railroad (determined without regard to any consideration for such expenditure given by the Class II or Class III railroad which made the assignment of such track).[99]

An eligible taxpayer means any Class II or Class III railroad, and any person who transports property using the rail facilities of a Class II or Class III railroad or who furnishes railroad-related property or services to a Class II or Class III railroad, but only with respect to miles of railroad track assigned to such person by such railroad under the provision.[100]

The terms Class II or Class III railroad have the meanings given by the Surface Transportation Board.[101]

The provision applies to qualified railroad track maintenance expenditures paid or incurred during taxable years beginning after December 31, 2004, and before January 1, 2008.

Explanation of Provision

The provision extends the present law provision for two years, for qualified railroad track maintenance expenditures paid or incurred before January 1, 2010.

Effective Date

The provision is effective for expenditures paid or incurred during taxable years beginning after December 31, 2007.

[Law at ¶ 5095. CCH Explanation at ¶ 415.]

---

[97] Sec. 45G(a).
[98] Sec. 45G(b)(1).
[99] Sec. 45G(d).

[100] Sec. 45G(c).
[101] Sec. 45G(e)(1).

[¶10,550] Act Sec. C317. Seven-year recovery period for motorsports racing track facility

Joint Committee on Taxation (J.C.T. REP. NO. JCX-75-08)

[Code Sec. 168]

Present Law

A taxpayer generally must capitalize the cost of property used in a trade or business and recover such cost over time through annual deductions for depreciation or amortization. Tangible property generally is depreciated under the modified accelerated cost recovery system ("MACRS"), which determines depreciation by applying specific recovery periods, placed-in-service conventions, and depreciation methods to the cost of various types of depreciable property.[103] The cost of nonresidential real property is recovered using the straight-line method of depreciation and a recovery period of 39 years. Nonresidential real property is subject to the mid-month placed-in-service convention. Under the mid-month convention, the depreciation allowance for the first year property is placed in service is based on the number of months the property was in service, and property placed in service at any time during a month is treated as having been placed in service in the middle of the month. Land improvements (such as roads and fences) are recovered over 15 years. An exception exists for the theme and amusement park industry, whose assets are assigned a recovery period of seven years. Additionally, a motorsports entertainment complex placed in service before December 31, 2007 is assigned a recovery period of seven years.[104] For these purposes, a motorsports entertainment complex means a racing track facility which is permanently situated on land that during the 36 month period following its placed in service date it hosts a racing event.[105] The term motorsports entertainment complex also includes ancillary facilities, land improvements (e.g., parking lots, sidewalks, fences), support facilities (e.g., food and beverage retailing, souvenir vending), and appurtenances associated with such facilities (e.g., ticket booths, grandstands).

Explanation of Provision

The provision extends the present law seven year recovery period for two years through December 31, 2009.

Effective Date

The provision is effective for property placed in service after December 31, 2007.

[Law at ¶5230. CCH Explanation at ¶325.]

[¶10,560] Act Sec. C318. Expensing of environmental remediation costs

Joint Committee on Taxation (J.C.T. REP. NO. JCX-75-08)

[Code Sec. 198]

Present Law

Present law allows a deduction for ordinary and necessary expenses paid or incurred in carrying on any trade or business.[109] Treasury regulations provide that the cost of incidental repairs that neither materially add to the value of property nor appreciably prolong its life, but keep it in an ordinarily efficient operating condition, may be deducted currently as a business expense. Section 263(a)(1) limits the scope of section 162 by prohibiting a current deduction for certain capital expenditures. Treasury regulations define "capital expenditures" as amounts paid or incurred to materially add to the value, or substantially prolong the useful life, of property owned by the taxpayer, or to adapt property to a new or different use. Amounts paid for repairs and maintenance do not constitute capital expenditures. The determination of whether an expense is deductible or capitalizable is based on the facts and circumstances of each case.

Taxpayers may elect to treat certain environmental remediation expenditures paid or incurred before January 1, 2008, that would otherwise be chargeable to capital account as

---

[103] Sec. 168.
[104] Sec. 168(e)(3)(C)(ii).

[105] Sec. 168(i)(15).
[109] Sec. 162.

deductible in the year paid or incurred.[110] The deduction applies for both regular and alternative minimum tax purposes. The expenditure must be incurred in connection with the abatement or control of hazardous substances at a qualified contaminated site. In general, any expenditure for the acquisition of depreciable property used in connection with the abatement or control of hazardous substances at a qualified contaminated site does not constitute a qualified environmental remediation expenditure. However, depreciation deductions allowable for such property, which would otherwise be allocated to the site under the principles set forth in Commissioner v. Idaho Power Co.[111] and section 263A, are treated as qualified environmental remediation expenditures.

A "qualified contaminated site" (a so-called "brownfield") generally is any property that is held for use in a trade or business, for the production of income, or as inventory and is certified by the appropriate State environmental agency to be an area at or on which there has been a release (or threat of release) or disposal of a hazardous substance. Both urban and rural property may qualify. However, sites that are identified on the national priorities list under the Comprehensive Environmental Response, Compensation, and Liability Act of 1980 ("CERCLA")[112] cannot qualify as targeted areas. Hazardous substances generally are defined by reference to sections 101(14) and 102 of CERCLA, subject to additional limitations applicable to asbestos and similar substances within buildings, certain naturally occurring substances such as radon, and certain other substances released into drinking water supplies due to deterioration through ordinary use, as well as petroleum products defined in section 4612(a)(3) of the Code.

In the case of property to which a qualified environmental remediation expenditure otherwise would have been capitalized, any deduction allowed under section 198 is treated as a depreciation deduction and the property is treated as section 1245 property. Thus, deductions for qualified environmental remediation expenditures are subject to recapture as ordinary income upon a sale or other disposition of the property. In addition, sections 280B (demolition of structures) and 468 (special rules for mining and solid waste reclamation and closing costs) do not apply to amounts that are treated as expenses under this provision.

Section 1400N(g) permits the expensing of environmental remediation expenditures paid or incurred on or after August 28, 2005, and before January 1, 2008, to abate contamination at qualified contaminated sites located in the Gulf Opportunity Zone.

Explanation of Provision

The provision extends the present law expensing provision under section 198 for two years through December 31, 2009.

Effective Date

The provision is effective for expenditures paid or incurred after December 31, 2007.

[Law at ¶ 5270. CCH Explanation at ¶ 340.]

[¶10,570] Act Sec. C319. Extension of the Hurricane Katrina work opportunity tax credit

Joint Committee on Taxation (J.C.T. REP. NO. JCX-75-08)

[Act Sec. C319]

Present Law

Work opportunity tax credit

In general

The work opportunity tax credit is available on an elective basis for employers hiring individuals from one or more of nine targeted groups. The amount of the credit available to an employer is determined by the amount of qualified wages paid by the employer. Generally, qualified wages consist of wages attributable to service rendered by a member of a targeted group during the one-year period beginning with the day the individual begins work for the employer (two years in the case of an individual in the long-term family assistance recipient category).

Targeted groups eligible for the credit

Generally an employer is eligible for the credit only for qualified wages paid to members of a targeted group. There are nine targeted groups: (1) families receiving Temporary Assis-

---

[110] Sec. 198.
[111] 418 U.S. 1 (1974).

[112] Pub. L. No. 96-510 (1980).

tance for Needy Families Program ("TANF"); (2) qualified veterans; (3) qualified ex-felons; (4) designated community residents; (5) vocational rehabilitation referrals; (6) qualified summer youth employees; (7) qualified food stamp recipients; (8) qualified supplemental security income ("SSI") benefit recipients; and (9) qualified long-term family assistance recipients.

Qualified wages

Generally, qualified wages are defined as cash wages paid by the employer to a member of a targeted group. The employer's deduction for wages is reduced by the amount of the credit.

For purposes of the credit, generally, wages are defined by reference to the FUTA definition of wages contained in sec. 3306(b) (without regard to the dollar limitation therein contained). Special rules apply in the case of certain agricultural labor and certain railroad labor.

Calculation of the credit

The credit available to an employer for qualified wages paid to members of all targeted groups except for long-term family assistance recipients equals 40 percent (25 percent for employment of 400 hours or less) of qualified first-year wages. Generally, qualified first-year wages are qualified wages (not in excess of $6,000) attributable to service rendered by a member of a targeted group during the one-year period beginning with the day the individual began work for the employer. Therefore, the maximum credit per employee is $2,400 (40 percent of the first $6,000 of qualified first-year wages). There are two exceptions to this general rule. First, with respect to qualified summer youth employees, the maximum credit is $1,200 (40 percent of the first $3,000 of qualified first-year wages). Second, with respect to qualified veterans who are entitled to compensation for a service-connected disability, the maximum credit is $4,800 because qualified first-year wages are $12,000 rather than $6,000 for such individuals.[161] Except for long-term family assistance recipients, no credit is allowed for second-year wages.

In the case of long-term family assistance recipients, the credit equals 40 percent (25 percent for employment of 400 hours or less) of $10,000 for qualified first-year wages and 50 percent of the first $10,000 of qualified second-year wages. Generally, qualified second-year wages are qualified wages (not in excess of $10,000) attributable to service rendered by a member of the long-term family assistance category during the one-year period beginning on the day after the one-year period beginning with the day the individual began work for the employer. Therefore, the maximum credit per employee is $9,000 (40 percent of the first $10,000 of qualified first-year wages plus 50 percent of the first $10,000 of qualified second-year wages).

Certification rules

An individual is not treated as a member of a targeted group unless: (1) on or before the day on which an individual begins work for an employer, the employer has received a certification from a designated local agency that such individual is a member of a targeted group; or (2) on or before the day an individual is offered employment with the employer, a pre-screening notice is completed by the employer with respect to such individual, and not later than the 28th day after the individual begins work for the employer, the employer submits such notice, signed by the employer and the individual under penalties of perjury, to the designated local agency as part of a written request for certification. For these purposes, a pre-screening notice is a document (in such form as the Secretary may prescribe) which contains information provided by the individual on the basis of which the employer believes that the individual is a member of a targeted group.

Minimum employment period

No credit is allowed for qualified wages paid to employees who work less than 120 hours in the first year of employment.

Other rules

The work opportunity tax credit is not allowed for wages paid to a relative or dependent of the taxpayer. No credit is allowed for wages paid to an individual who is a more than fifty-percent owner of the entity. Similarly, wages paid to replacement workers during a strike or lockout are not eligible for the work opportunity tax credit. Wages paid to any employee during any period for which the employer received on-the-job training program payments with respect to that employee are not eligible for the work opportunity tax credit. The work opportunity tax credit generally is not allowed for wages paid to individuals who had previously been employed by the employer. In addition, many other technical rules apply.

---

[161] The expanded definition of qualified first-year wages does not apply to the veterans qualified with reference to a food stamp program, as defined under present law.

Expiration

The work opportunity tax credit is not available for individuals who begin work for an employer after August 31, 2011.

Work opportunity tax credit for Hurricane Katrina employees

In general

The Katrina Emergency Tax Relief Act of 2005 provided that a Hurricane Katrina employee is treated as a member of a targeted group for purposes of the work opportunity tax credit. A Hurricane Katrina employee was: (1) an individual who on August 28, 2005, had a principal place of abode in the core disaster area and was hired during the two-year period beginning on such date for a position, the principal place of employment of which was located in the core disaster area; and (2) an individual who on August 28, 2005, had a principal place of abode in the core disaster area, who was displaced from such abode by reason of Hurricane Katrina and was hired during the period beginning on such date and ending on December 31, 2005 without regard to whether the new principal place of employment is in the core disaster area.

The present-law WOTC certification requirement was waived for such individuals. In lieu of the certification requirement, an individual may have provided to the employer reasonable evidence that the individual is a Hurricane Katrina employee.

The present-law rule that denies the credit with respect to wages of employees who had been previously employed by the employer was waived for the first hire of such employee as a Hurricane Katrina employee unless such employee was an employee of the employer on August 28, 2005.

Definitions

The term "Hurricane Katrina disaster area" means an area with respect to which a major disaster has been declared by the President before September 14, 2005 under section 401 of the Robert T. Stafford Disaster Relief and Emergency Assistance Act.

The term "core disaster area" means that portion of the Hurricane Katrina disaster area determined by the President to warrant individual or individual and public assistance from the Federal Government under the Robert T. Stafford Disaster Relief and Emergency Assistance Act.

Explanation of Provision

The provision extends through August 28, 2009, the work opportunity tax credit for certain Hurricane Katrina employees employed within the core disaster area. For this purpose, a Hurricane Katrina employee employed within the core disaster area is an individual who on August 28, 2005, had a principal place of abode in the core disaster area and is hired on or after August 28, 2005 and before August 29, 2009 for a position, the principal place of employment of which was located in the core disaster area.[162] The other special rules (e.g., certification and previous employment) for Hurricane Katrina employees apply.

Effective Date

The provision is effective for individuals hired after August 28, 2007, and before August 29, 2009.

[Law at ¶7156. CCH Explanation at ¶635.]

[¶10,580] Act Sec. C321. Extension of the enhanced charitable deduction for contributions of computer technology and equipment

Joint Committee on Taxation (J.C.T. REP. NO. JCX-75-08)

[Code Sec. 170

Present Law

In the case of a charitable contribution of inventory or other ordinary-income or short-term capital gain property, the amount of the charitable deduction generally is limited to the taxpayer's basis in the property. In the case of a charitable contribution of tangible personal property, the deduction is limited to the tax-

---

[162] The prior-law work opportunity tax credit for Katrina employees hired to a new place of employment outside of the core disaster area is not extended by this provision.

payer's basis in such property if the use by the recipient charitable organization is unrelated to the organization's tax-exempt purpose. In cases involving contributions to a private foundation (other than certain private operating foundations), the amount of the deduction is limited to the taxpayer's basis in the property.[154]

Under present law, a taxpayer's deduction for charitable contributions of computer technology and equipment generally is limited to the taxpayer's basis (typically, cost) in the property. However, certain corporations may claim a deduction in excess of basis for a "qualified computer contribution."[155] This enhanced deduction is equal to the lesser of (1) basis plus one-half of the item's appreciation (i.e., basis plus one half of fair market value in excess of basis) or (2) two times basis. The enhanced deduction for qualified computer contributions expires for any contribution made during any taxable year beginning after December 31, 2007.

A qualified computer contribution means a charitable contribution of any computer technology or equipment, which meets standards of functionality and suitability as established by the Secretary of the Treasury. The contribution must be to certain educational organizations or public libraries and made not later than three years after the taxpayer acquired the property or, if the taxpayer constructed or assembled the property, not later than the date construction or assembly of the property is substantially completed.[156] The original use of the property must be by the donor or the donee,[157] and in the case of the donee, must be used substantially for educational purposes related to the function or purpose of the donee. The property must fit productively into the donee's education plan. The donee may not transfer the property in exchange for money, other property, or services, except for shipping, installation, and transfer costs. To determine whether property is constructed or assembled by the taxpayer, the rules applicable to qualified research contributions apply. Contributions may be made to private foundations under certain conditions.[158]

Explanation of Provision

The provision extends the enhanced deduction for computer technology and equipment for one year to apply to contributions made during any taxable year beginning after December 31, 2007, and before January 1, 2010.

Effective Date

The provision is effective for taxable years beginning after December 31, 2007.

[Law at ¶ 5235. CCH Explanation at ¶ 440.]

[¶ 10,590] Act Sec. C322. Tax incentives for investment in the District of Columbia

Joint Committee on Taxation (J.C.T. REP. No. JCX-75-08)

[Code Secs. 1400, 1400A, 1400B and 1400C]

Present Law

In general

The Taxpayer Relief Act of 1997 designated certain economically depressed census tracts within the District of Columbia as the District of Columbia Enterprise Zone (the "D.C. Zone"), within which businesses and individual residents are eligible for special tax incentives. The census tracts that compose the D.C. Zone are (1) all census tracts that presently are part of the D.C. enterprise community designated under section 1391 (i.e., portions of Anacostia, Mt. Pleasant, Chinatown, and the easternmost part of the District), and (2) all additional census tracts within the District of Columbia where the poverty rate is not less than 20 percent. The D.C. Zone designation remained in effect for the period from January 1, 1998, through December 31, 2007. In general, the tax incentives available in connection with the D.C. Zone are a 20-percent wage credit, an additional $35,000 of section 179 expensing for qualified zone property, expanded tax-exempt financing for certain zone facilities, and a zero-percent capital gains rate from the sale of certain qualified D.C. zone assets.

---

[154] Sec. 170(e)(1).

[155] Secs. 170(e)(4) and 170(e)(6).

[156] If the taxpayer constructed the property and reacquired such property, the contribution must be within three years of the date the original construction was substantially completed. Sec. 170(e)(6)(D)(i).

[157] This requirement does not apply if the property was reacquired by the manufacturer and contributed. Sec. 170(e)(6)(D)(ii).

[158] Sec. 170(e)(6)(C).

Wage credit

A 20-percent wage credit is available to employers for the first $15,000 of qualified wages paid to each employee (i.e., a maximum credit of $3,000 with respect to each qualified employee) who (1) is a resident of the D.C. Zone, and (2) performs substantially all employment services within the D.C. Zone in a trade or business of the employer.

Wages paid to a qualified employee who earns more than $15,000 are eligible for the wage credit (although only the first $15,000 of wages is eligible for the credit). The wage credit is available with respect to a qualified full-time or part-time employee (employed for at least 90 days), regardless of the number of other employees who work for the employer. In general, any taxable business carrying out activities in the D.C. Zone may claim the wage credit, regardless of whether the employer meets the definition of a "D.C. Zone business."[129]

An employer's deduction otherwise allowed for wages paid is reduced by the amount of wage credit claimed for that taxable year.[130] Wages are not to be taken into account for purposes of the wage credit if taken into account in determining the employer's work opportunity tax credit under section 51 or the welfare-to-work credit under section 51A.[131] In addition, the $15,000 cap is reduced by any wages taken into account in computing the work opportunity tax credit or the welfare-to-work credit.[132] The wage credit may be used to offset up to 25 percent of alternative minimum tax liability.[133]

Section 179 expensing

In general, a D.C. Zone business is allowed an additional $35,000 of section 179 expensing for qualifying property placed in service by a D.C. Zone business.[134] The section 179 expensing allowed to a taxpayer is phased out by the amount by which 50 percent of the cost of qualified zone property placed in service during the year by the taxpayer exceeds $200,000 ($500,000 for taxable years beginning after 2006 and before 2011). The term "qualified zone property" is defined as depreciable tangible property (including

buildings), provided that (1) the property is acquired by the taxpayer (from an unrelated party) after the designation took effect, (2) the original use of the property in the D.C. Zone commences with the taxpayer, and (3) substantially all of the use of the property is in the D.C. Zone in the active conduct of a trade or business by the taxpayer.[135] Special rules are provided in the case of property that is substantially renovated by the taxpayer.

Tax-exempt financing

A qualified D.C. Zone business is permitted to borrow proceeds from tax-exempt qualified enterprise zone facility bonds (as defined in section 1394) issued by the District of Columbia.[136] Such bonds are subject to the District of Columbia's annual private activity bond volume limitation. Generally, qualified enterprise zone facility bonds for the District of Columbia are bonds 95 percent or more of the net proceeds of which are used to finance certain facilities within the D.C. Zone. The aggregate face amount of all outstanding qualified enterprise zone facility bonds per qualified D.C. Zone business may not exceed $15 million and may be issued only while the D.C. Zone designation is in effect.

Zero-percent capital gains

A zero-percent capital gains rate applies to capital gains from the sale of certain qualified D.C. Zone assets held for more than five years.[137] In general, a qualified "D.C. Zone asset" means stock or partnership interests held in, or tangible property held by, a D.C. Zone business. For purposes of the zero-percent capital gains rate, the D.C. Enterprise Zone is defined to include all census tracts within the District of Columbia where the poverty rate is not less than 10 percent.

In general, gain eligible for the zero-percent tax rate means gain from the sale or exchange of a qualified D.C. Zone asset that is (1) a capital asset or property used in the trade or business as defined in section 1231(b), and (2) acquired before January 1, 2008. Gain that is attributable to real property, or to intangible assets, qualifies

---

[129] However, the wage credit is not available for wages paid in connection with certain business activities described in section 144(c)(6)(B) or certain farming activities. In addition, wages are not eligible for the wage credit if paid to (1) a person who owns more than five percent of the stock (or capital or profits interests) of the employer, (2) certain relatives of the employer, or (3) if the employer is a corporation or partnership, certain relatives of a person who owns more than 50 percent of the business.

[130] Sec. 280C(a).

[131] Secs. 1400H(a), 1396(c)(3)(A) and 51A(d)(2).
[132] Secs. 1400H(a), 1396(c)(3)(B) and 51A(d)(2).
[133] Sec. 38(c)(2).
[134] Sec. 1397A.
[135] Sec. 1397D.
[136] Sec. 1400A.
[137] Sec. 1400B.

for the zero-percent rate, provided that such real property or intangible asset is an integral part of a qualified D.C. Zone business.[138] However, no gain attributable to periods before January 1, 1998, and after December 31, 2012, is qualified capital gain.

District of Columbia homebuyer tax credit

First-time homebuyers of a principal residence in the District of Columbia are eligible for a nonrefundable tax credit of up to $5,000 of the amount of the purchase price. The $5,000 maximum credit applies both to individuals and married couples. Married individuals filing separately can claim a maximum credit of $2,500 each. The credit phases out for individual taxpayers with adjusted gross income between $70,000 and $90,000 ($110,000-$130,000 for joint filers). For purposes of eligibility, "first-time homebuyer" means any individual if such individual did not have a present ownership interest in a principal residence in the District of Columbia in the one-year period ending on the date of the purchase of the residence to which the credit applies. The credit expired for purchases after December 31, 2007.[139]

Explanation of Provision

The provision extends the designation of the D.C. Zone for two years (through December 31, 2009), thus extending the wage credit and section 179 expensing for two years.

The provision extends the tax-exempt financing authority for two years, applying to bonds issued during the period beginning on January 1, 1998, and ending on December 31, 2009.

The provision extends the zero-percent capital gains rate applicable to capital gains from the sale of certain qualified D.C. Zone assets for two years.

The provision extends the first-time homebuyer credit for two years, through December 31, 2009.

Effective Date

The provision is effective for periods beginning after, bonds issued after, acquisitions after, and property purchased after December 31, 2007.

[Law at ¶5370, ¶5375, ¶5380, ¶5385 and ¶5390. CCH Explanation at ¶365.]

[¶10,600] Act Sec. C323. Extension of the enhanced charitable deduction for contributions of food inventory

Joint Committee on Taxation (J.C.T. REP. NO. JCX-75-08)

[Code Sec. 170]

Present Law

General rules regarding contributions of food inventory

Under present law, a taxpayer's deduction for charitable contributions of inventory generally is limited to the taxpayer's basis (typically, cost) in the inventory, or if less the fair market value of the inventory.

For certain contributions of inventory, C corporations may claim an enhanced deduction equal to the lesser of (1) basis plus one-half of the item's appreciation (i.e., basis plus one-half of fair market value in excess of basis) or (2) two times basis.[145] In general, a C corporation's charitable contribution deductions for a year may not exceed 10 percent of the corporation's taxable income.[146] To be eligible for the enhanced deduction, the contributed property generally must be inventory of the taxpayer, contributed to a charitable organization described in section 501(c)(3) (except for private nonoperating foundations), and the donee must (1) use the property consistent with the donee's exempt purpose solely for the care of the ill, the needy, or infants, (2) not transfer the property in exchange for money, other property, or services, and (3) provide the taxpayer a written statement that the donee's use of the property will be consistent with such requirements. In the case of contributed property subject to the Federal Food, Drug, and Cosmetic Act, the property must satisfy the applicable requirements of such Act on the date of transfer and for 180 days prior to the transfer.

A donor making a charitable contribution of inventory must make a corresponding adjust-

---

[138] However, sole proprietorships and other taxpayers selling assets directly cannot claim the zero-percent rate on capital gain from the sale of any intangible property (i.e., the integrally related test does not apply).

[139] Sec. 1400C(i).
[145] Sec. 170(e)(3).
[146] Sec. 170(b)(2).

ment to the cost of goods sold by decreasing the cost of goods sold by the lesser of the fair market value of the property or the donor's basis with respect to the inventory.[147] Accordingly, if the allowable charitable deduction for inventory is the fair market value of the inventory, the donor reduces its cost of goods sold by such value, with the result that the difference between the fair market value and the donor's basis may still be recovered by the donor other than as a charitable contribution.

To use the enhanced deduction, the taxpayer must establish that the fair market value of the donated item exceeds basis. The valuation of food inventory has been the subject of disputes between taxpayers and the IRS.[148]

Temporary rule expanding and modifying the enhanced deduction for contributions of food inventory

Under a temporary provision enacted as part of the Katrina Emergency Tax Relief Act of 2005 and extended by the Pension Protection Act of 2006, any taxpayer, whether or not a C corporation, engaged in a trade or business is eligible to claim the enhanced deduction for donations of food inventory.[149] For taxpayers other than C corporations, the total deduction for donations of food inventory in a taxable year generally may not exceed 10 percent of the taxpayer's net income for such taxable year from all sole proprietorships, S corporations, or partnerships (or other non C corporation) from which contributions of apparently wholesome food are made. For example, if a taxpayer is a sole proprietor, a shareholder in an S corporation, and a partner in a partnership, and each business makes charitable contributions of food inventory, the taxpayer's deduction for donations of food inventory is limited to 10 percent of the taxpayer's net income from the sole proprietorship and the taxpayer's interests in the S corporation and partnership. However, if only the sole proprietorship and the S corporation made charitable contributions of food inventory, the taxpayer's deduction would be limited to 10 percent of the net income from the trade or business of the sole proprietorship and the taxpayer's interest in the S corporation, but not the taxpayer's interest in the partnership.[150]

Under the temporary provision, the enhanced deduction for food is available only for food that qualifies as "apparently wholesome food." "Apparently wholesome food" is defined as food intended for human consumption that meets all quality and labeling standards imposed by Federal, State, and local laws and regulations even though the food may not be readily marketable due to appearance, age, freshness, grade, size, surplus, or other conditions.

The temporary provision does not apply to contributions made after December 31, 2007.

Explanation of Provision

The provision extends the expansion of, and modifications to, the enhanced deduction for charitable contributions of food inventory to contributions made before January 1, 2010.

Effective Date

The provision is effective for contributions made after December 31, 2007.

[Law at ¶5235. CCH Explanation at ¶445.]

---

[147] Treas. Reg. sec. 1.170A-4A(c)(3).

[148] *Lucky Stores Inc. v. Commissioner*, 105 T.C. 420 (1995) (holding that the value of surplus bread inventory donated to charity was the full retail price of the bread rather than half the retail price, as the IRS asserted).

[149] Sec. 170(e)(3)(C).

[150] The 10 percent limitation does not affect the application of the generally applicable percentage limitations. For example, if 10 percent of a sole proprietor's net income from the proprietor's trade or business was greater than 50 percent of the proprietor's contribution base, the available deduction for the taxable year (with respect to contributions to public charities) would be 50 percent of the proprietor's contribution base. Consistent with present law, such contributions may be carried forward because they exceed the 50 percent limitation. Contributions of food inventory by a taxpayer that is not a C corporation that exceed the 10 percent limitation but not the 50 percent limitation could not be carried forward.

[¶10,610] Act Sec. C324. Extension of the enhanced charitable deduction for contributions of book inventory

Joint Committee on Taxation (J.C.T. REP. No. JCX-75-08)

[Code Sec. 170]

Present Law

Under present law, a taxpayer's deduction for charitable contributions of inventory generally is limited to the taxpayer's basis (typically, cost) in the inventory, or, if less, the fair market value of the inventory.

In general, for certain contributions of inventory, C corporations may claim an enhanced deduction equal to the lesser of (1) basis plus one-half of the item's appreciation (i.e., basis plus one-half of fair market value in excess of basis) or (2) two times basis.[151] In general, a C corporation's charitable contribution deductions for a year may not exceed 10 percent of the corporation's taxable income.[152] To be eligible for the enhanced deduction, the contributed property generally must be inventory of the taxpayer contributed to a charitable organization described in section 501(c)(3) (except for private nonoperating foundations), and the donee must (1) use the property consistent with the donee's exempt purpose solely for the care of the ill, the needy, or infants, (2) not transfer the property in exchange for money, other property, or services, and (3) provide the taxpayer a written statement that the donee's use of the property will be consistent with such requirements. In the case of contributed property subject to the Federal Food, Drug, and Cosmetic Act, the property must satisfy the applicable requirements of such Act on the date of transfer and for 180 days prior to the transfer.

A donor making a charitable contribution of inventory must make a corresponding adjustment to the cost of goods sold by decreasing the cost of goods sold by the lesser of the fair market value of the property or the donor's basis with respect to the inventory.[153] Accordingly, if the allowable charitable deduction for inventory is the fair market value of the inventory, the donor reduces its cost of goods sold by such value, with the result that the difference between the fair market value and the donor's basis may still be recovered by the donor other than as a charitable contribution.

To use the enhanced deduction, the taxpayer must establish that the fair market value of the donated item exceeds basis.

The Katrina Emergency Tax Relief Act of 2005 expanded the generally applicable enhanced deduction for C corporations to certain qualified book contributions made after August 28, 2005, and before January 1, 2006. The Pension Protection Act of 2006 extended the deduction for qualified book contributions to contributions made before January 1, 2008. A qualified book contribution means a charitable contribution of books to a public school that provides elementary education or secondary education (kindergarten through grade 12) and that is an educational organization that normally maintains a regular faculty and curriculum and normally has a regularly enrolled body of pupils or students in attendance at the place where its educational activities are regularly carried on. The enhanced deduction for qualified book contributions is not allowed unless the donee organization certifies in writing that the contributed books are suitable, in terms of currency, content, and quantity, for use in the donee's educational programs and that the donee will use the books in such educational programs. The donee also must make the certifications required for the generally applicable enhanced deduction, i.e., the donee will (1) use the property consistent with the donee's exempt purpose solely for the care of the ill, the needy, or infants, (2) not transfer the property in exchange for money, other property, or services, and (3) provide the taxpayer a written statement that the donee's use of the property will be consistent with such requirements.

Explanation of Provision

The provision extends the enhanced deduction for contributions of book inventory to contributions made before January 1, 2010.

Effective Date

The provision is effective for contributions made after December 31, 2007.

[Law at ¶5235. CCH Explanation at ¶450.]

---

[151] Sec. 170(e)(3).
[152] Sec. 170(b)(2).

[153] Treas. Reg. sec. 1.170A-4A(c)(3).

[¶10,620] Act Sec. C401. Extension of IRS authority to fund undercover operations

Joint Committee on Taxation (J.C.T. REP. NO. JCX-75-08)

[Code Sec. 7608]

Present Law

IRS undercover operations are statutorily[179] exempt from the generally applicable restrictions controlling the use of Government funds (which generally provide that all receipts must be deposited in the general fund of the Treasury and all expenses be paid out of appropriated funds). In general, the Code permits the IRS to use proceeds from an undercover operation to pay additional expenses incurred in the undercover operation, through 2007. The IRS is required to conduct a detailed financial audit of large undercover operations in which the IRS is churning funds and to provide an annual audit report to the Congress on all such large undercover operations.

Explanation of Provision

The provision makes permanent the IRS's authority to use proceeds from an undercover operation to pay additional expenses incurred in the undercover operation.

Effective Date

The provision shall take effect on January 1, 2008.

[Law at ¶5485. CCH Explanation at ¶720.]

[¶10,630] Act Sec. C402. Authority to disclose information related to terrorist activity made permanent

Joint Committee on Taxation (J.C.T. REP. NO. JCX-75-08)

[Code Sec. 6103]

Present Law

In general

Section 6103 provides that returns and return information may not be disclosed by the IRS, other Federal employees, State employees, and certain others having access to the information except as provided in the Internal Revenue Code. Section 6103 contains a number of exceptions to this general rule of nondisclosure that authorize disclosure in specifically identified circumstances (including nontax criminal investigations) when certain conditions are satisfied.

Disclosure provisions relating to emergency circumstances

The IRS is authorized to disclose return information to apprise Federal law enforcement agencies of danger of death or physical injury to an individual or to apprise Federal law enforcement agencies of imminent flight of an individual from Federal prosecution.[176] This authority has been used in connection with the investigation of terrorist activity.[177]

Disclosure provisions relating specifically to terrorist activity

Also among the disclosures permitted under the Code is disclosure of returns and return information for purposes of investigating terrorist incidents, threats, or activities, and for analyzing intelligence concerning terrorist incidents, threats, or activities. The term "terrorist incident, threat, or activity" is statutorily defined to mean an incident, threat, or activity involving an act of domestic terrorism or international terrorism.[178]

The term "international terrorism" means activities that involve violent acts or acts dangerous to human life that are a violation of the criminal laws of the United States or of any State, or that would be a criminal violation if committed within the jurisdiction of the United States or of any State; appear to be intended to intimidate or coerce a civilian population, to influence the policy of a government by intimida-

---

[179] Sec. 7608(c).

[176] Sec. 6103(i)(3)(B).

[177] See, Joint Committee on Taxation, *Disclosure Report for Public Inspection Pursuant to Internal Revenue Code Section 6103(p)(3)(C) for Calendar Year 2002 (JCX-29-04)* April 6, 2004.

[178] Sec. 6103(b)(11). For this purpose, "domestic terrorism" is defined in 18 U.S.C. sec. 2331(5) and "international terrorism" is defined in 18 U.S.C. sec. 2331(1).

tion or coercion, or to affect the conduct of a government by mass destruction, assassination, or kidnapping; and occur primarily outside the territorial jurisdiction of the United States, or transcend national boundaries in terms of the means by which they are accomplished, the persons they appear intended to intimidate or coerce, or the locale in which their perpetrators operate or seek asylum. The term "domestic terrorism" means activities that involve acts dangerous to human life that are a violation of the criminal laws of the United States or of any State; appear to be intended to intimidate or coerce a civilian population, to influence the policy of a government by intimidation or coercion or to affect the conduct of a government by mass destruction, assassination, or kidnapping; and occur primarily within the territorial jurisdiction of the United States.

In general, returns and taxpayer return information must be obtained pursuant to an ex parte court order. Return information, other than taxpayer return information, generally is available upon a written request meeting specific requirements. The IRS also is permitted to make limited disclosures of such information on its own initiative to the appropriate Federal law enforcement agency.

No disclosures may be made under these provisions after December 31, 2007. The procedures applicable to these provisions are described in detail below.

Disclosure of returns and return information - by ex parte court order

Ex parte court orders sought by Federal law enforcement and Federal intelligence agencies

The Code permits, pursuant to an ex parte court order, the disclosure of returns and return information (including taxpayer return information) to certain officers and employees of a Federal law enforcement agency or Federal intelligence agency. These officers and employees are required to be personally and directly engaged in any investigation of, response to, or analysis of intelligence and counterintelligence information concerning any terrorist incident, threat, or activity. These officers and employees are permitted to use this information solely for their use in the investigation, response, or analysis, and in any judicial, administrative, or grand jury proceeding, pertaining to any such terrorist incident, threat, or activity.

The Attorney General, Deputy Attorney General, Associate Attorney General, an Assistant Attorney General, or a United States attorney, may authorize the application for the ex

parte court order to be submitted to a Federal district court judge or magistrate. The Federal district court judge or magistrate would grant the order if based on the facts submitted he or she determines that: (1) there is reasonable cause to believe, based upon information believed to be reliable, that the return or return information may be relevant to a matter relating to such terrorist incident, threat, or activity; and (2) the return or return information is sought exclusively for the use in a Federal investigation, analysis, or proceeding concerning any terrorist incident, threat, or activity.

Special rule for ex parte court ordered disclosure initiated by the IRS

If the Secretary of the Treasury (or his delegate) possesses returns or return information that may be related to a terrorist incident, threat, or activity, the Secretary may, on his own initiative, authorize an application for an ex parte court order to permit disclosure to Federal law enforcement. In order to grant the order, the Federal district court judge or magistrate must determine that there is reasonable cause to believe, based upon information believed to be reliable, that the return or return information may be relevant to a matter relating to such terrorist incident, threat, or activity. The information may be disclosed only to the extent necessary to apprise the appropriate Federal law enforcement agency responsible for investigating or responding to a terrorist incident, threat, or activity and for officers and employees of that agency to investigate or respond to such terrorist incident, threat, or activity. Further, use of the information is limited to use in a Federal investigation, analysis, or proceeding concerning a terrorist incident, threat, or activity. Because the Department of Justice represents the Secretary in Federal district court, the Secretary is permitted to disclose returns and return information to the Department of Justice as necessary and solely for the purpose of obtaining the special IRS ex parte court order.

Disclosure of return information other than by ex parte court order

Disclosure by the IRS without a request

The Code permits the IRS to disclose return information, other than taxpayer return information, related to a terrorist incident, threat, or activity to the extent necessary to apprise the head of the appropriate Federal law enforcement agency responsible for investigating or responding to such terrorist incident, threat, or activity. The IRS on its own initiative and without a written request may make this disclosure. The head of the Federal law enforcement agency may disclose information to officers and employees of such agency to the extent necessary to investigate or respond to such terrorist incident, threat, or activity. A taxpayer's identity is not treated as return information supplied by the taxpayer or his or her representative.

Disclosure upon written request of a Federal law enforcement agency

The Code permits the IRS to disclose return information, other than taxpayer return information, to officers and employees of Federal law enforcement upon a written request satisfying certain requirements. The request must: (1) be made by the head of the Federal law enforcement agency (or his delegate) involved in the response to or investigation of terrorist incidents, threats, or activities, and (2) set forth the specific reason or reasons why such disclosure may be relevant to a terrorist incident, threat, or activity. The information is to be disclosed to officers and employees of the Federal law enforcement agency who would be personally and directly involved in the response to or investigation of terrorist incidents, threats, or activities. The information is to be used by such officers and employees solely for such response or investigation.

The Code permits the redisclosure by a Federal law enforcement agency to officers and employees of State and local law enforcement personally and directly engaged in the response to or investigation of the terrorist incident, threat, or activity. The State or local law enforcement agency must be part of an investigative or response team with the Federal law enforcement agency for these disclosures to be made.

Disclosure upon request from the Departments of Justice or the Treasury for intelligence analysis of terrorist activity

Upon written request satisfying certain requirements discussed below, the IRS is to disclose return information (other than taxpayer return information) to officers and employees of the Department of Justice, Department of the Treasury, and other Federal intelligence agencies, who are personally and directly engaged in the collection or analysis of intelligence and counterintelligence or investigation concerning terrorist incidents, threats, or activities. Use of the information is limited to use by such officers and employees in such investigation, collection, or analysis.

The written request is to set forth the specific reasons why the information to be disclosed is relevant to a terrorist incident, threat, or activity. The request is to be made by an individual who is: (1) an officer or employee of the Department of Justice or the Department of the Treasury, (2) appointed by the President with the advice and consent of the Senate, and (3) responsible for the collection, and analysis of intelligence and counterintelligence information concerning terrorist incidents, threats, or activities. The Director of the United States Secret Service also is an authorized requester.

Explanation of Provision

The provision makes permanent the present-law disclosure authority relating to terrorist activities.

Effective Date

The provision is effective for disclosures made on or after the date of enactment.

[Law at ¶5450. CCH Explanation at ¶715.]

[¶10,640] Act Sec. C501. Refundable child credit

Joint Committee on Taxation (J.C.T. REP. NO. JCX-75-08)

[Code Sec. 24(d)]

Present Law

An individual may claim a tax credit for each qualifying child under the age of 17. The amount of the credit per child is $1,000 through 2010, and $500 thereafter. A child who is not a citizen, national, or resident of the United States cannot be a qualifying child.

The credit is phased out for individuals with income over certain threshold amounts. Specifically, the otherwise allowable child tax credit is reduced by $50 for each $1,000 (or fraction thereof) of modified adjusted gross income over $75,000 for single individuals or heads of households, $110,000 for married individuals filing joint returns, and $55,000 for married individuals filing separate returns. For purposes of this limitation, modified adjusted gross income includes certain otherwise excludable income earned by U.S. citizens or residents living abroad or in certain U.S. territories.

The credit is allowable against the regular tax and the alternative minimum tax. To the extent the child credit exceeds the taxpayer's tax liability, the taxpayer is eligible for a refundable credit (the additional child tax credit) equal to 15 percent of earned income in excess of a threshold dollar amount (the "earned income" formula). The threshold dollar amount is $12,050 (2008), and is indexed for inflation.

Families with three or more children may determine the additional child tax credit using the "alternative formula," if this results in a larger credit than determined under the earned income formula. Under the alternative formula, the additional child tax credit equals the amount by which the taxpayer's social security taxes exceed the taxpayer's earned income credit ("EIC").

Earned income is defined as the sum of wages, salaries, tips, and other taxable employee compensation plus net self-employment earnings. Unlike the EIC, which also includes the preceding items in its definition of earned income, the additional child tax credit is based only on earned income to the extent it is in-cluded in computing taxable income. For example, some ministers' parsonage allowances are considered self-employment income, and thus are considered earned income for purposes of computing the EIC, but the allowances are excluded from gross income for individual income tax purposes, and thus are not considered earned income for purposes of the additional child tax credit since the income is not included in taxable income.

Explanation of Provision

The provision modifies the earned income formula for the determination of the refundable child credit to apply to 15 percent of earned income in excess of $8,500 for taxable years beginning in 2009.

Effective Date

The provision is effective for taxable years beginning in 2009.

[Law at ¶5010. CCH Explanation at ¶255.]

[¶10,650] Act Sec. C502a. Expensing for certain qualified film and television productions

Joint Committee on Taxation (J.C.T. REP. NO. JCX-75-08)

[Code Sec. 181]

Present Law

The modified Accelerated Cost Recovery System ("MACRS") does not apply to certain property, including any motion picture film, video tape, or sound recording, or to any other property if the taxpayer elects to exclude such property from MACRS and the taxpayer properly applies a unit-of-production method or other method of depreciation not expressed in a term of years. Section 197 does not apply to certain intangible property, including property produced by the taxpayer or any interest in a film, sound recording, video tape, book or similar property not acquired in a transaction (or a series of related transactions) involving the acquisition of assets constituting a trade or business or substantial portion thereof. Thus, the recovery of the cost of a film, video tape, or similar property that is produced by the taxpayer or is acquired on a "stand-alone" basis by the taxpayer may not be determined under ei-ther the MACRS depreciation provisions or under the section 197 amortization provisions. The cost recovery of such property may be determined under section 167, which allows a depreciation deduction for the reasonable allowance for the exhaustion, wear and tear, or obsolescence of the property. A taxpayer is allowed to recover, through annual depreciation deductions, the cost of certain property used in a trade or business or for the production of income. Section 167(g) provides that the cost of motion picture films, sound recordings, copyrights, books, and patents are eligible to be recovered using the income forecast method of depreciation.

Under section 181, taxpayers may elect[167] to deduct the cost of any qualifying film and television production, commencing prior to January 1, 2009, in the year the expenditure is incurred in lieu of capitalizing the cost and recovering it through depreciation allowances.[168] A qualified film or television production is one in which the

---

[167] See Treas. Reg. section 1.181-2T for rules on making an election under this section.

[168] For this purpose, a production is treated as commencing on the first date of principal photography.

aggregate cost is $15 million or less.[169] The threshold is increased to $20 million if a significant amount of the production expenditures are incurred in areas eligible for designation as a low-income community or eligible for designation by the Delta Regional Authority as a distressed county or isolated area of distress.[170]

A qualified film or television production means any production of a motion picture (whether released theatrically or directly to video cassette or any other format) or television program if at least 75 percent of the total compensation expended on the production is for services performed in the United States by actors, directors, producers, and other relevant production personnel.[171] The term "compensation" does not include participations and residuals (as defined in section 167(g)(7)(B)).[172] With respect to property which is one or more episodes in a television series, each episode is treated as a separate production and only the first 44 episodes qualify under the provision.[173] Qualified property does not include sexually explicit productions as defined by section 2257 of title 18 of the U.S. Code.[174]

For purposes of recapture under section 1245, any deduction allowed under section 181 is treated as if it were a deduction allowable for amortization.[175]

Explanation of Provision

The provision extends the provision for one year, to qualified film and television productions commencing prior to January 1, 2010.

Effective Date

The provision applies to qualified film and television productions commencing after December 31, 2008.

[Law at ¶5265. CCH Explanation at ¶345.]

[¶10,660] Act Sec. C502b. Modification of expensing for certain qualified film and television production

Joint Committee on Taxation (J.C.T. REP. No. JCX-75-08)

[Code Sec. 181]

Present Law

The modified Accelerated Cost Recovery System ("MACRS") does not apply to certain property, including any motion picture film, video tape, or sound recording, or to any other property if the taxpayer elects to exclude such property from MACRS and the taxpayer properly applies a unit-of-production method or other method of depreciation not expressed in a term of years. Section 197 does not apply to certain intangible property, including property produced by the taxpayer or any interest in a film, sound recording, video tape, book or similar property not acquired in a transaction (or a series of related transactions) involving the acquisition of assets constituting a trade or business or substantial portion thereof. Thus, the recovery of the cost of a film, video tape, or similar property that is produced by the taxpayer or is acquired on a "stand-alone" basis by the taxpayer may not be determined under either the MACRS depreciation provisions or under the section 197 amortization provisions. The cost recovery of such property may be determined under section 167, which allows a depreciation deduction for the reasonable allowance for the exhaustion, wear and tear, or obsolescence of the property. A taxpayer is allowed to recover, through annual depreciation deductions, the cost of certain property used in a trade or business or for the production of income. Section 167(g) provides that the cost of motion picture films, sound recordings, copyrights, books, and patents are eligible to be recovered using the income forecast method of depreciation.

Under section 181, taxpayers may elect[186] to deduct the cost of any qualifying film and television production, commencing prior to January 1, 2009, in the year the expenditure is incurred in lieu of capitalizing the cost and recovering it

---

[169] Sec. 181(a)(2)(A). A qualifying film or television production that is co-produced is eligible for the benefits of the provision only if its aggregate cost, regardless of funding source, does not exceed the threshold.

[170] Sec. 181(a)(2)(B).

[171] Sec. 181(d)(3)(A).

[172] Sec. 181(d)(3)(B).

[173] Sec. 181(d)(2)(B).

[174] Sec. 181(d)(2)(C).

[175] Sec. 1245(a)(2)(C).

[186] See Treas. Reg. section 1.181-2T for rules on making an election under this section.

through depreciation allowances.[187] A qualified film or television production is one in which the aggregate cost is $15 million or less.[188] The threshold is increased to $20 million if a significant amount of the production expenditures are incurred in areas eligible for designation as a low-income community or eligible for designation by the Delta Regional Authority as a distressed county or isolated area of distress.[189]

A qualified film or television production means any production of a motion picture (whether released theatrically or directly to video cassette or any other format) or television program if at least 75 percent of the total compensation expended on the production is for services performed in the United States by actors, directors, producers, and other relevant production personnel.[190] The term "compensation" does not include participations and residuals (as defined in section 167(g)(7)(B)).[191] With respect to property which is one or more episodes in a television series, each episode is treated as a separate production and only the first 44 episodes qualify under the provision.[192] Qualified property does not include sexually explicit productions as defined by section 2257 of title 18 of the U.S. Code.[193]

For purposes of recapture under section 1245, any deduction allowed under section 181 is treated as if it were a deduction allowable for amortization.[194]

Explanation of Provision

The provision modifies the dollar limitation so that the first $15 million ($20 million for productions in low income communities or distressed area or isolated area of distress) of an otherwise qualified film or television production may be treated as an expense in cases where the aggregate cost of the production exceeds the dollar limitation. The cost of the production in excess of the dollar limitation is capitalized and recovered under the taxpayer's method of accounting for the recovery of such property.

Effective Date

The provision applies to qualified film and television productions commencing after December 31, 2007.

[Law at ¶ 5265. CCH Explanation at ¶ 345.]

[¶ 10,670] Act Sec. C502c. Modification of domestic production activities deduction for film production

Joint Committee on Taxation (J.C.T. REP. No. JCX-75-08)

[Code Sec. 199]

Present Law

In general

Section 199 of the Code provides a deduction from taxable income (or, in the case of an individual, adjusted gross income) that is equal to a portion of the taxpayer's qualified production activities income. For taxable years beginning after 2009, the deduction is nine percent of such income. For taxable years beginning in 2008 and 2009, the deduction is six percent of such

income. The deduction for a taxable year is limited to 50 percent of the wages properly allocable to domestic production gross receipts paid by the taxpayer during the calendar year that ends in such taxable year.[195]

Qualified production activities income

In general, qualified production activities income ("QPAI") is equal to domestic production gross receipts ("DPGR"), reduced by the sum of: (1) the costs of goods sold that are allocable to such receipts; (2) other expenses, losses, or de-

---

[187] For this purpose, a production is treated as commencing on the first date of principal photography.

[188] Sec. 181(a)(2)(A). A qualifying film or television production that is co-produced is eligible for the benefits of the provision only if its aggregate cost, regardless of funding source, does not exceed the threshold.

[189] Sec. 181(a)(2)(B).

[190] Sec. 181(d)(3)(A).

[191] Sec. 181(d)(3)(B).

[192] Sec. 181(d)(2)(B).

[193] Sec. 181(d)(2)(C).

[194] Sec. 1245(a)(2)(C).

[195] For purposes of the provision, "wages" include the sum of the amounts of wages as defined in section 3401(a) and elective deferrals that the taxpayer properly reports to the Social Security Administration with respect to the employment of employees of the taxpayer during the calendar year ending during the taxpayer's taxable year. Elective deferrals include elective deferrals as defined in section 402(g)(3), amounts deferred under section 457, and, designated Roth contributions (as defined in section 402A).

ductions which are properly allocable to such receipts.[196]

Domestic production gross receipts

DPGR generally are gross receipts of a taxpayer that are derived from: (1) any sale, exchange or other disposition, or any lease, rental or license, of qualifying production property ("QPP") that was manufactured, produced, grown or extracted ("MPGE") by the taxpayer in whole or in significant part within the United States;[197] (2) any sale, exchange or other disposition, or any lease, rental or license, of qualified film produced by the taxpayer; (3) any sale, exchange or other disposition of electricity, natural gas, or potable water produced by the taxpayer in the United States; (4) in the case of a taxpayer engaged in the active conduct of a construction trade or business, construction of real property performed in the United States by the taxpayer in the ordinary course of such trade or business;[198] or (5) in the case of a taxpayer engaged in the active conduct of an engineering or architectural services trade or business, engineering or architectural services performed in the United States by the taxpayer in the ordinary course of such trade or business with respect to the construction of real property in the United States.[199]

Domestic production gross receipts do not include any gross receipts of the taxpayer that are derived from: (1) the sale of food or beverages prepared by the taxpayer at a retail establishment; (2) the transmission or distribution of electricity, natural gas, or potable water; or (3) the lease, rental, license, sale, exchange, or other disposition of land.[200]

A special rule for government contracts provides that property that is manufactured or produced by the taxpayer pursuant to a contract with the Federal Government is considered to be DPGR even if title or risk of loss is transferred to the Federal Government before the manufacture or production of such property is complete to the extent required by the Federal Acquisition Regulation.[201]

For purposes of determining DPGR of a partnership and its partners, provided all of the interests in the capital and profits of the partnership are owned by members of the same expanded affiliated group ("EAG") at all times during the taxable year of the partnership, then the partnership and all members of that EAG are treated as a single taxpayer during such period.[202]

Qualifying production property and qualified film

QPP generally includes any tangible personal property, computer software, or sound recordings. "Qualified film" includes any motion picture film or videotape[203] (including live or delayed television programming, but not including certain sexually explicit productions) if 50 percent or more of the total compensation relating to the production of such film (including compensation in the form of residuals and participations)[204] constitutes compensation for services performed in the United States by actors, production personnel, directors, and producers.[205]

Other rules

Qualified production activities income of partnerships and S corporations

With respect to the domestic production activities of a partnership or S corporation, the deduction under section 199 is determined at the partner or shareholder level.[206] In performing the calculation, each partner or shareholder generally will take into account such person's allocable share of the components of the calculation (including domestic production gross receipts; the cost of goods sold allocable to such receipts;

---

[196] Sec. 199(c)(1).

[197] Domestic production gross receipts include gross receipts of a taxpayer derived from any sale, exchange or other disposition of agricultural products with respect to which the taxpayer performs storage, handling or other processing activities (other than transportation activities) within the United States, provided such products are consumed in connection with, or incorporated into, the manufacturing, production, growth or extraction of qualifying production property (whether or not by the taxpayer).

[198] For this purpose, construction activities include activities that are directly related to the erection or substantial renovation of residential and commercial buildings and infrastructure. Substantial renovation would include structural improvements, but not mere cosmetic changes, such as painting, that is not performed in connection with activities that otherwise constitute substantial renovation.

[199] Sec. 199(c)(4)(A).

[200] Sec. 199(c)(4)(B).

[201] Sec. 199(c)(4)(C).

[202] Sec. 199(c)(4)(D).

[203] The nature of the material on which properties described in section 168(f)(3) are embodied and the methods and means of distribution of such properties does not affect their qualification under this provision.

[204] To the extent that a taxpayer has included an estimate of participations and/or residuals in its income forecast calculation under section 167(g), the taxpayer must use the same estimate of participations and/or residuals for purposes of determining total compensation.

[205] Sec. 199(c)(6).

[206] Sec. 199(d)(1)(A)(i).

and other expenses, losses, or deductions allocable to such receipts) from the partnership or S corporation as well as any items relating to the partner or shareholder's own qualified production activities, if any.[207] Each partner or shareholder is treated as having W-2 wages for the taxable year in an amount equal to such person's allocable share of the W-2 wages of the partnership or S corporation for the taxable year.[208]

The Treasury regulations provide that, except for certain qualifying in-kind partnerships and EAG partnerships, an owner of a pass-thru entity is not treated as conducting the qualified production activities of the of the pass-thru entity, and vice versa.[209]

Alternative minimum tax

The deduction under section 199 is allowed for purposes of computing alternative minimum taxable income (including adjusted current earnings), without regard to alternative minimum tax adjustments.[210] The deduction in computing alternative minimum taxable income is determined by reference to the lesser of the qualified production activities income (as determined for the regular tax) or the alternative minimum taxable income (in the case of an individual, adjusted gross income as determined for the regular tax) without regard to this deduction.[211]

Explanation of Provision

The provision modifies the W-2 wage limitation by defining the term "W-2 wages" for qualified films to include any compensation for services performed in the United States by actors, production personnel, directors, and producers. Thus, compensation is not restricted to W-2 wages for the limitation of qualified films.

The provision provides that a qualified film includes any copyrights, trademarks, and other intangibles with respect to the film.

The provision provides that the deduction under section 199 for qualified films is not affected by the methods and means of distributing an otherwise qualified film.[212] For example, the distribution of a qualified film via the internet (whether the film is viewed online or downloaded or whether or not there is a fee charged) is considered to be a disposition of the film for purposes of determining DPGR. Likewise, the distribution of a qualified film through an open air (free of charge) broadcast is considered a disposition of the film for these purposes.

The provision modifies the application of section 199 to partnerships and S corporations. First, the provision provides that each partner with at least a 20 percent capital interest or shareholder with at least a 20 percent ownership interest, either directly or indirectly, in such entity is treated as having engaged directly in any film produced by the partnership or S corporation. For example, Studio A and Studio B form a partnership in which each is a 50-percent partner to produce a qualified film. Studio A has the rights to distribute the film domestically and Studio B has the rights to distribute the film outside the United States. Under the provision, the production activities of the partnership are attributed to each partner, and thus each partner's revenue from the distribution of the qualified film is not treated as non-DPGR solely because neither Studio A nor Studio B produced the qualified film itself. Additionally, a partnership or S corporation is treated as having engaged directly in any film produced by any partner with at least a 20 percent capital interest or shareholder with at least a 20 percent ownership interest, either directly or indirectly, in the partnership or S corporation. For example, Studio A and Studio B form a partnership in which each is a 50-percent partner to distribute a qualified film. Studio A produced the film and contributes it to the partnership and Studio B contributes distribution services to the partnership. Under the provision, the production activities of Studio A are attributed to the partnership, and thus the partnership's revenue from the distribution of the qualified film is not treated as non-DPGR solely because the partnership did not produce the qualified film. Thus, the Treasury regulation providing that an owner of a pass-thru entity is not treated as conducting the qualified production activities of the of the pass-thru entity, and vice versa,[213] does not apply to situations to which this provision applies.

Effective Date

The provision is effective for taxable years beginning after December 31, 2007.

[Law at ¶ 5280. CCH Explanation at ¶ 368.]

---

[207] Sec. 199(d)(1)(A)(ii).

[208] Sec. 199(d)(1)(A)(iii).

[209] Treas. Reg. sec. 1.199-5T(g).

[210] Sec. 199(d)(6)(A).

[211] Sec. 199(d)(6)(A).

[212] This provision is consistent with H.R. Conf. Rep. No. 108-755, at 262, Footnote 30 (2004).

[213] Treas. Reg. sec. 1.199-5T(g).

[¶10,680] Act Sec. C503. Exemption from excise tax for certain wooden and fiberglass arrows designed for use by children

Joint Committee on Taxation (J.C.T. REP. NO. JCX-75-08)

[Code Sec. 4161]

Present Law

Under present law, section 4161(b)(2) of the Code imposes an excise tax of 39 cents, adjusted for inflation, on the first sale by the manufacturer, producer, or importer of any shaft (whether sold separately or incorporated as part of a finished or unfinished product) used to produce certain types of arrows.[214] These taxes support the Federal Aid to Wildlife Restoration Fund.[215]

Explanation of Provision

The provision exempts from the excise tax on arrow shafts certain shafts (whether sold sep-arately or incorporated as part of a finished or unfinished product) that are all fiberglass and hollow, or made of all natural wood. The shaft cannot be in excess of 5/16 of an inch in diameter and cannot have any laminations or artificial means of enhancing the spine of the shaft. The shaft must be of a type used in the manufacture of an arrow which after its assembly is not suitable for use with a bow that has a peak draw weight of 30 pounds or more.

Effective Date

This provision applies to shafts first sold after the date of enactment.

[Law at ¶5420. CCH Explanation at ¶840.]

[¶10,690] Act Sec. C506. Modified standard for imposition of tax return preparer penalties

Joint Committee on Taxation (J.C.T. REP. NO. JCX-75-08)

[Code Sec. 6694]

Present Law

The provision revises the definition of an "unreasonable position" and changes the standards for imposition of the tax return preparer penalty. The preparer standard for undisclosed positions is reduced to "substantial authority," which conforms to the taxpayer standard. The preparer standard for disclosed positions is set at "reasonable basis." The preparer standard for reportable transactions, to which section 6662A applies (i.e., listed transactions and reportable transactions with significant avoidance or evasion purposes), remains unchanged. For reportable transactions the preparer must have a reasonable belief that the position would more likely than not be sustained on its merits.

Prior to enactment of the Small Business and Work Opportunity Tax Act of 2007, an income tax return preparer who prepared a tax return with respect to which there was an understatement of tax that was due to an undisclosed position for which there was not a realistic possibility of being sustained on its merits was liable for a $250 penalty. For a disclosed position, the preparer was liable only if the position was frivolous.

Legislation enacted as part of the Small Business and Work Opportunity Tax Act of 2007 broadened the scope of the preparer penalty by applying it to all tax return preparers and altered the standards of conduct a tax return preparer is required to meet in order to avoid the imposition of penalties for the preparation of a return with respect to which there is an understatement of tax. A tax return preparer now can be penalized for preparing a return on which there is an understatement of tax liability as a result of an "unreasonable position." Any position that a return preparer does not reasonably believe is more likely than not to be sustained on its merits is an "unreasonable position" unless the position is disclosed on the return and there is a reasonable basis for the position.

In general, the term "tax return preparer" is broadly defined as any person who prepares for compensation, or who employs one or more persons to prepare for compensation, any return of

---

[214] The tax on arrow shafts is 43 cents per arrow shaft beginning January 1, 2008.

[215] 16 U.S.C. sec. 669b

tax or any claim for refund of tax.[216] Preparation of a substantial portion of a return is treated as if it were the preparation of such return.

Explanation of Provision

The provision revises the definition of an "unreasonable position" and changes the standards for imposition of the tax return preparer penalty. The preparer standard for undisclosed positions is reduced to "substantial authority," which conforms to the taxpayer standard. The preparer standard for disclosed positions is set at "reasonable basis." The preparer standard for reportable transactions, to which section 6662A applies (i.e., listed transactions and reportable

transactions with significant avoidance or evasion purposes), remains unchanged. For reportable transactions the preparer must have a reasonable belief that the position would more likely than not be sustained on its merits.

Effective Date

The provision generally is effective with respect to returns prepared after May 25, 2007. In the case of reportable transactions, the provision is effective for returns prepared for taxable years beginning after the date of enactment.

[Law at ¶ 5470. CCH Explanation at ¶ 705.]

[¶ 10,700] Act Sec. C704. Additional low-income housing credit allocations for disaster areas

Joint Committee on Taxation (J.C.T. Rep. No. JCX-73-08)

[Code Sec. 42(h)]

Present Law

In general

The low-income housing credit may be claimed over a 10-year period by owners of certain residential rental property for the cost of rental housing occupied by tenants having incomes below specified levels (sec. 42). The amount of the credit for any taxable year in the credit period is the applicable percentage of the qualified basis of each qualified low-income building. The qualified basis of any qualified low-income building for any taxable year equals the applicable fraction of the eligible basis of the building.

Volume limits

A low-income housing credit is allowable only if the owner of a qualified building receives a housing credit allocation from the State or local housing credit agency. Generally, the aggregate credit authority provided annually to each State for calendar years 2008 and 2009 is $2.20 per resident, with a minimum annual cap for certain small population States. In 2010, the volume limits will return to lower prescribed levels. These amounts are indexed for inflation. Projects that also receive financing with proceeds of tax-exempt bonds issued subject to the private activity bond volume limit do not require an allocation of the low-income housing credit.

Certain distressed areas

Special allocations of the low income credit are not provided for distressed areas on a regular basis but rather must be separately enacted on a case-by-case basis (e.g., Gulf Opportunity Zones).

Explanation of Provision

The provision provides a National pool of additional low-income credit allocations for Federally declared disaster areas. The total amount of these additional allocations is capped at $190 million. All allocations under the provision must be made by the Secretary of the Treasury (the "Secretary") after consultation with the Director of the Federal Emergency Management Agency (e.g., providing information to help verify that areas satisfy the requirements necessary to be a housing loss disaster area). The allocations must be made ratably over the four-year period 2008-2011 unless the Secretary determines that a different allocation is warranted by the severity or frequency of Federally declared disasters in the period. A State must apply for these allocations to be eligible.

An allocation under this provision is available only to States which include a disaster area. In making these allocations the Secretary is to give priority to housing loss disaster areas but may also provide allocations in respect to other buildings in the disaster area but outside of the

---

[216] Sec. 7701(a)(36)(A).

housing loss disaster areas. If a priority allocation is made then such priority allocation must be used in the housing loss disaster area pursuant to the terms of the priority allocation. For these purposes, a housing loss disaster area is a county or municipality: (1) where the lesser of 1,000 dwelling units or ten percent of the total dwelling units in such county or municipality have been rendered uninhabitable by reason of damage or destruction caused by a Federally declared disaster area; and (2) located in a Federally declared disaster area.[26]

Any allocation made by the Secretary which is subsequently terminated by the Secretary (e.g., because of lack of use) shall not be treated like other allocation amounts under the present-law

housing credit dollar rules but rather shall be eligible for reallocation by the Secretary pursuant to the otherwise applicable rules of the provision.

The additional allocations allowed under the provision may only be made with respect to disasters occurring after December 31, 2007 and before January 1, 2012. No allocations under this provision may be made after December 31, 2012.

Effective Date

The provision applies to credit allocations made after the date of enactment.

[Law at ¶7183. CCH Explanation at ¶650.]

[¶10,710] Act Sec. C706. Losses attributable to federally declared disasters

Joint Committee on Taxation (J.C.T. REP. NO. JCX-73-08)

[Code Secs. 63 and 165]

Present Law

Casualty losses

Under present law, a taxpayer may generally claim a deduction for any loss sustained during the taxable year and not compensated by insurance or otherwise.[2] For individual taxpayers, deductible losses must be incurred in a trade or business or other profit-seeking activity or consist of property losses arising from fire, storm, shipwreck, or other casualty, or from theft. Personal casualty or theft losses for the taxable year are allowable only if they exceed a $100 limitation per casualty or theft.[3] In addition, aggregate net casualty and theft losses are deductible only to the extent they exceed 10 percent of an individual taxpayer's adjusted gross income.[4] If the disaster occurs in a Presidentially declared disaster area, the taxpayer may elect to take into account the casualty loss in the taxable year immediately preceding the taxable year in which the disaster occurs.[5]

Standard deduction

An individual taxpayer's taxable income is computed by reducing adjusted gross income either by a standard deduction or, if the taxpayer elects, by the taxpayer's itemized deductions.

Unless an individual elects, no itemized deductions are allowed for the taxable year. The deduction for casualty losses is an itemized deduction.

Explanation of Provision

Waiver of adjusted gross income limitation for personal casualty losses

The provision waives the 10 percent of adjusted gross income limitation for a "net disaster loss." The term "net disaster loss" means the excess of personal casualty losses attributable to a "Federally declared disaster" occurring after December 31, 2007, and before January 1, 2012, occurring in a "disaster area," over personal casualty gains. The term "Federally declared disaster" means any disaster subsequently determined by the President of the United States to warrant assistance by the Federal Government under the Robert T. Stafford Disaster Relief and Emergency Assistance Act. The term "disaster area" means the area so determined to warrant assistance.

Net disaster losses are deductible without regard to whether aggregate net casualty losses exceed 10 percent of a taxpayer's adjusted gross income. For purposes of applying the 10-percent limitation to other personal casualty or theft

---

[26] See section 2 of this bill for this definition of Federally declared disaster.

[2] Sec. 165.

[3] Sec. 165(h)(1).

[4] Sec. 165(h)(2).

[5] Sec. 165(i).

losses, losses deductible under this provision are disregarded. Thus, the provision has the effect of treating net disaster losses attributable to Federally declared disasters as a deduction separate from all other non-disaster casualty and theft losses.

The following examples show the application of the provision.

Example 1.-An individual taxpayer with $100,000 of adjusted gross income has the following personal casualty items during the taxable year: $5,000 personal casualty gain, $30,000 allowable personal casualty loss attributable to a Federally declared disaster, and a $7,000 allowable personal casualty loss.[6] The deductible net disaster loss is $25,000 ($30,000 disaster casualty loss less the $5,000 personal casualty gain). The deductible non-disaster casualty loss is $0 ($7,000 non-disaster casualty loss less $10,000 (10 percent of adjusted gross income)) limitation. The taxpayer's deductible net personal casualty loss for the taxable year is $25,000 (the sum of the net disaster loss and the excess of the other casualty losses over the 10-percent limitation).

Example 2.-An individual taxpayer with $100,000 of adjusted gross income has the following personal casualty items during the taxable year: $5,000 personal casualty gain, $30,000 allowable personal casualty loss attributable to a Federally declared disaster, and a $12,000 allowable personal casualty loss.[7] The deductible net disaster loss is $25,000 ($30,000 disaster casualty loss less the $5,000 personal casualty gain). The deductible non-disaster casualty loss is $2,000 ($12,000 non-disaster casualty loss less $10,000

(10 percent of adjusted gross income)) limitation. The taxpayer's deductible net personal casualty loss for the taxable year is $27,000 (the sum of the net disaster loss and the excess of the other casualty losses over the 10-percent limitation).

Increase of standard deduction

The provision increases an individual taxpayer's standard deduction by the "disaster loss deduction." The "disaster loss deduction" is defined as the net disaster loss.

Increase of limitation per casualty

The provision increases the $100 limitation per casualty to $500 for taxable years beginning after December 31, 2008, and before January 1, 2012.

Effective Dates

The provision generally applies to taxable years beginning after December 31, 2007.

The provision applies to the taxpayer's last taxable year beginning before January 1, 2008, solely for purposes of determining the amount allowable as a deduction with respect to any net disaster loss for such year by reason of an election under section 165(i).

The portion of the provision increasing the limitation per casualty to $500 applies to taxable years beginning after December 31, 2008, and before January 1, 2012.

[Law at ¶5175, ¶5185, ¶5200, ¶5225, ¶5240, ¶5355,¶5480 and ¶7186. CCH Explanation at ¶605.]

[¶10,720] Act Sec. C707. Expensing of qualified disaster expenses

Joint Committee on Taxation (J.C.T. REP. NO. JCX-73-08)

[New Code Sec. 198A]

Present Law

In general

Present law allows a deduction for ordinary and necessary expenses paid or incurred in carrying on any trade or business.[8] Section 263(a)(1) limits the scope of section 162 by prohibiting a current deduction for certain capital expendi-

tures. Treasury regulations define "capital expenditures" as amounts paid or incurred to add to the value, or substantially prolong the useful life, of property owned by the taxpayer, or to adapt property to a new or different use.[9] Amounts paid or incurred for incidental repairs and maintenance of property that neither materially add to the value of the property nor appreciably prolong its life are not considered to be

---

[6] The allowable casualty losses are after application of the limitation per casualty (the limitation per casualty under section 165(h)(1).

[7] *Id.*

[8] Sec. 162.

[9] Treas. Reg. sec. 1.263(a)-1(b).

capital expenditures and may be deducted currently.[10] The determination of whether an expense is deductible or capitalizable is based on the facts and circumstances of each case.

Environmental remediation costs

Taxpayers may elect to treat certain environmental remediation expenditures paid or incurred before January 1, 2008, that would otherwise be chargeable to capital account as deductible in the year paid or incurred.[11] The deduction applies for both regular and alternative minimum tax purposes. The expenditure must be incurred in connection with the abatement or control of hazardous substances at a qualified contaminated site. In general, any expenditure for the acquisition of depreciable property used in connection with the abatement or control of hazardous substances at a qualified contaminated site does not constitute a qualified environmental remediation expenditure. However, depreciation deductions allowable for such property, which would otherwise be allocated to the site under the principles set forth in Commissioner v. Idaho Power Co.[12] and section 263A, are treated as qualified environmental remediation expenditures.

A "qualified contaminated site" (a so-called "brownfield") generally is any property that is held for use in a trade or business, for the production of income, or as inventory and is certified by the appropriate State environmental agency to be an area at or on which there has been a release (or threat of release) or disposal of a hazardous substance. Both urban and rural property may qualify. However, sites that are identified on the national priorities list under the Comprehensive Environmental Response, Compensation, and Liability Act of 1980 ("CERCLA")[13] cannot qualify as targeted areas. Hazardous substances generally are defined by reference to sections 101(14) and 102 of CERCLA, subject to additional limitations applicable to asbestos and similar substances within buildings, certain naturally occurring substances such as radon, and certain other substances released into drinking water supplies due to deterioration through ordinary use, as well as petroleum products defined in section 4612(a)(3) of the Code.

In the case of property to which a qualified environmental remediation expenditure otherwise would have been capitalized, any deduction allowed under section 198 is treated as a depreciation deduction and the property is treated as section 1245 property. Thus, deductions for qualified environmental remediation expenditures are subject to recapture as ordinary income upon a sale or other disposition of the property. In addition, sections 280B (demolition of structures) and 468 (special rules for mining and solid waste reclamation and closing costs) do not apply to amounts that are treated as expenses under this provision.

Section 1400N(g) permits the expensing of environmental remediation expenditures paid or incurred on or after August 28, 2005, and before January 1, 2008, to abate contamination at qualified contaminated sites located in the Gulf Opportunity Zone.

Debris removal and demolition of structures

Under present law, the cost of demolishing a structure is generally capitalized into the taxpayer's basis in the land on which the structure is located.[14] Land is not subject to an allowance for depreciation or amortization.

The treatment of the cost of debris removal depends on the nature of the costs incurred. For example, the cost of debris removal after a storm may in some cases constitute an ordinary and necessary business expense which is deductible in the year paid or incurred. In other cases, debris removal costs may be in the nature of replacement of part of the property that was damaged. In such cases, the costs are capitalized and added to the taxpayer's basis in the property. For example, Revenue Ruling 71-161[15] permits the use of clean-up costs as a measure of casualty loss but requires that such costs be added to the post-casualty basis of the property.

Section 1400N(f) provides a special rule for certain demolition and clean-up costs. Under the provision, a taxpayer is permitted a deduction for 50 percent of any qualified Gulf Opportunity Zone clean-up cost paid or incurred on or after August 28, 2005, and before January 1, 2008. The remaining 50 percent is capitalized and treated under the general rules. A qualified Gulf Opportunity Zone clean-up cost is an amount paid or incurred for the removal of debris from, or the demolition of structures on, real property located in the Gulf Opportunity Zone to the extent that the amount would otherwise be capitalized. In order to qualify, the property must be held for use in a trade or business, for the production of income, or as inventory. This special rule also

---

[10] Treas. Reg. sec. 1.162-4 and 1.263(a)-1(b).

[11] Sec. 198.

[12] 418 U.S. 1 (1974).

[13] Pub. L. No. 96-510 (1980).

[14] Sec. 280B.

[15] 1971-1 C.B. 76.

applies to the Kansas disaster area, as added by the Heartland, Habitat, Harvest, and Horticulture Act of 2008.[16]

Repair of business property

As described above, the cost of incidental repairs that neither materially add to the value of property nor appreciably prolong its life, but keep it in an ordinarily efficient operating condition, may be deducted currently as a business expense. In the case of repair expenditures incurred subsequent to a casualty event, the IRS ruled in 1999 that the costs of restoring uninsured property damage caused by severe flooding was that the determination of whether the costs are deductible as repairs or capital expenditures "turns on the taxpayer's particular set of facts."[17] In other words, the treatment of the costs to restore the property after a casualty is determined based on the general treatment of such costs, regardless of the fact that such costs are incurred as a result of a casualty event. In August 2006, Treasury issued proposed regulations with a different view, providing that amounts paid or incurred to restore property are required to be capitalized to the extent the taxpayer deducts a casualty loss under section 165 with respect to the same property.[18] This proposes mandatory capitalization of costs incurred by a taxpayer to repair property after suffering a casualty loss. In an internal legal memorandum issued after the proposed Treasury regulations were issued, the IRS stated that the proposed regulations, which contained a prospective effective date when finalized, were "essentially reflective of current law."[19] In March 2008, Treasury reissued the proposed regulations with the same treatment of restoration expenditures of property destroyed in a casualty.

Explanation of Provision

Under the provision, a taxpayer may elect to treat any qualified disaster expense that is paid or incurred by the taxpayer as a deduction for the taxable year in which paid or incurred. For purposes of the provision, a qualified disaster expense is any otherwise capitalizable expenditure paid or incurred in connection with a trade or business or with business-related property that is: (1) for the abatement or control of hazardous substances that were released on account of a Federally declared disaster;[20] (2) for the removal of debris from, or the demolition of structures on, real property damaged or destroyed as a result of a Federally declared disaster; or (3) for the repair of business-related property damaged as a result of a Federally declared disaster. No inference is intended as to the proper present law treatment of expenditures to repair business-related property damaged in a casualty event. The purpose of this provision is to provide that, in any case in which such costs are otherwise required to be capitalized, the costs may be deducted in the taxable year paid or incurred to the extent incurred as a result of a Federally declared disaster.

For purposes of this provision, "business-related property" is property held by the taxpayer for use in a trade or business, for the production of income, or as inventory, and a Federally declared disaster is any disaster occurring after December 31, 2007, and before January 1, 2012, that is subsequently determined by the President of the United States to warrant assistance by the Federal Government under the Robert T. Stafford Disaster Relief and Emergency Assistance Act.

For purposes of recapture as ordinary income, any deduction allowed under this provision is treated as a deduction for depreciation and section 1245 property for purposes or depreciation recapture.

Effective Date

The provision is effective for amounts paid or incurred after December 31, 2007.

[Law at ¶5275 and ¶7186. CCH Explanation at ¶615.]

---

[16] Pub. L. No. 110-234, sec. 15345(a)(3) (2008).

[17] CCA 199903030.

[18] Prop. Reg. sec. 1.263(a)-3(f)(3)(iv). 2006-2 C.B. 532.

[19] AM 2006-006, footnote 2.

[20] See section 2 of this bill for the definition of Federally declared disaster.

[¶10,730] Act Sec. C708. Net operating losses attributable to federally declared disasters

Joint Committee on Taxation (J.C.T. Rep. No. JCX-73-08)

[Code Sec. 172]

Present Law

Under present law, a net operating loss ("NOL") is, generally, the amount by which a taxpayer's business deductions exceed its gross income. In general, an NOL may be carried back two years and carried over 20 years to offset taxable income in such years.[21] NOLs offset taxable income in the order of the taxable years to which the NOL may be carried.[22]

Different rules apply with respect to NOLs arising in certain circumstances. A three-year carryback applies with respect to NOLs (1) arising from casualty or theft losses of individuals, or (2) attributable to Presidentially declared disasters for taxpayers engaged in a farming business or a small business. A five-year carryback applies to NOLs (1) arising from a farming loss (regardless of whether the loss was incurred in a Presidentially declared disaster area), or (2) certain amounts related to the Gulf Opportunity Zone and Kansas disaster area. Special rules also apply to real estate investment trusts (no carryback), specified liability losses (10-year carryback), and excess interest losses (no carryback to any year preceding a corporate equity reduction transaction). Additionally, a special rule applies to certain electric utility companies.

Explanation of Provision

The provision provides a special five-year carryback period for NOLs to the extent of a qualified disaster loss. For purposes of the provision, a qualified disaster loss is the lesser of: (1) the sum of (a) section 165 losses for the taxable year attributable to a Federally declared disaster[23] occurring after December 31, 2007, and before January 1, 2012, and occurring in a disaster area,[24] and (b) the deduction for the taxable year for qualified disaster expenses allowable under section 198A(a)[25] or which would be allowable as a deduction under that section if not treated as an expense in another section of the Code; or (2) the NOL for the taxable year.

The amount of the NOL to which the five-year carryback period applies is limited to the amount of the corporation's overall NOL for the taxable year. Any remaining portion of the taxpayer's NOL is subject to the general two-year carryback period. Ordering rules similar to those for specified liability losses apply to losses carried back under the provision.

Any taxpayer entitled to the five-year carryback under this provision may elect to have the carryback period determined without regard to this provision. In addition, the general rule which limits a taxpayer's NOL deduction to 90 percent of AMTI does not apply to any NOL to which the five-year carryback period applies under the provision. Instead, a taxpayer may apply such NOL carrybacks to offset up to 100 percent of AMTI.

Effective Date

The provision is effective for net operating losses for taxable years beginning after December 31, 2007.

[Law at ¶5175, ¶5240 and ¶7186. CCH Explanation at ¶610.]

---

[21] Sec. 172(b)(1)(A).

[22] Sec. 172(b)(2).

[23] See section 2 of this bill for the definition of Federally declared disaster.

[24] See section 2 of this bill for the definition of disaster area.

[25] See section 3 of this bill.

[¶10,740] Act Sec. C709. Special rules for mortgage revenue bonds in federally declared disaster areas

Joint Committee on Taxation (J.C.T. REP. NO. JCX-73-08)

[Code Sec. 143]

Present Law

In general

Under present law, gross income does not include interest on State or local bonds (sec. 103). State and local bonds are classified generally as either governmental bonds or private activity bonds. Governmental bonds are bonds which are primarily used to finance governmental functions or which are repaid with governmental funds. Private activity bonds are bonds with respect to which the State or local government serves as a conduit providing financing to nongovernmental persons (e.g., private businesses or individuals). The exclusion from income for State and local bonds does not apply to private activity bonds, unless the bonds are issued for certain permitted purposes ("qualified private activity bonds") (secs. 103(b)(1) and 141).

Qualified mortgage bonds

Generally

The definition of a qualified private activity bond includes a qualified mortgage bond (sec. 143). Qualified mortgage bonds are issued to make mortgage loans to qualified mortgagors for the purchase, improvement, or rehabilitation of owner-occupied residences. Rehabilitation loans are eligible for such financing if: (1) the mortgagor receiving the financing is the first resident after the completion of the rehabilitation; (2) at least 20 years have elapsed between the first use of the residence and the start of the physical work of the rehabilitation; (3) certain percentages of internal and external walls are retained after the rehabilitation; and (4) rehabilitation expenditures equal at least 25 percent of the taxpayer's adjusted basis in the residence after such rehabilitation (sec. 141 (k)(5)).

The Code imposes several limitations on qualified mortgage bonds, including purchase price limitations for the home financed with bond proceeds and income limitations for homebuyers. In general the purchase price limitation is met if the acquisition cost of each residence financed does not exceed 90 percent of the average area purchase applicable to the residence (i.e., the average single-family residence purchase price purchased during the one-year period in the statistical area in which the resi-

dence is located) (sec. 141(e)). Also, the income limitation generally is met if all the owner-financing provided under the issue is provided to individuals who have family income of 115 percent of the applicable median family income (sec. 141(f)).

First-time homebuyers

In addition to the purchase price and income limitations, qualified mortgage bonds generally cannot be used to finance a mortgage for a homebuyer who had an ownership interest in a principal residence in the three years preceding the execution of the mortgage (the "first-time homebuyer" requirement) (sec. 141 (d)). The first-time homebuyer requirement does not apply to targeted area residences (described below).

Special rules for targeted area residences

A targeted area residence is one located in either (1) a census tract in which at least 70 percent of the families have an income which is 80 percent or less of the state-wide median income or (2) an area of chronic economic distress (sec. 141(j)).

In addition to the waiver of the first-time homebuyer rule, targeted area residences have special purchase price limitations and income limitations. For targeted area residences, the purchase price limitation is applied by substituting 110 percent for 90 percent. (i.e., the purchase price limitation is met if the acquisition cost of each residence financed does not exceed 110 percent of the average area purchase applicable to the residence). For targeted area residences, the income limitation generally is met if at least two-thirds of all the owner-financing provided under the issue is provided to individuals who have family income of 140 percent of the applicable median family income. The other third is not subject to an income limitation.

Special rules for Federally disaster areas

A temporary provision waives the first-time homebuyer requirement for residences located in Federally declared disaster areas (sec. 143(k)(11)). Also, under the provision, residences located in Federally declared disaster areas are treated as targeted area residences for purposes of the income and purchase price limitations. The special rules for residences located in Federally declared disaster areas applies to bonds issued after May 1, 2008 and before January 1, 2010.

Explanation of Provision

The provision replaces the temporary present-law provision for residences located in Federally declared disaster areas with: (1) a waiver of the first-time homebuyer requirement; and (2) the purchase price limitation otherwise applicable to targeted area residences (i.e., the purchase price limitation is met if the acquisition cost of each residence financed does not exceed 110 percent of the average area purchase applicable to the residence). The provision applies for the two-year period beginning on the date of the disaster, when the principal residence of a taxpayer is: (1) rendered unsafe for use by reason of a Federally declared disaster, or (2) demolished or relocated by reason of an order of the government of a State of political subdivision thereof on account of a Federally declared disaster.

Also, the provision expands the definition of rehabilitation loans to include the cost of repair or reconstruction of a taxpayer's principal residence for damage from a Federally declared disaster regardless of whether the present-law rehabilitation requirements are satisfied. Such rehabilitation loans are limited to the lesser of $150,000 or the cost of repair or reconstruction.

For purposes of the provision, the term Federally declared disaster has the same definition as in section 2 of this bill except that it does not apply to any disaster occurring before January 1, 2008, or after December 31, 2011.

Effective Date

The provision is effective for bonds issued after the date of enactment.

[Law at ¶5210 and ¶7186. CCH Explanation at ¶645.]

[¶10,750] Act Sec. C801. Modify tax treatment of nonqualified deferred compensation from certain tax indifferent parties

Joint Committee on Taxation (J.C.T. REP. NO. JCX-75-08)

[New Code Sec. 457A]

Present Law

In general

Under present law, the determination of when amounts deferred under a nonqualified deferred compensation arrangement are includible in the gross income of the person earning the compensation depends on the facts and circumstances of the arrangement. A variety of tax principles and Code provisions may be relevant in making this determination, including the doctrine of constructive receipt, the economic benefit doctrine,[269] the provisions of section 83 relating generally to transfers of property in connection with the performance of services, provisions relating specifically to nonexempt employee trusts (sec. 402(b)) and nonqualified annuities (sec. 403(c)), and the requirements of section 409A.

In general, the time for income inclusion of nonqualified deferred compensation depends on whether the arrangement is unfunded or funded. If the arrangement is unfunded, then the

compensation generally is includible in income by a cash-basis taxpayer when it is actually or constructively received. If the arrangement is funded, then income is includible for the year in which the individual's rights are transferable or not subject to a substantial risk of forfeiture.

An arrangement generally is considered funded if there has been a transfer of property under section 83. Under that section, a transfer of property occurs when a person acquires a beneficial ownership interest in such property. The term "property" is defined very broadly for purposes of section 83.[270] Property includes real and personal property other than money or an unfunded and unsecured promise to pay money in the future. Property also includes a beneficial interest in assets (including money) that are transferred or set aside from claims of the creditors of the transferor; for example, in a trust or escrow account. Accordingly, if, in connection with the performance of services, vested contributions are made to a trust on an individual's behalf and the trust assets may be used solely to provide future payments to the individual, the

---

[269] See, e.g., *Sproull v. Commissioner*, 16 T.C. 244 (1951), aff'd, per curiam, 194 F.2d 541 (6th Cir. 1952); Rev. Rul. 60-31, 1960-1 C.B. 174.

[270] Treas. Reg. sec. 1.83-3(e). This definition, in part, reflects previous IRS rulings on nonqualified deferred compensation.

payment of the contributions to the trust constitutes a transfer of property to the individual that is taxable under section 83. On the other hand, deferred amounts generally are not includible in income if nonqualified deferred compensation is payable from general corporate funds that are subject to the claims of general creditors, as such amounts are treated as unfunded and unsecured promises to pay money or property in the future.

As discussed above, if the arrangement is unfunded, then the compensation generally is includible in income by a cash-basis taxpayer when it is actually or constructively received under section 451.[271] Income is constructively received when it is credited to a person's account, set apart, or otherwise made available so that it may be drawn on at any time. Income is not constructively received if the taxpayer's control of its receipt is subject to substantial limitations or restrictions. A requirement to relinquish a valuable right in order to make withdrawals is generally treated as a substantial limitation or restriction.

Prior to the enactment of section 409A, arrangements had developed in an effort to provide employees with security for nonqualified deferred compensation, while still allowing deferral of income inclusion under the constructive receipt doctrine (which applies to unfunded arrangements). One such arrangement is a "rabbi trust." A rabbi trust is a trust or other fund established by the employer to hold assets from which nonqualified deferred compensation payments will be made. The trust or fund is generally irrevocable and does not permit the employer to use the assets for purposes other than to provide nonqualified deferred compensation, except that the terms of the trust or fund provide that the assets are subject to the claims of the employer's creditors in the case of insolvency or bankruptcy. In the case of a rabbi trust, these terms had been the basis for the conclusion that the creation of a rabbi trust does not cause the related nonqualified deferred compensation arrangement to be funded for income tax purposes.[272] As a result, no amount was included in income by reason of the rabbi trust; generally income inclusion occurs as payments are made from the trust.

Section 409A

Reason for enactment

The Congress enacted section 409A[273] because it was concerned that many nonqualified deferred compensation arrangements had developed which allowed improper deferral of income. Executives often used arrangements that allowed deferral of income, but also provided security of future payment and control over amounts deferred. For example, nonqualified deferred compensation arrangements often contained provisions that allowed participants to receive distributions upon request, subject to forfeiture of a minimal amount (i.e., a "haircut" provision). In addition, Congress was aware that since the concept of a rabbi trust was developed, techniques had been used that attempted to protect the assets from creditors despite the terms of the trust. For example, the trust or fund would be located in a foreign jurisdiction, making it difficult or impossible for creditors to reach the assets.

Prior to the enactment of section 409A, while the general tax principles governing deferred compensation were well established, the determination whether a particular arrangement effectively allowed deferral of income was generally made on a facts and circumstances basis. There was limited specific guidance with respect to common deferral arrangements. The Congress believed that it was appropriate to provide specific rules regarding whether deferral of income inclusion should be permitted and to provide a clear set of rules that would apply to these arrangements. The Congress believed that certain arrangements that allow participants inappropriate levels of control or access to amounts deferred should not result in deferral of income inclusion. The Congress also believed that certain arrangements, such as offshore trusts, which effectively protect assets from creditors of the employer, should be treated as funded and not result in deferral of income inclusion to the extent the amounts are vested.

General requirements of section 409A

In general.-Under section 409A, all amounts deferred by a service provider under a nonquali-

---

[271] Treas. Reg. secs. 1.451-1 and 1.451-2.

[272] This conclusion was first provided in a 1980 private ruling issued by the IRS with respect to an arrangement covering a rabbi; hence, the popular name "rabbi trust." Priv. Ltr. Rul. 8113107 (Dec. 31, 1980).

[273] Section 409A was added to the Code by section 885 of the American Job Creation Act of 2004, Pub. L. No. 108-357.

fied deferred compensation plan[274] for all taxable years are currently includible in gross income of the service provider to the extent such amounts are not subject to a substantial risk of forfeiture[275] and not previously included in gross income, unless certain requirements are satisfied. If the requirements of section 409A are not satisfied, in addition to current income inclusion, interest at the rate applicable to underpayments of tax plus one percentage point is imposed on the underpayments that would have occurred had the compensation been includible in income when first deferred, or if later, when not subject to a substantial risk of forfeiture. The amount required to be included in income is also subject to a 20-percent additional tax. Section 409A does not limit the amount that may be deferred under a nonqualified deferred compensation plan.

The Secretary of the Treasury is authorized to prescribe regulations as are necessary or appropriate to carry out the purposes of section 409A. The Secretary of the Treasury published final regulations under section 409A on April 17, 2007.[276] Under these regulations, the term "service provider" includes an individual, corporation, subchapter S corporation, partnership, personal service corporation (as defined in section 269A(b)(1)), noncorporate entity that would be a personal service corporation if it were a corporation, or qualified personal service corporation (as defined in section 448(d)(2)) for any taxable year in which such individual or entity accounts for gross income from the performance of services under the cash receipts and disbursements method of accounting.[277] Section 409A does not apply to a service provider that provides significant services to at least two service recipients that are not related to each other or the service provider. This exclusion does not apply to a service provider who is an employee or a director of a corporation (or similar position in the case of an entity that is not a corporation).[278] In addition, the exclusion does not apply to an entity that operates as the manager of a hedge fund or private equity fund. This is because the exclusion does not apply to the extent that a service provider provides management services to a service recipient. Management services for this purpose means services that involve the actual or de facto direction or control of the financial or operational aspects of a trade or business of the service recipient or investment management or advisory services provided to a service recipient whose primary trade or business includes the investment of financial assets, such as a hedge fund.[279]

Permissible distribution events.-Under section 409A, distributions from a nonqualified deferred compensation plan may be allowed only upon separation from service (as determined by the Secretary of the Treasury), death, a specified time (or pursuant to a fixed schedule), change in control of a corporation (to the extent provided by the Secretary of the Treasury), occurrence of an unforeseeable emergency, or if the service provider becomes disabled. A nonqualified deferred compensation plan may not allow distributions other than upon the permissible distribution events and, except as provided in regulations by the Secretary of the Treasury, may not permit acceleration of a distribution. In the case of a specified employee who separates from service, distributions may not be made earlier than six months after the date of the separation from service or upon death. Specified employees are key employees[280] of publicly-traded corporations.

Elections.-Section 409A requires that a plan must provide that compensation for services performed during a taxable year may be deferred at the service provider's election only if the election to defer is made no later than the close of the preceding taxable year, or at such other time as provided in Treasury regulations. In the case of any performance-based compensation based on services performed over a period of at least 12 months, such election may be made no later than six months before the end of the service period. The time and form of distributions must be specified at the time of initial deferral. A plan may allow changes in the time and form of distributions subject to certain requirements.

---

[274] A plan includes an agreement or arrangement, including an agreement or arrangement that includes one person. Amounts deferred also include actual or notional earnings.

[275] The rights of a person to compensation are subject to a substantial risk of forfeiture if the person's rights to such compensation are conditioned upon the performance of substantial services by any individual.

[276] On October 22, 2007, the IRS announced that during 2008, taxpayers are not required to comply with the final regulations. Instead, taxpayers must operate a plan in compliance with section 409A and the otherwise applicable guidance. To the extent an issue is not addressed, a reasonable, good faith interpretation of the statute must be used. Notice 2007-86.

[277] Treas. Reg. sec. 1.409A-1(f)(1).

[278] Treas. Reg. sec. 1.409A-1(f)(2).

[279] Treas. Reg. sec. 1.409A-1(f)(2)(iv).

[280] Key employees are defined in section 416(i) and generally include officers (limited to 50 employees) having annual compensation greater than $150,000 (for 2008), five percent owners, and one percent owners having annual compensation from the employer greater than $150,000.

Back-to-back arrangements.-Back-to-back service recipients (i.e., situations under which an entity receives services from a service provider such as an employee, and the entity in turn provides services to a client) that involve back-to-back nonqualified deferred compensation arrangements (i.e., the fees payable by the client are deferred at both the entity level and the employee level) are subject to special rules under section 409A. For example, the final regulations generally permit the deferral agreement between the entity and its client to treat as a permissible distribution event those events that are specified as distribution events in the deferral agreement between the entity and its employee. Thus, if separation from employment is a specified distribution event between the entity and the employee, the employee's separation generally is a permissible distribution event for the deferral agreement between the entity and its client.[281]

Offshore funding arrangements.-Section 409A requires current income inclusion in the case of certain offshore funding of nonqualified deferred compensation. Under section 409A, in the case of assets set aside (directly or indirectly) in a trust (or other arrangement determined by the Secretary of the Treasury) for purposes of paying nonqualified deferred compensation, such assets are treated as property transferred in connection with the performance of services under section 83 (whether or not such assets are available to satisfy the claims of general creditors) at the time set aside if such assets are located outside of the United States or at the time transferred if such assets are subsequently transferred outside of the United States. Any subsequent increases in the value of, or any earnings with respect to, such assets are treated as additional transfers of property.

Interest at the underpayment rate plus one percentage point is imposed on the underpayments of tax that would have occurred had the amounts set aside been includible in income for the taxable year in which first deferred or, if later, the first taxable year not subject to a substantial risk of forfeiture. The amount required to be included in income also is subject to an additional 20-percent tax.

The special funding rule does not apply to assets located in a foreign jurisdiction if substantially all of the services to which the nonqualified deferred compensation relates are performed in such foreign jurisdiction. The Sec-

retary of the Treasury has authority to exempt arrangements from the provision if the arrangements do not result in an improper deferral of U.S. tax and will not result in assets being effectively beyond the reach of creditors.

Definition of substantial risk of forfeiture

Under the Treasury regulations, compensation is subject to a substantial risk of forfeiture if entitlement to the amount is conditioned upon either the performance of substantial future services by any person or the occurrence of a condition related to a purpose of the compensation, provided that the possibility of forfeiture is substantial.[282]

Definition of nonqualified deferred compensation

Under section 409A, a nonqualified deferred compensation plan generally includes any plan that provides for the deferral of compensation other than a qualified employer plan or any bona fide vacation leave, sick leave, compensatory time, disability pay, or death benefit plan. A qualified employer plan means a qualified retirement plan, tax-deferred annuity, simplified employee pension, and SIMPLE. A qualified governmental excess benefit arrangement (sec. 415(m)) and an eligible deferred compensation plan (sec. 457(b)) is a qualified employer plan.

The Treasury regulations also provide that certain other types of plans are not considered deferred compensation, and thus are not subject to section 409A. For example, if a service recipient transfers property to a service provider, there is no deferral of compensation merely because the value of the property is either not includible in income under section 83 by reason of the property being substantially nonvested or is includible in income because of a valid section 83(b) election.[283] Special rules apply in the case of stock options.[284] Another exception applies to amounts that are not deferred beyond a short period of time after the amount is no longer subject to a substantial risk of forfeiture.[285] Under this exception, there generally is no deferral for purposes of section 409A if the service provider actually or constructively receives the amount on or before the last day of the applicable 2½ month period. The applicable 2½ month period is the period ending on the later of the 15th day of the third month following the end of: (1) the service provider's first taxable year in

---

[281] Treas. Reg. sec. 1.409A-3(i)(6).
[282] Treas. Reg. sec. 1.409A-1(d)(1).
[283] Treas. Reg. Sec. 1.409A-1(b)(6).

[284] Treas. Reg. Sec. 1.409A-1(b)(5).
[285] Treas. Reg. sec. 1.409A-1(b)(4).

which the right to the payment is no longer subject to a substantial risk of forfeiture; or (2) the service recipient's first taxable year in which the right to the payment is no longer subject to a substantial risk of forfeiture.

Special rules apply in the case of stock appreciation rights ("SARs").[286] Under the final Treasury regulations, a SAR is a right to compensation based on the appreciation in value of a specified number of shares of service recipient stock occurring between the date of grant and the date of exercise of such right. The final regulations generally provide that a SAR does not result in a deferral of compensation for purposes of section 409A (and thus is not subject to section 409A) if the compensation payable under the SAR is not greater than the excess of the fair market value of the underlying stock on the date the SAR is exercised over the fair market value of the underlying stock on the date the SAR is granted.[287]

The Treasury regulations provide exclusions from the definition of nonqualified deferred compensation in the case of services performed by individuals who participate in certain foreign plans, including plans covered by an applicable treaty and broad-based foreign retirement plans.[288] In the case of a U.S. citizen or lawful permanent alien, nonqualified deferred compensation plan does not include a broad-based foreign retirement plan, but only with respect to the portion of the plan that provides for nonelective deferral of foreign earned income and subject to limitations on the annual amount deferred under the plan or the annual amount payable under the plan. In general, foreign earned income refers to amounts received by an individual from sources within a foreign country that constitutes earned income attributable to services.

Timing of the service recipient's deduction

Special statutory provisions govern the timing of the deduction for nonqualified deferred compensation, regardless of whether the arrangement covers employees or nonemployees and regardless of whether the arrangement is funded or unfunded.[289] Under these provisions, the amount of nonqualified deferred compensation that is includible in the income of the service provider is deductible by the service recipient for the taxable year in which the amount is includible in the service provider's income.[290] Thus, for example, in the case of an unfunded nonqualified deferred compensation plan, a deduction to the taxable service recipient is deferred until the deferred compensation is actually paid or made available to the service provider.

Section 457

Special income recognition rules apply in the case of a participant in a deferred compensation plan that is sponsored by a State or local government or an organization that is exempt from Federal income tax under section 501(a). Section 457 provides for different income inclusion rules for two basic types of deferred compensation arrangements: (1) arrangements that limit the amount of compensation that may be deferred (generally, $15,500 in 2007) and that meet certain other requirements specified in section 457(b) (referred to as a "section 457(b) plan" or an "eligible deferred compensation plan"); and (2) arrangements that do not satisfy the requirements of section 457(b) (referred to as a "section 457(f) plan" or an "ineligible deferred compensation plan"). Section 457 does not provide a limit on the amount of compensation that may be deferred under a section 457(f) plan.

A participant in a section 457(b) plan does not recognize income with respect to the participant's interest in such plan until the time of actual distribution (or, if earlier, the time the participant's interest is made available to the participant, but only in the case of a section 457(b) plan maintained by a tax-exempt sponsor other than a State or local government). In contrast, a participant in a section 457(f) plan must

---

[286] Treas. Reg. sec. 1.409A-1(b)(5).

[287] Treas. Reg. sec. 1.409A-1(b)(5)(i)(B).

[288] Treas. Reg. sec. 1.409A-1(a)(3).

[289] Secs. 404(a)(5), (b) and (d) and sec. 83(h).

[290] In the case of a publicly held corporation, no deduction is allowed for a taxable year for remuneration with respect to a covered employee to the extent that the remuneration exceeds $1 million. Code sec. 162(m). The Code defines the term "covered employee" in part by reference to Federal securities law. In light of changes to Federal securities law, the Internal Revenue Service interprets the term covered employee as the principal executive officer of the taxpayer as of the close of the taxable year or the three most highly compensated employees of the taxpayer for the taxa-

ble year whose compensation must be disclosed to the taxpayer's shareholders (other than the principal executive officer or the principal financial officer). Notice 2007-49, 2007-25 I.R.B. 1429. For purposes of the deduction limit, remuneration generally includes all remuneration for which a deduction is otherwise allowable, although commission-based compensation and certain performance-based compensation are not subject to the limit. Remuneration does not include compensation for which a deduction is allowable after a covered employee ceases to be a covered employee. Thus, the deduction limitation often does not apply to deferred compensation that is otherwise subject to the deduction limitation (e.g., is not performance-based compensation) because the payment of the compensation is deferred until after termination of employment.

include amounts deferred under such a plan in gross income for the first taxable year in which there is no substantial risk of forfeiture of the rights to such compensation.

Explanation of Provision

In general

Under the provision, any compensation of a service provider that is deferred under a nonqualified deferred compensation plan of a nonqualified entity is includible in gross income by the service provider when there is no substantial risk of forfeiture of the service provider's rights to such compensation. The provision applies in addition to the requirements of section 409A (or any other provision of the Code or general tax law principle) with respect to nonqualified deferred compensation. The term service provider has the same meaning as under the regulations under section 409A except that whether a person is a service provider is determined without regard to the person's method of accounting.

Nonqualified deferred compensation

For purposes of the provision, the term nonqualified deferred compensation plan is defined in the same manner as for purposes of section 409A. As under section 409A, the term nonqualified deferred compensation includes earnings with respect to previously deferred amounts. Earnings are treated in the same manner as the amount deferred to which the earnings relate.

Under the provision, nonqualified deferred compensation includes any arrangement under which compensation is based on the increase in value of a specified number of equity units of the service recipient. Thus, stock appreciation rights (SARs) are treated as nonqualified deferred compensation under the provision, regardless of the exercise price of the SAR. It is not intended that the term nonqualified deferred compensation plan include an arrangement taxable under section 83 providing for the grant of an option on employer stock with an exercise price that is not less than the fair market value of the underlying stock on the date of grant if such arrangement does not include a deferral feature other than the feature that the option holder has the right to exercise the option in the future. The provision is not intended to change the tax treatment of incentive stock options meeting the requirements of section 422 or options granted under an employee stock purchase plan meeting the requirements of section 423. Similarly, nonqualified deferred compensation for purposes of the provision does not include a transfer of property to which section 83 is applicable (such as a transfer of restricted stock), provided that the arrangement does not include a deferral feature. However, it is not intended that the provision be avoided through the use of an instrument (such as an option or a notional principal contract) held or entered into directly or indirectly by a service provider, the value of which is determined in whole or part by reference to the profits or value (or any increase or decrease in the profits or value) of the business of the entity for which the services are effectively provided, particularly when the value of such instrument is not determinable at the time it is granted or received. Similarly, it is not intended that the purposes of the provision be avoided through the use of "springing" partnerships or other entities or rights that come into existence in the future and serve a function similar to a conversion right.

Compensation is not treated as deferred for purposes of the provision if the service provider receives payment of the compensation not later than 12 months after the end of the first taxable year of the service recipient during which the right to the payment of such compensation is no longer subject to a substantial risk of forfeiture.

Nonqualified entity

The term nonqualified entity includes certain foreign corporations and certain partnerships (either domestic or foreign). A foreign corporation is a nonqualified entity unless substantially all of its income is effectively connected with the conduct of a United States trade or business or is subject to a comprehensive foreign income tax. A partnership is a nonqualified entity unless substantially all of its income is, directly or indirectly, allocated to (1) United States persons (other than persons exempt from U.S. income tax); (2) foreign persons with respect to whom such income is subject to a comprehensive foreign income tax; (3) foreign persons with respect to whom such income is effectively connected with the conduct of a United States trade or business and a withholding tax is paid under section 1446 with respect to such income; or (4) organizations which are exempt from US income tax if such income is unrelated business taxable income (as defined in section 512) with respect to such organization. It is intended that substantially all the income of a partnership—whether allocated directly, or, in the case of tiered partnerships, indirectly—be taxed in the hands of partners under the U.S. income tax, or be subject to a comprehensive foreign income tax, for the partnership not to be treated as a nonqualified entity. It is not intended that tiered partnerships, or intermediate entities, be used to achieve deferral of compensation that would otherwise not be permitted under the provision.

The term comprehensive foreign income tax means with respect to a foreign person, the income tax of a foreign country if (1) such person is eligible for the benefits of a comprehensive income tax treaty between such foreign county and the United States, or (2) such person demonstrates to the satisfaction of the Secretary of the Treasury that such foreign country has a comprehensive income tax.

The Secretary may provide guidance concerning the case of a corporation resident in a country that has an income tax treaty with the United States but that does not generally tax the foreign-source income of its residents (a "territorial country"). This guidance may address the question whether, or in which circumstances, substantially all the income of such a corporation will be considered to be subject to a comprehensive income tax if the corporation derives income not only from its country of residence but also from one or more countries that may or may not have tax treaties with the United States. For example, it is intended that if a corporation resident in a territorial country that has an income tax treaty with the United States derives a portion of its income from dividends paid by a subsidiary organized in another country that also has an income tax treaty with the United States, and the dividends are paid out of income that is subject to tax by that other treaty country, the Secretary may provide guidance under which the dividend income is considered subject to a comprehensive income tax in determining whether substantially all of the income of the recipient corporation is subject to a comprehensive income tax.

In the case of a foreign corporation with income that is taxable under section 882, the provision does not apply to compensation which, had such compensation been paid in cash on the date that such compensation ceased to be subject to a substantial risk of forfeiture, would have been deductible by such foreign corporation against such income. The provision does not apply to a nonqualified deferred compensation plan of a nonqualified entity if such compensation is payable to an employee of a domestic subsidiary of such entity and such compensation is reasonably expected to be deductible by such subsidiary under section 404(a)(5) when such compensation is includible in income by such employee.

Additional rules

For purposes of the provision, compensation of a service provider is subject to a substantial risk of forfeiture only if such person's right to the compensation is conditioned upon the future performance of substantial services by any person. Thus, compensation is subject to a substantial risk of forfeiture only if entitlement to the compensation is conditioned on the performance of substantial future services and the possibility of forfeiture is substantial. Substantial risk of forfeiture does not include a condition related to a purpose of the compensation (other than future performance of substantial services), regardless of whether the possibility of forfeiture is substantial.

To the extent provided in regulations prescribed by the Secretary, if compensation is determined solely by reference to the amount of gain recognized on the disposition of an investment asset, such compensation is treated as subject to a substantial risk of forfeiture until the date of such disposition. Investment asset means any single asset (other than an investment fund or similar entity) (1) acquired directly by an investment fund or similar entity, (2) with respect to which such entity does not (nor does any person related to such entity) participate in the active management of such asset (or if such asset is an interest in an entity, in the active management of the assets of such entity), and (3) substantially all of any gain on the disposition of which (other than the nonqualified deferred compensation) is allocated to investors of such entity. The rule only applies if the compensation is determined solely by reference to the gain upon the disposition of an investment asset. Thus, for example, the rule does not apply in the case of an arrangement under which the amount of this compensation is reduced for losses on the disposition of any other asset. With respect to any gain attributable to the period before the asset is treated as no longer subject to a substantial risk of forfeiture, it is intended that Treasury regulations will limit the application of this rule to gain attributable to the period that the service provider is performing services.

The rule is intended to apply to compensation contingent on the disposition of a single asset held as a long-term investment, provided that the service provider does not actively manage the asset (other than the decision to purchase or sell the investment). If the asset is an interest in an entity (such as a company that produces products or services), the rule does not apply if the service provider actively participates in the management of the entity. Active management is intended to include participation in the day-to-day activities of the asset, but does not include the election of a director or other voting rights exercised by shareholders.

The rule is intended to apply solely to compensation arrangements relating to passive investments by an investment fund in a single asset. For example, if an investment fund acquires XYZ operating corporation, the rule is intended to apply to an arrangement that the fund manager receive 20 percent of the gain from the disposition of XYZ operating corporation if the fund manager does not actively participate in the management of XYZ operating corporation. In contrast, the rule does not apply if the investment fund holds two or more operating corporations and the fund manager's compensation is based on the net gain resulting from the disposition of the operating corporations. The rule does not apply to the disposition of a foreign subsidiary which holds a variety of assets the investment of which is managed by the service provider.

Under the provision, if the amount of any deferred compensation is not determinable at the time that such compensation is otherwise required to be taken into account into income under the provision, the amount is taken into account when such amount becomes determinable. This rule applies in lieu of the general rule of the provision, under which deferred compensation is taken into account in income when such compensation is no longer subject to a substantial risk of forfeiture. In addition, the income tax with respect to such amount is increased by the sum of (1) an interest charge, and (2) an amount equal to 20 percent of such compensation. The interest charge is equal to the interest at the rate applicable to underpayments of tax plus one percentage point imposed on the underpayments that would have occurred had the compensation been includible in income when first deferred, or if later, when not subject to a substantial risk of forfeiture.

Treasury regulations

It is intended that the Secretary of the Treasury issue regulations as to when an amount is not determinable for purposes of the provision. It is intended that an amount of deferred compensation is not determinable at the time the amount is no longer subject to a substantial risk of forfeiture if the amount varies depending on the satisfaction of an objective condition. For example, if a deferred amount varies depending on the satisfaction of an objective condition at the time the amount is no longer subject to substantial risk of forfeiture (e.g., no amount is paid unless a certain threshold is achieved, 100 percent is paid if the threshold is achieved, and 200 percent is paid if a higher threshold is achieved), the amount deferred is not determinable.

The Secretary of the Treasury is authorized to issue such regulations as may be necessary or appropriate to carry out the purposes of the provision, including regulations disregarding a substantial risk of forfeiture as necessary to carry out such purposes and regulations that provide appropriate treatment where an individual who was employed by an employer which is not a nonqualified entity is temporarily employed by a nonqualified entity which is related to such employer.

Under the provision, aggregation rules similar to those that apply under section 409A apply for purposes of determining whether a plan sponsor is a nonqualified entity. It is intended, however, that such aggregation rules are limited by the Secretary to operate in accordance with the purposes of the provision. For example, it is intended that that the aggregation rules do not result in the application of the provision to a nonqualified deferred compensation plan of a foreign corporation that is not a nonqualified entity (disregarding the aggregation rule) to the extent of deferred compensation expenses that are properly allocable to such corporation, despite the fact that such corporation is aggregated with a nonqualified entity.

Effective Date

The provision is effective with respect to amounts deferred which are attributable to services performed after December 31, 2008. In the case of an amount deferred which is attributable to services performed on or before December 31, 2008, to the extent such amount is not includible in gross income in a taxable year beginning before 2018, then such amount is includible in gross income in the later of (1) the last taxable year beginning before 2018, or (2) the taxable year in which there is no substantial risk of forfeiture of the rights to such compensation. Earnings on amounts deferred which are attributable to services performed on or before December 31, 2008, are subject to the provision only to the extent that the amounts to which such earnings relate are subject to the provision.

No later than 120 days after date of enactment, the Secretary shall issue guidance providing a limited period of time during which a nonqualified deferred compensation arrangement attributable to services performed on or before December 31, 2008, may, without violating the requirements of section 409A(a), be amended to conform the date of distribution to the date the amounts are required to be included in income. If the taxpayer is also a service recipient and maintains one or more nonqualified deferred compensation arrangements for its service providers under which any amount is attributable to services performed on or before December 31, 2008, the guidance shall permit such arrangements to be amended to conform the dates of distribution under the arrangement to the date amounts are required to be included in income of the taxpayer under the provision. An amendment made pursuant to the Treasury guidance will not be treated as a material modification of the arrangement for purposes of section 409A.

A special transition rule applies to nonqualified deferred compensation that is determined based on gain recognized on the disposition of a specified asset held by a service recipient on the date of enactment. Under this rule, if any portion of compensation payable under a binding written contract entered into on or before December 31, 2007, is determined as a portion of the amount of gain recognized on the disposition during such period of the specified asset, the provision will not apply to the portion of compensation attributable to such disposition even though such portion of compensation may be reduced by realized losses or depreciation in the value of other assets during such period or a prior period or be attributable in part to services performed after December 31, 2008. However, this rule only applies if payment of such portion of compensation is received by the service provider and included in its gross income no later than the earlier of 12 months after the end of the taxable year of the service recipient during which the disposition of the specified asset occurs and the last taxable year of the service provider beginning before January 1, 2018.

[Law at ¶5035 and ¶5305. CCH Explanation at ¶455.]

Committee Reports

Michelle's Law

¶15,001 Introduction

The Act entitled "Michelle's Law" amends the Employee Retirement Income Security Act of 1974 (ERISA), the Public Health Service Act, and the Internal Revenue Code of 1986. The purpose of the law is to insure that dependent students who take a medically necessary leave of absence do not lose health insurance coverage. The House Committee Report accompanying H.R. 2851 explains the intent of Congress regarding the provisions in the Act. At the end of the Committee Report text, references are provided to corresponding explanations and Code provisions. Subscribers to the electronic version can link from these references to the corresponding material. *The pertinent text of the Committee Report appears at ¶15,010.*

¶15,005 Background

The bill, H.R. 2851, entitled Michelle's Law, was introduced in the House of Representatives on June 25, 2007. It was passed by the House by voice vote on July 30, 2008. It was then passed, without amendment and by unanimous consent, by the Senate on September 25, 2008. On September 30, 2008, it was presented to the President for his signature.

References are to the following report:

• Report to accompany H.R. 2851 from the House of Representatives Committee on Energy and Commerce (H. R. REP. NO. 110-806).

[¶15,010] Act Sec. 2(c). Michelle's law

House Committee Report (H. Rep. No. 110-806)

[New Code Sec. 9813]

Purpose and Summary

The purpose of H.R. 2851, Michelle's Law, is to ensure continuity of health coverage for students, who because of a serious illness or injury, can no longer maintain student status.

Background and Need for Legislation

Michelle Morse was a full-time college student at Plymouth State University in New Hampshire who was diagnosed with colon cancer in 2003. Her doctors recommended that she cut back her college course load while undergoing chemotherapy treatment. She was informed, however, that if she cut back her classroom hours, she would lose her health insurance coverage because she would no longer qualify as a dependent on her parents' health insurance plan.

Other health insurance coverage options were unaffordable. As a result, she was forced to remain in school as a full-time student while undergoing 14 rounds of chemotherapy. In 2005, she succumbed to her illness. The case spurred interest in protections that would extend the definition of dependents to allow college students needing medical leaves of absence from class work to retain health insurance coverage on their parents' policies.

Private health insurance contracts define when a person can be considered to be a "dependent" for the purpose of purchasing a family health insurance plan. It is common practice, although far from universal, that dependents are considered to include college- age students as long as those students are enrolled in college full- time. Many States also have legislation that impacts how those dependents can be defined. At least six States—Maine, New Hampshire, New York, Vermont, Virginia, and Wisconsin— have enacted laws similar to Michelle's Law. Those State laws extend the ability of dependents to remain on their parents' plan for a limited period of time during a medical leave from full-time student status.[1] Four States—Maryland,

Michigan, Rhode Island, and Texas—require insurers to allow college-age dependents who are enrolled part-time in school to remain on their parent's health insurance plan.[2] At least nine additional States—Colorado, Florida, Indiana, Massachusetts, Missouri, Montana, New Jersey, New Mexico, and Utah—have enacted laws that would define dependents to include those older than 18 (the exact age varies) regardless of student status.[3]

States' laws, however, have limited applicability. States can enact laws that apply to individually-offered health insurance (not offered through employment) and to employment-based coverage as long as it is coverage that is comprised of an insurance product offered by companies in the business of selling insurance (including health maintenance organizations.)

If an employer self-insures (funds and retains the risk that the premiums collected may not cover the cost of medical benefits provided) its employees, State laws regulating the business of insurance do not apply. Over one-half of all employees are covered by self-insured employment-based coverage that is exempt from State insurance laws according to the Department of Labor.[4]

Thus to protect individuals across all plan types, Federal action is needed. H.R. 2851, or Michelle's Law, was introduced in the House of Representatives by Representative Hodes. The bill would extend the ability of dependents to remain on their parents' plan for a limited period of time during a medical leave from student status and would apply to all health insurance products, whether sold to individuals or offered as a workplace benefit, and whether or not the employer plan is self-insured. More protective State laws would continue to remain in effect. The bill does not disturb underlying Federal protections relating to rights and responsibilities of plans, issuers, or individuals. The American Cancer Society estimates that this bill could im-

---

[1] Based on a CRS review of State statutes and "The Changing Definition of 'Dependent': Who is Insured and For How Long?"—National Conference of State Legislatures, Updated February 2008.

[2] Based on a CRS review of State statutes and "The Changing Definition of 'Dependent': Who is Insured and For How Long?"—National Conference of State Legislatures, Updated February 2008.

[3] Based on a CRS review of State statutes and "The Changing Definition of 'Dependent': Who is Insured and For How Long?"—National Conference of State Legislatures, Updated February 2008.

[4] About 54 percent of workers were enrolled in employment-based coverage that was self-insured in CY 2005. Unpublished Department of Labor estimates based on March 2006 CPS.

pact about 2,400 college-age students who will be diagnosed with cancer each year.

A similar bill, S. 400, was introduced in the Senate on January 25, 2007, by Senators Sununu, Gregg, and Clinton. That bill would have a more limited scope than H.R. 2851, however, in that it would only apply to employer-provided health insurance. It was referred to the Committee on Health, Education, Labor, and Pensions. No further action has been taken on S. 400.

* * *

Section-by-Section Analysis of the Legislation

Section 1. Short title

This section establishes the short title of the legislation as "Michelle's Law".

Section 2. Coverage of dependent students on medically necessary leave of absence

(a) Amendments of ERISA

This provision would add a new section to the Employee Retirement Income Security Act of 1974 (ERISA) requiring all employer- provided health insurance plans (whether insured or self-insured) to continue coverage for a child dependent on a medically necessary leave of absence for a period of up to one year after the first day of the leave of absence or the date on which such coverage would otherwise terminate under the terms of the plan, whichever is earlier. Very small employer plans, those with fewer than 2 participants, are exempted from this requirement. A dependent child is described as a dependent under the terms of the plan who was enrolled in the plan on the first day of the medically necessary leave of absence and was enrolled as a full-time student at a postsecondary education institution until the first day of the medically necessary leave of absence.

A medically necessary leave of absence is defined as a leave of absence (or any other change in enrollment) from a post secondary education institution that (1) begins while the child is suffering from a severe illness or injury, (2) is medically necessary, and (3) causes the child to lose full-time student status under the terms of the plan. The bill would require a certification by the child's attending physician be submitted to the plan or issuer stating that the dependent is suffering from a severe illness or injury and that the leave of absence is medically necessary..The bill provides that if the child's attending physician has made this certification, for purposes of an administrative or judicial proceeding there shall be a rebuttable presumption that the child has met the first two criteria for a medically necessary leave of absence.

The bill states that breaks in the school semester can not disqualify a dependent from protection against disenrollment. The bill states that benefits cannot be reduced during the medically necessary leave of absence. Ordinary rights under ERISA pertaining to items such as appeals, notice, denials, and continuation of COBRA coverage would continue to apply.

(b) Amendments to the Public Health Service Act

Similar provisions are added to the Public Health Service Act, ensuring applicability of the law to insurance carriers and other entities in the business of selling health coverage both to employers and to individuals. The provisions differ from the ERISA provisions described above in the following ways:

• It clarifies that the protections of the legislation apply to dependents who qualify under the plan as students, not solely those who lose full-time student status. This would not require plans to cover any particular class of dependent, but only ensure that all classes of student dependents covered under a plan would receive the protections of the legislation. A plan would not be required to cover a full time student as a dependent. Only that if the plan did cover a full time student as a dependent than the provisions of the bill apply. Similarly, the bill does not require a plan to cover a part time student as a dependent.

• It modifies the definition of medical leave to be the result of a "serious illness or injury" instead of a "severe illness or injury."

• It modifies the requirement to provide a physician certification so that the child's "treating" physician must provide such certification instead of the child's attending physician.

• It adds a requirement that insofar as plans provide notice of the availability of coverage of dependent students, the notice describes that such coverage remains available during medical leave.

• It removes provisions regarding intra-semester breaks and the presumption relating to the burden of proof in legal and administrative proceedings.

• It ensures that certification by the treating physician is sufficient proof of serious illness or injury and the medical necessity of the student's leave of absence for the protections of the bill to apply.

(c) Amendments to the Internal Revenue Code

Provisions identical to the ERISA amendments are added to the Internal Revenue Code, ensuring the applicability of the law to certain types of health coverage that is not employer sponsored nor sold by entities in the business of selling health insurance or health coverage; such as church-sponsored plans. In addition, these provisions ensure that certain penalties for non-compliance described in the Internal Revenue Code are applicable for entities that are found to be in violation of the provisions.

Effective Date

The bill would become effective for plan years beginning on or after one year after the date of enactment.

[Law at ¶ 5505. CCH Explanation at ¶ 885.]

¶20,001 Effective Dates

Emergency Economic Stabilization Act of 2008

This CCH-prepared table presents the general effective dates for major law provisions added, amended or repealed by the Emergency Economic Stabilization Act of 2008 (P.L. 110-343), enacted October 3, 2008. Entries are listed in Code Section order.

Code Sec.	Act Sec.	Act Provision Subject	Effective Date
23(b)(4)(B)	106(e)(2)(A)	Division B—Credit for Residential Energy Efficient Property—Credit Allowed Against Alternative Minimum Tax—Conforming Amendments	Tax years beginning after December 31, 2007
24(b)(3)(B)	106(e)(2)(B)	Division B—Credit for Residential Energy Efficient Property—Credit Allowed Against Alternative Minimum Tax—Conforming Amendments	Tax years beginning after December 31, 2007
24(b)(3)(B)	205(d)(1)(A)	Division B—Credit for New Qualified Plug-In Electric Drive Motor Vehicles—Conforming Amendments	Tax years beginning after December 31, 2008
24(d)(4)	501(a)	Division C—$8,500 Income Threshold Used to Calculate Refundable Portion of Child Tax Credit	Tax years beginning after December 31, 2007
25(e)(1)(C)(ii)	205(d)(1)(B)	Division B—Credit for New Qualified Plug-In Electric Drive Motor Vehicles—Conforming Amendments	Tax years beginning after December 31, 2008
25B(g)(2)	106(e)(2)(C)	Division B—Credit for Residential Energy Efficient Property—Credit Allowed Against Alternative Minimum Tax—Conforming Amendments	Tax years beginning after December 31, 2007
25B(g)(2)	205(d)(1)(C)	Division B—Credit for New Qualified Plug-In Electric Drive Motor Vehicles—Conforming Amendments	Tax years beginning after December 31, 2008
25C(c)(1)	302(e)(1)	Division B—Credit for Nonbusiness Energy Property—Modification of Qualified Energy Efficiency Improvements	Property placed in service after October 3, 2008
25C(c)(2)(D)	302(e)(2)(A)-(B)	Division B—Credit for Nonbusiness Energy Property—Modification of Qualified Energy Efficiency Improvements—Building Envelope Component	Property placed in service after October 3, 2008
25C(d)(2)(C)	302(d)(2)	Division B—Credit for Nonbusiness Energy Property—Qualified Biomass Fuel Property—Coordination with Credit for Qualified Geothermal Heat Pump Property Expenditures—Conforming Amendment	Expenditures made after December 31, 2008

Code Sec.	Act Sec.	Act Provision Subject	Effective Date
25C(d)(3)(C)-(F)	302(d)(1)	Division B—Credit for Nonbusiness Energy Property—Qualified Biomass Fuel Property—Coordination with Credit for Qualified Geothermal Heat Pump Property Expenditures	Expenditures made after December 31, 2008
25C(d)(3)(D)-(F)	302(b)(1)(A)-(C)	Division B—Credit for Nonbusiness Energy Property—Qualified Biomass Fuel Property	Expenditures made after December 31, 2008
25C(d)(3)(E)	302(c)	Division B—Credit for Nonbusiness Energy Property—Qualified Biomass Fuel Property—Modification of Water Heater Requirement	Expenditures made after December 31, 2008
25C(d)(6)	302(b)(2)	Division B—Credit for Nonbusiness Energy Property—Qualified Biomass Fuel Property—Biomass Fuel	Expenditures made after December 31, 2008
25C(g)	302(a)	Division B—Credit for Nonbusiness Energy Property—Extension of Credit	Expenditures made after December 31, 2008
25D(a)(2)-(4)	106(c)(1)	Division B—Credit for Residential Energy Efficient Property—Credit for Residential Wind Property	Tax years beginning after December 31, 2007
25D(a)(3)-(5)	106(d)(1)	Division B—Credit for Residential Energy Efficient Property—Credit for Geothermal Heat Pump Systems	Tax years beginning after December 31, 2007
25D(b)(1)(A)-(E)	106(b)(1)(A)-(B)	Division B—Credit for Residential Energy Efficient Property—Removal of Limitation for Solar Electric Property	Tax years beginning after December 31, 2008
25D(b)(1)(B)-(D)	106(c)(2)	Division B—Credit for Residential Energy Efficient Property—Credit for Residential Wind Property—Limitation	Tax years beginning after December 31, 2007
25D(b)(1)(C)-(E)	106(d)(2)	Division B—Credit for Residential Energy Efficient Property—Credit for Geothermal Heat Pump Systems—Limitation	Tax years beginning after December 31, 2007
25D(c)	106(e)(1)	Division B—Credit for Residential Energy Efficient Property—Credit Allowed Against Alternative Minimum Tax	Tax years beginning after December 31, 2007
25D(d)(4)	106(c)(3)(A)	Division B—Credit for Residential Energy Efficient Property—Credit for Residential Wind Property—Qualified Small Wind Energy Property Expenditures	Tax years beginning after December 31, 2007
25D(d)(5)	106(d)(3)	Division B—Credit for Residential Energy Efficient Property—Credit for Geothermal Heat Pump Systems—Qualified Geothermal Heat Pump Property Expenditure	Tax years beginning after December 31, 2007
25D(e)(4)(A)(i)-(v)	106(b)(2)(A)-(B)	Division B—Credit for Residential Energy Efficient Property—Removal of Limitation for Solar Electric Property—Conforming Amendment	Tax years beginning after December 31, 2008

¶20,001

Code Sec.	Act Sec.	Act Provision Subject	Effective Date
25D(e)(4)(A)(ii)-(iv)	106(c)(4)	Division B—Credit for Residential Energy Efficient Property—Credit for Residential Wind Property—Maximum Expenditures in Case of Joint Occupancy	Tax years beginning after December 31, 2007
25D(e)(4)(A)(iii)-(v)	106(d)(4)	Division B—Credit for Residential Energy Efficient Property—Credit for Geothermal Heat Pump Systems—Maximum Expenditures in Case of Joint Occupancy	Tax years beginning after December 31, 2007
25D(g)	106(a)	Division B—Credit for Residential Energy Efficient Property—Extension	Tax years beginning after December 31, 2007
26(a)(1)	106(e)(2)(D)	Division B—Credit for Residential Energy Efficient Property—Credit Allowed Against Alternative Minimum Tax—Conforming Amendments	Tax years beginning after December 31, 2007
26(a)(1)	205(d)(1)(D)	Division B—Credit for New Qualified Plug-In Electric Drive Motor Vehicles—Conforming Amendments	Tax years beginning after December 31, 2008
26(a)(2)	101(a)(1)-(2)	Division C—Extension of Alternative Minimum Tax Relief for Nonrefundable Personal Credits	Tax years beginning after December 31, 2007
26(b)(2)(V)-(X)	801(b)	Division C—Nonqualified Deferred Compensation From Certain Tax Indifferent Parties—Conforming Amendment	Amounts deferred which are attributable to services performed after December 31, 2008, generally
30B(d)(3)(D)	205(b)	Division B—Credit for New Qualified Plug-In Electric Drive Motor Vehicles—Coordination with Alternative Motor Vehicle Credit	Tax years beginning after December 31, 2008
30C(c)(2)	207(b)	Division B—Alternative Fuel Vehicle Refueling Property Credit—Inclusion of Electricity as a Clean-Burning Fuel	Property placed in service after October 3, 2008, in tax years ending after such date
30C(g)(2)	207(a)	Division B—Alternative Fuel Vehicle Refueling Property Credit—Extension of Credit	Property placed in service after October 3, 2008, in tax years ending after such date
30D	205(a)	Division B—Credit for New Qualified Plug-In Electric Drive Motor Vehicles	Tax years beginning after December 31, 2008
38(b)(32)-(34)	115(b)	Division B—Tax Credit for Carbon Dioxide Sequestration—Conforming Amendment	Carbon dioxide captured after October 3, 2008
38(b)(32)-(35)	205(c)	Division B—Credit for New Qualified Plug-In Electric Drive Motor Vehicles—Credit Made Part of General Business Credit	Tax years beginning after December 31, 2008
38(c)(4)(B)(v)-(vii)	103(b)(1)	Division B—Energy Credit-Allowance of Energy Credit Against Alternative Minimum Tax	Credits determined under Code Sec. 46 in tax years beginning after October 3, 2008 and to carrybacks of such credits

Code Sec.	Act Sec.	Act Provision Subject	Effective Date
38(c)(4)(B)(v)-(viii)	316(b)(1)-(2)	Division C—Railroad Track Maintenance—Credit Allowed Against Alternative Minimum Tax	Credits determined under Code Sec. 45G in tax years beginning after December 31, 2007, and to carrybacks of such credits
38(c)(4)(B)(vi)	103(b)(2)	Division B—Energy Credit-Allowance of Energy Credit Against Alternative Minimum Tax—Technical Amendment	Credits determined under Code Sec. 46 in tax years beginning after October 3, 2008 and to carrybacks of such credits
40(d)(7)	203(a)	Division B—Clarification that Credits for Fuel are Designed to Provide an Incentive for United States Production—Alcohol Fuels Credit	Claims for credit or payment made on or after May 15, 2008
40A(b)(1)-(2)	202(b)(1)	Division B—Credits for Biodiesel and Renewable Diesel—Increase in Rate of Credit—Income Tax Credit	Fuel produced and sold or used after December 31, 2008
40A(b)(3)-(5)	202(b)(3)(A)	Division B—Credits for Biodiesel and Renewable Diesel—Increase in Rate of Credit—Conforming Amendments	Fuel produced and sold or used after December 31, 2008
40A(d)(2)	202(f)	Division B—Credits for Biodiesel and Renewable Diesel—Modification Relating to Definition of Agri-Biodiesel	Fuel produced and sold or used after December 31, 2008
40A(d)(3)(C)(ii)	202(b)(3)(D)	Division B—Credits for Biodiesel and Renewable Diesel—Increase in Rate of Credit—Conforming Amendments	Fuel produced and sold or used after December 31, 2008
40A(d)(5)	203(b)	Division B—Clarification that Credits for Fuel are Designed to Provide an Incentive for United States Production—Biodiesel Fuel Credit	Claims for credit or payment made on or after May 15, 2008
40A(e)(2)-(3)	202(b)(3)(C)	Division B—Credits for Biodiesel and Renewable Diesel—Increase in Rate of Credit—Conforming Amendments	Fuel produced and sold or used after December 31, 2008
40A(f)(2)	202(b)(3)(B)	Division B—Credits for Biodiesel and Renewable Diesel—Increase in Rate of Credit—Conforming Amendments	Fuel produced and sold or used after December 31, 2008
40A(f)(3)	202(c)(1)-(3)	Division B—Credits for Biodiesel and Renewable Diesel—Uniform Treatment of Diesel Produced from Biomass	Fuel produced and sold or used after December 31, 2008
40A(f)(3)	202(d)(1)	Division B—Credits for Biodiesel and Renewable Diesel—Coproduction of Renewable Diesel With Petroleum Feedstock	Fuel produced and sold or used after October 3, 2008
40A(f)(3)	202(d)(2)	Division B—Credits for Biodiesel and Renewable Diesel—Coproduction of Renewable Diesel With Petroleum Feedstock—Conforming Amendment	Fuel produced and sold or used after October 3, 2008
40A(f)(4)	202(e)	Division B—Credits for Biodiesel and Renewable Diesel—Eligibility of Certain Aviation Fuel	Fuel produced and sold or used after December 31, 2008

Code Sec.	Act Sec.	Act Provision Subject	Effective Date
40A(g)	202(a)	Division B—Credits for Biodiesel and Renewable Diesel	Fuel produced and sold or used after December 31, 2008
41(c)(5)(A)	301(c)	Division C—Extension and Modification of Research Credit—Modification of Alternative Simplified Credit	Tax years beginning after December 31, 2007
41(h)	301(a)(1)	Division C—Extension and Modification of Research Credit—Extension	Amounts paid or incurred after December 31, 2007
41(h)(2)-(3)	301(b)	Division C—Extension and Modification of Research Credit—Termination of Alternative Incremental Credit	Tax years beginning after December 31, 2007
41(h)(2)-(3)	301(d)	Division C—Extension and Modification of Research Credit—Technical Correction	Tax years beginning after December 31, 2007
45(b)(2)	108(b)(2)	Division B—Credit for Steel Industry Fuel—Credit Amount—Inflation Adjustment	Fuel produced and sold after September 30, 2008
45(b)(4)(A)	102(d)	Division B—Production Credit for Electricity Produced from Marine Renewables—Credit Rate	Electricity produced and sold after October 3, 2008, in tax years ending after such date
45(c)(1)(G)-(I)	102(a)	Division B—Production Credit for Electricity Produced from Marine Renewables	Electricity produced and sold after October 3, 2008, in tax years ending after such date
45(c)(7)(A)	108(a)(1)	Division B—Credit for Steel Industry Fuel—Treatment for Refined Coal	Fuel produced and sold after September 30, 2008
45(c)(7)(A)(i)	101(b)(1)(A)-(C)	Division B—Renewable Energy Credit—Modification of Refined Coal as a Qualified Energy Resource—Elimination of Increased Market Value Test	Coal produced and sold from facilities placed in service after December 31, 2008
45(c)(7)(B)	101(b)(2)	Division B—Renewable Energy Credit—Modification of Refined Coal as a Qualified Energy Resource—Increase in Required Emission Reduction	Coal produced and sold from facilities placed in service after December 31, 2008
45(c)(7)(C)	108(a)(2)	Division B—Credit for Steel Industry Fuel—Treatment for Refined Coal—Steel Industry Fuel Defined	Fuel produced and sold after September 30, 2008
45(c)(8)(C)	101(e)	Division B—Renewable Energy Credit—Modification of Rules for Hydropower Production	Property originally placed in service after December 31, 2008
45(c)(10)	102(b)	Division B—Production Credit for Electricity Produced from Marine Renewables—Marine Renewables	Electricity produced and sold after October 3, 2008, in tax years ending after such date

Code Sec.	Act Sec.	Act Provision Subject	Effective Date
45(d)	101(a)(1)	Division B—Renewable Energy Credit—Extension of Credit—1-Year Extension for Wind and Refined Coal Facilities	Property originally placed in service after December 31, 2008
45(d)(1)	106(c)(3)(B)	Division B—Credit for Residential Energy Efficient Property—Credit for Residential Wind Property—Qualified Small Wind Energy Property Expenditures—No Double Benefit	Tax years beginning after December 31, 2007
45(d)(2)(A)(i)-(ii)	101(a)(2)(A)	Division B—Renewable Energy Credit—Extension of Credit—2-Year Extension for Certain Other Facilities	Property originally placed in service after December 31, 2008
45(d)(2)(B)-(C)	101(d)(2)	Division B—Renewable Energy Credit—Expansion of Biomass Facilities—Closed-Loop Biomass Facilities	Property placed in service after October 3, 2008
45(d)(3)(A)(i)-(ii)	101(a)(2)(B)	Division B—Renewable Energy Credit—Extension of Credit—2-Year Extension for Certain Other Facilities	Property originally placed in service after December 31, 2008
45(d)(3)(B)-(C)	101(d)(1)	Division B—Renewable Energy Credit—Expansion of Biomass Facilities—Open-Loop Biomass Facilities	Property placed in service after October 3, 2008
45(d)(4)	101(a)(2)(C)	Division B—Renewable Energy Credit—Extension of Credit—2-Year Extension for Certain Other Facilities	Property originally placed in service after December 31, 2008
45(d)(5)	101(a)(2)(D)	Division B—Renewable Energy Credit—Extension of Credit—2-Year Extension for Certain Other Facilities	Property originally placed in service after December 31, 2008
45(d)(5)	102(e)	Division B—Production Credit for Electricity Produced from Marine Renewables—Coordination with Small Irrigation Power	Electricity produced and sold after October 3, 2008, in tax years ending after such date
45(d)(6)	101(a)(2)(E)	Division B—Renewable Energy Credit—Extension of Credit—2-Year Extension for Certain Other Facilities	Property originally placed in service after December 31, 2008
45(d)(7)	101(a)(2)(F)	Division B—Renewable Energy Credit—Extension of Credit—2-Year Extension for Certain Other Facilities	Property originally placed in service after December 31, 2008
45(d)(7)	101(c)(1)-(2)	Division B—Renewable Energy Credit—Trash Facility Clarification	Electricity produced and sold after October 3, 2008
45(d)(8)	108(c)	Division B—Credit for Steel Industry Fuel—Termination	Fuel produced and sold after September 30, 2008
45(d)(9)(A)-(B)	101(a)(2)(G)	Division B—Renewable Energy Credit—Extension of Credit—2-Year Extension for Certain Other Facilities	Property originally placed in service after December 31, 2008

Code Sec.	Act Sec.	Act Provision Subject	Effective Date
45(d)(11)	102(c)	Division B—Production Credit for Electricity Produced from Marine Renewables—Definition of Facility	Electricity produced and sold after October 3, 2008, in tax years ending after such date
45(e)(8)(D)	108(b)(1)	Division B—Credit for Steel Industry Fuel—Credit Amount	Fuel produced and sold after September 30, 2008
45(e)(9)(B)	108(d)(1)A)-(B)	Division B—Credit for Steel Industry Fuel—Coordination with Credit for Producing Fuel from a Nonconventional Source	Fuel produced and sold after September 30, 2008
45A(f)	314(a)	Division C—Indian Employment Credit	Tax years beginning after December 31, 2007
45C(b)(1)(D)	301(a)(2)	Division C—Extension and Modification of Research Credit—Extension—Conforming Amendment	Amounts paid or incurred after December 31, 2007
45D(f)(1)(D)	302	Division C—New Markets Credit	October 3, 2008
45G(f)	316(a)	Division C—Railroad Track Maintenance	Expenditures paid or incurred during tax years beginning after December 31, 2007
45K(g)(2)(E)	108(d)(2)	Division B—Credit for Steel Industry Fuel—Coordination with Credit for Producing Fuel from a Nonconventional Source—No Double Benefit	Fuel produced and sold after September 30, 2008
45L(g)	304	Division B—New Energy Efficient Home Credit	October 3, 2008
45M(b)	305(a)	Division B—Modifications of Energy Efficient Appliance Credit for Appliances Produced After 2007	Appliances produced after December 31, 2007
45M(c)	305(b)(1)(A)-(D)	Division B—Modifications of Energy Efficient Appliance Credit for Appliances Produced After 2007—Eligible Production—Similar Treatment for all Appliances	Appliances produced after December 31, 2007
45M(c)(2)	305(b)(2)	Division B—Modifications of Energy Efficient Appliance Credit for Appliances Produced After 2007—Eligible Production—Modification of Base Period	Appliances produced after December 31, 2007
45M(d)	305(c)	Division B—Modifications of Energy Efficient Appliance Credit for Appliances Produced After 2007—Types of Energy Efficient Appliances	Appliances produced after December 31, 2007
45M(e)(1)	305(d)(1)	Division B—Modifications of Energy Efficient Appliance Credit for Appliances Produced After 2007—Aggregate Credit Amount Allowed—Increase in Limit	Appliances produced after December 31, 2007

Code Sec.	Act Sec.	Act Provision Subject	Effective Date
45M(e)(2)	305(d)(2)	Division B—Modifications of Energy Efficient Appliance Credit for Appliances Produced After 2007—Aggregate Credit Amount Allowed—Exception for Certain Refrigerator and Clothes Washers	Appliances produced after December 31, 2007
45M(f)(1)	305(e)(1)	Division B—Modifications of Energy Efficient Appliance Credit for Appliances Produced After 2007—Qualified Energy Efficient Appliances	Appliances produced after December 31, 2007
45M(f)(3)	305(e)(2)	Division B—Modifications of Energy Efficient Appliance Credit for Appliances Produced After 2007—Qualified Energy Efficient Appliances—Clothes Washer	Appliances produced after December 31, 2007
45M(f)(4)-(8)	305(e)(3)	Division B—Modifications of Energy Efficient Appliance Credit for Appliances Produced After 2007—Qualified Energy Efficient Appliances—Top-Loading Clothes Washer	Appliances produced after December 31, 2007
45M(f)(6)	305(e)(4)	Division B—Modifications of Energy Efficient Appliance Credit for Appliances Produced After 2007—Qualified Energy Efficient Appliances—Replacement of Energy Factor	Appliances produced after December 31, 2007
45M(f)(9)-(10)	305(e)(5)	Division B—Modifications of Energy Efficient Appliance Credit for Appliances Produced After 2007—Qualified Energy Efficient Appliances—Gallons Per Cycle; Water Consumption Factor	Appliances produced after December 31, 2007
45N(e)	310	Division C—Extension of Mine Rescue Team Training Credit	October 3, 2008
45Q	115(a)	Division B—Tax Credit for Carbon Dioxide Sequestration	Carbon dioxide captured after October 3, 2008
48(a)(1)	103(c)(3)	Division B—Energy Credit-Energy Credit for Combined Heat and Power System Property—Conforming Amendment	Periods after October 3, 2008, in tax years ending after such date, generally
48(a)(1)	104(d)	Division B—Energy Credit for Small Wind Property—Conforming Amendment	Periods after October 3, 2008, in tax years ending after such date, generally
48(a)(2)(A)(i)	104(b)	Division B—Energy Credit for Small Wind Property—30 Percent Credit	Periods after October 3, 2008, in tax years ending after such date, generally
48(a)(2)-(3)	103(a)(1)	Division B—Energy Credit-Extension of Credit—Solar Energy Power	October 3, 2008
48(a)(3)(A)(iii)-(v)	103(c)(1)	Division B—Energy Credit-Energy Credit for Combined Heat and Power System Property	Periods after October 3, 2008, in tax years ending after such date, generally

Code Sec.	Act Sec.	Act Provision Subject	Effective Date
48(a)(3)(A)(iv)-(vi)	104(a)	Division B—Energy Credit for Small Wind Property	Periods after October 3, 2008, in tax years ending after such date, generally
48(a)(3)(A)(v)-(vii)	105(a)	Division B—Energy Credit for Geothermal Heat Pump Systems	Periods after October 3, 2008, in tax years ending after such date, generally
48(a)(3)	103(e)(1)	Division B—Energy Credit—Public Utility Property Taken Into Account	Periods after February 13, 2008, in tax years ending after such date, generally
48(c)(1)(B)	103(d)	Division B—Energy Credit-Increase of Credit Limitation for Fuel Cell Property	Periods after October 3, 2008, in tax years ending after such date, generally
48(c)(1)(D)-(E)	103(e)(2)(A)	Division B—Energy Credit—Public Utility Property Taken Into Account—Conforming Amendments	Periods after February 13, 2008, in tax years ending after such date, generally
48(c)(1)(E)	103(a)(2)	Division B—Energy Credit-Extension of Credit—Fuel Cell Property	October 3, 2008
48(c)(2)(D)-(E)	103(e)(2)(B)	Division B—Energy Credit—Public Utility Property Taken Into Account—Conforming Amendments	Periods after February 13, 2008, in tax years ending after such date, generally
48(c)(2)(E)	103(a)(3)	Division B—Energy Credit-Extension of Credit—Microturbine Property	October 3, 2008
48(c)(4)	104(c)	Division B—Energy Credit for Small Wind Property—Qualified Small Wind Energy Property	Periods after October 3, 2008, in tax years ending after such date, generally
48(c)	103(c)(2)(A)-(B)	Division B—Energy Credit-Energy Credit for Combined Heat and Power System Property—Combined Heat and Power System Property	Periods after October 3, 2008, in tax years ending after such date, generally
48A(a)(1)-(3)	111(a)	Division B—Expansion and Modification of Advanced Coal Project Investment Credit—Modification of Credit	Credits the application for which is submitted during the period described in Code Sec. 48A(d)(2)(A)(ii) and which are allocated or reallocated after October 3, 2008
48A(d)(2)(A)	111(c)(2)	Division B—Expansion and Modification of Advanced Coal Project Investment Credit—Authorization of Additional Projects—Application Period for Additional Projects	Credits the application for which is submitted during the period described in Code Sec. 48A(d)(2)(A)(ii) and which are allocated or reallocated after October 3, 2008

Code Sec.	Act Sec.	Act Provision Subject	Effective Date
48A(d)(3)(A)	111(b)	Division B—Expansion and Modification of Advanced Coal Project Investment Credit—Expansion of Aggregate Credits	Credits the application for which is submitted during the period described in Code Sec. 48A(d)(2)(A)(ii) and which are allocated or reallocated after October 3, 2008
48A(d)(3)(B)	111(c)(1)	Division B—Expansion and Modification of Advanced Coal Project Investment Credit—Authorization of Additional Projects	Credits the application for which is submitted during the period described in Code Sec. 48A(d)(2)(A)(ii) and which are allocated or reallocated after October 3, 2008
48A(d)(5)	111(d)	Division B—Expansion and Modification of Advanced Coal Project Investment Credit—Disclosure of Allocations	Certifications after October 3, 2008
48A(e)(1)(E)-(G)	111(c)(3)(A)	Division B—Expansion and Modification of Advanced Coal Project Investment Credit—Authorization of Additional Projects—Capture and Sequestration of Carbon Dioxide Emissions Requirement	Credits the application for which is submitted during the period described in Code Sec. 48A(d)(2)(A)(ii) and which are allocated or reallocated after October 3, 2008
48A(e)(3)	111(c)(5)	Division B—Expansion and Modification of Advanced Coal Project Investment Credit—Authorization of Additional Projects...Clerical Amendment	Periods after August 8, 2005, generally
48A(e)(3)(A)-(C)	111(c)(3)(B)	Division B—Expansion and Modification of Advanced Coal Project Investment Credit—Authorization of Additional Projects—Capture and Sequestration of Carbon Dioxide Emissions Requirement—Highest Priority for Projects Which Sequester Carbon Dioxide Emissions	Credits the application for which is submitted during the period described in Code Sec. 48A(d)(2)(A)(ii) and which are allocated or reallocated after October 3, 2008
48A(e)(3)(B)(ii)-(iv)	111(c)(4)(A)-(C)	Division B—Expansion and Modification of Advanced Coal Project Investment Credit—Authorization of Additional Projects—Additional Priority for Research Partnerships	Credits the application for which is submitted during the period described in Code Sec. 48A(d)(2)(A)(ii) and which are allocated or reallocated after October 3, 2008
48A(i)	111(c)(3)(C)	Division B—Expansion and Modification of Advanced Coal Project Investment Credit—Authorization of Additional Projects—Capture and Sequestration of Carbon Dioxide Emissions Requirement—Recapture of Credit for Failure to Sequester	Credits the application for which is submitted during the period described in Code Sec. 48A(d)(2)(A)(ii) and which are allocated or reallocated after October 3, 2008

¶20,001

Code Sec.	Act Sec.	Act Provision Subject	Effective Date
48B(a)	112(a)	Division B—Expansion and Modification of Coal Gasification Investment Credit—Modification of Credit Amount	Credits described in Code Sec. 48B(d)(1)(B) which are allocated or reallocated after October 3, 2008
48B(c)(7)(F)-(H)	112(e)	Division B—Expansion and Modification of Coal Gasification Investment Credit—Eligible Projects Include Transportation Grade Liquid Fuels	Credits described in Code Sec. 48B(d)(1)(B) which are allocated or reallocated after October 3, 2008
48B(d)(1)	112(b)	Division B—Expansion and Modification of Coal Gasification Investment Credit—Expansion of Aggregate Credits	Credits described in Code Sec. 48B(d)(1)(B) which are allocated or reallocated after October 3, 2008
48B(d)(4)	112(d)	Division B—Expansion and Modification of Coal Gasification Investment Credit—Selection Priorities	Credits described in Code Sec. 48B(d)(1)(B) which are allocated or reallocated after October 3, 2008
48B(f)	112(c)	Division B—Expansion and Modification of Coal Gasification Investment Credit—Recapture of Credit for Failure to Sequester	Credits described in Code Sec. 48B(d)(1)(B) which are allocated or reallocated after October 3, 2008
53(e)(2)	103(a)	Division C—Increase of AMT Refundable Credit Amount for Individuals with Long-Term Unused Credits for Prior Year Minimum Tax Liability, Etc.	Tax years beginning after December 31, 2007
53(f)	103(b)	Division C—Increase of AMT Refundable Credit Amount for Individuals with Long-Term Unused Credits for Prior Year Minimum Tax Liability, Etc.—Treatment of Certain Underpayments, Interest, and Penalties Attributable to the Treatment of Incentive Stock Options	Tax years beginning after December 31, 2007 except Code Sec. 53(f)(1) effective October 3 2008
54(m)	107(c)	Division B—New Clean Renewable Energy Bonds—Extension for Clean Renewable Energy Bonds	Obligations issued after October 3, 2008
54A(d)(1)	107(b)(1)	Division B—New Clean Renewable Energy Bonds—Conforming Amendments	Obligations issued after October 3, 2008
54A(d)(1)	301(b)(1)	Division B—Qualified Energy Conservation Bonds—Conforming Amendments	Obligations issued after October 3, 2008
54A(d)(1)(B)-(D)	313(b)(1)	Division C—Qualified Zone Academy Bonds—Conforming Amendments	Obligations issued after October 3, 2008
54A(d)(2)(C)	107(b)(2)	Division B—New Clean Renewable Energy Bonds—Conforming Amendments	Obligations issued after October 3, 2008
54A(d)(2)(C)	301(b)(2)	Division B—Qualified Energy Conservation Bonds—Conforming Amendments	Obligations issued after October 3, 2008

Code Sec.	Act Sec.	Act Provision Subject	Effective Date
54A(d)(2)(C)(ii)-(iv)	313(b)(2)	Division C—Qualified Zone Academy Bonds—Conforming Amendments	Obligations issued after October 3, 2008
54C	107(a)	Division B—New Clean Renewable Energy Bonds	Obligations issued after October 3, 2008
54D	301(a)	Division B—Qualified Energy Conservation Bonds	Obligations issued after October 3, 2008
54E	313(a)	Division C—Qualified Zone Academy Bonds	Obligations issued after October 3, 2008
55(d)(1)(A)-(B)	102(a)(1)-(2)	Division C—Extension of Increased Alternative Minimum Tax Exemption Amount	Tax years beginning after December 31, 2007
56(b)(1)(E)	706(b)(3)	Division C—Losses Attributable to Federally Declared Disasters—Increase in Standard Deduction by Disaster Casualty Loss—Allowance in Computing Alternative Minimum Taxable Income	Disasters declared in tax years beginning after December 31, 2007
56(d)(3)	708(c)	Division C—Net Operating Losses Attributable to Federally Declared Disasters—Loss Deduction Allowed in Computing Alternative Minimum Taxable Income	Losses arising in tax years beginning after December 31 2007, in connection with disasters declared after such date
62(a)(2)(D)	203(a)	Division C—Deduction for Certain Expenses of Elementary and Secondary School Teachers	Tax years beginning after December 31, 2007
63(c)(1)(B)-(D)	706(b)(1)	Division C—Losses Attributable to Federally Declared Disasters—Increase in Standard Deduction by Disaster Casualty Loss	Disasters declared in tax years beginning after December 31, 2007
63(c)(1)(C)	204(a)	Division C—Additional Standard Deduction for Real Property Taxes for Nonitemizers	Tax years beginning after December 31, 2008
63(c)(8)	706(b)(2)	Division C—Losses Attributable to Federally Declared Disasters—Increase in Standard Deduction by Disaster Casualty Loss—Disaster Loss Deduction	Disasters declared in tax years beginning after December 31, 2007
108(a)(1)(E)	303(a)	Division A—Extension of Exclusion of Income from Discharge of Qualified Principal Residence Indebtedness-Extension	Discharges of indebtedness occurring on or after January 1, 2010
132(f)(1)(D)	211(a)	Division B—Transportation Fringe Benefit to Bicycle Commuters	Tax years beginning after December 31, 2008
132(f)(2)(A)-(C)	211(b)	Division B—Transportation Fringe Benefit to Bicycle Commuters—Limitation on Exclusion	Tax years beginning after December 31, 2008
132(f)(4)	211(d)	Division B—Transportation Fringe Benefit to Bicycle Commuters—Constructive Receipt Benefit	Tax years beginning after December 31, 2008
132(f)(5)(F)	211(c)	Division B—Transportation Fringe Benefit to Bicycle Commuters—Definitions	Tax years beginning after December 31, 2008

Code Sec.	Act Sec.	Act Provision Subject	Effective Date
139(c)(2)	706(a)(2)(D)(iv)	Division C—Losses Attributable to Federally Declared Disasters—Waiver of Adjusted Gross Income Limitation—Conforming Amendments	Disasters declared in tax years beginning after December 31, 2007
142(l)(8)	307(a)	Division B—Qualified Green Building and Sustainable Design Projects	October 3, 2008
142(l)(9)	307(b)	Division B—Qualified Green Building and Sustainable Design Projects—Treatment of Current Refunding Bonds	October 3, 2008
143(k)(12)	709(a)	Division C—Waiver of Certain Mortgage Revenue Bond Requirements Following Federally Declared Disasters	Disasters occurring after December 31, 2007
162(m)(5)	302(a)	Division A—Special Rules for Tax Treatment of Executive Compensation of Employers Participating in the Troubled Assets Relief Program—Denial of Deduction	Tax years ending on or after October 3, 2008
164(b)(5)(I)	201(a)	Division C—Deduction for State and Local Sales Taxes	Tax years beginning after December 31, 2007
1033(h)	706(a)(2)(D)(i)	Division C—Losses Attributable to Federally Declared Disasters—Waiver of Adjusted Gross Income Limitation—Conforming Amendments	Disasters declared in tax years beginning after December 31, 2007
165(h)(1)	706(c)	Division C—Losses Attributable to Federally Declared Disasters—Increase in Standard Deduction by Disaster Casualty Loss—Increase in Limitation on Individual Loss Per Casualty	Tax years beginning after December 31, 2008
165(h)(3)-(5)	706(a)(1)	Division C—Losses Attributable to Federally Declared Disasters—Waiver of Adjusted Gross Income Limitation	Disasters declared in tax years beginning after December 31, 2007
165(h)(4)(B)	706(a)(2)(A)	Division C—Losses Attributable to Federally Declared Disasters—Waiver of Adjusted Gross Income Limitation—Conforming Amendments	Disasters declared in tax years beginning after December 31, 2007
165(i)(1)	706(a)(2)(B)	Division C—Losses Attributable to Federally Declared Disasters—Waiver of Adjusted Gross Income Limitation—Conforming Amendments	Disasters declared in tax years beginning after December 31, 2007
165(i)(4)	706(a)(2)(C)	Division C—Losses Attributable to Federally Declared Disasters—Waiver of Adjusted Gross Income Limitation—Conforming Amendments	Disasters declared in tax years beginning after December 31, 2007
168(b)(2)(B)-(D)	306(c)	Division B—Accelerated Recovery Period for Depreciation of Smart Meters and Smart Grid Systems—Continued Application of 150 Percent Declining Balance Method	Property placed in service after October 3, 2008

¶20,001

Code Sec.	Act Sec.	Act Provision Subject	Effective Date
168(b)(3)(I)	305(c)(3)	Division C—Extension of 15-Year Straight-Line Cost Recovery for Qualified Leasehold Improvements and Qualified Restaurant Improvements; 15-Year Straight-Line Cost Recovery for Certain Improvements to Retail Space—Recovery Period for Depreciation of Certain Improvements to Retail Space—Requirement to Use Straight-Line Method	Property placed in service after December 31, 2008
168(e)(3)(B)(v)-(vii)	505(a)	Division C—Certain Farming Business Machinery and Equipment Treated as 5-Year Property	Property placed in service after December 31, 2008
168(e)(3)(D)(i)-(iv)	306(a)	Division B—Accelerated Recovery Period for Depreciation of Smart Meters and Smart Grid Systems	Property placed in service after October 3, 2008
168(e)(3)(E)(iv)-(v)	305(a)(1)	Division C—Extension of 15-Year Straight-Line Cost Recovery for Qualified Leasehold Improvements and Qualified Restaurant Improvements; 15-Year Straight-Line Cost Recovery for Certain Improvements to Retail Space—Extension of Leasehold and Restaurant Improvements	Property placed in service after December 31, 2007
168(e)(3)(E)(vii)-(ix)	305(c)(1)	Division C—Extension of 15-Year Straight-Line Cost Recovery for Qualified Leasehold Improvements and Qualified Restaurant Improvements; 15-Year Straight-Line Cost Recovery for Certain Improvements to Retail Space—Recovery Period for Depreciation of Certain Improvements to Retail Space—15-Year Recovery Period	Property placed in service after December 31, 2008
168(e)(7)	305(b)(1)	Division C—Extension of 15-Year Straight-Line Cost Recovery for Qualified Leasehold Improvements and Qualified Restaurant Improvements; 15-Year Straight-Line Cost Recovery for Certain Improvements to Retail Space—Treatment to Include New Construction	Property placed in service after December 31, 2008
168(e)(8)	305(c)(2)	Division C—Extension of 15-Year Straight-Line Cost Recovery for Qualified Leasehold Improvements and Qualified Restaurant Improvements; 15-Year Straight-Line Cost Recovery for Certain Improvements to Retail Space—Recovery Period for Depreciation of Certain Improvements to Retail Space—Qualified Retail Improvement Property	Property placed in service after December 31, 2008

Code Sec.	Act Sec.	Act Provision Subject	Effective Date
168(g)(3)(B)	305(c)(4)	Division C—Extension of 15-Year Straight-Line Cost Recovery for Qualified Leasehold Improvements and Qualified Restaurant Improvements; 15-Year Straight-Line Cost Recovery for Certain Improvements to Retail Space—Recovery Period for Depreciation of Certain Improvements to Retail Space—Alternate System	Property placed in service after December 31, 2008
168(g)(3)(B)	505(b)	Division C—Certain Farming Business Machinery and Equipment Treated as 5-Year Property—Alternative System	Property placed in service after December 31, 2008
168(i)(15)(D)	317(a)	Division C—Seven-Year Cost Recovery Period for Motorsports Racing Track Facility	Property placed in service after December 31, 2007
168(i)(18)-(19)	306(b)	Division B—Accelerated Recovery Period for Depreciation of Smart Meters and Smart Grid Systems—Definitions	Property placed in service after October 3, 2008
168(j)(8)	315(a)	Division C—Accelerated Depreciation for Business Property on Indian Reservations	Property placed in service after December 31, 2007
168(l)	201(b)(1)-(3)	Division B—Inclusion of Cellulosic Biofuel in Bonus Depreciation for Biomass Ethanol Plant Property—Conforming Amendments	Property placed in service after October 3, 2008, in tax years ending after such date
168(l)(3)	201(a)	Division B—Inclusion of Cellulosic Biofuel in Bonus Depreciation for Biomass Ethanol Plant Property	Property placed in service after October 3, 2008, in tax years ending after such date
168(m)	308(a)	Division B—Special Depreciation Allowance for Certain Refuse and Recycling Property	Property placed in service after August 31, 2008
168(n)	710(a)	Division C—Special Depreciation Allowance for Qualified Disaster Property	Property placed in service after December 31, 2007, with respect to disasters declared after such date
170(b)(3)	323(b)(1)	Division C—Enhanced Charitable Deductions for Contributions of Food Inventory—Temporary Suspension of Limitations on Charitable Contributions	Tax years ending after October 3, 2008
170(e)(3)(C)(iv)	323(a)(1)	Division C—Enhanced Charitable Deductions for Contributions of Food Inventory—Increased Amount of Deduction	Contributions made after December 31, 2007
170(e)(3)(D)(iii)	324(b)	Division C—Extension of Enhanced Charitable Deduction for Contributions of Book Inventory-Clerical Amendment	Contributions made after December 31, 2007
170(e)(3)(D)(iv)	324(a)	Division C—Extension of Enhanced Charitable Deduction for Contributions of Book Inventory-Extension	Contributions made after December 31, 2007

Code Sec.	Act Sec.	Act Provision Subject	Effective Date
170(e)(6)(G)	321(a)	Division C—Enhanced Deduction for Qualified Computer Contributions	Contributions made during tax years beginning after December 31, 2007
172(b)(1)(F)(ii)	708(d)(1)	Division C—Net Operating Losses Attributable to Federally Declared Disasters—Conforming Amendments	Losses arising in tax years beginning after December 31, 2007, in connection with disasters declared after such date
172(b)(1)(F)(ii)(II)	706(a)(2)(D)(v)	Division C—Losses Attributable to Federally Declared Disasters—Waiver of Adjusted Gross Income Limitation—Conforming Amendments	Disasters declared in tax years beginning after December 31, 2007
172(b)(1)(F)(ii)(III)	706(a)(2)(D)(vi)	Division C—Losses Attributable to Federally Declared Disasters—Waiver of Adjusted Gross Income Limitation—Conforming Amendments	Disasters declared in tax years beginning after December 31, 2007
172(b)(1)(J)	708(a)	Division C—Net Operating Losses Attributable to Federally Declared Disasters	Losses arising in tax years beginning after December 31, 2007, in connection with disasters declared after such date
172(i)(1)	708(d)(2)	Division C—Net Operating Losses Attributable to Federally Declared Disasters—Conforming Amendments	Losses arising in tax years beginning after December 31, 2007, in connection with disasters declared after such date
172(j)-(l)	708(b)	Division C—Net Operating Losses Attributable to Federally Declared Disasters—Qualified Disaster Loss	Losses arising in tax years beginning after December 31, 2007, in connection with disasters declared after such date
179(e)	711(a)	Division C—Increased Expensing for Qualified Disaster Assistance Property	Property placed in service after December 31, 2007, with respect to disasters declared after such date
179C(c)(1)	209(a)(1)-(2)	Division B—Extension and Modification of Election Expense Certain Refineries—Extension	Property placed in service after October 3, 2008
179C(d)	209(b)(1)	Division B—Extension and Modification of Election Expense Certain Refineries—Inclusion of Fuel Derived From Shale and Tar Sand	Property placed in service after October 3, 2008
179C(e)(2)	209(b)(2)	Division B—Extension and Modification of Election Expense Certain Refineries—Inclusion of Fuel Derived From Shale and Tar Sand—Conforming Amendment	Property placed in service after October 3, 2008
179D(h)	303	Division B—Energy Efficient Commercial Building Deduction	October 3, 2008

¶20,001

Code Sec.	Act Sec.	Act Provision Subject	Effective Date
179E(g)	311	Division C—Extension of Election to Expense Advanced Mine Safety Equipment	October 3, 2008
181(a)(2)(A)	502(b)	Division C—Provisions Related to Film and Television Productions—Modification of Limitation on Expensing	Qualified film and television productions commencing after December 31, 2007
181(d)(3)(A)	502(d)	Division C—Provisions Related to Film and Television Productions—Conforming Amendment	Qualified film and television productions commencing after December 31, 2007
181(f)	502(a)	Division C—Provisions Related to Film and Television Productions—Extension of Expensing Rules for Qualified Film and Television Productions	Qualified film and television productions commencing after December 31, 2007
198(h)	318(a)	Division C—Expensing of Environmental Remediation Costs	Expenditures paid or incurred after December 31, 2007
198A	707(a)	Division C—Expensing of Qualified Disaster Expenses	Amounts paid or incurred after December 31, 2007 in connection with disaster declared after such date
199(b)(2)(D)	502(c)(1)	Division C—Provisions Related to Film and Television Productions—Modifications to Deduction for Domestic Activities	Tax years beginning after December 31, 2007
199(c)(6)	502(c)(2)	Division C—Provisions Related to Film and Television Productions—Modifications to Deduction for Domestic Activities—Definition of Qualified Film	Tax years beginning after December 31, 2007
199(d)(1)(A)(ii)-(iv)	502(c)(3)	Division C—Provisions Related to Film and Television Productions—Modifications to Deduction for Domestic Activities—Partnerships	Tax years beginning after December 31, 2007
199(d)(2)	401(b)	Division B—Limitation of Deduction for Income Attributable to Domestic Production of Oil, Gas, or Primary Products Thereof—Conforming Amendment	Tax years beginning after December 31, 2008
199(d)(8)(C)	312(a)(1)-(2)	Division C—Deduction Allowable with Respect to Income Attributable to Domestic Production Activities in Puerto Rico	Tax years beginning after December 31, 2007
199(d)(9)-(10)	401(a)	Division B—Limitation of Deduction for Income Attributable to Domestic Production of Oil, Gas, or Primary Products Thereof	Tax years beginning after December 31, 2008
222(e)	202(a)	Division C—Deduction of Qualified Tuition and Related Expenses	Tax years beginning after December 31, 2007

Code Sec.	Act Sec.	Act Provision Subject	Effective Date
280G(e)-(f)	302(b)(1)-(2)	Division A—Special Rules for Tax Treatment of Executive Compensation of Employers Participating in the Troubled Assets Relief Program—Golden Parachute Rule	Payments with respect to severances occurring during the period during which the authorities under the Troubled Asset Relief Program are in effect (October 3, 2008 through December 31, 2009)
408(d)(8)(F)	205(a)	Division C—Tax-Free Distributions from Individual Retirement Plans for Charitable Purposes	Distributions made in Tax years beginning after December 31, 2007
451(i)(3)	109(a)(1)	Division B—Special Rule to Implement FERC and State Electric Restructuring Policy—Extension for Qualified Electric Utilities	Transactions after December 31, 2007
451(i)(4)(B)(ii)	109(b)	Division B—Special Rule to Implement FERC and State Electric Restructuring Policy—Extension of Period for Transfer of Operational Control Authorized by FERC	Transactions occurring after October 22, 2004, in tax years ending after such date
451(i)(5)(C)	109(c)	Division B—Special Rule to Implement FERC and State Electric Restructuring Policy—Property Located Outside the United States Not Treated as Exempt Utility Property	Transactions after October 3, 2008
451(i)(6)-(11)	109(a)(2)	Division B—Special Rule to Implement FERC and State Electric Restructuring Policy—Extension for Qualified Electric Utilities—Qualified Electric Utility	Transactions after December 31, 2007
457A	801(a)	Division C—Nonqualified Deferred Compensation From Certain Tax Indifferent Parties	Amounts deferred which are attributable to services performed after December 31, 2008, generally
512(b)(13)(E)(iv)	306(a)	Division C—Modification of Tax Treatment of Certain Payments to Controlling Exempt Organizations	Payments received or accrued after December 31, 2007
613A(c)(6)(H)	210	Division B—Extension of Suspension of Taxable Income Limit on Percentage Depletion for Oil and Natural Gas Produced from Marginal Properties	October 3, 2008
871(k)(1)(C)	206(a)	Division C—Treatment of Certain Dividends of Regulated Investment Companies—Interest-Related Dividends	Tax years of regulated investment companies beginning after December 31, 2007
871(k)(2)(C)	206(b)	Division C—Treatment of Certain Dividends of Regulated Investment Companies—Short-Term Capital Gain Dividends	Tax years of regulated investment companies beginning after December 31, 2007
897(h)(4)(A)(ii)	208(a)	Division C—Qualified Investment Entities	January 1, 2008

Code Sec.	Act Sec.	Act Provision Subject	Effective Date
907(a)-(b)	402(a)	Division B—Elimination of the Different Treatment of Foreign Oil and Gas Extraction Income and Foreign Oil Related Income for Purposes of the Foreign Tax Credit	Tax years beginning after December 31, 2008
907(c)(4)	402(b)	Division B—Elimination of the Different Treatment of Foreign Oil and Gas Extraction Income and Foreign Oil Related Income for Purposes of the Foreign Tax Credit—Recapture of Foreign Oil and Gas Losses	Tax years beginning after December 31, 2008
907(f)	402(c)(1)-(2)	Division B—Elimination of the Different Treatment of Foreign Oil and Gas Extraction Income and Foreign Oil Related Income for Purposes of the Foreign Tax Credit—Carryback and Carryover of Disallowed Credits	Tax years beginning after December 31, 2008
953(e)(10)	303(a)(1)-(2)	Division C-Subpart F Exception for Active Financing Income—Exempt Insurance Income	October 3, 2008
954(c)(6)(C)	304(a)	Division C—Extension of Look-Thru Rule for Related Controlled Foreign Corporations	Tax years of foreign corporations beginning after December 31, 2007, and to tax years of United States shareholders with or within which such tax years of foreign corporations end.
954(h)(9)	303(b)	Division C-Subpart F Exception for Active Financing Income—Exception to Treatment as Foreign Personal Holding Company Income	October 3, 2008
1012	403(b)(1)-(3)	Division B—Broker Reporting of Customer's Basis in Securities Transactions—Determination of Basis of Certain Securities on Account by Account or Average Basis Method	January 1, 2011
1016(a)(35)-(37)	205(d)(2)	Division B—Credit for New Qualified Plug-In Electric Drive Motor Vehicles—Conforming Amendments	Tax years beginning after December 31, 2008
1033(h)(2)	706(a)(2)(D)(ii)	Division C—Losses Attributable to Federally Declared Disasters—Waiver of Adjusted Gross Income Limitation—Conforming Amendments	Disasters declared in tax years beginning after December 31, 2007
1033(h)(3)	706(a)(2)(D)(iii)	Division C—Losses Attributable to Federally Declared Disasters—Waiver of Adjusted Gross Income Limitation—Conforming Amendments	Disasters declared in tax years beginning after December 31, 2007
1367(a)(2)	307(a)	Division C—Basis Adjustment to Stock of S Corporations Making Charitable Contributions of Property	Contributions made in tax years beginning after December 31, 2007
1397E(m)	313(b)(3)	Division C—Qualified Zone Academy Bonds—Conforming Amendments	Obligations issued after October 3, 2008

¶20,001

Code Sec.	Act Sec.	Act Provision Subject	Effective Date
1400(f)	322(a)(1)	Division C—Tax Incentives for Investment in the District of Columbia—Designation of Zone	Periods beginning after December 31, 2007
1400A(b)	322(b)(1)	Division C—Tax Incentives for Investment in the District of Columbia—Tax-Exempt Economic Development Bonds	Bonds issued after December 31, 2007
1400B(b)	322(c)(1)	Division C—Tax Incentives for Investment in the District of Columbia—Zero-Percent Capital Gains Rate	Acquisitions after December 31, 2007
1400B(e)(2)	322(c)(2)(A)(i)-(ii)	Division C—Tax Incentives for Investment in the District of Columbia—Zero-Percent Capital Gains Rate—Conforming Amendments	October 3, 2008
1400B(g)(2)	322(c)(2)(B)	Division C—Tax Incentives for Investment in the District of Columbia—Zero-Percent Capital Gains Rate—Conforming Amendments	October 3, 2008
1400C(d)(2)	205(d)(1)(E)	Division B—Credit for New Qualified Plug-In Electric Drive Motor Vehicles—Conforming Amendments	Tax years beginning after December 31, 2008
1400C(i)	322(d)	Division C—Tax Incentives for Investment in the District of Columbia—First-Time Homebuyer Credit	Property purchased after December 31, 2007
1400F(d)	322(c)(2)(C)	Division C—Tax Incentives for Investment in the District of Columbia—Zero-Percent Capital Gains Rate—Conforming Amendments	October 3, 2008
1400N(h)	320(a)	Division C—Extension of Increased Rehabilitation Credit for Structures in the Gulf Opportunity Zone	Expenditures paid or incurred after October 3, 2008
2105(d)(3)	207(a)	Division C—Stock in RIC for Purposes of Determining Estates of Nonresidents Not Citizens	Decedents dying after December 31, 2007
3301	404(a)(1)-(2)	Division B—0.2 Percent FUTA Surtax	Wages paid after December 31, 2008
4053(9)-(10)	206(a)	Division B—Exclusion from Heavy Truck Tax for Idling Reduction Units and Advanced Insulation	Sales or installations after October 3, 2008
4121(e)(2)(A)-(B)	113(a)(1)-(2)	Division B—Temporary Increase in Coal Excise Tax; Funding of Black Lung Disability Trust Fund—Extension of Temporary Increase	October 3, 2008
4161(b)(2)(B)-(C)	503(a)	Division C—Exemption from Excise Tax for Certain Wooden Arrows Designed for Use by Children	Shafts first sold after October 3, 2008
4611(c)(2)(B)	405(a)(1)	Division B—Increase and Extension of Oil Spill Liability Trust Fund Tax—Increase in Rate	On and after the first day of the first calendar quarter beginning more than 60 days after October 3, 2008
4611(f)(1)	405(b)(2)	Division B—Increase and Extension of Oil Spill Liability Trust Fund Tax—Extension—Conforming Amendment	October 3, 2008

Code Sec.	Act Sec.	Act Provision Subject	Effective Date
4611(f)(2)-(3)	405(b)(1)	Division B—Increase and Extension of Oil Spill Liability Trust Fund Tax—Extension	October 3, 2008
6033(b)(13)-(15)	703(a)	Division C—Reporting Requirements Relating to Disaster Relief Contributions	Returns for which the due date occurs after December 31, 2008
6045(b)	403(a)(3)(A)	Division B—Broker Reporting of Customer's Basis in Securities Transactions—Extension of Period for Statements Sent to Customers	Statements required to be furnished after December 31, 2008
6045(b)	403(a)(3)(C)	Division B—Broker Reporting of Customer's Basis in Securities Transactions—Extension of Period for Statements Sent to Customers—Other Statements	Statements required to be furnished after December 31, 2008
6045(d)	403(a)(3)(B)(i)-(ii)	Division B—Broker Reporting of Customer's Basis in Securities Transactions—Extension of Period for Statements Sent to Customers—Statements Related to Substitute Payments	Statements required to be furnished after December 31, 2008
6045(g)	403(a)(1)	Division B—Broker Reporting of Customer's Basis in Securities Transactions	January 1, 2011
6045(h)	403(a)(2)	Division B—Broker Reporting of Customer's Basis in Securities Transactions—Broker Information Required with Respect to Options	January 1, 2011
6045A	403(c)(1)	Division B—Broker Reporting of Customer's Basis in Securities Transactions—Information by Transferors to Aid Brokers	January 1, 2011
6045B	403(d)(1)	Division B—Broker Reporting of Customer's Basis in Securities Transactions—Additional Issuer Information to Aid Brokers	January 1, 2011
6103(i)(3)(C)(iv)	402(a)	Division C—Permanent Authority for Disclosure of Information Relating to Terrorist Activities—Disclosure of Return Information to Apprise Appropriate Officials of Terrorist Activities	Disclosures after October 3, 2008
6103(i)(7)(E)	402(b)	Division C—Permanent Authority for Disclosure of Information Relating to Terrorist Activities—Disclosure Upon Request of Information Relating to Terrorist Activities	Disclosures after October 3, 2008
6426(c)(2)	202(b)(2)	Division B—Credits for Biodiesel and Renewable Diesel—Increase in Rate of Credit—Excise Tax Credit	Fuel produced and sold or used after December 31, 2008
6426(c)(6)	202(a)	Division B—Credits for Biodiesel and Renewable Diesel	Fuel produced and sold or used after December 31, 2008

Code Sec.	Act Sec.	Act Provision Subject	Effective Date
6426(d)(1)	204(b)(2)	Division B—Extension and Modification of Alternative Fuel Credit—Modifications—Credit Allowed for Aviation Use of Fuel	Fuel sold or used after October 3, 2008
6426(d)(2)(E)	204(c)(2)	Division B—Extension and Modification of Alternative Fuel Credit—Carbon Capture Requirement for Certain Fuels-Conforming Amendment	Fuel sold or used after October 3, 2008
6426(d)(2)(E)-(G)	204(b)(1)	Division B—Extension and Modification of Alternative Fuel Credit—Modifications—Alternative Fuel to Include Compressed or Liquified Biomass Gas	Fuel sold or used after October 3, 2008
6426(d)(4)-(5)	204(c)(1)	Division B—Extension and Modification of Alternative Fuel Credit—Carbon Capture Requirement for Certain Fuels	Fuel sold or used after October 3, 2008
6426(d)(4)	204(a)(1)	Division B—Extension and Modification of Alternative Fuel Credit—Extension—Alternative Fuel Credit	Fuel sold or used after October 3, 2008
6426(e)(3)	204(a)(2)	Division B—Extension and Modification of Alternative Fuel Credit—Extension—Alternative Fuel Mixture Credit	Fuel sold or used after October 3, 2008
6426(i)	203(c)(1)	Division B—Clarification that Credits for Fuel are Designed to Provide an Incentive for United States Production—Excise Tax Credit	Claims for credit or payment made on or after May 15, 2008
6427(e)(5)(B)	202(a)	Division B—Credits for Biodiesel and Renewable Diesel	Fuel produced and sold or used after December 31, 2008
6427(e)(5)(C)	204(a)(3)	Division B—Extension and Modification of Alternative Fuel Credit—Extension—Payments	Fuel sold or used after October 3, 2008
6427(e)(5)-(6)	203(c)(2)	Division B—Clarification that Credits for Fuel are Designed to Provide an Incentive for United States Production—Excise Tax Credit—Conforming Amendment	Claims for credit or payment made on or after May 15, 2008
6501(i)	402(d)	Division B—Elimination of the Different Treatment of Foreign Oil and Gas Extraction Income and Foreign Oil Related Income for Purposes of the Foreign Tax Credit—Conforming Amendment	Tax years beginning after December 31, 2008
6501(m)	205(d)(3)	Division B—Credit for New Qualified Plug-In Electric Drive Motor Vehicles—Conforming Amendments	Tax years beginning after December 31, 2008

Code Sec.	Act Sec.	Act Provision Subject	Effective Date
6694(a)	506(a)	Division C—Modification of Penalty on Understatement of Taxpayer's Liability by Tax Return Preparer	Positions other than as described in Code Sec. 6694(a)(2)(C), to returns prepared after May 25, 2007; and for positions described in Code Sec. 6694(a)(2)(C), to returns prepared for tax years ending after October 3, 2008
6724(d)(1)(B)(iv)-(xxiii)	403(d)(2)(A)	Division B—Broker Reporting of Customer's Basis in Securities Transactions—Additional Issuer Information to Aid Brokers—Assessable Penalties	January 1, 2011
6724(d)(2)(I)-(EE)	403(c)(2)	Division B—Broker Reporting of Customer's Basis in Securities Transactions—Information by Transferors to Aid Brokers—Assessable Penalties	January 1, 2011
6724(d)(2)(J)-(FF)	403(d)(2)(B)	Division B—Broker Reporting of Customer's Basis in Securities Transactions—Additional Issuer Information to Aid Brokers—Assessable Penalties	January 1, 2011
7508A(a)	706(a)(2)(D)(vii)	Division C—Losses Attributable to Federally Declared Disasters—Waiver of Adjusted Gross Income Limitation—Conforming Amendments	Disasters declared in tax years beginning after December 31, 2007
7608(c)(6)	401(a)	Division C—Permanent Authority for Undercover Operations	Operations conducted after October 3, 2008
7652(f)(1)	308(a)	Division C—Increase in Limit on Cover Over of Rum Excise Tax to Puerto Rico and the Virgin Islands	Distilled spirits brought into the United States after December 31, 2007
7704(d)(1)(E)	116(a)	Division B—Certain Income and Gains Relating to Industrial Source Carbon Dioxide Treated as Qualifying Income for Publicly Traded Partnerships	October 3, 2008, in tax years ending after such date
7704(d)(1)(E)	208(a)	Division B—Certain Income and Gains Relating to Alcohol Fuels and Mixtures, Biodiesel Fuels and Mixtures, and Alternative Fuels and Mixtures Treated as Qualifying Income for Publicly Traded Partnerships	October 3, 2008, in tax years ending after such date
9812	512(c)(1)-(7)	Divisions C—Mental Health Parity—Amendments to Internal Revenue Code	Group health plans for plan years beginning after October 2, 2009 generally
9812	512(g)(3)(A)	Divisions C—Mental Health Parity—Amendments to Internal Revenue Code	Group health plans for plan years beginning after October 2, 2009 generally

¶20,001

Code Sec.	Act Sec.	Act Provision Subject	Effective Date
...	113(b)(1)(A)-(F)	Division B—Temporary Increase in Coal Excise Tax; Funding of Black Lung Disability Trust Fund—Restructuring of Trust Fund Debt—Definitions	October 3, 2008
...	113(b)(2)(A)-(C)	Division B—Temporary Increase in Coal Excise Tax; Funding of Black Lung Disability Trust Fund—Refinancing of Outstanding Principal of Repayable Advances and Unpaid Interest on such Advances—Transfer to General Fund	October 3, 2008
...	113(b)(4)	Division B—Temporary Increase in Coal Excise Tax; Funding of Black Lung Disability Trust Fund—Restructuring of Trust Fund Debt—Prepayment of Trust Fund Obligations	October 3, 2008
...	114(a)(1)(A)-(B)	Division B—Special Rules for Refund of the Coal Excise Tax to Certain Coal Producers and Reporters—Refund—Coal Producers	October 3, 2008
...	114(a)(2)	Division B—Special Rules for Refund of the Coal Excise Tax to Certain Coal Producers and Reporters—Refund—Exporters	October 3, 2008
...	114(b)	Division B—Special Rules for Refund of the Coal Excise Tax to Certain Coal Producers and Reporters—Limitations	October 3, 2008
...	114(c)	Division B—Special Rules for Refund of the Coal Excise Tax to Certain Coal Producers and Reporters—Subsequent Refund Prohibited	October 3, 2008
...	114(e)	Division B—Special Rules for Refund of the Coal Excise Tax to Certain Coal Producers and Reporters—Timing of Refund	October 3, 2008
...	114(f)	Division B—Special Rules for Refund of the Coal Excise Tax to Certain Coal Producers and Reporters—Interest	October 3, 2008
...	114(g)(1)-(2)	Division B—Special Rules for Refund of the Coal Excise Tax to Certain Coal Producers and Reporters—Denial of Double Benefit	October 3, 2008
...	114(h)	Division B—Special Rules for Refund of the Coal Excise Tax to Certain Coal Producers and Reporters—Application of Section	October 3, 2008
...	114(i)(1)-(2)	Division B—Special Rules for Refund of the Coal Excise Tax to Certain Coal Producers and Reporters—Standing Not Conferred	October 3, 2008
...	115(c)	Division B—Tax Credit for Carbon Dioxide Sequestration-Clerical Amendment	October 3, 2008

Code Sec.	Act Sec.	Act Provision Subject	Effective Date
...	205(d)(4)	Division B—Credit for New Qualified Plug-In Electric Drive Motor Vehicles—Conforming Amendments	Tax years beginning after December 31, 2008
...	301(b)(3)	Division B—Qualified Energy Conservation Bonds—Conforming Amendments	Obligations issued after October 3, 2008
...	307(c)	Division B—Qualified Green Building and Sustainable Design Projects—Accountability	October 3, 2008
...	309(a)(1)-(2)	Division C—Extension of Economic Development Credit for American Somoa	Tax years beginning after December 31, 2007
...	313(b)(4)	Division C—Qualified Zone Academy Bonds—Conforming Amendments	October 3, 2008
...	319(a)	Division C—Extension of Work Opportunity Tax Credit for Hurricane Katrina Employees	Individuals hired after August 27, 2007
...	325(a)	Division C—Extension and Modification of Duty Suspension on Wool Products; Wool Research Fund; Wool Duty Refunds—Extension of Temporary Duty Reductions	October 3, 2008
...	325(b)(1)-(2)	Division C—Extension and Modification of Duty Suspension on Wool Products; Wool Research Fund; Wool Duty Refunds—Extension of Duty Refunds and Wool Research Trust Fund	October 3, 2008
...	403(d)(3)	Division B—Broker Reporting of Customer's Basis in Securities Transactions—Additional Issuer Information to Aid Brokers—Clerical Amendment	January 1, 2011
...	504(a)(1)-(2)	Division C—Income Averaging for Amounts Received In connection with the Exxon Valdez Litigation—Income Averaging Amounts Received from the Exxon Valdez Litigation	October 3, 2008
...	504(b)(1)-(5)	Division C—Income Averaging for Amounts Received In connection with the Exxon Valdez Litigation—Contributions of Amounts Received to Retirement Accounts	October 3, 2008
...	504(c)(1)-(2)	Division C—Income Averaging for Amounts Received In connection with the Exxon Valdez Litigation—Treatment of Qualified Settlement Income Under Employment Taxes	October 3, 2008
...	504(d)(1)-(2)	Division C—Income Averaging for Amounts Received In connection with the Exxon Valdez Litigation—Qualified Taxpayer	October 3, 2008

Code Sec.	Act Sec.	Act Provision Subject	Effective Date
...	504(e)(1)-(2)	Division C—Income Averaging for Amounts Received In connection with the Exxon Valdez Litigation—Qualified Settlement Income	October 3, 2008
...	707(b)	Division C—Expensing of Qualified Disaster Expenses—Clerical Amendment	October 3, 2008
...	801(c)	Division C—Nonqualified Deferred Compensation From Certain Tax Indifferent Parties—Clerical Amendment	October 3, 2008
...	403(c)(3)	Division B—Broker Reporting of Customer's Basis in Securities Transactions—Information by Transferors to Aid Brokers—Clerical Amendment	January 1, 2011
...	107(b)(3)	Division B—New Clean Renewable Energy Bonds—Conforming Amendments	Obligations issued after October 3, 2008
...	113(b)(3)(A)-(B)	Division B—Temporary Increase in Coal Excise Tax; Funding of Black Lung Disability Trust Fund—One-Time Appropriation	October 3, 2008
...	114(d)(1)-(4)	Division B—Special Rules for Refund of the Coal Excise Tax to Certain Coal Producers and Reporters—Definitions	October 3, 2008
...	117(a)	Division B-Carbon Audit of the Tax Code-Study	October 3, 2008
...	117(b)	Division B—Carbon Audit of the Tax Code—Report	October 3, 2008
...	117(c)	Division B—Carbon Audit of the Tax Code—Authorization of Appropriations	October 3, 2008

¶20,001

¶20,005 Effective Dates

Federal Aviation Administration Extension Act of 2008, Part II

This CCH-prepared table presents the general effective dates for major law provisions added, amended or repealed by the Federal Aviation Administration Extension Act of 2008 (P.L. 110-330), enacted September 30, 2008. Entries are listed in Code Section order.

Code Sec.	Act Sec.	Act Provision Subject	Effective Date
4081(d)(2)(B)	2(a)	Extension of Taxes Funding Airport and Airway Trust Fund—Fuel Taxes	October 1, 2008
4261(j)(1)(A)(ii)	2(b)(1)	Extension of Taxes Funding Airport and Airway Trust Fund—Ticket Taxes	October 1, 2008
4271(d)(1)(A)(ii)	2(b)(2)	Extension of Taxes Funding Airport and Airway Trust Fund—Ticket Taxes	October 1, 2008
9502(d)(1)(A)	3(a)(2)	Extension of Airport and Airway Trust Fund Expenditure Authority	October 1, 2008
9502(d)(1)	3(a)(1)	Extension of Airport and Airway Trust Fund Expenditure Authority	October 1, 2008
9502(e)(2)	3(b)	Extension of Airport and Airway Trust Fund Expenditure Authority—Conforming Amendment	October 1, 2008
...	4(a)(1)(A)-(C)	Extension of Airport Improvement Program—Authorization of Appropriations	September 30, 2008
...	4(a)(2)	Extension of Airport Improvement Program—Authorization of Appropriations—Obligation of Amounts	September 30, 2008
...	4(a)(3)(A)-(B)	Extension of Airport Improvement Program—Authorization of Appropriations—Program Implementation	September 30, 2008
...	4(b)	Extension of Airport Improvement Program—Project Grant Authority	September 30, 2008
...	5(a)-(k)	Extension of Expiring Authorities	October 1, 2008
..	6(1)-(3)	Federal Aviation Administration Operations	September 30, 2008
...	7(1)-(3)	Air Navigation Facilities and Equipment	September 30, 2008
...	8(1)-(3)	Research, Engineering, and Development	September 30, 2008

¶20,010 Effective Dates

Fostering Connections to Success and Increasing Adoptions Act of 2008

This CCH-prepared table presents the general effective dates for major law provisions added, amended or repealed by the Fostering Connections to Success and Increasing Adoptions Act of 2008 (P.L. 100-351) , enacted October 7, 2008. Entries are listed in Code Section order.

Code Sec.	Act Sec.	Act Provision Subject	Effective Date
24(a)	501(c)(1)	Clarification of Uniform Definition of Child—Restrict Qualifying Child Tax Benefits to Child's Parent—Child Tax Credit	Tax years beginning after December 31, 2008
152(c)(1)	501(b)	Clarification of Uniform Definition of Child—Child Must be Unmarried	Tax years beginning after December 31, 2008
152(c)(3)(A)	501(a)	Clarification of Uniform Definition of Child—Child Must be Younger than Claimant	Tax years beginning after December 31, 2008
152(c)(4)	501(c)(2)(B)(ii)	Clarification of Uniform Definition of Child—Restrict Qualifying Child Tax Benefits to Child's Parent—Persons Other Than Parents Claiming Qualifying Child—Conforming Amendments	Tax years beginning after December 31, 2008
152(c)(4)(A)	501(c)(2)(B)(i)	Clarification of Uniform Definition of Child—Restrict Qualifying Child Tax Benefits to Child's Parent—Persons Other Than Parents Claiming Qualifying Child—Conforming Amendments	Tax years beginning after December 31, 2008
152(c)(4)(C)	501(c)(2)(A)	Clarification of Uniform Definition of Child—Restrict Qualifying Child Tax Benefits to Child's Parent—Persons Other Than Parents Claiming Qualifying Child	Tax years beginning after December 31, 2008
...	502	Investment of Operating Cash	Date of enactment
...	503	No Federal Funding to Unlawfully Present Individuals	Date of enactment

¶20,015 Effective Dates

Inmate Tax Fraud Prevention Act

This CCH-prepared table presents the general effective dates for major law provisions added, amended or repealed by the Inmate Tax Fraud Prevention Act of 2008 (H.R. 7082). Entries are listed in Code Section order.

Code Sec.	Act Sec.	Act Provision Subject	Effective Date
6103(k)(10)	2(a)	Disclosure of Prisoner Return Information to Federal Bureau of Prisons	Disclosures made after December 31, 2008
6103(p)(4)	2(b)	Disclosure of Prisoner Return Information to Federal Bureau of Prisons—Recordkeeping	Disclosures made after December 31, 2008
7803(d)(3)(A)-(C)	2(c)	Disclosure of Prisoner Return Information to Federal Bureau of Prisons—Evaluation by Treasury Inspector General for Tax Administration	Disclosures made after December 31, 2008
...	3(a)	Restoration of Certain Judicial Survivors' Annuities	The first day of the first month beginning at least 30 days after September 30, 2008 and shall apply in the case of a remarriage which is dissolved by death, divorce, or annulment on or after such first day, generally
...	3(b)	Restoration of Certain Judicial Survivors' Annuities—Conforming Amendment	The first day of the first month beginning at least 30 days after September 30, 2008 and shall apply in the case of a remarriage which is dissolved by death, divorce, or annulment on or after such first day, generally

¶20,020 Effective Dates

SSI Extension for Elderly and Disabled Refugees Act of 2008

This CCH-prepared table presents the general effective dates for major law provisions added, amended or repealed by the SSI Extension for Elderly and Disabled Refugees Act of 2008 (P.L. 110-328), enacted September 30, 2008. Entries are listed in Code Section order.

Code Sec.	Act Sec.	Act Provision Subject	Effective Date
3304(a)(4)(E)-(G)	3(c)(1)-(3)	Collection of Unemployment Compensation Debts Resulting from Fraud—Expenditures from State Fund	Refunds payable under Code Sec 6402 on or after September 30, 2008
6103(a)(3)	3(b)(1)	Collection of Unemployment Compensation Debts Resulting from Fraud—Disclosure of Certain Information to States Requesting Refund Offsets for Legally Enforceable State Unemployment Compensation Debt Resulting from Fraud	Refunds payable under Code Sec 6402 on or after September 30, 2008
6103(l)(10)	3(b)(2)(A)-(C)	Collection of Unemployment Compensation Debts Resulting from Fraud—Disclosure of Certain Information to States Requesting Refund Offsets for Legally Enforceable State Unemployment Compensation Debt Resulting from Fraud—Disclosure to Department of Labor and Its Agent	Refunds payable under Code Sec 6402 on or after September 30, 2008
6103(p)(4)	3(b)(3)(A)-(C)	Collection of Unemployment Compensation Debts Resulting from Fraud—Disclosure of Certain Information to States Requesting Refund Offsets for Legally Enforceable State Unemployment Compensation Debt Resulting from Fraud—Safeguards	Refunds payable under Code Sec 6402 on or after September 30, 2008
6402(a)	3(d)(1)	Collection of Unemployment Compensation Debts Resulting from Fraud—Conforming Amendments	Refunds payable under Code Sec 6402 on or after September 30, 2008
6402(d)(2)	3(d)(2)	Collection of Unemployment Compensation Debts Resulting from Fraud—Conforming Amendments	Refunds payable under Code Sec 6402 on or after September 30, 2008
6402(e)(3)	3(d)(3)	Collection of Unemployment Compensation Debts Resulting from Fraud—Conforming Amendments	Refunds payable under Code Sec 6402 on or after September 30, 2008
6402(f)-(l)	3(a)	Collection of Unemployment Compensation Debts Resulting from Fraud	Refunds payable under Code Sec 6402 on or after September 30, 2008

Code Sec.	Act Sec.	Act Provision Subject	Effective Date
6402(g)	3(d)(4)	Collection of Unemployment Compensation Debts Resulting from Fraud—Conforming Amendments	Refunds payable under Code Sec 6402 on or after September 30, 2008
6402(i)	3(d)(5)	Collection of Unemployment Compensation Debts Resulting from Fraud—Conforming Amendments	Refunds payable under Code Sec 6402 on or after September 30, 2008

¶20,025 Effective Dates

Michelle's Law

This CCH-prepared table presents the general effective dates for major law provisions added, amended or repealed by Michelle's Law (P.L. 110-381), enacted October 9, 2008. Entries are listed in Code Section order.

Code Sec.	Act Sec.	Act Provision Subject	Effective Date
9813	2(c)(1)	Coverage of Dependent Students on Medically Necessary Leave of Absence--Amendments to the Internal Revenue Code	Plan years beginning on or after the date that is one year after the date of enactment and to medically necessary leaves of absence beginning during such plan years
...	2(c)(2)	Coverage of Dependent Students on Medically Necessary Leave of Absence--Amendments to the Internal Revenue Code--Conforming Amendment	Date of enactment

¶25,001 Code Section to Explanation Table

¶25,005 Code Sections Added, Amended or Repealed

The list below notes all the Code Sections or subsections of the Internal Revenue Code that were added, amended or repealed by the Emergency Economic Stabilization Act of 2008 (P.L. 110-343), enacted October 3, 2008, the Fostering Connections to Success and Increasing Adoptions Act of 2008 (P.L. 110-351), the SSI Extension for Elderly and Disabled Refugees Act (P.L. 110-328), enacted September 30, 2008, the Federal Aviation Administration Extension Act of 2008, Part II (P.L. 110-330), enacted September 30, 2008, the Inmate Tax Fraud Prevention Act (H.R. 7082), and Michelle's Law (P.L. 110-381), enacted October 9, 2008. The first column indicates the Code Section added, amended or repealed, and the second column indicates the Act Section.

Emergency Economic Stabilization Act of 2008

Code Sec.	Act Sec.	Code Sec.	Act Sec.
23(b)(4)(B)	106(e)(2)(A), Div. B	30C(g)(2)	207(a), Div. B
24(b)(3)(B)	106(e)(2)(B), Div. B	30D	205(a), Div. B
24(b)(3)(B)	205(d)(1)(A), Div. B	38(b)(32)-(34)	115(b), Div. B
24(d)(4)	501(a), Div. C	38(b)(33)-(35)	205(c), Div. B
25(e)(1)(C)(ii)	205(d)(1)(B), Div. B	38(c)(4)(B)[v]-(vii)	103(b)(1), Div. B
25B(g)(2)	106(e)(2)(C), Div. B	38(c)(4)(B)(v)-(viii)	316(b)(1)-(2), Div. C
25B(g)(2)	205(d)(1)(C), Div. B	38(c)(4)(B)(vi)	103(b)(2), Div. B
25C(c)(1)	302(e)(1), Div. B	40(d)(7)	203(a), Div. B
25C(c)(2)(D)	302(e)(2)(A)-(B), Div. B	40A(b)(1)-(2)	202(b)(1), Div. B
25C(d)(2)(C)	302(d)(2), Div. B	40A(b)(3)-(5)	202(b)(3)(A), Div. B
25C(d)(3)(C)-(F)	302(d)(1), Div. B	40A(d)(2)	202(f), Div. B
25C(d)(3)(D)-(F)	302(b)(1)(A)-(C), Div. B	40A(d)(3)(C)(ii)	202(b)(3)(D), Div. B
25C(d)(3)(E)	302(c), Div. B	40A(d)(5)	203(b), Div. B
25C(d)(6)	302(b)(2), Div. B	40A(e)(2)-(3)	202(b)(3)(C), Div. B
25C(g)	302(a), Div. B	40A(f)(2)	202(b)(3)(B), Div. B
25D(a)(2)-(4)	106(c)(1), Div. B	40A(f)(3)	202(c)(1)-(3), Div. B
25D(a)(3)-(5)	106(d)(1), Div. B	40A(f)(3)	202(d)(1), Div. B
25D(b)(1)(A)-(E)	106(b)(1)(A)-(B), Div. B	40A(f)(3)	202(d)(2), Div. B
25D(b)(1)(B)-(D)	106(c)(2), Div. B	40A(f)(4)	202(e), Div. B
25D(b)(1)(C)-(E)	106(d)(2), Div. B	40A(g)	202(a), Div. B
25D(c)	106(e)(1), Div. B	41(c)(5)(A)	301(c), Div. C
25D(d)(4)	106(c)(3)(A), Div. B	41(h)	301(a)(1), Div. C
25D(d)(5)	106(d)(3), Div. B	41(h)(2)-(3)	301(b), Div. C
25D(e)(4)(A)(i)-(v)	106(b)(2)(A)-(B), Div. B	41(h)(2)-(3)	301(d), Div. C
25D(e)(4)(A)(ii)-(iv)	106(c)(4), Div. B	45(b)(2)	108(b)(2), Div. B
25D(e)(4)(A)(iii)-(v)	106(d)(4), Div. B	45(b)(4)(A)	102(d), Div. B
25D(g)	106(a), Div. B	45(c)(1)(G)-(I)	102(a), Div. B
26(a)(1)	106(e)(2)(D), Div. B	45(c)(7)(A)	108(a)(1), Div. B
26(a)(1)	205(d)(1)(D), Div. B	45(c)(7)(A)(i)	101(b)(1)(A)-(C), Div. B
26(a)(2)	101(a)(1)-(2), Div. C	45(c)(7)(B)	101(b)(2), Div. B
26(b)(2)(V)-(X)	801(b), Div. C	45(c)(7)(C)	108(a)(2), Div. B
30B(d)(3)(D)	205(b), Div. B	45(c)(8)(C)	101(e), Div. B
30C(c)(2)(C)	207(b), Div. B	45(c)(10)	102(b), Div. B

Code Sec.	Act Sec.	Code Sec.	Act Sec.
45(d)	101(a)(1), Div. B	48A(d)(2)(A)	111(c)(2), Div. B
45(d)(1)	106(c)(3)(B), Div. B	48A(d)(3)(A)	111(b), Div. B
45(d)(2)(A)(i)-(ii)	101(a)(2)(A), Div. B	48A(d)(3)(B)	111(c)(1), Div. B
45(d)(2)(B)-(C)	101(d)(2), Div. B	48A(d)(5)	111(d), Div. B
45(d)(3)(A)(i)-(ii)	101(a)(2)(B), Div. B	48A(e)(1)(E)-(G)	111(c)(3)(A), Div. B
45(d)(3)(B)-(C)	101(d)(1), Div. B	48A(e)(3)	111(c)(5), Div. B
45(d)(4)	101(a)(2)(C), Div. B	48A(e)(3)(A)-(C)	111(c)(3)(B), Div. B
45(d)(5)	101(a)(2)(D), Div. B	48A(e)(3)(B)(ii)-(iv)	111(c)(4)(A)-(C), Div. B
45(d)(5)	102(e), Div. B	48A(i)	111(c)(3)(C), Div. B
45(d)(6)	101(a)(2)(E), Div. B	48B(a)	112(a), Div. B
45(d)(7)	101(a)(2)(F), Div. B	48B(c)(7)(F)-(H)	112(e), Div. B
45(d)(7)	101(c)(1)-(2), Div. B	48B(d)(1)	112(b), Div. B
45(d)(8)	108(c), Div. B	48B(d)(4)	112(d), Div. B
45(d)(9)(A)-(B)	101(a)(2)(G), Div. B	48B(f)	112(c), Div. B
45(d)(11)	102(c), Div. B	53(e)(2)	103(a), Div. C
45(e)(8)(D)	108(b)(1), Div. B	53(f)	103(b), Div. C
45(e)(9)(B)	108(d)(1)(A)-(B), Div. B	54(m)	107(c), Div. B
45A(f)	314(a), Div. C	54A(d)(1)	107(b)(1), Div. B
45C(b)(1)(D)	301(a)(2), Div. C	54A(d)(1)	301(b)(1), Div. B
45D(f)(1)(D)	302, Div. C	54A(d)(1)(B)-(D)	313(b)(1), Div. C
45G(f)	316(a), Div. C	54A(d)(2)(C)	107(b)(2), Div. B
45K(g)(2)(E)	108(d)(2), Div. B	54A(d)(2)(C)	301(b)(2), Div. B
45L(g)	304, Div. B	54A(d)(2)(C)(ii)-(iv)	313(b)(2), Div. C
45M(b)	305(a), Div. B	54C	107(a), Div. B
45M(c)	305(b)(1)(A)-(D), Div. B	54D	301(a), Div. B
45M(c)(2)	305(b)(2), Div. B	54E	313(a), Div. C
45M(d)	305(c), Div. B	55(d)(1)(A)-(B)	102(a)(1)-(2), Div. C
45M(e)(1)	305(d)(1), Div. B	56(b)(1)(E)	706(b)(3), Div. C
45M(e)(2)	305(d)(2), Div. B	56(d)(3)	708(c), Div. C
45M(f)(1)	305(e)(1), Div. B	62(a)(2)(D)	203(a), Div. C
45M(f)(3)	305(e)(2), Div. B	63(c)(1)(B)-(D)	706(b)(1), Div. C
45M(f)(4)-(8)	305(e)(3), Div. B	63(c)(1)(C)	204(a), Div. C
45M(f)(6)	305(e)(4), Div. B	63(c)(8)	706(b)(2), Div. C
45M(f)(9)-(10)	305(e)(5), Div. B	108(a)(1)(E)	303(a), Div. A
45N(e)	310, Div. C	132(f)(1)(D)	211(a), Div. B
45Q	115(a), Div. B	132(f)(2)(A)-(C)	211(b), Div. B
48(a)(1)	103(c)(3), Div. B	132(f)(4)	211(d), Div. B
48(a)(1)	104(d), Div. B	132(f)(5)(F)	211(c), Div. B
48(a)(2)(A)(i)	104(b), Div. B	139(c)(2)	706(a)(2)(D)(iv), Div. C
48(a)(2)-(3)	103(a)(1), Div. B	142(l)(8)	307(a), Div. B
48(a)(3)	103(e)(1), Div. B	142(l)(9)	307(b), Div. B
48(a)(3)(A)(iii)-(v)	103(c)(1), Div. B	143(k)(12)[13]	709(a), Div. C
48(a)(3)(A)(iv)-(vi)	104(a), Div. B	162(m)(5)	302(a), Div. A
48(a)(3)(A)(v)-(vii)	105(a), Div. B	164(b)(5)(I)	201(a), Div. C
48(c)	103(c)(2)(A)-(B), Div. B	165(h)(1)	706(c), Div. C
48(c)(1)(B)	103(d), Div. B	165(h)(3)-(5)	706(a)(1), Div. C
48(c)(1)(D)-(E)	103(e)(2)(A), Div. B	165(h)(4)(B)	706(a)(2)(A), Div. C
48(c)(1)(E)	103(a)(2), Div. B	165(i)(1)	706(a)(2)(B), Div. C
48(c)(2)(D)-(E)	103(e)(2)(B), Div. B	165(i)(4)	706(a)(2)(C), Div. C
48(c)(2)(E)	103(a)(3), Div. B	168(b)(2)(B)-(D)	306(c), Div. B
48(c)(4)	104(c), Div. B	168(b)(3)(I)	305(c)(3), Div. C
48A(a)(1)-(3)	111(a), Div. B	168(e)(3)(B)(v)-(vii)	505(a), Div. C

Code Sec.	Act Sec.	Code Sec.	Act Sec.
168(e)(3)(D)(i)-(iv)	306(a), Div. B	871(k)(1)(C)	206(a), Div. C
168(e)(3)(E)(iv)-(v)	305(a)(1), Div. C	871(k)(2)(C)	206(b), Div. C
168(e)(3)(E)(vii)-(ix)	305(c)(1), Div. C	897(h)(4)(A)(ii)	208(a), Div. C
168(e)(7)	305(b)(1), Div. C	907(a)-(b)	402(a), Div. B
168(e)(8)	305(c)(2), Div. C	907(c)(4)	402(b), Div. B
168(g)(3)(B)	305(c)(4), Div. C	907(f)	402(c)(1)-(2), Div. B
168(g)(3)(B)	505(b), Div. C	953(e)(10)	303(a)(1)-(2), Div. C
168(i)(15)(D)	317(a), Div. C	954(c)(6)(C)	304(a), Div. C
168(i)(18)-(19)	306(b), Div. B	954(h)(9)	303(b), Div. C
168(j)(8)	315(a), Div. C	1012	403(b)(1)-(3), Div. B
168(l)	201(b)(1)-(3), Div. B	1016(a)(35)-(37)	205(d)(2), Div. B
168(l)(3)	201(a), Div. B	1033(h)	706(a)(2)(D)(i), Div. C
168(m)	308(a), Div. B	1033(h)(2)	706(a)(2)(D)(ii), Div. C
168(n)	710(a), Div. C	1033(h)(3)	706(a)(2)(D)(iii), Div. C
170(b)(3)	323(b)(1), Div. C	1367(a)(2)	307(a), Div. C
170(e)(3)(C)(iv)	323(a)(1), Div. C	1397E(m)	313(b)(3), Div. C
170(e)(3)(D)	324(a), Div. C	1400(f)	322(a)(1), Div. C
170(e)(3)(D)(iii)	324(b), Div. C	1400A(b)	322(b)(1), Div. C
170(e)(6)(G)	321(a), Div. C	1400B(b)	322(c)(1), Div. C
172(b)(1)(F)(ii)	708(d)(1), Div. C	1400B(e)(2)	322(c)(2)(A)(i)-(ii), Div. C
172(b)(1)(F)(ii)(II)	706(a)(2)(D)(v), Div. C		
172(b)(1)(F)(ii)(III)	706(a)(2)(D)(vi), Div. C	1400B(g)(2)	322(c)(2)(B), Div. C
172(b)(1)(J)	708(a), Div. C	1400C(d)(2)	205(d)(1)(E), Div. B
172(i)(1)	708(d)(2), Div. C	1400C(i)	322(d), Div. C
172(j)-(l)	708(b), Div. C	1400F(d)	322(c)(2)(C), Div. C
179(e)	711(a), Div. C	1400N(h)	320(a), Div. C
179C(c)(1)	209(a)(1)-(2), Div. B	2105(d)(3)	207(a), Div. C
179C(d)	209(b)(1), Div. B	3301	404(a)(1)-(2), Div. B
179C(e)(2)	209(b)(2), Div. B	4053(9)-(10)	206(a), Div. B
179D(h)	303, Div. B	4121(e)(2)(A)-(B)	113(a)(1)-(2), Div. B
179E(g)	311, Div. C	4161(b)(2)(B)-(C)	503(a), Div. C
181(a)(2)(A)	502(b), Div. C	4611(c)(2)(B)	405(a)(1), Div. B
181(d)(3)(A)	502(d), Div. C	4611(f)(1)	405(b)(2), Div. B
181(f)	502(a), Div. C	4611(f)(2)-(3)	405(b)(1), Div. B
198(h)	318(a), Div. C	6033(b)(14)-(15)	703(a), Div. C
198A	707(a), Div. C	6045(b)	403(a)(3)(A), Div. B
199(b)(2)(D)	502(c)(1), Div. C	6045(b)	403(a)(3)(C), Div. B
199(c)(6)	502(c)(2), Div. C	6045(d)	403(a)(3)(B)(i)-(ii), Div. B
199(d)(1)(A)(ii)-(iv)	502(c)(3), Div. C		
199(d)(2)	401(b), Div. B	6045(g)	403(a)(1), Div. B
199(d)(8)(C)	312(a)(1)-(2), Div. C	6045(h)	403(a)(2), Div. B
199(d)(9)-(10)	401(a), Div. B	6045A	403(c)(1), Div. B
222(e)	202(a), Div. C	6045B	403(d)(1), Div. B
280G(e)-(f)	302(b)(1)-(2), Div. A	6103(i)(3)(C)	402(a), Div. C
408(d)(8)(F)	205(a), Div. C	6103(i)(7)(E)	402(b), Div. C
451(i)(3)	109(a)(1), Div. B	6426(c)(2)	202(b)(2), Div. B
451(i)(4)(B)(ii)	109(b), Div. B	6426(c)(6)	202(a), Div. B
451(i)(5)(C)	109(c), Div. B	6426(d)(1)	204(b)(2), Div. B
451(i)(6)-(11)	109(a)(2), Div. B	6426(d)(2)(E)	204(c)(2), Div. B
457A	801(a), Div. C	6426(d)(2)(E)-(G)	204(b)(1), Div. B
512(b)(13)(E)	306(a), Div. C	6426(d)(4)	204(a)(1), Div. B
613A(c)(6)(H)	210, Div. B	6426(d)(4)-(5)	204(c)(1), Div. B

Code Sec.	Act Sec.	Code Sec.	Act Sec.
6426(e)(3)	204(a)(2), Div. B	6724(d)(2)(I)-(EE)	403(c)(2), Div. B
6426(i)	203(c)(1), Div. B	6724(d)(2)(J)-(FF)	403(d)(2)(B), Div. B
6427(e)(5)(B)	202(a), Div. B	7508A(a)	706(a)(2)(D)(vii), Div. C
6427(e)(5)(C)	204(a)(3), Div. B	7608(c)(6)	401(a), Div. C
6427(e)(5)-(6)	203(c)(2), Div. B	7652(f)(1)	308(a), Div. C
6501(i)	402(d), Div. B	7704(d)(1)(E)	116(a), Div. B
6501(m)	205(d)(3), Div. B	7704(d)(1)(E)	208(a), Div. B
6694(a)	506(a), Div. C	9812	512(c)(1)-(7), Div. C
6724(d)(1)(B)(iv)-(xxiii)	403(d)(2)(A), Div. B	9812	512(g)(3)(A), Div. C

Fostering Connections to Success and Increasing Adoptions Act of 2008

Code Sec.	Act Sec.	Code Sec.	Act Sec.
24(a)	501(c)	152(c)(4)	501(c)(2)(B)(ii)
152(c)(1)(C)-(E)	501(b)	152(c)(4)(A)	501(c)(2)(B)(i)
152(c)(3)(A)	501(a)	152(c)(4)(C)	501(c)(2)(A)

SSI Extension for Elderly and Disabled Refugees Act

Code Sec.	Act Sec.	Code Sec.	Act Sec.
3304(a)(4)(E)-(G)	3(c)(1)-(3)	6402(d)(2)	3(d)(2)
6103(a)(3)	3(b)(1)	6402(e)(3)	3(d)(3)
6103(l)(10)	3(b)(2)(A)-(C)	6402(f)-(l)	3(a)
6103(p)(4)	3(b)(3)(A)-(C)	6402(g)	6402(g)
6402(a)	3(d)(1)	6402(i)	6402(i)

Federal Aviation Administration Extension Act of 2008, Part II

Code Sec.	Act Sec.	Code Sec.	Act Sec.
4081(d)(2)(B)	2(a)	9502(d)(1)	3(a)(1)-(2)
4261(j)(1)(A)(ii)	2(b)(1)	9502(e)(2)	3(b)
4271(d)(1)(A)(ii)	2(b)(2)		

Inmate Tax Fraud Prevention Act

Code Sec.	Act Sec.	Code Sec.	Act Sec.
6103(k)(10)	2(a)	7803(d)(3)(A)-(C)	2(c)
6103(p)(4)	2(b)		

Michelle's Law

Code Sec.	Act Sec.
9813	2(c)(1)

¶25,005

¶25,010 Table of Amendments to Other Acts

Emergency Economic Stabilization Act of 2008

Amended Act Sec.	H.R. 1424 Sec.	Par. (¶)	Amended Act Sec.	H.R. 1424 Sec.	Par. (¶)
			American Jobs Creation Act of 2004		
Title 5, United States Code			701(d)	307, Div. B	¶7147
5315	101(a)(B)(i), Div. A	¶7012	**Tax Relief and Health Care Act of 2006**		
Title 31, United States Code			119(d)	309, Div. C	¶7153
301(e)	101(a)(B)(ii), Div. A	¶7012	**Katrina Emergency Tax Relief Act of 2005**		
1105(a)(35)	203(a), Div. A	¶7126			
3101(b)	122, Div. A	¶7075			
6906	601(c)(1)-(2), Div. C	¶7171	201(b)(1)	319, Div. C	¶7156
National Housing Act			**Harmonized Tariff Schedule**		
257(e)(1)(B)	124(1)(A), Div. A	¶7081	9902.51	325(a), Div. C	¶7159
257(e)(2)(B)	124(1)(B), Div. A	¶7081			
257(e)(4)(A)	124(1)(C)(i)-(ii), Div. A	¶7081	**Wool Suit and Textile Trade Extension Act of 2004**		
257(w)	124(2), Div. A	¶7081	4002(c)(3)(C)	325(b)(1)(A), Div. C	¶7159
Federal Deposit Insurance Act			4002(c)(6)(A)	325(b)(1)(B), Div. C	¶7159
8(c)(4)	126(b), Div. A	¶7087	**Trade and Development Act of 2000**		
13(c)(11)	126(c), Div. A	¶7087			
18(a)	126(d)(2), Div. A	¶7087	506(f)	325(b)(2), Div. C	¶7159
18(a)(3)	126(d)(1)(A)-(B), Div. A	¶7087	**Employee Retirement Income Security Act of 1974**		
18(a)(4)	126(a), Div. A	¶7087	712	512(a)(8), Div. C	¶7168
Financial Services Regulatory Relief Act of 2006			712	512(g)(1)(A)-(B), Div. C	¶7168
203	128, Div. A	¶7093	712(a)(1)(B)(i)	512(a)(7), Div. C	¶7168
			712(a)(1)(C)	512(a)(7), Div. C	¶7168
Truth in Lending Act			712(a)(2)(B)(i)	512(a)(7), Div. C	¶7168
128(b)(2)	130, Div. A	¶7099	712(a)(2)(C)	512(a)(7), Div. C	¶7168

Amended Act Sec.	H.R. 1424 Sec.	Par. (¶)	Amended Act Sec.	H.R. 1424 Sec.	Par. (¶)
712(a)(3)-(5)	512(a)(1), Div. C	¶7168	2705(e)(4)-(5)	512(b)(4), Div. C	¶7168
712(b)(2)	512(a)(2), Div. C	¶7168	2705(f)	512(b)(5), Div. C	¶7168
712(c)(1)(B)	512(a)(3)(A), Div. C	¶7168			
712(c)(2)	512(a)(3)(B), Div. C	¶7168			
712(e)(4)-(5)	512(a)(4), Div. C	¶7168			
712(f)	512(a)(5), Div. C	¶7168			
712(f)-(g)	512(a)(6), Div. C	¶7168			

Secure Rural Schools and Community Self-Determination Act of 2000

1-403	601(a), Div. C	¶7171

Public Health Service Act

2705	512(b)(7), Div. C	¶7168
2705	512(g)(2), Div. C	¶7168
2705(a)(1)(B)(i)	512(b)(6), Div. C	¶7168
2705(a)(1)(C)	512(b)(6), Div. C	¶7168
2705(a)(2)(B)(i)	512(b)(6), Div. C	¶7168
2705(a)(2)(C)	512(b)(6), Div. C	¶7168
2705(a)(3)-(5)	512(b)(1), Div. C	¶7168
2705(b)(2)	512(b)(2), Div. C	¶7168
2705(c)(1)	512(b)(3)(A), Div. C	¶7168
2705(c)(2)	512(b)(3)(B), Div. C	¶7168

Act of May 23, 1908

. . .	601(b)(1), Div. C	¶7171

Act of March 1, 1911

13	601(b)(2), Div. C	¶7171

Surface Mining Control and Reclamation Act of 1977

402(i)(1)(C)	602, Div. C	¶7174

¶25,015 Table of Act Sections Not Amending Internal Revenue Code Sections

Emergency Economic Stabilization Act of 2008

¶25,020 Act Sections Amending Code Sections

Emergency Economic Stabilization Act of 2008

Act Sec.	Code Sec.	Act Sec.	Code Sec.
101(a)(1), Div. B	45(d)	106(b)(2)(A)-(B), Div. B	25D(e)(4)(A)(i)-(v)
101(a)(1)-(2), Div. C	26(a)(2)		
101(a)(2)(A), Div. B	45(d)(2)(A)(i)-(ii)	106(c)(1), Div. B	25D(a)(2)-(4)
101(a)(2)(B), Div. B	45(d)(3)(A)(i)-(ii)	106(c)(2), Div. B	25D(b)(1)(B)-(D)
101(a)(2)(C), Div. B	45(d)(4)	106(c)(3)(A), Div. B	25D(d)(4)
101(a)(2)(D), Div. B	45(d)(5)	106(c)(3)(B), Div. B	45(d)(1)
101(a)(2)(E), Div. B	45(d)(6)	106(c)(4), Div. B	25D(e)(4)(A)(ii)-(iv)
101(a)(2)(F), Div. B	45(d)(7)	106(d)(1), Div. B	25D(a)(3)-(5)
101(a)(2)(G), Div. B	45(d)(9)(A)-(B)	106(d)(2), Div. B	25D(b)(1)(C)-(E)
101(b)(1)(A)-(C), Div. B	45(c)(7)(A)(i)	106(d)(3), Div. B	25D(d)(5)
		106(d)(4), Div. B	25D(e)(4)(A)(iii)-(v)
101(b)(2), Div. B	45(c)(7)(B)	106(e)(1), Div. B	25D(c)
101(c)(1)-(2), Div. B	45(d)(7)	106(e)(2)(A), Div. B	23(b)(4)(B)
101(d)(1), Div. B	45(d)(3)(B)-(C)	106(e)(2)(B), Div. B	24(b)(3)(B)
101(d)(2), Div. B	45(d)(2)(B)-(C)	106(e)(2)(C), Div. B	25B(g)(2)
101(e), Div. B	45(c)(8)(C)	106(e)(2)(D), Div. B	26(a)(1)
102(a)(1)-(2), Div. C	55(d)(1)(A)-(B)	107(a), Div. B	54C
102(a), Div. B	45(c)(1)(G)-(I)	107(b)(1), Div. B	54A(d)(1)
102(b), Div. B	45(c)(10)	107(b)(2), Div. B	54A(d)(2)(C)
102(c), Div. B	45(d)(11)	107(c), Div. B	54(m)
102(d), Div. B	45(b)(4)(A)	108(a)(1), Div. B	45(c)(7)(A)
102(e), Div. B	45(d)(5)	108(a)(2), Div. B	45(c)(7)(C)
103(a)(1), Div. B	48(a)(2)-(3)	108(b)(1), Div. B	45(e)(8)(D)
103(a)(2), Div. B	48(c)(1)(E)	108(b)(2), Div. B	45(b)(2)
103(a)(3), Div. B	48(c)(2)(E)	108(c), Div. B	45(d)(8)
103(a), Div. C	53(e)(2)	108(d)(1)(A)-(B), Div. B	45(e)(9)(B)
103(b)(1), Div. B	38(c)(4)(B)[v]-(vii)		
103(b)(2), Div. B	38(c)(4)(B)(vi)	108(d)(2), Div. B	45K(g)(2)(E)
103(b), Div. C	53(f)	109(a)(1), Div. B	45I(i)(3)
103(c)(1), Div. B	48(a)(3)(A)(iii)-(v)	109(a)(2), Div. B	45I(i)(6)-(11)
103(c)(2)(A)-(B), Div. B	48(c)	109(b), Div. B	45I(i)(4)(B)(ii)
		109(c), Div. B	45I(i)(5)(C)
103(c)(3), Div. B	48(a)(1)	111(a), Div. B	48A(a)(1)-(3)
103(d), Div. B	48(c)(1)(B)	111(b), Div. B	48A(d)(3)(A)
103(e)(1), Div. B	48(a)(3)	111(c)(1), Div. B	48A(d)(3)(B)
103(e)(2)(A), Div. B	48(c)(1)(D)-(E)	111(c)(2), Div. B	48A(d)(2)(A)
103(e)(2)(B), Div. B	48(c)(2)(D)-(E)	111(c)(3)(A), Div. B	48A(e)(1)(E)-(G)
104(a), Div. B	48(a)(3)(A)(iv)-(vi)	111(c)(3)(B), Div. B	48A(e)(3)(A)-(C)
104(b), Div. B	48(a)(2)(A)(i)	111(c)(3)(C), Div. B	48A(i)
104(c), Div. B	48(c)(4)	111(c)(4)(A)-(C), Div. B	48A(e)(3)(B)(ii)-(iv)
104(d), Div. B	48(a)(1)		
105(a), Div. B	48(a)(3)(A)(v)-(vii)	111(c)(5), Div. B	48A(e)(3)
106(a), Div. B	25D(g)	111(d), Div. B	48A(d)(5)
106(b)(1)(A)-(B), Div. B	25D(b)(1)(A)-(E)	112(a), Div. B	48B(a)
		112(b), Div. B	48B(d)(1)

Act Sec.	Code Sec.	Act Sec.	Code Sec.
112(c), Div. B	48B(f)	207(a), Div. B	30C(g)(2)
112(d), Div. B	48B(d)(4)	207(a), Div. C	2105(d)(3)
112(e), Div. B	48B(c)(7)(F)-(H)	207(b), Div. B	30C(c)(2)(C)
113(a)(1)-(2), Div. B	4121(e)(2)(A)-(B)	208(a), Div. B	7704(d)(1)(E)
115(a), Div. B	45Q	208(a), Div. C	897(h)(4)(A)(ii)
115(b), Div. B	38(b)(32)-(34)	209(a)(1)-(2), Div. B	179C(c)(1)
116(a), Div. B	7704(d)(1)(E)	209(b)(1), Div. B	179C(d)
201(a), Div. B	168(l)(3)	209(b)(2), Div. B	179C(e)(2)
201(a), Div. C	164(b)(5)(I)	210, Div. B	613A(c)(6)(H)
201(b)(1)-(3), Div. B	168(l)	211(a), Div. B	132(f)(1)(D)
202(a), Div. B	40A(g)	211(b), Div. B	132(f)(2)(A)-(C)
202(a), Div. B	6426(c)(6)	211(c), Div. B	132(f)(5)(F)
202(a), Div. B	6427(e)(5)(B)	211(d), Div. B	132(f)(4)
202(a), Div. C	222(e)	301(a)(1), Div. C	41(h)
202(b)(1), Div. B	40A(b)(1)-(2)	301(a)(2), Div. C	45C(b)(1)(D)
202(b)(2), Div. B	6426(c)(2)	301(a), Div. B	54D
202(b)(3)(A), Div. B	40A(b)(3)-(5)	301(b)(1), Div. B	54A(d)(1)
202(b)(3)(B), Div. B	40A(f)(2)	301(b)(2), Div. B	54A(d)(2)(C)
202(b)(3)(C), Div. B	40A(e)(2)-(3)	301(b), Div. C	41(h)(2)-(3)
202(b)(3)(D), Div. B	40A(d)(3)(C)(ii)	301(c), Div. C	41(c)(5)(A)
202(c)(1)-(3), Div. B	40A(f)(3)	301(d), Div. C	41(h)(2)-(3)
202(d)(1), Div. B	40A(f)(3)	302(a), Div. A	162(m)(5)
202(d)(2), Div. B	40A(f)(3)	302(a), Div. B	25C(g)
202(e), Div. B	40A(f)(4)	302(b)(1)(A)-(C), Div. B	25C(d)(3)(D)-(F)
202(f), Div. B	40A(d)(2)		
203(a), Div. B	40(d)(7)	302(b)(1)-(2), Div. A	280G(e)-(f)
203(a), Div. C	62(a)(2)(D)	302(b)(2), Div. B	25C(d)(6)
203(b), Div. B	40A(d)(5)	302(c), Div. B	25C(d)(3)(E)
203(c)(1), Div. B	6426(i)	302(d)(1), Div. B	25C(d)(3)(C)-(F)
203(c)(2), Div. B	6427(e)(5)-(6)	302(d)(2), Div. B	25C(d)(2)(C)
204(a)(1), Div. B	6426(d)(4)	302(e)(1), Div. B	25C(c)(1)
204(a)(2), Div. B	6426(e)(3)	302(e)(2)(A)-(B), Div. B	25C(c)(2)(D)
204(a)(3), Div. B	6427(e)(5)(C)		
204(a), Div. C	63(c)(1)(C)	302, Div. C	45D(f)(1)(D)
204(b)(1), Div. B	6426(d)(2)(E)-(G)	303(a)(1)-(2), Div. C	953(e)(10)
204(b)(2), Div. B	6426(d)(1)	303(a), Div. A	108(a)(1)(E)
204(c)(1), Div. B	6426(d)(4)-(5)	303(b), Div. C	954(h)(9)
204(c)(2), Div. B	6426(d)(2)(E)	303, Div. B	179D(h)
205(a), Div. B	30D	304(a), Div. C	954(c)(6)(C)
205(a), Div. C	408(d)(8)(F)	304, Div. B	45L(g)
205(b), Div. B	30B(d)(3)(D)	305(a)(1), Div. C	168(e)(3)(E)(iv)-(v)
205(c), Div. B	38(b)(33)-(35)	305(a), Div. B	45M(b)
205(d)(1)(A),.Div.B	24(b)(3)(B)	305(b)(1)(A)-(D), Div. B	45M(c)
205(d)(1)(B), Div. B	25(e)(1)(C)(ii)		
205(d)(1)(C), Div. B	25B(g)(2)	305(b)(1), Div. C	168(e)(7)
205(d)(1)(D), Div. B	26(a)(1)	305(b)(2), Div. B	45M(c)(2)
205(d)(1)(E), Div. B	1400C(d)(2)	305(c)(1), Div. C	168(e)(3)(E)(vii)-(ix)
205(d)(2), Div. B	1016(a)(35)-(37)	305(c)(2), Div. C	168(e)(8)
205(d)(3), Div. B	6501(m)	305(c)(3), Div. C	168(b)(3)(I)
206(a), Div. B	4053(9)-(10)	305(c)(4), Div. C	168(g)(3)(B)
206(a), Div. C	871(k)(1)(C)	305(c), Div. B	45M(d)
206(b), Div. C	871(k)(2)(C)	305(d)(1), Div. B	45M(e)(1)

Act Sec.	Code Sec.	Act Sec.	Code Sec.
305(d)(2), Div. B	45M(e)(2)	403(a)(2), Div. B	6045(h)
305(e)(1), Div. B	45M(f)(1)	403(a)(3)(A), Div. B	6045(b)
305(e)(2), Div. B	45M(f)(3)	403(a)(3)(B)(i)-(ii),	6045(d)
305(e)(3), Div. B	45M(f)(4)-(8)	Div. B	
305(e)(4), Div. B	45M(f)(6)	403(a)(3)(C), Div. B	6045(b)
305(e)(5), Div. B	45M(f)(9)-(10)	403(b)(1)-(3), Div. B	1012
306(a), Div. B	168(e)(3)(D)(i)-(iv)	403(c)(1), Div. B	6045A
306(a), Div. C	512(b)(13)(E)	403(c)(2), Div. B	6724(d)(2)(I)-(EE)
306(b), Div. B	168(i)(18)-(19)	403(d)(1), Div. B	6045B
306(c), Div. B	168(b)(2)(B)-(D)	403(d)(2)(A), Div. B	6724(d)(1)(B)(iv)-(xxiii)
307(a), Div. B	142(l)(8)	403(d)(2)(B), Div. B	6724(d)(2)(J)-(FF)
307(a), Div. C	1367(a)(2)	404(a)(1)-(2), Div. B	3301
307(b), Div. B	142(l)(9)	405(a)(1), Div. B	4611(c)(2)(B)
308(a), Div. B	168(m)	405(b)(1), Div. B	4611(f)(2)-(3)
308(a), Div. C	7652(f)(1)	405(b)(2), Div. B	4611(f)(1)
310, Div. C	45N(e)	501(a), Div. C	24(d)(4)
311, Div. C	179E(g)	502(a), Div. C	181(f)
312(a)(1)-(2), Div. C	199(d)(8)(C)	502(b), Div. C	181(a)(2)(A)
313(a), Div. C	54E	502(c)(1), Div. C	199(b)(2)(D)
313(b)(1), Div. C	54A(d)(1)(B)-(D)	502(c)(2), Div. C	199(c)(6)
313(b)(2), Div. C	54A(d)(2)(C)(ii)-(iv)	502(c)(3), Div. C	199(d)(1)(A)(ii)-(iv)
313(b)(3), Div. C	1397E(m)	502(d), Div. C	181(d)(3)(A)
314(a), Div. C	45A(f)	503(a), Div. C	4161(b)(2)(B)-(C)
315(a), Div. C	168(j)(8)	505(a), Div. C	168(e)(3)(B)(v)-(vii)
316(a), Div. C	45G(f)	505(b), Div. C	168(g)(3)(B)
316(b)(1)-(2), Div. C	38(c)(4)(B)(v)-(viii)	506(a), Div. C	6694(a)
317(a), Div. C	168(i)(15)(D)	512(c)(1)-(7), Div. C	9812
318(a), Div. C	198(h)	512(g)(3)(A), Div. C	9812
320(a), Div. C	1400N(h)	703(a), Div. C	6033(b)(14)-(15)
321(a), Div. C	170(e)(6)(G)	706(a)(1), Div. C	165(h)(3)-(5)
322(a)(1), Div. C	1400(f)	706(a)(2)(A), Div. C	165(h)(4)(B)
322(b)(1), Div. C	1400A(b)	706(a)(2)(B), Div. C	165(i)(1)
322(c)(1), Div. C	1400B(b)	706(a)(2)(C), Div. C	165(i)(4)
322(c)(2)(A)(i)-(ii),	1400B(e)(2)	706(a)(2)(D)(i), Div. C	1033(h)
Div. C			
322(c)(2)(B), Div. C	1400B(g)(2)	706(a)(2)(D)(ii), Div. C	1033(h)(2)
322(c)(2)(C), Div. C	1400F(d)		
322(d), Div. C	1400C(i)	706(a)(2)(D)(iii), Div. C	1033(h)(3)
323(a)(1), Div. C	170(e)(3)(C)(iv)		
323(b)(1), Div. C	170(b)(3)	706(a)(2)(D)(iv), Div. C	139(c)(2)
324(a), Div. C	170(e)(3)(D)		
324(b), Div. C	170(e)(3)(D)(iii)	706(a)(2)(D)(v), Div. C	172(b)(1)(F)(ii)(II)
401(a), Div. B	199(d)(9)-(10)		
401(a), Div. C	7608(c)(6)	706(a)(2)(D)(vi), Div. C	172(b)(1)(F)(ii)(III)
401(b), Div. B	199(d)(2)		
402(a), Div. B	907(a)-(b)	706(a)(2)(D)(vii), Div. C	7508A(a)
402(a), Div. C	6103(i)(3)(C)		
402(b), Div. B	907(c)(4)	706(b)(1), Div. C	63(c)(1)(B)-(D)
402(b), Div. C	6103(i)(7)(E)	706(b)(2), Div. C	63(c)(8)
402(c)(1)-(2), Div. B	907(f)	706(b)(3), Div. C	56(b)(1)(E)
402(d), Div. B	6501(i)	706(c), Div. C	165(h)(1)
403(a)(1), Div. B	6045(g)	707(a), Div. C	198A

Act Sec.	Code Sec.	Act Sec.	Code Sec.
708(a), Div. C	172(b)(1)(J)	709(a), Div. C	143(k)(12)[13]
708(b), Div. C	172(j)-(l)	710(a), Div. C	168(n)
708(c), Div. C	56(d)(3)	711(a), Div. C	179(e)
708(d)(1), Div. C	172(b)(1)(F)(ii)	801(a), Div. C	457A
708(d)(2), Div. C	172(i)(1)	801(b), Div. C	26(b)(2)(V)-(X)

Fostering Connections to Success and Increasing Adoptions Act of 2008

Act Sec.	Code Sec.	Act Sec.	Code Sec.
501(a)	152(c)(3)(A)	501(c)(2)(A)	152(c)(4)(C)
501(b)	152(c)(1)(C)-(E)	501(c)(2)(B)(i)	152(c)(4)(A)
501(c)	24(a)	501(c)(2)(B)(ii)	152(c)(4)

SSI Extension for Elderly and Disabled Refugees Act

Act Sec.	Code Sec.	Act Sec.	Code Sec.
3(a)	6402(f)-(l)	3(d)(1)	6402(a)
3(b)(1)	6103(a)(3)	3(d)(2)	6402(d)(2)
3(b)(2)(A)-(C)	6103(l)(10)	3(d)(3)	6402(e)(3)
3(b)(3)(A)-(C)	6103(p)(4)	6402(g)	6402(g)
3(c)(1)-(3)	3304(a)(4)(E)-(G)	6402(i)	6402(i)

Federal Aviation Administration Extension Act of 2008, Part II

Act Sec.	Code Sec.	Act Sec.	Code Sec.
2(a)	4081(d)(2)(B)	3(a)(1)-(2)	9502(d)(1)
2(b)(1)	4261(j)(1)(A)(ii)	3(b)	9502(e)(2)
2(b)(2)	4271(d)(1)(A)(ii)		

Inmate Tax Fraud Prevention Act

Act Sec.	Code Sec.	Act Sec.	Code Sec.
2(a)	6103(k)(10)	2(c)	7803(d)(3)(A)-(C)
2(b)	6103(p)(4)		

Michelle's Law

Act Sec.	Code Sec.
2(c)(1)	9813

¶25,020

¶27,001 Client Letters

CLIENT LETTER #1

Re: Emergency Economic Stabilization Act of 2008: General Explanation of Tax Changes

Congress has just passed, and President Bush has signed, a massive rescue plan to help restore confidence in the financial markets. The new law includes more than $150 billion in tax incentives as well as some important revenue raisers. Practitioners can send or email this letter to clients to alert them about the new law, invite them to discuss the tax incentives and develop a tax strategy.

Dear Client:

The crisis in the financial markets, the housing slump and the credit crunch are straining our fragile economy. Consumer and business spending is down and everyone it seems is looking for ways to make their money go further. On October 3, the President signed into law a $850 billion financial markets rescue package, the *Emergency Economic Stabilization Act of 2008* with more than $150 billion in tax incentives.

Troubled Assets Relief Program. Congress gave the Treasury Department sweeping powers to purchase "troubled assets" from banks and other institutions. Many of these troubled assets are linked to home mortgages. However, the housing slump has sent millions of homeowners into foreclosure, making these assets much less valuable.

If a bank or other institution seeks to participate in the rescue program, it must agree to new curbs on executive compensation. In some situations, the Treasury Department can set limits on the compensation of an entity's executives. On other cases, the Treasury Department can limit how much the company deducts for executive compensation. Congress also authorized the Treasury Department to prohibit or limit golden parachute payments.

Tax cuts. Originally, the rescue package did not include the "extenders," energy incentives and disaster relief. Only after the House defeated the original rescue package on September 30 did the Senate add these "sweeteners" to win more support for the rescue plan. The Senate's strategy worked. On October 3, the House passed the Senate's version of the rescue plan including the tax incentives. President Bush signed the bill into law later that day.

Many of the tax incentives in the rescue are commonly known as extenders. These are popular but temporary tax breaks which expire every year or two years unless Congress extends them. Some of these temporary tax cuts have been extended so many times that individuals and businesses mistakenly believe they are permanent when, in reality, they are still temporary. The temporary nature of these incentives makes tax planning challenging because you may be able to take a credit or deduction in one year but not in a future year. Fortunately, the extenders under the new law have been passed soon enough to enable use of year-end tax planning strategies that can maximize 2008 tax savings retroactively to the start of 2008, as well as 2009 tax breaks right from the start of the new year.

Individual incentives. Many of individual incentives are familiar. The new law extends the state and local sales tax deduction (which you can take in lieu of deducting state and local income taxes); higher education tuition deduction, teachers' classroom expense deduction, and tax-free distributions from IRAs for charitable purposes. In all, more than a dozen important tax breaks has been given new life by being extended. These incentives are now available for 2008 and 2009.

The rescue package includes good news for individuals who pay alternative minimum tax (AMT). Congress has authorized an AMT "patch" for 2008 to help keep middle-income individuals out of the reach of the AMT by giving them higher exemption amounts and allowing taxpayers to take nonrefundable personal credits to reduce their AMT liability. The 2008 exemption amounts are $69,950 for married couples filing jointly and surviving spouses, $46,200 for single taxpayers and heads of household and $34,975 for married couples filing separately for 2008.

New to the AMT patch for 2008 is targeted help for individuals with worthless stock options. At the height of the dot.com boom, many individuals received incentive stock options (ISOs) that were valuable at that time but became worthless after the dot.com bubble burst. The rescue plan abates AMT liability stemming from the exercise of incentive ISOs along with interest and penalties on the unpaid amounts. Additionally, all individuals, including those who paid their ISO AMT liabilities, may accelerate the refund of the minimum tax credit that has not been used.

Earlier this year, Congress created new tax incentives to help homeowners: the first-time homebuyer's tax credit and the additional standard deduction for real property taxes. Individuals who do not itemize their deductions may be eligible for the additional standard deduction for real property taxes. This deduction was originally available only for 2008. The rescue package extends the deduction through 2009. However, the rescue package does not extend the first-time homebuyer's tax credit.

When a lender forecloses on property, sells the home for less than the borrower's outstanding mortgage and forgives all or part of the excess mortgage debt, the Tax Code treats the cancelled debt as taxable income to the homeowner. The *Mortgage Forgiveness Debt Relief Act*, enacted in late 2007, excludes from federal tax those discharges involving up to $2 million of indebtedness ($1 million for a married taxpayer filing a separate return) secured by a principal residence and incurred in the acquisition, construction or substantial improvement of the residence. The new law extends this treatment from the end of 2009 through 2012.

Additionally, the rescue package enhances the child tax credit. Before the new law, the child tax credit was refundable to the extent of 15 percent of the taxpayer's earned income in excess of approximately $12,050 (reflecting inflation adjustments from the original floor of $10,000). Under the new law, the floor falls to $8,500. Additionally, the rescue plan changes the definition of a "qualifying child" with respect to age and joint returns, clarifies certain tiebreaker rules and ties the child tax credit to the child dependency exemption.

If you install qualifying energy conservation property, such as exterior windows and doors, in your home you may be eligible to a tax break. The new law extends a number of energy conservation tax incentives and creates a new tax credit for individuals who purchase a plug-in electric vehicle. Solar power, too, has been given

¶27,001

a tremendous boost. Both the availability of an unlimited credit for its installation and extensive tax breaks for the solar industry as a whole will drive down energy costs for everyone but especially those with homes that "go solar," at least in part.

Business tax incentives. The business tax incentives in the rescue package are extensive. The largest business extender is the research tax credit. This credit is available for qualifying research expenses, including wages. The rescue package extends the research tax credit to amounts paid or incurred in 2008 and 2009. It also increases the alternative simplified research credit to 14 percent starting next year, a tremendous incentive now for smaller firms to finally use the research credit to grow their business.

Many businesses remodel or otherwise make improvements to their facilities on a regular schedule. These improvements are usually depreciated over 39 years. The rescue package shortens that period to 15 years for qualifying leasehold, restaurant and retail improvements. However, this special treatment is temporary, so timing these improvements becomes critical.

Businesses that donate food to charitable organizations and books and computers to schools may be eligible for a tax deduction. The rescue package extends these tax breaks through 2009.

Employees may exclude certain employer-paid transportation fringe benefits from their incomes. The rescue package adds commuting by bicycle to types of commuting eligible for the exclusion.

Producers of alternative energy, such as electricity from solar power, biomass and wind facilities also benefit under the rescue package. Congress extended and enhanced various alternative energy tax incentives. Tax breaks for energy efficient improvements to commercial buildings and energy efficient appliances likewise are extended and in some cases enhanced. With the price of heating and air conditioning steadily rising, these tax breaks should considerably reduce the pay-back time for these improvements.

Other business incentives in the rescue package include extensions of the New Markets Tax Credit, enhanced depreciation of leasehold, restaurant and retail improvements, brownfield remediation, Indian employment credit, subpart F active financing, look-through treatment of payments between related controlled foreign corporations (CFCs), and enhanced expensing for U.S. film and television production. The business incentives in the rescue package are not only targeted, however; they are also complex. Please contact our office if you have any questions.

Disaster relief. The rescue package helps individuals and businesses recovering from storms and tornadoes that hit the Mid-West earlier this year. Individuals in 10 Mid-West states may be eligible for special tax incentives, such as enhanced casualty loss deductions, expensing and depreciation. The rescue plan also includes more limited tax incentives to help victims of Hurricane Ike in Louisiana and Texas along with temporary national disaster relief.

Revenue raisers. To pay for a portion of these tax incentives, Congress included several revenue raisers in the rescue package. For those affected, they also are being referred to as "tax increases."

¶27,001

One of the most wide-reaching is broker basis reporting. The rescue package requires brokers to report the adjusted basis of publicly-traded securities and indicate whether gain is long-term or short-term. Securities subject to the new reporting requirement include stocks, bonds, debentures, commodities, derivatives, and other financial instruments designated by Treasury. The reporting requirement takes effect for stocks acquired in 2011, mutual funds acquired in 2012, and other securities acquired in 2013.

Another revenue raiser targets foreign deferred compensation. It closes a loophole through which Nonqualified deferred compensation plans maintained by foreign corporations will generally become taxable, unless the compensation is deferred 12 months or less after the end of the year that the compensation vests. Deferred compensation would be taxable when the amount is determinable. If the compensation is not determinable when it was deferred, the individual must pay a 20 percent surtax, plus interest, when the amount is determinable. The provision does not apply to an entity whose income is taxable in the U.S. or subject to a "comprehensive foreign income tax."

The rescue package also caps the Code Sec. 199 domestic production activities deduction for oil and gas companies. Additionally, it tightens the rules oil and gas companies to pay taxes on overseas income. Two special taxes, the oil spill tax and the FUTA surtax, are extended under the new law.

Time for planning. The *Emergency Economic Stabilization Act of 2008* is one of the largest tax laws in recent years. You may be able to take advantage of one or more the tax incentives. There is still time in 2008 to utilize these incentives in your strategic tax planning. Planning to take maximum advantage of these incentives in 2009 also should start now. Please call or email our office so we can discuss these opportunities in more detail.

Sincerely yours,

CLIENT LETTER #2

Re: Emergency Economic Stabilization Act of 2008: Tax Changes Affecting Individuals

Congress has just passed, and President Bush has signed, a massive rescue plan to help restore confidence in the financial markets. The new law includes more than $150 billion in tax incentives as well as some important revenue raisers. Practitioners can send or email this letter to clients to alert them about the individual tax incentives in the rescue package.

Dear Client:

On October 3, President Bush signed into law a $ 850 billion financial markets rescue package. The rescue plan is designed to restore liquidity to the financial markets. At the same time, it includes some valuable individual tax incentives we want you to know about. The tax incentives cover a wide spectrum of activities. They are designed to put money back into the pockets of individual taxpayers during these difficult days. In this letter, we highlight some of the key incentives and invite you to discuss them with us in more detail.

AMT. The rescue package has some good news for individuals who are liable for alternative minimum tax (AMT) The AMT was created nearly 40 years ago as an alternative tax to the regular income tax to ensure that very wealthy individuals pay their fair share of taxes. However, the AMT was not indexed for inflation and it is ensnaring middle-income taxpayers. To prevent this, Congress created an AMT "patch." The 2008 patch is similar to past patches but with some important differences.

The 2008 patch raises the AMT exemption amounts to $69,950 for married couples filing jointly and surviving spouses, $46,200 for single taxpayers and heads of household and $34,975 for married couples filing separately. The rescue package also allows taxpayers to take nonrefundable personal credits to reduce their AMT liability. Additionally, and this is a new feature to the patch, the rescue plan abates AMT liability stemming from the exercise of incentive stock options along with interest and penalties on the unpaid amounts. The rescue package also allows individuals, including those who paid their ISO AMT liabilities, to accelerate the refund of the minimum tax credit that has not been used.

Homeowners. When a lender forecloses on property, sells the home for less than the borrower's outstanding mortgage and forgives all or part of the excess mortgage debt, the Tax Code treats the cancelled debt as taxable income to the homeowner. The *Mortgage Forgiveness Debt Relief Act*, enacted in late 2007, excludes from federal tax discharges involving up to $2 million of indebtedness ($1 million for a married taxpayer filing a separate return) secured by a principal residence and incurred in the acquisition, construction or substantial improvement of the residence. The new law extends this treatment from the end of 2009 through 2012.

The rescue package also extends the additional standard deduction for real property taxes. Individuals who do not itemize their deductions may take this deduction in 2008 and 2009. This deduction is not an above the line deduction that lowers your adjusted gross income. It is an addition to the standard deduction, and can reduce your taxable income by as much as $500 ($1,000 for those filing joint returns).

¶27,001

Child tax credit. The rescue package also enhances the child tax credit. Before the new law, the child tax credit was refundable to the extent of 15 percent of the taxpayer's earned income in excess of approximately $12,050 (reflecting inflation adjustments from the original floor of $10,000). Under the new law, the floor falls to $8,500. This treatment will result in an increase in the amount of the refundable credit for more taxpayers. Additionally, the rescue plan changes the definition of a "qualifying child" with respect to age and joint returns, clarifies the tiebreaker rules and ties the child tax credit to the child dependency exemption.

Charity. In 2008 and 2009, an individual age 70 1/2 or older can distribute up to $100,000 of his or her IRA balance to charitable organizations, including churches, without recognizing income and without taking a charitable deduction. This special tax break had expired at the end of 2007. The rescue package also includes some provisions related to donations to charities helping victims in disaster areas.

Energy. Rising fuel costs are pinching many people's wallets. If you install qualifying energy conservation property, such as exterior windows and doors, in your home you may be eligible to a tax break. The new law extends a number of energy conservation tax incentives and creates a new tax credit for individuals who purchase a plug-in electrical vehicle. Significant take breaks for "going solar" are also available in connection with home improvements.

State and local taxes. The rescue package gives individuals who itemize their deductions the option of deducting state and local income taxes or deducting state and local general sales taxes. This election was available in past years but expired at the end of 2007. The new law makes it retroactive to January 1, 2008, and extends it for 2009.

Education. The Tax Code provides many incentives to help individuals with educational expenses. The higher education tuition deduction is one of the most popular. The rescue package extends it but does not make it permanent. Nonetheless, it can be a valuable incentive. As previously, however, the amount of the deduction depends on your adjusted gross income.

Teachers. The Tax Code also gives teachers and other education workers a special deduction. Teachers may deduct up to $250 of qualified classroom expenses above-the-line. This special treatment expired at the end of 2007. The rescue package makes it retroactive to January 1, 2008, and extends it through 2009.

Disasters. Many individuals across the country are recovering from tornadoes, hurricanes and other natural disasters in 2008. The rescue package targets tax relief for individuals affected by flooding and tornadoes in 10 states and also helps victims of Hurricane Ike in Louisiana and Texas. For the first time, Congress authorized temporary national disaster relief.

Broker basis reporting. Starting in 2011, brokers will be required to report to the IRS not only their customers' gross proceeds from the sale of most corporate stocks but also the investor's cost basis in those shares. This will encourage the more accurate computation of capital gains each year. Broker basis reporting is expected to raise $6 billion over 10 years to partially offset the cost of the tax incentives in the rescue package. The reporting requirement takes effect for stocks acquired in 2011, mutual funds acquired in 2012, and other securities acquired in 2013.

¶27,001

We encourage you to call or email our office to discuss these tax breaks and the many other incentives and new tax rules created under the rescue package. You may be able to realize some tax savings this year. Don't put off contacting us; we can help you develop a strategy that maximizes your tax savings.

Sincerely yours,

CLIENT LETTER #3

Re: Emergency Economic Stabilization Act of 2008: Tax Changes Affecting Businesses

Congress has just passed, and President Bush has signed, a massive rescue plan to help restore confidence in the financial markets. The new law includes more than $150 billion in tax incentives as well as some important revenue raisers. Practitioners can send or email this letter to clients to alert them about the business tax incentives in the rescue package.

Dear Client:

On October 3, President Bush signed into law a $850 billion financial markets rescue package. The rescue plan—called the *Emergency Economic Stabilization Act of 2008*—is designed to restore liquidity to the financial markets. At the same time, it includes some valuable individual and business tax incentives that also will serve to help revive our economy.

The business tax incentives in the *Emergency Economic Stabilization Act of 2008* cover a wide range of activities and industries. As with most tax incentives, however, they can be realized only if you take the time and effort to plan for them. In this letter, we highlight some of the key incentives and invite you to discuss them with us in more detail.

Research Tax Credit. The rescue package extends the research tax credit to amounts paid or incurred in 2008 and 2009. It also increases the alternative simplified research credit to 14 percent starting next year, a tremendous incentive now for smaller firms to finally use the research credit to grow their businesses.

Leasehold improvements. Many businesses remodel or otherwise make improvements to their facilities on a regular schedule. Under the new law, qualifying restaurant improvements and leasehold improvements will be eligible for 15-year cost recovery rather than a 39-year period for two more years, through December 31, 2009. Similarly, Congress authorized a 15-year recovery period for depreciation of certain improvements to retail space. This treatment is extended through December 31, 2009. It applies to both owner-occupied businesses and restaurants, as well as leased establishments.

Energy conservation. The new law extends a host of energy tax incentives, some targeted to consumers (including businesses) and others to producers and manufacturers. Many of the extensions go beyond the one or two year periods that Congress authorized for non-energy extenders. Most notable are the extension of the special deduction for energy efficient commercial buildings, through December 31, 2013; and the substantial, long-term tax breaks given to businesses that develop or use solar energy. For businesses in urban areas, a $20/month transportation fringe benefit may be set up for employees who bicycle to work.

Charitable contributions. The Tax Code gives businesses enhanced deductions for contributions of food to charitable organizations, as well as contributions of books and computer equipment to qualifying schools. The new law extends these tax breaks through December 31, 2009. Additionally, Congress extended the temporary suspension of limitations on charitable contributions in the case of a qualified farmer or rancher contributing food before January 1, 2009.

¶27,001

S corporation shareholders are also eligible for special tax treatment when making charitable contributions of qualifying property. The new law extends, through December 31, 2009, the special rule allowing S corp shareholders to take into account their pro-rata share of charitable deductions even if such deductions would exceed such shareholder's adjusted basis in his or her S corporation.

New Markets Tax Credit. The new law extends the New Markets Tax Credit through December 31, 2009. The New Markets Tax Credit is one of the few incentives in the Tax Code to encourage taxpayers to invest in or make loans to small businesses in economically distressed areas. In today's credit crunch, extension of the New Markets Tax Credit may help small businesses secure financing that otherwise would not be available.

Disaster relief. The new law provides temporary, but significant, tax relief to victims of the recent severe storms, tornadoes, and flooding that hit the Midwest and, to a somewhat lesser extent, victims of Hurricane Ike in Texas. Additionally, Congress authorized national relief for locations declared disaster areas by the president in tax years beginning after December 31, 2007. Exceptions do apply, so we are advising affected clients to contact our offices for further assistance.

Other business extenders. The rescue package also targets a whole host of extended, enhanced and expanded tax breaks to certain specific businesses. If your operations touch upon one of these areas, please contact our offices for further details. These targeted tax breaks includes:

- Farming business machinery and equipment treated as five-year property;
- Brownfield remediation;
- The Code Sec. 199 domestic production activities deduction for qualifying activities in Puerto Rico;
- Qualified Zone Academy Bonds;
- The Subpart F active financing exception;
- Look-through treatment of payments between related controlled foreign corporations (CFCs);
- Enhanced expensing for U.S. film and television production;
- District of Columbia first-time homebuyer tax credit;
- . . . and over ten other targeted measures ranging from tax breaks for mine safety, to special deductions for NASCAR racetracks, to an excise tax exemption for manufacturers of wooden arrows.

In addition to tax breaks only available to businesses, the *Emergency Economic Stabilization Act of 2008* also provides tax relief to individuals in their capacities as business owners or shareholders. All told, the *Emergency Economic Stabilization Act of 2008* is one of the largest tax laws in recent years, containing something for almost everyone. Some of these breaks, however, require quick action before the 2008 tax year ends; others call for careful coordination with standard year-end tax strategies; and still others require planning now to maximize the benefits available in 2009 and beyond. We encourage you to call or email our office to discuss in more detail how the new *Emergency Economic Stabilization Act of 2008* applies to you and your business

Sincerely yours,

¶27,001

CLIENT LETTER #4

Re: Emergency Economic Stabilization Act of 2008: Mortgage Debt Forgiveness Relief Extended

Dear Client:

The *Emergency Economic Stabilization Act of 2008* (2008 Stabilization Act) includes a provision that temporarily extends an exclusion from income for the forgiveness of debt on a principal residence. Debt forgiveness relief was originally granted to taxpayers through the Mortgage Forgiveness Debt Relief Act of 2007 (2007 Mortgage Act), effective for debts discharged after January 1, 2007 and before January 1, 2010. The 2008 Stabilization Act extends this relief to debts discharged before January 1, 2013. This provision creates an additional three-year exclusion so that homeowners caught in the current subprime mortgage crisis do not have to pay taxes for debt forgiveness on their troubled home loans.

In general, the amount of the forgiveness of debt on a principal residence that is included in income is equal to the difference between the amount of the debt being cancelled and the amount used to satisfy the debt. These rules generally apply to foreclosure or the exchange of an old obligation for a new obligation. For example, assume a taxpayer who is not bankrupt or insolvent owns a principal residence subject to a $200,000 mortgage. If the creditor forecloses and the home is sold for $180,000 in satisfaction of the debt, without this exclusion, the taxpayer has $20,000 of income from the discharge of indebtedness. Likewise, if the creditor restructures the loan and reduces the principal balance amount to $180,000, the taxpayer would also have $20,000 of income from the discharge of indebtedness.

The tax on this income would have created an additional burden to taxpayers already struggling financially. The 2008 Stabilization Act provides relief from this burden so that taxpayers can recover faster.

If you have any questions regarding this provision or if you have concerns regarding a home foreclosure, we can answer any questions and discuss your options in greater detail. Please call our office at your earliest convenience to arrange an appointment.

Sincerely yours,

CLIENT LETTER #5

Re: Emergency Economic Stabilization Act of 2008: Property Tax Deduction for Nonitemizers

Dear Client:

If you are a homeowner who pays real estate taxes, but who generally uses the standard deduction in computing taxable income, you often have not been able to take advantage of one of the more significant benefits of home ownership, that is, the ability to itemize deductions.

As part of the overall effort to provide relief to homeowners in a difficult economy, Congress previously enacted The Housing Assistance Tax Act of 2008, which provided an increase in the standard deduction for state and local real property taxes for homeowners who do not itemize deductions. This increase was effective for the 2008 tax year. To provide additional relief to homeowners, Congress has enacted the *Emergency Economic Stabilization Act of 2008*, extending the additional standard deduction for the 2009 tax year.

Under these provisions, the standard deduction is increased by the lesser of (1) the amount otherwise allowable to an individual as a deduction for state and local real property taxes, or (2) $500 ($1,000 in the case of married taxpayers filing jointly).

The increased deduction may be of real assistance to you. Please call our offices to discuss how this benefit, and other benefits of the *Emergency Economic Stabilization Act of 2008*, can help your overall tax situation.

Sincerely yours,

¶27,001

CLIENT LETTER #6

Re: Emergency Economic Stabilization Act of 2008: Reduced Recovery Periods for Restaurants, Retailers and Leaseholds

Dear Client:

The American Jobs Creation Act of 2004 created a 15-year recovery period under the Modified Adjusted Cost Recovery System (MACRS) for qualified leasehold improvement property and qualified restaurant property placed in service after October 22, 2004, and before January 1, 2006. Taxpayers using this recovery period were required to use the straight-line method and the half-year convention (unless the mid-quarter convention applies). The Tax Relief and Health Care Act of 2006 extended these provisions to property placed in service prior to January 1, 2008.

The *Emergency Economic Stabilization Act of 2008* generally extends the placed in service date through January 1, 2010, and provides affected taxpayers an additional two years to take advantage of the reduced recovery period for restaurant and leasehold improvement property. Fifteen-year treatment is also extended to certain new construction, as well as to certain improvements to retail space placed in service after December 31, 2008, and before January 1, 2010.

If your business reported restaurant, retail or leasehold improvement property in prior years, you may want to note this favorable tax development when planning to acquire qualified restaurant, retail or leasehold property. The specific requirements for qualification of the improvement property for 15-year treatment are somewhat detailed and complex, and we would be happy to assist you in ensuring that your tax benefits from use of such property are maximized.

If you would like additional information on whether or not your anticipated purchases qualify for this favorable tax provision, please call our office at your earliest convenience.

Sincerely yours,

CLIENT LETTER #7

Re: Emergency Economic Stabilization Act of 2008: Deduction for Higher Education

Dear Client:

The popular above-the-line higher education tuition deduction has been extended through 2009 by the *Emergency Economic Stabilization Act of 2008*. If you have reported higher education expenses in the past or have dependents that are of college age, you may be interested to learn that this deduction is still available.

As an above-the-line deduction, the deduction for qualified tuition and related expenses can be taken even if you do not itemize deductions, and it is not subject to the two-percent floor or the overall limitation on itemized deductions. However, the amount of the deduction is limited depending on your adjusted gross income and the tax year in which the deduction is claimed.

For 2008, a $4,000 above-the-line education deduction is available to single taxpayers with adjusted gross incomes (AGI) of $65,000 or less ($130,000 for joint filers). A $2,000 above-the-line education deduction is available to single taxpayers with adjusted gross incomes up to $80,000 ($160,000 for joint filers). These are the same levels set for the deduction as in 2004 through 2007.

Qualified tuition and related éxpenses are tuition and fees required for the enrollment or attendance of you, your spouse, or any dependent at an eligible educational institution for courses of instruction. Generally, any accredited public, nonprofit, or proprietary post-secondary institution is an eligible educational institution.

Depending on the school's deadline for payment, you may want to consider delaying or accelerating your deduction by paying tuition and fees for the spring semester before or after the end of the year. We can help you plan for the maximum tax advantage. Please call our office at your earliest convenience to discuss your options.

Sincerely yours,

CLIENT LETTER #8

Re: Emergency Economic Stabilization Act of 2008: Extension and Modification of Research Credit

Dear Client:

The *Emergency Economic Stabilization Act of 2008* extends the research credit that was due to expire at the end 2007 until December 31, 2009. In addition, the rates used for the alternative simplified method of computing the credit are increased. However, a taxpayer may no longer use the alternative incremental method for tax years ending after December 31, 2008.

The research credit was provided to encourage taxpayers to increase their research expenditures. The credit is equal to the sum of 20 percent of the excess of qualified research expenses over the amounts paid in prior years, plus 20 percent of the basic research payments made to qualified organizations to perform basic research. Because of the complexity of the computation for the credit, taxpayers were able to elect to compute the credit under an alternative incremental method for tax years beginning after June 30, 1996. This method is no longer available after 2008. However, the *Emergency Economic Stabilization Act of 2008* increases the rate allowed under the alternative simplified method from 12 percent to 14 percent for tax years ending after December 31, 2008.

The good news is that if you claimed a research credit in prior tax years, you may continue to do so for two more years. However, the changes to the available methods for computing the credit may have the potential to significantly affect the amount of the credit you may claim. If you would like additional information, please call us at your earliest opportunity to arrange an appointment.

Sincerely yours,

¶27,001

CLIENT LETTER #9

Re: Emergency Economic Stabilization Act of 2008: Food and Book Inventory Contributions

Dear Client:

The *Emergency Economic Stabilization Act of 2008* (2008 Stabilization Act) extends the enhanced deduction for donations of certain inventory. The enhanced deduction is equal to the lesser of: the cost of producing the item (or basis) plus one-half of the item's appreciated value; or twice the basis.

[This paragraph applies to businesses other than C corporations. Delete if not applicable.] Prior to the *Katrina Emergency Tax Relief Act of 2005* (Katrina Act), only C corporations could claim an enhanced deduction for donations of food. Non-C corporations (S corporations, partnerships, and sole proprietors) were limited to claiming a deduction equal to their basis in the item. The Katrina Act expanded the deduction for non C corporations through December 31, 2005. The Pension Act of 2006 extended the expanded enhanced deduction through December 31, 2007. The 2008 Stabilization Act extends the enhanced deduction through December 31, 2009

[This paragraph applies to businesses other than C corporations. Delete if not applicable.] Donated food inventories must consist of "apparently wholesome food." "Apparently wholesome food" is defined as food intended for human consumption that meets all quality and labeling standards imposed by federal, state, and local laws and regulations even though the food may not be readily marketable due to appearance, age, freshness, grade, size, surplus, or other conditions.

[This paragraph applies to C corporations only. Delete if not applicable.] The 2008 Stabilization Act extends the enhanced deduction of qualified donations of book inventory to public schools for C corporations. Prior to the Katrina Act, C corporations could claim an enhanced deduction for inventory contributed to a qualified charity or private operating foundation for use in the care of the ill, the needy or infants. The Katrina Act expanded the enhanced deduction for C corporations to include the donations of book inventories to public schools through December 31, 2005. The Pension Act extended the enhanced deduction for C corporations to public schools through December 31, 2007. The 2008 Stabilization Act extends the enhanced deduction through December 31, 2009.

[This paragraph applies to C corporations only. Delete if not applicable.] A qualified book contribution means a charitable contribution of books to a public school that provides elementary or secondary education (kindergarten through grade 12) and maintains a regular facility and curriculum with a regular enrolled student body In addition, the donee educational institution must certify in writing that the books are suitable in terms of currency, content and quality for use in the school's educational programs, and the school will actually use the books in its educational programs.

Although the Katrina Act was enacted in response to the hurricane disasters along the Gulf coast in 2005, donations do not have to be targeted specifically for hurricane disaster relief efforts in order to be eligible for the enhanced deduction.

¶27,001

If you would like more information regarding the extension of the enhanced deduction, or other provisions of the Pension Act, please call our office at your earliest convenience.

Sincerely yours,

CLIENT LETTER #10

Re: Emergency Economic Stabilization Act of 2008: Extension of Sales Tax Deduction

Dear Client:

The *Emergency Economic Stabilization Act of 2008* (2008 Stabilization Act) extends the election to deduct state and local general sales taxes in lieu of state and local income taxes through 2009. The extension applies to tax years beginning after December 31, 2007, when the previous extension expired.

It is possible that you may be eligible to take advantage of this opportunity. If you qualify, one of three options may be used to determine the amount of your sales tax deduction. You may:

- add up the total amount of sales tax actually paid if you save your receipts throughout the year; or
- use the sales tax tables available in the Instructions for Schedules A & B (Form 1040); or
- use the "Sales Tax Deduction Calculator" available on the IRS website (www.irs.gov).

You may want to accelerate the purchase of big ticket items in order to claim a larger sales tax deduction in the current year. However, if claiming the sales tax deduction triggers alternative minimum tax, you may lose most or all of the advantage of this election. Please call our office at your earliest convenience to review your tax options.

Sincerely yours,

CLIENT LETTER #11

Re: Emergency Economic Stabilization Act of 2008: Tax-Free IRA Distributions to Charity Extended

Dear Client:

The *Emergency Economic Stabilization Act of 2008* (2008 Stabilization Act) extends through 2009 the provision which allows individuals who are at least 70 by the end of the year to exclude from gross income qualified charitable distributions up to $100,000 from a traditional or Roth IRA, which would otherwise be included in income. Married individuals filing a joint return are allowed to exclude a maximum of $200,000 for these distributions ($100,000 per individual IRA owner). A review of your tax return indicates that you may be eligible to take advantage of this opportunity.

As you may know, taxpayers cannot keep funds in traditional IRAs indefinitely. IRA owners must either withdraw the entire balance or start receiving periodic distributions from their traditional IRAs by April 1 of the year following the year in which they reach age 70. The minimum distribution that is required each year is computed by dividing the IRA account balance as of the close of business on December 31 of the preceding year by the applicable life expectancy. An IRA owner who does not make the required withdrawals may be subject to a 50-percent excise tax on the amount not withdrawn.

Many taxpayers who receive taxable distributions also contribute to charitable organizations. If that is true for you, you can reduce your taxable income by excluding up to $100,000 of your IRA distribution from gross income when you transfer it directly to a charitable organization. This exclusion is available for taxable Roth IRA distributions as well as minimum required distributions from a traditional IRA.

Although a charitable contribution may be motivated by humanitarian reasons rather than by tax considerations, it is, nevertheless, wise to take tax considerations into account when making a contribution. Since this distribution must be made by the IRA trustee directly to a qualified (i.e., 50-percent) charitable organization, you should review your charitable tax giving as soon as possible. Please call our office at your earliest convenience to discuss this new development.

Sincerely yours,

Topical Index

References are to paragraph (¶) numbers

References are to paragraph (¶) numbers

References are to paragraph (¶) numbers

MOD

References are to paragraph (¶) numbers